The Complete Results & Line-ups of the European Cup-Winners' Cup 1960-1999

Romeo Ionescu

About the author

Romeo Ionescu was born in Ploiesti, Romania, on 19th December 1962. He fell in love with football statistics the first time he held a sports newspaper in 1970 and since then has collected a great number of sports newspapers, magazines and books, now possessing around 20,000 items. He began to collate statistics when he was a schoolboy and continued as a student in Bucuresti, where he completed his Romanian football statistics, spending hundreds of hours in two national libraries. Romeo began to exchange magazines and footballing material with other enthusiasts overseas in 1985 including his Dutch friend Kees Doeleman. Kees sparked Romeo's interest with European Cup line-ups and provided a lot of match details, which eventually led to production of a book about this competition. After collaborating on several books including *The European Football Yearbook, Annuario del Calcio Mondiale,* and a Romanian yearbook, Romeo published his first book, *An Encyclopedia of Romanian Football,* in 2000, followed by books on The European Cup and The European Championship amongst others. By profession a mechanical engineer, he now works as a full-time football statistician and is seeking an appointment with an international agency.

British Library Cataloguing in Publication Data
A catalogue record for this book is available from the British Library

ISBN 1-86223-087-0

Copyright © 2004, SOCCER BOOKS LIMITED. (01472 696226)
72 St. Peter's Avenue, Cleethorpes, N.E. Lincolnshire, DN35 8HU, England

All rights are reserved. No part of this publication may be reproduced, stored in a retrieval system or transmitted, in any form or by any means, electronic, mechanical, photocopying, recording, or otherwise, without the prior written permission of Soccer Books Limited.

Printed by 4edge Ltd. www.4edge.co.uk

INTRODUCTION

The Cup-Winners' Cup, known as *Coupe des vainquers des Coupe* in French and *Coppa delle Coppe* in Italian, was the last of the three European club competitions to be founded.

The first of these European competitions was the Inter-Cities Fairs Cup which commenced on 4th June 1955. Many of the entrants in the first years of this competition were combined teams made up of players from different clubs within individual cities although some actual teams such as FC Barcelona and Internazionale Milan did also take part. In later years City teams ceased competing as the event became entirely club-based. The Fairs Cup was replaced in 1971 by the UEFA Cup which runs to this day.

Shortly after the inception of the Fairs Cup, the second, and most prestigious club competition began. The new European football body, UEFA, founded the European Champion Clubs' Cup, a knock-out competition to be played between the Club Champions of each of its members. The first match in this Cup was played on 4th September 1955 and the competition still exists to this day, albeit in the altered Champions League format.

The first match in the last of the three European club competitions to commence, the Cup-Winners' Cup, was played on 31st July 1960. This competition was played on a knock-out basis between the domestic Cup winners of UEFA's member countries. At the time of it's inception, the Cup-Winners' Cup was conceived as being second in prestige only to the Champions' Cup and this was a problem for five of the UEFA member countries who didn't have a domestic Cup! To this end, Belgium, Cyprus, Czechoslovakia, Poland and Sweden immediately started up domestic Cup competitions to enable their teams to have an extra chance to compete against other European teams.

Throughout it's life, the Cup-Winners' Cup proved to be a more difficult trophy to retain than any of the other European competitions. Indeed, no team ever succeeded in retaining the trophy even though the winner automatically qualified for the next year's event. Anderlecht perhaps came the closest by appearing in three consecutive finals from 1976 to 1978, winning the first and third respectively. As an overall record, FC Barcelona had the most success in the competition winning the trophy on no less than four separate occasions. AC Milan, Chelsea, Dinamo Kiev, Anderlecht all won the trophy twice and Fiorentina, Atlético Madrid, Tottenham Hotspur, Sporting Lisbon, West Ham United, Borussia Dortmund, Bayern Munich, Slovan Bratislava, Manchester City, Glasgow Rangers, 1.FC Magdeburg, Hamburger SV, CF Valencia, Dinamo Tbilisi, Aberdeen, Juventus, Everton, Ajax, KV Mechelen, Sampdoria, Manchester United, Werder Bremen, AC Parma, Arsenal, Real Zaragoza, Paris St. Germain and Lazio complete an illustrious line-up of teams to win the trophy once.

The final match of the tournament was played on 19th May 1999 when Lazio beat Real Mallorca 2-1 in the Final at Villa Park in Birmingham to win the trophy outright. The inception of the UEFA Champions League in 1991 as a replacement for the old European Club Champions' Cup had led to the Cup-Winners' Cup becoming an increasingly less attractive competition for the big clubs and it was decided that the tournament should end. The number of entrants into the UEFA Cup was increased to compensate with more teams given the chance to qualify for this competition.

This book

The statistical information contained in this book is a result of 10 years work during which time I have referenced thousands of pages in newspapers and books and I was also helped by many other statisticians. Special thanks are reserved for Kees Doeleman from Almere in Holland for the line-ups, first names of players and photocopies he sent me over a period of many years. Thanks also go to Rien Buikema and Dirk Karsdorp from Holland, Santiago Velasco from Spain, Andrew Cuthew from England and Soccer Books Limited who now publish this book. From the many books I have used as a reference, special mention goes to *The European Football Yearbook*, *Annuario del Calcio Mondiale*, *Memo Foot*, the books of Andrew Cuthew and the Greek yearbook *Gkol*.

I have endeavoured to make the contents of this book as accurate as possible but often, checking two different sources leads to different information for the same match. In cases such as this I have used the most trustworthy information I could find.

Thoughout this book, rather than use English spellings, I have used the correct spelling of Club names and places as used in the country of origin. For example, Rome is Roma, Copenhagen is København etc. If a club's name does not include the name of the town or city from which they originate, this name has been appended. For example, Chelsea and Heart of Midlothian become Chelsea London and Heart of Midlothian Edinburgh accordingly.

Romeo Ionescu

CUP WINNERS' CUP 1960-61

FIRST ROUND

ZASK VORWÄRTS BERLIN
v RUDÁ HVEZDA BRNO 2-1 (1-0)
Friedrich Ludwig Jahn Sportpark, Berlin 31.07.1960
Referee: Friedrich Seipelt (AUS)   Attendance: 8,000
VORWÄRTS: Karl-Heinz Spickenagel; Peter Kalinke, Werner Unger, Dieter Krampe; Hans-Georg Kiupel (Cap), Gerhard Reichelt; Rainer Nachtigall, Gerhard Vogt, Lothar Meyer, Jürgen Nöldner, Horst Kohle.   Trainer: Harald Seeger
RUDÁ HVEZDA: František Schmucker; Karel Kohlík, Bohumil Sláma, Jiří Navrátil; Jan Král, František Són, Karel Komárek; Karel Lichtnégl, Jozef Bomba, Vlastimil Bubník (Cap), Josef Majer.   Trainer: Josef Eremiás
Goals: Kohle (42), Nöldner (48), Bubník (77)

RUDÁ HVEZDA BRNO
v ZASK VORWÄRTS BERLIN 2-0 (2-0)
Stadion Za Luzánkami, Brno 11.08.1960
Referee: Erich Steiner (AUS)   Attendance: 15,000
RUDÁ HVEZDA: František Schmucker; Karel Kohlík, Bohumil Sláma, Jiří Navrátil; Jan Král, Zdenek Machovsky; Karel Kolácek, Karel Lichtnégl, Vlastimil Bubník (Cap), Bronislav Danda, Karel Komárek.   Trainer: Josef Eremiás
VORWÄRTS: Karl-Heiz Spickenagel; Peter Kalinke, Werner Unger, Dieter Krampe; Hans-Georg Kiupel (Cap), Gerhard Reichelt; Raier Nachtigall, Lothar Meyer, Gerhard Vogt, Peter Schaarschmidt, Horst Kohle.   Trainer: Harald Seeger
Goals: Bubník (31), Komárek (43)

GLASGOW RANGERS
v FERENCVÁROS BUDAPEST 4-2 (0-1)
Ibrox stadium, Glasgow 28.09.1960
Referee: Václav Korelus (CZE)   Attendance: 36,000
RANGERS: William Ritchie; Robert Shearer, Eric Caldow (Cap); Harold Davis, William Paterson, James Baxter; Alexander Scott, Joh Ian McMillan, James Millar, Ralph Brand, David Wilson.   Manager: James Scotland Symon
FERENCVÁROS: György Horváth; Antal Thomann, András Gerendás, László Kiss III; Oszkár Vileszál, György Kocsis; Zoltán Friedmanszky, Pal Orosz, Flórián Albert, Gyula Rákosi, Máté Fenyvesi (Cap).   Trainer: Sándor Tátrai
Goals: Orosz (17), Davis (52), Millar (57, 86), Brand (73), Friedmanszky (79)

FERENCVÁROS BUDAPEST
v GLASGOW RANGERS 2-1 (1-0)
Népstadion, Budapest 12.10.1960
Referee: Erich Steiner (AUS)   Attendance: 25,000
FERENCVÁROS: György Horváth; László Kiss III, András Gerendás, Jenő Dalnoki I; Oszkár Vileszál, György Kocsis; József Dálnoki II, Pál Orosz, Zoltán Friedmanszky, Gyula Rákosi, Máté Fenyvesi (Cap).   Trainer: Sándor Tátrai
RANGERS: William Ritchie; Robert Shearer, Eric Caldow (Cap); Harold Davis, William Paterson, James Baxter; Alexander Scott, John Ian McMillan, James Millar, Ralph Brand, David Wilson.   Manager: James Scotland Symon
Goals: Orosz (18), Friedmanszky (48), Wilson (61)

QUARTER-FINALS

RUDA HVEZDA BRNO v DINAMO ZAGREB 0-0
Stadion Za Luzánkami, Brno 28.09.1960
Referee: István Zsolt (HUN)   Attendance: 7,000
RUDA HVEZDA: František Schmucker; Karel Kohlik, Jiří Navratil; Jan Král, Jozef Bomba, Zdenek Machovsky; Karel Kolácek, Karel Lichtnégl, Karel Komárek, Vlastimil Bubník (Cap), Josef Majer.   Trainer: Josef Eremias
DINAMO: Mirko Stojanović; Josip Sikić, Vlatko Marković; Ivan Santek, Tomislav Crnković (Cap), Željko Perusić; Ivica Cvitković, Dragan Blazić, Željko Matuš, Stjepan Lamza, Ilijas Pasić.   Trainer: Milan Antolković

DINAMO ZAGREB
v RUDÁ HVEZDA BRNO 2-0 (2-0)
Maksimir, Zagreb 26.10.1960
Referee: Andor Dorogi (HUN)   Attendance: 11,500
DINAMO: Gordan Irović; Josip Sikić, Vlatko Markovic; Ivan Santek, Tomislav Crnković (Cap), Željko Perusić; Vladimir Conc, Drazen Jerković, Željko Matuš, Stjepan Lamza, Ilijas Pasić.   Trainer: Milan Antolković
RUDA HVEZDA: František Schmucker; Jozef Bomba, Bohumil Sláma (Cap), Jiří Navratil; Jan Král, František Són; Jiří Milka, Karel Komárek, Karel Lichtnégl, Miroslav Hradsky, Josef Majer.   Trainer: Josef Eremiás
Goals: Matus (10), Jerkovic (15)

FK AUSTRIA WIEN
v WOLVERHAMPTON WANDERERS 2-0 (0-0)

Prater, Wien   12.10.1960

Referee: Albert Dusch (W. GER)   Attendance: 20,000

AUSTRIA: Herbert Gartner; Oskar Fischer, Karl Stotz (Cap), Franz Swoboda; Erich Medveth, Horst Paproth; Horst Hirnschrodt, Johann Riegler, Horst Nemec, Ernst Fiala, Werner Huschek.   Trainer: Karl Schlechta

WOLVERHAMPTON: Geoffrey Sidebottom; Philip Kelly, George Showell; John Kirkham, Edward Stuart, Ronald Flowers (Cap); Gerard Mannion, James Murray, James Edward Farmer, Peter Frank Broadbent, Norman Victor Deeley.   Manager: Stanley Cullis

Goals: Riegler (71), Huschek (86)

GLASGOW RANGERS
v BORUSSIA MONCHENGLADBACH 8-0 (5-0)

Ibrox Park, Glasgow   30.11.1960

Referee: Gino Rigato (ITA)   Attendance: 38,174

RANGERS: George Niven; Robert Shearer, Eric Caldow (Cap); Harod Davis, William Paterson, James Baxter; Alexander Scott, John McMillan, James Millar, Ralph Brand, David Wilson.   Manager: James Scotland Symon

BORUSSIA: Günter Jansen; Bert Pfeiffer, Heinz de Lange; Albert Jansen, Hans Göbbels, Friedhelm Frontzeck; Franz Brungs, Albert Brülls (Cap), Ulrich Kohn, Karl-Heinz Mülhausen, Helmut Fendel.   Trainer: Bernd Oles

Goals: Baxter (2), Brand (17, 44, 51), Pfeiffer (36 og), Millar (45, 53), Davis (65)

WOLVERHAMPTON WANDERERS
v FK AUSTRIA WIEN 5-0 (3-0)

Molineux Ground, Wolverhampton   30.11.1960

Referee: Josef Gulde (SWI)   Attendance: 31,699

WOLVERHAMPTON: Geoffrey Sidebottom; Edward Stuart, Gerald Harris; Edward Clamp, William John Slater (C), John Kirkham; Norman Victor Deeley, Robert Mason, James Edward Farmer, Peter Frank Broadbent, Clifford Durandt.   Manager: Stanley Cullis

AUSTRIA: Herbert Gartner; Johann Löser, Karl Stotz (Cap), Franz Swoboda; Erich Medveth, Horst Paproth; Horst Hirnschrodt, Johann Riegler, Horst Nemec, Ernst Fiala, Walter Schleger.   Trainer: Karl Schlechta

Goals: Kirkham (1, 26), Mason (35), Broadbent (71, 74)

FC LUZERN
v AC FIORENTINA FIRENZE 0-3 (0-2)

Stadion Allmend, Luzern   23.11.1960

Referee: Kurt Tschenscher (W. GER)   Attendance: 11,000

FC LUZERN: Antonio Permunian; Walter Schumacher, Paul Stehrenberger, Werner Hofmann, Henri Cerutti, Rudolf Arn; Walter Baerli, Erich Hahn, Walter Wüest, Paul Wolfisberg (Cap), Werner Frey.   Trainer: Rudolf Gutendorf

FIORENTINA: Enrico Albertosi; Saul Malatrasi, Enzo Robotti; Dante Micheli, Alberto Orzan (Cap), Claudio Rimbaldo; Kurt Hamrin, Dino Da Costa, Angeli Benedicto António Antoninho, Luigi Milan, Gianfranco Petris.   Trainers: Lajos Czeizler & Nándor Hidegkuti

Goals: Hamrin (32, 35, 81)

VfL BORUSSIA MÖNCHENGLADBACH
v GLASGOW RANGERS 0-3 (0-2)

Rheinstadion, Düsseldirf   15.11.1960.

Referee: Ezio Damiani (YUG)   Attendance: 50,000

BORUSSIA: Friedel Dresbach; Bert Pfeiffer, Heinz de Lange; Karl-Heinz Mülhausen, Friedhelm Frontzeck, Egmont Kablitz; Fraanz Brungs, Albert Brülls (Cap), Ulrich Kohn, Helmut Fendel, Dieter Bedürftig.   Trainer: Bernd Oles

RANGERS: George Niven; Robert Shearer, Eric Caldow (Cap); Harod Davis, William Paterson, James Baxter; Alexander Scott, John McMillan, James Millar, Ralph Brand, David Wilson.   Manager: James Scotland Symon

Goals: Millar (23), Scott (25), McMillan (58)

AC FIORENTINA FIRENZE
v FC LUZERN 6-2 (3-1)

Stadio Comunale, Firenze   28.12.1960

Referee: Alois Obtulovič (CZE)   Attendance: 5,000

FIORENTINA: Giuliano Sarti; Enzo Robotti, Sergio Castelletti; Dante Micheli, Alberto Orzan (Cap), Reanto Benaglia; Kurt Hamrin, Dino Da Costa, Angeli Benedicto António Antoninho, Luigi Milan, Gianfranco Petris.   Trainers: Lajos Czeizler & Nándor Hidegkuti

FC LUZERN: Antonio Permunian; René Glaus, Paul Stehrenberger; Werner Hofmann, Henri Cerutti (Cap), Rudolf Arn; Walter Baerli, Erich Hahn, Walter Wüest, Rolf Künzli, Werner Frey.   Trainer: Rudolf Gutendorf

Goals: Antoninho (28, 52, 75), Hamrin (33 pen, 46), Milan (38), Frey (43), Hahn (55)

SEMI-FINALS

**AC FIORENTINA FIRENZE
v DINAMO ZAGREB 3-0** (1-0)

Stadio Comunale, Firenze   22.03.1961

Referee: Josef Kandlbinder (W. GER)   Attendance: 5,000

FIORENTINA: Enrico Albertosi; Piero Gonfiantini, Enzo Robotti; Renato Benaglia, Alberto Orzan (Cap), Claudio Rimbaldo; Kurt Hamrin, Paolo Lazzotti, Angeli Benedicto António Antoninho, Dino Da Costa, Gianfranco Petris. Trainers: Lajos Czeizler & Nándor Hidegkuti

DINAMO: Gordan Irović; Josip Sikić, Vladimir Bolfek; Ivan Santek, Vlatko Marković, Željko Perusić; Ivica Cvitković, Slaven Zambata (Cap), Vladimir Conc, Željko Matuš, Dragan Blazić. Traier: Milan Antolković

Goals: Antoninho (40), Da Costa (69), Lazzotti (80)

**DINAMO ZAGREB
v AC FIORENTINA FIRENZE 2-1** (2-0)

Maksimir, Zagreb   12.04.1961

Referee: Jan Kment (CZE)   Attendance: 20,000

DINAMO: Gordan Irović; Josip Sikić, Stjepan Lamza; Ivan Santek, Vlatko Marković, Željko Perusić; Ivica Cvitković, Vladimir Conc, Zlatko Haramincić, Željko Matuš (Cap), Dragan Blazić.   Trainer: Milan Antolković

FIORENTINA: Enrico Albertosi; Enzo Robotti, Sergio Castelletti; Renato Benaglia, Alberto Orzan (Cap), Rino Marchesi; Kurt Hamrin, Paolo Lazzotti, Dino Da Costa, Luigi Milan, Gianfranco Petris.
Trainers: Lajos Czeizler & Nándor Hidegkuti

Goals: Matus (15), Haramincic (18), Petris (50)

**GLASGOW RANGERS
v WOLVERHAMPTON WANDERERS 2-0** (1-0)

Ibrox Stadium, Glasgow   29.03.1961

Referee: Cesare Jonni (ITA)   Attendance: 80,000

RANGERS: William Ritchie; Robert Shearer, Eric Caldow (Cap); Harold Davis, William Paterson, James Curran Baxter; Alexander Silcock Scott, David Wilson, Douglas Baillie, Ralph Laidlaw Brand, Robert Hume.
Manager: James Scotland Symon

WOLVERHAMPTON: Malcolm Finlayson; Edward Stuart, George Showell; Edward Clamp, William John Slater, Ronald Flowers (Cap); Norman Victor Deeley, James Murray, James Edward Farmer, Robert Mason, Clifford Durandt.
Manager: Stanley Cullis

Goals: Scott (33), Brand (84)

**WOLVERHAMPTON WANDERERS
v GLASGOW RANGERS 1-1** (0-1)

Molineux Ground, Wolverhampton   19.04.1961

Referee: Gottfried Dienst (SWI)   Attendance: 45,163

WOLVERHAMPTON: Malcolm Finlayson; Edward Stuart, George Showell; Edward Clamp, William Slater, Ronald Flowers (Cap); Norman Deeley, Robert Mason, James Murray, Peter Broadbent, Clifford Durandt.   Manager: Stanley Cullis

RANGERS: William Ritchie; Robert Shearer, Eric Caldow (Cap); Harold Davis, William Paterson, James Curran Baxter; Alexander Silcock Scott, David Wilson, Ian McMillan, Ralph Laidlaw Brand, Robert Hume.
Manager: James Scotland Symon

Goals: Scott (45), Broadbent (65)

FINAL

**GLASGOW RANGERS
v AC FIORENTINA FIRENZE 0-2** (0-1)

Ibrox Stadium, Glasgow   17.05.1961

Referee: Erich Steiner (AUS)   Attendance: 80,000

RANGERS: William Ritchie; Robert Shearer, Eric Caldow (Cap); Harold Davis, Wiliam Paterson, James Curran Baxter; David Wilson, John Livingstone McMillan, Alexander Silcock Scott, Ralph Laidlaw Brand, Robert Hume.
Manager: James Scotland Symon

FIORENTINA: Enrico Albertosi; Vincenzo Robotti, Sergio Castelletti; Piero Gonfiantini, Alberto Orzan (Cap), Claudio Rimbaldo; Kurt Hamrin, Dante Micheli, Dino da Costa, Luigi Milan, Gianfranco Petris.   Trainer: Nándor Hidegkuti

Goals: Milan (12, 88)

**AC FIORENTINA FIRENZE
v GLASGOW RANGERS 2-1** (1-0)

Stadio Comunale, Firenze   27.05.1961

Referee: Vilmos Hernádi (HUN)   Attendance: 27,000

FIORENTINA: Enrico Albertosi; Vincenzo Robotti, Sergio Castelletti; Piero Gonfiantini, Alberto Orzan (Cap), Claudio Rimbaldo; Kurt Hamrin, Dante Micheli, Dino Da Costa, Luigi Milan, Gianfranco Petris.   Trainer: Nándor Hidegkuti

RANGERS: William Ritchie; Robert Shearer, Eric Caldow (Cap); Harold Davis, William Paterson, James Curran Baxter; Alexander Scott, John McMillan, James Millar, Ralph Brand, David Wilson.   Manager:

Goals: Milan (12), Scott (60), Hamrin (86)

Goalscorers European Cup-Winners' Cup 1960-61:

6 goals: Kurt Hamrin (Fiorentina Firenze)
5 goals: Ralph Brand, James Millar (Rangers)
4 goals: Alexander Scott (Rangers), Luigi Milan, Angeli Benedicto António Antoninho (Fiorentina)
3 goals: Peter Broadbent (Wolverhampton)
2 goals: Vlastimil Bubnik (Ruda Hvezda), Harold Davis (Rangers), Pál Orosz, Zoltán Friedmanszky (Ferencváros), Željko Matus (Dinamo), John Kirkham (Wolverhampton)
1 goal: Horst Kohle, Jürgen Nöldner (Vorwärts), Karel Komárek (RH), David Wilson, John McMillan, James Baxter (Rangers), Zlatko Haramincic, Drazen Jerkovic (Dinamo), Johann Riegler, Werner Huschek (Austria), Robert Mason (Wolverhampton), Dino Da Costa, Paolo Lazzoti, Gianfranco Petris (Fiorentina), Werner Frey, Erich Hahn (Luzern)

Own goal: Pfeiffer (Borussia Mönchengladbach) for Glasgow Rangers

CUP WINNERS' CUP 1961-62

FIRST ROUND

FC LA CHAUX DE FONDS
v LEIXÕES PORTO 6-2 (2-1)
Charriere, La Chaux de Fonds 7.09.1961

Referee: Pierre Schwinte (FRA)   Attendance: 3,194

FC LA CHAUX DE FONDS: Leo Eichmann; Kurt Leuenberger, Jean-Claude Deforel; Raymond Aubert, Willy Kernen (Cap), Gabriel Morel; André Brossard, Kurt Sommerlatt, Heinz Bertschi, Richard Jäger, Charles Antenen. Trainer: Kurt Sommerlatt

LEIXÕES: José Nunes-Rosas; Eduardo MENDES Santana, Joaquim Pacheco; Jacinto Santos, RAÚL Martins MACHADO (Cap), MÁRIO Soares VENTURA; ANTÓNIO José Santos MEDEIROS, MANUEL OLIVEIRA Santos, Osvaldo Silva, Manuel Patela, José Matos Jaburu.
Trainer: Nelson Filipo Nuñez

Goals: Antenen (9), Sommerlatt (23), Bertschi (51, 67), Jäger (52, 57), Manuel Oliveira (42, 85)

LEIXÕES PORTO
v FC LA CHAUX DE FONDS 5-0 (2-0)
Campo do Santana, Matosinhos 5.10.1961

Referee: Jean Tricot (FRA)   Attendance: 3,747

LEIXÕES: MÁRIO ROLDÃO; Eduardo MENDES Santana, Jacinto Santos, RAÚL Martins MACHADO (Cap), Joaquim Pacheco; MÁRIO Soares VENTURA, ANTÓNIO José Santos MEDEIROS, EDUARDO Oliveira GOMES; MANUEL OLIVEIRA Santos, Osvaldo Silva, Manuel Patela.
Trainer: Nelson Filipo Nuñez

LA CHAUX DE FONDS: Leo Eichmann; Kurt Leuenberger, Jean-Claude Deforel; Raymond Aubert, Willy Kernen (Cap), Gabriel Morel; André Brossard, Kurt Sommerlatt, Roberto Frigeiro, Heinz Bertschi, Charles Antenen.
Trainer: Kurt Sommerlatt

Goals: Osvaldo Silva (24, 30), Oliveira (46, 71), Mario Ventura (52)

DUNFERMLINE ATHLETIC FC
v ST. PATRICK'S ATHLETIC DUBLIN 4-1 (3-1)
East End Park, Dunfermline 12.09.1961

Referee: Arthur Holland (ENG)   Attendance: 10,890

DUNFERMLINE ATHLETIC: Edward Connachan; Cameron Fraser, William Cunningham (Cap); Roland Mailer, George Miller, John Duffy; Thomas McDonald, Alexander Smith, Charles Dickson, George Peebles, Harold Melrose.
Manager: John Stein

ST. PATRICK'S: Denis Lowry; John White, Thomas Dunne (Cap), Joseph Clarke, Seán McCarthy, Vincent O'Reilly; Brian Treacy, Patrick O'Rourke, James Redmond, Ronald Whelan, William Peyton.   Manager: James Collins

Goals: Melrose (15), Peebles (23), Dickson (28), O'Rourke (38), McDonald (87)

ST. PATRICK'S ATHLETIC
v DUNFERMLINE ATHLETIC FC 0-4 (0-3)
Tolka Park, Dublin 27.09.1961

Referee: George McCabe (ENG)   Attendance: 6,220

ST. PATRICK'S: Denis Lowry; Thomas Dunne (Cap), John White; Joseph Clarke, Seán McCarthy, Vincent O'Reilly; John McGeehan, Patrick O'Rourke, James Redmond, Ronald Whelan, William Peyton.   Manager: James Collins

DUNFERMLINE ATHLETIC: Edward Connachan; Cameron Fraser, William Cunningham (Cap); Ronald Mailer, John Williamson, George Miller; Thomas McDonald, Alexander Smith, Charles Dickson, George Peebles, Harold Melrose.   Manager: John Stein

Goals: Peebles (1, 80), Dickson (25, 31)

RAPID WIEN v SPARTAK VARNA 0-0

Prater-stadion, Wien   13.09.1961

Referee: Pietro Bonetto (ITA)   Attendance: 23,301

RAPID: Ludwig Huyer; Paul Halla, Walter Glechner, Josef Höltl; Gerhard Hanappi (Cap), Karl Giesser; Max Schmid, Walter Seitl, Robert Dienst, Rudolf Flögel, Branko Milanovic.   Trainer: Robert Körner

SPARTAK: Hristo Valtschanov; Vasil Nenov, Spiridon Filipov; Biser Dimitrov (Cap), Ilia Kirtschev, Nikola Jivkov; Gerasim Kalugerov, Blagoi Yanev, Liuben Kostov, Hristo Nikolov, Stefan Stefanov.   Trainer: Toma Zahariev

SPARTAK VARNA v RAPID WIEN 2-5 (0-2)

Iuri Gagarin stadion, Varna   27.09.1961

Referee: Giuseppe Adami (ITA)   Attendance: 18,000

SPARTAK: Hristo Valtschanov; Vasil Nenov, Spiridon Filipov; Biser Dimitrov (Cap), Ilia Kirtschev, Nikola Jivkov; Gerasim Kalugerov, Blagoi Yanev, Liuben Kostov, Hristo Nikolov, Stefan Stefanov.   Trainer: Toma Zahariev

RAPID: Ludwig Huyer; Paul Halla, Wilhelm Zaglitsch, Josef Höltl; Gerhard Hanappi (Cap), Karl Giesser; Franz Wolny, Walter Skocik, Max Schmid, Rudolf Flögel, Branko Milanovic.   Trainer: Robert Körner

Goals: Schmid (7, 84), Skocik (30), Flögel (46), Milanovic (56), Kostov (63 pen, 68)

**GLENAVON LURGAN
v LEICESTER CITY 1-4** (1-3)

Mourneview Park, Belfast   13.09.1961

Referee: George Bowman (SCO)   Attendance: 7,084

GLENAVON: Joseph Kinkead; Robert Armstrong, Edward Johnston; John Duggan, Desmond Anderson (Cap), Jackie Hughes; Samuel Wilson, William Johnston, James Jones, Stewart Campbell, Sydney Weatherup.
Manager: James McAlinden

LEICESTER: Gordon Banks; Leonard Chalmers, Richard Norman; Ian White, John King, Colin Appleton (Cap); Howard Riley, James Walsh, Kenneth Keyworth, Graham Frederick Cross, Gordon Wills.   Manager: Matthew Muirhead Gillies

Goals: Jones (14), Walsh (36, 42), Appleton (37), Keyworth (62)

**LEICESTER CITY
v GLENAVON BELFAST 3-1** (0-0)

Filbert Street stadium, Leicester   27.09.1961

Referee: Thomas Kenneth Wharton (SCO)   Att: 10,445

LEICESTER: Gordon Banks; Leonard Chalmers, Richard Norman; Ian White, John King, Colin Appleton (Cap); Howard Riley, Albert Cheesebrough, Hugh McIlmoyle, Kenneth Keyworth, Gordon Wills.
Manager: Matthew Muirhead Gillies

GLENAVON: Roy Rea; Robert Armstrong, Edward Johnston; John Duggan, Desmond Anderson (Cap), Jackie Hughes; Samuel Wilson, William Johnston, James Jones, Stewart Campbell, Sydney Weatherup.   Manager: James McAlinden

Goals: Wills (55), Keyworth (70), Wilson (74), McIlmoyle (82)

**UNION ASSOCIATION SEDAN-TORCY
v ATLÉTICO MADRID 2-3** (0-3)

Stade Emile Albeau, Sedan   13.09.1961

Referee: Johannes Malka (W. GER)   Attendance: 8,225

UA SEDAN: Jean Wyra; Maryan Synakowski, Zacharie Noah, Pierre Michelin, Louis Lemasson, Marcel Mouchel (Cap), Guy Hatchi; Maxime Fulgenzy, Faustino Silva Pinto, Claude Brény, Yannick Lebert.   Trainer: Louis Dugauguez

ATLÉTICO: Edgardo Mario MADINABEYTIA Bassi; Feliciano RIVILLA Muñoz, Jorge Bernardo GRIFFA Monferoni, Alberto CALLEJO Román (Cap); RAMIRO Rodríguez Valente, Jesús GLARÍA Roldán; Antonio DOMÍNGUEZ Martínez, ADELARDO Rodríguez Sánchez, Jorge Alberto MENDONÇA Paulino, Joaquín PEIRÓ Lucas, Enrique COLLAR Monterrubio.
Trainer: José VILLALONGA Llorente

Goals: Collar (13), Adelardo (17), Mendonça (38), Hatchi (51), Fulgenzy (76)

**ATLÉTICO MADRID
v UA SEDAN-TORCY 4-1** (3-0)

Estadio Metropolitano, Madrid   27.09.1961

Referee: Albert Dusch (W. GER)   Attendance: 32,578

ATLÉTICO: Edgardo Mario MADINABEYTIA Bassi; Isacio CALLEJA García, Jorge Bernardo GRIFFA Monferoni, Alberto CALLEJO Román (Cap); RAMIRO Rodríguez Valente, Jesús GLARÍA Roldán; Miguel JONES del Castillo, ADELARDO Rodríguez Sánchez, Jorge Alberto MENDONÇA Paulino, Joaquín PEIRÓ Lucas, Enrique COLLAR Monterrubio.
Trainer: José VILLALONGA Llorente

UA SEDAN: Alexandre Roszak; Maxime Fulgenzy, Zacharie Noah; Pierre Michelin, Maryan Synakowski, Marcel Mouchel (Cap); Emilio Salaber, Claude Brény, Faustino Silva Pinto, Guy Hatchi, Yannick Lebert.   Trainer: Louis Dugauguez

Goals: Peiró (25, 38), Mendonça (27), Adelardo (75), Salaber (89)

FLORIANA FC
v ÚJPESTI DOZSA BUDAPEST 2-5 (0-3)
Empire Stadium, Valletta 17.09.1961
Referee: Raoul Righi (ITA)   Attendance: 11,581
FLORIANA: Joseph Alamango; Emmanuel Debattista, Edward Azzopardi; Joseph Farrugia, Lino Farrugia, Emmanuel Borg (Cap); Charles McKay, Nazzareno Alamango, William Dalli, Anthony Cauchi, Publius D'Emanuelle.
Trainer: James Wilson
ÚJPESTI DOZSA: Gábor Török; Károly Rajna (Cap), György Borsányi, Kálmán Sóvári; Benő Káposzta, József Szini; Sándor Lenkei, János Göröcs, Ernö Solymosi, Béla Kuharszki, Ferenc Rossi.   Trainer: Géza Kalocsay
Goals: Göröcs (7), Rossi (16), Kuharszki (30, 74), Cauchi (63, 87), Solymosi (85)

ÚJPEST DOZSA BUDAPEST
v FLORIANA FC 10-2 (5-1)
Népstadion, Budapest 27.09.1961
Referee: Panagiotis Nikiforakis (GRE)   Attendance: 10,000
ÚJPESTI DOZSA: Gábor Török; Károly Rajna (Cap), Pál Várhidi (Cap), Kálmán Sóvári; József Szini, György Borsányi; Ferenc Bene, János Göröcs, Ernö Solymosi, Béla Kuharszki, László Bacskay.   Trainer: Géza Kalocsay
FLORIANA: Joseph Alamango; Emmanuel Debattista, Edward Azzopardi; Charles McKay, Lino Farrugia, James Alfred Vella; Nazzareno Alamango, Emmanuel Borg (Cap), Anthony Cauchi, William Dalli, Anthony Sultana.
Trainer: James Wilson
Goals: Göröcs (13, 43, 47, 58), Solymosi (22, 63, 71, 87), Kuharszki (29, 38), Dalli (41), Cauchi (69)

SWANSEA TOWN v MOTOR JENA 2-2 (1-2)
LASK-Platz, Linz 16.10.1961
Referee: Friedrich Seipelt (AUS)   Attendance: 3,643
SWANSEA TOWN: Noel Dwyer; Alan Sanders, Harold Griffiths; Michael Johnson, Melvyn Tudor George Nurse (Cap), Brian Hughes; Barrie Jones, Reginald Davies, Brayley Reynolds, Herbert John Williams, Colin Webster.
Manager: Trevor Morris
MOTOR: Harald Fritzsche; Hilmar Ahnert, Siegfried Woitzat (Cap); Heinz Marx, Dieter Stricksner, Waldemar Eglmeyer; Roland Ducke, Helmut Müller, Peter Ducke, Franz Röhrer, Dieter Lange.   Trainer: Georg Buschner
Sent off: Webster (71)
Goals: Lange (14), Reynolds (26), R. Ducke (32), Nurse (70 pen)

MOTOR JENA v SWANSEA TOWN 5-1 (2-1)
Ernst Abbé Sportfeld, Jena 18.10.1961
Referee: Leopold Silvayn Horn (HOL)   Attendance: 14,749
MOTOR: Harald Fritzsche; Hans-Joachim Otto, Siegfried Woitzat (Cap); Heinz Marx, Dieter Stricksner, Waldemar Eglmeyer; Roland Ducke, Helmut Müller, Peter Ducke, Franz Röhrer, Dieter Lange.   Trainer: Georg Buschner
SWANSEA TOWN: Noel Dwyer; Alan Sanders, Harold Griffiths; Michael Johnson, Melvyn Tudor George Nurse (Cap), Brian Hughes; Reginald Davies, Herbert John Williams, Brayley Reynolds, Graham Williams, Barrie Jones.
Manager: Trevor Morris
Goals: Reynolds (8), Müller (15, 26), Lange (61), P. Ducke (75), R. Ducke (80)

SECOND ROUND

WERDER BREMEN v ÅRHUS GF 2-0 (1-0)
Weserstadion, Bremen 25.10.1961
Referee: Erik L. Johansson (SWE)   Attendance: 18,570
WERDER: Heinrich Kokartis; Edmund Rupoczinski, Walter Nachtwey; Helmut Schimeczek, Arnold Schütz, Helmut Jagielski; Max Lorenz, Willi Schröder (Cap), Horst Barth, Willi Soya, Klaus Hänel.   Trainer: Georg Knöpfle
ÅRHUS GF: Lars Windeløv; Kaj Christensen, Arne Sørensen; Bruno Jensen, Hans Christian Nielsen, Jörgen Olesen; Thorkild Rydahl, Leif Nielsen, John Amdisen (Cap), Aage Rou Jensen, Torsten Lindvald.   Trainer: Géza Toldi
Goals: Barth (7), Schütz (76)

ÅRHUS GF v WERDER BREMEN 2-3 (0-1)
Idraetspark, Århus 1.11.1961
Referee: Erik L. Johansson (SWE)   Attendance: 6,810
ÅRHUS GF: Lars Windeløv; Kaj Christensen, Arne Sørensen; Bruno Jensen, Hans Christian Nielsen, Jörgen Olesen; John Jensen, John Amdisen (Cap), Leif Nielsen, Aage Rou Jensen, Torsten Lindvald.   Trainer: Géza Toldi
WERDER: Heinrich Kokartis; Josef Piontek, Walter Nachtwey; Helmut Schimeczek, Arnold Schütz, Helmut Jagielski; Max Lorenz, Willi Schröder (Cap), Horst Barth, Willi Soya, Klaus Hänel.   Trainer: Georg Knöpfle
Goals: Barth (36), Hänel (49), Amdisen (66), Lorenz (71), Bruno Jensen (87)

**DUNFERMLINE ATHLETIC FC FIFE
v FK VARDAR SKOPLJE 5-0** (3-0)
East End Park, Dunfermline 25.10.1961

Referee: Jozef Casteleyn (BEL)   Attendance: 11,958

DUNFERMLINE ATHLETIC: Edward Connachan; Cameron Fraser, William Cunningham (Cap); Ronald Mailer, John Williamson, George Miller; Thomas McDonald, Alexander Smith, Charles Dickson, George Peebles, Harald Melrose.   Manager: John Stein

VARDAR: Kosta Milosevski; Branko Hristovski, Caslav Bozinovski, Ilija Moisov; Slavko Dacevski, Dragan Trajcevski; Mirko Ilijevski, Vladimir Zelenika, Andon Doncevski (Cap), Petar Sulincevski, Tome Jakimovski.
Trainer: Kiril Simonovski

Sent off: Trajcevski (63)

Goals: Smith (7), Dickson (28, 43), Melrose (56), Peebles (84)

ATLÉTICO MADRID v LEICESTER CITY 2-0 (0-0)
Estadio Metropolitano, Madrid 15.11.1961

Referee: Michel Kitabdjian (FRA)   Attendance: 27,460

ATLÉTICO: Edgardo Mario MADINABEYTIA Bassi; Feliciano RIVILLA Muñoz, Jorge Bernardo GRIFFA Monferoni, José Antonio RODRÍGUEZ López; Alberto CALLEJO Román (Cap), Isacio CALLEJA García; Vicente MEDINA García, ADELARDO Rodríguez Sánchez, Miguel JONES del Castillo, Jorge Alberto MENDONÇA Paulino, Enrique COLLAR Monterrubio.
Trainer: José VILLALONGA Llorente

LEICESTER CITY: Gordon Banks; John King, Richard Norman; Leonard Chalmers, Graham Frederick Cross, Ian White; Howard Riley, Kenneth Keyworth, Gordon Wills, Colin Appleton (Cap), John Mitten.
Manager: Matthew Muirhead Gillies

Goals: Collar (60 pen), Jones (75)

**VARDAR SKOPLJE
v DUNFERMLINE ATHLETIC 2-0** (1-0)
Gradski, Skoplje 8.11.1961

Referee: Dimitar A. Rumenchev (BUL)   Attendance: 6,700

VARDAR: Perko Perkovski; Nikola Bosalevski, Caslav Bozinovski, Petar Andjusev; Zivko Popovski, Slavko Dacevski (Cap); Mirko Ilijevski, Vladimir Zelenika, Petar Sulincevski, Dragoljub Lakic, Tome Jakimovski.   Trainer: Kiril Simonovski

DUNFERMLINE ATHLETIC: Edward Connachan; Cameron Fraser, William Cunningham (Cap); Ronald Mailer, John Williamson, George Miller; Thomas McDonald, Alexander Smith, Charles Dickson, George Peebles, Harold Melrose.   Manager: John Stein

Goals: Sulincevski (11), Jakimovski (75)

**AC FIORENTINA FIRENZE
v RAPID WIEN 3-1** (1-0)
Stadio Comunale, Firenze 25.10.1961

Referee: Gottfried Dienst (SWI)   Attendance: 6,828

FIORENTINA: Enrico Albertosi; Saul Malatrasi, Enzo Robotti; Amilcare Ferretti, Alberto Orzan (Cap), Rino Marchesi; Kurt Hamrin, Torbjörn Jonsson, Aurelio Milani, Luigi Milan, Gianfranco Petris.   Trainer: Nándor Hidegkuti

RAPID: Ludwig Huyer; Paul Halla, Walter Glechner, Josef Höltl; Gerhard Hanappi (Cap), Karl Giesser; Walter Seitl, Walter Skocik, Max Schmid, Rudolf Flögel, Branko Milanovic.
Trainer: Robert Körner

Goals: Milani (13), Hamrin (50), Jonsson (67), Seitl (81)

LEICESTER CITY v ATLÉTICO MADRID 1-1 (0-0)
Filbert Street, Leicester 25.10.1961

Referee: Pierre Schwinte (FRA)   Attendance: 25,527

LEICESTER CITY: Gordon Banks; Leonard Chalmers, Richard Norman; Frank McLintock, John King, Ian White; Howard Riley, Kenneth Keyworth, Gordon Wills, Colin Appleton (Cap), John Mitten.
Manager: Matthew Muirhead Gillies

ATLÉTICO: Edgardo Mario MADINABEYTIA Bassi; Feliciano RIVILLA Muñoz, Jorge Bernardo GRIFFA Monferoni, Isacio CALLEJA García; RAMIRO Rodríguez Valente, Alberto CALLEJO Román (Cap); José Antonio RODRÍGUEZ López, Vicente MEDINA García, Jorge Alberto MENDONÇA Paulino, Joaquín PEIRÓ Lucas, Enrique COLLAR Monterrubio.   Trainer: José VILLALONGA Llorente

Goals: Keyworth (56), Mendonça (89)

**RAPID WIEN
v AC FIORENTINA FIRENZE 2-6** (0-2)
Prater, Wien 22.11.1961

Referee: Daniel Mellet (SWI)   Attendance: 16,798

RAPID: Ludwig Huyer; Johann Steup, Walter Glechner, Josef Höltl; Gerhard Hanappi (Cap), Karl Giesser; Paul Halla, Walter Skocik, Max Schmid, Rudolf Flögel, Josef Bertalan.
Trainer: Robert Körner

FIORENTINA: Enrico Albertosi; Saul Malatrasi, Sergio Castelletti; Amilcare Ferretti, Alberto Orzan (Cap), Rino Marchesi; Kurt Hamrin, Torbjörn Jonsson, Aurelio Milani, Lucio dell'Angelo, Gianfranco Petris.
Trainer: Nándor Hidegkuti

Goals: Milani (28, 59, 70), dell'Angelo (40), Jonsson (50), Hamrin (66), Schmid (85, 89)

**AJAX AMSTERDAM v
ÚJPEST DOZSA BUDAPEST 2-1** (2-0)

Olympisch, Amsterdam   2.11.1961

Referee: Werner Treichel (W. GER)   Attendance: 16,358

AJAX: Lambert Jacobus Hoogerman; Pieter Ouderland, Anton Pronk; Gerrit Van Mourik (Cap), Werner Schaaphok, Bernardus Muller; Jesaia Swart, Hendrik Groot, Cornelis Groot, Jacobus Theodorus Prins, Peter Hendrik Petersen.   Trainer: Keith Spurgeon

ÚJPEST DOZSA: Gábor Török; Benő Káposzta, Károly Rajna (Cap), Kálmán Sóvári; Ernö Solymosi, György Borsányi; Sándor Lenkei, János Göröcs, István Halápi, Béla Kuharszky, Ferenc Rossi.   Trainer: Géza Kalocsay

Goals: H. Groot (3, 20), Kuharszky (81)

**DINAMO ZILINA
v OLIMPIAKOS PEIRAIAS 1-0** (1-0)

Pod Dubnom stadium, Zilina   30.11.1961

Referee: Gyula Gere (HUN)   Attendance: 8,512

DINAMO: František Plach; Anton Kopčan, Alexander Horváth, Ján Saga; Jozef Marusin, Ján Urbanic; Vladimír Pisárik, Július David, Viliam Jakubcik (Cap), Milan Mravec, Pavol Majercik.   Trainer: Ján Kluciar

OLIMPIAKOS: Stathis Tsanaktsis; Dimitris Plessas, Nikos Kambolis, Giagkos Simantiris; Savas Papazoglou, Kostas Polihroniou (Cap); Aristidis Papazoglou, Giorgos Sideris, Panagiotis Barbalias, Dimitris Stefanakos, Kostas Papazoglou.   Trainer: Kiril Simonovski (YUG)

Sent off: David (58), A. Papazoglou (59), Horváth (78), S. Papazoglou (78)

Goal: Pisárik (16)

**ÚJPEST DÓZSA BUDAPEST
v AJAX AMSTERDAM 3-1** (1-0)

Népstadion, Budapest   29.11.1961

Referee: Johannes Malka (W. GER)   Attendance: 3,178

ÚJPEST DÓZSA: Gábor Török; Benó Káposzta, Károly Rajna (Cap), Kálmán Sóvári; Ernö Solymosi, József Szini; Ferenc Bene, János Göröcs, Sándor Lenkei, Béla Kuharszky, Ferenc Rossi.   Trainer: Géza Kalocsay

AJAX: Lambert Jacobus Hoogerman; Pieter Ouderland, Anton Pronk; Gerrit Van Mourik (Cap), Bernardus Muller, Jan Dahrs; Adrianus Visser, Jesaia Swart, Hendrik Groot, Cornelis Groot, Peter Hendrik Petersen.   Trainer: Keith Spurgeon

Goals: Bene (15), Göröcs (65, 68), Petersen (82)

**LEIXÕES PORTO
v PROGRESUL BUCUREȘTI 1-1** (0-1)

Estádio José Alvalade, Lisboa   23.11.1961

Referee: Josef Stoll (AUS)   Attendance: 7,226

LEIXÕES: MÁRIO ROLDÃO; Eduardo MENDES Santana, RAÚL Martins MACHADO (Cap), MANUEL Fernando Martins MOREIRA; MÁRIO Soares VENTURA, JACINTO Santos; ANTÓNIO José Santos MEDEIROS, Osvaldo Silva, MANUEL OLIVEIRA Santos, EDUARDO Oliveira GOMES, Manuel Patela.   Trainer: Nelson Filipo Nuñez

PROGRESUL: Petre Mîndru; Ioan Nedelcu, Alexandru Karikas (Cap), Valeriu Soare; Nicolae Ioniță, Alexandru Pașcanu; Nicolae Oaidă, Șerban Protopopescu, Marin Voinea, George Marin, Dumitru Baboie.   Trainer: Ion Lupaș

Goals: Karikas (19), Osvaldo (52)

**OLYMPIAKOS PEIRAIAS
v DINAMO ZILINA 2-3** (1-2)

Karaiskaki, Athina   22.11.1961

Referee: Andor Dorogi (HUN)   Attendance: 7,424

OLIMPIAKOS: Savvas Theodoridis; Dimitris Plessas, Nikos Kambolis, Giagkos Simantiris; Savas Papazoglou, Kostas Polihroniou (Cap); Aristidis Papazoglou, Giorgos Sideris, Panagiotis Barbalias, Kiriakos Kalkitanidis, Panagiotis Spetseris.   Trainer: Kiril Simonovski (YUG)

DINAMO: František Plach; Anton Kopčan, Alexander Horváth, Ján Saga; Jozef Marusin, Ján Urbanic; Vladimír Pisárik, Július David, Viliam Jakubcik (Cap), Milan Mravec, Pavol Majercik.   Trainer: Ján Kluciar

Goals: Pisárik (4), Sideris (15, 49), Mravec (28), David (87)

**PROGRESUL BUCUREȘTI
v LEIXÕES PORTO 0-1** (0-0)

23 August, București   30.11.1961

Referee: Franz Mayer (AUS)   Attendance: 40,000

PROGRESUL: Petre Mîndru; Nicolae Smărăndescu, Alexandru Karikas (Cap), Ioan Nedelcu; Nicolae Ioniță, Alexandru Pașcanu; Nicolae Oaidă, Șerban Protopopescu, Marin Voinea, George Marin, Dumitru Baboie.   Trainer: Ion Lupaș

LEIXÕES: MÁRIO ROLDÃO; Eduardo MENDES Santana, MANUEL Fernando Martins MOREIRA, JACINTO Santos; RAÚL Martins MACHADO, JOAQUIM PACHECO (Cap); ANTÓNIO José Santos MEDEIROS, MÁRIO Soares VENTURA, Osvaldo Silva, MANUEL OLIVEIRA Santos, EDUARDO Oliveira GOMES.   Trainer: Nelson Filipo Nuñez

Goal: Osvaldo (61)

MOTOR JENA v ALIANCE DUDELANGE 7-0 (3-0)
Ernst-Abbé-Sportfeld, Jena   17.12.1961

Referee: Pieter Paulus Roomer (HOL)   Attendance: 6,250

MOTOR: Harald Fritzsche; Hans-Joachim Otto, Hilmar Ahnert; Heinz Marx, Dieter Stricksner, Waldemar Eglmeyer; Roland Ducke, Helmut Müller, Peter Ducke, Dieter Lange, Horst Kirsch (Cap).   Trainer: Georg Buschner

ALIANCE: Bruno Zangarini; Dino Piccinini, Fernand Meneghetti; Jules Zambon, Louis Dickers, Pierre Capitani; Alfiero Venanzi, Jacques Bellion, Henri Cirelli (Cap), Guerino Capitani, Narcisse De Paoli.   Trainer: Benny Michaux

Goals: Kirsch (1, 28), Müller (41), Lange (47, 64), P. Ducke (63), Piccinini (72 og)

ALIANCE DUDELANGE v MOTOR JENA 2-2 (1-0)
Georgi Dimitroff stadium, Erfurt   19.12.1961

Referee: Pieter Paulus Roomer (HOL)   Attendance: 1,383

ALIANCE: Bruno Zangarini; Dino Piccinini, Fernand Meneghetti; Jules Zambon, Louis Dickers, Pierre Capitani; Alfiero Venanzi, Jacques Bellion, Jos Luzzi (Cap), Henri Cirelli, Narcisse De Paoli.   Trainer: Benny Michaux

MOTOR: Harald Fritzsche; Heinz Wilsch, Hilmar Ahnert; Heinz Marx, Dieter Stricksner, Waldemar Eglmeyer; Peter Rock, Helmut Müller, Peter Ducke, Dieter Lange, Horst Kirsch (Cap).   Trainer: Georg Buschner

Goals: Cirelli (39), Bellion (53), Kirsch (72), P. Ducke (76)

QUARTER-FINALS

**WERDER BREMEN
v ATLÉTICO MADRID 1-1** (0-0)
Weserstadion, Bremen   17.01.1962

Referee: Marcel Raeymaekers (BEL)   Attendance: 23,705

WERDER: Heinrich Kokartis; Josef Piontek, Helmut Jagielski, Walter Nachtwey; Max Lorenz, Helmut Schimeczek; Gerhard Zebrowski, Arnold Schütz (Cap), Horst Barth, Willi Soya, Klaus Hänel.   Trainer: Georg Knöpfle

ATLÉTICO: Edgardo Mario MADINABEYTIA Bassi; Feliciano RIVILLA Muñoz, Antonio González Álvarez "CHUZO", Isacio CALLEJA García; Amador CORTÉS García, Manuel Bermúdez Arias "POLO"; Miguel JONES del Castillo, ADELARDO Rodríguez Sánchez, Jorge Alberto MENDONÇA Paulino, Joaquín PEIRÓ Lucas, Enrique COLLAR Monterrubio (Cap).   Trainer: José VILLALONGA Llorente

Goals: Jones (71), Soya (85)

**ATLÉTICO MADRID
v WERDER BREMEN 3-1** (2-1)
Estadio Metropolitano, Madrid   28.02.1962

Referee: Josef Gulde (SWI)   Attendance: 27,692

ATLÉTICO: Manuel Pazos; Feliciano RIVILLA Muñoz, Alberto CALLEJO Román (Cap), Isacio CALLEJA García; RAMIRO Rodríguez Valente, Jesús GLARÍA Roldán; José RIBES Flores, ADELARDO Rodríguez Sánchez, Miguel JONES del Castillo, Joaquín PEIRÓ Lucas, Enrique COLLAR Monterrubio.   Trainer: José VILLALONGA Llorente

WERDER: Heinrich Kokartis; Josef Piontek, Helmut Jagielski, Walter Nachtwey; Max Lorenz, Helmut Schimeczek; Gerhard Zebrowski, Willi Schröder (Cap), Arnold Schütz, Willi Soya, Horst Barth.   Trainer: Georg Knöpfle

Goals: Jagielski (2 og), Peiró (30), Schröder (37), Adelardo (61)

**ÚJPESTI DÓZSA BUDAPEST
v ATHLETIC DUNFERMLINE 4-3** (2-2)
Népstadion, Budapest   13.02.1962

Referee: Trajan Ivanovski (YUG)   Attendance: 15,000

ÚJPESTI DÓZSA: Ferenc Lung; Benő Káposzta, Károly Rajna (Cap), Kálmán Sóvári; Ernö Solymosi, György Borsányi; Ferenc Bene, János Göröcs, Sándor Lenkei, Béla Kuharszki, Ferenc Rossi.   Trainer: Géza Kalocsay

ATHLETIC DUNFERMLINE: Edward Connachan; James Thomson, William Cunningham (Cap); Ronald Mailer, John Williamson, George Miller; Thomas McDonald, Alexander Smith, Charles Dickson, Harold Melrose, George Peebles.   Manager: John Stein

Goals: Smith (1), McDonald (8, 85), Bene (29), Lenkei (30), Solymosi (74 pen), Göröcs (81)

**DUNFERMLINE ATHLETIC
v ÚJPESTI DÓZSA BUDAPEST 0-1** (0-0)
East End Park, Dunfermline   20.02.1962

Referee: Tage Sørensen (DEN)   Attendance: 24,049

ATHLETIC DUNFERMLINE: Edward Connachan; Cameron Fraser, John Williamson, William Cunningham (Cap); James Thomson, George Miller; Thomas McDonald, Alexander Smith, Charles Dickson, Harold Melrose, George Peebles.   Manager: John Stein

ÚJPESTI DÓZSA: Ferenc Lung; Benő Káposzta, Károly Rajna (Cap), Kálmán Sóvári; Ernö Solymosi, György Borsányi; Ferenc Bene, János Göröcs, Sándor Lenkei, Béla Kuharszki, Ferenc Rossi.   Trainer: Géza Kalocsay

Goal: Bene (51)

**DINAMO ZILINA
v AC FIORENTINA FIRENZE 3-2** (2-0)
Pod Dubnom stadion, Zilina 21.02.1962
Referee: Kurt Tschenscher (W. GER)   Attendance: 9,543
DINAMO: František Plach; Ján Urbanic, Ján Saga; Vladimír Minarech, Anton Kopčan, Jozef Marusin; Vladimír Pisárik, Pavol Majercik, Viliam Jakubcik (Cap), Milan Mravec, Eduard Hancin.   Trainer: Ján Kluciar

FIORENTINA: Enrico Albertosi; Saul Malatrasi, Enzo Robotti; Amilcare Ferretti, Alberto Orzan (Cap), Claudio Rimbaldo; Fernando Veneranda, Lucio dell'Angelo, Aurelio Milani, Luigi Milan, Gianfranco Petris.
Trainer: Nándor Hidegkuti

Goals: Jakubcik (7, 63), Majercik (42), Milan (50), dell'Angelo (85)

LEIXÕES PORTO v MOTOR JENA 1-3 (0-1)
Freundschaft, Gera 25.02.1962
Referee: Stanislav Fencl (CZE)   Attendance: 9,738
LEIXÕES: MÁRIO ROLDÃO; Eduardo MENDES Santana, JOAQUIM PACHECO (Cap); MÁRIO Soares VENTURA, RAÚL Martins MACHADO, JACINTO Santos; Francisco Carlos Correia de Lima "CHICO", Osvaldo Silva, MANUEL OLIVEIRA Santos, EDUARDO Oliveira GOMES, ANTÓNIO José Santos MEDEIROS.   Trainer: Nelson Filipo Nuñez

MOTOR: Harald Fritzsche; Hans-Joachim Otto, Hilmar Ahnert; Heinz Marx, Dieter Stricksner, Waldemar Eglmeyer; Roland Ducke, Helmut Müller, Horst Kirsch (Cap), Franz Röhrer, Dieter Lange.   Trainer: Georg Buschner

Goals: Kirsch (8), Osvaldo Silva (56), Lange (59), Röhrer (80)

SEMI-FINALS

**AC FIORENTINA FIRENZE
v DINAMO ZILINA 2-0** (2-0)
Stadio Comunale, Firenze 27.02.1962
Referee: Friedrich Seipelt (AUS)   Attendance: 8,117
FIORENTINA: Enrico Albertosi; Enzo Robotti, Sergio Castelletti; Amilcare Ferretti, Alberto Orzan (Cap), Piero Gonfiantini; Kurt Hamrin, Rino Marchesi, Luigi Milan, Lucio dell'Angelo, Gianfranco Petris.   Trainer: Nándor Hidegkuti
DINAMO: František Plach; Ján Urbanic, Ján Saga; Alexander Horváth, Anton Kopčan, Jozef Marusin; Vladimír Pisarik, Pavol Majercik, Viliam Jakubcik (Cap), Milan Mravec, Eduard Hancin.   Trainer: Ján Kluciar

Goals: Ferretti (38), Hamrin (41)

**FIORENTINA FIRENZE
v ÚJPEST DOZSA BUDAPEST 2-0** (1-0)
Stadio Comunale, Firenze 21.03.1962
Referee: John Kelly (ENG)   Attendance: 4,143
FIORENTINA: Giuliano Sarti; Enzo Robotti, Sergio Castelletti; Amilcare Ferretti, Alberto Orzan (Cap), Piero Gonfiantini; Kurt Hamrin, Luigi Milan, Aurelio Milani, Lucio dell'Angelo, Can Bartu.   Trainer: Nándor Hidegkuti
ÚJPEST DÓZSA: Ferenc Lung; Pál Várhidi, Károly Rajna (Cap), Kálmán Sóvári; Benő Káposzta, György Borsányi; Ferenc Bene, János Göröcs, József Szini, Béla Kuharszky, Ferenc Rossi.   Trainer: Géza Kalocsay

Goals: Hamrin (6, 47)

MOTOR JENA v LEIXÕES PORTO 1-1 (0-1)
Ernst Abbé Sportfeld, Jena 22.02.1962
Referee: Milan Kusak (CZE)   Attendance: 14,273
MOTOR: Harald Fritzsche; Hans-Joachim Otto, Hilmar Ahnert; Heinz Marx, Dieter Stricksner, Waldemar Eglmeyer; Roland Ducke, Helmut Müller, Horst Kirsch (Cap), Franz Röhrer, Dieter Lange.   Trainer: Georg Buschner
LEIXÕES: MÁRIO ROLDÃO; Eduardo MENDES Santana, RAÚL Martins MACHADO (Cap), JACINTO Santos; MÁRIO Soares VENTURA, Raúl Oliveira; Francisco Carlos Correia de Lima "CHICO"; Osvaldo Silva, MANUEL OLIVEIRA Santos, EDUARDO Oliveira GOMES, ANTÓNIO José Santos MEDEIROS.   Trainer: Nelson Filipo Nuñez

Goals: Manuel Oliveira (44), Marx (89)

**ÚJPESTI DÓZSA BUDAPEST
v FIORENTINA FIRENZE 0-1** (0-0)
Népstadion, Budapest 11.04.1962
Referee: Friedrich Mayer (AUS)   Attendance: 21,277
ÚJPEST DÓZSA: Ferenc Lung; Benó Káposzta, Pál Várhidi (Cap), Kálman Sóvári; Ernö Solymosi, József Szini; Ferenc Bene, János Göröcs, István Halápi, Béla Kuharszky, Ferenc Rossi.   Trainer: Géza Kalocsay
FIORENTINA: Enrico Albertosi; Enzo Robotti (Cap), Sergio Castelletti; Amilcare Ferretti, Piero Gonfiantini, Claudio Rimbaldo; Kurt Hamrin, Can Bartu, Luigi Milan, Lucio dell'Angelo, Gianfraco Petris.   Trainer: Nándor Hidegkuti

Sent off: Milan (40) and Szini (40)

Goal: Bartu (56)

MOTOR JENA v ATLÉTICO MADRID 0-1 (0-0)
Ernst Abbe Sportfeld, Jena   28.03.1962
Referee: Bengt Lundell (SWE)   Attendance: 22,523
MOTOR: Harald Fritzsche; Hans-Joachim Otto, Dieter Stricksner, Hilmar Ahnert; Heinz Marx, Waldemar Eglmeyer; Roland Ducke, Helmut Müller, Peter Ducke, Dieter Lange, Horst Kirsch (Cap).   Trainer: Georg Buschner
ATLÉTICO: Edgardo Mario MADINABEYTIA Bassi; Feliciano RIVILLA Muñoz, Antonio González Álvarez "CHUZO", Isacio CALLEJA García; RAMIRO Rodríguez Valente, Jesús GLARÍA Roldán; Miguel JONES del Castillo, ADELARDO Rodríguez Sánchez, Jorge Alberto MENDONÇA Paulino, Joaquín PEIRÓ Lucas, Enrique COLLAR Monterrubio (Cap).   Trainer: José VILLALONGA Llorente

Goal: Peiró (61)

ATLÉTICO MADRID v MOTOR JENA 4-0 (2-0)
Malmö Stadion   11.04.1962
Referee: Lucien van Nuffel (BEL)   Attendance: 4,605
ATLÉTICO: Edgardo Mario MADINABEYTIA Bassi; Feliciano RIVILLA Muñoz, Antonio González Álvarez "CHUZO", Isacio CALLEJA García; RAMIRO Rodríguez Valente, Jesús GLARÍA Roldán; Miguel JONES del Castillo, ADELARDO Rodríguez Sánchez, Jorge Alberto MENDONÇA Paulino, Joaquín PEIRÓ Lucas, Enrique COLLAR Monterrubio (Cap).   Trainer: José VILLALONGA Llorente
MOTOR: Harald Fritzsche; Hans-Joachim Otto, Dieter Stricksner, Hilmar Ahnert; Siegfried Woitzat (Cap), Waldemar Eglmeyer; Roland Ducke, Helmut Müller, Peter Ducke, Dieter Lange, Horst Kirsch.   Trainer: Georg Buschner

Goals: Mendonça (14, 60), Jones (18, 54)

FINAL

CLUB ATLÉTICO MADRID
v AC FIORENTINA FIRENZE 1-1 (1-1)
Hampden Park, Glasgow   10.05.1962
Referee: Thomas Kenneth Wharton (SCO)   Att: 29,066
ATLÉTICO: Edgardo Mario MADINABEYTIA Bassi; Feliciano RIVILLA Muñoz, Antonio González Álvarez "CHUZO", Isacio CALLEJA García; RAMIRO Rodríguez Valente, Jesús Jordan GLARÍA Roldán, Miguel JONES del Castillo, ADELARDO Rodríguez Sánchez, Jorge Alberto MENDONÇA Paulino, Joaquín PEIRÓ Lucas, Enrique COLLAR Monterrubio (Cap).
Trainer: José VILLALONGA Llorente
FIORENTINA: Giuliano Sarti; Alberto Orzan (Cap), Sergio Castelletti; Amilcare Ferretti, Piero Gonfiantini, Claudio Rimbaldo; Kurt Hamrin, Can Bartu, Aurelio Milani, Lucio dell'Angelo, Gianfranco Petris.   Trainer: Nándor Hidegkuti

Goals: Peiró (11), Hamrin (27)

FINAL REPLAY

CLUB ATLÉTICO MADRID
v AC FIORENTINA FIRENZE 3-0 (2-0)
Neckarstadion, Stuttgart   5.09.1962
Referee: Kurt Tschenscher (W. GER)   Attendance: 38,120
ATLÉTICO: Edgardo Mario MADINABEYTIA Bassi; Feliciano RIVILLA Muñoz, Isacio CALLEJA García, RAMIRO Rodríguez Valente, Jorge Bernardo GRIFFA Monferoni, Jesús GLARÍA Roldán, Miguel JONES del Castillo, ADELARDO Rodríguez Sánchez, Jorge Alberto MENDONÇA Paulino, Joaquín PEIRÓ Lucas, Enrique COLLAR Monterrubio (Cap).
Trainer: José VILLALONGA Llorente

FIORENTINA: Enrico Albertosi; Enzo Robotti, Sergio Castelletti; Saul Malatrasi, Alberto Orzan (Cap), Rino Marchesi; Kurt Hamrin, Amilcare Ferretti, Aurelio Milani, Lucio dell'Angelo, Gianfranco Petris.
Trainer: Nándor Hidegkuti

Goals: Jones (8), Mendonça (26), Peiró (58)

Goalscorers Cup-Winners' Cup 1961-62:

8 goals: János Göröcs (Újpesti Dózsa Budapest)

6 goals: Kurt Hamrin (Fiorentina Firenze), Ernö Solymosi (Újpesti Dózsa), Jorge Alberto MENDONÇA Paulino, Joaquín PEIRÓ Lucas (Atlético Madrid)

5 goals: Charles Dickson (Dunfermline), Manuel Oliveira, Osvaldo Silva (Leixões Porto), Miguel JONES del Castillo (Atlético Madrid), Béla Kuharszky (Újpesti Dózsa), Dieter Lange (Motor Jena)

4 goals: Max Schmid (Rapid Wien), Horst Kirsch (Motor Jena), Aurelio Milani (Fiorentina), G. Peebles (Dunfermline)

3 goals: Cauchi (Floriana), Keyworth (Leicester), McDonald (Dunfermline), Adelardo (Atlético Madrid), Bene (Újpesti), Müller, P. Ducke (Motor Jena)

2 goals: Bertschi, Jäger (La Chaux de Fonds), Kostov (Spartak Varna), Walsh (Leicester), H.Groot (Ajax Amsterdam), Sideris (Olimpiakos Pireas), Barth (Werder Bremen), Melrose, Smith (Athletic Dunfermline), Jakubcik, Pisárik (Dinamo Zilina), Collar (Atlético Madrid), R. Ducke (Motor Jena), dell'Angelo, Jonsson (Fiorentina)

1 goal: Antenen, Sommerlatt (La Chaux de Fonds), O'Rourke (St.Patrick's), Wilson, Jones (Glenavon), Hatchi, Fulgenzy, Salaber (Sedan), Dalli (Floriana), G.Williams, Reynolds, Nurse (Swansea), Amdisen, Bruno Jensen (Århus), Sulincevski, Jakimovski (Vardar), Wills, McIlmoyle, Appleton (Leicester), Seitl (Rapid Wien), Petersen (Ajax Amsterdam), Karikas (Progresul Buc), Cirelli, Bellion (Aliance Dudelange), Soya, Schröder, Schütz, Hänel, Lorenz (Werder), Skocik, Flögel, Milanovic (Rapid Wien), Majercik, Mravec, David (Dinamo Zilina), Mario Ventura (Leixões), Lenkei, Rossi (Újpesti), Marx, Röhrer (Motor Jena), Bartu, Milan, Ferretti (Fiorentina)

Own goals: Piccinini (Aliance Dudelange) for (Motor Jena), Jagielski (Werder Bremen) for Atlético Madrid

CUP WINNERS' CUP 1962-63

FIRST ROUND

**CERCLE SPORTIF ALLIANCE DUDELANGE
v BOLDKLUBBEN 1909 ODENSE 1-1** (0-0)
Emile Mayrisch, Esch-sur-Alzette 5.09.1962
Referee: Joseph Hannet (BEL)   Attendance: 1,109
CS ALLIANCE: Bruno Zangarini; Dino Piccinini, Fernand Meneghetti; Jos Luzzi, Louis Dickers (Cap), Pierre Capitani; Paul Strasser, Alfiero Venanzi, Jules Zambon, Jacques Bellion, Narcisse De Paoli.   Trainer: Benny Michaux
BK 1909: Svend Aage Rask; Erling Linde Larsen, Bent Nielsen; Boris Christensen, Bruno Eliasen (Cap), Per Jacobsen; Palle Kähler, John Danielsen, Jörgen Petersen, Palle Hansen, Mogens Berg.   Trainer: Alfons Ramlein
Goals: Petersen (50), Zambon (55)

**BK 1909 ODENSE
v CS ALIANCE DUDELANGE 8-1** (2-1)
Odense stadion 18.09.1962
Referee: Gerhard Schulenburg (W. GER)   Attendance: 5,105
BK 1909: Svend Aage Rask; Erling Linde Larsen, Jörgen Rask; Hans Madsen, Bruno Eliasen (Cap), Boris Christensen; Mogens Engström, Erling Nielsen, Arno Hansen, John Danielsen, Mogens Berg.   Trainer: Alfons Ramlein
CS ALLIANCE: Bruno Zangarini; Erny Fattebene, Fernand Meneghetti; Dino Piccinini, Louis Dickers (Cap), Jos Luzzi; Paul Strasser, Jules Zambon, Alfiero Venanzi, Narcisse De Paoli, Guerino Capitani.   Trainer: Benny Michaux
Goals: Madsen (10), Zambon (35), Danielsen (43, 71), Christensen (60), A. Hansen (74, 90), E. Nielsen (80), Berg (87)

**OMLADINSKI FUDBALSKI KLUB BEOGRAD
v SPORT-CLUB CHEMIE HALLE 2-0** (1-0)
Omladinski, Beograd 5.09.1962
Referee: Lajos Aranyossi (HUN)   Attendance: 1,800
OFK: Stanoje Miloradović; Miroslav Milovanović, Momcilo Gavrić; Milorad Popov, Djordje Cokić, Zoran Dakić; Spasoje Samardzić, Sava Antić (Cap), Stojan Milosev, Srdjan Cebinac, Josip Skoblar.   Trainer: Milovan Ciric
CHEMIE: Helmut Wilk; Klaus Urbanczyk, Klaus Hoffmann (Cap), Robert Heyer; Günter Hoffmann, Heinz Walter; Achim Schimpf, Wolfgang Meissner, Erhard Heilemann, Helmut Stein, Rainer Topf.   Trainer: Heinz Krügel
Goals: Milosev (27), Antic (55)

**SPORT-CLUB CHEMIE HALLE v OMLADINSKI
FUDBALSKI KLUB BEOGRAD 3-3** (2-3)
Kurt-Wabbel, Halle 19.09.1962
Referee: Stanislav Fencl (CZE)   Attendance: 18,587
CHEMIE: Freimut Bott; Klaus Urbanczyk, Klaus Hoffmann (Cap), Werner Okupniak; Heinz Walter, Günter Hoffmann; Werner Lehrmann, Wolfgang Meissner, Helmut Stein, Rainer Topf, Günther Busch.   Trainer: Heinz Krügel
OFK: Stanoje Miloradović; Miroslav Milovanović, Momčilo Gavrić; Milorad Popov, Djordje Cokić, Zoran Dakić; Spasoje Samardzić, Sreten Banović, Stojan Milosev, Sava Antić (Cap), Josip Skoblar.   Trainer: Milovan Ciric
Goals: Antić (5), Busch (15, 87 pen), K. Hoffmann (17 og), Stein (28), Skoblar (35)

**GLASGOW RANGERS FOOTBALL CLUB
v SEVILLA CLUB DE FÚTBOL 4-0** (2-0)
Ibrox stadium, Glasgow 5.09.1962
Referee: Tage Sørensen (DEN)   Attendance: 60,500
RANGERS: William Ritchie; Robert Shearer (Cap), Eric Caldow; Harold Davis, Ronald McKinnon, James Baxter; William Henderson, John Greig, James Millar, Ralph Brand, David Wilson.   Manager: James Scotland Symon
SEVILLA CF: Salvador MUT; JUAN MANUEL, Marcelino Vaquero González del Río "CAMPANAL" (Cap), José Aragón LUQUE; Manuel RUIZ-SOSA, Ignacio ACHÚCARRO Ayala; Darcy Silvera dos Santos "CANARIO", José Carlos DIÉGUEZ Bravo, José Luis ARETA Vélez, Enrique MATEOS Mancebo, José Manuel MOYA.   Trainer: Antonio Barrios
Goals: Millar (14, 17, 63), Brand (64)

SEVILLA CF v GLASGOW RANGERS FC 2-0 (1-0)
Estadio Ramón Sánchez Pizjuán, Sevilla 26.09.1962
Referee: Décio de Freitas (POR)   Attendance: 35,000
SEVILLA CF: Salvador MUT; JUAN MANUEL, Marcelino Vaquero González del Río "CAMPANAL" (Cap), José Aragón LUQUE; José Luis ARETA Vélez, Ignacio ACHÚCARRO Ayala; Ángel OLIVEROS Jiménez, José Carlos DIÉGUEZ Bravo, Cesáreo RIVERA Pérez, Enrique MATEOS Mancebo, Darcy Silveira dos Santos "CANARIO".   Trainer: Antonio Barrios
RANGERS: William Ritchie; Robert Shearer (Cap), Eric Caldow; Harold Davis, Ronald McKinnon, James Baxter; William Henderson, John Greig, James Millar, Ralph Brand, David Wilson.   Manager: James Scotland Symon
Goals: Diéguez (16), Mateos (48)

BANGOR CITY FOOTBALL CLUB
v NAPOLI ASSOCIAZIONE CALCIO 2-0 (1-0)

Farrar Road, Bangor   5.09.1962

Referee: Johan Heinrich Martens (HOL)   Attendance: 6,500

BANGOR: Len Davies; William Souter, Iorys Griffiths; Kenneth Birch (Cap), Edward Murphy, Barry Wilkinson; Roy Matthews, Brian Ellis, Edward Brown, James McAllister, Reginald Hunter.   Trainer: Thomas George Jones

NAPOLI: Walter Pontel; Giovanni Molino, Dolo Mistone; Pier Luigi Ronzon, Rosario Rivellino, Achille Fraschini; Amos Mariani (Cap), Humberto Jorge Rosa, Ugo Tomeazzi, Gianni Corelli, Juan Carlos Tacchi.   Trainer: Eraldo Monzeglio

Goals: Matthews (43), Birch (82 pen)

ÚJPESTI DÓZSA BUDAPEST
v ZAGLEBIE SOSNOWIEC 5-0 (2-0)

Megyeri út, Budapest   12.09.1962

Referee: Josef Stoll (AUS)   Attendance: 8,000

ÚJPESTI DÓZSA: Ferenc Lung; Benő Káposzta, Károly Rajna (Cap), Kálmán Sóvári; Ernö Solymosi, József Szini; Sándor Lenkei, János Göröcs, Ferenc Bene, Béla Kuharszky, Ferenc Rossi.   Trainer: Gyula Szűcs

ZAGLEBIE: Aleksander Dziurowicz; Franciszek Skiba, Roman Bazan, Wlodzimierz Spiewak; Alojzy Fulczyk, Witold Majewski; József Galeczka, Czeslaw Uznanski (Cap), Zenon Kosider, Zbigniew Myga, Ginter Piecyk.
Trainer: Teodor Wieczorek

Goals: Bene (3), Göröcs (41, 64), Solymosi (66), Sovari (87)

NAPOLI AC v BANGOR CITY FC 3-1 (1-0)

San Paolo, Napoli   26.09.1962

Referee: Daniel Mellet (SWI)   Attendance: 13,477

NAPOLI: Walter Pontel; Giovanni Molino, Dolo Mistone; Luigi Bodi, Mauro Gatti, Antonio Girardo; Amos Mariani (Cap), Pier Luigi Ronzon, Giovanni Fanello, Humberto Jorge Rosa, Juan Carlos Tacchi.   Trainer: Eraldo Monzeglio

BANGOR: Len Davies; William Souter, Iorys Griffiths; Kenneth Birch (Cap), Edward Murphy, Barry Wilkinson; Roy Matthews, Brian Ellis, Edward Brown, James McAllister, Reginald Hunter.   Trainer: Thomas George Jones

Goals: Mariani (29), Tacchi (54), McAllister (71), Fanello (84)

ZAGLEBIE SOSNOWIEC
v ÚJPESTI DÓZSA BUDAPEST 0-0

Ludowy, Sosnowiec   26.09.1962

Referee: Walter Meissner (E. GER)   Attendance: 15,000

ZAGLEBIE: Witold Szygula; Franciszek Skiba, Roman Strzalkowski, Wlodzimierz Spiewak; Witold Majewski, Alojzy Fulczyk; József Galeczka, Czeslaw Uznanski (Cap), Zenon Kosider, Zbigniew Myga, Ginter Piecyk.
Trainer: Teodor Wieczorek

ÚJPESTI DÓZSA: Ferenc Lung; Benő Káposzta, Pál Várhidi (Cap), Kálmán Sóvári; Ernö Solymosi, József Szini; Sándor Lenkei, János Göröcs, Ferenc Bene, Béla Kuharszky, Ferenc Rossi.   Trainer: Gyula Szűcs

NAPOLI AC v BANGOR CITY FC 2-1 (1-0)

Highbury, London   10.10.1962

Referee: Arthur Holland (ENG)   Attendance: 21,895

NAPOLI: Pacifico Cuman; Giovanni Molino, Antonio Girardo; Gianni Corelli, Rosario Rivellino, Achille Fraschini; Amos Mariani (Cap), Humberto Jorge Rosa, Giovanni Fanello, Pier Luigi Ronzon, Juan Carlos Tacchi.
Trainer: Eraldo Monzeglio

BANGOR: Len Davies; William Souter, Iorys Griffiths; Kenneth Birch (Cap), Edward Murphy, Barry Wilkinson; Roy Matthews, Brian Ellis, Edward Brown, James McAllister, Reginald Hunter.   Trainer: Thomas George Jones

Goals: Rosa (37, 85), McAllister (70)

STEAUA BUCUREȘTI
v BOTEV PLOVDIV 3-2 (1-1)

23 August, București   13.09.1962

Referee: Borce Nedelkovski (YUG)   Attendance: 35,000

STEAUA: Dumitru Eremia; Vasile Zavoda, Bujor Hălmăgeanu, Traian Ivănescu; Emeric Jenei, Ion Crișan; Carol Creiniceanu, Gheorghe Constantin (Cap), Florea Voinea, Gavril Raksi, Nicolae Tătaru.   Trainer: Ștefan Onisie

BOTEV: Mihail Karushkov; Raino Panaiotov, Georgi Chakarov (Cap), Viden Apostolov; Raiko Stoinov, Ivan Zanev; Dinko Dermendjiev, Stoichko Peshev, Georgi Haralampiev, Georgi Asparuhov, Georgi Popov.   Trainer: Georgi Genov

Goals: Asparuhov (33, 48), Voinea (43), Constantin (67), Crisan (86)

BOTEV PLOVDIV
v STEAUA BUCUREŞTI 5-1 (4-0)

Municipal, Plovdiv   19.09.1962

Referee: Petros Tsouvaras (GRE)   Attendance: 18,614

BOTEV: Mihail Karushkov; Raino Panaiotov, Georgi Chakarov (Cap), Viden Apostolov; Raiko Stoinov, Ivan Zanev; Dinko Dermendjiev, Georgi Haralampiev, Georgi Asparuhov, Ivan Sotirov, Georgi Popov.   Trainer: Georgi Genov

STEAUA: Dumitru Eremia; Vasile Zavoda, Dragoş Cojocaru, Gheorghe Staicu; Emeric Jenei, Ion Crişan; Gavril Raksi, Gheorghe Constantin (Cap), Florea Voinea, Traian Ivănescu, Nicolae Tătaru.   Trainer: Ştefan Onisie

Goals: Apostolov (9), Asparuhov (14, 28, 39), Tătaru (50), Dermendjiev (56)

AS SAINT ETIENNE
v VITÓRIA FUTEBOL CLUBE SETUBAL 1-1 (0-0)

Stade Geoffroy Guichard, St.Etienne   20.09.1962.

Referee: Gennaro Marchese (ITA)   Attendance: 11,983

AS ST.ETIENNE: Robert Philippe; Régis Courbon, Georges Polny; René Domingo (Cap), Richard Tylinski, Jean Bordas; Jean-Claude Baulu, Roland Mitoraj, Jacques Faivre, René Ferrier, Manuel Balboa.   Trainer: François Wicart

VITÓRIA: José Felix Mourinho (Cap); Francisco Polido, Manuel Joaquim Coelho; Emidio Graça, João Resende, Alfredo Moreira; Manuel Mateus, Mário Silva «Pepe», Manuel Pompeu, Jaime Graça, Julio Teixeira.
Trainer: Nelson Filipo Nuñez

Goals: Mateus (57 pen), Mitoraj (72)

LAUSANNE SPORTS
v SPARTA ROTTERDAM 3-0 (1-0)

Stade Olympique de la Pontaise, Lausanne   19.09.1962

Referee: Henri Faucheux (FRA)   Attendance: 7,931

LAUSANNE SPORTS: René Künzi; André Grobéty (Cap), Kurt Hunziker; Richard Dürr, Ely Tacchella, Gilbert Rey; Zdravko Rajkov, Roger Vonlanthen, Roberto Frigerio, Robert Hosp, Charles Hertig.   Trainer: Jean Luciano (FRA)

SPARTA: Willem Doesburg; Piet De Groot, Frederik van der Lee; Ad Verhoeven (Cap), Gerrie Ter Horst, Jacobus Johannes de Koning; Anthony van Ede, Béla Bodnár, Carl Wilson, Martinus Bosselaar, Pieter Gijsbertus de Vries.
Trainer: Denis Neville

Goals: Vonlanthen (12), Frigerio (55), Ter (64 og)

VITÓRIA FC SETÚBAL v AS ST.ETIENNE 0-3 (0-1)

Estádio do Bonfim, Setúbal   23.09.1962

Referee: Juan Gardeazabal Garay (SPA)   Attendance: 5,346

VITÓRIA: José Felix Mourinho (Cap); Francisco Polido, Manuel Joaquim Coelho; Herculano Santos, João Resende, Alfredo Moreira; Manuel Mateus, Mario Silva "Pepe", Manuel Pompeu, Jaime Graça, Julio Teixeira.
Trainer: Nelson Filipo Nuñez

AS ST.ETIENNE: Robert Philippe; Régis Courbon, Georges Polny; René Domingo (Cap), Richard Tylinski, Jean Bordas; Jean-Claude Baulu, Roland Mitoraj, Jacques Faivre, René Ferrier, Jean Masson.   Trainer: François Wicart

Goals: Faivre (44, 55), Baulu (72)

SECOND ROUND

SPARTA ROTTERDAM
v LAUSANNE SPORTS 4-2 (1-0)

Feyenoord, Rotterdam   3.10.1962

Referee: Kewin Howley (ENG)   Attendance: 25,000

SPARTA: Willem Doesburg; Piet De Groot, Frederik van der Lee; Ad Verhoeven (Cap), Gerrie Ter Horst, Jacobus Johannes de Koning; Anthony van Ede, Piet van Miert, Carl Wilson, Martinus Bosselaar, Cor Adelaar.   Trainer: Denis Neville

LAUSANNE SPORTS: René Künzi; André Grobéty (Cap), Kurt Hunziker; Richard Dürr, Ely Tacchella, Gilbert Rey; Zdravko Rajkov, Roger Vonlanthen, Roberto Frigerio, Kurt Armbruster, Charles Hertig.   Trainer: Jean Luciano

Goals: Wilson (42, 51, 57), Dürr (78 pen), Hertig (83), Van Miert (87)

AS ST.ETIENNE v 1.FC NÜRNBERG 0-0

Stade Geoffroy Guichard, St.Etienne   18.10.1962

Referee: Daniel Zariquiegui (SPA)   Attendance: 20,561

AS ST.ETIENNE: Robert Philippe; Régis Courbon, Richard Tylinski, Jean Bordas, Georges Polny; Robert Herbin, René Domingo (Cap), René Ferrier; Jean-Claude Baulu, Jacques Faivre, Roland Mitoraj.   Trainer: François Wicart

FC NÜRNBERG: Roland Wabra; Paul Derbfuss, Ferdinand Wenauer (Cap), Helmut Hilpert; Gustav Flachenecker, Stefan Reisch; Kurt Haseneder, Reinhold Gettinger, Heinz Strehl, Tasso Wild, Richard Albrecht.   Trainer: Herbert Widmayer

1.FC NÜRNBERG v AS ST.ETIENNE 3-0 (1-0)

Zerzabelshof, Nürnberg 14.11.1962

Referee: Karol Galba (CZE)   Attendance: 28,506

FC NÜRNBERG: Roland Wabra; Horst Leupold, Ferdinand Wenauer (Cap), Helmut Hilpert; Gustav Flachenecker, Stefan Reisch; Richard Albrecht, Tasso Wild, Heinz Strehl, Kurt Haseneder, Peter Engler.   Trainer: Herbert Widmayer

AS ST.ETIENNE: Robert Philippe; Antonello Sbaiz, Richard Tylinski, Robert Herbin, Georges Polny; René Domingo (Cap), René Ferrier, Jean Oleksiak; Jean-Claude Baulu, Jacques Foik, Jacques Faivre.   Trainer: François Wicart

Sent off: Sbaiz & Haseneder (76)

Goals: Strehl (27), Wild (63), Haseneder (73)

SHAMROCK ROVERS FC DUBLIN v BOTEV PLOVDIV 0-4 (0-1)

Dalymount Park, Dublin 24.10.1962

Referee: Andries van Leeuwen (HOL)   Attendance: 20,315

SHAMROCK ROVERS: Patrick Dunne; John Keogh, Michael Cahill, Patrick Courtney; Ronald Nolan (Cap), John Fullam; Francis O'Neill, John Mooney, Edward Bailham, Eamonn Farrell, Anthony O'Connell.   Trainer: Sean Thomas

BOTEV: Georgi Naidenov; Raino Panaiotov, Georgi Chakarov (Cap), Viden Apostolov; Raiko Stoinov, Georgi Razlojki; Dinko Dermendjiev, Georgi Haralampiev, Georgi Asparuhov, Stoichko Peshev, Georgi Popov.   Trainer: Georgi Genov

Goals: Asparuhov (2), Peshev (47), Popov (70, 78)

CLUB ATLÉTICO DE MADRID v HIBERNIANS FOOTBALL CLUB PAOLA 4-0 (2-0)

Estadio Metropolitano, Madrid 24.10.1962

Referee: Abel Da Costa (POR)   Attendance: 23,405

ATLÉTICO: Edgardo Mario MADINABEYTIA Bassi; José Antonio RODRÍGUEZ López, Antonio González Álvarez "CHUZO", Isacio CALLEJA García; RAMIRO Rodríguez Valente, Jesús GLARÍA Roldán; Miguel JONES del Castillo, Vicente MEDINA García, Jorge Alberto MENDONÇA Paulino, ADELARDO Rodríguez Sánchez, Enrique COLLAR Monterrubio (Cap).   Trainer: Rafael Tinte

HIBERNIAN: Alfred Mizzi; John Privitera, Emanuel Attard, Edward Gatt; Joseph Attard, Louis Theobald (Cap); Victor Cassar, Edward Theobald, James Mizzi, Francis Xuereb, Emanuel Sultana.   Trainer: Salvino Cuschieri

Goals: Mendonça (12), Medina (27), Collar (60 pen), Ramiro (83)

BOTEV PLOVDIV v SHAMROCK ROVERS FC DUBLIN 1-0 (1-0)

Gradski, Plovdiv 14.11.1962

Referee: Aleksandar Škorić (YUG)   Attendance: 17,694

BOTEV: Mihail Karushkov; Raino Panaiotov, Georgi Chakarov (Cap), Viden Apostolov; Georgi Razlojki, Raiko Stoinov; Dinko Dermendjiev, Ivan Sotirov, Georgi Asparuhov, Stoichko Peshev, Georgi Popov.   Trainer: Georgi Genov

SHAMROCK ROVERS: Patrick Dunne; John Keogh, Michael Cahill, Patrick Courtney; Ronald Nolan (Cap), John Fullam; Francis O'Neill, John Mooney, Edward Bailham, Anthony O'Connell, Patrick Ambrose.   Trainer: Sean Thomas

Goal: Peshev (5)

HIBERNIANS FC PAOLA v CLUB ATLÉTICO DE MADRID 0-1 (0-1)

The Empire Stadium, Valletta 7.11.1962

Referee: Cesare Jonni (ITA)   Attendance: 10,807

HIBERNIAN: Alfred Mizzi; John Privitera, Emanuel Attard, Edward Gatt; Joseph Attard, Louis Theobald (Cap); Victor Cassar, Edward Theobald, James Mizzi, Francis Xuereb, Emanuel Sultana.   Trainer: James Davidson

ATLÉTICO: Edgardo Mario MADINABEYTIA Bassi; Feliciano RIVILLA Muñoz, Jesús MARTÍNEZ JAYO, Isacio CALLEJA García; RAMIRO Rodríguez Valente, Jesús GLARÍA Roldán; Miguel JONES del Castillo, José RIBES Flores, Jorge Alberto MENDONÇA Paulino, Amador CORTÉS García, Enrique COLLAR Monterrubio (Cap).   Trainer: Rafael Tinte

Goal: Jones (24)

GRAZER ATLETIK-KLUB v BOLDKLUBBEN 1909 ODENSE 1-1 (0-1)

Bundesstadion Graz-Libenau, Graz 30.10.1962

Referee: Dittmar Huber (SWI)   Attendance: 6,004

GAK: Erik Welk; Erwin Ninaus, Erich Frisch, Alfred Kölly; Helmut Loske, Hermann Stessl; Walter Koleznik (Cap), Walter Loske, Johannes Jank, Johann Egger, Wilhelm Sgerm.   Trainer: Stefan Kölly

BK 1909: Svend Aage Rask; Flemming Johansen, Bruno Eliasen (Cap), Jörgen Rask; Erling Nielsen, Hans Madsen; Mogens Berg, Mogens Engström, Arno Hansen, John Danielsen, Palle Hansen.   Trainer: Alfons Ramlein

Goals: A. Hansen (38), Jank (89)

BK 1909 ODENSE v GRAZER AK 5-3 (3-3)

Odense stadion   14.11.1962

Referee: Hugh Phillips (SCO)   Attendance: 5,401

BK 1909: Svend Aage Rask; Erling Linde Larsen, Bruno Eliasen (Cap), Jörgen Rask; Erling Nielsen, Hans Madsen; Mogens Berg, Arno Hansen, Jörgen Petersen, John Danielsen, Palle Hansen.   Trainer: Alfons Ramlein

GAK: Erich Welk; Günther Stangl, Erwin Ninaus, Alfred Kölly; Gerald Erkinger, Helmut Loske; Walter Koleznik (Cap), Hermann Stessl, Walter Loske, Johann Egger, Wilhelm Sgerm.   Trainer: Stefan Kölly

Goals: Petersen (5, 33, 38, 57), Koleznik (28), W. Loske (30), Stessl (43), Berg (75)

OFK BEOGRAD v PORTADOWN FC 5-1 (2-0)

Omladinski, Beograd   7.11.1962

Referee: Lajos Horvath (HUN)   Attendance: 2,015

OFK: Slobodan Veljković; Miroslav Milovanović, Milos Grujić; Milorad Popov, Djordje Cokić, Dragan Djukić; Dragan Gugleta, Srdjan Cebinac, Josip Skoblar (Cap), Stojan Milosev, Sreten Banović.   Trainer: Milovan Ciric

PORTADOWN: Frank Connor; Robin Burke, Alan Loughlin; Wilbur Cush (Cap), Kenneth Beattie, Walter Thompson; Peter Gillespie, James McMillan, James Jones, Eamonn Gorman, David Clements.   Trainer: Gibby McKenzie

Goals: Djukic (3), Skoblar (22, 78), Gugleta (50), Cebinac (56), Clements (58)

**TOTTENHAM HOTSPUR FC LONDON
v GLASGOW RANGERS FC 5-2** (4-2)

White Hart Lane, London   31.10.1962

Referee: Kurt Tschenscher (W. GER)   Attendance: 58,859

TOTTENHAM: William Dallas Fyfe Brown; Peter Russell Barker Baker, Ronald Patrick Henry; Robert Daniel Blanchflower (Cap), Maurice Norman, David Craig Mackay; Terence Cameron Medwin, John Anderson White, Leslie Allen, James Peter Greaves, Clifford William Jones.
Trainer: William Edward Nicholson

RANGERS: William Ritchie; Robert Shearer (Cap), Eric Caldow; Harold Davis, Ronald McKinnon, James Baxter; William Henderson, John Ian McMillan, James Millar, Ralph Brand, David Wilson.   Manager: James Scotland Symon

Goals: White (4), Brand (9), Greaves (23), Allen (37), Shearer (43 og), Millar (44), Norman (78)

PORTADOWN FC v OFK BEOGRAD 3-2 (2-0)

Windsor Park, Belfast   21.11.1962

Referee: Einar Poulsen (DEN)   Attendance: 5,000

PORTADOWN: Frank Connor; Robin Burke, Brian Campbell; Wilbur Cush (Cap), Kenneth Beattie, Walter Thompson; James McMillan, Eamonn Gorman, James Jones, David Clements, Alan Loughlin.   Trainer: Gibby McKenzie

OFK: Slobodan Veljković; Miroslav Milovanović, Momcilo Gavrić; Milorad Popov, Djordje Cokić, Milos Grujić; Spasoje Samardzić, Dragan Gugleta, Stojan Milosev, Sreten Banović, Josip Skoblar (Cap).   Trainer: Milovan Ciric

Goals: Burke (17), Jones (32), Popov (60), Skoblar (65), Cush (88)

**GLASGOW RANGERS FC
v TOTTENHAM HOTSPUR FC LONDON 2-3** (0-1)

Ibrox Stadium, Glasgow   11.12.1962

Referee: Marcel du Bois (FRA)   Attendance: 78,642

RANGERS: William Ritchie; Robert Shearer (Cap), Eric Caldow; Harold Davis, Ronald McKinnon, James Baxter; William Henderson, John Ian McMillan, James Millar, Ralph Brand, David Wilson.   Manager: James Scotland Symon

TOTTENHAM: William Dallas Fyfe Brown; Peter Russell Barker Baker, Ronald Patrick Henry; Robert Daniel Blanchflower (Cap), Maurice Norman, David Craig Mackay; Terence Cameron Medwin, John Anderson White, Robert Alfred Smith, James Peter Greaves, Clifford William Jones.
Trainer: William Edward Nicholson

Goals: Greaves (8), Brand (47), Smith (50, 89), Wilson (74)

**LAUSANNE SPORTS
v SLOVAN BRATISLAVA 1-1** (1-0)

Stade Olympique de la Pontaise, Lausanne   14.11.1962

Referee: Alfeo Grignani (ITA)   Attendance: 11,875

LAUSANNE: René Künzi; André Grobéty (Cap), Kurt Hunziker; Richard Dürr, Ely Tacchella, Gilbert Rey; Zdravko Rajkov, Roger Vonlanthen, Kurt Armbruster, Robert Hosp, Charles Hertig.   Trainer: Jean Luciano (FRA)

SLOVAN: Viliam Schrojf; Anton Urban, Vojtech Jankovic; Stefan Král, Ján Popluhár (Cap), Jozef Venglos; Zdenek Velecky, Anton Moravcík, Pavol Molnár, Jozéf Obert, Ludovít Cvetler.   Trainer: Anton Bulla

Goals: Hosp (40), Moravcík (52)

**SLOVAN BRATISLAVA
v LAUSANNE SPORTS 1-0** (0-0)

Stadion Tehelné pole, Bratislava   28.11.1962

Referee: Friedrich Seipelt (AUS)   Attendance: 5,314

SLOVAN: Viliam Schrojf; Vojtech Jankovic, Anton Urban, Ján Slosiarik; Jozef Venglos, Stefan Král; Zdenek Velecky, Anton Moravcík, Pavol Molnár (Cap), Jozéf Obert, Ludovít Cvetler. Trainer: Anton Bulla

LAUSANNE: René Künzi; André Grobéty (Cap), Kurt Hunziker; Richard Dürr, Ely Tacchella, Gilbert Rey; Zdravko Rajkov, Roger Vonlanthen, Roberto Frigerio, Kurt Armbruster, Charles Hertig.   Trainer: Jean Luciano (FRA)

Goal: Moravcík (86)

**NAPOLI AC
v ÚJPESTI DOZSA BUDAPEST 3-1** (3-0)

Stade Olympique de la Pontaise, Lausanne   4.12.1962

Referee: Daniel Mellet (SWI)   Attendance: 3,171

NAPOLI: Walter Pontel; Giovanni Molino, Dolo Mistone; Mauro Gatti, Rosario Rivellino, Antonio Girardo; Amos Mariani (Cap), Pier Luigi Ronzon, Giovanni Fanello, Ugo Tomeazzi, Juan Carlos Tacchi.   Trainer: Eraldo Monzeglio

ÚJPESTI DÓZSA: Ferenc Lung; Benö Káposzta, Pál Várhidi (Cap), József Györvári; Ernö Solymosi, József Szini; Ferenc Rossi, Ferenc Bene, Sándor Lenkei, Béla Kuharszky, Mihály Tóth.   Trainer: Gyula Szűcs

Goals: Fanello (5), Ronzon (10), Tacchi (34), Kuharszky (52)

QUARTER-FINALS

**ÚJPESTI DÓZSA BUDAPEST
v NAPOLI AC 1-1** (1-0)

Megyeri út, Budapest   14.11.1962

Referee: Paul Schiller (AUS)   Attendance: 10,153

ÚJPESTI DÓZSA: Ferenc Lung; Benö Káposzta, Pál Várhidi (Cap), Kálmán Sóvári; Ernö Solymosi, József Szini; Sándor Lenkei, János Göröcs, Ferenc Bene, Béla Kuharszky, Ferenc Rossi.   Trainer: Gyula Szűcs

NAPOLI: Walter Pontel; Giovanni Molino, Dolo Mistone; Mauro Gatti, Rosario Rivellino, Antonio Girardo; Amos Mariani (Cap), Pier Luigi Ronzon, Ugo Tomeazzi, Achille Fraschini, Antonio Juliano.   Trainer: Eraldo Monzeglio

Goals: Bene (1), Fraschini (60)

OFK BEOGRAD v AC NAPOLI 2-0 (0-0)

Crvena Zvezda, Beograd   6.02.1963

Referee: István Zsolt (HUN)   Attendance: 7,693

OFK: Blagoje Vidinić; Miroslav Milovanović, Momčilo Gavrić; Dragoljub Marić, Djordje Cokić, Dragan Gugleta; Spasoje Samardžić, Milorad Popov, Srdjan Cebinac, Sreten Banović, Josip Skoblar (Cap).   Trainer: Milovan Ciríc

NAPOLI: Pacifico Cuman; Giovanni Molino, Dolo Mistone; Gianni Corelli, Rosario Rivellino, Vincenzo Montefusco; Amos Mariani (Cap), Pier Luigi Ronzon, Ugo Tomeazzi, Achille Fraschini, Antonio Juliano.

Trainers: Bruno Pesaola & Eraldo Monzeglio

Goals: Samardzić (78), Popov (88)

**NAPOLI AC
v ÚJPESTI DOZSA BUDAPEST 1-1** (1-1)

Stadio San Paolo, Napoli   28.11.1962

Referee: Arthur Lentini (MAL)   Attendance: 17,185

NAPOLI: Walter Pontel; Giovanni Molino, Dolo Mistone; Mauro Gatti, Rosario Rivellino, Antonio Girardo; Amos Mariani (Cap), Ugo Tomeazzi, Giovanni Fanello, Pier Luigi Ronzon, Juan Carlos Tacchi.   Trainer: Eraldo Monzeglio

ÚJPESTI DÓZSA: Ferenc Lung; Benö Káposzta, Pál Várhidi (Cap), József Györvári; Ernö Solymosi, József Szini; Sándor Lenkei, János Göröcs, Ferenc Bene, Béla Kuharszky, Ferenc Rossi.   Trainer: Gyula Szűcs

Goals: Tomeazzi (33), Solymosi (36)

AC NAPOLI v OFK BEOGRAD 3-1 (1-1)

Stadio San Paolo, Napoli   20.03.1963

Referee: Albert Guinnard (SWI)   Attendance: 15,463

NAPOLI: Walter Pontel; Mauro Gatti, Dolo Mistone; Antonio Girardo, Rosario Rivellino, Pier Luigi Ronzon; Amos Mariani (Cap), Achille Fraschini, Giovanni Fanello, Jarbas Faustinho Cané, Ugo Tomeazzi.

Trainers: Bruno Pesaola & Eraldo Monzeglio

OFK: Blagoje Vidinić; Miroslav Milovanović, Momčilo Gavrić; Dragoljub Marić, Djordje Cokić, Dragan Gugleta; Spasoje Samardžić, Milorad Popov, Srdjan Cebinac, Sava Antić (Cap), Josip Skoblar.   Trainer: Milovan Ciríc

Goals: Cané (12), Samardzic (43), Fanello (56), Mariani (65)

OFK BEOGRAD v AC NAPOLI 3-1 (1-1)

Stade Velodrome, Marseille 3.04.1963

Referee: Joseph Barbéran (FRA)   Attendance: 8,956

OFK: Blagoje Vidinić; Miroslav Milovanović, Momcilo Gavrić; Dragoljub Marić, Blagomir Krivokuca, Djordje Cokić; Spasoje Samardzić, Dragan Gugleta, Milorad Popov, Sreten Banović, Josip Skoblar (Cap). Trainer: Milovan Cirić

NAPOLI: Walter Pontel; Giovanni Molino, Mauro Gatti; Pier Luigi Ronzon, Rosario Rivellino, Antonio Girardo; Amos Mariani (Cap), Achille Fraschini, Giovanni Fanello, Jarbas Faustinho Cané, Ugo Tomeazzi.
Trainers: Bruno Pesaola & Eraldo Monzeglio

Sent off: Fanello (36)

Goals: Samardzic (19, 83), Cané (23), Popov (53)

**SLOVAN BRATISLAVA
v TOTTENHAM HOTSPUR FC LONDON 2-0** (1-0)

Stadion Tehelné pole, Bratislava 5.03.1963

Referee: Ryszard Banasiuk (POL)   Attendance: 32,000

SLOVAN: Viliam Schrojf; Anton Urban, Ján Popluhár (Cap), Vojtech Jankovic; Jozef Venglos, Stefan Král; Ivan Mráz, Anton Moravcík, Ivan Hrdlicka, Jozef Obert, Ludovít Cvetler.
Trainer: Anton Bulla

TOTTENHAM: William Dallas Fyfe Brown; Peter Russell Barker Baker, Ronald Patrick Henry; Anthony Marchi, Maurice Norman, David Craig Mackay (Cap); Frank Lander Saul, John Anderson White, Robert Alfred Smith, James Peter Greaves, Clifford William Jones.
Trainer: William Edward Nicholson

Goals: Cvetler (30), Moravcík (54)

**BOTEV PLOVDIV
v CLUB ATLÉTICO DE MADRID 1-1** (1-0)

Botev, Plovdiv 27.02.1963

Referee: Branko Tešanić (YUG)   Attendance: 11,814

BOTEV: Georgi Naidenov; Raino Panaiotov, Georgi Chakarov (Cap), Viden Apostolov; Georgi Razlojki, Raiko Stoinov; Dinko Dermendjiev, Georgi Haralampiev, Georgi Asparuhov, Stoichko Peshev, Georgi Popov. Trainer: Georgi Genov

ATLÉTICO: Edgardo Mario MADINABEYTIA Bassi; Feliciano RIVILLA Muñoz, Jorge Bernardo GRIFFA Monferoni, José Antonio RODRÍGUEZ López; RAMIRO Rodríguez Valente, Jesús GLARÍA Roldán; Miguel JONES del Castillo, ADELARDO Rodríguez Sánchez, Antonio González Álvarez "CHUZO", Jorge Alberto MENDONÇA Paulino, Enrique COLLAR Monterrubio (Cap). Trainer: Rafael Tinte

Goals: Peshev (16), Ramiro (74)

**TOTTENHAM HOTSPUR FC LONDON
v SLOVAN BRATISLAVA 6-0** (3-0)

White Hart Lane, London 14.03.1963

Referee: Leopold Sylvain Horn (HOL)   Attendance: 61,504

TOTTENHAM: William Dallas Fyfe Brown; Melvyn Hopkins, Ronald Patrick Henry; Anthony Marchi, Maurice Norman, David Craig Mackay (Cap); Frank Lander Saul, John Anderson White, Robert Alfred Smith, James Peter Greaves, Clifford William Jones. Trainer: William Edward Nicholson

SLOVAN: Viliam Schrojf; Anton Urban, Ján Popluhár (Cap), Vojtech Jankovic; Jozef Venglos, Ivan Hrdlicka; Zdenek Velecky, Anton Moravcík, Pavol Molnár, Jozef Obert, Ludovít Cvetler. Trainer: Anton Bulla

Goals: Mackay (31), Greaves (44, 65), Smith (45), Jones (75), White (85)

**CLUB ATLÉTICO DE MADRID
v BOTEV PLOVDIV 4-0** (2-0)

Estadio Metropolitano, Madrid 13.03.1963

Referee: Marcel Bois (FRA)   Attendance: 36,523

ATLÉTICO: Edgardo Mario MADINABEYTIA Bassi; Feliciano RIVILLA Muñoz, Jorge Bernardo GRIFFA Monferoni, José Antonio RODRÍGUEZ López; RAMIRO Rodríguez Valente, Jesús GLARÍA Roldán; Miguel JONES del Castillo, ADELARDO Rodríguez Sánchez, Antonio González Álvarez "CHUZO", Jorge Alberto MENDONÇA Paulino, Enrique COLLAR Monterrubio (Cap). Trainer: Rafael Tinte

BOTEV: Georgi Naidenov; Raino Panaiotov, Georgi Chakarov (Cap), Viden Apostolov; Georgi Razlojki, Raiko Stoinov; Dinko Dermendjiev, Georgi Haralampiev, Georgi Asparuhov, Stoichko Peshev, Georgi Popov. Trainer: Georgi Genov

Goals: Adelardo (10), Chuzo (30, 76), Collar (69)

BK 1909 ODENSE v 1.FC NÜRNBERG 0-1 (0-0)

Rosenau, Augsburg 21.03.1963

Referee: John Taylor (ENG)   Attendance: 25,366

BK 1909: Svend Aage Rask; Leif Hartwig, Bruno Eliasen (Cap), Jörgen Rask; Erling Nielsen, Per Jacobsen; Mogens Berg, Mogens Engström, Mogens Haastrup, Arno Hansen, Palle Hansen. Trainer: Alfons Ramlein

FC NÜRNBERG: Roland Wabra; Horst Leupold, Ferdinand Wenauer (Cap), Helmut Hilpert; Gustav Flachenecker, Stefan Reisch; Peter Engler, Max Morlock, Heinz Strehl, Tasso Wild, Kurt Dachlauer. Trainer: Herbert Widmayer

Goal: Flachenecker (60 pen)

1.FC NÜRNBERG v B 1909 ODENSE 6-0 (3-0)

Zerzabelshof, Nürnberg   24.03.1963

Referee: Dimitros Wlachoyannis (AUS)   Attendance: 24,525

FC NÜRNBERG: Roland Wabra; Horst Leupold, Ferdinand Wenauer (Cap), Helmut Hilpert; Gustav Flachenecker, Stefan Reisch; Peter Engler, Max Morlock, Tasso Wild, Kurt Haseneder, Kurt Dachlauer.   Trainer: Herbert Widmayer

BK 1909: Svend Aage Rask; Flemming Johansen, Erling Nielsen (Cap), Jörgen Rask; Per Jacobsen, Leif Hartwig; Mogens Engström, Arno Hansen, Mogens Haastrup, John Danielsen, Palle Hansen.   Trainer: Alfons Ramlein

Goals: Morlock (34, 40), Dachlauer (38), Wild (64), Engler (84 pen), Haseneder (89)

SEMI-FINALS

1.FC NÜRNBERG v CLUB ATLÉTICO DE MADRID 2-1 (1-1)

Zerzabelshof, Nürnberg   10.04.1963

Referee: Clive W. Kingston (WAL)   Attendance: 44,140

FC NÜRNBERG: Roland Wabra; Horst Leupold, Ferdinand Wenauer (Cap), Helmut Hilpert; Gustav Flachenecker, Stefan Reisch; Peter Engler, Max Morlock, Heinz Strehl, Tasso Wild, Kurt Dachlauer.   Trainer: Herbert Widmayer

ATLÉTICO: Edgardo Mario MADINABEYTIA Bassi; Feliciano RIVILLA Muñoz, Jorge Bernardo GRIFFA Monferoni, José Antonio RODRÍGUEZ López; RAMIRO Rodríguez Valente, Jesús GLARÍA Roldán; Miguel JONES del Castillo, ADELARDO Rodríguez Sánchez, Jesús MARTÍNEZ JAYO, Amador CORTÉS García, Enrique COLLAR Monterrubio (Cap).   Trainer: Rafael Tinte

Goals: Jones (24), Wild (31, 70)

CLUB ATLÉTICO DE MADRID v 1.FC NÜRNBERG 2-0 (1-0)

Estadio Santiago Bernabéu, Madrid   24.04.1963

Referee: Dittmar Huber (SWI)   Attendance: 86,130

ATLÉTICO: Edgardo Mario MADINABEYTIA Bassi; Feliciano RIVILLA Muñoz, Jorge Bernardo GRIFFA Monferoni, José Antonio RODRÍGUEZ López; Amador CORTÉS García, Jesús GLARÍA Roldán; Miguel JONES del Castillo, ADELARDO Rodríguez Sánchez, Antonio González Álvarez "CHUZO", Jorge Alberto MENDONÇA Paulino, Enrique COLLAR Monterrubio (Cap).   Trainer: Rafael Tinte

FC NÜRNBERG: Roland Wabra; Horst Leupold, Ferdinand Wenauer (Cap), Helmut Hilpert; Gustav Flachenecker, Stefan Reisch; Peter Engler, Max Morlock, Heinz Strehl, Tasso Wild, Kurt Dachlauer.   Trainer: Herbert Widmayer

Goals: Chuzo (45), Mendonça (54)

OFK BEOGRAD v TOTTENHAM HOTSPUR FC LONDON 1-2 (1-1)

Crvena Zvezda, Beograd   24.04.1963

Referee: Lajos Aranyossi (HUN)   Attendance: 45,000

OFK: Blagoje Vidinić; Miroslav Milovanović, Blagomir Krivokuca, Momčilo Gavrić; Dragoljub Marić, Dragan Gugleta; Spasoje Samardzić, Milorad Popov, Sava Antić (Cap), Sreten Banović, Josip Skoblar.   Trainer: Milovan Cirić

TOTTENHAM: William Dallas Fyfe Brown; Peter Russell Barker Baker, Ronald Patrick Henry; Anthony Marchi (Cap), Maurice Norman, David Craig Mackay; James Peter Greaves, John Smith, Robert Alfred Smith, John Anderson White, Terence Kent Dyson.   Trainer: William Edward Nicholson

Sent off: Greaves (54)

Goals: White (27), Popov (36 pen), Dyson (75)

TOTTENHAM HOTSPUR FC LONDON v OFK BEOGRAD 3-1 (2-1)

White Hart Lane, London   1.05.1963

Referee: Tage Sørensen (DEN)   Attendance: 59,736

TOTTENHAM: William Dallas Fyfe Brown; Peter Russell Barker Baker, Ronald Patrick Henry; Robert Daniel Blanchflower (Cap), Maurice Norman, Anthony Marchi; Clifford William Jones, John Anderson White, Robert Alfred Smith, David Craig Mackay, Terence Kent Dyson. Trainer: William Edward Nicholson

OFK: Blagoje Vidinić; Miroslav Milovanović, Blagomir Krivokuca, Momčilo Gavrić; Dragoljub Marić, Dragan Gugleta; Spasoje Samardzić, Milorad Popov, Stojan Milosev, Sreten Banović, Josip Skoblar (Cap).   Trainer: Milovan Cirić

Goals: Mackay (23), Skoblar (28), Jones (43), R. Smith (49)

FINAL

TOTTENHAM HOTSPUR FC LONDON v CLUB ATLÉTICO DE MADRID 5-1 (2-0)

Feyenoord, Rotterdam   15.05.1963

Referee: Andries Van Leeuwen (HOL)   Attendance: 49,143

TOTTENHAM: William Dallas Fyfe Brown; Peter Russell Barker Baker, Ronald Patrick Henry; Robert Daniel Blanchflower (Cap), Maurice Norman, Anthony Marchi; Clifford William Jones, John Anderson White, Robert Alfred Smith, James Peter Greaves, Terence Kent Dyson.   Trainer: William Edward Nicholson

ATLÉTICO: Edgardo Mario MADINABEYTIA Bassi; Feliciano RIVILLA Muñoz, José Antonio RODRÍGUEZ López; RAMIRO Rodríguez Valente, Jorge Bernardo GRIFFA Monferoni, Jesús GLARÍA Roldán; Miguel JONES del Castillo, ADELARDO Rodríguez Sánchez, Antonio González Álvarez "CHUZO", Jorge Alberto MENDONÇA Paulino, Enrique COLLAR Monterrubio (Cap).   Trainer: J. Villalonga Llorente

Goals: Greaves (16, 80), White (35), Collar (47 pen), Dyson (67, 85)

Goalscorers European Cup-Winners' Cup 1962-63:

6 goals: Georgi Asparuhov (Botev Plovdiv), James Peter Greaves (Tottenham)

5 goals: Jörgen Petersen (BK 1909 Odense), Josip Skoblar (OFK Beograd)

4 goals: James Millar (Rangers), Robert Alfred Smith, John Anderson White (Tottenham), Tasso Wild (FC Nürnberg), Spasoje Samardzic, Milorad Popov (OFK Beograd)

3 goals: Wilson (Sparta Rotterdam), Moravcik (Slovan Bratislava), Giovanni Fanello (Napoli), Stoichko Peshev (Botev Plovdiv), A.Hansen (BK 1909 Odense), Dyson (Tottenham), Chuzo, Collar (Atlético Madrid)

2 goals: Zambon (Alliance Dudelange), Busch (Chemie Halle), McAllister (Bangor City), Faivre (AS St.Etienne), Brand (Rangers), Cané, Mariani, Rosa, Tacchi (Napoli), Popov (Botev Plovdiv), Bene, Göröcs, Solymosi (Újpesti Dózsa), Berg, Danielsen (BK 1909 Odense), Haseneder, Morlock (FC Nürnberg), Antic (OFK Beograd), Mackay, Jones (Tottenham), Jones, Mendonça, Ramiro (Atlético Madrid)

1 goal: Stein (Chemie Halle), Diéguez, Mateos (Sevilla), Matthews, Birch (Bangor City), Tataru, Voinea, Constantin, Crisan (Steaua), Van Miert (Sparta Rotterdam), Mateus (Vitoria Setubal), Baulu, Mitoraj (St.Etienne), Koleznik, W.Loske, Stessl, Jank (AK Graz), Henderson, Wilson (Rangers), Clements, Burke, Jones, Cush (Portadown), Hosp, Hertig, Vonlanthen, Frigerio, Dürr (Lausanne), Kuharszky, Sovari (Újpesti Dózsa), Tomeazzi, Fraschini, Ronzon (Napoli), Cvetler (Slovan Bratislava), Apostolov, Dermendjiev (Botev Plovdiv), H.Madsen, Christensen, E.Nielsen (BK 1909 Odense), Flachenecker, Dachlauer, Engler, Strehl (FC Nürnberg), Djukic, Gugleta, Cebinac, Milosev (OFK), Leslie Allen, Norman (Tottenham), Adelardo, Medina (Atlético Madrid)

Own goals: Ter (Sparta Rotterdam) for Lausanne Sports, Shearer (Rangers) for Tottenham, K.Hoffmann (Chemie Halle) for OFK Beograd

CUP WINNERS' CUP 1963-64

FIRST ROUND

ATALANTA BERGAMASCA CALCIO
v SPORTING LISBOA 2-0 (0-0)
Stadio Comunale Beumana, Bergamo   4.09.1963
Referee: Josef Stoll (AUS)   Attendance: 8,548
ATALANTA: Pier-Luigi Pizzaballa; Alfredo Pesenti, Franco Nodari; Flemming Nielsen, Pietro Gardoni (Cap), Umberto Colombo; Angelo Domenghini, Luigi Milan, Salvatore Calvanese, Mario Mereghetti, Kurt Christensen.
Trainer: Carlo Alberto Quario
SPORTING: Joaquim da Silva CARVALHO; Mário Lino, Hilário da Conceição (Cap); Fernando Mendes, Lúcio Soares, David Júlio; Augusto Martins, Roberto Bocaleri Bé, Domingos António da Silva Mascarenhas, Alexandre Baptista, João Morais. Trainer: Gentil Cardoso
Goals: Calvanese (74), Domenghini (86)

SPORTING CP LISBOA
v ATALANTA BERGAMO 3-1 (1-1)
Estádio José de Alvalade, Lisboa   9.10.1963
Referee: Dittmar Huber (SWI)   Attendance: 37,943
SPORTING: Joaquim da Silva CARVALHO; Mário Lino, Hilário da Conceição (Cap); Fernando Mendes, Lúcio Soares, David Júlio; Domingos António da Silva Mascarenhas, Roberto Bocaleri Bé, Ernesto Figueiredo, Geraldo de Carvalho Géo, João Morais. Trainer: Gentil Cardoso
ATALANTA: Pier-Luigi Pizzaballa; Alfredo Pesenti, Franco Nodari; Flemming Nielsen, Pietro Gardoni (Cap), Umberto Colombo; Angelo Domenghini, Luigi Milan, Salvatore Calvanese, Mario Mereghetti, Kurt Christensen.
Trainer: Carlo Alberto Quario
Goals: Figueiredo (5), Christensen (17), Mascarenhas (63), Bé (76)

SPORTING CP LISBOA
v ATALANTA BERGAMO 3-1 (1-1, 1-1) (AET)
Estadio Sarria, Barcelona   14.10.1963
Referee: Manuel Gómes Arribas (SPA)   Attendance: 4,860
SPORTING: Joaquim da Silva CARVALHO; Mário Lino, Hilário da Conceição (Cap); Fernando Mendes, Lúcio Soares, David Júlio; João Morais, Domingos António da Silva Mascarenhas, Ernesto Figueiredo, Geraldo de Carvalho Géo, Artur Louro. Trainer: Gentil Cardoso
ATALANTA: Zaccaria Cometti; Alfredo Pesenti, Franco Nodari; Flemming Nielsen, Pietro Gardoni (Cap), Umberto Colombo; Angelo Domenghini, Luigi Milan, Salvatore Calvanese, Mario Mereghetti, Enrico Nova.
Trainer: Carlo Alberto Quario
Goals: Nova (21), Mascarenhas (24, 115), Lúcio (98)

APOEL FC NICOSIA v GJØVIK/LYN 6-0 (1-0)

Nicosia 8.09.1963

Referee: Cezmi Basar (TUR)   Attendance: 7,100

APOEL: Antonis Mavroudis; Stavros Nathanael, Dimitris Hiotis; Savvas Partakis (Cap), Stelios Haritakis, Pantelas Konstantinidis; Nikos Kantzilieris, Takis Hailis, Nikos Agathokleous, Andreas Tassouris, Marios Papallos. Trainer: Neil Franklin

GJØVIK/LYN: Per Sandli; Rolf Hagen, Arne Amundsen; Knut Iversen, Odd Hermansen, Knut Kolberg; Björn Rime, Håkon Skattum, Rolf Bjørn Bache (Cap), Erik Johansen, Knut Solbrekken.   Trainer: Torbjørn Lønstad

Goals: T. Hailis (15, 61, 80), Agathokleous (67), Papallos (78), Kantzileris (86)

**PETROLUL PLOIEŞTI
v FENERBAHÇE SK ISTANBUL 1-0** (1-0)

Petrolul, Ploieşti 16.10.1963

Referee: Giannis Mihailidis (GRE)   Attendance: 13,800

PETROLUL: Mihai Ionescu; Gheorghe Pahonţu (Cap), Dumitru Nicolae, Gheorghe Florea; Dumitru Munteanu, Marin Marcel; Alexandru Badea, Eduard Juhasz, Mircea Dridea, Anton Munteanu, Constantin Moldoveanu. Trainer: Ilie Oană

FENERBAHÇE: Hazim Canitez; Atilla Altaş, Ismail Kurt; Ali Ihsan Okçuoglu; Özer Kanra, Seref Has (Cap); Lefter Küçükandonyadis, Nedim Dogan, Senol Birol, Birol Pekel, Selim Soydan.   Trainer: Naci Erdem

Goal: M. Dridea (16)

GJØVIK/LYN v APOEL FC NICOSIA 0-1 (0-0)

Gjøvik stadion 29.09.1963

Referee: Gunnar Michaelsen (DEN)   Attendance: 5,756

GJØVIK/LYN: Stein Morris Mellum; Rolf Hagen, Svein Frydenlund; Knut Kolberg, Odd Hermansen, Knut Iversen; Arild Törud, Knut Solbrekken, Rolf Bjørn Bache (Cap), Erik Johansen, Björn Rime.   Trainer: Torbjørn Lønstad

APOEL: Antonis Mavroudis; Stavros Nathanael, Dimitris Hiotis; Savvas Partakis (Cap), Stelios Haritakis, Pantelas Konstantinidis; Nikos Kantzilieris, Takis Hailis, Nikos Agathokleous, Andreas Tassouris, Marios Papallos. Trainer: Neil Franklin

Goal: Partakis (48 pen)

**SLIEMA WANDERERS FC
v BOROUGH UNITED FC 0-0**

The Empire stadium, Gzira 15.09.1963

Referee: Antonio Sbardella (ITA)   Attendance: 9,786

SLIEMA: Alfred Debono; Vincent "Lino" Falzon, Joseph Aquilina; Charles Spiteri, Saviour Bonnici, Robert Buttigieg (Cap); Ronald Cocks, Edward Aquilina, Joseph Cini, George Cuschieri, Samuel Nicholl.   Trainer: Salvino Schembri

BOROUGH: Dave Walker; Eric Morris, Frank Harrison (Cap); Harry Hodges, Derek Owen, Brian Clowry; Michael Pritchard, Keith Pritchard, Gerry Duffy, Willy Russel, Derek Bolton.

**FENERBAHÇE SK ISTANBUL
v PETROLUL PLOIEŞTI 4-1** (0-0)

Dolmabahçe, Istanbul 12.09.1963

Referee: Petros Tsouvaras (GRE)   Attendance: 23,000

FENERBAHÇE: Hazim Canitez; Tuncay Becedek, Özkan Köksoy; Seref Has (Cap), Özer Kanra, Ali Ihsan Okçuoglu; Lefter Küçükandonyadis, Nedim Dogan, Senol Birol, Birol Pekel, Selim Soydan.   Trainer: Naci Erdem

PETROLUL: Vasile Sfetcu; Gheorghe Pahonţu (Cap), Dumitru Nicolae, Gheorghe Florea; Alexandru Fronea, Marin Marcel; Alexandru Badea, Dumitru Munteanu, Mircea Dridea, Anton Munteanu, Constantin Moldoveanu. Trainer: Ilie Oană

Goals: Birol (55), Selim (56), Senol (68), Nedim (70), Dridea (74)

**BOROUGH UNITED FC
v SLIEMA WANDERERS FC 2-0** (1-0)

Racecourse, Wrexham 3.10.1963

Referee: Gerhard Schulenburg (W. GER)   Att: 17,613

BOROUGH: Dave Walker; Eric Morris, Frank Harrison (Cap); Harry Hodges, Derek Owen, Brian Clowry; Michael Pritchard, Keith Pritchard, Gerry Duffy, Willy Russel, Joseph Bebb.

SLIEMA: Alfred Debono; Joseph Bonnici, Joseph Aquilina; Vincent "Lino" Falzon, Saviour Bonnici, George Cuschieri; Ronald Cocks, Charles Spiteri, Joseph Cini, Robert Buttigieg (Cap), Samuel Nicholl.   Trainer: Salvino Schembri

Goals: Duffy (35), M. Pritchard (57)

**HELSINGIN PALLOSEURA
v SLOVAN BRATISLAVA 1-4** (0-3)

Pallokenttä, Helsinki   15.09.1963

Referee: Rudolf Glöckner (E. GER)   Attendance: 2,934

PALLOSEURA: Matti Korhonen; Matti Raitio, Nils-Erik Vilen (Cap), Henry Kiviniemi; Pentti Rautiainen, Kaj Österberg; Erkki Mustakari, Vilho Raatikainen, Urho Laakso, Raimo Elo, Taisto Lintunen.   Trainer: Alpo Lintamo

SLOVAN: Ferdinand Hason; Anton Urban, Ján Slosiarik; Jozef Venglos, Ján Popluhár (Cap), Ivan Hrdlicka; Zdenek Velecky, Jozef Obert, Pavol Molnár, Anton Moravcík, Peter Molnár (62 Stefan Král).   Trainer: Leopold Stastny

Goals: Pavol Molnár (7), Obert (15, 19), Velecky (51), Rautiainen (72)

**SLOVAN BRATISLAVA
v HELSINGIN PALLOSEURA 8-1** (1-0)

Tehelné pole, Bratislava   19.10.1963

Referee: Józef Kowal (POL)   Attedance: 5,119

SLOVAN: Viliam Schrojf; Anton Urban (Cap), Ján Slosiarik; Ivan Hrdlicka, Jozef Venglos, Peter Molnár; Zdenek Velecky, Anton Moravcík, Jozef Obert, Karol Jokl, Ludovít Cvetler.   Trainer: Leopold Stastny

PALLOSEURA: Matti Korhonen; Matti Raitio, Nils-Erik Vilen (Cap), Henry Kiviniemi; Pentti Rautiainen, Kaj Österberg; Erkki Mustakari, Vilho Raatikainen, Urho Laakso, Raimo Elo, Taisto Lintunen.   Trainer: Alpo Lintamo

Goals: Obert (20, 81), Moravcík (56, 57), Cvetler (62), Velecky (65, 76), Hrdlicka (70), Raatikainen (84)

FC BASEL v CELTIC FC GLASGOW 1-5 (0-2)

St. Jakob, Basel   17.09.1963

Referee: Manuel Gomez Arribas (SPA)   Attendance: 14,300

FC BASEL: Kurt Stettler; Peter Füri, Bruno Michaud (Cap); Hanspeter Stocker, Hans Weber, Carlo Porlezza; Raymond Simonet, Karl Odermatt, Markus Pfirter, Heinz Blumer, Walter Baumann.   Trainer: Jiří Sobotka

CELTIC: Frank Haffey; Duncan MacKay, Thomas Gemmell; John McNamee, William McNeill (Cap), John Clark; Robert Lennox, Stephen Chalmers, John Hughes, John Divers, Frank Brogan.   Manager: James McGrory

Goals: Divers (21), Hughes (42, 65, 78), Lennox (53), Blumer (79)

CELTIC FC GLASGOW v FC BASEL 5-0 (2-0)

Celtic Park, Glasgow   9.10.1963

Referee: Valdemar Hansen (DEN)   Attendance: 7,909

CELTIC: Frank Haffey; Ian Young, William McNeill (Cap), Thomas Gemmell; Duncan MacKay, James Kennedy; James Johnstone, Robert Murdoch, Stephen Chalmers, John Divers, John Hughes.   Manager: James McGrory

FC BASEL: Kurt Stettler; Peter Füri, Bruno Michaud (Cap); Hanspeter Stocker, René Burri, Carlo Porlezza; Erdmann Lüthi, Karl Odermatt, Markus Pfirter, Walter Löffel, Enrico Mazzola.   Trainer: Jiří Sobotka

Goals: Johnston (2), Divers (41, 89), Murdoch (62), Chalmers (78)

**SHELBOURNE FC DUBLIN
v CF BARCELONA 0-2** (0-1)

Dalymount Park, Dublin   24.09.1963

Referee: Leopold Sylvain Horn (HOL)   Attendance: 19,493

SHELBOURNE: John Heavey; Patrick Bonham, Brendan O'Brien; Patrick Roberts, Frederick Strahan (Cap), Anthony Corrigan; Joseph Wilson, Brendan Hannigan, Eric Barber, John Hennessy, Oliver Conroy.   Manager: Gerard Doyle

CF BARCELONA: Salvador SADURNÍ Urpi; Fernando OLIVELLA Pons, ELADIO Silvestre Graells; Juan SEGARRA Iraceta (Cap), Jesús GARAY Vicino, Enrique GENSANA Meroles; Pedro María ZABALLA Barquín, Jesús María PEREDA Ruiz de Temiño, José Antonio ZALDÚA Urdanavia, Fernand Goyvaerts, José María FUSTÉ Blanch.   Trainer: César Rodríguez

Goals: Zaldúa (45), Pereda (77)

**CF BARCELONA
v SHELBOURNE FC DUBLIN 3-1** (1-1)

Camp Nou, Barcelona   15.10.1963

Referee: Concetto lo Bello (ITA)   Attendance: 18,694

CF BARCELONA: José Manuel PESUDO Soler; Alfonso María Rodríguez Salas "FONCHO", Francisco Rodríguez García "RODRI", Sigfrido GRACIA Royo (Cap); Martín VERGÉS Massa, Enrique GENSANA Meroles; Pedro María ZABALLA Barquín, Sándor Kocsis, Cayetano RE Rodríguez, Fernand Goyvaerts, José María FUSTÉ Blanch.   Trainer: César Rodríguez

SHELBOURNE: John Heavey; Patrick Bonham, Patrick Roberts, Theo Dunne (Cap), Brendan O'Brien; Anthony Corrigan; Brendan Hannigan, John Hennessy; Joseph Wilson, Eric Barber, Joseph Boyce.   Manager: Gerard Doyle

Goals: Bonham (30 pen), Kocsis (36), Fusté (79), Re (80)

HAMBURGER SV
v UNION SPORTIVE LUXEMBOURG 4-0 (3-0)

Volksparkstadion, Hamburg   25.09.1963

Referee: Alois Obtulovič (CZE)   Attendance: 17,935

HAMBURGER SV: Horst Schnoor; Gerhard Krug, Jürgen Kurbjuhn; Harry Bähre, Hubert Stapelfeldt, Dieter Seeler (Cap); Fritz Wilhelm Friedrich Boyens, Willi Giesemann, Uwe Seeler, Ernst Kreuz, Gert Dörfel.   Trainer: Martin Wilke

US LUXEMBOURG: Nico Schmitt; Ady Colas, Roland Christen; Mathias Ewen, Romain Kies, Paul Ries (Cap); Constant Winandy, René Schneider, Johny Leonard, Guy Bernardin, Jean-Pierre Hemmerling.   Trainer: Georges Berry

Goals: Boyens (28, 32, 63), U. Seeler (38)

UNION SPORTIVE LUXEMBOURG
v HAMBURGER SV 2-3 (0-1)

Stade Municipal, Luxembourg   2.10.1963

Referee: Pieter Paulus Roomer (HOL)   Attendance: 7,939

US LUXEMBOURG: Nico Schmitt (Cap); Ady Colas, Roland Christen; Jean-Pierre Mertl, Mathias Ewen, René Schneider; Gaston Bauer, Constant Winandy, Johny Leonard, Guy Bernardin, Jean-Pierre Hemmerling.   Trainer: Georges Berry

HAMBURGER SV: Horst Schnoor; Lothar Kröpelin, Jürgen Kurbjuhn; Erwin Piechowiak, Hubert Stapelfeldt, Dieter Seeler (Cap); Fritz Wilhelm Friedrich Boyens, Willi Giesemann, Horst Dehn, Ernst Kreuz, Uwe Reuter.   Trainer: Martin Wilke

Goals: Giesemann (20, 62), Winandy (70), Kurbjuhn (83), Bernardin (88)

OLYMPIAKOS SINDESMOS FILATHLON PEIRAIAS v ZAGLEBIE SOSNOWIEC 2-1 (0-0)

Neas Filadelfeias, Athina   25.09.1963

Referee: Mustafa Gerçeker (TUR)   Attendance: 15,000

OLYMPIAKOS: Stathis Tsanaktsis; Giagkos Simantiris, Dimitris Stefanakos, Orestis Pavlidis; Kostas Polihroniou (Cap), Giannis Gkaitatzis; Paulos Vasileiou, Giorgos Sideris, Pavlos Grigoriadis, Panagiotis Kiprianidis, Nikos Tzinis. Trainer: András Dolgos (HUN)

ZAGLEBIE: Witold Szygula; Franciszek Skiba, Roman Bazan, Wlodzimierz Spiewak; Witold Majewski, Alojzy Fulczyk; Józef Galeczka, Ryszard Krawiarz, Andrzej Jarosik, Czeslaw Uznanski (Cap), Ginter Piecyk.   Trainer: Teodor Wieczorek

Goals: G. Sideris (47, 63), Piecyk (86)

ZAGLEBIE SOSNOWIEC
v OLYMPIAKOS SF PEIRAIAS 1-0 (1-0)

Ludowy, Sosnowiec   2.10.1963

Referee: Johannes Malka (W. GER)   Attendance: 20,479

ZAGLEBIE: Witold Szygula; Franciszek Skiba, Roman Bazan; Wlodzimierz Spiewak, Witold Majewski (Cap), Alojzy Fulczyk; Józef Galeczka, Ryszard Krawiarz, Zenon Kosider, Zbigniew Myga, Ginter Piecyk.   Trainer: Teodor Wieczorek

OLYMPIAKOS: Stathis Tsanaktsis; Giagkos Simantiris, Dimitris Stefanakos, Paulos Vasileiou; Kostas Polihroniou (Cap/), Orestis Pavlidis; Argirios Neofotistos, Panagiotis Kiprianidis, Giannis Gkaitatzis, Pavlos Grigoriadis, Giorgos Sideris (/Cap).   Trainer: András Dolgos

Sent off: Polihroniou (46)

Goal: Krawiarz (40)

OLYMPIAKOS SF PEIRAIAS
v ZAGLEBIE SOSNOWIEC 2-0 (1-0)

Hohe Warte, Wien   23.10.1963

Referee: Josef Stoll (AUS)   Attendance: 3,000

OLYMPIAKOS: Stathis Tsanaktsis; Giagkos Simantiris, Dimitris Stefanakos; Orestis Pavlidis, Nikos Sideris; Argirios Neofotistos, Giannis Gkaitatzis, Panagiotis Kiprianidis, Nikos Tzinis, Dimitris Plessas, Giorgos Sideris (Cap). Trainer: András Dolgos (HUN)

ZAGLEBIE: Witold Szygula; Franciszek Skiba, Roman Bazan; Wlodzimierz Spiewak, Roman Strzalkowski, Witold Majewski (Cap); Józef Galeczka, Ryszard Krawiarz, Andrzej Jarosik, Zbigniew Myga, Ginter Piecyk.   Trainer: Teodor Wieczorek

Goals: G. Sideris (38), Tzinis (52)

WILLEM II TILBURG
v MANCHESTER UNITED FC 1-1 (1-1)

Feyenoord, Rotterdam   25.09.1963

Referee: Jean Tricot (FRA)   Attendance: 16,000

WILLEM II: René Dijckmans; Theodorus Josephus Ferdinand van Doremalen, Johannes Cornelis Brooijmans (Cap), Johannes Adrianus Walhout, Henricus Lodevicus Adrianus Antonius Vriens; Gerrit De Wit, Wilhelmus Adrianus Senders; Gábor Keresztes, Cornelis Jan Marinus Koopal, Piet Timmermans, Frederikus Johannes Louer.
Trainer: Jaap van der Leck

MANCHESTER UNITED: Harold Gregg; Anthony Patrick Dunne, Noel Cornelious Cantwell, Patrick Timothy Crerand, William Anthony Foulkes (Cap), Maurice Edgar Setters; David George Herd, John Philip Chisnall, David Sadler, Denis Law, Robert Charlton.   Manager: Matthew Busby

Sent off: Herd (80)

Goals: Louer (9), Herd (11)

**MANCHESTER UNITED FC
v WILLEM II TILBURG 6-1** (3-1)

Old Trafford, Manchester   15.10.1963

Referee: Henri Faucheux (FRA)   Attendance: 42,672

MANCHESTER UNITED: Harold Gregg; Anthony Patrick Dunne, Noel Cornelious Cantwell; Patrick Timothy Crerand, William Anthony Foulkes (Cap), Maurice Edgar Setters; Albert Quixhall, John Philip Chisnall, David George Herd, Denis Law, Robert Charlton.   Manager: Matthew Busby

WILLEM II: René Dijckmans; Theodorus Josephus Ferdinand van Doremalen, Johannes Cornelis Brooijmans (Cap), Johannes Adrianus Walhout, Henricus Lodevicus Adrianus Antonius Vriens; Gerrit De Wit, Wilhelmus Adrianus Senders; Gábor Keresztes, Cornelis Jan Marinus Koopal, Piet Timmermans, Frederikus Johannes Louer.
Trainer: Jaap van der Leck

Goals: Setters (7), Law (12, 32, 70), Cantwell (36 og), Charlton (63), Herd (80)

**MAGYAR TESTGYAKORLÓK KÖRE BUDAPEST
v SLAVIA SOFIA 1-0** (1-0)

Hungária körut, Budapest   2.10.1963

Referee: Eduard Babauczek (AUS)   Attendance: 10,000

MTK: Ferenc Kovalik; György Keszei, József Danszky, István Jenei; István Nagy, Ferenc Kovács III; Károly Sándor (Cap), László Bánkuti, László Bödör, Mihály Laczkó, István Szimcsák.
Trainer: Imre Kovács

SLAVIA: Stefan Pasholov; Stoian Aleksiev, Petar Velichkov, Petar Panagonov; Ivan Davidov, Petar Petrov; Mihail Mishev, Emanuil Manolov, Anton Krastev, Aleksandar Vasilev (Cap), Georgi Gugalov.   Trainer: Anastas Kovachev

Goal: Sándor (8)

SLAVIA SOFIA v MTK BUDAPEST 1-1 (1-1)

Vasil Levski, Sofia   9.10.1963

Referee: Bozidar Gugić (YUG)   Attendance: 25,000

SLAVIA: Stefan Pasholov; Stoian Aleksiev, Petar Velichkov, Petar Panagonov; Ivan Davidov, Petar Petrov; Mihail Mishev, Emanuil Manolov, Anton Krastev, Georgi Haralampiev, Aleksandar Vasilev (Cap).   Trainer: Anastas Kovachev

MTK: Ferenc Kovalik; György Keszei, József Danszky, István Jenei; István Nagy, Ferenc Kovács III; Károly Sándor (Cap), Mihály Vasas, István Kuti, Mihály Laczkó, László Bödör.
Trainer: Imre Kovács

Goals: Mishev (6), Kuti (36)

LINZER ASK v NK DINAMO ZAGREB 1-0 (1-0)

Linzer stadion, Linz   9.10.1963

Referee: István Zsolt (HUN)   Attendance: 5,410

LASK: Helmut Kitzmüller; Heribert Trubrig, Manfred Pichler, Julius Szabó; Adolf Blutsch, Gerhard Sturmberger (Cap); Luka Liposinovic, Hermann Fürst, László Nemeth, Rudolf Sabetzer, Carlos Lima Chico.   Trainer: Karl Schlechta

DINAMO: Branko Crnković; Rudolf Belin, Željko Perusić; Vlatko Marković, Mirko Braun, Atko Kasumović; Zdenko Kobešćak, Slaven Zambata (Cap), Zlatko Haramincić, Zdravko Raus, Stjepan Lamza.   Trainer: Milan Antolković

Sent off: Braun (69), Sturmberger (74), Zambata (74)

Goal: Fürst (32)

NK DINAMO ZAGREB v LINZER ASK 1-0 (0-0)

Maksimir, Zagreb   16.10.1963

Referee: Béla Balla (HUN)   Attendance: 6,030

DINAMO: Branko Crnković; Rudolf Belin (Cap), Marijan Biscan; Vlatko Marković, Atko Kasumović, Željko Perusić; Zdenko Kobešćak, Tomislav Knez, Zdravko Raus, Zlatko Haramincić, Stjepan Lamza.   Trainer: Milan Antolković

LASK: Helmut Kitzmüller; Heribert Trubrig, Manfred Pichler (Cap); Clemens Lusenberger, Adolf Blutsch, Rudolf Sabetzer; Walter Rautmann, Carlos Lima Chico, László Nemeth, Janos Kondert, Ferdinand Zechmeister.   Trainer: Karl Schlechta

Goal: Lamza (48)

**LINZER ASK
v NK DINAMO ZAGREB 1-1** (0-1, 1-1) (AET)

Linzer Stadion   23.10.1963

Referee: Albert Guinnard (SWI)   Attendance: 11,212

LASK: Helmut Kitzmüller; Heribert Trubrig, Manfred Pichler, Julius Szabó; Adolf Blutsch, Gerhard Sturmberger (Cap); Janos Kondert, Carlos Lima Chico, László Nemeth, Rudolf Sabetzer, Walter Rautmann.   Trainer: Karl Schlecht

DINAMO: Branko Crnković; Rudolf Belin, Željko Perusić; Vlatko Marković, Mirko Braun, Atko Kasumović; Zdenko Kobešćak, Slaven Zambata (Cap), Zdravko Raus, Tomislav Knez, Stjepan Lamza.   Trainer: Milan Antolković

Goals: Raus (38), Nemeth (49)

Dinamo Zagreb won on the toss of a coin

OLYMPIQUE LYONNAIS
v BOLDKLUBBEN 1913 ODENSE 3-1 (2-1)

Stade Gerland, Lyon   9.10.1963

Referee: Josef Heymann (SWI)   Attendance: 9,815

OLYMPIQUE: Marcel Aubour; Jean Djorkaeff, Aimé Mignot (Cap); Roger Duffez, Thadée Polak, Guy Hatchi; Fleury Di Nallo, Georges Taberner, Nestor Combin, Jean-Louis Rivoire, Angel Rambert.   Trainer: Lucien Jasseron

B 1913: Erik Lykke Sørensen; Ib Mortensen, Finn Helweg; Kurt Grønning Hansen, Erik Nielsen, Ole Steffensen; Jörgen Rasmussen, Erik Dyrholm, Eigil Misser (Cap), Palle Bruun, Ole Knudsen.   Trainer: Jack Johnsen

Goals: Combin (10), Di Nallo (14), Rasmussen (44), Taberner (55).

LINFIELD AFC BELFAST
v FENERBAHÇE SK ISTANBUL 2-0 (1-0)

Windsor Park, Belfast   11.12.1963

Referee: Erling Rolf Olsen (NOR)   Attendance: 7,863

LINFIELD: Iam McFaul; Kenneth Gilliland, John Graham; Isaac Andrews, Samuel Hatton, William Wilson; Thomas Stewart, Philip Scott, Thomas Dickson (Cap), William Craig, William Ferguson.   Trainer: Thomas Dickson

FENERBAHÇE: Hazim Canitez; Atilla Altaş, Ismail Kurt; Seref Has (Cap), Özer Kanra, Ali Ihsan Okçuoglu; Lefter Kücükandonyadis, Nedim Dogan, Senol Birol, Birol Pekel, Aydin Yelken.   Trainer: Naci Erdem

Goals: Craig (11), Ferguson (80).

BOLDKLUBBEN 1913 ODENSE
v OLYMPIQUE LYONNAIS 1-3 (1-2)

Odense stadion   16.10.1963

Referee: William Clements (ENG)   Attendance: 9,938

B 1913: Erik Lykke Sørensen; Ib Mortensen, Finn Helweg; Kurt Grønning Hansen, Knud Naeshave, Ole Steffensen; Erik Dyrholm, Jörgen Rasmussen, Eigil Misser (Cap), Kurt Larsen, Ole Knudsen.   Trainer: Jack Johnsen

OLYMPIQUE: Marcel Aubour; Guy Hatchi, Aimé Mignot (Cap); Roger Duffez, Thadée Polak, Michel Bossy; Jean Dumas, Fleury Di Nallo, Nestor Combin, Angel Rambert, Georges Taberner.   Trainer: Lucien Jasseron

Goals: Hansen (10), Di Nallo (15), Combin (20, 87).

SPORTING CP LISBOA
v APOEL FC NICOSIA 16-1 (6-1)

Estádio José Alvalade, Lisboa   13.11.1963

Referee: James Finney (ENG)   Attendance: 5,111

SPORTING: Joaquim da Silva CARVALHO; Mário Lino, Pedro Gomes; José Perides, Alfredo Moreira, Fernando Mendes; Ernesto Figueiredo, Fernando Ferreira Pinto, Domingos António da Silva Mascarenhas (Cap), Augusto Martins, Artur Louro.   Trainer: Gentil Cardoso

APOEL: Antonis Mavroudis; Stavros Nathanael, Dimitris Hiotis; Andreas Antoniadis, Stelios Haritakis, Savvas Partakis (Cap); Nicos Kantzileris, Solis Andreou, Nicos Agathokleous, Andreas Tassouris, Andreas Stylianou.   Trainer: Neil Franklin

Goals: Mascarenhas (5, 20, 27, 57, 84, 88), Ferreira Pinto (7, 65), Andreou (24), Lino (35), Louro (36), Pérides (48), Augusto (64, 81), Figueiredo (67, 72, 76).

SECOND ROUND

FENERBAHÇE SK ISTANBUL
v LINFIELD ATHLETIC FC BELFAST 4-1 (2-0)

Mithatpaşa, Istanbul   13.11.1963

Referee: Paul Bonett (MAL)   Attendance: 50,000

FENERBAHÇE: Hazim Canitez; Atilla Altaş, Ismail Kurt; Seref Has (Cap), Özer Kanra, Ali Ihsan Okçuoglu; Ogün Altiparmak, Nedim Dogan, Senol Birol, Birol Pekel, Aydin Yelken.   Trainer: Naci Erdem

LINFIELD: Iam McFaul; Kenneth Gilliland, John Graham; Isaac Andrews, Samuel Hatton, William Wilson; Thomas Stewart, Philip Scott, George McCleery, William Craig, Thomas Dickson (Cap).   Trainer: Thomas Dickson

Goals: Ogün (4), Senol (34, 52, 76), Dickson (85).

SPORTING CP LISBOA
v APOEL FC NICOSIA 2-0 (1-0)

Estádio José Alvalade, Lisboa   20.11.1963

Referee: Daniel Zariquiegui (SPA)   Attendance: 8,534

SPORTING: Joaquim da Silva CARVALHO; Mário Lino, Pedro Gomes; José Perides, Alfredo Moreira, Fernando Mendes; Ernesto Figueiredo, José Monteiro, Domingos António da Silva Mascarenhas (Cap), Augusto Martins, João Morais.   Trainer: Gentil Cardoso

APOEL: Andreas Aloneftis; Stavros Assiotis, Dimitris Hiotis; Savvas Partakis (Cap), Stelios Haritakis, Pantelas Konstantinidis; Marios Pappalos, Andreas Antoniadis, Takis Hailis, Andreas Tassouris, Spyros Kettenis.   Trainer: Neil Franklin

Goals: Augusto (37), Mascarenhas (54).

MOTOR ZWICKAU v MTK BUDAPEST 1-0 (0-0)
Georgi Dimitroff stadion, Zwickau 20.11.1963
Referee: Martti Hirviniemi (FIN)   Attendance: 20,000
MOTOR: Peter Meyer; Alois Glaubitz, Albert Beier, Werner Wilde; Helmut Gruner (Cap), Armin Schäfer; Dieter Jakob, Eberhard Franz, Horst Jura, Peter Henschel, Hans Speth. Trainer: Karl Dittes
MTK: Ferenc Kovalik; György Keszei, József Danszky, István Jenei; István Nagy, Ferenc Kovács III (Cap); Mihály Laczkó, Mihály Vasas, István Kuti, István Halápi, László Bödör. Trainer: Imre Kovács
Goal: Jakob (51)

OLYMPIAKOS PEIRAIAS v OLYMPIQUE LYONNAIS 2-1 (1-0)
Neas Filadelfeias Football Ground, Athina 4.12.1963
Referee: Atanas Stavrev (BUL)   Attendance: 33,060
OLYMPIAKOS: Stathis Tsanaktsis; Giagkos Simantiris, Dimitris Stefanakos, Kostas Polihroniou (Cap), Aristidis Papazoglou; Giorgos Sideris, Orestis Pavlidis; Pavlos Grigoriadis, Giannis Gkaitatzis, Panagiotis Kiprianidis, Nikos Tzinis. Trainer: András Dolgos
OLYMPIQUE: Marcel Aubour; Jean Djorkaeff, Aimé Mignot (Cap); Roger Duffez, Thadée Polak, Marcel Le Borgne; Jean Dumas, Fleury Di Nallo, Nestor Combin, Guy Hatchi, Angel Rambert. Trainer: Lucien Jasseron
Goals: G. Sideris (16), Kiprianidis (55), Combin (85)

MTK BUDAPEST v MOTOR ZWICKAU 2-0 (0-0)
Hungária körut, Budapest 30.11.1963
Referee: Aleksandar Škorić (YUG)   Attendance: 5,000
MTK: Ferenc Kovalik; György Keszei, József Danszky, István Jenei; István Nagy, Ferenc Kovács III (Cap); József Török, Mihály Vasas, István Kuti, Mihály Laczkó, László Bödör. Trainer: Imre Kovács
MOTOR: Peter Meyer; Alois Glaubitz, Albert Beier, Wolfgang Schneider; Helmut Gruner (Cap), Armin Schäfer; Eberhard Franz, Werner Baumann, Horst Jura, Peter Henschel, Hans Speth. Trainer: Karl Dittes
Sent off: Franz (60)
Goals: Kovács (61 pen), Bödör (71)

CF BARCELONA v HAMBURGER SV 4-4 (2-2)
Nou Camp, Barcelona 20.11.1963
Referee: Gennaro Marchese (ITA)   Attendance: 49,942
CF BARCELONA: José Manuel PESUDO Soler; Alfonso María Rodríguez Salas "FONCHO", ELADIO Silvestre Graells; Juan SEGARRA Iraceta (Cap), Fernando OLIVELLA Pons, José María FUSTÉ Blanch; Pedro María ZABALLA Barquín, Jesús María PEREDA Ruiz de Temiño, Cayetano RE Rodríguez, Sándor Kocsis, Luis Alberto CUBILLA Almeyda. Trainer: César Rodríguez
HAMBURGER SV: Horst Schnoor; Gerhard Krug, Jürgen Kurbjuhn; Harry Bähre, Willi Giesemann, Dieter Seeler (Cap); Horst Dehn, Uwe Seeler, Fritz Wilhelm Friedrich Boyens, Ernst Kreuz, Gert Dörfel.   Trainer: Martin Wilke
Goals: U. Seeler (18, 71), Pereda (24), G. Dörfel (33), Fusté (37 pen, 82), Zaballa (50), Eladio (61 og)

OLYMPIQUE LYONNAIS v OLYMPIAKOS PEIRAIAS 4-1 (2-1)
Stade Gerland, Lyon 20.11.1963
Referee: Günther Baumgärtel (W. GER)   Attendance: 12,000
OLYMPIQUE: Marcel Aubour; Jean Djorkaeff, Aimé Mignot (Cap); Roger Duffez, Thadée Polak, Marcel Le Borgne; Jean Dumas, Fleury Di Nallo, Nestor Combin, Jean-Louis Rivoire, Angel Rambert. Trainer: Lucien Jasseron
OLYMPIAKOS: Parashos Avgitidis; Giagkos Simantiris, Kostas Polihroniou (Cap), Aristidis Papazoglou, Pavlos Grigoriadis; Orestis Pavlidis, Giannis Gkaitatzis; Paulos Vasileiou, Panagiotis Kiprianidis, Giorgos Sideris, Dimitris Plessas. Trainer: András Dolgos
Goals: Combin (19, 33, 54 pen), Papazoglou (22), Le Borgne (89)

HAMBURGER SV v CF BARCELONA 0-0
Volksparkstadion, Hamburg 11.12.1963
Referee: Dittmar Huber (SWI)   Attendance: 62,035
HAMBURGER SV: Horst Schnoor; Gerhard Krug, Jürgen Kurbjuhn; Harry Bähre; Willi Giesemann, Dieter Seeler (Cap); Bernd Dörfel, Uwe Seeler, Fritz Wilhelm Friedrich Boyens, Ernst Kreuz, Gert Dörfel.   Trainer: Martin Wilke
CF BARCELONA: José Manuel PESUDO Soler; Alfonso María Rodríguez Salas "FONCHO", ELADIO Silvestre Graells; Juan SEGARRA Iraceta (Cap), Fernando OLIVELLA Pons, Sigfrido GRACIA Royo; Fernand Goyvaerts, Sándor Kocsis, Cayetano RE Rodríguez, Martín VERGÉS Massa, José María FUSTÉ Blanch.   Trainer: César Rodríguez

HAMBURGER SV v CF BARCELONA 3-2 (0-0)

Stade Olympique de la Pontaise, Lausanne 18.12.1963

Referee: Daniel Mellet (SWI)   Attendance: 14,759

HAMBURGER SV: Horst Schnoor; Gerhard Krug, Jürgen Kurbjuhn; Harry Bähre, Willi Giesemann, Erwin Piechowiak; Fritz Wilhelm Friedrich Boyens, Horst Dehn, Uwe Seeler (Cap), Ernst Kreuz, Gert Dörfel.   Trainer: Martin Wilke

CF BARCELONA: José Manuel PESUDO Soler; Alfonso María Rodríguez Salas "FONCHO", Fernando OLIVELLA Pons, Sigfrido GRACIA Royo; Martín VERGÉS Massa, Juan SEGARRA Iraceta (Cap); Pedro María ZABALLA Barquín, Sándor Kocsis, Fernand Goyvaerts, Cayetano RE Rodríguez, José María FUSTÉ Blanch.   Trainer: César Rodríguez

Goals: Bähre (52), Kocsis (62, 64), Seeler (66, 83)

**CELTIC FC GLASGOW
v NK DINAMO ZAGREB 3-0** (2-0)

Celtic Park, Glasgow 4.12.1963

Referee: Pieter Paulus Roomer (HOL)   Attendance: 42,000

CELTIC: John Fallon; Ian Young, Thomas Gemmell; John Clark, William McNeill (Cap), James Kennedy; James Johnstone, Robert Murdoch, Stephen Chalmers, John Divers, John Hughes.   Manager: James McGrory

DINAMO: Branko Crnković; Rudolf Belin, Mirko Braun; Atko Kasumović, Vlatko Marković, Nikola Benko; Zdenko Kobešćak, Slaven Zambata (Cap), Zdravko Raus, Stjepan Lamza, Berislav Ribić.   Trainer: Milan Antolković

Goals: Chalmers (10, 13), Hughes (62)

**TOTTENHAM HOTSPUR FC LONDON
v MANCHESTER UNITED FC 2-0** (0-0)

White Hart Lane, London 3.12.1963

Referee: Hugh Phillips (SCO)   Attendance: 57,447

TOTTENHAM: William Dallas Fyfe Brown; Peter Russell Barker Baker, Ronald Patrick Henry; Anthony Marchi, Maurice Norman, David Craig Mackay (Cap); Clifford William Jones, John Anderson White, Robert Alfred Smith, James Peter Greaves, Terence Kent Dyson.
Manager: William Edward Nicholson

MANCHESTER: David John Gaskell; Anthony Patrick Dunne, Noel Cornelious Cantwell; Patrick Timothy Crerand, William Anthony Foulkes (Cap), Maurice Edgar Setters; Albert Quixhall, Norbert Peter Stiles, David George Herd, Denis Law, Robert Charlton.   Manager: Matthew Busby

Goals: MacKay (67), Dyson (86)

**NK DINAMO ZAGREB
v CELTIC FC GLASGOW 2-1** (0-1)

Maksimir, Zagreb 11.12.1963

Referee: Lajos Horvath (HUN)   Attendance: 6,490

DINAMO: Zlatko Škorić; Rudolf Belin, Mladen Ramljak; Atko Kasumović, Mirko Braun, Nikola Benco; Zdenko Kobešćak, Slaven Zambata (Cap), Zdravko Raus, Stjepan Lamza, Berislav Ribić.   Trainer: Milan Antolković

CELTIC: John Fallon; Ian Young, Thomas Gemmell; John Clark, William McNeill (Cap), James Kennedy; James Johnstone, Robert Murdoch, Stephen Chalmers, John Divers, John Hughes.   Manager: James McGrory

Goals: Murdoch (40), Lamza (63), Zambata (85)

**MANCHESTER UNITED FC
v TOTTENHAM HOTSPUR FC LONDON 4-1** (1-0)

Old Trafford, Manchester 10.12.1963

Referee: Leo Callaghan (WAL)   Attendance: 48,639

MANCHESTER: David John Gaskell; Anthony Patrick Dunne, Noel Cornelious Cantwell; Patrick Timothy Crerand, William Anthony Foulkes (Cap), Maurice Edgar Setters; Albert Quixhall, John Philip Chisnall, David George Herd, Denis Law, Robert Charlton.   Manager: Matthew Busby

TOTTENHAM: William Dallas Fyfe Brown; Peter Russell Barker Baker, Ronald Patrick Henry; Anthony Marchi, Maurice Norman, David Craig Mackay (Cap); Clifford William Jones, John Anderson White, Robert Alfred Smith, James Peter Greaves, Terence Kent Dyson.
Manager: William Edward Nicholson

Goals: Herd (6, 54), Greaves (59), R. Charlton (77, 83)

**BOROUGH UNITED FC
v SLOVAN BRATISLAVA 0-1** (0-0)

Racecourse, Wrexham 11.12.1963

Referee: Henri Faucheux (FRA)   Attendance: 10,196

BOROUGH: Dave Walker; Eric Morris, Frank Harrison (Cap); Harry Hodges, Derek Owen, Brian Clowry; Michael Pritchard, Keith Pritchard, Gerry Duffy, Willy Russell, Joseph Bebb.

SLOVAN: Ferdinand Hason; Anton Urban, Jozef Fillo; Jozef Venglos, Ján Popluhár (Cap), Stefan Kral; Anton Moravcík, Jozef Obert, Ivan Hrdlicka, Pavel Molnár, Karol Jokl.
Trainer: Leopold Stastny

Goal: Pavel Molnár (51)

**SLOVAN BRATISLAVA
v BOROUGH UNITED FC 3-0** (0-0)

Tehelné pole, Bratislava   15.12.1963

Referee: Marian Koczner (POL)   Attendance: 3,653

SLOVAN: Viliam Schrojf; Anton Urban, Jozef Fillo; Jozef Venglos, Ján Popluhár (Cap), Peter Molnár; Anton Moravcík, Jozef Obert, Pavol Molnár, Ivan Hrdlicka, Karol Jokl. Trainer: Leopold Stastny

BOROUGH: Dave Walker; Eric Morris, Frank Harrison (Cap); Harry Hodges, Derek Owen, Brian Clowry; Michael Pritchard, Keith Pritchard, Gerry Duffy, Brian Hallett, Joseph Bebb.

Goals: Pavel Molnár (52, 59), Moravcík (73)

**MANCHESTER UNITED FC v SPORTING CLUBE
DE PORTUGAL LISBOA 4-1** (2-0)

Old Trafford, Manchester   26.02.1964

Referee: Johan Heinrich Martens (HOL)   Att: 60,207

MANCHESTER: David John Gaskell; Seamus Anthony Brennan, Anthony Patrick Dunne; Patrick Timothy Crerand, William Anthony Foulkes (Cap), Maurice Edgar Setters; David George Herd, Norbert Peter Stiles, Robert Charlton, Denis Law, George Best.   Manager: Matthew Busby

SPORTING: Joaquim da Silva CARVALHO; Pedro Gomes, Hilário da Conceição; José Carlos, Alexandre Baptista, Alfredo Moreira; Osvaldo Silva, Fernando Mendes (Cap), Ernesto Figueiredo, Geraldo de Carvalho Géo, João Morais. Trainers: Gentil Cardoso & Anselmo Fernández

Goals: Law (22, 60, 73), Charlton (40), Osvaldo Silva (65)

QUARTER-FINALS

**CELTIC FC GLASGOW
v SLOVAN BRATISLAVA 1-0** (0-0)

Celtic Park, Glasgow   26.02.1964

Referee: Hubert Burguet (BEL)   Attendance: 52,000

CELTIC: John Fallon; Ian Young, Thomas Gemmell; John Clark, William McNeill (Cap), James Kennedy; James Johnstone, Robert Murdoch, Stephen Chalmers, John Divers, John Hughes.   Manager: James McGrory

SLOVAN: Viliam Schrojf; Anton Urban, Jozef Fillo; Alexander Horváth, Ján Popluhár (Cap), Peter Molnár; Ludovít Cvetler, Jozef Obert, Ivan Hrdlicka, Pavol Molnár, Karol Jokl. Trainer: Leopold Stastny

Goal: Murdoch (71 pen)

**SPORTING CP LISBOA
v MANCHESTER UNITED FC 5-0** (2-0)

Estádio José Alvalade, Lisboa   18.03.1964

Referee: Michel Kitabdjian (FRA)   Attendance: 30,000

SPORTING: Joaquim da Silva CARVALHO; Pedro Gomes, Hilário da Conceição; Fernando Mendes (Cap), Alexandre Baptista, José Carlos; Ernesto Figueiredo, Osvaldo Silva, Domingos António da Silva Mascarenhas, Geraldo de Carvalho Géo, João Morais.
Trainer: Francisco Reboredo & Anselmo Fernández

MANCHESTER: David John Gaskell; Seamus Anthony Brennan, Anthony Patrick Dunne; Patrick Timothy Crerand, William Anthony Foulkes (Cap), Maurice Edgar Setters; David George Herd, John Philip Chisnall, Robert Charlton, Denis Law, George Best.   Manager: Matthew Busby

Goals: Osvaldo Silva (3, 12, 54), Géo (47), Morais (52)

**SLOVAN BRATISLAVA
v CELTIC FC GLASGOW 0-1** (0-0)

Tehelné pole, Bratislava   4.03.1964

Referee: Werner Treichel (W. GER)   Attendance: 29,000

SLOVAN: Viliam Schrojf; Anton Urban, Jozef Fillo; Alexander Horváth, Ján Popluhár (Cap), Peter Molnár; Anton Moravcík, Jozef Obert, Pavol Molnár, Ivan Hrdlicka, Ludovít Cvetler. Trainer: Leopold Stastny

CELTIC: John Fallon; Ian Young, Thomas Gemmell; John Clark, William McNeill (Cap), James Kennedy; James Johnstone, Robert Murdoch, Stephen Chalmers, John Divers, John Hughes.   Manager: James McGrory

Goal: Hughes (58)

**MTK BUDAPEST
v FENERBAHÇE SK ISTANBUL 2-0** (0-0)

Hungária körut, Budapest   27.02.1964

Referee: Eduard Babauczek (AUS)   Attendance: 20,000

MTK: Ferenc Kovalik; György Keszei, József Danszky, István Jenei; István Nagy, Ferenc Kovács III (Cap); József Török, Mihály Laczkó, Mihály Vasas, István Halápi, László Bödör. Trainer: Imre Kovács

FENERBAHÇE: Hazim Canitez; Özcan Köksoy, Özer Kanra, Ismail Kurt; Ali Ihsan Okçuoglu, Seref Has (Cap); Ogün Altiparmak, Mustafa Güven, Senol Birol, Huseyin Yazici, Aydin Yelken.   Trainer: Naci Erdem

Sent off: Has (76)

Goals: Vasas (77 pen), Bödör (82)

FENERBAHÇE SK ISTANBUL
v MTK BUDAPEST 3-1 (1-0)

Mithat Paşa, Istanbul   7.03.1964

Referee: Konstantin Zecević (YUG)   Attendance: 30,000

FENERBAHÇE: Hazim Canitez; Atilla Altaş, Özer Kanra, Ismail Kurt (Cap); Hüseyin Yazici, Ali Ihsan Okçuoglu; Ogün Altiparmak, Birol Pekel, Senol Birol, Selim Soydan, Aydin Yelken.   Trainer: Naci Erdem

MTK: Ferenc Kovalik; György Keszei, József Danszky, István Jenei; István Nagy, Ferenc Kovács III (Cap); József Török, Mihály Laczkó, István Halápi, Mihály Vasas, László Bödör. Trainer: Imre Kovács

Goals: Ogün (6, 76), Selim (66), Bödör (80)

OLYMPIQUE LYONNAIS
v HAMBURGER SV 2-0 (1-0)

Stade Gerland, Lyon   18.03.1964

Referee: Daniel Mellet (SWI)   Attendance: 26,805

OLYMPIQUE: Marcel Aubour; Jean Djorkaeff, Aimé Mignot (Cap); Lucien Degeorges, Thadée Polak, Marcel Le Borgne; Jean Dumas, Fleury Di Nallo, Nestor Combin, Guy Hatchi, Angel Rambert.   Trainer: Lucien Jasseron

HAMBURGER SV: Horst Schnoor; Gerhard Krug, Jürgen Kurbjuhn; Willi Giesemann, Hubert Stapelfeldt, Dieter Seeler (Cap); Helmut Sandmann, Harry Bähre, Uwe Seeler, Ernst Kreuz, Gert Dörfel.   Trainer: Martin Wilke

Sent off: Combin (75)

Goals: Combin (15, 62)

MTK BUDAPEST
v FENERBAHÇE SK ISTANBUL 1-0 (0-0)

Stadio Flaminio, Roma   18.03.1964

Referee: Cesare Jonni (ITA)   Attendance: 7,000

MTK: Ferenc Kovalik; György Keszei, József Danszky, István Jenei; István Nagy (Cap), Ferenc Kovács III; József Török, László Takács, István Kuti, Mihály Laczkó, László Bödör. Trainer: Imre Kovács

FENERBAHÇE: Hazim Canitez; Atilla Altaş, Özer Kanra, Ismail Kurt; Seref Has (Cap), Ali Ihsan Okçuoglu; Ogün Altiparmak, Birol Pekel, Senol Birol, Selim Soydan, Aydin Yelken.   Trainer: Naci Erdem

Goal: Kuti (86)

SEMI-FINALS

OLYMPIQUE LYONNAIS
v SPORTING CP LISBOA 0-0

Stade Gerland, Lyon   8.04.1964

Referee: Pieter Paulus Roomer (HOL)   Attendance: 28,053

OLYMPIQUE: Marcel Aubour; Jean Djorkaeff, Aimé Mignot (Cap); Lucien Degeorges, Thadée Polak, Marcel Le Borgne; Jean Dumas, Fleury Di Nallo, Jean-Louis Rivoire, Guy Hatchi, Angel Rambert.   Trainer: Lucien Jasseron

SPORTING: Joaquim da Silva CARVALHO; Pedro Gomes, Hilário da Conceição; Fernando Mendes (Cap), Alexandre Baptista, José Carlos; Ernesto Figueiredo, Osvaldo Silva, Domingos António da Silva Mascarenhas, Geraldo de Carvalho "GÉO", João Morais.
Trainers: Francisco Reboredo & Anselmo Fernández

HAMBURGER SV
v OLYMPIQUE LYONNAIS 1-1 (1-1)

Volksparkstadion, Hamburg   4.03.1964

Referee: Cesare Jonni (ITA)   Attendance: 35,018

HAMBURGER SV: Horst Schnoor; Gerhard Krug, Jürgen Kurbjuhn; Harry Bähre, Willi Giesemann, Erwin Piechowiak; Fritz Wilhelm Friedrich Boyens, Bernd Dörfel, Uwe Seeler (Cap), Ernst Kreuz, Gert Dörfel.   Trainer: Martin Wilke

OLYMPIQUE: Marcel Aubour; Jean Djorkaeff, Aimé Mignot (Cap); Lucien Degeorges, Thadée Polak, Marcel Le Borgne; Jean Dumas, Angel Rambert, Nestor Combin, Guy Hatchi, Georges Taberner.   Trainer: Lucien Jasseron

Goals: Mignot (11), G. Dörfel (22)

SPORTING CP LISBOA
v OLYMPIQUE LYONNAIS 1-1 (0-1)

Estádio José Alvalade, Lisboa   21.04.1964

Referee: Kurt Tschenscher (W. GER)   Attendance: 40,749

SPORTING: Joaquim da Silva CARVALHO; Pedro Gomes, Hilário da Conceição; Fernando Mendes (Cap), Alexandre Baptista, José Carlos; Ernesto Figueiredo, Osvaldo Silva, Domingos António da Silva Mascarenhas, Geraldo de Carvalho "GÉO", João Morais.
Trainer: Francisco Reboredo & Anselmo Fernández

OLYMPIQUE: Marcel Aubour; Aimé Mignot (Cap), Jean Djorkaeff; Lucien Degeorges, Thadée Polak, Marcel Le Borgne; Jean Dumas, Fleury Di Nallo, Nestor Combin, Guy Hatchi, Georges Taberner.   Trainer: Lucien Jasseron

Goals: Combin (13), Géo (48)

SPORTING CP LISBOA
v OLYMPIQUE LYONNAIS 1-0 (0-0)

Estadio Metropolitano, Madrid   5.05.1964

Referee: José González Echeverría (SPA)   Att: 20,000

SPORTING: Joaquim da Silva CARVALHO, Pedro Gomes, Hilário da Conceição; Fernando Mendes (Cap), Alexandre Baptista, José Carlos; José Perides, Osvaldo Silva, Domingos António da Silva Mascarenhas, Geraldo de Carvalho "GÉO", João Morais.
Trainers: Francisco Reboredo & Anselmo Fernández

OLYMPIQUE: Marcel Aubour; Jean Djorkaeff, Aimé Mignot (Cap); Jacques Glyczinski, Thadée Polak, Lucien Degeorges; Jean Dumas, Fleury Di Nallo, Nestor Combin, Guy Hatchi, Angel Rambert.   Trainer: Lucien Jasseron

Sent off: Dumas (70)

Goal: Osvaldo (64)

CELTIC FC GLASGOW
v MTK BUDAPEST 3-0 (1-0)

Celtic Park, Glasgow   15.04.1964

Referee: Giulio Campanati (ITA)   Attendance: 51,000

CELTIC: John Fallon; Ian Young, Thomas Gemmell; John Clark, William McNeill (Cap), James Kennedy; James Johnstone, Robert Murdoch, Stephen Chalmers, Charles Gallacher, John Hughes.   Manager: James McGrory

MTK: Ferenc Kovalik; György Keszei, József Danszky, István Jenei; István Nagy (Cap), Mihály Vasas; József Török, László Takács, László Bödör, István Kuti, Illés Dinnyés.
Trainer: Imre Kovács

Goals: Johnstone (41), Chalmers (65, 76)

MTK BUDAPEST
v CELTIC FC GLASGOW 4-0 (1-0)

Népstadion, Budapest   29.04.1964

Referee: Dimitris Wlachojanis (AUS)   Attendance: 15,000

MTK: Ferenc Kovalik; György Keszei, József Danszky, István Jenei; István Nagy, Mihály Vasas; Károly Sándor (Cap), László Takács, László Bödör, István Kuti, István Halápi.
Trainer: Imre Kovács

CELTIC: John Fallon; Ian Young, Thomas Gemmell; John Clark, William McNeill (Cap), James Kennedy; James Johnstone, Robert Murdoch, Stephen Chalmers, Charles Gallacher, John Hughes.   Manager: James McGrory

Goals: Kuti (11, 71), Vasas (47), Sándor (61)

FINAL

SPORTING LISBOA
v MTK BUDAPEST 3-3 (1-1, 3-3) (AET)

Heysel, Bruxelles   13.05.1964

Referee: Lucien Van Nuffel (BEL)   Attendance: 3,208

SPORTING: Joaquim da Silva CARVALHO; Pedro Gomes, Alexandre Baptista, José Carlos; João Morais, Fernando Mendes (Cap); Osvaldo Silva, Domingos António da Silva "Mascarenhas", Ernesto Figueiredo, Geraldo de Carvalho "GÉO", Roberto Bocaleri "BÉ".   Trainer: Anselmo Fernándes

MTK: Ferenc Kovalik; György Keszei, József Danszky, István Jenei; István Nagy, Ferenc Kovács III; Károly Sándor (Cap), Mihály Vasas, László Bödör, István Kuti, István Halápi.
Trainer: Béla Volentik

Goals: Sándor (19, 72), Mascarenhas (40), Figueiredo (48, 81), Kuti (70)

FINAL REPLAY

SPORTING LISBOA v MTK BUDAPEST 1-0 (1-0)

Boschuil Deurne, Antwerp   15.05.1964

Referee: Gérard Versyp (BEL)   Attendance: 13,924

SPORTING: Joaquim da Silva CARVALHO; Pedro Gomes, Alexandre Baptista, José Carlos; José Perides, Fernando Mendes (Cap); Osvaldo Silva, Domingos António da Silva "Mascarenhas", Ernesto Figueiredo, Geraldo de Carvalho "GÉO", João Morais.   Trainer: Anselmo Fernándes

MTK: Ferenc Kovalik; György Keszei, József Danszky, István Jenei; István Nagy, Ferenc Kovács III; Károly Sándor (Cap), Mihály Vasas, László Bödör, István Kuti, István Halápi.
Trainer: Béla Volentik

Goal: Morais (20)

Goalscorers European Cup-Winners' Cup 1963-64:

11 goals: Domingos António da Silva Mascarenhas (Sporting Lisboa)

10 goals: Nestor Combin (Olympique Lyonnais)

6 goals: Denis Law (Manchester United), Ernesto Figueiredo (Sporting Lisboa)

5 goals: Uwe Seeler (Hamburger SV), Osvaldo Silva (Sporting Lisboa), Stephen Chalmers, John Hughes (Celtic Glasgow), István Kuti (MTK Budapest)

4 goals: Giorgos Sideris (Olympiakos Pireas), David George Herd, Robert Charlton (Manchester United), Károly Sándor (MTK Budapest), Senol Birol (Fenerbahçe Istanbul), Pavol Molnar, Jozef Obert (Slovan Bratislava)

3 goals: Takis Hailis (Apoel Nicosia), Fusté, Kocsis (CF Barcelona), Moravcík, Velecky (Slovan), Ogün (Fenerbahçe), Boyens (Hamburger SV), Divers, Murdoch (Celtic), Bödör (MTK Budapest), Augusto (Sporting CP Lisboa)

2 goals: M. Dridea (Petrolul), Pereda (CF Barcelona), Lamza (Dinamo Zagreb), Selim (Fenerbahçe), G.Dörfel, Giesemann (Hamburger SV), Di Nallo (Olympique Lyonnais), Johnstone (Celtic), Vasas (MTK Budapest), Ferreira Pinto, Géo, Morais (Sporting CP Lisboa)

1 goal: Calvanese, Domenghini, Christensen, Nova (Atalanta), Rautiainen, Raatikaincn (HPS), Blumer (FC Basel), Bonham (Shelbourne), Winandy, Bernardin (US Luxembourg), Piecyk, Krawiarz (Zaglebie Sosnowiec), Louer (Willem II Tilburg), Mishev (Slavia Sofia), Fürst, Nemeth (LASK), Rasmussen, Hansen (B 1913 Odense), Dickson, Craig, Ferguson (Linfield), Andreou, Agathokleous, Papallos, Kantzileris, Partakis (Apoel), Jakob (Motor Zwickau), Papazoglou, Kiprianidis, Tzinis (Olympiakos), Zaballa, Re, Zaldúa (CF Barcelona), MacKay, Dyson, Greaves (Tottenham), Zambata, Raus (Dinamo Zagreb), Cvetler, Hrdlicka (Slovan), Setters (Manchester), Birol, Nedim (Fenerbahçe), Duffy, M.Pritchard (Borough), Bähre, Kurbjuhn (Hamburger SV), Mignot, Le Borgne, Taberner (Olympique Lyonnais), Lennox (Celtic), Kovács (MTK Budapest), Lino, Louro, Pérides, Bé, Lúcio (Sporting Lisboa)

Own goals: Cantwell (Manchester United) for Willem II Tilburg, Eladio (CF Barcelona) for Hamburger SV

CUP WINNERS' CUP 1964-65

FIRST ROUND

LAUSANNE SPORTS v HONVÉD BUDAPEST 2-0 (0-0)
Stade Olympique de la Pontaise, Lausanne 2.09.1964
Referee: Kurt Tschenscher (W. GER)   Attendance: 12,910
SPORTS: René Künzi; André Grobéty (Cap), Kurt Hunziker; Heinz Schneiter, Ely Tacchella, Richard Dürr; Pieter Johannes Elisabeth Kerkhoffs, Robert Hosp, Norbert Eschmann, Kurt Armbruster, Charles Hertig.   Trainer: Karl Rappan
HONVÉD: Béla Takács; László Marosi, Zoltán Dudás; Ferenc Nógrádi, Ferenc Sipos, István Vági; György Nagy, Imre Komora, Lajos Tichy (Cap), Antal Nagy, Sándor Katona.   Trainer: Mihály Kispéter
Goals: Kerkhoffs (62, 70)

HONVÉD BUDAPEST v LAUSANNE SPORTS 1-0 (1-0)
Népstadion, Budapest 9.09.1964
Referee: Alois Obtulovič (CZE)   Attendance: 45,000
HONVÉD: Béla Takács; László Marosi, Ferenc Sipos; Boldizsár Mihalecz, Ferenc Nógrádi, István Vági; Antal Nagy, Károly Balogh, Lajos Tichy (Cap), Kálmán Tóth, Sándor Katona.   Trainer: Mihály Kispéter
SPORTS: René Künzi; André Grobéty (Cap), Kurt Hunziker; Richard Dürr, Ely Tacchella, Heinz Schneiter; Norbert Eschmann, Pieter Johannes Elisabeth Kerkhoffs, Kurt Armbruster, Robert Hosp, Charles Hertig.   Trainer: Karl Rappan
Goal: Vági (27)

UNION SPORTIVE LUXEMBOURG v TSV MÜNCHEN 1860 0-4 (0-3)
Stade Municipal, Luxembourg 2.09.1964
Referee: Josef Stoll (AUS)   Attendance: 6,000
US LUXEMBOURG: Nico Schmitt; Ady Colas, Roland Christen; Romain Kies, Mathias Ewen, Paul Ries (Cap); Gaston Bauer, René Schneider, Johny Leonard, Guy Bernardin, Jean-Pierre Hemmerling.   Trainer: Georges Berry
TSV MÜNCHEN: Petar Radenkovic; Rudolf Steiner, Bernd Patzke; Rudolf Zeiser, Hans Reich, Otto Luttrop; Engelbert Kraus, Peter Grosser, Rudolf Brunnenmeier (Cap), Hans Küppers, Alfred Heiss.   Trainer: Max Merkel
Goals: Brunnenmeier (6, 26), Küppers (12), Luttrop (81)

TSV MÜNCHEN 1860
v UNION SPORTIVE LUXEMBOURG 6-0 (1-0)
Stadion Grünwalder str. München 9.09.1964
Referee: Eduard Babauczek (AUS)   Attendance: 14,316
TSV MÜNCHEN: Petar Radenkovic; Bernd Patzke, Rudolf Steiner; Rudolf Zeiser, Hans Reich, Otto Luttrop; Hans Rebele, Wilfried Kohlars, Rudolf Brunnenmeier (Cap), Hans Küppers, Peter Grosser.   Trainer: Max Merkel
US LUXEMBOURG: Armand Olinger; Ady Colas, Roland Christen; Romain Kies, Mathias Ewen, Paul Ries (Cap); Gaston Bauer, Jean-Pierre Mertl, Johny Leonard, René Schneider, Pierre Hemmerling.   Trainer: Georges Berry
Goals: Brunnenmeier (11, 46), Luttrop (54), Rebele (60, 74), Grosser (69)

FC VALLETTA v REAL ZARAGOZA 0-3 (0-1)
The Empire Stadium, Valletta 6.09.1964
Referee: Raoul Righi (ITA)   Attendance: 6,748
FC VALLETTA: Thomas Taylor; Joseph Attard, Vincent Gauci; Charles Williams, Joseph Cilia (Cap), Frank Zammit; Anthony Calleja, Joseph Urpani, Joseph Zarb, Edward Vella, Paul Gauci.   Trainer: Carm Borg
REAL ZARAGOZA CD: Enrique YARZA Sorlauce (Cap); Joaquín CORTIZO Rosendo, Severino REIJA Vázquez; Santiago ISASI Salazar, Francisco SANTAMARÍA Briones, José Cuéllar González "PEPÍN"; Darcy Silveira Dos Santos "CANARIO", Eleuterio SANTOS Brito, MARCELINO Martínez Cao, Juan Manuel VILLA Gutiérrez, Carlos LAPETRA Coarasa.   Trainer: Roque Olsen
Goals: Marcelino (16, 48), Canario (80)

FC ADMIRA ENERGIE WIEN
v LEGIA WARSZAWA 1-3 (0-1)
Prater, Wien 2.09.1964
Referee: Erwin Vetter (E. GER)   Attendance: 11,405
ADMIRA: Karl Sandner; Michael Breibert, Johann Pesser, Johann Szauer; Bohumil Hruska (Cap), Walter Stamm; Gerhard Pinisch, Peter Reiter, Felix Latzke, Günther Kaltenbrunner, Karl Skerlan.
Trainer: Franz Pelikan, Johann Pesser
LEGIA: Stanislaw Foltyn; Antoni Mahseli, Henryk Grzybowski, Antoni Trzaskowski, Jacek Gmoch; Bernard Blaut, Janusz Zmijewski, Lucjan Brychczy (Cap), Henryk Apostel, Wieslaw Korzeniowski, Edward Biernacki.
Trainer: Virgil Popescu (ROM)
Goals: Brychczy (12), Kaltenbrunner (69), Zmijewski (73, 75)

REAL ZARAGOZA v FC VALLETTA 5-1 (3-1)
Estadio de La Romareda, Zaragoza 14.10.1964
Referee: Gino Rigato (ITA)   Attendance: 11,174
REAL ZARAGOZA CD: Vicente CARDOSO; Joaquín CORTIZO Rosendo, José Luis VIOLETA Lajusticia; Antonio PAÍS Castroagudín, Francisco SANTAMARÍA Briones (Cap), Eduardo Bibiano ENDÉRIZ Cortajarena; Darcy Silveira Dos Santos "CANARIO", Eleuterio SANTOS Brito, MARCELINO Martínez Cao, José Sigfredo Martínez "SIGI", José María ENCONTRA Tolosana.   Trainer: Roque Olsen
FC VALLETTA: Alfred Stivala; Joseph Attard, Vincent Gauci; Charles Williams, Leonard Mizzi, Edward Vella; Anthony Calleja, Joseph Urpani (Cap), Alfred Connor, Frank Zammit, Paul Gauci.   Trainer: Carm Borg
Goals: Sigi (2, 27, 85), Marcelino (17), P. Gauci (29), Santos (53)

LEGIA WARSZAWA
v ADMIRA ENERGIE WIEN 1-0 (1-0)
Wojska Polskiego, Warszawa 23.09.1964
Referee: Helmut Köhler (E. GER)   Attendance: 4,613
LEGIA: Stanislaw Foltyn; Antoni Mahseli, Henryk Grzybowski, Antoni Trzaskowski, Jacek Gmoch; Bernard Blaut, Janusz Zmijewski, Lucjan Brychczy (Cap), Henryk Apostel, Wieslaw Korzeniowski, Edward Biernacki.
Trainer: Virgil Popescu
ADMIRA: Karl Sandner; Alexander Zelesnik, Josef Wahl, Michael Breibert; Werner Bedernik, Walter Stamm; Karl Skerlan, Peter Reiter (Cap), Gerhard Pinisch, Felix Latzke, Johann Szauer.   Trainer: Franz Pelikan
Goal: Brychczy (11)

STEAUA BUCUREŞTI v DERRY CITY FC 3-0 (1-0)
23 August, Bucureşti 9.09.1964
Referee: Alexandros Monastiriotis (GRE)   Att: 20,000
STEAUA: Dumitru Eremia; Mircea Georgescu, Dumitru Nicolae, Mircea Petescu, Dragoş Cojocaru; Emerich Jenei, Constantin Koszka; Sorin Avram, Gheorghe Constantin (Cap), Cornel Pavlovici, Carol Creiniceanu.   Trainer: Ilie Savu
DERRY CITY: Edward Mahon; Frank Campbell, William Cathcart; James McGeough, James Crossan, Douglas Wood (Cap); John McKenzie, Matthew Doherty, Francis Coyle, Joseph Wilson, Roy Seddon.   Manager: Willie Ross
Goals: Pavlovici (9, 80), Constantin (68 pen)

DERRY CITY FC v STEAUA BUCUREŞTI 0-2 (0-0)

The Brandywell, Derry   16.09.1964

Referee: George McCabe (ENG)   Attendance: 7,426

DERRY CITY: Edward Mahon; Frank Campbell, William Cathcart; James McGeough, James Crossan, Douglas Wood (Cap); John McKenzie, Matthew Doherty, Roy Seddon, Joseph Wilson, Ronald Wood.   Manager: Willie Ross

STEAUA: Dumitru Eremia; Mircea Georgescu, Dumitru Nicolae, Mircea Petescu, Dragoş Cojocaru; Emerich Jenei, Constantin Koszka; Sorin Avram, Gheorghe Constantin (Cap), Cornel Pavlovici, Carol Creiniceanu.   Trainer: Ilie Savu

Goals: Creiniceanu (48, 57)

**SC AUFBAU MAGDEBURG
v GALATASARAY SK ISTANBUL 1-1** (1-0)

Ernst-Grube-Stadion, Magdeburg   9.09.1964

Referee: Pieter Paulus Roomer (HOL)   Attendance: 19,385

AUFBAU: Wolfgang Blochwitz; Rainer Wiedemann, Rolf Retschlag; Günter Kubisch, Manfred Zapf, Günter Fronzeck; Winfried Klingbiel, Günter Hirschmann, Hans-Joachim Walter, Peter Heuer, Hermann Stöcker (Cap).
Trainer: Ernst Kümmel

GALATASARAY: Bülent Gürbüz; Dogan Sel, Ahmet Berman; Ismet Yurtsu, Naci Erdem, Talat Özkarsli; Yilmaz Gökdel, Turan Dogangün, Metin Oktay (Cap), Tarik Kutver, Ugur Kökten.   Trainer: Coşkun Özari

Goals: Heuer (13), Turan (52)

**ATHLITIKI ENOSIS KONSTANDINOUPOLI
ATHINA v DINAMO ZAGREB 2-0** (0-0)

Neas Filadelfeias, Athina   9.09.1964

Referee: Mihai Popa (ROM)   Attendance: 23,650

AEK: Stelios Serafeidis; Giorgos Kefalidis, Alexandros Iordanou; Alekos Sofianidis, Stelios Skevofilax, Andreas Stamatiadis (Cap); Fotios Balopoulos, Giorgos Petridis, Kostas Nestoridis, Dimitris Papaioannou, Spiros Pomonis. Trainer: Mirko Kokotović

DINAMO: Zlatko Škorić; Marijan Krizaj, Rudolf Belin; Mladen Ramljak, Atko Kasumović, Miljenko Puljcan; Zdenko Kobešćak, Slaven Zambata (Cap), Drazen Jerković, Stjepan Lamza, Krasnodar Rora.   Trainer: Vlatko Konjevod.

Sent off: Kobešćak (67).

Goals: Papaioannou (75), Nestoridis (80)

**GALATASARAY SK ISTANBUL
v SC AUFBAU MAGDEBURG 1-1** (1-0,1-1)

Ali Sami Yen, Istanbul   17.09.1964

Referee: Vladimír Stanković (YUG)   Attendance: 26,347

GALATASARAY: Bülent Gürbüz; Dogan Sel, Ahmet Berman; Ismet Yurtsu, Naci Erdem, Talat Özkarsli; Yilmaz Gökdel, Tarik Kutver, Metin Oktay (Cap), Turan Dogangün, Ugur Kökten.
Trainer: Coşkun Özari

AUFBAU: Wolfgang Blochwitz; Rainer Wiedemann, Rolf Retschlag; Günter Kubisch, Manfred Zapf, Wolfgang Seguin; Wilfried Klingbiel, Günter Hirschmann, Hans-Joachim Walter, Peter Heuer, Hermann Stöcker (Cap).
Trainer: Ernst Kümmel

Goals: Ugür (26), Heuer (74)

DINAMO ZAGREB v AEK ATHINA 3-0 (1-0)

Maksimir, Zagreb   16.09.1964

Referee: Petre Sotir (ROM)   Attendance: 10,418

DINAMO: Zlatko Škorić; Zlatko Mesić, Miljenko Puljcan; Atko Kasumović, Mladen Ramljak, Rudolf Belin; Stjepan Lamza, Slaven Zambata (Cap), Drazen Jerković, Željko Matuš, Krasnodar Rora.   Trainer: Vlatko Konjevod

AEK: Stelios Serafeidis; Giorgos Kefalidis, Alexandros Iordanou; Alekos Sofianidis, Fotios Balopoulos, Stelios Skevofilax; Andreas Stamatiadis (Cap), Giorgos Petridis, Kostas Nestoridis, Spiros Pomonis, Theofanis Tasinos. Trainer: Mirko Kokotović

Sent off: Zambata (85) & Pomonis (78)

Goals: Lamza (45), Zambata (50), Jerković (57)

**GALATASARAY ISTANBUL
v AUFBAU MAGDEBURG 1-1** (0-0,1-1)

Hohe Warte, Wien   7.10.1964

Referee: Alfred Haberfellner (AUS)   Attendance: 1,000

AUFBAU: Wolfgang Blochwitz; Günter Kubisch, Rolf Retschlag; Wolfgang Seguin, Manfred Zapf, Günter Fronzeck; Rainer Wiedemann, Günter Hirschmann (Cap), Hans-Joachim Walter, Peter Heuer, Wilfried Klingbiel.
Trainer: Ernst Kümmel

GALATASARAY: Turgay Şeren (Cap); Candemir Berkman, Dogan Sel; Naci Erdem, Talat Özkarsli, Ahmet Berman; Yilmaz Gökdel, Tarik Kutver, Metin Oktay, Turan Dogangün, Ugur Kökten.   Trainer: Coşkun Özari

Goals: Klingbiel (62), Metin (81)

Galatasaray won on the toss of coin

**ESBJERG FORENEDE BOLDKLUBBER
v CARDIFF CITY AFC 0-0**
Idraetspark, Esbjerg   9.09.1964
Referee: Joseph Hannet (BEL)   Attendance: 7,093
ESBJERG FB: Erik Gaardhøje; Jens Jørgen Hansen, Preben Jensen; Finn Nielsen, John Madsen, Jens Petersen; Knud Petersen, Carl Emil Christiansen (Cap), Palle Bruun, Egon Jensen, Bjarne Kikkenborg.   Trainer: Arne Sørensen
CARDIFF CITY: Dilwyn John; Peter Rodrigues, Trevor Peck; Gareth Williams, John Charles, Barrington Gerald Hole; Peter King, Melvyn Charles, Thomas Halliday, Ivor John Allchurch (Cap), Greg Farrell.   Manager: James Scoular

HAKA VALKEAKOSKEN v SKEID OSLO 2-0 (0-0)
Tehtaan kenttä, Valkeakoski   7.10.1964
Referee: Vagn Bramming Sørensen (DEN)   Att: 1,379
HAKA: Martti Halme; Olli Mäkinen, Pentti Niittymäki; Antti Nieminen, Veijo Valtonen (Cap), Markku Lahti; Esko Malm, Mauri Tuuri, Timo Paimander, Juhani Peltonen, Mauri Paavilainen.   Trainer: Aimo Pulkkinen
SKEID: Kjell Kaspersen; Kjell Wangen, Finn Tøråsen; Björn Elvenes, Finn Thorsen, Erik Mejlo; Jan Gulbrandsen (Cap), Frank Olafsen, Jan Mathisen, Päl Saetrang, Terje Kristoffersen.   Trainer: Brede Borgen
Goals: Paimander (67), Peltonen (81)

CARDIFF CITY v ESBJERG FBK 1-0 (0-0)
Ninian Park, Cardiff   13.10.1964
Referee: Vital Loraux (BEL)   Attendance: 8,084
CARDIFF CITY: Dilwyn John; Peter Rodrigues, Trevor Peck; Gareth Williams, Donald Murray (Cap), Barrington Gerald Hole; Greg Farrell, Peter King, Derek Tapscott, Mel Charles, Bernard Lewis.   Manager: James Scoular
ESBJERG: Erik Gaardhøje; Jens Jørgen Hansen, Preben Jensen; Egon Jensen, John Madsen, Jens Petersen; Knud Petersen, Carl Emil Christiansen (Cap), Peter Thøgersen, Finn Nielsen, Bjarne Kikkenborg.   Trainer: Arne Sørensen
Goal: King (57)

**SPARTA PRAHA
v ANORTHOSIS FAMAGUSTA 10-0** (5-0)
Letná, Praha   16.09.1964
Referee: Werner Treichel (W. GER)   Attendance: 8,981
SPARTA: Antonín Kramerius; Milan Kollár, Vladimír Táborsky; Jiří Gura, Jiří Tichy (Cap), Karel Steiningel; Pavel Dyba, Ivan Mráz, Tadeás Kraus, Václav Masek, Václav Vrána.   Trainer: Václav Jezek
ANORTHOSIS: Andreas Hatzikonstandi; Hristofis Hristofi, Mihail Giasemi (Cap); Thomas, Antonis Tsoukas, Andreas Konstantinou; Dimitris Zagkylos, Kostas Pieris, Mavrikios Asprou, Kostas Kokkinis, Antonakis Kafas.   Trainer: Reyner
Goals: Masek (15 pen, 32, 49), Mráz (17, 21, 34, 55, 80), Steiningel (75), Kraus (83)

SKEID OSLO v HAKA VALKEAKOSKEN 1-0 (1-0)
Bislett, Oslo   15.09.1964
Referee: Carl W. Hansen (DEN)   Attendance: 11,306
SKEID: Kjell Kaspersen; Kjell Wangen, Finn Tøråsen; Jan Gulbrandsen (Cap), Björn Elvenes, Erik Mejlo; Terje Kristoffersen, Frank Olafsen, Jan Mathisen, Päl Saetrang, Trond Börresen.   Trainer: Brede Borgen
HAKA: Martti Halme; Oli Mäkinen, Pentti Niittymäki; Antti Nieminen, Veijo Valtonen (Cap), Markku Lahti; Esko Malm, Mauri Tuuri, Timo Paimander, Juhani Peltonen, Mauri Paavilainen.   Trainer: Aimo Pulkkinen
Goal: Mathisen (38)

**ANORTHOSIS FAMAGUSTA
v SPARTA PRAHA 0-6** (0-2)
Stadion Štruncovy sady, Plzen   20.09.1964
Referee: Waclaw Majdan (POL)   Attendance: 9,514
ANORTHOSIS: Alexandros Papiros; Hristofis Hristofi, Antonis Tsoukas, Mihail Giasemi (Cap); Thomas, Andreas Konstantinou; Dimitris Zagkylos, Kostas Pieris, Mavrikos Asprou, Kostas Kokkinis, Antonakis Kafas.   Trainer: Reyner
SPARTA: Antonín Kramerius; Milan Kollár, Vladimír Táborsky; Jiří Gura, Jiří Tichy (Cap), Karel Steiningel; Pavel Dyba; Ivan Mráz, Tadeás Kraus, Václav Masek, Václav Vrána.   Trainer: Václav Jezek
Goals: Vrána (36), Kraus (40, 84), Dyba (67), Masek (82, 90)

FC PORTO v OLYMPIQUE LYONNAIS 3-0 (1-0)

Estádio Das Antas, Porto 16.09.1964

Referee: Daniel Zariquiegui (SPA)   Attendance: 18,115

FC PORTO: AMERICO Ferreira Lopes (Cap); Alberto Festa, João Luís Pinto ALMEIDA; António Manuel PAULA, José ROLANDO Andrade Gonçalves, JOAQUIM Antonio JORGE; JAIME Ferreira Silva, Custódio Pinto, VALDIR Araújo Sousa, Carlos Baptista, Francisco Lage Pereira da NOBREGA. Trainer: Otto Glória

OLYMPIQUE: Marcel Aubour; Jean Djorkaeff, Aimé Mignot (Cap); Lucien Degeorges, Marcel Le Borgne, Guy Hatchi; Michel Margottin, Fleury Di Nallo, Jean Dumas, Jean-Louis Rivoire, Angel Rambert.   Trainer: Lucien Jasseron

Goals: Pinto (41, 72), Baptista (60)

WEST HAM UNITED LONDON v A.R.A. LA GANTOISE 1-1 (1-1)

Upton Park, London 7.10.1964

Referee: Rolf Erling Olsen (NOR)   Attendance: 24,101

WEST HAM UNITED: Alan Dickie; John Frederick Bond, Martin Stanford Peters; Edward Bovington, Kenneth Brown, Robert Frederick Moore (Cap); Peter Brabrook, Ronald William Boyce, John Joseph Byrne, Geoffrey Charles Hurst, John Leslie Sissons.   Manager: Ronald Greenwood

ARA LA GANTOISE: Armand Seghers (Cap); Noël Van de Velde, Richard De Nayer, Antoine Devreese; Robert Mahieu, Lucien Ghellynck; Albert Mayama, Urbain Seghers, Eric Lambert, Cyprien Bula, James Storme. Trainer: Max Schirschin

Goals: Peters (33 og), Byrne (43)

OLYMPIQUE LYONNAIS v FC PORTO 0-1 (0-0)

Stade Gerland, Lyon 14.10.1964

Referee: Juan Gardeazabal Garay (SPA)   Attendance: 19,162

OLYMPIQUE: Marcel Aubour; Jean Djorkaeff, Aimé Mignot (Cap); Lucien Degeorges, Thadée Polak, Marcel Le Borgne; Michel Margottin, Fleury Di Nallo, Stéphane Bruey, Guy Hatchi, Angel Rambert.   Trainer: Lucien Jasseron

FC PORTO: AMERICO Ferreira Lopes; Alberto Festa, João Eleutério Luis ATRACA; José ROLANDO Andrade Gonçalves, João Luís Pinto ALMEIDA, António Manuel PAULA (Cap); José Duarte RICO, Carlos Baptista, VALDIR Araújo Sousa, Custódio Pinto, Francisco Lage Pereira da NOBREGA. Trainer: Otto Glória

Goal: Valdir (89)

AC TORINO v FORTUNA GELEEN 3-1 (1-1)

Stadio Comunale, Torino 23.09.1964

Referee: Joseph Heymann (SWI)   Attendance: 11,091

AC TORINO: Lido Vieri; Fabrizio Poletti, Natalino Fossati; Giancarlo Cella, Roberto Rosato, Giorgio Puia; Luigi Simoni, Giorgio Ferrini (Cap), Gerald Archibald Hitchens, Luigi Meroni, Gianbattista Moschino.   Trainer: Nereo Rocco

FORTUNA: Piet Vogels; Harry Rosie Marie Brüll, Willem Hubert Quaedackers; Petrus Barbera Beenen, Cornelis van der Hart (Cap), Pierre Kusters; Aleksandar Petakovic, Eugene Maria Gerards, Antoine Kohn, Pieter van Rhijn, Bart Carlier. Trainer: Willem Latten

Goals: Kohn (15), Hitchens (45), Moschino (50 pen), Meroni (63)

ASSOCIATION ROYALE ATHLÉTIQUE LA GANTOISE v WEST HAM UNITED LONDON 0-1 (0-0)

Jules Otten, Gent 23.09.1964

Referee: Birger Nilsen (NOR)   Attendance: 5,173

ARA LA GANTOISE: Armand Seghers (Cap); Antoine Devreese, Richard De Nayer; Norbert Delmulle, Roger Debaets, Lucien Ghellynck; Robert Mahieu, Urbain Seghers, Eric Lambert, Albert Mayama, James Storme. Trainer: Max Schirschin

WEST HAM UNITED: James Standen; John Frederick Bond, Martin Stanford Peters; Edward Bovington, Kenneth Brown, Robert Frederick Moore (Cap); Peter Brabrook, Ronald William Boyce, John Joseph Byrne, Geoffrey Charles Hurst, John Leslie Sissons.   Manager: Ronald Greenwood

Goal: Boyce (51)

FORTUNA GELEEN v AC TORINO 2-2 (0-1)

Mauritspark, Geleen 7.10.1964

Referee: Daniel Mellet (SWI)   Attendance: 10,523

FORTUNA: Piet Vogels; Harry Rosie Marie Brüll, Willem Hubert Quaedackers; Petrus Barbera Benen, Cornelis van der Hart (Cap), Pierre Kusters; Aleksandar Petakovic, André Thomas Piters, Antoine Kohn, Pieter van Rhijn, Bart Carlier. Trainer: Willem Latten

AC TORINO: Lido Vieri; Fabrizio Poletti, Luciano Teneggi; Giorgio Puia, Remo Lancioni, Amilcare Ferretti; Carlo Crippa, Giorgio Ferrini (Cap), Gerald Archibald Hitchens, Luigi Meroni, Gianbattista Moschino.   Trainer: Nereo Rocco

Goals: Hitchens (5), Brüll (53og), Van Rhijn (59), Beenen (66 pen)

SLAVIA SOFIA v CORK CELTIC FC 1-1 (0-0)
Vasil Levski, Sofia   30.09.1964

Referee: Gyula Gere (HUN)   Attendance: 10,940

SLAVIA: Stefan Pascholov; Aleksandar Shalamanov, Petar Panagonov; Dimitar Largov (Cap), Dimitar Kostov, Petar Velichkov; Mihail Mishev, Georgi Haralampiev, Anton Krastev, Petar Hristov, Georgi Gugalov.   Trainer: Dobromir Tashkov

CELTIC: Kevin Blount; Liam O'Flynn, Patrick O'Mahony; Michael Millington, John Clifford, Raymond Cowhie; Paul O'Donovan, Austin Noonan (Cap), Donal Leahy, Alexander Casey, Francis McCarthy.   Manager: Seamus Madden

Goals: Krastev (54), Leahy (83)

AC TORINO v HAKA VALKEAKOSKI 5-0 (3-0)
Stadio Comunale, Torino   6.12.1964

Referee: Dittmar Huber (SWI)   Attendance: 6,381

AC TORINO: Lido Vieri; Fabrizio Poletti, Luciano Buzzacchera; Giorgio Puia, Giancarlo Cella, Roberto Rosato; Luigi Simoni, Giorgio Ferrini (Cap), Gerald Archibald Hitchens, Luigi Meroni, Gianbattista Moschino.   Trainer: Nereo Rocco

HAKA: Martti Halme; Olli Mäkinen, Pentti Niittymäki; Antti Nieminen, Veijo Valtonen (Cap), Markku Lahti; Harri Eerola, Esko Malm, Asko Mäkilä, Timo Paimander, Mauri Paavilainen.   Trainer: Aimo Pulkkinen

Goals: Simoni (6), Hitchens (9), Meroni (33, 59), Puia (61)

CORK CELTIC v SLAVIA SOFIA 0-2 (0-1)
Flower Lodge, Cork   7.10.1964

Referee: Robert Lacoste (FRA)   Attendance: 10,237

CELTIC: Kevin Blount; Liam O'Flynn, Patrick O'Mahoney; Raymond Cowhie, John Clifford, Michael Millington; Paul O'Donovan, Austin Noonan (Cap), Donal Leahy, Alexander Casey, Francis McCarthy.   Manager: Seamus Madden

SLAVIA: Simeon Simeonov; Aleksandar Shalamanov, Petar Panagonov; Dimitar Largov (Cap), Petar Velichkov, Emanuil Manolov; Georgi Haralampiev, Petar Hristov, Anton Krastev, Georgi Gugalov, Mihail Mishev.   Trainer: Dobromir Tashkov

Goals: Mishev (8), Hristov (86)

LEGIA WARSZAWA v GALATASARAY ISTANBUL 2-1 (0-0)
Wojska Polskiego, Warszawa   18.11.1964

Referee: Gábor Soós (HUN)   Attendance: 2,259

LEGIA: Ignacy Penconek; Antoni Mahseli, Henryk Grzybowski, Antoni Trzaskowski; Jacek Gmoch, Antoni Piechniczek, Janusz Zmijewski, Lucjan Brychczy (Cap), Bernard Blaut, Wieslaw Korzeniowski, Kazmierz Frackiewicz.   Trainer: Virgil Popescu

GALATASARAY: Bülent Gürbüz; Candemir Berkman, Naci Erdem, Dogan Sel; Talat Özkarsli, Kadri Aytaç; Tarik Kutver, Mustafa Yürür, Metin Oktay (Cap), Ahmet Berman, Ugur Kökten.   Trainer: Gündüz Kiliç

Goals: Gmoch (69, 88), Metin (73)

SECOND ROUND

HAKA VALKEAKOSKEN v AC TORINO 0-1 (0-1)
Tehtaankenttä, Valkeakoski   11.11.1964

Referee: Samuel H. Carswell (NIR)   Attendance: 2,023

HAKA: Martti Halme; Olli Mäkinen, Pentti Niittymäki; Antti Nieminen, Veijo Valtonen (Cap), Markku Lahti; Harri Eerola, Esko Malm, Asko Mäkilä, Timo Paimander, Mauri Paavilainen.   Trainer: Aimo Pulkkinen

AC TORINO: Lido Vieri; Fabrizio Poletti, Luciano Buzzacchera; Giorgio Puia, Roberto Rosato, Natalino Fossati; Enrico Albrigi, Giorgio Ferrini (Cap), Gerald Archibald Hitchens, Luigi Meroni, Carlo Crippa.   Trainer: Nereo Rocco

Goal: Albrigi (25)

GALATASARAY ISTANBUL v LEGIA WARSZAWA 1-0 (1-0)
Ali Sami Yen, Istanbul   3.12.1964

Referee: Franz Mayer (AUS)   Attendance: 22,442

GALATASARAY: Turgay Şeren (Cap); Candemir Berkman, Dogan Sel; Naci Erdem, Talat Özkarsli, Kadri Aytaç; Yilmaz Gökdel, Mustafa Yürür, Tarik Kutver, Metin Oktay, Ugur Kökten.   Trainer: Gündüz Kiliç

LEGIA: Ignacy Penconek; Antoni Mahseli, Antoni Piechniczek, Henryk Grzybowski, Antoni Trzaskowski, Jacek Gmoch, Bernard Blaut; Janusz Zmijewski, Lucjan Brychczy (Cap), Wieslaw Korzeniowski, Kazmierz Frackiewicz.   Trainer: Virgil Popescu

Goal: Metin (22)

**LEGIA WARSZAWA
v GALATASARAY ISTANBUL 1-0** (1-0)
23 August, București 10.12.1964
Referee: Nicolae Mihăilescu (ROM)   Attendance: 5,000
LEGIA: Ignacy Penconek; Antoni Mahseli, Jacek Gmoch, Antoni Piechniczek, Antoni Trzaskowski, Wieslaw Korzeniowski, Bernard Blaut, Janusz Zmijewski, Lucjan Brychczy (Cap), Henryk Apostel, Kazmierz Frackiewicz.
Trainer: Virgil Popescu
GALATASARAY: Turgay Şeren (Cap); Candemir Berkman, Ahmet Berman; Naci Erdem, Dogan Sel, Kadri Aytaç; Tarik Kutver, Mustafa Yürür, Metin Oktay, Turan Dogangün, Ugur Kökten.   Trainer: Gündüz Kiliç

Goal: Apostel (14)

LAUSANNE SPORTS v SLAVIA SOFIA 3-2 (2-1)
Flaminio, Roma   29.12.1964
Referee: Antonio Sbardella (ITA)   Attendance: 1,000
LAUSANNE SPORTS: René Künzi; André Grobéty (Cap), Kurt Hunziker; Heinz Schneiter, Ely Tacchella, Richard Dürr; Norbert Eschmann, Pieter Johannes Elisabeth Kerkhoffs, Kurt Armbruster, Robert Hosp, Charles Hertig.
Trainer: Karl Rappan
SLAVIA: Simeon Simeonov; Aleksandar Shalamanov, Petar Panagonov; Dimitar Largov (Cap), Petar Velichkov, Emanuil Manolov; Georgi Haralampiev, Anton Krastev, Aleksandar Vasilev, Georgi Gugalov, Petar Hristov.
Trainer: Dobromir Tashkov

Goals: Hristov (15), Eschmann (30), Kerkhoffs (35, 80), Gugalov (70)

SLAVIA SOFIA v LAUSANNE SPORTS 1-0 (0-0)
Vasil Levski, Sofia   18.11.1964
Referee: Paul Bonett (MAL)   Attendance: 13,410
SLAVIA: Simeon Simeonov; Aleksandar Shalamanov, Petar Panagonov; Dimitar Largov (Cap), Petar Velichkov, Emanuil Manolov; Georgi Haralampiev, Anton Krastev, Aleksandar Vasilev, Georgi Gugalov, Mihail Mishev.
Trainer: Dobromir Tashkov
LAUSANNE SPORTS: René Künzi; André Grobéty (Cap), Kurt Hunziker; Richard Dürr, Heinz Schneiter, Ely Tacchella; Kurt Armbruster, Pieter Johannes Elisabeth Kerkhoffs, Norbert Eschmann, Charles Hertig, Robert Hosp.
Trainer: Karl Rappan

Goal: Vasilev (50)

DUNDEE FC v REAL ZARAGOZA 2-2 (1-2)
Dens Park, Dundee   18.11.1964
Referee: Andries van Leeuwen (HOL)   Attendance: 20,000
DUNDEE: Alistair Donaldson; Alexander Hamilton, Robert Cox (Cap); Alan Cousin, Norman Beattie, Alexander Stuart; Stephen Murray, Andrew Penman, Robert Waddell, Douglas Houston, Hugh Robertson.   Manager: Robert Shankly
REAL ZARAGOZA: Enrique YARZA Sorlauce (Cap); Joaquín CORTIZO Rosendo, Severino REIJA Vázquez; Santiago ISASI Salazar, Francisco SANTAMARÍA Briones, José Cuéllar González "PEPÍN"; Darcy Silveira Dos Santos "CANARIO", Eleuterio SANTOS Brito, MARCELINO Martínez Cao, Juan Manuel VILLA Gutiérrez, Carlos LAPETRA Coarasa.
Trainer: Roque Olsen

Goals: Murray (2), Santos (23), Villa (26), Houston (89)

LAUSANNE SPORTS v SLAVIA SOFIA 2-1 (2-1)
Stade Olympique de la Pontaise, Lausanne   6.12.1964
Referee: Wlodzimierz Storoniak (POL)   Attendance: 7,568
LAUSANNE SPORTS: René Künzi; André Grobéty (Cap), Kurt Hunziker; Richard Dürr, Ely Tacchella, Heinz Schneiter; Norbert Eschmann, Pieter Johannes Elisabeth Kerkhoffs, Kurt Armbruster, Robert Hosp, Charles Hertig.
Trainer: Karl Rappan
SLAVIA: Simeon Simeonov; Aleksandar Shalamanov, Petar Panagonov; Dimitar Largov (Cap), Petar Velichkov, Emanuil Manolov; Georgi Haralampiev, Petar Hristov, Anton Krastev, Georgi Gugalov, Aleksandar Vasilev.
Trainer: Dobromir Tashkov

Goals: Kerkhoffs (7), Krastev (20), Hosp (43)

REAL ZARAGOZA v DUNDEE FC 2-1 (2-1)
Estadio La Romareda, Zaragoza   8.12.1964
Referee: Francesco Francescon (ITA)   Attendance: 24,531
REAL ZARAGOZA: Enrique YARZA Sorlauce (Cap); Joaquín CORTIZO Rosendo, Severino REIJA Vázquez; Santiago ISASI Salazar, Francisco SANTAMARÍA Briones, José Luis VIOLETA Lajusticia; Darcy Silveira Dos Santos "CANARIO", Eleuterio SANTOS Brito, MARCELINO Martínez Cao, Juan Manuel VILLA Gutiérrez, Carlos LAPETRA Coarasa.
Trainer: Roque Olsen
DUNDEE: Alistair Donaldson; Alexander Hamilton, Robert Cox (Cap); Alan Cousin, George Ryden, Alexander Stuart; Stephen Murray, Andrew Penman, Kenneth Cameron, Douglas Houston, Hugh Robertson.   Manager: Robert Shankly

Goals: Robertson (18), Lapetra (40, 42)

**WEST HAM UNITED LONDON
v SPARTA PRAHA 2-0** (0-0)

Upton Park, London 25.11.1964

Referee: José Maria Ortiz de Mendíbil (SPA)   Att: 27,590

WEST HAM UNITED: James Standen; John Frederick Bond, John Burkett; Edward Bovington, Kenneth Brown (Cap), Martin Stanford Peters; Alan Sealey, Ronald William Boyce, John Joseph Byrne, Geoffrey Charles Hurst, John Leslie Sissons.   Manager: Ronald Greenwood

SPARTA: Antonín Kramerius; Jiří Gura, Vladimír Táborsky; Karel Steiningel, Josef Vojta, Vladimír Kos; Pavel Dyba, Ivan Mráz, Andrej Kvasnák, Tadeáš Kraus (Cap), Václav Masek.   Trainer: Václav Jezek

Goals: Bond (57), Sealey (82)

TSV 1860 MÜNCHEN v FC PORTO 1-1 (1-1)

Stadion Grünwalder str., München 16.12.1964

Referee: Konstantin Zecević (YUG)   Attendance: 36,430

TSV MÜNCHEN: Petar Radenkovic; Bernd Patzke, Rudolf Steiner; Otto Luttrop, Hans Reich, Rudolf Zeiser; Alfred Heiss, Wilfried Kohlars, Rudolf Brunnenmeier (Cap), Peter Grosser, Stefan Bena.   Trainer: Max Merkel

FC PORTO: RUI Fernando Sousa Teixeira; Alberto Festa, João Eleutério Luis ATRACA; José ROLANDO Andrade Gonçalves, Miguel Arcanjo, ALÍPIO Vasconcelos Monteiro; JAIME Ferreira Silva, Custódio Pinto (Cap), VALDIR Araújo Sousa, JOAQUIM Antonio JORGE, Francisco Lage Pereira da NOBREGA.   Trainer: Otto Glória

Goals: Heiss (37), Valdir (44)

SPARTA PRAHA v WEST HAM UNITED 2-1 (0-1)

Letná, Praha 9.12.1964

Referee: Konstantin Dinov (BUL)   Attendance: 20,462

SPARTA: Antonín Kramerius; Jiří Gura, Vladimír Táborsky; Jiří Tichy, Vladimír Kos, Josef Vojta; Pavel Dyba, Ivan Mráz, Andrej Kvasnák, Václav Masek, Tadeáš Kraus (Cap).   Trainer: Václav Jezek

WEST HAM UNITED: James Standen; John Frederick Bond, John Burkett; Edward Bovington, Kenneth Brown (Cap), Martin Stanford Peters; Alan Sealey, Ronald William Boyce, John Joseph Byrne, Geoffrey Charles Hurst, John Leslie Sissons.   Manager: Ronald Greenwood

Goals: Sissons (14), Masek (68), Mráz (88)

**STEAUA BUCUREŞTI
v DINAMO ZAGREB 1-3** (1-1)

23 August, Bucureşti 9.12.1964

Referee: Zdenek Vales (CZE)   Attendance: 12,676

STEAUA: Carol Haidu; Mircea Georgescu, Dumitru Nicolae, Mircea Petescu, Vasile Dumbravă; Vasile Negrea, Gavril Raksi; Sorin Avram, Gheorghe Constantin (Cap), Florea Voinea, Carol Creiniceanu.   Trainer: Ilie Savu

DINAMO: Zlatko Škorić; Mladen Ramljak, Zlatko Mesić; Miljenko Puljcan, Atko Kasumović, Rudolf Belin; Zdenko Kobešćak, Andjelko Pavić, Stjepan Lamza, Željko Matuš (Cap), Krasnodar Rora.   Trainer: Vlatko Konjevod

Goals: Raksi (20), Matuš (35), Pavić (61), Kobešćak (87)

FC PORTO v TSV MÜNCHEN 1860 0-1 (0-1)

Estádio Das Antas, Porto 2.12.1964

Referee: Joseph Barbéran (FRA)   Attendance: 11,643

FC PORTO: AMERICO Ferreira Lopes; Alberto Festa, João Eleutério Luis ATRACA; JOAQUIM Antonio JORGE, João Luís Pinto ALMEIDA, ALÍPIO Vasconcelos Monteiro; JAIME Ferreira Silva, Custódio Pinto (Cap), VALDIR Araújo Sousa, Carlos Baptista, Francisco Lage Pereira da NOBREGA.   Trainer: Otto Glória

TSV MÜNCHEN: Petar Radenkovic; Bernd Patzke, Rudolf Steiner; Rudolf Zeiser, Hans Reich, Otto Luttrop; Alfred Heiss, Wilfried Kohlars, Rudolf Brunnenmeier (Cap), Peter Grosser, Stefan Bena.   Trainer: Max Merkel

Goal: Heiss (22)

**DINAMO ZAGREB
v STEAUA BUCUREŞTI 2-0** (1-0)

Maksimir, Zagreb 16.12.1964

Referee: Rudolf Glöckner (E. GER)   Attendance: 5,784

DINAMO: Zlatko Škorić; Mladen Ramljak, Zlatko Mesić; Miljenko Puljcan, Atko Kasumović, Rudolf Belin; Zdenko Kobešćak, Andjelko Pavić, Stjepan Lamza, Željko Matuš (Cap), Krasnodar Rora.   Trainer: Vlatko Konjevod

STEAUA: Carol Haidu; Mircea Georgescu, Emerich Jenei (Cap), Mircea Petescu, Vasile Dumbravă; Ion Crişan, Constantin Koszka; Gavril Raksi, Florea Voinea, Vasile Negrea, Carol Creiniceanu.   Trainer: Ilie Savu

Goals: Pavić (2), Ramljak (62)

SPORTING LISBOA v CARDIFF CITY 1-2 (0-1)

Estádio José Alvalade, Lisboa 16.12.1964

Referee: Rudolf Kreitlein (W. GER)   Attendance: 15,311

SPORTING: Joaquim da Silva CARVALHO; Pedro Gomes, Alfredo Moreiro; José Carlos, Hilário da Conceição, Fernando Mendes (Cap); Fernando Ferreira Pinto, Roberto Bocareli Bé, Osvaldo Silva, Ernesto Figueireido, João Moraes. Trainer: Júlio Cernades Pereira "JUCA"

CARDIFF CITY: Dilwyn John; Alan Harrington, Peter Rodrigues; John Charles, Donald Murray (Cap), Barrington Gerald Hole; Greg Farrell, Gareth Williams, Derek Tapscott, Peter King, Bernard Lewis.   Manager: James Scoular

Goals: Farrell (31), Tapscott (65), Figueiredo (81)

CARDIFF CITY v SPORTING LISBOA 0-0

Ninian Park, Cardiff 23.12.1964

Referee: Robert Schaut (BEL)   Attendance: 23,800

CARDIFF CITY: Dilwyn John; Alan Harrington, Peter Rodrigues; John Charles, Donald Murray (Cap), Barrington Gerald Hole; Greg Farrell, Gareth Williams, Derek Tapscott, Peter King, Bernard Lewis.   Manager: James Scoular

SPORTING: Joaquim da Silva CARVALHO; Pedro Gomes, Alfredo Moreira; Hilário da Conceição, Fernando Mendes (Cap), José Carlos; Lourenço Sitoe, Osvaldo Silva, Ernesto Figuereido, Fernando Ferreira Pinto, João Morais. Trainer: Júlio Cernades Pereira "JUCA"

QUARTER-FINALS

REAL ZARAGOZA v CARDIFF CITY 2-2 (2-2)

Estadio La Romareda, Zaragoza 20.01.1965

Referee: Dittmar Huber (SWI)   Attendance: 22,780

REAL ZARAGOZA: Enrique YARZA Sorlauce (Cap); José Cuéllar González "PEPÍN", Severino REIJA Vázquez; Antonio PAÍS Castroagudin, Francisco SANTAMARÍA Briones, José Luis VIOLETA Lajusticia; Darcy Silveira Dos Santos "CANARIO", Eleuterio SANTOS Brito, MARCELINO Martínez Cao, Carlos LAPETRA Coarasa, José María ENCONTRA Tolosana. Trainer: Roque Olsen

CARDIFF CITY: Robert Wilson; Alan Harrington, Peter Rodrigues; John Charles, Donald Murray (Cap), Barrington Gerald Hole; Greg Farrell, Gareth Williams, Derek Tapscott, Peter King, Bernard Lewis.   Manager: James Scoular

Goals: Lapetra (2), País (10), Williams (15), King (38)

CARDIFF CITY v REAL ZARAGOZA 0-1 (0-0)

Ninian Park, Cardiff 3.02.1965

Referee: André Hauben (BEL)   Attendance: 38,458

CARDIFF CITY: Robert Wilson; Alan Harrington, Peter Rodrigues; John Charles, Donald Murray (Cap), Barrington Gerald Hole; Greg Farrell, Gareth Williams, Derek Tapscott, Peter King, Bernard Lewis.   Manager: James Scoular

REAL ZARAGOZA: Enrique YARZA Sorlauce (Cap); Joaquín CORTIZO Rosendo, Severino REIJA Vázquez; Santiago ISASI Salazar, Francisco SANTAMARÍA Briones, José Luis VIOLETA Lajusticia; Darcy Silveira Dos Santos "CANARIO", Eleuterio SANTOS Brito, MARCELINO Martínez Cao, Antonio PAÍS Castroagudin, Carlos LAPETRA Coarasa.

Trainer: Roque Olsen

Goal: Canario (75)

AC TORINO v DINAMO ZAGREB 1-1 (1-0)

Stadio Comunale, Torino 3.03.1965

Referee: Günther Baumgärtel (W. GER)   Attendance: 6,911

AC TORINO: Lido Vieri; Fabrizio Poletti, Luciano Buzzacchera; Giorgio Puia, Giancarlo Cella, Roberto Rosato; Luigi Meroni, Giorgio Ferrini (Cap), Gerald Archibald Hitchens, Gianbattista Moschino, Luigi Simoni. Trainer: Nereo Rocco

DINAMO: Zlatko Škorić; Mladen Ramljak, Zlatko Mesić; Rudolf Belin, Atko Kasumović, Ivan Sestanj; Stjepan Lamza, Slaven Zambata, Josip Gucmirtl, Željko Matuš, Drazen Jerković (Cap), Krasnodar Rora.   Trainer: Vlatko Konjevod

Goals: Simoni (43), Lamza (48)

DINAMO ZAGREB v AC TORINO 1-2 (0-2)

Maksimir, Zagreb 17.03.1965

Referee: József Fehérvári (HUN)   Attendance: 17,576

DINAMO: Zlatko Škorić; Mladen Ramljak, Zlatko Mesić, Rudolf Belin; Atko Kasumović, Ivan Sestanj; Stjepan Lamza, Slaven Zambata, Drazen Jerković (Cap), Željko Matuš, Krasnodar Rora.   Trainer: Vlatko Konjevod

AC TORINO: Lido Vieri; Fabrizio Poletti, Luciano Buzzacchera; Giorgio Puia, Giancarlo Cella, Roberto Rosato; Luigi Meroni, Giorgio Ferrini (Cap), Gerald Archibald Hitchens, Amilcare Ferretti, Alberto Carelli. Trainer: Nereo Rocco

Goals: Poletti (14), Hitchens (44), Jerkovic (81)

LEGIA WARSZAWA
v TSV 1860 MÜNCHEN 0-4 (0-0)

Wojska Polskiego, Warszawa   3.03.1965

Referee: John Adair (NIrl)   Attendance: 4,033

LEGIA: Ignacy Penconek; Antoni Mahseli, Antoni Trzaskowski, Jerzy Wozniak; Jacek Gmoch, Bernard Blaut; Janusz Zmijewski, Lucjan Brychczy (Cap), Henryk Apostel, Wieslaw Korzeniowski, Kazmierz Frackiewicz.
Trainer: Virgil Popescu

TSV MÜNCHEN: Petar Radenkovic; Rudolf Steiner, Hans Reich, Bernd Patzke; Rudolf Zeiser, Otto Luttrop; Alfred Heiss, Hans Küppers, Rudolf Brunnenmeier (Cap), Peter Grosser, Manfred Wagner.   Trainer: Max Merkel

Goals: Grosser (69), Küppers (73), Heiss (75, 87)

TSV 1860 MÜNCHEN v LEGIA WARSZAWA 0-0

Stadion Grünwalder str., München   17.03.1965

Referee: Stjepan Varaždinec (YUG)   Attendance: 30,278

TSV MÜNCHEN: Petar Radenkovic; Rudolf Steiner, Hans Reich, Bernd Patzke; Rudolf Zeiser, Manfred Wagner; Alfred Heiss (Cap), Hans Küppers, Otto Luttrop, Peter Grosser, Hans Rebele.   Trainer: Max Merkel

LEGIA: Wladyslaw Grotynski; Antoni Mahseli, Antoni Piechniczek; Antoni Trzaskowski, Jacek Gmoch, Bernard Blaut; Janusz Zmijewski, Lucjan Brychczy (Cap), Henryk Apostel, Wieslaw Korzeniowski, Kazmierz Frackiewicz.
Trainer: Virgil Popescu

LAUSANNE SPORTS
v WEST HAM UNITED LONDON 1-2 (0-1)

Stade Olympique de la Pontaise, Lausanne   16.03.1965

Referee: Paul Schiller (AUS)   Attendance: 18,546

LAUSANNE SPORTS: René Künzi; André Grobéty (Cap), Kurt Hunziker; Heinz Schneiter, Ely Tacchella, Richard Dürr; Norbert Eschmann, Pieter Johannes Elisabeth Kerkhoffs, Kurt Armbruster, Robert Hosp, Charles Hertig.
Trainer: Karl Rappan

WEST HAM UNITED: James Standen; Joseph Kirkup, Martin Stanford Peters; Ronald William Boyce, Kenneth Brown, Robert Frederick Moore (Cap); Alan Sealey, Geoffrey Charles Hurst, John Joseph Byrne, Brian Dear, John Leslie Sissons.   Manager: Ronald Greenwood

Goals: Dear (33), Byrne (55), Hosp (80)

WEST HAM UNITED LONDON v
LAUSANNE SPORTS 4-3 (2-1)

Upton Park, London   23.03.1964

Referee: Pieter Paulus Roomer (HOL)   Attendance: 31,780

WEST HAM UNITED: James Standen; Joseph Kirkup, Martin Stanford Peters; Ronald William Boyce, Kenneth Brown, Robert Frederick Moore (Cap); Alan Sealey, Geoffrey Charles Hurst, John Joseph Byrne, Brian Dear, John Leslie Sissons.   Manager: Ronald Greenwood

LAUSANNE SPORTS: René Künzi; André Grobéty (Cap), Kurt Hunziker; Heinz Schneiter, Ely Tacchella, Richard Dürr; Norbert Eschmann, Pieter Johannes Elisabeth Kerkhoffs, Kurt Armbruster, Robert Hosp, Charles Hertig.
Trainer: Karl Rappan

Goals: Kerkhoffs (37), Tacchella (41 og), Dear (45, 89), Hertig (49), Peters (60), Eschmann (80)

SEMI-FINALS

WEST HAM UNITED LONDON
v REAL ZARAGOZA 2-1 (2-0)

Upton Park, London   7.04.1965

Referee: Robert Lacoste (FRA)   Attendance: 34,864

WEST HAM UNITED: James Standen; Joseph Kirkup, John Burkett; Martin Stanford Peters, Kenneth Brown, Robert Frederick Moore (Cap); Ronald William Boyce, Brian Dear, John Joseph Byrne, Geoffrey Charles Hurst, John Leslie Sissons.   Trainer: Ronald Greenwood

REAL ZARAGOZA: Enrique YARZA Sorlauce (Cap); Joaquín CORTIZO Rosendo, Severino REIJA Vázquez; Santiago ISASI Salazar, Francisco SANTAMARÍA Briones, José Luis VIOLETA Lajustica; Darcy Silveira Dos Santos "CANARIO", Eleuterio SANTOS Brito, MARCELINO Martínez Cao, Eduardo Bibiano ENDÉRIZ Cortajarena, Carlos LAPETRA Coarasa.
Trainer: Roque Olsen

Goals: Dear (8), Byrne (28), Canario (54)

REAL ZARAGOZA
v WEST HAM UNITED LONDON 1-1 (1-0)

Estadio La Romareda, Zaragoza   28.04.1965

Referee: Leopold Sylvain Horn (HOL)   Attendance: 29,421

REAL ZARAGOZA: Enrique YARZA Sorlauce (Cap); Joaquín CORTIZO Rosendo, Severino REIJA Vázquez; Eduardo Bibiano ENDÉRIZ Cortajarena, Francisco SANTAMARÍA Briones, José Luis VIOLETA Lajustica; Darcy Silveira Dos Santos "CANARIO", Eleuterio SANTOS Brito, MARCELINO Martínez Cao, Juan Manuel VILLA Gutiérrez, Carlos LAPETRA Coarasa.   Trainer: Roque Olsen

WEST HAM UNITED: James Standen; Joseph Kirkup, John Burkett; Martin Stanford Peters, Kenneth Brown, Robert Frederick Moore (Cap); Ronald William Boyce, Alan Sealey, Geoffrey Charles Hurst, Brian Dear, John Leslie Sissons.

Goals: Lapetra (22), Sissons (54)

AC TORINO v TSV 1860 MÜNCHEN 2-0 (2-0)

Stadio Comunale, Torino   20.04.1965

Referee: Alfred Haberfellner (AUS)   Attendance: 22,977

AC TORINO: Lido Vieri; Fabrizio Poletti, Natalino Fossati; Giorgio Puia, Giancarlo Cella, Roberto Rosato; Luigi Meroni, Giorgio Ferrini (Cap), Gerald Archibald Hitchens, Gianbattista Moschino, Luigi Simoni.   Trainer: Nereo Rocco

TSV MÜNCHEN: Petar Radenkovic; Wilfried Kohlars, Bernd Patzke; Stefan Bena, Hans Reich, Otto Luttrop; Alfred Heiss, Hans Küppers, Rudolf Brunnenmeier (Cap), Peter Grosser, Hans Rebele.   Trainer: Max Merkel

Goals: Rosato (9), Luttrop (41 og)

TSV 1860 MÜNCHEN v AC TORINO 3-1 (2-0)

Stadion Grünwalder str., München   27.04.1965

Referee: Zdenek Vales (CZE)   Attendance: 33,134

TSV MÜNCHEN: Petar Radenkovic; Manfred Wagner, Wilfried Kohlars; Stefan Bena, Hans Reich, Otto Luttrop; Alfred Heiss, Hans Küppers, Rudolf Brunnenmeier (Cap), Peter Grosser, Hans Rebele.   Trainer: Max Merkel

AC TORINO: Lido Vieri; Fabrizio Poletti, Natalino Fossati; Giorgio Puia, Remo Lancioni, Roberto Rosato; Luigi Meroni, Giorgio Ferrini (Cap), Gerald Archibald Hitchens, Gianbattista Moschino, Luigi Simoni.   Trainer: Nereo Rocco

Goals: Luttrop (12, 52 pen), Heiss (25), Lancioni (74)

TSV MÜNCHEN 1860 v AC TORINO 2-0 (0-0)

Letzigrund, Zürich   5.05.1965

Referee: Dittmar Huber (SWI)   Attendance: 22,977

TSV MÜNCHEN: Petar Radenkovic; Manfred Wagner, Wilfried Kohlars; Stefan Bena, Hans Reich, Otto Luttrop; Alfred Heiss, Hans Küppers, Rudolf Brunnenmeier (Cap), Peter Grosser, Hans Rebele.   Trainer: Max Merkel

AC TORINO: Lido Vieri; Fabrizio Poletti, Natalino Fossati; Giorgio Puia, Giancarlo Cella, Roberto Rosato; Luigi Meroni, Giorgio Ferrini (Cap), Gerald Archibald Hitchens, Gianbattista Moschino, Luigi Simoni.   Trainer: Nereo Rocco

Goals: Rebele (59), Luttrop (90 pen)

FINAL

WEST HAM UNITED LONDON v TSV MÜNCHEN 1860 2-0 (0-0)

Wembley, London   19.05.1965

Referee: István Zsolt (HUN)   Attendance: 97,974

WEST HAM UNITED: James Standen; Joseph Kirkup, Kenneth Brown, John Burkett; Martin Stanford Peters, Robert Frederick Moore (Cap); Alan Sealey, Ronald William Boyce, Geoffrey Charles Hurst, Brian Dear, John Leslie Sissons.   Trainer: Ronald Greenwood

TSV MÜNCHEN: Petar Radenkovic; Manfred Wagner, Hans Reich, Wilfried Kohlars; Stefan Bena, Otto Luttrop; Alfred Heiss, Hans Küppers, Rudolf Brunnenmeier (Cap), Peter Grosser, Hans Rebele.   Trainer: Max Merkel (AUS)

Goals: Sealey (69, 71)

Goalscorers European Cup-Winners' Cup 1964-65:

6 goals: Václav Masek, Ivan Mráz (Sparta Praha), Pierre Kerkhoffs (Lausanne Sports)

5 goals: Alfred Heiss, Otto Luttrop (TSV München 1860)

4 goals: Brian Dear (West Ham), Carlos LAPETRA Coarasa (Real Zaragoza), Rudolf Brunnenmeier (TSV München 1860), Gerry Hitchens (AC Torino)

3 goals: Metin (Galatasaray), Kraus (Sparta Praha), Canario, Marcelino, Sigi (Real Zaragoza), Meroni (Torino), Rebele (TSV München), Brne, Sealey (West Ham United)

2 goals: Heuer (Aufbau), Hristov, Krastev (Slavia), Valdir, Pinto (FC Porto), Creiniceanu, Pavlovici (Steaua), King (Cardiff City), Jerkovic, Lamza, Pavic (Dinamo Zagreb), Brychczy, Gmoch, Zmijevski (Legia Warszawa), Eschmann, Hosp (Lausanne), Santos (Real Zaragoza), Simoni (Torino), Grosser, Küppers (München 1860), Sissons (West Ham United)

1 goal: Vági (Honvéd), Kaltenbrunner (Admira), P.Gauci (FC Valletta), Klingbiel (Aufbau), Papaioannou, Nestoridis (ΛΕΚ Athina), Mathisen (Skeid Oslo), Kohn, Van Rhijn, Beenen (Fortuna Geleen), Leahy (Cork Celtic), Paimander, Peltonen (Haka Valkeakosken), Turan, Uğur (Galatasaray), Gugalov, Vasilev, Mishev (Slavia), Murray, Houston, Robertson (Dundee FC), Steiningel, Vrána, Dyba (Sparta Praha), Baptista (FC Porto), Raksi, Constantin (Steaua), Figueiredo (Sporting), Williams, Farrell, Tapscott (Cardiff City), Ramljak, Matus, Kobeščak, Zambata (Dinamo Zagreb), Apostel (Legia), Hertig (Lausanne), País, Villa (Real Zaragoza), Rosato, Lancioni, Poletti, Albrigi, Puia, Moschino (Torino), Peters, Bond, Boyce (West Ham United)

Own goals: Peters (West Ham) for La Gantoise, Brüll (Fortuna) for Torino, Tacchella (Lausanne) for West Ham, Luttrop (München 1860) for Torino

CUP WINNERS' CUP 1965-66

FIRST ROUND

KNATTSPYRNUFÉLAG REYKJAVIK v ROSENBORG BALLKLUBB TRONDHEIM 1-3 (0-1)

Laugardalsvöllur, Reykjavik   24.08.1965

Referee: William Joseph Mullan (SCO)   Attendance: 3,270

KR REYKJAVIK: Heimir Gudjónsson; Arsaell Kjartansson, Bjarni Felixson; Thórdur Jónsson, Thorgeir Gudmundsson, Sveinn Jónsson; Gunnar Felixson, Saemundur Bjarkan Arelíusson, Baldvin Baldvinsson, Ellert Schram (Cap), Gunnard Gudmannsson.   Trainer: Gudbjörn Jónsson

ROSENBORG: Tor Røste Fossen; Knut Jenssen, Kjell Hvidsand; Svein Haagenrud, Käre Rönnes (Cap), Egil Nygärd; Tore Pedersen, Birger Thingstad, Tore Lindvåg, Eldar Hansen, Tor Kleveland.   Trainer: Knut Naess

Goals: Kieveland (9, 77), Schram (70), T. Pedersen (84)

ROSENBORG BK TRONDHEIM v K.R. REYKJAVIK 3-1 (0-0)

Lerkendal, Trondheim   12.09.1965

Referee: John Adair (NIR)   Attendance: 9,002

ROSENBORG: Tor Røste Fossen; Knut Jenssen, Kjell Hvidsand; Käre Rönnes (Cap), Harald Gulbrandsen, Egil Nygärd; Tore Pedersen, Birger Thingstad, Tore Lindvåg, Svein Haagenrud, Odd Iversen.   Trainer: Knut Naess

K.R.REYKJAVIK: Heimir Gudjónsson; Arsaell Kjartansson, Bjarni Felixson; Kristinn Jónsson, Hördur Felixson, Sveinn Jónsson; Gunnar Felixson, Einar Isfeld, Baldvin Baldvinsson, Ellert Schram (Cap), Gudmundur Haraldsson.   Trainer: Gudbjörn Jónsson

Goals: Haagenrud (49), T. Pedersen (66), Isfeld (75), Lindvåg (81)

ÅRHUS GF v VITÓRIA SETÚBAL 2-1 (1-1)

Idraetspark, Århus   25.08.1965

Referee: George T. Powell (WAL)   Attendance: 13,500

ÅRHUS GF: John Leo Jensen; Arne Sørensen, Søren Pedersen; John Amdisen (Cap), Bent Wolmar, Ove Sørensen; Poul Erik Baekgaard, Kjeld Jensen, Jørn Bjerregaard, Henning Enoksen, Verner Hermansen.   Trainer: Henry From

VITÓRIA: José Félix Mourinho; Joaquim Conceição, Herculano Santos, Manuel Santos Carriço; Carlos Cardoso, Carlos TORPES Junior, Armando Bonjour, Jaime Graça (Cap), José Maria Junior, Augusto Martins, Joaquim Ventura da Silva Quim.   Trainer: Fernando Vaz

Goals: Bjerregaard (16), Joaquim Silva Quim (35), K. Jensen (80)

VITÓRIA SETÚBAL v ÅRHUS GF 1-2 (0-0)

Parque do Bonfim, Setúbal   19.09.1965

Referee: Robert Schaut (BEL)   Attendance: 8,053

VITÓRIA: José Félix Mourinho; Joaquim Conceição, Herculano Santos, Manuel Santos Carriço; Carlos Cardoso, Carlos TORPES Junior, Jaime Graça (Cap), OSVALDO Martins, José Maria Junior, Augusto Martins, Joaquim Ventura da Silva Quim.   Trainer: Fernando Vaz

ÅRHUS: Bent Martin; Arne Sørensen, Søren Pedersen; John Amdisen (Cap), Bent Wolmar, Kaj Mikkelsen; Jørn Bjerregaard, Kjeld Jensen, Ove Sørensen, Karten Petersen, Henning Enoksen.   Trainer: Henry From

Goals: Enoksen (56), Graça (68), K. Jensen (70)

LAHDEN REIPAS v HONVÉD BUDAPEST 2-10 (1-3)

Kisapuisto, Lahti   25.08.1965

Referee: Ivan Lukianov (USSR)   Attendance: 4,200

REIPAS: Risto Remes; Sakari Pihlamo, Raimo Piira, Timo Kautonen (Cap); Matti Haahti, Olli Heinonen; Pekka Leivolahti, Timo Salonen, Martti Hyvärinen, Kalevi Nupponen, Semi Nuoranen.   Trainer: Aarre Lievonen

HONVÉD: Béla Takács; Zoltán Dudás, Ferenc Sipos, Boldizsár Mihalecz; Antal Tussinger, István Vági; György Nagy, Ferenc Nógrádi, Lajos Tichy (Cap), Kálmán Tóth, Sándor Katona.   Trainer: Mihály Kispéter

Goals: Tóth (20, 38, 52, 62, 88), Tichy (34, 84), Hyvärinen (35), Nagy (47), Nógrádi (61), Katona (79), Kautonen (87)

HONVÉD BUDAPEST v LAHDEN REIPAS 6-0 (2-0)

Népstadion, Budapest   13.10.1965

Referee: Josef Tittl (AUS)   Attendance: 40,000

HONVÉD: Béla Takács; László Marosi, Ferenc Sipos, Boldizsár Mihalecz; József Dorogi, István Vági; György Nagy, Imre Komora, Lajos Tichy (Cap), Kálmán Tóth, Sándor Katona.   Trainer: Mihály Kispéter

REIPAS: Markku Talsi; Sakari Pihlamo, Raimo Piira; Timo Kautonen (Cap); Matti Haahti, Olli Heinonen; Keijo Voutilainen, Pekka Kosonen, Kalevi Nupponen, Martti Hyvärinen, Semi Nouranen.   Trainer: Aarre Lievonen

Goals: Komora (3, 65), Tichy (40, 69), Talsi (72 og), Nagy (76)

1. WIENER NEUSTÄDTER SK v ŞTIINŢA CLUJ 0-1 (0-0)

Wiener Neustädt 1.09.1965

Referee: György Vadas (HUN)   Attendance: 6,521

WIENER NEUSTÄDT: Josef Schneider; Herbert Ofenbach, Hubert Hutfless (Cap); Rudolf Neudauer, Manfred Fenz, Josef Fresser; Herbert Lenzinger; Alfred Seidl, Friedrich Tiefenbrunner, Karl Schatzer, Heinz Artner.
Trainer: Adolf Patek

ŞTIINŢA: Vasile Gaboraş; Paul Marcu, Mircea Neşu, Paul Grăjdeanu, Remus Cîmpeanu; Vasile Alexandru, Werner Pexa; Zoltan Ivansuc, Traian Georgescu (Cap), Mihai Adam, Nicolae Szabo.   Trainers: Andrei Sepci & Robert Cosmoc

Goal: Ivansuc (70)

DINAMO KIEV v COLERAINE FC 4-0 (3-0)

Republikanskiy, Kiev 8.09.1965

Referee: Alexandru Toth (ROM)   Attendance: 52,000

DINAMO: Viktor Bannikov; Vladimir Schegolkov, Vadim Sosnikhin, Leonid Ostrovski; Iosif Sabo, Vasili Turianchik; Oleg Bazilevich, Viktor Serebrianikov, Fiedor Medvid, Andrei Biba (Cap), Vitali Khmelnitski.   Trainer: Viktor Maslov

COLERAINE: Victor Hunter; John McCurdy, Alan Campbell; Ivan Murray, Alan Hunter, Robert Peacock (Cap); Thomas Kinsella, Anthony Curley, Kenneth Halliday, Seamus Doherty, David Irwin.   Trainer: Robert Peacock

Goals: Biba (5), Bazilevich (17, 43), Khmelnitski (89)

ŞTIINŢA CLUJ v 1. WIENER NEUSTÄDTER SK 2-0 (1-0)

Municipal, Cluj 6.10.1965

Referee: Josef Krnávek (CZE)   Attendance: 10,000

ŞTIINŢA: Vasile Gaboraş, Iosif Szőke, Mircea Neşu, Paul Grăjdeanu, Remus Cîmpeanu (Cap); Vasile Alexandru, Werner Pexa; Zoltan Ivansuc, Paul Marcu, Mihai Adam, Nicolae Szabo.
Trainer: Andrei Sepci

WIENER NEUSTÄDT: Josef Schneider; Herbert Ofenbach, Hubert Hutfless (Cap); Rudolf Neudauer, Manfred Fenz, Josef Fresser; Herbert Lenzinger; Josef Bierbaumer, Friedrich Tiefenbrunner, Alfred Hoffmann, Karl Schatzer.
Trainer: Adolf Patek

Goals: Ivansuc (9), Adam (86)

CARDIFF CITY v STANDARD LIÈGE 1-2 (1-1)

Ninian Park, Cardiff 8.09.1965

Referee: Adrianus Aalbrecht (HOL)   Attendance: 12,738

CITY: Robert Wilson; Alan Harrington, Peter Rodrigues, Gareth Williams; Donald Murray (Cap), Barrie Gerald Hole; Greg Farrell, George Johnston, John Charles, Terry Harkin, Bernard Lewis.   Trainer: James Scoular

STANDARD: Jean Nicolay; Jozef Vliers, Jean-Pierre Marchal, Jacques Beurlet, Lucien Spronck (Cap), Guillaume Raskin, Léon Semmeling, Marcel Paeschen, Roger Claessen, Velimir Naumovic, James Storme.   Trainer: Milorad Pavić

Goals: Johnston (30), Claessen (40), Semmeling (68)

COLERAINE v DYNAMO KIEV 1-6 (0-4)

The Showgrounds, Coleraine 2.09.1965

Referee: Johannes Malka (W. GER)   Attendance: 5,281

COLERAINE: Victor Hunter; John McCurdy, Alan Campbell; Ivan Murray, Alan Hunter, Robert Peacock (Cap); Thomas Kinsella, Anthony Curley, Kenneth Halliday, Sean Dunlop, David Irwin.   Trainer: Robert Peacock

DINAMO: Viktor Bannikov; Vladimir Schegolkov, Leonid Ostrovski, Vadim Sosnikhin, Vasili Turianchik, Iosif Sabo, Oleg Bazilevich, Viktor Serebrianikov, Vladimir Levchenko, Andrei Biba (Cap), Vitali Khmelnitski.   Trainer: Viktor Maslov

Goals: Biba (14, 52), Bazilevich (34), Khmelnitski (40), Serebrianikov (44, 63), Curley (72)

STANDARD LIÈGE v CARDIFF CITY FC 1-0 (0-0)

Stede de Sclessin, Liège 20.10.1965

Referee: Francisco Gonçalves Guerra (POR)   Att: 17,985

STANDARD: Jean Nicolay; Jozef Vliers, Jacques Beurlet, Louis Pilot, Lucien Spronck (Cap), Paul Vandenberg, Léon Semmeling, Nicolas Dewalque, Roger Claessen, Casimir Jurkiewicz, James Storme.   Trainer: Milorad Pavić

CITY: Robert Wilson; Alan Harrington, Peter Rodrigues, David Summerhayes, Donald Murray (Cap), Barrie Gerald Hole, Greg Farrell, George Johnston, John Charles, Peter King, Bernard Lewis.   Manager: James Scoular

Goal: Storme (48)

ATLÉTICO MADRID
v DINAMO ZAGREB 4-0 (2-0)
Estadio Metropolitano, Madrid 15.09.1965
Referee: George McCabe (ENG)   Attendance: 31,787
ATLÉTICO: Edgardo Mario MADINABEYTIA Bassi; Feliciano RIVILLA Muñoz (Cap), Jorge Bernardo GRIFFA Monferoni, Isacio CALLEJA García, Manuel RUIZ-SOSA, Jesús MARTÍNEZ JAYO; José Armando UFARTE Ventoso, ADELARDO Rodríguez Sánchez, Jorge Alberto MENDONÇA Paulino, LUIS Aragonés Suarez, José Enrique CARDONA Gutiérrez.   Trainer: Domingo Balmanya
DINAMO: Zlatko Škorić; Mladen Ramljak, Petar Lončarić; Zlatko Mesić, Vlatko Marković, Rudolf Belin; Zdenko Kobešćak, Slaven Zambata (Cap), Željko Matuš, Ivica Kiš, Krasnodar Rora.   Trainer: Milan Antolković
Goals: Mendonça (10, 21, 85), Luis (65)

DINAMO ZAGREB
v ATLÉTICO MADRID 0-1 (0-0)
Maksimir, Zagreb 22.09.1965
Referee: Gerhard Schulenburg (W. GER)   Att: 14,660
DINAMO: Zlatko Škorić; Mladen Ramljak, Petar Lončarić; Rudolf Belin, Vlatko Marković, Zlatko Mesić; Zdenko Kobešćak, Slaven Zambata (Cap), Ivica Kiš, Stjepan Lamza, Krasnodar Rora.   Trainer: Ivan Jazbinsek
ATLÉTICO: Edgardo Mario MADINABEYTIA Bassi; Julio Santaella Benitez "COLO", Jorge Bernardo GRIFFA Monferoni, Jesús MARTÍNEZ JAYO; Feliciano RIVILLA Muñoz (Cap), Jesús GLARÍA Roldán; Miguel JONES del Castillo, ADELARDO Rodríguez Sánchez, Jorge Alberto MENDONÇA Paulino, LUIS Aragonés Suarez, José Enrique CARDONA Gutiérrez.   Trainer: Domingo Balmanya
Goal: Adelardo (80)

FC SION v GALATASARAY ISTANBUL 5-1 (1-1)
Parc des Sports, Sion 15.09.1965
Referee: Alessandro d'Agostini (ITA)   Attendance: 7,558
FC SION: Blagoje Vidinic; Jean-Pierre Jungo, Peter Roesch, André Germanier, Georges Perroud (Cap); Claude Sixt, Franz Stockbauer, Norbert Eschmann, Michel Desbiolles, René Quentin, Roger Gasser.   Trainer: Lav Mantula
GALATASARAY: Bülent Gürbüz; Bahri Altintabak, Ismet Yurtsu, Ahmet Berman; Naci Erdem, Talat Özkarsli (Cap); Yilmaz Gökdel, Ayhan Elmastaşoglu, Tarik Kutver, Turan Dogangün, Ugur Kökten.   Trainer: Gündüz Kiliç
Goals: Eschmann (12, 50), Quentin (55), Stockbauer (80, 89), Tarik (43)

GALATASARAY ISTANBUL v FC SION 2-1 (1-0)
Ali Sami Yen, Istanbul 29.09.1965
Referee: Zivko Bajić (YUG)   Attendance: 20,065
GALATASARAY: Bülent Gürbüz; Bahri Altintabak, Dogan Sel, Naci Erdem, Talat Özkarsli, Mustafa Yürür, Tarik Kutver, Turan Dogangün, Ayhan Elmastaşoglu, Metin Oktay, Ugur Kökten.   Trainer: Gündüz Kiliç
FC SION: Blagoje Vidinić; Jean-Pierre Jungo, Peter Roesch, André Germanier, Georges Perroud; Claude Sixt, Franz Stockbauer, Norbert Eschmann, Michel Desbiolles, René Quentin, Roger Gasser.   Trainer: Lav Mantula
Goals: Ugur (33), Sixt (50), Ayhan (59)

DUKLA PRAHA v STADE RENNAIS 2-0 (1-0)
Juliska, Praha 22.09.1965
Referee: Erwin Vetter (E. GER)   Attendance: 5,498
DUKLA: Ivo Viktor; Karel Dvorak, Ladislav Novák, Ján Geleta, Jiří Čadek; Josef Masopust (Cap), Jan Brumovský, Ján Strausz, Josef Vacenovský, František Knebort, Josef Jelínek.   Trainer: Jaroslav Vejvoda
STADE RENNAIS: Georges Lamia; Jean-Pierre Darchen, Louis Cardiet, Yves Boutet (Cap), René Cédolin; Marcel Loncle, Louis Floch, André Ascensio, Daniel Rodighiero, Claude Dubaële, Jean-François Prigent.   Trainer: Jean Prouff
Goals: Strausz (35), Knebort (83)

STADE RENNAIS v DUKLA PRAHA 0-0
Route de Lorient, Rennes 29.09.1965
Referee: José Plaza Pedraz (SPA)   Attendance: 13,495
STADE RENNAIS: Georges Lamia; Jean-Pierre Darchen, Louis Cardiet, Yves Boutet, Marcel Loncle, René Cédolin, Jean-François Prigent, André Ascensio, Daniel Rodighiero, Giovanni Pellegrini, Claude Dubaële.   Trainer: Jean Prouff
DUKLA: Ivo Viktor; Miroslav Cmarada, Ladislav Novák, Ivo Novák, Jiří Čadek; Josef Masopust, Jan Brumovský, Josef Vacenovský, Ján Geleta, František Knebort, Josef Jelinek.   Trainer: Jaroslav Vejvoda

1.FC MAGDEBURG
v CA SPORA LUXEMBURG 1-0 (1-0)
Ernst Grube, Magdeburg 22.09.1965
Referee: Marian Koczner (POL)   Attendance: 14,304
1.FC MAGDEBURG: Wolfgang Blochwitz; Rainer Wiedemann, Manfred Zapf, Rolf Retschlag; Ingolf Ruhloff, Wolfgang Seguin; Günter Kubisch, Peter Heuer, Hans-Joachim Walter, Rainer Segger, Hermann Stöcker (Cap).
Trainer: Ernst Kümmel
SPORA: Friedhelm Jesse; Ernest Royer, Fernand Brosius (Cap), Mario Morocutti, Paul Ludwig, Victor Nürenberg, Emile Meyer, Carlo Bofferding, Jean Hardt, Walter Glinski, Norry Wampach.   Trainer: Victor Nürenberg
Goal: Seguin (24)

**CA SPORA LUXEMBURG
v 1.FC MAGDEBURG 0-2** (0-1)

Stade Municipal, Luxembourg 13.10.1965

Referee: Pierre Schwinté (FRA)   Attendance: 3,255

SPORA: Friedhelm Jesse; Mario Morocutti, Bernard Ruetze; Paul Ludwig, Fernand Brosius (Cap), Jean Hardt; Emile Meyer, Carlo Bofferding, Victor Nürenberg, Erwin Kariko, Norry Wampach.   Trainer: Victor Nürenberg

1.FC MAGDEBURG: Wolfgang Blochwitz; Rainer Wiedemann, Manfred Zapf, Rolf Retschlag; Wolfgang Seguin, Ingolf Ruhloff; Günter Kubisch, Hans-Joachim Walter, Manfred Eckardt, Rainer Segger, Hermann Stöcker (Cap). Trainer: Ernst Kümmel

Goals: Kubisch (5), Seguin (80)

**GO AHEAD EAGLES DEVENTER
v CELTIC GLASGOW 0-6** (0-2)

Stadion aan de Vetkampstraat, Deventer 29.09.1965

Referee: Antoine Queudeville (LUX)   Attendance: 18,223

GO AHEAD: Nicolaas Van Zoghel; Rolf Thiemann, Johan Butter, Hendrik Kanselaar, Hendrik Warnas, Gerhardus Johannes Somer (Cap), Roelof Greving, Wietse Harm Veenstra, Jan Boekestein, Gerrit Niehaus, Cor Adelaar. Trainer: František Fadhronc

CELTIC: Ronald Simpson; Ian Young, Thomas Gemmell; Robert Murdoch, William McNeill (Cap), John Clark; James Johnstone, Charles Gallacher, Robert Lennox, Stephen Chalmers, John Hughes.   Manager: John Stein

Goals: Lennox (26, 56, 70), Hughes (29), Johnstone (47, 78)

**OMONOIA NICOSIA
v OLYMPIAKOS PEIRAIAS 0-1** (0-1)

Makareio, Nicosia 26.09.1965

Referee: Arthur Lentini (MAL)   Attendance: 11,787

OMONOIA: Nikos Eleytheriadis; Kostas Hristou, Akis Ioannou; Stefanos Stefanou, Kostas Panagiotou, Ploutis Pallas; Drosos Kalotheou, Antonis Kyriakou, Giorgos Hristoforou (Cap), Melis Asprou, Andreas Konstantinou.
Trainer: Georgi Ivanov Pavecev

OLYMPIAKOS: Parashos Avgitidis; Alexandros Livadas, Orestis Pavlidis, Kostas Polihroniou (Cap), Giannis Gkaitatzis, Antonis Dermatis, Paulos Vasileiou, Giorgos Sideris, Nikos Sideris, Nikos Gioutsos, Vasilis Botinos.
Trainer: Marton Bukovi

Goal: Botinos (5)

**CELTIC GLASGOW
v GO AHEAD EAGLES DEVENTER 1-0** (1-0)

Celtic Park, Glasgow 7.10.1965

Referee: Hannes Th. Sigurdsson (ICE)   Attendance: 14,723

CELTIC: Ronald Simpson; James Craig, Thomas Gemmell; Robert Murdoch, William McNeill (Cap), John Clark; James Johnstone, Stephen Chalmers, Joseph McBride, John Hughes, Robert Lennox.   Manager: John Stein

GO AHEAD: Nicolaas Van Zoghel; Johan Butter, Hendrik Warnas; Rolf Thiemann, Hendrik Kanselaar, Gerhardus Johannes Somer (Cap); Gerhardus Wüstfeld, Gerrit J. Niehaus, Roelof Greving, Wietse Harm Veenstra, Cor W. Adelaar. Trainer: František Fadhronc

Goal: McBride (12)

**OLYMPIAKOS PEIRAIAS
v OMONOIA NICOSIA 1-1** (1-1)

Karaiskaki, Peiraias 10.10.1965

Referee: Dimitar Rumentchev (BUL)   Attendance: 22,699

OLYMPIAKOS: Parashos Avgitidis; Orestis Pavlidis, Giagkos Simantiris, Kostas Polihroniou (Cap), Antonis Dermatis, Giannis Gkaitatzis, Nikos Gioutsos, Vasilis Botinos, Dimitris Sinatkas, Aristidis Papazoglou, Paulos Vasileiou.
Trainer: Marton Bukovi

OMONOIA: Nikos Eleytheriadis; Kostas Hristou, Akis Ioannou; Stefanos Stefanou, Kostas Panagiotou, Ploutis Pallas; Antonis Kyriakou, Drosos Kalotheou, Giorgos Hristoforou (Cap), Melis Asprou, Andreas Konstantinou.
Trainer: Georgi Ivanov Pavecev

Sent off: Papazoglou (57)

Goals: Grigoriou (17), Papazoglou (20)

**FLORIANA FC VALLETTA
v BORUSSIA DORTMUND 1-5** (1-1)

The Manoel Island Sports Ground, Gzira 29.09.1965

Referee: Raoul Righi (ITA)   Attendance: 6,630

FLORIANA FC: Anthony Borg; Alfred Debono, Joseph Grima; Edward Azzopardi, Emmanuel Debattista, Frank Micallef; Charles Chircop, Nazzareno Alamango, Anthony Cauchi, Charles Buttigieg, Emmanuel Borg (Cap).
Trainer: Emmanuel Borg

BORUSSIA: Hans Tilkowski; Reinhold Wosab, Theo Redder; Dieter Kurrat, Wolfgang Paul (Cap), Rudolf Assauer; Reinhard Libuda, Jürgen Weber, Siegfried Held, Wilhelm Sturm, Lothar Emmerich.   Trainer: Willi Multhaup

Goals: Emmerich (27), Chircop (30), Wosab (58, 65), Held (62, 64)

**BORUSSIA DORTMUND
v FLORIANA FC VALLETTA 8-0** (3-0)

Rote Erde, Dortmund 10.10.1965

Referee: John Meighan (IRL)   Attendance: 8,870

BORUSSIA: Bernhard Wessel; Theo Redder, Reinhold Wosab; Friedhelm Groppe, Wolfgang Paul (Cap), Dieter Kurrat; Reinhard Libuda, Alfred Schmidt, Siegfried Held, Wilhelm Sturm, Lothar Emmerich.   Trainer: Willi Multhaup

FLORIANA FC: Anthony Borg; Edward Azzopardi, Joseph Grima; Anthony Cauchi, Emmanuel Debattista, Alfred Debono; Emmanuel Borg (Cap), Charles Chircop, Nazzareno Alamango, Charles Buttigieg, Hugh Caruana. Trainer: Emmanuel Borg

Goals: Emmerich (5 pen, 37, 52, 58, 67, 74), Schmidt (26, 63)

JUVENTUS v LIVERPOOL FC 1-0 (0-0)

Stadio Comunale, Torino 29.09.1965

Referee: István Zsolt (HUN)   Attendance: 9,242

JUVENTUS: Roberto Anzolin; Adolfo Gori, Gianfranco Leoncini; Giancarlo Bercellino, Sandro Salvadore, Bruno Mazzia; Gino Stacchini, Luis Del Sol (Cap), Silvio Bercellino, Sidney Cunha Cinesinho, Giampaolo Menichelli. Trainer: Heriberto Herrera

LIVERPOOL: Thomas Lawrence; Geoffrey Strong, Gerald Byrne, Alfred Arrowsmith, Ronald Yeats (Cap), William Stevenson, Ian Robert Callaghan, Roger Hunt, Ian St. John, Thomas Smith, Peter Thompson.   Manager: William Shankly

Goal: Leoncini (81)

LIVERPOOL FC v JUVENTUS TORINO 2-0 (2-0)

Anfield Road, Liverpool 13.10.1965

Referee: Joseph Heymann (SWI)   Attendance: 51,055

LIVERPOOL: Thomas Lawrence; Christopher Lawler, Gerald Byrne, Geoffrey Strong, Ronald Yeats (Cap), William Stevenson, Ian Robert Callaghan, Roger Hunt, Ian St. John, Thomas Smith, Peter Thompson.   Manager: William Shankly

JUVENTUS: Roberto Anzolin; Adolfo Gori, Benito Sarti; Giancarlo Bercellino, Sandro Salvadore, Gianfranco Leoncini; Bruno Mazzia, Luis Del Sol (Cap), Vincenzo Traspedini, Sidney Cunha Cinesinho, Giampaolo Menichelli. Trainer: Heriberto Herrera

Goals: Lawler (20), Strong (25)

FC LIMERICK v CSKA SOFIA 1-2 (1-2)

Dalymount Park, Dublin 7.10.1965

Referee: Ivar Hornslien (NOR)   Attendance: 10,620

LIMERICK: Kevin Fitzpatrick; Joseph Casey, Vincent Quinn, Desmond McNamara, Alexander Ewan Fenton (Cap), Alphonsus Finucane, Richard O'Connor, Thomas Hamilton, Peter Mitchell, Joseph O'Brien, Pascal Curtin. Manager: Alexander Ewan Fenton

CSKA: Stoian Iordanov; Ivan Vasilev, Hristo Marinchev, Boris Stankov, Boris Gaganelov, Dimitar Penev, Evgeni Kamenov, Nikola Tsanev (Cap), Dimitar Iakimov, Ianko Kirilov, Ivan Kolev.   Trainer: Grigori Pinaichev

Goals: Tsanev (6), O'Connor (18), Kamenov (22)

CSKA SOFIA v FC LIMERICK 2-0 (0-0)

Narodna Armia, Sofia 13.10.1965

Referee: Faruk Talu (TUR)   Attendance: 14,561

CSKA: Stoian Iordanov; Ivan Vasilev, Dimitar Penev, Stefan Iliev, Hristo Marinchev; Boris Stankov, Ianko Kirilov; Evgeni Kamenov, Nikola Tsanev (Cap), Dimitar Iakimov, Ivan Kolev. Trainer: Grigori Pinaichev

LIMERICK: Kevin Fitzpatrick; Vincent Quinn, Joseph Casey; Desmond McNamara, Alexander Ewan Fenton (Cap), Alphonsus Finucane; Richard O'Connor, Thomas Hamilton, Peter Mitchell, Joseph O'Brien, Pascal Curtin. Manager: Alexander Ewan Fenton

Goals: Kolev (53), Kamenov (73)

SECOND ROUND

**ROSENBORG TRONDHEIM
v DINAMO KIEV 1-4** (0-3)

Lerkendal, Trondheim 24.10.1965

Referee: Adrianus Aalbrecht (HOL)   Attendance: 10,435

ROSENBORG BK: Tor Røste Fossen; Knut Jenssen, Kjell Hvidsand; Kåre Rønnes (Cap), Harald Gulbrandsen, Egil Nygård; Eldar Hansen, Birger Thingstad, Odd Iversen, Svein Haagenrud, Tor Kleveland.   Trainer: Knut Naess

DINAMO: Viktor Bannikov; Vladimir Schegolkov, Vadim Sosnikhin, Sergei Krulikovski, Leonid Ostrovski; Iosif Sabo, Vasili Turianchik; Anatoli Puzach, Viktor Serebrianikov, Andrei Biba (Cap), Vitali Khmelnitski.
Trainer: Viktor Maslov

Goals: Biba (7), Khmelnitski (20), Puzach (42, 62), E. Hansen (61)

**DINAMO KIEV
v ROSENBORG TRONDHEIM 2-0** (2-0)

Republikanskiy, Kiev   28.10.1965

Referee: Ferdinand Marschall (AUS)   Attendance: 10,102

DINAMO: Viktor Bannikov; Vladimir Schegolkov, Vadim Sosnikhin, Leonid Ostrovski; Iosif Sabo, Vasili Turianchik (Cap); Oleg Bazilevich, Viktor Serebrjanikov, Fiedor Medvid, Anatoli Puzach, Vitali Khmelnitski.   Trainer: Viktor Maslov

ROSENBORG BK: Tor Røste Fossen; Knut Jenssen, Kjell Hvidsand; Kåre Rønnes (Cap), Harald Gulbrandsen, Egil Nygård; Eldar Hansen, Birger Thingstad, Odd Iversen, Svein Haagenrud, Tor Kleveland.   Trainer: Knut Naess

Goals: Khmelnitski (5), Bazilevich (29)

ÅRHUS GF v CELTIC GLASGOW 0-1 (0-1)

Århus Stadion   3.11.1965

Referee: Hubert Burguet (BEL)   Attendance: 10,831

ÅRHUS GF: Bent Martin; Arne Sørensen, Erik Nielsen; Søren Pedersen, Bent Wolmar, John Amdisen (Cap); Kjeld Jensen, Jørn Bjerregaard, Henning Enoksen, Ove Sørensen, Verner Hermansen.   Trainer: Henry From

CELTIC: Ronald Simpson; Ian Young, Thomas Gemmell; Robert Murdoch, William McNeill (Cap), John Clark; James Johnstone, Charles Gallacher, Joseph McBride, Robert Lennox, John Hughes.   Manager: John Stein

Goal: McBride (22)

DUKLA PRAHA v HONVED BUDAPEST 2-3 (1-3)

Juliska, Praha   3.11.1965

Referee: Kurt Tschenscher (W. GER)   Attendance: 4,035

DUKLA: Ivo Viktor; Milan Dvorak, Jiří Čadek, Ladislav Novák; Ján Geleta, Josef Masopust (Cap); Stanislav Strunc, Josef Vacenovský, František Knebort, Miroslav Rödr, Josef Jelínek.   Trainer: Jaroslav Vejvoda

HONVÉD: Béla Takács; Zoltán Dudás, Ferenc Sipos, Boldizsár Mihalecz; József Dorogi, Imre Komora; György Nagy, Ferenc Nógrádi, Lajos Tichy (Cap), Kálmán Tóth, Sándor Katona.   Trainer: Mihály Kispéter

Goals: Rödr (6), Tichy (12, 39, 41), Strunc (74)

CELTIC GLASGOW v ÅRHUS GF 2-0 (2-0)

Celtic Park, Glasgow   17.11.1965

Referee: Johan Riseth (NOR)   Attendance: 23,079

CELTIC: Ronald Simpson; James Craig, Thomas Gemmell; Robert Murdoch, William McNeill (Cap), John Clark; James Johnstone, Charles Gallacher, Joseph McBride, Robert Lennox, John Hughes.   Manager: John Stein

ÅRHUS GF: Bent Martin; Ole Laursen, Arne Sørensen; John Amdisen (Cap), Bent Wolmar, Søren Pedersen; Kjeld Jensen, Jørn Bjerregaard, Henning Enoksen, Ove Sørensen, Verner Hermansen.   Trainer: Henry From

Goals: McNeill (7), Johnstone (40)

HONVED BUDAPEST v DUKLA PRAHA 1-2 (1-0)

Népstadion, Budapest   10.11.1965

Referee: Konstantin Dinov (BUL)   Attendance: 12,278

HONVÉD: Béla Takács; László Marosi, Ferenc Sipos, Boldizsár Mihalecz; József Dorogi, István Vági; György Nagy, Ferenc Nógrádi, Lajos Tichy (Cap), Imre Komora, Sándor Katona.   Trainer: Mihály Kispéter

DUKLA: Ivo Viktor; Milan Dvorak, Ladislav Novák, Ivo Novák, Jiří Čadek; Josef Masopust (Cap), Ján Geleta; Stanislav Strunc, František Knebort, Miroslav Rödr, Josef Vacenovský.   Trainer: Jaroslav Vejvoda

Goals: Dorogi (22), Masopust (75), Knebort (87)

BORUSSIA DORTMUND v CSKA SOFIA 3-0 (2-0)

Rote Erde, Dortmund   10.11.1965

Referee: Gyula Emsberger (HUN)   Attendance: 18,522

BORUSSIA: Bernhard Wessel; Reinhold Wosab, Theo Redder; Dieter Kurrat, Wolfgang Paul (Cap), Rudolf Assauer; Reinhard Libuda, Alfred Schmidt, Siegfried Held, Wilhelm Sturm, Lothar Emmerich.   Trainer: Willi Multhaup

CSKA: Stoian Iordanov; Ivan Vasilev, Stefan Iliev, Boris Stankov, Boris Gaganelov, Dimitar Penev, Nikola Tsanev (Cap), Vasil Romanov, Dimitar Iakimov, Stoichko Peshev, Ivan Kolev.   Trainer: Grigori Pinaichev

Goals: Sturm (17), Held (24), Schmidt (54)

CSKA SOFIA v BORUSSIA DORTMUND 4-2 (2-2)
Vasil Levski, Sofia 24.11.1965

Referee: Muzafer Sarvan (TUR) Attendance: 19,150

CSKA: Stoian Iordanov; Ivan Vasilev, Hristo Marinchev; Boris Stankov, Boris Gaganelov (Cap), Dimitar Penev; Vasil Romanov, Stefan Iliev, Dimitar Iakimov, Asparuh Nikodimov, Ivan Kolev. Trainer: Grigori Pinaichev

BORUSSIA: Hans Tilkowski; Reinhold Wosab, Theo Redder, Dieter Kurrat, Wolfgang Paul (Cap), Friedhelm Groppe, Reinhard Libuda, Alfred Schmidt, Siegfried Held, Wilhelm Sturm, Lothar Emmerich. Trainer: Willi Multhaup

Sent off: Kurrat (87)

Goals: Romanov (7, 43, 68), Held (24), Emmerich (39), Vasilev (74 pen)

ŞTIINŢA CLUJ v ATLÉTICO MADRID 0-2 (0-0)
Municipal, Cluj 17.11.1965

Referee: Alois Obtulovič (CZE) Attendance: 9,000

ŞTIINŢA: Cristian Ringheanu; Paul Marcu, Mircea Neşu, Paul Grăjdeanu, Remus Cîmpeanu; Vasile Alexandru, Traian Georgescu (Cap); Nicolae Szabo, Zoltan Ivansuc, Mihai Adam, Ioan Suciu. Trainer: Andrei Sepci

ATLÉTICO: Edgardo Mario MADINABEYTIA Bassi; Julio Santaella Benítez "COLO", Jorge Bernardo GRIFFA Monferoni, Jesús GLARÍA Roldán, Feliciano RIVILLA Muñoz; Manuel RUIZ-SOSA, ADELARDO Rodríguez Sánchez; José Armando UFARTE Ventoso, Jorge Alberto MENDONÇA Paulino, LUIS Aragonés Suarez, Enrique COLLAR Monterrubio (Cap). Trainer: Domingo Balmanya

Goals: Collar (67), Adelardo (85)

1.FC MAGDEBURG v FC SION 8-1 (3-1)
Ernst-Grube, Magdeburg 17.11.1965

Referee: Toimi Olkku (FIN) Attendance: 8,720

1.FC MAGDEBURG: Wolfgang Blochwitz; Manfred Zapf, Günter Fronzeck, Rolf Retschlag; Günter Kubisch, Wolfgang Seguin; Rainer Wiedemann, Hans-Joachim Walter, Manfred Eckardt, Wilfried Klingbiel, Hermann Stöcker (Cap). Trainer: Ernst Kümmel

FC SION: Blagoje Vidinic; Jean-Pierre Jungo, Peter Roesch, André Germanier, Georges Perroud (Cap), Claude Sixt, Franz Stockbauer, Lav Mantula, Norbert Eschmann, Michel Desbiolles, René Quentin. Trainer: Lav Mantula

Goals: Eckardt (9, 25), Eschmann (35), Stöcker (45, 57), Kubisch (53, 63), Walter (69, 77)

ATLÉTICO MADRID v ŞTIINŢA CLUJ 4-0 (2-0)
Estadio Metropolitano, Madrid 15.12.1965

Referee: James Finney (ENG) Attendance: 9,383

ATLÉTICO: Roberto Rodríguez García; Julio Santaella Benítez "COLO", Jorge Bernardo GRIFFA Monferoni, Jesús GLARÍA Roldán, Jesús MARTÍNEZ JAYO; Manuel RUIZ-SOSA, VÍCTOR Díaz Gutiérrez; José Enrique CARDONA Gutiérrez, Jorge Alberto MENDONÇA Paulino, LUIS Aragonés Suarez, Enrique COLLAR Monterrubio (Cap). Trainer: Domingo Balmanya

ŞTIINŢA: Cristian Ringheanu; Iosif Szőke, Mircea Neşu, Paul Grăjdeanu, Remus Cîmpeanu; Vasile Alexandru, Traian Georgescu (Cap), Werner Pexa; Zoltan Ivansuc, Paul Marcu, Mihai Adam. Trainer: Andrei Sepci

Goals: Mendonça (26, 60), Víctor (40), Luis (80 pen)

FC SION v 1.FC MAGDEBURG 2-2 (0-2)
Parc des Sports, Sion 8.12.1965

Referee: Stjepan Varaždinec (YUG) Attendance: 2,979

FC SION: Blagoje Vidinic; Jean-Pierre Jungo, Peter Roesch, André Germanier, Georges Perroud (Cap); Joseph Antonelli, Claude Sixt; Franz Stockbauer, Michel Desbiolles, René Quentin, Lav Mantula. Trainer: Lav Mantula

1.FC MAGDEBURG: Wolfgang Blochwitz; Manfred Zapf, Günter Fronzeck, Rolf Retschlag, Günter Kubisch, Wolfgang Seguin, Rainer Wiedemann, Hans-Joachim Walter, Wilfried Klingbiel, Hermann Stöcker (Cap), Günter Hirschmann. Trainer: Ernst Kümmel

Sent off: Hirschmann (48), Antonelli (84)

Goals: Wiedemann (1, 35), Desbiolles (56, 72)

WEST HAM UNITED LONDON v OLYMPIAKOS PEIRAIAS 4-0 (2-0)
Upton Park, London 24.11.1965

Referee: Karl Keller (SWI) Attendance: 27,250

WEST HAM: James Standen; Joseph Kirkup, John Charles, Edward Bovington, Kenneth Brown; Robert Frederick Moore, Peter Brabrook, Martin Stanford Peters; John Joseph Byrne (Cap), Geoffrey Charles Hurst, John Leslie Sissons. Manager: Ronald Greenwood

OLYMPIAKOS: Giannis Fronimidis; Orestis Pavlidis, Dimitris Stefanakos, Kostas Polihroniou (Cap), Paulos Vasileiou; Giorgos Sideris, Nikos Gioutsos; Vasilis Botinos, Giannis Gkaitatzis, Dimitris Plessas, Hristos Zanteroglou. Trainer: Marton Bukovi

Goals: Hurst (23, 43), Byrne (65), Brabrook (82)

**OLYMPIAKOS PEIRAIAS
v WEST HAM UNITED LONDON 2-2** (0-1)

Karaiskaki, Peiraias 1.12.1965

Referee: Tofik Bakhramov (USSR)   Attendance: 32,826

OLYMPIAKOS: Giannis Fronimidis; Dimitris Stefanakos, Evangelos Milisis, Kostas Polihroniou (Cap), Paulos Vasileiou; Nikos Gioutsos, Aristidis Papazoglou; Vasilis Botinos, Giannis Gkaitatzis, Dimitris Plessas, Grigoris Aganian. Trainer: Marton Bukovi

WEST HAM: James Standen; Joseph Kirkup, John Charles, Edward Bovington, Kenneth Brown; Robert Frederick Moore, Peter Brabrook, Martin Stanford Peters, John Joseph Byrne (Cap), Geoffrey Charles Hurst, John Leslie Sissons. Manager: Ronald Greenwood

Goals: Peters (28, 53), Bovington (57 og), Polihroniou (81 pen)

LIVERPOOL FC v STANDARD LIÈGE 3-1 (1-0)

Anfield Road, Liverpool 1.12.1965

Referee: Robert Lacoste (FRA)   Attendance: 46,112

LIVERPOOL FC: Thomas Lawrence; Christopher Lawler, Gerald Byrne, Gordon Milne, Ronald Yeats (Cap), William Stevenson, Ian Robert Callaghan, Roger Hunt, Ian St. John, Thomas Smith, Peter Thompson.   Manager: William Shankly

STANDARD: Jean Nicolay; Jozef Vliers, Jacques Beurlet, Louis Pilot, Lucien Spronck (Cap), Guillaume Raskin, Léon Semmeling, Nicolas Dewalque, Roger Claessen, Velimir Naumovic, James Storme.   Trainer: Milorad Pavić

Goals: Lawler (27, 50), Storme (57), Thompson (60)

STANDARD LIÈGE v LIVERPOOL FC 1-2 (1-0)

Stade Maurice Dufrasne - Sclessin, Liège 15.12.1965

Referee: Ryszard Banasiuk (POL)   Attendance: 29,534

STANDARD: Jean Nicolay; Jozef Vliers, Jacques Beurlet, Louis Pilot, Lucien Spronck (Cap), Léon Semmeling, Victor Wégria, Nicolas Dewalque, Roger Claessen, Velimir Naumovic, James Storme.   Trainer: Milorad Pavić

LIVERPOOL FC: Thomas Lawrence; Christopher Lawler, Gerald Byrne, Geoffrey Strong, Ronald Yeats (Cap), William Stevenson, Ian Robert Callaghan, Roger Hunt, Ian St. John, Thomas Smith, Peter Thompson.   Manager: William Shankly

Goals: Claessen (43), Hunt (51), St. John (57)

QUARTER-FINALS

CELTIC GLASGOW v DINAMO KIEV 3-0 (1-0)

Celtic Park, Glasgow 12.01.1966

Referee: Günther Baumgärtel (W. GER)   Attendance: 64,363

CELTIC: Ronald Simpson; James Craig, Thomas Gemmell; Robert Murdoch (Cap), John Cushley, John Clark; James Johnstone, Charles Gallacher, Joseph McBride, Stephen Chalmers, John Hughes.   Manager: John Stein

DINAMO: Viktor Bannikov; Vladimir Schegolkov, Vadim Sosnikhin, Leonid Ostrovski; Fiedor Medvid, Vasili Turianchik; Oleg Bazilevich, Viktor Serebrianikov, Anatoli Puzach, Andrei Biba (Cap), Vitali Khmelnitski. Trainer: Viktor Maslov

Goals: Gemmell (27), Murdoch (63, 85)

DINAMO KIEV v CELTIC GLASGOW 1-1 (1-1)

Dinamo, Tbilisi 26.01.1966

Referee: Antonio Sbardella (ITA)   Attendance: 30,516

DINAMO: Viktor Bannikov; Vladimir Schegolkov, Vadim Sosnikhin, Vladimir Levchenko; Iosif Sabo, Vasili Turianchik; Oleg Bazilevich, Viktor Serebrianikov, Fiedor Medvid, Andrei Biba (Cap), Vitali Khmelnitski.   Trainer: Viktor Maslov

CELTIC: Ronald Simpson; James Craig, Thomas Gemmell; William McNeill (Cap), John Cushley, John Clark; James Johnstone, Robert Murdoch, Joseph McBride, Stephen Chalmers, John Hughes.   Manager: John Stein

Sent off: Craig & Khmelnitski (66)

Goals: Sabo (21), Gemmell (30)

**ATLÉTICO MADRID
v BORUSSIA DORTMUND 1-1** (0-0)

Estadio del Manzanares, Madrid 16.02.1966

Referee: William Clements (ENG)   Attendance: 19,960

ATLÉTICO: Roberto Rodríguez García; Feliciano RIVILLA Muñoz, Jesús MARTÍNEZ JAYO, Jesús GLARÍA Roldán, Jorge Bernardo GRIFFA Monferoni; ADELARDO Rodríguez Sánchez, José Armando UFARTE Ventoso, LUIS Aragonés Suarez, Jorge Alberto MENDONÇA Paulino, Miguel JONES del Castillo, Enrique COLLAR Monterrubio (Cap). Trainer: Domingo Balmanya

BORUSSIA: Hans Tilkowski; Gerhard Cyliax, Theo Redder, Dieter Kurrat, Wolfgang Paul (Cap), Friedhelm Groppe, Reinhard Libuda, Alfred Schmidt, Siegfried Held, Wilhelm Sturm, Lothar Emmerich.   Trainer: Willi Multhaup

Goals: Emmerich (58), Mendonça (86)

**BORUSSIA DORTMUND
v ATLÉTICO MADRID 1-0** (1-0)

Rote Erde, Dortmund   2.03.1966

Referee: Lajos Aranyosi (HUN)   Attendance: 32,516

BORUSSIA: Hans Tilkowski; Gerhard Cyliax, Theo Redder, Dieter Kurrat, Wolfgang Paul (Cap), Friedhelm Groppe, Reinhard Libuda, Alfred Schmidt, Siegfried Held, Wilhelm Sturm, Lothar Emmerich.   Trainer: Willi Multhaup

ATLÉTICO: Roberto Rodríguez García; Julio Santaella Benitez "COLO", Jesús MARTÍNEZ JAYO, Feliciano RIVILLA Muñoz; Francisco GARCÍA, Jesús GLARÍA Roldán; José Armando UFARTE Ventoso, LUIS Aragonés Suarez, Miguel JONES del Castillo, ADELARDO Rodríguez Sánchez, Enrique COLLAR Monterrubio (Cap).   Trainer: Domingo Balmanya

Goal: Emmerich (16)

**WEST HAM UNITED
v 1.FC MAGDEBURG 1-0** (0-0)

Upton Park, London   2.03.1966

Referee: Jean Tricot (FRA)   Attendance: 30,620

WEST HAM: James Standen; Dennis Burnett, John Burkett, Martin Stanford Peters, Kenneth Brown, Robert Frederick Moore; Peter Brabrook, Ronald William Boyce, John Joseph Byrne (Cap), Geoffrey Charles Hurst, John Leslie Sissons.
Manager: Ronald Greenwood

1.FC MAGDEBURG: Wolfgang Blochwitz; Rainer Wiedemann, Manfred Zapf, Günter Kubisch, Dieter Busch, Günter Fronzeck, Wilfried Klingbiel, Wolfgang Seguin, Rainer Geschke, Rainer Segger, Hermann Stöcker (Cap).
Trainer: Ernst Kümmel

Goal: Byrne (46)

**1.FC MAGDEBURG
v WEST HAM UNITED 1-1** (0-0)

Ernst Grube, Magdeburg   16.03.1966

Referee: Vital Loraux (BEL)   Attendance: 30,926

1.FC MAGDEBURG: Wolfgang Blochwitz; Rainer Wiedemann, Günter Fronzeck, Manfred Zapf; Günter Kubisch, Günter Hirschmann; Wilfried Klingbiel, Jürgen Sparwasser, Hans-Joachim Walter, Wolfgang Seguin, Hermann Stöcker (Cap).   Trainer: Ernst Kümmel

WEST HAM: James Standen; Dennis Burnett, John Burkett, Edward Bovington, Kenneth Brown; Robert Frederick Moore (Cap), Peter Brabrook, Ronald William Boyce, Geoffrey Charles Hurst, Martin Stanford Peters, John Leslie Sissons.
Manager: Ronald Greenwood

Goals: Walter (76), Sissons (77)

HONVÉD BUDAPEST v LIVERPOOL FC 0-0

Népstadion, Budapest   1.03.1966

Referee: Dimitris Wlachojanis (AUS)   Attendance: 16,163

HONVÉD: Béla Takács; Zoltán Dudás, Ferenc Sipos, Boldizsár Mihalecz; Antal Tussinger, Ferenc Nógrádi; György Nagy, Imre Komora, Lajos Tichy (Cap), Kálmán Tóth, Sándor Katona.   Trainer: József Bozsik

LIVERPOOL: Thomas Lawrence; Christopher Lawler, Gerald Byrne; Gordon Milne, Ronald Yeats (Cap), William Stevenson; Ian Robert Callaghan, Roger Hunt, Ian St. John, Thomas Smith, Peter Thompson.   Manager: William Shankly

SEMI-FINALS

LIVERPOOL FC v HONVÉD BUDAPEST 2-0 (2-0)

Anfield Road, Liverpool   8.03.1966

Referee: Anton Bucheli (SWI)   Attendance: 54,631

LIVERPOOL: Thomas Lawrence; Christopher Lawler, Gerald Byrne; Gordon Milne, Ronald Yeats (Cap), William Stevenson; Ian Robert Callaghan, Roger Hunt, Ian St.John, Thomas Smith, Peter Thompson.   Manager: William Shankly

HONVÉD: Béla Takács; Zoltán Dudás, Ferenc Sipos, Boldizsár Mihalecz; Antal Tussinger, Ferenc Nógrádi; József Dorogi, Imre Komora, Lajos Tichy (Cap), György Nagy, Sándor Katona.   Trainer: József Bozsik

Goals: Lawler (12), St. John (44)

**WEST HAM UNITED
v BORUSSIA DORTMUND 1-2** (0-0)

Upton Park, London   5.04.1966

Referee: José María Ortiz de Mendíbil (SPA)   Att: 28,130

WEST HAM: James Standen; Kenneth Brown, John Charles, Robert Frederick Moore, Ronald William Boyce, Martin Stanford Peters, Peter Brabrook, James Bloomfield, John Joseph Byrne (Cap), Geoffrey Charles Hurst, Brian Dear.
Manager: Ronald Greenwood

BORUSSIA: Hans Tilkowski; Gerhard Cyliax, Theo Redder, Dieter Kurrat, Wolfgang Paul (Cap), Rudolf Assauer, Reinhard Libuda, Alfred Schmidt, Siegfried Held, Wilhelm Sturm, Lothar Emmerich.   Trainer: Willi Multhaup

Goals: Peters (52), Emmerich (80, 82)

**BORUSSIA DORTMUND
v WEST HAM UNITED 3-1** (2-1)

Rote Erde, Dortmund 13.04.1966

Referee: Julio Campanati (ITA)   Attendance: 33,052

BORUSSIA: Hans Tilkowski; Gerhard Cyliax, Theo Redder, Dieter Kurrat, Wolfgang Paul (Cap), Rudolf Assauer, Reinhard Libuda, Alfred Schmidt, Siegfried Held, Wilhelm Sturm, Lothar Emmerich.   Trainer: Willi Multhaup

WEST HAM: James Standen; Edward Bovington, John Charles, Martin Stanford Peters, Kenneth Brown, Robert Frederick Moore, Peter Brabrook, Ronald William Boyce, John Joseph Byrne (Cap), Geoffrey Charles Hurst, James Bloomfield.   Manager: Ronald Greenwood

Goals: Emmerich (1, 28), Byrne (43), Cyliax (86)

CELTIC GLASGOW v LIVERPOOL FC 1-0 (0-0)

Celtic Park (Parkhead), Glasgow 14.04.1966

Referee: Rudolf Glöckner (E. GER)   Attendance: 76,446

CELTIC: Ronald Simpson; Ian Young, Thomas Gemmell; Robert Murdoch, William McNeill (Cap), John Clark; James Johnstone, Joseph McBride, Stephen Chalmers, Robert Lennox, Robert Auld.   Manager: John Stein

LIVERPOOL: Thomas Lawrence; Christopher Lawler, Gerald Byrne, Gordon Milne, Ronald Yeats (Cap), William Stevenson, Ian Robert Callaghan, John Philip Chisnall, Ian St. John, Thomas Smith, Peter Thompson.   Manager: William Shankly

Goal: Lennox (52)

LIVERPOOL FC v CELTIC GLASGOW 2-0 (0-0)

Anfield Road, Liverpool 19.04.1966

Referee: Joseph Hannet (BEL)   Attendance: 54,208

LIVERPOOL: Thomas Lawrence; Christopher Lawler, Gerald Byrne, Gordon Milne, Ronald Yeats (Cap), William Stevenson, Ian Robert Callaghan, Geoffrey Strong, Ian St. John, Thomas Smith, Peter Thompson.   Manager: William Shankly

CELTIC: Ronald Simpson; Ian Young, Thomas Gemmell; Robert Murdoch, William McNeill (Cap), John Clark; Robert Lennox, Joseph McBride, Stephen Chalmers, Robert Auld, John Hughes.   Manager: John Stein

Goals: Smith (59), Strong (65)

FINAL

**BORUSSIA DORTMUND
v LIVERPOOL FC 2-1** (0-0, 1-1) (AET)

Hampden Park, Glasgow 5.05.1966

Referee: Pierre Schwinté (FRA)   Attendance: 41,657

BORUSSIA: Hans Tilkowski; Gerhard Cyliax, Wolfgang Paul (Cap), Dieter Kurrat, Theo Redder; Alfred Schmidt, Rudolf Assauer; Reinhard Libuda, Siegfried Held, Wilhelm Sturm, Lothar Emmerich.   Trainer: Willi Multhaup

LIVERPOOL FC: Thomas Lawrence; Christopher Lawler, Gordon Milne, Ronald Yeats (Cap), Gerald Byrne; William Stevenson, Thomas Smith; Ian Robert Callaghan, Roger Hunt, Ian St. John, Peter Thompson.   Manager: William Shankly.

Goals: Held (61), Hunt (68), Libuda (109)

Goalscorers Cup-Winners' Cup 1965-66:

14 goals: Lothar Emmerich (BV Borussia Dortmund)

7 goals: Lajos Tichy (Budapesti Honvéd)

6 goals: J. Alberto MENDONÇA Paulino (Atlético Madrid)

5 goals: Kálmán Tóth (Budapesti Honvéd), Siegfried Held (Borussia Dortmund)

4 goals: Oleg Bazilevich, Andrej Biba, Vitali Khmelnitski (Dinamo Kiev), Robert Lennox (Celtic Glasgow), Christopher Lawler (Liverpool FC)

3 goals: Romanov (CSKA Sofia), Eschmann (FC Sion), Kubisch, Walter (FC Magdeburg), Byrne, Peters (West Ham), Johnstone (Celtic), Schmidt (Borussia Dortmund)

2 goals: Knebort (Dukla Praha), Kieveland, T. Pedersen (Rosenborg), Ivansuc (Știința Cluj), K.Jensen (Århus), Komora, Nagy (Honvéd), Kamenov (CSKA Sofia), Stockbauer, Desbiolles (FC Sion), Storme, Claessen (Standard Liége), Serebrianikov, Puzach (Dinamo Kiev), Luis, Adelardo (Atlético Madrid), Eckardt, Stöcker, Wiedemann, Seguin (FC Magdeburg), Hurst (West Ham), McBride, Murdoch, Gemmell (Celtic), Hunt, St. John, Strong (Liverpool), Wosab (Borussia Dortmund)

1 goal: Leoncini (Juventus), O'Connor (Limerick), Chircop (Floriana), Botinos, Papazoglou, Polihroniou (Olympiakos), Grigoriou (Omonoia), Strausz, Rödr, Strunc, Masopust (Dukla Praha), Tarik, Ugur, Ayhan (Galatasaray), Schram, Isfeld (KR Reykjavik), Haagenrud, Lindvåg, E.Hansen (Rosenborg), Joaquim Silva Quim, Graça (Vitória Setubal), Johnston (Cardiff City), Curley (Coleraine), Adam (Știința Cluj), Hyvärinen, Kautonen (Lahden Reipas), Bjerregaard, Enoksen (Århus), Nógrádi, Katona, Dorogi (Honvéd), Tsanev, Kolev, Vasilev (CSKA Sofia), Sixt, Quentin (FC Sion), Semmeling (Standard Liége), Sabo (Dinamo Kiev), Collar, Víctor (Atlético Madrid), Brabrook, Sissons (West Ham), Hughes, McNeill (Celtic), Thompson, Smith (Liverpool), Sturm, Cyliax, Libuda (Borussia Dortmund)

Own goals: Bovington (West Ham) for Olympiakos, Talsi (Lahden Reipas) for Honvéd

CUP WINNERS' CUP 1966-67

PRELIMINARY ROUND

**VALUR REYKJAVÍK
v STANDARD LIÈGE 1-1** (0-0)

Laugardalsvöllur, Reykjavík 22.08.1966

Referee: John Adair (NIR)   Attendance: 3,233

VALUR: Sigurdur Dagsson; Arni Njálsson (Cap), Halldór Einarsson; Hans Gudmundsson, Björn Júlíusson, Sigurjón Gíslason; Gunnsteinn Skúlason, Bergsveinn Alfonsson, Hermann Gunnarsson, Ingvar Elísson, Bergsteinn Magnússon.   Trainer: Oli Jónsson

STANDARD: Jean Nicolay; Hans Wackerle, Jacques Beurlet; Louis Pilot, Lucien Spronck, Guillaume Raskin; Léon Semmeling (Cap), Nicolas Dewalque, Roger Claessen, Velimir Naumovic, James Storme.   Trainer: Milorad Pavić

Goals: Elísson (58), Claessen (65).

**STANDARD LIEGE
v VALUR REYKJAVIK 8-1** (5-1)

Stade Maurice Dufrasne, Liège 31.08.1966

Referee: Adrianus Boogaerts (HOL)   Attendance: 9,214

STANDARD: Jean Nicolay; Guillaume Raskin, Jacques Beurlet; Tony Van Schoonbeek, Lucien Spronck, Louis Pilot; Léon Semmeling (Cap), Nicolas Dewalque, Roger Claessen, Paul Vandenberg, José Germano de Sales.   Trainer: Milorad Pavić

VALUR: Sigurdur Dagsson; Arni Njálsson (Cap), Halldór Einarsson; Hans Gudmundsson, Björn Júlíusson, Sigurjón Gíslason; Gunnsteinn Skúlason, Bergsveinn Alfonsson, Hermann Gunnarsson, Ingvar Elísson, Bergsteinn Magnússon.   Trainer: Oli Jónsson

Goals: Claessen (6, 10, 18, 61, 76), Dewalque (8, 59), Pilot (15), Júlíusson (32).

FIRST ROUND

**RAPID WIEN
v GALATASARAY ISTANBUL 4-0** (3-0)

Prater, Wien 24.08.1966

Referee: Karl Göppel (SWI)   Attendance: 21,213

RAPID: Roman Pichler; Walter Gebhardt, Walter Glechner (Cap), Walter Baier; Walter Skocik, Ewald Ullmann; Anton Fritsch, Franz Hasil, Jørn Bjerregaard, Rudolf Flögel, Walter Seitl.   Trainer: Rudolf Vytlacil

GALATASARAY: Turgay Şeren (Cap); Bekir Türkgeldi, Tuncer Ince; Mustafa Yürür, Talat Özkarsli, Turan Dogangün; Yilmaz Gökdel, Ayhan Elmastaşoglu, Ergin Gürses, Ugur Kökten, Ergün Acuner.   Trainer: Gündüz Kiliç

Goals: Seitl (7, 21), Flögel (33), Bjerregaard (63).

**GALATASARAY ISTANBUL
v RAPID WIEN 3-5** (2-3)

Ali Sami-Yen, Istanbul 7.09.1966

Referee: Kestutis Andziulis (USSR)   Attendance: 15,580

GALATASARAY: Turgay Şeren (Cap); Bekir Türkgeldi, Tuncer Ince; Mustafa Yürür, Talat Özkarsli, Turan Dogangün; Yilmaz Gökdel, Ergin Gürses, Ayhan Elmastaşoglu, Ugur Kökten, Ergün Acuner.   Trainer: Gündüz Kiliç

RAPID: Roman Pichler; Walter Gebhardt, Walter Baier; Walter Skocik, Walter Glechner (Cap), Ewald Ullmann; Anton Fritsch, Leopold Grausam, Jørn Bjerregaard, Rudolf Flögel, Walter Seitl.   Trainer: Rudolf Vytlacil

Goals: Ayhan (17), Bjerregaard (21, 60), Fritsch (27), Seitl (36, 46), Ergun (43), Yilmaz (88).

SKEID OSLO v REAL ZARAGOZA CD 3-2 (1-0)

Bislett, Oslo 30.08.1966

Referee: John K.Taylor (ENG)   Attendance: 14,774

SKEID: Kjell Kaspersen; Ragnar Naess, Kjell Wangen; Erik Mejlo, Finn Thorsen (Cap), Trygve Bornø; Tom Weinholdt, Frank Olafsen, Kai Sjøberg, Pål Saetrang, Terje Kristoffersen.   Trainer: Brede Borgen

REAL ZARAGOZA: Enrique YARZA Sorlauce (Cap); José Ramón IRUSQUIETA García, Severino REIJA Vázquez; Antonio PAÍS Castroagudin, Francisco SANTAMARÍA Briones, José Luis VIOLETA Lajusticia; Darcy Silveira Dos Santos "CANARIO", Eleuterio SANTOS Brito, MARCELINO Martínez Cao, Juan Manuel VILLA Gutiérrez, Carlos LAPETRA Coarasa.   Trainer: Fernando Daučik

Goals: Sjøberg (3, 81), Reija (65), Canario (75), Kristoffersen (86).

REAL ZARAGOZA CD v SKEID OSLO 3-1 (1-0)

La Romareda, Zaragoza 12.10.1966

Referee: William A.O'Neill (IRL)   Attendance: 15,365

REAL ZARAGOZA: Enrique YARZA Sorlauce (Cap); José Ramón IRUSQUIETA García, Severino REIJA Vázquez; Antonio PAÍS Castroagudin, Francisco SANTAMARÍA Briones, José Luis VIOLETA Lajusticia; Darcy Silveira Dos Santos "CANARIO", Eleuterio SANTOS Brito, MARCELINO Martínez, Juan Manuel VILLA Gutiérrez, Carlos LAPETRA Coarasa.   Trainer: Fernando Daučik

SKEID: Kjell Kaspersen; Ragnar Naess, Erik Becklund; Frank Olafsen, Finn Thorsen (Cap), Erik Mejlo; Tom Weinholdt, Kjell Wangen, Kai Sjøberg, Pål Saetrang, Terje Kristoffersen.   Trainer: Brede Borgen

Goals: Santos (17), País (54), Thorsen (84 pen), Marcelino (85).

SERVETTE GENÈVE
v AIF KAMRATERNA TURKU 1-1 (1-0)
Stade des Charmilles, Genève   14.09.1966

Referee: Gyula Emsberger (HUN)   Attendance: 3,617

SERVETTE: Jacques Barlie; Raymond Maffiolo (Cap), Georges Martignano; Bernard Mocellin, Michel Fatton, Péter Pázmándy; Valér Németh, Antonio Conti, Michel Desbiolles, Jürgen Sundermann, Jean-Claude Schindelholz. Trainer: Roger Vonlanthen

AIFK: Teemu Koskikuusi; Timo Niemi, Pekka Laakso, Thor-Björn Lundqvist; Erik Lönnfors, Bengt Boman; Aulis Laine (Cap), Sauli Lehtinen, Raimo Ojanen, Hans Martin, Caj Stjärnstedt.   Trainer: Reino Koskinen

Goals: Conti (43), Laine (65)

SPARTA ROTTERDAM
v FLORIANA FC 6-0 (3-0)
De Kuip, Rotterdam   5.10.1966

Referee: Hadyn D. Davies (WAL)   Attendance: 13,000

SPARTA: Willem Doesburg; Hans Buitendijk, Hans Johannes Antonius Eijkenbroek (Cap), Matheus Wilhelmus Theodorus Laseroms, Hans Bentzon, Ben Bosma, Ton Kemper; Jan Bouman, Ole Madsen, "Henk" Hendrik Willem Bosveld, Ad Vermolen.   Trainer: Wiel Coerver

FLORIANA: Alfred Borg; Alfred Debono, Joseph Grima; Charles Galea, Emmanuel Debattista, Frank Micallef; Saviour Borg, Emmanuel Borg, Anthony Cauchi, Edward Philips (Cap), Hugh Caruana.   Trainer: Edward Philips

Goals: Kemper (16, 83), Vermolen (21, 62), Bosveld (40), Bouman (78)

AIF KAMRATERNA TURKU
v SERVETTE GENÈVE 1-2 (0-1)
Olympiastadion, Helsinki   5.10.1966

Referee: Aage Poulsen (DEN)   Attendance: 1,987

AIFK: Teemu Koskikuusi; Pekka Laakso, Bengt Boman; Thor-Björn Lundqvist, Timo Niemi, Erik Lönnfors; Rolf Engström, Aulis Laine (Cap), Hans Martin, Sauli Lehtinen, Caj Stjärnstedt.   Trainer: Reino Koskinen

SERVETTE: Jacques Barlie; Raymond Maffiolo (Cap), Bernard Mocellin; Jürgen Sundermann, Georges Martignano, Péter Pázmándy; Valér Németh, Pierre Georgy, Antonio Conti, Dezső Makay, Jean-Claude Schindelholz. Trainer: Béla Guttmann

Goals: Németh (43), Laine (51), Schindelholz (67)

STANDARD LIEGE
v APOLLON LIMASSOL 5-1 (2-1)
Stade Maurice Dufrasne, Liège   21.09.1966

Referee: Hans Granlund (NOR)   Attendance: 9,178

STANDARD: Jean Nicolay; Léon Jeck, Jacques Beurlet; Tony Van Schoonbeeck, Lucien Spronck, Louis Pilot (Cap); Wilhelm Bleser, Nicolas Dewalque, Roger Claessen, Velimir Naumovic, José Germano de Sales.   Trainer: Milorad Pavić

APOLLON: Evagoras Vasileiou; Hristos Polycarpou, Dimos Kavazis; Mihalis Konstantinou, Andreas Georgiou, Andreas Themistokleous; Dimitris Hristofi, Panikos Krystallis (Cap), Kostas Ioanou, Panagiotis Poliviou, Antros Konstantinou. Trainer: János Zsolnay

Goals: Claessen (25), Bleser (43), Dewalque (46, 52), Germano (50), Ioanou (80)

FLORIANA FC v SPARTA ROTTERDAM 1-1 (0-1)
The Empire Stadium, Gzira   18.09.1966

Referee: Antonio Sbardella (ITA)   Attendance: 8,883

FLORIANA: Charles Zerafa; Alfred Debono, Joseph Grima; Charles Galea, Emmanuel Debattista, Frank Micallef; Emmanuel Borg, Emmanuel Aquilina, Anthony Cauchi, Edward Philips (Cap), Hugh Caruana.   Trainer: Edward Philips

SPARTA: Willem Doesburg; Hans Buitendijk, Hans Johannes Antonius Eijkenbroek (Cap), Matheus Wilhelmus Theodorus Laseroms, Hans Bentzon, Jan Bouman, Ton Kemper, Ben Bosma, Ole Madsen, «Henk» Hendrik Willem Bosveld, Ad Vermolen.   Trainer: Wiel Coerver

Goals: Kemper (28), Philips (65)

APOLLON LIMASSOL
v STANDARD LIEGE 0-1 (0-0)
Stade Communal, Jambes   28.09.1966

Referee: Hans-Joachim Weyland (W. GER)   Att: 5,534

APOLLON: Evagoras Vasileiou; Hristos Polycarpou, Dimos Kavazis; Mihalis Konstantinou, Panikos Giolitis, Andreas Themistokleous; Antros Konstantinou, Kostas Vasiliadis, Panikos Krystallis (Cap), Antonis Panagidis, Kostas Ioanou. Trainer: János Zsolnay

STANDARD: Jean Nicolay; Jacques Beurlet, Hans Wackerle; Louis Pilot (Cap), Lucien Spronck, Guillaume Raskin; James Storme, Nicolas Dewalque, Roger Claessen, Jean Thissen, Tony Van Schoonbeek.   Trainer: Milorad Pavić

Goal: Claessen (78)

SWANSEA TOWN v SLAVIA SOFIA 1-1 (0-0)

Vetch Field, Swansea 21.09.1966

Referee: Magnús Vignir Pétursson (ICE)   Att: 12,107

SWANSEA: George Heyes; Roy Evans, Victor Gomersall; Alan Jones, Brian Purcell, Brian Hughes; William Humphries, James McLaughlin, Keith Todd, Ivor John Allchurch, Brian Evans.   Manager: Glyn Davies

SLAVIA: Simeon Simeonov; Aleksandar Shalamanov, Dimitar Kostov; Stoian Aleksiev, Dimitar Largov, Petar Petrov; Liuben Tasev, Georgi Haralampiev, Emanuil Manolov, Stoian Vrajev, Aleksandar Vasilev (Cap).   Trainer: Dobromir Tashkov

Goals: Todd (60), Tasev (80)

**GLASGOW RANGERS
v GLENTORAN BELFAST 4-0** (2-0)

Ibrox, Glasgow 5.10.1966

Referee: José María Ortiz de Mendíbil (SPA)   Att: 33,473

RANGERS: William Ritchie; Kai Johansen, David Provan; John Greig (Cap), Ronald McKinnon, David Smith; William Henderson, Alexander Smith, George McLean, Dennis Setterrington, William Johnston.   Manager: James Scotland Symon

GLENTORAN: Albert Finlay; Harold Creighton, William McKeag; Walter Bruce, William McCullough, Arthur Stewart; Gerard Conroy, William Sinclair, Trevor Thompson, John Colrain (Cap), Eric Ross.   Manager: John Colrain

Goals: Johnston (9), D. Smith (44), Setterrington (70), McLean (77)

SLAVIA SOFIA v SWANSEA TOWN 4-0 (1-0)

Slavia, Sofia 5.10.1966

Referee: Dogan Babaçan (TUR)   Attendance: 16,723

SLAVIA: Simeon Simeonov; Aleksandar Shalamanov, Dimitar Kostov; Stoian Aleksiev, Petar Petrov, Ivan Davidov; Liuben Tasev, Georgi Haralampiev, Stoian Vrajev, Emanuil Manolov, Aleksandar Vasilev (Cap).   Trainer: Dobromir Tashkov

SWANSEA: George Heyes; Roy Evans, Victor Gomersall; Alan Jones, Brian Purcell, Herbert Williams (Cap); William Humphries, James McLaughlin, Keith Todd, Ivor John Allchurch, Brian Evans.   Manager: Glyn Davies

Goals: Tasev (6, 68, 87), Vrajev (46)

**TATRAN PREŠOV
v BAYERN MÜNCHEN 1-1** (1-1)

Tatran, Prešov 28.09.1966

Referee: Waclaw Majdan (POL)   Attendance: 3,587

TATRAN: Július Holes; Dušan Gabalec, Jozef Bomba (Cap); Juraj Husár, Stefan Páll, Tomás Dzurej; Jozef Milko, Ján Turcányi, Stefan Caban, Lubos Holuj, Anton Kozman.   Trainer: Gejza Sabanos

BAYERN: Josef Maier; Hans Nowak, Werner Olk (Cap); Peter Werner, Franz Beckenbauer, Hans Rigotti; Rudolf Nafziger, Rainer Ohlhauser, Gerhard Müller, Franz Roth, Dieter Brenninger.   Trainer: Zlatko Čajkovski

Goals: Caban (13), Roth (21)

**GLENTORAN FC BELFAST
v GLASGOW RANGERS 1-1** (0-1)

The Oval, Belfast 27.09.1966

Referee: Vital Loraux (BEL)   Attendance: 29,421

GLENTORAN: Albert Finlay; Harold Creighton, William McKeag; Walter Bruce, William McCullough, Arthur Stewart; Gerard Conroy, William Sinclair, Trevor Thompson, John Colrain (Cap), Eric Ross.   Manager: John Colrain

RANGERS: William Ritchie; Kai Johansen, David Provan; James Millar, Ronald McKinnon, David Smith; William Henderson, John Greig (Cap), George McLean, Alexander Smith, William Johnston.   Manager: James Scotland Symon

Goals: McLean (16), Sinclair (90)

**BAYERN MÜNCHEN
v TATRAN PREŠOV 3-2** (1-0)

Stadion Grünwalder Str., München 5.10.1966

Referee: Antonio Sbardella (ITA)   Attendance: 14,416

BAYERN: Josef Maier; Peter Kupferschmidt, Werner Olk (Cap); Adolf Kunstwadl, Franz Beckenbauer, Peter Werner; Rudolf Nafziger, Gerhard Müller, Dieter Koulmann, Rainer Ohlhauser, Dieter Brenninger.   Trainer: Zlatko Čajkovski

TATRAN: Július Holes; Dušan Gabalec, Stefan Pall; Juraj Husár, Jozef Bomba (Cap), Tomás Dzurej; Jozef Milko, Karol Kocúrek, Stefan Caban, Rudolf Pavlovic, Ján Turcányi.   Trainer: Gejza Sabanos

Goals: Brenninger (32), Pavlovic (56, 84), Müller (72, 73)

AEK ATHINA
v SPORTING CLUBE DE BRAGA 0-1 (0-1)

Neas Filadelfeias, Athina   28.09.1966

Referee: Lajos Horváth (HUN)   Attendance: 23,207

AEK: Theodoros Maniateas; Nikos Stathopoulos, Tasos Vasileiou; Alekos Sofianidis, Fotios Balopoulos, Stelios Skevofilax; Vasilis Mastrakoulis, Kostandinos Nikolaidis, Giorgos Karafeskos, Dimitris Papaioannou (Cap), Spiros Pomonis.   Trainer: Trifon Tzanetis

SPORTING: Armando Pereira da Silva; José Maria Silva Azevedo (Cap), José Manuel Gouveia; Agostinho Pereira Ribeiro, Mário Manuel Jardim Rodrigues, Joaquim Ferreira Coimbra; Albino Aguiar de Sousa, José António Conceição Neto, Miguel Angel Perrichon, Luciano Marques da Silva, Estevao António Mansidao.   Trainer: Fernando Caiado

Goal: Luciano da Silva (26)

GYÖRI VASAS ETO
v FIORENTINA FIRENZE 4-2 (2-2)

ETO, Györ   5.10.1966

Referee: Friedrich Mayer (AUS)   Attendance: 20,000

VASAS ETO: Lajos Tóth; János Szániel, László Izsáki; Károly Palotai (Cap), Arpád Orbán, Zoltán Kiss; János Stolcz, Tibor Varsányi, József Szaló, József Somogyi, László Keglovich.   Trainer: Ferenc Szusza

FIORENTINA: Enrico Albertosi; Bernardo Rogora, Giampiero Vitali; Mario Bertini, Ugo Ferrante, Pietro Lenzi; Kurt Hamrin (Cap), Claudio Merlo, Mario Brugnera, Giancarlo De Sisti, Luciano Chiarugi.   Trainer: Giuseppe Chiapella

Goals: Stolcz (10, 59), Bertini (20), De Sisti (31), Varsányi (37), Orbán (85)

SPORTING BRAGA v AEK ATHINA 3-2 (2-1)

Estádio do 28 de Maio, Braga   5.10.1966

Referee: John Adair (NIR)   Attendance: 13,892

SPORTING: Armando Pereira da Silva; José Maria Silva Azevedo (Cap), José Manuel Gouveia; Agostinho Pereira Ribeiro, Mário Manuel Jardim Rodrigues, Joaquim Ferreira Coimbra; Albino Aguiar de Sousa, José António Conceição Neto, Miguel Angel Perrichon, Luciano Marques da Silva, Estevao António Mansidao.   Trainer: Fernando Caiado

AEK: Theodoros Maniateas (31 Evangelos Petrakis); Alekos Sofianidis, Tasos Vasileiou; Apostolos Fragoudakis, Fotios Balopoulos, Stelios Skevofilax; Andreas Stamatiadis, Kostas Papageorgiou, Giorgos Karafeskos, Dimitris Papaioannou (Cap), Vasilis Mastrakoulis.   Trainer: Trifon Tzanetis

Goals: Papaioannou (6), Mário (15), Perrichon (30, 44), Coimbra (87 og)

OFK BEOGRAD v SPARTAK MOSKVA 1-3 (0-3)

JNA, Beograd   28.09.1966

Referee: Erwin Vetter (E. GER)   Attendance: 3,944

OFK: Stanoje Miloradović; Miroslav Milovanović, Momčilo Gavrić; Blagomir Krivokuca, Miodrag Radosević (Cap), Todor Grujić; Spasoje Samardzić, Bogdan Turudija, Slobodan Santrac, Ilija Mitić, Branislav Mihajlović.   Trainer: Zarko Mihajlović

SPARTAK: Vladimir Maslachenko; Vladimir Petrov, Valeri Dikarev; Alexei Korneiev, Anatoli Krutikov, Viacheslav Ambartsumian; Valeri Reingold, Nikolai Osianin, Gennadi Logofet (Cap), Yuri Siemin, Galimzian Khusainov.   Trainer: Nikolai Guljaev

Goals: Siemin (10, 16), G. Logofet (36), Krivocuca (52)

FIORENTINA FIRENZE
v GYÖRI VASAS ETO 1-0 (0-0)

Comunale, Firenze   28.09.1966

Referee: Gerhard Schulenburg (W. GER)   Attendance: 10,858

FIORENTINA: Enrico Albertosi; Bernardo Rogora, Giampiero Vitali; Mario Bertini, Ugo Ferrante, Pietro Lenzi; Kurt Hamrin (Cap), Claudio Merlo, Mario Brugnera, Giancarlo De Sisti, Luciano Chiarugi.   Trainer: Giuseppe Chiapella

VASAS ETO: Lajos Tóth; János Szániel, László Izsáki; Károly Palotai (Cap), Arpád Orbán, Zoltán Kiss; János Stolcz, Tibor Varsányi, József Szaló, József Somogyi, László Keglovich.   Trainer: Ferenc Szusza

Goal: Chiarugi (62)

SPARTAK MOSKVA v OFK BEOGRAD 3-0 (0-0)

Lenin, Moskva   5.10.1966

Referee: Nicolae Mihăilescu (ROM)   Attendance: 41,000

SPARTAK: Vladimir Maslachenko; Vladimir Petrov, Valeri Dikarev; Aleksei Korneev, Anatoli Krutikov, Viacheslav Ambartsumian; Gennadi Logofet (Cap), Vladimir Yanischevski, Yuri Siemin, Galimzian Khusainov, Valeri Bokatov.   Trainer: Nikolai Guljaev

OFK: Bratislav Djordjević; Miroslav Milovanović, Momčilo Gavrić; Zdravko Jokić, Miodrag Radosević (Cap), Todor Grujić; Bogdan Turudija, Blagomir Krivokuca, Slobodan Santrac, Ilija Mitić, Branislav Stevanović.   Trainer: Zarko Mihajlović

Goals: Siemin (55), Khusainov (59), Bokatov (79)

**SHAMROCK ROVERS FC
v CA SPORA LUXEMBOURG 4-1** (2-1)

Dalymount Park, Dublin   28.09.1966

Referee: Robert Lacoste (FRA)   Attendance: 12,321

SHAMROCK ROVERS: Michael Smyth; Patrick Mulligan, Patrick Courtney; Seán Core, Ronald Nolan, John Fullam; Francis O'Neill, William Dixon, Robert Gilbert, William Tuohy (Cap), Michael Kearin.   Trainer: William Tuohy

SPORA: Friedhelm Jesse; Walter Glinski, Mario Morocutti; René Schmitt, Fernand Brosius (Cap), Mathias Ewen; Emile Meyer, Domingos Da Fonseca, François Lacour, Jean Kremer, Armand Weis.   Trainers: Johny Fonck & Robert Geib

Goals: Fullam (8), Weis (28), Dixon (29), Kearin (55), O'Neill (74 pen)

EVERTON LIVERPOOL v AALBORG BK 2-1 (0-0)

Goodison Park, Liverpool   11.10.1966

Referee: Anibal da Silva Oliveira (POR)   Attendance: 36,628

EVERTON: Gordon West; Thomas James Wright, Ramon "Ray" Wilson; James Gabriel, Brian Leslie Labone (Cap), James Colin Harvey; James Husband, Alan James Ball, Alexander Young, Derek William Temple, John Morrissey.   Manager: Harry Catterick

AALBORG: Kurt Sørensen; Preben Larsen, Jørgen Christensen; Leif Skov (Cap), Henning Munk Jensen, Heini Hald; Kurt Berthelsen, Kjeld Thorst, Jimmy Nielsen, Bjarne Lildballe, Finn Andersen.   Trainer: Kaarlo Niilonen

Sent off: Larsen (86)

Goals: Morrissey (57), Lildballe (69), Ball (71)

**CA SPORA LUXEMBOURG
v SHAMROCK ROVERS FC 1-4** (1-2)

Stade Municipal, Luxembourg   5.10.1966

Referee: Kurt Handwerker (W. GER)   Attendance: 1,238

SPORA: Friedhelm Jesse; Walter Glinski, Mario Morocutti; René Schmitt, Mathias Ewen, Jean Kremer (Cap); Emile Meyer, Domingos Da Fonseca, François Lacour, Joseph Krier, Armand Weis.   Trainers: Johny Fonck & Robert Geib

SHAMROCK ROVERS: Michael Smyth; Patrick Mulligan, Patrick Courtney; Seán Core, Ronald Nolan, John Fullam; Francis O'Neill, William Dixon, Robert Gilbert, William Tuohy (Cap), Michael Kearin.   Trainer: William Tuohy

Goals: Kearin (17), Krier (35), Dixon (42, 75), O'Neill (69)

CHEMIE LEIPZIG v LEGIA WARSZAWA 3-0 (0-0)

Zentralstadion, Leipzig   28.09.1966

Referee: Pieter Paulus Roomer (HOL)   Attendance: 10,634

CHEMIE: Klaus Günther; Bernd Herzog, Heinz Herrmann; Manfred Walter (Cap), Wolfgang Krause, Horst Slaby; Helmut Schmidt, Hans-Bert Matoul, Dieter Scherbarth, Bernd Bauchspiess, Klaus Lisiewicz.   Trainer: Alfred Kunze

LEGIA: Wladyslaw Grotynski; Antoni Mahseli, Andrzej Zygmunt; Jacek Gmoch, Feliks Niedziólka, Bernard Blaut; Kazmierz Frąckiewicz, Wieslaw Korzeniowski, Lucjan Brychczy (Cap), Henryk Apostel, Janusz Zmijewski.   Trainer: Jaroslav Vejvoda

Goals: Bauchspiess (58, 85), Scherbarth (78)

**AALBORG BOLDSPILKLUB
v EVERTON LIVERPOOL 0-0**

Aalborg Stadion   28.09.1966

Referee: Antoine Queudeville (LUX)   Attendance: 11,385

AALBORG: Kurt Sørensen; Kjeld Gregersen, Jørgen Christensen; Leif Skov (Cap), Henning Munk Jensen, Heini Hald; Kurt Berthelsen, Kjeld Thorst, Jimmy Nielsen, Bjarne Lildballe, Finn Andersen.   Trainer: Kaarlo Niilonen

EVERTON: Gordon West; Thomas James Wright, Ramon "Ray" Wilson; James Gabriel, Brian Leslie Labone (Cap); James Colin Harvey; Alan James Ball, Derek William Temple, Alexander Young, Michael Trebilcock, John Morrissey.   Manager: Harry Catterick

LEGIA WARSZAWA v CHEMIE LEIPZIG 2-2 (1-2)

Wojska Polskiego, Warszawa   12.10.1966

Referee: Erik Beijar (FIN)   Attendance: 7,000

LEGIA: Wladyslaw Grotynski; Antoni Mahseli, Andrzej Zygmunt; Jacek Gmoch, Henryk Grzybowski, Kazmierz Frąckiewicz; Henryk Apostel, Wieslaw Korzeniowski, Lucjan Brychczy (Cap), Bernard Blaut, Janusz Zmijewski.   Trainer: Jaroslav Vejvoda

CHEMIE: Klaus Günther; Bernd Herzog, Heinz Herrmann; Manfred Walter (Cap), Wolfgang Krause, Volker Trojan; Manfred Richter, Hans-Bert Matoul, Dieter Scherbarth, Bernd Bauchspiess, Wolfgang Behla.   Trainer: Alfred Kunze

Goals: Bauchspiess (17, 29), Korzeniowski (40), Zmijewski (88)

RACING CLUB STRASBOURG
v STEAUA BUCUREŞTI 1-0 (0-0)

Meinau, Strasbourg   5.10.1966

Referee: Thomas Kenneth Wharton (SCO)   Att: 14,204

RACING: Johnny Schuth; René Hauss (Cap), Roland Merschel, Pierre Sbaiz; Marcel Lazarus, Raymond Stieber; Ruben Muñoz, Ramon Muller, José Farias, Robert Szczepaniak, Gilbert Heiné.   Trainer: Walter Presch

STEAUA: Vasile Suciu; Mircea Petescu, Emerich Jenei, Dumitru Nicolae, Lajos Sătmăreanu; Vasile Negrea, Dumitru Popescu; Sorin Avram, Gheorghe Constantin (Cap), Florea Voinea, Gavril Raksi.   Trainer: Ilie Savu

Goal: Muller (56)

STEAUA BUCUREŞTI
v RACING CLUB STRASBOURG 1-1 (0-0)

23 August, Bucureşti   12.10.1966

Referee: Michalakis Kirikiades (CYP)   Attendance: 5,406

STEAUA: Vasile Suciu; Mircea Petescu, Emerich Jenei, Dumitru Nicolae, Lajos Sătmăreanu; Vasile Negrea, Dumitru Popescu; Sorin Avram, Gheorghe Constantin (Cap), Florea Voinea, Gavril Raksi.   Trainer: Ilie Savu

RACING: Johnny Schuth; René Hauss (Cap), Roland Merschel, Pierre Sbaiz; Marcel Lazarus, Raymond Stieber; Ruben Muñoz, Ramon Muller, José Farias, Robert Szczepaniak, Gérard Hausser.   Trainer: Walter Presch

Goals: Hausser (61), Avram (68)

SECOND ROUND

SERVETTE GENÈVE
v SPARTA ROTTERDAM 2-0 (1-0)

Stade des Charmilles, Genève   9.11.1966

Referee: Francesco Francescon (ITA)   Attendance: 6,794

SERVETTE: Jacques Barlie; Raymond Maffiolo (Cap), Roger Piguet; Bernard Mocellin, Jürgen Sundermann, Georges Martignano; Valér Németh, Walter Heuri, Michel Desbiolles, Dezső Makay, Jean-Claude Schindelholz.
Trainer: Béla Guttmann

SPARTA: Willem Doesburg; Hans Buitendijk, "Hans" Johannes Antonius Eijkenbroek (Cap); Gerrie Ter Horst, Hans Bentzon, Matheus Wilhelmus Theodorus Laseroms; Ton Kemper, Ben Bosma, Jan Bouman, "Henk" Hendrik Willem Bosveld, Ad Vermolen.   Trainer: Wiel Coerver

Sent off: Heuri (85)

Goals: Schindelholz (5, 62)

SPARTA ROTTERDAM
v SERVETTE GENÈVE 1-0 (1-0)

De Kuip, Rotterdam   16.11.1966

Referee: Norman C.H.Burtenshaw (ENG)   Att: 18,706

SPARTA: Willem Doesburg; Gerrie Ter Horst, "Hans" Johannes Antonius Eijkenbroek (Cap); Matheus Wilhelmus Theodorus Laseroms, Hans Bentzon, Ben Bosma; Co Onsman, Ton Kemper, Jan Bouman, "Henk" Hendrik Willem Bosveld, Ad Vermolen.   Trainer: Wiel Coerver

SERVETTE: Jacques Barlie; Raymond Maffiolo (Cap), Roger Piguet; Bernard Mocellin, Georges Martignano, Péter Pázmándy; Valér Németh, Jürgen Sundermann, Michel Desbiolles, Dezső Makay, Jean-Claude Schindelholz.
Trainer: Béla Guttmann

Goal: Laseroms (19)

SHAMROCK ROVERS DUBLIN
v BAYERN MÜNCHEN 1-1 (0-1)

Dalymount Park, Dublin   9.11.1966

Referee: Laurens van Ravens (HOL)   Attendance: 15,462

SHAMROCK: Michael Smyth; John Keogh, Patrick Courtney; Seán Core, Ronald Nolan, John Fullam; Francis O'Neill, Patrick Mulligan, Michael Kearin, William Tuohy (Cap), William Dixon.   Trainer: William Tuohy

BAYERN: Josef Maier; Hans Nowak, Franz Beckenbauer, Werner Olk (Cap), Rudolf Nafziger, Peter Kupferschmidt, Gerhard Müller, Rainer Ohlhauser, Dieter Brenninger, Dieter Koulmann, Peter Werner.   Trainer: Zlatko Čajkovski

Goals: Koulmann (17), Dixon (61)

BAYERN MÜNCHEN
v SHAMROCK ROVERS DUBLIN 3-2 (2-0)

Stadion Grünwalder Str., München   23.11.1966

Referee: Konstantin Zecević (YUG)   Attendance: 11,586

BAYERN: Josef Maier; Peter Kupferschmidt, Franz Beckenbauer, Georg Schwarzenbeck, Rudolf Nafziger, Gerhard Müller, Werner Olk (Cap), Rainer Ohlhauser, Dieter Koulmann, Dieter Brenninger, Franz Roth.
Trainer: Zlatko Čajkovski

SHAMROCK: Michael Smyth; Mick Kearin, Ronald Nolan, Patrick Courtney; Patrick Mulligan, John Fullam; Francis O'Neill, William Dixon, William Tuohy (Cap), John Keogh, Robert Gilbert.   Trainer: William Tuohy

Goals: Brenninger (5), Ohlhauser (8), Gilbert (55), Tuohy (58), Müller (86)

**REAL ZARAGOZA CD
v EVERTON LIVERPOOL 2-0** (1-0)

La Romareda, Zaragoza 9.11.1966

Referee: Dittmar Huber (SWI)   Attendance: 14,364

REAL ZARAGOZA: José María GOICOECHEA Ibarguren; José Manuel GONZÁLEZ López, Severino REIJA Vázquez; José Luis VIOLETA Lajusticia, Francisco SANTAMARÍA Briones, Antonio PAÍS Castroagudin; Darcy Silveira Dos Santos "CANARIO", Eleuterio SANTOS Brito, MARCELINO Martínez Cao, Juan Manuel VILLA Gutiérrez, Carlos LAPETRA Coarasa (Cap).   Trainer: Fernando Daučik

EVERTON: Gordon West; Thomas James Wright, Ramon "Ray" Wilson; James Gabriel, Brian Leslie Labone (Cap), James Colin Harvey; Alexander Silcock Scott, Alan James Ball, Alexander Young, Derek William Temple, John Morrissey. Manager: Harry Catterick

Sent off: Morrissey (44)

Goals: Santos (13), Marcelino (63)

**EVERTON LIVERPOOL
v REAL ZARAGOZA CD 1-0** (0-0)

Goodison Park, Liverpool 23.11.1966

Referee: Hans-Joachim Weyland (W. GER)   Att: 55,077

EVERTON: Gordon West; Thomas James Wright, Ramon "Ray" Wilson; James Gabriel, Brian Leslie Labone (Cap), James Colin Harvey; Alexander Silcock Scott, Alan James Ball, Alexander Young, Alexander Brown, Derek William Temple. Manager: Harry Catterick

REAL ZARAGOZA: Enrique YARZA Sorlauce (Cap); José Manuel GONZÁLEZ López, Severino REIJA Vázquez; José Luis VIOLETA Lajusticia, Francisco SANTAMARÍA Briones, Antonio PAÍS Castroagudin; Darcy Silveira Dos Santos "CANARIO", Eleuterio SANTOS Brito, MARCELINO Martínez Cao, Juan Manuel VILLA Gutiérrez, Santiago ISASI Salazar. Trainer: Fernando Daučik

Goal: Brown (80)

SPARTAK MOSKVA v RAPID WIEN 1-1 (1-1)

Lenin, Moskva 9.11.1966

Referee: Ryszard Banasiuk (POL)   Attendance: 16,000

SPARTAK: Vladimir Maslachenko; Vladimir Petrov, Valeri Dikarev, Aleksei Korneev, Anatoli Krutikov, Viacheslav Ambartsumian; Gennadi Logofet (Cap), Valeri Reingold, Nikolai Osianin, Yuri Siemin, Galimzian Khusainov. Trainer: Nikolai Guljaev

RAPID: Roman Pichler; Walter Gebhardt, Erich Fak; Franz Hasil, Walter Glechner (Cap), Walter Skocik; Anton Fritsch, August Starek, Jørn Bjerregaard, Walter Seitl, Tomislav Knez. Trainer: Rudolf Vytlacil

Goals: Bjerregaard (23), Khusainov (40)

RAPID WIEN v SPARTAK MOSKVA 1-0 (0-0)

Prater, Wien 8.12.1966

Referee: Michel Kitabdjian (FRA)   Attendance: 34,273

RAPID: Roman Pichler; Walter Gebhardt, Erich Fak; Franz Hasil, Walter Skocik, Ewald Ullmann; Anton Fritsch, August Starek, Jørn Bjerregaard, Rudolf Flögel (Cap), Tomislav Knez. Trainer: Rudolf Vytlacil

SPARTAK: Vladimir Maslachenko; Vladimir Petrov, Valeri Dikarev; Vladimir Mescheriakov, Vajdotas Zhitkus, Vladimir Yankin; Gennadi Logofet (Cap), Valeri Reingold, Nikolai Osianin, Valeri Bokatov, Galimzian Khusainov. Trainer: Nikolai Guljaev

Goal: Starek (49)

**GYÖRI VASAS ETO
v SPORTING CLUBE DE BRAGA 3-0** (1-0)

ETO, Györ 9.11.1966

Referee: Fritz Köpcke (E. GER)   Attendance: 20,000

VASAS ETO: Lajos Tóth; János Szániel, László Izsáki; Károly Palotai (Cap), Arpád Orbán, Zoltán Kiss; János Stolcz, Tibor Varsányi, József Szaló, József Somogyi, László Keglovich. Trainer: Ferenc Szusza

SPORTING: Armando Pereira da Silva; José Maria Silva Azevedo (Cap), José Manuel Gouveia; Joaquim Ferreira Coimbra, Agostinho Pereira Ribeiro, Mário Manuel Jardim Rodrigues; Luciano Marques da Silva, Albino Aguiar da Sousa, Miguel Angel Perrichon, Adao António Craveiro, Estevao António Mansidao.   Trainer: Fernando Caiado

Goals: Szaló (3, 73), Ribeiro (72 og)

**SPORTING CLUBE DE BRAGA
v GYÖRI VASAS ETO 2-0** (1-0)

Estádio 1º Maio, Braga 8.12.1966

Referee: Vital Loraux (BEL)   Attendance: 15,565

SPORTING: Armando Pereira da Silva; Juvenal Silva Costa, Agostinho Pereira Ribeiro, Joaquim Ferreira Coimbra (Cap), José Manuel Gouveia; Luciano Marques da Silva, Mário Manuel Jardim Rodrigues, Albino Aguiar de Sousa, Miguel Angel Perrichon, Adao António Craveiro, Estevao António Mansidao.   Trainer: Fernando Caiado

VASAS ETO: Lajos Tóth; János Szániel, László Izsáki; Lajos Nell, Arpád Orbán (Cap), Zoltán Kiss; János Stolcz, Tibor Varsányi, József Szaló, József Somogyi, László Keglovich. Trainer: Ferenc Szusza

Goals: Perrichon (42) Adao (83)

**RACING CLUB STRASBOURG
v SLAVIA SOFIA 1-0** (1-0)

Meinau, Strasbourg   23.11.1966

Referee: Robert Holley Davidson (SCO)   Att: 11,404

RC STRASBOURG: Johnny Schuth; René Hauss (Cap), Pierre Sbaiz; Marcel Lazarus, Roland Merschel, Raymond Stieber; Rubén Muñoz, Ramon Muller, José Farias, Robert Szczepaniak, Gérard Hausser.   Trainer: Walter Presch

SLAVIA: Simeon Simeonov; Aleksandar Shalamanov (Cap), Dimitar Kostov; Stoian Aleksiev, Petar Petrov, Ivan Davidov; Liuben Tasev, Georgi Haralampiev, Stoian Vrajev, Emanuil Manolov, Aleksandar Vasilev.   Trainer: Dobromir Tashkov

Goal: Hausser (37)

**BORUSSIA DORTMUND v
GLASGOW RANGERS 0-0**

Kampfbahn Rode Erde, Dortmund   6.12.1966

Referee: Dimitar A. Rumentchev (BUL)   Attendance: 36,486

BORUSSIA: Bernhard Wessel; Gerhard Cyliax, Gerhard Peehs; Dieter Kurrat, Wolfgang Paul (Cap), Wilhelm Sturm; Reinhard Libuda, Horst Trimhold, Siegfried Held, Rudolf Assauer, Lothar Emmerich.   Trainer: Heinz Murach

RANGERS: Norman Martin; Kai Johansen, David Provan; John Greig (Cap), Ronald McKinnon, David Smith; William Henderson, Robert Watson, James Forrest, Alexander Smith, William Johnston.   Manager: James Scotland Symon

**SLAVIA SOFIA
v RACING CLUB STRASBOURG 2-0** (1-0)

Vasil Levski, Sofia   30.11.1966

Referee: Dimitris Wlachojanis (AUS)   Attendance: 10,004

SLAVIA: Simeon Simeonov; Aleksandar Shalamanov (Cap), Dimitar Kostov; Stoian Aleksiev, Petar Petrov, Ivan Davidov; Liuben Tasev, Georgi Haralampiev, Stoian Vrajev, Aleksandar Vasilev, Mihail Mishev.   Trainer: Dobromir Tashkov

RC STRASBOURG: Johnny Schuth; René Hauss (Cap), Pierre Sbaiz; Gérard Burcklé, Roland Merschel, Raymond Stieber; Rubén Muñoz, Marcel Lazarus, José Farias, Robert Szczepaniak, Gérard Hausser.   Trainer: Walter Presch

Goals: Vrajev (42), Mishev (49)

CHEMIE LEIPZIG v STANDARD LIEGE 2-1 (2-1)

Zentralstadion, Leipzig   30.11.1966

Referee: Gyula Gere (HUN)   Attendance: 10,711

CHEMIE: Klaus Günther; Heinz Herrmann, Wolfgang Krause, Bernd Herzog, Manfred Walter (Cap), Manfred Richter; Helmut Schmidt, Bernd Bauchspiess, Dieter Scherbarth, Wolfgang Behla, Hans-Bert Matoul. Trainer: Alfred Kunze

STANDARD: Jean Nicolay; Léon Jeck, Jacques Beurlet; Guillaume Raskin, Lucien Spronck, Louis Pilot; Léon Semmeling (Cap), Roger Claessen, Milan Galic, Velimir Naumovic, James Storme.   Trainer: Milorad Pavić

Goals: Behla (4), Schmidt (23), Galic (43)

**GLASGOW RANGERS
v BORUSSIA DORTMUND 2-1** (1-1)

Ibrox Park, Glasgow   23.11.1966

Referee: Daniel M. Zariquiegui (SPA)   Attendance: 63,917

RANGERS: Norman Martin; Kai Johansen, David Provan; John Greig (Cap), Ronald McKinnon, David Smith; William Henderson, Robert Watson, James Forrest, Alexander Smith, William Johnston.   Manager: James Scotland Symon

BORUSSIA: Bernhard Wessel; Gerhard Peehs, Gerhard Cyliax; Dieter Kurrat, Wolfgang Paul (Cap), Rudolf Assauer; Reinhold Wosab, Horst Trimhold, Siegfried Held, Lothar Emmerich, Willi Neuberger.   Trainer: Heinz Murach

Goals: Johansen (12), Trimhold (31), A. Smith (75)

STANDARD LIEGE v CHEMIE LEIPZIG 1-0 (0-0)

Stade Maurice Dufrasne, Liège   14.12.1966

Referee: John Adair (NIR)   Attendance: 18,856

STANDARD: Jean Nicolay; Léon Jeck, Jacques Beurlet; Louis Pilot, Lucien Spronck, Guillaume Raskin; Léon Semmeling (Cap), Velimir Naumovic, Roger Claessen, Milan Galic, James Storme.   Trainer: Milorad Pavić

CHEMIE: Klaus Günther; Wolfgang Krause, Heinz Herrmann; Bernd Herzog, Manfred Walter (Cap), Manfred Richter; Helmut Schmidt, Wolfgang Behla, Dieter Scherbarth, Bernd Bauchspiess, Klaus Lisiewicz.   Trainer: Alfred Kunze

Goal: Claessen (57)

QUARTER-FINALS

RAPID WIEN v BAYERN MÜNCHEN 1-0 (0-0)
Prater, Wien   15.02.1967
Referee: Joseph Hannet (BEL)   Attendance: 43,825
RAPID: Roman Pichler; Walter Gebhardt, Walter Glechner (Cap), Erich Fak; Franz Hasil, Walter Skocik; Walter Seitl, August Starek, Tomislav Knez, Jørn Bjerregaard, Rudolf Flögel. Trainer: Rudolf Vytlacil
BAYERN: Josef Maier; Franz Roth, Werner Olk (Cap); Franz Beckenbauer, Rainer Ohlhauser, Rudolf Nafziger, Peter Kupferschmidt, Gerhard Müller, Dieter Koulmann, Dieter Brenninger, Hans Rigotti.   Trainer: Zlatko Čajkovski
Goal: Starek (48)

SLAVIA SOFIA v SERVETTE GENÉVE 3-0 (1-0)
Vasil Levski, Sofia   8.03.1967
Referee: Alessandro d'Agostini (ITA)   Attendance: 26,470
SLAVIA: Simeon Simeonov; Aleksandar Shalamanov (Cap), Petar Petrov; Stoian Aleksiev, Ivan Davidov, Emanuil Manolov; Liuben Tasev, Georgi Haralampiev, Stoian Vrajev, Aleksandar Vasilev, Mihail Mishev.   Trainer: Dobromir Tashkov
SERVETTE: Jacques Barlie; Raymond Maffiolo (Cap), Roger Piguet; Bernard Mocellin, Jürgen Sundermann, Georges Martignano; Antonio Conti, Michel Desbiolles, Charles Kvicinsky, Dezső Makay, Jean-Claude Schindelholz. Trainer: Béla Guttmann
Goals: Mishev (43), Haralampiev (53), Piguet (86 og)

BAYERN MÜNCHEN v RAPID WIEN 2-0 (0-0,1-0)
Grünwalder Str., München   8.03.1967
Referee: Thomas Kenneth Wharton (SCO)   Att: 37,413
BAYERN: Josef Maier; Peter Kupferschmidt, Werner Olk (Cap); Franz Roth, Franz Beckenbauer, Hans Rigotti; Rudolf Nafziger, Rainer Ohlhauser, Gerhard Müller, Dieter Koulmann, Dieter Brenninger.   Trainer: Zlatko Čajkovski
RAPID: Roman Pichler; Walter Gebhardt, Erich Fak; Walter Skocik, Walter Glechner (Cap), Ewald Ullmann; Walter Seitl, Franz Hasil, Jørn Bjerregaard, Rudolf Flögel, August Starek. Trainer: Rudolf Vytlacil
Sent off: Seitl (62)
Goals: Ohlhauser (59), Müller (106)

GYÖRI VASAS ETO v STANDARD LIEGE 2-1 (2-0)
ETO, Györ   1.03.1967
Referee: George McCabe (ENG)   Attendance: 13,352
VASAS ETO: Lajos Tóth; János Szániel, Arpád Orbán, László Tamás; Károly Palotai (Cap), Zoltán Kiss; János Stolcz, László Györffi, József Szaló, József Somogyi, László Keglovich. Trainer: Ferenc Szusza
STANDARD: Jean Nicolay; Léon Jeck, Jacques Beurlet; Nicolas Dewalque, Lucien Spronck, Louis Pilot; Léon Semmeling (Cap), Paul Vandenberg; Roger Claessen, Velimir Naumovic, Casimir Jurkiewicz.   Trainer: Milorad Pavić
Goals: Stolcz (34), Szaló (44), Semmeling (85)

SERVETTE GENÈVE v SLAVIA SOFIA 1-0 (0-0)
Stade des Charmilles, Genève   26.02.1967
Referee: Josef Krnavek (CZE)   Attendance: 8,330
SERVETTE: Jacques Barlie; Raymond Maffiolo (Cap), Roger Piguet; Bernard Mocellin, Jürgen Sundermann, Péter Pázmándy; Antonio Conti, Michel Desbiolles, Charles Kvicinsky, Dezső Makay, Jean-Claude Schindelholz. Trainer: Béla Guttmann
SLAVIA: Simeon Simeonov; Aleksandar Shalamanov (Cap), Petar Petrov; Stoian Aleksiev, Dimitar Largov, Emanuil Manolov; Emil Lukach, Georgi Haralampiev, Stoian Vrajev, Petar Hristov, Aleksandar Vasilev.
Trainer: Dobromir Tashkov
Goal: Desbiolles (57)

STANDARD LIEGE v GYÖRI VASAS ETO 2-0 (0-0)
Maurice Dufrasne, Liège   8.03.1967
Referee: Daniel Zariquiegui (SPA)   Attendance: 28,445
STANDARD: Jean Nicolay; Léon Jeck, Jacques Beurlet; Nicolas Dewalque, Lucien Spronck, Louis Pilot; Léon Semmeling (Cap), Velimir Naumovic, Roger Claessen, Milan Galic, Casimir Jurkiewicz.   Trainer: Milorad Pavić
VASAS ETO: Lajos Tóth; Ferenc Soproni, László Izsáki, Lajos Nell, Arpád Orbán (Cap), Zoltán Kiss; János Stolcz, Tibor Varsányi, József Szaló, József Somogyi, László Keglovich. Trainer: Ferenc Szusza
Goals: Claessen (55), Jurkiewicz (58)

**GLASGOW RANGERS
v REAL ZARAGOZA 2-0** (2-0)

Ibrox Park, Glasgow   1.03.1967

Referee: Laurens van Ravens (HOL)   Attendance: 60,531

RANGERS: Norman Martin; Kai Johansen, David Provan; William Jardine, Ronald McKinnon, John Greig (Cap); William Henderson, Alexander Willoughby, Alexander Smith, David Smith, David Wilson.   Manager: James Scotland Symon

REAL ZARAGOZA: Enrique YARZA Sorlauce (Cap); José Ramón IRUSQUIETA García, Severino REIJA Vázquez; José Luis VIOLETA Lajusticia, José Manuel GONZÁLEZ López, Antonio PAÍS Castroagudin; Darcy Silveira Dos Santos "CANARIO", Eleuterio SANTOS Brito, MARCELINO Martínez Cao, Juan Manuel VILLA Gutiérrez, Carlos LAPETRA Coarasa.   Trainer: Fernando Daučik

Goals: D. Smith (9), Willoughby (27)

**REAL ZARAGOZA CD
v GLASGOW RANGERS 2-0** (1-0, 2-0) (AET)

La Romareda, Zaragoza   22.03.1967

Referee: Michel Kitabdjian (FRA)   Attendance: 35,000

REAL ZARAGOZA: Enrique YARZA Sorlauce (Cap); José Ramón IRUSQUIETA García, Severino REIJA Vázquez; José Luis VIOLETA Lajusticia, José Manuel GONZÁLEZ López, Antonio PAÍS Castroagudin; Juan Manuel VILLA Gutiérrez, Eleuterio SANTOS Brito, Miguel Ángel BUSTILLO Lafoz, MARCELINO Martínez Cao, Carlos LAPETRA Coarasa.   Trainer: Fernando Daučik

RANGERS: Norman Martin; Kai Johansen, David Provan; William Jardine, Colin Jackson, John Greig (Cap); William Henderson, Alexander Willoughby, Alexander Smith, David Smith, David Wilson.   Manager: James Scotland Symon

Goals: Lapetra (24), Santos (86 pen)

Glasgow Rangers FC won on the toss of a coin.

SEMI-FINALS

**BAYERN MÜNCHEN
v STANDARD LIÈGE 2-0** (2-0)

Grünwalder Str., München   11.04.1967

Referee: István Zsolt (HUN)   Attendance: 37,543

BAYERN: Josef Maier; Peter Kupferschmidt, Georg Schwarzenbeck; Franz Beckenbauer, Franz Roth, Gerhard Müller, Werner Olk (Cap), Rudolf Nafziger, Rainer Ohlhauser, Dieter Koulmann, Dieter Brenninger.   Trainer: Zlatko Čajkovski

STANDARD: Jean Nicolay; Léon Jeck, Jacques Beurlet; Nicolas Dewalque, Lucien Spronck, Louis Pilot; Léon Semmeling (Cap), Velimir Naumovic, Roger Claessen, Milan Galic, Casimir Jurkiewicz.   Trainer: Milorad Pavić

Goals: Müller (2), Kupferschmidt (10)

**STANDARD LIÈGE
v BAYERN MÜNCHEN 1-3** (1-1)

Stade Maurice Dufrasne, Liège   26.04.1967

Referee: Bertil Lööw (SWE)   Attendance: 32,000

STANDARD: Jean Nicolay; Léon Jeck, Jacques Beurlet; Nicolas Dewalque, Lucien Spronck, Louis Pilot; Léon Semmeling (Cap), Milan Galic, Velimir Naumovic, Roger Claessen, José Germano de Sales.   Trainer: Milorad Pavić

BAYERN: Josef Maier; Hans Nowak, Peter Kupferschmidt; Franz Beckenbauer, Franz Roth, Werner Olk (Cap); Rudolf Nafziger, Rainer Ohlhauser, Gerhard Müller, Dieter Koulmann, Dieter Brenninger.   Trainer: Zlatko Čajkovski

Goals: Müller (27, 73, 83), Galic (32)

SLAVIA SOFIA v GLASGOW RANGERS 0-1 (0-1)

Vasil Levski, Sofia   19.04.1967

Referee: Tofik Bakhramov (USSR)   Attendance: 20,000

SLAVIA: Simeon Simeonov; Aleksandar Shalamanov (Cap), Petar Petrov; Stoian Aleksiev, Emanuil Manolov, Ivan Davidov; Emil Lukach, Georgi Haralampiev, Stoian Vrajev, Aleksandar Vasilev, Mihail Mishev.   Trainer: Dobromir Tashkov

RANGERS: Norman Martin; Kai Johansen, David Provan; William Jardine, Ronald McKinnon, John Greig (Cap); William Henderson, Alexander Willoughby, Alexander Smith, David Smith, David Wilson.   Manager: James Scotland Symon

Goal: Wilson (31)

GLASGOW RANGERS v SLAVIA SOFIA 1-0 (1-0)

Ibrox Park, Glasgow   3.05.1967

Referee: Pierre Schwinté (FRA)   Attendance: 70,000

RANGERS: Norman Martin; Kai Johansen, David Provan; William Jardine, Ronald McKinnon, John Greig (Cap); William Henderson, Alexander Smith, Roger Hynd, David Smith, William Johnston.   Manager: James Scotland Symon

SLAVIA: Simeon Simeonov; Aleksandar Shalamanov (Cap), Petar Petrov; Stoian Aleksiev, Dimitar Largov, Emanuil Manolov; Stoian Vrajev, Georgi Haralampiev, Aleksandar Vasilev, Ivan Davidov, Mihail Mishev.   Trainer: Dobromir Tashkov

Goal: Henderson (32)

FINAL

**BAYERN MÜNCHEN
v GLASGOW RANGERS 1-0** (0-0, 0-0) (AET)
Stadion am Dutzendteich, Nürnberg 31.05.1967
Referee: Concetto Lo Bello (ITA) Attendance: 69,480

BAYERN: Josef Maier; Hans Nowak, Werner Olk (Cap), Franz Beckenbauer, Peter Kupferschmidt; Franz Roth, Dieter Koulmann, Rudolf Nafziger, Rainer Ohlhauser, Gerhard Müller, Dieter Brenninger. Trainer: Zlatko Čajkovski

RANGERS: Norman Martin; Kai Johansen, William Jardine, Ronald McKinnon, David Provan; Alexander Smith, John Greig (Cap); William Henderson, Roger Hynd, David Smith, William Johnston. Trainer: James Scotland Symon

Goal: Roth (108)

Goalscorers Cup-Winners' Cup 1966-67:

10 goals: Roger Claessen (Standard Liège)

8 goals: Gerhard Müller (Bayern München)

4 goals: Bernd Bauchspiess (Chemie Leipzig), William Dixon (Shamrock Rovers), Walter Seitl, Jørn Bjerregaard (Rapid Wien), Liuben Tasev (Slavia Sofia), Nicolas Dewalque (Standard Liège)

3 goals: Santos (Zaragoza), Schindelholz (Servette), Kemper (Sparta Rotterdam), Perrichon (Sporting Braga), Stolcz, Szaló (Vasas ETO), Siemin (Spartak Moskva)

2 goals: Sjøberg (Skeid Oslo), Pavlovic (Tatran Prešov), Brenninger, Ohlhauser, Roth (Bayern), Kearin, O'Neill (Shamrock Rovers), Flögel (Rapid), Vrajev, Mishev (Slavia), Marcelino (Zaragoza), Laine (AIFK Turku), Vermolen (Sparta), McLean, D.Smith (Rangers), Hausser (Strasbourg), Khusainov (Spartak Moskva), Galic (Standard)

1 goal: Elísson, Júlíusson (Valur Reykjavik), Trimhold (Borussia), Ayhan, Ergun, Yilmaz (Galatasaray), Kristoffersen, Thorsen (Skeid Oslo), Pilot, Semmeling, Jurkiewicz, Bleser, Germano (Standard), Ioanou (Apollon Limassol), Caban (Tatran Prešov), Koulmann, Kupferschmidt (Bayern), Scherbarth, Behla, Schmidt (Chemie), Korzeniowski, Zmijewski (Legia), Weis, Krier (Spora Luxembourg), Fullam, Gilbert, Tuohy (Shamrock Rovers), Starek, Fritsch (Rapid), Todd (Swansea), Haralampiev (Slavia), Reija, Canario, País, Lapetra (Zaragoza), Conti, Németh, Desbiolles (Servette), Philips (Floriana), Bosveld, Bouman, Laseroms (Sparta), Johansen, A.Smith, Wilson, Willoughby, Henderson, Johnston, Setterington (Rangers), Sinclair (Glentoran), Papaioannou (AEK Athina), Luciano, Mário, Adao (Sporting Braga), Chiarugi, Bertini, De Sisti (Fiorentina), Varsányi, Orbán (Vasas ETO), Avram (Steaua), Muller (Strasbourg), Lildballe (Aalborg), Morrissey, Ball, Brown (Everton), Krivocuca (OFK Beograd), G.Logofet, Bokatov (Spartak Moskva)

Own goals: Piguet (Servette) for Slavia Sofia, Ribeiro (Braga) for Vasas ETO, Coimbra (Sporting Braga) for AEK Athina

CUP WINNERS' CUP 1967-68

FIRST ROUND

ABERDEEN FC v KR REYKJAVÍK 10-0 (4-0)
Pittodrie, Aberdeen 6.09.1967
Referee: Adrianus Aalbrecht (HOL) Attendance: 14,784

ABERDEEN FC: Robert Clark; James Whyte, Alistair Shewan, Jens Petersen, Thomas McMillan; Martin Buchan, James Wilson, Francis Munro; James Storrie (Cap), James Smith, Ian Taylor. Manager: Edward Turnbull

KR: Gudmundur Pétursson; Kristinn Jónsson, Bjarni Felixson; Thórdur Jónsson, Ellert Schram (Cap), Arsaell Kjartansson; Hördur Markan, Gunnar Felixson, Baldvin Baldvinsson, Eyleifur Hafsteinsson, Sigurthór Jakobsson. Trainer: Sveinn Jónsson

Goals: Munro (19, 52, 61), Storrie (21, 56), Smith (31, 76), McMillan (45), Taylor (48), Petersen (72)

KR REYKJAVÍK v ABERDEEN FC 1-4 (0-2)
Laugardalsvöllur, Reykjavík 13.09.1967
Referee: Ivar Hornslien (NOR) Attendance: 1,242

KR: Gudmundur Pétursson; Bjarni Felixson, Kristinn Jónsson; Thorgeir Gudmundsson, Ellert Schram (Cap), Arsaell Kjartansson; Gunnar Felixson, Thórdur Jónsson, Baldvin Baldvinsson, Eyleifur Hafsteinsson, Olafur Lárusson. Trainer: Sveinn Jónsson

ABERDEEN FC: Robert Clark; James Whyte, Alistair Shewan, Francis Munro, Thomas McMillan; James Kirkland, James Wilson, James Smith; James Storrie (Cap), Martin Buchan, Ian Taylor. Manager: Edward Turnbull

Goals: Storrie (43, 58), Buchan (44), Munro (48), Hafsteinsson (72)

HAMBURGER SV v RANDERS FREJA 5-3 (2-1)
Volksparkstadion, Hamburg 6.09.1967
Referee: Peter Coates (IRL) Attendance: 14,787

HAMBURGER SV: Erhard Schwerin; Dieter Strauss, Jürgen Kurbjuhn; Peter Rohrschneider, Egon Horst, Willi Schulz; Bernd Dörfel, Franz-Josef Hönig, Uwe Seeler (Cap), Werner Krämer, Hans Schulz. Trainer: Kurt Koch

RANDERS FREJA: Alfred Mogensen; Mogens Kaarup, Jørgen Rasmussen, Per Lykke, Ole Nielsen, Knud Olesen (Cap), Erik Sørensen, Per Gaardsøe, John Andreasen, René Møller, Hans Berg Andersen. Trainer: Kaj Christiansen

Goals: Seeler (3, 28, 83), Andreasen (18), Krämer (55), Hönig (64), Sørensen (68), Gaardsøe (90)

RANDERS FREJA v HAMBURGER SV 0-2 (0-2)
Randers, Freja   20.09.1967
Referee: Birger Nilsen (NOR)   Attendance: 14,882
RANDERS FREJA: Alfred Mogensen; Mogens Kaarup, Jørgen Rasmussen, Per Lykke, Johannes Enevoldsen, Knud Olesen (Cap), Erik Sørensen, Ole Nielsen, John Andreasen, René Møller, Hans Berg Andersen.   Trainer: Kaj Christiansen
HAMBURGER SV: Özcan Arkoç; Helmut Sandmann, Jürgen Kurbjuhn, Willi Giesemann, Willi Schulz, Egon Horst, Peter Rohrschneider, Werner Krämer, Uwe Seeler (Cap), Hans Schulz, Holger Dieckmann.   Trainer: Kurt Koch
Goals: Kurbjuhn (2), Dieckmann (21)

GYÖRI VASAS ETO
v APOLLON LIMASSOL 5-0 (2-0)
ETO, Györ   20.09.1967
Referee: Paul Schiller (AUS)   Attendance: 10,000
VASAS ETO: Lajos Tóth; László Keglovich, Arpád Orbán (Cap), László Izsáki; Lajos Nell, Zoltán Kiss; János Stolcz, Tibor Varsányi, László Györffi, József Somogyi, József Szaló. Trainer: Ferenc Szusza
APOLLON: Evagoras Vasileiou; Mihail Gavalas, Hristos Polikarpou Fazoulis, Andreas Georgiou, Andreas Themistokleous; Dimos Kavazis, Dimitris Antoniou; Panikos Krystallis (Cap), Kostas Vasiliadis, Giannis Vasiliadis, Andreas Konstantinou.   Trainer: Panikos Krystallis
Goals: Nell (19), Györffi (25), Varsányi (48), Szaló (80, 83)

FK AUSTRIA WIEN
v STEAUA BUCUREŞTI 0-2 (0-1)
Prater-stadion, Wien   13.09.1967
Referee: Ivan Placek (CZE)   Attendance: 14,433
AUSTRIA: Josef Schneider; Heinz Novy, Johann Frank, Karl Fröhlich; Adolf Knoll, Alfons Dirnberger; Thomas Parits, Herbert Poindl, Vlatko Markovic, Walter Hiesel, Ernst Fiala (Cap).   Trainers: Heinrich Müller & Leopold Vogel
STEAUA: Carol Haidu; Lajos Sătmăreanu, Bujor Hălmăgeanu, Dumitru Nicolae, Radu Rotaru; Vasile Negrea, Dumitru Popescu; Sorin Avram, Gheorghe Constantin (Cap), Vasile Soo, Florea Voinea.   Trainer: Ştefan Kovacs
Goals: Soo (42), Avram (70)

APOLLON LIMASSOL
v GYÖRI VASAS ETO 0-4 (0-0)
Sóstói, Székesfehérvár   23.09.1967
Referee: Paul Schiller (AUS)   Attendance: 4,000
APOLLON: Giannis Papaioannou; Hristos Polikarpou Fazoulis, Dimos Kavazis, Andreas Themistokleous, Andreas Georgiou, Panagiotis Poliviou, Dimitris Antoniou, Panikos Giolitis, Panikos Krystallis, Kostas Vasiliadis, Andreas Konstantinou.   Trainer: Panikos Krystallis
VASAS ETO: Lajos Tóth; László Keglovich, László Izsáki; Lajos Nell, Arpád Orbán, Zoltán Kiss; János Stolcz, Tibor Varsányi, László Györffi, József Somogyi, József Szaló. Trainer: Ferenc Szusza
Goals: Kiss (63), Szaló (65), Varsányi (72), Stolcz (79)

STEAUA BUCUREŞTI
v FK AUSTRIA WIEN 2-1 (1-1)
Republicii, Bucureşti   27.09.1967
Referee: Timoleon Latsios (GRE)   Attendance: 9,101
STEAUA: Carol Haidu; Lajos Sătmăreanu, Bujor Hălmăgeanu, Dumitru Nicolae, Radu Rotaru; Vasile Negrea, Dumitru Popescu; Sorin Avram, Gheorghe Constantin (Cap), Florea Voinea, Dumitru Manea.   Trainer: Ştefan Kovacs
AUSTRIA: Rudolf Szanwald; Heinz Novy, Johann Frank, Karl Fröhlich; Adolf Knoll, Alfons Dirnberger; Thomas Parits, Herbert Poindl, Vlatko Markovic, Josef Hickersberger, Ernst Fiala (Cap).   Trainers: Heinrich Müller & Leopold Vogel
Goals: Manea (24), Markovic (37), Negrea (85)

HAJDUK SPLIT
v TOTTENHAM HOTSPUR LONDON 0-2 (0-1)
Hajduk, Split   20.09.1967
Referee: Todor P. Betchirov (BUL)   Attendance: 25,000
HAJDUK: Radomir Vukčević; Milutin Folić, Aleksandar Ristić; Dragomir Slisković, Dragan Holcer (Cap), Miroslav Bosković; Miroslav Ferić, Miroslav Vardić, Petar Nadoveza, Zlatomir Obradov, Ivica Hlevnjak.   Trainer: Dušan Nenković
TOTTENHAM: Patrick Jennings; Joseph Kinnear, Cyril Barry Knowles; Alan Patrick Mullery (Cap), Harold Michael England, Philip Beal; James Gillen Robertson, James Peter Greaves, Alan John Gilzean, Terence Frederick Venables, Frank Saul.   Manager: William Edward Nicholson
Goals: Robertson (4), Greaves (88)

**TOTTENHAM HOTSPUR LONDON
v HAJDUK SPLIT 4-3** (3-0)
White Hart Lane, London 27.09.1967
Referee: Joaquim Fernandes Campos (POR)   Att: 38,623
TOTTENHAM: Patrick Jennings; Joseph Kinnear, Cyril Barry Knowles; Alan Patrick Mullery (Cap), Harold Michael England, Philip Beal; James Gillen Robertson, James Peter Greaves, Alan John Gilzean, Terence Frederick Venables, Clifford William Jones.   Manager: William Edward Nicholson
HAJDUK: Radomir Vukčević; Miroslav Bosković, Aleksandar Ristić; Dragomir Slisković, Dragan Holcer (Cap), Ante Zaja; Dzemaludin Musović, Miroslav Vardić, Zlatomir Obradov, Petar Nadoveza, Ivica Hlevnjak.   Trainer: Dušan Nenković
Goals: Robertson (23, 83), Gilzean (30), Venables (38), Vardic (81), Musovic (82), Hlevnjak (89 pen)

**ARIS BONNEVOIE
v OLYMPIQUE LYONNAIS 0-3** (0-2)
Stade Municipal, Luxembourg 20.09.1967
Referee: Hans-Joachim Weyland (W. GER)   Att: 1,803
ARIS: Jean Leonard; Emile Wagner, Paul Hoscheit; Joseph Kunnert, Jean-Pierre Hoffstetter (Cap), Nicolas Hoffmann; Johny Schreiner, Paul Lang, Bertrand Heger, Marco Maas, Josy Kirchens.   Trainer: Rainer Gawell
OLYMPIQUE: Yves Chauveau; Erwin Kuffer, Jacques Glyczinski, Marcel Le Borgne, René Rocco; Hector Maison, Robert Nouzaret; Mohamed Lekkak, Jacques Pin, Fleury Di Nallo (Cap), Angel Rambert.   Trainer: Louis Hon
Goals: Pin (22), Di Nallo (39, 63)

SHAMROCK ROVERS v CARDIFF CITY 1-1 (1-0)
Dalymount Park, Dublin 20.09.1967
Referee: Pieter Paulus Roomer (HOL)   Attendance: 21,883
SHAMROCK ROVERS: Michael Smyth; Patrick Courtney, Patrick Mulligan, Michael Kearin, Ronald Nolan (Cap), John Fullam, Francis O'Neill, William Dixon, Robert Gilbert, Michael Leech, Thomas Kinsella.   Trainer: William Tuohy
CITY: Robert Wilson; Graham Coldrick, Robert Ferguson; Gareth Williams, Donald Murray (Cap), Brian Harris; Barrie Spencer Jones, John Toshack, Peter King, Malcolm Clarke, Ronald Bird.   Manager: James Scoular
Goals: Gilbert (16), King (48)

**OLYMPIQUE LYONNAIS
v ARIS BONNEVOIE 2-1** (2-0)
Stade Gerland, Lyon 4.10.1967
Referee: John Robertson P. Gordon (SCO)   Att: 5,058
OLYMPIQUE: Yves Chauveau (46 Michel Zewulko); Erwin Kuffer, Jacques Glyczinski, René Rocco, Bernard Lhomme; Hector Maison, Raymond Schwinn; Mohamed Lekkak, Jacques Pin, Fleury Di Nallo (Cap), Angel Rambert.   Trainer: Louis Hon
ARIS: Théo Stendebach; Emile Wagner, Paul Hoscheit; Nicolas Hoffmann, Jean-Pierre Hoffstetter (Cap), Joseph Kunnert; Joseph Pesch, Paul Lang, Bertrand Heger, Morry Wampach, Josy Kirchens.   Trainer: Jim Kremer
Goals: Pin (5), Maison (28 pen), Heger (79)

CARDIFF CITY v SHAMROCK ROVERS 2-0 (1-0)
Ninian Park, Cardiff 4.10.1967
Referee: Vital Loraux (BEL)   Attendance: 14,180
CITY: Robert Wilson; Graham Coldrick, David Carver; Gareth Williams, Donald Murray (Cap), Brian Harris; Barrie Spencer Jones, Robert Brown, John Toshack, Peter King, Ronald Bird.   Manager: James Scoular
SHAMROCK ROVERS: Michael Smyth; Patrick Courtney, Thomas Kelly, Michael Kearin, Ronald Nolan, William Dixon, Francis O'Neill, Michael Leech, Damien Richardson, William Tuohy (Cap), Thomas Kinsella.   Trainer: William Tuohy
Goals: Toshack (30), Brown (74 pen)

TORPEDO MOSKVA v MOTOR ZWICKAU 0-0
Central V.I.Lenin, Moskva 20.09.1967
Referee: Pekka Aho (FIN)   Attendance: 15,000
TORPEDO: Anzor Kavazashvili; Vladimir Saraev, Viktor Shustikov, Aleksandr Chumakov; Valeri Voronin (Cap), Evgeni Vasiliev; Aleksandr Leniev, Eduard Streltsov, Vladimir Scherbakov, Mikhail Gershkovich, David Pais.   Trainer: Valentin Ivanov
MOTOR: Jürgen Croy; Harald Söldner, Alois Glaubitz, Albert Beier, Volkmar Resch; Harald Irmscher, Horst Jura (Cap), Gerd Mattern; Hartmut Rentzsch, Peter Henschel, Erwin Erdmann.   Trainer: Horst Oettler

MOTOR ZWICKAU
v TORPEDO MOSKVA 0-1 (0-0)
Georgi Dimitroff, Zwickau   4.10.1967
Referee: Ryszard Banasiuk (POL)   Attendance: 12,214
MOTOR: Jürgen Croy; Harald Söldner, Alois Glaubitz, Albert Beier, Erwin Erdmann; Heinz Dietzsch, Horst Jura (Cap), Harald Irmscher; Hartmut Rentzsch, Peter Henschel, Hartmut Hoffmann.   Trainer: Horst Oettler
TORPEDO: Anzor Kavazashvili; Aleksandr Leniev, Leonid Pakhomov, Viktor Shustikov, Vladimir Saraev; Valeri Voronin (Cap), Aleksandr Chumakov; Eduard Streltsov, Vladimir Scherbakov, Vladimir Brednev, David Pais.
Trainer: Valentin Ivanov
Goal: Streltsov (68)

HJK HELSINKI v WISLA KRAKÓW 1-4 (0-3)
Olympiastadion, Helsinki   20.09.1967
Referee: Erwin Vetter (E. GER)   Attendance: 4,172
HJK: Leo Ristlakki (46 Paavo Heinonen); Reijo Jalava (Cap), Ari Ojala, Bo Sjöstedt, Pentti Kokko, Kaj Österberg, Erkki Jauhiainen, Timo Rahja, Pekka Talaslahti, Kai Pahlman, Raimo Pajo.   Trainer: Aulis Rytkönen
WISLA: Henryk Stroniarz; Fryderyk Monica, Wladyslaw Kawula (Cap), Adam Musial, Tadeusz Polak; Ryszard Wójcik, Wieslaw Lendzion, Józef Gach, Andrzej Sykta, Ireneusz Adamus, Hubert Skupnik.   Trainer: Mieczyslaw Gracz
Goals: Skupnik (10), Lendzion (14, 27), Sykta (66), Pajo (76)

WISLA KRAKÓW v HJK HELSINKI 4-0 (2-0)
Wisla, Kraków   4.10.1967
Referee: Anvar Zverev (USSR)   Attendance: 10,000
WISLA: Henryk Stroniarz; Fryderyk Monica, Wladyslaw Kawula (Cap), Adam Musial; Tadeusz Polak, Ryszard Wójcik, Wieslaw Lendzion, Józef Gach, Andrzej Sykta, Ireneusz Adamus, Hubert Skupnik.   Trainer: Mieczyslaw Gracz
HJK: Paavo Heinonen; Eero Rainiala, Ari Ojala; Bo Sjöstedt, Pentti Kokko (Cap), Raimo Marttinen; Erkki Jauhiainen, Kaj Österberg, Timo Rahja, Jaakko Murtovaara, Raimo Pajo.
Trainer: Aulis Rytkönen
Goals: Rainiala (25 og), Skupnik (44), Wójcik (60), Sykta (79)

FREDRIKSTAD FK v VITÓRIA SETÚBAL 1-5 (0-3)
Fredrikstad stadium   20.09.1967
Referee: Gunnar Michaelsen (DEN)   Attendance: 5,204
FK FREDRIKSTAD: Per Mosgaard; Kjell Andreassen, Jan Hermansen, Asle Arntzen, Roar Johansen (Cap), Thor Spydevold, Bjørn Borgen, Jan Fuglset, Knut Spydevold, Per Kristoffersen, Jan Aas.   Trainer: Bjørn Spydevold
VITÓRIA: Dinis Martins Vital; Joaquim Adrião José CONCEIÇÃO (Cap), Manuel Jesus Pereira LEIRIA, HERCULANO Carmo Santos, Manuel Luís dos Santos CARRIÇO, ARMANDO Bronze Bonjour; José Maria Freitas Pereira PEDRAS, Fernando Massano Tomé, Félix Marques Guerreiro, JOSÉ MARIA Júnior, Jacinto João.
Trainer: Fernando Vaz
Goals: Pedras (20, 33), José Maria (43), Guerreiro (63, 78), Fuglset (72)

VITÓRIA SETÚBAL v FREDRIKSTAD FK 2-1 (1-0)
Estádio do Bonfim, Setúbal   5.10.1967
Referee: Daniel Zariquiegui (SPA)   Attendance: 6,546
VITÓRIA: Dinis Martins Vital; Joaquim Adrião José CONCEIÇÃO (Cap), Manuel Luís dos Santos CARRIÇO; Fernando Massano Tomé, Manuel Jesus Pereira LEIRIA, HERCULANO Carmo Santos, ARMANDO Bronze Bonjour; José Maria Freitas Pereira PEDRAS, Félix Marques Guerreiro, JOSÉ MARIA Júnior, Jacinto João.   Trainer: Fernando Vaz
FK FREDRIKSTAD: Per Mosgaard (10 Vidar Svendsen); Kjell Andreassen, Jan Hermansen, Asle Arntzen, Thor Spydevold, Roar Johansen (Cap), Bjørn Borgen, Per Kristoffersen, Jan Fuglset, Kai Nilsen, Knut Spydevold.
Trainer: Bjørn Spydevold
Goals: Pedras (5), Armando (50), Arntzen (59)

VALENCIA CF
v CRUSADERS BELFAST FC 4-0 (3-0)
Luís Casanova, Valencia   20.09.1967
Referee: Roger Machin (FRA)   Attendance: 20,000
VALENCIA: Ángel ABELARDO González Bernardo; Juan Cruz SOL Oria, Francisco VIDAGAÑY Hernández, Francisco García Goméz "PAQUITO", Manuel MESTRE Torres (Cap), ROBERTO Gil Esteve, SALVADOR Terol, WALDO Machado da Silva, Fernando ANSOLA Sanmartín, José CLARAMUNT Torres, Vicente Anastasio JARA Segovia.
Trainer: Edmundo Suárez Mundo
CRUSADERS: Terence Nicholson; Joseph Patterson, Derek Lewis; Samuel McCullough, Albert Campbell (Cap), John McPolin; Mervyn Law, Danny Trainor, Joseph Meldrum, Thanny Brush, Liam Wilson.   Trainer: Edward Smyth
Goals: Ansola (2, 13), Jara (28 pen), Waldo (55)

**CRUSADERS BELFAST FC
v VALENCIA CF** 2-4 (1-3)
The Oval, Belfast   11.10.1967
Referee: Joseph Hannet (BEL)   Attendance: 6,391
CRUSADERS: Derek Humphries; Joseph Patterson, Derek Lewis; Samuel McCullough, Albert Campbell (Cap), John McPolin; Mervyn Law, Danny Trainor, Edward Magill, Joseph Meldrum, Liam Wilson.   Trainer: Edward Smyth
VALENCIA: Ángel ABELARDO González Bernardo; José Antonio García TATONO, Francisco VIDAGAÑY Hernández; Antonio CATALÁ Benet, Luis VILAR Botet, ROBERTO Gil Esteve (Cap); José CLARAMUNT Torres, WALDO Machado da Silva, Fernando ANSOLA Sanmartín, Francisco García Gómez "PAQUITO", Vicente Anastasio JARA Segovia. Trainer: Edmundo Suárez Mundo
Goals: Trainor (3), Paquito (14, 33, 63), Ansola (41), Magill (69)

**LAUSANNE SPORTS
v SPARTAK TRNAVA** 3-2 (2-2)
Stade Olympique de la Pontaise, Lausanne   20.09.1967
Referee: Ronald P. Jones (WAL)   Attendance: 7,625
LAUSANNE SPORTS: René Schneider; Christian Delay, Kurt Hunziker, Kurt Armbruster, Richard Dürr, Ely Tacchella (Cap), Anton Weibel, Pierre Kerkhoffs, Georges Vuilleumier, Robert Hosp, Charles Hertig.   Trainer: Roger Vonlanthen
SPARTAK: Josef Geryk; Karol Dobias, Stanislav Jarábek (Cap), Ján Zlocha, Vladimír Hagara; Anton Hrušecký, Emil Brumovský, Valerian Svec, Ladislav Kuna, Jozef Adamec, Dušan Kabát.   Trainer: Anton Malatinsky
Goals: Svec (8, 17), Kerkhoffs (33, 43), Armbruster (90)

**SPARTAK TRNAVA
v LAUSANNE SPORTS** 2-0 (1-0)
Spartak, Trnava   11.10.1967
Referee: Karl Riegg (W. GER)   Attendance: 9,588
SPARTAK: František Kozinka; Karol Dobias, Vladimír Hagara, Ján Zlocha, Stanislav Jarábek (Cap); Jaroslav Kravárik, Stanislav Martinkovic, Anton Hrušecký, Ladislav Kuna, Jozef Adamec, Dušan Kabát.   Trainer: Anton Malatinsky
LAUSANNE SPORTS: René Schneider; André Grobéty (Cap), Kurt Hunziker, Christian Delay, Ely Tacchella, Anton Weibel, Robert Hosp, André Bosson, Georges Vuilleumier, Richard Dürr, Pierre Kerkhoffs.   Trainer: Roger Vonlanthen
Goals: Adamec (25), Martinkovic (90)

MILAN AC v LEVSKI SOFIA 5-1 (0-0)
Stadio San Siro, Milano   20.09.1967
Referee: Konstantin Zecević (YUG)   Attendance: 39,779
AC MILAN: Fabio Cudicini; Angelo Anquilletti, Karl-Heinz Schnellinger; Roberto Rosato, Saul Malatrasi, Giovanni Trapattoni; Kurt Hamrin, Giovanni Lodetti, Angelo Benedicto Sormani, Gianni Rivera (Cap), Bruno Mora.
Trainer: Nereo Rocco
LEVSKI: Biser Mihailov; Stoicho Peshev, Ivan Zdravkov, Ivan Vutsov, Georgi Georgiev; Kiril Ivkov, Ianko Kirilov; Georgi Sokolov, Georgi Asparuhov, Hristo Iliev (Cap), Aleksandar Kostov.   Trainer: Krastyo Chakarov
Goals: Sormani (51), Hamrin (53, 70), Asparuhov (63), Anquilletti (83, 86)

LEVSKI SOFIA v AC MILAN 1-1 (0-1)
Vasil Levski, Sofia   11.10.1967
Referee: Faruk Talu (TUR)   Attendance: 24,864
LEVSKI: Biser Mihailov; Stoichko Peshev, Ivan Vutsov (Cap), Ivan Zdravkov, Kiril Ivkov, Georgi Georgiev, Tsvetan Veselinov, Ianko Kirilov, Georgi Asparuhov, Aleksandar Kostov, Georgi Sokolov.   Trainer: Krastyo Chakarov
AC MILAN: Pier-Angelo Belli; Angelo Anquilletti, Karl-Heinz Schnellinger; Roberto Rosato, Saul Malatrasi, Giovanni Trapattoni; Kurt Hamrin, Giovanni Lodetti, Angelo Benedicto Sormani, Gianni Rivera (Cap), Pierino Prati.
Trainer: Nereo Rocco
Goals: Sormani (11), Asparuhov (74)

**ALTAY GENCLIK IZMIR
v STANDARD LIÈGE** 2-3 (2-1)
Alsançak, Izmir   20.09.1967
Referee: Vasile Dumitrescu (ROM)   Attendance: 12,728
ALTAY: Varol Ürkmez (Cap); Yilmaz Canlisoy, Necdet Tunca; Enver Katip, A. Riza Şenol, Ayfer Elmastasogu; Ender İçten, Dogan Aki, Feridun Öztürk, Oguz Böke, Aydin Yelken. Trainer: Bülent Eken
STANDARD: Jean Nicolay (46 Daniel Mathy); Jacques Beurlet, Jean Thissen; Nicolas Dewalque, Léon Jeck, Louis Pilot; Léon Semmeling (Cap), Drago Smajlovic, Roger Claessen, Milan Galic, Jean-Paul Colonval.
Trainer: Milorad Pavić
Goals: Colonval (11), Aki Dogan (23), Ender (42), Claessen (72, 82)

STANDARD LIÈGE v ALTAY GENCLIK IZMIR 0-0
Stade Maurice Dufrasne, Liège 18.10.1967

Referee: Gottfried Dienst (SWI)   Attendance: 12,781

STANDARD: Jean Nicolay; Jacques Beurlet, Jean Thissen, Nicolas Dewalque, Léon Jeck; Julien Onclin, Léon Semmeling (Cap), Drago Smajlovic, Roger Claessen, Milan Galic, Casimir Jurkiewicz.   Trainer: Milorad Pavić

ALTAY: Varol Ürkmez (Cap); Yilmaz Canlisoy, Zinnur Sari, Enver Katip; A.Riza Şenol, Necdet Tunca; Aytekin Erhanoglu, Dogan Aki, Behzat Çinar, Oguz Böke, Ender Içten. Trainer: Bülent Eken

BAYERN MÜNCHEN v PANATHINAIKOS ATHINA 5-0 (3-0)
Grünwalder strasse, München 20.09.1967

Referee: Kenneth Dagnall (ENG)   Attendance: 21,750

BAYERN: Josef Maier; Peter Kupferschmidt, Georg Schwarzenbeck, Franz Roth, Franz Beckenbauer, Werner Olk (Cap), Gerhard Müller, Rudolf Nafziger, Gustav Jung, Horst Schauss, Dieter Brenninger.   Trainer: Zlatko Čajkovski

PANATHINAIKOS: Takis Oikonomopoulos; Aristidis Kamaras, Mihalis Bellis, Zaharias Pitihoutis, Takis Loukanidis, Fragkiskos Sourpis, Pavlos Kopsaheilis, Giannis Kalaitzidis, Mimis Domazos (Cap), Andreas Papaemmanouil, Giorgos Rokidis.   Trainer: Béla Guttmann

Goals: Müller (13 pen, 46), Kupferschmidt (25), Beckenbauer (32), Jung (57)

PANATHINAIKOS ATHINA v BAYERN MÜNCHEN 1-2 (0-1)
PAO – Leoforou Alexandras, Athina 18.10.1967

Referee: Jacques Colling (LUX)   Attendance: 20,665

PANATHINAIKOS: Takis Oikonomopoulos; Aristidis Kamaras, Mihalis Bellis, Zaharias Pitihoutis, Takis Loukanidis, Fragkiskos Sourpis, Pavlos Kopsaheilis, Giannis Kalaitzidis, Mimis Domazos (Cap), Andreas Papaemmanouil, Harilaos Grammos.   Trainer: Béla Guttmann

BAYERN: Josef Maier; Hans Nowak, Georg Schwarzenbeck, Franz Roth, Werner Olk (Cap), Peter Kupferschmidt, Rudolf Nafziger, Gerhard Müller, Rainer Ohlhauser, Dieter Koulmann, Dieter Brenninger.   Trainer: Zlatko Čajkovski

Goals: Müller (8), Kalaitzidis (68), Koulmann (89)

FLORIANA FC v NOAD ADVENDO COMBINATIE BREDA 1-2 (0-0)
The Empire Stadium, Gzira 21.09.1967

Referee: Francesco Francescon (ITA)   Attendance: 8,000

FLORIANA: Anthony Borg; Charles Farrugia, Frank Micallef; Anton Camilleri, Alfred Debono, Charles Grech; Saviour Borg, William Vassallo, Charles Buttigieg, Publius Micallef, Hugh Caruana.   Trainer: Emmanuel Borg

NAC: Petrus van de Merwe (Cap); Johannes Adrianus Antonius van Gorp, Frederikus Johannes van Ierland, Antonius Martinus Wilhelmus Maria Graaumans, Adrianus Antonius Maria Pelkmans; Reinier Johannes Maria Rijnders, Franciscus Cornelis Johannes Vermeulen; Ferdinand Peter Jan Pirard, Jacobus Marinus Petrus Visschers, Martin Snoeck, Godefridus Francisca Johannes Antonius Nouwens. Trainer: Robert Janse

Goals: Visschers (48, 69), Buttigieg (49)

NAC BREDA v FLORIANA FC 1-0 (0-0)
Philips Sportpark, Eindhoven 12.10.1967

Referee: John Adair (NIR)   Attendance: 8,000

NAC: Petrus van de Merwe (Cap); Johannes Adrianus Antonius van Gorp, Frederikus Johannes van Ierland, Antonius Martinus Wilhelmus Maria Graaumans, Adrianus Antonius Maria Pelkmans; Reinier Johannes Maria Rijnders, Franciscus Cornelis Johannes Vermeulen; Martin Snoeck, Jacobus Marinus Petrus Visschers, Ferdinand Peter Jan Pirard, Franciscus Bouwmeester sr.   Trainer: Robert Janse

FLORIANA: Charles Zerafa; Charles Galea, Charles Farrugia; Anton Camilleri, Alfred Debono (Cap), Publius Micallef; Frank Micallef, Willie Vassallo, Charles Buttigieg, Louis Arpa, Hugh Caruana.   Trainer: Emmanuel Borg

Goal: Pirard (56)

SECOND ROUND

BAYERN MÜNCHEN v VITÓRIA SETÚBAL 6-2 (3-1)
Grünwalder strasse, München 8.11.1967

Referee: Kevin Howley (ENG)   Attendance: 18,341

BAYERN: Josef Maier; Peter Kupferschmidt, Georg Schwarzenbeck, Hans Nowak, Franz Beckenbauer, Werner Olk, Gerhard Müller, Rudolf Nafziger, Rainer Ohlhauser, Dieter Koulmann, Dieter Brenninger.   Trainer: Zlatko Čajkovski

VITÓRIA: Dinis Martins VITAL; Joaquim Adrião José CONCEIÇÃO, Manuel Luíz dos Santos CARRIÇO, Fernando Massano Tomé, Manuel Jesus Pereira LEIRIA, HERCULANO Carmo Santos, ARMANDO Bronze Bonjour, Félix Marques Guerreiro, CARLOS MANUEL Ferreira Cordeiro, José Maria Freitas Pereira PEDRAS, Jacinto João.   Trainer: Fernando Vaz

Goals: Pedras (7), Müller (8, 59, 89 pen), Brenninger (20), Ohlhauser (27), Nafziger (50), Tomé (81)

VITÓRIA SETÚBAL v BAYERN MÜNCHEN 1-1 (0-0)

Estádio do Bonfim, Setúbal   14.11.1967

Referee: Roger Barde (FRA)   Attendance: 5,259

VITÓRIA: Dinis Martins VITAL; Joaquim Adrião José CONCEIÇÃO (Cap), Manuel Luíz dos Santos CARRIÇO, Fernando Massano Tomé, Manuel Jesus Pereira LEIRIA, HERCULANO Carmo Santos, VíTOR Manuel Ferreira BAPTISTA, Félix Marques Guerreiro, José Maria Freitas Pereira PEDRAS, JOSÉ MARIA Júnior, Jacinto João.   Trainer: Fernando Vaz

BAYERN: Josef Maier; Werner Olk (Cap), Franz Roth, Horst Schauss, Franz Beckenbauer, Georg Schwarzenbeck, Peter Kupferschmidt, Rudolf Nafziger, Herbert Stöckl, Rainer Ohlhauser, Gerhard Müller.   Trainer: Zlatko Čajkovski

Goals: Pedras (68), Ohlhauser (75)

NAC BREDA v CARDIFF CITY 1-1 (1-0)

Philips, Eindhoven   15.11.1967

Referee: Kåre Sirevag (NOR)   Attendance: 7,618

NAC: Petrus van de Merwe (Cap); Johannes Adrianus Antonius van Gorp, Frederikus Johannes van Ierland, Franciscus Cornelis Johannes Vermeulen, Adrianus Antonius Maria Pelkmans; Reinier Johannes Maria Rijnders; Martin Snoeck, Franciscus Bouwmeester sr., Jacobus Marinus Petrus Visschers, Ferdinand Peter Jan Pirard, Godefridus Francisca Johannes Antonius Nouwens.   Trainer: Robert Janse

CITY: Robert Wilson; Stephen Clifford Derrett, Robert Ferguson; Malcolm Clarke, Donald Murray (Cap), Brian Harris; Barrie Spencer Jones, Robert Brown, Peter King, John Toshack, Ronald Bird.   Manager: James Scoular

Goals: Visschers (9), King (68)

CARDIFF CITY v NAC BREDA 4-1 (2-1)

Ninian Park, Cardiff   29.11.1967

Referee: Gunnar Michaelsen (DEN)   Attendance: 16,411

CITY: Robert Wilson; Graham Coldrick, Robert Ferguson; Malcolm Clarke, Donald Murray (Cap), Brian Harris; Barrie Spencer Jones, Robert Brown, Peter King, John Toshack, Gary Bell.   Manager: James Scoular

NAC: Petrus van de Merwe (Cap); Johannes Adrianus Antonius van Gorp, Frederikus Johannes van Ierland, Franciscus Cornelis Johannes Vermeulen, Adrianus Antonius Maria Pelkmans; Reinier Johannes Maria Rijnders, Franciscus Bouwmeester jr.; Ferdinand Peter Jan Pirard, Jacobus Marinus Petrus Visschers, Godefridus Francisca Johannes Antonius Nouwens, Martins Snoeck.   Trainer: Robert Janse

Goals: Brown (2), Barrie Jones (19), Nouwens (29), Clarke (66), Toshack (67)

WISLA KRAKÓW v HAMBURGER SV 0-1 (0-0)

Wisla, Kraków   15.11.1967

Referee: Gocho Rusev (BUL)   Attendance: 5,000

WISLA: Henryk Stroniarz; Fryderyk Monica, Wladyslaw Kawula (Cap), Ryszard Wójcik; Tadeusz Kotlarczyk, Józef Gach; Wieslaw Lendzion, Andrzej Sykta, Zygmunt Pietraszewski, Czeslaw Studnicki, Hubert Skupnik.   Trainer: Mieczyslaw Gracz

HAMBURGER SV: Özcan Arkoç; Helmut Sandmann, Jürgen Kurbjuhn, Reinhard Löffler, Willi Schulz, Holger Dieckmann, Hans Schulz, Franz-Josef Hönig, Uwe Seeler (Cap), Werner Krämer, Gert Dörfel.   Trainer: Kurt Koch

Goal: Seeler (82)

HAMBURGER SV v WISLA KRAKÓW 4-0 (3-0)

Volksparkstadion, Hamburg   29.11.1967

Referee: Patrick J. Graham (EIR)   Attendance: 8,038

HAMBURGER SV: Özcan Arkoç; Helmut Sandmann, Jürgen Kurbjuhn; Reinhard Löffler, Egon Horst, Willi Schulz, Holger Dieckmann, Hans Schulz, Uwe Seeler (Cap), Werner Krämer, Gert Dörfel.   Trainer: Kurt Koch

WISLA: Henryk Stroniarz; Fryderyk Monica, Ryszard Wójcik; Tadeusz Kotlarczyk, Wladyslaw Kawula (Cap), Tadeusz Polak; Wieslaw Lendzion, Czeslaw Studnicki, Andrzej Sykta, Józef Gach, Zygmunt Pietraszewski.   Trainer: Mieczyslaw Gracz

Goals: H. Schulz (24, 43), Kurbjuhn (41), Seeler (57)

GYÖRI VASAS ETO v AC MILAN 2-2 (1-1)

ETO, Györ   22.11.1967

Referee: Gottfried Dienst (SWI)   Attendance: 15,533

VASAS ETO: Lajos Tóth; László Keglovich, Arpád Orbán (Cap), László Izsáki; Lajos Nell, Zoltán Kiss; János Stolcz, Tibor Varsányi, László Györffi, József Somogyi, József Szaló.   Trainer: Ferenc Szusza

AC MILAN: Pier-Angelo Belli; Angelo Anquilletti, Karl-Heinz Schnellinger; Giovanni Trapattoni, Saul Malatrasi, Roberto Rosato; Kurt Hamrin, Giovanni Lodetti, Angelo Benedicto Sormani, Gianni Rivera (Cap), Giorgio Rognoni.   Trainer: Nereo Rocco

Goals: Sormani (19, 81), Györffi (29, 80)

AC MILAN v GYÖRI VASAS ETO 1-1 (1-1)
San Siro, Milano 7.12.1967
Referee: Helmut Fritz (W. GER)   Attendance: 17,757

AC MILAN: Pier-Angelo Belli; Angelo Anquilletti, Karl-Heinz Schnellinger; Giovanni Trapattoni, Saul Malatrasi, Roberto Rosato; Kurt Hamrin, Giovanni Lodetti, Pierino Prati, Gianni Rivera (Cap), Giorgio Rognoni.   Trainer: Nereo Rocco

VASAS ETO: Lajos Tóth; László Keglovich, Arpád Orbán (Cap), László Izsáki; Zoltán Kiss, Lajos Nell, János Stolcz; Tibor Varsányi, László Györffi, József Somogyi, József Szaló.   Trainer: Ferenc Szusza

Goals: Szaló (6), Prati (22)

STANDARD LIÈGE v ABERDEEN FC 3-0 (2-0)
Stade Maurice Dufrasne, Liège 29.11.1967
Referee: Salvador H. García (POR)   Attendance: 17,039

STANDARD: Jean Nicolay; Julien Onclin, Jacques Beurlet, Nicolas Dewalque, Léon Jeck; Louis Pilot, Léon Semmeling (Cap), Velimir Naumovic, Roger Claessen, Milan Galic, Casimir Jurkiewicz.   Trainer: Milorad Pavić

ABERDEEN: Robert Clark; James Whyte, Alistair Shewan, Francis Munro, Thomas McMillan; Jens Petersen, David Johnston, James Smith, David Robb, Harold Melrose (Cap), James Wilson.   Manager: Edward Turnbull

Goals: Claessen (6), Jurkiewicz (11), Pilot (66)

TORPEDO MOSKVA v SPARTAK TRNAVA 3-0 (2-0)
Pakhtakor, Tashkent 25.11.1967
Referee: Ferdinand Marschall (AUS)   Attendance: 35,432

TORPEDO: Anzor Kavazashvili; Aleksandr Leniev, Leonid Pakhomov, Aleksandr Chumakov; Valeri Voronin, Viktor Shustikov (Cap); Gennadi Schalimov, Eduard Streltsov, Vladimir Scherbakov, Vladimir Brednev, David Pais.   Trainer: Valentin Ivanov

SPARTAK: František Kozinka (46 Jozef Geryk); Karol Dobias, Stanislav Jarábek (Cap), Vladimír Hagara, Ján Zlocha; Anton Hrušecký, Stanislav Martinkovic, Jaroslav Kravárik, Ladislav Kuna, Jozef Adamec, Dušan Kabát.   Trainer: Anton Malatinsky

Goals: Scherbakov (17), Pakhomov (41), Voronin (62)

ABERDEEN FC v STANDARD LIÈGE 2-0 (1-0)
Pittodrie, Aberdeen 6.12.1967
Referee: Magnur Petursson (ICE)   Attendance: 12,785

ABERDEEN: Robert Clark; James Whyte, Alistair Shewan, Francis Munro, Thomas McMillan; Jens Petersen, William Little, James Smith; David Robb, Harold Melrose (Cap), James Wilson.   Manager: Edward Turnbull

STANDARD: Jean Nicolay; Léon Semmeling (Cap), Roger Claessen, Louis Pilot, Jacques Beurlet, Velimir Naumovic, Nicolas Dewalque, Léon Jeck, Jean Thissen, Milan Galic, Casimir Jurkiewicz.   Trainer: Milorad Pavić

Goals: Munro (20), Melrose (66)

SPARTAK TRNAVA v TORPEDO MOSKVA 1-3 (0-2)
Spartak, Trnava 30.11.1967
Referee: Adrianus Aalbrecht (HOL)   Attendance: 13,571

SPARTAK: František Kozinka; Karol Dobias, Stanislav Jarábek, Ján Zlocha, Vladimír Hagara; Anton Hrušecký, Stanislav Martinkovic, Jaroslav Kravárik, Ladislav Kuna, Jozef Adamec, Dušan Kabát.   Trainer: Anton Malatinsky

TORPEDO: Anzor Kavazashvili; Aleksandr Leniev, Leonid Pakhomov, Aleksandr Chumakov, Vladimir Saraev, Valeri Voronin, Viktor Shustikov, Valeri Stafirov, Eduard Streltsov, Vladimir Scherbakov, David Pais.   Trainer: Valentin Ivanov

Goals: Pais (10), Streltsov (16, 57), Kuna (63)

OLYMPIQUE LYONNAIS v TOTTENHAM HOTSPUR LONDON 1-0 (0-0)
Stade Gerland, Lyon 29.11.1967
Referee: Josef Krnávek (CZE)   Attendance: 10,997

OLYMPIQUE: Yves Chauveau; Erwin Kuffer, René Rocco, Yves Flohic, Bernard Lhomme; Hector Maison, Raymond Schwinn; Mohamed Lekkak, André Guy, Fleury Di Nallo (Cap), Angel Rambert.   Trainer: Louis Hon

TOTTENHAM: Patrick Jennings; Joseph Kinnear, Cyril Barry Knowles, Alan Patrick Mullery (Cap), Roger E. Hoy, David Craig Mackay, James Gillen Robertson, James Peter Greaves, Alan John Gilzean, Terence Frederick Venables, Clifford William Jones.   Manager: William Edward Nicholson

Sent off: Mullery & Guy (34)

Goal: Di Nallo (75)

**TOTTENHAM HOTSPUR LONDON
v OLYMPIQUE LYONNAIS 4-3 (2-0)**

White Hart Lane, London   13.12.1967

Referee: José María Ortiz de Mendíbil (SPA)   Att: 41,895

TOTTENHAM: Patrick Jennings; Joseph Kinnear, Cyril Barry Knowles, Dennis Bond, Roger E. Hoy, David Craig Mackay (Cap), James Gillen Robertson, James Peter Greaves, Alan John Gilzean, Terence Frederick Venables, Clifford William Jones. Manager: William Edward Nicholson

OLYMPIQUE: Yves Chauveau; Erwin Kuffer, René Rocco, Yves Flohic, Bernard Lhomme, Hector Maison, Raymond Schwinn, Jacques Pin, Mohammed Bouassa; Fleury Di Nallo (Cap), Angel Rambert.   Trainer: Louis Hon

Goals: Greaves (20, 45 pen), Di Nallo (54), Jones (55), Rambert (57), Gilzean (69), Bouassa (79)

VALENCIA CF v STEAUA BUCUREȘTI 3-0 (2-0)

Estadio Luis Casanova, Valencia   30.11.1967

Referee: Francesco Francescon (ITA)   Attendance: 22049

VALENCIA: Ángel ABELARDO González Bernardo; José Antonio García TATONO, Francisco VIDAGAÑY Hernández, Jorge CAYUELA Peiró, Manuel MESTRE Torres (Cap); ROBERTO Gil Esteve, Vicente GUILLOT Fabián; WALDO Machado da Silva, Fernando ANSOLA Sanmartín, Francisco García Gómez "PAQUITO", José CLARAMUNT Torres. Trainer: Edmundo Suárez "MUNDO"

STEAUA: Carol Haidu; Lajos Sătmăreanu, Emerich Jenei, Dumitru Nicolae, Bujor Hălmăgeanu; Vasile Negrea, Dumitru Popescu; Sorin Avram, Gheorghe Constantin (Cap), Vasile Soo, Florea Voinea.   Trainer: Ștefan Kovacs

Goals: Claramunt (1), Ansola (41, 73)

STEAUA BUCUREȘTI v VALENCIA CF 1-0 (1-0)

Republicii, București   14.12.1967

Referee: Milivoje Gugulović (YUG)   Attendance: 10,000

STEAUA: Vasile Suciu; Lajos Sătmăreanu, Emerich Jenei, Dumitru Nicolae, Bujor Hălmăgeanu; Vasile Negrea, Dumitru Popescu; Sorin Avram, Gheorghe Constantin (Cap), Vasile Soo, Florea Voinea.   Trainer: Ștefan Kovacs

VALENCIA: Ángel ABELARDO González Bernardo; Alberto ARNAL Andrés, Manuel MESTRE Torres (Cap), ROBERTO Gil Esteve, Francisco VIDAGAÑY Hernández; Luis VILAR Botet, Francisco García Gómez "PAQUITO"; Vicente GUILLOT Fabián, WALDO Machado da Silva, Fernando ANSOLA Sanmartín, José CLARAMUNT Torres. Trainer: Edmundo Suárez "MUNDO"

Goal: Constantin (12)

QUARTER-FINALS

FC VALENCIA v BAYERN MÜNCHEN 1-1 (1-0)

Estadio Luis Casanova, Valencia   14.02.1968

Referee: Michel Kitabdjian (FRA)   Attendance: 48,191

VALENCIA CF: Ángel ABELARDO González Bernardo; José Antonio García TATONO, Francisco VIDAGAÑY Hernández, ROBERTO Gil, Manuel MESTRE Torres (Cap), Luis VILAR Botet, SALVADOR Terol, Fernando ANSOLA Sanmartín, WALDO Machado da Silva, Francisco García Gómez "PAQUITO", José CLARAMUNT Torres. Trainer: Edmundo Suárez "MUNDO"

BAYERN: Josef Maier; Peter Kupferschmidt, Franz Beckenbauer, Georg Schwarzenbeck, Werner Olk (Cap); Hans Nowak, Rudolf Nafziger, Franz Roth, Rainer Ohlhauser, Gerhard Müller, Dieter Brenninger. Trainer: Zlatko Čajkovski

Goals: Vilar (6), Mestre (77 og)

BAYERN MÜNCHEN v FC VALENCIA 1-0 (1-0)

Stadion an der Grünwalder Strasse, München   13.03.1968

Referee: Kenneth Dagnall (ENG)   Attendance: 18,973

BAYERN: Josef Maier; Peter Kupferschmidt, Franz Beckenbauer, Franz Roth, Georg Schwarzenbeck, Werner Olk (Cap), Gustav Jung, Rainer Ohlhauser, Gerhard Müller, Dieter Koulmann, Dieter Brenninger.   Trainer: Zlatko Čajkovski

VALENCIA CF: Ángel ABELARDO González Bernardo; José Antonio García TATONO, Francisco VIDAGAÑY Hernández, Luis VILAR Botet, Manuel MESTRE Torres (Cap), ROBERTO Gil Esteve, Manuel Polinario Muñoz "POLI", Jorge CAYUELA Peiró, WALDO Machado da Silva, José CLARAMUNT Torres, Francisco García Gómez "PAQUITO". Trainer: Edmundo Suárez "MUNDO"

Goal: Müller (3)

**HAMBURGER SV
v OLYMPIQUE LYONNAIS 2-0 (0-0)**

Volksparkstadion, Hamburg   21.02.1968

Referee: Anvar Zverev (USSR)   Attendance: 31,675

HAMBURGER SV: Özcan Arkoç; Helmut Sandmann, Jürgen Kurbjuhn, Holger Dieckmann, Egon Horst; Willi Schulz, Hans-Jürgen Hellfritz, Hans Schulz, Uwe Seeler (Cap), Franz-Josef Hönig, Gert Dörfel.   Trainer: Kurt Koch

OLYMPIQUE: Yves Chauveau; Erwin Kuffer, Bernard Lhomme, Yves Flohic, Marcel Le Borgne, Hector Maison, Raymond Schwinn, Mohammed Bouassa; André Guy, Fleury Di Nallo (Cap), Angel Rambert.   Trainer: Louis Hon

Goals: Dieckmann (81), Dörfel (82)

**OLYMPIQUE LYONNAIS
v HAMBURGER SV 2-0** (1-0)
Stade Gerland, Lyon   13.03.1968
Referee: Thomas Kenneth Wharton (SCO)   Att: 21,425
OLYMPIQUE: Yves Chauveau; Erwin Kuffer, Yves Flohic, Marcel Le Borgne, René Rocco, Robert Nouzaret, Raymond Schwinn, Jacques Pin, André Guy, Fleury Di Nallo (Cap), Angel Rambert.   Trainer: Louis Hon
HAMBURGER SV: Özcan Arkoç; Helmut Sandmann, Jürgen Kurbjuhn, Holger Dieckmann, Egon Horst, Willi Schulz, Hans-Jürgen Hellfritz, Franz-Josef Hönig, Uwe Seeler (Cap), Werner Krämer, Hans Schulz.   Trainer: Kurt Koch
Goals: Di Nallo (19, 82)

AC MILAN v STANDARD LIÈGE 1-1 (1-0)
San Siro, Milano   13.03.1968
Referee: Juan Gardeazabal Garay (SPA)   Attendance: 55,146
AC MILAN: Fabio Cudicini; Angelo Anquilletti, Karl-Heinz Schnellinger; Giovanni Trapattoni, Saul Malatrasi, Roberto Rosato; Giorgio Rognoni, Giovanni Lodetti, Angelo Benedicto Sormani, Gianni Rivera (Cap), Pierino Prati.
Trainer: Nereo Rocco
STANDARD: Jean Nicolay; Jacques Beurlet, Jean Thissen, Nicolas Dewalque, Léon Jeck, Louis Pilot, Léon Semmeling (Cap), Velimir Naumovic, Roger Claessen, Jean-Paul Colonval, Casimir Jurkiewicz.   Trainer: Milorad Pavić
Goals: Rognoni (40), Jurkiewicz (73)

**HAMBURGER SV
v OLYMPIQUE LYONNAIS 2-0** (0-0)
Volksparkstadion, Hamburg   20.03.1968
Referee: Adrianus Aalbrecht (HOL)   Attendance: 59,174
HAMBURGER SV: Özcan Arkoç; Helmut Sandmann, Jürgen Kurbjuhn; Willi Schulz, Egon Horst, Hans Schulz; Holger Dieckmann, Franz-Josef Hönig, Uwe Seeler (Cap), Werner Krämer, Gert Dörfel.   Trainer: Kurt Koch
OLYMPIQUE: Yves Chauveau; Erwin Kuffer, Yves Flohic, Marcel Le Borgne, René Rocco, Robert Nouzaret, Raymond Schwinn, Jacques Pin, Fleury Di Nallo (Cap), Angel Rambert, Hector Maison.   Trainer: Louis Hon
Goals: Seeler (47, 59 pen)

AC MILAN v STANDARD LIÈGE 2-0 (1-0)
San Siro, Milano   20.03.1968
Referee: Roger Barde (FRA)   Attendance: 40,362
AC MILAN: Fabio Cudicini; Angelo Anquilletti, Karl-Heinz Schnellinger; Roberto Rosato, Saul Malatrasi, Nevio Scala; Kurt Hamrin, Giovanni Lodetti, Angelo Benedicto Sormani, Gianni Rivera (Cap), Pierino Prati.   Trainer: Nereo Rocco
STANDARD: Jean Nicolay; Jacques Beurlet, Jean Thissen, Nicolas Dewalque, Léon Jeck, Louis Pilot, Léon Semmeling (Cap), Velimir Naumovic, Roger Claessen, Drago Smajlovic, Casimir Jurkiewicz.   Trainer: Milorad Pavić
Goals: Prati (2), Rivera (48)

STANDARD LIÈGE v AC MILAN 1-1 (1-1)
Stade Maurice Dufrasne, Liège   28.02.1968
Referee: István Zsolt (HUN)   Attendance: 28,730
STANDARD: Jean Nicolay; Jacques Beurlet, Jean Thissen, Nicolas Dewalque, Léon Jeck; Louis Pilot, Léon Semmeling (Cap), Velimir Naumovic, Roger Claessen, Drago Smajlovic, Jean-Paul Colonval.   Trainer: Milorad Pavić
AC MILAN: Fabio Cudicini; Angelo Anquilletti, Karl-Heinz Schnellinger; Giovanni Trapattoni, Bruno Bavoni, Roberto Rosato; Nevio Scala, Giovanni Lodetti, Angelo Benedicto Sormani, Gianni Rivera (Cap), Pierino Prati.
Trainer: Nereo Rocco
Goals: Prati (20), Claessen (33)

CARDIFF CITY v TORPEDO MOSKVA 1-0 (1-0)
Ninian Park, Cardiff   6.03.1968
Referee: Robert Schaut (BEL)   Attendance: 30,526
CITY: Robert Wilson; Stephen Clifford Derrett, Robert Ferguson; Malcolm Clarke, Donald Murray (Cap), Brian Harris; Barrie Spencer Jones, Bryn Jones, Peter King, John Toshack, Ronald Bird.   Manager: James Scoular
TORPEDO: Anzor Kavazashvili; Grigori Yanets, Leonid Pakhomov, Vladimir Nepomiluev, Aleksandr Chumakov; Viktor Shustikov (Cap), Aleksandr Leniev, Eduard Streltsov, Vladimir Scherbakov, Vladimir Brednev, David Pais.
Trainer: Valentin Ivanov
Goal: Barrie Jones (44)

TORPEDO MOSKVA v CARDIFF CITY 1-0 (1-0)

Pakhtakor, Tashkent   19.03.1968

Referee: Bertil Lööw (SWE)   Attendance: 37,049

TORPEDO: Anzor Kavazashvili; Aleksandr Chumakov, Leonid Pakhomov, Viktor Shustikov (Cap), Grigori Yanets, Aleksandr Leniev, Aleksandr Stenischev, Vladimir Scherbakov, Eduard Streltsov, Mikhail Gershkovich, David Pais. Trainer: Valentin Ivanov

CITY: Robert Wilson; Stephen Clifford Derrett, Robert Ferguson; Malcolm Clarke, Donald Murray (Cap), Brian Harris; Barrie Spencer Jones, Norman Dean, Peter King, John Toshack, Ronald Bird.   Manager: James Scoular

Goal: Gershkovich (43)

CARDIFF CITY v HAMBURGER SV 2-3 (1-1)

Ninian Park, Cardiff   1.05.1968

Referee: Laurens van Ravens (HOL)   Attendance: 43,070

CARDIFF CITY: Robert Wilson; David Carver, Robert Ferguson; Norman Dean, Donald Murray (Cap), Brian Harris; Barrie Spencer Jones, Malcolm Clarke, Peter King, John Toshack, Leslie Lea.   Manager: James Scoular

HAMBURGER SV: Özcan Arkoç; Helmut Sandmann, Jürgen Kurbjuhn; Hans Schulz, Egon Horst, Hans-Jürgen Hellfritz; Holger Dieckmann, Werner Krämer, Uwe Seeler (Cap), Franz-Josef Hönig, Gert Dörfel.   Trainer: Kurt Koch

Goals: Dean (11), Hönig (15, 90), Seeler (57), Harris (78)

CARDIFF CITY v TORPEDO MOSKVA 1-0 (1-0)

Rosenau, Augsburg   3.04.1968

Referee: Helmut Fritz (W. GER)   Attendance: 28,581

CITY: Robert Wilson; Graham Coldrick, Robert Ferguson; Malcolm Clarke, Richard Morgan, Brian Harris (Cap); Barrie Spencer Jones, Norman Dean, Peter King, John Toshack, Ronald Bird.   Manager: James Scoular

TORPEDO: Anzor Kavazashvili; Vladimir Nepomiluev, Leonid Pakhomov, Grigori Yanets, Valeri Voronin, Viktor Shustikov (Cap); Aleksandr Leniev, Aleksandr Stenischev, Mikhail Gershkovich, Eduard Streltsov, Vladimir Scherbakov. Trainer: Valentin Ivanov

Goal: Dean (42)

AC MILAN v BAYERN MÜNCHEN 2-0 (0-0)

Stadio San Siro, Milano   1.05.1968

Referee: Salvador Campos García (POR)   Att: 70,158

AC MILAN: Fabio Cudicini, Angelo Anquilletti, Karl-Heinz Schnellinger; Giovanni Trapattoni, Saul Malatrasi, Roberto Rosato; Giovanni Lodetti, Kurt Hamrin, Angelo Benedicto Sormani, Gianni Rivera (Cap), Pierino Prati. Trainer: Nereo Rocco

BAYERN: Josef Maier; Peter Kupferschmidt, Georg Schwarzenbeck, Werner Olk (Cap), Peter Werner, Franz Beckenbauer, Gustav Jung, Rainer Ohlhauser, Gerhard Müller, Franz Roth, Dieter Brenninger.   Trainer: Zlatko Čajkovski

Goals: Sormani (51), Prati (74)

SEMI-FINALS

HAMBURGER SV v CARDIFF CITY 1-1 (0-1)

Volksparkstadion, Hamburg   24.04.1968

Referee: José María Ortiz de Mendíbil (SPA)   Att: 64,410

HAMBURGER SV: Özcan Arkoç; Helmut Sandmann, Jürgen Kurbjuhn; Hans-Jürgen Hellfritz, Egon Horst, Holger Dieckmann; Hans Schulz, Werner Krämer, Heinz Libuda, Franz-Josef Hönig, Gert Dörfel (Cap).   Trainer: Kurt Koch

CARDIFF CITY: Robert Wilson; David Carver, Robert Ferguson; Norman Dean, Donald Murray (Cap), Brian Harris; Barrie Spencer Jones, Malcolm Clarke, Peter King, John Toshack, Leslie Lea.   Manager: James Scoular

Goals: Dean (5), Sandmann (69)

BAYERN MÜNCHEN v AC MILAN 0-0

Grünwalder Strasse, München   8.05.1968

Referee: Gottfried Dienst (SWI)   Attendance: 39,061

BAYERN: Josef Maier; Peter Kupferschmidt, Georg Schwarzenbeck, Werner Olk (Cap); Peter Werner, Franz Beckenbauer; Gustav Jung, Rainer Ohlhauser, Gerhard Müller, Franz Roth, Dieter Brenninger.   Trainer: Zlatko Čajkovski

AC MILAN: Fabio Cudicini, Saul Malatrasi, Angelo Anquilletti, Roberto Rosato, Karl-Heinz Schnellinger; Giovanni Trapattoni, Kurt Hamrin, Giovanni Lodetti, Angelo Benedicto Sormani, Gianni Rivera (Cap), Pierino Prati. Trainer: Nereo Rocco

FINAL

AC MILAN v HAMBURGER SV 2-0 (2-0)

Feyenoord, Rotterdam   23.05.1968

Referee: José María Ortiz de Mendíbil (SPA)   Att: 53,276

AC MILAN: Fabio Cudicini; Angelo Anquilletti, Roberto Rosato, Giovanni Trapattoni, Karl-Heinz Schnellinger; Giovanni Lodetti, Gianni Rivera (Cap), Nevio Scala; Kurt Hamrin, Angelo Benedicto Sormani, Pierino Prati. Trainer: Nereo Rocco

HAMBURGER SV: Özcan Arkoç; Helmut Sandmann, Willi Schulz, Holger Dieckmann, Jürgen Kurbjuhn; Werner Krämer, Egon Horst; Bernd Dörfel, Uwe Seeler (Cap), Franz-Josef Hönig, Gert Dörfel.   Trainer: Kurt Koch

Goals: Hamrin (3, 19)

(Panathinaikos), Buttigieg (Floriana), Tomé, José Maria, Armando (Vitória Setúbal), Nouwens, Pirard (NAC Breda), Wójcik (Wisla), Nell, Kiss, Stolcz (Vasas ETO), Kuna, Adamec, Martinkovic (Spartak Trnava), Melrose, Buchan, McMillan, Taylor, Petersen (Aberdeen), Jones, Venables (Tottenham), Constantin, Manea, Negrea, Soo, Avram (Steaua București), Vilar, Claramunt, Jara, Waldo (Valencia), Rambert, Bouassa, Maison (Olympique Lyon), Pilot, Colonval (Standard), Gershkovich, Pais, Scherbakov, Pakhomov, Voronin (Torpedo Moskva), Harris, Clarke (Cardiff City), Brenninger, Nafziger, Kupferschmidt, Beckenbauer, Jung, Koulmann (Bayern), Rognoni, Rivera (Milan), Sandmann, Dörfel, Krämer (Hamburger SV)

Own goals: Rainiala (HJK) for Wisla, Mestre (Valencia) for Bayern

Goalscorers European Cup-Winners' Cup 1967-68:

8 goals: Uwe Seeler (Hamburger SV)

7 goals: Gerhard Müller (Bayern München)

6 goals: Fleury Di Nallo (Olympique Lyonnais)

5 goals: Francis Munro (Aberdeen), Fernando ANSOLA Sanmartín (Valencia CF), José Maria Freitas Pereira PEDRAS (Vitória Setúbal), Angelo Sormani (Milan)

4 goals: James Storrie (Aberdeen), József Szaló (Györi Vasas ETO), Roger Claessen (Standard Liége), Kurt Hamrin, Pierino Prati (Milan)

3 goals: Jacobus Visschers (NAC Breda), László Györffi (Vasas ETO), James Greaves, James Robertson (Tottenham), Francisco García Paquito (Valencia), Eduard Streltsov (Torpedo Moskva), Norman Dean (Cardiff City), Franz-Josef Hönig (Hamburger SV)

2 goals: Kerkhoffs (Lausanne), Asparuhov (Levski), Guerreiro (Vitória Setúbal), Lendzion, Sykta, Skupnik (Wisla), Varsányi (Vasas ETO), Svec (Spartak Trnava), Smith (Aberdeen), Gilzean (Tottenham), Pin (Olympique Lyon), Jurkiewicz (Standard Liége), Barrie Jones, King, Brown, Toshack (Cardiff City), Ohlhauser (Bayern), Anquilletti (Milan), Dieckmann, H.Schulz, Kurbjuhn (Hamburger SV)

1 goal: Hafsteinsson (KR Reykjavík), Andreasen, Sørensen, Gaardsøe (Randers), Markovic (Austria Wien), Vardic, Musovic, Hlevnjak (Hajduk Split), Gilbert (Shamrock Rovers), Heger (Aris Bonnevoie), Pajo (HJK Helsinki), Fuglset, Arntzen (Fredrikstad), Trainor, Magill (Crusaders), Armbruster (Lausanne), Aki Dogan, Ender (Altay Izmir), Kalaitzidis

CUP WINNERS' CUP 1968-69

FIRST ROUND

Spartak Sofia (BUL), Union Berlin (GDR), Górnik Zabrze (POL), Dynamo Moscow (USSR) and Vasas ETO Györ (HUN) withdrew from the competition due to the political situation in Czechoslovakia.

**UNION SPORTIVE RUMELANGE
v SLIEMA WANDERERS 2-1** (1-0)
Stade de la Frontière, Esch-sur-Alzette 18.09.1968
Referee: Alfred Ott (W. GER)   Attendance: 2,199
US RUMELANGE: Ferrero; Jean Schlutter, Eisenbarth, Marcel Bertoldo, Maiolatesi, Bordignon, Kerschen, René Cardoni, Norbert Lesczcynski, Furio Cardoni, Wantz.
SLIEMA: Michael Sultana; Vincent "Lino" Falzon, Joseph Aquilina, Franz Falzon, George Micallef, Edward Darmanin, Ronald Cocks, Robert Buttigieg, Joseph Cini, John Bonett, Vincent Vassallo (.. Charles Spiteri).
Goals: Lesczcynski (21, 48), Cocks (58)

**SLIEMA WANDERERS
v UNION SPORTIVE RUMELANGE 1-0** (0-0)
The Empire Stadium, Valletta 29.09.1968
Referee: Alessandro d'Agostini (ITA)   Attendance: 12,929
SLIEMA: Michael Sultana; Vincent "Lino" Falzon, Joseph Aquilina, Robert Buttigieg, George Micallef, Edward Darmanin, Ronald Cocks, Franz Falzon, Joseph Cini, Joe Serge (.. Vincent Vassallo), John Bonett.
US RUMELANGE: Ferrero; Jean Schlutter (.. Jean Halsdorf), Eisenbarth, Pierre Turci, Maiolatesi, Bordignon, Keuschen (.. Marcel Bertoldo), René Cardoni, Norbert Lesczcynski, Furio Cardoni, Wantz.
Goal: F. Falzon (67)

ALTAY IZMIR v LYN OSLO 3-1 (1-0)
Alsançak, Izmir 18.09.1968
Referee: Iosif Ritter (ROM)   Attendance: 12,184
ALTAY: Sencer Tanzer; Yilmaz Canlisoy, Zinnur Sari; Enver Katip, Riza Senol, Ayfer Elmastasoglu; Behzat Cinar (.. Aydin Yelken), Aytekin Erhanoglu, Mustafa Denizli (.. Oğuz Boke), Feridun Öztürk, Roland Magnusson.
LYN: Svein Bjørn Olsen; Jan Rodvang, Helge Østvold, Andreas Morisbak, Trygve Christophersen, Sveinung Aarnseth, Knut Berg, Karl Johan Johannessen, Jan Berg, Ola Dybwad Olsen, Jon Palmer Austnes.   Trainer: Knut Osnet
Goals: Feridun (17), Austnes (62), Aytekin (83, 89)

LYN OSLO v ALTAY IZMIR 4-1 (2-0)
Ullevål, Oslo 2.10.1968
Referee: Gudmundsson (ICE)   Attendance: 13,768
LYN: Svein Bjørn Olsen; Jan Rodvang, Helge Østvold, Andreas Morisbak, Knut Kolle; Knut Berg, Trygve Christophersen, Jan Berg, Karl Johan Johannessen, Ola Dybwad Olsen, Jon Palmer Austnes.   Trainer: Knut Osnet
ALTAY: Sencer Tanzer; Yilmaz Canlisoy, Zinnur Sari; Enver Katip, Riza Senol, Necdet Tunca; Ayfer Elmastasoglu (.. Behzat Cinar, .. Oguz Boke), Aytekin Erhanoglu, Feridun Öztürk, Roland Magnusson, Mustafa Denizli.
Goals: K. Berg (40), K.J. Johannessen (44, 70), Mustafa (54), J. Berg (89)

CARDIFF CITY v FC PORTO 2-2 (1-0)
Ninian Park, Cardiff 18.09.1968
Referee: Gáspar Pintado Víu (SPA)   Attendance: 19,202
CARDIFF CITY: Frederick Davies; Stephen Derrett, Gary Bell, Melwyn Sutton, Donald Murray, Brian Harris, Barrie Jones, Brian Clark, Peter King, John Toshack, Ronald Bird.   Manager: James Scoular
FC PORTO: Américo Lopes; David Sucena, Bernardo da Velha, Valdemar Pacheco, ACÁCIO Carneiro, José ROLANDO Andrade Gonçalves, Fernando Neves Pavao (25 João CUSTÓDIO PINTO), Bernardo Francisco "CHICO" GORDO, Djalma Freitas, Eduardo GOMES, Francisco Lage Pereira da NOBREGA.   Trainer: José Maria PEDROTO
Goals: Toshack (24), Bird (50 pen), Custódio Pinto (60, 68)

FC PORTO v CARDIFF CITY 2-1 (1-0)
Estádio das Antas, Porto 2.10.1968
Referee: Robert Hélies (FRA)   Attendance: 55,000
FC PORTO: Américo Lopes; Bernardo da Velha, Valdemar Pacheco, João Eleutério Luis ATRACA, David Sucena, LISBOA Alberto Dias, Fernando Neves PAVÃO (60 José ROLANDO Andrade Gonçalves), João Custódio Pinto, Djalma Freitas (80 Malagueta Serafim MESQUITA), Eduardo GOMES, Francisco Lage Pereira da NOBREGA.   Trainer: José Maria PEDROTO
CARDIFF CITY: Frederick Davies; Graham Coldrick, Gary Bell, Melwyn Sutton, Donald Murray, Stephen Derrett, Barrie Jones, Brian Clark, Peter King, John Toshack, Leslie Lea (54 Leighton Phillips, 80 Ronald Bird).   Manager: James Scoular
Goals: Pavao (9), Toshack (51), Custódio Pinto (76)

PARTIZANI TIRANË v AC TORINO 1-0 (0-0)
Qemal Stafa, Tiranë 18.09.1968
Referee: Milivoje Gugulović (YUG)   Attendance: 19,000
PARTIZANI: Mikel Janku; Mihal Gjika, S.Gjika, Teodor Vaso, Ramazan Rragami, Lin Shllaku, Neptun Bajko, Xhevdet Shaqiri, Sabah Bizi, Panajot Pano, Robert Jashari (45 Ciraku).   Trainer: Loro Boriçi
AC TORINO: Lido Vieri; Fabrizio Poletti, Natalino Fossati, Giorgio Puia, Angelo Cereser, Bruno Bolchi, Alberto Carelli (30 Emiliano Mondonico), Giorgio Ferrini, Piero Baisi, Gianbattista Moschino, Carlo Facchin (56 Renzo Corni).   Trainer: Edmondo Fabbri
Goal: Shaqiri (46)

AC TORINO v PARTIZANI TIRANË 3-1 (2-0)
Stadio Comunale, Torino 2.10.1968
Referee: Josef Krnavec (CZE)   Attendance: 22,408
AC TORINO: Lido Vieri; Mario Trebbi, Natalino Fossati, Giorgio Puia, Angelo Cereser, Bruno Bolchi (10 Alberto Carelli), Emiliano Mondonico (70 Renzo Corni), Aldo Agroppi, Nestor Combin, Gianbattista Moschino, Carlo Facchin.   Trainer: Edmondo Fabbri
PARTIZANI: Mikel Janku; Mihal Gjika, S.Gjika, Teodor Vaso, Shule, Lin Shllaku, Neptun Bajko, Ramazan Rragami, Sabah Bizi, Panajot Pano (76 Ciraku), Xhevdet Shaqiri.   Trainer: Loro Boriçi
Goals: Carelli (22), Facchin (28), Mondonico (59), Bajko (85)

GIRONDINS de BORDEAUX v 1.FC KÖLN 2-1 (1-1)
Stade Municipal, Bordeaux 18.09.1968
Referee: Jef F. Dorpmans (HOL)   Attendance: 18,385
GIRONDINS: Christian Montes; Robert Peri, André Chorda, Bernard Baudet, Didier Desremeaux, Guy Calleja, Jean-Louis Massé, Felix Burdino, Didier Couécou, Jacques Simon, Claude Petyt (90 Gabriel Abossolo).   Trainer: Jean-Pierre Bakrim
1.FC KÖLN: Paul Heyeres; Fritz Pott, Matthias Hemmersbach, Peter Blusch, Wolfgang Weber, Heinz Simmet, Karl-Heinz Rühl, Werner Biskup, Heinz Flohe, Wolfgang Overath, Heinz Hornig.   Trainer: Hans Merkle
Goals: Petyt (19), Rühl (26), Massé (56)

1.FC KÖLN v GIRONDINS de BORDEAUX 3-0 (2-0)
Müngersdorferstadion, Köln 2.10.1968
Referee: Leo Callaghan (WAL)   Attendance: 22,976
1.FC KÖLN: Paul Heyeres; Karl-Heinz Thielen, Matthias Hemmersbach, Peter Blusch, Wolfgang Weber, Werner Biskup, Heinz Flohe, Heinz Simmet, Karl-Heinz Rühl, Wolfgang Overath, Heinz Hornig.   Trainer: Hans Merkle
GIRONDINS: Christian Montes; Robert Peri, André Chorda, Bernard Baudet, Didier Desremeaux (60 Edouard Wojciak), Guy Calleja, Jean-Louis Massé (.. Gérard Papin), Felix Burdino, Didier Couécou, Jacques Simon, Claude Petyt.   Trainer: Jean-Pierre Bakrim
Goals: Blusch (20), Overath (22), Rühl (53 pen)

SLOVAN BRATISLAVA v FK BOR 3-0 (0-0)
Tehelné pole, Bratislava 18.09.1968
Referee: Ferdinand Marschall (AUS)   Attendance: 5,942
SLOVAN: Alexander Vencel; Peter Mutkovic, Ján Zlocha, Ľudevít Zlocha, Alexander Horváth, Milan Sokol, Ludovit Cvetler, Ladislav Móder (.. Bohumil Bizon), Ivan Hrdlička, Karol Jokl, Ján Čapkovič.   Trainer: Michal Vičan
FK BOR: Jovan Hajduković; Desimir Ranković, Perić, Perisić, Radulović, Rajzner, Petrović, Dušan Sopić, Mitrović, Slobodan Tomić, Pogarcić (.. Sorban).   Trainer: Zigante
Goals: Jokl (48, 69), Hrdlička (80)

FK BOR v SLOVAN BRATISLAVA 2-0 (1-0)
Gradski, Bor 2.10.1968
Referee: Efstathios Papavasiliou (GRE)   Attendance: 2,740
FK BOR: Jovan Hajduković; Desimir Ranković, Perić, V. Petrović (.. Stevan Komljenović), Radulović, Rajzner, T. Petrović, Dušan Sopić, Mitrović, Slobodan Tomić, Pogarcić.   Trainer: Zigante
SLOVAN: Kontir; Ľudevít Zlocha, Ján Popluhár, Ján Zlocha, Alexander Horváth, Milan Sokol, Ludovit Cvetler, Jozef Čapkovič, Ivan Hrdlička, Karol Jokl (.. Ladislav Móder), Ján Čapkovič.   Trainer: Michal Vičan
Goals: Ranković (42 pen), Tomić (59)

**DUNFERMLINE ATHLETIC
v APOEL NICOSIA 10-1** (5-0)
East End Park, Dunfermline 18.09.1968
Referee: Kare Sirevaag (NOR)   Attendance: 7,167
DUNFERMLINE: Bent Martin, William Callaghan, John Lunn, John McGarty, Roy Barry, Willie Renton, Hugh Robertson, Robert Paton (..Thomas Callaghan), Alexander Edwards, Ian Lister (.. Ian Cowan), Pat Gardner. Manager: George Farm
APOEL: Theodoros Theodorides; Lefteris Poulias, Dimitris Hiotis, Solis Andreou, Stelios Haritakis, Stefanis Mihail, Nikos Kantzilieris, Andreas Antoniadis (.. Spyros Kettenis), Nikos Agathokleous, Andreas Hristodoulou (.. Papageorgiou), Andres Stylianou.
Goals: Robertson (9, 46), Barry (17), Gardner (19), Renton (26, 86), Edwards (44), W. Callaghan (57, 65), Th. Callaghan (70), Stylianou (74)

**APOEL NICOSIA
v DUNFERMLINE ATHLETIC 0-2** (0-0)
Makarios Athletic Centre, Nicosia 2.10.1968
Referee: Francesco Francescon (ITA)   Attendance: 3,200
APOEL: Kostas Vasileiou; Lefteris Poulias, Mihalis Kolokasis, Solis Andreou, Stelios Haritakis, Stefanis Mihail, Nikos Kantzilieris, Andreas Stylianou, Leonidas Leonidou, Andreas Hristodoulou, Spyros Kettenis.
DUNFERMLINE: Bent Martin; William Callaghan, John Lunn, Jim Fraser, James Thomson, Willie Renton, Hugh Robertson (.. George McKimmie), Robert Paton, Alexander Edwards, Pat Gardner, Ian Lister.   Manager: George Farm
Goals: Gardner (57), W. Callaghan (84)

**CLUB BRUGGE KV
v WEST BROMWICH ALBION 3-1** (1-1)
Albert Dyserynckstadion, Brugge 18.09.1968
Referee: Frede Hansen (DEN)   Attendance: 14,724
CLUB BRUGGE: Fernand Boone; Freddy Hinderijckx, John Moelaert, Gilbert Marmenout, Kurt Axelsson, Erwin Vandendaele, Johnny Thio, Stefan Reisch, Pierre Carteus, Raoul Lambert, Tom Turesson (65 Gilbert Bailliu). Trainer: Milorad Pavić
WEST BROMWICH ALBION: John Osborne, Douglas Fraser, Graham Williams, Anthony Brown, John Talbut, John Kaye, Ronald Rees, Asa Hartford, Jeffrey Astle (57 Graham Lovett), Robert Hope, Clive Clark.   Manager: Alan Ashman
Goals: Thio (26), Hartford (34), Lambert (51), Bailliu (73)

**WEST BROMWICH ALBION
v CLUB BRUGGE KV 2-0** (2-0)
The Hawthorns, West Bromwich 2.10.1968
Referee: Einar Boström (SWE)   Attendance: 33,747
WEST BROMWICH ALBION: John Osborne; Douglas Fraser, Graham Williams, Anthony Brown, John Talbut, John Kaye, Ronald Rees, Asa Hartford (65 Ian Collard), Jeffrey Astle, Robert Hope, Clive Clark.   Manager: Alan Ashman
CLUB BRUGGE: Fernand Boone; Freddy Hinderijckx, John Moelaert, Gilbert Marmenout, Kurt Axelsson, Erwin Vandendaele, Johnny Thio, Stefan Reisch (57 André Vanderlinden), Pierre Carteus, Raoul Lambert, Walter Loske (70 Gilbert Bailliu).   Trainer: Milorad Pavić
Goals: Brown (14), Hartford (43)

FC LUGANO v FC BARCELONA 0-1 (0-0)
Stadio Comunale di Cornaredo, Lugano 18.09.1968
Referee: Roger Machin (FRA)   Attendance: 9,541
FC LUGANO: Mario Prosperi; Bernard Mocellin (79 Simonetto Simonetti), Ernesto Indemini, Flavio Signorelli, Remo Pullica, Adriano Coduri, Vicenzo Brenna, Gérard Coinçon (81 Gerhard Lusenti), Heinz Blumer, Otto Luttrop, Antonio Chiesa.   Trainer: Louis Maurer
FC BARCELONA: Salvador SADURNÍ Urpi; Antonio TORRES García, ELADIO Silvestre Graells, P.FERNÁNDEZ, Francisco Fernández Rodríguez "GALLEGO", Pedro María ZABALZA Inda, Juan Díaz Sánchez "JUANITO" (46 Ángel OLIVEROS Jiménez), Carlos PELLICER Vázquez, Jorge Alberto MENDOZA Paulino, Jesús María PEREDA Ruiz de Temiño, Carlos REXACH Cerdá.   Trainer: Salvador Artigas
Goal: Zabalza (76)

FC BARCELONA v FC LUGANO 3-0 (0-0)
Camp Nou, Barcelona 2.10.1968
Referee: John Wright Paterson (SCO)   Attendance: 38,740
FC BARCELONA: Salvador SADURNÍ Urpi; Antonio TORRES García, ELADIO Silvestre Graells, P. FERNÁNDEZ (46 Jesús María PEREDA Ruiz de Temiño), Francisco Fernández Rodríguez "GALLEGO", Pedro María ZABALZA Inda, Juan Díaz Sánchez "JUANITO", José Antonio ZALDÚA Urdanavia, Jorge Alberto MENDOZA Paulino, José María FUSTÉ Blanch (85 Carlos PELLICER Vázquez), Carlos REXACH Cerdá.   Trainer: Salvador Artigas
FC LUGANO: Mario Prosperi; Bernard Mocellin, Ernesto Indemini, Flavio Signorelli, Remo Pullica, Adriano Coduri, Vicenzo Brenna, Gérard Coinçon (53 Gerhard Lusenti), Heinz Blumer, Otto Luttrop, Antonio Chiesa.   Trainer: Louis Maurer
Goals: Mendoza (75, 90), Zaldúa (83)

CRUSADERS BELFAST
v IFK NORRKÖPING 2-2 (1-1)

Seaview, Belfast   18.09.1968

Referee: Vital Loraux (BEL)   Attendance: 8,000

CRUSADERS: Terry Nicholson; James McGuinness, William Cathcart, Walter McFarland (.. Alex Anderson), Albert Campbell, John McPolin, Frank McArdle (.. James Burke), John Jamison, Joseph Meldrum, Ivan Parke, Liam Wilson.

IFK: Bengt Lindström; Bert-Ottar Blom, Roland Pressfeldt, Torbjörn Jonsson, Björn Nordqvist, Björn Franzen, Hans Larsson, Christer Hult (..Krister Norblad), Ulf Hultberg, Sven Evert Hesselgren, Lars Berglund.   Trainer: Gunnar Nordahl

Goals: Hult (42), Hultberg (53), Jamison (40), Parke (77)

SHAMROCK ROVERS
v RANDERS FREJA 1-2 (0-1)

Glenmalure Park, Dublin   2.10.1968

Referee: Michel Kitabdjian (FRA)   Attendance: 15,818

SHAMROCK ROVERS: Michael Smyth; James Gregg, Patrick Courtney (.. Thomas Kinsella), Damien Richardson, John Fullam, Frank Brady, Francis O'Neill, William Dixon, Robert Gilbert, Michael Leech (.. William Tuohy), Michael Lawlor.

RANDERS FREJA: Alfred Mogensen; Mogens Kaarup, Jørgen Rasmussen, Per Lykke, Ole Nielsen, Helge Vonsyld, Erik Sørensen, John Andreasen, Per Gaardsøe, Hans Berg Andersen, Anders Bødker.   Trainer: Juan Ramón Rodríguez

Goals: Gaardsøe (22), Fullam (53), Andreasen (57)

IFK NORRKÖPING
v CRUSADERS BELFAST 4-1 (3-0)

Idrottsparken, Norrköping   2.10.1968

Referee: Tage Sørensen (DEN)   Attendance: 8,000

IFK: Bengt Lindström; Bert-Ottar Blom, Roland Pressfeldt, Torbjörn Jonsson, Björn Franzen, Björn Nordqvist, Hans Larsson, Krister Norblad, Ulf Hultberg (.. Bo La Fleur, .. Christer Hult), Sven Evert Hesselgren, Lars Berglund.
Trainer: Gunnar Nordahl

CRUSADERS: Terry Nicholson; Alex Anderson, James McGuinness (.. Jackie Bell), Walter McFarland (.. James Hume), Albert Campbell, John McPolin, Frank McArdle, John Jamison, Ivan Parke, Joseph Meldrum, Liam Wilson.

Goals: Norblad (10, 37), Hultberg (21, 54), McPolin (55)

ADO Den HAAG v GRAZER AK 4-1 (1-1)

Zuiderpark, Den Haag   19.09.1968

Referee: Antoine Quedeville (LUX)   Attendance: 26,000

ADO: Ton Thie; Theo Van den Burch, Kees Weimar, Aad Mansveld, Harry Vos, Joop Jochems (.. Dick Advocaat), Piet De Zoete, Piet Giesen, Harry Heijnen, Lex Schoenmaker, Kees Aarts.   Trainer: Eddie Hartmann

GAK: Gerfried Hodschar (60 Rumpf); Gerald Erkinger, Erich Frisch, Erwin Ninaus, Günther Klug; Hermann Stessl, Heinz Schilcher, Walter Koleznik, Josef Stering (.. Weiss), Erwin Hohenwarter, Stovic.   Trainer: Fritz Kominek

Goals: Hohenwarter (40), Giesen (41, 69), Schoenmaker (53), Aarts (57)

RANDERS FREJA
v SHAMROCK ROVERS DUBLIN 1-0 (0-0)

Randers stadion, Freja   18.09.1968

Referee: Hans Joachim Weyland (W. GER)   Att: 9,029

RANDERS FREJA: Alfred Mogensen; Mogens Kaarup, Jørgen Rasmussen, Per Lykke, Ole Nielsen, Helge Vonsyld, John Andreasen (.. Petersen), Anders Bødker, Per Gaardsøe, Hans Berg Andersen, Erik Sørensen.
Trainer: Juan Ramón Rodríguez

SHAMROCK ROVERS: Michael Smyth; Patrick Courtney, James Gregg, William Dixon, Frank Brady, John Fullam, Thomas Kinsella, Michael Leech, Robert Gilbert, Francis O'Neill, Damien Richardson.

Goal: Gaardsøe (88)

GRAZER AK v ADO Den HAAG 0-2 (0-1)

Bundesstadion Liebenau, Graz   3.10.1968

Referee: Othmar Huber (SWI)   Attendance: 3,000

GAK: Rumpf; Gerald Erkinger (86 Weiss), Erich Frisch, Erwin Ninaus, Günther Klug; Walter Koleznik, Ferdinand Eckhart, Heinz Schilcher, Gerhard Krois, Erwin Hohenwarter, Stovic (55 Karl Phillipp).   Trainer: Fritz Kominek

ADO: Ton Thie; Theo Van den Burch, Kees Weimar (56 Joop Jochems), Aad Mansveld, Harry Vos, Jan Van den Oever, Piet De Zoete, Piet Giesen, Harry Heijnen, Lex Schoenmaker, Kees Aarts.   Trainer: Eddie Hartmann

Goals: Heijnen (16, 89)

**OLYMPIAKOS PEIRAIAS
v KR REYKJAVÍK 2-0** (1-0)

Karaiskaki, Athina 20.09.1968

Referee: Konstantin Dinov (BUL) Attendance: 22,000

OLYMPIAKOS: Nikos Tsortsis; Giannis Gkaitatzis, Orestis Pavlidis, Grigorois Aganian (46 Vasilis Siokos), Hristos Zanteroglou, Nikos Sideris, Paulos Vasileiou, Giorgos Sideris, Giorgos Stolingas, Nikos Gioutsos, Vasilis Botinos. Trainer: Ljubisa Spajić

KR: Gudmundur Pétursson; Björn Arnason, Arsaell Kjartansson, Kristinn Jónsson, Ellert Schram, Halldór Björnsson, Hördur Markan, Eyleifur Hafsteinsson, Olafur Lárusson, Thorolfur Beck, Gunnar Felixson

Goals: Botinos (45), Zanteroglou (90)

IFK NORRKÖPING v LYN OSLO 3-2 (1-1)

Idrottspark, Norrköping 17.11.1968

Referee: Martti Hirviniemi (FIN) Attendance: 2,275

IFK: Bengt Lindström; Bert-Ottar Blom, Roland Pressfeldt, Bill Björklund, Björn Nordqvist, Hans Larsson, Bo La Fleur (..Krister Norblad), Torbjörn Jonsson, Ulf Hultberg, Sven Evert Hesselgren, Lars Berglund. Trainer: Gunnar Nordahl

LYN: Svein Bjørn Olsen; Jan Rodvang, Helge Østvold, Andreas Morisbak, Knut Kolle, Knut Berg, Karl Johan Johannessen, Jan Berg, Harald Berg, Ola Dybwad Olsen, Jon Palmer Austnes. Trainer: Knut Osnet

Goals: Hultberg (1, 51), H. Berg (40), Austnes (50), Hesselgren (65)

**KR REYKJAVÍK
v OLYMPIAKOS PEIRAIAS 0-2** (0-1)

Kautatzogleio, Thessaloniki 22.09.1968

Referee: Konstantin Dinov (BUL) Attendance: 8,000

KR: Gudmundur Pétursson; Arsaell Kjartansson, Gunnarsson, Kristinn Jónsson, Ellert Schram, Halldór Björnsson, Hördur Markan, Eyleifur Hafsteinsson, Olafur Lárusson, Thorolfur Beck, Gunnar Felixson

OLYMPIAKOS: Nikos Tsortsis; Giannis Gkaitatzis, Orestis Pavlidis, Vasilis Siokos, Hristos Zanteroglou, Nikos Sideris, Paulos Vasileiou (46 Vasilis Liakos), Giorgos Sideris, Giorgos Stolingas, Nikos Gioutsos, Vasilis Botinos. Trainer: Ljubisa Spajić

Goals: Gioutsos (23), Stolingas (60)

ADO Den HAAG v FC KÖLN 0-1 (0-0)

Zuiderpark, Den Haag 12.11.1968

Referee: Roger Machin (FRA) Attendance: 23,246

ADO: Ton Thie; Theo Van den Burch, Jan Van den Oever, Kees Weimar, Harry Vos, Piet De Zoete, Lex Schoenmaker, Piet Giesen, Harry Heijnen, Lambert Maassen, Kees Aarts. Trainer: Eddie Hartmann

FC KÖLN: Paul Heyeres; Karl-Heinz Thielen, Wolfgang Weber, Werner Biskup, Peter Blusch, Heinz Simmet, Wolfgang Overath, Heinz Flohe, Johannes Löhr (70 Jürgen Jendrossek), Bernhard Hermes, Heinz Hornig. Trainer: Hans Merkle

Goal: Jendrossek (88)

SECOND ROUND

LYN OSLO v IFK NORRKÖPING 2-0 (1-0)

Ullevål, Oslo 31.10.1968

Referee: Vital Loraux (BEL) Attendance: 4,912

LYN: Svein Bjørn Olsen; Jan Rodvang, Helge Østvold, Andreas Morisbak, Knut Kolle, Knut Berg, Karl Johan Johannessen, Jan Berg, Harald Berg, Ola Dybwad Olsen, Jon Palmer Austnes. Trainer: Knut Osnet

IFK: Bengt Lindström; Bert-Ottar Blom, Roland Pressfeldt, Björn Franzen, Björn Nordqvist, Hans Larsson, Torbjörn Jonsson, Bo La Fleur (..Krister Norblad), Ulf Hultberg, Christer Hult (..Sven Evert Hesselgren), Lars Berglund. Trainer: Gunnar Nordahl

Goals: K. Berg (40), H. Berg (57)

FC KÖLN v ADO Den HAAG 3-0 (1-0)

Müngersdorferstadion, Köln 27.11.1968

Referee: Ronald J.P.Jones (WAL) Attendance: 23,304

FC KÖLN: Paul Heyeres; Karl-Heinz Thielen, Heinz Simmet, Wolfgang Weber, Werner Biskup, Peter Blusch, Wolfgang Overath, Bernhard Hermes, Karl-Heinz Rühl (30 Jürgen Jendrossek), Johannes Löhr, Heinz Hornig (45 Matthias Hemmersbach). Trainer: Hans Merkle

ADO: Ton Thie; Theo Van den Burch, Aad Mansveld, Jan Van den Oever, Harry Vos, Piet De Zoete, Lex Schoenmaker, Piet Giesen, Harry Heijnen, Lambert Maassen, Kees Aarts. Trainer: Eddie Hartmann

Goals: Löhr (3, 53), Blusch (72)

DINAMO BUCUREȘTI
v WEST BROMWICH ALBION 1-1 (1-1)

23 August, București   13.11.1968

Referee: Hans-Joachim Weyland (GER)   Attendance: 15,000

DINAMO: Ilie Datcu; Cornel Popa, Alexandru Boc, Cornel Dinu, Constantin Ștefan; Vasile Gergely (78 Viorel Sălceanu), Mircea Stoenescu, Ion Pîrcălab, Mircea Lucescu, Florea Dumitrache, Ion Haidu (56 Radu Nunweiller).
Trainer: Bazil Marian

W.B.A.: John Osborne; Douglas Fraser, Ramon „Ray" Wilson, Anthony Brown, John Talbut, John Kaye (84 Graham Lovett), Ronald Rees, Ian Collard, Jeffrey Astle, Robert Hope, Asa Hartford.   Manager: Alan Ashman

Sent off: Rees (75)

Goals: Dumitrache (23), Hartford (28)

WEST BROMWICH ALBION
v DINAMO BUCUREȘTI 4-0 (2-0)

The Hawthorns, West Bromwich   27.11.1968

Referee: Robert Héliès (FRA)   Attendance: 33,059

WBA: John Osborne; Douglas Fraser, Ramon „Ray" Wilson, Anthony Brown, John Talbut, John Kaye, Clive Clark, Graham Lovett, Jeffrey Astle, Robert Hope, Asa Hartford.
Manager: Alan Ashman

DINAMO: Ilie Datcu, Cornel Popa, Alexandru Boc, Cornel Dinu, Constantin Ștefan; Vasile Gergely, Mircea Stoenescu, Ion Pîrcălab (52 Viorel Sălceanu), Radu Nunweiller, Florea Dumitrache, Ion Haidu (76 Constantin Frățilă).
Trainer: Bazil Marian

Goals: Lovett (35), Brown (44, 52 pen), Astle (72)

RANDERS FREJA FC
v SLIEMA WANDERERS 6-0 (2-0)

Randers stadion, Freja   13.11.1968

Referee: Jacques Colling (LUX)   Attendance: 7,120

RANDERS FREJA: Alfred Mogensen; Mogens Kaarup, Jørgen Rasmussen, Per Lykke, Ole Nielsen, Knud Olesen, Erik Sørensen, Anders Bødker, Per Gaardsøe (.. John Andreasen), Hans Berg Andersen, Petersen.
Trainer: Juan Ramón Rodríguez

SLIEMA: Alfred Vella (46 Michael Sultana); Charles Spiteri, Joseph Aquilina, Robert Buttigieg, George Micallef, Edward Darmanin, Ronald Cocks, Joe Serge, Joseph Cini, John Bonett, Franz Falzon.

Goals: Andersen (3, 85), Olesen (35), Bødker (53), Sørensen (55), Lykke (65 pen)

SLIEMA WANDERERS
v RANDERS FREJA 0-2 (0-1)

The Empire Stadium, Valletta   27.11.1968

Referee: Antonio Sbardella (ITA)   Attendance: 3,996

SLIEMA: Michael Sultana; Vincent "Lino" Falzon, Charles Spiteri, Bernard Sultana, George Micallef, Robert Buttigieg, Ronald Cocks, John Bonett, Joseph Farrugia (.. Lawrence Borg), Joe Serge, Vincent Vassallo.

RANDERS FREJA: Alfred Mogensen; Mogens Kaarup, Jørgen Rasmussen, Per Lykke, Ole Nielsen, Knud Olesen (.. Leo Jensen), Erik Sørensen, Helge Vonsyld, Per Gaardsøe, Hans Berg Andersen, Anders Bødker.
Trainer: Juan Ramón Rodríguez

Goals: Gaardsøe (23, 65)

FC PORTO v SLOVAN BRATISLAVA 1-0 (1-0)

Estádio das Antas, Porto   13.11.1968

Referee: Malcolm Wright (NIR)   Attendance: 20,748

FC PORTO: Américo Lopes; Bernardo da Velha, Valdemar Pacheco, João Eleutério Luis ATRACA, ACÁCIO Carneiro, José ROLANDO Andrade Gonçalves, João Custódio Pinto, Humberto FRANCISCO BAPTISTA Silva (46 VÍTOR GOMES), Djalma Freitas, Eduardo GOMES (46 Bernardo Francisco "CHICO" GORDO), Francisco Lage Pereira da NOBREGA.
Trainer: José Maria PEDROTO

SLOVAN: Alexander Vencel; Ľudevít Zlocha (46 Vladimir Hrivňák), Ján Popluhár, Ján Zlocha, Alexander Horváth, Ivan Hrdlička, Bohumil Bizon, Ludovit Cvetler, Jozef Čapkovič, Karol Jokl, Ján Čapkovič.   Trainer: Michal Vičan

Goal: Custódio Pinto (34)

SLOVAN BRATISLAVA v FC PORTO 4-0 (1-0)

Tehelné pole, Bratislava   27.11.1968

Referee: Dogan Babacan (TUR)   Attendance: 7,776

SLOVAN: Alexander Vencel; Peter Mutkovic, Vladimir Hrivňák, Ján Zlocha, Alexander Horváth, Jozef Čapkovič (86 Bohumil Bizon), Ludovit Cvetler, Karol Jokl, Ivan Hrdlička, Ladislav Móder, Ján Čapkovič.   Trainer: Michal Vičan

FC PORTO: Américo Lopes; Bernardo da Velha, Valdemar Pacheco, João Eleutério Luis ATRACA, David Sucena, José ROLANDO Andrade Gonçalves, João CUSTÓDIO PINTO, LISBOA Alberto Dias (55 VÍTOR GOMES), Djalma Freitas, Fernando Neves Pavao, Francisco Lage Pereira da NOBREGA.
Trainer: José Maria PEDROTO

Goals: Ján Čapkovič (22), Jokl (48, 88 pen), Jozef Čapkovič (84)

DUNFERMLINE ATHLETIC
v OLYMPIAKOS PEIRAIAS 4-0 (0-0)
East End Park, Dunfermline   13.11.1968

Referee: Henry Öberg (NOR)   Attendance: 7,000

DUNFERMLINE: Bent Martin; William Callaghan, John Lunn, Jim Fraser, Roy Barry, Willie Renton, Hugh Robertson (.. Ian Lister), Robert Paton (..Thomas Callaghan), Alexander Edwards, Pat Gardner, Barrie Mitchell.
Manager: George Farm

OLYMPIAKOS: Dimitris Xarhakos; Hristos Zanteroglou, Giannis Gkaitatzis, Orestis Pavlidis, Grigoris Aganian, Vasilis Siokos, Paulos Vasileiou, Giorgos Sideris, Giorgos Stolingas, Nikos Gioutsos, Vasilis Botinos.   Trainer: Ljubisa Spajić

Goals: Mitchell (48), Edwards (55, 77), Fraser (80)

OLYMPIAKOS PEIRAIAS
v DUNFERMLINE ATHLETIC 3-0 (3-0)
Karaiskaki, Peiraias   27.11.1968

Referee: Josef Krnavek (CZE)   Attendance: 20,000

OLYMPIAKOS: Dimitris Xarhakos; Hristos Zanteroglou, Giannis Gkaitatzis, Orestis Pavlidis, Grigorois Aganian, Vasilis Siokos, Paulos Vasileiou, Giorgos Sideris, Giorgos Stolingas, Nikos Gioutsos (78 Miltiadis Koumarias), Vasilis Botinos.
Trainer: Ljubisa Spajić

DUNFERMLINE: Bent Martin, William Callaghan, John Lunn, Jim Fraser, Roy Barry (.. James Thomson), Willie Renton, Hugh Robertson (.. Alex Totten), Barrie Mitchell, Alexander Edwards, Pat Gardner, Ian Lister.
Manager: George Farm

Goals: Stolingas (10), Botinos (29), Vasileiou (32)

QUARTER-FINALS

DUNFERMLINE ATHLETIC
v WEST BROMWICH ALBION 0-0
East End Park, Dunfermline   15.01.1969

Referee: Helmut Fritz (W. GER)   Attendance: 22,000

DUNFERMLINE: William Duff; Alex Totten (58 James Thomson), John Lunn, Jim Fraser, Roy Barry, Willie Renton, Hugh Robertson, Robert Paton, Alexander Edwards, Pat Gardner, Ian Lister.   Manager: George Farm

WEST BROMWICH ALBION: John Osborne; Douglas Fraser, Ramon „Ray" Wilson, Anthony Brown, John Talbut, John Kaye, Robert Hope, Graham Lovett, Jeffrey Astle, Ian Collard, Asa Hartford (90 Richard Krzywicki).
Manager: Alan Ashman

WEST BROMWICH ALBION
v DUNFERMLINE ATHLETIC 0-1 (0-1)
The Hawthorns, West Bromwich   19.02.1969

Referee: William A. O'Neill (IRE)   Attendance: 32,269

WEST BROMWICH ALBION: John Osborne; Douglas Fraser, Ramon „Ray" Wilson, Anthony Brown, John Talbut, John Kaye, Dennis Martin, Graham Lovett, Jeffrey Astle, Ian Collard, Asa Hartford.   Manager: Alan Ashman

DUNFERMLINE: William Duff; William Callaghan, John Lunn, Jim Fraser, Roy Barry, James Thomson, Hugh Robertson, Robert Paton, Alexander Edwards, Willie Renton, Pat Gardner.   Manager: George Farm

Goal: Gardner (2)

LYN OSLO v FC BARCELONA 2-3 (0-0)
Camp Nou, Barcelona   30.01.1969

Referee: James Finney (ENG)   Attendance: 4,486

LYN: Svein Bjørn Olsen; Jan Rodvang, Helge Østvold, Andreas Morisbak, Knut Kolle (.. Trygve Christophersen), Knut Berg, Karl Johan Johannessen, Jan Berg, Harald Berg, Ola Dybwad Olsen, Jon Palmer Austnes.   Trainer: Knut Osnet

FC BARCELONA: Salvador SADURNÍ Urpi; José FRANCH Xargay, Francisco Fernández Rodríguez "GALLEGO", ELADIO Silvestre Graells, Antonio TORRES García, José María FUSTÉ Blanch (46 Pedro María ZABALZA Inda), Carlos PELLICER Vázquez, Jesús María PEREDA Ruiz de Temiño, José Antonio ZALDÚA Urdanavia, JUAN CARLOS Perez López, Joaquín RIFÉ Climent (75 José PALAU Busquet).
Trainer: Salvador Artigas

Goals: Zaldúa (11), Pellicer (24), H. Berg (38), Gallego (60), O.D. Olsen (78)

FC BARCELONA v LYN OSLO 2-2 (0-1)
Camp Nou, Barcelona   5.02.1969

Referee: Robert Hélies (FRA)   Attendance: 11,602

FC BARCELONA: Miguel REINA Santos; José FRANCH Xargay, Francisco Fernández Rodríguez "GALLEGO", ELADIO Silvestre Graells, Antonio TORRES García, Pedro María ZABALZA Inda, Carlos PELLICER Vázquez, Jesús María PEREDA Ruiz de Temiño, José PALAU Busquet (65 Fernando OLIVELLA Pons), JUAN CARLOS Perez López (65 P.FERNÁNDEZ), Joaquín RIFÉ Climent.
Trainer: Salvador Artigas

LYN: Svein Bjørn Olsen; Jan Rodvang, Helge Østvold, Andreas Morisbak, Knut Kolle (.. Trygve Christophersen), Knut Berg, Karl Johan Johannessen, Jan Berg, Harald Berg, Ola Dybwad Olsen, Jon Palmer Austnes.   Trainer: Knut Osnet

Goals: Johannessen (29, 54), Gallego (75, 83)

AC TORINO v SLOVAN BRATISLAVA 0-1 (0-0)
Stadio Comunale, Torino   19.02.1969
Referee: Antonio Saldanha Ribeiro (POR)   Att: 15,974
AC TORINO: Lido Vieri; Fabrizio Poletti, Natalino Fossati (59 Bruno Bolchi), Giorgio Puia, Angelo Cereser, Aldo Agroppi, Alberto Carelli, Giorgio Ferrini, Nestor Combin, Gianbattista Moschino, Carlo Facchin (59 Emiliano Mondonico). Trainer: Edmondo Fabbri
SLOVAN: Alexander Vencel; Ľudevít Zlocha, Vladimir Hrivňák, Alexander Horváth, Ján Zlocha, Ivan Hrdlička, Ludovit Cvetler, Jozef Čapkovič, Karol Jokl, Hlavenka, Ján Čapkovič.   Trainer: Michal Vičan
Goal: Jokl (54)

RANDERS FREJA v 1.FC KÖLN 0-3 (0-1)
Randers stadion, Freja   12.03.1969
Referee: Hubert Burguet (BEL)   Attendance: 15,838
RANDERS FREJA: Alfred Mogensen; Mogens Kaarup, Jørgen Rasmussen, Per Lykke, Ole Nielsen (46 John Andreasen), Knud Olesen, Erik Sørensen, Helge Vonsyld, Per Gaardsøe, Hans Berg Andersen, Anders Bødker.
Trainer: Juan Ramón Rodríguez
1.FC KÖLN: Paul Heyeres; Karl-Heinz Thielen, Fritz Pott, Peter Blusch, Wolfgang Weber, Werner Biskup, Karl-Heinz Rühl, Heinz Simmet, Jürgen Jendrossek, Wolfgang Overath, Heinz Hornig.   Trainer: Hans Merkle
Goals: Biskup (24), Rühl (70, 83)

SEMI-FINALS

SLOVAN BRATISLAVA v AC TORINO 2-1 (1-0)
Tehelné pole, Bratislava   5.03.1969
Referee: Paul Schiller (AUS)   Attendance: 20,633
SLOVAN: Alexander Vencel; Ľudevít Zlocha, Vladimir Hrivňák, Alexander Horváth, Ján Zlocha (79 Jozef Fillo), Ivan Hrdlička, Ludovit Cvetler, Ladislav Móder, Jozef Čapkovič, Karol Jokl (55 Hlavenka), Ján Čapkovič.
Trainer: Michal Vičan
AC TORINO: Lido Vieri (4 Francesco Sattolo); Fabrizio Poletti, Natalino Fossati, Giorgio Puia, Angelo Cereser, Aldo Agroppi, Alberto Carelli, Giorgio Ferrini, Nestor Combin, Gianbattista Moschino, Carlo Facchin.
Trainer: Edmondo Fabbri
Goals: Horváth (26), Hlavenka (62), Carelli (89)

1.FC KÖLN v FC BARCELONA 2-2 (1-1)
Müngersdorferstadion, Köln   2.04.1969
Referee: Leo Callaghan (WAL)   Attendance: 45,678
1.FC KÖLN: Paul Heyeres (81 Rolf Birkhölzer); Karl-Heinz Thielen (32 Matthias Hemmersbach), Fritz Pott, Peter Blusch, Wolfgang Weber, Werner Biskup, Karl-Heinz Rühl, Heinz Simmet, Johannes Löhr, Wolfgang Overath, Heinz Hornig.   Trainer: Hans Merkle
FC BARCELONA: Salvador SADURNÍ Urpi; José FRANCH Xargay, Antonio TORRES García, Pedro María ZABALZA Inda, Francisco Fernández Rodríguez "GALLEGO" (71 Fernando OLIVELLA Pons), José María FUSTÉ Blanch, Joaquín RIFÉ Climent, José Antonio ZALDÚA Urdanavia (46 Santiago CASTRO Anido), Narciso MARTÍ FILOSÍA, Carlos PELLICER Vázquez, Carlos REXACH Cerdá.
Trainer: Salvador Artigas
Goals: Löhr (7), Zabalza (23), Rühl (75), Fusté (79)

1.FC KÖLN v RANDERS FREJA 2-1 (1-1)
Müngersdorferstadion, Köln   5.03.1969
Referee: Josef Krnavek (CZE)   Attendance: 15,311
1.FC KÖLN: Paul Heyeres; Karl-Heinz Thielen, Heinz Simmet, Werner Biskup, Wolfgang Weber, Peter Blusch, Karl-Heinz Rühl, Heinz Flohe (58 Bernhard Hermes), Jürgen Jendrossek, Wolfgang Overath, Heinz Hornig.
Trainer: Hans Merkle
RANDERS FREJA: Alfred Mogensen; Mogens Kaarup, Jørgen Rasmussen, Per Lykke, Ole Nielsen, Knud Olesen (.. John Andreasen), Erik Sørensen, Helge Vonsyld, Per Gaardsøe, Hans Berg Andersen, Anders Bødker.
Trainer: Juan Ramón Rodríguez
Goals: Jendrossek (34), Gaardsøe (42), Biskup (89)

FC BARCELONA v 1.FC KÖLN 4-1 (1-1)
Camp Nou, Barcelona   19.04.1969
Referee: Antonio Sbardella (ITA)   Attendance: 56,864
FC BARCELONA: Salvador SADURNÍ Urpi; José FRANCH Xargay, ELADIO Silvestre Graells, Joaquín RIFÉ Climent, Antonio TORRES García, Pedro María ZABALZA Inda, Carlos PELLICER Vázquez (80 Jesús María PEREDA Ruiz de Temiño), José Antonio ZALDÚA Urdanavia, Narciso MARTÍ FILOSÍA, José María FUSTÉ Blanch, Carlos REXACH Cerdá.
Trainer: Salvador Artigas
1.FC KÖLN: Rolf Birkhölzer; Karl-Heinz Thielen, Fritz Pott, Peter Blusch, Wolfgang Weber, Werner Biskup, Karl-Heinz Rühl, Heinz Simmet, Johannes Löhr (58 Jürgen Jendrossek), Wolfgang Overath, Heinz Hornig.   Trainer: Hans Merkle
Goals: Martí Filosía (6), Rühl (17), Fusté (53, 67, 80)

DUNFERMLINE ATHLETIC
v SLOVAN BRATISLAVA 1-1 (1-0)

East End Park, Dunfermline 9.04.1969

Referee: Kurt Tschenscher (W. GER)   Attendance: 16,559

DUNFERMLINE: William Duff; William Callaghan, John Lunn, Jim Fraser, Roy Barry, Willie Renton (.. Edward Ferguson), Hugh Robertson, Robert Paton, Alexander Edwards, Pat Gardner, Ian Lister.   Manager: George Farm

SLOVAN: Alexander Vencel; Jozef Fillo, Vladimir Hrivňák, Zlocha, Alexander Horváth, Jozef Hatar, Ludovit Cvetler, Ladislav Móder, Jozef Čapkovič, Karol Jokl, Ján Čapkovič.   Trainer: Michal Vičan

Goals: Fraser (44), Ján Čapkovič (83)

SLOVAN BRATISLAVA
v DUNFERMLINE ATHLETIC 1-0 (1-0)

Tehelné pole, Bratislava 23.04.1969

Referee: Josip Horvath (YUG)   Attendance: 15,000

SLOVAN: Alexander Vencel; Jozef Fillo, Vladimir Hrivňák, Zlocha, Alexander Horváth, Ivan Hrdlička, Ludovit Cvetler, Ladislav Móder, Jozef Čapkovič, Karol Jokl (.. Jozef Hatar), Ján Čapkovič.   Trainer: Michal Vičan

ATHLETIC: William Duff; William Callaghan, John Lunn, Jim Fraser, Roy Barry, Willie Renton, Barrie Mitchell (.. George McKimmie), Robert Paton, Alexander Edwards, James Thomson (.. Ian Lister), Pat Gardner.   Manager: George Farm

Goal: Ján Čapkovič (23)

FINAL

TJ SLOVAN BRATISLAVA
v FC BARCELONA 3-2 (3-1)

Sankt Jakob-Stadion, Basel 21.05.1969

Referee: Laurens van Ravens (HOL)   Attendance: 19,478

SLOVAN: Alexander Vencel; Jozef Fillo, Vladimir Hrivňák, Alexander Horváth (Cap), Ján Zlocha; Ludovit Cvetler, Jozef Čapkovič, Ivan Hrdlička, Karol Jokl; Ladislav Móder (68 Jozef Hatar), Ján Čapkovič.   Trainer: Michal Vičan

CF BARCELONA: Salvador SADURNÍ Urpi; José FRANCH Xargay (12 Jesús María PEREDA Ruiz de Temiño), Joaquín RIFÉ Climent, Fernando OLIVELLA Pons (Cap), ELADIO Silvestre Graells; Pedro María ZABALZA Inda, Carlos PELLICER Vázquez, Santiago CASTRO Anido (46 Jorge Alberto MENDOZA Paulino), José María FUSTÉ Blanch; José Antonio ZALDÚA Urdanavia, Carlos REXACH Cerdá.
Trainer: Salvador Artigas

Goals: Cvetler (2), Zaldúa (16), Hrivňák (29), Ján Čapkovič (42), Rexach (52)

Goalscorers European Cup-Winners' Cup 1968-69:

6 goals: Karl-Heinz Rühl (FC Köln)

5 goals: Ulf Hultberg (IFK Norrköping), Per Gaardsøe (Randers Freja), Karol Jokl (Slovan Bratislava)

4 goals: João Custódio Pinto (FC Porto), Karl Johan Johannessen (Lyn Oslo), José María FUSTÉ (Barcelona), Ján Čapkovič (Slovan Bratislava)

3 goals: Anthony Brown, Asa Hartford (West Bromwich Albion), Harald Berg (Lyn Oslo), Johannes Löhr (FC Köln), Alexander Edwards, Pat Gardner, William Callaghan (Dunfermline), José Antonio ZALDÚA (Barcelona)

2 goals: Lesczcynski (US Rumelange), Aytekin (Altay Izmir), Toshack (Cardiff City), Norblad (IFK Norrköping), Giesen, Heijnen (ADO den Haag), Cocks (Sliema), Botinos, Stolingas (Olympiakos), Austnes, K.Berg (Lyn Oslo), Carelli (Torino), Andersen (Randers Freja), Biskup, Blusch, Jendrossek (FC Köln), Fraser, Renton, Robertson (Dunfermline), Gallego, Mendoza, Pellicer, Zabalza (Barcelona)

1 goal: Feridun, Mustafa (Altay Izmir), Bird (Cardiff City), Bajko, Shaqiri (Partizani Tiranë), Petyt, Massé (Bordeaux), Ranković, Tomić (FK Bor), Stylianou (Apoel Nicosia), Thio, Lambert, Bailliu (Club Brugge), Jamison, Parke, McPolin (Crusaders), Fullam (Shamrock Rovers), Hohenwarter (Grazer AK), Hesselgren, Hult (IFK Norrköping), Aarts, Schoenmaker (ADO den Haag), Dumitrache (Dinamo Bucureşti), Pavao (FC Porto), Vasileiou, Zanteroglou, Gioutsos (Olympiakos), Lovett, Astle (West Bromwich Albion), O.D.Olsen, J.Berg (Lyn Oslo), Facchin, Mondonico (Torino), Olesen, Bødker, Sørensen, Lykke, Andreasen (Randers Freja), Overath (FC Köln), Mitchell, Barry, Th.Callaghan (Dunfermline), Rexach, Marti-Filosia (Barcelona), Cvetler, Hrivňák, Horváth, Hlavenka, Jozef Čapkovič, Hrdlička (Slovan)

CUP WINNERS' CUP 1969-70

PRELIMINARY ROUND

RAPID WIEN v TORPEDO MOSKVA 0-0
Prater, Wien 27.08.1969
Referee: Laurens van Ravens (HOL)   Attendance: 20,000
RAPID: Gerald Fuchsbichler; Walter Gebhardt, Walter Glechner, Christoph Wirth; Johann Eigenstiller, Alois Jagodic; Josef Hartl (46 Anton Fritsch), Jörn Bjerregaard, Geza Gallos (61 Leopold Grausam), Rudolf Flögel, Helmut Redl.
Trainer: Karl Rappan
TORPEDO: Laimonia Laizan; Grigori Yanets, Leonid Pakhomov, Vladimir Krasnov, Aleksandr Chumakov, Viktor Shustikov, Aleksandr Leniev, Yuri Savchenko (72 Valentin Spiridonov), Vadim Nikonov, Mikhail Gershkovich, Vladimir Mikhailov.   Trainer: Valentin Ivanov

TORPEDO MOSKVA v RAPID WIEN 1-1 (0-0)
Lenin, Moskva 3.09.1969
Referee: Antonio Sbardella (ITA)   Attendance: 80,000
TORPEDO: Laimonia Laizan; Grigori Yanets, Leonid Pakhomov, Vladimir Krasnov, Aleksandr Chumakov, Viktor Shustikov, Aleksandr Leniev, David Pais (46 Yuri Savchenko), Vadim Nikonov, Mikhail Gershkovich, Vladimir Mikhailov.
Trainer: Valentin Ivanov
RAPID: Gerald Fuchsbichler; Walter Gebhardt, Walter Glechner, Johann Eigenstiller; Alois Jagodic, Ewald Ullmann; Anton Fritsch (71 Geza Gallos), Jörn Bjerregaard, Leopold Grausam, Rudolf Flögel, Helmut Redl.   Trainer: Karl Rappan
Goals: Redl (53), Gershkovich (88)

FIRST ROUND

ÍB VESTMANNAEYJAR v LEVSKI SPARTAK SOFIA 0-4 (0-4)
Vestmannaeyjavöllur, Vestmannaeyjarr 30.08.1969
Referee: Henry Öberg (NOR)   Attendance: 2,384
ÍB: Páll Palmason; Olafur Sigurvinsson, Magnusson, Fridfinnur Finnbogason, Helgason, Andersen, S.Palmason, Oskar Valtysson, Saevar Tryggvason, Haraldur Júliusson, Tómas Pálsson.
LEVSKI SPARTAK: Biser Mihailov; Milko Gaidarski, Dobromir Jechev, Stefan Aladjov, Kiril Ivkov, Stefan Pavlov (.. Nikola Kotkov), Tsvetan Veselinov, Pavel Panov, Georgi Asparuhov, Ianko Kirilov, Aleksandar Kostov (.. Vasil Mitkov).   Trainer: Krastyo Chakarov
Goals: Veselinov (7), J. Kirilov (..), Kotkov (..), Mitkov (..)

LEVSKI SPARTAK SOFIA v ÍB VESTMANNAEYJAR 4-0 (1-0)
Vasil Levski, Sofia 1.10.1969
Referee: Jacques Colling (LUX)   Attendance: 13,499
LEVSKI SPARTAK: Biser Mihailov; Milko Gaidarski, Georgi Todorov (46 Dobromir Jechev), Stefan Aladjov, Kiril Ivkov, Peshev, Petar Kirilov, Ivan Stoianov, Georgi Asparuhov (46 Pavel Panov), Nikola Kotkov, Vasil Mitkov.
Trainer: Krastyo Chakarov
ÍB: Páll Palmason; Olafur Sigurvinsson (.. Steingrimsson), Magnusson, Einar Fridthjófsson, Helgason, Andersen, S.Palmason, Oskar Valtysson, Saevar Tryggvason, Haraldur Júliusson, Tómas Pálsson.
Goals: Kotkov (17, 48, 50), Gaidarski (67)

K LIERSE SK v APOEL NICOSIA 10-1 (5-0)
Stadion aan het Lisp, Lier 17.09.1969
Referee: Marian Srodecki (POL)   Attendance: 7,004
LIERSE SK: Carl Engelen; Gustaaf Van den Eynde, Walter Boogaerts, Ronny Michielsens, Eddy Lodewijckx, Robert Willems, Frans Vermeyen, François Janssens, Corneel De Ceulaer, André Denul, René Van Opstal (46 Edwig Put).
Trainer: Gustaaf van den Bergh
APOEL: Elias Papageorgiou; Stavros Assiotis, Dimitris Hiotis, Stelios Haritakis, Pantelas Konstantinides, Solis Andreou, Leonidas Leonidou, Andreas Hristodoulou, Nikos Agathokleous, Andreas Stylianou, Spyros Kettenis (.. Nikos Kantzilieris).
Goals: Vermeyen (10, 21, 43, 49), Denul (20, 27, 75, 87), Put (55), Agathokleous (65), Janssens (80)

APOEL NICOSIA v LIERSE SK 0-1 (0-1)
Stadion aan het Lisp, Lier 24.09.1969
Referee: Anton Bucheli (SWI)   Attendance: 3,271
APOEL: Elias Papageorgiou; Stavros Assiotis, Dimitris Hiotis, Stelios Haritakis, Pantelas Konstantinides, Solis Andreou, Leonidas Leonidou, Andreas Hristodoulou, Nikos Agathokleous, Andreas Stylianou, Spyros Kettenis.
LIERSE SK: Carl Engelen; Roger Dierckx, Walter Boogaerts, Ronny Michielsens, Frans Laeremans, Robert Willems, René Van Opstal, François Janssens, Frans Vermeyen, André Denul (74 Leo Hendrickx), Marc Vermeylen.
Trainer: Gustaaf van den Bergh
Goal: Denul (15)

IFK NORRKÖPING
v SLIEMA WANDERERS 5-1 (3-1)

Idrottspark, Norrköpping 17.09.1969

Referee: Magnus Petursson (ICE)   Attendance: 3,652

IFK: Lennart Andersson; Bo La Fleur, Lennart Carlsson, Björn Nordqvist, Roland Pressfeldt, Christer Hult, Hans Larsson, Ulf Jansson, Ulf Hultberg (.. Lars Berglund), Torbjörn Jonsson, Krister Norblad.   Trainer: Gunnar Nordahl

SLIEMA: Michael Sultana; Lawrence Borg (.. John Borg), Joseph Aquilina, Vincent "Lino" Falzon, George Micallef, Bernard Sultana, Ronald Cocks, Joe Serge, John Bonett, Carmel Camenzuli (.. Tony Griffiths), Vincent Vassallo.

Goals: J. Bonnet (8), Hultberg (9, 19), Pressfeldt (38), Norblad (58), Jonsson (75)

SLIEMA WANDERERS
v IFK NORRKÖPING 1-0 (0-0)

The Empire Stadium, Valletta 30.09.1969

Referee: Kevin Howley (ENG)   Attendance: 5,037

SLIEMA: Alfred Vella; Bernard Sultana, Joseph Aquilina, John Borg, George Micallef, Vincent "Lino" Falzon, Ronald Cocks, Joe Serge (75 Tony Griffiths), John Bonett, Carmel Camenzuli (.. Robert Buttigieg), Vincent Vassallo.

IFK: Bengt Lindström; Bo La Fleur, Lennart Carlsson, Björn Nordqvist, Roland Pressfeldt, Christer Hult, Hans Larsson, Ulf Jansson, Krister Norblad, Torbjörn Jonsson, Sven Evert Hesselgren.   Trainer: Gunnar Nordahl

Goal: Griffiths (87)

ATHLETIC CLUB BILBAO
v MANCHESTER CITY 3-3 (2-1)

Estadio San Mamés, Bilbao 17.09.1969

Referee: Ferdinand Marschall (AUS)   Attendance: 41,400

ATHLETIC: José Angel IRIBAR Cortajarena; José Ignacio SÁEZ, Jesús ARANGUREN Merino, José María IGARTUA Mendizábal, Luis María ECHEBERRÍA Igartua, José Ramón Martínez LARRAURI, José María ARGOITIA Acha, Fidel URIARTE Macho, Antonio María ARIETA Araunabeña Piedra (67 Jesús María Saenz ORTUONDO), Javier CLEMENTE Lazaro (63 Nicolás ESTÉFANO Montalbán), José Francisco ROJO Arroitia.   Trainer: Ronnie Allen

MANCHESTER CITY: Joseph Corrigan; Anthony Book, Glyn Pardoe, Michael Doyle, Thomas Booth, Alan Oakes, Michael Summerbee, Colin Bell, Francis Lee, Neil Young, Ian Bowyer. Manager: Joe Mercer

Goals: Argoitia (9), Clemente (12), Young (42), Uriarte (57), Booth (68), Echeberría (86 og)

MANCHESTER CITY
v ATHLETIC CLUB BILBAO 3-0 (0-0)

Maine Road, Manchester 1.10.1969

Referee: István Zsolt (HUN)   Attendance: 49,665

MANCHESTER CITY: Joseph Corrigan; Anthony Book, Glyn Pardoe, Michael Doyle, Thomas Booth, Alan Oakes, Michael Summerbee, Colin Bell, Francis Lee, Neil Young, Ian Bowyer. Manager: Joe Mercer

ATHLETIC: José Ángel IRÍBAR Cortajarena; Luis María ZUGAZAGA Martínez, Jesús ARANGUREN Merino, José María IGARTUA Mendizábal, Luis María ECHEBERRÍA Igartua, José Ramón Martínez LARRAURI, José María ARGOITIA Acha, José Ramón BETZUÉN Urquiza (46 Jesús María Saenz ORTUONDO), Antonio María ARIETA Araunabeña Piedra, Javier CLEMENTE Lazaro, José Francisco ROJO Arroitia.   Trainer: Ronnie Allen

Goals: Oakes (58), Bell (66), Bowyer (85)

GLASGOW RANGERS
v STEAUA BUCUREŞTI 2-0 (2-0)

Ibrox, Glasgow 17.09.1969

Referee's: José María Ortiz De Mendibil; Francisc Cardos, Joaquin Vilamaa (SPA).   Attendance: 60,000

RANGERS: Gerhardt Neef; Kai Johansen, David Provan; John Greig (Cap), Ronald McKinnon, James Baxter; William Henderson, William Jardine, Colin Stein, William Johnston, Orjan Persson (37 David Smith).   Manager: David White

STEAUA: Vasile Suciu; Gheorghe Cristache, Lajos Sătmăreanu, Bujor Hălmăgeanu, Iosif Vigu; Vasile Negrea, Dumitru Dumitriu; Nicolae Pantea, Gheorghe Tătaru, Florea Voinea (Cap), Carol Creiniceanu (18 Dumitru Manea). Trainer: Ştefan Kovacs

Goals: Johnston (40, 43)

STEAUA BUCUREŞTI v GLASGOW RANGERS 0-0

23 August, Bucureşti 1.10.1969

Referee: Leonidas Vamvakopoulos (GRE).   Att: 70,000

STEAUA: Vasile Suciu; Gheorghe Cristache, Lajos Sătmăreanu, Bujor Hălmăgeanu (Cap), Iosif Vigu; Vasile Negrea, Dumitru Dumitriu (65 Dumitru Nicolae); Nicolae Pantea, Gheorghe Tătaru, Florea Voinea, Dumitru Manea (57 Costică Ştefănescu).   Trainer: Ştefan Kovacs

RANGERS: Gerhardt Neef; Kai Johansen, David Provan; John Greig (Cap), Ronald McKinnon, James Baxter; William Henderson, Robert Watson (72 David Smith), Colin Stein, William Jardine, William Johnston.   Manager: David White

SHAMROCK ROVERS DUBLIN
v SCHALKE 04 GELSENKIRCHEN 2-1 (0-1)

Dalymount Park, Dublin   17.09.1969

Referee: Carl-Waldemar Hansen (DEN)   Att: 12,747

SHAMROCK ROVERS: Michael Smyth; James Gregg, Christy Canavan, Michael Kearin, Patrick Mulligan (.. Joe Haverty), Damien Richardson, Francis O'Neill, Michael Leech, Brendan Hannigan, Eric Barber, William Dixon. Trainer: Fitzsimons

SCHALKE 04: Norbert Nigbur; Hans-Jürgen Becher, Klaus Senger (.. Klaus Scheer), Alban Wüst, Heinz Van Haaren, Klaus Fichtel, Reinhard Libuda, Manfred Pohlschmidt, Gerd Neuser, Hans-Jürgen Wittkamp, Hans Pirkner. Trainer: Rudi Gutendorf

Goals: Pirkner (35), Barber (71, 72)

FC SANKT GALLEN
v FREM KØBENHAVN 1-0 (0-0)

Stade Espenmoos, Sankt-Gallen   1.10.1969

Referee: János Biroczki (HUN)   Attendance: 4,157

FC ST GALLEN: Jean-Paul Biaggi; Heinz Rütti, Kurt Brander, Heinz Ziehmann, Markus Pfirter, Hansruedi Fuhrer, Aldo Moscatelli, Rudolf Nafziger, Louis Frei (.. Herbert Frei), Fritz Rafreider, Marcel Cornioley.   Trainer: Albert Sing

FREM: Curlei Nielsen; Hardy Hansen, Flemming Ahlberg, Stegler, Finn Bøje (.. Birger Larsen), Jensen (.. Finn Hansen), Jørn Jeppesen, Ole Mørch, Jan Poulsen, Henning Hansen, Leif Printzlau.

Goal: Cornioley (53)

SCHALKE 04 GELSENKIRCHEN
v SHAMROCK ROVERS 3-0 (1-0)

Glückauf Kampfbahn, Gelsenkirchen   1.10.1969

Referee: Pavel Kazakov (USSR)   Attendance: 30,244

SCHALKE 04: Norbert Nigbur; Hans-Jürgen Becher, Klaus Senger, Hans-Jürgen Wittkamp, Klaus Fichtel, Heinz Van Haaren, Reinhard Libuda, Gerd Neuser, Hans Pirkner, Manfred Pohlschmidt, Alban Wüst (4 Hermann Erlhoff). Trainer: Rudi Gutendorf

SHAMROCK ROVERS: Michael Smyth; James Gregg, Patrick Courtney, Michael Kearin, Patrick Mulligan, Damien Richardson, Francis O'Neill, Michael Leech, Brendan Hannigan (71 Mick Lawlor), Eric Barber, Joe Haverty (60 William Dixon).   Trainer: Fitzsimons

Goals: Libuda (7), Pirkner (57), Wittkamp (80)

GÖZTEPE IZMIR
v UNION SPORTIVE LUXEMBOURG 3-0 (1-0)

Alsançak, Izmir   17.09.1969

Referee: Pavel Spotak (CZE)   Attendance: 15,384

GÖZTEPE: Güngör Celikciler; Mehmet Işikal, Caglayan Derebasi, Özer Yurteri, Mehmet Aydin, Nevzat Güzelirmak, Fadil Özduran (60 Halil Artuner), Ertan Öznur, Fevzi Zemzem, Gürsel Aksel (.. Okcu Oglu), Mehmet Türkan.

US: Roland Pletschette, Gruneisen, Jacques Mousel, Mathias Ewen (.. Paul Goedert), René Schneider, Portz, Jean-Pierre Hemmerling, Jean-Paul Martin, Pierre Weis, Guy Bernardin, Nico Braun.

Goals: Gürsel Aksel (7), Fadil (58), Halil Artuner (67)

FREM KØBENHAVN
v FC SANKT GALLEN 2-1 (1-1)

Valby Idraetspark, København   17.09.1969

Referee: Curt F.W.Liedberg (SWE)   Attendance: 4,567

FREM: Curlei Nielsen; Hardy Hansen, Flemming Ahlberg, Bent Hougaard, Finn Bøje, Jensen, Jørn Jeppesen, Henning Hansen, Jan Poulsen, Ole Mørch, Leif Printzlau.

FC ST GALLEN: Jean-Paul Biaggi; Heinz Rütti, Peter Riehn, Markus Pfirter, Heinz Ziehmann, Hansruedi Fuhrer, Aldo Moscatelli, Rudolf Nafziger, Renato Pellegrini, Fritz Rafreider, Marcel Cornioley.   Trainer: Albert Sing

Goals: Nafziger (15), Henning Hansen (21, 54)

UNION SPORTIVE LUXEMBOURG
v GÖZTEPE IZMIR 2-3 (0-2)

Luxembourg   1.10.1969

Referee: Gilbert Droz (SWI)   Attendance: 1,060

US: Roland Pletschette; Gruneisen, Jacques Mousel, Mathias Ewen, René Schneider, Portz, Jean-Pierre Hemmerling (.. Pierre Weis), Jean-Paul Martin, Nico Braun, Guy Bernardin, Raymond Clemen.

GÖZTEPE: Güngör Celikciler; Mehmet Işikal, Caglayan Derebasi, Okcu Oglu, Mehmet Aydin (.. Halil Kiraz), Nevzat Güzelirmak, Ertan Öznur, Flemming Nielsen, Fevzi Zemzem, Gürsel Aksel, Mehmet Türkan.

Goals: Fevzi (15), Nielsen (33, 67), Bernardin (75), Weiss (88)

1.FC MAGDEBURG v MTK BUDAPEST 1-0 (1-0)
Ernst Grube, Magdeburg 17.09.1969
Referee: William Anderson (SCO)   Attendance: 20,945

1.FC MAGDEBURG: Kurt Erler; Jörg Ohm, Günter Fronzeck, Manfred Zapf, Rolf Retschlag; Günter Kubisch, Wolfgang Seguin; Heinz Oelze (57 Manfred Briebach), Joachim Walter, Jürgen Sparwasser, Wolfgang Abraham.
Trainer: Heinz Krügel

MTK: Sándor Lanczkor; Sándor Oborzil, Lajos Dunai, Csaba Csetényi, György Keszei (78 Tibor Szántó); István Salánki, László Strasszer, András Szucsányi; József Török, István Sárközi, László Takács (57 Tibor Kiss).
Trainer: Ferenc Kovács

Goal: Sparwasser (30)

CARDIFF CITY v MJØNDALEN IF 5-1 (4-1)
Ninian Park, Cardiff 1.10.1969
Referee: Günter Männig (E. GER)   Attendance: 14,730

CITY: Frederick Davies; David Carver, Gary Bell, Melwyn Sutton, Donald Murray; Terence Lewis, Barrie Jones, Brian Clark, Alexander Allan, John Toshack (.. Leslie Lea), Peter King.   Trainer: James Scoular

MJØNDALEN IF: J.Larsen; Brock, Jensrud, Ole Kristian Olsen, Torbjørn Loe, Terje Svendsen, Brede Skistad, Kristiansen (.. Sven Larsen), Egil Solberg, Jan Erik Holmen (.. K. Solberg), John Olsen.

Goals: King (16, 68), Allan (36, 38, 43), Solberg (37)

MTK BUDAPEST v 1.FC MAGDEBURG 1-1 (1-0, 1-0) (AET)
Hungária krt, Budapest 1.10.1969
Referee: Michel Kitabdjian (FRA)   Attendance: 8,000

MTK: Sándor Lanczkor; Sándor Oborzil, Lajos Dunai, György Keszei, István Salánki; István Sárközi, András Szucsányi; József Török, László Takács, Sándor Mártha, József Becsei (72 Tibor Kiss).   Trainer: Ferenc Kovács

1.FC MAGDEBURG: Ulrich Schulze; Peter Sykora, Günter Fronzeck, Manfred Zapf, Rolf Retschlag; Wolfgang Seguin, Jörg Ohm; Hans-Jürgen Hermann (93 Wolfgang Abraham), Joachim Walter, Jürgen Sparwasser, Günter Kubisch.
Trainer: Heinz Krügel

Goals: Takács (7), Sparwasser (112)

ARDS NEWTONARDS v AS ROMA 0-0
The Oval, Belfast 17.09.1969
Referee: Robert Schaut (BEL)   Attendance: 3,167

ARDS: Sam Kydd; David McCoy, George Crothers, Alan Bell, William Stewart, William Nixon, William Humphries, William McAvoy, Ronnie McAteer, James Burke (46 Richard Sands), Roy Welsh.   Trainer: George Eastham

AS ROMA: Alberto Ginulfi; Aldo Bet, Francesco Carpenetti, Luciano Spinosi, Francesco Cappelli, Sergio Santarini, Joaquim Lucas Peiro, Giorgio Braglia (68 Fabio Enzo), Fausto Landini, Fabio Capello, Francesco Scaratti.   Trainer: Helenio Herrera

MJØNDALEN IF v CARDIFF CITY 1-7 (1-3)
Neder Eiker, Oslo 17.09.1969
Referee: Joseph Hannet (BEL)   Attendance: 18,000

MJØNDALEN IF: Runar Nilsen; Brock (.. Kristian), Jensrud, Torbjørn Loe, Terje Svendsen, Brede Skistad, Kristiansen, Egil Solberg, Jan Erik Holmen (.. Sven Larsen), Bo. Skistad, John Olsen.

CITY: Frederick Davies; Stephen Derrett, David Carver, Melwyn Sutton, Donald Murray, Brian Harris, Leighton Phillips (.. Barrie Jones), Brian Clark, Leslie Lea, John Toshack, Peter King.   Trainer: James Scoular

Goals: Clark (4, 35), Toshack (43, 87), J. Olsen (44), Lea (67), Sutton (74), King (77)

AS ROMA v ARDS NEWTONARDS 3-1 (1-0)
Stadio Olimpico, Roma 1.10.1969
Referee: Erich Linemayr (AUS)   Attendance: 13,287

AS ROMA: Alberto Ginulfi; Aldo Bet, Sergio Petrelli, Elvio Salvori, Francesco Cappelli, Sergio Santarini, Lucio Bertogna, Renato Cappellini (55 Fausto Landini), Joaquim Lucas Peiro, Fabio Capello, Franco Cordova.   Trainer: Helenio Herrera

ARDS: Sam Kydd; David McCoy, George Crothers, Alan Bell, William Stewart, William Nixon, William Humphries, William McAvoy, Ronnie McAteer, John Anderson (73 Barry Brown), Roy Welsh (46 Richard Sands).   Trainer: George Eastham

Goals: Salvori (20, 55), Peiro (53), Crothers (79)

**OLYMPIAKOS PEIRAIAS
v GÓRNIK ZABRZE 2-2** (0-2)

PAO, Athina   17.09.1969

Referee: Milivoje Gugulović (YUG)   Attendance: 25,000

OLYMPIAKOS: Evangelos Liadelis; Giannis Gkaitatzis, Orestis Pavlidis, Nikos Sideris (46 Dimitris Plessas), Hristos Zanteroglou, Grigorois Aganian, Paulos Vasileiou, Giorgos Sideris, Dimitris Miler, Miltiadis Koumarias, Athanasios Aggelis (46 Nikos Gioutsos).   Trainer: Stefan Bobek

GÓRNIK: Hubert Kostka (65 Jan Gomola); Rainer Kuchta, Stanislaw Oslizlo, Henryk Latocha, Stefan Florenski, Alojzy Deja, Erwin Wilczek, Alfred Olek, Zygfryd Szoltysik, Wlodzimierz Lubanski, Hubert Skowronek.
Trainer: H. Hostka

Goals: Wilczek (8, 36), Gioutsos (55), G.Sideris (84)

PSV EINDHOVEN v RAPID WIEN 4-2 (2-1)

Philips, Eindhoven   1.10.1969

Referee: Joaquim Fernendes Campos (POR)   Att: 18,247

PSV: Pim Doesburg (2 Willy Heijink); Wim Van den Dungen, Pleun Strik, Lazar Radovic, Jef Blatter (16 Peter Kemper), Kresten Bjerre, Jacques van Stippent, Bent Schmidt-Hansen, Willy Van der Kuylen, Wietze Veenstra, Peter Ressel.
Trainer: Kurt Linder

RAPID: Gerald Fuchsbichler; Walter Glechner, Johann Eigenstiller (40 Alois Jagodic), Ewald Ullmann, Walter Gebhardt, Jörn Bjerregaard, Rudolf Flögel, Leopold Grausam (.. Geza Gallos), Erich Fak, Josef Hartl, Helmut Redl.
Trainer: Karl Rappan

Goals: Van der Kuylen (17), Flögel (25), Veenstra (38), Schmidt-Hansen (68, 71), Bjerregaard (76)

**GÓRNIK ZABRZE
v OLYMPIAKOS PEIRAIAS 5-0** (1-0)

Slaski, Chorzów   1.10.1969

Referee: John Wright Paterson (SCO)   Attendance: 30,000

GÓRNIK: Hubert Kostka; Henryk Latocha (.. Rainer Kuchta), Stanislaw Oslizlo, Jerzy Gorgon, Stefan Florenski, Zygfryd Szoltysik, Erwin Wilczek, Alfred Olek (.. Hubert Skowronek), Jan Banas, Wlodzimierz Lubanski, Wladyslaw Szarynski.
Trainer: H. Hostka

OLYMPIAKOS: Evangelos Liadelis; Giannis Gkaitatzis, Orestis Pavlidis, Dimitris Plessas, Grigorois Aganian, Vasilis Siokos, Paulos Vasileiou, Giorgos Sideris, Dimitris Miler, Nikos Gioutsos (46 Miltiadis Koumarias), Vasilis Botinos (58 Giorgos Stolingas).   Trainer: Stefan Bobek

Goals: Wilczek (1), Skowronek (62), Szoltysik (70), Banas (82 pen, 84)

**DUKLA PRAHA
v OLYMPIQUE MARSEILLE 1-0** (1-0)

Letna, Praha   17.09.1969

Referee: Rudolf Scheurer (SWI)   Attendance: 1,615

DUKLA: Ivo Viktor; Karel Dvorák, Václav Samek, Bendl, Ivan Novák, Miroslav Vojkurka, Stanislav Strunc, Josef Nedorost, Ján Geleta, Milan Hudec (.. Jaroslav Melichár), Viliam Lasso.
Trainer: V. Pavlis

OLYMPIQUE: Jean-Paul Escale; Jean-Pierre Lopez, Jean-Louis Hodoul, Jules Zvunka, Jean Djorkaeff, Jacky Novi, Roland Merschel, Roger Magnusson, Joseph Bonnel, Yegba-Maya Joseph, Charles Loubet.   Trainer: Mario Zatelli

Goal: Hudec (33)

RAPID WIEN v PSV EINDHOVEN 1-2 (1-2)

Prater, Wien   17.09.1969

Referee: Eric T. Jennings (ENG)   Attendance: 65,000

RAPID: Gerald Fuchsbichler; Walter Gebhardt, Walter Glechner, Johann Eigenstiller (.. Christoph Wirth); Alois Jagodic (72 Geza Gallos), Ewald Ullmann; Jörn Bjerregaard, Rudolf Flögel, Leopold Grausam, Anton Fritsch, Helmut Redl.
Trainer: Karl Rappan

PSV: Pim Doesburg; Jef Blatter, Pleun Strik, Lazar Radovic, Kresten Bjerre, Wim Van den Dungen, Jacques van Stippent, Wietze Veenstra, Bent Schmidt-Hansen, Willy Van der Kuylen, Gerard Weber.   Trainer: Kurt Linder

Goals: Veenstra (5), Schmidt-Hansen (15), Flögel (20)

**OLYMPIQUE MARSEILLE
v DUKLA PRAHA 2-0** (1-0, 1-0) (AET)

Stade Vélodrome, Marseille   1.10.1969

Referee: Gaspar Pintado Viu (SPA)   Attendance: 26,313

OLYMPIQUE: Jean-Paul Escale; Jean-Pierre Lopez, Jean-Louis Hodoul, Jules Zvunka, Jean Djorkaeff, Jacky Novi, Roland Merschel (106 Jacques Casolari), Roger Magnusson, Joseph Yegba-Maya (60 Didier Couécou), Joseph Bonnel, Charles Loubet.   Trainer: Mario Zatelli

DUKLA: Ivo Viktor; Karel Dvorák, Jiří Čadek, Bendl, Ivan Novák, Stanislav Kocourek, Stanislav Strunc (60 Miroslav Vojkurka), Ján Geleta, Milan Hudec (79 Jan Brumovský), Josef Nedorost, Jaroslav Melichár.   Trainer: V. Pavlis

Goals: Loubet (15, 91)

DINAMO ZAGREB
v SLOVAN BRATISLAVA 3-0 (1-0)

Maksimir, Zagreb   17.09.1969

Referee: Antonio Saldanha Ribeiro (POR)   Att: 8,459

DINAMO: Fahrija Dautbegović; Rudolf Cvek, Branko Gracanin, Rudolf Belin, Mladen Ramljak, Filip Blasković, Marijan Cercek, Ivica Miljković, Marijan Novak, Josip Gucmirtl, Krasnodar Rora.   Trainer: Ivica Horvath

SLOVAN: Alexander Vencel; Jozef Fillo (.. Kovarik), Vladimír Hrivňák, Peter Mutkovic, Alexander Horváth, Anton Skorupa, Ivan Hrdlička (.. Posa), Ladislav Móder, Jozef Čapkovič, Karol Jokl, Ján Čapkovič.   Trainer: Michal Vičan.

Goals: Miljkovic (2), Novak (51), Gucmirtl (58)

SLOVAN BRATISLAVA v DINAMO ZAGREB 0-0

Tehelné pole, Bratislava   1.10.1969

Referee: Francesco Francescon (ITA)   Attendance: 15,269

SLOVAN: Alexander Vencel; Zlocha, Vladimír Hrivňák, Jozef Fillo, Alexander Horváth, Ivan Hrdlička, Stefan Bodnár, Ladislav Móder (.. Bohumil Bizon), Jozef Čapkovič, Karol Jokl, Ján Čapkovič.   Trainer: Michal Vičan

DINAMO: Fahrija Dautbegović; Rudolf Cvek, Damir Valec, Rudolf Belin, Mladen Ramljak, Filip Blasković, Marijan Cercek, Ivica Miljković, Marijan Novak, Josip Gucmirtl, Krasnodar Rora.   Trainer: Ivica Horvath

ACADEMICA COIBRA
v KUOPION PALLOSEURA 0-0

Estádio Municipal Calhabe, Coimbra   17.09.1969

Referee: Hans-Joachim Weyland (W. GER)   Att: 6,742

ACADEMICA: Francisco Domingues Ricardo ABREU; António José CURADO, Armando Manuel Matos ARAÚJO, RUI Gouveia Pinto RODRIGUES (58 Augusto Francisco ROCHA), Carlos Alexandre Fortes ALHINHO, João António Pinho BELO, MÁRIO Alberto Domingos CAMPOS, MANUEL ANTÓNIO Da Silva, Modesto Luis Hortiz Sousa Neves «NENÉ», Vasco Manuel Vieira Pereira GERVÁSIO, VÍTOR José Domingos CAMPOS (57 VÍTOR Manuel Silva Correia GOMES).   Trainer: Francisco ANDRADE

KUPS: Pertti Hänninen; Hannu Raatikainen, Jaakko Marttila, Matti Väänänen, Matti Terästö, Eero Rissanen, Ari Savolainen, Antero Kostilainen, Janne Ilvetsalo, Teuvo Korpinen (76 Matti Tirkkonen), Pekka Louesalo.

KUOPION PALLOSEURA
v ACADEMICA COIMBRA 0-1 (0-0)

Väinölänniemi, Kuopio   1.10.1969

Referee: Jef F.Dorpmans (HOL)   Attendance: 2,693

KUPS: Pertti Hänninen; Hannu Raatikainen, Jouko Suomalainen, Jaakko Martilla (59 Aki Heiskanen), Matti Terästö, Eero Rissanen, Matti Väänänen, Antero Kostilainen, Janne Ilvetsalo, Jarmo Flink (59 Veli Pohjolainen), Pekka Louesalo.

ACADEMICA: Francisco Domingues Ricardo ABREU (79 António Alberto BRASSARD); António José CURADO, Armando Manuel Matos ARAÚJO, RUI Gouveia Pinto RODRIGUES, Carlos Alexandre Fortes ALHINHO, João António Pinho BELO, VÍTOR Manuel Silva Correia GOMES, MANUEL ANTÓNIO Da Silva, Modesto Luis Hortiz Sousa Neves "NENÉ", Vasco Manuel Vieira Pereira GERVÁSIO, MÁRIO Alberto Domingos CAMPOS.   Trainer: Francisco ANDRADE

Goal: Nené (65)

SECOND ROUND

IFK NORRKÖPING
v SCHALKE 04 GELSENKIRCHEN 0-0

Idrottspark, Norrköping   12.11.1969

Referee: William John Gow (WAL)   Attendance: 2,343

IFK: Andersson; Bo La Fleur, Lennart Carlsson, Björn Nordqvist, Roland Pressfeldt, Christer Hult, Hans Larsson, Ulf Jansson, Krister Norblad (73 Håkan Forsberg), Sven Evert Hesselgren (59 Benny Wendt), Lars Berglund.   Trainer: Gunnar Nordahl

SCHALKE 04: Josef Elting; Waldemar Slomiany, Friedel Rausch, Hans-Jürgen Wittkamp, Klaus Fichtel, Hermann Erlhoff, Reinhard Libuda, Gerd Neuser, Hans Pirkner, Heinz Van Haaren, Herbert Lütkebohmert.   Trainer: Rudi Gutendorf

SCHALKE 04 GELSENKIRCHEN
v IFK NORRKÖPING 1-0 (1-0)

Glückauf Kampfbahn, Gelsenkirchen   26.11.1969

Referee: Stanislaw Eksztajn (POL)   Attendance: 17,489

SCHALKE 04: Josef Elting; Waldemar Slomiany, Friedel Rausch, Gerd Neuser (38 Hans-Jürgen Wittkamp), Klaus Fichtel, Heinz Van Haaren, Reinhard Libuda, Klaus Scheer, Manfred Pohlschmidt, Herbert Lütkebohmert, Hans Pirkner.   Trainer: Rudi Gutendorf

IFK: Andersson; Bert-Ottar Blom, Lennart Carlsson, Björn Nordqvist (48 Håkan Forsberg), Roland Pressfeldt, Christer Hult, Hans Larsson, Bo La Fleur, Lars Berglund, Torbjörn Jonsson, Benny Wendt.   Trainer: Gunnar Nordahl

Goal: Scheer (25)

**OLYMPIQUE MARSEILLE
v DINAMO ZAGREB 1-1** (1-0)

Stade Vélodrome, Marseille   12.11.1969

Referee: Kevin Howley (ENG)   Attendance: 32,689

OLYMPIQUE: Jean-Paul Escale; Jean-Pierre Lopez, Jean-Louis Hodoul, Jules Zvunka, Jean Djorkaeff, Jacky Novi, Roland Merschel, Roger Magnusson, Joseph Bonnel, Yegba-Maya JOSEPH, Charles Loubet.   Trainer: Mario Zatelli

DINAMO: Fahrija Dautbegović; Rudolf Cvek, Branko Gracanin, Rudolf Belin, Mladen Ramljak, Filip Blasković, Marijan Cercek, Daniel Pirić, Marijan Novak, Ivica Kiš, Krasnodar Rora.   Trainer: Ivica Horvath

Goals: Loubet (28), Cercek (80)

FC ST. GALLEN v LEVSKI SPARTAK SOFIA 0-0

Espenmoos, Sankt-Gallen   26.11.1969

Referee: Pavel Spotak (CZE)   Attendance: 1,530

FC ST. GALLEN: Rolf Fischer; Heinz Rütti, Guido Schüwig, Walter Kaspar, Marcel Tanner, Berthold Rotert, Peter Riehn, Rudolf Nafziger, Louis Frei, Fritz Rafreider, Marcel Cornioley.   Trainer: Albert Sing

LEVSKI SPARTAK: Biser Mihailov; Milko Gaidarski, Georgi Todorov, Stefan Aladjov, Kiril Ivkov, Stefan Pavlov, Petar Kirilov, Ianko Kirilov (73 Tsvetan Veselinov), Pavel Panov, Nikola Kotkov (46 Ivan Stoianov), Aleksandar Kostov.   Trainer: Krastyo Chakarov

**DINAMO ZAGREB
v OLYMPIQUE MARSEILLE 2-0** (0-0)

Maksimir, Zagreb   26.11.1969

Referee: Gocho Rusev (BUL)   Attendance: 2,241

DINAMO: Fahrija Dautbegović; Rudolf Cvek, Branko Gracanin, Rudolf Belin, Mladen Ramljak, Filip Blasković, Drago Vabec, Daniel Pirić, Marijan Novak, Josip Gucmirtl, Krasnodar Rora.   Trainer: Ivica Horvath

OLYMPIQUE: Jean-Paul Escale; Jean-Pierre Lopez, Jean-Louis Hodoul, Jules Zvunka, Jean Djorkaeff, Jacky Novi, Roland Merschel, Charles Loubet, Joseph Bonnel, Yegba-Maya JOSEPH, Jean-Pierre Destrumelle.   Trainer: Mario Zatelli

Goals: Novak (52, 90)

LIERSE SK v MANCHESTER CITY 0-3 (0-3)

Stadion aan het Lisp, Lier   12.11.1969

Referee: Gerhard Schulenburg (W. GER)   Att: 15,348

LIERSE SK: Carl Engelen; Roger Dierckx, Walter Boogaerts, Ronny Michielsens, Gustaaf Van den Eynde (70 Frans Laeremans), Robert Willems, Frans Vermeyen (54 Edwig Put), René Van Opstal, André Denul, Corneel De Ceulaer, François Janssens.   Trainer: Gustaaf van den Bergh

MANCHESTER CITY: Joseph Corrigan; Anthony Book, Glyn Pardoe, Michael Doyle (37 George Heslop), Thomas Booth, Alan Oakes, Michael Summerbee, Colin Bell, Francis Lee, Neil Young, Ian Bowyer.   Manager: Joe Mercer

Goals: Lee (5, 35), Bell (45)

**LEVSKI SPARTAK SOFIA
v FC ST. GALLEN 4-0** (2-0)

Vasil Levski, Sofia   12.11.1969

Referee: Erich Linemayr (AUS)   Attendance: 15,155

LEVSKI SPARTAK: Biser Mihailov; Peshev, Dobromir Jechev, Milko Gaidarski, Kiril Ivkov, Ianko Kirilov, Tsvetan Veselinov, Vasil Mitkov (74 Petar Kirilov), Pavel Panov, Nikola Kotkov, Aleksandar Kostov.   Trainer: Krastyo Chakarov

FC ST. GALLEN: Jean-Paul Biaggi; Guido Schüwig, Markus Pfirter, Walter Kaspar, Heinz Rütti, Hansruedi Fuhrer, Kurt Brander, Rudolf Nafziger, Louis Frei, Herbert Frei, Marcel Turin.   Trainer: Albert Sing

Goals: Kostov (11), Panov (34), Mitkov (62), I. Kirilov (73)

MANCHESTER CITY v LIERSE SK 5-0 (1-0)

Maine Road, Manchester   26.11.1969

Referee: Rudolf Glöckner (E. GER)   Attendance: 26,486

MANCHESTER CITY: Kenneth Mulhearn; Anthony Book, Glyn Pardoe, Michael Doyle, Thomas Booth, Alan Oakes (75 Anthony Towers), Michael Summerbee, Colin Bell, Francis Lee, Derek Jeffries, Ian Bowyer.   Manager: Joe Merce

LIERSE SK: Carl Engelen; Gustaaf Van den Eynde, Walter Boogaerts, Ronny Michielsens (77 Frans Laeremans), Walter Mertens, Robert Willems, René Van Opstal, François Janssens, Corneel De Ceulaer, André Denul, Raymond Min (65 Edwig Put).   Trainer: Gustaaf van den Bergh

Goals: Summerbee (22), Lee (48, 55), Bell (60, 71)

AS ROMA v PSV EINDHOVEN 1-0 (0-0)
Stadio Olimpico, Roma 12.11.1969
Referee: Robert Hélies (FRA) Attendance: 26,814
AS ROMA: Alberto Ginulfi; Francesco Scaratti, Aldo Bet, Luciano Spinosi, Elvio Salvori, Sergio Santarini, Fabio Capello, Franco Cordova (70 Walter Franzot), Fausto Landini, Renato Cappellini (59 Giorgio Braglia), Joaquim Lucas Peiro. Trainer: Helenio Herrera
PSV: Pim Doesburg; Wim Van den Dungen, Lazar Radovic, Pleun Strik, Peter Kemper, Kresten Bjerre, Jacques van Stippent, Wietze Veenstra, Bent Schmidt-Hansen, Willy Van der Kuylen, Peter Ressel. Trainer: Kurt Linder
Goal: Capello (87 pen)

PSV EINDHOVEN v AS ROMA 1-0 (0-0, 1-0) (AET)
Phillips, Eindhoven 26.11.1969
Referee: Gyula Emsberger (HUN) Attendance: 18,305
PSV: Pim Doesburg; Wim Van den Dungen, Lazar Radovic, Pleun Strik, Peter Kemper, Kresten Bjerre, Jacques van Stippent, Willy Van der Kuylen, Bent Schmidt-Hansen, Nico Mares, Peter Ressel (.. Jef Blatter). Trainer: Kurt Linder
AS ROMA: Alberto Ginulfi; Francesco Cappelli, Sergio Santarini, Aldo Bet, Luciano Spinosi, Elvio Salvori, Francesco Scaratti, Franco Cordova, Joaquim Lucas Peiro, Renato Cappellini (95 Giovanni Bertini), Giorgio Braglia (91 Walter Franzot). Trainer: Helenio Herrera
Goal: Van der Kuylen (64 pen)
AS Roma won on the toss of coin.

GÖZTEPE IZMIR v CARDIFF CITY 3-0 (3-0)
Alsançak, Izmir 12.11.1969
Referee: Lado Jakse (YUG) Attendance: 25,000
GÖZTEPE: Ali Artuner; Mehmet Işikal, Caglayan Derebasi, Özer Yurteri (.. Nevzat Güzelirmak), Mehmet Aydin, Okcu Oglu, Fevzi Zemzem, Ertan Öznur, Flemming Nielsen, Gürsel Aksel, Mehmet Türkan.
CITY: Frederick Davies; David Carver, Gary Bell, Melwyn Sutton, Donald Murray, Brian Harris, Leslie Lea, Brian Clark, Peter King, John Toshack, Frank Sharp (.. Alexander Allan). Trainer: James Scoular
Goals: Fevzi Zemzem (14), Ertan Öznu (30), Nielsen (33)

CARDIFF CITY v GÖZTEPE IZMIR 1-0 (0-0)
Ninian Park, Cardiff 26.11.1969
Referee: Gilbert Droz (SWI) Attendance: 17,866
CITY: Frederick Davies; David Carver, Gary Bell, Melwyn Sutton, Donald Murray, Brian Harris, Alexander Allan, Brian Clark, Leslie Lea (.. Ronald Bird), John Toshack (.. Graham Coldrick), Peter King. Trainer: James Scoular
GÖZTEPE: Ali Artuner; Mehmet Işikal, Caglayan Derebasi, Özer Yurteri, Mehmet Aydin, Nevzat Güzelirmak, Fevzi Zemzem, Ertan Öznur, Flemming Nielsen (.. Kartal), Gürsel Aksel, Mehmet Türkan.
Goal: Bird (78)

**1.FC MAGDEBURG
v ACADEMICA COIMBRA 1-0** (1-0)
Ernst Grube, Magdeburg 12.11.1969
Referee: Freder Hansen (DEN) Attendance: 14,038
1.FC MAGDEBURG: Hans-Georg Moldenhauer; Peter Sykora (73 Heinz Oelze), Günter Fronzeck, Jörg Ohm, Rolf Retschlag, Günter Kubisch, Wolfgang Seguin, Hans-Jürgen Hermann, Joachim Walter, Jürgen Sparwasser, Wolfgang Abraham. Trainer: Heinz Krügel
ACADEMICA: Armelim Ferreira VIEGAS; ARTUR Manuel Soares CORREIA, Carlos Alexandre Fortes ALHINHO, RUI Gouveia Pinto RODRIGUES, João António Pinho BELO, Armando Manuel Matos ARAÚJO, Vasco Manuel Vieira Pereira GERVÁSIO, MÁRIO Alberto Domingos CAMPOS, MANUEL ANTÓNIO da Silva, Modesto Luis Hortiz Sousa Neves "NENÉ", VÍTOR José Domingos CAMPOS. Trainer: Francisco ANDRADE
Goal: Sparwasser (41)

**ACADEMICA COIMBRA
v FC MAGDEBURG 2-0** (0-0)
Estádio Municipal Calhabe, Coimbra 26.11.1969
Referee: Francesco Francescon (ITA) Attendance: 9,335
ACADEMICA: Armelim Ferreira VIEGAS; ARTUR Manuel Soares CORREIA, Carlos Alexandre Fortes ALHINHO, RUI Gouveia Pinto RODRIGUES (.. Augusto Francisco ROCHA), Armando Manuel Matos ARAÚJO, Vasco Manuel Vieira Pereira GERVÁSIO, VÍTOR José Domingos CAMPOS, MÁRIO Alberto Domingos CAMPOS, MANUEL ANTÓNIO da Silva, Modesto Luis Hortiz Sousa Neves "NENÉ", Manuel SERAFIM Monteiro Pereira. Trainer: Francisco ANDRADE
FC MAGDEBURG: Hans-Georg Moldenhauer; Günter Kubisch, Manfred Zapf, Peter Sykora, Günter Fronzeck, Jörg Ohm, Detlef Enge (85 Heinz Oelze), Hans-Jürgen Hermann, Joachim Walter, Jürgen Sparwasser, Wolfgang Abraham. Trainer: Heinz Krügel
Goals: Alhinho (57), Mario Campos (85)

GÓRNIK ZABRZE
v GLASGOW RANGERS 3-1 (2-0)

Slaski, Chorzów   12.11.1969

Referee: Joseph Hannet (BEL)   Attendance: 80,000

GÓRNIK: Hubert Kostka; Henryk Latocha, Stanislaw Oslizlo, Jerzy Gorgon, Stefan Florenski, Zygfryd Szoltysik, Erwin Wilczek, Alfred Olek (.. Hubert Skowronek), Jan Banas, Wlodzimierz Lubanski, Wladyslaw Szarynski.
Trainer: Geza Kalocsai

RANGERS: Gerhardt Neef; Kai Johansen, Brian Heron, John Greig, Ronald McKinnon, James Baxter, William Henderson, Andrew Penman, Colin Stein, William Johnston, Orjan Persson.   Manager: David White

Goals: Lubanski (5, 87), Szarynski (11), Persson (55)

GLASGOW RANGERS
v GÓRNIK ZABRZE 1-3 (1-0)

Ibrox, Glasgow   26.11.1969

Referee: Bertil Lööw (SWE)   Attendance: 62,935

RANGERS: Gerhardt Neef; Kai Johansen (.. William Jardine), Brian Heron, John Greig, Ronald McKinnon, James Baxter, William Henderson, Andrew Penman, Colin Stein, William Johnston, Orjan Persson (.. Alex MacDonald).
Manager: David White

GÓRNIK: Hubert Kostka; Rainer Kuchta, Stanislaw Oslizlo, Henryk Latocha, Jerzy Gorgon, Zygfryd Szoltysik, Erwin Wilczek, Alfred Olek, Jan Banas, Wlodzimierz Lubanski, Wladyslaw Szarynski (46 Hubert Skowronek).
Trainer: Geza Kalocsai

Goals: Baxter (17), Olek (63), Lubanski (77), Skowronek (81)

QUARTER-FINALS

ACADEMICA COIMBRA
v MANCHESTER CITY 0-0

Estádio Municipal Calhabe, Coimbra   4.03.1970

Referee: Robert Schaut (BEL)   Attendance: 8,206

ACADEMICA: Rogério Manuel Leal CARDOSO; ARTUR Manuel Soares CORREIA, Carlos Alexandre Fortes ALHINHO, RUI Gouveia Pinto RODRIGUES, António Pereira MARQUES, Augusto Francisco ROCHA, VÍTOR José Domingos CAMPOS (64 Vasco Manuel Vieira Pereira GERVÁSIO), Modesto Luis Hortiz Sousa Neves "NENÉ", MÁRIO Alberto Domingos CAMPOS, ANTÓNIO JORGE Tavares de Almeida, Manuel SERAFIM Monteiro Pereira.
Trainer: Julio Carnadas Pereira "JUCA"

MANCHESTER CITY: Joseph Corrigan; Anthony Book (69 George Heslop), Arthur Mann, Glyn Pardoe, Michael Doyle, Thomas Booth, Alan Oakes, Neil Young, Michael Summerbee, Colin Bell, Francis Lee.   Manager: Joe Mercer

MANCHESTER CITY
v ACADEMICA COIMBRA 1-0 (0-0, 0-0) (AET)

Maine Road, Manchester   18.03.1970

Referee: Gocho Rusev (BUL)   Attendance: 36,111

MANCHESTER CITY: Joseph Corrigan; Anthony Book, Thomas Booth, Alan Oakes, Arthur Mann, George Heslop (46 Anthony Towers), Michael Doyle, Colin Bell (73 Christopher Glennon), Francis Lee, Neil Young, Glyn Pardoe.
Manager: Joe Mercer

ACADEMICA: Rogério Manuel Leal CARDOSO; ARTUR Manuel Soares CORREIA, Carlos Alexandre Fortes ALHINHO, RUI Gouveia Pinto RODRIGUES, António Pereira MARQUES, Augusto Francisco ROCHA (94 Vasco Manuel Vieire Pereira GERVÁSIO), MÁRIO Alberto Domingos CAMPOS (102 ANTÓNIO JORGE Tavares de Almeida), VÍTOR José Domingos CAMPOS, MANUEL ANTÓNIO da Silva, Modesto Luis Hortiz Sousa Neves "NENÉ", Manuel SERAFIM Monteiro Pereira.   Trainer: Julio Carnadas Pereira "JUCA"

Goal: Towers (120)

AS ROMA v GÖZTEPE IZMIR 2-0 (1-0)

Stadio Olimpico, Roma   4.03.1970

Referee: Stanislaw Eksztajn (POL)   Attendance: 15,461

AS ROMA: Alberto Ginulfi; Aldo Bet, Luciano Spinosi, Elvio Salvori, Francesco Cappelli, Sergio Santarini, Renato Cappellini (81 Giorgio Braglia), Fausto Landini, Joaquim Lucas Peiro, Fabio Capello, Franco Cordova.
Trainer: Helenio Herrera

GÖZTEPE: Ali Artuner; Mehmet Işikal, Caglayan Derebasi, Özer Yurteri (83 Hüseyin Yazici, 86 Halil Kiraz), Mehmet Aydin, Nevzat Güzelirmak, Okcu Oglu, Ertan Öznur, Flemming Nielsen, Fevzi Zemzem, Gürsel Aksel.

Goals: Landini (32), Capelli (76)

GÖZTEPE IZMIR v AS ROMA 0-0

Alsançak, Izmir   18.03.1970

Referee: Laurens van Ravens (HOL)   Attendance: 21,917

GÖZTEPE: Ali Artuner; Mehmet Işikal, Caglayan Derebasi, Özer Yurteri, Mehmet Aydin, Nevzat Güzelirmak (46 Okcu Oglu), Halil Kiraz, Ertan Öznur, Fevzi Zemzem, Gürsel Aksel, Mehmet Türkan.

AS ROMA: Alberto Ginulfi; Aldo Bet, Francesco Scaratti, Luciano Spinosi, Francesco Cappelli, Sergio Santarini, Renato Cappellini, Fausto Landini, Joaquim Lucas Peiro, Fabio Capello, Franco Cordova.   Trainer: Helenio Herrera

LEVSKI SPARTAK SOFIA
v GÓRNIK ZABRZE 3-2 (2-1)

Vasil Levski, Sofia 4.03.1970

Referee: István Zsolt (HUN)   Attendance: 60,000

LEVSKI SPARTAK: Georgi Kamenski; Peshev, Dobromir Jechev, Stefan Aladjov, Kiril Ivkov, Ianko Kirilov, Petar Kirilov, Pavel Panov, Georgi Asparuhov, Nikola Kotkov, Vasil Mitkov (46 Aleksandar Kostov).   Trainer: Krastyo Chakarov

GÓRNIK: Hubert Kostka; Rainer Kuchta, Stanislaw Oslizlo, Henryk Latocha (16 Stefan Florenski), Jerzy Gorgon, Zygfryd Szoltysik, Erwin Wilczek, Alfred Olek, Jan Banas, Wlodzimierz Lubanski, Alojzy Deja.

Goals: Szoltysik (5), Asparuhov (30, 89), Panov (36), Banas (52)

SCHALKE 04 GELSENKIRCHEN
v DINAMO ZAGREB 1-0 (0-0)

Glückauf Kampfbahn, Gelsenkirchen   18.03.1970

Referee: Cornel Nițescu (ROM)   Attendance: 21,175

SCHALKE 04: Norbert Nigbur; Hans-Jürgen Becher, Friedel Rausch, Rolf Rüssmann, Klaus Fichtel, Heinz Van Haaren, Reinhard Libuda, Gerd Neuser, Alban Wüst (73 Klaus Scheer), Manfred Pohlschmidt, Hans Pirkner.
Trainer: Rudi Gutendorf

DINAMO: Fahrija Dautbegović; Rudolf Cvek (21 Drago Vabec), Branko Gracanin, Rudolf Belin, Mladen Ramljak, Ivica Miljković, Marijan Cercek, Daniel Pirić, Marijan Novak, Josip Gucmirtl, Krasnodar Rora.   Trainer: Ivica Horvath

Goal: Scheer (73)

SEMI-FINALS

GÓRNIK ZABRZE
v LEVSKI SPARTAK SOFIA 2-1 (1-0)

Slaski, Chorzów 18.03.1970

Referee: Hans-Joachim Weyland (W. GER)   Att: 100,000

GÓRNIK: Jan Gomola; Rainer Kuchta, Stanislaw Oslizlo, Henryk Latocha, Jerzy Gorgon, Zygfryd Szoltysik, Erwin Wilczek, Alfred Olek, Jan Banas, Wlodzimierz Lubanski, Alojzy Deja.

LEVSKI SPARTAK: Georgi Kamenski; Milko Gaidarski, Dobromir Jechev, Stefan Aladjov, Kiril Ivkov, Peshev (.. Pavel Panov), Tsvetan Veselinov, Ivan Stoianov, Georgi Asparuhov, Ianko Kirilov, Petar Kirilov.   Trainer: Krastyo Chakarov

Goals: Lubanski (44), Banas (56), P. Kirilov (59)

SCHALKE 04 GELSENKIRCHEN
v MANCHESTER CITY 1-0 (0-0)

Glückauf Kampfbahn, Gelsenkirchen   1.04.1970

Referee: Milivoje Gugulović (YUG)   Attendance: 27,429

SCHALKE 04: Norbert Nigbur; Waldemar Slomiany, Hans-Jürgen Becher (70 Alban Wüst), Hermann Erlhoff, Klaus Fichtel, Heinz Van Haaren, Reinhard Libuda, Gerd Neuser, Manfred Pohlschmidt, Hans-Jürgen Wittkamp (46 Klaus Scheer), Hans Pirkner.   Trainer: Rudi Gutendorf

MANCHESTER CITY: Joseph Corrigan; Anthony Book, Glyn Pardoe, Michael Doyle, Derek Jeffries, Alan Oakes, Thomas Booth, Colin Bell, Francis Lee, Neil Young, Michael Summerbee.   Manager: Joe Mercer

Goal: Libuda (76)

MANCHESTER CITY
v SCHALKE 04 GELSENKIRCHEN 5-1 (3-0)

Maine Road, Manchester   15.04.1970

Referee: Laurens van Ravens (HOL)   Attendance: 46,361

MANCHESTER CITY: Joseph Corrigan; Anthony Book, Glyn Pardoe, Michael Doyle (86 George Heslop), Thomas Booth, Alan Oakes, Anthony Towers, Colin Bell, Michael Summerbee (68 Francis Carrodus), Francis Lee, Neil Young.
Manager: Joe Mercer

SCHALKE 04: Norbert Nigbur; Waldemar Slomiany, Hans-Jürgen Becher, Rolf Rüssmann, Klaus Fichtel, Hans-Jürgen Wittkamp (63 Herbert Lütkebohmert), Reinhard Libuda, Gerd Neuser, Manfred Pohlschmidt, Hermann Erlhoff (46 Alban Wüst), Heinz Van Haaren.   Trainer: Rudi Gutendorf

Goals: Doyle (8), Young (14, 28), Lee (50), Bell (81), Libuda (89)

DINAMO ZAGREB
v SCHALKE 04 GELSENKIRCHEN 1-3 (0-1)

Maksimir, Zagreb 4.03.1970

Referee: Erich Linemayr (AUS)   Attendance: 2,593

DINAMO: Željko Stinčić; Rudolf Cvek, Damir Valec, Rudolf Belin, Mladen Ramljak, Filip Blasković, Marijan Cercek, Daniel Pirić, Marijan Novak, Josip Gucmirtl, Krasnodar Rora.   Trainer: Ivica Horvath

SCHALKE 04: Norbert Nigbur; Hans-Jürgen Becher, Friedel Rausch, Rolf Rüssmann, Klaus Fichtel, Klaus Senger (30 Hermann Erlhoff), Hans Pirkner, Jürgen Sobieray, Manfred Pohlschmidt, Heinz Van Haaren, Alban Wüst (.. Herbert Lütkebohmert).   Trainer: Rudi Gutendorf

Goals: Pirkner (42), Cercek (65), Fichtel (69), Becher (86)

AS ROMA v GÓRNIK ZABRZE 1-1 (0-1)

Stadio Olimpico, Roma   1.04.1970

Referee: Todor P.Betchkirov (BUL)   Attendance: 46,681

AS ROMA: Alberto Ginulfi; Luciano Spinosi, Aldo Bet, Elvio Salvori (67 Francesco Scaratti), Francesco Cappelli, Sergio Santarini, Renato Cappellini (85 Giorgio Braglia), Franco Cordova, Joaquim Lucas Peiro, Fabio Capello, Fausto Landini.   Trainer: Helenio Herrera

GÓRNIK: Hubert Kostka; Rainer Kuchta, Stanislaw Oslizlo, Henryk Latocha, Jerzy Gorgon, Zygfryd Szoltysik, Erwin Wilczek, Alfred Olek, Jan Banas, Wlodzimierz Lubanski, Alojzy Deja.   Trainer: Michal Matyas

Goals: Banas (29), Salvori (53)

GÓRNIK ZABRZE v AS ROMA 2-2 (0-1, 1-1) (AET)

Slaski, Chorzów   15.04.1970

Referee: José María Ortiz de Mendibil (SPA)   Att: 90,000

GÓRNIK: Hubert Kostka; Rainer Kuchta, Stanislaw Oslizlo, Henryk Latocha, Jerzy Gorgon, Zygfryd Szoltysik, Erwin Wilczek, Alfred Olek, Jan Banas, Wlodzimierz Lubanski, Alojzy Deja (46 Wladyslaw Szarynski).   Trainer: Michal Matyas

AS ROMA: Alberto Ginulfi; Francesco Scaratti, Aldo Bet, Elvio Salvori, Luciano Spinosi, Sergio Santarini, Renato Cappellini (106 Giacomo La Rosa), Fausto Landini (106 Giorgio Braglia), Joaquim Lucas Peiro, Fabio Capello, Walter Franzot.   Trainer: Helenio Herrera

Goals: Capello (9 pen), Lubanski (90 pen, 93), Scaratti (120)

REPLAY

AS ROMA v GÓRNIK ZABRZE 1-1 (0-1, 1-1) (AET)

Stade de la Meinau, Strasbourg   22.04.1970

Referee: Roger Machin (FRA)   Attendance: 9,949

AS ROMA: Alberto Ginulfi; Francesco Scaratti (46 Morales Victor Benitez), Aldo Bet, Elvio Salvori, Luciano Spinosi, Sergio Santarini, Renato Cappellini (93 Giacomo La Rosa), Fausto Landini, Joaquim Lucas Peiro, Fabio Capello, Sergio Petrelli.   Trainer: Helenio Herrera

GÓRNIK: Hubert Kostka; Stefan Florenski, Stanislaw Oslizlo, Henryk Latocha, Jerzy Gorgon, Zygfryd Szoltysik, Erwin Wilczek (91 Alojzy Deja), Alfred Olek, Jan Banas, Wlodzimierz Lubanski, Wladyslaw Szarynski (106 Jerzy Musialek).   Trainer: Michal Matyas

Goals: Lubanski (42), Capello (57 pen)

Górnik Zabrze won on the toss of a coin.

FINAL

MANCHESTER CITY v KS GÓRNIK ZABRZE 2-1 (2-0)

Prater, Wien   29.04.1970

Referee: Paul Schiller (AUS)   Attendance: 7,968

MANCHESTER CITY: Joseph Corrigan; Anthony Book (Cap), Thomas Booth, George Heslop, Glyn Pardoe; Michael Doyle (24 Ian Bowyer), Alan Oakes; Colin Bell, Francis Lee, Neil Young, Anthony Towers.   Manager: Joe Mercer

GÓRNIK: Hubert Kostka; Jerzy Gorgon, Stanislaw Oslizlo (Cap), Stefan Florenski (83 Alojzy Deja), Henryk Latocha; Alfred Olek, Zygrfyd Szoltysik, Erwin Wilczek (75 Hubert Skowronek); Jan Banas, Wlodzimierz Lubanski, Wladyslaw Szarynski.   Trainer: Michal Matyas

Goals: Young (12), Lee (43 pen), Oslizlo (68)

Goalscorers Cup-Winners' Cup 1969-70:

7 goals: Wlodzimierz Lubanski (Górnik Zabrze)

6 goals: Francis Lee (Manchester City)

5 goals: André Denul (Lierse), Colin Bell (Manchester City), Jan Banas (Górnik Zabrze)

4 goals: Frans Vermeyen (Lierse), Nikola Kotkov (Levski Spartak Sofia), Neil Young (Manchester City)

3 goals: Charles Loubet (Marseille), Bent Schmidt-Hansen (PSV Eindhoven), Alexander Allan, Peter King (Cardiff City), Jürgen Sparwasser (FC Magdeburg), Flemming Nielsen (Göztepe), Marijan Novak (Dinamo Zagreb), Reinhard Libuda, Hans Pirkner (Schalke), Fabio Capello, Elvio Salvori (Roma), Erwin Wilczek (Górnik Zabrze)

2 goals: Barber (Sharock Rovers), Henning Hansen (Frem), Flögel (Rapid Wien), Hultberg (IFK Norrköping), Van der Kuylen, Veenstra (PSV Eindhoven), Clark, Toshack (Cardiff City), Johnston (Glasgow Rangers), Fevzi Zemzem (Göztepe), Asparuhov, I.Kirilov, Mitkov, Panov (Levski Spartak Sofia), Cercek (Dinamo Zagreb), Scheer (Schalke 04), Skowronek, Szoltysik (Górnik Zabrze)

1 goal: Gershkovich (Torpedo Moskva), Agathokleous (Apoel Nicosia), Bonnet, Serge (Sliema), Argoitia, Clemente, Uriarte (Athletic Bilbao), Bernardin, Weiss (US Luxembourg), Takács (MTK Budapest), J.Olsen, Solberg (Mjøndalen), Crothers (Ards), Gioutsos, Y.Sideris (Olympiakos), Bjerregaard, Redl (Rapid Wien), Hudec (Dukla Praha), Pressfeldt, Norblad, Jönsson (IFK Norrköping), Nafziger, Cornioley (St. Gallen), Put, Janssens (Lierse), Bird, Lea, Sutton (Cardiff City), Persson, Baxter (Glasgow Rangers), Alhinho, Mario Campos, Nené (Academica Coimbra), Ertan Özner, Gürsel Aksel, Fadil Özduran, Halil Artuner (Göztepe), P.Kirilov, Kostov, Veselinov, Gaidarski (Levski Spartak Sofia), Miljkovic, Josip Gucmirtl (Dinamo Zagreb), Fichtel, Becher, Wittkamp (Schalke 04), Cappelli, Scaratti, Landini, Peiro (Roma), Doyle, Towers, Summerbee, Booth, Oakes, Bowyer (Manchester City), Oslizlo, Szarynski, Olek (Górnik Zabrze)

Own goal: Echeberría (Athletic Bilbao) for Manchester City

CUP WINNERS' CUP 1970-71

PRELIMINARY ROUND

ÅTVIDABERG FF v PARTIZANI TIRANË 1-1 (0-1)
Kopparvallen, Åtvidaberg   23.08.1970
Referee: Robert Schaut (BEL)   Attendance: 2,146
ÅTVIDABERG: Ulf Blomberg, Jan Olsson, Kent Karlsson, Örjan Johansson, Conny Gustafsson, Bo Augustsson, Conny Torstensson (46 Leif Schenell), Anders Ljungberg, Lars Göran Andersson, Ove Eklund, Leif Franzen.
Trainer: Bengt Gustavsson
PARTIZANI: Baskim Muhedini, Sotir Seferaj, Safet Berisha, Astrit Ziu, Bujar Cani, Lin Shllaku (70 Thaka), Vladimir Balluku, Ragami, Sabah Bizi (85 Shehu), Panayot Pano, Mikel Janku.
Goals: Johansson (2 og), Franzen (61)

PARTIZANI TIRANË v ÅTVIDABERG FF 2-0 (2-0)
Qemal Stafa, Tiranë   2.09.1970
Referee: Dogan Babacan (TUR)   Attendance: 17,000
PARTIZANI: Baskim Muhedini, Sotir Seferaj, Safet Berisha, Astrit Ziu, Bujar Cani, Lin Shllaku, Vladimir Balluku (66 Thaka), Ragami, Sabah Bizi, Pano, Janku.
ÅTVIDABERG: Ulf Blomberg, Jan Olsson, Kent Karlsson, Sten-Åke Andersson, Conny Gustafsson, Bo Augustsson (55 Leif Franzen), Lars Göran Andersson, Anders Ljungberg, Veine Wallinder, Ove Eklund, Roland Sandberg (80 Örjan Johansson).   Trainer: Bengt Gustavsson
Goals: Pano (14), Ragami (35)

**BOHEMIANS DUBLIN
v TJ GOTTWALDOV 1-2** (1-0)
Dalymount Park, Dublin   26.08.1970
Referee: Frede Hansen (DEN)   Attendance: 8,544
BOHEMIANS: Denis Lowry, John Doran, David Parkes, John Fullam, Ronald Nolan, John Conway, Fran Swan (79 Byrne), Tommy Kelly, Anthony O'Connell, Noel Dunne, Mick Kelly.
TJ GOTTWALDOV: Jurasek, Zakopal, Klimes, František Hojsik, Ondra, Jugas, Ernest Malazsky, František Cipro, Zdenek Nehoda, Josef Jencik, Ján Urban.
Goals: Swan (22 pen), Urban (67), Nehoda (84)

**TJ GOTTWALDOV
v BOHEMIANS DUBLIN 2-2** (2-1)
Stadión Gottwaldov   2.09.1970
Referee: Gilbert Droz (SWI)   Attendance: 2,095
TJ GOTTWALDOV: Jurasek, Zakopal, František Hojsik, Klimes, Ondra, Jugas, Ernest Malazsky, František Cipro, Zdenek Nehoda (79 Zavadil), Josef Jencik, Ján Urban (72 Brezik).
BOHEMIANS: Denis Lowry, John Doran, David Parkes, John Fullam, Ronald Nolan, John Conway, Ben O'Sullivan, Tommy Kelly, Anthony O'Connell, Noel Dunne (79 Fran Swan), Mick Kelly.
Goals: Hojsik (5), Jencik (25), O'Connell (39), Dunne (64)

FIRST ROUND

FC ZÜRICH v IB AKUREYRI 7-1 (3-0)
Letzigrund, Zürich   16.09.1970
Referee: Alexandru Pîrvu (ROM)   Attendance: 5,700
IB AKUREYRI: Johansson, Sigurgeirsson, Sigurdsson, Austfjörd, Thorsteinsson, Fridriksson (80 S.Jonatansson), Magnús Jónatansson, Augustsson, Einarsson (46 Gudni Jónsson), Hermann Gunnarsson, Kari Arnason.
FC ZÜRICH: Karl Grob; Konrad Baumgartner, Hubert Münch (80 Daniel Steiger), Konrad Kyburz, Pirmin Stierli, Jakob Kuhn, Rosario Martinelli (46 Heinz Kissling), Kurt Grünig, Georg Volkert, Fritz Künzli, René-Pierre Quentin.
Goals: P. Stierli (1), Martinelli (34), Volkert (44, 49, 62), Künzli (52, 69), Arnason (71)

FC ZÜRICH v IB AKUREYRI 7-0 (4-0)
Stade Espenmoos, St.Gallen   22.09.1970
Referee: Cornel Nițescu (ROM)   Attendance: 1,975
FC ZÜRICH: Karl Grob, Konrad Baumgartner, René Hasler, Konrad Kyburz, Pirmin Stierli (46 Daniel Steiger), Jakob Kuhn (46 Heinz Kissling), Kurt Grünig, René-Pierre Quentin, Max Heer, Fritz Künzli, Georg Volkert.
IB AKUREYRI: Johansson, Sigurgeirsson, Sigurdsson, Austfjörd, Thorarinsson (58 Thorsteinsson), Fridriksson, Magnús Jónatansson, Augustsson, Kari Arnason, Hermann Gunnarsson, Gudni Jónsson.
Goals: Künzli (6, 13, 19), Volkert (17, 55), Heer (83), Grünig (87)

98

**GÖZTEPE IZMIR
v UNION SPORTIVE LUXEMBOURG 5-0** (3-0)

Alsançak, Izmir 16.09.1970

Referee: Prlja (ALB)   Attendance: 13,691

GÖZTEPE: Ali Artuner, Ayhan, Işikal Mehmet, Aydin Mehmet, Güzelirmak Nevzat, John Nielsen, Ertan Öznur, Fevzi Zemzem, Gürsel Aksel (60 Kiraz Halil), Cudi, Türkan Mehmet (60 Ali Ihsan Okçuoglu).

US: Roland Pletschette, Jean Hardt, René Schneider, Mathias Ewen, Johny Hoffmann, Portz, Jean Klein (46 Bertrand Heger), Guy Bernardin, Schuler, Nico Braun, Pierre Weis.

Goals: Ertan (18, 26, 57), Nevzat (21), Nielsen (90)

**UNION SPORTIVE LUXEMBOURG
v GÖZTEPE IZMIR 1-0** (1-0)

Stade Municipal, Luxembourg 23.09.1970

Referee: Hiqmet Kuka (ALB)   Attendance: 1,842

US: Roland Pletschette, Jean Hardt, Portz, Johny Hoffmann, René Schneider, Mathias Ewen, Schuler, Jean Klein, Nico Braun, Guy Bernardin, Pierre Weis.

GÖZTEPE: Ali Artuner, Ayhan, Cudi, Işikal Mehmet, Aydin Mehmet, Güzelirmak Nevzat, Ertan Öznur, John Nielsen, Fevzi Zemzem, Gürsel Aksel, Türkan Mehmet.

Goal: Braun (15)

**FC WACKER INNSBRUCK
v PARTIZANI TIRANI 3-2** (1-2)

Tivoli, Innsbruck 16.09.1970

Referee: Milivoje Gugulović (YUG)   Attendance: 7,944

WACKER: Herbert Rettensteiner (30 Leo Tschenett); Roland Eschlmüller, Heinz Binder, Peter Werner, Helmut Voggenberger; Johann Eigenstiller, Josip Francescin, Josef Obert (60 Helmut Senekowitsch), Leopold Grausam, Johannes Ettmayer, Kurt Jara.   Trainer: Branko Elsner

PARTIZANI: Baskim Muhedini, Sotir Seferaj, Safet Berisha, Astrit Ziu, Bujar Cani, Lin Shllaku, Vladimir Balluku, Ragami, Sabah Bizi, Panayot Pano, Mikel Janku.

Goals: Pano (22), Janku (23), Ettmayer (40 pen), Obert (52), Franceskin (83)

**PARTIZANI TIRANË
v FC WACKER INNSBRUCK 1-2** (1-1)

Qemal Stafa, Tiranë 30.09.1970

Referee: Rudolf Scheurer (SWI)   Attendance: 17,508

PARTIZANI: Baskim Muhedini, Sotir Seferaj, Safet Berisha, Astrit Ziu, Bujar Cani, Lin Shllaku, Vladimir Balluku, Ragami, Sabah Bizi, Panayot Pano, Mikel Janku (79 Fatmir Ismaili).

WACKER: Herbert Rettensteiner; Roland Eschlmüller, Werner, Johann Eigenstiller, Werner Kriess; Helmut Senekowitsch, Josip Francescin, Josef Obert, Leopold Grausam, Johannes Ettmayer, Kurt Jara.   Trainer: B. Elsner

Goals: Ragami (24), Grausam (38, 67)

VORWÄRTS BERLIN v AC BOLOGNA 0-0

Friedrich Ludwig Jahn Stadion, Berlin 16.09.1970

Referee: Adrianus Boogaerts (HOL)   Attendance: 17,372

VORWÄRTS: Alfred Zulkowski, Otto Frässdorf, Manfred Müller, Rainer Withulz (89 Heinz Dietzsch), Erich Hamann, Gerhard Körner, Jürgen Pfefferkorn (80 Wolfgang Strübing), Horst Wruck, Jürgen Nöldner, Horst Begerad, Jürgen Piepenburg.   Trainer: Hans-Georg Kiupel

BOLOGNA: Giuseppe Vavassori, Tazio Roversi, Adriano Fedele, Franco Cresci, Francesco Janich, Ivan Gregori, Francesco Liguori (85 Roberto Prini), Francesco Rizzo, Giuseppe Savoldi, Giacomo Bulgarelli, Bruno Pace.   Trainer: Juan Carlos Lorenzo

**AC BOLOGNA
v VORWÄRTS BERLIN 1-1** (0-0, 0-0) (AET)

Stadio Comunale, Bologna 30.09.1970

Referee: Robert Hélies (FRA)   Attendance: 16,568

BOLOGNA: Giuseppe Vavassori, Tazio Roversi, Adriano Fedele, Franco Cresci, Francesco Janich, Ivan Gregori, Marino Perani (46 Francesco Liguori), Francesco Rizzo, Giuseppe Savoldi, Giacomo Bulgarelli (89 Augusto Scala), Bruno Pace.   Trainer: Juan Carlos Lorenzo

VORWÄRTS: Alfred Zulkowski, Otto Frässdorf, Manfred Müller, Rainer Withulz (60 Norbert Meyer), Erich Hamann, Gerhard Körner, Horst Wruck (87 Jürgen Pfefferkorn), Wolfgang Strübing, Jürgen Nöldner, Horst Begerad, Jürgen Piepenburg.   Trainer: Hans-Georg Kiupel

Goals: Savoldi (106), Begerad (112)

TJ GOTTWALDOV v PSV EINDHOVEN 2-1 (1-0)

Stadión Gottwaldov 16.09.1970

Referee: Erich Linemayr (AUS)   Attendance: 4,000

TJ GOTTWALDOV: Hastik, Zakopal, Klimes, František Hojsik, Nemec, Zavadil (80 Malits), Kucera, František Cipro, Zdenek Nehoda, Josef Jencik, Ján Urban.

PSV: Jan van Beveren, Wim van den Dungen, Henning Munk Jensen, Pleun Strik, Harry Vos, Gerrit van Tilburg (41 Jac van Stippent), Guus Hiddink (46 Eef Mulders), Bengt Schmidt-Hansen, Johan Devrindt, Willy van der Kuylen, Wietse Veenstra.   Trainer: Kurt Linder

Goals: Urban (2), Nehoda (53), Devrindt (88)

PSV EINDHOVEN v TJ GOTTWALDOV 1-0 (0-0)
Philips, Eindhoven   30.09.1970
Referee: Kåre Sirevaag (NOR)   Attendance: 15,500
PSV: Jan van Beveren, Peter Kemper, Lazar Radović, Henning Munk Jensen, Pleun Strik, Harry Vos (87 Guus Hiddink), Wim van den Dungen, Bengt Schmidt-Hansen, Eef Mulders, Willy van der Kuylen (87 Johan Devrindt), Wietse Veenstra.   Trainer: Kurt Linder
TJ GOTTWALDOV: Hastik, Zakopal, Ernest Malazsky, František Hojsik, Nemec, Kucera, Jugas, František Cipro, Zdenek Nehoda, Josef Jencik, Ján Urban.
Goal: Veenstra (46)

KARPATI LVOV v STEAUA BUCUREŞTI 0-1 (0-0)
Druzba, Lvov   16.09.1970
Referee: István Zsolt (HUN)   Attendance: 48,000
KARPATI: Gavriil Vajda; Ivan Gereg, Rostislav Potochniak, Pietr Danilchuk, Valeri Sirov; Lev Brovarski (81 Vladimir Bulgakov), Bogdan Greschak, Ostap Savka, Yanosch Gabovda (57 Vladimir Daniliuk), Igor Kulcitski, Gennadi Likhachiov.   Trainer: Ernest Just
STEAUA: Vasile Suciu; Lajos Sătmăreanu, Marius Ciugarin, Iosif Vigu, Costică Ştefănescu, Bujor Hălmăgeanu, Nicolae Pantea, Gheorghe Tătaru, Dumitru Dumitriu III, Ion Naom, Dumitru Manea.   Trainer: Ştefan Kovacs
Goal: Tătaru (88)

HIBERNIANS PAOLA v REAL MADRID 0-0
Empire Stadium, Valletta   16.09.1970
Referee: Leo Callaghan (WAL)   Attendance: 16,056
HIBERNIANS: Alfred Mizzi, John Privitera, Alfred Mallia, Edward Theobald, Edgar Azzopardi, Alfred Delia, Charlie Micallef, Salvu Gatt, Salvu Bonello, Norman Buckle, Lawrence Young (70 Blacklock).   Trainer: Stanley Matthews
REAL: MIGUEL ÁNGEL González Suarez, JOSÉ LUIS López Peinado, Manuel SANCHIS Martínez, José Antonio GRANDE Cereijo, Pedro DE FELIPE Cortés, Gregorio BENITO Rubio, José Martínez Sánchez "PIRRI", Manuel VELÁZQUEZ Villaverde, AMANCIO Amaro Varela, Juan Bautista PLANELLES Marco, Francisco GENTO López (46 Sebastián FLEITAS Miranda).   Trainer: Miguel MUÑOZ Mozún

STEAUA BUCUREŞTI v KARPATI LVOV 3-3 (2-2)
Republicii, Bucureşti   30.09.1970
Referee: Günter Männig (E. GER)   Attendance: 12,000
STEAUA: Vasile Suciu; Lajos Sătmăreanu, Bujor Hălmăgeanu, Marius Ciugarin, Iosif Vigu; Dumitru Dumitriu (69 Ion Naom), Costică Ştefănescu (80 Vasile Negrea); Nicolae Pantea, Gheorghe Tătaru, Anghel Iordănescu, Dumitru Manea.   Trainer: Ştefan Kovacs
KARPATI: Mikhail Luppol; Ivan Gereg, Rostislav Potochniak, Pietr Danilchuk, Valeri Sirov; Lev Brovarski (81 Vladimir Bulgakov), Igor Kulchitski, Bogdan Greschak, Ostap Savka, Yanosch Gabovda, Gennadi Likhachiov (83 Vladimir Daniliuk).   Trainer: Ernest Just
Goals: Kulchitski (13), Dumitriu III (16), Gabovda (24), Tătaru (27 pen), Ştefănescu (69), Greschak (90)

REAL MADRID v HIBERNIANS PAOLA 5-0 (1-0)
Estadio Santiago Bernabéu, Madrid   30.09.1970
Referee: Joaquim Fernandes de Campos (POR)   Att: 16,469
REAL: MIGUEL ÁNGEL González Suarez, JOSÉ LUIS López Peinado, Gregorio BENITO Rubio, Manuel SANCHIS Martínez, José Antonio GRANDE Cereijo, Ignacio ZOCO Esparza, AMANCIO Amaro Varela, José Martínez Sánchez "PIRRI" (46 Rafael Pérez González "MARAÑON"), Juan Bautista PLANELLES Marco, Manuel VELÁZQUEZ Villaverde, Francisco GENTO López (61 Manuel BUENO Cabral).   Trainer: Miguel MUÑOZ Mozún
HIBERNIANS: Alfred Mizzi, John Privitera, Edgar Azzopardi, Alfred Delia, Salvu Gatt, Alfred Mallia, Edward Theobald, Lawrence Young, Charlie Micallef, Salvu Bonello, Norman Buckle (57 Tony Zerafa).   Trainer: Stanley Matthews
Goals: Pirri (1), Planelles (8, 54, 82), Marañon (51)

AALBORG BK v GÓRNIK ZABRZE 0-1 (0-1)
Aalborg stadium   16.09.1970
Referee: William Mullan (SCO)   Attendance: 4,700
AALBORG: Kaj Poulsen, J.Andersen, Claus Johansen (75 Karsten Holm Jensen), Arne Toft, Jørgen Christensen, Kurt Berthelsen, Børge Bach, Ove Flindt Bjerg, Ole Storch, Finn Jønsson, Erling Andersen (71 Per Haugaard).
GÓRNIK: Hubert Kostka, Jan Wrazy (71 Rainer Kuchta), Stanislaw Oslizlo, Henryk Latocha, Jerzy Gorgon, Zygfryd Szoltysik, Alfred Olek, Hubert Skowronek, Jerzy Wilim, Włodzimierz Lubanski, Wladyslaw Szarynski.   Trainer: Géza Kalocsay
Goal: Lubanski (28)

GÓRNIK ZABRZE v AALBORG BK 8-1 (3-1)
Górnik, Zabrze 30.09.1970
Referee: Tofik Bakhramov (USSR)   Attendance: 10,000
GÓRNIK: Jan Gomola, Rainer Kuchta, Stanislaw Oslizlo, Jan Wrazy, Jerzy Gorgon, Zygfryd Szoltysik, Erwin Wilczek (.. Jerzy Kowalik), Alfred Olek, Jerzy Wilim, Włodzimierz Lubanski, Wladyslaw Szarynski.   Trainer: Géza Kalocsay
AALBORG: Kaj Poulsen, J. Andersen, Jørgen Christensen, Kurt Berthelsen, Arne Toft, Claus Johansen, Ole Storch, Børge Bach, Jønsson (70 Simonsen), Erling Andersen (51 Karsten Holm Jensen), Ove Flindt Bjerg.
Goals: Szarynski (1), Olek (8, 84), Wilim (15, 58), E. Andersen (27), Lubanski (46, 74 pen), Szoltysik (51)

STRØMSGODSET IF DRAMMEN
v FC NANTES 0-5 (0-2)
Marienlyst, Drammen 16.09.1970
Referee: Curt F. Liedberg (SWE)   Attendance: 6,000
STRØMSGODSET: Inge Thun; Per Rune Wøllner, Arild Mathisen, Tor Alsaker Nøstdahl, Erik Eriksen; Odd Arild Amundsen (46 Johnny vidar Pedersen), Jan Kristiansen; Egil Olsen (82 Ole Jonny Friise), Bjørn Odmar Andersen, Steinar Pettersen, Thorodd Presberg.
FC NANTES: Jean-Michel Fouché; Roger Lemerre, Jean-Claude Osman, Patrice Rio, Gabriel De Michele; Henri Michel, Claude Arribas; Bernard Blanchet, Philippe Gondet, Allan Michaelsen, Philippe Levavasseur.   Trainer: José Arribas
Goals: Gondet (30), Levavasseur (42, 64), Arribas (62), Michel (90)

ABERDEEN v HONVÉD BUDAPEST 3-1 (2-1)
Pittodrie, Aberdeen 16.09.1970
Referee: Anton Bucheli (SWI)   Attendance: 21,500
ABERDEEN: Robert Clark; Hermiston, George Murray (75 James Hamilton), Stephen Murray, Henning Boel; Martin Buchan, Arthur Graham; Derek McKay (68 George Buchan), Robb, James Forrest, Joseph Harper.
HONVÉD: Bertalan Bicskei; László Molnár, József Ruzsinszki, József Tajti, Pal Vári; Imre Komora, István Vági; László Pusztai (75 Sándor Pintér), Gyula Tóth, Lajos Kocsis, Lajos Szurgent.   Trainer: Kálmán Preiner
Goals: Pusztai (7), Graham (12), Harper (32), S. Murray (83)

FC NANTES
v STRØMSGODSET IF DRAMMEN 2-3 (0-0)
Stade Marcel-Saupin, Nantes 30.09.1970
Referee: Mariano Medina Iglesias (SPA)   Attendance: 6,000
FC NANTES: Jean-Michel Fouché; Roger Lemerre, Jean-Claude Osman, Patrice Rio (57 Jacques Le Bourgocq), Gabriel De Michele; Claude Arribas (46 Michel Pech), Henri Michel; Bernard Blanchet, Philippe Gondet, Allan Michaelsen, Philippe Levavasseur.   Trainer: José Arribas
STRØMSGODSET: Inge Thun; Arild Mathisen, Jan Kristiansen, Tor Alsaker Nøstdahl, Erik Eriksen; Johnny Vidar Pedersen (34 Håvard Beckstrøm), Odd Arild Amundsen; Bjørn Odmar Andersen, Steinar Pettersen, V. Pettersen, Ingar Pettersen (69 Per Rune Wøllner)
Goals: I. Pettersen (50), S. Pettersen (53, 55), Levavasseur (70), Blanchet (85)

HONVÉD BUDAPEST
v ABERDEEN 3-1 (1-0, 3-1) (AET)
Kispest, Budapest 30.09.1970
Referee: Concetto Lo Bello (ITA)   Attendance: 5,000
HONVÉD: Bertalan Bicskei; József Tajti, József Ruzsinszki, Pal Vári (46 Gyula Tóth), László Marosi; Lajos Kocsis, István Vági; László Pusztai, Sándor Pintér, Mihály Kozma, József Karakas (61 Lajos Tichy).   Trainer: Kálmán Preiner
ABERDEEN: Robert Clark; Henning Boel, William Young (46 Alexander Willoughby), Hermiston, George Murray, Joseph Harper, Martin Buchan, Robb, James Forrest, Stephen Murray, Arthur Graham.
Goals: Kocsis (19, 69), Kozma (58), S. Murray (78)
Penalties: 0-1 Murray, 1-1 Tichy, 1-2 Harper, 2-2 Kocsis, Forrest, 3-2 Marosi, 3-3 Hermiston, 4-3 Vagi, 4-4 Willoughby, 5-4 Bicskei

ARIS THESSALONIKI
v CHELSEA LONDON 1-1 (0-0)
Kautatzogleio Thessaloniki 16.09.1970
Referee: Gyula Emsberger (HUN)   Attendance: 42,103
ARIS: Nikos Hristidis, Theodoros Pallas, Hristos Nalbantis, Sofoklis Semertzis, Aggelos Spiridon, Takis Loukanidis, Giorgos Konstantinidis, Manolis Keramidas, Alekos Alexiadis, Vaggelis Siropoulos, Kostas Papaioannou.
Trainer: Milovan Cirić
CHELSEA: Peter Bonetti, Patrick Mulligan, Ronald Harris, John Hollins, John Dempsey, David Webb, Keith Weller, Alan Hudson, Peter Osgood, Ian Hutchinson, Charles Cooke.
Manager: Dave Sexton
Sent off: Dempsey (40)
Goals: Alexiadis (51), Hutchinson (75)

CHELSEA LONDON
v ARIS THESSALONIKI 5-1 (3-0)

Stamford Bridge, London 30.09.1970

Referee: Martti Hirviniemi (FIN)   Attendance: 40,425

CHELSEA: Peter Bonetti, Patrick Mulligan, Ronald Harris, John Hollins, Marvin Hinton, David Webb, Keith Weller, Alan Hudson, Peter Osgood (90 Thomas Baldwin), Ian Hutchinson, Peter Houseman.   Manager: Dave Sexton

ARIS: Nikos Hristidis, Hristos Nalbantis, Klimis Gounaris, Giannis Balafas, Dimitris Raptopoulos, Sofoklis Semertzis, Takis Loukanidis (32 Giorgos Konstantinidis), Alekos Alexiadis, Zisis Mittas, Vaggelis Siropoulos, Kostas Papaioannou.   Trainer: Milovan Ćirić

Goals: Hollins (7, 27), Hutchinson (20, 56), Hinton (52), Alexiadis (85)

KICKERS OFFENBACH
v CLUB BRUGGE 2-1 (0-1)

Biebererbergstadion, Offenbach 16.09.1970

Referee: Bertil Lööw (SWE)   Attendance: 17,422

KICKERS: Karl-Heinz Volz, Josef Weilbächer, Roland Weida, Hans Reich, Helmut Kremers, Walter Bechtold, Egon Schmitt, Winfried Schäfer (65 Gerhard Kraft), Horst Gecks, Klaus Winkler, Helmut Nerlinger.   Trainer: Alfred Schmidt

CLUB BRUGGE: Luc Sanders, Alfons Bastijns, Kurt Axelsson, Erwin Vandendaele, Freddy Hinderijckx (62 John Moulaert), Henk Houwaart, Pierre Carteus, Gilbert Marmenout, Johnny Thio, Raoul Lambert, Rob Rensenbrink.
Trainer: Frans de Munck

Goals: Lambert (33), H. Kremers (48 pen, 67)

OLIMPIA LJUBLJANA
v BENFICA LISBOA 1-1 (0-1)

Central, Ljubljana 16.09.1970

Referee: Paul Bonett (MAL)   Attendance: 11,951

OLIMPIJA: Zlatko Škorić; Andjelo Milevoj (46 Radoslav Bečejac), Miloš Šoškić, Dragan Popadić, Dragan Rogić; Zlatko Klampfer, Marjan Golac; Danilo Popivoda, Ivan Pejović, Viliam Ameršek, Branko Oblak.

BENFICA: JOSÉ HENRIQUE Rodrigues Marques, António José MALTA da SILVA, HUMBERTO Manuel Jesus COELHO, José Cavaco "Zeca", António Monteiro Teixeira de BARROS; JAIME da Silva GRAÇA (88 Tamagnini Manuel Gomes Baptista NENÉ), Augusto MATINE, VITOR Manuel Rosa MARTINS ; Artur Jorge, EUSÉBIO da Silva Ferreira, Antonio José SIMÕES da Costa.   Trainer: James Hagan

Goals: Eusébio (30), Pejović (53)

CLUB BRUGGE
v KICKERS OFFENBACH 2-0 (1-0)

Albert Dyserynck Stadion, Brugge 30.09.1970

Referee: Fernando Santos Leite (POR)   Attendance: 20,000

CLUB BRUGGE: Luc Sanders, Alfons Bastijns, Kurt Axelsson, Erwin Vandendaele, John Moulaert (86 Freddy Hinderijckx), Henk Houwaart, Pierre Carteus, Gilbert Marmenout, Johnny Thio, Raoul Lambert, Rob Rensenbrink.
Trainer: Frans de Munck

KICKERS: Karl-Heinz Volz, Josef Weilbächer, Egon Schmitt (46 Nikolaus Semlitsch), Hans Reich (84 Heinz Schönberger), Helmut Kremers, Roland Weida, Walter Bechtold, Winfried Schäfer, Helmut Schmidt, Horst Gecks, Klaus Winkler.
Trainer: Rudi Gutendorf

Goals: Marmenout (30), Hinderijckx (90)

BENFICA LISBOA
v OLIMPIA LJUBLJANA 8-1 (3-0)

Estádio da Luz, Lisboa 30.09.1970

Referee: Antoine Queudeville (LUX)   Attendance: 38,760

BENFICA: JOSÉ HENRIQUE Rodrigues Marques, António José MALTA da SILVA, HUMBERTO Manuel Jesus COELHO, José Cavaco "ZECA", António José da Conceição Oliveira "TONI" (80 António Monteiro Teixeira de BARROS); JAIME da Silva GRAÇA, Augusto MATINE, Antonio José SIMÕES da Costa; Artur Jorge, José Torres, EUSÉBIO da Silva Ferreira.   Trainer: James Hagan

OLIMPIJA: Zlatko Škorić; Atanas Djorlev, Dragan Rogić, Zlatko Klampfer, Miloš Šoškić; Dragan Popadić, Danilo Popivoda; Marjan Golac (46 Mahmut Kapidžić), Radoslav Bečejac, Viliam Ameršek, Branko Oblak.

Goals: Eusebio (26, 30, 32, 71, 83), Zeca (47), Artur Jorge (67), Graça (83), Ameršek (51)

MANCHESTER CITY
v LINFIELD BELFAST 1-0 (0-0)

Maine Road, Manchester 16.09.1970

Referee: Gudmundur Haraldsson (ICE)   Attendance: 25,184

CITY: Joseph Corrigan, Anthony Book, Glyn Pardoe, Mike Doyle, Thomas Booth, Alan Oakes, Michael Summerbee, Colin Bell, Francis Lee, Neil Young, Anthony Towers.
Manager: Joseph Mercer

LINFIELD: Derek Humphries, Alan Fraser, John Patterson, Isaac Andrews (78 Ronnie McAteer), Ivan McAllister, Eric Bowyer, William Millen (.. Phil Scott), Eric Magee, Bryan Hamilton, William Sinclair, Des Cathcart.
Manager: William Bingham

Goal: Bell (83)

**LINFIELD BELFAST
v MANCHESTER CITY 2-1** (1-1)
Windsor Park, Belfast   30.09.1970
Referee: William J. Gow (WAL)   Attendance: 25,000
LINFIELD: Derek Humphries, Alan Fraser, John Patterson, Eric Bowyer, Isaac Andrews, Ivan McAllister, William Sinclair, William Millen, Eric Magee, Bryan Hamilton, Des Cathcart.   Manager: William Bingham
CITY: Joseph Corrigan, Anthony Book, Derek Jeffries, Alan Oakes, Glyn Pardoe, Michael Doyle, Colin Bell, Neil Young, Michael Summerbee, Francis Lee (19 Ian Bowyer), Anthony Towers.   Manager: Joseph Mercer
Goals: Millen (4, 56), Lee (6)

CSKA SOFIA v HAKA VALKEAKOSKI 9-0 (5-0)
Narodna Armia, Sofia   16.09.1970
Referee: Nejat Sener (TUR)   Attendance: 20,182
CSKA: Iordan Filipov; Ivan Zafirov, Kiril Stankov, Plamen Iankov, Georgi Denev, Dimitar Penev (46 Ivan Tishanski), Tsvetan Atanasov, Asparuh Nikodimov, Petar Jekov, Dimitar Iakimov, Dimitar Marashliev.   Trainer: Manol Manolov
HAKA: Martti Halme, Markku Närvä, Jorma Huovinen, Antti Nieminen, Hannu Asikainen (46 Markku Eloranta), Seppo And, Juhani Haavisto, Esko Malm, Juhani Peltonen, Juhani Tapola (75 Mauri Paavilainen), Jukka Pirinen.
Goals: Iakimov (7, 30, 68), Nikodimov (15, 37), Asikainen (43 og), Jekov (61, 81), Marashliev (77)

HAKA VALKEAKOSKI v CSKA SOFIA 1-2 (0-0)
Tehtaankenttä, Valkeakoski   30.09.1970
Referee: Erwin Vetter (E. GER)   Attendance: 627
HAKA: Martti Halme, Juhani Haavisto, Jorma Huovinen, Antti Nieminen, Markku Eloranta, Seppo And, Esko Malm, Juhani Tapola, Juhani Peltonen (75 Hannu Asikainen), Jukka Pirinen, Markku Närvä.
CSKA: Iordan Filipov; Ivan Zafirov, Boris Gaganelov, Plamen Iankov, Georgi Denev (65 Kiril Liubomirov), Dimitar Penev, Tsvetan Atanasov, Asparuh Nikodimov, Petar Jekov, Dimitar Iakimov, Dimitar Marashliev (55 Ivan Tishanski).   Trainer: Manol Manolov
Goals: Iakimov (50, 56), Malm (88)

**CARDIFF CITY
v PEZOPORIKOS LARNACA 8-0** (5-0)
Ninian Park, Cardiff   16.09.1970
Referee: Jacques Colling (LUX)   Attendance: 12,984
CITY: Frank Parsons, David Carver, Gary Bell, Melwin Sutton, Donald Murray, Brian Harris, Ian Gibson, Brian Clark, Robert Woodruff, John Benjamin Toshack, Peter King.   Trainer: James Scoular
PEZOPORIKOS: Takis Palmiris, Giannis Petrou, Giannis Paridis, Kallis Konstantinou, Stelios Kyriakou, Dinos Hatzistillis, Giorgos Kounnidis, Antonis Karapittas, Hristos Loizou, Grigoris Filiastidis, Stavrinos Konstantinou.
Goals: Sutton (18), Gibson (33), King (36), Woodruff (40), Clark (44, 60), Toshack (54, 82)

SECOND ROUND

CARDIFF CITY v FC NANTES 5-1 (3-1)
Ninian Park, Cardiff   21.10.1970
Referee: Wolfgang Riedel (E. GER)   Attendance: 17,905
CITY: James Eadie; David Carver, Gary Bell, Melwin Sutton, Donald Murray, Brian Harris, Ian Gibson, Brian Clark (78 Leighton Phillips), Robert Woodruff, John Benjamin Toshack, Peter King.   Manager: James Scoular
FC NANTES: Jean-Michel Fouché; Roger Lemerre, Gabriel De Michele, Jean-Claude Osman, Patrice Rio, Allan Michaelsen, Bernard Blanchet, Henri Michel, Patrice Kervarrec, Philippe Gondet, Michel Pech (67 Joël Audiger).   Trainer: José Arribas
Goals: Gondet (2), Toshack (8, 37), Gibson (9), King (76), Phillips (82)

PEZOPORIKOS LARNACA v CARDIFF CITY 0-0
GSZ, Larnaca   30.09.1970
Referee: Petar Nikolov (BUL)   Attendance: 2,100
PEZOPORIKOS: Takis Palmiris, Giannis Petrou, Giannis Paridis, Kallis Konstantinou, Stelios Kyriakou, Dinos Hatzistillis, Giorgos Kounnidis, Antonis Karapittas, Hristos Loizou, Grigoris Filiastidis, Stavrinos Konstantinou.
CITY: Frank Parsons; David Carver, Gary Bell, Melwin Sutton; Donald Murray, Brian Harris; Ian Gibson, Brian Clark, Robert Woodruff, John Benjamin Toshack (68 Leighton Phillips), Peter King.   Trainer: James Scoular

FC NANTES v CARDIFF CITY 1-2 (0-1)

Stade Marcel Saupin, Nantes   4.11.1970

Referee: Timoleon Latsios (GRE)   Attendance: 10,000

FC NANTES: Jean-Michel Fouché; Roger Lemerre, Gabriel De Michele, Patrice Rio, Bernard Gardon; Henri Michel, Allan Michaelsen; Bernard Blanchet, Patrice Kervarrec, Michel Pech (70 Michel Albaladejo), Joël Audiger.   Trainer: José Arribas

CITY: James Eadie; David Carver, Gary Bell, Melwin Sutton, Donald Murray, Brian Harris, Ian Gibson, John Benjamin Toshack, Leighton Phillips (.. Brian Clark), Robert Woodruff, Peter King.   Manager: James Scoular

Goals: Toshack (13), Clark (76), Blanchet (85)

HONVÉD BUDAPEST v MANCHESTER CITY 0-1 (0-0)

Kispest, Budapest   21.10.1970

Referee: Mariano Medina Iglesias (SPA)   Att: 10,000

HONVÉD: Bertalan Bicskei; József Tajti, József Ruzsinszki, László Marosi, Pal Vári; Lajos Kocsis, Imre Komora, István Vági (67 Gyula Tóth); László Pusztai, Lajos Tichy (46 József Karakas), Mihály Kozma.   Trainer: Kálmán Preiner

CITY: Joseph Corrigan, Anthony Book, Glyn Pardoe, Mike Doyle, George Heslop, Derek Jeffries, Michael Summerbee, Colin Bell, Francis Lee, Freddie Hill, Anthony Towers.
Manager: Joseph Mercer

Goal: Lee (65)

REAL MADRID v WACKER INNSBRUCK 0-1 (0-1)

Estadio SantiagoBernabeu, Madrid   21.10.1970

Referee: Laurens van Ravens (HOL)   Attendance: 18,353

REAL: MIGUEL ÁNGEL González Suarez; JOSÉ LUIS López Peinado, Manuel SANCHIS Martínez (72 MIGUEL Ángel PÉREZ Pilipuix), José Antonio GRANDE Cereijo (46 Ferando ORTUÑO Blasco), Pedro DE FELIPE Cortés, Gregorio BENITO Rubio, AMANCIO Amaro Varela, José Martínez Sánchez "PIRRI", Rafael Pérez González "MARAÑON", Manuel VELÁZQUEZ Villaverde, Manuel BUENO Cabral.
Trainer: Miguel MUÑOZ Mozún

WACKER: Herbert Rettensteiner; Roland Eschlmüller, Werner, Johann Eigenstiller, Werner Kriess; Heinz Binder, Josip Francescin, Josef Obert, Leopold Grausam, Johannes Ettmayer, Kurt Jara (61 Franz Wolny).   Trainer: Branko Elsner

Goal: Grausam (1)

MANCHESTER CITY v HONVÉD BUDAPEST 2-0 (1-0)

Maine Road, Manchester   4.11.1970

Referee: Fernando Nunes Santos Leite (POR)   Att: 28,770

CITY: Joseph Corrigan, Anthony Book, Glyn Pardoe, Mike Doyle, George Heslop; Alan Oakes, Michael Summerbee, Colin Bell, Francis Lee, Freddie Hill, Anthony Towers.
Manager: Joseph Mercer

HONVÉD: Bertalan Bicskei; József Tajti, József Ruzsinszki, István Vági, László Marosi; Gyula Tóth (32 Pal Vári), Lajos Kocsis, Imre Komora; Sándor Pintér (60 László Pusztai), Mihály Kozma, Lajos Szurgent.   Trainer: Kálmán Preiner

Goals: Bell (10), Lee (67)

WACKER INNSBRUCK v REAL MADRID 0-2 (0-0)

Tivoli, Innsbruck   4.11.1970

Referee: István Zsolt (HUN)   Attendance: 15,048

WACKER: Herbert Rettensteiner; Roland Eschlmüller, Werner, Johann Eigenstiller, Werner Kriess; Heinz Binder, Josip Francescin (72 Franz Wolny), Josef Obert, Leopold Grausam, Johannes Ettmayer, Kurt Jara (80 Boris Sikic).
Trainer: Branko Elsner

REAL: MIGUEL ÁNGEL González Suarez; JOSÉ LUIS López Peinado, Manuel SANCHIS Martínez, José Antonio GRANDE Cereijo, Gregorio BENITO Rubio, Ignacio ZOCO Esparza, MIGUEL Ángel PÉREZ Pilipuix, José Martínez Sánchez "PIRRI", Sebastián FLEITAS Miranda, Manuel VELÁZQUEZ Villaverde, Manuel BUENO Cabral.
Trainer: Miguel MUÑOZ Mozún

Goals: Grande (76), Bueno (83)

PSV EINDHOVEN v STEAUA BUCUREȘTI 4-0 (1-0)

Philips Sportpark, Eindhoven   21.10.1970

Referee: Gerhard Schulenburg (W. GER)   Att: 19,500

PSV: Jan Van Beveren; Wim Van den Dungen, Pleun Strik, Lazar Radović, Peter Kemper; Guus Hiddink (65 Johan Devrindt), Harry Vos; Wietze Veenstra, Bent Schmidt-Hansen, Willy Van der Kuylen, Eef Mulders.   Trainer: Kurt Linder

STEAUA: Vasile Suciu; Lajos Sătmăreanu, Marius Ciugarin, Iosif Vigu; Dumitru Dumitriu, Bujor Hămăgeanu, Nicolae Pantea, Gheorghe Tătaru, Anghel Iordănescu, Costică Ștefănescu, Mihai Mirăuță (73 Dumitru Manea).
Trainer: Ștefan Kovacs

Goals: Veenstra (32), Devrindt (67, 87), Mulders (68)

**STEAUA BUCUREȘTI
v PSV EINDHOVEN 0-3** (0-1)

23 August, București   4.11.1970

Referee: James Finney (ENG)   Attendance: 50,000

STEAUA: Vasile Suciu; Mihai Mirăuță, Lajos Sătmăreanu, Bujor Hălmăgeanu, Iosif Vigu; Dumitru Dumitriu, Costică Ștefănescu; Nicolae Pantea, Gheorghe Tătaru (25 Ion Naom), Anghel Iordănescu, Dumitru Manea.   Trainer: Ștefan Kovacs

PSV: Jan Van Beveren; Wim Van Den Dungen, Lazar Radović, Pleun Strik, Peter Kemper (31 Henning Munk Jensen); Harry Vos, Guus Hiddink; Wietze Veenstra, Willy Van der Kuylen, Bent Schmidt-Hansen (60 Johan Devrindt), Eef Mulders.   Trainer: Kurt Linder

Goals: Veenstra (45, 53), Van der Kuylen (79)

GÖZTEPE IZMIR v GÓRNIK ZABRZE 0-1 (0-1)

Alsançak, Izmir   21.10.1970

Referee: Robert Schaut (BEL)   Attendance: 25,000

GÖZTEPE: Ali Artuner, Işikal Mehmet, Cudi, Yurteri Özer, Aydin Mehmet, Güzelirmak Nevzat, Ertan Öznur, Ayhan (46 John Nielsen), Fevzi Zemzem (60 Halil Kiraz), Gürsel Aksel, Türkan Mehmet.

GÓRNIK: Jan Gomola, Jan Wrazy (46 Rainer Kuchta), Stanislaw Oslizlo, Henryk Latocha, Jerzy Gorgon, Hubert Skowronek, Erwin Wilczek, Alfred Olek, Alojzy Deja, Włodzimierz Lubanski, Wladyslaw Szarynski.
Trainer: Géza Kalocsay

Goal: Lubanski (28)

CLUB BRUGGE v FC ZÜRICH 2-0 (2-0)

Albert Dyserynck Stadion, Brugge   21.10.1970

Referee: Brunon Piotrowicz (POL)   Attendance: 12,267

CLUB BRUGGE: Luc Sanders, Alfons Bastijns, Kurt Axelsson, Erwin Vandendaele, John Moulaert, Henk Houwaart, Pierre Carteus, Johnny Thio, Gilbert Marmenout, Raoul Lambert (60 Freddy Hinderijckx), Rob Rensenbrink.
Trainer: Frans de Munck

FC ZÜRICH: Karl Grob, René Hasler, Pirmin Stierli, Hubert Münch, Konrad Baumgartner, Konrad Kyburz, Max Heer (50 René-Pierre Quentin), Rosario Martinelli, Fritz Künzli, Jakob Kuhn, Georg Volkert.

Goals: Rensenbrink (18), Carteus (37)

GÓRNIK ZABRZE v GÖZTEPE IZMIR 3-0 (3-0)

Górnik, Zabrze   4.11.1970

Referee: Michel Kitabdjian (FRA)   Attendance: 20,000

GÓRNIK: Jan Gomola, Jan Wrazy, Jerzy Gorgon, Henryk Latocha (6 Stefan Florenski), Stanislaw Oslizlo, Alojzy Deja, Erwin Wilczek, Zygfryd Szoltysik, Jan Banas, Włodzimierz Lubanski, Wladyslaw Szarynski.   Trainer: Géza Kalocsay

GÖZTEPE: Ali Artuner, Ayhan, Çaglayan Derebaşi, Yurteri Özer, Aydin Mehmet, Güzelirmak Nevzat, John Nielsen, Ertan Öznur, Fevzi Zemzem, Gürsel Aksel, Türkan Mehmet.

Goals: Lubanski (28, 33), Banas (30)

FC ZÜRICH v CLUB BRUGGE 3-2 (1-1)

Letzigrund, Zürich   4.11.1970

Referee: Ertugrul Dilek (TUR)   Attendance: 11,500

FC ZÜRICH: Karl Grob; Hubert Münch, Pirmin Stierli, Konrad Kyburz (25 René Hasler), Konrad Baumgartner, Jakob Kuhn, Georg Volkert, Rosario Martinelli, Fritz Künzli, Kurt Grünig, René-Pierre Quentin.

CLUB BRUGGE: Luc Sanders, Alfons Bastijns, Kurt Axelsson, Erwin Vandendaele, John Moulaert, Henk Houwaart, Pierre Carteus, Johnny Thio, Gilbert Marmenout, Freddy Hinderijckx, Rob Rensenbrink.   Trainer: Frans de Munck

Goals: Carteus (4), Axelsson (21 og), Grünig (55), Rensenbrink (74), Künzli (83)

CSKA SOFIA v CHELSEA LONDON 0-1 (0-1)

Vasil Levski, Sofia   21.10.1970

Referee: Rudolf Scheurer (SWI)   Attendance: 45,000

CSKA: Iordan Filipov, Ivan Zafirov, Bojil Kolev, Plamen Iankov (46 Boris Gaganelov), Georgi Denev, Dimitar Penev, Tsvetan Atanasov, Asparuh Nikodimov, Petar Jekov, Dimitar Marashliev, Dimitar Iakimov.   Trainer: Manol Manolov

CHELSEA: Peter Bonetti, Patrick Mulligan, Ronald Harris, John Hollins, Marvin Hinton, David Webb, Keith Weller, Alan Hudson, Peter Osgood, Thomas Baldwin, Peter Houseman.
Manager: Dave Sexton

Goal: Baldwin (43)

CHELSEA LONDON v CSKA SOFIA 1-0 (1-0)
Stamford Bridge, London   4.11.1970
Referee: Paul Schiller (AUS)   Attendance: 41,613

CHELSEA: Peter Bonetti, Patrick Mulligan (30 John Boyle), Ronald Harris, John Hollins, Marvin Hinton, David Webb, Keith Weller, Charles Cooke, Peter Osgood, Ian Hutchinson, Peter Houseman.   Manager: Dave Sexton

CSKA: Iordan Filipov; Ivan Zafirov, Bojil Kolev, Boris Gaganelov, Kiril Stankov, Dimitar Penev, Tsvetan Atanasov, Asparuh Nikodimov, Petar Jekov (70 Vladimir Danchev), Dimitar Iakimov, Georgi Denev.   Trainer: Manol Manolov

Sent off: Stankov (80)

Goal: Webb (43)

BENFICA LISBOA
v VORWÄRTS BERLIN 2-0 (1-0)
Estádio Da Luz, Lisboa   21.10.1970
Referee: Dragutin Josip Horvath (YUG)   Att: 29,796

BENFICA: JOSÉ HENRIQUE Rodrigues Marques; António José MALTA da SILVA, HUMBERTO Manuel Jesus COELHO; José Cavaco "ZECA", António José da Conceição Oliveira "TONI""; Augusto MATINE (28 VITOR Manuel Rosa MARTINS), JAIME da Silva GRAÇA, José Torres (60 ADOLFO António da Cruz Calisto), Artur Jorge, EUSÉBIO da Silva Ferreira, DIAMANTINO José Vieira COSTA.   Trainer: James Hagan

VORWÄRTS: Alfred Zulkowski, Otto Frässdorf, Manfred Müller, Rainer Withulz, Erich Hamann, Gerhard Körner, Wolfgang Andressen (46 Horst Wruck), Wolfgang Strübing (73 Norbert Meyer), Jürgen Nöldner, Horst Begerad, Jürgen Piepenburg.   Trainer: Hans-Georg Kiupel

Goals: Eusébio (3), Diamantino (66)

VORWÄRTS BERLIN
v BENFICA LISBOA 2-0 (1-0, 2-0) (AET)
Friedrich-Ludwig-Jahn-Stadion, Berlin   4.11.1970
Referee: John Adair (NIR)   Attendance: 10,533

VORWÄRTS: Alfred Zulkowski, Otto Frässdorf, Wolfgang Andressen, Rainer Withulz, Erich Hamann (105 Heinz Dietzsch), Gerhard Körner, Horst Wruck (90 Lothar Schulz), Wolfgang Strübing, Jürgen Nöldner, Horst Begerad, Jürgen Piepenburg.   Trainer: Hans-Georg Kiupel

BENFICA: JOSÉ HENRIQUE Rodrigues Marques; António José MALTA da SILVA, HUMBERTO Manuel Jesus COELHO, José Cavaco "ZECA", António José da Conceição Oliveira "TONI""; Jorge Calado, VITOR Manuel Rosa MARTINS, JAIME da Silva GRAÇA, Artur Jorge, Tamagnini Manuel Gomes Baptista NENÉ, DIAMANTINO José Vieira COSTA (107 RAUL António ÁGUAS).   Trainer: James Hagan

Goals: Wruck (25), Frässdorf (67)

Penalties: 1-0 Dietzsch, 1-1 A. Jorge, 2-1 Körner, V. Martins (miss), 3-1 Nöldner, 3-2 Toni, 4-2 Frassdorf, 4-3 Águas, 5-3 Strübring

QUARTER-FINALS

CLUB BRUGGE v CHELSEA LONDON 2-0 (2-0)
Albert Dyserynck Stadion, Brugge   10.03.1971
Referee: Gotcho Rusev (BUL)   Attendance: 23,000

CLUB BRUGGE: Luc Sanders, Alfons Bastijns, Kurt Axelsson, Erwin Vandendaele, Norbert Denaeghel, Henk Houwaart, Pierre Carteus, Gilbert Marmenout, Johnny Thio, Raoul Lambert (43 Freddy De Coninck), Rob Rensenbrink.   Trainer: Frans de Munck

CHELSEA: John Phillips; John Boyle, John Hollins; John Dempsey, Edward McCreadie, David Webb; Derek Smethurst, Charles Cooke, Thomas Baldwin, Alan Hudson, Keith Weller.   Manager: Dave Sexton

Goals: Lambert (4), Marmenout (40)

CHELSEA LONDON
v CLUB BRUGGE 4-0 (1-0, 2-0) (AET)
Stamford Bridge, Lonon   24.03.1971
Referee: Petar Kostovski (YUG)   Attendance: 45,558

CHELSEA: John Phillips; Ronald Harris, John Hollins; John Dempsey (46 John Boyle), Edward McCreadie, David Webb; Alan Hudson, Thomas Baldwin, Charles Cooke, Peter Osgood, Peter Houseman.   Manager: Dave Sexton

CLUB BRUGGE: Luc Sanders, Alfons Bastijns, Kurt Axelsson, Erwin Vandendaele, Norbert Denaeghel, Henk Houwaart, Pierre Carteus, Gilbert Marmenout, Johnny Thio, Raoul Lambert (46 John Moulaert), Rob Rensenbrink.   Trainer: Frans de Munck

Goals: Houseman (20), Osgood (82, 114), Baldwin (117)

CARDIFF CITY v REAL MADRID 1-0 (1-0)
Ninian Park, Cardiff   10.03.1971
Referee: Vital Loraux (BEL)   Attendance: 47,500

CITY: James Eadie, David Carver, Donald Murray, Leighton Phillips, Gary Bell, Melwin Sutton, Ian Gibson, Peter King, Brian Clark, Robert Woodruff, Nigel Rees.   Manager: James Scoular

REAL: José Luis BORJA Alarcon, Fernando ZUNZUNEGUI Rodríguez (46 JOSÉ LUIS López Peinado), Manuel SANCHIS Martínez, José Antonio GRANDE Cereijo, Gregorio BENITO Rubio, José Martínez Sánchez "PIRRI", Ignacio ZOCO Esparza, Manuel VELÁZQUEZ Villaverde, AMANCIO Amaro Varela, Ramón Moreno GROSSO (75 Sebastián FLEITAS Miranda), MIGUEL Ángel PÉREZ Pilipuix.   Trainer: Miguel MUÑOZ Mozún

Goal: Clark (32)

REAL MADRID v CARDIFF CITY 2-0 (0-0)

Estadio Santiago Bernabéu, Madrid 24.03.1971

Referee: Karol Sarka (CZE)   Attendance: 60,000

REAL: Andrés Avelino Zapico JUNQUERA, Fernando ZUNZUNEGUI Rodríguez, Manuel SANCHIS Martínez, José Antonio GRANDE Cereijo, Gregorio BENITO Rubio, José Martínez Sánchez "PIRRI", Ignacio ZOCO Esparza, Manuel VELÁZQUEZ Villaverde, AMANCIO Amaro Varela (88 MIGUEL Ángel PÉREZ Pilipuix), Ramón Moreno GROSSO, Rafael Pérez González "MARAÑON" (46 Sebastián FLEITAS Miranda).   Trainer: Miguel MUÑOZ Mozún

CITY: James Eadie, David Carver, Donald Murray, Leighton Phillips, Gary Bell, Melwin Sutton, Ian Gibson, Peter King, Brian Clark, Robert Woodruff, Nigel Rees (66 Brian Harris). Manager: James Scoular

Goals: Velazquez (50), Fleitas (51)

**PSV EINDHOVEN
v VORWÄRTS BERLIN 2-0** (0-0)

Philips, Eindhoven 10.03.1971

Referee: Gyula Emsberger (HUN)   Attendance: 24,000

PSV: Jan van Beveren, Wim van den Dungen, Lazar Radović (68 Jac van Stippent), Pleun Strik, Henning Munk Jensen, Wietse Veenstra, Harry Vos, Willy van der Kuylen, Bengt Schmidt-Hansen, Johan Devrindt, Eef Mulders.
Trainer: Kurt Linder

VORWÄRTS: Alfred Zulkowski, Otto Frässdorf, Erich Hamann, Horst Begerad, Rainer Withulz, Gerhard Körner, Horst Wruck (84 Wolfgang Andressen), Wolfgang Strübing (85 Manfred Müller), Jürgen Nöldner, Jürgen Grossheim, Jürgen Piepenburg.   Trainer: Hans-Georg Kiupel

Goals: Devrindt (47), Van den Dungen (80)

**VORWÄRTS BERLIN
v PSV EINDHOVEN 1-0** (1-0)

Friedrich Ludwig Jahn Stadion, Berlin 24.03.1971

Referee: Gaspar Pintado Viu (SPA)   Attendance: 16,000

VORWÄRTS: Alfred Zulkowski, Wolfgang Andressen, Erich Hamann, Horst Begerad, Rainer Withulz, Gerhard Körner, Horst Wruck, Wolfgang Strübing (46 Jürgen Grossheim), Otto Frässdorf, Jürgen Nöldner, Jürgen Piepenburg.
Trainer: Hans-Georg Kiupel

PSV: Jan van Beveren, Wim van den Dungen, Lazar Radović, Pleun Strik, Harry Vos, Wietse Veenstra, Gerrit van Tilburg, Henning Munk Jensen, Willy van der Kuylen (60 Bengt Schmidt-Hansen), Johan Devrindt, Eef Mulders.
Trainer: Kurt Linder

Goal: Frässdorf (17)

**GÓRNIK ZABRZE
v MANCHESTER CITY 2-0** (2-0)

Slaski, Chrozów 10.03.1971

Referee: Leonidas Vamvakopoulos (GRE)   Att: 90,000

GÓRNIK: Hubert Kostka, Jan Wrazy, Henryk Latocha, Jerzy Gorgon, Stanislaw Oslizlo, Zygfryd Szoltysik, Erwin Wilczek, Jan Banas, Włodzimierz Lubanski (25 Wladyslaw Szarynski), Jerzy Wilim, Hubert Skowronek.   Trainer: Géza Kalocsay

CITY: Joseph Corrigan, Anthony Book, Mike Doyle, Thomas Booth, Anthony Towers, Alan Oakes, Colin Bell, Derek Jeffries, Michael Summerbee, Francis Lee, Neil Young.
Manager: Joseph Mercer

Goals: Lubanski (34), Wilczek (40)

**MANCHESTER CITY
v GÓRNIK ZABRZE 2-0** (1-0)

Maine Road, Manchester 24.03.1971

Referee: Anton Bucheli (SWI)   Attendance: 31,950

CITY: Ronald Healey, David Connor, Thomas Booth, William Donachie, Anthony Towers, Mike Doyle, Colin Bell, Neil Young (96 Arthur Mann), Derek Jeffries, Francis Lee, Ian Mellor (78 Ian Bowyer).   Manager: Joseph Mercer

GÓRNIK: Jan Gomola, Jan Wrazy, Henryk Latocha (22 Rainer Kuchta), Jerzy Gorgon, Stanislaw Oslizlo, Zygfryd Szoltysik, Erwin Wilczek (7 Alfred Olek), Hubert Skowronek, Jan Banas, Włodzimierz Lubanski, Alojzy Deja.
Trainer: Géza Kalocsay

Goals: Mellor (40), Doyle (66)

**MANCHESTER CITY
v GÓRNIK ZABRZE 3-1** (2-0)

Idraetspark, København 31.03.1971

Referee: Gunnar Michaelsen (DEN)   Attendance: 12,100

CITY: Ronald Healey, Anthony Towers, David Connor, Mike Doyle, Thomas Booth, William Donachie, Derek Jeffries, Colin Bell, Francis Lee, Neil Young, Freddie Hill.
Manager: Joseph Mercer

GORNIK: Hubert Kostka, Jan Wrazy (65 Alfred Olek), Stanislaw Oslizlo, Henryk Latocha, Jerzy Gorgon, Zygfryd Szoltysik, Alojzy Deja, Hubert Skowronek, Jan Banas, Włodzimierz Lubanski, Wladyslaw Szarynski (46 Jerzy Wilim).   Trainer: Géza Kalocsay

Goals: Young (20), Booth (38), Lubanski (57), Lee (65)

SEMI-FINALS

**CHELSEA LONDON
v MANCHESTER CITY 1-0** (0-0)
Stamford Bridge, London   14.04.1971
Referee: Pavel Kazakov (USSR)   Attendance: 45,595
CHELSEA: John Phillips; John Boyle, John Dempsey, David Webb, Ronald Harris, Michael Droy, John Hollins, Alan Hudson, Charles Cooke (46 Keith Weller), Derek Smethurst (82 Thomas Baldwin), Peter Houseman.
Manager: Dave Sexton
CITY: Joseph Corrigan, Anthony Book, David Connor, Anthony Towers, Thomas Booth, William Donachie, Freddie Hill, Neil Young, Jeffrey Johnson, Francis Lee, Arthur Mann.
Manager: Joseph Mercer
Goal: Smethurst (46)

**MANCHESTER CITY
v CHELSEA LONDON 0-1** (0-1)
Maine Road, Manchester   28.04.1971
Referee: István Zsolt (HUN)   Attendance: 43,663
CITY: Ronald Healey, Anthony Book, George Heslop, David Connor, Anthony Towers, Derek Jeffries, Ian Bowyer, Neil Young, Michael Summerbee (75 Steve Carter), Francis Lee, Jeffrey Johnson (46 William Donachie).
Manager: Joseph Mercer
CHELSEA: John Phillips; Patrick Mulligan, John Dempsey, David Webb, Ronald Harris, Charles Cooke, John Boyle, Alan Hudson, Keith Weller, Derek Smethurst, Peter Houseman.
Manager: Dave Sexton
Goal: Weller (43)

PSV EINDHOVEN v REAL MADRID 0-0
Philips, Eindhoven   14.04.1971
Referee: William A. O'Neill (IRL)   Attendance: 24,000
PSV: Jan van Beveren, Wim van den Dungen, Lazar Radović, Pleun Strik, Harry Vos, Gerrit van Tilburg, Wietse Veenstra, Willy van der Kuylen (70 Henning Munk Jensen), Bengt Schmidt-Hansen, Johan Devrindt, Eef Mulders.
Trainer: Kurt Linder
REAL: Andrés Avelino Zapico JUNQUERA (14 Antonio BETANCORT Barrera), Fernando ZUNZUNEGUI Rodríguez, Gregorio BENITO Rubio, Ignacio ZOCO Esparza, Manuel SANCHIS Martínez, José Antonio GRANDE Cereijo, Manuel VELÁZQUEZ Villaverde, Ramón Moreno GROSSO, AMANCIO Amaro Varela, José Martínez Sánchez "PIRRI", Francisco GENTO López.   Trainer: Miguel MUÑOZ Mozún

REAL MADRID v PSV EINDHOVEN 2-1 (1-0)
Estadio Santiago Bernabéu, Madrid   28.04.1971
Referee: Michel Kitabdjian (FRA)   Attendance: 25,000
REAL: José Luis BORJA Alarcon, Fernando ZUNZUNEGUI Rodríguez, Manuel SANCHIS Martínez (74 Manuel BUENO Cabral), Gregorio BENITO Rubio, José Antonio GRANDE Cereijo (64 Sebastián FLEITAS Miranda), Ignacio ZOCO Esparza, AMANCIO Amaro Varela, José Martínez Sánchez "PIRRI", Ramón Moreno GROSSO, Manuel VELÁZQUEZ Villaverde, Francisco GENTO López.
Trainer: Miguel MUÑOZ Mozún
PSV: Jan van Beveren, Wim van den Dungen, Lazar Radović, Pleun Strik, Harry Vos, Jac van Stippent (46 Willy van der Kuylen), Wietse Veenstra (68 Henning Munk Jensen), Gerrit van Tilburg, Bengt Schmidt-Hansen, Johan Devrindt, Eef Mulders.   Trainer: Kurt Linder
Sent off: van Tilburg (74)
Goals: Zoco (33), Van den Dungen (58), Pirri (82)

FINAL

**CHELSEA LONDON
v REAL MADRID 1-1** (0-0, 1-1) (AET)
Karaiskaki, Athina   19.05.1971
Refere: Rudolf Scheurer (SWI)   Attendance: 42,000
CHELSEA: Peter Bonetti; John Boyle, John Dempsey, John Hollins (91 Patrick Mulligan), Ronald Harris (Cap); Keith Weller, Charles Cooke, David Webb; Alan Hudson, Peter Osgood (86 Thomas Baldwin), Peter Houseman.
Trainer: Dave Sexton
REAL: José Luis BORJA Alarcon; JOSÉ LUIS López Peinado, Gregorio BENITO Rubio, Ignacio ZOCO Esparza, Fernando ZUNZUNEGUI Rodríguez; José Martínez Sánchez "PIRRI", Manuel VELÁZQUEZ Villaverde, MIGUEL Ángel PÉREZ Pilipuix (65 Sebastián FLEITAS Miranda); AMANCIO Amaro Varela, Ramón Moreno GROSSO, Francisco GENTO López (Cap) (76 José Antonio GRANDE Cereijo).
Trainer: Miguel MUÑOZ Mozún
Goals: Osgood (56), Zoco (90)

FINAL REPLAY

CHELSEA LONDON v REAL MADRID 2-1 (2-0)
Karaiskaki, Athina 21.05.1971
Referee: Anton Bucheli (SWI) Attendance: 19,917
CHELSEA: Peter Bonetti; John Boyle, John Dempsey, Charles Cooke, Ronald Harris (Cap); Keith Weller, Thomas Baldwin, David Webb; Alan Hudson, Peter Osgood (73 Derek Smethurst), Peter Houseman. Manager: Dave Sexton.
REAL: José Luis BORJA Alarcon; JOSÉ LUIS López Peinado, Gregorio BENITO Rubio, Ignacio ZOCO Esparza, Fernando ZUNZUNEGUI Rodríguez; José Martínez Sánchez "PIRRI" (Cap), Manuel VELÁZQUEZ Villaverde (75 Francisco GENTO López), Sebastián FLEITAS Miranda; AMANCIO Amaro Varela, Ramón Moreno GROSSO, Manuel BUENO Cabral (52 José Antonio GRANDE Cereijo).
Trainer: Miguel MUÑOZ Mozún
Goals: Dempsey (31), Osgood (39), Fleitas (75)

1 goal: Franzen (Åtvidaberg), Swan, O'Connell, Dunne (Bohemians Dublin), Arnason (IB Akureyri), Braun (US Luxembourg), Janku (Partizani Tiranë), Savoldi (Bologna), Hojsik, Jencik (TJ Gottwaldow), Gabovda, Greschak, Kulchitski (Karpati Lvov), E.Andersen (Aalborg), Graham, Harper (Aberdeen), I.Pettersen (Strømsgodset), Pejović, Ameršek (Olimpia Ljubljana), Malm (Haka Valkeakoski), Arribas, Michel (FC Nantes), Ettmayer, Obert, Franceskin (Wacker Innsbruck), Pusztai, Kozma (Honvéd Budapest), D.Dumitriu, Ştefănescu (Steaua Bucureşti), P.Stierli, Martinelli, Heer (FC Zürich), Nevzat, Nielsen (Göztepe Izmir), Marashliev (CSKA Sofia), Diamantino, Zeca, Artur Jorge, Graça (Benfica Lisboa), Hinderijckx (Club Brugge), Phillips, Sutton, Woodruff (Cardiff City), Wruck, Begerad (Vorwärts Berlin), Wilczek, Banas, Szarynski, Szoltysik (Górnik Zabrze), Young, Booth (Manchester City), Mellor, Doyle (Manchester City), Van der Kuylen, Mulders (PSV Eindhoven), Velázquez, Grande, Bueno, Marañon (Real Madrid), Dempsey, Weller, Smethurst, Houseman, Webb, Hinton (Chelsea London)

Own goals: Johansson (Åtvidaberg) for Partizani Tiranë, Asikainen (Haka Valkeakoski) for CSKA Sofia, Axelsson (Club Brugge) for FC Zürich

Goalscorers European Cup-Winners' Cup 1970-71:

8 goals: Włodzimierz Lubanski (Górnik Zabrze),

7 goals: EUSÉBIO da Silva Ferreira (Benfica Lisboa)

6 goals: Fritz Künzli (FC Zürich)

5 goals: Georg Volkert (FC Zürich), Dimitar Iakimov (CSKA Sofia), John Toshack (Cardiff City)

4 goals: Brian Clark (Cardiff City), Francis Lee (Manchester City), Johan Devrindt, Wietse Veenstra (PSV Eindhoven), Peter Osgood (Chelsea London)

3 goals: Levavasseur (FC Nantes), Grausam (Wacker Innsbruck), Ertan (Göztepe Izmir), Planelles (Real Madrid), Hutchinson (Chelsea London),

2 goals: Pano, Ragami (Partizani Tiranë), Urban, Nehoda (TJ Gottwaldow), S.Murray (Aberdeen), S.Pettersen (Strømsgodset), Alexiadis (Aris Thessaloniki), H.Kremers (Kickers Offenbach), Millen (Linfield Belfast), Gondet, Blanchet (FC Nantes), Kocsis (Honvéd Budapest), Tătaru (Steaua Bucureşti), Grünig (FC Zürich), Nikodimov, Jekov (CSKA Sofia), Lambert (Club Brugge), Marmenout, Carteus, Rensenbrink (Club Brugge), Gibson, King (Cardiff City), Frässdorf (Vorwärts Berlin), Olek, Wilim (Górnik Zabrze), Bell (Manchester City), Van den Dungen (PSV Eindhoven), Fleitas, Pirri, Zoco (Real Madrid), Baldwin, Hollins (Chelsea London),

CUP WINNERS' CUP 1971-72

PRELIMINARY ROUND

B 1909 ODENSE v AUSTRIA WIEN 4-2 (0-1)

Odense stadion 18.08.1971

Referee: Erik Axelryd (SWE)   Attendance: 10,561

B 1909: From, Bjarne Nielsen, Viggo Jensen, Arno Hansen, Mogens Berg, Jens Andersen, Hugo Andersen, Walther Richter, Pedersen, Niels Thorn, Bent Outzen.

AUSTRIA: Steinböck (57 Dieter Feller); Robert Sara, Eduard Krieger, Karl Weber; Johann Geyer, Alfons Dirnberger, Kurt Foka, Josef Hickersberger, Josef Gallautz, Ernst Fiala, Helmut Köglberger.

Goals: Foka (37, 60), Thorn (47), Richter (57 pen), Berg (75), H. Andersen (80).

AUSTRIA WIEN v B 1909 ODENSE 2-0 (2-0)

Prater, Wien 25.08.1971

Referee: Sándor Petri (HUN)   Attendance: 7,873

AUSTRIA: Dieter Feller; Robert Sara, Eduard Krieger, Karl Weber, Johann Geyer, Erich Obermayer, Helmut Köglberger, Josef Hickersberger (76 Helmut Weigl), Josef Gallautz, Ernst Fiala (88 Molnár), Kurt Foka.

B 1909: From, Bjarne Nielsen, Viggo Jensen, Arno Hansen, Mogens Berg, Jens Andersen, Hugo Andersen, Walther Richter, Pedersen (46 Mogens Haastrup), Niels Thorn, Bent Outzen (70 Sørensen or Laysen).

Goals: Foka (21), Köglberger (41).

HIBERNIANS PAOLA
v FRAM REYKJAVIK 3-0 (0-0)

Empire Stadium, Valletta 28.08.1971

Referee: Paolo Toselli (ITA)   Attendance: 3,383

HIBERNIANS: Alfred Mizzi, Tony Zerafa, John Privitera, Edward Theobald, Zarb, Alfred Delia, Edgar Caruana, Borg, Joseph Cini, Charlie Micallef, Salvu Bonello.

FRAM: Helgason, Schering, Arason, Gunnar Gudmundsson, Marteinn Geirsson, Sigurbergur Sigsteinsson, Gudlaugsson (24 Snorri Hauksson), Förundsson, Erlandur Magnusson, Asgeir Eliasson, Kjartansson (46 August Gudmundsson)

Goals: Cini (65), Micallef (70, 75).

FRAM REYKJAVIK
v HIBERNIANS PAOLA 2-0 (1-0)

Empire Stadium, Valletta 1.09.1971

Referee: Francesco Francescon (ITA)   Attendance: 2,194

FRAM: Helgason, Schering, Jón Petursson, Gunnar Gudmundsson, Marteinn Geirsson, Sigurbergur Sigsteinsson, Haraldsson, Förundsson, Erlandur Magnusson, Asgeir Eliasson, August Gudmundsson (60 Snorri Hauksson).

HIBERNIANS: Alfred Mizzi, Tony Zerafa, John Privitera (46 Francis Mifsud), Edward Theobald, Zarb, Alfred Delia, Edgar Caruana, Borg, Zammit (60 Joseph Cini), Charlie Micallef, Salvu Bonello.

Goals: E. Magnusson (22, 67)

FIRST ROUND

FC HIBERNIANS PAOLA
v STEAUA BUCUREŞTI 0-0

Empire Stadium, Valletta 14.09.1971

Referee: Josip Strmecki (YUG)   Attendance: 10,000

HIBERNIANS: Alfred Mizzi; John Privitera, Francis Mifsud, Tony Zerafa, Edgar Caruana; Charles Micallef, H. Mifsud (77 Zammit); Edward Theobald, Salvu Bonello, Joseph Cini, Borg.

STEAUA: Narcis Coman; Lajos Sătmăreanu, Viorel Smarandache, Vasile Negrea, Gheorghe Cristache; Ion Naom, Iosif Vigu; Nicolae Pantea, Gheorghe Tătaru (56 Vasile Aelenei), Anghel Iordănescu, Viorel Năstase.

Trainer: Valentin Stănescu

STEAUA BUCUREŞTI
v FC HIBERNIANS PAOLA 1-0 (1-0)

Republicii, Bucureşi 29.09.1971

Referee: Muzafer Sarvan (TUR)   Attendance: 15,000

STEAUA: Narcis Coman; Lajos Sătmăreanu, Viorel Smarandache, Vasile Negrea, Bujor Hălmăgeanu; Iosif Vigu, Ion Naom; Nicolae Pantea (56 Costică Ştefănescu), Gheorghe Tătaru (56 Vasile Aelenei), Anghel Iordănescu, Viorel Năstase.

Trainer: Valentin Stănescu

HIBERNIANS: Alfred Mizzi; John Privitera, Francis Mifsud, Tony Zerafa, Edgar Caruana; Alfred Delia, Charles Micallef; Edward Theobald, Salvu Bonello, Joseph Cini, Borg (46 Zammit).

Goal: Caruana (9 og)

STADE de RENNES
v GLASGOW RANGERS 1-1 (0-0)

Stade de la Route-de-Lorient, Rennes 15.09.1971

Referee: Ferdinand Marschall (AUS)   Attendance: 20,000

STADE de RENNES: Marcel Aubour; Alain Cosnard, René Cédolin, Sygmunt Chlosta, Louis Cardiet; Pierre Garcia (58 Philippe Redon), Raymond Kéruzoré; Philippe Terrier, Sokrat Mojsov (46 Daniel Périault), André Betta, Serge Lenoir. Trainer: René Cedolin

RANGERS: Peter McCloy; William Jardine, Ronald McKinnon, Colin Jackson, William Mathieson, John Greig, Andrew Penman; Alexander MacDonald, Thomas McLean, Colin Stein (76 Jim Denny), William Johnston. Manager: William Waddell

Goals: W. Johnston (68), Redon (77)

ÅTVIDABERG
v ZAGLEBIE SOSNOWIEC 1-1 (1-1)

Kopparvallen, Åtvidaberg 29.09.1971

Referee: Kaj Rasmussen (DEN)   Attendance: 2,678

ÅTVIDABERG: Ulf Blomberg; Jan Olsson, Kent Karlsson, Sten-Åke Andersson, Conny Gustafsson, Anders Ljungberg, Lars-Göran Andersson, Conny Torstensson (73 Bo Augustsson), Veine Wallinder, Roland Sandberg, Ralf Edström. Trainer: Sven-Agne Larsson

ZAGLEBIE: Jerzy Urbanski, Jan Leszczynski, Roman Bazan, Eugeniusz Szmidt, Wojciech Rudy, Zbigniew Seweryn, Wieslaw Ambrozy, Józef Galeczka, Stanislaw Gzil, Andrzej Jarosik, József Kowalczyk.

Goals: Jarosik (7), Ljungberg (15)

GLASGOW RANGERS
v STADE de RENNES 1-0 (1-0)

Ibrox, Glasgow 28.09.1971

Referee: Sergio Gonella (ITA)   Attendance: 40,000

RANGERS: Peter McCloy; William Jardine, John Greig, Ronald McKinnon, William Mathieson; Colin Jackson, Alfred Conn; William Henderson, Colin Stein, Alexander MacDonald, William Johnston.   Manager: William Waddell

STADE de RENNES: Marcel Aubour; Alain Cosnard, René Cédolin, Sygmunt Chlosta, Louis Cardiet, Pierre Garcia, Hector Toublanc; Raymond Kéruzoré (83 Philippe Redon), Philippe Terrier (54 Sokrat Mojsov), André Betta, Serge Lenoir.   Trainer: René Cedolin

Goal: MacDonald (37)

KOMLÓ BSE
v CRVENA ZVEZDA BEOGRAD 2-7 (2-3)

Pécsi ú, Komló 15.09.1971

Referee: Francisco S. Marques Lobo (POR)   Att: 6,000

KOMLÓ: György Buús (45 István Erdösi); István Kótai, Lajos Kovács, István Csordás, László Horváth (55 Imre Mohácsik), Balász Makrai, Lajos Bordács, Tibor Juhász, Gyula Solymosi, József Orsós, Vilmos Bencsik.   Trainer: Mihály Lantos

CRVENA ZVEZDA: Ratomir Dujković; Milovan Djorić, Petar Krivokuča, Zoran Antonijević, Vladislav Bogićević (46 Sead Sušić), Miroslav Pavlović, Branko Klenkovski (27 Mihalj Keri), Stanislav Karasi, Zoran Filipović, Jovan Aćimović, Mile Novković.

Goals: Juhász (14), Karasi (19), Filipovic (33, 53, 58, 71), Antonijević (41), Horváth (44), Krivokuča (62)

ZAGLEBIE SOSNOWIEC
v ÅTVIDABERG 3-4 (1-1)

Stadion Ludow, Sosnowiec 15.09.1971

Referee: Tsvetan P.Stanev (BUL)   Attendance: 15,000

ZAGLEBIE: Jerzy Urbanski, Jan Leszczynski, Roman Bazan, Eugeniusz Szmidt, Jan Czerniak (46 Jerzy Pielok), Stanislaw Gzil, József Kowalczyk, József Galeczka, Zbigniew Seweryn, Andrzej Jarosik, Wieslaw Ambrozy.

ÅTVIDABERG: Ulf Blomberg, Jan Olsson, Kent Karlsson, Sten-Åke Andersson, Örjan Johansson, Anders Ljungberg, Lars-Göran Andersson (57 Nils Nilsson), Conny Torstensson, Veine Wallinder, Roland Sandberg, Ralf Edström (57 Bo Augustsson).   Trainer: Sven-Agne Larsson

Goals: Jarosik (15), Gzil (50), Galeczka (82), Sandberg (30 pen, 47), Torstensson (62), Edström (71)

CRVENA ZVEZDA BEOGRAD
v KOMLÓ BSE 1-2 (1-1)

Crvena Zvezda, Beograd 29.09.1971

Referee: Valentin Lipatov (USSR)   Attendance: 5,000

CRVENA ZVEZDA: Ratomir Dujković; Branko Radović, Petar Krivokuča, Mile Novković; Mihalj Keri, Miroslav Pavlović; Slobodan Janković, Stanislav Karasi, Jovan Aćimović (66 Dušan Nikolić), Trifun Mihajlović, Dragan Džajić (46 Sead Sušić).

KOMLÓ: György Buús; Szokratesz Lazaridisz, Lajos Kovács, István Csordás, László Horváth, Balász Makrai, Tibor Juhász, Lajos Bordács, Gyula Solymosi, József Orsós (46 Imre Mohácsik), Vilmos Bencsik.   Trainer: Mihály Lantos

Goals: Acimović (25), Juhász (35), Bencsik (60)

MIKKELIN PALLOILIJAT v ESKIŞEHIRSPOR 0-0

Urheilupuisto, Mikkeli   15.09.1971

Referee: Erik Axelryd (SWE)   Attendance: 3,796

PALLOILIJAT: Risto Remes, Rainer Jungman, Heikki Valjakka, Eero Karppinen (78 Kari Mutanen), Raimo Marttinen, Seppo Günther, Pauli Sinkko, Matti Vanhanen (81 Heikki Kangaskorpi), Antero Hyttinen, Antero Nikkanen, Pentti Toivola.

ESKIŞEHIRSPOR: Taskin Yilmaz, Ilhan Çolak, Abdurrahman Temel, Burhan Tözer, Ismail Arca, Kamuran Yavuz, Halil Gundögan, Vahap Özbayar, Fethi Heper, Burhan Isin, Şevki Şenlen.

**ESKIŞEHIRSPOR
v MIKKELIN PALLOILIJAT 4-0** (3-0)

Atatürk, Eskişehir   29.09.1971

Referee: Constantin Bărbulescu (ROM)   Attendance: 11,935

ESKIŞEHIRSPOR: Taskin Yilmaz, Ilhan Çolak, Faik Sentasler, Burhan Tözer, Ismail Arca, Kamuran Yavuz (76 Süreyya), Halil Gundögan, Vahap Özbayar, Fethi Heper, Burhan Isin, Şevki Şenlen (36 Nihat Atacan).

PALLOILIJAT: Risto Remes, Rainer Jungman, Heikki Valjakka, Eero Karppinen, Raimo Marttinen (46 Kari Mutanen, 80 Kyösti Vilhunen), Seppo Günther, Jouko Vuori, Matti Vanhanen, Antero Hyttinen, Antero Nikkanen, Pentti Toivola.

Goals: Fethi (8, 15, 40, 80)

DINAMO TIRANË v AUSTRIA WIEN 1-1 (0-0)

Qemal Stafa, Tiranë   15.09.1971

Referee: Günter Männig (E. GER)   Attendance: 18,051

DINAMO: Ahmet Ahmedani, Gjinali, Faruk Sejdini, Kodra, Enver Ibershimi, Astrit Hafizi (60 Jani Rama), Ilir Pernaska, Iljaz Ceco, Ciraku, Cutra, Hysi (46 Shapllo).

AUSTRIA: Dieter Feller; Robert Sara, Eduard Krieger, Karl Weber, Johann Geyer, Alfons Dirnberger, Helmut Köglberger, Helmut Weigl, Josef Gallautz (27 Molnar), Ernst Fiala, Kurt Foka.

Goals: Dirnberger (64), I. Ceco (70 pen)

AUSTRIA WIEN v DINAMO TIRANË 1-0 (1-0)

Prater, Wien   29.09.1971

Referee: Josef Poucek (CZE)   Attendance: 1,425

AUSTRIA: Dieter Feller; Robert Sara, Eduard Krieger, Karl Weber, Helmut Weigl, Alfons Dirnberger, Kurt Foka (72 Josef Gallautz), Josef Hickersberger (46 Karl Fröhlich), Helmut Köglberger, Johann Geyer, Alfred Riedl.

DINAMO: Ahmet Ahmedani; Gjinali, Faruk Sejdini, Kodra, Enver Ibershimi, A. Xhafa, Ilir Pernaska, Iljaz Ceco, Ciraku, Cutra (65 Hysi), Astrit Hafizi (58 Hoxha).

Goal: Riedl (22)

ŠKODA PLZEN v BAYERN MÜNCHEN 0-1 (0-1)

Struncovy Stadion, Plzen   15.09.1971

Referee: Kostas Xanthoulis (CYP)   Attendance: 30,000

ŠKODA: František Caloun, Spinka, František Plass, Zdenek Michalek, Zdenek Plesko, Karel Süss, Vaclav Kamir, Bachner (72 Hofman), František Sudik, Ivan Bican, Miroslav Ziegler.

BAYERN: Josef Maier, Johnny Hansen, Georg Schwarzenbeck, Franz Beckenbauer, Paul Breitner, Rainer Zobel, Franz Roth, Edgar Schneider, Uli Hoeness, Gerhard Müller, Wolfgang Sühnholz.   Trainer: Udo Lattek

Goal: Sühnholz (77)

BAYERN MÜNCHEN v ŠKODA PLZEN 6-1 (2-1)

Stadion an der Grünwalder strasse, München   29.09.1971

Referee: Hristo Mihas (GRE)   Attendance: 6,000

BAYERN: Josef Maier; Johnny Hansen, Georg Schwarzenbeck, Paul Breitner, Franz Roth, Rainer Zobel, Uli Hoeness (34 Herward Koppenhöfer), Franz Krauthausen, Edgar Schneider (46 Wilhelm Hoffmann), Gerhard Müller, Wolfgang Sühnholz.   Trainer: Udo Lattek

ŠKODA: František Caloun, Spinka, František Plass, Vaclav Korinek (78 Vaclav Kamir), Zdenek Plesko, Karel Süss, Ivan Bican, Bachner, František Sudik, Zdenek Michalek, Miroslav Ziegler.

Goals: Müller (1, 74 pen), Bican (4), Krauthausen (17), Hoffmann (50, 80), Roth (87)

**DISTILLERY BELFAST
v CF BARCELONA 1-3** (0-1)

Windsor Park, Belfast   15.09.1971

Referee: Antoine Queudeville (LUX)   Attendance: 3,000

DISTILLERY: Roy McDonald, Raymond White, Derek Meldrum, Thomas Brannigan, Peter Rafferty, Martin Donnelly, Mervyn Law, Peter Watson, James Savage, Martin O'Neill, Sean Quinn (65 Alan McCaroll).   Trainer: McAlinden

CF BARCELONA: Miguel REINA Santos, Joaquín RIFÉ Climent, Francisco Fernández Rodríguez "GALLEGO", Antonio TORRES García, ELADIO Silvestre Graells, Enrique Álvarez COSTAS, JUAN CARLOS Pérez López, Pedro María ZABALZA Inda, Carlos REXACH Cerdá, Ramón ALFONSEDA Pous (55 Miguel Ángel BUSTILLO Lafoz), Juan Manuel ASENSI Ripoll.   Trainer: Rinus Michels

Goals: Alfonseda (44), Asensi (57, 85), O'Neill (77)

**CF BARCELONA
v DISTILLERY BELFAST 4-0** (2-0)

Camp Nou, Barcelona 29.09.1971

Referee: Paul Bonett (MAL)   Attendance: 15,000

CF BARCELONA: Salvador SADURNÍ Urpi; Joaquín RIFÉ Climent, Francisco Fernández Rodríguez "GALLEGO" (83 José María FUSTÉ Blanch), Antonio TORRES García, ELADIO Silvestre Graells, Enrique Álvarez COSTAS, Carlos REXACH Cerdá (65 Ramón ALFONSEDA Pous), MARCIAL Pina Morales, Teófilo DUEÑAS Samper, Juan Manuel ASENSI Ripoll, JUAN CARLOS Pérez López.   Trainer: Rinus Michels

DISTILLERY: Roy McDonald, Raymond White, Derek Meldrum, Thomas Brannigan, Peter Rafferty, Martin Donnelly, Mervyn Law, Peter Watson (83 Alan McCaroll), James Savage, Martin O'Neill, Sean Quinn (89 Roy Welsh).
Trainer: McAlinden

Goals: Marcial (4, 29, 51, 66)

DYNAMO BERLIN v CARDIFF CITY 1-1 (0-0)

Sportforum, Berlin 15.09.1971

Referee: Rolf Nyhus (NOR)   Attendance: 11,651

DYNAMO: Werner Lihsa, Dieter Stumpf, Bernd Brillat, Jürgen Hübner, Joachim Hall, Peter Rohde, Frank Terletzki, Manfred Becker, Harald Schütze, Dieter Labes, Norbert Johannsen.   Trainer: Johannes Geitel

CITY: James Eadie, Kenneth Jones, Gary Bell, Melwin Sutton, Donald Murray, Leighton Phillips, Peter King, Brian Clark, Robert Woodruff, Alan Warboys, Ian Gibson.

Goals: Gibson (75), Schütze (90)

**CARDIFF CITY
v DYNAMO BERLIN 1-1** (0-0, 0-0) (AET)

Ninian Park, Cardiff 29.09.1971

Referee: Franz Geluck (BEL)   Attendance: 12,676

CITY: James Eadie; Kenneth Jones, Gary Bell; Melwin Sutton, Donald Murray, Leighton Phillips; Peter King, Brian Clark, Robert Woodruff (91 Alan Foggon), Alan Warboys, Ian Gibson.

DYNAMO: Werner Lihsa, Dieter Stumpf (62 Jürgen Hübner), Jochen Carow, Wilfried Trümpler, Joachim Hall, Peter Rohde, Frank Terletzki, Manfred Becker, Harald Schütze (70 Ralf Schulenberg), Dieter Labes, Norbert Johannsen.
Trainer: Johannes Geitel

Goals: Clark (59), Labes (62)

Penalties: 1-0 Gibson, 1-1 Johannsen, Murray (miss), 1-2 Terletzki, 2-2 King, 2-3 Carow, 3-3 Bell, 3-4 Becker, 4-4 Woodruff, 4-5 Labes

LIMERICK AFC v AC TORINO 0-1 (0-1)

Thomond Park, Limerick 15.09.1971

Referee: Alistair McKenzie (SCO)   Attendance: 3,329

LIMERICK: Kevin Fitzpatrick, Vincent Quinn, Sean Byrnes, Richard Hall, Alphonsus Finucane, Joe O'Mahony, Paddy Shortt (84 Eddie O'Donovan), Andrew McEvoy, Davy Barrett, Seamus Coad, Tony Meaney.

AC TORINO: Luciano Castellini, Natalino Fossati, Roberto Mozzini, Luciano Zecchini, Angelo Cereser, Aldo Agroppi, Rosario Rampanti, Giorgio Ferrini, Paolo Pulici (65 Giovanni Pui), Claudio Sala (76 Alessandro Crivelli), Giovanni Toschi.
Trainer: Gustavo Giagnoni

Goal: Rampanti (8)

AC TORINO v LIMERICK AFC 4-0 (0-0)

Stadio Comunale, Torino 29.09.1971

Referee: Leonidas Vamvakopoulos (GRE)   Att: 15,934

AC TORINO: Luciano Castellini, Natalino Fossati, Roberto Mozzini, Luciano Zecchini, Angelo Cereser, Aldo Agroppi, Rosario Rampanti, Giorgio Ferrini, Paolo Pulici (60 Livio Luppi), Claudio Sala, Giovanni Toschi.
Trainer: Gustavo Giagnoni

LIMERICK: Kevin Fitzpatrick, Vincent Quinn, Sean Byrnes, Richard Hall, Alphonsus Finucane, Joe O'Mahony, Paddy Shortt (71 Eddie O'Donovan), Andrew McEvoy, Davy Barrett, Seamus Coad, Tony Meaney.

Goals: Toschi (46, 74, 83), Luppi (80)

SERVETTE GENÈVE v LIVERPOOL FC 2-1 (1-0)

Stade des Charmilles, Genève 15.09.1971

Referee: Robert Wurtz (FRA)   Attendance: 21,000

SERVETTE: Jacques Barlie; Christian Morgenegg, Ueli Wegmann, Gilbert Guyot, Georges Perroud, André Bosson, Valer Nemeth, Bernd Dörfel, Michel Desbiolles (67 Eduardo Manzoni), Franco Marchi, Frantz Barriquand.
Trainer: Jean Snella

LIVERPOOL: Raymond Clemence, Christopher Lawler, Alec Lindsay, Ian Ross, Larry Lloyd, Emlyn Hughes, Robert Graham, Brian Hall (55 Peter Thompson), Steve Heighway, John Toshack (85 Alun Evans), Ian Callaghan.
Manager: William Shankly

Goals: Dörfel (25), Barriquand (48), Lawler (80)

LIVERPOOL FC v SERVETTE GENÈVE 2-0 (1-0)
Anfield Road, Liverpool   29.09.1971
Referee: Rudolf Glöckner (E. GER)   Attendance: 38,591
LIVERPOOL: Raymond Clemence, Christopher Lawler, Alec Lindsay, Thomas Smith (85 Ian Ross), Larry Lloyd, Emlyn Hughes, Kevin Keegan (70 John Toshack), Brian Hall, Steve Heighway, Robert Graham, Ian Callaghan.
Manager: William Shankly
SERVETTE: Jacques Barlie; Christian Morgenegg, Ueli Wegmann, Gilbert Guyot, Georges Perroud, Franco Marchi (75 Jean-Pierre Kurz), Valer Nemeth, Bernd Dörfel, Michel Desbiolles, André Bosson, Frantz Barriquand.
Trainer: Jean Snella
Goals: Hughes (27), Heighway (59)

SPORTING LISBOA v S & FK LYN OSLO 4-0 (2-0)
Estádio José Alvalade, Lisboa   15.09.1971
Referee: Francesco Francescon (ITA)   Attendance: 17,022
SPORTING: Vítor Manuel Afonso DAMAS de Oliveira, Manuel PEDRO GOMES, HILÁRIO Rosário da Conceição, VAGNER Canotilho (18 Vítor GONÇALVES), Francisco CALÓ, João Gonçalves LARANJEIRA, FRANCISCO DELFIM DIAS FARIA CHICO (30 MARIO DA SILVA MATEUS "MÁRINHO"), João de Matos Moura LOURENÇO, Hector YAZALDE, NÉLSON Fernandes, Joaquim DINIS.
LYN: Svein Bjørn Olsen, Jan Rodvang, Tore Børrehaug, Helge Østvold, Svein Gjedrem, Knut Kolle (8 Arne Amundsen), Knut Iversen (35 Arild Gulden), Tor Fuglset, Ola Dybwad Olsen, Trygve Christophersen, Sven Otto Birkeland.
Goals: Yazalde (8), Lourenço (20, 90), Marinho (88)

**JEUNESSE HAUTCHARAGE
v CHELSEA LONDON 0-8** (0-6)
Stade Municipal, Luxembourg   15.09.1971
Referee: Ferdinand Biwersi (W. GER)   Attendance: 13,000
JEUNESSE: Lucien Fusulier, Jean-Pierre Poos, Eddy Welscher, Romain Schoder, Fernand Felten (67 Raymond Welscher), Jean-Pierre Welscher (57 Robert Battello), René Frantzen, Lucien Welscher, André Schrobiltgen, Guy Thill, Romain Kaiser.   Trainer: Romain Schoder
CHELSEA: Peter Bonetti; John Boyle, John Dempsey (46 Marvin Hinton), David Webb, Ronald Harris, Charles Cooke, Alan Hudson, John Hollins, Thomas Baldwin, Peter Osgood, Peter Houseman.   Manager: Dave Sexton
Goals: Osgood (2, 28, 42), Houseman (9, 29), Hollins (37), Baldwin (74), Webb (81)

S & FK LYN OSLO v SPORTING LISBOA 0-3 (0-2)
Ullevål, Oslo   29.09.1971
Referee: Magnus Petursson (ICE)   Attendance: 3,214
LYN: Svein Bjørn Olsen, Jan Rodvang, Tore Børrehaug, Helge Østvold, Svein Gjedrem, Knut Iversen, Svein Bredo Østlien, Tor Fuglset, Trygve Christophersen, Ola Dybwad Olsen, Sven Otto Birkeland.
SPORTING: Vítor Manuel Afonso DAMAS de Oliveira, Manuel PEDRO GOMES, HILÁRIO Rosário da Conceição, Vítor GONÇALVES, Francisco CALÓ, João Gonçalves LARANJEIRA (75 FRANCISCO DELFIM DIAS FARIA CHICO), NÉLSON Fernandes, João de Matos Moura LOURENÇO (46 CARLOS ALBERTO MANACA DIAS), Hector YAZALDE, VAGNER Canotilho, Joaquim DINIS.
Goals: Yazalde (35, 70), Dinis (42)

**CHELSEA LONDON
v JEUNESSE HAUTCHARAGE 13-0** (6-0)
Stamford Bridge, London   29.09.1971
Referee: Richard Stagno Navarra
(MAL)   Attendance: 27,621
CHELSEA: Peter Bonetti; John Boyle, Ronald Harris, John Hollins, David Webb, Marvin Hinton, Charles Cooke, Thomas Baldwin, Peter Osgood, Alan Hudson, Peter Houseman.
Manager: Dave Sexton
JEUNESSE: Lucien Fusulier, Lucien Welscher, René Frantzen, Eddy Welscher, Romain Schoder, Robert Battello, Raymond Welscher (70 Jean-Marie Thill), Jean-Pierre Welscher, André Schrobiltgen (81 Paul Simon), Guy Thill, Romain Kaiser.
Trainer: Romain Schoder
Goals: Osgood (4, 6, 63, 81, 85), Hudson (12), Hollins (13 pen), Webb (22), Harris (43), Baldwin (61, 69, 90), Houseman (78)

**OLYMPIAKOS PEIRAIAS
v DINAMO MOSKVA 0-2** (0-0)
Karaiskaki, Athina   15.09.1971
Referee: Gerhard Künze (E. GER)   Attendance: 41,817
OLYMPIAKOS: Mihalis Milonas, Giannis Gkaitatzis, Athanasios Aggelis, Miltiadis Koumarias, Vasilios Siokos, Takis Synetopoulos, Papadopoulos, Persidis, Nikos Gioutsos, Giorgos Delikaris, Petros Karavitis (46 Giotis Papadimitriou).
Trainer: Alan Asman
DINAMO: Vladimir Pilgui, Vladimir Schtapov, Viktor Anichkin, Valeri Zikov, Valeri Maslov, Evgeni Zhukov, Vladimir Eshtrekov (68 Vladimir Kozlov), Iosif Sabo, Anatoli Kozhemiakin (76 Aleksandr Grebnev), Aleksandr Makhovikov, Gennadi Evriuzhikhin.   Trainer: Lev Yashin
Goals: Kozlov (83, 87)

**DINAMO MOSKVA
v OLYMPIAKOS PEIRAIAS 1-2** (1-2)
Dinamo, Moskva 30.09.1971
Referee: Anton Bucheli (SWI)   Attendance: 22,000
DINAMO: Vladimir Pilgui, Vladimir Schtapov, Viktor Anichkin, Valeri Zikov (46 Vladimir Basalaev), Valeri Maslov, Evgeni Zhukov, Vladimir Eshtrekov, Iosif Sabo, Anatoli Kozhemiakin (55 Vladimir Kozlov), Aleksandr Makhovikov, Gennadi Evriuzhikhin.   Trainer: Lev Yashin
OLYMPIAKOS: Karipidis, Giannis Gkaitatzis, Zoanos, Persidis, Kiriakos Koureas, Takis Synetopoulos, Petros Karavitis (70 Pampoulis), Nikos Gioutsos, Yves Triantafillos, Roman Argiroudis (60 Sotiris Pappas), Giotis Papadimitiou. Trainer: Alan Asman
Goals: Triantafilos (6), Sabo (15), Gkaitatzis (45)

**BEERSCHOT ANTWERP
v ANORTHOSIS FAMAGUSTA 7-0** (3-0)
Stedelijk Olympisch Stadion, Antwerp 23.09.1971
Referee: Norbert Rolles (LUX)   Attendance: 5,587
BEERSCHOT: Helmut Brösch, Roland Coclet (65 Leo de Smet), Robert Dalving, Rudolf Belin, Julien van Opdorp, Jean-Pierre Kasprzak, Guido Mallants, Arto Tolsa, Chris Stroybant, Roger Claessen, Peter Suykerbuyk.
ANORTHOSIS: Fanos Stylianou, Sotos Andreou, Vasos Larkou, Stefanos Lysandrou, Dimitris Sialis, Hristofis Hristofi, Hristos Soleas, Giannis Hristou "Mantis", Kostas Rouvalis (46 Andreas Hatzigiannis), Antonakis Kafas, Giorgos Panagidis.
Goals: Tolsa (8, 29), Van Opdorp (21), Suykerbuyck (60), Mertakkas (74 og), Claessen (76), Mallants (87)

**ANORTHOSIS FAMAGUSTA
v BEERSCHOT ANTWERP 0-1** (0-0)
Stedelijk Olympisch Stadion, Antwerp 29.09.1971
Referee: Marcel Herrmann (LUX)   Attendance: 2,089
ANORTHOSIS: Fanos Stylianou, Giannis Mertakkas, Vasos Larkou, Stefanos Lysandrou, Dimitris Sialis, Artemis Theoharous (46 Sotos Andreou), Hristos Soleas (.. Stelios Vafopoulos), Giannis Hristou "Mantis", Kostas Rouvalis, Antonakis Kafas, Giorgos Panagidis.
BEERSCHOT: Helmut Brösch, Roland Coclet, Robert Dalving, Rudolf Belin, Julien van Opdorp, Chris Stroybant, Jean-Pierre Kasprzak, Herman Houben (46 Arto Tolsa), Peter Suykerbuyk, Roger Claessen, Guido Mallants (35 Luigi Levantaci).
Goal: Kasprzak (90 pen)

**LEVSKI SPARTAK SOFIA
v SPARTA ROTTERDAM 1-1** (1-0)
Vasil Levski, Sofia 16.09.1971
Referee: Timoleon Latsios (GRE)   Attendance: 8,000
LEVSKI SPARTAK: Biser Mihailov, Milko Gaidarski, Dobromir Jechev, Kiril Ivkov, Stefan Aladjov, Ivan Stoianov, Ianko Kirilov, Tsvetan Veselinov, Georgi Tzvetkov, Pavel Panov, Petar Kirilov (60 Voin Voinov).
SPARTA: Pim Doesburg, Hans Venneker, Gerrie Ter Horst, Hans Eijkenbroek, Dries Visser, Stef Walbeek, Henk Bosveld (75 Hans Bentzon), Jan van der Veen, Nol Heijerman, Jan Klijnjan, Jørgen Kristensen.   Trainer: Elek Schwartz
Goals: Panov (40), Bosveld (81)

SECOND ROUND

**SPARTA ROTTERDAM
v LEVSKI SPARTAK SOFIA 2-0** (1-0)
Het Kasteel, Rotterdam 29.09.1971
Referee: William J. Mullan (SCO)   Attendance: 22,000
SPARTA: Pim Doesburg, Hans Venneker, Gerrie Ter Horst, Hans Eijkenbroek, Dries Visser, Stef Walbeek, Henk Bosveld (71 Jan van der Veen), Jan Klijnjan, Nol Heijerman, Janusz Kowalik, Jørgen Kristensen.   Trainer: Elek Schwartz
LEVSKI SPARTAK: Biser Mihailov, Milko Gaidarski, Dobromir Jechev, Kiril Ivkov, Stefan Aladjov, Ivan Stoianov, Ianko Kirilov, Tsvetan Veselinov, Georgi Tzvetkov, Pavel Panov, Petar Kirilov (62 Iosif Haralambiev).
Goals: Kristensen (5), Kowalik (49)

LIVERPOOL FC v BAYERN MÜNCHEN 0-0
Anfield Road, Liverpool 20.10.1971
Referee: Sergio Gonella (ITA)   Attendance: 42,949
LIVERPOOL: Raymond Clemence, Larry Lloyd, Christopher Lawler, Thomas Smith, Ian Ross, Emlyn Hughes, Brian Hall (70 Peter Thompson), Alun Evans, Kevin Keegan, Steve Heighway, Ian Callaghan.   Manager: William Shankly
BAYERN: Josef Maier, Franz Beckenbauer, Herward Koppenhöfer, Uli Hoeness, Georg Schwarzenbeck, Paul Breitner, Franz Roth, Edgar Schneider, Gerhard Müller, Franz Krauthausen, Wolfgang Sühnholz.   Trainer: Udo Lattek

BAYERN MÜNCHEN v LIVERPOOL FC 3-1 (2-1)
Grünwalderstadion, München 3.11.1971
Referee: Pavel Kazakov (USSR) Attendance: 40,000
BAYERN: Josef Maier, Johnny Hansen, Georg Schwarzenbeck, Franz Beckenbauer, Paul Breitner, Franz Roth, Rainer Zobel, Uli Hoeness, Franz Krauthausen, Gerhard Müller, Wolfgang Sühnholz. Trainer: Udo Lattek
LIVERPOOL: Raymond Clemence, Emlyn Hughes, Thomas Smith, Larry Lloyd, Christopher Lawler, Ian Callaghan, Robert Graham, Ian Ross, Kevin Keegan, Alun Evans, Steve Heighway. Manager: William Shankly
Goals: Müller (25, 27), Evans (38), U. Hoeness (58)

CF BARCELONA v STEAUA BUCUREŞTI 0-1 (0-1)
Camp Nou Barcelona 20.10.1971
Referee: Desmott Barett (IRL) Attendance: 40,000
CF BARCELONA: Salvador SADURNÍ Urpi; Joaquín RIFÉ Climent, Francisco Fernández Rodríguez "GALLEGO", Antonio TORRES García, Enrique Álvarez COSTAS; José María FUSTÉ Blanch, MARCIAL Pina Morales; Narciso MARTÍ FILOSÍA, Teófilo DUEÑAS Samper (46 Ramón ALFONSEDA Pous), Carlos REXACH Cerdá, Juan Manuel ASENSI Ripoll (69 Pedro María ZABALZA Inda). Trainer: Rinus Michels
STEAUA: Narcis Coman (46 Carol Haidu); Lajos Sătmăreanu, Viorel Smarandache, Vasile Negrea, Gheorghe Cristache; Ion Naom, Iosif Vigu, Dumitru Dumitriu; Nicolae Pantea, Anghel Iordănescu, Viorel Năstase. Trainer: Valentin Stănescu
Goal: Năstase (12)

AC TORINO v AUSTRIA WIEN 1-0 (0-0)
Stadio Filadelfia, Torino 20.10.1971
Referee: Hans-Joachim Weyland (W. GER) Att: 22,521
AC TORINO: Luciano Castellini, Marino Lombardo, Natalino Fossati, Luciano Zecchini, Angelo Cereser, Aldo Agroppi, Rosario Rampanti, Giorgio Ferrini, Paolo Pulici, Claudio Sala (68 Ferdinando Rossi), Giovanni Toschi (37 Livio Luppi). Trainer: Gustavo Giagnoni
AUSTRIA: Dieter Feller; Robert Sara, Eduard Krieger, Karl Weber, Johann Geyer, Alfons Dirnberger, Helmut Köglberger, Zeger, Josef Gallautz (60 Kurt Foka), Ernst Fiala, Alfred Riedl.
Goal: Agroppi (81)

STEAUA BUCUREŞTI v CF BARCELONA 2-1 (0-0)
23 August, Bucureşti 3.11.1971
Referee: Pius Kamber (SWI) Attendance: 5,000
STEAUA: Carol Haidu; Lajos Sătmăreanu, Viorel Smarandache, Vasile Negrea, Gheorghe Cristache; Ion Naom, Iosif Vigu; Nicolae Pantea (68 Costică Ştefănescu), Anghel Iordănescu, Viorel Năstase, Dumitru Marcu. Trainer: Valentin Stănescu
CF BARCELONA: Miguel REINA Santos; Joaquín RIFÉ Climent, Francisco Fernández Rodríguez "GALLEGO", Antonio TORRES García, ELADIO Silvestre Graells; Enrique Álvarez COSTAS, Juan Manuel ASENSI Ripoll; Ramón ALFONSEDA Pous, MARCIAL Pina Morales, Carlos REXACH Cerdá, José María FUSTÉ Blanch (46 Teófilo DUEÑAS Samper). Trainer: Rinus Michels
Goals: Asensi (50), Năstase (53 pen, 60)

AUSTRIA WIEN v AC TORINO 0-0
Prater, Wien 3.11.1971
Referee: Robert Hélies (FRA) Attendance: 10,092
AUSTRIA: Dieter Feller; Helmut Weigl (85 Josef Gallautz), Eduard Krieger, Karl Fröhlich, Johann Geyer, Alfons Dirnberger, Kurt Foka, Robert Sara, Helmut Köglberger, Zeger, Alfred Riedl.
AC TORINO: Luciano Castellini, Marino Lombardo, Natalino Fossati, Luciano Zecchini, Angelo Cereser, Aldo Agroppi, Alessandro Crivelli, Giorgio Ferrini, Paolo Pulici (59 Rosario Rampanti), Claudio Sala, Livio Luppi (80 Ferdinando Rossi). Trainer: Gustavo Giagnoni

SPARTA ROTTERDAM v CRVENA ZVEZDA BEOGRAD 1-1 (0-1)
Het Kasteel, Rotterdam 20.10.1971
Referee: Einar J. Boström (SWE) Attendance: 13,051
SPARTA: Pim Doesburg, Hans Venneker, Gerrie Ter Horst, Hans Eijkenbroek, Stef Walbeek, Jan van der Veen, Jan Klijnjan, Henk Bosveld (85 Aad Koudijzer), Nol Heijerman, Janusz Kowalik, Jørgen Kristensen. Trainer: Elek Schwartz
CRVENA ZVEZDA: Ratomir Dujković; Milovan Djorić (56 Mihalj Keri), Zoran Antonijević, Vladislav Bogicević, Petar Krivokuča, Miroslav Pavlović, Slobodan Janković, Stanislav Karasi (81 Mile Novković), Zoran Filipović, Jovan Acimović, Dragan Džajić (Cap).
Goals: Janković (17), Bosveld (47)

**CRVENA ZVEZDA BEOGRAD
v SPARTA ROTTERDAM 2-1** (1-0)

Crvena Zvezda, Beograd 3.11.1971

Referee: José Maria Ortiz de Mendibil (SPA) Att: 10,000

CRVENA ZVEZDA: Ratomir Dujković; Mihalj Keri, Zoran Antonijević, Vladislav Bogicević, Petar Krivokuča, Miroslav Pavlović, Branko Radović, Stanislav Karasi, Zoran Filipović, Jovan Acimović, Mile Novković.

SPARTA: Pim Doesburg, Hans Venneker, Gerrie Ter Horst, Hans Eijkenbroek, Stef Walbeek, Jan van der Veen, Jan Klijnjan, Henk Bosveld, Nol Heijerman, Aad Koudijzer, Jørgen Kristensen. Trainer: Elek Schwartz

Goals: Karasi (36), Klijnjan (51), Antonijević (82)

**BEERSCHOT ANTWERP
v DYNAMO BERLIN 1-3** (0-0)

Stedelijk Olympisch stadion, Antwerp 20.10.1971

Referee: Francisco S. Marques Lobo (POR) Att: 6,118

BEERSCHOT: Helmut Brösch, Roland Coclet, Robert Dalving, Jan Van Gucht, Julien van Opdorp, Chris Stroybant, Rudolf Belin, Jean-Pierre Kasprzak, Herman Houben, Peter Suykerbuyk, Guido Mallants.

DYNAMO: Werner Lihsa, Dieter Stumpf (69 Jürgen Hübner), Jochen Carow, Wilfried Trümpler, Joachim Hall, Peter Rohde, Frank Terletzki, Manfred Becker, Harald Schütze, Dieter Labes, Norbert Johannsen. Trainer: Johannes Geitel

Goals: Schütze (60), Suykerbuyck (62), Johannsen (80), P. Rohde (89)

ÅTVIDABERG FF v CHELSEA LONDON 0-0

Kopparvallen, Åtvidaberg 20.10.1971

Referee: Henry Öberg (NOR) Attendance: 10,209

ÅTVIDABERG: Ulf Blomberg; Jan Olsson, Kent Karlsson, Sten-Åke Andersson, Conny Gustafsson, Anders Ljungberg, Lars-Göran Andersson, Conny Torstensson, Veine Wallinder, Roland Sandberg, Ralf Edström. Trainer: Sven-Agne Larsson

CHELSEA: Peter Bonetti; Edward McCreadie (47 Patrick Mulligan), Ronald Harris, John Boyle, David Webb, Marvin Hinton, Charles Cooke, Thomas Baldwin, John Hollins, Peter Osgood, Alan Hudson. Manager: Dave Sexton

**DYNAMO BERLIN
v BEERSCHOT ANTWERP 3-1** (1-0)

Sportforum, Berlin 3.11.1971

Referee: Ib Nielsen (DEN) Attendance: 8,304

DYNAMO: Werner Lihsa, Dieter Stumpf, Jochen Carow, Wilfried Trümpler, Joachim Hall, Peter Rohde, Frank Terletzki, Manfred Becker, Norbert Johannsen, Harald Schütze, Dieter Labes. Trainer: Johannes Geitel

BEERSCHOT: Helmut Brösch, Roland Coclet (55 Jean-Pierre Kasprzak), Yves Baré, Robert Dalving, Julien van Opdorp, Chris Stroybant, Jan Van Gucht, Herman Houben, Peter Suykerbuyk, Arto Tolsa, Guido Mallants.

Goals: Johannsen (25), Labes (74), Kasprzak (76), Becker (85)

**GLASGOW RANGERS
v SPORTING LISBOA 3-2** (3-0)

Ibrox, Glasgow 20.10.1971

Referee: Rudolf Glöckner (E. GER) Attendance: 40,000

RANGERS: Peter McCloy, John Greig, William Mathieson, William Jardine, Ronald McKinnon, David Smith, William Henderson, Andrew Penman (13 Alfred Conn), Colin Stein, Graham Fyfe, Alexander MacDonald.
Manager: William Waddell

SPORTING: Vítor Manuel Afonso DAMAS de Oliveira, João Gonçalves LARANJEIRA (46 Manuel PEDRO GOMES), HILÁRIO Rosário da Conceição, Vítor GONÇALVES (35 João de Matos Moura LOURENÇO), Francisco CALÓ, JOSÉ CARLOS da Silva José, Francisco Delfim Dias Faria "CHICO", NÉLSON Fernandes, Hector YAZALDE, VAGNER Canotilho, Joaquim DINIS.

Goals: Stein (5, 10), Henderson (30), Chico (67), Vagner (88)

CHELSEA LONDON v ÅTVIDABERG FF 1-1 (0-0)

Stamford Bridge, London 3.11.1971

Referee: Jacques Colling (LUX) Attendance: 28,071

CHELSEA: Peter Bonetti; Patrick Mulligan (46 Marvin Hinton), Ronald Harris, John Boyle, John Dempsey, David Webb, Charles Cooke, John Hollins, Peter Osgood, Alan Hudson, Peter Houseman. Manager: Dave Sexton

ÅTVIDABERG: Ulf Blomberg; Jan Olsson, Kent Karlsson, Sten-Åke Andersson, Conny Gustafsson, Anders Ljungberg, Lars-Göran Andersson, Conny Torstensson, Veine Wallinder (57 Benno Magnusson), Roland Sandberg, Ralf Edström. Trainer: Sven-Agne Larsson

Goals: Hudson (46), Sandberg (67)

**SPORTING LISBOA
v GLASGOW RANGERS 4-3** (2-1, 3-2) (AET)

Estádio José Alvalade, Lisboa   3.11.1971

Referee: Laurens van Ravens (HOL)   Attendance: 20,000

SPORTING: Vítor Manuel Afonso DAMAS de Oliveira, Manuel PEDRO GOMES, Francisco CALÓ, João Gonçalves LARANJEIRA, HILÁRIO Rosário da Conceição, VAGNER Canotilho, Fernando PERES, Fernando Massano TOMÉ (46 NÉLSON Fernandes), João de Matos Moura LOURENÇO, Hector YAZALDE, Joaquim DINIS
(46 Mario da Silva Mateus "MÁRINHO").

RANGERS: Peter McCloy, John Greig, William Mathieson, William Jardine, Ronald McKinnon (46 David Smith), Colin Jackson, William Henderson, William Johnston (46 Thomas McLean), Colin Stein, Alfred Conn, Alexander MacDonald.
Manager: William Waddell

Goals: Yazalde (25), Stein (26, 46), Laranjeira (38), Pedro Gomes (87), Henderson (100), Peres (115)

The referee mistakenly ordered penalties to be taken (Rangers had already won on the Away Goals rule!)

Penalties: 1-0 Caló, Jardine (miss), 2-0 Yazalde, Newton (miss), 3-0 ...., MacDonald (miss), 4-0 ...., Stein (miss)

ESKİŞEHIRSPOR v DINAMO MOSKVA 0-1 (0-1)

Atatürk, Eskişehir   20.10.1971

Referee: Paul Bonett (MAL)   Attendance: 15,000

ESKİŞEHIRSPOR: Taskin Yilmaz, Abdurrahman Temel, Ismail Arca, Kamuran Yavuz, Faik Sentasler, K.Burhan, Vahap Özbayar, V.Burhan (65 Ilhan Çolak), Halil Gundögan, Fethi Heper, Şevki Şenlen.

DINAMO: Vladimir Pilgui, Vladimir Basalaev, Aleksandr Grebnev, Viktor Anichkin, Vladimir Dolbonosov, Aleksandr Makhovikov, Evgeni Zhukov, Yuri Siemin, Anatoli Baydachnyi, Vladimir Kozlov, Gennadi Evriuzhikhin (46 Anatoli Kozhemiakin).   Trainer: Konstantin Boshkov

Goal: Kozlov (6)

DINAMO MOSKVA v ESKİŞEHIRSPOR 1-0 (1-0)

Dinamo, Moskva   3.11.1971

Referee: Martti Hirviniemi (FIN)   Attendance: 12,000

DINAMO: Valeri Baliasnikov, Vladimir Basalaev, Viktor Anichkin, Valeri Zikov, Vladimir Dolbonosov, Evgeni Zhukov, Vladimir Eshtrekov (60 Anatoli Piskunov), Iosif Sabo, Vladimir Kozlov, Aleksandr Makhovikov, Gennadi Evriuzhikhin (46 Vladimir Larin).
Trainer: Konstantin Boshkov

ESKİŞEHIRSPOR: Taskin Yilmaz, Ilhan Çolak, Faik Sentasler, K. Burhan (37 Nihat Atacan, 65 V. Burhan), Ismail Arca, Abdurrahman Temel, Halil Gundögan, Kamuran Yavuz, Fethi Heper, Vahap Özbayar, S. Mehmet.

Goal: Kozlov (8)

QUARTER-FINALS

AC TORINO v GLASGOW RANGERS 1-1 (0-1)

Stadio Comunale, Torino   8.03.1972

Referee: Pius Kamber (SWI)   Attendance: 30,000

AC TORINO: Luciano Castellini, Angelo Cereser, Roberto Mozzini, Luciano Zecchini, Natalino Fossati (60 Giovanni Toschi), Giorgio Ferrini, Claudio Sala, Aldo Agroppi, Rosario Rampanti (67 Livio Luppi), Paolo Pulici, Giovanni Bui.
Trainer: Gustavo Giagnoni

RANGERS: Peter McCloy, John Greig, William Jardine, William Mathieson, Colin Jackson, David Smith, Alexander MacDonald, Thomas McLean, Derek Johnstone, Colin Stein, William Johnston.   Manager: William Waddell

Goals: Johnston (12), Pulici (61)

GLASGOW RANGERS v AC TORINO 1-0 (0-0)

Ibrox, Glasgow   22.03.1972

Referee: Francisco S. Marques Lobo (POR)   Att: 65,000

RANGERS: Peter McCloy, Colin Jackson, William Jardine, William Mathieson, John Greig, David Smith, Thomas McLean, Derek Johnstone, Colin Stein, Alexander MacDonald, William Johnston.   Manager: William Waddell

AC TORINO: Luciano Castellini, Marino Lombardo, Natalino Fossati (46 Mario Barbaresi), Giorgio Puia, Angelo Cereser, Giorgio Ferrini, Livio Luppi, Alessandro Crivelli, Giovanni Bui (47 Ferdinando Rossi), Rosario Rampanti, Giovanni Toschi.
Trainer: Gustavo Giagnoni

Goal: MacDonald (46)

ÅTVIDABERG IF v DYNAMO BERLIN 0-2 (0-1)

Kopparvallen, Åtvidaberg   8.03.1972

Referee: Francesco Francescon (ITA)   Attendance: 5,000

ÅTVIDABERG: Ulf Blomberg; Sten-Åke Andersson, Jan Olsson, Kent Karlsson, Conny Gustafsson, Lars-Göran Andersson, Ralf Edström, Conny Torstensson (55 Bo Augustsson), Benno Magnusson, Roland Sandberg, Veine Wallinder.   Trainer: Sven-Agne Larsson

DYNAMO: Werner Lihsa, Jochen Carow, Dieter Stumpf, Wilfried Trümpler, Jürgen Hübner, Frank Terletzki, Peter Rohde, Harald Schütze, Norbert Johannsen (65 Dieter Labes), Wolf-Rüdiger Netz, Ralf Schulenberg.
Trainer: Johannes Geitel

Goals: Netz (36, 58)

DYNAMO BERLIN v ÅTVIDABERG IF 2-2 (1-2)
Sportforum, Berlin 22.03.1972
Referee: Robert Holley Davidson (SCO) Attendance: 30,000
DYNAMO: Werner Lihsa, Jochen Carow, Dieter Stumpf, Wilfried Trümpler, Jürgen Hübner, Peter Rohde, Harald Schütze, Frank Terletzki, Norbert Johannsen, Wolf-Rüdiger Netz, Ralf Schulenberg. Trainer: Johannes Geitel
ÅTVIDABERG: Ulf Blomberg; Sten-Åke Andersson, Jan Olsson, Kent Karlsson, Conny Gustafsson, Bo Augustsson, Conny Torstensson, Veine Wallinder, Benno Magnusson (74 Lars-Göran Andersson), Roland Sandberg, Ralf Edström. Trainer: Sven-Agne Larsson
Goals: Schulenberg (11), Wallinder (29), Sandberg (31), Netz (38)

CRVENA ZVEZDA BEOGRAD
v DINAMO MOSKVA 1-2 (0-1)
Crvena Zvezda, Beograd 8.03.1972
Referee: Kenneth Howard Burns (ENG) Attendance: 40,000
CRVENA ZVEZDA: Ratomir Dujković; Branko Klenkovski, Vladislav Bogicević (46 Petar Krivokuča), Miroslav Pavlović, Kiril Dojčinovski, Mihalj Keri, Slobodan Janković, Stanislav Karasi (52 Nikola Jovanović), Zoran Filipović, Jovan Acimović, Sead Sušić.
DINAMO: Vladimir Pilgui, Vladimir Basalaev, Oleg Dolmatov, Valeri Zikov, Iosif Sabo, Evgeni Zhukov, Anatoli Baydachnyi (81 Mikhail Gershkovich), Andrei Yakubik, Anatoli Kozhemiakin, Aleksandr Makhovikov, Gennadi Evriuzhikhin (66 Vladimir Kozlov).
Trainer: Konstantin Boshkov
Goals: Kozhemiakin (45), Filipović (88), Gershkovich (90)

DINAMO MOSKVA
v CRVENA ZVEZDA BEOGRAD 1-1 (0-0)
Pakhtakor, Tashkent 22.03.1972
Referee: Roger Machin (FRA) Attendance: 55,000
DINAMO: Vladimir Pilgui, Vladimir Basalaev, Oleg Dolmatov, Valeri Zikov, Vladimir Dolbonosov, Evgeni Zhukov, Anatoli Baydachnyi, Andrei Yakubik, Anatoli Kozhemiakin, Aleksandr Makhovikov, Gennadi Evriuzhikhin.
Trainer: Konstantin Boshkov
CRVENA ZVEZDA: Ratomir Dujković; Milovan Djorić, Vladislav Bogicević, Miroslav Pavlović, Kiril Dojčinovski, Petar Krivokuča, Mile Novković, Zoran Antonijević, Aleksandar Panajotović, Jovan Acimović, Stanislav Karasi.
Goals: Krivokuča (65), Kozhemiakin (75)

STEAUA BUCUREŞTI
v BAYERN MÜNCHEN 1-1 (1-0)
23 August, Bucureşti 8.03.1972
Referee: Adrianus Bogaerts (HOL) Attendance: 40,000
STEAUA: Carol Haidu; Lajos Sătmăreanu, Viorel Smarandache, Bujor Hălmăgeanu, Gheorghe Cristache; Iosif Vigu, Ion Naom; Nicolae Pantea, Gheorghe Tătaru, Anghel Iordănescu (39 Vasile Aelenei), Viorel Năstase.
Trainer: Valentin Stănescu
BAYERN: Josef Maier; Johnny Hansen, Georg Schwarzenbeck, Franz Beckenbauer, Paul Breitner; Franz Roth, Rainer Zobel, Uli Hoeness; Edgar Schneider (55 Franz Krauthausen), Gerhard Müller, Wolfgang Sühnholz.
Trainer: Udo Lattek
Goals: Tătaru (17), Müller (70)

SEMI-FINALS

BAYERN MÜNCHEN v STEAUA BUCUREŞTI 0-0
Grünwalderstadion, München 22.03.1972
Referee: Jozef Krnavec (CZE) Attendance: 40,000
BAYERN: Josef Maier; Johnny Hansen, Georg Schwarzenbeck, Franz Beckenbauer, Paul Breitner; Franz Roth, Franz Krauthausen, Rainer Zobel; Gerhard Müller, Uli Hoeness, Wolfgang Sühnholz. Trainer: Udo Lattek
STEAUA: Narcis Coman; Lajos Sătmăreanu, Viorel Smarandache, Bujor Hălmăgeanu, Gheorghe Cristache; Vasile Negrea, Iosif Vigu; Nicolae Pantea, Gheorghe Tătaru, Anghel Iordănescu, Costică Ştefănescu. Trainer: Valentin Stănescu

BAYERN MÜNCHEN
v GLASGOW RANGERS 1-1 (1-0)
Stadion am der Grünwalder Strasse, München 5.04.1972
Referee: Liuben Radunchev (BUL) Attendance: 40,000
BAYERN: Josef Maier, Franz Beckenbauer, Johnny Hansen, Georg Schwarzenbeck, Paul Breitner, Uli Hoeness, Rainer Zobel, Franz Roth (61 Edgar Schneider), Franz Krauthausen, Gerhard Müller, Wolfgang Sühnholz. Trainer: Udo Lattek
RANGERS: Peter McCloy, David Smith, William Jardine, Colin Jackson, William Mathieson, John Greig, Alexander MacDonald, Thomas McLean, Derek Johnstone, Colin Stein, William Johnston. Manager: William Waddell
Goals: Breitner (21), Zobel (47 og)

**GLASGOW RANGERS
v BAYERN MÜNCHEN 2-0** (2-0)

Ibrox, Glasgow   19.04.1972

Referee: Francesco Francescon (ITA)   Attendance: 80,000

RANGERS: Peter McCloy, William Jardine, Colin Jackson, David Smith, William Mathieson, Derek Parlane, Derek Johnstone, Alexander MacDonald, Thomas McLean, Colin Stein, William Johnston.   Manager: William Waddell

BAYERN: Josef Maier, Herward Koppenhöfer, Georg Schwarzenbeck, Franz Beckenbauer, Paul Breitner (29 Günther Rybarczyk), Franz Roth, Johnny Hansen, Rainer Zobel, Uli Hoeness, Gerhard Müller, Edgar Schneider.   Trainer: Udo Lattek

Goals: Jardine (1), Parlane (22)

DYNAMO BERLIN v DINAMO MOSKVA 1-1 (0-0)

Sportforum, Berlin   5.04.1972

Referee: Gusztáv Bircsak (HUN)   Attendance: 30,000

DYNAMO: Werner Lihsa, Dieter Stumpf, Jochen Carow, Wilfried Trümpler, Jürgen Hübner, Peter Rohde, Frank Terletzki, Harald Schütze, Ralf Schulenberg, Wolf-Rüdiger Netz, Norbert Johannsen.   Trainer: Johannes Geitel

DINAMO: Vladimir Pilgui, Vladimir Basalaev, Iosif Sabo, Oleg Dolmatov, Valeri Zikov, Andrei Yakubik, Evgeni Zhukov, Aleksandr Makhovikov, Anatoli Baydachnyi, Anatoli Kozhemiakin, Gennadi Evriuzhikhin.
Trainer: Konstantin Boshkov

Goals: Evriuzhikhin (54), Johannsen (83 pen).

**DINAMO MOSKVA
v DYNAMO BERLIN 1-1** (0-1, 1-1) (AET)

Druzba, Lvov   20.04.1972

Referee: Einar J.Boström (SWE)   Attendance: 30,000

DINAMO: Vladimir Pilgui, Vladimir Basalaev, Iosif Sabo, Oleg Dolmatov, Valeri Zikov, Andrei Yakubik (60 Viktor Anichkin), Evgeni Zhukov, Aleksandr Makhovikov, Anatoli Baydachnyi, Anatoli Kozhemiakin (48 Mikhail Gershkovich), Gennadi Evriuzhikhin.   Trainer: Konstantin Boshkov

DYNAMO: Werner Lihsa, Jochen Carow, Dieter Stumpf, Wilfried Trümpler, Jürgen Hübner, Peter Rohde, Harald Schütze (112 Manfred Becker), Frank Terletzki, Norbert Johannsen, Wolf-Rüdiger Netz (112 Bernd Brillat), Ralf Schulenberg.   Trainer: Johannes Geitel

Goals: Netz (37), Evriuzhikhin (58)

Penalties: 1-0 Dolmatov, Johannsen (miss), 2-0 Baidachny, Terletzki (miss), 3-0 Evriuzhikhin, 3-1 Carow, 4-1 Makhovikov.

FINAL

**GLASGOW RANGERS
v DINAMO MOSKVA 3-2** (2-0)

Camp Nou Barcelona   24.05.1972

Referee: José Maria Ortiz de Mendibil Monasterio (SPA)
Attendance: 24,701

RANGERS: Peter McCloy; William Pullar Jardine, John Greig (Cap), Derek Johnstone, William Mathieson; David Bruce Smith, Alfred James Conn, Alexander MacDonald; Thomas McLean, Colin Stein, William Johnston.
Manager: William Waddell

DINAMO: Vladimir Pilgui; Vladimir Basalaev, Iosif Sabo (Cap), Evgeni Zhukov, Vladimir Dolbonosov (68 Mikhail Gershkovich); Valeri Zikov, Oleg Dolmatov, Aleksandr Makhovikov; Anatoli Baydachnyi, Andrei Yakubik (57 Vladimir Eshtrekov), Gennadi Evriuzhikhin.
Trainer: Konstantin Boshkov

Goals: Stein (24), Johnston (40, 49), Eshtrekov (60), Makhovikov (86)

Goalscorers European Cup-Winners' Cup 1971-72:

8 goals: Peter Osgood (Chelsea London)

5 goals: Zoran Filipović (Crvena Zvezda Beograd), Gerhard Müller (Bayern München), Colin Stein (Glasgow Rangers)

4 goals: MARCIAL Pina Morales (CF Barcelona), Thomas Baldwin (Chelsea London), Hector Yazalde (Sporting Lisboa), Fethi Heper (Eskişehirspor), Roland Sandberg (Åtvidaberg), Wolf-Rüdiger Netz (Dynamo Berlin), Vladimir Kozlov (Dinamo Moskva)

3 goals: Kurt Foka (Austria Wien), Juan Manuel ASENSI Ripoll (CF Barcelona), Peter Houseman (Chelsea London), Giovanni Toschi (Torino), Viorel Năstase (Steaua Bucureşti), Norbert Johannsen (Dynamo Berlin)

2 goals: E. Magnusson (Fram Reykjavík), Jarosik (Zaglebie Sosnowiec), Juhász (Komló BSE), Bosveld (Sparta Rotterdam), Micallef (Hibernians), Hudson, Hollins, Webb (Chelsea London), Kasprzak, Suykerbuyck, Tolsa (Beerschot), Lourenço (Sporting Lisboa), Antonijević, Karasi, Krivokuča (Crvena Zvezda), Hoffmann (Bayern), Evriuzhikhin, Kozhemiakin (Dinamo Moskva), Labes, Schütze (Dynamo Berlin), Henderson, MacDonald (Glasgow Rangers), Johnstone, Johnston (Glasgow Rangers)

1 goal: Thorn, Richter, Berg, H.Andersen (B 1909 Odense), Redon (Stade Rennes), Gzil, Galeczka (Zaglebie Sosnowiec), Horváth, Bencsik (Komló BSE), Ceco (Dinamo Tiranë), Bican (Škoda Plzeň), O'Neill (Distillery Belfast), Gibson, Clark (Cardiff City), Dörfel, Barriquand (Servette Genève), Triantafilos, Gkaitatzis (Olympiakos Peiraias), Panov (Levski Spartak Sofia), Evans, Hughes, Heighway, Lawler (Liverpool), Dirnberger, Riedl, Köglberger (Austria Wien), Alfonseda (CF Barcelona), Klijnjan, Kristensen, Kowalik (Sparta Rotterdam), Cini (Hibernians Paola), Harris (Chelsea London), Van Opdorp, Claessen, Mallants (Beerschot), Laranjeira, Pedro Gomes, Peres, Chico, Vagner, Marinho, Dinis (Sporting Lisboa), Pulici, Agroppi, Rampanti, Luppi (Torino), Wallinder, Torstensson, Edström, Ljungberg (Åtvidaberg), Tătaru (Steaua București), Janković, Aćimović (Crvena Zvezda Beograd), Breitner, Hoeness, Sühnholz, Krauthausen, Roth (Bayern München), Schulenberg, P.Rohde, Becker (Dynamo Berlin), Eshtrekov, Makhovikov, Gershkovich, Sabo (Dinamo Moskva), Jardine, Parlane (Glasgow Rangers)

Own goals: Caruana (Hibernians Paola) for Steaua București, Mertakkas (Anorthosis Famagusta) for Beerschot Antwerp, Zobel (Bayern) for Glasgow Rangers

CUP WINNERS' CUP 1972-73

FIRST ROUND

RED BOYS DIFFERDANGE v MILAN AC 1-4 (0-3)

Thillenberg Stadium, Differdange 6.09.1972

Referee: Robert Wurtz (FRA)   Attendance: 5,200

RED BOYS: Giacomini, Johny Kirsch, René Flenghi, Gabriel Christophe, Jean Welter, Jean Paul Goerres (46 Jean Calmes), Berkefeld, Carlevaris, Gilbert Dussier, Giardin, M. Klein (60 Henri Klein).

AC MILAN: William Vecchi, Angelo Anquilletti, Giuseppe Sabadini, Roberto Rosato, Karl-Heinz Schnellinger, Maurizio Turone, Luciano Chiarugi, Giorgio Biasiolo, Pierino Prati (22 Carlo Tresoldi), Gianni Rivera, Lino Golin.
Trainer: Nereo Rocco

Goals: Prati (4, 17), Golin (19), Chiarugi (83), H. Klein (90)

MILAN AC v RED BOYS DIFFERDANGE 3-0 (2-0)

San Siro, Milano 27.09.1972

Referee: Richard Casha (MAL)   Attendance: 30,000

AC MILAN: William Vecchi, Angelo Anquilletti, Giulio Zignoli, Dario Dolci, Karl-Heinz Schnellinger, Giorgio Biasiolo (46 Maurizio Turone), Lino Golin (46 Guido Magherini), Romeo Benetti, Alberto Bigon, Gianni Rivera, Luciano Chiarugi.   Trainer: Nereo Rocco

RED BOYS: Norbert Wampach, Johny Kirsch, Jean Welter, Gabriel Christophe, René Flenghi, Jean Calmes, Berkefeld, Gilbert Dussier, Henri Klein (46 Jean Paul Goerres), Giardin (63 Lamberty), M. Klein.

Goals: Chiarugi (4, 66), Benetti (33)

**PEZOPORIKOS LARNACA
v CORK HIBERNIANS 1-2** (0-1)

Flower Lodge, Cork 10.09.1972

Referee: Gudmundur Haraldsson (ICE)   Attendance: 5,653

PEZOPORIKOS: Takis Palmiris, Andreas Yakavou, Giannis Paridis, Iakovos Filippou, Kallis Konstantinou, Stelios Kyriakou, Hristos Loizou (50 Giorgos Kounnidis), Stavros Papadopoulos, Melis Asprou, Keith Miller, William Duffy.

HIBERNIANS: Joe O'Grady, David Bacuzzi, Frank Connolly, Martin Sheehan, John Herrick, John Lawson, Sonny Sweeney, Matthew Donovan, Jerry Finnegan (65 Donie Madden), Jeremiah Dennehy, David Wigginton.

Goals: Lawson (25 pen), Duffy (57), Sheehan (75)

**CORK HIBERNIANS
v PEZOPORIKOS LARNACA 4-1** (2-0)

Flower Lodge, Cork   13.09.1972

Referee: E.H. Hjartarsson (ICE)   Attendance: 5,000

HIBERNIANS: Joe O'Grady, David Bacuzzi, Martin Sheehan, Frank Connolly, John Herrick, John Lawson, Sonny Sweeney, Matthew Donovan, David Wigginton, Jeremiah Dennehy, Donald Wallace.

PEZOPORIKOS: Takis Palmiris, Andreas Yakavou, Giannis Paridis, Iakovos Filippou, Kallis Konstantinou, Stelios Kyriakou, Hristos Loizou (.. Giorgos Kounnidis), Satvros Papadopoulos, Melis Asprou, Keith Miller, William Duffy.

Goals: Wallace (21), Lawson (45, 72), Miller (70), Dennehy (85)

**SPORTING CLUBE DO PORTUGAL LISBOA
v HIBERNIAN EDINBURGH 2-1** (0-0)

Estádio José Alvalade, Lisboa   13.09.1972

Referee: Arie van Gemert (HOL)   Attendance: 30,000

SPORTING: Vítor Manuel Afonso DAMAS de Oliveira, Manuel PEDRO GOMES, CARLOS Eduardo da Silva PEREIRA, Carlos Alberto MANACA Dias, João Gonçalves LARANJEIRA, Vítorino Manuel Antunes BASTOS, Mario da Silva Mateus "MÁRINHO", Samuel Ferreira FRAGUITO, Hector YAZALDE, NÉLSON Fernandes, VAGNER Canotilho (77 Francisco Delfim Dias Faria CHICO).

HIBERNIAN: James Herriot, John Brownlie, Erich Schaedler, Patrick Stanton, James Black, John Blackley, Alexander Edwards, James O'Rourke, Alan Gordon, Alexander Cropley, Arthur Duncan.

Goals: Fraguito (59), Manaca (61), Duncan (69)

HIBERNIAN EDINBURGH v SPORTING CLUBE de PORTUGAL LISBOA 6-1 (1-1)

Easter Road Park, Edinburgh   27.09.1972

Referee: Günter Männig (E. GER)   Attendance: 26,041

HIBERNIAN: James Herriot, John Brownlie, Erich Schaedler, Patrick Stanton, James Black, John Blackley, Alexander Edwards, James O'Rourke, Alan Gordon, Alexander Cropley, Arthur Duncan.

SPORTING: Vítor Manuel Afonso DAMAS de Oliveira, Manuel PEDRO GOMES, CARLOS Eduardo da Silva PEREIRA, Francisco Delfim Dias Faria CHICO (73 Joaquim DINIS), Carlos Alberto MANACA Dias, João Gonçalves LARANJEIRA, Mario da Silva Mateus "MÁRINHO", Samuel Ferreira FRAGUITO, Hector YAZALDE, NÉLSON Fernandes, VAGNER Canotilho (75 Fernando Massano TOMÉ).

Goals: Gordon (28, 59), O'Rourke (55, 63, 80 pen), Manaca (87 og), Yazalde (42)

**FREMAD AMAGER KØBENHAVN
v BESA KAVAJE DURRES 1-1** (0-1)

Sundby, København   13.09.1972

Referee: Jan Lazowski (POL)   Attendance: 2,365

FREMAD AMAGER: Larsen, Skytte, Jacobsen, Hansen, Poul Mathiasen, E.Andersen, Kristensen, Ivel (46 A.Andersen), F.Nielsen (65 Salomonsen), Erik Erik Ryde, Lerch.

BESA: Arkaxhiu, Mullalhui, Kapedani, N.Ushi, Qerolli (50 Dyli), Kujtim Pagria, Kashami, Maksut Leshteni, Nimet Merhori (78 Naim Allaj), Muharrem Kariqi, Bishtaja.

Goals: Merhori (15), Ryde (67)

**BESA KAVAJE DURRES
v FREMAD AMAGER KØBENHAVN 0-0**

Lokomotiva, Durres   27.09.1972

Referee: Josip Strmecki (YUG)   Attendance: 12,000

BESA: Arkaxhiu, Mullalhui, Kapedani, N.Ushi, Dyli (63 Dedej), Muharrem Kariqi, Kashami, Maksut Leshteni, Kujtim Pagria (37 Qerolli), Nimet Merhori, Bishtaja.

FREMAD AMAGER: Larsen, Skytte, Jacobsen, J. Madsen, Poul Mathiasen, Kristensen, Ivel, Tommy Nielsen, F. Nielsen, Erik Ryde (64 P. Madsen), Lerch (58 Salomonsen).

STANDARD LIÈGE v SPARTA PRAHA 1-0 (0-0)

Stade Maurice Dufrasne Sclessin, Liège   13.09.1972

Referee: William A. O'Neill (IRL)   Attendance: 30,000

STANDARD: Christian Piot (37 Zdravko Brkljacic), Jacques Beurlet, Leo Dolmans, Jean Thissen, Léon Jeck, Christian Labarbe, Léon Semmeling, Nico Dewalque, Vahdin Musovic (84 Wolfgang John), Roger Henrotay, Silvester Takac.

SPARTA: Vladimir Brabec, Jan Tenner, Tomás Stránsky, Vladimír Táborsky, Oldrich Urban, František Chovanec, Jaroslav Barton, Václav Masek, Vladimir Kara, Josef Jurkanin, Josef Pesice.   Trainer: T. Kraus

Goal: Dewalque (69)

SPARTA PRAHA v STANDARD LIÈGE 4-2 (1-1)

Stadión na Letnej, Praha   27.09.1972

Referee: Ferdinand Marschall (AUS)   Attendance: 14,575

SPARTA: Vladimir Brabec, Jan Tenner, Tomás Stránsky, Vladimír Táborsky, Oldrich Urban, František Chovanec, Jaroslav Barton, Václav Masek, Vladimir Kara (87 Josef Pesice), Josef Jurkanin, Svatopluk Bouska.   Trainer: T. Kraus

STANDARD: Christian Piot, Jacques Beurlet, Leo Dolmans, Nico Dewalque, Léon Jeck (73 Charles Ernotte), Christian Labarbe, Léon Semmeling, Tommy Svensson, Vahdin Musovic (67 Wolfgang John), Roger Henrotay, Silvester Takac.

Goals: Kara (17, 60, 69), Takac (21), Urban (73 pen), Henrotay (87)

HAJDUK SPLIT v FK FREDRIKSTAD 1-0 (1-0)
Plinada stadion, Split   13.09.1972

Referee: Faik Bajrami (ALB)   Attendance: 15,000

HAJDUK: Ante Sirković; Vilson Džoni, Mario Boljat, Dražen Mužinić, Miroslav Bošković, Luka Peruzović, Ivica Hlevnjak, Jure Jerković, Petar Nadoveza, Micun Jovanić (46 Josko Gluić), Ivan Šurjak.   Trainer: Branko Zebec

FREDRIKSTAD: Per Haftorsen, Tom Zakariassen, Knut Røragen, Bjørn Drillestad, Erik Karlsen, Robert Nilsson, Frithjof Gjermundsen, Terje Høili, Kai Nilsen, Jan Fuglset, Bjørge Sandhaug.

Goal: Nadoveza (19)

LANDSKRONA BOYS v RAPID BUCUREȘTI 1-0 (1-0)
Carlslunds Idrottspark, Landskrona   27.09.1972

Referee: John Wright Paterson (SCO)   Attendance: 10,000

BoYs: Christer Olsson; Gert-Inge Svensson, Roger Karlsson, Kenneth Dahlgren, Jerry Rosengren (45 Torbjörn Lindström); Christer Lindgren, Kenneth Berg, Bo Nilsson (60 Tommy Gustavsson); Claes Cronqvist, Sune "Sonny" Johansson, Dan Brzokoupil.   Trainer: Rolf Svensson

RAPID: Răducanu Necula; Vasile Ștefan, Alexandru Boc, Alexandru Grigoraș, Gheorghe Codrea; Marin Stelian, Iordan Angelescu; Mircea Savu, Constantin Năsturescu (69 Marian Petreanu), Alexandru Neagu, Dumitru Dumitriu.   Trainer: Bazil Marian

Goal: Lindgren (32)

FK FREDRIKSTAD v HAJDUK SPLIT 0-1 (0-1)
Fredrikstad Stadion   27.09.1972

Referee: Kaj Rasmussen (DEN)   Attendance: 7,781

FK FREDRIKSTAD: Per Haftorsen, Tom Zakariassen, Bjørn Drillestad, Knut Røragen, Erik Karlsen, Kai Nilsen, Frithjof Gjermundsen, Robert Nilsson, Terje Høili, Jan Fuglset, Bjørge Sandhaug.

HAJDUK: Ante Sirković; Vilson Džoni, Mario Boljat, Miroslav Bošković, Dražen Mužinić, Luka Peruzović, Ivica Hlevnjak, Jure Jerković, Petar Nadoveza, Micun Jovanić, Ivan Šurjak (65 Josko Gluić).   Trainer: Branko Zebec

Goal: Nadoveza (25)

FC ZÜRICH v WREXHAM 1-1 (0-0)
Letzigrund, Zürich   13.09.1972

Referee: Petar Kostovski (YUG)   Attendance: 20,000

FC ZÜRICH: Karl Grob; Max Heer, Hilmar Zigerlig, Hubert Münch, Renzo Bionda, Jakob Kuhn, Erwin Schweizer (46 Timo Konietzka), Rosario Martinelli (60 Pirmin Stierli), Fritz Künzli, Rudolf Brunnenmeier, Daniel Jeandupeux.

WREXHAM: Brian Lloyd; Stuart Mason, David Fogg, Gareth Davis, Edward May, Michael Evans, Brian Tinnion, Melvyn Sutton, William Ashcroft, Albert Kinsey, Michael Thomas.

Goals: Künzli (47), Kinsey (48)

RAPID BUCUREȘTI v LANDSKRONA BOYS 3-0 (1-0)
23 August, București   13.09.1972

Referee: Franz Wöhrer (AUS)   Attendance: 4,986

RAPID: Răducanu Necula; Vasile Ștefan, Alexandru Boc, Alexandru Grigoraș, Gheorghe Codrea; Ion Naom (67 Mircea Savu), Iordan Angelescu; Marian Petreanu (60 Constantin Năsturescu), Marin Stelian, Alexandru Neagu, Dumitru Dumitriu.   Trainer: Bazil Marian

BoYs: Christer Olsson; Gert-Inge Svensson, Roger Karlsson, Kenneth Dahlgren, Jerry Rosengren; Kenneth Berg, Claes Cronqvist, Lars Nilsson (75 Tommy Gustavsson); Torbjörn Lindström (46 Christer Lindgren), Sune "Sonny" Johansson, Dan Brzokoupil.   Trainer: Rolf Svensson

Goals: M. Stelian (43, 70), Năsturescu (82)

WREXHAM v FC ZÜRICH 2-1 (0-0)
Racecourse Ground, Wrexham   27.09.1972

Referee: Rolf Nyhus (NOR)   Attendance: 18,189

WREXHAM: Brian Lloyd, Stuart Mason, David Fogg, Gareth Davis, Edward May, Michael Evans, Brian Tinnion, Melvyn Sutton, William Ashcroft, Albert Kinsey (46 Roger Mostyn), Michael Thomas.

FC ZÜRICH: Karl Grob; Max Heer, Pirmin Stierli, Hilmar Zigerlig, Renzo Bionda, Rudolf Brunnenmeier, Erwin Schweizer, Rosario Martinelli, Fritz Künzli, Timo Konietzka, Daniel Jeandupeux.

Goals: Martinelli (48), Ashcroft (63), Sutton (74)

RAPID WIEN v PAOK THESSALONIKI 0-0

Prater, Wien   13.09.1972

Referee: Francesco Francescon (ITA)   Attendance: 10,000

RAPID: Erwin Fuchsbichler; Ewald Ullmann, Werner, Erich Fak, Norbert Hof, Egon Pajenk, Bernhard Lorenz, Jürgen Ey (60 Karl Müller), Johann Krankl (46 Stanislaus Kastner), Werner Walzer, Geza Gallos.

PAOK: Apostolos Savvoulidis, Giannis Gounaris, Aristarhos Fountoukidis, Kostas Iosifidis, P.Papadopoulos, Hristos Terzanidis, Dimitris Paridis, Mihalis Bellis, Kiriakos Apostolidis, Giorgos Koudas, Ahilleas Aslanidis.
Trainer: Les Sanon

PAOK THESSALONIKI v RAPID WIEN 2-2 (1-2)

Toumpas, Thessaloniki   27.09.1972

Referee: Károly Palotai (HUN)   Attendance: 40,000

PAOK: Giannis Stefas, Giannis Gounaris, Aristarhos Fountoukidis, Kostas Iosifidis, P.Papadopoulos, Hristos Terzanidis, Dimitris Paridis, Stavros Sarafis, Vasilis Lazos, Kiriakos Apostolidis, Ahilleas Aslanidis.   Trainer: Les Sanon

RAPID: Erwin Fuchsbichler; Ewald Ullmann, Werner, Erich Fak, Norbert Hof, Egon Pajenk, Stanislaus Kastner (62 Roman Groll), Werner Walzer, Johann Krankl, Bernhard Lorenz, Geza Gallos.

Goals: Gallos (22), Sarafis (32 pen), Krankl (43), Aslanidis (90)

ANKARAGÜCÜ v LEEDS UNITED 1-1 (0-1)

19 Mayis, Ankara   13.09.1972

Referee: Kevorc Ghemigean (ROM)   Attendance: 20,000

ANKARAGÜCÜ: Aydin Tohumcu, Remzi Hotlar (50 Mehmet Aktan), Ismail Dilber, Erman Toroğlu, Mujdat Yalman, Zafer Göncüler, Metin Yilmaz, Selçuk Yalçintaş, Melih Atacan, Coskun Ferman, Köksal Mesci.   Trainer: Ziya Taner

UNITED: David Harvey, Paul Reaney, Trevor Cherry, William Bremner, Roy Ellam, Norman Hunter, Peter Lorimer, Christopher Galvin (44 Terence Yorath), Joseph Jordan, John Giles, Paul Madeley.   Manager: Don Revie

Goals: Jordan (45), Zafer (50 pen)

LEEDS UNITED v ANKARAGÜCÜ 1-0 (0-0)

Elland Road, Leeds   27.09.1972

Referee: Klaus Ohmsen (W. GER)   Attendance: 22,411

UNITED: David Harvey, Paul Reaney, Trevor Cherry, William Bremner, Roy Ellam, Norman Hunter, Peter Lorimer, Allan Clarke, Michael Jones, John Giles, Michael Bates.
Manager: Don Revie

ANKARAGÜCÜ: Aydin Tohumcu, Remzi Hotlar, Ismail Dilber, Erman Toroğlu, Mujdat Yalman, Mehmet Aktan, Selçuk Yalçintaş, Metin Yilmaz (9 Zafer Göncüler), Behzat, Coskun Ferman, Köksal Mesci.   Trainer: Ziya Taner

Goal: Jones (68)

SPARTAK MOSKVA v FC DEN HAAG 1-0 (0-0)

Lenin, Moskva   13.09.1972

Referee: Bertil Lööw (SWE)   Attendance: 28,000

SPARTAK: Yuri Darvin, Gennadi Logofet, Sergei Olshanski, Nikolai Abramov, Evgeni Lovchev, Mikhail Bulgakov, Vitali Mirzoev, Aleksandr Piskarev, Viktor Papaev, Valeri Andreev (74 Aleksandr Minaev), Vladimir Redin.
Trainer: Nikita Simonian

FC DEN HAAG: Ton Thie; Thijs Wijngaarde, Aad Mansveld, Kees Weimar, Joop Korevaar, Piet De Zoete, Dick Advocaat, Aad Kila, Harald Berg, Kees Bregman, Paul Roodnat.
Trainer: Vaclav Jezek

Goal: Bulgakov (55)

FC DEN HAAG v SPARTAK MOSKVA 0-0

Zuiderpark, Den Haag   27.09.1972

Referee: Antonio Saldanha Ribeiro (POR)   Att: 21,000

FC DEN HAAG: Ton Thie; Leo De Caluwe, Aad Mansveld, Piet De Zoete, Joop Korevaar, Aad Kila, Dick Advocaat, Harald Berg, Kees Bregman (45 Paul Roodnat), Tor Fuglset, Hans Bres.   Trainer: Vaclav Jezek

SPARTAK: Yuri Darvin, Gennadi Logofet, Sergei Olshanski, Nikolai Abramov, Evgeni Lovchev, Mikhail Bulgakov, Vitali Mirzoev, Aleksandr Piskarev, Viktor Papaev, Valeri Zenkov, Vladimir Redin.   Trainer: Nikita Simonian

**VIKINGUR FC REYKJAVÍK
v LEGIA WARSZAWA 0-2** (0-0)

Laugardalsvöllur, Reykjavík   13.09.1972

Referee: Alistair MacKenzie (SCO)   Attendance: 4,000

VIKINGUR FC: Didrik Olafsson, Jón Olafsson, Magnus Thorvaldsson, Bjarni Gunnarsson, Páll Björgvinsson, Gunnar Gunnarsson, Gudgeir Leifsson, Johannes Bardarsson, Haflidi Pétursson, Eirikur Thorsteinsson (76 Stefán Halldórsson), Gunnar Orn Kristjansson (.. Olafur Thorsteinsson).

LEGIA: Piotr Mowlik, Wladyslaw Stachurski, Zygfryd Blaut, Antoni Trzaskowski, Andrzej Zygmunt, Bernard Blaut, Tadeusz Nowak, Stefan Balcerzak, Stefan Bialas, Jan Pieszko, Tadeusz Cypka.

Goals: Bialas (60), Balcerzak (62)

LEGIA WARSZAWA
v VIKINGUR FC REYKJAVÍK 9-0 (3-0)

Stadion Wojska Polskiego, Warszawa 27.09.1972

Referee: Pavel Kazakov (USSR)   Attendance: 7,000

LEGIA: Wieslaw Surlit, Wladyslaw Stachurski, Feliks Niedziolka, Antoni Trzaskowski, Andrzej Zygmunt, Jan Pieszko, Tadeusz Nowak, Leslaw Cmikiewicz, Stefan Bialas, Kazimierz Deyna, Robert Gadocha (65 Tadeusz Cypka).

VIKINGUR FC: Didrik Olafsson, Oskar Pétur Tomasson, Magnus Thorvaldsson, Páll Björgvinsson, Jón Olafsson, Bjarni Gunnarsson, Gudgeir Leifsson, Jonasson, Haflidi Pétursson (75 Olafur Thorsteinsson), Eirikur Thorsteinsson (70 Stefán Halldórsson), Gunnar Orn Kristjansson.

Goals: Bialas (6, 44), Pieszko (17, 47, 67), Stachurski (46), Deyna (60, 85 pen), Cmikiewicz (84).

SCHALKE 04 GELSENKIRCHEN
v SLAVIA SOFIA 2-1 (1-0)

Parkstadion, Gelsenkirchen 13.09.1972

Referee: Robert Holley Davidson (SCO)   Att: 20,000

SCHALKE 04: Norbert Nigbur, Hartmut Huhse, Helmut Kremers, Rolf Rüssmann, Klaus Fichtel, Herbert Lütkebohmert, Paul Holz, Karl-Heinz Frey (70 Ulrich van den Berg), Klaus Fischer, Klaus Scheer (45 Nico Braun), Erwin Kremers.   Trainer: Ivica Horvat

SLAVIA: Petar Tsolov; Aleksandar Shalamanov, Liudmil Topusov, Viktor Ionov, Nikola Krastev, Liuben Tasev, Atanas Aleksandrov (78 Tsvetan Slavchev), Stefan Pavlov, Bozhidar Grigorov, Andrei Jeliazkov, Georgi Georgiev.

Goals: Rüssmann (8), Fischer (52), Georgiev (58)

FC CARL ZEISS JENA
v MIKKELIN PALLOILIJAT 6-1 (1-1)

Ernst Abbe Sportfeld, Jena 13.09.1972

Referee: William John Gow (WAL)   Attendance: 12,000

FC CARL ZEISS: Wolfgang Blochwitz, Gerhard Hoppe, Peter Rock (23 Michael Strempel), Lothar Kurbjuweit, Harald Irmscher, Konrad Weise, Rainer Schlutter, Helmut Stein, Peter Ducke, Norbert Schumann, Eberhard Vogel.
Trainer: Hans-Joachim Meyer

PALLOILIJAT: Risto Remes, Rainer Jungman, Heikki Valjakka, Eero Karppinen, Vilho Rajantie, Antti Rusanen, Kari Pasanen (65 Kari Mutanen), Matti Vanhanen, Antero Hyttinen, Markku Kääriäinen, Pentti Toivola (72 Heikki Kangaskorpi).

Goals: Vogel (13, 49, 79 pen), Stein (82, 87, 90), Kääriäinen (18)

SLAVIA SOFIA
v SCHALKE 04 GELSENKIRCHEN 2-1 (1-1)

Slavia, Sofia 27.09.1972

Referee: Rudolf Scheurer (SWI)   Attendance: 4,500

SLAVIA: Georgi Gugalov; Krumov, Liudmil Topusov, Viktor Ionov, Nikola Krastev, Liuben Tasev, Atanas Aleksandrov, Stefan Pavlov, Bozhidar Grigorov, Andrei Jeliazkov, Stoian Kotzev.

SCHALKE 04: Norbert Nigbur, Helmut Manns, Hartmut Huhse, Rolf Rüssmann, Klaus Fichtel, Herbert Lütkebohmert, Klaus Scheer, Karl-Heinz Frey, Nico Braun, Helmut Kremers, Erwin Kremers.   Trainer: Ivica Horvat

Goals: H. Kremers (4), Jeleaskov (39), Tasev (62).

This game was stopped after 65 minutes due to bad weather conditions and replayed the following day.

MIKKELIN PALLOILIJAT
v CARL ZEISS JENA 3-2 (2-1)

Urheilupuisto, Mikkeli 27.09.1972

Referee: Sven Jonsson (SWE)   Attendance: 2,500

PALLOILIJAT: Risto Remes, Rainer Jungman, Heikki Valjakka, Eero Karpinen, Vilho Rajantie, Antti Rusanen, Heikki Kangaskorpi (80 Markku Kääriäinen), Matti Vanhanen, Antero Hyttinen, Antero Nikkanen, Pentti Toivola.

FC CARL ZEISS: Wolfgang Blochwitz, Gerhard Hoppe, Michael Strempel, Konrad Weise (72 Peter Rock), Lothar Kurbjuweit, Harald Irmscher, Rainer Schlutter, Helmut Stein, Peter Ducke, Dieter Scheitler, Eberhard Vogel (60 Martin Göbel).   Trainer: Hans-Joachim Meyer

Goals: Kangaskorpi (12), Vanhanen (29), Vogel (36), Toivola (69), Scheitler (73)

SLAVIA SOFIA
v SCHALKE 04 GELSENKIRCHEN 1-3 (0-2)

Slavia, Sofia 28.09.1972

Referee: Rudolf Scheurer (SWI)   Attendance: 4,840

SLAVIA: Georgi Gugalov; Krumov (46 Georgi Georgiev), Topusov, Viktor Ionov, Nikola Krastev, Liuben Tasev, Atanas Aleksandrov, Stefan Pavlov, Bozhidar Grigorov (66 Atanas Mihailov), Andrei Jeliazkov, Stoian Kotzev.

SCHALKE 04: Norbert Nigbur, Helmut Manns, Hartmut Huhse, Rolf Rüssmann, Klaus Fichtel, Herbert Lütkebohmert, Klaus Scheer, Karl-Heinz Frey, Nico Braun, Helmut Kremers, Erwin Kremers.   Trainer: Ivica Horvat

Goals: Braun (4), Scheer (32), Lütkebohmert (73), Mihailov (90)

SEC BASTIA v ATLÉTICO MADRID 0-0

Stade François Coty, Ajaccio   14.09.1972

Referee: Robert Schaut (BEL)   Attendance: 8,000

SEC BASTIA: Ilija Pantelić; Victor Mosa, Jean-Claude Tosi, Jean-Louis Luccini, Cvetko Savkovic; Denis Bauda, Jean-Pierre Giordani, Serge Lenoir, François Felix, Claude Papi, Marc Case "Kanyan".   Trainer: Pierre Cahuzac

ATLÉTICO: Roberto Rodríguez García "RODRI", Francisco Delgado MELO, José Luis CAPÓN González, ADELARDO Rodríguez Sánchez, Iselín Santos OVEJERO Maya; Julio IGLESIAS Santamaría, José Armando UFARTE Ventoso, Ignacio Manuel SALCEDO Sánchez Blanca, Domingo BENEGAS Jiménez, Javier Iruretagoyena Amiano "IRURETA", ALBERTO Fernández Fernández.   Trainer: Max Merkel

ATLÉTICO MADRID v SEC BASTIA 2-1 (1-1)

Estadio Vicente Calderón, Madrid   26.09.1972

Referee: Sergio Gonella (ITA)   Attendance: 30,000

ATLÉTICO: Roberto Rodríguez García "RODRI", Francisco Delgado MELO, José Luis CAPÓN González, ADELARDO Rodríguez Sánchez (66 EUSEBIO Bejarano Vilaroz), Jesús MARTÍNEZ JAYO, Domingo BENEGAS Jiménez, José Armando UFARTE Ventoso, Ignacio Manuel SALCEDO Sánchez Blanca, LUIS Aragonés Suarez, Javier Iruretagoyena Amiano "IRURETA", Heraldo BECERRA Nuñes.   Trainer: Max Merkel

SEC BASTIA: Ilija Pantelić; Victor Mosa, Jean-Louis Hodoul, Jean-Louis Luccini (63 Jean Claude Tosi), Cvetko Savkovic, Georges Calmettes, Jean-Pierre Giordani, Denis Bauda, François Felix, Serge Lenoir, Marc Case "Kanyan".   Trainer: Pierre Cahuzac

Goals: Felix (21), Salcedo (33), Luis (58)

FLORIANA FC v FERENCVÁROS TC BUDAPEST 1-0 (1-0)

Valletta   20.09.1972

Referee: Leonidas Vamvakopoulos (GRE)   Att: 3,000

FLORIANA: A.Farrugia, George Ciantar, Edwin Farrugia, John Holland, Alfred Debono; Frank Micallef, Salvu Bonello; William Vassallo, Raymond Xuereb, Louis Arpa, George Xuereb.

FTC: István Géczi; János Füsi, Miklós Páncsics, Arpad Horváth, Péter Vépi; István Juhász, Lajos Kü; István Szőke, László Branikovits, Flórián Albert, József Mucha (73 Gyözö Martos).   Trainer: Ferenc Csanádi

Goal: Arpa (2)

FERENCVÁROSI TC BUDAPEST v FLORIANA FC LA VALLETTA 6-0 (3-0)

Népstadion, Budapest   27.09.1972

Referee: Aurel Bentu (ROM)   Attendance: 18,000

FTC: István Géczi; János Füsi, Miklós Páncsics, László Bálint, Péter Vépi; István Juhász, Lajos Kü; István Szőke (63 Lajos Bányai), László Branikovits (64 István Megyesi), Flórián Albert, József Mucha.   Trainer: Ferenc Csanádi

FLORIANA: A.Farrugia, George Ciantar, Edwin Farrugia, John Holland, Alfred Debono; Frank Micallef, Salvu Bonello; William Vassallo, Raymond Xuereb, Louis Arpa, George Xuereb.

Goals: Kü (28, 76), Branikovits (36, 53), Szőke (43), Mucha (47)

SECOND ROUND

RAPID WIEN v RAPID BUCUREŞTI 1-1 (1-0)

Prater, Wien   25.10.1972

Referee: Vital Loraux (BEL)   Attendance: 12,000

RAPID WIEN: Adolf Antrich; Ewald Ullmann, Werner, Egon Pajenk; Erich Fak; Werner Walzer, Günter Scheffl, Norbert Hof (59 Jürgen Ey); Bernhard Lorenz, Johann Krankl, Geza Gallos.

RAPID BUCUREŞTI: Răducanu Necula; Vasile Ştefan, Alexandru Boc, Alexandru Grigoraş, Gheorghe Codrea; Marin Stelian, Iordan Angelescu; Constantin Năsturescu, Dumitru Dumitriu (46 Mircea Savu), Alexandru Neagu, Marian Petreanu (83 Teofil Codreanu).   Trainer: Bazil Marian

Goals: Gallos (10), Neagu (66)

RAPID BUCUREŞTI v RAPID WIEN 3-1 (1-0)

23 August, Bucureşti   8.11.1972

Referee: Dogan Babacan (TUR)   Attendance: 15,000

RAPID BUCUREŞTI: Răducanu Necula; Ion Pop, Alexandru Boc, Alexandru Grigoraş, Gheorghe Codrea; Mircea Savu, Iordan Angelescu; Constantin Năsturescu (42 Dumitru Dumitriu), Marin Stelian, Alexandru Neagu, Marian Petreanu.   Trainer: Bazil Marian

RAPID WIEN: Adolf Antrich; Werner Walzer, Egon Pajenk, Erich Fak, Norbert Hof; Ewald Ullmann, Jürgen Ey (46 Karl Müller), Günter Scheffl; Bernhard Lorenz, Johann Krankl, Geza Gallos.

Goals: Krankl (40 og), Hof (50), Boc (75), Petreanu (85)

FC CARL ZEISS JENA v LEEDS UNITED 0-0
Ernst Abbe Sportfeld, Jena   25.10.1972
Referee: Leo W. van der Kroft (HOL)   Attendance: 13,724
FC CARL ZEISS: Wolfgang Blochwitz, Gerhard Hoppe, Michael Strempel, Konrad Weise (46 Peter Rock), Lothar Kurbjuweit, Harald Irmscher, Martin Göbel, Rainer Schlutter, Peter Ducke, Dieter Scheitler, Eberhard Vogel (75 Norbert Schumann).   Trainer: Hans-Joachim Meyer
UNITED: David Harvey, Paul Madeley, Trevor Cherry, William Bremner, John Charlton, Norman Hunter, Peter Lorimer, Allan Clarke, Joseph Jordan, Michael Bates, Edward Gray.   Manager: Don Revie

LEEDS UNITED v FC CARL ZEISS JENA 2-0 (0-0)
Elland Road, Leeds   8.11.1972
Referee: Concetto Lo Bello (ITA)   Attendance: 26,885
UNITED: David Harvey, Paul Reaney, Trevor Cherry, William Bremner, John Charlton, Norman Hunter, Peter Lorimer, Allan Clarke, Michael Jones, Michael Bates (80 John Giles), Terence Yorath.   Manager: Don Revie
FC CARL ZEISS: Wolfgang Blochwitz, Gerhard Hoppe, Peter Rock, Konrad Weise, Lothar Kurbjuweit, Michael Strempel, Rainer Schlutter, Martin Göbel, Peter Ducke (70 Dieter Scheitler), Harald Irmscher, Eberhard Vogel.
Trainer: Hans-Joachim Meyer
Goals: Cherry (55), Jones (63)

WREXHAM v HAJDUK SPLIT 3-1 (3-0)
Racecourse Ground, Wrexham   25.10.1972
Referee: Paul Bonett (MAL)   Attendance: 19,013
WREXHAM: Brian Lloyd, Stuart Mason, David Fogg, Michael Evans, Gareth Davis, Michael Thomas, David Smallman, Melvyn Sutton, William Ashcroft, Brian Tinnion, Arfon Griffiths.
HAJDUK: R. Vukcević, Vilson Džoni, Mario Boljat, Dražen Mužinić, Dragan Holcer, Miroslav Bošković, Josko Gluić, Jure Jerković, Petar Nadoveza, Micun Jovanić, Ivan Šurjak
Goals: Tinnion (14), Smallman (15), Mužinić (40 og), Jovanić (84)

HAJDUK SPLIT v WREXHAM 2-0 (2-0)
Plinada stadion, Split   8.11.1972
Referee: Stanislaw Ekstajn (POL)   Attendance: 22,000
HAJDUK: Radomir Vukcević, Vilson Džoni, Ivan Buljan, Dražen Mužinić, Dragan Holcer, Miroslav Bošković, Ivica Hlevnjak, Jure Jerković, Petar Nadoveza, Micun Jovanić, Ivan Šurjak.
WREXHAM: Brian Lloyd, Stuart Mason, David Fogg, Gareth Davis, Edward May, Michael Evans, Brian Tinnion, Melvyn Sutton, William Ashcroft (69 Michael McBurney), Michael Thomas, Albert Kinsey (53 David Smallman).
Goals: Nadoveza (13, 28 pen)

CORK HIBERNIANS
v SCHALKE 04 GELSENKIRCHEN 0-0
Flower Lodge, Cork   25.10.1972
Referee: Michel Kitabdjian (FRA)   Attendance: 8,000
HIBERNIANS: Declan O'Mahony, David Bacuzzi, Martin Sheehan, Frank Connolly, John Brohan, John Lawson, Sonny Sweeney, Matthew Donovan, Jeremiah Dennehy, David Wigginton, Donald Wallace.
SCHALKE 04: Norbert Nigbur, Helmut Manns, Hartmut Huhse, Rolf Rüssmann, Klaus Fichtel, Herbert Lütkebohmert, Nico Braun, Karl-Heinz Frey, Peter Ehmke, Klaus Scheer, Erwin Kremers.   Trainer: Ivica Horvat

SCHALKE 04 GELSENKIRCHEN
v CORK HIBERNIANS 3-0 (2-0)
Parkstadion, Gelsenkirchen   8.11.1972
Referee: Károly Palotai (HUN)   Attendance: 12,000
SCHALKE 04: Norbert Nigbur, Hartmut Huhse, Helmut Kremers (46 Ulrich van den Berg), Rolf Rüssmann, Klaus Fichtel, Herbert Lütkebohmert, Paul Holz, Peter Ehmke, Nico Braun (70 Helmut Manns), Klaus Beverungen, Erwin Kremers.   Trainer: Ivica Horvat
HIBERNIANS: Declan O'Mahony, David Bacuzzi, Martin Sheehan, Frank Connolly, John Herrick, John Lawson, Sonny Sweeney, Matthew Donovan (70 Don Kenny), Jeremiah Dennehy, David Wigginton, Donald Wallace (70 John Brohan).
Goals: Ehmke (14), Braun (15), E. Kremers (68 pen).

ATLÉTICO MADRID
v SPARTAK MOSKVA 3-4 (0-1)
Estadio Vicente Calderón, Madrid   25.10.1972
Referee: Rudolf Glöckner (E. GER)   Attendance: 22,673
ATLÉTICO: Roberto Rodríguez García "RODRI", José Luis CAPÓN González, Enrique Vicente Hernandez "QUIQUE", ADELARDO Rodríguez Sánchez, Iselín Santos OVEJERO Maya, Domingo BENEGAS Jiménez, José Armando UFARTE Ventoso (75 ALBERTO Fernández Fernández), Ignacio Manuel SALCEDO Sánchez Blanca, LUIS Aragonés Suarez, Javier Iruretagoyena Amiano "IRURETA", Heraldo BECERRA Nuñes.   Trainer: Max Merkel
SPARTAK: Yuri Darvin, Gennadi Logofet, Sergei Olshanski, Evgeni Lovchev, Nikolai Abramov, Valeri Zenkov, Mikhail Bulgakov, Galimzian Khusainov, Aleksandr Piskarev, Viktor Papaev, Vladimir Redin.   Trainer: Nikita Simonian
Goals: Redin (42, 87), Piskarev (59), Bulgakov (77), Luis (79 pen), Ovejero (86), Becerra (89)

SPARTAK MOSKVA
v ATLÉTICO MADRID 1-2 (0-1)
Dinamo, Moskva 8.11.1972
Referee: Erich Linemayr (AUS)   Attendance: 13,614
SPARTAK: Yuri Darvin, Vladimir Bukievski, Sergei Olshanski, Evgeni Lovchev, Nikolai Abramov, Valeri Zenkov, Mikhail Bulgakov, Galimzian Khusainov, Aleksandr Piskarev, Viktor Papaev, Vladimir Redin.   Trainer: Nikita Simonian
ATLÉTICO: Roberto Rodríguez García "RODRI", Francisco Delgado MELO, Enrique Vicente Hernandez "QUIQUE", Julio IGLESIAS Santamaría, Domingo BENEGAS Jiménez, EUSEBIO Bejarano Vilaroz, Ignacio Manuel SALCEDO Sánchez Blanca, LUIS Aragonés Suarez, Eugenio LEAL Vargas, Javier Iruretagoyena Amiano "IRURETA", ALBERTO Fernández Fernández.   Trainer: Max Merkel
Goals: Salcedo (11, 55), Khusainov (59)

FERENCVÁROS TC BUDAPEST
v SPARTA PRAHA 2-0 (0-0)
Népstadion, Budapest 25.10.1972
Referee: Tzvetan P. Stanev (BUL)   Attendance: 14,000
FTC: István Géczi; János Füsi, László Bálint, Péter Vépi, István Megyesi; István Juhász (63 Arpad Horváth), Lajos Kü; István Szőke, László Branikovits, Flórián Albert, József Mucha. Trainer: Ferenc Csanádi
SPARTA: Vladimir Brabec; Tibor Semendák, Tomás Stránsky, Vladimír Táborsky, Oldrich Urban, František Chovanec, Bohumil Vesely, Václav Masek, Jaroslav Barton, Josef Jurkanin, Josef Pesice.   Trainer: T. Kraus
Goals: Kü (46), Mucha (72)

HIBERNIAN EDINBURGH
v BESA KAVAJË 7-1 (2-0)
Easter Road Park, Edinburgh 25.10.1972
Referee: Rolf Nyhus (NOR)   Attendance: 20,000
HIBERNIAN: James Herriot, John Brownlie, Erich Schaedler (.. John Hamilton), Patrick Stanton, James Black, John Blackley, Alexander Edwards, James O'Rourke, Alan Gordon, Alexander Cropley, Arthur Duncan.
BESA: Arkaxhiu, Mullalhui, Kapedani, Hushi, Naim Allaj, Qerolli, Kashami (14 Dyli), Maksut Leshteni, Muharrem Kariqi, Nimet Merhori, Bishtaja (57 Feshti).
Goals: Cropley (12), O'Rourke (14, 52, 61), Brownlie (55), Duncan (57, 64), Kariqi (72)

SPARTA PRAHA
v FERENCVÁROS TC BUDAPEST 4-1 (2-1)
Stadión na Letnej, Praha 8.11.1972
Referee: Gerhard Künze (E. GER)   Attendance: 20,000
SPARTA: Vladimir Brabec, Tibor Semendák (55 Jan Tenner), Svatopluk Bouska (62 Tomás Stránsky), Vladimír Táborsky, Oldrich Urban, František Chovanec, Bohumil Vesely, Václav Masek, Vladimir Kara, Josef Jurkanin, Jaroslav Barton. Trainer: T. Kraus
FTC: István Géczi; Péter Vépi, Arpad Horváth, László Bálint, István Megyesi; István Juhász, Lajos Kü, József Mucha; István Szőke (59 János Bartosik), László Branikovits, János Füsi. Trainer: Ferenc Csanádi
Goals: Barton (6, 53), Mucha (33), Kara (45), Urban (80 pen)

BESA KAVAJË
v HIBERNIAN EDINBURGH 1-1 (0-0)
Lokomotiva, Durres 8.11.1972
Referee: Karl Keller (SWI)   Attendance: 20,000
BESA: Arkaxhiu, Mullalhui, Kapedani, Hushi, Naim Allaj, Nimet Merhori, Kujtim Pagria, Kashami, Muharrem Kariqi, Maksut Leshteni, Bishtaja.
HIBERNIAN: James Herriot (70 Robert Robertson), John Brownlie, Erich Schaedler, Patrick Stanton, James Black, John Blackley, Alexander Edwards, James O'Rourke, Alan Gordon, Alexander Cropley, Arthur Duncan.
Goals: Pagria (54), Gordon (60)

LEGIA WARSZAWA v MILAN AC 1-1 (0-0)
Stadion Wojska Polskiego, Warszawa 25.10.1972
Referee: Hristo Mihas (GRE)   Attendance: 50,000
LEGIA: Piotr Mowlik, Wladyslaw Stachurski, Zygfryd Blaut, Andrzej Zygmunt, Antoni Trzaskowski, Leslaw Cmikiewicz, Kazimierz Deyna, Jan Pieszko, Tadeusz Nowak, Stefan Bialas, Robert Gadocha.
MILAN AC: Pierangelo Belli, Angelo Anquilletti, Giuseppe Sabadini, Roberto Rosato (81 Giulio Zignoli), Karl-Heinz Schnellinger, Giorgio Biasiolo, Alberto Bigon, Romeo Benetti, Pierino Prati, Gianni Rivera, Guido Magherini (70 Lino Golin).   Trainer: Nereo Rocco
Goals: Golin (74), Deyna (78)

MILAN AC
v LEGIA WARSZAWA 2-1 (1-1, 1-1) (AET)
Stadio San Siro, Milano   8.11.1972
Referee: Kurt Tschenscher (W. GER)   Attendance: 35,000
MILAN AC: Pierangelo Belli, Angelo Anquilletti, Giulio Zignoli, Dario Dolci (46 Giorgio Biasiolo), Karl-Heinz Schnellinger, Roberto Rosato (78 Maurizio Turone), Alberto Bigon, Romeo Benetti, Pierino Prati, Gianni Rivera, Luciano Chiarugi.   Trainer: Nereo Rocco
LEGIA: Piotr Mowlik, Wladyslaw Stachurski, Zygfryd Blaut, Andrzej Zygmunt, Antoni Trzaskowski, Leslaw Cmikiewicz, Kazimierz Deyna, Jan Pieszko, Tadeusz Nowak (112 Zbigniew Stawiszynski), Wladyslaw Dabrowski, Robert Gadocha.
Goals: Zignoli (10), Pieszko (44), Chiarugi (118)

HIBERNIAN EDINBURGH
v HAJDUK SPLIT 4-2 (2-1)
Easter Road Park, Edinburgh   7.03.1973
Referee: Antonio Camacho Jiménez (SPA)   Att: 28,424
HIBERNIAN: James Herriot, Desmond Bremner, Erich Schaedler, Patrick Stanton, James Black, John Blackley, Alexander Edwards, Tony Higgins (79 James O'Rourke), Alan Gordon, Alexander Cropley, Arthur Duncan.
HAJDUK: Ante Sirković, Vilson Džoni, Dražen Mužinić, Ivan Buljan, Dragan Holcer, Luka Peruzović, Ivica Hlevnjak, Miroslav Bošković, Micun Jovanić, Jure Jerković, Ivan Šurjak.   Trainer: Branko Zebec
Goals: Gordon (7, 26, 60), Duncan (47), Hlevnjak (38, 77)

QUARTER-FINALS

LEEDS UNITED v RAPID BUCUREŞTI 5-0 (3-0)
Elland Road, Leeds   7.03.1973
Referee: Bohumil Smejkal (CZE)   Attendance: 25,702
UNITED: David Harvey; Paul Reaney, Gordon McQueen (83 Terence Yorath), Norman Hunter, Trevor Cherry; William Bremner, John Giles, Peter Lorimer; Allan Clarke, Joseph Jordan, Paul Madeley.   Manager: Don Revie
RAPID: Răducanu Necula; Ion Pop, Alexandru Grigoraş, Constantin Muşat, Gheorghe Codrea; Marin Stelian, Marin Florin; Mircea Savu, Constantin Năsturescu (74 Ion Naom), Alexandru Neagu, Dumitru Dumitriu.   Trainer: Bazil Marian
Goals: Giles (14), Clarke (25), Lorimer (32, 57), Jordan (65)

HAJDUK SPLIT
v HIBERNIAN EDINBURGH 3-0 (2-0)
Plinada stadion, Split   21.03.1973
Referee: Hristo Mihas (GRE)   Attendance: 25,000
HAJDUK: Radomir Vukcević, Miroslav Bošković, Dražen Mužinić, Luka Peruzović, Dragan Holcer, Ivan Buljan, Ivica Hlevnjak, Jure Jerković, Petar Nadoveza (62 Vilson Džoni), Micun Jovanić, Ivan Šurjak.   Trainer: Branko Zebec
HIBERNIAN: James Herriot, Desmond Bremner (52 Robert Smith), Erich Schaedler, Patrick Stanton, James Black, John Blackley, Alexander Edwards, Tony Higgins (46 James O'Rourke), Alan Gordon, Alexander Cropley, Arthur Duncan.
Goals: Bošković (16), Hlevnjak (23), Blackley (53 og)

RAPID BUCUREŞTI v LEEDS UNITED 1-3 (0-2)
Republicii, Bucureşti   21.03.1973
Referee: Ove Dahlberg (SWE)   Attendance: 30,000
RAPID: Răducanu Necula; Ion Pop, Alexandru Grigoraş, Constantin Muşat, Gheorghe Codrea; Marin Stelian, Mircea Savu; Constantin Năsturescu, Emil Dumitriu (46 Dumitru Dumitriu), Alexandru Neagu, Marian Petreanu.   Trainer: Bazil Marian
UNITED: David Harvey; Paul Reaney, Gordon McQueen, Norman Hunter, Paul Madeley; Michael Bates (9 Terence Yorath), John Giles (76 Frank Gray), Eddie Gray; Peter Lorimer, Michael Jones, Joseph Jordan.   Manager: Don Revie
Goals: Bates (2), Jones (23), D. Dumitriu (59), Jordan (65)

SCHALKE 04 GELSENKIRCHEN
v SPARTA PRAHA 2-1 (2-1)
Parkstadion, Gelsenkirchen   7.03.1973
Referee: Nicolae Rainea (ROM)   Attendance: 12,000
SCHALKE 04: Norbert Nigbur, Hartmut Huhse, Ulrich van den Berg, Rolf Rüssmann, Klaus Fichtel, Herbert Lütkebohmert, Klaus Scheer, Peter Ehmke, Rainer Budde, Helmut Kremers, Erwin Kremers.   Trainer: Ivica Horvat
SPARTA: Vladimir Brabec, Jan Tenner (23 Antonin Princ), Oldrich Urban, František Chovanec, Vladimír Táborsky, Svatopluk Bouska, Tomás Stránsky, Václav Masek, Bohumil Vesely, Josef Jurkanin, Jaroslav Barton.   Trainer: T. Kraus
Goals: Barton (21), Ehmke (41), Rüssmann (44)

SEMI-FINALS

SPARTA PRAHA
v SCHALKE 04 GELSENKIRCHEN 3-0 (1-0)
Stadión na Letnej, Praha   21.03.1973
Referee: Clive Thomas (WAL)   Attendance: 34,000
SPARTA: Vladimir Brabec, Svatopluk Bouska, Antonin Princ, Vladimír Táborsky, Oldrich Urban, František Chovanec, Bohumil Vesely, Václav Masek, Vladimir Kara, Josef Jurkanin, Jaroslav Barton.   Trainer: T. Kraus
SCHALKE 04: Norbert Nigbur, Jürgen Klein, Hartmut Huhse, Rüßmann, Klaus Fichtel, Herbert Lütkebohmert, Klaus Scheer, Klaus Beverungen (65 Helmut Manns), Peter Ehmke, Helmut Kremers, Erwin Kremers.   Trainer: Ivica Horvat
Goals: Jurkanin (1), Kara (63), Barton (82)

LEEDS UNITED v HAJDUK SPLIT 1-0 (1-0)
Elland Road, Leeds   11.04.1973
Referee: Gyula Emsberger (HUN)   Attendance: 32,051
LEEDS UNITED: David Harvey, Paul Reaney, Trevor Cherry, William Bremner, Terence Yorath, Norman Hunter, Peter Lorimer, Allan Clarke, Michael Jones, John Giles, Michael Bates (66 Joseph Jordan).   Manager: Don Revie
HAJDUK: Radomir Vukčević; Vilson Džoni, Miroslav Bošković, Luka Peruzović, Dragan Holcer, Ivan Buljan, Ivica Hlevnjak, Mario Boljat, Mičun Jovanić, Jurica Jerković, Ivan Šurjak.   Trainer: Branko Zebec
Sent off: Clarke (72).
Goal: Clarke (20)

SPARTAK MOSKVA v MILAN AC 0-1 (0-0)
Sochi   7.03.1973
Referee: John K. Taylor (ENG)   Attendance: 14,153
SPARTAK: Aleksandr Prokhorov, Gennadi Logofet, Evgeni Lovchev, Mikhail Bulgakov, Sergei Olshanski, Nikolai Abramov, Aleksandr Minaev, Aleksandr Kokorev, Aleksandr Piskarev, Galimzian Khusainov (75 Vitali Mirzoev), Vladimir Redin.   Trainer: Nikita Simonian
MILAN AC: Pierangelo Belli, Angelo Anquilletti, Giuseppe Sabadini, Dario Dolci, Karl-Heinz Schnellinger, Giorgio Biasiolo, Riccardo Sogliano, Romeo Benetti, Alberto Bigon, Gianni Rivera, Luciano Chiarugi (74 Lino Golin).   Trainer: Nereo Rocco
Goals: Benetti (62).

HAJDUK SPLIT v LEEDS UNITED 0-0
Plinada stadion, Split   25.04.1973
Referee: Robert Héliès (FRA)   Attendance: 30,000
HAJDUK: Ante Sirković; Vilson Džoni, Miroslav Bošković, Dragan Holcer, Mario Boljat (79 Luka Peruzović), Jurica Jerković, Ivan Buljan, Mičun Jovanić (54 Dražen Mužinić), Ivica Hlevnjak, Petar Nadoveza, Ivan Šurjak.
Trainer: Branko Zebec
LEEDS UNITED: David Harvey, Paul Reaney, Terence Yorath, Norman Hunter, Trevor Cherry, William Bremner, John Giles, Paul Madeley, Peter Lorimer, Michael Jones, Joseph Jordan.

MILAN AC v SPARTAK MOSKVA 1-1 (1-1)
Stadio San Siro, Milano   21.03.1973
Referee: Milivoje Gugulović (YUG)   Attendance: 40,000
MILAN AC: Pierangelo Belli, Giulio Zignoli, Giuseppe Sabadini, Dario Dolci, Roberto Rosato, Riccardo Sogliano, Luciano Chiarugi (46 Lino Golin, 80 Roberto Casone), Romeo Benetti, Alberto Bigon, Gianni Rivera, Pierino Prati.   Trainer: Nereo Rocco
SPARTAK: Yuri Darvin, Gennadi Logofet, Evgeni Lovchev, Sergei Olshanski, Vladimir Bukievski, Mikhail Bulgakov, Aleksandr Minaev, Valeri Zenkov, Aleksandr Piskarev, Viktor Papaev, Vladimir Redin.   Trainer: Nikita Simonian
Goals: Bigon (2), Piskarev (7).

MILAN AC v SPARTA PRAHA 1-0 (0-0)
Stadio San Siro, Milano   11.04.1973
Referee: John Wright Paterson (SCO)   Attendance: 45,000
MILAN AC: Pierangelo Belli, Angelo Anquilletti, Giuseppe Sabadini (15 Giulio Zignoli), Dario Dolci, Karl-Heinz Schnellinger, Giorgio Biasiolo, Riccardo Sogliano (46 Lino Golin), Romeo Benetti, Alberto Bigon, Gianni Rivera, Luciano Chiarugi.   Trainer: Nereo Rocco
SPARTA: Vladimir Brabec, Jan Tenner, Tomás Stránsky, Vladimír Táborsky, Oldrich Urban, František Chovanec, Bohumil Vesely, Václav Masek, Vladimir Kara (81 Vaclav Hladik), Svatopluk Bouska, Josef Vesely.   Trainer: T. Kraus
Goal: Chiarugi (69).

SPARTA PRAHA v MILAN AC 0-1 (0-0)
Stadión na Letnej, Praha   25.04.1973
Referee: Pablo Augusto Sánchez Ibanez (SPA)   Att: 37,000

SPARTA: Vladimir Brabec, Antonin Princ, Vladimír Táborsky, Oldrich Urban, František Chovanec, Svatopluk Bouska, Tomás Stránsky, Václav Masek, Bohumil Vesely, Vladimir Kara, Jaroslav Barton.   Trainer: T. Kraus

MILAN AC: William Vecchi, Angelo Anquilletti, Giulio Zignoli, Dario Dolci, Karl-Heinz Schnellinger, Roberto Rosato, Maurizio Turone, Giorgio Biasiolo (89 Guido Magherini), Alberto Bigon, Gianni Rivera, Luciano Chiarugi.   Trainer: Nereo Rocco

Goal: Chiarugi (73)

FINAL

AC MILAN v LEEDS UNITED 1-0 (1-0)
Kautatzogleio, Thessaloniki   16.05.1973
Referee: Hristo Mihas (GRE)   Attendance: 40,154

AC MILAN: William Vecchi; Giuseppe Sabadini, Angelo Anquilletti, Roberto Rosato (58 Dario Dolci), Giulio Zignoli; Maurizio Turone, Riccardo Sogliano, Gianni Rivera (Cap), Romeo Benetti; Alberto Bigon, Luciano Chiarugi.   Trainer: Nereo Rocco

UNITED: David Harvey; Paul Reaney, Paul Madeley, Trevor Cherry, Frankie Gray; Michael Bates, Norman Hunter, Michael Jones, Terence Yorath (54 Gordon McQueen); Peter Lorimer, Joseph Jordan.   Trainer: Don Revie.

Sent off: Sogliano (88), Hunter (88).

Goal: Chiarugi (3)

Goalscorers European Cup-Winners' Cup 1972-73:

7 goals: Luciano Chiarugi (AC Milan)

6 goals: Gordon, O'Rourke (Hibernian Edinburgh),

5 goals: Vladimir Kara (Sparta Praha)

4 goals: Vogel (FC Carl Zeiss Jena), Pieszko (Legia Warszawa), Duncan (Hibernian Edinburgh), Petar Nadoveza (Hajduk Split), Barton (Sparta Praha),

3 goals: Lawson (Cork Hibernians), Stein (FC Carl Zeiss Jena), Salcedo (Atlético Madrid), Kü, Mucha (Ferencváros Budapest), Bialas, Deyna (Legia Warszawa), Ivica Hlevnjak (Hajduk Split), Jones, Jordan (Leeds United),

2 goals: Gallos (Rapid Wien), Luis (Atlético Madrid), Branikovits (Ferencváros Budapest), M.Stelian (Rapid București), Ehmke, Rüssmann (Schalke 04), Bulgakov, Piskarev, Redin (Spartak Moskva), Urban (Sparta Praha), Benetti, Golin, Prati (AC Milan), Clarke, Lorimer (Leeds United)

1 goal: H. Klein (Red Boys Differdange), Duffy, Miller (Pezoporikos Larnaca), Wallace, Dennehy, Sheehan (Cork Hibernians), Fraguito, Manaca, Yazalde (Sporting Lisboa), Ryde (Fremad Amager), Merhori, Kariqi, Pagria (Bessa Kavajë), Takac, Henrotay, Dewalque (Standard Liège), Lindgren (Landskrona BoYs), Künzli, Martinelli (FC Zürich), Sarafis, Aslanidis (PAOK Thessaloniki), Zafer (Ankaragücü), Kääriäinen, Kangaskorpi, Vanhanen, Toivola (Mikkelin Palloilijat), Georgiev, Mihailov (Slavia Sofia), Felix (Bastia), Arpa (Floriana Valletta), Hof, Krankl (Rapid Wien), Scheitler (FC Carl Zeiss Jena), Tinnion, Smallman, Ashcroft, Sutton, Kinsey (Wrexham), Ovejero, Becerra (Atlético Madrid), Szőke (Ferencváros Budapest), Stachurski, Cmikiewicz, Balcerzak (Legia Warszawa), Cropley, Brownlie (Hibernian Edinburgh), Braun, E.Kremers, Fischer, Braun, Scheer, Lütkebohmert (Schalke 04), D.Dumitriu, Boc, Petreanu, Neagu, Năsturescu (Rapid București), Khusainov (Spartak Moskva), Bošković, Jovanić (Hajduk Split), Jurkanin (Sparta Praha), Bigon, Zignoli (AC Milan), Giles, Bates, Cherry (Leeds United)

Own goals: Manaca (Sporting Lisboa) for Hibernian Edinburgh, Krankl (Rapid Wien) for Rapid București, Mužinić (Hajduk Split) for Wrexham, Blackley (Hibernian Edinburgh) for Hajduk Split

CUP WINNERS' CUP 1973-74

FIRST ROUND

NAC BREDA v FC MAGDEBURG 0-0
Feyenoord, Rotterdam   13.09.1973
Referee: Malcolm Wright (NIR)   Attendance: 6,000
NAC: Jan De Jong, Jan Blom, Ad Graaumans, Gerard Van den Dries, Ad Bakker, Theo Dierickx, Bertus Quaars, Frans Bouwmeester jr (86 Chris Bouman), Martin Vreijsen, Piet Van Dijk, Ad Brouwers.   Trainer: Henk Wullems
FC MAGDEBURG: Ulrich Schulze, Klaus Decker, Manfred Zapf, Wolfgang Abraham, Jörg Ohm, Axel Tyll, Wolfgang Seguin, Jürgen Pommerenke, Martin Hoffmann, Jürgen Sparwasser, Siegmund Mewes (66 Hans-Jürgen Herrmann).   Trainer: Heinz Krügel

FC MAGDEBURG v NAC BREDA 2-0 (0-0)
Ernst-Grube-Stadion, Magdeburg   3.10.1973
Referee: Georg Krurtelev (FIN)   Attendance: 25,000
FC MAGDEBURG: Ulrich Schulze, Klaus Decker, Manfred Zapf, Jürgen Achtel, Wolfgang Abraham, Axel Tyll, Wolfgang Seguin, Jürgen Pommerenke, Hans-Jürgen Herrmann, Jürgen Sparwasser, Martin Hoffmann.   Trainer: Heinz Krügel
NAC: Jan De Jong, Jan Blom (85 Chris Bouman), Ad Graaumans, Frans Vermeulen, Gerard Van den Dries, Ad Bakker, Theo Dierickx, Bertus Quaars, Frans Bouwmeester jr, Martin Vreijsen (77 Piet Van Dijk), Ad Brouwers.   Trainer: Henk Wullems
Goals: Tyll (60), Hoffmann (63).

BEROE STARA ZAGORA v FOLA ESCH 7-0 (4-0)
Gradski, Stara Zagora   19.09.1973
Referee: Karlo Kruashvili (USSR)   Attendance: 5,077
BEROE: Todor Krastev, Hristo Belchev, Hristo Todorov, Boris Tasev, Nikola Kordov, Jeko Jelev (46 Ivan Vutsov), Metodi Bonchev, Georgi Stoianov (46 Evgeni Ianchovski), Petko Petkov, Dimitar Dimitrov, Georgi Belchev.   Trainer: Ivan Tanev
FOLA: Ferrero (83 Klein), Hummer, Joubert, Ronconi, Weyrich, Josy Melde, Durain, Tonnar, Thorn, Hopp (78 Wagner), Martini.
Goals: Bonchev (1, 26, 68, 80), Stoianov (24), Petkov (43, 50)

FOLA ESCH v BEROE STARA ZAGORA 1-4 (0-1)
Gradski, Stara Zagora   22.09.1973
Referee: Tofik Bakhramov (USSR)   Attendance: 5,010
FOLA: Ferrero, Hummer, Joubert, Ronconi, Weyrich (70 Wagner), Josy Melde, Durain, Tonnar, Thorn, Hopp, Martini.
BEROE: Dimitar Vichev (46 Todor Krastev), Hristo Belchev, Hristo Todorov, Georgiev, Stefan Ivanov, Jeko Jelev, Metodi Bonchev, Georgi Stoianov, Petko Petkov (46 Nikola Kordov), Boris Kirov, Georgi Belchev.   Trainer: Ivan Tanev
Goals: Petkov (10), Belchev (50), Todorov (60), Kirov (68), Melde (89)

LAHDEN REIPAS v OLYMPIQUE LYON 0-0
Keskusurheilukenttä, Lahti   19.09.1973
Referee: Valentin Lipatov (USSR)   Attendance: 1,804
REIPAS: Harri Holli; Pekka Kosonen, Mikko Kautonen, Erkki Lehtinen, Markku Repo; Raimo Hukka, Urho Partanen (63 Matti Sandberg), Jorma Salonen; Timo Kautonen, Olavi Litmanen, Juha Peltomaa.
OLYMPIQUE: Yves Chauveau; Raymond Domenech, Ljubomir Mihajlovic, Jean Baeza, Bernard Lhomme; Robert Cacchioni, Daniel Ravier, Serge Chiesa, Bernard Lacombe, Fleury Di Nallo, Yves Mariot.   Trainer: Aimé Mignot

OLYMPIQUE LYON v LAHDEN REIPAS 2-0 (1-0)
Stade Gerland, Lyon   3.10.1973
Referee: Fernando Santos Leite (POR)   Attendance: 12,784
OLYMPIQUE: Yves Chauveau; Raymond Domenech, Ljubomir Mihajlovic, Jean Baeza, Bernard Lhomme; Aimé Jacquet, Daniel Ravier; Serge Chiesa, Bernard Lacombe, Fleury Di Nallo, Yves Mariot.   Trainer: Aimé Mignot
REIPAS: Harri Holli; Pekka Kosonen, Mikko Kautonen, Erkki Lehtinen (65 Juha Peltomaa), Markku Repo; Urho Partanen, Timo Kautonen, Raimo Hukka (75 Matti Sandberg), Jorma Salonen, Olavi Litmanen, Pertti Jantunen.
Goals: Di Nallo (30, 67)

RANDERS FREJA v RAPID WIEN 0-0
Randers stadion Freja   19.09.1973
Referee: John Carpenter (IRL)   Attendance: 11,000
FREJA: Ebbe Andersen; Leif Raaby, Helge Vonsyld, Steen Danielsen, Jørgen Rasmussen; Per Lykke, Hansen, Steenberg, Erik Sørensen (80 Bødker), Gert Nielsen, Christian Mouritzen.
RAPID: Adolf Antrich; Peter Latocha, Gerhard Sturmberger, Norbert Hof, Egon Pajenk; Werner Walzer, Herbert Gronen, Karl Ritter, Johann Krankl, August Starek, Bernhard Lorenz.   Trainer: Ernst Hlozek

RAPID WIEN v RANDERS FREJA 2-1 (1-0)
Prater, Wien   3.10.1973
Referee: Milos Cajić (YUG)   Attendance: 7,000
RAPID: Peter Barthold; Peter Latocha, Gerhard Sturmberger, Norbert Hof, Egon Pajenk; Werner Walzer, Herbert Gronen (70 Günter Scheffl), Karl Ritter, Johann Krankl, August Starek, Bernhard Lorenz.   Trainer: Ernst Hlozek
FREJA: Ebbe Andersen, Leif Raaby, Helge Vonsyld, Steen Danielsen, Jørgen Rasmussen; Per Lykke, Hansen, Steenberg, Erik Sørensen, Christian Mouritzen, Carsten Brandenborg (.. Gert Nielsen).
Goals: Krankl (14), Lorenz (57), Lykke (60)

AC MILAN v DINAMO ZAGREB 3-1 (2-0)
Stadio San Siro, Milano   19.09.1973
Referee: Walter Eschweiler (W. GER)   Attendance: 47,428
AC MILAN: William Vecchi, Angelo Anquilletti, Giulio Zignoli, Dario Dolci, Karl-Heinz Schnellinger, Ottavio Bianchi, Mario Bergamaschi, Romeo Benetti, Alberto Bigon, Gianni Rivera, Luciano Chiarugi.   Trainer: Nereo Rocco
DINAMO: Zeljko Stincić, Damir Valec, Mladen Ramljak, Veljko Tuksa (46 Josip Kuze), Ivica Miljković, Filip Blaskovic, Mario Bonic, Josip Lalić, Fikret Mujkić, Drago Vabec, Srecko Huljić (46 Zdenko Kafka).   Trainer: Ivan Marković
Goals: Bigon (10, 53), Chiarugi (16), Lalić (70)

DINAMO ZAGREB v AC MILAN 0-1 (0-1)
Maksimir, Zagreb   3.10.1973
Referee: Alois Kessler (AUS)   Attendance: 23,776
DINAMO: Zeljko Stincić, Damir Valec, Ivan Car, Josip Kuze, Ivica Miljković, Mladen Ramljak, Mario Bonić, Josip Lalić, Fikret Mujkić (64 Veljko Tuksa), Drago Vabec, Srecko Huljić.
AC MILAN: William Vecchi, Angelo Anquilletti, Giulio Zignoli, Dario Dolci, Karl-Heinz Schnellinger, Ottavio Bianchi, Mario Bergamaschi, Romeo Benetti, Alberto Bigon, Gianni Rivera, Luciano Chiarugi.   Trainer: Nereo Rocco
Goal: Chiarugi (7)

GZIRA UNITED v BRANN BERGEN 0-2 (0-1)
Empire Stadium, Valletta   19.09.1973
Referee: Antonio Camacho Jiménez (SPA)   Att: 1,914
GZIRA UNITED: Michael Sultana (46 J. Scerri), Joe Bartolo, Caruana, Charles Zammit, Vincent Borg, George Cuschieri, Albert Cristiano, Paul Portelli, Eric Schembri, Tony Bonello (55 Martin Vidal), Ronnie Schembri.
BRANN: Tor Enge, Helge Karlsen (75 Atle Bilsback), Bjørn Dahl, Rune Pedersen, Erling Mikkelsen, Arnfinn Espeseth, Torgeir Hauge, Tore Nordtvedt, Jan Erik Osland (85 Kjell Øyasaether), Endre Blindheim, Roald Jensen.
Goals: Blindheim (22, 89)

BRANN BERGEN v GZIRA UNITED 7-0 (1-0)
Brann stadion, Bergen   3.10.1973
Referee: Kaj Tage Sørensen (DEN)   Attendance: 8,403
BRANN: Tor Enge, Helge Karlsen, Rune Pedersen, Bjørn Dahl, Tore Nordtvedt, Torgeir Hauge, Jan Erik Osland (36 Frode Larsen), Arnfinn Espeseth, Kjell Øyasaether, Endre Blindheim, Roald Jensen (46 Atle Hellesø).
GZIRA UNITED: J. Scerri, Joe Bartolo, Paul Portelli (81 Galdes), Charles Zammitt, Caruana, George Cuschieri, Eric Schembri, Albert Cristiano, Tony Bonello, Martin Vidal, Ronnie Schembri (49 Vincent Borg).
Goals: Hauge (4), Osland (47), Espeseth (50, 84), Blindheim (57), Øyasaether (75), F. Larsen (89)

**CHIMIA RÎMNICU VÎLCEA
v GLENTORAN BELFAST 2-2** (2-1)
1 Mai, Rm. Vîlcea   19.09.1973
Referee: Kostas Xanthoulis (CYP)   Attendance: 5,000
CHIMIA: Ştefan Stana; Marian Cincă, Constantin Pintilie, Miron Borz, Gheorghe Lepădatu; Ion Haidu, Costică Donose, Ion Ionescu; Filip Şutru, Gheorghe Gojgaru, Vasile Iordache (85 Iulian Orovitz).
Trainers: Gheorghe Nuţescu & Dumitru Anescu
GLENTORAN: Alan Paterson; John Hill, Roy Stewart, William McCullough, Geoff Gorman (46 Roy Walsh); Rab McCreery, Andrew Dougan, John Anderson; John Jamison, James Hall, Warren Feeney.   Trainer: Bobby McGregor
Goals: Gojgaru (9, 28), McCreery (27), Jamison (74)

**GLENTORAN BELFAST
v CHIMIA RÎMNICU VÎLCEA 2-0** (1-0)
The Oval, Belfast   3.10.1973
Referee: Henk Pijper (HOL)   Attendance: 5,000
GLENTORAN: Alan Paterson; James McIlwaine, Geoff Gorman; Roy Stewart, William McCullough, Andrew Dougan; James Weatherup, Rab McCreery, John Jamison, John Anderson; Warren Feeney (46 Thomas Craig).
Trainer: Bobby McGregor
CHIMIA: Ştefan Stana; Marian Cincă, Miron Borz (46 Constantin Pintilie), Teodor Ciobanu, Gheorghe Lepădatu; Ion Haidu, Costică Donose, Ion Ionescu (46 Ion Crăciunescu); Gheorghe Gojgaru, Vasile Iordache, Filip Şutru.
Trainers: Gheorghe Nuţescu & Dumitru Anescu
Goals: Jamison (19), T. Craig (86)

**TORPEDO MOSKVA
v ATHLETIC CLUB BILBAO 0-0**
Lenin stadion, Moskva 19.09.1973
Referee: Alois Kessler (AUS)   Attendance: 13,278
TORPEDO: Aleksandr Rakitski, Vladimir Krasnov, Leonid Pakhomov, Vladimir Buturlakin (46 Valeri Abramov), Grigori Yanets, Ivan Zabiniak, Vladimir Yurin, Vadim Nikonov, Anatoli Soloviov, Anatoli Degtiariev (72 Gennadi Schalimov), Anatoli Fetisov.   Trainer: Aleksandr Ivanov
ATHLETIC: José Ángel IRÍBAR Cortajarena, José Ignacio SÁEZ Ruiz, Félix ZUBIAGA Acha, Agustín GUISASOLA Zabala, Daniel ASTRAIN Eqozcue, José Ángel ROJO Arroitia, José María LASA Ibarguren (80 CARLOS Ruiz Hierro), Ángel María VILLAR Llona, Antonio María ARIETA Araunabeña Piedra, Fidel URIARTE Macho (64 José María IGARTUA Mendizábal), José Francisco ROJO Arroitia.
Trainer: Milorad Pavlić

**ATHLETIC CLUB BILBAO
v TORPEDO MOSKVA 2-0** (1-0)
Estadio San Mamés, Bilbao 3.10.1973
Referee: Heinz Aldinger (W. GER)   Attendance: 38,208
ATHLETIC: José Ángel IRÍBAR Cortajarena, José Ignacio SÁEZ Ruiz, Félix ZUBIAGA Acha, Agustín GUISASOLA Zabala, Daniel ASTRAIN Eqozcue (42 José Ramón Martínez LARRAURI), José Ángel ROJO Arroitia, José María LASA Ibarguren, Ángel María VILLAR Llona, Antonio María ARIETA Araunabeña Piedra (60 José María IGARTUA Mendizábal), Fidel URIARTE Macho, José Francisco ROJO Arroitia.   Trainer: Milorad Pavlić
TORPEDO: Aleksandr Rakitski, Vladimir Krasnov, Leonid Pakhomov, Aleksandr Tukmanov (55 Valeri Abramov), Grigori Yanets, Ivan Zabiniak, Vladimir Yurin, Vadim Nikonov, Anatoli Soloviov, Yuri Smirnov, Anatoli Fetisov.
Trainer: Aleksandr Ivanov
Goals: Astrain (30), Lasa (49)

VASAS BUDAPEST v SUNDERLAND 0-2 (0-0)
Népstadion, Budapest 19.09.1973
Referee: Sergio Gonella (ITA)   Attendance: 27,130
VASAS: Ferenc Mészáros; Peter Török, Tibor Fábián, Csaba Vidáts, Mihály Kántor; Lajos Lakinger (65 István Gass), Sándor Müller, Bálint Tóth, Béla Váradi, István Kovács, József Sipöcz.   Trainer: Lajos Baróti
SUNDERLAND: James Montgomery, Richard Malone, Ronald Guthrie, Michael Horswill, David Watson, Richard Pitt, Robert Kerr, William Hughes, Victor Halom (78 David Young), Ian Porterfield, Dennis Tueart.   Manager: Bob Stokoe
Goals: Hughes (68), Tueart (89)

SUNDERLAND v VASAS BUDAPEST 1-0 (0-0)
Roker Park, Sunderland 3.10.1973
Referee: Francisco S. Marques Lobo (POR)   Att: 22,462
SUNDERLAND: James Montgomery, Richard Malone, Ronald Guthrie, Michael Horswill, David Watson, David Young, Robert Kerr, William Hughes, Victor Halom, Ian Porterfield, Dennis Tueart.   Manager: Bob Stokoe
VASAS: Ferenc Mészáros; Peter Török, Tibor Fábián, Mihály Kántor; Bálint Tóth, Csaba Vidáts, Sándor Müller, András Komjáti (64 Attila Földi), István Gass, Lajos Lakinger, Béla Váradi (40 István Szőke).   Trainer: Lajos Baróti
Goal: Tueart (58 pen)

**LEGIA WARSZAWA
v PAOK THESSALONIKI 1-1** (0-0)
Wojska Polskiego, Warszawa 19.09.1973
Referee: Josef Bucek (AUS)   Attendance: 12,047
LEGIA: Piotr Mowlik, Adam Topolski, Feliks Niedziolka, Andrzej Zygmunt, Jan Pieszko, Tadeusz Nowak (74 Stawiszynski), Leslaw Cmikiewicz, Wladyslaw Dabrowski, Jan Samek, Kazimierz Deyna, Robert Gadocha.   Trainer: Vejvoda
PAOK: Giannis Stefas, Giannis Gounaris, Aristarhos Fountoukidis, Kostas Iosifidis, Filotas Pellios, Hristos Terzanidis, Dimitris Paridis, Stavros Sarafis, Kiriakos Apostolidis, Vasilis Lazos, Ahilleas Aslanidis.
Trainer: Les Sanon
Goals: Terzanidis (51), Pieszko (59)

**P.A.O.K. THESSALONIKI
v LEGIA WARSZAWA 1-0** (0-0)
Toumpas, Thessaloniki 3.10.1973
Referee: Gheorghe Limona (ROM)   Attendance: 28,795
PAOK: Giannis Stefas, Giannis Gounaris, Aristarhos Fountoukidis, Kostas Iosifidis, Filotas Pellios, Hristos Terzanidis, Dimitris Paridis, Stavros Sarafis, Kiriakos Apostolidis, Vasilis Lazos, Ahilleas Aslanidis.
Trainer: Les Sanon
LEGIA: Piotr Mowlik, Adam Topolski, Feliks Niedziolka, Jan Samek, Andrzej Zygmunt, Jan Pieszko, Wieslaw Pacocha (76 Wladyslaw Dabrowski), Leslaw Cmikiewicz, Stefan Bialas, Kazimierz Deyna, Robert Gadocha.   Trainer: Vejvoda
Goal: Paridis (80)

PEZOPORIKOS LARNACA v MALMÖ FF 0-0

Zenon, Larnaca   19.09.1973

Referee: Milos Cajić (YUG)   Attendance: 1,200

PEZOPORIKOS: Mihalis Kyriakides, Iakovos Philippou, Andreas Pastellidis, Kostas Alexandrou, Kallis Konstantinou, Karapittas (.. Leonidas Xenofontos), Giorgos Kounnidis, Stavros Papadopoulos, Hristos Loizou, William Duffy, Andreas Alexandrou (.. Nikos Papantoniou).

MALMÖ FF: Jan Möller, Krister Kristensson, Roland Andersson, Roy Andersson, Staffan Tapper, Harry Jönsson, Anders Ljungberg (.. Jan-Åke Svensson), Tommy Larsson, Tommy Andersson, Conny Andersson, Tore Cervin (.. Bo Larsson).   Trainer: Karl Erik Hult

SPORTING CLUBE DO PORTUGAL LISBOA v CARDIFF CITY 2-1 (1-1)

Estádio José Alvalade, Lisboa   3.10.1973

Referee: Jacques Colling (LUX)   Attendance: 40,000

SPORTING: Vítor Manuel Afonso DAMAS de Oliveira (Cap), Carlos Alberto MANACA Dias, CARLOS Eduardo da Silva PEREIRA, Samuel Ferreira FRAGUITO, João Gonçalves LARANJEIRA, Carlos Alexandre Fortes ALHINHO, Mario da Silva Mateus "MÁRINHO", NÉLSON Fernandes, Hector YAZALDE, Fernando Massano TOMÉ (67 Francisco Delfim Dias Faria CHICO), Joaquim DINIS.   Trainer: Mario Lino

CITY: William Irwin, Philip Dwyer, Gary Bell, Robert Woodruff, Donald Murray (Cap), Leighton Phillips, Anthony Villars (87 Gilbert Reece), Andrew McCulloch, Derek Showers, John Vincent, Peter King.

Goals: Yazalde (23), Villars (39), Fraguito (50)

MALMÖ FF v PEZOPORIKOS LARNACA 11-0 (6-0)

Malmö Stadion   3.10.1973

Referee: John Robertson P. Gordon (SCO)   Att: 4,048

MALMÖ FF: Jan Möller, Roland Andersson, Krister Kristensson, Roy Andersson, Harry Jönsson, Conny Andersson, Staffan Tapper, Curt Olsberg, Björn Friberg, Bo Larsson, Tore Cervin.   Trainer: Karl Erik Hult

PEZOPORIKOS: Mihalis Kyriakides, Stelios Kyriakou, Andreas Pastellidis, Iakovos Philippou (46 Papantoniou), Kallis Konstantinou, Kostas Alexandrou, Leonidas Xenophontos, Melis Asprou (75 Andreas Iakovou), Hristos Loizou, William Duffy, Andreas Alexandrou.

Goals: Cervin (9, 15, 33, 89), Tapper (61, 74, 76), Kristensson (10), C. Andersson (35), Olsberg (13), Bo Larsson (50)

BANÍK OSTRAVA v CORK HIBERNIANS 1-0 (1-0)

Stadión na Bazaloch, Ostrava   19.09.1973

Referee: György Müncz (HUN)   Attendance: 7,388

BANÍK: Ivancik, Lumír Mochel, Rostislav Vojácek, Jiří Hudecek, Miroslav Vojkuvka, Jozef Hatar, Miroslav Micka, Josef Tondra, Lubomír Knapp, Jiří Klement, Milan Albrecht.   Trainer: Tomáš Pospíchal

HIBERNIANS: Peter Gregson, David Bacuzzi, Noel O'Mahony, Martin Sheehan, John Brohan, Frank Connolly, Sonny Sweeney, John Lawson, Denis Allen, Jimmy Lumsden, Carl Humphries.

Goal: Albrecht (25)

CARDIFF CITY v SPORTING CLUBE DO PORTUGAL LISBOA 0-0

Ninian Park, Cardiff   19.09.1973

Referee: Anthony Briguglio (MAL)   Attendance: 13,300

CITY: William Irwin, Philip Dwyer, Gary Bell, George Smith, Donald Murray (Cap), Leighton Phillips, Anthony Villars (63 Peter King), Andrew McCulloch, Robert Woodruff, John Vincent, William Anderson.

SPORTING: Vítor Manuel Afonso DAMAS de Oliveira (Cap), Carlos Alberto MANACA Dias, CARLOS Eduardo da Silva PEREIRA, Samuel Ferreira FRAGUITO, João Gonçalves LARANJEIRA, Carlos Alexandre Fortes ALHINHO, Mario da Silva Mateus "MÁRINHO", NÉLSON Fernandes, Hector YAZALDE, VAGNER Canotilho, Joaquim DINIS.   Trainer: Mario Lino

CORK HIBERNIANS v BANÍK OSTRAVA 1-2 (0-1)

Flower Lodge, Cork   3.10.1973

Referee: William John Gow (WAL)   Attendance: 4,519

HIBERNIANS: Peter Gregson, David Bacuzzi, Noel O'Mahony, Martin Sheehan, John Brohan, John Lawson, Sonny Sweeney, Jimmy Lumsden, Denis Allen, Carl Humphries, Jerry Finnegan (67 Jerry Coyne).

BANÍK: Frantisek Schmucker, Lumír Mochel, Rostislav Vojácek, Jiří Hudecek (67 Frantisek Huml), Miroslav Vojkuvka, Arnost Kvasnica, Miroslav Micka (46 Jozef Hatar), Josef Tondra, Lubomír Knapp, Jiří Klement, Milan Albrecht.   Trainer: Tomáš Pospíchal

Goals: Tondra (23), Humphreys (67), Klement (68)

ANKARAGÜCÜ v GLASGOW RANGERS 0-2 (0-1)
19 Mayis, Ankara   19.09.1973
Referee: Jan Lazowski (POL)   Attendance: 30,000
ANKARAGÜCÜ: Baskin, Hotlar Remzi, Ismail Dilber, Mehmet Aktan, Yalman Müjdat, Zafer Göncüler, Metin Yilmaz, Yalçintaş Selçuk, Melih Atacan, Ali Osman, H.Tahsin.
RANGERS: Peter McCloy, William Jardine, William Mathieson, John Greig, Colin Jackson, David Smith, Thomas McLean, Thomas Forsyth, Derek Parlane, Alfred Conn (.. Ally Scott), Quinton Young.   Manager: John Wallace
Goals: McLean (23), Conn (68)

GLASGOW RANGERS v ANKARAGÜCÜ 4-0 (1-0)
Ibrox, Glasgow   3.10.1973
Referee: Rolf Nyhus (NOR)   Attendance: 21,040
RANGERS: Peter McCloy, William Jardine, William Mathieson, John Greig, Derek Johnstone, Alexander MacDonald, Thomas McLean, Thomas Forsyth, Alex O'Hara, Alfred Conn, Douglas Houston.   Manager: John Wallace
ANKARAGÜCÜ: Baskin, Hotlar Remzi, Ismail Dilber (75 Z.Osman), Toroğlu Erman, Yalman Müjdat, Zafer Göncüler, Mehmet Aktan, Metin Yilmaz, Melih Atacan, Ferman Coskun, Tahsin.
Goals: Greig (15, 20), Johnstone (35), O'Hara (68)

ANDERLECHT BRUSSEL v FC ZÜRICH 3-2 (0-2)
Parc Astrid, Brussel   19.09.1973
Referee: Alistair MacKenzie (SCO)   Attendance: 14,729
ANDERLECHT: Jan Ruiter, François van der Elst, Jos Volders, Gilbert van Binst (46 Ludo Coeck), Hugo Broos; Jean Dockx, Jan Verheyen (61 Eddy de Bolle); André De Nul, Attila Ladinszky, Paul van Himst, Rob Rensenbrink.
FC ZÜRICH: Karl Grob; Max Heer, Ernst Rutschmann, Hilmar Zigerlig, Renzo Bionda; Jakob Kuhn, Rosario Martinelli, Ilija Katic; Daniel Jeandupeux (44 Peter Marti), Pirmin Stierli, René Botteron.   Trainer: Timo Konietzka
Goals: Stierli (25), Katic (29), Rensenbrink (49, 54, 57)

FC ZÜRICH v ANDERLECHT BRUSSEL 1-0 (1-0)
Letzigrund, Zürich   3.10.1973
Referee: Antonio Rigo Sureda (SPA)   Attendance: 19,658
FC ZÜRICH: Karl Grob, Max Heer (40 Walter Iselin), Ernst Rutschnamm, Hilmar Zigerlig, Renzo Bionda, Jakob Kuhn, Rosario Martinelli, Ilija Katic; Daniel Jeandupeux, Pirmin Stierli, René Botteron.   Trainer: Timo Konietzka
ANDERLECHT: Jan Ruiter; Gilbert van Binst, Jean Dockx, Hugo Broos, Jos Volders; François van der Elst, Jan Verheyen, Ludo Coeck (75 Eddy de Bolle); André De Nul, Attila Ladinszky, Rob Rensenbrink (46 Inge Ejderstedt)
Goal: Rutschmann (29 pen)

ÍB VESTMANNAEYJAR v BORUSSIA MÖNCHENGLADBACH 0-7 (0-3)
Laugardalsvöllur, Reykjavík   20.09.1973
Referee: Patrick Partridge (ENG)   Attendance: 2,742
ÍBV: Arsaell Sveinsson, Olafur Sigurvinsson, Einar Fridthjófsson, Thordur Hallgrimsson, Fridfinnur Finnbogasson, Snorri Rútsson, Orn Oskarsson, Oskar Valtysson, Tómas Pálsson, Haraldur Júliusson, Sigurgeirsson.
BORUSSIA: Wolfgang Kleff, Dietmar Danner, Hans-Hubert Vogts, Klaus-Dieter Sieloff, Hans Klinkhammer, Heinz Michallik, Jensen (46 Allan Simonsen), Horst Köppel, Bernd Rupp, Christian Kulik (64 Lorenz-Günter Köstner), Josef Heynckes.   Trainer: Hennes Weisweiler
Goals: Heynckes (8, 56, 75), Sigurgeirsson (37 og), Kulik (39, 48), Finnbogasson (62 og)

BORUSSIA MÖNCHENGLADBACH v ÍB VESTMANNAEYJAR 9-1 (6-0)
Bökelberg, Mönchengladbach   3.10.1973
Referee: Robert Wurtz (FRA)   Attendance: 4,838
BORUSSIA: Wolfgang Kleff, Dietmar Danner (46 Lorenz-Günter Köstner), Heinz Michallik, Klaus-Dieter Sieloff, Hans Klinkhammer, Ulrich Stielike, Allan Simonsen, Christian Kulik (75 Bernd Rupp), Horst Köppel, Herbert Wimmer, Josef Heynckes.   Trainer: Hennes Weisweiler
ÍBV: Arsaell Sveinsson, Olafur Sigurvinsson, Einar Fridthjófsson, Thordur Hallgrimsson, Fridfinnur Finnbogasson, Snorri Rútsson, Orn Oskarsson, Oskar Valtysson, Tómas Pálsson, Haraldur Júliusson (60 Vidar Elíasson), Sigurgeirsson.
Goals: Wimmer (3, 56), Valtysson (23 og), Simonsen (28, 33, 68), Köppel (34, 39), Oskarsson (65), Rupp (81)

SECOND ROUND

FC ZÜRICH v MALMÖ FF 0-0
Letzigrund, Zürich   23.10.1973
Referee: Antoine Queudeville (LUX)   Attendance: 10,957
FC ZÜRICH: Karl Grob; Max Heer, Ernst Rutschmann, Hilmar Zigerlig (59 Peter Marti), Renzo Bionda, Jakob Kuhn, Rosario Martinelli, Ilija Katic, Daniel Jeandupeux, Pirmin Stierli, René Botteron.   Trainer: Timo Konietzka
MALMÖ FF: Jan Möller, Roland Andersson, Krister Kristensson, Roy Andersson, Staffan Tapper, Harry Jönsson, Björn Friberg, Bo Larsson, Conny Andersson, Curt Olsberg, Tommy Andersson (68 Sten Sternqvist).
Trainer: Karl Erik Hult

MALMÖ FF v FC ZÜRICH 1-1 (1-0)
Malmö Stadion 4.11.1973
Referee: Günter Männig (E. GER)   Attendance: 7,469
MALMÖ FF: Jan Möller, Roland Andersson, Krister Kristensson (60 Anders Ljungberg), Roy Andersson, Staffan Tapper, Harry Jönsson, Curt Olsberg, Björn Friberg, Conny Andersson (75 Sten Sternqvist), Bo Larsson, Christer Malmberg.   Trainer: Karl Erik Hult
FC ZÜRICH: Karl Grob; Max Heer, Walter Iselin (46 Peter Marti), Hilmar Zigerlig, Renzo Bionda, Jakob Kuhn, Rosario Martinelli, Ilija Katic, Daniel Jeandupeux, Pirmin Stierli, René Botteron.   Trainer: Timo Konietzka
Goals: Malmberg (23), Katic (68)

SUNDERLAND v SPORTING CLUBE DO PORTUGAL LISBOA 2-1 (1-0)
Roker Park, Sunderland   24.10.1973
Referee: Michel Kitabdjian (FRA)   Attendance: 31,568
SUNDERLAND: James Montgomery, Richard Malone, Joseph Bolton, Michael Horswill, David Watson, David Young, Robert Kerr (Cap), William Hughes, Victor Halom, Ian Porterfield, Dennis Tueart.   Manager: Bob Stokoe
SPORTING: Vítor Manuel Afonso DAMAS de Oliveira (Cap), Carlos Alberto MANACA Dias, CARLOS Eduardo da Silva PEREIRA, Samuel Ferreira FRAGUITO, João Gonçalves LARANJEIRA, Carlos Alexandre Fortes ALHINHO, Francisco Delfim Dias Faria CHICO, NÉLSON Fernandes, Hector YAZALDE, VAGNER Canotilho, Armando Manuel de Sousa Machado "NANDO" (74 Fernando Massano TOMÉ). Trainer: Mario Lino
Goals: Kerr (32), Horswill (64), Yazalde (85)

SPORTING CLUBE DO PORTUGAL LISBOA v SUNDERLAND 2-0 (1-0)
Estádio de José Alvalade, Lisboa   7.11.1973
Referee: Rudolf Scheurer (SWI)   Attendance: 41,434
SPORTING: Vítor Manuel Afonso DAMAS de Oliveira (Cap), Carlos Alberto MANACA Dias, CARLOS Eduardo da Silva PEREIRA, Samuel Ferreira FRAGUITO, João Gonçalves LARANJEIRA, Carlos Alexandre Fortes ALHINHO, Francisco Delfim Dias Faria CHICO, NÉLSON Fernandes, Hector YAZALDE (64 Fernando Massano TOMÉ), VAGNER Canotilho, Mario da Silva Mateus "MÁRINHO" (76 Armando Manuel de Sousa Machado "NANDO").   Trainer: Mario Lino
SUNDERLAND: James Montgomery, Richard Malone, Joseph Bolton, Michael Horswill (73 John Lathan), Dave Watson, David Young, Robert Kerr (Cap), William Hughes (84 Ronald Guthrie), Victor Halom, Ian Porterfield, Dennis Tueart.   Manager: Bob Stokoe
Goals: Yazalde (26), Fraguito (69)

AC MILAN v RAPID WIEN 0-0
Stadio San Siro, Milano   24.10.1973
Referee: Alistair MacKenzie (SCO)   Attendance: 17,896
AC MILAN: William Vecchi, Giuseppe Sabadini, Giulio Zignoli, Angelo Anquilletti, Maurizio Turone, Ottavio Bianchi, Mario Bergamaschi (59 Alessandro Turini), Romeo Benetti, Alberto Bigon, Giorgio Biasiolo, Luciano Chiarugi.
Trainer: Nereo Rocco
RAPID: Peter Barthold; Emil Krause, Gerhard Sturmberger, Peter Latocha, Egon Pajenk, Werner Walzer, Herbert Gronen, Günter Scheffl, Johann Krankl, Bernhard Lorenz (72 Karl Ritter), Norbert Hof.   Trainer: Ernst Hlozek

RAPID WIEN v AC MILAN 0-2 (0-2)
Rapid-Platz Hütteldorf, Wien   7.11.1973
Referee: Pavel Kazakov (USSR)   Attendance: 3,486
RAPID: Peter Barthold; Emil Krause, Gerhard Sturmberger, Peter Latocha, Egon Pajenk (46 Aufgeweckt); Werner Walzer, Bernhard Lorenz, Günter Scheffl, Johann Krankl, August Starek, Norbert Hof.   Trainer: Ernst Hlozek
AC MILAN: William Vecchi, Angelo Anquilletti, Giulio Zignoli, Dario Dolci, Karl-Heinz Schnellinger, Giorgio Biasiolo, Giuseppe Sabadini, Romeo Benetti, Alberto Bigon, Gianni Rivera, Mario Bergamaschi.   Trainer: Nereo Rocco
Goals: Bigon (26, 41)

BORUSSIA MÖNCHENGLADBACH v GLASGOW RANGERS 3-0 (1-0)
Bökelberg, Mönchengladbach   24.10.1973
Referee: Robert Schaut (BEL)   Attendance: 33,000
BORUSSIA: Wolfgang Kleff, Dietmar Danner, Hans-Hubert Vogts, Klaus-Dieter Sieloff, Rainer Bonhof, Christian Kulik, Henning Jensen, Horst Köppel, Bernd Rupp, Herbert Wimmer, Josef Heynckes.   Trainer: Hennes Weisweiler
RANGERS: Peter McCloy, William Jardine, William Mathieson, John Greig, Derek Johnstone, Alexander MacDonald, Thomas McLean, Thomas Forsyth, Derek Parlane (63 Alex O'Hara), Alfred Conn, Douglas Houston.   Manager: John Wallace
Goals: Heynckes (21, 64), Rupp (87)

**GLASGOW RANGERS
v BORUSSIA MÖNCHENGLADBACH 3-2** (2-1)

Ibrox, Glasgow   7.11.1973

Referee: Francisco S.Marques Lobo (POR)   Att: 40,000

RANGERS: Peter McCloy, William Jardine, William Mathieson, John Greig, Colin Jackson, Alexander MacDonald, Thomas McLean, Thomas Forsyth (60 Quinton Young), Alex O'Hara, Alfred Conn, Douglas Houston.
Manager: John Wallace

BORUSSIA: Wolfgang Kleff, Dietmar Danner, Hans-Hubert Vogts, Klaus-Dieter Sieloff, Rainer Bonhof, Christian Kulik, Henning Jensen, Horst Köppel, Bernd Rupp, Herbert Wimmer, Josef Heynckes.   Trainer: Hennes Weisweiler

Goals: Conn (11), Jensen (27, 71), Jackson (32), A. MacDonald (61).

**BEROE STARA ZAGORA
v ATHLETIC CLUB BILBAO 3-0** (1-0)

Gradski, Stara Zagora   24.10.1973

Referee: Giorgos Katsoras (GRE)   Attendance: 20,527

BEROE: Todor Krastev; Hristo Belchev, Hristo Todorov, Boris Tasev, Nikola Kordov, Jeko Jelev, Boris Kirov, Evgeni Ianchovski, Petko Petkov, Dimitar Dimitrov, Georgi Belchev (68 Metodi Bonchev).   Trainer: Ivan Tanev

ATHLETIC: José Ángel IRÍBAR Cortajarena, José Ignacio SÁEZ Ruiz, Félix ZUBIAGA Acha, Agustín GUISASOLA Zabala, José Ramón Martínez LARRAURI, José Ángel ROJO Arroitia, José María LASA Ibarguren, Ángel María VILLAR Llona, Antonio María ARIETA Araunabeña Piedra (77 José María AMORRORTU Prieto), Fidel URIARTE Macho, José Francisco ROJO Arroitia.   Trainer: Milorad Pavlić

Sent off: Zubiaga (59)

Goals: Dimitrov (26), Jelev (56), Bonchev (80)

**ATHLETIC CLUB BILBAO
v BEROE STARA ZAGORA 1-0** (1-0)

Estadio San Mamés, Bilbao   7.11.1973

Referee: Sándor Petri (HUN)   Attendance: 33,839

ATHLETIC: José Ángel IRÍBAR Cortajarena, José Ignacio SÁEZ Ruiz, Jesús ARANGUREN Merino, Agustín GUISASOLA Zabala, Daniel ASTRAIN Eqozcue (86 José Ramón Martínez LARRAURI), José Ángel ROJO Arroitia (80 José María IGARTUA Mendizábal), José María LASA Ibarguren, Ángel María VILLAR Llona, Antonio María ARIETA Araunabeña Piedra, Fidel URIARTE Macho, José Francisco ROJO Arroitia.
Trainer: Milorad Pavlić

BEROE: Todor Krastev; Hristo Belchev, Hristo Todorov, Boris Tasev, Nikola Kordov, Jeko Jelev, Boris Kirov, Evgeni Ianchovski, Petko Petkov, Dimitar Dimitrov (86 Stefan Ivanov), Georgi Belchev (30 Metodi Bonchev).
Trainer: Ivan Tanev

Goal: Lasa (30)

**BRANN BERGEN
v GLENTORAN BELFAST 1-1** (1-0)

Brann, Bergen   24.10.1973

Referee: Martti Hirviniemi (FIN)   Attendance: 9,832

BRANN: Tor Enge, Helge Karlsen, Bjørn Dahl, Rune Pedersen, Erling Mikkelsen (72 Atle Bilsback), Torgeir Hauge, Jan Erik Osland, Tore Nordtvedt, Arnfinn Espeseth (5 Kjell Øyasaether), Endre Blindheim, Roald Jensen.

GLENTORAN: Trevor McCullough, James McIlwaine, Geoff Gorman, Roy Stewart, William Walker, William McCullough, James Weatherup, Rab McCreery (80 Roy Walsh), John Jamison, John Anderson (46 Andrew Dougan), Warren Feeney.
Trainer: Bobby McGregor

Goals: R. Jensen (10), Feeney (79)

**GLENTORAN BELFAST
v BRANN BERGEN 3-1** (2-0)

The Oval, Belfast   7.11.1973

Referee: Hans-Joachim Weyland (W. GER)   Att: 5,000

GLENTORAN: Trevor McCullough, James McIlwaine, Geoff Gorman (85 Roy Walsh), Roy Stewart, William Walker, William McCullough, James Weatherup, Andrew Dougan, John Jamison, John Anderson, Warren Feeney.
Trainer: Bobby McGregor

BRANN: Tor Enge, Helge Karlsen, Rune Pedersen, Ole Kobbeltveldt, Erling Mikkelsen, Torgeir Hauge (78 Atle Bilsback), Jan Erik Osland, Tore Nordtvedt, Arnfinn Espeseth (72 Kjell Øyasaether), Endre Blindheim, Roald Jensen.

Goals: Feeney (7), Jamison (14, 67), Osland (50)

BANÍK OSTRAVA v 1.FC MAGDEBURG 2-0 (1-0)

Stadión na Bazaloch, Ostrava   24.10.1973

Referee: Atanas P. Mateev (BUL)   Attendance: 4,834

BANÍK: Frantisek Schmucker, Arnost Kvasnica (56 Jiří Hudecek), Rostislav Vojácek, Frantisek Huml, Miroslav Vojkuvka, Jozef Hatar, Miroslav Micka, Josef Tondra, Lubomír Knapp, Jiří Klement, Milan Albrecht.
Trainer: Tomáš Pospíchal

1.FC MAGDEBURG: Ulrich Schulze, Klaus Decker, Manfred Zapf, Jürgen Achtel (69 Detlef Enge), Wolfgang Abraham, Axel Tyll, Wolfgang Seguin, Jürgen Pommerenke, Siegmund Mewes, Jürgen Sparwasser, Martin Hoffmann (80 Hans-Jürgen Herrmann).   Trainer: Heinz Krügel

Goals: Albrecht (16), Klement (68)

1.FC MAGDEBURG v BANÍK OSTRAVA 3-0 (1-0)
Ernst-Grube-Stadion, Magdeburg   7.11.1973
Referee: Pablo Augusto Sánchez Ibañez (SPA)   Att: 12,015
1.FC MAGDEBURG: Ulrich Schulze, Detlef Enge, Manfred Zapf, Wolfgang Abraham, Klaus Decker, Jürgen Pommerenke, Wolfgang Seguin, Axel Tyll, Hans-Jürgen Herrmann, Jürgen Sparwasser, Martin Hoffmann.   Trainer: Heinz Krügel
BANÍK: Frantisek Schmucker, Lubomír Knapp (20 Miroslav Jirousek), Rostislav Vojácek, Frantisek Huml, Miroslav Vojkuvka, Jiří Hudecek, Miroslav Micka, Josef Tondra, Jozef Hatar, Jiří Klement, Milan Albrecht.
Trainer: Tomáš Pospíchal
Goals: Abraham (30 pen), Hoffmann (84), Sparwasser (104)

OLYMPIQUE LYON
v P.AOK THESSALONIKI 3-3 (1-1)
Stade Gerland, Lyon   24.10.1973
Referee: Malcolm Wright (NIR)   Attendance: 26,250
OLYMPIQUE: Yves Chauveau; Raymond Domenech, Ljubomir Mihajlovic, Jean Baeza, Bernard Lhomme; Aimé Jacquet, Daniel Ravier; Serge Chiesa, Bernard Lacombe, Fleury Di Nallo, Yves Mariot.   Trainer: Aimé Mignot
PAOK: Giannis Stefas; Giannis Gounaris, Aristarhos Fountoukidis, Kostas Iosifidis, Filotas Pellios; Hristos Terzanidis, Dimitris Paridis, Stavros Sarafis, Kiriakos Apostolidis, Vasilis Lazos, Ahilleas Aslanidis.
Trainer: Les Sanon
Goals: Lacombe (10), Aslanidis (45), Terzanidis (50), Di Nallo (51), Ravier (67), Sarafis (81)

PAOK THESSALONIKI
v OLYMPIQUE LYON 4-0 (2-0)
Toumpas, Thessaloniki   7.11.1973
Referee: Sergio Gonella (ITA)   Attendance: 35,000
PAOK: Giannis Stefas, Giannis Gounaris, Aristarhos Fountoukidis, Kostas Iosifidis, Filotas Pellios; Hristos Terzanidis, Dimitris Paridis, Stavros Sarafis (81 Vasilis Lazos), Kiriakos Apostolidis, Giorgos Koudas, Ahilleas Aslanidis (68 Panagiotis Kermanidis).   Trainer: Les Sanon
OLYMPIQUE: Yves Chauveau; Robert Valette, Ljubomir Mihajlovic, Jean Baeza, Bernard Lhomme; Aimé Jacquet, Robert Cacchioni; Serge Chiesa, Daniel Ravier, Fleury Di Nallo, Bernard Lacombe.   Trainer: Aimé Mignot
Goals: Paridis (26, 61), Aslanidis (38 pen), Sarafis (85)

QUARTER-FINALS

GLENTORAN BELFAST
v BORUSSIA MÖNCHENGLADBACH 0-2 (0-1)
The Oval, Belfast   5.03.1974
Referee: Anton Bucheli (SWI)   Attendance: 7,066
GLENTORAN: Trevor McCullough, John Hill, William McKeag, William McCullough, William Walker (39 John Anderson), Roy Walsh, Robin Clarke (51 James Weatherup), Roy Stewart, Warren Feeney, Andrew Dougan, Victor Hooks.
Trainer: Bobby McGregor
BORUSSIA: Wolfgang Kleff, Hans-Hubert Vogts (82 Heinz Michallik), Dietmar Danner, Klaus-Dieter Sieloff, Rainer Bonhof, Ulrich Stielike, Lorenz-Günter Köstner, Christian Kulik, Henning Jensen (18 Horst Köppel), Herbert Wimmer, Josef Heynckes.   Trainer: Hennes Weisweiler
Goals: Heynckes (8), Köppel (70).

BORUSSIA MÖNCHENGLADBACH
v GLENTORAN BELFAST 5-0 (2-0)
Bökelberg Mönchengladbach 20.03.1974
Referee: Bohumil Kopcio (CZE)   Attendance: 11,332
BORUSSIA: Wolfgang Kleff, Hans-Hubert Vogts, Hans Klinkhammer (53 Christian Kulik), Klaus-Dieter Sieloff (73 Lorenz-Günter Köstner), Rainer Bonhof, Dietmar Danner, Ulrich Stielike, Horst Köppel, Bernd Rupp, Herbert Wimmer, Josef Heynckes.   Trainer: Hennes Weisweiler
GLENTORAN: Trevor McCullough, John Hill, William McKeag, William Stewart, William McCullough, Roy Walsh, John Jamison (70 James Weatherup), Victor Hooks (46 Peter Dickenson), Warren Feeney, Robin Clarke, Andrew Dougan.
Trainer: Bobby McGregor
Goals: Wimmer (20), Heynckes (22, 63), Köppel (57), Vogts (60),

1.FC MAGDEBURG
v BEROE STARA ZAGORA 2-0 (0-0)
Ernst-Grube-Stadion, Magdeburg   6.03.1974
Referee: Alistair MacKenzie (SCO)   Attendance: 20,352
1.FC MAGDEBURG: Ulrich Schulze, Detlef Enge, Manfred Zapf, Helmut Gaube, Axel Tyll, Jürgen Pommerenke, Wolfgang Seguin, Hans-Jürgen Herrmann, Martin Hoffmann, Jürgen Sparwasser, Siegmund Mewes.   Trainer: Heinz Krügel
BEROE: Todor Krastev; Hristo Belchev, Hristo Todorov, Boris Tasev, Nikola Kordov, Tenio Minchev, Boris Kirov (77 Yusein Ahmedov), Ivan Vutsov, Dimitar Dimitrov, Jeko Jelev, Metodi Bonchev.   Trainer: Ivan Tanev
Goals: Hermann (70), Mewes (73)

FC BEROE STARA ZAGORA
v 1.FC MAGDEBURG 1-1 (0-0)
Beroe, Stara Zagora 20.03.1974
Referee: Ertugrul Dilek (TUR)   Attendance: 13,995
BEROE: Todor Krastev; Hristo Belchev, Hristo Todorov, Boris Tasev, Nikola Kordov, Tenio Minchev, Stefan Ivanov (46 Kancho Kasherov), Evgeni Ianchovski (75 Georgi Stoianov), Dimitar Dimitrov, Ivan Vutsov, Metodi Bonchev.
Trainer: Ivan Tanev
1.FC MAGDEBURG: Ulrich Schulze, Detlef Enge, Manfred Zapf, Klaus Decker, Jürgen Pommerenke, Axel Tyll, Wolfgang Seguin, Hans-Jürgen Herrmann, Siegmund Mewes, Jürgen Sparwasser, Martin Hoffmann.   Trainer: Heinz Krügel
Goals: Ivan Vutsov (72 pen), Hermann (81)

SPORTING CLUBE DO PORTUGAL
v FC ZÜRICH 3-0 (0-0)
Estádio José Alvalade, Lisboa 6.03.1974
Referee: Hans Joachim Weyland (W. GER)   Att: 41,280
SPORTING: Vítor Manuel Afonso DAMAS de Oliveira (Cap); Carlos Alberto MANACA Dias, CARLOS Eduardo da Silva PEREIRA, VAGNER Canotilho, Vítorino Manuel Antunes BASTOS, Carlos Alexandre Fortes ALHINHO, Mario da Silva Mateus "MÁRINHO", NÉLSON Fernandes, Hector YAZALDE, Vítor Manuel Jesus Gonçalves "BALTASAR", Francisco Delfim Dias Faria CHICO.   Trainer: Mario Lino
FC ZÜRICH: Karl Grob; Max Heer, Ernst Rutschmann (88 Peter Marti), Hilmar Zigerlig, Renzo Bionda, Jakob Kuhn (Cap), Rosario Martinelli, Ilija Katic, Daniel Jeandupeux, Pirmin Stierli, René Botteron.   Trainer: Timo Konietzka
Goals: Nélson (55), Marinho (57), Yazalde (80 pen)

FC ZÜRICH
v SPORTING CLUBE DO PORTUGAL 1-1 (1-1)
Letzigrund, Zürich 20.03.1974
Referee: György Müncz (HUN)   Attendance: 13,697
FC ZÜRICH: Karl Grob; Max Heer (62 Pius Senn), Peter Marti, Hilmar Zigerlig (46 Ernst Rutschmann), Renzo Bionda, Jakob Kuhn (Cap), Rosario Martinelli, Ilija Katic, Daniel Jeandupeux, Pirmin Stierli, René Botteron.
Trainer: Timo Konietzka
SPORTING: Vítor Manuel Afonso DAMAS de Oliveira (Cap), JOSÉ CARLOS da Silva José, CARLOS Eduardo da Silva PEREIRA, VAGNER Canotilho (79 Francisco Delfim Dias Faria CHICO), Vítorino Manuel Antunes BASTOS, Carlos Alexandre Fortes ALHINHO, Mario da Silva Mateus "MÁRINHO", NÉLSON Fernandes, Hector YAZALDE, Vítor Manuel Jesus Gonçalves "BALTASAR" (81 Samuel Ferreira FRAGUITO), Joaquim DINIS.   Trainer: Mario Lino
Goals: Botteron (7), Baltasar (18)

AC MILAN v PAOK THESSALONIKI 3-0 (2-0)
Stadio San Siro, Milano 13.03.1974
Referee: Paul Bonett (MAL)   Attendance: 25,963
AC MILAN: William Vecchi, Angelo Anquilletti, Giuseppe Sabadini, Giorgio Biasiolo, Karl-Heinz Schnellinger, Aldo Maldera III, Carlo Tresoldi (72 Alessandro Turini), Romeo Benetti, Alberto Bigon, Gianni Rivera, Luciano Chiarugi.
Trainer: Nereo Rocco
PAOK: Savvas Hatzioannou, Giannis Hatziantoniou, Aristarhos Fountoukidis, Kostas Iosifidis, Filotas Pellios, Hristos Terzanidis (38 Vasilis Lazos), Dimitris Paridis (78 Panagiotis Kermanidis), Stavros Sarafis, P. Papadopoulos, Giorgos Koudas, Ahilleas Aslanidis.   Trainer: Les Sanon
Goals: Bigon (13), Benetti (38), Chiarugi (86)

PAOK THESSALONIKI v AC MILAN 2-2 (1-0)
Toumpas, Thessaloniki 20.03.1974
Referee: Vital Loraux (BEL)   Attendance: 28,350
PAOK: Savvas Hatzioannou, Giannis Hatziantoniou, Filotas Pellios, Kostas Iosifidis, Takis Tsiligkiridis, Dimitris Paridis, Hristos Terzanidis, Stavros Sarafis, Kiriakos Apostolidis, Giorgos Koudas, Ahilleas Aslanidis (66 Panagiotis Kermanidis).   Trainer: Les Sanon
AC MILAN: William Vecchi, Giuseppe Sabadini, Giulio Zignoli, Angelo Anquilletti, Karl-Heinz Schnellinger, Aldo Maldera III, Mario Bergamaschi (74 Carlo Tresoldi), Giorgio Biasiolo, Alberto Bigon, Gianni Rivera, Luciano Chiarugi.
Trainer: Nereo Rocco
Goals: Sarafis (29, 72), Bigon (54), Tresoldi (78)

SEMI-FINALS

SPORTING CLUBE DO PORTUGAL LISBOA
v 1.FC MAGDEBURG 1-1 (0-0)
Estádio José Alvalade, Lisboa 10.04.1974
Referee: Petar Nikolov (BUL)   Attendance: 29,422
SPORTING: Vítor Manuel Afonso DAMAS de Oliveira (Cap), Carlos Alexandre Fortes ALHINHO, Carlos Alberto MANACA Dias, Vítorino Manuel Antunes BASTOS, CARLOS Eduardo da Silva PEREIRA (73 JOAQUIM Teixeira da ROCHA), PAULO José ROCHA Beldroegas (73 Fernando Massano TOMÉ), VAGNER Canotilho, Vítor Manuel Jesus Gonçalves "BALTASAR", Mario da Silva Mateus "MÁRINHO", Francisco Delfim Dias Faria CHICO, Joaquim DINIS.
Trainer: Mario Lino
1.FC MAGDEBURG: Ulrich Schulze; Manfred Zapf (Cap), Detlef Enge, Wolfgang Abraham, Klaus Decker; Detlef Raugust, Axel Tyll, Wolfgang Seguin; Siegmund Mewes (78 Hans-Jürgen Herrmann), Jürgen Sparwasser, Martin Hoffmann.   Trainer: Heinz Krügel
Goals: Sparwasser (62), Manaca (76)

1.FC MAGDEBURG v SPORTING CLUBE DO PORTUGAL LISBOA 2-1 (1-0)

Ernst-Grube-Stadion, Magdeburg   24.04.1974

Referee: John K. Taylor (ENG)   Attendance: 34,643

1.FC MAGDEBURG: Ulrich Schulze, Manfred Zapf (Cap), Detlef Enge, Wolfgang Abraham, Klaus Decker; Wolfgang Seguin, Jürgen Pommerenke, Axel Tyll; Detlef Raugust (77 Hans-Jürgen Herrmann), Jürgen Sparwasser, Martin Hoffmann.   Trainer: Heinz Krügel

SPORTING: Vítor Manuel Afonso DAMAS de Oliveira (Cap), Vítorino Manuel Antunes BASTOS, Carlos Alberto MANACA Dias, Carlos Alexandre Fortes ALHINHO, CARLOS Eduardo da Silva PEREIRA (63 JOAQUIM Teixeira da ROCHA), PAULO José ROCHA Beldroegas (70 Fernando Massano TOMÉ), NÉLSON Fernandes, VAGNER Canotilho, Vítor Manuel Jesus Gonçalves "BALTASAR", Mario da Silva Mateus "MÁRINHO", Francisco Delfim Dias Faria CHICO. Trainer: Mario Lino

Goals: Pommerenke (9), Sparwasser (70), Marinho (78)

AC MILAN v BORUSSIA MÖNCHENGLADBACH 2-0 (1-0)

Stadio San Siro, Milano   10.04.1974

Referee: Erich Linemayr (AUS)   Attendance: 61,285

AC MILAN: Pier Luigi Pizzaballa, Maurizio Turone, Angelo Anquilletti, Enrico Lanzi, Giuseppe Sabadini, Aldo Maldera III, Romeo Benetti, Ottavio Bianchi, Mario Bergamaschi (72 Alessandro Turini), Alberto Bigon, Luciano Chiarugi. Trainer: Nereo Rocco

BORUSSIA: Wolfgang Kleff, Klaus-Dieter Sieloff, Hans-Hubert Vogts, Rainer Bonhof, Dietmar Danner (75 Allan Simonsen), Horst Köppel (65 Christian Kulik), Herbert Wimmer, Ulrich Stielike, Henning Jensen, Bernd Rupp, Josef Heynckes.   Trainer: Hennes Weisweiler

Goals: Bigon (18), Chiarugi (58)

BORUSSIA MÖNCHENGLADBACH v AC MILAN 1-0 (1-0)

Rheinstadion, Düsseldorf   24.04.1974

Referee: Ángel Franco Martínez (SPA)   Attendance: 67,081

BORUSSIA: Wolfgang Kleff, Klaus-Dieter Sieloff, Rainer Bonhof, Hans-Hubert Vogts, Ulrich Stielike, Lorenz-Günter Köstner, Christian Kulik (49 Heinz Michallik), Herbert Wimmer, Allan Simonsen, Horst Köppel, Bernd Rupp. Trainer: Hennes Weisweiler

AC MILAN: Pier Luigi Pizzaballa, Karl-Heinz Schnellinger (71 Giorgio Biasiolo), Giuseppe Sabadini, Enrico Lanzi, Angelo Anquilletti, Mario Bergamaschi, Romeo Benetti, Aldo Maldera III, Ottavio Bianchi, Alberto Bigon, Luciano Chiarugi. Trainer: Nereo Rocco

Goal: Sabadini (28 og)

FINAL

FC MAGDEBURG v AC MILAN 2-0 (1-0)

Feyenoord, Rotterdam   8.05.1974

Referee: Arendt van Gemert (HOL)   Attendance: 4,641

FC MAGDEBURG: Ulrich Schulze; Manfred Zapf (Cap), Axel Tyll, Wolfgang Abraham, Detlef Enge; Helmut Gaube, Wolfgang Seguin, Jürgen Pommerenke, Detlef Raugust; Jürgen Sparwasser, Martin Hoffmann.   Trainer: Heinz Krügel

AC MILAN: Pier Luigi Pizzaballa; Angelo Anquilletti, Aldo Maldera III, Karl-Heinz Schnellinger, Enrico Lanzi; Giuseppe Sabadini, Carlo Tresoldi, Gianni Rivera (Cap), Romeo Benetti; Alberto Bigon, Mario Bergamaschi (60 Alessandro Turini). Trainer: Nereo Rocco.

Goals: Lanzi (42 og), Seguin (75)

Goalscorers Cup-Winners' Cup 1973-74:

8 goals: Josef Heynckes (Borussia Mönchengladbach)

7 goals: Alberto Bigon (AC Milan)

5 goals: Metodi Bonchev (Beroe Stara Zagora)

4 goals: Tore Cervin (Malmö FF), Jamison (Glentoran Belfast), Hector Yazalde (Sporting Lisboa), Luciano Chiarugi (Milan AC), Horst Köppel (Borussia), Sarafis (PAOK)

3 goals: Rob Rensenbrink (Anderlecht), Staffan Tapper (Malmö FF), Endre Blindheim (Brann Bergen), Albrecht (Baník Ostrava), Di Nallo (Olympique Lyon), Petkov (Beroe), Paridis (PAOK), Jürgen Sparwasser (FC Magdeburg), Wimmer, Simonsen (Borussia)

2 goals: Gojgaru (Chimia Rm.Vîlcea), Tueart (Sunderland), Conn, Greig (Rangers), Lasa (Athletic Bilbao), Espeseth, Osland (Brann Bergen), Aslanidis, Terzanidis (PAOK), Feeney (Glentoran), Katic (FC Zürich), Marinho, Fraguito (Sporting Lisboa), Hermann, Hoffmann (FC Magdeburg), Rupp, Jensen, Kulik (Borussia)

1 goal: Melde (Fola Esch), Lykke (Randers Freja), Lalic (Dinamo Zagreb), Pieszko (Legia), Villars (Cardiff City), Humphreys (Cork Hibernians), Oskarsson (Vestmannaeyjar), Malmberg, Kristensson, C.Andersson, Olsberg, Bo Larsson (Malmö FF), Kerr, Horswill, Hughes (Sunderland), Krankl, Lorenz (Rapid Wien), Jackson, A.MacDonald, McLean, Johnstone, O'Hara (Rangers), Astrain (Athletic Bilbao), R.Jensen, Hauge, Öyasäther, F.Larsen (Brann Bergen), Klement, Tondra (Baník Ostrava), Lacombe, Ravier (Olympique Lyon), McCreery, Craig (Glentoran), Vutsov, Dimitrov, Jelev, Belchev, Todorov, Kirov, Stoianov (Beroe), Botteron, Stierli, Rutschmann (FC Zürich), Manaca, Baltasar, Nélson (Sporting Lisboa), Tresoldi, Benetti (AC Milan), Mewes, Tyll, Pommerenke, Abraham, Seguin (FC Magdeburg), Vogts (Borussia)

Own goals: Sigurgeirsson (IBV), Finnbogasson (IBV), Valtysson (IBV) for Borussia, Sabadini (Milan) for Borussia, Lanzi (Milan) for FC Magdeburg

CUP WINNERS' CUP 1974-75

FIRST ROUND

LIVERPOOL FC
v STRØMSGODSET IF DRAMMEN 11-0 (5-0)
Anfield Road, Liverpool   17.09.1974

Referee: Edwin Borg (MAL)   Attendance: 24,743

LIVERPOOL FC: Raymond Clemence, Thomas Smith, Alec Lindsay, Philip Thompson, Peter Cormack, Emlyn Hughes, Philip Boersma, Brian Hall, Steve Heighway, Raymond Kennedy, Ian Callaghan.   Manager: Robert Paisley

STRØMSGODSET IF: Inge Thun; Per Rune Wølmer, Helge Karlsen, Tor Alsaker-Nøstdahl, Johnny Vidar Pedersen, Odd Arild Amundsen (75 Øivind Wibe), Egil Olsen, Tor Henriksen, Bjørn Erik Halvorsen, Steinar Pettersen, Trond Olsen (69 Finn Aksel Olsen).   Trainer: Erik Eriksen

Goals: Lindsay (3 pen), Boersma (13, 35), Philip Thompson (30, 74), Heighway (42), Cormack (65), Hughes (76), Smith (85), Callaghan (87), R. Kennedy (88)

STRØMSGODSET IF DRAMMEN
v LIVERPOOL FC 0-1 (0-1)
Ullevål, Oslo   1.10.1974

Referee: Erik Axelryd (SWE)   Attendance: 16,346

STRØMSGODSET IF: Inge Thun; Per Rune Wølmer, Helge Karlsen, Tor Alsaker-Nøstdahl, Øyvind Wibe, Odd Arild Amundsen (73 Vidar Nyseter), Egil Olsen, Tor Henriksen, Bjørn Erik Halvorsen, Finn Aksel Olsen, Ingar Pettersen (87 Trond Olsen).   Trainer: Erik Eriksen

LIVERPOOL FC: Raymond Clemence, Thomas Smith, Alec Lindsay, Christopher Lawler, Philip Boersma, Emlyn Hughes, Kevin Keegan, Brian Hall, Steve Heighway, Raymond Kennedy, Ian Callaghan.   Manager: Robert Paisley

Goal: R. Kennedy (17)

EINTRACHT FRANKFURT am MAIN
v AS MONACO 3-0 (2-0)
Waldstadion, Frankfurt   17.09.1974

Referee: Sándor Petri (HUN)   Attendance: 19,035

EINTRACHT: Peter Kunter, Peter Reichel, Gert Trinklein, Karl-Heinz Körbel, Klaus Beverungen; Wolfgang Kraus, Bernd Nickel; Roland Weidle, Bernd Hölzenbein, Jürgen Grabowski, Thomas Rohrbach.   Trainer: Dietrich Weise

AS MONACO: Christian Montes; Jean-Louis Samuel, Serge Perruchini, André Guesdon, Georges Prost; Jean Petit (79 Bernard Guignedoux), Gérard Burklé, Omar Pastoriza; Christian Dalger, Delio Onnis, Anibal Roberto TARAVINI Duvalle (79 Michel Rouquette).   Trainer: Albert Muro

Goals: Hölzenbein (8, 57), Rohrbach (26)

AS MONACO
v EINTRACHT FRANKFURT am MAIN 2-2 (0-2)
Louis II, Monaco   2.10.1974

Referee: Ángel Franco Martínez (SPA)   Attendance: 5,000

AS MONACO: Christian Montes; Jean-Louis Samuel, Gérard Burklé, André Guesdon, Georges Prost; Jean Petit, Bernard Guignedoux, Omar Pastoriza; Christian Dalger (46 Michel Rouquette), Delio Onnis (63 Yvon Chomet), Anibal Roberto TARAVINI Duvalle.   Trainer: Albert Muro

EINTRACHT: Günther Wienhold; Peter Reichel, Gert Trinklein, Karl-Heinz Körbel, Klaus Beverungen; Helmut Müller, Bernd Nickel, Jürgen Grabowski, Roland Weidle, Thomas Rohrbach, Bernd Lorenz.   Trainer: Dietrich Weise

Goals: Beverungen (4), Nickel (7), Onnis (49), Petit (51)

SLIEMA WANDERERS
v LAHDEN REIPAS 2-0 (1-0)
Empire Stadium, Gzira   18.09.1974

Referee: Cesare Gussoni (ITA)   Attendance: 8,612

SLIEMA WANDERERS: Charles Sciberras, Lawrence Borg, Gennaro Camilleri, David Azzopardi, Mario Schembri, Edward Darmanin, Ronald Cocks, Emanuel Fabri, Anton Camilleri (66 Joseph Vella), Richard Aquilina, Edward Aquilina (83 Mario Zammit).

REIPAS: Harri Holli, Pekka Kosonen, Mikko Kautonen, Jorma Salonen, Markku Repo, Urho Partanen, Lauri Riutto (66 Seppo Nordman), Raimo Hukka, Pertti Jantunen, Olavi Litmanen, Matti Sandberg (69 Risto Rautemaa).

Goal: Camilleri (23, 55)

LAHDEN REIPAS
v SLIEMA WANDERERS 4-1 (3-0)
Keskusurheilukenttä, Lahti   1.10.1974

Referee: Henry Öberg (NOR)   Attendance: 638

REIPAS: Harri Holli, Pekka Kosonen, Mikko Kautonen, Jorma Salonen, Markku Repo, Urho Partanen, Harri Toivanen (65 Seppo Nordman), Raimo Hukka, Pertti Jantunen, Olavi Litmanen, Matti Sandberg.

SLIEMA WANDERERS: Charles Sciberras, Lawrence Borg, Gennaro Camilleri, David Azzopardi (62 Emanuel Micallef), Mario Schembri (68 Mario Zammit), Edward Darmanin, Ronald Cocks, Richard Aquilina, Anton Camilleri, Emanuel Fabri, Edward Aquilina.

Goals: Sandberg (15, 30), Salonen (45), Kosonen (68), R. Aquilina (89)

GWARDIA WARSZAWA v BOLOGNA 2-1 (0-1)
Gwardia, Warszawa   18.09.1974
Referee: Ferdinand Biwersi (W. GER)   Attendance: 3,114
GWARDIA: Andrzej Sikorski I, Jan Sroka, Ryszard Kielak, Krystian Michalik, Stanislaw Dawidczynski, Jerzy Kraska, Miroslaw Polakow, Edward Lipinski, Dariusz Sledziewski, Wlodzimierz Siudek (75 Zenon Smialek), Stanislaw Terlecki (75 Bogdan Nowicki).
BOLOGNA: Sergio Buso, Tazio Roversi, Francesco Cresci, Francesco Battisodo, Bellugi, Claudio Maselli, Piero Ghetti, Giacomo Bulgarelli, Giuseppe Savoldi, Lionello Massimelli (69 Roberto Vieri), Fausto Landini II.   Trainer: Bruno Pesaola
Goals: Savoldi (42), Sroka (47 pen), Kraska (80)

ARDS NEWTONARDS
v PSV EINDHOVEN 1-4 (1-2)
Castlereagh Park, Newtonards   2.10.1974
Referee: Kaj Rasmussen (DEN)   Attendance: 1,474
ARDS: Robert McKenzie, Syd Patterson, Ronald Cromie, David McCoy, William Nixon, Thomas Moffatt, David Graham, William Humphries, Maxie Patton (75 Trevor Best), William McAvoy, Denis Guy.
PSV: André Van Gerven, Kees Krijgh, Björn Nordqvist, Adri van Kraay, Gerrie Deijkers, Willy van de Kerkhof, Pleun Strik, Bertus Quaars, Willy van der Kuylen, Ralf Edström, Peter Dahlqvist.   Trainer: Kees Rijvers
Goals: Van der Kuylen (6), Edström (20), Guy (40), Dahlqvist (77, 86)

BOLOGNA
v GWARDIA WARSZAWA 2-1 (2-1, 2-1) (AET)
Stadio Comunale, Bologna   2.10.1974
Referee: Erich Linemayr (AUS)   Attendance: 16,038
BOLOGNA: Sergio Buso, Tazio Roversi, Francesco Cresci, Francesco Battisodo, Bellugi (77 Vittorio Caporale), Claudio Maselli, Mario Brugnera (40 Eraldo Pecci), Lionello Massimelli, Giuseppe Savoldi, Piero Ghetti, Fausto Landini II. Trainer: Bruno Pesaola
GWARDIA: Andrzej Sikorski I, Jan Sroka (102 Adam Lipinski), Ryszard Kielak, Krystian Michalik, Stanislaw Dawidczynski, Jerzy Kraska, Miroslaw Polakow, Edward Lipinski (91 Dariusz Sledziewski), Jan Malkiewicz, Stanislaw Terlecki, Andrzej Wisniewski.
Goals: Savoldi (8, 43), Terlecki (20)
Penalties: 0-1 Malkiewicz, 1-1 Landini, 1-2 Dawidczynski, 2-2 Savoldi, 2-3 Sledziewski, 3-3 Ghetti, 3-4 Michalik, Massimelli (miss), 3-5 Polakow

DINAMO KIEV v CSKA SOFIA 1-0 (0-0)
Republikanski, Kiev   18.09.1974
Referee: Orhan Cebe (TUR)   Attendance: 75,000
DINAMO: Evgeni Rudakov, Anatoli Schepel, Viktor Matvienko, Mikhail Fomenko, Stefan Reschko, Vladimir Troshkin (62 Viktor Maslov), Vladimir Muntian, Vladimir Onischenko, Viktor Kolotov, Vladimir Veremeev, Oleg Blohin. Trainer: Valeriy Lobanovskiy
CSKA: Stoian Iordanov; Ivan Zafirov, Kiril Stankov, Tsono Vasilev, Bojil Kolev, Dimitar Penev, Borislav Sredkov (81 Kevork Takmisian), Asparuh Nikodimov, Petar Jekov (70 Todor Simov), Georgi Denev, Dimitar Marashliev.
Goal: Blohin (57)

PSV EINDHOVEN
v ARDS NEWTONARDS 10-0 (5-0)
Philips, Eindhoven   18.09.1974
Referee: Sven Jonsson (SWE)   Attendance: 12,000
PSV: Jan van Beveren, Kees Krijgh, Björn Nordqvist, Adri van Kraay, Peter Kemper (46 Peter Dahlqvist), Bertus Quaars, Pleun Strik, Gerrie Deijkers, Harrie Lubse, Ralf Edström, Willy van der Kuylen.   Trainer: Kees Rijvers
ARDS: Robert McKenzie, Syd Patterson, Ronald Cromie, David McCoy, William Nixon, Thomas Moffatt, David Graham, William Humphries, Maxie Patton, William McAvoy, Denis Guy.
Goals: Van der Kuylen (5, 68, 83), Lubse (13, 37, 76), Kemper (26), Deijkers (28), Edström (50), Van Kraay (82).

CSKA SOFIA v DINAMO KIEV 0-1 (0-0)
Vasil Levski, Sofia   2.10.1974
Referee: Günter Männig (E. GER)   Attendance: 20,293
CSKA: Stoian Iordanov; Ivan Zafirov, Tsono Vasilev, Stefan Velichkov, Bojil Kolev, Dimitar Penev, Borislav Sredkov, Kevork Takmisian (50 Kiril Liubomirov), Stefan Mihailov, Georgi Denev, Dimitar Marashliev (18 Stoil Trankov).
DINAMO: Evgeni Rudakov, Leonid Buriak, Viktor Matvienko, Mikhail Fomenko, Stefan Reschko, Valeri Zuev, Anatoli Schepel, Vladimir Onischenko, Viktor Kolotov, Vladimir Veremeev, Oleg Blohin.   Trainer: Valeriy Lobanovskiy
Goal: Blohin (81)

BENFICA LISBOA v VANLØSE IF 4-0 (2-0)
Estádio da Luz, Lisboa 18.09.1974
Referee: Pablo Augusto Sánchez Ibañez (SPA)   Att: 40,000
BENFICA: JOSÉ HENRIQUE Rodrigues Marques; ARTUR Manuel Soares CORREIA, HUMBERTO Manuel Jesus COELHO, MESSIAS Julio Tímula, ADOLFO António da Cruz Calisto; JAIME da Silva GRAÇA (80 José Pedro), VITOR Manuel Rosa MARTINS, Antonio José SIMÕES da Costa (Cap), Tamagnini Manuel Gomes Baptista NENÉ (76 Mario Jorge MOINHOS de Matos), Rui Manuel da Trindade JORDÃO, VÍTOR Manuel Ferreira BAPTISTA.
VANLØSE IF: Jan Madsen, Erik Eriksen, Bo Strøm, Mogens Westergaard, Poul Søborg, Steen Madsen, Allan Jensen, Birger Mauritsen, Tommy Kristiansen, Jacob Rossander, Bjarne Pettersson.
Goals: H. Coelho (26), Nené (43), Jordão (65, 89)

**CARDIFF CITY
v FERENCVÁROS TC BUDAPEST 1-4** (0-0)
Ninian Park, Cardiff 2.10.1974
Referee: Francis Rion (BEL)   Attendance: 4,088
CITY: Ronald Healey, Philip Dwyer, Frederick Pethard, Anthony Villars (46 John Farrington), Donald Murray, David Powell, William Anderson, George Smith, Derek Showers, Gilbert Reece (46 John Impey), John Vincent.
FERENCVÁROS: István Géczi; Ferenc Eipel, László Bálint, József Mucha, István Megyesi; László Takács, Gusztav Kelemen, László Pusztai, Ferenc Szabó, Zoltán Ebedli (46 Tibor Onhausz), János Máté.   Trainer: Jenő Dálnoki
Goals: Takács (53), Szabó (59), Pusztai (69), Dwyer (80), Máté (85)

VANLØSE IF v SL BENFICA LISBOA 1-4 (1-3)
Idraetsparken, København 2.10.1974
Referee: Eric Smyton (NIR)   Attendance: 3,100
VANLØSE IF: Jan Madsen, Erik Eriksen, Bo Strøm, Mogens Westergaard, Poul Søborg, Steen Madsen, Allan Jensen, Birger Mauritsen (76 Kim Frandsen), Tommy Kristiansen (76 Allan Lundgren), Jacob Rossander, Bjarne Pettersson.
BENFICA: JOSÉ HENRIQUE Rodrigues Marques (59 Manuel Galrinho BENTO), ARTUR Manuel Soares CORREIA, HUMBERTO Manuel Jesus COELHO, António Monteiro Teixeira de BARROS, ADOLFO António da Cruz Calisto; António José da Conceição Oliveira "TONI", VITOR Manuel Rosa MARTINS, Antonio José SIMÕES da Costa (Cap); Tamagnini Manuel Gomes Baptista NENÉ (46 Mario Jorge MOINHOS de Matos), Rui Manuel da Trindade JORDÃO, VÍTOR Manuel Ferreira BAPTISTA.
Goals: Pettersson (15), Nené (27), Jordão (29, 43), Barros (86)

KSV WAREGEM v AUSTRIA WIEN 2-1 (1-1)
Regenboog, Waregem 18.09.1974
Referee: Dominic Vincent Byrne (IRL)   Attendance: 18,000
WAREGEM: Philip Mesmaeckers, John Bogaert, Norbert Deviaene, Luc Millecamps, Marc Devolder, Marc Millecamps, Alex Saelen, Jaak Dreesen (79 Rudy Haleydt), Eduardo Giba, Aad Koudijzer, Hervé Delesie.   Trainer: Mathys
AUSTRIA: Hubert Baumgartner; Robert Sara, Erich Obermayer, Herbert Prohaska (13 Alberto Martínez), Helmut Weigl, Eduard Krieger, Helmut Köglberger, Julio Cesar Morales, Hans Pirkner, Ernst Fiala, Karl Daxbacher.
Trainer: Robert Dienst
Goals: Pirkner (22), Delesie (45, 85)

**FERENCVÁROS TC BUDAPEST
v CARDIFF CITY 2-0** (1-0)
Üllői út, Budapest 18.09.1974
Referee: Josef Bucek (AUS)   Attendance: 25,000
FERENCVÁROS: István Géczi, Tamás Viczkó, László Bálint, István Megyesi, József Mucha; László Takács, Tibor Nyilasi, László Pusztai, Gusztav Kelemen (64 Zoltán Ebedli), Ferenc Szabó, János Máté.   Trainer: Jenő Dálnoki
CITY: Ronald Healey; Albert Larmour (46 John Impey), Frederick Pethard, Anthony Villars, Donald Murray, David Powell, John Farrington, Clive Charles, Derek Showers, James McInch, William Anderson.
Goals: Nyilasi (14), Szabó (79)

AUSTRIA WIEN v KSV WAREGEM 4-1 (1-0)
Bundesstadion Südstadt, Wien 2.10.1974
Referee: Otto Anderco (ROM)   Attendance: 5,000
AUSTRIA: Hubert Baumgartner, Robert Sara, Erich Obermayer, Helmut Weigl, Karl Daxbacher, Eduard Krieger, Helmut Köglberger, Julio Cesar Morales, Hans Pirkner, Ernst Fiala, Alberto Martínez.   Trainer: Robert Dienst
WAREGEM: Philip Mesmaeckers, John Bogaert, Norbert Deviaene, Luc Millecamps, Marc Devolder, Marc Millecamps, Alex Saelen (69 Nico Veeken), Jaak Dreesen, Rudy Haleydt (54 Eduardo Giba), Aad Koudijzer, Hervé Delesie.
Trainer: Mathys
Goals: Pirkner (24, 79), Weigl (58), Koudijzer (81), Fiala (87)

**BURSASPOR
v FINN HARPS BALLYBOFEY 4-2** (1-1)

Atatürk, Bursa 18.09.1974

Referee: Marijan Rauš (YUG)   Attendance: 11,946

BURSASPOR: Rasim Kara, Kemal Batmaz, Orhan Ozselek, Ihsan, Gürol, Vahit Dogan, Sedat Ozen (46 Ismail), Vahap Cemil, Ali Kahraman, Sinan Bürr, Turan Karadogan.

FINN HARPS: Joe Harper, Declan McDowell, Peter Hutton, Anthony O'Doherty, James Sheridan, Paddy McGrory, Jim Smith, Sean McLaughlin (52 Gerry Doherty), Brendan Bradley, Hilary Carlyle (75 Paul McGee), Charles Ferry.

Goals: Ali (19), Turan (58, 80), Sinan (52 pen), Ferry (39), Bradley (69)

FINN HARPS BALLYBOFEY v BURSASPOR 0-0

Finn Park, Ballybofey 2.10.1974

Referee: John David Williams (WAL)   Attendance: 2,766

FINN HARPS: Gerald Murray, Declan McDowell, Peter Hutton, Anthony O'Doherty, James Sheridan, Paddy McGrory, Jim Smith, Gerry Doherty (70 Gerry McGranaghan), Brendan Bradley, Hilary Carlyle, Charles Ferry.

BURSASPOR: Rasim Kara, Ihsan, Yusuf, Gürol, Ismail, Sacit Karabas, Ali Kahraman, Vahap Cemil, Beyku Tüyüz, Vahit Dogan, Turan Karadogan.

DUNDEE UNITED v JIUL PETROŞANI 3-0 (2-0)

Tannadice Park, Dundee 18.09.1974

Referee: Theo Boosten (HOL)   Attendance: 7,787

UNITED: Hamish McAlpine; Andy Rolland, Frank Kopel, Jack Copland, Douglas Smith; David Narey, Douglas Houston (62 Paul Sturrock), Patrick Gardner; Andy Gray, George Fleming (85 Duncan McLeod), Iain McDonald.
Manager: Jim McLean

JIUL: Gabriel Ion (80 Dorin Naste); Ion Niţu, Gogu Tonca, Andrei Stocker, Constantin Muşat; Adrian Dodu, Petre Libardi, Alexandru Nagy; Mihai Stoichiţă, Adalbert Rozsnyai, Gheorghe Mulţescu.   Trainer: Titus Ozon

Goals: Narey (34), Copland (37), Gardner (70)

JIUL PETROŞANI v DUNDEE UNITED 2-0 (2-0)

Jiul, Petroşani 2.10.1974

Referee: Nikolas Zlatanos (GRE)   Attendance: 15,000

JIUL: Dorin Naste; Sturza Rusu, Gogu Tonca (84 Constantin Muşat), Andrei Stocker, Adrian Dodu; Alexandru Nagy, Petre Libardi (60 Gheorghe Fildiroiu), Gabriel Stan; Mihai Stoichiţă, Adalbert Rozsnyai, Gheorghe Mulţescu.   Trainer: Titus Ozon

UNITED: Hamish McAlpine; Andy Rolland, Frank Kopel, Jack Copland, Douglas Smith; David Narey, Patrick Gardner, George Fleming (63 Thomas Traynor); Archie Knox, Andy Gray, Iain McDonald.   Manager: Jim McLean

Goals: Rozsnyai (15), Tonca (36)

MALMÖ FF v FC SION 1-0 (1-0)

Malmö Stadion 18.09.1974

Referee: John Robertson P. Gordon (SCO)   Att: 5.19908

MALMÖ FF: Jan Möller, Christer Malmberg (82 Kent Jönsson), Krister Kristensson, Roy Andersson, Harry Jönsson, Staffan Tapper (51 Sten Sternqvist), Anders Ljungberg, Claes Malmberg, Tore Cervin, Thomas Sjöberg, Tommy Larsson.
Trainer: Robert Houghton

FC SION: Jean-Claude Donze; Jean-Yves Valentini, Serge Trinchero, Milenko Bajic, Pierre-Antoine Dayen, Günter Herrmann, Umberto Barberis, Philippe Pillet, Fernand Luisier, Franco Cucinotta, René-Pierre Quentin.

Goal: Cervin (21)

FC SION v MALMÖ FF 1-0 (0-0, 1-0) (AET)

Stade de Tourbillon, Sion 2.10.1974

Referee: René Vigliani (FRA)   Attendance: 9,485

FC SION: Jean-Claude Donze; Jean-Yves Valentini, Serge Trinchero, Milenko Bajic, Pierre-Antoine Dayen, Günter Herrmann (105 Lucien Schürmann), Umberto Barberis, Philippe Pillet (90 Alvaro Lopez), Fernand Luisier, Franco Cucinotta, René-Pierre Quentin.

MALMÖ FF: Jan Möller, Roland Andersson, Krister Kristensson, Roy Andersson, Harry Jönsson, Staffan Tapper, Anders Ljungberg, Claes Malmberg (105 Christer Malmberg), Tommy Andersson (78 Kent Jönsson), Thomas Sjöberg, Tommy Larsson.   Trainer: Robert Houghton

Goal: Cucinotta (82)

Penalties: 1-0 Ljungberg, 1-1 Luisier, 2-1 Tapper, 2-2 Quentin, 3-2 T. Larsson, 3-3 Dayen, 4-3 Roland Andersson, 4-4 Trinchero, 5-4 Roy Andersson, Lopez (miss)

SLAVIA PRAHA v FC CARL ZEISS JENA 1-0 (0-0)

Dr. Vacka Stadium, Praha 18.09.1974

Referee: György Müncz (HUN)   Attendance: 7,207

SLAVIA: Miroslav Stárek, Pavel Biros, Jan Mares, Bohumil Smolik, Josef Jebavy (76 Vaclav Bouska), Zdenek Peclinovsky, Frantisek Vesely (61 Hlavnicka), František Cipro, Robert Segmüller, Zdenek Klimes, Dušan Herda.
Trainer: Jaroslav Jareš

FC CARL ZEISS: Hans-Ulrich Grapenthin, Gert Brauer, Helmut Stein, Konrad Weise, Lothar Kurbjuweit, Ulrich Göhr, Harald Irmscher, Martin Goebel, Norbert Schumann, Dietmar Sengewald, Eberhard Vogel.   Trainer: Hans-Joachim Meyer

Goal: D. Herda (90)

**FC CARL ZEISS JENA
v SLAVIA PRAHA 1-0** (1-0, 1-0) (AET)
Ernst Abbe Sportfeld, Jena 2.10.1974
Referee: Anatoli Milchenko (USSR)   Attendance: 9,169
FC CARL ZEISS: Hans-Ulrich Grapenthin, Gert Brauer, Helmut Stein, Konrad Weise, Lothar Kurbjuweit, Ulrich Göhr, Harald Irmscher, Rainer Schlutter, Peter Ducke, Norbert Schumann, Harry Kunze.   Trainer: Hans-Joachim Meyer
SLAVIA: Miroslav Stárek, Pavol Biros (97 Petr Ondrásek), Jan Mares, Bohumil Smolik, Josef Jebavy, Zdenek Peclinovsky, Frantisek Vesely (118 Jiří Grospic), František Cipro, Robert Segmüller, Dušan Herda, Peter Herda.   Trainer: Jaroslav Jareš
Goal: Stein (23)
Penalties: Irmscher (miss), 0-1 D. Herda, 1-1 Kurbjuweit, 1-2 Cipro, 2-2 Schlutter, Segmüller (miss), 3-2 P. Ducke, Jebavy (miss), Weise (miss), P. Herda (miss)

**PAOK THESSALONIKI
v CRVENA ZVEZDA BEOGRAD 1-0** (0-0)
Toumpas, Thessaloniki 18.09.1974
Referee: Domenico Serafino (ITA)   Attendance: 20,427
PAOK: René Deck, Giannis Gounaris, Takis Tsiligkiridis, Kostas Iosifidis, Filotas Pellios, Hristos Terzanidis, Neto Gkouerino (73 Panagiotis Kermanidis), Stavros Sarafis, Kiriakos Apostolidis, Giorgos Koudas, Ahilleas Aslanidis.   Trainer: Les Sanon
CRVENA ZVEZDA: Ognjen Petrović; Zoran Jelikić, Živorad Jevtić, Petar Baralić, Mihalj Keri, Branko Radović, Radivoje Ratković, Vladimir Petrović, Dušan Savić, Zoran Antonijević, Aleksandar Panajotović (73 Milos Šestić).   Trainer: Miljenko Mihić
Goal: Terzanidis (67)

**CRVENA ZVEZDA BEOGRAD
v PAOK THESSALONIKI 2-0** (0-0, 1-0) (AET)
Crvena Zvezda, Beograd 2.10.1974
Referee: Anton Bucheli (SWI)   Attendance: 50,000
CRVENA ZVEZDA: Ognjen Petrović; Zoran Jelikić, Živorad Jevtić, Petar Baralić, Mihalj Keri, Branko Radović, Radivoje Ratković (46 Aleksandar Panajotović), Vladimir Petrović, Dušan Savić, Zoran Antonijević (57 Sead Sušić), Dragan Džajić.   Trainer: Miljenko Mihić
PAOK: René Deck, Takis Tsiligkiridis (75 Giannis Gounaris), Aristarhos Fountoukidis, Kostas Iosifidis, Filotas Pellios, Aggelos Anastasiadis, Panagiotis Kermanidis, Stavros Sarafis, Kiriakos Apostolidis, Giorgos Koudas, Ahilleas Aslanidis.   Trainer: Les Sanon
Goals: V. Petrović (58), Savić (103)

FRAM REYKJAVIK v REAL MADRID CF 0-2 (0-1)
Laugardalsvöllur, Reykjavik 19.09.1974
Referee: Derry Barrett (IRL)   Attendance: 7,252
FRAM: Thorbergur Atlason, Jón Pétursson, August Gudmundsson, Gunnar Gudmundsson, Marteinn Geirsson, Sigurbegur Sigsteinsson, Gudgeir Leifsson, Kristinn Jörundsson, Runar Gíslason, Ásgeir Eliasson, Eggert Steingrimsson.   Trainer: Johannes Atlasson
REAL: MIGUEL ÁNGEL González Suarez, JOSÉ LUIS López Peinado, José Antonio CAMACHO Alfaro, José Martínez Sánchez "PIRRI", Gregorio BENITO Rubio, Alberto VITORIA Soria, Juan ROBERTO MARTÍNEZ Martínez, Paul Breitner, Vicente DEL BOSQUE González, Gunter Netzer, José MACANÁS Pérez.   Trainer: Miljan Miljanić
Goals: Roberto Martínez (10, 54)

REAL MADRID v FRAM REYKJAVIK 6-0 (3-0)
Estadio Santiago Bernabéu, Madrid 1.10.1974
Referee: Antonio José da Silva Garrido (POR)   Att: 34,822
REAL: MIGUEL ÁNGEL González Suarez, JOSÉ LUIS López Peinado, José Antonio CAMACHO Alfaro, José Martínez Sánchez "PIRRI", Gregorio BENITO Rubio (29 Benito RUBIÑAN Soutullo), Alberto VITORIA Soria (69 Ramón Moreno GROSSO), Francisco AGUILAR García, Paul Breitner, Carlos Alonso González "SANTILLANA", Gunter Netzer, José MACANÁS Pérez.   Trainer: Miljan Miljanić
FRAM: Arni Stefansson, Jón Pétursson, August Gudmundsson, Gunnar Gudmundsson, Marteinn Geirsson, Sigurbegur Sigsteinsson, Gudgeir Leifsson, Kristinn Jörundsson, Runar Gíslason, Ásgeir Eliasson, Eggert Steingrimsson (69 Snorri Hauksson).   Trainer: Johannes Atlasson
Goals: Santillana (13), Pirri (19, 59), Netzer (28), Macanás (76), Aguilar (86)

SECOND ROUND

MALMÖ FF v LAHDEN REIPAS 3-1 (1-1)
Malmö Stadion 23.10.1974
Referee: Wieslaw Karolak (POL)   Attendance: 4,321
MALMÖ FF: Jan Möller, Roland Andersson, Krister Kristensson, Roy Andersson, Harry Jönsson, Staffan Tapper, Anders Ljungberg, Bo Larsson, Thomas Sjöberg, Tore Cervin (69 Tommy Andersson), Tommy Larsson.
Trainer: Robert Houghton
REIPAS: Harri Holli, Pekka Kosonen, Harri Toivanen, Markku Repo, Lauri Riutto, Urho Partanen, Mikko Kautonen, Raimo Hukka (84 Risto Rautemaa), Pertti Jantunen, Ari Tupasela, Matti Sandberg.
Goals: Hukka (3), Bo Larsson (35, 87), Sjöberg (80)

LAHDEN REIPAS v MALMÖ FF 0-0
Urheilukeskus, Lahti   3.11.1974
Referee: Edgar H. Pedersen (DEN)   Attendance: 1,663
REIPAS: Harri Holli, Pekka Kosonen, Mikko Kautonen, Markku Repo, Harri Toivanen, Urho Partanen (75 Jorma Salonen), Lauri Riutto, Raimo Hukka (46 Timo Kautonen), Pertti Jantunen, Olavi Litmanen, Matti Sandberg.
MALMÖ FF: Jan Möller, Roland Andersson (88 Christer Malmberg), Krister Kristensson, Roy Andersson, Harry Jönsson, Staffan Tapper, Anders Ljungberg, Bo Larsson, Thomas Sjöberg, Tore Cervin, Claes Malmberg.
Trainer: Robert Houghton

EINTRACHT FRANKFURT
v DINAMO KIEV 2-3 (1-1)
Waldstadion, Frankfurt   23.10.1974
Referee: César da Luz Dias Correia (POR)   Att: 21,282
EINTRACHT: Peter Kunter, Helmut Müller, Gert Trinklein, Karl-Heinz Körbel, Jürgen Kalb, Klaus Beverungen, Bernd Nickel, Roland Weidle (68 Wolfgang Kraus), Bernd Hölzenbein, Jürgen Grabowski, Thomas Rohrbach.
Trainer: Dietrich Weise
DINAMO: Evgeni Rudakov, Valeri Zuev, Viktor Matvienko, Mikhail Fomenko, Stefan Reschko, Viktor Maslov, Vladimir Muntian, Vladimir Onischenko, Viktor Kolotov, Vladimir Veremeev, Oleg Blohin.   Trainer: Valeriy Lobanovskiy
Goals: Nickel (2), Onischenko (32), Körbel (64 pen), Blohin (83), Muntian (87)

LIVERPOOL FC
v FERENCVÁROS TC BUDAPEST 1-1 (1-0)
Anfield Road, Liverpool   23.10.1974
Referee: Pablo Augusto Sánchez Ibañez (SPA)   Att: 35,027
LIVERPOOL FC: Raymond Clemence, Thomas Smith, Alec Lindsay, Christopher Lawler, Brian Hall (50 John Toshack), Emlyn Hughes, Philip Boersma, Kevin Keegan, Ian Callaghan, Raymond Kennedy (66 Peter Cormack), Steve Heighway.
Manager: Robert Paisley
FERENCVÁROS: István Géczi; Miklós Pataki, László Bálint, István Megyesi, Tibor Rab (56 Tibor Onhausz), József Mucha, László Pusztai, Gusztav Kelemen, Ferenc Szabó (55 István Magyar), László Takács, János Máté.   Trainer: Jenő Dalnoki
Goals: Keegan (37), Máté (90)

DINAMO KIEV
v EINTRACHT FRANKFURT 2-1 (2-0)
Republikanskiy, Kiev   5.11.1974
Referee: Martti Hirviniemi (FIN)   Attendance: 60,000
DINAMO: Evgeni Rudakov, Leonid Buriak, Viktor Matvienko, Mikhail Fomenko, Stefan Reschko, Vladimir Troshkin, Vladimir Muntian, Vladimir Onischenko, Viktor Kolotov, Vladimir Veremeev, Oleg Blohin.
Trainer: Valeriy Lobanovskiy
EINTRACHT: Günther Wienhold, Helmut Müller, Gert Trinklein, Gerd Simons, Jürgen Kalb, Klaus Beverungen, Wolfgang Kraus, Karl-Heinz Körbel (46 Thomas Rohrbach), Bernd Nickel, Jürgen Grabowski, Bernd Hölzenbein.
Trainer: Dietrich Weise
Goals: Onischenko (1, 37), Rohrbach (46)

FERENCVÁROS TC BUDAPEST
v LIVERPOOL FC 0-0 (AET)
Üllöi út, Budapest   5.11.1974
Referee: René Vigliani (FRA)   Attendance: 30,000
FERENCVÁROS: István Géczi; Gyözö Martos, László Bálint, István Megyesi, Tibor Rab, József Mucha; László Pusztai (71 Zoltán Ebedli), Tibor Nyilasi, Gusztav Kelemen, István Magyar (60 Ferenc Szabó), János Máté.   Trainer: Jenő Dalnoki
LIVERPOOL FC: Raymond Clemence, Thomas Smith, Alec Lindsay, Christopher Lawler, Philip Boersma, Emlyn Hughes, Kevin Keegan, Brian Hall, Steve Heighway (71 Peter Cormack), Raymond Kennedy (78 John Toshack), Ian Callaghan.
Manager: Robert Paisley

GWARDIA WARSZAWA
v PSV EINDHOVEN 1-5 (0-3)
Gwardia, Warszawa   23.10.1974
Referee: Nikolaos Zlatanos (GRE)   Attendance: 5,000
GWARDIA: Andrzej Sikorski I, Jan Sroka, Ryszard Kielak, Krystian Michalik, Stanislaw Dawidczynski, Andrzej Sikorski II (74 Wlodzimierz Siudek), Miroslaw Polakow, Adam Lipinski, Jan Malkiewicz, Zenon Smialek (72 Andrzej Wisniewski), Stanislaw Terlecki.
PSV: André Van Gerven, Kees Krijgh, Björn Nordqvist, Adri van Kraay, Gerrie Deijkers, Willy van de Kerkhof, Pleun Strik, Willy van der Kuylen, Ralf Edström, Harrie Lubse, Peter Dahlqvist.   Trainer: Kees Rijvers
Goals: Deijkers (15), Lubse (17), W. van de Kerkhof (20), Van der Kuylen (60), Kielak (70 og), Malkiewicz (73).

PSV EINDHOVEN
v GWARDIA WARSZAWA 3-0 (2-0)

Philip, Eindhoven 6.11.1974

Referee: Milivoje Gugulović (YUG)   Attendance: 16,000

PSV: Jan van Beveren, Kees Krijgh, Björn Nordqvist, Adri van Kraay, Gerrie Deijkers, Willy Van de Kerkhof, Pleun Strik (46 Bertus Quaars), Willy van der Kuylen, Harrie Lubse, Ralf Edström, Peter Dahlqvist (72 Peter Kemper).
Trainer: Kees Rijvers

GWARDIA: Andrzej Sikorski I, Jan Sroka, Ryszard Kielak, Krystian Michalik, Stanislaw Dawidczynski, Andrzej Sikorsky II, Jerzy Kraska, Miroslaw Polakow, Jan Malkiewicz, Stanislaw Terlecki, Andrzej Wisniewski (57 Edward Lipinski).

Goals: Van der Kuylen (34, 36), Lubse (89).

DUNDEE UNITED v BURSASPOR 0-0

Tannadice Park, Dundee 23.10.1974

Referee: Rolf Arnshed (SWE)   Attendance: 8,675

UNITED: Hamish McAlpine; Andy Rolland, Frank Kopel, Jack Copland, Douglas Smith, Douglas Houston, Thomas Traynor, David Narey, Andy Gray, Archie Knox (68 Graeme Payne), Iain McDonald. Manager: Jim McLean

BURSASPOR: Rasim Kara, Kemal Batmaz, Orhan Ozselek, Gürol, Ismail, Hayrettin, Vahap Cemil, Ali Kahraman, Sinan Bürr, Beyku Tüyüz, Vahit Dogan.

BURSASPOR v DUNDEE UNITED 1-0 (1-0)

Atatürk, Bursa 6.11.1974

Referee: Paul Schiller (AUS)   Attendance: 11,594

BURSASPOR: Rasim Kara, Kemal Batmaz, Orhan Ozselek, Gürol, Ismail (5 Ceki), Hayrettin, Beyku Tüyüz, Vahap Cemil, Sinan Bürr, Vahit Dogan, Ali Kahraman.

UNITED: Hamish McAlpine; Andy Rolland, Frank Kopel, Jack Copland, Douglas Smith, Douglas Houston, Graeme Payne (46 Iain McDonald), Walter Smith (76 David Narey), Andy Gray, George Fleming, Thomas Traynor. Manager: Jim McLean

Goal: Vahit (10)

FC CARL ZEISS JENA
v SL BENFICA LISBOA 1-1 (0-1)

Ernst Abbe Sportfeld, Jena 23.10.1974

Referee: Walter Hungerbühler (SWI)   Attendance: 13,049

FC CARL ZEISS: Hans-Ulrich Grapenthin, Gert Brauer, Helmut Stein, Konrad Weise, Lothar Kurbjuweit, Ulrich Göhr, Harald Irmscher, Rainer Schlutter; Peter Ducke, Norbert Schumann (62 Harry Kunze), Eberhard Vogel.
Trainer: Hans-Joachim Meyer

BENFICA: Manuel Galrinho BENTO, António José MALTA da SILVA, HUMBERTO Manuel Jesus COELHO, António Monteiro Teixeira de BARROS, ARTUR Manuel Soares CORREIA; António José da Conceição Oliveira "TONI", EUSÉBIO da Silva Ferreira, VITOR Manuel Rosa MARTINS, Antonio José SIMÕES da Costa (Cap) (80 JAIME da Silva GRAÇA), Tamagnini Manuel Gomes Baptista NENÉ, VÍTOR Manuel Ferreira BAPTISTA.

Goals: Nene (20), Vogel (76)

SL BENFICA LISBOA v FC CARL ZEISS JENA 0-0

Estádio da Luz, Lisboa 6.11.1974

Referee: Patrick Partridge (ENG)   Attendance: 40,348

BENFICA: Manuel Galrinho BENTO, António José MALTA da SILVA, HUMBERTO Manuel Jesus COELHO, António Monteiro Teixeira de BARROS, ARTUR Manuel Soares CORREIA; António José da Conceição Oliveira "TONI", EUSÉBIO da Silva Ferreira (Cap) (77 JAIME da Silva GRAÇA), VITOR Manuel Rosa MARTINS; Tamagnini Manuel Gomes Baptista NENÉ, VÍTOR Manuel Ferreira BAPTISTA (46 Antonio José SIMÕES da Costa), Mario Jorge MOINHOS de Matos.

FC CARL ZEISS: Hans-Ulrich Grapenthin, Gert Brauer, Helmut Stein, Konrad Weise, Lothar Kurbjuweit, Ulrich Göhr, Harald Irmscher, Rainer Schlutter, Peter Ducke, Norbert Schumann (77 Harry Kunze), Martin Goebel.
Trainer: Hans-Joachim Meyer

AVENIR BEGGEN
v CRVENA ZVEZDA BEOGRAD 1-6 (0-3)

Stade Municipal, Luxembourg 23.10.1974

Referee: Robert Wurtz (FRA)   Attendance: 1,376

AVENIR: Jeannot Moes, Marc Jungbluth, Jean-Pierre Zender, Steichen, Pierre Wohlfart, Jean Hansen, Chahbi (61 Achille Sinner), Gilbert Dresch, Gilbert Zender (46 Kempis), Quaring, Carlo Bamberg.

CRVENA ZVEZDA: Ognjen Petrović (70 Bosko Kajganić); Bratislav Djordjević, Živorad Jevtić, Petar Baralić, Mihalj Keri, Branko Radović, Radivoje Ratković, Dragoslav Stepanović, Zoran Filipović, Zoran Antonijević, Milos Šestić.
Trainer: Miljenko Mihić

Goals: Šestić (1, 29, 73), Filipović (3, 56), Ratković (62), Sinner (76)

**CRVENA ZVEZDA BEOGRAD
v AVENIR BEGGEN 5-1** (3-0)

Crvena Zvezda, Beograd 6.11.1974

Referee: Paul Bonett (MAL)   Attendance: 4,000

CRVENA ZVEZDA: Ognjen Petrović; Bratislav Djordjević, Živorad Jevtić, Dragoslav Stepanović, Branko Radović, Zoran Antonijević, Radivoje Ratković, Aleksandar Panajotović, Dušan Savić, Zoran Filipović (73 Dragan Nikitović), Miloš Šestić.   Trainer: Miljenko Mihić

AVENIR: Jeannot Moes, Marc Jungbluth (87 Guy Wohlfart), Jean-Pierre Zender, Kempis, Pierre Wohlfart, Steichen, Braun (45 Cirelli), Gilbert Dresch, Jean Hansen, Quaring, Achille Sinner.

Goals: Filipović (1), Ratković (7, 58), Šestić (25), Savić (65), Dresch (86)

REAL MADRID v AUSTRIA WAC WIEN 3-0 (3-0)

Estadio Santiago Bernabeu, Madrid 23.10.1974

Referee: Vital Loraux (BEL)   Attendance: 45,720

REAL: MIGUEL ÁNGEL González Suarez, Juan Carlos TOURIÑO Cancela, Benito RUBIÑAN Soutullo, José Martínez Sánchez "PIRRI", Gregorio BENITO Rubio, José Antonio CAMACHO Alfaro, Juan ROBERTO MARTÍNEZ Martínez, Paul Breitner, Carlos Alonso González "SANTILLANA", Gunter Netzer, José MACANÁS Pérez (63 AMANCIO Amaro Varela).   Trainer: Miljan Miljanić

AUSTRIA: Hubert Baumgartner, Robert Sara, Erich Obermayer, Alberto Martínez, Karl Daxbacher (79 Heinz Hengster), Eduard Krieger, Helmut Weigl, Julio César Morales, Hans Pirkner (46 Ernst Fiala), Herbert Prohaska, Helmut Köglberger.   Trainer: Robert Dienst

Goals: Pirri (35), Santillana (40), Roberto Martínez (43)

AUSTRIA WAC WIEN v REAL MADRID 2-2 (1-1)

Prater, Wien 6.11.1974

Referee: Sergio Gonella (ITA)   Attendance: 3,006

AUSTRIA: Igor Vukman, Robert Sara, Erich Obermayer, Herbert Prohaska, Karl Daxbacher, Eduard Krieger, Helmut Köglberger (15 Heinz Hengster), Julio Cesar Morales, Hans Pirkner, Ernst Fiala, Alberto Martínez.   Trainer: Robert Dienst

REAL: MIGUEL ÁNGEL González Suarez, Juan Carlos TOURIÑO Cancela, José Antonio CAMACHO Alfaro, José Martínez Sánchez "PIRRI" (46 Manuel VELÁZQUEZ Villaverde), Gregorio BENITO Rubio (28 Benito RUBIÑAN Soutullo), Ramón Moreno GROSSO, Juan ROBERTO MARTÍNEZ Martínez, Paul Breitner, Vicente DEL BOSQUE González, Gunter Netzer, Francisco AGUILAR García.   Trainer: Miljan Miljanić

Goals: Roberto Martínez (18), Pirkner (40), Fiala (70 pen), Netzer (75)

QUARTER-FINALS

**REAL MADRID
v CRVENA ZVEZDA BEOGRAD 2-0** (1-0)

Estadio Santiago Bernabeu, Madrid 5.03.1975

Referee: Michel Kitabdjian (FRA)   Attendance: 125,000

REAL: MIGUEL ÁNGEL González Suarez, Gregorio BENITO Rubio, José Antonio CAMACHO Alfaro, Vicente DEL BOSQUE González, Benito RUBIÑAN Soutullo, Manuel VELÁZQUEZ Villaverde, Paul Breitner, Gunter Netzer, AMANCIO Amaro Varela (61 Francisco AGUILAR García), Carlos Alonso González "SANTILLANA", Juan ROBERTO MARTÍNEZ Martínez (70 José MACANÁS Pérez).
Trainer: Miljan Miljanić

CRVENA ZVEZDA: Ognjen Petrović; Mihalj Keri, Bratislav Djordjević, Petar Baralić, Živorad Jevtić, Branko Radović, Vladimir Petrović, Zoran Antonijević, Radivoje Ratković, Slobodan Janković (61 Dušan Savić), Dragan Džajić.
Trainer: Miljenko Mihić

Goals: Santillana (34), Netzer (65)

**CRVENA ZVEZDA BEOGRAD
v REAL MADRID 2-0** (1-0, 2-0) (AET)

Crvena Zvezda, Beograd 19.03.1975

Referee: Kenneth Howard Burns (ENG)   Att: 100,000

CRVENA ZVEZDA: Ognjen Petrović; Bratislav Djordjević, Dragan Nikitović, Petar Baralić, Mihalj Keri, Branko Radović, Vladimir Petrović, Sead Sušić (74 Radivoje Ratković), Slobodan Janković, Dušan Savić, Dragan Džajić (84 Zoran Filipović).   Trainer: Miljenko Mihić

REAL: MIGUEL ÁNGEL González Suarez, Gregorio BENITO Rubio, José Antonio CAMACHO Alfaro, Benito RUBIÑAN Soutullo, Vicente DEL BOSQUE González, Manuel VELÁZQUEZ Villaverde, Paul Breitner, Gunter Netzer, Francisco AGUILAR García, Carlos Alonso González "SANTILLANA", José MACANÁS Pérez (64 Juan ROBERTO MARTÍNEZ Martínez).   Trainer: Antonio RUIZ

Goals: Džajić (35), O. Petrović (55 pen)

Penalties: 1-0 Keri, 1-1 Del Bosque, 2-1 Filipović, 2-2 Netzer, 3-2 Baralić, 3-3 Aguilar, 4-3 Savić, 4-4 Breitner, 5-4 O. Petrović, 5-5 Rubiñan, Djordjević (miss), Benito (miss), 6-5 V. Petrović, Santillana (saved)

MALMÖ FF
v FERENCVÁROS TC BUDAPEST 1-3 (0-1)

Malmö Stadion   5.03.1975

Referee: Francisco S.Marques Lobo (POR)   Att: 6,000

MALMÖ FF: Jan Möller, Roland Andersson, Krister Kristensson, Roy Andersson, Harry Jönsson; Staffan Tapper (80 Claes Malmberg), Anders Ljungberg (55 Tore Cervin), Bo Larsson, Tommy Larsson, Conny Andersson, Thomas Sjöberg. Trainer: Robert Houghton

FERENCVÁROS: István Géczi; Győző Martos, László Bálint, József Mucha, István Megyesi; Tibor Nyilasi, István Juhász, László Branikovits, László Pusztai, János Máté, István Magyar. Trainer: Jenő Dalnoki

Goals: Nyilasi (11), Jönsson (57 og), Máté (60), Sjöberg (90)

FERENCVÁROS TC BUDAPEST
v MALMÖ FF 1-1 (0-1)

Üllői út, Budapest   19.03.1975

Referee: Hilmi Ok (TUR)   Attendance: 27,559

FERENCVÁROS: István Géczi; Győző Martos, László Bálint, József Mucha (60 Tibor Rab), István Megyesi; István Juhász, Tibor Nyilasi, László Branikovits (50 Tibor Onhausz); László Pusztai, János Máté, István Magyar.   Trainer: Jenő Dalnoki

MALMÖ FF: Jan Möller, Christer Malmberg, Krister Kristensson, Roy Andersson, Harry Jönsson, Staffan Tapper, Anders Ljungberg, Bo Larsson; Tore Cervin, Thomas Sjöberg, Tommy Larsson.   Trainer: Robert Houghton

Sent off: Larsson (63)

Goals: Sjöberg (19), Máté (49)

PSV EINDHOVEN v BENFICA LISBOA 0-0

Philips, Eindhoven   5.03.1975

Referee: Alberto Michelotti (ITA)   Attendance: 26,000

PSV: Jan van Beveren, Kees Krijgh, Adri van Kraay, Björn Nordqvist, Gerrie Deijkers, Willy van de Kerkhof (62 Peter Dahlqvist), Pleun Strik, Willy van der Kuylen, René van de Kerkhof, Harrie Lubse, Ralf Edström.   Trainer: Kees Rijvers

BENFICA: JOSÉ HENRIQUE Rodrigues Marques (52 Manuel Galrinho BENTO), ARTUR Manuel Soares CORREIA, António Monteiro Teixeira de BARROS, HUMBERTO Manuel Jesus COELHO, MESSIAS Julio Tímula, VITOR Manuel Rosa MARTINS, António José da Conceição Oliveira "TONI", Tamagnini Manuel Gomes Baptista NENÉ, Mario Jorge MOINHOS de Matos, EUSÉBIO da Silva Ferreira, Antonio José SIMÕES da Costa (Cap).

BENFICA LISBOA v PSV EINDHOVEN 1-2 (1-1)

Estadio da Luz, Lisboa   19.03.1975

Referee: John Wright Paterson (SCO)   Attendance: 70,000

BENFICA: JOSÉ HENRIQUE Rodrigues Marques, ARTUR Manuel Soares CORREIA, António Monteiro Teixeira de BARROS, HUMBERTO Manuel Jesus COELHO, MESSIAS Julio Tímula, VITOR Manuel Rosa MARTINS (73 Antonio José SIMÕES da Costa), António José da Conceição Oliveira "TONI", EUSÉBIO da Silva Ferreira (Cap), VÍTOR Manuel Ferreira BAPTISTA, Mario Jorge MOINHOS de Matos, DIAMANTINO José Vieira COSTA.

PSV: Jan van Beveren, Kees Krijgh, Adri van Kraay, Björn Nordqvist, Gerrie Deijkers, Willy van de Kerkhof, Pleun Strik, Willy van der Kuylen, René van de Kerkhof (74 Peter Dahlqvist), Harrie Lubse, Ralf Edström (14 Bertus Quaars).   Trainer: Kees Rijvers

Goals: W. van de Kerkhof (11), Humberto (17), Van der Kuylen (85).

BURSASPOR v DINAMO KIEV 0-1 (0-1)

Atatürk, Bursa   5.03.1975

Referee: Tzvetan P.Stanev (BUL)   Attendance: 16,765

BURSASPOR: Rasim Kara, Orhan Ozselek, Kemal Batmaz, Hayrettin, Ihsan, Feridun, Vahit Dogan, Ceki (55 Beyku Tüyüz), Vahap Cemil, Ali Kahraman, Sinan Bürr.

DINAMO: Evgeni Rudakov, Vladimir Troshkin, Viktor Matvienko, Mikhail Fomenko, Stefan Reschko, Anatoli Konkov, Vladimir Muntian, Vladimir Veremeev, Viktor Kolotov, Vladimir Onischenko, Oleg Blohin. Trainer: Valeriy Lobanovskiy

Goal: Onischenko (21).

DINAMO KIEV v BURSASPOR 2-0 (0-0)

Republikanskiy, Kiev   19.03.1975

Referee: Kurt Tschenscher (W. GER)   Attendance: 71,926

DINAMO: Evgeni Rudakov, Anatoli Konkov, Viktor Matvienko, Mikhail Fomenko, Stefan Reschko, Vladimir Troshkin, Vladimir Muntian, Vladimir Onischenko, Viktor Kolotov, Vladimir Veremeev (74 Leonid Buriak), Oleg Blohin. Trainer: Valeriy Lobanovskiy

BURSASPOR: Rasim Kara, Kemal Batmaz, Ihsan, Orhan Ozselek, Hayrettin, Vahap Cemil, Ali Kahraman, Feridun, Sedat Ozen, Vahit Dogan, Beyku Tüyüz.

Goals: Kolotov (72 pen), Muntian (87).

SEMI-FINALS

**FERENCVÁROS TC BUDAPEST
v CRVENA ZVEZDA BEOGRAD 2-1** (1-0)
Népstadion, Budapest 9.04.1975
Referee: Nicolae Rainea (ROM) Attendance: 55,000
FERENCVÁROS TC: István Géczi; Györö Martos, László Bálint, Tibor Rab, István Megyesi; István Juhász (75 Ferenc Szabó), László Branikovits, József Mucha (71 Tibor Onhausz), Guzstav Kelemen, János Máté, István Magyar.
Trainer: Jenő Dalnoki
CRVENA ZVEZDA: Ognjen Petrović; Zoran Jelikić, Dragan Nikitović, Mihalj Keri, Branko Radović, Petar Baralić, Radivoje Ratković (75 Milos Šestić), Sead Sušić (80 Mile Novković), Vladimir Petrović, Dušan Savić, Dušan Nikolić.
Trainer: Miljenko Mihić
Goals: Branikovits (44), Savić (56), Magyar (77)

**CRVENA ZVEZDA BEOGRAD
v FERENCVÁROS TC BUDAPEST 2-2** (0-1)
Crvena Zvezda, Beograd 23.04.1975
Referee: Walter Eschweiler (W. GER) Attendance: 100,000
CRVENA ZVEZDA: Ognjen Petrović; Bratislav Djordjević, Mihalj Keri, Branko Radović, Dragan Nikitović, Petar Baralić, Slobodan Janković, Sead Sušić, Vladimir Petrović, Dušan Savić, Zoran Antonijević (37 Zoran Filipović).
Trainer: Miljenko Mihić
FERENCVÁROS: István Géczi; Györö Martos (89 Gusztav Kelemen), László Bálint, Tibor Rab, István Megyesi, István Juhász, Tibor Onhausz (53 László Takács), József Mucha, László Pusztai, János Máté, István Magyar.
Trainer: Jenő Dalnoki
Sent off: Bálint (70)
Goals: Pusztai (7), Keri (50), Filipović (77), Megyesi (83 pen)

DINAMO KIEV v PSV EINDHOVEN 3-0 (2-0)
Republikanskiy, Kiev 9.04.1975
Referee: Patrick Partridge (ENG) Attendance: 100,000
DINAMO: Evgeni Rudakov, Vladimir Troshkin, Viktor Matvienko, Mikhail Fomenko, Stefan Reschko, Anatoli Konkov, Vladimir Muntian, Vladimir Onischenko (74 Sergei Kuznetsov), Viktor Kolotov, Leonid Buriak, Oleg Blohin.
Trainer: Valeriy Lobanovskiy
PSV: Jan van Beveren, Kees Krijgh, Adri van Kraay, Björn Nordqvist, Gerrie Deijkers, Willy van de Kerkhof, Bertus Quaars, Willy van der Kuylen, René van de Kerkhof, Harrie Lubse, Ralf Edström. Trainer: Kees Rijvers
Goals: Kolotov (17), Onischenko (32), Blohin (56)

PSV EINDHOVEN v DINAMO KIEV 2-1 (1-0)
Philips, Eindhoven 23.04.1975
Referee: Pablo Augusto Sánchez Ibanez (SPA) Att: 24,000
PSV: Jan van Beveren, Kees Krijgh, Adri van Kraay, Björn Nordqvist, Gerrie Deijkers, Willy van de Kerkhof, Pleun Strik, Willy van der Kuylen (46 Harrie Lubse), Bengt Schmidt-Hansen, Ralf Edström, René van de Kerkhof.
Trainer: Kees Rijvers
DINAMO: Evgeni Rudakov, Vladimir Troshkin, Viktor Matvienko, Mikhail Fomenko, Stefan Reschko, Anatoli Konkov, Vladimir Muntian (70 Leonid Buriak), Vladimir Onischenko, Viktor Kolotov, Vladimir Veremeev, Oleg Blohin.
Trainer: Valeriy Lobanovskiy
Goals: Edström (24, 86), Buriak (77)

FINAL

**DINAMO KIEV
v FERENCVÁROS BUDAPEST 3-0** (2-0)
Sankt Jakob Basel 14.05.1975
Referee: Robert Holley Davidson (SCO) Att: 10,897
DINAMO: Evgeni Rudakov; Anatoli Konkov, Stefan Reschko, Mikhail Fomenko, Viktor Matvienko; Vladimir Troshkin, Vladimir Muntian, Viktor Kolotov (Cap); Vladimir Onischenko, Leonid Buriak, Oleg Blohin.
Trainer: Valeriy Lobanovskiy
FERENCVÁROS: István Géczi (Cap); Györö Martos, Miklós Pataki, Tibor Rab, István Megyesi; István Juhász, Tibor Nyilasi (60 Tibor Onhausz), József Mucha; Ferenc Szabó, János Máté, István Magyar. Trainer: Jenő Dalnoki
Goals: Onischenko (18, 39), Blohin (67)

Goalscorers European Cup-Winners' Cup 1974-75:

8 goals: Van der Kuylen (PSV Eindhoven)
7 goals: Onischenko (Dinamo Kiev)
5 goals: Lubse (PSV Eindhoven), Oleg Blohin (Dinamo Kiev)
4 goals: Pirkner (Austria Wien), Roberto Martínez (Real Madrid), Jordão (Benfica Lisboa), Filipović (Crvena Zvezda), Šestić (Crvena Zvezda), Edström (PSV Eindhoven), Máté (Ferencváros Budapest)
3 goals: Savoldi (Bologna), Boersma, R. Kennedy, Philip Thompson (Liverpool), Netzer, Pirri, Santillana (Real Madrid), Sjöberg (Malmö FF), Nené (Benfica Lisboa), Ratković, Savić (Crvena Zvezda)

2 goals: Camilleri (Sliema Wanderers), Delesie (SV Waregem), Sandberg (Lahden Reipas), Nickel, Hölzenbein, Rohrbach (Eintracht Frankfurt), Fiala (Austria Wien), Humberto Coelho (Benfica Lisboa), Turan (Bursaspor), Bo Larsson (Malmö FF), Dahlqvist, Deijkers, W.van de Kerkhof (PSV Eindhoven), Pusztai, Nyilasi, Szabó (Ferencváros Budapest), Kolotov, Muntian (Dinamo Kiev),

1 goal: Onnis, Petit (AS Monaco), R.Aquilina (Sliema Wanderers), Guy (Ards Newtonards), Pettersson (Vanløse IF), Dwyer (Cardiff City), Koudijzer (SV Waregem), Ferry, Bradley (Finn Harps), Rozsnyai, Tonca (Jiul Petroşani), Cucinotta (FC Sion), D.Herda (Slavia Praha), Terzanidis (PAOK Thessaloniki), Hukka, Salonen, Kosonen (Lahden Reipas), Keegan, Lindsay, Heighway, Cormack, Hughes, Smith, Callaghan (Liverpool), Körbel, Beverungen (Eintracht Frankfurt), Malkiewicz (Gwardia Warszawa), Narey, Copland, Gardner (Dundee United), Vogel, Stein (FC Carl Zeiss Jena), Sinner, Dresch (Avenir Beggen), Weigl (Austria Wien), Macaná, Aguilar (Real Madrid), Barros (Benfica Lisboa), Vahit, Ali, Sinan (Bursaspor), Cervin (Malmö FF), Terlecki, Sroka, Kraska (Gwardia Warszawa), Keri, Džajić, O.Petrović, V.Petrović (Crvena Zvezda), Kemper, Van Kraay (PSV Eindhoven), Megyesi, Branikovits, Magyar, Takács (Ferencváros Budapest), Buriak (Dinamo Kiev)

Own goals: Kielak (Gwardia Warszawa) for PSV Eindhoven, Jönsson (Malmö FF) for Ferencváros Budapest

CUP WINNERS' CUP 1975-76

FIRST ROUND

EINTRACHT FRANKFURT
v COLERAINE 5-1 (5-0)
Waldstadion, Frankfurt   16.09.1975
Referee: György Müncz (HUN)   Attendance: 11,225
EINTRACHT: Günther Wienhold, Peter Reichel, Willi Neuberger, Peter Krobbach, Helmut Müller, Karl-Heinz Körbel, Klaus Beverungen, Bernd Hölzenbein (46 Rüdiger Wenzel), Jürgen Grabowski (52 Winfried Stradt), Bernd Nickel, Bernd Lorenz.   Trainer: Dietrich Weise
COLERAINE: Vincent Magee, David Gordon (46 Hugh McIntyre), Eygene McNutt, Liam Beckett, David Jackson, Ivan Murray, Terry Cochrane, Brian Jennings, Michael Guy (65 Frank Moffatt), Des Dickson, Alan Simpson.
Goals: Körbel (13), Beverungen (22), Hölzenbein (28), Nickel (32, 41), Cochrane (80)

COLERAINE
v EINTRACHT FRANKFURT/MAIN 2-6 (1-3)
The Showgrounds, Coleraine   30.09.1975
Referee: Jan F.Beck (HOL)   Attendance: 3,500
COLERAINE: Vincent Magee, William McCurdy, Eygene McNutt, Liam Beckett, David Jackson, Alan Simpson (68 David Gordon), Terry Cochrane, Brian Jennings, Michael Guy, Des Dickson, Frank Moffatt (53 Peter Tweed).
EINTRACHT: Peter Kunter, Helmut Müller, Karl-Heinz Körbel, Klaus Beverungen, Willi Neuberger, Roland Weidle, Jürgen Grabowski, Rüdiger Wenzel (53 Winfried Stradt), Bernd Hölzenbein, Bernd Nickel, Bernd Lorenz. Trainer: Dietrich Weise
Goals: McCurdy (20), Grabowski (21, 65, 90), Nickel (27), Lorenz (35), Cochrane (75), Hölzenbein (84).

VALUR REYKJAVÍK
v CELTIC GLASGOW 0-2 (0-1)
Laugardalsvöllur, Reykjavík   16.09.1975
Referee: Malcolm Wright (NIR)   Attendance: 9,000
VALUR: Sigurdur Dagsson, Bergsveinn Alfonsson, Grimur Saemundsen, Gudmundur Kjartansson, Dyri Gudmundsson, Magnus Bergs, Gudmundur Thorbjörnsson, Hordur Hilmarsson, Hermann Gunnarsson, Ingi Björn Albertsson, Atli Edvaldsson (.. Albert Gudmundsson).
CELTIC: Peter Latchford, Danny McGrain, Andy Lynch, Patrick McCluskey, Rodney McDonald, Johannes Edvaldsson, Henry Anthony Hood (80 Ronald Glavin), Jackie McNamara, Kenneth Dalglish, Thomas Callaghan, Paul Wilson.
Manager: Jock Stein
Goals: Wilson (6), McDonald (65)

**CELTIC GLASGOW
v VALUR REYKJAVÍK 7-0** (5-0)

Celtic Park, Glasgow   1.10.1975

Referee: Patrick Mullhall (IRE)   Attendance: 16,000

CELTIC: Peter Latchford, Danny McGrain, Andy Lynch, Johannes Edvaldsson, Rodney McDonald, Patrick McCluskey, Paul Wilson (45 George McCluskey), Kenneth Dalglish, John Deans, Thomas Callaghan (68 James Casey), Henry Anthony Hood. Manager: Jock Stein

VALUR: Sigurdur Dagsson, Bergsveinn Alfonsson, Grimur Saemundsen, Gudmundur Kjartansson, Dyri Gudmundsson, Magnus Bergs, Gudmundur Thorbjörnsson, Hordur Hilmarsson, Hermann Gunnarsson, Ingi Bjorn Albertsson (.. Haraldsson), Atli Edvaldsson.

Goals: A. Edvaldsson (6), Dalglish (11), P. McCluskey (30 pen), Hood (37, 81), Deans (42), Callaghan (49)

**HALADAS VASUTAS SE SZOMBATHELY
v FC LA VALLETTA 7-0** (1-0)

Rohonczi út, Szombathely   17.09.1975

Referee: D. Stec (POL)   Attendance: 18,000

HALADÁS: Vilmos Békei; Lzló Fischer, Arpad Horváth, Zoltán Kereki, György Kiss; Zoltán Halmosi, Sándor Fedor, Sándor Szabó (75 Lajos Dobány), László Farkas, Ferenc Király, Zoltán Horváth (75 Ferenc Kulcsár).

FC VALLETTA: Alfred Debono; Vincent Gauci, Joe Borg, Tony Ciantar, Edward Vella; Dennis Fenech, Charles Agius, Tony Giglio (60 Joe Abdilla); Vincent Magro, Norman Darmanin-Demajo (60 Micallef), Carlo Seychell.

Goals: Fedor (3, 46), Király (68), A. Horváth (49, 87), Farkas (74), Halmosi (81)

**FC VALLETTA
v HALADAS SZOMBATHELY 1-1** (0-1)

Empire Stadium, Valletta   30.09.1975

Referee: Bruno Della Bruna (SWI)   Attendance: 3,000

FC VALLETTA: Alfred Debono; Micallef, Edward Vella, Joe Abdilla, Dennis Fenech; Norman Darmanin-Demajo, Leonard Farrugia, Vincent Magro; Charles Agius, Tony Giglio, Carlo Seychell.

HALADAS: Vilmos Békei; László Fischer, Arpad Horváth, Zoltán Kereki, László Kovács; Zoltán Halmosi (75 Miklós Bokor), Sándor Fedor, Ferenc Kulcsár; Sándor Szabó, László Farkas (58 Lajos Nemeth), Zoltán Horváth.

Goals: Kereki (22), Giglio (75)

SKEID OSLO v STAL RZESZÓW 1-4 (0-1)

Ullevål, Oslo   17.09.1975

Referee: Martti Hirviniemi (FIN)   Attendance: 5,000

SKEID: Per Egil Nygard, Per Kåre Hagen, Per Christian Olsen (61 Georg Hammer), Børge Josefsen (46 Eistein Berge), Jan Birkelund, Trygve Bornø, Tor Egil Johansen, Odd Pedersen, Bjørn Skjønsberg, Kai Arild Lund, Trond Hasund.

STAL: Henryk Jalocha, Stanislaw Sieniawski (75 Piotr Blaga), Józef Rosól, Boleslaw Biel, Jan Gawlik, Tadeusz Michaliszyn, Marian Kozerski, Stanislaw Curylo, Janusz Krawczyk, Zdzislaw Napieracz (63 Tadeusz Krysinski), Czeslaw Miler.

Goals: Kozerski (30, 48), Curylo (67), Miler (77), Skjønsberg (90)

STAL RZESZÓW v SKEID OSLO 4-0 (3-0)

Stal, Rzeszów   1.10.1975

Referee: Talat Tokat (TUR)   Attendance: 15,000

STAL: Henryk Jalocha, Stanislaw Sieniawski, Józef Rosól, Boleslaw Biel, Jan Gawlik, Tadeusz Michaliszyn, Marian Kozerski (63 Stanislaw Urban), Stanislaw Curylo (65 Andrzej Dziama), Janusz Krawczyk, Zdzislaw Napieracz, Czeslaw Miler.

SKEID: Per Egil Nygard, Per Kåre Hagen, Per Christian Olsen, Jan Birkelund, Børge Josefsen, Trygve Bornø, Tor Egil Johansen, Georg Hammer, Bjørn Skjønsberg, Kai Arild Lund, Eivind Garberg.

Goals: Kozerski (7), Miler (16), Krawczyk (44), Napieracz (67)

**RAPID BUCUREŞTI
v ANDERLECHT BRUSSEL 1-0** (1-0)

23 August, Bucureşti   17.09.1975

Referee: Josef Bucek (AUS)   Att: 25,000

RAPID: Marian Ioniţă; Octavian Niţă, Alexandru Grigoraş, Florin Marin, Gheorghe Iordan; Iordan Angelescu, Mircea Savu (60 Marinel Rîşniţă); Marin Stelian, Nicolae Manea, Alexandru Neagu, Eduard Bartales.
Trainer: Ion Motroc, Vasile Copil

ANDERLECHT: Jacky Munaron; Gilbert Van Binst, Jean Dockx, Erwin Vandendaele, Jean Thissen; Arie Haan, Michel De Groote, Ludo Coeck; Peter Ressel, Torsten Frank Andersen (66 Ronny Van Poucke), Rob Rensenbrink.
Trainer: Hans Croon

Goal: Thissen (20 og)

**ANDERLECHT BRUSSEL
v RAPID BUCUREȘTI 2-0** (1-0)
Parc Astrid, Brussel   1.10.1975
Referee: Michal Jursa (CZE)   Attendance: 17,361
ANDERLECHT: Jacky Munaron; François van der Elst, Jean Dockx, Erwin Vandendaele, Michel Lomme; Arie Haan, Ludo Coeck; Michel De Groote, Torsten Frank Andersen, Gilbert Van Binst (78 Peter Ressel), Rob Rensenbrink.
Trainer: Hans Croon
RAPID: Marian Ioniță; Ion Pop, Alexandru Grigoraș, Florin Marin, Octavian Niță; Marin Stelian (54 Gabriel Petcu), Iordan Angelescu; Mircea Savu, Viorel Leșeanu, Alexandru Neagu (60 Ilie Rontea), Nicolae Manea.   Trainer: Ion Motroc
Goals: Van Binst (38), Rensenbrink (50 pen)

**ARARAT EREVAN
v ANORTHOSIS FAMAGUSTA 9-0** (2-0)
Razdan, Erevan   17.09.1975
Referee: Belá Nagy (HUN)   Attendance: 12,893
ARARAT: Aleksei Abramian (65 Norik Demirchian), Suren Martirosian, Armen Sarkisian, Aleksandr Mirzoian (80 Aram Parsadanian), Norik Mesropian, Sanasar Gevorkian, Sergei Bondarenko, Samuel Petrosian, Eduard Markarov, Khoren Oganesian, Nazar Petrosian.   Trainer: Viktor Maslov
ANORTHOSIS: Mihalis Pamporis, Hristos Kovis, Nikos Nikolaou, Stefanos Lysandrou, Kostas Konstantinou (46 Ahilleas Nikolaou), Giorgos Theoharides (60 Artemis Theoharous), Hristos Soleas, Giannis Hristou "Mantis", Antonakis Kafas, Mihalis Athinodorou "Tartaros", Fivos Vrahimis.
Goals: Markarov (4 pen, 14, 16, 70, 80), Oganesian (52, 84), N. Petrosian (72), Bondarenko (87)

**ANORTHOSIS FAMAGUSTA
v ARARAT EREVAN 1-1** (0-0)
Famagusta   1.10.1975
Referee: Constantin Ghiță (ROM)   Attendance: 1,700
ANORTHOSIS: Mihalis Pamporis, Artemis Theoharous (80 Ahilleas Nikolaou), Nikos Nikolaou, Stefanos Lysandrou, Kostas Konstantinou, Giorgos Theoharides, Hristos Soleas (80 Fotos Hatzidimitriou), Giannis Hristou "Mantis", Antonakis Kafas, Mihalis Athinodorou "Tartaros", Fivos Vrahimis.
ARARAT: Aleksei Abramian, Suren Martirosian, Armen Sarkisian, Aleksandr Mirzoian, Norik Mesropian, Sanasar Gevorkian, Arkadi Andreasian, Sergei Bondarenko, Eduard Markarov, Khoren Oganesian, Nazar Petrosian.
Trainer: Viktor Maslov
Goals: Bondarenko (65), Vrahimis (66 pen)

FC BASEL v ATLÉTICO MADRID 1-2 (1-0)
Sankt Jakob, Basel   17.09.1975
Referee: Robert Wurtz (FRA)   Attendance: 32,647
FC BASEL: Hans Müller, Jörg Stohler (74 Walter Geisser), Walter Mundschin, Peter Ramseier, Paul Fischli, Markus Tanner (74 Otto Demarmels), Peter Marti, Roland Schönenberger, Serge Muhmenthaler, René Hasler, Eigil Nielsen.   Trainer: Helmut Benthaus (GER)
ATLÉTICO: José PACHECO Gómez, Francisco Delgado MELO, José Luis CAPÓN González, ADELARDO Rodríguez Sánchez (74 Heraldo BECERRA Nuñes), Rubén Osvaldo "PANADERO" DÍAZ Figueroa, EUSEBIO Bejarano Vilaroz, Eugenio LEAL Vargas, Ignacio Manuel SALCEDO Sánchez Blanca, José Eulogio GÁRATE Ormaechea (80 MARCELINO Pérez Ayllón), ALBERTO Fernández Fernández, Rubén Hugo AYALA Zanabria.   Trainer: LUIS Aragonés
Goals: Schönenberger (3), Gárate (65), Ayala (68)

ATLÉTICO MADRID v FC BASEL 1-1 (0-0)
Vicente Calderón, Madrid   1.10.1975
Referee: Paul Schiller (AUS)   Attendance: 25,000
ATLÉTICO: Miguel REINA Santos, MARCELINO Pérez Ayllón, Rubén Osvaldo "PANADERO" DÍAZ Figueroa, ADELARDO Rodríguez Sánchez (46 Francisco Javier BERMEJO Caballero), Ramón Armando HEREDIA Dionisio, EUSEBIO Bejarano Vilaroz, Rubén Hugo AYALA Zanabria, Eugenio LEAL Vargas, José Eulogio GÁRATE Ormaechea (83 Francisco BAENA Jiménez), ALBERTO Fernández Fernández, Heraldo BECERRA Nuñes.   Trainer: LUIS Aragonés
FC BASEL: Hans Müller, Jörg Stohler, Walter Mundschin, Peter Ramseier, Paul Fischli, Otto Demarmels, Peter Marti, Roland Schönenberger, Serge Muhmenthaler, Markus Tanner, Eigil Nielsen.   Trainer: Helmut Benthaus
Goals: Becerra (74), Demarmels (89)

**PANATHINAIKOS ATHINA
v SACHSENRING ZWICKAU 0-0**
Panahaikis, Patra   17.09.1975
Referee: Cesare Gussoni (ITA)   Attendance: 13,468
PANATHINAIKOS: Vasilis Konstantinou, Nikos Karamanlis, Anthimos Kapsis, Giorgos Gonios, Giorgos Vlahos, Dimitris Dimitriou, Harilaos Grammos (46 Panagiotis Papadimitriou), Georgevic, Antonis Antoniadis (61 Oikonomou), Spiros Livathinos, Odiseas Vakalis.   Trainer: Aimore Moreira
SACHSENRING: Jürgen Croy, Roland Stemmler, Hans Schykowski, Peter Henschel, Andreas Reichelt, Joachim Schykowski, Michael Braun, Ludwig Blank (83 Claus Schwemmer), Werner Bräutigam (46 Dieter Leuschner), Heinz Dietzsch, Peter Nestler.   Trainer: Karl-Heinz Kluge

SACHSENRING ZWICKAU
v PANATHINAIKOS ATHINA 2-0 (1-0)

Sachsenring, Zwickau   1.10.1975

Referee: Kenneth Howard Burns (ENG)   Att: 33,217

SACHSENRING: Jürgen Croy, Roland Stemmler, Hans Schykowski, Peter Henschel, Günter Lippmann (48 Claus Schwemmer, 70 Uwe Fuchs), Dieter Leuschner, Joachim Schykowski, Andreas Reichelt, Werner Bräutigam, Heinz Dietzsch, Michael Braun.   Trainer: Karl-Heinz Kluge

PANATHINAIKOS: Vasilis Konstantinou, Nikos Karamanlis, Anthimos Kapsis, Giorgos Gonios, Giorgos Vlahos, Dimitris Dimitriou, Harilaos Grammos, Georgevic (64 Agis Panopoulos), Antonis Antoniadis, Dimitris Domazos, Odiseas Vakalis (46 Spiros Livathinos).   Trainer: Aimore Moreira

Goals: J. Schykowski (37), Dietzsch (58 pen)

BEŞIKTAŞ ISTANBUL
v FIORENTINA FIRENZE 0-3 (0-1)

Istanbul   17.09.1975

Referee: Constantin Petrea (ROM)   Attendance: 17,765

BEŞIKTAŞ: Mustafa Güngören, Ahmet Dogan Börtücere, Zekeriya Alp, Niko Kovi, Turgut Erkut, Lütfü Isigöllü, Ceyhun Güney, Hayri Kol (46 Yusuf Tanaoglu), Sinan Alayoglu, Bülent Taskin (64 Terzcan), Melih Atakan.

FIORENTINA: Francesco Superchi, Bruno Beatrice, Moreno Roggi, Ennio Pellegrini, Mauro Della Martira, Vincenzo Guerini, Domenico Caso (72 Paolo Rosi), Claudio Merlo, Gianfranco Casarsa (83 Claudio Desolati), Giancarlo Antognoni, Walter Speggiorin I.   Trainer: Carlo Mazzone

Goals: Caso (42, 49), Casarsa (76)

WREXHAM UNITED
v DJURGÅRDEN IF STOCKHOLM 2-1 (1-1)

Racecourse Ground, Wrexham   17.09.1975

Referee: B. Nielsen (DEN)   Attendance: 9,002

WREXHAM: Brian Lloyd, Alan Hill, David Fogg (67 John Lyons), Michael Evans, Edward May, Gareth Davis, Brian Tinnion, Melvyn Sutton, William Ashcroft, Alan Dwyer, Arfon Griffiths.

DJURGÅRDEN: Björn Alkeby, Roland Andersson, Tommy Davidsson, Berger Jacobsson, Tommy Berggren, Sven Lindman, Kjell Samuelsson, Harry Svensson, Lars Stenbäck, Kjell Karlsson, Sven Krantz.

Goals: Griffiths (33), Krantz (52), Davis (89)

FIORENTINA FIRENZE
v BEŞIKTAŞ ISTANBUL 3-0 (2-0)

Stadio Comunale, Firenze   1.10.1975

Referee: Heinz Aldinger (W. GER)   Attendance: 10,621

FIORENTINA: Francesco Superchi, Giancarlo Galdiolo, Bruno Beatrice, Ennio Pellegrini, Mauro Della Martira, Vincenzo Guerini, Domenico Caso (46 Paolo Rosi), Claudio Merlo, Gianfranco Casarsa, Giancarlo Antognoni, Walter Speggiorin (57 Carlo Bresciani).   Trainer: Carlo Mazzone

BEŞIKTAŞ: Mete Bozkurt, Ahmet Dogan Börtücere, Zekeriya Alp, Vedat Okyar, Lütfü Isigöllü, Gürol Arkan, Adem Kurukaya (73 Melih Atakan), Bülent Taskin (79 Ünal Tombulel), Tezcan Özan, Hayri Kol, Kahraman Kartaloglu.

Goals: Caso (32, 36), Casarsa (88)

DJURGÅRDEN STOCKHOLM
v WREXHAM UNITED 1-1 (0-1)

Olympiastadion, Stockholm   1.10.1975

Referee: Wolfgang Riedel (E. GER)   Attendance: 1,769

DJURGÅRDEN: Björn Alkeby, Per-Olof Erixon, Tommy Berggren, Tommy Davidsson, Berger Jacobsson, Per Lövfors, Sven Lindman, Kjell Samuelsson, Kjell Karlsson (46 Curt Olsberg), Harry Svensson, Sven Krantz (64 Lars Stenbäck).

WREXHAM: Brian Lloyd, Alan Hill, Michael Evans, Gareth Davis, Edward May, Michael Thomas, Brian Tinnion, Melvyn Sutton, Geoffrey Davies, Graham Whittle, Arfon Griffiths.

Goals: Whittle (20), Lövfors (70)

HOME FARM DUBLIN
v RACING CLUB LENS 1-1 (1-1)

Tolka Park, Dublin   17.09.1975

Referee: Jean Claude Jourquin (BEL)   Attendance: 1,000

HOME FARM: Jim Grace; Brian Daly, Donal Cregan, Shay Kelly, Michael Brophy; Tom O'Dea, David Hughes, Noel King, Tony Higgins, Frank Devlin, Martin Murray.

RC LENS: André Lannoy; Alain Hopquin, Walter Winkler, Jean Cieselski, Júan Martín Mujica; Didier Notheaux, Daniel Leclercq, Slobodan Jankovic, Jean Marie Elie, Fares Bousdira, Alfred Kaiser.   Trainer: Arnold Sowinski

Goals: Hopquin (11), Brophy (20)

**RACING CLUB LENS
v HOME FARM DUBLIN 6-0** (3-0)
Félix Bollaert, Lens   1.10.1975

Referee: Cézar de Luiz Dias Correia (POR)   Att: 18,173

RC LENS: André Lannoy; Alain Hopquin, Walter Winkler, Alexandre Stassievitch (45 Jean Cieselski), Júan Martín Mujica; Jean Marie Elie, Daniel Leclercq; Slobodan Jankovic, Didier Notheaux (25 Robert Llorens), Fares Bousdira, Alfred Kaiser.   Trainer: Arnold Sowinski

HOME FARM: Jim Grace; Brian Daly, Donal Cregan, Frank Devlin, Michael Brophy; Tom O'Dea, David Hughes; Noel King, Tony Higgins, Cormac Breslin (46 Mike O'Grady), Martin Murray.

Goals: Notheaux (10), Mujica (20 pen), Kaiser (30, 60, 62), Llorens (80)

SPARTAK TRNAVA v BOAVISTA PORTO 0-0
Spartak, Trnava   17.09.1975

Referee: Ernst Dörflinger (SWI)   Attendance: 14,890

SPARTAK: Dušan Kéketi, Pavol Benčo, Alojz Fandel, Milan Zvarík, Dušan Kabát, Michal Gasparík (66 Jozef Dian), Tibor Jancula, Jaroslav Masrna, Ladislav Kúna, Jozef Adamec, Ludovít Badura (72 Rudolf Kramolis).
Trainer: Anton Malatinský

BOAVISTA: António José da Silva BOTELHO, Leonel TRINDADE, MARIO JOÃO, António Carlos Sousa Laranjeira "TAÍ", Manuel José Ferreira da Silva BARBOSA, ALVES, CELSO Luis de Matos, FRANCISCO MÁRIO P. Silva, SALVADOR Luis Almeida, Alvaro CAROLINO Nascimento, ACÁCIO Casimiro (72 JORGE Manuel Freitas ALMEIDA).

**REIPAS LAHTI
v WEST HAM UNITED LONDON 2-2** (1-1)
Olympiastadion, Lahti   17.09.1975

Referee: Ulf Eriksson (SWE)   Attendance: 4,587

REIPAS: Harri Holli, Pekka Kosonen, Mikko Kautonen, Lauri Riutto, Markku Repo, Harri Toivanen, Timo Kautonen, Ari Tupasela, Pertti Jantunen, Hannu Hämäläinen, Harri Lindholm.   Trainer: Keijo Voutilainen

WEST HAM: Mervyn Day, John McDowell, Frank Lampard, William Bonds, Thomas Taylor, Kevin Lock, Patrick Holland, Graham Paddon, Alan Taylor, Trevor Brooking, Keith Robson (70 William Jennings).   Manager: John Lyall

Goals: Lindholm (4), Brooking (29), Tupasela (53), Bonds (76)

BOAVISTA PORTO v SPARTAK TRNAVA 3-0 (1-0)
Estádio do Bessa, Porto   1.10.1975

Referee: Jacques Van Melkebeeke (BEL)   Attendance: 9,387

BOAVISTA: António José da Silva BOTELHO, Leonel TRINDADE, MARIO JOÃO, Alvaro CAROLINO Nascimento, António Carlos Sousa Laranjeira "TAÍ", CELSO Luis de Matos, ALVES, FRANCISCO MÁRIO P. Silva, Manuel Chagas "MANÉ", SALVADOR Luis Almeida, ACÁCIO Casimiro.

SPARTAK: Dušan Kéketi, Karol Dobias, Alojz Fandel, Milan Zvarík, Pavol Benčo, Michal Gasparík, Daniel Kolenic, Jaroslav Masrna, Ladislav Kúna, Frantisek Horváth, Ludovít Badura.
Trainer: Anton Malatinský

Goals: Mané (35), Celso (62), Salvador (79)

**WEST HAM UNITED LONDON
v REIPAS LAHTI 3-0** (0-0)
Boleyn Ground Upton Park, London   1.10.1975

Referee: Anthony Briguglio (MAL)   Attendance: 24,131

WEST HAM: Mervyn Day, John McDowell, Frank Lampard, William Bonds, Thomas Taylor, Kevin Lock, Alan Taylor (73 William Jennings), Graham Paddon, Keith Robson, Trevor Brooking, Patrick Holland.   Manager: John Lyall

REIPAS: Harri Holli, Pekka Kosonen, Mikko Kautonen, Lauri Riutto, Markku Repo, Harri Toivanen (73 Seppo Nordman), Timo Kautonen, Ari Tupasela, Pertti Jantunen, Hannu Hämäläinen, Harri Lindholm.   Trainer: Keijo Voutilainen

Goals: Robson (59), Holland (88), Jennings (90)

VEJLE BK v FC DEN HAAG 0-2 (0-1)
Vejle Stadion   17.09.1975

Referee: Antoine Queudeville (LUX)   Attendance: 5,300

VEJLE: Niels Wodskou, Jens Jørn Jensen, Jan Knudsen, Knud Herbert Sørensen, Flemming Serritslev, Ole Fritsen, Poul Erik Ostergaard (75 Iver Schriver), Gert Eg (65 Finn Johansen), Karl Aage Damsgaard, Ulrich Thychosen, Ib Jacquet.

FC DEN HAAG: Ton Thie, Leo de Caluwé, Aad Mansveld, Simon van Vliet, Joop Korevaar, Aad Kila (75 Roger Albertsen), Lex Schoenmaker, Dojcin Perazic, Martin Jol, Henk van Leeuwen, Hans Bres.   Trainer: Vujadin Boskov

Goals: Jol (19), Van Leeuwen (78)

FC DEN HAAG v VEJLE BK 2-0 (1-0)

Zuiderparkstadion, Den Haag   1.10.1975

Referee: César da Luz Dias Correia (POR)   Att: 8,000

FC DEN HAAG: Ton Thie, Rob Ouwehand (61 Leo de Caluwé), Aad Mansveld, Simon van Vliet, Joop Korevaar, Aad Kila, Lex Schoenmaker, Dojcin Perazic, Ronnie Van Baaren (66 Roger Albertsen), Henk van Leeuwen, Hans Bres. Trainer: Vujadin Boskov

VEJLE: Niels Wodskou, Jens Jørn Jensen, Jan Knudsen, Knud Herbert Sørensen, Flemming Serritslev, Jørgen Nielsen, Gert Eg (70 Knud Nøregaard), Ole Fritsen, Karl Aage Damsgaard, Poul Erik Ostergaard, Ib Jacquet (62 Finn Johansen).

Goals: Perazic (28), Mansveld (55)

BORAC BANJA LUKA
v US RUMELANGE 9-0 (3-0)

BNA, Banja Luka   17.09.1975

Referee: Richard Casha (MAL)   Attendance: 6,270

BORAC: Petar Adjanski, Vukelja (64 Dragan Marjanović), Kusmić, Zvonko Vidacak, Brnjac, Miloš Cetina, Culafić (56 Dušan Jurkovic), Zoran Smileski, Muhamed Ibrahimbegovic, Dzevad Kreso, Abid Kovacević.

US RUMELANGE: Bodson, Jean Schlutter, Marius Pawlowski, Norbert Leszczynski, Eisenbarth, Pierre Turci, René Cardoni, Fumanti (52 Anelli), Armand Lambert, Furio Cardoni, Julian Bauer (64 Nico Rohmann).

Goals: Cetina (6, 16, 60), Ibrahimbegović (14, 48, 57, 58, 86), Jurković (82)

STURM GRAZ v SLAVIA SOFIA 3-1 (3-0)

Bundesstadion Liebenau, Graz   17.09.1975

Referee: Leonidas Vamvakopoulos (GRE)   Att: 8,000

STURM: Walter Saria; Manfred Wirth, Heinz Russ, Gustav Thaler, Helmut Huberts; Manfred Steiner, Hubert Kulmer (77 Walter Gruber), Anton Pichler, Kurt Stendal, Heribert Weber, Heinz Zamut (67 Gernot Jurtin).

SLAVIA: Petar Tsolov; Ivan Chakarov, Milcho Evtimov, Bozhidar Grigorov, Ivan Iliev, Vanio Kostov, Atanas Aleksandrov, Kostas Isakidis (68 Ivan Nenchev), Andrei Jeliazkov, Georgi Minchev, Chavdar Tzvetkov.

Goals: Stendal (18 pen, 26 pen), Kulmer (32), Kostov (50)

US RUMELANGE
v BORAC BANJA LUKA 1-5 (0-2)

Esch sur Alzette   2.10.1975

Referee: Georges Konrath (FRA)   Attendance: 836

US RUMELANGE: Bodson, Julian Bauer, Pierre Turci, Nico Rohmann, Eisenbarth, René Cardoni, Anelli, Armand Lambert, Fumenti (27 Wagener), Jean Carlo Scarpellini (46 Norbert Leszczynski), Furio Cardoni.

BORAC: Marijan Jantoljak, Bogojević, Kusmić, Zvonko Vidacak, Vukelja, Miloš Cetina, Dušan Jurkovic, Zoran Smileski, Muhamed Ibrahimbegovic, Dzevad Kreso (38 Dragan Marjanovic), Abid Kovacević (62 Culafić).

Goals: Smileski (8), Kreso (23), Kovacević (51), Vidacak (58), Rohmann (79), Marjanović (85)

SECOND ROUND

SLAVIA SOFIA v STURM GRAZ 1-0 (0-0)

Slavia, Sofia   1.10.1975

Referee: Rudolf Frickel (W. GER)   Attendance: 30,000

Slavia: Petar Tsolov; Ivan Chakarov, Milcho Evtimov, Bozhidar Grigorov, Ivan Iliev, Vanio Kostov, Atanas Aleksandrov, Kostas Isakidis (65 Ivan Nenchev), Andrei Jeliazkov, Georgi Minchev (75 Vesko Ganchev), Chavdar Tzvetkov.

STRUM: Refik Muftic, Manfred Wirth, Heinz Russ, Gustav Thaler, Helmut Huberts; Manfred Steiner, Hubert Kulmer (70 Gernot Jurtin), Anton Pichler, Kurt Stendal, Heribert Weber, Heinz Zamut (73 Walter Gruber).

Goal: Ganchev (76)

WREXHAM v STAL RZESZÓW 2-0 (2-0)

Racecourse Ground, Wrexham   22.10.1975

Referee: Erik Axelryd (SWE)   Attendance: 9,598

WREXHAM: Brian Lloyd, Alan Hill, Michael Evans, Gareth Davis, Edward May, Michael Thomas (75 Alan Dwyer), Brian Tinnion, Melvyn Sutton, William Ashcroft, Graham Whittle, Arfon Griffiths.

STAL: Henryk Jalocha, Stanislaw Sieniawski, Stefan Kawalec, Boleslaw Biel, Jan Gawlik, Tadeusz Michaliszyn, Marian Kozierski, Stanislaw Curylo, Janusz Krawczyk, Zdzislaw Napieracz (80 Józef Janiszewski), Czeslaw Miler.

Goals: Ashcroft (10, 34)

STAL RZESZÓW v WREXHAM 1-1 (0-0)

Stal, Rzeszów   5.11.1975

Referee: Antoine Quedeville (LUX)   Attendance: 20,000

STAL: Henryk Jalocha, Piotr Blaga, Józef Rosól, Boleslaw Biel, Jan Gawlik (69 Józef Janiszewski), Andrzej Dziama, Marian Kozerski, Stanislaw Curylo, Janusz Krawczyk, Zdzislaw Napieracz, Tadeusz Krysinski.

WREXHAM: Brian Lloyd, Alan Hill, Alan Dwyer, Gareth Davis, Edward May, Michael Evans, Brian Tinnion, Melvyn Sutton, William Ashcroft, Michael Thomas, Arfon Griffiths.

Goals: Kozerski (68), Sutton (83)

BOAVISTA PORTO v CELTIC GLASGOW 0-0

Estádio do Bessa, Porto   22.10.1975

Referee: Edgar H. Pedersen (DEN)   Attendance: 25,000

BOAVISTA: António José da Silva BOTELHO, Leonel TRINDADE, MÁRIO JOÃO, Alvaro CAROLINO Nascimento, António Carlos Sousa Laranjeira "TAÍ", CELSO Luis de Matos, ALVES, FRANCISCO MÁRIO P. Silva, Manuel Chagas "MANÉ", SALVADOR Luis Almeida, ACÁCIO Casimiro (70 RUFINO José Mendes).

CELTIC: Peter Latchford, Danny McGrain, Andy Lynch, Patrick McCluskey, Rodney McDonald, Johannes Edvaldsson, Thomas Callaghan, Jackie McNamara, Paul Wilson, Henry Anthony Hood, Robert Lennox.   Manager: Jock Stein

**ARARAT EREVAN
v WEST HAM UNITED LONDON 1-1** (0-0)

Razdan, Erevan   22.10.1975

Referee: Hans-Joachim Weyland (W. GER)   Att: 70,000

ARARAT: Aleksei Abramian, Suren Martirosian, Armen Sarkisian, Norik Mesropian, Armen Azarian (70 Sergei Bondarenko), Samuel Petrosian, Sanasar Gevorkian, Arkadi Andreasian, Nazar Petrosian (76 Sergei Pogosian), Eduard Markarov, Khoren Oganesian.   Trainer: Viktor Maslov

WEST HAM: Mervyn Day, John McDowell, Frank Lampard, William Bonds, Thomas Taylor, Keith Coleman, Alan Taylor, Graham Paddon, Robert Gould, Patrick Holland, Keith Robson.   Manager: John Lyall

Goals: A. Taylor (56), S. Petrosian (68)

CELTIC GLASGOW v BOAVISTA PORTO 3-1 (2-1)

Celtic Park, Glasgow   5.11.1975

Referee: Heinz Einbeck (E. GER)   Attendance: 37,000

CELTIC: Peter Latchford, Danny McGrain, Andy Lynch, Patrick McCluskey, Rodney McDonald, Johannes Edvaldsson, George McCluskey, Kenneth Dalglish, John Deans, Jackie McNamara, Thomas Callaghan (70 Robert Lennox).
Manager: Jock Stein

BOAVISTA: António José da Silva BOTELHO, Leonel TRINDADE, MÁRIO JOÃO, Alvaro CAROLINO Nascimento, António Carlos Sousa Laranjeira "TAÍ", Manuel José Ferreira da Silva BARBOSA (77 Mendes), ALVES, FRANCISCO MÁRIO P. Silva, Manuel Chagas "MANÉ", SALVADOR Luis Almeida, ACÁCIO Casimiro (46 José Marques Silva "ZÉZINHO").

Goals: Dalglish (1), Edvaldsson (21), Mané (39), Deans (85).

**WEST HAM UNITED LONDON
v ARARAT EREVAN 3-1** (2-0)

Boleyn Ground Upton Park, London   5.11.1975

Referee: Robert Héliès (FRA)   Attendance: 30,399

WEST HAM: Mervyn Day, John McDowell, Frank Lampard, William Bonds, Thomas Taylor, Keith Coleman, Alan Taylor, Graham Paddon, Patrick Holland, Trevor Brooking, Keith Robson.   Manager: John Lyall

ARARAT: Aleksei Abramian, Suren Martirosian, Armen Sarkisian, Norik Mesropian, Armen Azarian, Samuel Petrosian, Sanasar Gevorkian, Arkadi Andreasian, Khoren Oganesian, Eduard Markarov (70 Levon Ishtoian), Nazar Petrosian (70 Sergei Bondarenko).   Trainer: Viktor Maslov

Goals: Paddon (16), Robson (27), N. Petrosian (48), A. Taylor (59)

**ATLÉTICO MADRID
v EINTRACHT FRANKFURT/MAIN 1-2** (0-2)

Vicente Calderón, Madrid   22.10.1975

Referee: Kenneth Howard Burns (ENG)   Att: 31,147

ATLÉTICO: Miguel REINA Santos, José Luis CAPÓN González, Rubén Osvaldo "PANADERO" DÍAZ Figueroa, MARCELINO Pérez Ayllón, Ramón Armando HEREDIA Dionisio, EUSEBIO Bejarano Vilaroz, Francisco Javier BERMEJO Caballero, Rubén Hugo AYALA Zanabria, José Eulogio GÁRATE Ormaechea (46 Heraldo BECERRA Nuñes), Eugenio LEAL Vargas (46 Francisco BAENA Jiménez), Ignacio Manuel SALCEDO Sánchez Blanca.   Trainer: LUIS Aragonés

EINTRACHT: Günther Wienhold, Peter Reichel, Willi Neuberger, Karl-Heinz Körbel, Helmut Müller, Roland Weidle, Klaus Beverungen, Bernd Hölzenbein, Rüdiger Wenzel, Jürgen Grabowski, Bernd Nickel.   Trainer: Dietrich Weise

Goals: Hölzenbein (6, 14), Capón (50)

**EINTRACHT FRANKFURT/MAIN
v ATLÉTICO MADRID 1-0** (0-0)

Waldstadion, Frankfurt am Main   5.11.1975

Referee: Robert Schaut (BEL)   Attendance: 45,000

EINTRACHT: Günther Wienhold, Peter Reichel, Willi Neuberger, Karl-Heinz Körbel, Helmut Müller, Roland Weidle, Klaus Beverungen, Bernd Hölzenbein, Rüdiger Wenzel (72 Bernd Lorenz), Jürgen Grabowski, Bernd Nickel. Trainer: Dietrich Weise

ATLÉTICO: Miguel REINA Santos, Rafael Prado FRAGUAS, José Luis CAPÓN González, MARCELINO Pérez Ayllón (46 Eugenio LEAL Vargas), Rubén Osvaldo "PANADERO" DÍAZ Figueroa, EUSEBIO Bejarano Vilaroz, Francisco AGUILAR Fernández, Francisco Javier BERMEJO Caballero, Rubén Hugo AYALA Zanabria, ADELARDO Rodríguez Sánchez (72 Heraldo BECERRA Nuñes), Francisco BAENA Jiménez. Trainer: LUIS Aragonés

Goal: Reichel (88)

**FIORENTINA FIRENZE
v SACHSENRING ZWICKAU 1-0** (0-0)

Stadio Comunale, Firenze   22.10.1975

Referee: Milos Cajić (YUG)   Attendance: 12,871

FIORENTINA: Francesco Superchi, Bruno Beatrice, Moreno Roggi, Ennio Pellegrini, Mauro Della Martira, Vincenzo Guerini (65 Claudio Desolati), Domenico Caso, Claudio Merlo, Gianfranco Casarsa (46 Walter Speggiorin I), Giancarlo Antognoni, Carlo Bresciani.   Trainer: Carlo Mazzone

SACHSENRING: Jürgen Croy, Roland Stemmler, Hans Schykowski, Peter Henschel, Andreas Reichelt, Joachim Schykowski, Dieter Leuschner, Ludwig Blank, Werner Bräutigam, Heinz Dietzsch, Michael Braun. Trainer: Karl-Heinz Kluge

Goal: Speggiorin (70)

**SACHSENRING ZWICKAU
v FIORENTINA FIRENZE 1-0** (1-0, 1-0) (AET)

Sachsenring, Zwickau   5.11.1975

Referee: Nikolaos Zlatanos (GRE)   Attendance: 36,000

SACHSENRING: Jürgen Croy, Roland Stemmler, Hans Schykowski, Peter Henschel, Günter Lippmann, Dieter Leuschner, Joachim Schykowski, Ludwig Blank, Andreas Reichelt (73 Peter Nestler), Heinz Dietzsch, Michael Braun. Trainer: Karl-Heinz Kluge

FIORENTINA: Francesco Superchi, Giancarlo Galdiolo, Moreno Roggi, Ennio Pellegrini, Mauro Della Martira, Vincenzo Guerini, Domenico Caso, Bruno Beatrice, Gianfranco Casarsa (78 Claudio Desolati), Giancarlo Antognoni, Carlo Bresciani.   Trainer: Carlo Mazzone

Goal: J. Schykowski (30)

Penalties: 0-1 Caso, 1-1 J. Schykowski, 1-2 Guerini, 2-2 Leuschner, Antognoni (miss), 3-2 H. Schykowski, 3-3 Roggi, 4-3 Lippmann, 4-4 Bresciani, 5-4 Croy

FC DEN HAAG v RC LENS 3-2 (0-2)

Zuiderparkstadion, Den Haag   22.10.1975

Referee: John Carpenter (IRL)   Attendance: 18,000

FC DEN HAAG: Ton Thie; Leo de Caluwé, Aad Mansveld, Simon van Vliet, Joop Korevaar (70 Roger Albertsen); Aad Kila, Dojcin Perazic, Rob Ouwehand; Lex Schoenmaker, Martin Jol (46 Hans Bres), Henk van Leeuwen. Trainer: Vujadin Boskov

RC LENS: André Lannoy; Alain Hopquin, Jean Cieselski, Jacques Marie, Júan Martín Mujica; Jean Marie Elie, Fares Bousdira, Daniel Leclercq; Slobodan Jankovic, Didier Notheaux, Casimir Zuraszek (89 Alfred Kaiser). Trainer: Arnold Sowinski

Goals: Zuraszek (18), Jankovic (19), Schoenmaker (46), Van Vliet (49), Van Leeuwen (65)

RC LENS v FC DEN HAAG 1-3 (1-2)

Félix Bollaert, Lens   5.11.1975

Referee: Thomas H.C. Reynolds (WAL)   Attendance: 26,205

RC LENS: André Lannoy; Alain Hopquin, Walter Winkler, Jacques Marie, Júan Martín Mujica; Jean Marie Elie, Fares Bousdira, Daniel Leclercq; Slobodan Jankovic (77 Alfred Kaiser), Didier Notheaux, Casimir Zuraszek. Trainer: Arnold Sowinski

FC DEN HAAG: Ton Thie; Leo de Caluwé, Aad Mansveld, Simon van Vliet, Joop Korevaar; Roger Albertsen (50 Martin Jol), Dojcin Perazic (80 Aad Kila), Rob Ouwehand; Lex Schoenmaker, Henk van Leeuwen, Hans Bres. Trainer: Vujadin Boskov

Goals: Schoenmaker (28, 89), Van Leeuwen (29), Mujica (40 pen)

**ANDERLECHT BRUSSEL
v BORAC BANJA LUKA 3-0** (1-0)

Parc Astrid, Brussel   22.10.1975

Referee: Pablo Augusto Sánchez Ibañez (SPA)   Att: 20,789

ANDERLECHT: Jan Ruiter, François van der Elst, Michel Lomme, Erwin Vandendaele, Jean Dockx; Arie Haan, Michel de Groote; Torsten Frank Andersen (46 Peter Ressel), Gilbert van Binst, Ludo Coeck, Rob Rensenbrink. Trainer: Hans Croon

BORAC: Marijan Jantoljak; Kusmić, Lazić (46 Culafić), Zvonko Vidacak (77 Dragan Marjanović), Brnjac, Miloš Cetina, Vukelja, Zoran Smileski, Muhamed Ibrahimbegović, Dzevad Kreso, Abid Kovacević.

Goals: Rensenbrink (11, 55), Coeck (53)

BORAC BANJA LUKA
v ANDERLECHT BRUSSEL 1-0 (1-0)

BNA, Banja Luka   5.11.1975

Referee: Cesare Gussoni (ITA)   Attendance: 6,740

BORAC: Petar Adjanski, Kusmić, Lazić, Zvonko Vidacak, Brnjac (47 Crogojevic), Vukelja, Zoran Smileski, Bajekinovic, Muhamed Ibrahimbegović, Dušan Jurković (29 Culafić), Abid Kovacević.

ANDERLECHT: Jan Ruiter, François van der Elst, Michel Lomme, Erwin Vandendaele, Jean Dockx (46 Ronny van Poucke), Arie Haan, Michel de Groote, Peter Ressel, Gilbert van Binst, Ludo Coeck, Rob Rensenbrink.
Trainer: Hans Croon

Goal: Ibrahimbegović (37)

STURM GRAZ
v HALADÁS SZOMBATHELY 2-0 (0-0)

Bundesstadion Liebenau, Graz   22.10.1975

Referee: John K. Taylor (ENG)   Attendance: 9,000

STURM: Refik Muftić; Manfred Wirth, Heinz Russ, Heribert Weber, Gustav Thaler; Manfred Steiner, Hubert Kulmer, Anton Pichler, Kurt Stendal (82 Karl Hofmeister), Heinz Zamut (46 Anton Ringert), Gernot Jurtin.

HALADAS: Vilmos Békei; László Fischer, Arpad Horváth, Zoltán Kereki, György Kiss; Zoltán Halmosi, Sándor Fedor, Ferenc Kulcsár; Sándor Szabó, László Farkas, Ferenc Király.

Goals: Stendal (55), Steiner (67 pen)

HALADÁS SZOMBATHELY
v STURM GRAZ 1-1 (0-0)

Rohonczi út, Szombathely   5.11.1975

Referee: Dogan Babacan (TUR)   Attendance: 16,000

HALADAS: Vilmos Békei; László Fischer, Arpad Horváth, Zoltán Kereki, György Kiss; Zoltán Halmosi, Sándor Fedor, Zoltán Horváth (5 Ferenc Kulcsár); Sándor Szabó, László Farkas, Ferenc Király (46 Tibor Hauzer).

STURM: Refik Muftić; Manfred Wirth, Heinz Russ, Heribert Weber, Helmut Huberts; Manfred Steiner, Karl Hofmeister, Anton Pichler (69 Anton Ringert), Kurt Stendal (79 Heinz Zamut), Gustav Thaler, Gernot Jurtin.

Goals: A. Horváth (51), Jurtin (90)

QUARTER-FINALS

STURM GRAZ
v EINTRACHT FRANKFURT 0-2 (0-0)

Bundesstadion Liebenau, Graz   2.03.1976

Referee: Cesare Gussoni (ITA)   Attendance: 12,000

STURM: Refik Muftic; Manfred Wirth, Heinz Russ, Heribert Weber, Helmut Huberts; Manfred Steiner, Karl Hofmeister (65 Walter Gruber), Heinz Zamut (73 Gustav Thaler), Hubert Kulmer, Kurt Stendal, Gernot Jurtin.

EINTRACHT: Günther Wienhold, Peter Reichel, Willi Neuberger, Karl-Heinz Körbel, Helmut Müller, Roland Weidle, Klaus Beverungen, Jürgen Grabowski, Bernd Nickel, Bernd Hölzenbein, Rüdiger Wenzel.   Trainer: Dietrich Weise

Goals: Hölzenbein (74), Wenzel (87)

EINTRACHT FRANKFURT/MAIN
v STURM GRAZ 1-0 (0-0)

Waldstadion, Frankfurt   16.03.1976

Referee: Antonio José da Silva Garrido (POR)   Att: 17,022

EINTRACHT: Peter Kunter, Peter Reichel, Karl-Heinz Körbel, Willi Neuberger, Helmut Müller, Roland Weidle (85 Wolfgang Kraus), Jürgen Grabowski, Klaus Beverungen, Bernd Hölzenbein, Rüdiger Wenzel, Bernd Nickel.
Trainer: Dietrich Weise

STURM: Refik Muftic; Heribert Weber, Manfred Wirth, Heinz Russ, Helmut Huberts (72 Karl Hofmeister); Gustav Thaler, Anton Pichler, Heinz Zamut; Hubert Kulmer, Kurt Stendal, Gernot Jurtin.

Goal: Hölzenbein (85)

CELTIC GLASGOW
v SACHSENRING ZWICKAU 1-1 (1-0)

Celtic Park, Glasgow   3.03.1976

Referee: Erik Axelryd (SWE)   Attendance: 46,000

CELTIC: Peter Latchford, Patrick McCluskey, Danny McGrain, Roy Aitken, Andy Lynch, Johannes Edvaldsson, Kenneth Dalglish, Henry Anthony Hood, Paul Wilson, John Deans, Robert Lennox.   Manager: Jock Stein

SACHSENRING: Jürgen Croy, Günter Lippmann, Hans Schykowski, Roland Stemmler, Andreas Reichelt, Dieter Leuschner, Claus Schwemmer, Ludwig Blank, Joachim Schykowski, Heinz Dietzsch, Michael Braun (66 Bernd Wutzler).   Trainer: Karl-Heinz Kluge

Goals: Dalglish (41), Blank (89)

**SACHSENRING ZWICKAU
v CELTIC GLASGOW 1-0** (1-0)

Sachsenring, Zwickau 17.03.1976

Referee: Ángel Franco Martínez (SPA)   Attendance: 40,024

SACHSENRING: Jürgen Croy, Hans Schykowski, Joachim Schykowski, Roland Stemmler, Günter Lippmann, Dieter Leuschner, Heinz Dietzsch, Claus Schwemmer, Ludwig Blank, Werner Bräutigam (80 Andreas Reichelt), Michael Braun. Trainer: Karl-Heinz Kluge

CELTIC: Peter Latchford, Patrick McCluskey, Johannes Edvaldsson, Roy Aitken, Danny McGrain, Thomas Callaghan, Ronald Glavin (74 Jackie McNamara), Kenneth Dalglish, Henry Anthony Hood, Paul Wilson (67 James Casey), Rodney McDonald.   Manager: Jock Stein

Goal: Blank (4)

**FC DEN HAAG
v WEST HAM UNITED LONDON 4-2** (4-0)

Zuiderparkstadion, Den Haag 3.03.1976

Referee: Rudi Glöckner (E. GER)   Attendance: 26,000

FC DEN HAAG: Ton Thie, Leo de Caluwé, Aad Mansveld, Simon van Vliet, Joop Korevaar, Aad Kila, Dojcin Perazic, Rob Ouwehand, Lex Schoenmaker, Henk van Leeuwen, Leen Swanenburg.   Trainer: Vujadin Boskov

WEST HAM: Mervyn Day, Michael McGiven (46 Keith Coleman), Kevin Lock, Thomas Taylor, Frank Lampard, Graham Paddon, Alan Curbishley, William Bonds, William Jennings, Alan Taylor, Keith Robson.   Manager: John Lyall

Goals: Mansveld (12, 16 pen, 39 pen), Schoenmaker (44), Jennings (51, 59)

**WEST HAM UNITED LONDON
v FC DEN HAAG 3-1** (3-0)

Boleyn Ground Upton Park, London 17.03.1976

Referee: Károly Palotai (HUN)   Attendance: 29,829

WEST HAM: Mervyn Day, Keith Coleman, Thomas Taylor (65 Michael McGiven), Kevin Lock, Frank Lampard, William Bonds, Trevor Brooking, Graham Paddon (46 Alan Curbishley), Alan Taylor, William Jennings, Keith Robson. Manager: John Lyall

FC DEN HAAG: Ton Thie, Rob Ouwehand, Aad Mansveld, Simon van Vliet, Joop Korevaar, Aad Kila (75 Martin Jol), Roger Albertsen (65 Leen Swanenburg), Dojcin Perazić, Hans Bres, Henk van Leeuwen, Lex Schoenmaker.
Trainer: Vujadin Boskov

Goals: A. Taylor (29), Lampard (32), Bonds (35 pen), Schoenmaker (59)

ANDERLECHT BRUSSEL v WREXHAM 1-0 (1-0)

Parc Astrid, Brussel 3.03.1976

Referee: Marijan Rauš (YUG)   Attendance: 23,055

ANDERLECHT: Jan Ruiter; Jean Dockx, Michel Lomme, Erwin Vandendaele (46 Torsten Frank Andersen), Hugo Broos; François van der Elst, Arie Haan, Ludo Coeck (20 Michel de Groote); Peter Ressel, Gilbert van Binst, Rob Rensenbrink. Trainer: Hans Croon

WREXHAM: Brian Lloyd; Michael Evans, David Fogg, Gareth Davis, Edward May; Michael Thomas, Graham Whittle, Melvyn Sutton, Stuart Lee, William Ashcroft, Arfon Griffiths.

Goal: Van Binst (10)

SEMI-FINALS

**SACHSENRING ZWICKAU
v ANDERLECHT BRUSSEL 0-3** (0-2)

Sachsenring, Zwickau 31.03.1976

Referee: Robert Hélies (FRA)   Attendance: 36,246

SACHSENRING: Jürgen Croy; Hans Schykowski, Günter Lippmann, Roland Stemmler, Joachim Schykowski (56 Andreas Reichelt); Claus Schwemmer, Dieter Leuschner (10 Peter Nestler), Heinz Dietzsch, Ludwig Blank, Werner Bräutigam, Michael Braun.   Trainer: Karl-Heinz Kluge

ANDERLECHT: Jan Ruiter; Michel Lomme, Hugo Broos, Gilbert van Binst, Jean Thissen; Jean Dockx, François van der Elst, Arie Haan, Ludo Coeck; Peter Ressel, Rob Rensenbrink. Trainer: Hans Croon

Goals: Van der Elst (26, 38), Rensenbrink (67)

WREXHAM v ANDERLECHT BRUSSEL 1-1 (0-0)

Racecourse Ground, Wrexham 17.03.1976

Referee: Ferdinand Biwersi (W. GER)   Attendance: 19,668

WREXHAM: Brian Lloyd; Michael Evans, David Fogg, Gareth Davis, Edward May; Graham Whittle, Brian Tinnion, Melvyn Sutton, Stuart Lee, William Ashcroft, Arfon Griffiths.

ANDERLECHT: Jan Ruiter; Michel Lomme, Erwin Vandendaele, Hugo Broos, Jean Dockx; François van der Elst, Arie Haan, Ludo Coeck; Peter Ressel, Gilbert van Binst, Rob Rensenbrink.   Trainer: Hans Croon

Goals: Lee (60), Rensenbrink (76)

**ANDERLECHT BRUSSEL
v SACHSENRING ZWICKAU 2-0** (1-0)

Parc Astrid, Brussel 14.04.1976

Referee: Pablo Augusto Sánchez Ibanez (SPA)   Att: 25,000

ANDERLECHT: Jan Ruiter; Gilbert van Binst, Jean Dockx, Hugo Broos, Jean Thissen; Frank Vercauteren, François van der Elst, Ludo Coeck, Peter Ressel, Arie Haan, Rob Rensenbrink.   Trainer: Hans Croon

SACHSENRING: Jürgen Croy; Hans Schykowski, Andreas Reichelt, Roland Stemmler, Joachim Schykowski; Claus Schwemmer, Dieter Leuschner, Heinz Dietzsch, Michael Braun (63 Günter Lippmann), Peter Nestler, Werner Bräutigam.   Trainer: Karl-Heinz Kluge

Goals: Rensenbrink (43), Van der Elst (58)

**EINTRACHT FRANKFURT/MAIN
v WEST HAM UNITED LONDON 2-1** (1-1)

Waldstadion, Frankfurt/Main 31.03.1976

Referee: Vladimir Rudnev (USSR)   Attendance: 50,000

EINTRACHT: Peter Kunter, Peter Reichel, Willi Neuberger, Gerd Simons, Klaus Beverungen, Karl-Heinz Körbel, Wolfgang Kraus (70 Roland Weidle), Jürgen Grabowski, Bernd Nickel, Bernd Hölzenbein, Rüdiger Wenzel.   Trainer: Dietrich Weise

WEST HAM: Mervyn Day, Keith Coleman, Thomas Taylor, William Bonds, Frank Lampard, John McDowell, Patrick Holland, Graham Paddon, Trevor Brooking, William Jennings, Keith Robson.   Manager: John Lyall

Goals: Paddon (9), Neuberger (29), Kraus (47)

**WEST HAM UNITED LONDON
v EINTRACHT FRANKFURT/MAIN 3-1** (0-0)

Boleyn Ground Upton Park, London 14.04.1976

Referee: Walter Hungerbühler (SWI)   Attendance: 39,202

WEST HAM: Mervyn Day, Keith Coleman, Thomas Taylor, William Bonds, Frank Lampard, John McDowell, Graham Paddon, Trevor Brooking, Patrick Holland, William Jennings, Keith Robson.   Manager: John Lyall

EINTRACHT: Peter Kunter, Peter Reichel, Willi Neuberger, Bernd Lorenz, Klaus Beverungen, Roland Weidle, Karl-Heinz Körbel, Jürgen Grabowski, Bernd Nickel, Bernd Hölzenbein, Rüdiger Wenzel.   Trainer: Dietrich Weise

Goals: Brooking (49, 77), Robson (68), Beverungen (88)

FINAL

**ANDERLECHT BRUSSEL
v WEST HAM UNITED LONDON 4-2** (1-1)

Heysel, Brussel 5.05.1976

Referee: Robert Charles Paul Wurtz (FRA)   Att: 51,296

ANDERLECHT: Jan Ruiter, Michel Lomme, Gilbert Van Binst (Cap), Hugo Broos, Jean Thissen; François Van der Elst, Arendt Haan, Ludo Coeck (32 Frank Vercauteren), Jean Dockx; Peter Ressel, Pieter Robert Rob Rensenbrink.   Trainer: Hans Croon (HOL)

WEST HAM: Mervyn Day; Keith Coleman, Thomas Taylor, William Bonds (Cap), Frank Lampard (46 Alan Taylor); John McDowell, Graham Paddon, Trevor Brooking, Patrick Holland; William Jennings, Keith Robson.   Trainer: John Lyall

Goals: Holland (28), Rensenbrink (43, 73 pen), Van der Elst (48, 88), Robson (69)

Goalscorers European Cup-Winners' Cup 1975-76:

8 goals: Rob Rensenbrink (Anderlecht Brussel)

6 goals: Muhamed Ibrahimbegović (Borac Banja Luka), Bernd Hölzenbein (Eintracht Frankfurt)

5 goals: François van der Elst (Anderlecht), Lex Schoenmaker (FC den Haag), Markarov (Ararat Erevan),

4 goals: Aad Mansveld (FC den Haag), Domenico Caso (Fiorentina), Kozerski (Stal Rzeszow), Keith Robson (West Ham United)

3 goals: Cetina (Borac Banja Luka), Grabowski, Nickel (Eintracht Frankfurt), van Leeuwen (FC den Haag), Horváth (Szombathely Haladas), Kaiser (RC Lens), Dalglish (Celtic Glasgow), Stendal (Sturm Graz), Brooking, Jennings, A. Taylor (West Ham United)

2 goals: van Binst (Anderlecht), Cochrane (FC Coleraine), Beverungen (Eintracht Frankfurt), Casarsa (Fiorentina), Fedor (Szombathely Haladas), Mujica (RC Lens), Miler (Stal Rzeszow), Bondarenko, Oganesian, N. Petrosian (Ararat Erevan), Blanc, Schykowski (Sachsenring Zwickau), Mané (Boavista Porto), Edvaldsson, Deans, Hood (Celtic Glasgow), Ashcroft (Wrexham United), Bonds, Holland, Paddon (West Ham United)

1 goal: Coeck (Anderlecht Brussel), Vrahimis (Anorthosis), Jurković, Kovačević, Kreso, Smileski, Vidacak, Marjanović (Borac Banja Luka), Rohmann (US Rumelange), McCurdy (Coleraine), Körbel, Kraus, Lorenz, Neuberger, Reichel, Wenzel (Eintracht Frankfurt), Giglio (FC Valletta), Skjønsberg (Skeid Oslo), Schönenberger, Demarmels (FC Basel), Jol, Perazić, van Vliet (FC den Haag), Speggiorin (Fiorentina), Farkas, Halmosi, Kereki, Király (Szombathely Haladas), Brophy (Home Farm), Hopquin, Janković, Llorens, Notheaux, Zuraszek (RC Lens), Lindholm, Tupasela (Reipas Lahti), Krantz, Lövfors (Djurgården Stockholm), Ganchev, Kostov (Slavia Sofia), Curylo, Krawczyk, Napieracz (Stal Rzeszow), S.Petrosian (Ararat Erevan), Dietzsch (Sachsenring Zwickau), Celso, Salvador (Boavista Porto), Capón, Becerra, Gárate, Ayala (Atlético Madrid), P.McCluskey, Callaghan, Wilson, McDonald (Celtic Glasgow), Lee, Sutton, Whittle, Griffiths, Davis (Wrexham United), Steiner, Jurtin, Kulmer (Sturm Graz), Lampard (West Ham United)

Own goal: Thissen (Anderlecht) for Rapid București

CUP WINNERS' CUP 1976-77

PRELIMINARY ROUND

CARDIFF CITY v SERVETTE GENÈVE 1-0 (0-0)

Ninian Park, Cardiff 4.08.1976

Referee: Alexis Ponnet (BEL) Attendance: 10,266

CITY: Ronald Healey, Frederick Pethard, Clive Charles, Alan Campbell (56 David Giles), Richard Morgan, Albert Larmour, John Buchanan, Douglas Livermore, Anthony Evans, Adrian Alston, Derek Showers.

SERVETTE: Karl Engel, Marc Schnyder, Lucio Bizzini, Franco Marchi, Gilbert Guyot, Umberto Barberis, Hansjörg Pfister, Kurt Müller (64 Jean-Christian Thouvenel), Martin Chivers, Alfred Hussner, Jean-Ives Valentini. Trainer: Peter Pazmandy

Goal: Evans (88)

SERVETTE GENÈVE v CARDIFF CITY 2-1 (0-1)

Stade des Charmilles, Genève 11.08.1976

Referee: Heinz Aldinger (W. GER) Attendance: 21,500

SERVETTE: Karl Engel, Marc Schnyder (75 Frantz Barriquand), Lucio Bizzini, Franco Marchi, Gilbert Guyot, Umberto Barberis, Hansjörg Pfister, Kurt Müller, Martin Chivers, Alfred Hussner (58 Jean-Christian Thouvenel), Jean-Ives Valentini. Trainer: Peter Pazmandy

CITY: Ronald Healey, Frederick Pethard, Clive Charles, Alan Campbell, Richard Morgan (67 Keith Pontin), Albert Larmour, Peter Sayer, Douglas Livermore, Anthony Evans, Adrian Alston, Derek Showers (71 William Anderson).

Goals: Showers (34), Bizzini (63), Pfister (87)

FIRST ROUND

MTK BUDAPEST v SPARTA PRAHA 3-1 (1-1)

Hungária, Budapest 14.09.1976

Referee: Günter Männig (E. GER) Attendance: 2,500

MTK: Béla Hornyák; Tibor Palicskó, Csaba Csetényi, István Nyirö (72 András Szigeti), János Siklósi; Béla Kovács, István Köhalmi, János Borsó; László Takács (72 János Liptak), Tibor Kiss, Jenő Kunszt. Trainer: Mihály Keszthelyi

SPARTA: Jan Postulka; Pavel Melichár, Zdenek Caudr, Václav Kotal, Oldrich Urban (78 Pavel Stratil), Frantisek Chovanec, Jan Busek, Bohumil Vesely, Jiří Klement, Milan Cermák (78 Jiří Rosicky), Jiří Nevrly. Trainer: Dušan Uhrín

Goals: Kunszt (20), Cermák (32), Kovács (49), Borsó (70)

SPARTA PRAHA v MTK BUDAPEST 1-1 (0-1)
Stadión na Letnej, Praha   29.09.1976
Referee: Josef Bucek (AUS)   Attendance: 6,000
SPARTA: Jiří Kislinger; Pavel Melichár, Zdenek Caudr, Jiří Rosicky (46 Pavel Stratil), Oldrich Urban, Frantisek Chovanec, Jan Busek, Václav Kotal, Jiří Klement, Jiří Nevrly (81 Jan Houdek), Milan Vdovjak.   Trainer: Dušan Uhrín
MTK: József Gáspár; Tibor Palicskó, Csaba Csetényi, István Nyirö, László Csorna; Béla Kovács, László Takács (81 Lajos Koritár), János Siklósi, Tibor Kiss, János Borsó, Jenő Kunszt.   Trainer: Mihály Keszthelyi
Goals: Kunszt (25), Urban (72)

CARDIFF CITY v DINAMO TBILISI 1-0 (0-0)
Ninian Park, Cardiff   15.09.1976
Referee: Ole Amundsen (DEN)   Attendance: 11,181
CITY: William Irwin, Frederick Pethard, Clive Charles, Alan Campbell (60 Showers), Richard Morgan, Albert Larmour, John Buchanan, Douglas Livermore, Anthony Evans, Adrian Alston (75 Peter Sayer), William Anderson.
DINAMO: David Gogia; Nodar Khizanishvili, Peruz Kanteladze, Zarbeg Ebralidze, Shota Khinchagashvili, Aleksandr Chivadze, Manuchar Machaidze, Revaz Chelebadze, Vladimir Gutsaev, David Kipiani, Vakhtang Kopaleishvili.   Trainer: Nodari Parsadanovich Akhalkatsi
Goal: Alston (73)

LIERSE SK v NK HAJDUK SPLIT 1-0 (1-0)
Stadion aan het Lisp, Lier   14.09.1976
Referee: Giulio Ciacci (ITA)   Attendance: 15,000
LIERSE SK: Carl Engelen, Roger Dierckx (85 Luc Soons), Dragan Popadic, Raymond van der Borght, Walter Ceulemans, Gyula Visnyei, Herman Helleputte, Dimitrije Davidovic, François Janssens, Jan Ceulemans, Flor Van Uytsel (69 Roger Roebben).
HAJDUK: Ivan Katalinić, Marin Kurtela, Mario Boljat, Vedran Rozić, Drazen Muzinić, Sime Luketin, Borisav Djordjević, Ivan Šurjak, Slaviša Žungul, Jure Jerković, Ivica Kalinić.   Trainer: Josip Duvančić
Goal: J. Ceulemans (31)

DINAMO TBILISI v CARDIFF CITY 3-0 (1-0)
Dinamo, Tbilisi   29.09.1976
Referee: Werner Spiegl (AUS)   Attendance: 100,000
DINAMO: David Gogia; Nodar Khizanishvili, Peruz Kanteladze, Zarbeg Ebralidze, Shota Khinchagashvili, Gocha Machaidze, Manuchar Machaidze, Revaz Chelebadze, Vladimir Gutsaev (44 Zurab Tsereteli), David Kipiani, Vakhtang Kopaleishvili.   Trainer: Nodari Parsadanovich Akhalkatsi
CITY: William Irwin, Frederick Pethard, Clive Charles, Brian Attley, Philip Dwyer, Albert Larmour, John Buchanan, Douglas Livermore, Anthony Evans, Adrian Alston (72 Peter Sayer), Derek Showers (72 William Anderson).
Goals: Gutsaev (23), Kipiani (73), Kanteladze (80 pen).

NK HAJDUK SPLIT v LIERSE SK 3-0 (1-0)
Hajduk, Split   29.09.1976
Referee: Vladimir Rudnev (USSR)   Attendance: 15,000
HAJDUK: Ivan Katalinic, Vilson Dzoni, Mario Boljat, Vedran Rozić, Luka Peruzović, Drazen Muzinić, Slaviša Žungul, Goran Popović, Borisav Djordjević, Jure Jerković, Ivan Šurjak.   Trainer: Josip Duvančić
LIERSE SK: Carl Engelen, Roger Dierckx, Dragan Popadic (44 Eddy Smets), Raymond van der Borght, Walter Ceulemans, Gyula Visnyei, Herman Helleputte (62 Herman Stuyck), Luc Soons, François Janssens, Jan Ceulemans, Flor Van Uytsel.
Goals: Žungul (34, 46), Jerković (55)

CSU GALAȚI v BOAVISTA PORTO 2-3 (0-2)
Galați   15.09.1976
Referee: Kostas Xanthoulis (CYP)   Attendance: 12,000
CSU: Gheorghe Tănase; Pasquale, Mihai Olteanu, Marta, Șarpe; Florin Păunescu, Dobre (46 Mihail Bejenaru), Georgescu; Teodor Cotigă (78 Dandu Ustabacief), Petre Marinescu, Valentin Kramer.   Trainer: Ion Zaharia
BOAVISTA: António José da Silva BOTELHO; Leonel TRINDADE (75 CELSO Luis de Matos), MÁRIO JOÃO (Cap), ARTUR Nogueira Ferreira, Artur AMARAL Reis; Manuel José Ferreira da Silva BARBOSA, FRANCISCO MÁRIO Silva (63 Alvaro CAROLINO Nascimento), ALBERTINO Eduardo Pereira, NOGUEIRA; Manuel Chagas "MANÉ", SALVADOR Luis Almeida.   Trainer: Mario Wilson
Goals: Olteanu (17 og), Albertino (35), Marinescu (48), Kramer (53), Mané (67)

BOAVISTA PORTO v CSU GALAȚI 2-0 (2-0)
Estádio do Bessa Porto   29.09.1976
Referee: John Hunting (ENG)   Attendance: 8,000
BOAVISTA: António José da Silva BOTELHO; ALBERTO Teixeira, Alvaro CAROLINO Nascimento, ARTUR Nogueira Ferreira, Artur AMARAL Reis; Manuel José Ferreira da Silva BARBOSA, FRANCISCO MÁRIO Silva, ALBERTINO Eduardo Pereira; Manuel Chagas "MANÉ", CELSO Luis de Matos, NOGUEIRA.   Trainer: Mario Wilson
CSU: Chiriazic; Pasquale, Mihai Olteanu, Paul Enache, Șarpe; Florin Păunescu, Mihail Bejenaru, Georgescu (46 Dobre), Victor Angelescu; Valentin Kramer, Petre Marinescu.   Trainer: Ion Zaharia
Goals: Mané (7, 42)

IRAKLIS THESSALONIKI v APOEL NICOSIA   0-0
Kautatzogleio, Thessaloniki   15.09.1976
Referee: Otto Anderco (ROM)   Attendance: 10,000
IRAKLIS: Grigoris Fanaras, Giorgos Kakarinelis (50 Giorgos Orfanidis), Petar Krivokuča, Manolis Toumpoglou, Kostas Mihailidis, Thanasis Hristoforidis, Giorgos Pantazis (76 Apostolos Matsoukatidis), Vaggelis Kousoulakis, Dimitris Gkesios, Zoran Antonijević, Nikos Pontikis.
Trainer: Milan Rimbas
APOEL: Giorgos Pantziaras, Haralampous Menelaou, Mihalis Kolokasis, Hristos Lillos (..Totis Kyprianides), Nikos Pantziaras, Stefanis Mihail, Leonidas Leonidou, Markos Markou, Nikos Kritikos, Andreas Stylianou, Andreas Miamiliotis (79 Takis Antoniou).   Trainer: Kasinti

S&FK BODØ/GLIMT v SSC NAPOLI 0-2 (0-1)
Aspmyra stadion, Bodø   15.09.1976
Referee: Anders Mattsson (FIN)   Attendance: 2,000
S&FK BODØ/GLIMT: Jon Abrahamsen, Einar Kolstad (61 Arnfinn Helgesen), Truls Klausen, Ivar Pedersen, Trond Tidemann, Arild Olsen, Harald Berg, Jacob Klette, Sturla Solhaug, Arne Hanssen, Terje Mørkved.
NAPOLI: Pietro Carmignani, Giuseppe Bruscolotti, Antonio La Palma, Tarciso Burgnich, Giovanni Vavassori, Andrea Orlandini, Giuseppe Massa, Antonio Juliano, Giuseppe Savoldi, Claudio Vinazzani, Walter Speggiorin.
Trainer: Bruno Pesaola
Goals: Speggiorin (14, 57)

**APOEL NICOSIA
v IRAKLIS THESSALONIKI 2-0** (2-0)
Makareio, Nicosia   29.09.1976
Referee: Velibor Ljujić (YUG)   Attendance: 3,000
APOEL: Giorgos Pantziaras, Haralampous Menelaou, Mihalis Kolokasis, Hristos Lillos (65 Ioannou), Nikos Pantziaras, Stefanis Mihail (88 Andreas Hailis), Leonidas Leonidou, Markos Markou, Nikos Kritikos, Andreas Stylianou, Andreas Miamiliotis.   Trainer: Kasinti
IRAKLIS: Grigoris Fanaras, Giorgos Kakarinelis, Petar Krivokuča, Manolis Toumpoglou (67 Apostolos Matsoukatidis), Kostas Mihailidis, Giorgos Kalaitzidis (46 Thanasis Hristoforidis), Giorgos Pantazis, Vaggelis Kousoulakis, Dimitris Gkesios, Zoran Antonijević, Nikos Pontikis.   Trainer: Milan Rimbas
Goals: Markou (17, 40)

SSC NAPOLI v S&FK BODØ/GLIMT 1-0 (1-0)
Stadio San Paolo, Napoli   29.09.1976
Referee: Anthony Briguglio (MAL)   Attendance: 15,000
NAPOLI: Pietro Carmignani, Giuseppe Bruscolotti, Antonio La Palma; Tarciso Burgnich, Giovanni Vavassori, Andrea Orlandini; Giuseppe Massa, Antonio Juliano (71 Vincenzo Montefusco), Giuseppe Savoldi, Claudio Vinazzani, Luciano Chiarugi.   Trainer: Bruno Pesaola
S&FK BODØ/GLIMT: Jon Abrahamsen (77 Per Christian Størkersen), Arnfinn Helgesen, Truls Klausen, Ivar Pedersen, Trond Tidemann, Arild Olsen, Harald Berg, Jacob Klette (65 Einar Kolstad), Sturla Solhaug, Arne Hanssen, Terje Mørkved.
Goal: Massa (35)

HAMBURGER SV v ÍB KEFLAVIK 3-0 (2-0)
Volksparkstadion, Hamburg   15.09.1976
Referee: Miroslav Kopal (CZE)   Attendance: 8,000
HSV: Rudi Kargus, Manfred Kaltz, Hans-Jürgen Ripp, Ole Björnmose, Peter Hidien, Horst Blankenburg, Arno Steffenhagen, Klaus Zaczyk, Willi Reimann, Hans Ettmayer, Georg Volkert.   Trainer: Kuno Klötzer
ÍB KEFLAVIK: Thorsteinn Ólafsson, L. Gunnarsson (46 Gunnar Jónsson), Astradur Gunnarsson, Einar Gunnarsson, Gudni Kjartansson, Gísli Torfason, Sigurdur Björgvinsson, Olafur Júliusson, T. Jónsson, Steinar Jóhansson, Fridrik Ragnarsson.
Goals: Zaczyk (5), Reimann (8), Hidien (78)

ÍB KEFLAVIK v HAMBURGER SV 1-1 (0-1)

Laugardasvöllur, Reykjavík   29.09.1976

Referee: Thomas Perry (NIR)   Attendance: 2,000

ÍB KEFLAVIK: Thorsteinn Ólafsson, Gunnar Jónsson, Astradur Gunnarsson, Einar Gunnarsson, Gudni Kjartansson, Gísli Torfason, Sigurdur Björgvinsson, Olafur Júliusson, T.Jónsson (85 Einar Asbjörn Olafsson), Steinar Jóhannsson, Fridrik Ragnarsson (60 Thórir Sigfusson).

HSV: Rudi Kargus, Manfred Kaltz, Detlef Spincke, Ole Björnmose, Peter Hidien, Horst Blankenburg, Hans-Jürgen Sperlich, Klaus Zaczyk (65 Horst Bertl), Willi Reimann, Kurt Eigl, Arno Steffenhagen.   Trainer: Kuno Klötzer

Goals: Hidien (39), S. Johannsson (72)

**ANDERLECHT BRUSSEL
v RODA JC KERKRADE 2-1 (0-1)**

Parc Astrid, Brussel   15.09.1976

Referee: John Carpenter (IRL)   Attendance: 20,000

ANDERLECHT: Jan Ruiter, François van der Elst, Erwin Vandendaele, Hugo Broos, Jean Dockx, Arie Haan, Ludo Coeck, Frank Vercauteren, Peter Ressel, Duncan McKenzie (67 Guido Palmers), Rob Rensenbrink.
Trainer: Raymond Goethals

RODA JC: Bram Geilman (46 Jo Van de Mierden), Leo Ehlen, John Pfeiffer, Steen Ziegler, Jef Blatter, Johan Meuser, Johan Toonstra, Dick Advocaat, Gerard Van der Lem, Dick Nanninga, Pierre Vermeulen.   Trainer: Bert Jacobs

Goals: Toonstra (8), Vercauteren (88), Rensenbrink (89)

**RODA JC KERKRADE
v ANDERLECHT BRUSSEL 2-3 (1-0)**

Gemeentelijk Sportpark Kaalheide, Kerkrade   29.09.1976

Referee: Erik Axelryd (SWE)   Attendance: 23,000

RODA JC: Jo Van de Mierden, Leo Ehlen (68 André Broeks), John Pfeiffer, Steen Ziegler, Jef Blatter, Johan Meuser, Johan Toonstra, Dick Advocaat, Gerard Van der Lem, Dick Nanninga, Pierre Vermeulen.   Trainer: Bert Jacobs

ANDERLECHT: Jan Ruiter (47 Jacky Munaron), François van der Elst, Hugo Broos, Erwin Vandendaele, Jean Dockx, Arie Haan, Michel de Groote (46 Jean Thissen), Ludo Coeck, Peter Ressel, Duncan McKenzie, Rob Rensenbrink.
Trainer: Raymond Goethals

Goals: Vermeulen (34), Rensenbrink (67), Van der Lem (72 pen), van der Elst (82, 85)

RAPID WIEN v ATLÉTICO MADRID 1-2 (1-0)

Prater, Wien   15.09.1976

Referee: Alfred Delcourt (BEL)   Attendance: 60,000

RAPID: Herbert Feurer, Christian Kautzky, Peter Persidis, Egon Pajenk, Werner Zarbach; Helmut Kirisits, Kurt Widmann (72 Johann Krejcirik), Emil Krause, Johann Krankl, Johann Pregesbauer (63 August Starek), Rainer Schlagbauer.
Trainer: Anton Brzezanczyk

ATLÉTICO: Miguel REINA Santos, MARCELINO Pérez Ayllón, José Luis CAPÓN González, Ramón Armando HEREDIA Dionisio, LUIZ Edmundo PEREIRA Pereira, Domingo BENEGAS Jiménez, Francisco AGUILAR Fernández, Ignacio Manuel SALCEDO Sánchez Blanca, RUBÉN Andrés CANO Martínez (85 ALBERTO Fernández Fernández), Eugenio LEAL Vargas, Rubén Hugo AYALA Zanabria.
Trainer: LUIS Aragonés

Goals: Krankl (19), Cano (80), Ayala (87)

ATLÉTICO MADRID v RAPID WIEN 1-1 (0-0)

Vicente Calderón, Madrid   29.09.1976

Referee: Patrick Partridge (ENG)   Attendance: 45,000

ATLÉTICO: Miguel REINA Santos, José Luis CAPÓN González, Rubén Osvaldo "PANADERO" DÍAZ Figueroa, Valentín Jorge Sánchez "ROBI", LUIZ Edmundo PEREIRA Pereira, EUSEBIO Bejarano Vilaroz, Eugenio LEAL Vargas, João Leiva Campos "LEIVINHA", RUBÉN Andrés CANO Martínez, Ramón Armando HEREDIA Dionisio (80 MARCELINO Pérez Ayllón), Rubén Hugo AYALA Zanabria.
Trainer: LUIS Aragonés

RAPID: Peter Barthold, Christian Kautzky, Peter Persidis, Egon Pajenk, Werner Zarbach; Helmut Kirisits, Kurt Widmann, Emil Krause, Johann Krankl, Johann Pregesbauer (59 Johann Krejcirik), Rainer Schlagbauer.
Trainer: Anton Brzezanczyk

Goals: Leivinha (70), Krejcirik (79)

1.FC LOKOMOTIVE LEIPZIG v HEART OF MIDLOTHIAN EDINBURGH 2-0 (2-0)

Brune-Plache-Stadion, Leipzig   15.09.1976

Referee: Nicolaos Zlatanos (GRE)   Attendance: 25,000

1.FC LOKOMOTIVE: Werner Friese, Gunter Sekora, Roland Hammer, Wilfried Gröbner, Joachim Fritsche, Wolfgang Altmann (12 Klaus Lisiewicz), Lutz Moldt, Henning Frenzel, Andreas Roth, Wolfram Löwe, Dieter Kühn.
Trainer: Manfred Pfeifer

HEARTS: James Cruickshank, James Brown, Robert Kay, Ralph Callachan (81 Campbell Fraser), John Gallacher, Dave Clunie, Kenny Aird, Graham Shaw (62 William Gibson), Drew Busby, Donald Park, Robert Prentice.

Goals: Sekora (2), Fritsche (17)

166

HEART OF MIDLOTHIAN EDINBURGH
v 1.FC LOKOMOTIVE LEIPZIG 5-1 (2-1)

Tynecastle Park, Edinburgh   29.09.1976

Referee: Jean Dubach (SWI)   Attendance: 18,000

HEARTS: James Cruickshank, James Brown, Robert Kay, Ralph Callachan, John Gallacher (48 James Jeffries), Dave Clunie, Kenny Aird (65 Graham Shaw), Drew Busby, William Gibson, Donald Park, Robert Prentice.

1.FC LOKOMOTIVE: Werner Friese, Gunter Sekora, Roland Hammer, Wilfried Gröbner, Joachim Fritsche, Andreas Roth, Lutz Moldt, Henning Frenzel (51 Andreas Bornschein), Klaus Lisiewicz, Wolfram Löwe, Dieter Kühn (75 Jürgen Schubert). Trainer: Manfred Pfeifer

Goals: Kay (12), Gibson (29, 86), Fritsche (42), Brown (75), Busby (76)

SOUTHAMPTON
v OLYMPIQUE MARSEILLE 4-0 (3-0)

The Dell, Southampton   15.09.1976

Referee: Pedro M. Urrestarazu Elordi (SPA)   Att: 19,150

SOUTHAMPTON: Ian Turner, Peter Rodrigues, James Steele, Nick Holmes, Malcolm Waldron, Melvyn Blyth, Hugh Fisher, Michael Channon (86 Pat Earles), Peter Osgood, Robert Stokes, Steven Williams.   Manager: Lawrie McMenemy

OLYMPIQUE: Gérard Migeon; Michel Baulier, Marius Trésor, Victor Zvunka, François Bracci; Jean Fernandez (89 Michel Albaladéjo), Raoul Nogues, Albert Emon, Hector Yazalde, Norberto Alonso, Georges Bereta (83 Nebojsa Zlatarić). Trainer: José Arribas

Goals: Waldron (30), Channon (33, 70 pen), Osgood (35)

BOHEMIANS DUBLIN v ESBJERG BK 2-1 (1-0)

Dalymount Park, Dublin   15.09.1976

Referee: G.J. Berrevoets (HOL)   Attendance: 10,000

BOHEMIANS: Mick Smyth, Eamonn Gregg, Fran O'Brien, Tommy Kelly (61 Augustine Grimes), Joe Burke, Niall Shelly, Noel Mitten, Padraig O'Connoer, Turlough O'Connor, Pat Byrne, Gerald Ryan.

ESBJERG: Ole Kjaer, Jan Hansen, Torben Luxhøj, Bert Hansen, Erik Brock Petersen, Jens Jørn Bertelsen, Holm, Olesen (81 Søren Fisker), Jørgen Toft, Flemming Iversen, Henrik Nielsen (85 Mørup).

Goals: Ryan (44), H. Nielsen (59), B. Hansen (62 og)

OLYMPIQUE MARSEILLE
v SOUTHAMPTON 2-1 (1-0)

Stade Velodrome, Marseille   29.09.1976

Referee: Heinz Aldinger (W. GER)   Attendance: 17,834

OLYMPIQUE: Gérard Migeon; Michel Baulier, Marius Trésor, Victor Zvunka, François Bracci; Michel Albaladéjo, Nebojsa Zlatarić (60 Georges Bereta), Raoul Nogues, Hervé Flores, Norberto Alonso, Albert Emon.   Trainer: José Arribas

SOUTHAMPTON: Ian Turner, Peter Rodrigues, James Steele, Steven Williams (71 Paul Gilchrist), Malcolm Waldron, Melvyn Blyth, Hugh Fisher, Michael Channon, Peter Osgood, Robert Stokes, David Peach.   Manager: Lawrie McMenemy

Sent off: Emon (85), Fisher (85)

Goals: Nogues (25), Peach (66), Emon (80)

ESBJERG BK v BOHEMIANS DUBLIN 0-1 (0-0)

Esbjerg, Idraetspark   29.09.1976

Referee: Lars-Åke Björck (SWE)   Attendance: 6,300

ESBJERG: Ole Kjaer, Jan Hansen, Svend Aage Clausen, Bert Hansen, Erik Brock Petersen, Jens Jørn Bertelsen, Søren Fisker (25 Hans Aage Nielsen), Torben Luxhøj, Kristian Østergaard, Flemming Iversen, Henrik Nielsen.

BOHEMIANS: Mick Smyth, Eamonn Gregg, Fran O'Brien, Tommy Kelly, Joe Burke, Niall Shelly, Eddie Byrne, Padraig O'Connor, Turlough O'Connor (36 Noel Mitten), Pat Byrne, Gerald Ryan.

Goal: Mitten (70)

AIK SOLNA
v GALATASARAY ISTANBUL 1-2 (1-0)

Råsunda, Solna   15.09.1976

Referee: Svein Inge Thime (NOR)   Attendance: 2,230

AIK: Ronny Gustavsson, Göran Åberg, Claes Marklund, Jan Olof Wallgren, Sanny Åslund, Rolf Zetterlund, Göran Göransson, Björn Lundberg, Sven Dahlqvist (64 Stefan Lundin), Lars Karlsson, Yngve Leback.

GALATASARAY: Nihat Akbay, Bülent Under, Ali Elveren, Güngör Tekin, Fatih Terim, Zafer Dinçer, Sükrü C., Mehmet Özgul, Gökmen Ozdenak, K. Mehmet Oguz, Şevki Şenlen.

Goals: Wallgren (40), Gökmen (65), K. Mehmet (78)

**GALATASARAY ISTANBUL
v AIK SOLNA 1-1** (1-0)

Istanbul 29.09.1976

Referee: Nicolae Petriceanu (ROM)   Attendance: 25,000

GALATASARAY: Nihat Akbay, Bülent Under, Ali Elveren (72 Müfit Erkaçap), Güngör Tekin, Fatih Terim, Zafer Dinçer, Sükrü C., K.Mehmet Oguz, Gökmen Ozdenak, Şevki Şenlen (68 Engin Tuncer), Mehmet Özgul.

AIK: Ronny Gustavsson, Stefan Wallen, Claes Marklund, Jan Olof Wallgren, Lars Karlsson, Rolf Zetterlund, Bo Sjögren (58 Stefan Lundin), Göran Göransson (82 Manni Thofte), Tom Källström, Björn Lundberg, Yngve Leback.

Goals: Gökmen (30), Wallgren (80).

**LEVSKI-SPARTAK SOFIA
v LAHDEN REIPAS 12-2** (5-1)

Levski, Sofia 16.09.1976

Referee: Paul Bonett (MAL)   Attendance: 5,000

LEVSKI-SPARTAK: Stefan Staikov, Nikolai Grancharov, Ivan Tishanski, Stefan Aladjov, Kiril Ivkov (70 Milko Gaidarski), Todor Barzov, Voin Voinov, Iordan Iordanov, Kiril Milanov, Pavel Panov, Krasimir Borisov (46 Emil Spasov).
Trainer: Vasil Spasov

REIPAS: Harri Holli, Raimo Hukka, Mikko Kautonen, Markku Repo, Timo Kautonen, Seppo Nordman (46 Pekka Kosonen), Harri Lindholm (71 Risto Rautemaa), Pertti Jantunen, Matti Sandberg, Lauri Riutto, Ari Tupasela.

Goals: Iordanov (12, 16), Sandberg (22), Milanov (30, 45, 60, 64, 66, 88), Panov (44, 73), Spasov (57, 86), Tupasela (59)

**CARRICK RANGERS
v ARIS BONNEVOIE 3-1** (0-0)

Seaview, Belfast 15.09.1976

Referee: Erik Fredriksson (SWE)   Attendance: 3,000

CARRICK RANGERS: Geoff Cowan, Jimmy Hamilton, Albert Macklin, George Matchett, Ronnie Whiteside, Eddie Connors, Tom Cullen, Davy Allen, Davy McKenzie (58 Gary Erwin), Gary Prenter, Jim Brown (83 Gary Reid).
Trainer: Jim Brown

ARIS: Claude Birenbaum, Roger Fandel, Adrien Lorge, Kieffer, Baus, Guy Weis, Pierrot Langers, Brück, Albert Pissinger, Roland Kalte, Hauer.

Goals: Prenter (56, 85), Pissinger (76), Connors (89)

**LAHDEN REIPAS
v LEVSKI-SPARTAK SOFIA 1-7** (1-4)

Olympic, Helsinki 29.09.1976

Referee: Torben Mansson (DEN)   Attendance: 485

REIPAS: Risto Parkkonen, Lauri Riutto, Mikko Kautonen, Markku Repo, Heikki-Pekka Lampi, Timo Kautonen, Harri Lindholm, Pekka Kosonen, Matti Sandberg, Seppo Nordman, Ari Tupasela.

LEVSKI-SPARTAK: Nikolai Iliev; Nikolai Grancharov, Ivan Tishanski, Milko Gaidarski, Kiril Ivkov (46 Vladimir Nikolchev), Todor Barzov, Voin Voinov, Blagoi Krastanov, Kiril Milanov, Pavel Panov (46 Ivan Stoianov), Emil Spasov.
Trainer: Vasil Spasov

Goals: Panov (13), Milanov (18, 24 pen, 27, 59 pen), Sandberg (34), Spasov (63), Krastanov (75)

**ARIS BONNEVOIE
v CARRICK RANGERS 2-1** (1-0)

Luxembourg 6.10.1976

Referee: Michel Vautrot (FRA)   Attendance: 1,500

ARIS: Claude Birenbaum, Roger Fandel, Adrien Lorge, Claude Colling, Baus, Guy Weis, Pierrot Langers (75 Steil), Brück, Marcel Weber (80 Bausch), Albert Pissinger, Roland Kalte.

CARRICK RANGERS: Geoff Cowan; Jimmy Hamilton (55 Davy McKenzie), Albert Macklin, Jim Brown, George Matchett, Ronnie Whiteside, Davy Allen, Eddie Connors, Gary Erwin, Gary Prenter, Tom Cullen (60 Gary Reid).
Trainer: Jim Brown

Goals: Weber (8), Langers (48), Erwin (54)

FLORIANA FC v SLASK WROCLAW 1-4 (0-1)

Empire Stadium, Valletta 23.09.1976

Referee: Gianfranco Menegali (ITA)   Attendance: 2,000

FLORIANA: Anthony Sultana (80 Debattista), George Ciantar, Edwin Farrugia, John Holland, Anton Camilleri, Ray II Farrugia (47 D.Holland), Ray I Farrugia, William Vassallo, George Xuereb, Raymond Xuereb, Frank Micallef.

SLASK: Zygmunt Kalinowski (70 Zbigniew Dlugosz), Marian Balcerzak (47 Roman Faber), Henryk Kowalczyk, Krzysztof Karpinski, Mieczyslaw Kopycki, Mieczyslaw Olesiak, Tadeusz Pawlowski, Ireneusz Garlowski, Zygmunt Garlowski, Józef Kwiatkowski, Janusz Sybis.

Goals: Z. Garlowski (30 pen), Kwiatkowski (47, 74), I. Garlowski (57), Vassallo (80)

SLASK WROCLAW v FLORIANA FC 2-0 (0-0)
Slask, Wroclaw   29.09.1976
Referee: Constantin Ghiţă (ROM)   Attendance: 4,000

SLASK: Jacek Wisniewski, Krzysztof Karpinski, Henryk Kowalczyk, Ireneusz Garlowski (72 Miroslaw Mitka), Jan Erlich, Jacek Nocko, Tadeusz Pawlowski, Jerzy Szymonowicz, Zygmunt Garlowski (46 Mieczyslaw Olesiak), Józef Kwiatkowski, Janusz Sybis.

FLORIANA: Anthony Sultana, George Ciantar, Edwin Farrugia, John Holland, Anton Camilleri, Frank Micallef, Ray I Farrugia, William Vassallo, George Xuereb, Raymond Xuereb, Powie Micallef (65 D. Holland).

Goals: Pawlowski (60), Erlich (70).

DINAMO TBILISI v MTK BUDAPEST 1-4 (0-1)
Dinamo, Tbilisi   20.10.1976
Referee: Constantin Ghiţă (ROM)   Attendance: 80,000

DINAMO: David Gogia; Nodar Khizanishvili, Vakhtang Chelidze, Shota Khinchagashvili, Zarbeg Ebralidze, Vakhtang Kopaleishvili, Manuchar Machaidze, Vakhtang Koridze, Revaz Chelebadze (46 Tariel Dvalischvili), Vitali Daraselia, Zurab Tsereteli.   Trainer: Nodari Parsadanovich Akhalkatsi

MTK: József Gáspár; András Szigeti, Csaba Csetényi, István Nyirö, Béla Kovács, László Csorna, László Takács, János Siklósi, Tibor Kiss, János Borsó, Jenő Kunszt.
Trainer: Mihály Keszthelyi

Goals: Siklósi (31), Takács (51, 76), Kiss (87), M. Machaidze (89)

SECOND ROUND

**SLASK WROCLAW
v BOHEMIANS DUBLIN 3-0** (1-0)
Slask, Wroclaw   20.10.1976
Referee: Rolf Haugen (NOR)   Attendance: 12,000

SLASK: Zygmunt Kalinowski, Krzysztof Karpinski, Henryk Kowalczyk, Mieczyslaw Kopycki, Wladyslaw Zmuda, Zdzislaw Rybotycki (46 Mieczyslaw Olesiak), Tadeusz Pawlowski, Jan Erlich (62 Roman Faber), Zygmunt Garlowski, Józef Kwiatkowski, Janusz Sybis.

BOHEMIANS: Mick Smyth, Eamonn Gregg, Fran O'Brien, Tommy Kelly, Joe Burke, Niall Shelly, E. Byrne, Padraig O'Connor, Turlough O'Connor, P. Byrne, Gerald Ryan.

Goals: Kwiatkowski (1), Sybis (50, 52)

**BOHEMIANS DUBLIN
v SLASK WROCLAW 0-1** (0-1)
Dalymount Park, Dublin   3.11.1976
Referee: Jacques Colling (LUX)   Attendance: 2,000

BOHEMIANS: Mick Smyth, Eamonn Gregg, Austin Brady, Tommy Kelly, Joe Burke, E. Byrne, Padraig O'Connor, Augustine Grimes, Turlough O'Connor, P. Byrne, Gerald Ryan (65 Noel Mitten).

SLASK: Zygmunt Kalinowski, Marian Balcerzak, Wladyslaw Zmuda, Krzysztof Karpinski, Mieczyslaw Kopycki (78 Ireneusz Garlowski), Mieczyslaw Olesiak, Tadeusz Pawlowski, Jan Erlich, Zygmunt Garlowski, Józef Kwiatkowski (65 Zdzislaw Rybotycki), Janusz Sybis.

Goal: Pawlowski (31)

MTK BUDAPEST v DINAMO TBILISI 1-0 (0-0)
Népstadion, Budapest   3.11.1976
Referee: Nikos Zlatanos (GRE)   Attendance: 10,000

MTK: József Gáspár; Tibor Palicskó, Csaba Csetényi, István Nyirö; Béla Kovács, László Csorna, László Takács (75 Lajos Koritár), János Siklósi, Tibor Kiss, János Borsó (78 László Burg), Jenő Kunszt.   Trainer: Mihály Keszthelyi

DINAMO: David Gogia; Nodar Khizanishvili, Peruz Kanteladze, Shota Khinchagashvili, David Mudzhiri, Aleksandr Chivadze, Manuchar Machaidze, Vakhtang Kopaleishvili, Vladimir Gutsaev, Vitali Daraselia, Zurab Tsereteli.   Trainer: Nodari Parsadanovich Akhalkatsi

Goal: Koritar (89)

**BOAVISTA PORTO
v LEVSKI-SPARTAK SOFIA 3-1** (2-1)
Estádio do Bessa, Porto   20.10.1976
Referee: Clive Thomas (WAL)   Attendance: 10,000

BOAVISTA: António José da Silva BOTELHO, Leonel TRINDADE, MARIO JOÃO, Alvaro CAROLINO Nascimento, ARTUR Nogueira Ferreira, Manuel José Ferreira da Silva BARBOSA, FRANCISCO MÁRIO P. Silva, ALBERTINO Eduardo Pereira, Manuel Chagas "MANÉ" (90 JORGE GOMES da Silva Filho), CELSO Luis de Matos, NOGUEIRA.   Trainer: Mario Wilson

LEVSKI-SPARTAK: Stefan Staikov; Nikolai Grancharov, Ivan Tischanski, Stefan Aladjov, Kiril Ivkov, Todor Barzov, Voin Voinov, Blagoi Krastanov (63 Iordan Iordanov), Kiril Milanov, Pavel Panov, Emil Spasov.   Trainer: Vasil Spasov

Goals: Celso (16, 83), Milanov (28), Mané (43)

**LEVSKI - SPARTAK SOFIA
v BOAVISTA PORTO 2-0** (2-0)

Levski, Sofia 3.11.1976

Referee: Orhan Cebe (TUR)   Attendance: 40,000

LEVSKI-SPARTAK: Nikolai Iliev; Nikolai Grancharov, Ivan Tishanski, Stefan Aladjov, Kiril Ivkov, Todor Barzov, Voin Voinov (75 Krasimir Borisov), Iordan Iordanov (65 Stefan Pavlov), Kiril Milanov, Pavel Panov, Emil Spasov. Trainer: Vasil Spasov

BOAVISTA: António José da Silva BOTELHO, ALBERTO Teixeira (37 Leonel TRINDADE, 60 JORGE GOMES da Silva Filho), MARIO JOÃO, Alvaro CAROLINO Nascimento, ARTUR Nogueira Ferreira, Manuel José Ferreira da Silva BARBOSA, NOGUEIRA, FRANCISCO MÁRIO P. Silva, ALBERTINO Eduardo Pereira, CELSO Luis de Matos, Manuel Chagas "MANÉ".   Trainer: Mario Wilson

Goals: Panov (13), Milanov (30)

**RSC ANDERLECHT BRUSSEL
v GALATASARAY ISTANBUL 5-1** (2-0)

Parc Astrid, Brussel 20.10.1976

Referee: Wolfgang Riedel (E. GER)   Attendance: 30,000

ANDERLECHT: Jan Ruiter, Jean Dockx, Hugo Broos, Erwin Vandendaele, Jean Thissen, Frank Vercauteren, François van der Elst, Arie Haan, Peter Ressel, Ludo Coeck, Rob Rensenbrink.   Trainer: Raymond Goethals

GALATASARAY: Nihat Akbay, Ali Elveren, Bülent Under, Güngör Tekin, Fatih Terim, K.Mehmet Oguz, Öner Kiliç, Zafer Dinçer, Gökmen Ozdenak, Mehmet Özgul, Şevki Şenlen.

Goals: Coeck (10), Vercauteren (19), Gökmen (49), Rensenbrink (52 pen, 72), Van der Elst (81)

**GALATASARAY ISTANBUL
v RSC ANDERLECHT BRUSSEL 1-5** (1-2)

Ali Sami Yen, Istanbul 3.11.1976

Referee: Sándor Petri (HUN)   Attendance: 40,000

GALATASARAY: Nihat Akbay, Müfit Erkaçap, Ali Elveren, Engin Tuncer, Fatih Terim, Zafer Dinçer, K.Mehmet Oguz, Bülent Under, Gökmen Ozdenak, Mehmet Özgul, Şevki Şenlen.

ANDERLECHT: Jan Ruiter, Jean Dockx, Hugo Broos, Erwin Vandendaele, Jean Thissen, Frank Vercauteren, François van der Elst, Arie Haan, Peter Ressel, Ludo Coeck, Rob Rensenbrink.   Trainer: Raymond Goethals

Goals: Rensenbrink (25, 64), Gökmen (35), Haan (42), Ressel (70), Coeck (71)

**HAMBURGER SV v HEART OF MIDLOTHIAN
EDINBURGH 4-2** (2-1)

Volksparkstadion, Hamburg 20.10.1976

Referee: Jarkov (USSR)   Attendance: 22,000

HSV: Rudi Kargus, Manfred Kaltz, Hans-Jürgen Ripp, Ole Björnmose, Peter Hidien (46 Detlef Spincke), Klaus Winkler, Hans-Jürgen Sperlich, Klaus Zaczyk, Willi Reimann, Kurt Eigl, Arno Steffenhagen.   Trainer: Kuno Klötzer

HEARTS: Brian Wilson, James Brown, Robert Kay, James Jeffries, John Gallacher, Dave Clunie, Kenny Aird (75 Campbell Fraser), Donald Park, Graham Shaw, Drew Busby, Robert Prentice (78 William Gibson).

Goals: Björnmose (2), Park (15), Eigl (35), Reimann (59), Kaltz (68), Busby (89)

**HEART OF MIDLOTHIAN EDINBURGH
v HAMBURGER SV 1-4** (0-2)

Tynecastle Park, Edinburgh 3.11.1976

Referee: Robert Wurtz (FRA)   Attendance: 25,000

HEARTS: Brian Wilson, James Brown, Robert Kay, James Jeffries (46 Campbell Fraser), John Gallacher, Dave Clunie, Graham Shaw, Drew Busby, William Gibson, Donald Park, Robert Prentice (77 Eamonn Bannon).

HSV: Rudi Kargus, Manfred Kaltz, Hans-Jürgen Ripp, Ole Björnmose, Horst Bertl, Horst Blankenburg (80 Klaus Winkler), Arno Steffenhagen (80 Hans-Jürgen Sperlich), Klaus Zaczyk, Willi Reimann, Kurt Eigl, Felix Magath.   Trainer: Kuno Klötzer

Goals: Eigl (13, 71), Magath (31, 81), Gibson (69)

**CARRICK RANGERS
v SOUTHAMPTON FC 2-5** (0-1)

Seaview, Belfast 20.10.1976

Referee: Ole Amundsen (DEN)   Attendance: 6,500

CARRICK RANGERS: Geoff Cowan, Jimmy Hamilton, Albert Macklin, Jim Brown (30 Gary Reid), George Matchett, Ronnie Whiteside, Davy Allen, Eddie Connors, Gary Erwin, Gary Prenter, Tom Cullen (85 Davy McKenzie). Trainer: Jim Brown

SOUTHAMPTON FC: Stephen Middleton, Peter Rodrigues, David Peach, Nick Holmes, Malcolm Waldron, Melvyn Blyth, Steven Williams, Michael Channon, Peter Osgood, James McCalliog (80 Pat Earles), Robert Stokes. Manager: Lawrie McMenemy

Goals: Stokes (10), Erwin (52), Channon (61, 85), Osgood (80), McCalliog (67), Prenter (83)

**SOUTHAMPTON FC
v CARRICK RANGERS 4-1** (2-1)

The Dell, Southampton   3.11.1976

Referee: Frans P. Derks (HOL)   Attendance: 15,130

SOUTHAMPTON: Stephen Middleton, Stephenl Mills, David Peach, Nick Holmes, Malcolm Waldron, Melvyn Blyth, Steven Williams, Austin Hayes, Peter Osgood, James McCalliog, Robert Stokes.   Manager: Lawrie McMenemy

CARRICK RANGERS: Geoff Cowan, Jimmy Hamilton, Albert Macklin, George Matchett, Ronnie Whiteside, Eddie Connors, Tom Cullen, Davy Allen, Gary Erwin (79 Tommy Wallace), Gary Prenter, Gary Reid.   Trainer: Jim Brown

Goals: Williams (16), Reid (36), Hayes (31, 74), Stokes (68)

APOEL NICOSIA v NAPOLI 1-1 (1-0)

Makareio, Nicosia   20.10.1976

Referee: Dimitar Parmakov (BUL)   Attendance: 12,000

APOEL: Giorgos Pantziaras, Haralampous Menelaou, Mihalis Kolokasis, Hristos Lillos, Nikos Pantziaras, Stefanis Mihail, Leonidas Leonidou, Makos Markou, Nikos Kritikos, Andreas Stylianou, Andreas Miamiliotis (20 Andreas Hailis).

NAPOLI: Pietro Carmignani; Giuseppe Bruscolotti, Antonio La Palma; Tarciso Burgnich, Giovanni Vavassori, Andrea Orlandini; Giuseppe Massa, Antonio Juliano, Giuseppe Savoldi, Claudio Vinazzani, Walter Speggiorin.
Trainer: Bruno Pesaola

Goals: Leonidou (37), Savoldi (87 pen)

ATLÉTICO MADRID v HAJDUK SPLIT 1-0 (0-0)

Vicente Calderón, Madrid   20.10.1976

Referee: Rudolf Frickel (W. GER)   Attendance: 20,000

ATLÉTICO: Miguel REINA Santos, José Luis CAPÓN González, Rubén Osvaldo "PANADERO" DÍAZ Figueroa, ALBERTO Fernández Fernández, LUIZ Edmundo PEREIRA Pereira, EUSEBIO Bejarano Vilaroz, Eugenio LEAL Vargas, João Leiva Campos "LEIVINHA", RUBÉN Andrés CANO Martínez, Ramón Armando HEREDIA Dionisio, Rubén Hugo AYALA Zanabria.   Trainer: LUIS Aragonés

HAJDUK: Ivan Katalinić, Marin Kurtela, Mario Boljat, Vedran Rozić, Luka Peruzović, Sime Luketin (69 Goran Popović), Slaviša Žungul, Drazen Muzinić, Borisav Djordjević, Jure Jerković, Ivan Šurjak.   Trainer: Josip Duvančić

Goal: Cano (49)

NAPOLI v APOEL NICOSIA 2-0 (2-0)

Stadio San Paolo, Napoli   4.11.1976

Referee: Luis A. Porem (POR)   Attendance: 15,000

NAPOLI: Pietro Carmignani, Giuseppe Bruscolotti, Antonio La Palma, Tarciso Burgnich, Giovanni Vavassori, Andrea Orlandini, Giuseppe Massa, Antonio Juliano (46 Claudio Vinazzani), Giuseppe Savoldi, Salvatore Esposito, Walter Speggiorin.   Trainer: Bruno Pesaola

APOEL: Giorgos Pantziaras, Haralampous Menelaou, Mihalis Kolokasis, Hristos Lillos, Nikos Pantziaras, Takis Antoniou, Leonidas Leonidou, Markos Markou, Nikos Kritikos, Andreas Stylianou, Andreas Miamiliotis.

Goals: Speggiorin (9), Massa (25)

QUARTER-FINALS

HAJDUK SPLIT v ATLÉTICO MADRID 1-2 (1-0)

Plinada, Split   4.11.1976

Referee: John Wright Paterson (SCO)   Attendance: 25,000

HAJDUK: Ivan Katalinić, Marin Kurtela, Mario Boljat, Vedran Rozić, Luka Peruzović, Sime Luketin, Slaviša Žungul, Drazen Muzinić, Borisav Djordjević, Micun Jovanić (77 Goran Popović), Ivan Šurjak.   Trainer: Josip Duvančić

ATLÉTICO: Miguel REINA Santos, José Luis CAPÓN González, Rubén Osvaldo "PANADERO" DÍAZ Figueroa, ALBERTO Fernández Fernández, LUIZ Edmundo PEREIRA Pereira, EUSEBIO Bejarano Vilaroz, Eugenio LEAL Vargas, João Leiva Campos "LEIVINHA" (70 Valentín Jorge Sánchez "ROBI"), RUBÉN Andrés CANO Martínez, Ramón Armando HEREDIA Dionisio, Rubén Hugo AYALA Zanabria (26 Francisco AGUILAR Fernández).   Trainer: LUIS Aragonés

Goals: Žungul (16), Ayala (53), Leal (59)

SLASK WROCLAW v NAPOLI 0-0

Slask, Wroclaw   2.03.1977

Referee: Erik Fredriksson (SWE)   Attendance: 45,000

SLASK: Zygmunt Kalinowski, Mieczyslaw Kopycki, Henryk Kowalczyk, Wladyslaw Zmuda, Krzysztof Karpinski (46 Mieczyslaw Olesiak), Roman Faber, Zygmunt Garlowski, Zdzislaw Rybotycki, Janusz Sybis, Tadeusz Pawlowski, Józef Kwiatkowski.

NAPOLI: Nevio Favaro; Giuseppe Bruscolotti, Tarciso Burgnich, Giovanni Vavassori; Sauro Catellani, Andrea Orlandini; Antonio Juliano, Salvatore Esposito, Claudio Vinazzani, Giuseppe Savoldi, Luciano Chiarugi.
Trainer: Bruno Pesaola

NAPOLI v SLASK WROCLAW 2-0 (1-0)

Stadio San Paolo, Napoli   16.03.1977

Referee: Orhan Cebe (TUR)   Attendance: 60,000

NAPOLI: Pietro Carmignani; Giuseppe Bruscolotti, Giovanni Vavassori; Tarciso Burgnich, Sauro Catellani, Andrea Orlandini (27 Salvatore Esposito); Giuseppe Massa, Antonio Juliano, Giuseppe Savoldi, Claudio Vinazzani, Luciano Chiarugi.   Trainer: Bruno Pesaola

SLASK: Zygmunt Kalinowski, Marian Balcerzak, Jan Erlich, Wladyslaw Zmuda, Krzysztof Karpinski, Mieczyslaw Kopycki, Zygmunt Garlowski, Tadeusz Pawlowski (81 Zdzislaw Rybotycki), Mieczyslaw Olesiak, Janusz Sybis (46 Roman Faber), József Kwiatkowski.

Goals: Massa (10), Chiarugi (49)

MTK BUDAPEST v HAMBURGER SV 1-1 (0-0)

Hungária, Budapest   2.03.1977

Referee: Jean Dubach (SWI)   Attendance: 14,000

MTK: József Gáspár; Tibor Palicskó, Csaba Csetényi, János Siklósi, Sándor Szijjártó; Béla Kovács, Tibor Kiss, János Borsó; László Takács, Lajos Koritár, Jenő Kunszt (73 Mihály Tulipán).   Trainer: Mihály Keszthelyi

HSV: Rudi Kargus, Manfred Kaltz, Horst Blankenburg, Peter Nogly, Peter Hidien; Ole Björnmose, Horst Bertl, Felix Magath; Arno Steffenhagen, Willi Reimann, Georg Volkert.   Trainer: Kuno Klötzer

Goals: Volkert (61), Borso (78)

HAMBURGER SV v MTK BUDAPEST 4-1 (2-0)

Volksparkstadion, Hamburg   16.03.1977

Referee: Marijan Rauš (YUG)   Attendance: 37,000

HSV: Rudi Kargus; Manfred Kaltz, Hans-Jürgen Ripp, Peter Nogly (59 Horst Blankenburg), Peter Hidien; Ole Björnmose (24 Casper Memering), Klaus Zaczyk, Felix Magath; Arno Steffenhagen, Willi Reimann, Georg Volkert.   Trainer: Kuno Klötzer

MTK: József Gáspár, Sándor Szijjártó, Csaba Csetényi, László Burg, András Szigeti; Béla Kovács, János Siklósi, János Borsó (80 Tibor Kiss), László Takács (65 Lajos Koritár), Mihály Tulipán, Jenő Kunszt.   Trainer: Mihály Keszthelyi

Goals: Reimann (10, 19), Kaltz (46 pen), Zaczyk (63), Siklósi (76)

ANDERLECHT BRUSSEL v SOUTHAMPTON 2-0 (1-0)

Parc Astrid, Brussel   2.03.1977

Referee: Walter Hungerbühler (SWI)   Attendance: 35,000

ANDERLECHT: Jan Ruiter, Jean Dockx, Hugo Broos, Gilbert van Binst, Jean Thissen, François van der Elst, Arie Haan, Ludo Coeck, Frank Vercauteren, Peter Ressel, Rob Rensenbrink.   Trainer: Raymond Goethals

SOUTHAMPTON: Peter Wells, Manny Andruszewski, Nick Holmes, Melvyn Blyth, David Peach, James Steele, Steven Williams, James McCalliog, Michael Channon, Peter Osgood, Edward McDougall.   Manager: Lawrie McMenemy

Goals: Ressel (30), Rensenbrink (83)

SOUTHAMPTON v ANDERLECHT BRUSSEL 2-1 (0-0)

The Dell, Southampton   16.03.1977

Referee: Rudolf Glöckner (E. GER)   Attendance: 24,337

SOUTHAMPTON: Peter Wells, Manny Andrusewski (85 Robert Stokes), David Peach, Nick Holmes, Melvyn Blyth, James Steele, Steven Williams, Michael Channon, Peter Osgood, James McCalliog (50 Austin Hayes), Edward McDougall.   Manager: Lawrie McMenemy

ANDERLECHT: Jan Ruiter, Gilbert van Binst, Hugo Broos, Erwin Vandendaele, Jean Thissen, Jean Dockx, François van der Elst, Arie Haan, Ludo Coeck, Peter Ressel, Rob Rensenbrink.   Trainer: Raymond Goethals

Goals: Peach (61 pen), MacDougall (77), Van der Elst (83)

LEVSKI-SPARTAK SOFIA v ATLÉTICO MADRID 2-1 (2-0)

Vasil Levski, Sofia   2.03.1977

Referee: Sergio Gonella (ITA)   Attendance: 65,000

LEVSKI-SPARTAK: Stefan Staikov, Nikolai Grancharov, Kiril Ivkov, Stefan Aladjov, Ivan Tishanski, Todor Barzov, Emil Spasov (46 Voin Voinov), Iordan Iordanov (62 Stefan Pavlov), Kiril Milanov, Krasimir Borisov, Georgi Tzvetkov.   Trainer: Vasil Spasov

ATLÉTICO: José PACHECO Gómez, MARCELINO Pérez Ayllón, Domingo BENEGAS Jiménez, LUIZ Edmundo PEREIRA Pereira, José Luis CAPÓN González, Ignacio Manuel SALCEDO Sánchez Blanca (85 Ramón Armando HEREDIA Dionisio), Eugenio LEAL Vargas, ALBERTO Fernández Fernández, Rubén Hugo AYALA Zanabria, RUBÉN Andrés CANO Martínez, Francisco Javier BERMEJO Caballero (76 Francisco AGUILAR Fernández).   Trainer: LUIS Aragonés

Goals: Tzvetkov (9), Milanov (38), Ayala (68)

**ATLÉTICO MADRID
v LEVSKI-SPARTAK SOFIA 2-0** (1-0)

Vicente Calderón, Madrid 16.03.1977

Referee: John Carpenter (IRL)   Attendance: 55,000

ATLÉTICO: Miguel REINA Santos, MARCELINO Pérez Ayllón (82 Rubén Osvaldo "PANADERO" DÍAZ Figueroa), José Luis CAPÓN González, Valentín Jorge Sánchez "ROBI", LUIZ Edmundo PEREIRA Pereira, Domingo BENEGAS Jiménez, Eugenio LEAL Vargas, ALBERTO Fernández Fernández, RUBÉN Andrés CANO Martínez, Francisco Javier BERMEJO Caballero (85 Francisco AGUILAR Fernández), Rubén Hugo AYALA Zanabria.   Trainer: LUIS Aragonés

LEVSKI-SPARTAK: Stefan Staikov, Nikolai Grancharov, Ivan Tishanski, Stefan Aladjov, Kiril Ivkov, Todor Barzov, Voin Voinov (64 Georgi Tzvetkov), Iordan Iordanov (68 Milko Gaidarski), Kiril Milanov, Pavel Panov, Krasimir Borisov.   Trainer: Vasil Spasov

Goals: Ayala (5 pen, 69 pen)

SEMI-FINALS

ATLÉTICO MADRID v HAMBURGER SV 3-1 (0-0)

Vicente Calderón, Madrid 6.04.1977

Referee: Nicolae Rainea (ROM)   Attendance: 30,000

ATLÉTICO: Miguel REINA Santos, MARCELINO Pérez Ayllón, LUIZ Edmundo PEREIRA Pereira, Domingo BENEGAS Jiménez, José Luis CAPÓN González (85 EUSEBIO Bejarano Vilaroz), Valentín Jorge Sánchez "ROBI", ALBERTO Fernández Fernández, Eugenio LEAL Vargas, Francisco Javier BERMEJO Caballero, RUBÉN Andrés CANO Martínez (88 Francisco AGUILAR Fernández), Rubén Hugo AYALA Zanabria.   Trainer: LUIS Aragonés

HAMBURGER SV: Rudi Kargus, Manfred Kaltz, Hans-Jürgen Ripp, Peter Nogly, Peter Hidien, Casper Memering, Klaus Zaczyk, Felix Magath, Arno Steffenhagen, Willi Reimann, Georg Volkert.   Trainer: Kuno Klötzer

Goals: Cano (52, 69), Magath (56), Leal (60)

HAMBURGER SV v ATLÉTICO MADRID 3-0 (3-0)

Volksparkstadion, Hamburg 20.04.1977

Referee: Ulf Eriksson (SWE)   Attendance: 61,000

HAMBURGER SV: Rudi Kargus, Manfred Kaltz, Hans-Jürgen Ripp, Peter Nogly, Peter Hidien (74 Ole Björnmose), Casper Memering, Felix Magath, Willi Reimann, Arno Steffenhagen, Ferdinand Keller (78 Kurt Eigl), Georg Volkert.   Trainer: Kuno Klötzer

ATLÉTICO: Miguel REINA Santos, MARCELINO Pérez Ayllón, LUIZ Edmundo PEREIRA Pereira, Domingo BENEGAS Jiménez, José Luis CAPÓN González, EUSEBIO Bejarano Vilaroz (46 ALBERTO Fernández Fernández), Valentín Jorge Sánchez "ROBI", Eugenio LEAL Vargas, Francisco Javier BERMEJO Caballero, RUBÉN Andrés CANO Martínez, Rubén Hugo AYALA Zanabria (69 Francisco AGUILAR Fernández).   Trainer: LUIS Aragonés

Goals: Capón (19 og), Reimann (22), Keller (27)

NAPOLI v RSC ANDERLECHT BRUSSEL 1-0 (0-0)

Stadio San Paolo, Napoli 6.04.1977

Referee: Robert Hélies (FRA)   Attendance: 90,000

NAPOLI: Pietro Carmignani, Tarcisio Burgnich, Giuseppe Bruscolotti, Giovanni Vavassori, Sauro Catellani, Antonio La Palma, Giuseppe Massa (79 Andrea Orlandini), Antonio Juliano, Giuseppe Savoldi, Claudio Vinazzani, Luciano Chiarugi (21 Walter Speggiorin).   Trainer: Bruno Pesaola

ANDERLECHT: Jan Ruiter, Gilbert van Binst, Jean Dockx, Hugo Broos, Erwin Vandendaele, Jean Thissen, François van der Elst, Arie Haan, Ludo Coeck, Peter Ressel, Rob Rensenbrink.   Trainer: Raymond Goethals

Goal: Bruscolotti (81)

ANDERLECHT BRUSSEL v SSC NAPOLI 2-0 (1-0)

Parc Astrid, Brussel 20.04.1977

Referee: Robert Matthewson (ENG)   Attendance: 38,000

ANDERLECHT: Jan Ruiter, Gilbert van Binst, Hugo Broos, Erwin Vandendaele, Jean Thissen, François van der Elst, Ludo Coeck, Arie Haan, Jean Dockx, Peter Ressel, Rob Rensenbrink.   Trainer: Raymond Goethals

NAPOLI: Pietro Carmignani, Tarcisio Burgnich, Sauro Catellani, Giovanni Vavassori, Antonio La Palma, Salvatore Esposito, Antonio Juliano, Claudio Vinazzani (76 Andrea Orlandini), Walter Speggiorin, Giuseppe Massa, Giuseppe Savoldi.   Trainer: Bruno Pesaola

Goals: Thissen (20), Van der Elst (57)

FINAL

HAMBURGER S.V.
v RSC ANDERLECHT BRUSSEL 2-0 (0-0)
Olympisch, Amsterdam   11.05.1977
Referee: Patrick Partridge (ENG)   Attendance: 58,000
HAMBURGER SV: Rudi Kargus; Manfred Kaltz, Peter Nogly (Cap), Peter Hidien, Caspar Memering; Hans-Jürgen Ripp, Ferdinand Keller, Wolfgang Felix Magath; Arno Steffenhagen, Willi Reimann, Georg Volkert.   Trainer: Kuno Klötzer
ANDERLECHT: Jan Ruiter; Gilbert Van Binst, Hugo Broos, Erwin Vandendaele (Cap), Jean Thissen; François van der Elst, Arendt Haan, Ludo Coeck, Jean Dockx (81 Ronny van Poucke); Peter Ressel, Pieter Robert Rob Rensenbrink.
Trainer: Raymond Goethals
Sent off: Nogly, Vandendaele
Goals: Volkert (80 pen), Magath (90)

1 goal: Bizzini, Pfister (Servette Genève), Cermák, Urban (Sparta Praha), J.Ceulemans (Lierse SK), Alston, Evans, Showers (Cardiff City), Marinescu, Kramer (CSU Galați), S.Johannsson (ÍB Keflavík), Toonstra, Vermeulen, Van der Lem (Roda Kerkrade), Krejcirik, Krankl (Rapid Wien), Sekora (Lokomotiv Leipzig), H.Nielsen (Esbjerg), Nogues, Emon (Marseille), K.Mehmet Oguz (Galatasaray), Weber, Langers, Pissinger (Aris Bonnevoie), Haan, Thissen (Anderlecht), Leonidou (Apoel Nicosia), Leivinha (Atlético Madrid), Albertino (Boavista Porto), Ryan, Mitten (Bohemians Dublin), Connors, Reid (Carrick Rangers), Gutsaev, Kipiani, Kanteladze, Machaidze (Dinamo Tbilisi), Vassalo (Floriana), Jerković (Hajduk Split), Björnmose, Keller (Hamburger SV), Kay, Brown, Park (Hearts), Krastanov, Tzvetkov (Levski Spartak), Tupasela (Lahden Reipas), Z.Garlowski, I.Garlowski, Erlich (Slask Wroclaw), Kovács, Kiss, Koritár (MTK Budapest), Bruscolotti, Chiarugi, Savoldi (Napoli), Waldron, McDougall, Williams, McCalliog (Southampton)

Own goals: Olteanu (CSU Galați) for Boavista Porto, B. Hansen (Esbjerg) for Bohemians Dublin, Capón (Atlético Madrid) for Hamburger SV

Goalscorers European Cup-Winners' Cup 1976-77:

13 goals: Kiril Milanov (Levski Spartak Sofia)

7 goals: Rob Rensenbrink (Anderlecht Brussel)

5 goals: François van der Elst (Anderlecht), Rubén Ayala (Atlético Madrid), Willi Reimann (Hamburger SV)

4 goals: Rubén Cano (Atlético Madrid), Manuel Chagas "MANÉ" (Boavista Porto), Gökmen Özdenak (Galatasaray), Felix Magath (Hamburger SV), Pavel Panov (Levski Spartak Sofia), Michael Channon (Southampton)

3 goals: Prenter (Carrick Rangers), Žungul (Hajduk Split), Eigl (Hamburger SV), Gibson (Hearts), Spasov (Levski Spartak), Massa, Speggiorin (Napoli), Kwiatkowski (Slask Wroclaw)

2 goals: Fritsche (Lokomotiv Leipzig), Wallgren (AIK Solna), Coeck, Ressel, Vercauteren (Anderlecht), Markou (Apoel Nicosia), Leal (Atlético Madrid), Celso (Boavista Porto), Erwin (Carrick Rangers), Hidien, Kaltz, Volkert, Zaczyk (Hamburger SV), Busby (Hearts), Iordanov (Levski Spartak), Borsó, Kunszt, Siklósi, Takács (MTK Budapest), Sandberg (Reipas Lahti), Pawłowski, Sybis (Slask Wrocław), Hayes, Osgood, Peach, Stokes (Southampton)

CUP WINNERS' CUP 1977-78

PRELIMINARY ROUND

GLASGOW RANGERS
v YOUNG BOYS BERN 1-0 (1-0)

Ibrox, Glasgow 17.08.1977

Referee: Alexis Ponnet (BEL)   Attendance: 30,000

RANGERS: Peter McCloy, William Jardine, John Greig, Thomas Forsyth, Colin Jackson, Alexander MacDonald, Thomas McLean (75 William Mackay), Robert Russell, Derek Parlane (65 Gordon Smith), Chris Robertson, David Cooper.

YOUNG BOYS: Gérard Weissbaum, Jakob Brechbühl, Peter Burkhardt, Gérard Castella, Jean-Marie Conz, Jost Leuzinger, Bernd Lorenz, Kurt Müller, Karl Odermatt, Heinz Rebmann, Peter Mast.   Trainer: Kurt Linder

Goal: Greig (40)

YOUNG BOYS BERN
v GLASGOW RANGERS 2-2 (0-1)

Wankdorf, Bern 31.08.1977

Referee: Riccardo Lattanzi (ITA)   Attendance: 17,000

YOUNG BOYS: Walter Eichenberger, Jakob Brechbühl, Gérard Castella (76 René Schmid), Jean-Marie Conz, Joseph Küttel, Bernd Lorenz, Kurt Müller (46 Jost Leuzinger), Karl Odermatt, Heinz Rebmann, Martin Trümpler, Rolf Vögeli.   Trainer: Kurt Linder

RANGERS: Peter McCloy, William Jardine, John Greig, Thomas Forsyth, Colin Jackson, Alexander MacDonald, Thomas McLean (18 Robert McKean), Robert Russell (51 Alexander Miller), Derek Johnstone, Gordon Smith, David Cooper.

Goals: Johnstone (42), Jackson (48 og), Leuzinger (61), Smith (72)

FIRST ROUND

LOKOMOTIV SOFIA
v RSC ANDERLECHT BRUSSEL 1-6 (0-4)

Vasil Levski, Sofia 13.08.1977

Referee: Sergio Gonella (ITA)   Attendance; 35,000

LOKOMOTIV: Rumiancho Goranov, Georgi Stefanov, Borislav Dimitrov, Georgi Bonev, Iordan Stoikov, Ventsislav Arsov, Angel Kolev, Traiko Sokolov (78 Rumen Manolov), Boicho Velichkov, Atanas Mihailov, Liuben Traikov (66 Valentin Svilenov).   Trainer: Vasil Metodiev

ANDERLECHT: Nico de Bree, Gilbert van Binst, Hugo Broos, John Dusbaba, Jean Thissen, Jean Dockx, François van der Elst (66 Ronny van Poucke), Arie Haan, Peter Ressel, Benny Nielsen (79 Danny Degelaen), Frank Vercauteren.   Trainer: Raymond Goethals

Goals: Van der Elst (2, 6, 11 pen, 60), B. Nielsen (32), Kolev (57), Van Poucke (89)

RSC ANDERLECHT BRUSSEL
v LOKOMOTIV SOFIA 2-0 (1-0)

Constant vanden Stock, Brussel 28.09.1977

Referee: César da Luz Dias Correia (POR)   Att: 20,000

ANDERLECHT: Nico de Bree, Gilbert van Binst, Hugo Broos, John Dusbaba, Jean Thissen, Jean Dockx, François van der Elst, Arie Haan, Ronny van Poucke (60 Jean-Claude Bouvy), Benny Nielsen, Frank Vercauteren.   Trainer: Raymond Goethals

LOKOMOTIV: Rumiancho Goranov; Georgi Stefanov, Borislav Dimitrov, Georgi Bonev, Iordan Stoikov, Ventsislav Arsov, Angel Kolev, Traiko Sokolov, Boicho Velichkov, Atanas Mihailov, Liuben Traikov.   Trainer: Vasil Metodiev

Goals: Van der Elst (41), Bouvy (80)

BEŞIKTAŞ ISTANBUL
v DIOSGYÖRI VTK 2-0 (0-0)

Inönü, Istanbul 14.09.1977

Referee: Josef Bucek (AUS)   Attendance: 25,000

BEŞIKTAŞ: Mete Bozkurt, Ahmet Börtücere, Zekeriya Alp, Niko Kovi, Ali Coban, Kemal Kiliç, Resit Kaynak, Hayri Kol, Blagoje Paunović, Mehmet Akpinar (64 Mithat Mihçi), Saban Kartal.

DIOSGYÖRI VTK: György Veréb; Gabor Szántó, József Salamon, László Kutasi, Ferenc Oláh, Ottó Váradi, Bela Tokár, Tibor Tomesz, Balász Magyar, Sándor Fükö, László Fekete.

Goals: Zekeriya (2), Paunović (83)

DIOSGYÖRI VTK
v BEŞIKTAŞ SK ISTANBUL 5-0 (3-0)

Diósgyör, Miskolc 28.09.1977

Referee: Kenneth H.Burns (ENG)   Attendance: 20,000

DIOSGYÖRI VTK: György Veréb; Borisz Teodoru, József Salamon, László Kutasi, Ferenc Oláh, Ottó Váradi (87 Gyula Grolmusz), Sándor Fükö, Jánosz Kerekes, Balász Magyar (87 Tibor Tomesz), György Tatár, László Fekete.

BEŞIKTAŞ: Mete Bozkurt, Ahmet Börtücere, Zekeriya Alp, Ali Coban (68 Mehmet Akpinar), Niko Kovi, Mithat Mihçi, Resit Kaynak, Hayri Kol, Blagoje Paunović, Kemal Kiliç, Saban Kartal.

Goals: Fükö (15), Olah (34 pen, 67), Fekete (44, 85)

**PAOK THESSALONIKI
v ZAGLEBIE SOSNOWIEC 2-0** (1-0)

Toumpa, Thessaloniki   14.09.1977

Referee: Alberto Michelotti (ITA)   Attendance: 30,000

PAOK: Mladen Fortoula, Aggelos Anastasiadis, Kostas Iosifidis, Kiriakos Apostolidis, Filotas Pellios, Giannis Pathiakakis, Panagiotis Kermanidis, Giannis Damanakis, Giorgos Kostikos, Giorgos Koudas, Kostas Orfanos (60 Giannis Gounaris).   Trainer: Billy Bingham

ZAGLEBIE: Zdzislaw Kostrzewa, Jerzy Zarychta, Stanislaw Zuzok, Eugeniusz Wiencierz, Wojciech Rudy, Zbigniew Seweryn, Wojciech Saczek, Witold Kasperski, Wladyslaw Szarynski (65 Tadeusz Narbutowicz), Wlodzimierz Mazur, Jerzy Dworczyk (72 Zdzislaw Napieracz).

Goals: Pellios (25), Anastasiadis (72 pen)

**ZAGLEBIE SOSNOWIEC
v PAOK THESSALONIKI 0-2** (0-0)

Stadion Ludowy, Sosnowiec   28.09.1977

Referee: Brian McGinlay (SCO)   Attendance: 12,000

ZAGLEBIE: Zdzislaw Kostrzewa, Stanislaw Zuzok, Eugeniusz Wiencierz, Wojciech Rudy, Zbigniew Seweryn, Wojciech Saczek, Wladyslaw Szarynski, Witold Kasperski (64 Wladyslaw Starosciak), Jerzy Dworczyk, Wlodzimierz Mazur, Wojciech Rabenda (46 Tadeusz Narbutowicz).

PAOK: Mladen Fortoula, Giannis Gounaris, Kostas Iosifidis, Aggelos Anastasiadis (88 Dimitris Kapousouzis), Kiriakos Apostolidis, Giannis Pathiakakis, Panagiotis Kermanidis, Giannis Damanakis, Giorgos Kostikos, Giorgos Koudas, Kostas Orfanos.   Trainer: Billy Bingham

Goals: Kermanidis (48), Damanakis (70)

**GLASGOW RANGERS
v FC TWENTE ENSCHEDE 0-0**

Ibrox, Glasgow   14.09.1977

Referee: Wolfgang Riedl (E. GER)   Attendance: 18,000

RANGERS: Peter McCloy, William Jardine, Alexander Miller, Thomas Forsyth, Colin Jackson, Kenneth Watson, Robert McKean, Robert Russell, Martin Henderson, Gordon Smith, David Cooper.

TWENTE: André van Gerven, Kees van Ierssel, Epi Drost, Niels Overweg, Piet Wildschut, Frans Thijssen, Kick van der Vall, Arnold Mühren, Jaap Bos (86 Theo Pahlplatz), Ab Gritter, Hallvar Thoresen.   Trainer: Anton Spitz Kohn

**FC TWENTE ENSCHEDE
v GLASGOW RANGERS 3-0** (2-0)

Diekmann, Enschede   28.09.1977

Referee: Erich Linemayr (AUS)   Attendance: 17,500

TWENTE: André van Gerven, Kees van Ierssel, Epi Drost, Niels Overweg, Piet Wildschut, Frans Thijssen, Kick van der Vall, Arnold Mühren, Jaap Bos, Ab Gritter, Hallvar Thoresen. .   Trainer: Anton Spitz Kohn

RANGERS: Stewart Kennedy, William Jardine, Thomas Forsyth, Colin Jackson, Alexander Miller, Robert Russell, Alexander MacDonald, Robert McKean, Derek Parlane, Gordon Smith, David Cooper.

Goals: Gritter (33), A. Mühren (41), Van der Vall (65)

1.FC KÖLN v FC PORTO 2-2 (1-0)

Müngersdorfer stadion, Köln   14.09.1977

Referee: Clive Thomas (WAL)   Attendance: 21,000

1.FC KÖLN: Harald Schumacher, Jürgen Glowacz, Roland Gerber, Bernd Cullmann, Herbert Zimmermann, Heinz Simmet, Herbert Neumann, Heinz Flohe, Roger Van Gool, Dieter Müller, Johannes Löhr (57 Holger Willmer).   Trainer: Hennes Weisweiler

FC PORTO: João Francisco FONSECA dos Santos, GABRIEL Azevedo Mendes, Adelino de Jesus TEIXEIRA, Fernando José António FREITAS Alexandrino, Alfredo Manuel Ferreira Silva MURÇA; RODOLFO Reis Ferreira, CELSO Luis de Matos, OCTÁVIO Joaquim Coelho Machado; Arsénio Rodrigues Jardim "SÉNINHO" (80 Carlos António Fonseca SIMÕES), José Francisco Leandro Filho "DUDA" (85 Francisco António Lucas VITAL), António Luis Alves Ribeiro de OLIVEIRA.   Trainer: José Maria PEDROTO

Goals: Löhr (5), Gabriel (59), Müller (65), Octávio (69)

FC PORTO v 1.FC KÖLN 1-0 (0-0)

Coimbra   28.09.1977

Referee: Patrick Partridge (ENG)   Attendance: 30,000

FC PORTO: João Francisco FONSECA dos Santos; GABRIEL Azevedo Mendes, Carlos António Fonseca SIMÕES, Fernando José António FREITAS Alexandrino, Alfredo Manuel Ferreira Silva MURÇA; RODOLFO Reis Ferreira, CELSO Luis de Matos, OCTÁVIO Joaquim Coelho Machado; José Francisco Leandro Filho "DUDA", António Luis Alves Ribeiro de OLIVEIRA, Arsénio Rodrigues Jardim "SÉNINHO".   Trainer: José Maria PEDROTO

1.FC KÖLN: Harald Schumacher, Herbert Hein, Roland Gerber, Gerd Strack, Herbert Zimmermann, Heinz Simmet, Heinz Flohe, Herbert Neumann, Roger Van Gool, Dieter Müller, Johannes Löhr (70 Dieter Prestin).   Trainer: Hennes Weisweiler

Goal: Murça (57)

HAMBURGER SV v LAHDEN REIPAS 8-1 (4-0)
Volksparkstadion, Hamburg 14.09.1977
Referee: Alojzy Jarguz (POL)   Attendance: 7,000
HSV: Rudi Kargus, Hans-Jürgen Ripp, Manfred Kaltz, Ivan Buljan, Casper Memering, Kurt Eigl, Kevin Keegan, Ferdinand Keller, Arno Steffenhagen, Willi Reimann, Georg Volkert. Trainer: Rudi Gutendorf
REIPAS: Harri Holli, Kari Horelli (52 Lauri Riutto), Mikko Kautonen, Markku Repo, Timo Kautonen, Risto Rautemaa, Ari Tupasela, Pekka Kanerva, Erkki Vihtilä, Heikki-Pekka Lampi (46 Matti Sandberg), Harri Lindholm.
Goals: Keller (6, 34, 38, 73), Volkert (18 pen), Buljan (60), Steffenhagen (77), Reimann (83), Sandberg (88)

LAHDEN REIPAS v HAMBURGER SV 2-5 (0-1)
Kisapuisto, Lahti 28.09.1977
Referee: Rolf Nyhus (NOR)   Attendance: 3,000
REIPAS: Harri Holli, Pekka Kanerva, Mikko Kautonen, Markku Repo, Timo Kautonen, Risto Rautemaa, Ari Tupasela, Matti Sandberg (60 Heikki-Pekka Lampi), Erkki Vihtilä, Lauri Riutto, Harri Lindholm.
HSV: Jürgen Stars, Casper Memering, Manfred Kaltz, Peter Nogly, Peter Hidien, Kevin Keegan, Willi Reimann (46 Horst Bertl), Felix Magath, Arno Steffenhagen, Ferdinand Keller, Georg Volkert (46 Kurt Eigl).   Trainer: Rudi Gutendorf
Goals: Volkert (45 pen), Keegan (52), Riutto (56, 74), Magath (69), Keller (71), Steffenhagen (89)

FC DUNDALK v HAJDUK SPLIT 1-0 (0-0)
Oriel Park, Dundalk 14.09.1977
Referee: Jan Keiser (HOL)   Attendance: 7,000
DUNDALK: Richard Blackmore, Jack McManus (44 Derek O'Brien), Jim McLaughlin, Thomas McConville, Brian McConville, Synan Braddish, Seamus McDowell, Tony Cavanagh, Mick Lawlor, Terence Flanagan, James Dainty (87 Noel King).
HAJDUK: Ivan Katalinić, Zoran Vujović, Mario Boljat, Sime Luketin, Luka Peruzović, Vedran Rozić, Slaviša Žungul (80 Borisav Djordjević), Zeljko Nikolić, Zlatko Vujovic, Drago Rukljac, Ivan Šurjak.   Trainer: Vlatko Marković
Goal: Flanagan (85)

HAJDUK SPLIT v FC DUNDALK 4-0 (1-0)
Hajduk, Split 28.09.1977
Referee: Charles Scerri (MAL)   Attendance: 10,000
HAJDUK: Ivan Katalinić, Zoran Vujović, Mario Boljat, Sime Luketin, Luka Peruzović, Vedran Rozić, Slaviša Žungul, Borisav Djordjević, Zlatlo Vujović (77 Davor Cop), Drago Rukljac (84 Nenad Salov), Ivan Šurjak.
Trainer: Vlatko Marković
DUNDALK: Richard Blackmore, Derek O'Brien, Jim McLaughlin, Brian McConville, Jack McManus, Synan Braddish, Noel King, Seamus McDowell, Terence Flanagan, Mick Lawlor, James Dainty.
Goals: Zl. Vujović (29), McManus (54 og), Rukljac (80), B. McConville (84 og)

**REAL BETIS BALOMPIÉ SEVILLA
v AC MILAN 2-0** (1-0)
Estadio Benito Villamarín, Sevilla 14.09.1977
Referee: Michel Kitabdjian (FRA)   Attendance: 40,000
BETIS: José Ramón ESNAOLA Laburu, Francisco BIZCOCHO Estévez, Antonio BENÍTEZ Fernández, Francisco Javier LÓPEZ García, Antonio BIOSCA Pérez, Jaime SABATÉ Mercadé, Juan Antonio GARCÍA SORIANO, Sebastián ALABANDA Fernández, José Antonio EULATE, Julio CARDEÑOSA Rodríguez (84 Gerrie Mühren), Attila Ladinszky (65 Juan Manuel COBO González).
Trainer: Rafael IRIONDO Aurtenechea
AC MILAN: Enrico Albertosi, Giuseppe Sabadini, Aldo Maldera III, Giorgio Morini, Simone Boldini, Maurizio Turone, Ugo Tosetto (78 Roberto Antonelli), Fabio Capello, Alberto Bigon, Giorgio Biasiolo (66 Egidio Calloni), Ruben Buriani.
Trainer: Nils Liedholm
Goals: García Soriano (13), Eulate (71)

**AC MILAN
v REAL BETIS BALOMPIÉ SEVILLA 2-1** (1-0)
Stadio San Siro, Milano 28.09.1977
Referee: Orhan Cebe (TUR)   Attendance: 60,000
AC MILAN: Enrico Albertosi, Fulvio Collovati, Aldo Maldera III, Giorgio Morini (80 Roberto Antonelli), Aldo Bet, Maurizio Turone, Ugo Tosetto, Fabio Capello, Egidio Calloni, Gianni Rivera, Ruben Buriani.   Trainer: Nils Liedholm
BETIS: José Ramón ESNAOLA Laburu, Francisco BIZCOCHO Estevez, Antonio BENÍTEZ Fernández, Francisco Javier LÓPEZ García, Antonio BIOSCA Pérez, Jaime SABATÉ Mercadé, Juan Antonio GARCÍA SORIANO, Sebastián ALABANDA Fernández (70 Gerrie Mühren), José Antonio EULATE (46 Hugo Cabezas), Julio CARDEÑOSA Rodríguez, Rafael GORDILLO Vázquez.
Trainer: Rafael IRIONDO Aurtenechea
Goals: Tosetto (35), Capello (59), López (62)

COLERAINE FC
v 1.FC LOKOMOTIVE LEIPZIG 1-4 (0-3)
The Showgrounds, Coleraine 14.09.1977
Referee: Magnus V.Petursson (ICE)   Attendance: 7,000
COLERAINE FC: Vincent Magee, Anthony Hutton, Thomas Connell, Liam Beckett, David Jackson, Ivan Murray, Peter Tweed, Trevor Porter, Michael Guy, Des Dickson, Frank Moffatt (71 Terry Mullan).
1.FC LOKOMOTIVE: Werner Friese (80 Siegfried Stötzner), Gunter Sekora, Thomas Dennstedt, Wilfried Gröbner, Joachim Fritsche, Wolfgang Altmann, Lutz Moldt, Henning Frenzel (68 Matthias Liebers), Lutz Eichhorn, Wolfram Löwe, Dieter Kühn.   Trainer: Manfred Pfeifer
Goals: Eichhorn (2), Kühn (35), Löwe (44, 69), Tweed (53)

VEJLE BK v PROGRÈS NIEDERCORN 9-0 (3-0)
Vejle Stadion 28.09.1977
Referee: Svein Inge Thime (NOR)   Attendance: 8,400
VEJLE: Niels Wodskou, Per Jørgensen, Knud Herbert Sørensen, Johnny Hansen, Flemming Serritslev, Gert Eg (75 Sten Juulsen), Poul Erik Østergaard, Jørgen Markussen (65 Steen Thycosen), Knud Nørregaard, Ib Jacquet, Ulrik Le Fèvre.
PROGRÈS: Daman, Yves Schwachtgen, Garzitto, Jean-Louis Margue, Jean Paul Bossi, Henri Bossi (58 Maurice Rante), Claude Mirkes (46 Hubert Meunier), Emile Lahure, Roland Thill, Albert May, Camille Neumann.
Goals: K.H. Sørensen (15), Østergaard (19, 85), Eg (20), Nørregaard (50, 59, 64), Jacquet (77), Thychosen (80)

1.FC LOKOMOTIVE LEIPZIG
v COLERAINE FC 2-2 (2-1)
Brune-Plache-Stadion, Leipzig 28.09.1977
Referee: Albert Victor (LUX)   Attendance: 16,000
1.FC LOKOMOTIVE: Werner Friese, Gunter Sekora, Roland Hammer, Thomas Dennstedt, Joachim Fritsche, Wolfgang Altmann, Lutz Moldt, Henning Frenzel, Lutz Eichhorn (61 Matthias Liebers), Wolfram Löwe, Dieter Kühn.   Trainer: Manfred Pfeifer
COLERAINE: Vincent Magee, Anthony Hutton, Eygene McNutt, Liam Beckett, David Jackson, Ivan Murray, Thomas Connell, Trevor Porter, Michael Guy, Des Dickson, Peter Tweed.
Goals: Altmann (14), Fritsche (33 pen), Guy (38, 66)

BRANN BERGEN v ÍA AKRANES 1-0 (1-0)
Brann, Bergen 14.09.1977
Referee: Ole Amundsen (DEN)   Attendance: 7,000
BRANN: Jan Knudsen, Helge Karlsen, Rune Pedersen, Atle Bilsback, Tore Nordtvedt, Atle Hellesø (80 Frode Larsen), Egil Austbø, Neil MacLeod, Ingvald Haseklepp, Steinar Aase, Bjørn Tronstad.
ÍA AKRANES: Jón Thorbjornsson, Björn Lárusson, Gudjón Thórdarson, Hordur Kári Johannesson (75 Gudbjorn Trygvasson), Johannes Gudjónsson, Jón Gunnlaugsson, Jón Askelsson, Jón Alfredsson, Pétur Pétursson, Kristinn Björnsson, Árni Sveinsson.
Goal: Aase (37)

PROGRÈS NIEDERCORN v VEJLE BK 0-1 (0-0)
Jos Haupert, Niedercorn 14.09.1977
Referee: Jan Peeters (BEL)   Attendance: 1,100
PROGRÈS: Daman, Yves Schwachtgen, Garzitto, Jean-Louis Margue, Jean Paul Bossi, Henri Bossi (84 Maurice Rante), Claude Mirkes, Emile Lahure, Roland Thill, Albert May, Camille Neumann.
VEJLE: Niels Wodskou, Per Jørgensen, Knud Herbert Sørensen, Gert Jensen, Flemming Serritslev, Gert Eg, Poul Erik Østergaard, Steen Thychosen, Jørgen Markussen, Knud Nørregaard, Ulrik Le Fèvre.
Goal: Thychosen (70)

ÍA AKRANES v BRANN BERGEN 0-4 (0-1)
Akranesvöllur 28.09.1977
Referee: Thomas Perry (NIR)   Attendance: 1,800
ÍA AKRANES: Jón Thorbjornsson, Gudjón Thordarson (77 Björn Lárusson), Hordur Kári Johannesson (77 Gudbjörn Trygvasson), Johannes Gudjónsson, Jón Gunnlaugsson, Jón Askelsson, Karl Thórdarsson, Jón Alfredsson, Pétur Petursson, Kristinn Björnsson, Árni Sveinsson.
BRANN: Oddvar Traeen, Helge Karlsen, Rune Pedersen, Atle Bilsback, Tore Nordtvedt, Egil Austbø, Neil MacLeod, Ingvald Haseklepp (72 Ingvar Dalhaug), Atle Hellesø, Steinar Aase, Bjørn Tronstad.
Goals: Aase (36, 62), Dalhaug (82), Tronstad (90)

CARDIFF CITY v FK AUSTRIA WIEN 0-0
Ninian Park, Cardiff   14.09.1977
Referee: Ulf Eriksson (SWE)   Attendance: 3,631
CITY: William Irwin, Brian Attley, Gerald Byrne, Alan Campbell, Paul Went, Keith Pontin, Douglas Livermore, Peter Sayer, Anthony Evans, Philip Dwyer, David Giles (67 Stephen Grapes).
AUSTRIA: Hannes Weninger; Robert Sara, Erich Obermayer, Josef Sara, Ernst Baumeister; Thomas Parits, Karl Daxbacher, Felix Gasselich, Julio Cesar Morales (77 Fritz Drazan); Hans Pirkner, Franz Zach.   Trainer: Hermann Stessl

ÖSTERS IF VÄXJÖ
v LOKOMOTÍVA KOŠICE 2-2 (0-1)
Värendsvallen, Växjö   28.09.1977
Referee: Mauri Laakso (FIN)   Attendance: 3,100
ÖSTERS IF: Göran Hagberg, Jan-Ivar Bergqvist, Mats Nordenberg, Arvidsson, Karl Gunnar Björklund, Björn Andersson (28 Peter Svensson), Per Olof Bild, Andreas Ravelli, Mats Nordgren, Tommy Svensson (20 Johnny Gustavsson), Tommy Evesson.
LOKOMOTIVA: Stanislav Seman, Andrej Mantic, Jozef Suchánek, Vladimír Dobrovic, Pavol Pencak, Ján Kozák, Peter Jacko (87 Ľudovít Zitnár), Józef Moder, Ladislav Jozsa, Peter Fecko, Gejza Farkas (80 Dušan Ujhely).   Trainer: M. Baranék
Goals: Jozsa (28), Bild (52), Evesson (60), Dobrovic (63)

FK AUSTRIA WIEN v CARDIFF CITY 1-0 (0-0)
West-Stadion, Wien   28.09.1977
Referee: Marian Kuston (POL)   Attendance: 8,000
AUSTRIA: Hubert Baumgartner; Robert Sara, Erich Obermayer, Josef Sara, Ernst Baumeister; Felix Gasselich, Karl Daxbacher, Alberto Martínez (69 Fritz Drazan); Franz Zach, Hans Pirkner, Julio Cesar Morales.   Trainer: Hermann Stessl
CITY: William Irwin, Frederick Pethard, Brian Attley (73 Douglas Livermore), Alan Campbell, Paul Went, Keith Pontin, Gerald Byrne, John Buchanan, Anthony Evans, Philip Dwyer (77 Raymond Bishop), Peter Sayer.
Goal: Baumeister (52)

AS SAINT-ETIENNE
v MANCHESTER UNITED 1-1 (0-0)
Stade Geoffroy Guichard, St.Etienne   14.09.1977
Referee: Ferdinand Biwersi (W. GER)   Attendance: 33,678
AS SAINT-ETIENNE: Yvan Curković; Gérard Janvion, Gérard Farison, Osvaldo Piazza, Christian Lopez; Dominique Bathenay, Patrick Revelli, Jacques Santini, Jacques Barthelemy (62 Dominique Rocheteau), Christian Synaeghel, Christian Sarramagna.   Trainer: Robert Herbin
MANCHESTER UNITED: Alexander Stepney, James Nicholl, Arthur Albiston, Samuel McIlroy (83 Ashley Grimes), Brian Greenhoff (78 Stewart Houston), Martin Buchan, Chris McGrath, David McCreery, Stuart Pearson, Steve Coppell, Gordon Hill.   Manager: Dave Sexton
Goals: Hill (78), Synaeghel (80)

LOKOMOTÍVA KOŠICE v ÖSTERS IF VÄXJÖ 0-0
Jeho-Cermell-Stadion Košice   14.09.1977
Referee: John Bartley Homewood (ENG)   Att: 15,000
LOKOMOTIVA: Stanislav Seman, Andrej Mantic, Jozef Suchánek, Vladimír Dobrovic, Gejza Farkas, Ján Kozák, Peter Jacko (67 Ľudovít Zitnár), Józef Moder, Ladislav Jozsa, Peter Fecko (88 Pavol Pencak), Dušan Ujhely.   Trainer: M. Baranék
ÖSTERS IF: Göran Hagberg, Jan-Ivar Bergqvist, Mats Nordenberg, Johnny Gustavsson, Karl Gunnar Björklund, Björn Andersson, Per Olof Bild, Peter Svensson, Peter Strömberg, Tommy Svensson (80 Mats Nordgren), Tommy Evesson.

MANCHESTER UNITED
v AS SAINT-ETIENNE 2-0 (1-0)
Home Park, Plymouth   5.10.1977
Referee: Francis Rion (BEL)   Attendance: 31,634
MANCHESTER UNITED: Alexander Stepney, James Nicholl, Arthur Albiston, Samuel McIlroy, Brian Greenhoff, Martin Buchan, Steve Coppell, James Greenhoff, Stuart Pearson (38 Chris McGrath), Lou Macari, Gordon Hill.   Manager: Dave Sexton
AS SAINT-ETIENNE: Yvan Curković; Gérard Janvion, Gérard Farison, Osvaldo Piazza, Christian Lopez, Dominique Bathenay, Dominique Rocheteau, Jacques Santini, Patrick Revelli, Christian Synaeghel, Christian Sarramagna.   Trainer: Robert Herbin
Goals: Pearson (32), Coppell (65)

**OLYMPIAKOS NICOSIA
v UNIVERSITATEA CRAIOVA 1-6** (0-1)
GSP, Nicosia 15.09.1977
Referee: Dimitar Parmakov (BUL)   Attendance: 4,000
OLYMPIAKOS: Hris Adamou; Loukas Kosta, Panikos Georgiou, Filippos Kalotheou, Nikos Omirou "Mavris"; Hrysanthos Lagos "Faketti", Panagiotis Prodromou (32 Lakis Mitsides), Giorgos Aristeidou; Nikos Kikas, Panikos Konstantinou, Kostas Tsouris (54 Evangelou). Trainer: Elly Fuchs
UNIVERSITATEA: Silviu Lung; Nicolae Negrilă, Nicolae Tilihoi, Costică Ştefănescu, Petre Purima; Nicolae Ungureanu, Ilie Balaci, Aurel Ţicleanu (75 Mircea Irimescu); Zoltan Crişan, Sorin Cîrţu, Dumitru Marcu (64 Rodion Cămătaru). Trainer: Constantin Deliu
Goals: Balaci (12, 54), Cîrţu (51), Marcu (61), Crişan (81), Aristeidou (84 pen), Irimescu (86)

DINAMO MOSKVA v FC VALLETTA 5-0 (4-0)
Dinamo, Moskva 29.09.1977
Referee: Stefanos Hatzistefanou (CYP)   Attendance: 10,000
DINAMO: Nikolai Gontar, Anatoli Parov, Sergei Nikulin (46 Aleksandr Maksimenkov), Aleksandr Makhovikov, Aleksandr Bubnov, Aleksei Petruschin, Vladimir Kazachyenok (66 Mikhail Gershkovich), Oleg Dolmatov, Andrei Yakubik, Nikolai Kolesov, Aleksandr Minaev.   Trainer: K. Blinkov
FC VALLETTA: Alfred Debono, Vincent Gauci, Tony Galea, Joe Abdilla, Dennis Fenech, Emanuel Farrugia, Vincent Magro, Tony Giglio, Charles Agius, Leonard Farrugia, Carlo Seychell.
Goals: Kolesov (7, 10, 27), Yakubik (9), Kazachyenok (49)

SECOND ROUND

**UNIVERSITATEA CRAIOVA
v OLYMPIAKOS NICOSIA 2-0** (1-0)
Central, Craiova 28.09.1977
Referee: Vojtech Christov (CZE)   Attendance: 12,000
UNIVERSITATEA: Gabriel Boldici; Nicolae Negrilă (65 Sorin Cîrţu), Nicolae Tilihoi, Costică Ştefănescu, Petre Purima; Nicolae Ungureanu, Ilie Balaci, Aurel Ţicleanu (70 Mircea Irimescu); Zoltan Crişan, Rodion Cămătaru, Dumitru Marcu. Trainer: Constantin Deliu
OLYMPIAKOS: Loukas Andreou; Andreas Papageorgiou, Filippos Kalotheou, Hrysanthos Lagos "Faketti", Loukas Kosta; Giorgos Aristeidou, Nikos Omirou "Mavris", Panagiotis Prodromou; Panikos Konstantinou, Kostas Tsouris (84 Koulis Eliades), Lakis Mitsides (55 Nikos Kikas).   Trainer: Elly Fuchs
Goals: Marcu (15), Cîrţu (83)

**FK AUSTRIA WIEN
v TJ LOKOMOTIVA KOŠICE 0-0**
West-Stadion, Wien 19.10.1977
Referee: Nikolai M. Dudin (BUL)   Attendance: 8,500
AUSTRIA: Hubert Baumgartner; Robert Sara, Erich Obermayer, Josef Sara, Ernst Baumeister; Karl Daxbacher, Herbert Prohaska, Felix Gasselich; Fritz Drazan (54 Thomas Parits), Hans Pirkner, Julio Cesar Morales (77 Wilhelm Pöll). Trainer: Hermann Stessl
LOKOMOTIVA: Stanislav Seman, Andrej Mantic, Jozef Suchánek (40 Pavol Pencak), Vladimír Dobrovic, Gejza Farkas, Ján Kozák, Peter Jacko, Józef Moder, Ladislav Jozsa, Peter Fecko, Dušan Ujhely (88 Ľudovít Zitnár).
Trainer: M. Baranék

FC VALLETTA v DINAMO MOSKVA 0-2 (0-0)
Empire Stadium, Valletta 17.09.1977
Referee: Tome Manojlovski (YUG)   Attendance: 6,000
FC VALLETTA: Alfred Debono, Vincent Gauci, Emanuel Farrugia, Joe Abdilla, Tony Galea, Dennis Fenech, Vincent Magro, Norman Darmanin-Demajo (80 Tony Giglio), Charles Agius (68 Batada), Leonard Farrugia, Carlo Seychell.
DINAMO: Nikolai Gontar, Anatoli Parov, Sergei Nikulin, Aleksandr Makhovikov, Aleksandr Bubnov, Aleksei Petruschin, Mikhail Gershkovich (70 Andrei Yakubik), Oleg Dolmatov, Vladimir Kazachyenok (84 Nikolai Kolesov), Aleksandr Minaev, Aleksandr Maksimenkov. Trainer: K. Blinkov
Goals: Kazachyenok (55), Maksimenkov (60)

**TJ LOKOMOTIVA KOŠICE
v FK AUSTRIA WIEN 1-1** (0-0)
Jeho-Cermell-Stadion, Košice 2.11.1977
Referee: Georges Konrath (FRA)   Attendance: 15,000
LOKOMOTIVA: Stanislav Seman, Andrej Mantic, Jozef Suchánek, Vladimír Dobrovic, Gejza Farkas, Ján Kozák, Ľudovít Zitnár, Józef Moder (83 Jiří Repík), Ladislav Jozsa, Peter Fecko, Dušan Ujhely (78 Pavol Pencak).
Trainer: M. Baranék
AUSTRIA: Hubert Baumgartner; Robert Sara, Erich Obermayer, Josef Sara, Ernst Baumeister; Karl Daxbacher, Herbert Prohaska, Felix Gasselich (62 Fritz Drazan); Hans Pirkner, Thomas Parits, Julio Cesar Morales.
Trainer: Hermann Stessl
Goals: Farkas (51 pen), Morales (69)

HAMBURGER SV
v RSC ANDERLECHT BRUSSEL 1-2 (0-1)

Volksparkstadion, Hamburg 19.10.1977

Referee: Robert Wurtz (FRA) Attendance: 56,000

HSV: Rudi Kargus, Manfred Kaltz, Peter Nogly, Casper Memering, Peter Hidien, Felix Magath, Kevin Keegan, Arno Steffenhagen, Ferdinand Keller, Willi Reimann, Georg Volkert. Trainer: Rudi Gutendorf

ANDERLECHT: Nico de Bree, Gilbert van Binst, Hugo Broos, John Dusbaba, Jean Thissen, Frank Vercauteren, François van der Elst, Arie Haan, Benny Nielsen (65 Jean Dockx), Ludo Coeck, Rob Rensenbrink. Trainer: Raymond Goethals

Goals: Coeck (22), Keller (69), Rensenbrink (88)

RSC ANDERLECHT BRUSSEL
v HAMBURGER SV 1-1 (1-1)

Constant vanden Stock, Brussel 2.11.1977

Referee: Franz Wöhrer (AUS) Attendance: 37,000

ANDERLECHT: Nico de Bree, Gilbert van Binst, Hugo Broos, John Dusbaba, Jean Thissen, Frank Vercauteren, François van der Elst, Arie Haan, Peter Ressel (58 Benny Nielsen), Ludo Coeck, Rob Rensenbrink. Trainer: Raymond Goethals

HSV: Rudi Kargus, Hans-Jürgen Ripp, Manfred Kaltz, Peter Nogly, Peter Hidien, Casper Memering, Kurt Eigl, Felix Magath, Kevin Keegan, Ferdinand Keller, Georg Volkert. Trainer: Arkoç Özcan

Goals: Van der Elst (10), Keegan (41)

DINAMO MOSKVA
v UNIVERSITATEA CRAIOVA 2-0 (2-0)

Dinamo, Moskva 19.10.1977

Referee: Timoleon Latsios (GRE) Attendance: 5,000

DINAMO: Nikolai Gontar; Anatoli Parov, Aleksandr Novikov, Sergei Nikulin, Aleksandr Makhovikov; Mikhail Gershkovich (60 Andrei Yakubik, 80 Oleg Kramarenko), Nikolai Kolesov, Aleksandr Bubnov; Aleksandr Minaev, Vladimir Kazachyenok, Aleksei Petruschin. Trainer: K.Blinkov

UNIVERSITATEA: Gabriel Boldici; Nicolae Negrilă, Nicolae Tilihoi, Costică Ştefănescu, Petre Purima; Aurel Ţicleanu (66 Mircea Irimescu), Sorin Cîrţu (85 Nicolae Ungureanu), Ilie Balaci; Zoltan Crişan, Rodion Cămătaru, Dumitru Marcu. Trainer: Constantin Deliu

Goals: Kazachyenok (23), Minaev (39)

UNIVERSITATEA CRAIOVA
v DINAMO MOSKVA 2-0 (2-0 2-0) (AET)

Central, Craiova 2.11.1977

Referee: Marijan Rauš (YUG) Attendance: 25,000

UNIVERSITATEA: Gabriel Boldici (54 Silviu Lung); Nicolae Tilihoi, Costică Ştefănescu, Petre Purima; Aurel Ţicleanu, Ilie Balaci, Aurică Beldeanu; Zoltan Crişan (63 Nicolae Negrilă), Sorin Cîrţu, Rodion Cămătaru, Dumitru Marcu. Trainer: Constantin Deliu

DINAMO: Nikolai Gontar; Anatoli Parov, Aleksandr Novikov (34 Andrei Yakubik), Aleksandr Bubnov, Aleksandr Makhovikov; Oleg Dolmatov, Nikolai Kolesov (77 Mikhail Gershkovich), Aleksei Petruschin, Aleksandr Maksimenkov; Vladimir Kazachyenok, Aleksandr Minaev. Trainer: K. Blinkov

Goals: Cîrţu (18), Beldeanu (27)

Penalties: Beldeanu (miss), 0-1 Kazachyenok, Ştefănescu (miss), 0-2 Maksimenkov, Negrilă (miss), 0-3 Petruschin

DIOSGYÖRI VTK v HAJDUK SPLIT 2-1 (0-1)

Diósgyöri stadion 19.10.1977

Referee: Alojzy Jarguz (POL) Attendance: 13,000

DIOSGYÖRI VTK: György Veréb; Gabor Szántó, József Salamon, László Kutasi, Ferenc Oláh, Ottó Váradi, Sándor Fükö, Jánosz Kerekes (76 István Szalai), Balász Magyar, György Tatár, László Fekete.

HAJDUK: Ivan Katalinić, Zoran Vujović, Mario Boljat, Davor Cop, Luka Peruzović, Vedran Rozić, Slaviša Žungul, Drazen Muzinić, Zlatko Vujović, Drago Rukljac, Ivan Šurjak. Trainer: Vlatko Marković

Goals: Muzinić (21), Tatár (56), Váradi (64)

HAJDUK SPLIT
v DIOSGYÖRI VTK 2-1 (1-0, 2-1) (AET)

Hajduk, Split 2.11.1977

Referee: Otto Anderco (ROM) Attendance: 20,000

HAJDUK: Ivan Katalinić, Zoran Vujović, Mario Boljat, Zlatko Vujović, Luka Peruzović, Vedran Rozić, Slaviša Žungul, Drazen Muzinić (49 Nenad Salov), Borisav Djordjević, Drago Rukljac (89 Davor Cop), Ivan Šurjak. Trainer: Vlatko Marković

DIOSGYÖRI VTK: György Veréb; Gabor Szántó, József Salamon, László Kutasi, Ferenc Oláh, Ottó Váradi, István Szalai, Jánosz Kerekes (46 Balász Magyar), Sándor Fükö, György Tatár, László Fekete (113 Gyula Grolmusz).

Goals: Zl. Vujović (16), Tatár (81), Rukljac (85 pen),

Penalties: 1-0 Salov, 1-1 Fúkö, 2-1 Boljat, 2-2 Tatár, 3-2 Šurjak, 3-3 Oláh, 4-3 Žungul, Váradi (miss), ... (miss), Magyar (miss)

1.FC LOKOMOTIVE LEIPZIG v REAL BETIS BALOMPIÉ SEVILLA 1-1 (1-1)

Zentralstadion, Leipzig   19.10.1977

Referee: Ole Amundsen (DEN)   Attendance: 18,000

1.FC LOKOMOTIVE: Werner Friese, Gunter Sekora, Roland Hammer, Wilfried Gröbner, Joachim Fritsche, Wolfgang Altmann (46 Thomas Dennstedt), Lutz Moldt, Henning Frenzel (81 Andreas Bornschein), Matthias Liebers, Wolfram Löwe, Dieter Kühn.   Trainer: Manfred Pfeifer

BETIS: José Ramón ESNAOLA Laburu, Francisco BIZCOCHO Estevez (17 Juan Manuel COBO González), Antonio BENÍTEZ Fernández, Jaime SABATÉ Mercadé, Antonio BIOSCA Pérez, Gerrie Mühren, Juan Antonio GARCIA SORIANO, Francisco Javier LOPEZ García, Hugo Cabezas, Julio CARDEÑOSA Rodríguez (82 Sebastián ALABANDA Fernández), Rafael GORDILLO Vázquez.   Trainer: Rafael IRIONDO Aurtenechea

Goals: López (14), Gröbner (30)

PAOK THESSALONIKI v VEJLE BK 2-1 (1-0)

Toumpas, Thessaloniki   2.11.1977

Referee: Nicolae Rainea (ROM)   Attendance: 27,400

PAOK: Mladen Fortoula, Giannis Gounaris, Kostas Iosifidis, Giannis Damanakis, Filotas Pellios (76 Dimitris Kapousouzis), Giannis Pathiakakis, Panagiotis Kermanidis, Giorgos Kostikos (67 Aristarhos Fountoukidis), Neto Gkouerino, Giorgos Koudas, Kostas Orfanos.   Trainer: Billy Bingham

VEJLE: Niels Wodskou, Per Jørgensen, Knud Herbert Sørensen, Gert Jensen, Torben Sørensen, Jan Knudsen, Flemming Serritslev, Gert Eg, Poul Erik Østergaard (76 Peter Hansen), Jørgen Markussen (23 Steen Thychosen), Ib Jacquet.

Goals: Orfanos (22), Jacquet (74), Kermanidis (80)

REAL BETIS BALOMPIÉ SEVILLA v 1.FC LOKOMOTIVE LEIPZIG 2-1 (1-0)

Estadio Benito Villamarín, Sevilla   2.11.1977

Referee: Marcel van Langenhove (BEL)   Attendance: 35,000

BETIS: José Ramón ESNAOLA Laburu, Francisco BIZCOCHO Estevez, Antonio BENÍTEZ Fernández, Francisco Javier LOPEZ García, Antonio BIOSCA Pérez, Jaime SABATÉ Mercadé, Juan Antonio GARCIA SORIANO, Sebastián ALABANDA Fernández, Alfredo MEGIDO Sánchez, Julio CARDEÑOSA Rodríguez, Rafael GORDILLO Vázquez.   Trainer: Rafael IRIONDO Aurtenechea

1.FC LOKOMOTIVE: Werner Friese, Gunter Sekora, Roland Hammer, Wilfried Gröbner, Joachim Fritsche, Wolfgang Altmann, Thomas Dennstedt, Henning Frenzel, Matthias Liebers, Andreas Bornschein (59 Lutz Eichhorn), Dieter Kühn.   Trainer: Manfred Pfeifer

Goals: García Soriano (37, 75), Liebers (62)

FC TWENTE ENSCHEDE v BRANN BERGEN 2-0 (1-0)

Diekmann, Enschede   19.10.1977

Referee: Antoine Quedeville (LUX)   Attendance: 13,000

TWENTE: André van Gerven, Kees van Ierssel, Epi Drost, Niels Overweg, Piet Wildschut, Frans Thijssen, Kick van der Vall, Arnold Mühren, Jaap Bos (78 Theo Pahlplatz), Ab Gritter, Hallvar Thoresen.   Trainer: Anton Spitz Kohn

BRANN: Oddvar Traeen, Helge Karlsen, Tore Nordtvedt, Rune Pedersen, Atle Bilsback, Egil Austbø (78 Terje Rolland), Atle Hellesø, Ingvald Haseklepp (71 Idressen), Neil MacLeod, Steinar Aase, Bjørn Tronstad.

Goals: Gritter (42, 55)

VEJLE BK v PAOK THESSALONIKI 3-0 (1-0)

Vejle Stadion   19.10.1977

Referee: Ferdinand Biwersi (W. GER)   Attendance: 4,700

VEJLE: Niels Wodskou, Per Jørgensen, Knud Herbert Sørensen, Johnny Hansen, Torben Sørensen, Jan Knudsen, Flemming Serritslev, Gert Eg, Knud Nørregaard (70 Poul Erik Østergaard), Jørgen Markussen, Ib Jacquet.

PAOK: Mladen Fortoula, Giannis Gounaris, Kostas Iosifidis, Kiriakos Apostolidis, Aggelos Anastasiadis (85 Aristarhos Fountoukidis), Giannis Pathiakakis, Panagiotis Kermanidis, Neto Gkouerino, Giorgos Kostikos, Giorgos Koudas, Kostas Orfanos.   Trainer: Billy Bingham (IRE)

Goals: Eg (12), Jacquet (70), Østergaard (83)

BRANN BERGEN v FC TWENTE ENSCHEDE 1-2 (1-0)

Brann, Bergen   2.11.1977

Referee: Eysteinn Gudmundsson (ICE)   Attendance: 15,000

BRANN: Oddvar Traeen, Helge Karlsen, Tore Nordtvedt, Rune Pedersen, Atle Bilsback, Egil Austbø, Atle Hellesø, Ingvald Haseklepp, Neil MacLeod, Steinar Aase, Bjørn Tronstad (81 Ingvar Dalhaug).

TWENTE: André van Gerven, Kees van Ierssel, Epi Drost, Niels Overweg, Piet Wildschut, Frans Thijssen, Kick van der Vall, Arnold Mühren, Jaap Bos, Ab Gritter, Hallvar Thoresen.   Trainer: Anton Spitz Kohn

Goals: Tronstad (19), Gritter (55), Thoresen (86)

FC PORTO v MANCHESTER UNITED 4-0 (2-0)

Estádio Das Antas, Porto   19.10.1977

Referee: Ernst Dörflinger (SWI)   Attendance: 60,000

FC PORTO: João Francisco FONSECA dos Santos; GABRIEL Azevedo Mendes, Carlos António Fonseca SIMÕES, Fernando José António FREITAS Alexandrino, Alfredo Manuel Ferreira Silva MURÇA; RODOLFO Reis Ferreira, Adelino de Jesus TEIXEIRA, OCTÁVIO Joaquim Coelho Machado; Arsénio Rodrigues Jardim "SÉNINHO", José Francisco Leandro Filho "DUDA", António Luis Alves Ribeiro de OLIVEIRA.
Trainer: José Maria PEDROTO

MANCHESTER UNITED: Alexander Stepney, James Nicholl, Arthur Albiston, Samuel McIlroy, Stewart Houston (35 Alex Forsyth), Martin Buchan, Chris McGrath (59 Ashley Grimes), David McCreery, Steve Coppell, Lou Macari, Gordon Hill.
Manager: Dave Sexton

Goals: Duda (7, 26, 52), Oliveira (59)

MANCHESTER UNITED v FC PORTO 5-2 (3-1)

Old Trafford, Manchester   2.11.1977

Referee: Heinz Einbeck (E. GER)   Attendance: 52,375

MANCHESTER UNITED: Alexander Stepney, James Nicholl, Arthur Albiston, Samuel McIlroy, Stewart Houston, Martin Buchan, Chris McGrath, Steve Coppell, Stuart Pearson, David McCreery, Gordon Hill.   Manager: Dave Sexton

FC PORTO: João Francisco FONSECA dos Santos; GABRIEL Azevedo Mendes, Carlos António Fonseca SIMÕES, Fernando José António FREITAS Alexandrino, Alfredo Manuel Ferreira Silva MURÇA; RODOLFO Reis Ferreira, Adelino de Jesus TEIXEIRA, OCTÁVIO Joaquim Coelho Machado (86 Francisco António Lucas VITAL); Arsénio Rodrigues Jardim "SÉNINHO", António Luis Alves Ribeiro de OLIVEIRA (58 CELSO Luis de Matos), José Francisco Leandro Filho "DUDA".
Trainer: José Maria PEDROTO

Goals: Coppell (7, 65), Murça (39 og, 90 og), Nicholl (45), Séninho (29, 85)

QUARTER-FINALS

VEJLE BK v FC TWENTE ENSCHEDE 0-3 (0-1)

Vejle Stadion   1.03.1978

Referee: Vojtech Christov (CZE)   Attendance: 4,300

VEJLE BK: Alex Nielsen, Per Jørgensen, Per Sørensen, Johnny Hansen, Torben Sørensen, Gert Eg, Poul Erik Østergaard (46 Sten Juulsen), Ib Jacquet, Carsten Andersen, Jan Knudsen (46 Ulrik Le Fèvre), Steen Thychosen.

TWENTE: André van Gerven, Kees van Ierssel, Epi Drost, Niels Overweg, Piet Wildschut, Frans Thijssen, Kick van der Vall, Arnold Mühren, Jaap Bos, Ab Gritter, Hallvar Thoresen.
Trainer: Anton Spitz Kohn

Goals: A. Mühren (26), Gritter (77), Thijssen (86)

FC TWENTE ENSCHEDE v VEJLE BK 4-0 (3-0)

Diekmann, Enschede   15.03.1978

Referee: Alojzy Jarguz (POL)   Attendance: 12,000

TWENTE: André van Gerven, Kees van Ierssel, Epi Drost, Niels Overweg, Piet Wildschut, Frans Thijssen, Kick van der Vall, Arnold Mühren, Jaap Bos (.. Ron van Oostrom), Ab Gritter, Hallvar Thoresen (60 Theo Pahlplatz).
Trainer: Anton Spitz Kohn

VEJLE BK: Alex Nielsen, Per Jørgensen, Per Sørensen, Johnny Hansen, Torben Sørensen, Gert Eg, Steen Thychosen, Ib Jacquet, Carsten Andersen, Jan Knudsen, Ulrik Le Fèvre (46 Poul Erik Østergaard).

Goals: Thijssen (8), Overweg (15), Gritter (19), Van der Vall (89)

FK AUSTRIA WIEN v NK HAJDUK SPLIT 1-1 (0-0)

Prater, Wien   2.03.1978

Referee: Sergio Gonella (ITA)   Attendance: 13,000

AUSTRIA: Hubert Baumgartner; Robert Sara, Erich Obermayer, Josef Sara, Ernst Baumeister; Herbert Prohaska, Karl Daxbacher, Alberto Martínez (56 Felix Gasselich); Thomas Parits, Hans Pirkner, Julio Cesar Morales.
Trainer: Hermann Stessl

HAJDUK: Ivan Katalinić, Vilson Dzoni, Mario Boljat, Drazen Muzinić, Luka Peruzović, Vedran Rozić, Davor Cop, Jure Jerković, Borisav Djordjević, Drago Rukljac, Ivan Šurjak (74 Zoran Vujovic).   Trainer: Vlatko Marković

Goals: Parits (62), Šurjak (66)

HAJDUK SPLIT v AUSTRIA WIEN 1-1 (1-0, 1-1) (AET)

Hajduk, Split   15.03.1978

Referee: Ferdinand Biwersi (W. GER)   Attendance: 25,000

HAJDUK: Ivan Katalinić, Vilson Dzoni, Vedran Rozić, Marijan Zovko, Mario Boljat, Davor Cop, Jure Jerković, Drago Rukljac (91 Nenad Salov), Drazen Muzinić, Slaviša Žungul, Ivan Šurjak.   Trainer: Vlatko Marković

AUSTRIA: Hubert Baumgartner, Robert Sara, Erich Obermayer, Josef Sara, Ernst Baumeister; Karl Daxbacher, Herbert Prohaska, Felix Gasselich; Thomas Parits, Hans Pirkner (91 Fritz Drazan), Julio Cesar Morales.
Trainer: Hermann Stessl

Goals: Cop (20), Daxbacher (56)

Penalties: 0-1 Parits, Salov (miss), 0-2 Prohaska, Jerkovic (miss), 0-3 Drazan, Cop (miss)

**REAL BETIS BALOMPIÉ SEVILLA
v DINAMO MOSKVA 0-0**

Estadio Benito Villamarín, Sevilla 2.03.1978

Referee: Ian M.D. Foote (SCO)   Attendance: 50,000

BETIS: José Ramón ESNAOLA Laburu, Jaime SABATÉ Mercadé, Rafael GORDILLO Vázquez, Francisco Javier LÓPEZ García, Antonio BIOSCA Pérez, Gerrie Mühren (84 Francisco BIZCOCHO Estevez), Juan Antonio GARCÍA SORIANO (75 Rafael Sánchez DEL POZO), Sebastián ALABANDA Fernández, José Antonio EULATE, Julio CARDEÑOSA Rodríguez, Eduardo ANZARDA Álvarez.
Trainer: Rafael IRIONDO Aurtenechea

DINAMO: Nikolai Gontar, Anatoli Parov, Oleg Dolmatov, Aleksandr Bubnov, Aleksandr Novikov, Aleksandr Minaev, Aleksandr Maksimenkov, Aleksei Petruschin, Andrei Yakubik, Mikhail Gerschkovich, Vladimir Kazachyenok.
Trainer: Aleksandr Sevidov

DINAMO MOSKVA v REAL BETIS 3-0 (0-0)

Dinamo, Tbilisi 15.03.1978

Referee: Svein Inge Thime (NOR)   Attendance: 60,000

DINAMO: Nikolai Gontar (87 Vladimir Pilgui), Anatoli Parov (87 Sergei Nikulin), Vladimir Kazachyenok, Aleksandr Makhovikov, Aleksandr Bubnov, Aleksei Petruschin, Mikhail Gershkovich, Oleg Dolmatov, Andrei Yakubik, Aleksandr Maksimenkov, Aleksandr Minaev.   Trainer: A. Sevidov

BETIS: José Ramón ESNAOLA Laburu, Francisco BIZCOCHO Estevez, Juan Manuel COBO González (30 Rafael Sánchez DEL POZO), Gerrie Mühren, Antonio BIOSCA Pérez, Francisco Javier LÓPEZ García, Juan Antonio GARCÍA SORIANO (82 Eduardo ANZARDA Álvarez), Sebastián ALABANDA Fernández, Hugo Cabezas, Julio CARDEÑOSA Rodríguez, Rafael GORDILLO Vázquez.
Trainer: Rafael IRIONDO Aurtenechea

Goals: Gerschkovich (57), Kazachyenok (61), Maksimenkov (82)

FC PORTO v ANDERLECHT BRUSSEL 1-0 (1-0)

Torre das Antas, Porto 2.03.1978

Referee: John Carpenter (IRL)   Attendance: 55,000

FC PORTO: João Francisco FONSECA dos Santos; GABRIEL Azevedo Mendes, Adelino de Jesus TEIXEIRA, Carlos António Fonseca SIMÕES, Alfredo Manuel Ferreira Silva MURÇA; RODOLFO Reis Ferreira, António Luis Alves Ribeiro de OLIVEIRA, OCTÁVIO Joaquim Coelho Machado (62 Antonio Lima "TAÍ"); Arsénio Rodrigues Jardim "SÉNINHO", FERNANDO Mendes Soares GOMES, Francisco António Lucas VITAL (88 Antonio da Silva "TONINHO METRALHA").
Trainer: José Maria PEDROTO

ANDERLECHT: Nico de Bree, Gilbert van Binst, Hugo Broos, John Dusbaba, Jean Thissen, Arie Haan, François van der Elst, Ludo Coeck, Frank Vercauteren, Peter Ressel, Rob Rensenbrink.   Trainer: Raymond Goethals
Goal: Gomes (36)

ANDERLECHT BRUSSEL v FC PORTO 3-0 (2-0)

Constant vanden Stock, Brussel 15.03.1978

Referee: Walter Hungerbühler (SWI)   Attendance: 35,000

ANDERLECHT: Nico de Bree, Gilbert van Binst, Hugo Broos, John Dusbaba, Jean Thissen, Frank Vercauteren, François van der Elst, Arie Haan, Benny Nielsen, Ludo Coeck, Rob Rensenbrink.   Trainer: Raymond Goethals

FC PORTO: João Francisco FONSECA dos Santos; GABRIEL Azevedo Mendes, Adelino de Jesus TEIXEIRA, Carlos António Fonseca SIMÕES, Alfredo Manuel Ferreira Silva MURÇA; CELSO Luis de Matos (46 Fernando Mendes Soares GOMES), OCTÁVIO Joaquim Coelho Machado, ADEMIR Vieira, José Francisco Leandro Filho "DUDA"; António Luis Alves Ribeiro de OLIVEIRA, Arsénio Rodrigues Jardim "SÉNINHO" (65 Francisco António Lucas VITAL).
Trainer: José Maria PEDROTO

Goals: Rensenbrink (25 pen), Nielsen (33), Vercauteren (83)

SEMI-FINALS

**FC TWENTE ENSCHEDE
v ANDERLECHT BRUSSEL 0-1** (0-0)

Diekmann, Enschede 29.03.1978

Referee: Adolf Prokop (E. GER)   Attendance: 22,000

TWENTE: André van Gerven, Kees van Ierssel, Epi Drost, Niels Overweg, Piet Wildschut, Frans Thijssen, (.. Theo Pahlplatz), Kick van der Vall, Arnold Mühren, Jaap Bos, Ab Gritter, Hallvar Thoresen.   Trainer: Anton Spitz Kohn

ANDERLECHT: Nico de Bree, Gilbert van Binst, John Dusbaba, Jean Thissen, Hugo Broos, François van der Elst, Arie Haan, Frank Vercauteren, Benny Nielsen (.. Jean Dockx), Ludo Coeck, Rob Rensenbrink.   Trainer: Raymond Goethals

Goal: B. Nielsen (51)

**ANDERLECHT BRUSSEL
v FC TWENTE ENSCHEDE 2-0** (1-0)

Constant vanden Stock, Brussel 12.04.1978

Referee: Clive Thomas (WAL)   Attendance: 32,000

ANDERLECHT: Nico de Bree, Gilbert van Binst, John Dusbaba, Jean Thissen, Hugo Broos, François van der Elst, Arie Haan, Frank Vercauteren, Benny Nielsen, Ludo Coeck, Rob Rensenbrink.   Trainer: Raymond Goethals

TWENTE: André van Gerven, Kees van Ierssel, Epi Drost (68 Theo Pahlplatz), Niels Overweg, Harry Bruggink, Frans Thijssen, Kick van der Vall, Arnold Mühren, Piet Wildschut (.. Ron van Oostrom), Ab Gritter, Hallvar Thoresen.
Trainer: Anton Spitz Kohn

Goals: Haan (31), Rensenbrink (56 pen)

DINAMO MOSKVA v FK AUSTRIA WIEN 2-1 (0-1)
Dinamo, Tbilisi 29.03.1978
Referee: Dogan Babacan (TUR)   Attendance: 65,000

DINAMO: Nikolai Gontar, Anatoli Parov, Vladimir Kazachyenok, Aleksandr Makhovikov, Aleksandr Bubnov, Aleksei Petruschin (78 Aleksandr Novikov), Mikhail Gershkovich, Oleg Dolmatov, Andrei Yakubik (72 Zurab Tsereteli), Aleksandr Maksimenkov, Aleksandr Minaev. Trainer: Aleksandr Sevidov

AUSTRIA: Hubert Baumgartner; Erich Obermayer, Robert Sara, Karl Daxbacher, Ernst Baumeister; Herbert Prohaska, Alberto Martínez, Felix Gasselich; Julio Cesar Morales, Thomas Parits, Hans Pirkner.   Trainer: Hermann Stessl

Goals: Baumeister (26), Tsereteli (84), Gerschkovich (86)

**FK AUSTRIA WIEN
v DINAMO MOSKVA 2-1 (0-0, 2-1) (AET)**
Prater, Wien 12.04.1978
Referee: Antonio José da Silva Garrido (POR)   Att: 75,000

AUSTRIA: Hubert Baumgartner; Robert Sara, Erich Obermayer, Josef Sara, Ernst Baumeister; Herbert Prohaska, Julio Cesar Morales, Felix Gasselich (83 Alberto Martínez); Fritz Drazan (85 Günther Pospisil), Hans Pirkner, Thomas Parits.   Trainer: Hermann Stessl

DINAMO: Nikolai Gontar, Anatoli Parov (54 Zurab Tsereteli), Aleksandr Novikov, Aleksandr Makhovikov, Aleksandr Bubnov, Aleksei Petruschin, Mikhail Gershkovich (65 Andrei Yakubik), Oleg Dolmatov, Vladimir Kazachyenok, Aleksandr Maksimenkov, Aleksandr Minaev.
Trainer: Aleksandr Sevidov

Goals: Pirkner (49 pen), Morales (55), Yakubik (90)

Penalties: 0-1 Kazachyenok, 1-1 Parits, 1-2 Maksimenkov, 2-2 Pirkner, 2-3 Tsereteli, 3-3 Prohaska, 3-4 Yakubik, 4-4 Morales, Bubnov (miss), 5-4 Martínez

FINAL

ANDERLECHT BRUSSEL
v FK AUSTRIA WIEN 4-0 (3-0)
Parc des Princes, Paris 3.05.1978
Referee: Heinz Aldinger (W. GER)   Attendance: 48,679

ANDERLECHT: Nico de Bree; Gilbert Van Binst, John Dusbaba, Hugo Broos, Jean Thissen; François Van der Elst, Arendt Haan, Ludo Coeck, Frank Vercauteren (87 Jean Dockx); Benny Nielsen, Pieter Robert Rob Rensenbrink (Cap). Trainer: Raymond Goethals

AUSTRIA: Hubert Baumgartner; Robert Sara, Josef Sara, Erich Obermayer, Ernst Baumeister; Karl Daxbacher (60 Alberto Martínez), Herbert Prohaska, Felix Gasselich, Julio Cesar Morales (74 Fritz Drazan); Thomas Parits, Hans Pirkner. Trainer: Hermann Stessl.

Goals: Rensenbrink (13, 44), Van Binst (45, 82)

Goalscorers European Cup-Winners' Cup 1977-78:

6 goals: François van der Elst (Anderlecht Brussel), Ferdinand Keller (Hamburger SV), Ab Gritter (Twente Enschede)

5 goals: Rob Rensenbrink (Anderlecht)

4 goals: Vladimir Kazachyenok (Dinamo Moskva)

3 goals: B. Nielsen (Anderlecht), Garçia Soriano (Betis Sevilla), Kolesov (Dinamo Moskva), Duda (FC Porto), Coppell (Manchester United), Aase (Brann Bergen), Cîțu (Universitatea Craiova), Jacquet, Nørregaard, Østergaard (Vejle BK)

2 goals: Löwe (Lokomotiv Leipzig), van Binst (Anderlecht), Lopez (Betis Sevilla), Guy (Coleraine), Gershkovich, Maksimenkov, Yakubik (Dinamo Moskva), Fekete, Oláh, Tatár (Diosgyör VTK), Séninho (FC Porto), Baumeister, Morales (Austria Wien), Rukljak, Zl. Vujović (Hajduk Split), Keegan, Steffenhagen, Volkert (Hamburger SV), Kermanidis (PAOK Thessaloniki), Riutto (Reipas Lahti), Tronstad (Brann Bergen), Mühren, Thijssen, van der Vall (Twente Enschede), Balaci, Marcu (Universitatea Craiova), Eg, Thycosen (Vejle BK)

1 goal: Greig, Johnstone, Smith (Glasgow Rangers), Leuzinger (Young Boys Bern), K.H.Sørensen (Vejle BK), Beldeanu, Crişan, Irimescu (Universitatea Craiova), Overweg, Thoresen (Twente Enschede), Dalhaug (Brann Bergen), Sandberg (Lahden Reipas), Anastasiadis, Damanakis, Orfanos, Pellios (PAOK Thessaloniki), Bild, Evesson (Östers), Aristeidou (Olympiakos Nicosia), Hill, Nicholl, Pearson (Manchester United), Dobrovic, Farkas, Jozsa (Lokomotiva Košice), Kolev (Lokomotiv Sofia), Buljan, Reimann, Magath (Hamburger SV), Cop, Muzinić, Šurjak (Hajduk Split), Daxbacher, Parits, Pirkner (Austria Wien), Gomes, Oliveira, Murça, Gabriel, Octávio (FC Porto), Flanagan (Dundalk), Synaeghel (St. Etienne), Fükö, Váradi (Diosgyöri VTK), Minaev, Tsereteli (Dinamo Moskva), Tweed (Coleraine), Eulate (Betis Sevilla), Zekeriya, Paunović (Beşiktaş Istanbul), Coeck, Bouvy, Haan, Van Poucke, Vercauteren (Anderlecht Brussel), Tosetto, Capello (AC Milan), Liebers, Eichhorn, Kühn, Gröbner, Altmann, Fritsche (Lokomotive Leipzig), Löhr, Müller (FC Köln)

Own goals: Jackson (Glasgow Rangers) for Young Boys Bern, McManus (Dundalk) for Hajduk Split, B.McConville (Dundalk) for Hajduk Split, Murça (FC Porto) two for Manchester United

CUP WINNERS' CUP 1978-79

FIRST ROUND

SKI og FK BODØ/GLIMT
v US LUXEMBOURG 4-1 (0-1)

Aspmyra stadion, Bodø   27.08.1978

Referee: B. Nielsen (DEN)   Attendance: 5,000

SFK BODØ/GLIMT: Jon Abrahamsen, Ivar Pedersen (46 Trond Tidemann), Truls Klausen, Ernst Pedersen, Terje Mørkved, Arild Olsen, Harald Berg, Anders Farstad, Ove Andreassen (75 Jacob Klette), Arne Hanssen, Sturla Solhaug.

US LUXEMBOURG: Claude Schettgen, Jean-Paul Girres, Fernand Raths, Pasquini, Joseph Zangerle, Jean-Paul Martin (80 De Toffoli), Laurent Schonckert, Silvain Teitgen, Guy Fisch (50 Robert Langers), Romain Delhalt, Scheider.

Goals: Teitgen (1), Solhaug (57, 85), H. Berg (59), A. Hanssen (75)

US LUXEMBOURG
v SKI og FK BODØ/GLIMT 1-0 (1-0)

Luxembourg   12.09.1978

Referee: Gerard J.M. Geurts (HOL)   Attendance: 2,000

US LUXEMBOURG: Claude Schettgen, Jean-Paul Girres, Fernand Raths, Hellers, Pasquini (72 Laurent Schonkert), Scheider, Jean-Paul Martin, Silvain Teitgen, Guy Fisch, Robert Langers, De Toffoli.

SFK BODØ/GLIMT: Jon Abrahamsen, Trond Tidemann, Truls Klausen, Ernst Pedersen, Terje Mørkved, Arild Olsen, Harald Berg, Anders Farstad, Ove Andreassen (75 Jacob Klette), Arne Hanssen, Sturla Solhaug.

Goal: Teitgen (11)

ZAGLEBIE SOSNOWIEC
v SWW INNSBRUCK 2-3 (1-2)

Stadion Ludowy, Sosnowiec   13.09.1978

Referee: Lars Åke Björck (SWE)   Attendnace: 8,000

ZAGLEBIE: Krzysztof Slabik, Tadeusz Tlolka, Stanislaw Zuzok, Jerzy Zarychta, Janusz Koterwa, Wojciech Saczek, Marek Jedras (46 Krystian Pytel), Wladyslaw Szarynski, Wladyslaw Starosciak, Wlodzimierz Mazur, Jerzy Dworczyk.

SWW: Friedrich Koncilia; Werner Zanon (57 Robert Auer), Roland Freimüller, Boris Sikic, Gerhard Forstinger, Josef Hickersberger (46 Robert Hanschitz), Max Gartner, Peter Koncilia, Franz Oberacher, Günther Scharmann, Manfred Braschler.   Trainer: Hans Eigenstiller

Goals: Zarychta (10), P. Koncilia (20), Oberacher (38), Szarynski (57), Braschler (86)

SWW INNSBRUCK
v ZAGLEBIE SOSNOWIEC 1-1 (1-1)

Tivoli, Innsbruck   27.09.1978

Referee: Károly Palotai (HUN)   Attendance: 11,000

SWW: Friedrich Koncilia, Werner Zanon, Gerhard Forstinger, Dietmar Oberortner, Robert Auer, Werner Schwarz (59 Max Gartner), Robert Hanschitz, Peter Koncilia, Franz Oberacher, Günther Scharmann, Manfred Braschler (78 Wolfgang Schwarz).   Trainer: Hans Eigenstiller

ZAGLEBIE: Krzysztof Slabik; Jerzy Lula (63 Eugeniusz Wiencierz), Janusz Koterwa, Stanislaw Zuzok, Tadeusz Tlolka, Wojciech Saczek, Jerzy Zarychta, Wladyslaw Szarynski (78 Wladyslaw Starosciak), Marek Jedras, Wlodzimierz Mazur, Jerzy Dworczyk.

Goals: Koterwa (11 og), Dworczyk (26)

UNIVERSITATEA CRAIOVA
v FORTUNA DÜSSELDORF 3-4 (1-2)

Central, Craiova   13.09.1978

Referee: Ertugrul Dilek (TUR)   Attendance: 15,000

UNIVERSITATEA: Silviu Lung (46 Gabriel Boldici); Nicolae Ungureanu, Nicolae Tilihoi, Costică Ştefănescu, Petre Purima; Costică Donose (74 Nicolae Negrilă), Ilie Balaci, Aurică Beldeanu; Zoltan Crişan, Rodion Cămătaru, Dumitru Marcu.   Trainers: Ilie Oană & Constantin Deliu

FORTUNA: Wilfried Woyke; Dieter Brei, Gerd Zewe, Gerd Zimmermann, Heiner Baltes; Reinhold Fanz, Josef Weikl, Klaus Allofs (65 Herbert Zimmer); Emanuel Günther (77 Rudi Bommer), Fleming Lund, Wolfgang Seel.
Trainer: Dieter Tippenhauer

Goals: Cămătaru (13, 57), Zimmermann (24), Fanz (34, 85), Allofs (49), Crişan (80)

FORTUNA DÜSSELDORF
v UNIVERSITATEA CRAIOVA 1-1 (1-0)

Rheinstadion, Düsseldorf   27.09.1978

Referee: Dušan Krchnak (CZE)   Attendance: 7,000

FORTUNA: Wilfried Woyke; Josef Weikl, Gerd Zewe, Gerd Zimmermann, Heiner Baltes; Reinhold Fanz, Dieter Brei, Fleming Lund; Klaus Allofs, Rudi Bommer (83 Hubert Schmitz), Wolfgang Seel.   Trainer: Dieter Tippenhauer

UNIVERSITATEA: Silviu Lung; Nicolae Negrilă, Nicolae Tilihoi, Costică Ştefănescu, Petre Purima (46 Cornel Berneanu); Nicolae Ungureanu, Sorin Cîrţu, Aurică Beldeanu; Zoltan Crişan, Rodion Cămătaru, Dumitru Marcu.   Trainer: Ilie Oană

Goals: Bommer (38), Marcu (64)

FLORIANA FC
v INTERNAZIONALE MILANO 1-3 (0-1)
Empire Stadium, Valletta 13.09.1978
Referee: D.F. Reeves (ENG)   Attendance: 16,000

FLORIANA: Robert Gatt, George Ciantar, Edwin Farrugia, Ballani, V. Holland, George Xuereb, C. Micallef, Emanuel Azzopardi (64 Borg), Raymond Xuereb, Powie Micallef (67 G. Holland), R. Micallef.

INTER: Ivano Bordon, Giuseppe Baresi, Adriano Fedele, Giancarlo Pasinato, Nazzareno Canuti, Graziano Bini, Gabriele Oriali, Giampiero Marini, Alessandro Altobelli, Evaristo Beccalossi (66 Alessandro Scanziani), Carlo Muraro.   Trainer: Eugenio Bersellini

Goals: Altobelli (14, 80 pen, 90), R. Xuereb (47 pen)

KALMAR FF
v FERENCVÁROS TC BUDAPEST 2-2 (2-0)
Fredriksskans, Kalmar 27.09.1978
Referee: Anders Mattsson (FIN)   Attendance: 2,300

KALMAR FF: Leif Friberg; Christer Hult, Börje Axelsson, Ulf Ohlsson, Ronny Sörman; Benno Magnusson, Kjell Nyberg (50 Håkan Lindheim), Alf Nilsson; Tomas Sunesson (80 Stig Andreasson), Jan-Åke Lundberg, Johnny Erlandsson.

FERENCVÁROS: Gábor Zsiborás, Győző Martos, Péter Vépi, Ferenc Major, Ignác Tepszics, László Bálint, Pál Mészöly, Tibor Nyilasi, László Szokolai, Zoltán Ebedli, József Mucha (66 László Pogány).   Trainer: Zoltán Friedmanszky

Goals: Magnusson (18 pen), Nyberg (26), Ebedli (74), Szokolai (80)

INTERNAZIONALE MILANO
v FLORIANA FC 5-0 (2-0)
San Siro, Milano 27.09.1978
Referee: Andreas Kouniaides (CYP)   Attendance: 25,000

INTER: Ivano Bordon, Alessandro Scanziani, Adriano Fedele, Giancarlo Pasinato (65 Roberto Tricella), Giuseppe Baresi, Graziano Bini, Gabriele Oriali, Giampiero Marini, Alessandro Altobelli (71 Aldo Serena), Odoacre Chierico, Carlo Muraro.   Trainer: Eugenio Bersellini

FLORIANA: Robert Gatt, George Ciantar, Edwin Farrugia, V.Holland, Ballani, M.Micallef, C.Micallef (65 Borg), G.Holland, George Xuereb, Raymond Xuereb, Powie Micallef (82 Emanuel Azzopardi).

Goals: Muraro (32, 70), Chierico (33), Fedele (69, 90)

SPORTING CLUBE PORTUGAL
v BANÍK OSTRAVA OKD 0-1 (0-1)
Estádio José Alvalade, Lisboa 13.09.1978
Referee: Enzo Barbaresco (ITA)   Attendance: 45,000

SPORTING: António José da Silva BOTELHO, Artur, Augusto Soares INÁCIO, João Gonçalves LARANJEIRA, Francisco José Teles de Andrade "ZEZINHO", AILTON Ballesteros, VÍTOR MANUEL Soares Fernandes, MANOEL da Silva Costa, MANUEL José Tavares FERNANDES, Mário Abreu Alves da Silva "MÁRINHO" (73 ADEMAR Moreira Marques), Salif Keita (46 Pedro ZANDONAIDE Filho).

BANÍK: Pavol Michalík, Josef Foks, Rostislav Vojácek, Milan Albrecht, Zdenek Rygel, Libor Radimec, Augustín Antalík, Petr Nemec, Lubomír Knapp, Zdenek Sreiner, Werner Licka.   Trainer: Evzen Hadamczik

Goal: Antalik (30)

FERENCVÁROS TC BUDAPEST
v KALMAR FF 2-0 (2-0)
Üllői út, Budapest 13.09.1978
Referee: Nikolaos Lagogiannis (GRE)   Attendance: 25,000

FERENCVÁROS: Gábor Zsiborás; Ignác Tepszics, Péter Vépi, László Bálint, Ferenc Major; Győző Martos, Pál Mészöly (46 László Takács), Zoltán Ebedli; László Szokolai, Tibor Nyilasi, József Mucha (74 László Pogány).   Trainer: Zoltán Friedmanszky

KALMAR FF: Tony Ström; Stig Andreasson, Ulf Ohlsson, Börje Axelsson, Alf Nilsson; Tomas Sunesson, Kjell Nyberg, Kenneth Bojstedt, Benno Magnusson (86 Håkan Lindheim); Jan-Åke Lundberg, Johnny Erlandsson.

Goals: Nyilasi (16), Major (43)

BANÍK OSTRAVA OKD v SPORTING CLUBE DE PORTUGAL LISBOA 1-0 (0-0)
Stadión na Bazaloch, Ostrava 27.09.1978
Referee: John Hunting (ENG)   Attendance: 12,000

BANÍK: Pavol Michalík, Josef Foks, Rostislav Vojácek, Milan Albrecht, Zdenek Rygel, Libor Radimec, Augustín Antalík (84 Dušan Srubar), Petr Nemec, Lubomír Knapp, Zdenek Sreiner, Werner Licka.   Trainer: Evzen Hadamczik

SPORTING: António José da Silva BOTELHO, Artur (83 Vítorino Manuel Antunes BASTOS), Augusto Soares INÁCIO, João Gonçalves LARANJEIRA, Francisco José Teles de Andrade "ZEZINHO", Paulo MENESES, AILTON Ballesteros, MANOEL da Silva Costa, MANUEL José Tavares FERNANDES, Salif Keita, Pedro ZANDONAIDE Filho (65 VÍTOR MANUEL Soares Fernandes).

Goal: Licka (58)

VALUR REYKJAVÍK
v 1.FC MAGDEBURG 1-1 (0-0)
Laugardalsvöllur, Reykjavík   13.09.1978
Referee: Patrick Mulhall (IRL)   Attendance: 8,000

VALUR: Sigurdur Haraldsson, Magnus Bergs, Grimur Saemundssen, Hordur Hilmarsson (66 Jón Einarsson), Dyri Gudmundsson, Saevar Jónsson, Ingi Björn Albertsson (88 Magni Blondal Petursson), Atli Edvaldsson, Albert Gudmundsson, Thorbjörnsson, Hálfdan Orlygsson.

1.FC MAGDEBURG: Dirk Heine, Detlef Raugust, Manfred Zapf, Wolfgang Seguin, Klaus Decker, Siegmund Mewes, Jürgen Pommerenke (49 Axel Tyll), Wolfgang Steinbach, Joachim Streich, Jürgen Sparwasser, Martin Hoffmann.   Trainer: Klaus Urbanczyk

Goals: Steinbach (58), Albertsson (69 pen)

ABERDEEN FC
v MAREK STANKE DIMITROV 3-0 (0-0)
Pittodrie, Aberdeen   27.09.1978
Referee: Jan N.I. Keizer (HOL)   Attendance: 25,000

ABERDEEN FC: James Leighton, Stuart Kennedy, Charles McLelland, John McMaster, Alex McLeish, William Miller, Dominic Sullivan (58 Gordon Strachan), Steve Archibald, Joseph Harper, Andrew Jarvie, Ian Scanlon.

MAREK: Stoian Stoianov; Liuben Sevdin, Liuben Kolev, Roman Karakolev, Ivan Palev, Nikolai Vukov (72 Stefan Zlatkov), Sasho Pargov (59 Asen Tomov), Aleksandar Rainov, Ivan Petrov, Ventsislav Petrov, Emil Kiuchukov.   Trainer: Ianko Donkov

Goals: Strachan (63), Jarvie (75), Harper (81)

1.FC MAGDEBURG
v VALUR REYKJAVÍK 4-0 (3-0)
Ernst-Grube-Stadion, Magdeburg   27.09.1978
Referee: Aleksander Suchanek (POL)   Attendance: 15,000

1.FC MAGDEBURG: Dirk Heine, Detlef Raugust, Manfred Zapf, Wolfgang Seguin, Klaus Decker, Siegmund Mewes (83 Rainer Döbbel), Jürgen Pommerenke (70 Axel Tyll), Wolfgang Steinbach, Joachim Streich, Jürgen Sparwasser, Martin Hoffmann.   Trainer: Klaus Urbanczyk

VALUR: Sigurdur Haraldsson, Magnus Bergs (73 Gudmundur Kjartansson), Grimur Saemundssen, Hordur Hilmarsson, Dyri Gudmundsson, Saevar Jónsson, Ingi Björn Albertsson, Atli Edvaldsson, Albert Gudmundsson (77 Jón Einarsson), Thorbjörnsson, Hálfdan Orlygsson.

Goals: Seguin (6), Steinbach (43), Hoffmann (45), Streich (75)

SK BEVEREN v BALLYMENA UNITED 3-0 (2-0)
Freethiel, Beveren   13.09.1978
Referee: César da Luz Dias Correia (POR)   Att: 13,000

BEVEREN: Jean-Marie Pfaff, Eddy Jaspers, Paul van Genechten, Freddy Buyl, Marc Baecke, Wim Hofkens, Heinz Schönberger, Erwin Albert, Robert Stevens (60 Karl-Heinz Wissmann), Albert Cluytens, Jean Janssens (77 Florent Truyens).   Trainer: Robert Goethals

BALLYMENA UNITED: Robert Brown, Alex Donald, Liam Butcher, Ronald McCullough, David Jackson, David Shaw, Samuel McQuiston, John Sloan, Gerry Mullan, Alan Simpson, Jack McClean.

Goals: Albert (7), Stevens (30), Schönberger (60 pen)

MAREK STANKE DIMITROV
v ABERDEEN FC 3-2 (0-1)
Bonchuk, Stanke Dimitrov   13.09.1978
Referee: Jacques van Melkebeke (BEL)   Attendance: 20,000

MAREK: Stoian Stoianov; Liuben Sevdin, Liuben Kolev, Roman Karakolev, Ivan Palev (46 Emil Kiuchukov), Aleksandar Rainov, Sasho Pargov, Asen Tomov, Ivan Petrov, Ventsislav Petrov, Dimitar Dimitrov.   Trainer: Ianko Donkov

ABERDEEN FC: James Leighton, Stuart Kennedy, Charles McLelland, John McMaster, William Garner (55 Douglas Rougvie), William Miller, Dominic Sullivan, Steve Archibald, Joseph Harper, Andrew Jarvie, Ian Scanlon.

Goals: Jarvie (6), V. Petrov (67), Harper (76), I. Petrov (67, 89)

BALLYMENA UNITED
v SK BEVEREN-WAAS 0-3 (0-0)
The Showgrounds, Ballymena   27.09.1978
Referee: Eysteinn Gudmundsson (ICE)   Attendance: 5,000

BALLYMENA UNITED: Robert Brown, Alex Donald, Liam Butcher, Ronald McCullough, David Jackson, David Shaw (86 Kenny Spence), Samuel McQuiston, William McAvoy, Gerry Mullan, Alan Simpson, Jack McClean.

BEVEREN: Jean-Marie Pfaff, Eddy Jaspers, Paul van Genechten, Freddy Buyl, Marc Baecke, Wim Hofkens, Heinz Schönberger, Erwin Albert (82 Florent Truyens), Robert Stevens (76 Karl-Heinz Wissmann), Albert Cluytens, Jean Janssens.   Trainer: Robert Goethals

Goals: Janssens (76, 78), Wissmann (89)

**PAOK THESSALONIKI
v SERVETTE GENÈVE 2-0** (0-0)

Toumpas, Thessaloniki 13.09.1978

Referee: Constantin Bărbulescu (ROM)   Attendance: 20,000

PAOK: Mladen Fortoula; Giannis Gounaris, Kiriakos Apostolidis, Kostas Iosifidis, Theodoros Apostolidis, Giannis Damanakis, Panagiotis Kermanidis, Aggelos Anastasiadis (46 Stavros Sarafis), Neto Gkouerino (46 Giorgos Kostikos), Giorgos Koudas, Nikos Alavantas.   Trainer: Egon Pihatsek

SERVETTE: Karl Engel; Marc Schnyder, Lucio Bizzini, Serge Trinchero, Gilbert Guyot, Umberto Barberis, Hansjörg Pfister (75 Angelo Elia), Guy Dutoit, Piet Hamberg, Claude Andrey, Jean-Yves Valentini.   Trainer: Peter Pazmandy

Goals: Kermanidis (76), Sarafis (86)

**SERVETTE GENÈVE
v PAOK THESSALONIKI 4-0** (1-0)

Stade des Charmilles, Genève 27.09.1978

Referee: László Padar (HUN)   Attendance: 12,000

SERVETTE: Karl Engel; Marc Schnyder, Lucio Bizzini, Serge Trinchero, Gilbert Guyot, Umberto Barberis, Hansjörg Pfister, Franz Peterhans (46 Angelo Elia), Piet Hamberg, Claude Andrey, Jean-Yves Valentini.   Trainer: Peter Pazmandy

PAOK: Apostolos Filis; Giannis Gounaris, Kiriakos Apostolidis, Kostas Iosifidis, Filotas Pellios (87 Nikos Alavantas), Giannis Damanakis, Panagiotis Kermanidis, Stavros Sarafis, Neto Gkouerino (62 Giorgos Kostikos), Giorgos Koudas, Kostas Orfanos.   Trainer: Egon Pihatsek

Goals: Pfister (15), Hamberg (76), Elia (86, 89)

AZ 67 ALKMAAR v IPSWICH TOWN 0-0

Alkmaarderhout 13.09.1978

Referee: Jan Redelfs (W. GER)   Attendance: 14,000

AZ 67: Rizah Meskovic, Peter Arntz, John Metgod, Ronald Spelbos, Henk van Rijnsoever (84 Kees Tol), Jan Peters, Kristen Nygaard (56 Hugo Hovenkamp), Wim van Hanegem, Peter Ressel, Kees Kist, Jaan De Graaf.   Trainer: Georg Kessler

IPSWICH TOWN: Paul Cooper, George Burley, Russell Osman, Kevin Beattie, Michael Mills, Brian Talbot, John Wark, Les Tibbott, Paul Mariner, Trevor Whymark (86 David Geddis), Clive Woods.   Manager: Robert Robson

IPSWICH TOWN v AZ 67 ALKMAAR 2-0 (1-0)

Portman Road, Ipswich 27.09.1978

Referee: Marcel Van Langenhove (BEL)   Attendance: 21,330

IPSWICH TOWN: Paul Cooper, George Burley, Russell Osman, Kevin Beattie, Michael Mills, Brian Talbot, John Wark, Les Tibbott, Paul Mariner, Trevor Whymark, Clive Woods.   Manager: Robert Robson

AZ 67: Gerrit Vooys, Henk van Rijnsoever, John Metgod, Ronald Spelbos, Hugo Hovenkamp, Peter Arntz, Jan Peters, Wim van Hanegem, Peter Ressel, Kees Kist, Jaan De Graaf (75 Kristen Nygaard).   Trainer: Georg Kessler

Goals: Mariner (3), Wark (90 pen)

SHAMROCK ROVERS v APOEL NICOSIA 2-0 (1-0)

Milltown, Dublin 13.09.1978

Referee: Achille Verbecke (FRA)   Attendance: 8,000

SHAMROCK ROVERS: John Osborne, Michael Gannon, Pierce O'Leary, Eamon Dunphy, Noel Synnott, John Fullam, John Cervi, Stephen Lynex, Raymond Treacy, John Giles, Noel King.

APOEL: Herodotos Herodotou "Koupanos", Haralampos Menelaou, Mihalis Kolokasis, Andreas Stavrou, Nikos Pantziaras, Mihalis Hatzipieris, Andreas Miamiliotis (71 Giorgos Petrou), Markos Markou (46 Koulis Pantziaras), Takis Antoniou, Takis Timotheou, Petrakis Hatzithomas.

Goals: Giles (44), Lynex (67)

**APOEL NICOSIA
v SHAMROCK ROVERS 0-1** (0-0)

Nicosia 27.09.1978

Referee: Milorad Vlajić (YUG)   Attendance: 15,000

APOEL: Herodotos Herodotou "Koupanos", Stefanou, Mihalis Kolokasis (57 Andreas Miamiliotis), Andreas Stavrou, Nikos Pantziaras, Mihalis Hatzipieris, Leonidas Leonidou (63 Ermogenis Ermogenides), Takis Timotheou, Takis Antoniou, Koulis Pantziaras, Petrakis Hatzithomas.

SHAMROCK ROVERS: John Osborne, Michael Gannon, Pierce O'Leary, Noel King, John Burke, John Fullam, John Cervi, Stephen Lynex, Eddie Byrne, John Giles, Robert Tambling.

Goal: Lynex (88)

NK RIJEKA v WREXHAM 3-0 (2-0)
Kantrida, Rijeka   13.09.1978

Referee: Paolo Bergamo (ITA)   Attendance: 9,000

NK RIJEKA: Radojko Avramović (82 Mauro Ravnić), Sergio Makin, Miloš Hrstić, Nikica Cukrov, Zvjezdan Radin, Srećko Juričić, Salih Durkalić, Adrijano Fegić (77 Bursać), Edmond Tomić, Milan Ruzić, Damir Desnica.

WREXHAM: W. David Davies, Alan Hill, Graham Whittle, Gareth Davis, John Roberts, Michael Thomas, Robert Shinton, Melvyn Sutton, Richard McNeil (76 Peter Williams), John Lyons, Leslie Cartwright.

Goals: Tomić (35), Durkalić (43), Cukrov (72)

WREXHAM v NK RIJEKA 2-0 (0-0)
Racecourse Ground, Wrexham   27.09.1978

Referee: Norbert Rolles (LUX)   Attendance: 10,469

WREXHAM: W. David Davies, Alan Hill, Graham Whittle, Gareth Davis, Wayne Cegielski, Michael Thomas, Robert Shinton, Melvyn Sutton (60 John Lyons), Richard McNeil, Peter Williams (83 Arfon Griffiths), Leslie Cartwright.

NK RIJEKA: Radojko Avramović, Sergio Makin, Miloš Hrstić, Nikica Cukrov, Zvjezdan Radin, Srećko Juričić, Salih Durkalic (60 Ivan Car), Adrijano Fegic (77 Bursać), Edmond Tomić, Milan Ruzić, Damir Desnica.

Goals: McNeil (53), Cartwright (64)

CF BARCELONA v SHAKHTIOR DONETSK 3-0 (3-0)
Camp Nou, Barcelona   13.09.1978

Referee: Thomas Reynolds (WAL)   Attendance: 45,000

CF BARCELONA: Pedro María ARTOLA Urrutia, José Antonio RAMOS Huete, Miguel Bernardo Bianquetti "MIGUELI" (6 Enrique Álvarez COSTAS), Antonio OLMO Ramírez, Jesús Antonio DE LA CRUZ Gallego, Johan Neeskens, Carlos REXACH Cerdá, José Vicente SÁNCHEZ Felip, Johann Krankl, Juan Manuel ASENSI Ripoll (81 Francisco MARTÍNEZ Díaz), ESTEBAN Vigo Benítez.
Trainer: Lucien Muller

SHAKHTIOR: Yuri Degtyarev, Valeri Yaremchenko, Valeri Gorbunov, Viktor Kondratov, Vladimir Pianikh, Valeri Rudakov (60 Mikhail Sokolovski), Nikolai Latisch, Yuri Reznik, Vitali Starukhin, Yuri Dudinski (73 Nikolai Fedorenko), Vladimir Safonov.   Trainer: Vladimir Salkov

Goals: Krankl (1), Migueli (6), Sánchez (24)

SHAHTIOR DONETSK v CF BARCELONA 1-1 (1-1)
Lokomotiv, Donetsk   27.09.1978

Referee: Ulf Eriksson (SWE)   Attendance: 45,000

SHAKHTIOR: Yuri Degtyarev, Valeri Yaremchenko, Valeri Rudakov, Aleksei Varnavski, Vladimir Pianikh, Mikhail Sokolovski, Nikolai Latisch (46 Nikolai Fedorenko), Yuri Reznik, Vitali Starukhin, Yuri Dudinski (72 Evgeni Schaforostov), Vladimir Safonov.   Trainer: Vladimir Salkov

CF BARCELONA: Pedro María ARTOLA Urrutia, Jesús Antonio DE LA CRUZ Gallego, Miguel Bernardo Bianquetti "MIGUELI", Antonio OLMO Ramírez, Enrique Álvarez COSTAS, Johan Neeskens, Juan Carlos HEREDIA Alvarado, José Vicente SÁNCHEZ Felip, Johann Krankl, Juan Manuel ASENSI Ripoll, Francisco MARTÍNEZ Díaz.
Trainer: Lucien Muller

Goals: Reznik (1), Krankl (34)

FREM KØBENHAVN v AS NANCY-LORRAINE 2-0 (1-0)
Valby Idraetspark, København   13.09.1978

Referee: Malcolm Moffatt (NIR)   Attendance: 1,136

FREM: Per Wind, Mogens Nielsen, Lars Larsen, Henrik Thomsen, Flemming Ahlberg, Jesper Juul, Bjarne Andersen, Jacob Rossander (77 Henning Hansen), Jan Jacobsen (70 Brian Juul Nielsen), Ole Mørch, Frank Faber.

AS NANCY-LORRAINE: Jean-Michel Moutier; Jean-Pierre Raczynski, Jean-Claude Cloet (84 Joël Delpierrerre), Pierre Neubert, Carlos Curbelo, Jacques Perdrieau, Olivier Rouyer, Francisco Rubio, Robert Pintenat, Bernard Zenier, Rubén Umpierrez (67 Philippe Jeannol).
Trainer: Jean-Antoine Redin

Goals: Jacobsen (21), Hansen (82)

AS NANCY-LORRAINE v FREM KØBENHAVN 4-0 (1-0)
Stade Marcel Picot, Nancy   27.09.1978

Referee: J. Ignacio DE ALMEIRA (POR)   Att: 15,000

AS NANCY-LORRAINE: Jean-Michel Moutier, Jean-Claude Cloet, Joël Delpierrerre (69 Jean-Pierre Raczynski), Pierre Neubert, Carlos Curbelo, Philippe Jeannol, Olivier Rouyer, Jacques Perdrieau, Rubén Umpierrez, Francisco Rubio, Bernard Zenier.   Trainer: Jean-Antoine Redin

FREM: Per Wind, Mogens Nielsen, Lars Larsen, Henrik Thomsen, Henning Hansen, Jesper Juul, Bjarne Andersen, Jacob Rossander, Jan Jacobsen, Ole Mørch, Frank Faber (66 Brian Juul Nielsen).

Goals: Curbelo (2), Jeannol (70, 77), Zenier (86)

SECOND ROUND

INTERNAZIONALE MILANO
v SFK BODØ/GLIMT 5-0 (1-0)

San Siro, Milano   18.10.1978

Referee: Paul Bonett (MAL)   Attendance: 15,000

INTERNAZIONALE: Ivano Bordon, Giuseppe Baresi, Gabriele Oriali, Giancarlo Pasinato, Nazzareno Canuti, Graziano Bini, Odoacre Chierico, Giampiero Marini, Alessandro Altobelli, Evaristo Beccalossi (75 Alessandro Scanziani), Carlo Muraro.   Trainer: Eugenio Bersellini

SFK BODØ/GLIMT: Jon Abrahamsen, Ivar Pedersen (84 Trond Tidemann), Truls Klausen, Ernst Pedersen, Terje Mørkved, Arild Olsen, Harald Berg, Anders Farstad, Sturla Solhaug (78 Edd Meby), Arne Hanssen, Ove Andreassen.

Goals: Beccalossi (28), Altobelli (58, 60, 86), Muraro (89)

SFK BODØ GLIMT
v INTERNAZIONALE MILANO 1-2 (1-1)

Aspmyra stadion, Bodø   25.10.1978

Referee: Ian M.D. Foote (SCO)

SFK BODØ GLIMT: Jon Abrahamsen, Ivar Pedersen, Truls Klausen, Ernst Pedersen, Terje Mørkved, Arild Olsen, Harald Berg, Anders Farstad, Sturla Solhaug (84 Jacob Klette), Arne Hanssen (77 Edd Meby), Ove Andreassen.

INTERNAZIONALE: Ivano Bordon, Nazzareno Canuti (75 Roberto Tricella), Adriano Fedele, Giancarlo Pasinato, Silvano Fontolan, Graziano Bini, Gabriele Oriali, Giampiero Marini, Alessandro Altobelli, Alessandro Scanziani, Carlo Muraro.
Trainer: Eugenio Bersellini

Goals: Hanssen (40), Altobelli (45 pen), Scanziani (56)

BANÍK OSTRAVA
v SHAMROCK ROVERS 3-0 (2-0)

Stadión na Bazaloch, Ostrava   18.10.1978

Referee: Josef Bucek (AUS)   Attendance: 12,000

BANÍK: Pavol Michalík, Josef Foks, Rostislav Vojácek, Milan Albrecht, Zdenek Rygel, Libor Radimec, Augustín Antalík, Petr Nemec (65 Dušan Srubar), Lubomír Knapp, Zdenek Sreiner, Werner Licka.   Trainer: Evzen Hadamczik

SHAMROCK ROVERS: John Osborne, Michael Gannon, Pierce O'Leary (33 John Giles, 46 Gerry Clarke), Noel King, John Burke, John Fullam, John Cervi, Stephen Lynex, Raymond Treacy, Eamon Dunphy, Robert Tambling.

Goals: Knapp (5), Radimec (30), Rygel (57)

SHAMROCK ROVERS
v BANÍK OSTRAVA 1-3 (0-1)

Milltown, Dublin   1.11.1978

Referee: Jan N.I. Keizer (HOL)   Attendance: 3,000

SHAMROCK ROVERS: David Henderson, Michael Gannon, Gerry Clarke, Noel King, John Burke, John Fullam, John Cervi, Stephen Lynex, Raymond Treacy, John Giles, Richard Bayley.

BANÍK: Pavol Michalík, Josef Foks, Rostislav Vojácek, Milan Albrecht, Zdenek Rygel (81 Václav Pechácek), Libor Radimec, Augustín Antalík, Petr Nemec (69 Dušan Srubar), Lubomír Knapp, Zdenek Sreiner, Werner Licka.
Trainer: Evzen Hadamczik

Goals: Licka (37, 66), Albrecht (46), Giles (59)

IPSWICH TOWN v SWW INNSBRUCK 1-0 (0-0)

Portman Road, Ipswich   18.10.1978

Referee: Augusto Lamo Castillo (SPA)   Attendance: 20,394

IPSWICH TOWN: Paul Cooper, George Burley, Les Tibbott, Brian Talbot, Alan Hunter, Russell Osman, Michael Mills, John Wark, Paul Mariner (78 David Geddis), Trevor Whymark, Clive Woods.   Manager: Robert Robson

SWW: Friedrich Koncilia, Werner Zanon, Robert Auer, Boris Sikić, Werner Schwarz (75 Max Gartner), Günther Scharmann, Robert Hanschitz, Peter Koncilia, Franz Oberacher, Josef Hickersberger, Manfred Braschler (85 Wolfgang Auer).
Trainer: Hans Eigenstiller

Goal: Wark (60 pen)

SWW INNSBRUCK
v IPSWICH TOWN 1-1 (0-0, 1-0) (AET)

Tivoli, Innsbruck   1.11.1978

Referee: Alozjy Jarguz (POL)   Attendance: 18,000

SWW: Friedrich Koncilia, Werner Zanon, Gerhard Forstinger, Boris Sikić (60 Roland Freimüller), Robert Auer, Josef Hickersberger, Robert Hanschitz, Peter Koncilia, Franz Oberacher (100 Wolfgang Schwarz), Günther Scharmann, Manfred Braschler.   Trainer: Hans Eigenstiller

IPSWICH TOWN: Paul Cooper, George Burley, Les Tibbott, Brian Talbot, Alan Hunter, Russell Osman, Michael Mills, John Wark, Paul Mariner, David Geddis (80 Trevor Whymark), Clive Woods (80 Eric Gates).   Manager: Robert Robson

Goals: Oberacher (75), Burley (100)

SERVETTE GENÈVE
v AS NANCY-LORRAINE 2-1 (1-1)

Stade des Charmilles, Genève   18.10.1978

Referee: Vojtech Christov (CZE)   Attendance: 23,000

SERVETTE: Karl Engel; Marc Schnyder, Lucio Bizzini, Serge Trinchero, Gilbert Guyot, Umberto Barberis, Hansjörg Pfister, Angelo Elia (57 Hanspeter Weber), Piet Hamberg, Claude Andrey, Jean-Yves Valentini.   Trainer: Peter Pazmandy

AS NANCY-LORRAINE: Jean-Michel Moutier; Jean-Pierre Raczynski, Joël Delpierrerre, Pierre Neubert, Carlos Curbelo, Philippe Jeannol, Rubén Umpierrez (83 Bernard Zénier), Jacques Perdrieau, Robert Pintenat, Francisco Rubio, Olivier Rouyer.   Trainer: Jean-Antoine Redin

Goals: Hamberg (28), Rubio (39), Barberis (59)

AS NANCY-LORRAINE
v SERVETTE GENEVE 2-2 (0-0)

Stade Marcel Picot, Nancy   1.11.1978

Referee: Tome Manojlovski (YUG)   Attendance: 20,000

AS NANCY-LORRAINE: Jean-Michel Moutier; Jean-Pierre Raczynski, Joël Delpierrerre (75 Jean-Claude Cloet), Pierre Neubert, Carlos Curbelo, Philippe Jeannol, Olivier Rouyer, Jacques Perdrieau, Rubén Umpierrez, Francisco Rubio, Bernard Zénier.   Trainer: Jean-Antoine Redin

SERVETTE: Karl Engel; Marc Schnyder, Lucio Bizzini, Serge Trinchero, Gilbert Guyot, Umberto Barberis, Hansjörg Pfister, Angelo Elia, Piet Hamberg, Claude Andrey, Jean-Yves Valentini.   Trainer: Peter Pazmandy

Goals: Elia (68), Zénier (70 pen), Schnyder (76), Umpierrez (90)

RSC ANDERLECHT BRUSSEL
v CF BARCELONA 3-0 (1-0)

Constant vanden Stock, Brussel   18.10.1978

Referee: Riccardo Lattanzi (ITA)   Attendance: 35,000

ANDERLECHT: Nico de Bree, François van der Elst, Hugo Broos, John Dusbaba, Jean Thissen, Frank Vercauteren, Benny Nielsen, Ruud Geels, Arie Haan, Ludo Coeck, Rob Rensenbrink.   Trainer: Raymond Goethals

CF BARCELONA: Pedro María ARTOLA Urrutia, Rafael Ignacio ZUVIRÍA Rodríguez, Miguel Bernardo Bianquetti "MIGUELI", Antonio OLMO Ramírez, Jesús Antonio DE LA CRUZ Gallego, Johan Neeskens, José Vicente SÁNCHEZ Felip, Juan Carlos HEREDIA Alvarado, Johann Krankl, Juan Manuel ASENSI Ripoll, Francisco MARTÍNEZ Díaz (73 Carlos REXACH Cerdá).   Trainer: Lucien Muller

Sent off: Nielsen (82)

Goals: Van der Elst (19, 71), Coeck (47)

CF BARCELONA v RSC ANDERLECHT
BRUSSEL 3-0 (2-0, 3-0) (AET)

Camp Nou, Barcelona   1.11.1978

Referee: Walter Eschweiler (W. GER)   Attendance: 98,000

CF BARCELONA: Pedro María ARTOLA Urrutia, Rafael Ignacio ZUVIRÍA Rodríguez, Miguel Bernardo Bianquetti "MIGUELI", Antonio OLMO Ramírez (78 William Sílvio Modesto "BIO"), Jesús Antonio DE LA CRUZ Gallego, Johan Neeskens, José Vicente SÁNCHEZ Felip, Juan Carlos HEREDIA Alvarado (85 ESTEBAN Vigo Benítez), Johann Krankl, Juan Manuel ASENSI Ripoll, Carlos REXACH Cerdá.   Trainer: Lucien Muller

ANDERLECHT: Nico de Bree, Gilbert van Binst, Hugo Broos, John Dusbaba, Jean Thissen, Frank Vercauteren, François van der Elst, Ruud Geels, Arie Haan, Ludo Coeck, Rob Rensenbrink.   Trainer: Raymond Goethals

Sent off: Broos (76)

Goals: Krankl (8), Heredia (44), Zuviría (86)

Penalties: 1-0 Krankl, Van der Elst (saved), 2-0 Rexach, Geels (miss), 3-0 Bio, 3-1 Thissen, 4-1 Neeskens

FORTUNA DÜSSELDORF
v ABERDEEN FC 3-0 (1-0)

Rheinstadion, Düsseldorf   18.10.1978

Referee: Svein Inge Thime (NOR)   Attendance: 10,500

FORTUNA: Wilfried Woyke, Dieter Brei, Gerd Zewe, Gerd Zimmermann, Heiner Baltes, Egon Köhnen, Reinhold Fanz, Fleming Lund (58 Rudi Bommer), Emanuel Günther (83 Hubert Schmitz), Klaus Allofs, Wolfgang Seel.   Trainer: Dieter Tippenhauer

ABERDEEN FC: James Leighton, Stuart Kennedy, Charles McLelland, John McMaster (58 Ian Scanlon), Alex McLeish, William Miller, Douglas Rougvie, Steve Archibald, Joseph Harper, Andrew Jarvie (78 Gordon Strachan), Dominic Sullivan.

Goals: Günther (15, 58), Zimmermann (81)

ABERDEEN FC
v FORTUNA DÜSSELDORF 2-0 (0-0)

Pittodrie, Aberdeen   1.11.1978

Referee: César da Luz Dias Correia (POR)   Att: 16,800

ABERDEEN FC: Robert Clark, Douglas Rougvie, Charles McLelland, John McMaster (53 Ian Scanlon), Alex McLeish, William Miller, Dominic Sullivan, Steve Archibald, Joseph Harper, Andrew Jarvie, Gordon Strachan (77 Ian Fleming).

FORTUNA: Wilfried Woyke, Dieter Brei, Gerd Zewe, Gerd Zimmermann, Heiner Baltes, Egon Köhnen, Josef Weikl, Fleming Lund, Emanuel Günther, Klaus Allofs, Wolfgang Seel (12 Herbert Zimmer).   Trainer: Dieter Tippenhauer

Goals: McLelland (54), Jarvie (57)

NK RIJEKA v SK BEVEREN 0-0

Kantrida, Rijeka   18.10.1978

Referee: Nikolaos Lagogiannis (GRE)   Attendance: 8,000

NK RIJEKA: Radojko Avramović, Sergio Makin, Miloš Hrstić, Nikica Cukrov, Zvjezdan Radin, Srećko Juričić, Bursac (66 Ivan Jerolimov), Željko Mijač, Edmond Tomić (46 Salih Durkalić), Milan Ruzić, Damir Desnica.

BEVEREN: Jean-Marie Pfaff, Eddy Jaspers (46 Rudy van Goethem), Paul van Genechten, Freddy Buyl, Marc Baecke, Wim Hofkens, Heinz Schönberger, Erwin Albert, Florent Truyens, Albert Cluytens (83 Robert Stevens), Jean Janssens. Trainer: Robert Goethals

**FERENCVÁROS TC BUDAPEST
v 1.FC MAGDEBURG 2-1** (2-1)

Üllői út, Budapest   1.11.1978

Referee: Hilmi Ok (TUR)   Attendance: 30,000

FERENCVÁROS: Gábor Zsiborás; Ignác Tepszics, László Bálint, Péter Vépi, Győzö Martos; László Takács, Tibor Nyilasi, Zoltán Ebedli (85 László Csider); László Pusztai, László Szokolai, László Pogány (75 József Mucha). Trainer: Zoltán Friedmanszky

1.FC MAGDEBURG: Dirk Heine; Detlef Raugust, Manfred Zapf, Wolfgang Seguin, Klaus Decker; Axel Tyll, Jürgen Pommerenke, Wolfgang Steinbach; Joachim Streich, Dirk Stahmann, Martin Hoffmann.   Trainer: Klaus Urbanczyk

Goals: Stahmann (4), Pusztai (8), Szokolai (27)

SK BEVEREN v NK RIJEKA 2-0 (1-0)

Freethiel, Beveren   1.11.1978

Referee: Thomas Perry (NIR)   Attendance: 15,000

BEVEREN: Jean-Marie Pfaff, Eddy Jaspers, Paul van Genechten, Freddy Buyl, Marc Baecke, Wim Hofkens, Heinz Schönberger, Erwin Albert, Robert Stevens, Albert Cluytens, Jean Janssens.   Trainer: Robert Goethals

NK RIJEKA: Radojko Avramović, Sergio Makin, Miloš Hrstić, Nikica Cukrov, Zvjezdan Radin, Srećko Juričić, Bursac (63 Salih Durkalic), Adrijano Fegić, Ivan Jerolimov, Milan Ruzić, Damir Desnica.

Goals: Baecke (20, 65)

QUARTER-FINALS

1.FC MAGDEBURG v BANÍK OSTRAVA 2-1 (2-0)

Ernst-Grube-Stadion, Magdeburg   7.03.1979

Referee: Nikola M. Dudin (BUL)   Attendance: 15,000

1.FC MAGDEBURG: Dirk Heine, Detlef Raugust, Manfred Zapf, Wolfgang Seguin, Klaus Decker, Axel Tyll, Jürgen Pommerenke, Wolfgang Steinbach, Joachim Streich, Dirk Stahmann, Martin Hoffmann.   Trainer: Klaus Urbanczyk

BANÍK: Frantisek Schmucker (32 Pavel Macák), Josef Foks, Rostislav Vojácek, Milan Albrecht, Zdenek Rygel, Libor Radimec, Augustín Antalík, Dušan Srubar, Lubomír Knapp, Zdenek Sreiner, Werner Licka (85 Petr Zajaros). Trainer: Evzen Hadamczik

Goals: Streich (3, 30), Antalik (51)

**1.FC MAGDEBURG
v FERENCVÁROS TC BUDAPEST 1-0** (0-0)

Ernst-Grube-Stadion, Magdeburg   18.10.1978

Referee: Otto Anderco (ROM)   Attendance: 24,000

1.FC MAGDEBURG: Dirk Heine; Detlef Raugust, Manfred Zapf, Wolfgang Seguin, Klaus Decker; Siegmund Mewes, Jürgen Pommerenke, Wolfgang Steinbach; Joachim Streich, Jürgen Sparwasser (62 Axel Tyll), Martin Hoffmann. Trainer: Klaus Urbanczyk

FERENCVÁROS: Gábor Zsiborás; Ignác Tepszics, László Bálint, Ferenc Major, Péter Vépi; Győzö Martos, Tibor Nyilasi, László Takács; László Pusztai, László Szokolai, László Pogany (60 Zoltán Ebedli).   Trainer: Zoltán Friedmanszky

Goal: Streich (67)

BANÍK OSTRAVA v 1.FC MAGDEBURG 4-2 (2-0)

Stadión na Bazaloch, Ostrava   21.03.1979

Referee: John Carpenter (IRL)   Attendance: 25,000

BANÍK: Pavol Michalík, Josef Foks, Rostislav Vojácek, Milan Albrecht, Zdenek Rygel, Libor Radimec, Augustín Antalík, Petr Nemec, Lubomír Knapp, Zdenek Sreiner, Werner Licka (87 Dušan Srubar).   Trainer: Evzen Hadamczik

1.FC MAGDEBURG: Dirk Heine, Detlef Raugust, Manfred Zapf, Wolfgang Seguin, Klaus Decker, Dirk Stahmann, Jürgen Pommerenke, Wolfgang Steinbach, Joachim Streich (86 Rainer Döbbel), Jürgen Sparwasser, Martin Hoffmann. Trainer: Klaus Urbanczyk

Goals: Rygel (15, 86), Albrecht (42), Nemec (54), Sparwasser (70), Pommerenke (75)

INTERNAZIONALE MILANO v SK BEVEREN 0-0
Stadio Giuseppe Meazza, Milano   7.03.1979
Referee: Erich Linemayr (AUS)   Attendance: 55,000
INTER: Ivano Bordon, Roberto Tricella, Adriano Fedele (67 Odoacre Chierico), Gabriele Oriali, Silvano Fontolan, Graziano Bini, Alessandro Scanziani, Giampiero Marini, Alessandro Altobelli, Evaristo Beccalossi, Carlo Muraro (75 Aldo Serena). Trainer: Eugenio Bersellini
BEVEREN: Jean-Marie Pfaff, Eddy Jaspers, Paul Van Genechten, Freddy Buyl, Marc Baecke, Wim Hofkens, Heinz Schönberger, Erwin Albert, Robert Stevens (71 Florent Truyens), Albert Cluytens, Jean Janssens.
Trainer: Robert Goethals

**SERVETTE GENÈVE
v FORTUNA DÜSSELDORF 1-1** (0-1)
Stade des Charmilles, Genève   21.03.1979
Referee: Malcolm Wright (NIR)   Attendance: 23,000
SERVETTE: Karl Engel; Marc Schnyder, Lucio Bizzini, Serge Trinchero, Gilbert Guyot, Umberto Barberis, Hansjörg Pfister, Angelo Elia (75 Franz Peterhans), Piet Hamberg, Claude Andrey, Jean-Yves Valentini.   Trainer: Peter Pazmandy
FORTUNA: Jörg Daniel, Dieter Brei, Gerd Zewe, Gerd Zimmermann, Heiner Baltes, Reinhold Fanz, Thomas Allofs (47 Egon Köhnen), Hubert Schmitz, Fleming Lund, Klaus Allofs (29 Josef Weikl), Rudi Bommer.
Trainer: Dieter Tippenhauer
Goals: Bommer (4), Andrey (80).

**SK BEVEREN
v INTERNAZIONALE MILANO 1-0** (0-0)
Freethiel, Beveren   21.03.1979
Referee: André Daina (SWI)   Attendance: 22,000
BEVEREN: Jean-Marie Pfaff, Eddy Jaspers, Paul van Genechten, Freddy Buyl, Marc Baecke, Wim Hofkens, Heinz Schönberger, Erwin Albert, Robert Stevens, Albert Cluytens, Jean Janssens.   Trainer: Robert Goethals
INTER: Ivano Bordon, Nazzareno Canuti, Giuseppe Baresi, Gabriele Oriali (84 Odoacre Chierico), Silvano Fontolan, Graziano Bini, Alessandro Scanziani (62 Adriano Fedele), Giampiero Marini, Alessandro Altobelli, Evaristo Beccalossi, Carlo Muraro.   Trainer: Eugenio Bersellini
Goal: Stevens (85).

IPSWICH TOWN FC v CF BARCELONA 2-1 (0-0)
Portman Road, Ipswich   7.03.1979
Referee: Károly Palotai (HUN)   Attendance: 29,197
IPSWICH TOWN: Paul Cooper, George Burley, Les Tibbott, Michael Mills, Russell Osman, Terence Butcher, John Wark, Arnold Mühren, Alan Brazil, Eric Gates, David Geddis (81 Alan Hunter).   Manager: Robert Robson
CF BARCELONA: Pedro María ARTOLA Urrutia, Rafael Ignacio ZUVIRÍA Rodríguez, Miguel Bernardo Bianquetti "MIGUELI", Antonio OLMO Ramírez, Jesús Antonio DE LA CRUZ Gallego, Johan Neeskens (79 Enrique Álvarez COSTAS), ESTEBAN Vigo Benítez (86 José Joaquín ALBADALEJO Gispert), Juan Carlos HEREDIA Alvarado, Johann Krankl, Juan Manuel ASENSI Ripoll, Francisco MARTÍNEZ Díaz.
Trainer: Lucien Muller
Goals: Gates (52, 65), Esteban (53).

**FORTUNA DÜSSELDORF
v SERVETTE GENÈVE 0-0**
Rheinstadion, Düsseldorf   7.03.1979
Referee: Alojzy Jarguz (POL)   Attendance: 9,000
FORTUNA: Jörg Daniel, Dieter Brei, Gerd Zewe, Gerd Zimmermann, Heiner Baltes, Josef Weikl, Fleming Lund (65 Rudi Bommer), Hubert Schmitz, Emanuel Günther (74 Reinhold Fanz), Klaus Allofs, Wolfgang Seel.
Trainer: Dieter Tippenhauer
SERVETTE: Karl Engel; Marc Schnyder, Lucio Bizzini, Serge Trinchero, Gilbert Guyot, Umberto Barberis, Hansjörg Pfister, Guy Dutoit, Piet Hamberg, Claude Andrey, Jean-Yves Valentini.
Trainer: Peter Pazmandy

CF BARCELONA v IPSWICH TOWN 1-0 (1-0)
Camp Nou, Barcelona   21.03.1979
Referee: Eldar Asim-Zade (USSR)   Attendance: 100,000
CF BARCELONA: Pedro María ARTOLA Urrutia, Rafael Ignacio ZUVIRÍA Rodríguez, Miguel Bernardo Bianquetti "MIGUELI", Antonio OLMO Ramírez, José Joaquín ALBADALEJO Gispert, Johan Neeskens, Carlos REXACH Cerdá, Juan Carlos HEREDIA Alvarado, Johann Krankl, Juan Manuel ASENSI Ripoll, Francisco MARTÍNEZ Díaz.
Trainer: Lucien Muller
IPSWICH TOWN: Paul Cooper, George Burley, Kevin Beattie, Michael Mills, Russell Osman, Terence Butcher, John Wark (87 Thomas Parkin), Arnold Mühren, Alan Brazil, Eric Gates (68 David Geddis), Clive Woods.
Manager: Robert Robson
Goal: Migueli (42).

SEMI-FINALS

CF BARCELONA v SK BEVEREN 1-0 (0-0)
Camp Nou, Barcelona 11.04.1979
Referee: John Carpenter (IRL)   Attendance: 100,000

CF BARCELONA: Pedro María ARTOLA Urrutia, Rafael Ignacio ZUVIRÍA Rodríguez, Miguel Bernardo Bianquetti "MIGUELI", Antonio OLMO Ramírez, José Joaquín ALBADALEJO Gispert, Johan Neeskens, Carlos REXACH Cerdá, Juan Carlos HEREDIA Alvarado (84 Francisco José CARRASCO Hidalgo), Johann Krankl, Juan Manuel ASENSI Ripoll, Francisco MARTÍNEZ Díaz.   Trainer: Lucien Muller

BEVEREN: Jean-Marie Pfaff, Eddy Jaspers, Paul van Genechten, Freddy Buyl (86 Rudy van Goethem), Marc Baecke, Wim Hofkens, Heinz Schönberger (88 Florent Truyens), Erwin Albert, Robert Stevens, Albert Cluytens, Jean Janssens.   Manager: Robert Goethals.   Trainer: Henri Pauwels

Goal: Rexach (65 pen)

SK BEVEREN v CF BARCELONA 0-1 (0-0)
Freethiel, Beveren-Waas 25.04.1979
Referee: Patrick Partridge (ENG)   Attendance: 22,000

BEVEREN: Jean-Marie Pfaff, Eddy Jaspers, Paul van Genechten (83 Gustavo Lisazo), Freddy Buyl, Marc Baecke, Wim Hofkens, Heinz Schönberger, Erwin Albert, Robert Stevens, Albert Cluytens, Jean Janssens.   Manager: Robert Goethals.   Trainer: Henri Pauwels

CF BARCELONA: Pedro María ARTOLA Urrutia, Jesús Antonio DE LA CRUZ Gallego, Miguel Bernardo Bianquetti "MIGUELI", Enrique Álvarez COSTAS (70 Antonio OLMO Ramírez), José Joaquín ALBADALEJO Gispert, Johan Neeskens, José Vicente SÁNCHEZ Felip, Juan Carlos HEREDIA Alvarado (79 ESTEBAN Vigo Benítez), Juan Manuel ASENSI Ripoll, Johann Krankl, Carlos REXACH Cerdá.   Trainer: Joaquín RIFÉ Climent

Goal: Krankl (88 pen)

FORTUNA DÜSSELDORF
v BANÍK OSTRAVA OKD 3-1 (0-1)
Rheinstadion, Düsseldorf 11.04.1979
Referee: Augusto Lamo Castillo (SPA)   Attendance: 18,000

FORTUNA: Jörg Daniel, Dieter Brei, Gerd Zewe, Reinhold Fanz, Heiner Baltes, Josef Weikl, Rudi Bommer, Hubert Schmitz, Ralf Dusend (72 Fleming Lund), Klaus Allofs, Wolfgang Seel (76 Thomas Allofs).
Trainer: Dieter Tippenhauer

BANÍK: Pavol Michalík, Josef Foks, Rostislav Vojácek, Milan Albrecht, Zdenek Rygel, Libor Radimec, Augustín Antalík, Petr Nemec (82 Jozef Marchevsky), Lubomír Knapp, Zdenek Sreiner, Werner Licka.   Trainer: Evzen Hadamczik

Goals: Nemec (11), K. Allofs (54, 65), T. Allofs (90)

BANÍK OSTRAVA
v FORTUNA DÜSSELDORF 2-1 (0-1)
Stadión na Bazaloch, Ostrava 25.04.1979
Referee: Ernst Dörflinger (SWI)   Attendance: 33,000

BANÍK: Pavol Michalík, Josef Foks (69 Václav Pechácek), Rostislav Vojácek, Milan Albrecht, Zdenek Rygel, Libor Radimec, Augustín Antalík, Jozef Marchevsky (46 Petr Nemec), Lubomír Knapp, Zdenek Sreiner, Werner Licka.
Trainer: Evzen Hadamczik

FORTUNA: Jörg Daniel, Dieter Brei, Gerd Zewe, Gerd Zimmermann, Heiner Baltes (36 Josef Weikl), Reinhold Fanz, Egon Köhnen, Thomas Allofs, Rudi Bommer (41 Fleming Lund), Klaus Allofs, Wolfgang Seel.
Trainer: Dieter Tippenhauer

Goals: Zewe (31), Licka (65), Antalik (89)

FINAL

CF BARCELONA
v FORTUNA DÜSSELDORF 4-3 (2-2, 2-2) (AET)
St.Jakob, Basel 16.05.1979
Referee: Károly Palotai (HUN)   Attendance: 58,500

CF BARCELONA: Pedro Maria ARTOLA Urrutia; Rafael Ignacio ZUVIRÍA Rodríguez, Miguel Bernardo Bianquetti "MIGUELI", Enrique Álvarez COSTAS (66 Francisco MARTÍNEZ Díaz), José Joaquín ALBADALEJO Gispert (57 Jesús Antonio De la CRUZ Gallego); José Vicente SÁNCHEZ Felip, Johannes NEESKENS, Juan Manuel ASENSI Ripoll (Cap); Carlos REXACH Cerdá, Johann KRANKL, Francisco José CARRASCO Hidalgo.
Trainer: Joaquin Joaquín RIFÉ Climent

FORTUNA: Jörg Daniel; Dieter Brei (24 Josef Weikl), Gerd Zewe (Cap), Gerd Zimmermann (84 Fleming Lund), Heiner Baltes; Egon Köhnen, Hubert Schmitz, Thomas Allofs; Rudi Bommer, Klaus Allofs, Wolfgang Seel.
Trainer: Dieter Tippenhauer

Rexach had a penalty (12) saved by Daniel

Goals: Sánchez (5), T. Allofs (8), Asensi (34), Seel (41, 114), Rexach (103), Krankl (111)

Goalscorers European Cup-Winners' Cup 1978-79:

7 goals: Alessandro Altobelli (Inter Milano)

5 goals: Johann Krankl (FC Barcelona)

4 goals: Werner Lička (Baník Ostrava), Joachim Streich (FC Magdeburg)

3 goals: Jarvie (Aberdeen), Antalík, Rygel (Baník Ostrava), K. Allofs (Fortuna Düsseldorf), Muraro (Inter Milano), Elia (Servette Genève)

2 goals: Teitgen (US Luxembourg), Cămătaru (Universitatea Craiova), I. Petrov (Marek Stanke Dimitrov), Hanssen, Solhaug (FK Bodø/Glimt), Giles, Lynex (Shamrock Rovers), Oberacher (SWW Innsbruck), Jeannol, Zénier (AS Nancy), Van der Elst (Anderlecht), Harper (Aberdeen), Szokolai (Ferencváros Budapest), Steinbach (FC Magdeburg), Fedele (Inter Milano), Hamberg (Servette Genève), Gates, Wark (Ipswich Town), Baecke, Janssens, Stevens (Beveren), Nemec, Albrecht (Baník Ostrava), Bommer, Günther, Zimmermann, Fanz, Seel, T.Allofs (Fortuna Düsseldorf), Migueli, Rexach, Sánchez (CF Barcelona),

1 goal: Zarychta, Szarynski, Dworczyk (Zaglebie Sosnowiec), Crişan, Marcu (Universitatea Craiova), R.Xuereb (Floriana FC), Magnusson, Nyberg (Kalmar FF), Albertsson (Valur Reykjavík), V.Petrov (Marek Stanke Dimitrov), Kermanidis, Sarafis (PAOK Thessaloniki), McNeil, Cartwright (Wrexham), Reznik (Shahtior Donetsk), Jacobsen, Hansen (Frem København), H.Berg (Bodø/Glimt), P.Koncilia, Braschler (SWW Innsbruck), Rubio, Umpierrez, Curbelo (AS Nancy), Coeck (Anderlecht), McLelland, Strachan (Aberdeen), Tomić, Durkalić, Cukrov (NK Rijeka), Pusztai, Ebedli, Nyilasi, Major (Ferencváros Budapest), Sparwasser, Pommerenke, Stahmann, Seguin, Hoffmann (FC Magdeburg), Scanziani, Beccalossi, Chierico (Inter Milano), Andrey, Schnyder, Barberis, Pfister (Servette Genève), Burley, Mariner (Ipswich Town), Wissmann, Albert, Schönberger (Beveren), Knapp, Radimec (Baník Ostrava), Zewe (Fortuna Düsseldorf), Asensi, Esteban, Heredia, Zuviría (CF Barcelona)

Own goal: Koterwa (Zaglebie Sosnowiec) for SWW Innsbruck

CUP WINNERS' CUP 1979-80

PRELIMINARY ROUND

B1903 KØBENHAVN v APOEL NICOSIA 6-0 (2-0)

København 15.08.1979

Referee: Rolf Ericsson (SWE)   Attedance: 2,000

B 1903: Per Poulsen, Poul Kristiansen, Benny Johansen, Jörn Damm, John Andersen, Michael Sundby (46 Keld Kristiansen), Jörgen Lorentzen, Niels Haarbye, Thomas Larsen, Bent Kristiansen, Poul Erik Thygesen.

APOEL: Herodotos Herodotou "Koupanos", Haralampos Menelaou, Andreas Stefanou (79 Kostas Miamiliotis), Andreas Stavrou, Nikos Pantziaras, Koulis Pantziaras, Mihalis Hatzipieris, Takis Timotheou (54 Kyriakos Vasileiou), Petrakis Hatzithomas, Andreas Hailis, Takis Antoniou.

Goals: Haarby (12), Larsen (19), B. Kristiansen (47, 56), Thygesen (61, 88)

APOEL NICOSIA v B1903 KØBENHAVN 0-1 (0-0)

Nicosia 8.09.1979

Referee: Aleksandar Nikić (YUG)   Attendance: 2,500

APOEL: Herodotos Herodotou "Koupanos", Haralampos Menelaou, Andreas Stefanou, Andreas Stavrou, Kostas Miamiliotis, Koulis Pantziaras, Giorgos Petrou, Takis Timotheou (81 Ermogenis Ermogendes), Petrakis Hatzithomas, Takis Antoniou (70 Andreas Hailis), Mihalis Hatzipieris.

B 1903: Per Poulsen, John Andersen, Jørn Damm, Jørgen Lorentzen, Poul Kristiansen, Michael Sundby, Jens Sass Hansen, Keld Kristensen (63 Finn Schmidt Jensen), Benny Johansen, Niels Haarbye, Bent Kristiansen.

Goal: Damm (67)

GLASGOW RANGERS FC v LILLESTRØM SK 1-0 (1-0)

Ibrox Park, Glasgow 21.08.1979

Referee: Jan Beck (HOL)   Attendance: 25,000

RANGERS: Peter McCloy; William Jardine, Alistair Dawson, Gordon Smith, Colin Jackson, Kenneth Watson, Thomas McLean (85 John MacDonald), Robert Russell, Derek Johnstone (90 Chris Robertson), Alexander MacDonald, David Cooper.

LILLESTRØM SK: Arne Amundsen, Georg Hammer, Per Berg, Tore Kordahl, Leif Hansen, Frank Grønlund, Arne Erlandsen, Gunnar Lønstad, Arne Dokken, Terje Holt, Vidar Hansen.

Goal: Smith (12)

LILLESTRØM SK
v GLASGOW RANGERS FC 0-2 (0-1)
Ullevål, Oslo   5.09.1979
Referee: Olavi Peltola (FIN)   Attendance: 6,175

LILLESTRØM SK: Arne Amundsen, Georg Hammer, Per Berg, Tore Kordahl, Leif Hansen, Frank Grønlund, Arne Erlandsen, Gunnar Lønstad, Arne Dokken, Terje Holt, Vidar Hansen (.. Rolf Nordberg).

RANGERS: Peter McCloy, Alexander Miller, Alistair Dawson, William Jardine, Colin Jackson, Kenneth Watson, Thomas McLean (.. David Cooper), Robert Russell, Derek Johnstone, Alexander MacDonald, Gordon Smith.

Goals: A. MacDonald (45), Johnstone (89)

FIRST ROUND

SLIEMA WANDERERS
v BOAVISTA PORTO 2-1 (1-0)
Empire Stadium, Valletta   12.09.1979
Referee: Bruno Galler (SWI)   Attendance: 5,000

SLIEMA: Charles Sciberras, David Buckingham, Mario Schembri, Oliver Losco, Gennaro Camilleri, Fortell (84 John Caruana), Joseph Aquilina, Emanuel Fabri, Richard Aquilina, Tony Tabone, Steven Pandolfino (86 Spiteri).

BOAVISTA: Luís Filipe da Cruz MATOS, Manuel José Ferreira da Silva BARBOSA, Vitorino Oliveira BELINHA, ARTUR Nogueira Ferreira, António Carlos Sousa Laranjeira "TAÍ", ÓSCAR Vicente Martins Duarte, ELISEU Martins Ramalho, AILTON Ballesteros, Mario Jorge MOINHOS de Matos, JÚLIO Carlos da Costa Augusto, SALVADOR Luis Almeida.

Goals: Fortell (33 pen, 67 pen), Eliseu (78 pen).

BOAVISTA PORTO
v SLIEMA WANDERERS 8-0 (4-0)
Estádio do Bessa, Porto   5.10.1979
Referee: Antonio Tomeo Palanques (SPA)   Att: 25,000

BOAVISTA: Luís Filipe da Cruz MATOS, Manuel José Ferreira da Silva BARBOSA, ADÃO da Silva, ARTUR Nogueira Ferreira, António Carlos Sousa Laranjeira "TAÍ", Antonio Manuel dos Santos ALMEIDA, ELISEU Martins Ramalho (46 SALVADOR Luis Almeida), AILTON Ballesteros, Mario Jorge MOINHOS de Matos, JÚLIO Carlos da Costa Augusto (59 ÓSCAR Vicente Martins Duarte), Fernando Manuel Parada FOLHA.

SLIEMA: Charles Sciberras, David Buckingham, Emanuel Fabri, Mario Schembri, Oliver Losco, Gennaro Camilleri, Richard Aquilina (80 Lawrence Borg), Fortell, Joseph Aquilina, Tony Tabone (63 John Caruana), Eric Schembri.

Goals: Ailton (7), Julio (16, 28, 57), Moinhos (34), Salvador (53), Folha (63), Oscar (90)

YOUNG BOYS BERN
v STEAUA BUCUREŞTI 2-2 (1-2)
Wankdorf, Bern   19.09.1979
Referee: Sándor Kuti (HUN)   Attendance: 6,700

YOUNG BOYS: Walter Eichenberger; Jakob Brechbühl, Martin Weber, Jörg Schmidlin, Hansjörg Lüdi; Kurt Feuz, Charles Zwygart, Alfred Hussner, Thomas Zwahlen (75 Rolf Zahnd), Roland Schönenberger, Kurt Müller.
Trainer: Timo Konietzka

STEAUA: Vasile Iordache; Teodor Anghelini, Mario Agiu, Ştefan Sameş, Ion Niţu; Ion Dumitru, Tudorel Stoica, Anghel Iordănescu; Vasile Aelenei, Adrian Ionescu, Constantin Zamfir.
Trainer: Gheorghe Constantin

Goals: Stoica (38), Zwygart (42 pen), Iordănescu (44 pen), Schönenberger (78)

STEAUA BUCUREŞTI
v YOUNG BOYS BERN 6-0 (2-0)
Steaua, Bucureşti   3.10.1979
Referee: Talal Tokat (TUR)   Attendance: 6,700

STEAUA: Vasile Iordache (70 Răducanu Necula); Teodor Anghelini, Mario Agiu, Ştefan Sameş, Ion Niţu; Ion Dumitru, Tudorel Stoica, Vasile Aelenei; Marcel Răducanu, Adrian Ionescu, Constantin Zamfir (63 Gabriel Zahiu).
Trainer: Gheorghe Constantin

YOUNG BOYS: Walter Eichenberger; Jakob Brechbühl, Martin Weber, Alfred Hussner, Kurt Feuz; Rolf Zahnd (22 Jean-Marie Conz), Charles Zwygart, Hansjörg Lüdi; Thomas Zwahlen, Roland Schönenberger, Kurt Müller.
Trainer: Timo Konietzka

Goals: Niţu (2), Sameş (7, 65), Aelenei (47), M. Răducanu (56), Zahiu (72)

PANIONIOS ATHINA
v FC TWENTE ENSCHEDE 4-0 (1-0)
Neas Smirnis, Athina   19.09.1979
Referee: Alberto Michelotti (ITA)   Attendance: 6,800

PANIONIOS: Zafeiris Kakaris, Serafeim Zaharopoulos, Nikos Halkidis, Hristos Emboliadis, Giannis Grabanis, Vasilis Moraitelis, Giannis Pathiakakis (79 Carlos Felipe NUÑEZ), Leonido Lima, Nikos Anastopoulos, Dimitris Maurikis (72 Kostas Vallidis), Thomas Liolios.   Trainer: Z. Meltsik

TWENTE: Eddy Pasveer, Bert Strijdveen, Epi Drost, Niels Overweg, Romeo Zondervan, Aad Kila, Martin Jol, Hallvar Thoresen, Jaap Bos, Ab Gritter, Arie Van Staveren.
Trainer: Anton Spitz Kohn

Goals: Liolios (25, 48), Pathiakakis (78 pen), Anastopoulos (86)

**FC TWENTE ENSCHEDE
v PANIONIOS ATHINA 3-1** (2-0)
Diekmann, Enschede   3.10.1979
Referee: John Carpenter (IRL)   Attendance: 16,000
TWENTE: André van Gerven, John Scheve, Martin Jol, Tjalling Dilling, Romeo Zondervan, Heini Otto, Aad Kila (.. Epi Drost), Hallvar Thoresen, Jaap Bos, Sören Sören Lindsted (.. Arie Van Staveren), Ab Gritter.   Trainer: Anton Spitz Kohn
PANIONIOS: Zafeiris Kakaris, Serafeim Zaharopoulos, Giannis Grabanis, Nikos Halkidis, Hristos Emboliadis, Vasilis Moraitelis, Haralampos Saipas, Leonido Lima, Nikos Anastopoulos, Dimitris Maurikis (66 Harilaos Sofianos), Thomas Liolios.   Trainer: Z. Meltsik
Goals: Bos (2 pen), Lindsted (13), Jol (74), Anastopoulos (86)

REIPAS LAHTI v ARIS BONNEVOIE 0-1 (0-0)
Kisapuisto, Lahti   19.09.1979
Referee: Rolf Ericsson (SWE)   Attendance: 805
REIPAS: Risto Parkkonen, Vesa Pääkkönen, Risto Rautemaa (23 Jorma Salonen), Hannu Järvelin, Markku Repo, Hannu Hämäläinen (80 Juha Saarikunnas), Tarmo Haara, Pekka Kanerva, Heikki-Pekka Lampi, Seppo Nordman, Harri Lindholm.
ARIS: Claude Birenbaum, Roger Fandel, Baus, Fernand Jeitz, Marcel Weber, Wolfgang Tullius, André Vandivinit, Guy Weis, Roland Kalte, Carlo Bamberg, René Schiltz.   Trainer: Alfred Sbroglia
Goal: Schiltz (57)

**ARKA GDYNIA
v BEROE STARA ZAGORA 3-2** (1-1)
Arka, Gdynia   19.09.1979
Referee: Horst Di Carlo (E. GER)   Attendance: 20,000
ARKA: Wlodzimierz Zemojtel, Jacek Pietrzykowski, Zbigniew Bielinski, Franciszek Bochentyn, Tadeusz Krystyniak (80 Andrzej Bikiewicz), Andrzej Dybicz, Janusz Kupcewicz, Boguslaw Kaczmarek, Ryszard Kurzepa, Tomasz Korynt, Wieslaw Kwiatkowski.
BEROE: Kosta Kostov; Hristo Belchev, Tenio Minchev, Kancho Kasherov, Ilia Iliev, Georgi Stoianov (69 Tanko Tanev), Stefan Stefanov, Tanio Petrov (55 Stefan Naidenov), Petko Petkov, Tenio Tenev, Plamen Lipenski.   Trainer: Ivan Tanev
Goals: Kwiatkowski (19), Petkov (42), Korynt (46, 52), Lipenski (62)

ARIS BONNEVOIE v REIPAS LAHTI 1-0 (1-0)
Bonnevoie   3.10.1979
Referee: Louis Delsemme (BEL)   Attendance: 3,000
ARIS: Claude Birenbaum, Roger Fandel, Wolfgang Tullius, Baus, Marcel Weber, Claude Colling, Roland Kalte, Guy Weis, André Vandivinit, René Schiltz, Jean-Jacques Mathes.   Trainer: Alfred Sbroglia
REIPAS: Risto Parkkonen, Vesa Pääkkönen, Risto Rautemaa, Hannu Järvelin, Markku Repo, Hannu Hämäläinen, Ari Tupasela, Pekka Kanerva (.. Juha Saarikunnas), Heikki-Pekka Lampi, Seppo Nordman, Harri Lindholm.
Goal: Colling (32)

**BEROE STARA ZAGORA
v ARKA GDYNIA 2-0** (2-0)
Gradski, Stara Zagora   3.10.1979
Referee: Ermis Reires (CYP)   Attendance: 20,000
BEROE: Kosta Kostov; Mitkov, Dinko Dimitrov, Tenio Minhcev, Ilia Iliev, Georgi Stoianov, Stefan Naidenov (72 Tenio Tenev), Stefan Stefanov, Angel Yanev, Petko Petkov, Plamen Lipenski (74 Tanio Petrov).   Trainer: Ivan Tanev
ARKA: Wlodzimierz Zemojtel, Jacek Pietrzykowski, Zbigniew Bielinski, Franciszek Bochentyn, Adam Musial, Andrzej Dybicz, Janusz Kupcewicz, Boguslaw Kaczmarek, Ryszard Kurzepa, Tomasz Korynt, Wieslaw Kwiatkowski (78 Andrzej Bikiewicz).
Goals: Stoianov (31), Petkov (34)

**GLASGOW RANGERS
v FORTUNA DÜSSELDORF 2-1** (0-0)
Ibrox, Glasgow   19.09.1979
Referee: Achille Verbecke (FRA)   Attendance: 30,000
RANGERS: Peter McCloy, Alexander Miller, Alistair Dawson, William Jardine, Colin Jackson, Alexander MacDonald, Thomas McLean, Robert Russell (65 Kenneth Watson), Derek Johnstone, Gordon Smith, David Cooper.   Manager: John Greig
FORTUNA: Jörg Daniel, Josef Weikl, Gerd Zewe, Egon Köhnen, Heiner Baltes, Rüdiger Wenzel, Heinz Wirtz, Thomas Allofs (72 Hubert Schmitz), Rudi Bommer, Klaus Allofs, Wolfgang Seel.   Trainer: Dieter Tippenhauer
Goals: A. MacDonald (69), McLean (75), Wenzel (81)

**FORTUNA DÜSSELDORF
v GLASGOW RANGERS 0-0**
Rheinstadion, Düsseldorf   3.10.1979
Referee: Vojtech Christov (CZE)   Attendance: 40,000
FORTUNA: Jörg Daniel, Josef Weikl, Gerd Zewe, Heiner Baltes, Egon Köhnen, Heinz Wirtz (73 Ralf Dusend), Hubert Schmitz, Rudi Bommer, Rüdiger Wenzel, Klaus Allofs, Wolfgang Seel (46 Thomas Allofs).
Trainer: Dieter Tippenhauer
RANGERS: Peter McCloy, Alexander Miller (65 Alex Forsyth), Alistair Dawson, William Jardine, Colin Jackson, Kenneth Watson, Thomas McLean, Alexander MacDonald, Derek Johnstone, Gordon Smith (31 David Cooper), Derek Parlane.   Manager: John Greig

WREXHAM FC v 1.FC MAGDEBURG 3-2 (1-2)
Racecourse Ground, Wrexham   19.09.1979
Referee: Torben Mansson (DEN)   Attendance: 9,802
WREXHAM: David Davies, Joey Jones, Alan Dwyer, Gareth Davis, John Roberts, David Giles, Stephen Fox, Melvyn Sutton, Richard McNeil, Graham Whittle (57 Stephen Buxton), Alan Hill.
1.FC MAGDEBURG: Dirk Heine, Detlef Raugust, Rolf Döbbelin, Wolfgang Seguin, Klaus Decker, Jürgen Pommerenke, Wolfgang Steinbach (79 Axel Tyll), Joachim Streich, Siegmund Mewes, Martin Hoffmann, Heiner Thomas.
Trainer: Klaus Urbanczyk
Goals: McNeil (2), Streich (14), Steinbach (43), Fox (77), Buxton (84)

JUVENTUS TORINO v RABA ETO GYÖR 2-0 (0-0)
Stadio Comunale, Torino   19.09.1979
Referee: Klaus Scheurell (E. GER)   Attendance: 45,000
JUVENTUS: Dino Zoff; Claudio Gentile, Antonio Cabrini, Claudio Prandelli (65 Antonello Cuccureddu), Sergio Brio, Gaetano Scirea, Franco Causio, Marco Tardelli, Roberto Bettega, Roberto Tavola (55 Domenico Marocchino), Pietro Fanna.   Trainer: Giovanni Trapattoni
RABA ETO: Antal Palla; Gyula Csonka, Lajos Pozsgai, Ferenc Pásztor, Lajos Magyar; Péter Hannich, Tibor Onhausz, József Póczik (80 Lajos Jugovits); Ottó Szabó, Róbert Glázer (68 Sándor Mile), Gábor Pölöskei.   Trainer: Imre Kovács
Goals: Pozsgai (63 og), Cabrini (73 pen)

1.FC MAGDEBURG v WREXHAM FC 5-2 (1-2,3-2)
Ernst-Grube-Stadion, Magdeburg   3.10.1979
Referee: Svein Inge Thime (NOR)   Attendance: 15,000
1.FC MAGDEBURG: Dirk Heine, Detlef Raugust, Rolf Döbbelin (64 Axel Tyll), Wolfgang Seguin, Klaus Decker, Siegmund Mewes (96 Frank Siersleben), Jürgen Pommerenke, Wolfgang Steinbach, Joachim Streich, Heiner Thomas, Martin Hoffmann.   Trainer: Klaus Urbanczyk
WREXHAM: David Davies, Joey Jones, Gareth Davis, John Roberts, Alan Dwyer, David Giles (65 Graham Whittle), Alan Hill, Melvyn Sutton, Richard McNeil (.. Stephen Buxton), Stephen Fox, Michael Vinter.
Goals: Vinter (25), Hoffmann (28, 54 pen), Hill (34), Mewes (88), Steinbach (93 pen), Streich (115)

RABA ETO GYÖR v JUVENTUS TORINO 2-1 (2-0)
Györi stadion   3.10.1979
Referee: Emilio Carlos Guruceta Muro (SPA)   Att: 22,000
RABA ETO: Antal Palla; Gyula Csonka, Lajos Pozsgai, Ferenc Pásztor, Lajos Magyar; Péter Hannich, Tibor Onhausz, József Póczik; Ottó Szabó (79 Lajos Jugovits), Róbert Glázer (66 Sándor Mile), Gábor Pölöskei.   Trainer: Imre Kovács
JUVENTUS: Dino Zoff, Antonello Cuccureddu (77 Antonio Cabrini), Claudio Gentile, Giuseppe Furino, Sergio Brio, Gaetano Scirea; Marco Tardelli, Roberto Bettega, Roberto Tavola (46 Claudio Prandelli); Franco Causio, Pietro Fanna.
Trainer: Giovanni Trapattoni
Goals: Furino (6 og), Póczik (23), Causio (52)

**SWW INNSBRUCK
v LOKOMOTÍVA KOŠICE 1-2** (1-1)
Tivoli, Innsbruck   19.09.1979
Referee: Jan Keiser (HOL)   Attendance: 5,000
SWW: Norbert Schatz; Peter Schwartz, Robert Auer, Fernando Zappia, Walter Stöfflbauer; Josef Hickersberger (73 Robert Scheiber), Arnold Koreimann, Günther Kronsteiner (73 Roland Freimüller), Robert Hanschitz; Wilhelm Pöll, Francisco Castellano.   Trainer: Peter Velhorn
LOKOMOTÍVA: Stanislav Seman, Pavol Biros, Jozef Suchánek, Vladimír Dobrovic, Gejza Farkas, Ján Kozák, Peter Jacko, Józef Moder (32 Dušan Ujhely), Stanislav Strapek, Peter Fecko, Peter Lovacky.   Trainer: Jozef Jankech
Goals: Strapek (8), Pöll (16 pen), Jacko (63)

**LOKOMOTÍVA KOŠICE
v SWW INNSBRUCK 1-0** (1-0)

Jeho Cermell Stadion, Košice   3.10.1979

Referee: Jakob Baumann (SWI)   Attendance: 6,000

LOKOMOTÍVA: Stanislav Seman, Zdeno Kost, Jozef Suchánek, Vladimír Dobrovic, Gejza Farkas, Ján Kozák, Peter Jacko, Dušan Ujhely (74 Pavol Pizur), Stanislav Strapek, Peter Fecko, Peter Lovacky.   Trainer: Jozef Jankech

SWW: Egon Katnik; Peter Schwartz, Robert Auer, Fernando Zappia, Walter Stöfflbauer; Josef Hickersberger, Arnold Koreimann, Günther Kronsteiner, Francisco Castellano; Wilhelm Pöll, Manfred Braschler.   Trainer: Peter Velhorn

Goal: Kozák (6)

B 1903 KØBENHAVN v VALENCIA CF 2-2 (1-2)

Idraetspark, København   19.09.1979

Referee: Anders Mattsson (FIN)   Attendance: 11,800

B 1903: Per Poulsen, John Andersen, Jørn Damm, Jørgen Lorentzen, Poul Kristiansen, Michael Sundby, Benny Johansen, Thomas Larsen (59 Jens Sass Hansen), Keld Kristensen (84 Niels Haarbye), Bent Kristiansen, Poul Erik Thygesen.   Trainer: Erik Dennung

VALENCIA CF: Carlos Santiago PEREIRA, José CERVERO San Braulio, Daniel Cabezas "DANI", Manuel BOTUBOT Pereira, José PALMER, Enrique SAURA Gil, Rainer Bonhof (79 Pedro VILARRODÁ), Ángel CASTELLANOS Céspedes, Ricardo ARIAS Penella (54 Daniel SOLSONA Puig), Mario Alberto KEMPES Chiodi, Luis Dario FELMAN.   Trainer: Alfredo DI STEFANO Lahule

Goals: Thygesen (19), Arias (30), Hansen (73), Castellanos (38)

BEERSCHOT ANTWERP v NK RIJEKA 0-0

Stedelijk Olympisch Stadion, Antwerp   19.09.1979

Referee: Gianfranco Menegali (ITA)   Attendance: 14,000

BEERSCHOT: Jan Tomaszewski; Paul Beloy, Johnny Van Abbeny, Louis De Weerdt, Louis Van Gucht; Julien Cools, Frank Schrauwen, Juan Lozano (20 Jean Rylant), Stanislaw Gzil, René Mücher, Emmanuel Sanon (60 Rudi Van Landeghem).

NK RIJEKA: Mauro Ravnić; Sergio Makin, Miloš Hrstić, Zvjezdan Radin, Srećko Juričić, Nikica Cukrov, Milenković, Bacvarević (46 Edmond Tomić), Milan Radović, Milan Ruzić, Damir Desnica.   Trainer: Miroslav Blazević

VALENCIA CF v B.1903 KØBENHAVN 4-0 (1-0)

Estadio Luis Casanova, Valencia   3.10.1979

Referee: Ronald Bridges (WAL)   Attendance: 20,000

VALENCIA CF: Carlos Santiago PEREIRA, José CERVERO San Braulio, Daniel Cabezas "DANI", Manuel BOTUBOT Pereira, Enrique SAURA Gil, Ángel CASTELLANOS Céspedes, Daniel SOLSONA Puig, Ricardo ARIAS Penella, Luis Dario FELMAN (46 José PALMER), Mario Alberto KEMPES Chiodi, Orlando Ramón JIMÉNEZ (69 Pedro Vilarroda).   Trainer: Alfredo DI STEFANO Lahule

B 1903: Per Poulsen, John Andersen, Jørn Damm, Jørgen Lorentzen, Poul Kristiansen, Michael Sundby, Keld Kristensen, Benny Johansen, Bent Kristiansen, Niels Haarbye (57 Thomas Larsen), Poul Erik Thygesen (46 Finn Schmidt Jensen).   Trainer: Erik Dennung

Goals: Felman (44), Kempes (74, 89), Saura (86)

NK RIJEKA v BEERSCHOT ANTWERP 2-1 (1-1)

Kantrida, Rijeka   3.10.1979

Referee: René Vigliani (FRA)   Attendance: 12,000

NK RIJEKA: Mauro Ravnić; Sergio Makin, Miloš Hrstić, Zvjezdan Radin, Srećko Juričić; Nikica Cukrov, Milenković, Edmond Tomić (76 Ivan Jerolimov); Milan Ruzić, Milan Radović, Damir Desnica.   Trainer: Miroslav Blazević

BEERSCHOT: Jan Tomaszewski; Paul Beloy, Johnny Van Abbeny, Jean Rijlant, Louis Van Gucht; Julien Cools, Louis De Weerdt, Johan Coninx, Juan Lozano; René Mücher, Stanislaw Gzil.

Goals: Gzil (34), Radović (44, 89)

**ARSENAL LONDON
v FENERBAHÇE ISTANBUL 2-0** (1-0)

Arsenal Stadium Highbury, London   19.09.1979

Referee: Sigfried Kirschen (E. GER)   Attendance: 39,973

ARSENAL: Patrick Jennings, Patrick Rice, Samuel Nelson, Brian Talbot, David O'Leary, William Young, Liam Brady, Alan Sunderland, Francis Stapleton, John Hollins, Graham Rix.   Manager: Terence Neill

FENERBAHÇE: Adem Ibrahimoğlu, Emin Ilhan, Yenal Kaçira, Erol Togay, Cem Pamiroglu, Yasar Gosku (.. Tuna Guneysu), Şevki Şenlen, Onder Mustafaoğlu, Raşit Çetiner, Zafer Göncüler, Ali Kemal Denizci.   Trainer: Şükrü Ersoy

Goals: Sunderland (30), Young (85)

**FENERBAHÇE SK ISTANBUL
v ARSENAL FC LONDON 0-0**
İnönü, Istanbul 3.10.1979

Referee: Riccardo Lattanzi (ITA)   Attendance: 30,000

FENERBAHÇE: Adem Ibrahimoğlu, Şevki Şenlen, Yenal Kaçira, Erol Togay, Cem Pamiroglu, Yasar Gosku (55 Tuna Guneysu), Emin Ilhan, Onder Mustafaoğlu, Raşit Çetiner, Cemil Turan, Ali Kemal Denizci.   Trainer: Şükrü Ersoy

ARSENAL: Patrick Jennings, Patrick Rice, Samuel Nelson, Brian Talbot, David O'Leary, William Young, Liam Brady, Alan Sunderland, Francis Stapleton, John Hollins, Graham Rix.   Manager: Terence Neill

IFK GÖTEBORG v WATERFORD 1-0 (0-0)
Gamla Ullevi, Göteborg 19.09.1979

Referee: Albert Victor (LUX)   Attendance: 6,193

IFK: Odd Lindberg, Ruben Svensson, Reine Almqvist, Conny Karlsson, Reine Olausson, Olle Nordin, Tord Holmgren, Glenn Holm, Tommy Holmgren (.. Glenn Strömberg), Torbjörn Nilsson, Anders Ahlberg.   Trainer: Sven Göran Eriksson

WATERFORD: Peter Thomas, Brian Gardnier, Al.Finucane, Thomas Jackson, Martin Dunphy, Eamonn Coady (.. Tommy Keane), Brendan Carey, Mick Madigan, Vinny McCarthy, Sean Kiely, Tony Keane.

Goal: G. Holm (65 pen)

WATERFORD FC v IFK GÖTEBORG 1-1 (0-1)
Kilcohan Park, Waterford 3.10.1979

Referee: Gerd J.M. Geurds (HOL)   Attendance: 1,500

WATERFORD: Peter Thomas, Brian Gardiner, Al.Finucane, Thomas Jackson (.. Tony Dunphy), Martin Dunphy, Brendan Carey, Mick Madigan, Vinny McCarthy, Eamonn Coady, Sean Kiely, Tony Keane (.. Steve O'Halloran).

IFK: Odd Lindberg, Ruben Svensson, Glenn Hysén, Conny Karlsson, Reine Olausson, Glenn Schiller (.. Jerry Carlsson), Tord Holmgren, Glenn Strömberg, Olle Nordin, Tommy Holmgren (.. Erik Nilsson), Torbjörn Nilsson.   Trainer: Sven Göran Eriksson

Goals: Tord Holmgren (29), Tony Keane (68)

CLIFTONVILLE FC v FC NANTES 0-1 (0-1)
Solitude, Belfast 20.09.1979

Referee: Henning Lund-Sørensen (DEN)   Att: 3,500

CLIFTONVILLE: Brian Johnston, Brendan McGuicken (..John O'Connor), Eamon Largey, John Flanagan, Martin Quinn, Ciaran McCurry, Peter McCusker, John Hewitt, Walter Mills, John Platt (.. Michael Adair), Anthony Bell.

FC NANTES: Jean-Paul Bertrand-Demanes; Maxime Bossis, Thierry Tusseau, Patrice Rio, Henri Michel, Enzo Trossero, Bruno Baronchelli, Oscar Muller, Victor Trossero, Gilles Rampillon, Loic Amisse.   Trainer: Jean Vincent

Goal: Rampillon (26)

FC NANTES v CLIFTONVILLE FC 7-0 (4-0)
Marcel Saupin, Nantes 3.10.1979

Referee: J. Ignacio DE ALMEIRA (POR)   Att: 13,250

FC NANTES: Jean-Paul Bertrand-Demanes; Maxime Bossis, Patrice Rio, Henri Michel (46 William Ayache), Thierry Tusseau, Enzo Trossero, Oscar Muller, Gilles Rampillon, Victor Trossero, Loic Amisse (66 Fabrice Picot), Eric Pécout.   Trainer: Jean Vincent

CLIFTONVILLE: Brian Johnston, Walter Mills, John Flanagan, Martin Quinn, Eamon Largey (82 Brendan McGuicken), John Hewitt, John O'Connor, Ciaran McCurry (56 William Smyth), Peter McCusker, Michael Adair, Anthony Bell.

Goals: V. Trossero (3, 65), Pécout (19, 52, 85), Rampillon (29), Rio (41)

ÍA AKRANES v CF BARCELONA 0-1 (0-0)
Laugardalsvöllur, Reykjavík 26.09.1979

Referee: David Syme (SCO)   Attendance: 3,000

ÍA AKRANES: Bjarni Sigurdsson; Gudjón Thordarson, Jóhannes Gudjónsson, Sigurdur Lárusson; Sigurdur Haldórsson, Kristján Olgeirsson; Jón Gunnlaugsson, Jón Alfredsson, Arni Sveinsson, Sveinbjörn Hakonarsson (80 Kristinn Björnsson), Sigthór Omarsson (.. Gudbjörn Tryggvason).   Trainer: Klaus-Jürgen Hilpert

CF BARCELONA: Vicente AMIGÓ; Juan José ESTELLA Salas, Antonio OLMO Ramírez, José Cano "CANITO", Adjutorio SERRAT Giró; José Vicente SÁNCHEZ Felip (46 Francisco MARTÍNEZ Díaz), Jesús LANDÁBURU Sahuquillo, Rafael Ignacio ZUVIRÍA Rodríguez; Juan Carlos HEREDIA Alvarado (46 Carlos REXACH Cerdá), Johann Krankl, Allan Simonsen.   Trainer: Joaquin RIFE Climent

Goal: Rexach (55)

CF BARCELONA v ÍA AKRANES 5-0 (2-0)
Camp Nou, Barcelona 3.10.1979

Referee: Paul Bonett (MAL)   Attendance: 17,000

CF BARCELONA: Pedro María ARTOLA Urrutia, Juan José ESTELLA Salas, Miguel Bernardo Bianquetti "MIGUELI", José Cano "CANITO", Adjutorio SERRAT Giró, José Vicente SÁNCHEZ Felip, Juan Manuel ASENSI Ripoll, Jesús LANDÁBURU Sahuquillo, Carlos REXACH Cerdá, Johann Krankl (68 ESTEBAN Vigo Benítez), Allan Simonsen (46 Francisco José CARRASCO Hidalgo).   Trainer: Joaquin RIFE Climent

ÍA AKRANES: Bjarni Sigurdsson, Gudjón Thordarson, Jóhannes Gudjónsson, Sigurdur Lárusson, Sigurdur Haldórsson, Jón Gunnlaugsson, Jón Alfredsson, Arni Sveinsson, Kristján Olgeirsson, Sveinbjörn Hakonarsson, Sigthór Omarsson (72 Gudbjorn Tryggvason).   Trainer: Klaus-Jürgen Hilpert

Goals: Krankl (14), Simonsen (33), Rexach (53), Asensi (63), Carrasco (75)

Dynamo Moscow qualified for the next round, because KS Vllaznia Shkoder (ALB) refused to play in Russia.

SECOND ROUND

**ARSENAL FC LONDON
v 1.FC MAGDEBURG 2-1** (1-1)
Arsenal Stadium Highbury, London   24.10.1979
Referee: Horst Brummeier (AUS)   Attendance: 34,375
ARSENAL: Patrick Jennings, Patrick Rice, Samuel Nelson, Brian Talbot, David O'Leary, William Young, Liam Brady, Alan Sunderland, Francis Stapleton, John Hollins, Graham Rix.   Manager: Terence Neill
1.FC MAGDEBURG: Dirk Heine, Detlef Raugust, Axel Tyll, Wolfgang Seguin (55 Rolf Döbbelin), Klaus Decker, Siegmund Mewes, Jürgen Pommerenke, Wolfgang Steinbach, Joachim Streich, Dirk Stahmann, Martin Hoffmann.
Trainer: Klaus Urbanczyk

Goals: Young (4), Pommerenke (40), Sunderland (60)

**1.FC MAGDEBURG
v ARSENAL FC LONDON   2-2** (0-1)
Heinrich-Germer Stadion, Magdeburg   7.11.1979
Referee: Lars-Ake Björck (SWE)   Attendance: 18,000
1.FC MAGDEBURG: Dirk Heine, Detlef Raugust, Dirk Stahmann, Rolf Döbbelin, Klaus Decker, Siegmund Mewes, Jürgen Pommerenke (62 Wolfgang Seguin), Wolfgang Steinbach, Joachim Streich, Uwe Grüning, Rainer Döbbel (56 Axel Tyll).   Trainer: Klaus Urbanczyk
ARSENAL: Patrick Jennings, John Devine, Samuel Nelson (73 Stephen Walford), Brian Talbot, David O'Leary, William Young, Liam Brady, Stephen Gatting, Francis Stapleton, John Hollins (25 David Price), Graham Rix.   Manager: Terence Neill
Goals: Price (41), Streich (50 pen), Brady (85), Stahmann (88)

ARIS BONNEVOIE v CF BARCELONA   1-4 (0-0)
Stade Municipal, Luxembourg   24.10.1979
Referee: Jan Redelfs (W. GER)   Attendance: 6,000
ARIS: Claude Birenbaum, Roger Fandel, Marcel Weber, Baus, Wolfgang Tullius, Claude Colling, André Vandivinit, Guy Weis, René Schiltz, Roland Kalte (80 Carlo Bamberg), Jean-Jacques Mathes.   Trainer: Alfred Sbroglia
CF BARCELONA: Vicente AMIGO, Rafael Ignacio ZUVIRÍA Rodríguez, Miguel Bernardo Bianquetti "MIGUELI", Adjutorio SERRAT Giró, José Cano "CANITO",, Jesús LANDABURU Sahuquillo, Allan Simonsen, José Vicente SÁNCHEZ Felip, Francisco José CARRASCO Hidalgo, Juan Manuel ASENSI Ripoll, Carlos REXACH Cerdá.
Trainer: Joaquin RIFE Climent
Goals: Simonsen (53, 77, 90), Mathes (64), Rexach (66)

CF BARCELONA v ARIS BONNEVOIE 7-1 (4-0)
Camp Nou, Barcelona   7.11.1979
Referee: Mário da Silva (POR)   Attendance: 60,000
CF BARCELONA: Jaime HUGUET Gracia, Rafael Ignacio ZUVIRÍA Rodríguez, Miguel Bernardo Bianquetti "MIGUELI" (46 Enrique Álvarez COSTAS), Antonio OLMO Ramírez, Jesús Antonio DE LA CRUZ Gallego, Jesús LANDABURU Sahuquillo, José Vicente SÁNCHEZ Felip (21 Adjutorio SERRAT Giró), Juan Carlos HEREDIA Alvarado, Johann Krankl, José Cano "CANITO", Francisco José CARRASCO Hidalgo.   Trainer: Joaquin RIFE Climent
ARIS: Claude Birenbaum, Roger Fandel, Claude Colling, Baus, Wolfgang Tullius, André Vandivinit, Carlo Bamberg, Guy Weis (46 René Schiltz), Jean-Jacques Mathes, Roland Kalte (61 Schumacher), Marcel Weber.   Trainer: Alfred Sbroglia
Goals: Krankl (14, 27, 44), Heredia (16, 56), Schiltz (47), Carrasco (57), Canito (82)

PANIONIOS ATHINA v IFK GÖTEBORG 1-0 (0-0)
Neas Smirnis, Athina   24.10.1979
Referee: Brian McGinlay (SCO)   Attendance: 15,000
PANIONIOS: Zafeiris Kakaris, Giannis Grabanis (70 Nikos Pantelis), Haralampos Saipas, Dimitris Maurikis, Mihalis Beriel, Vasilis Moraitelis, Leonido Lima, Nikos Halkidis, Nikos Anastopoulos, Kostas Vallidis, Thomas Liolios (65 Giannis Pathiakakis).   Trainer: Z. Meltsik
IFK: Odd Lindberg, Ruben Svensson, Glenn Hysén, Conny Karlsson, Reine Olausson, Glenn Schiller (80 Reine Almqvist), Tord Holmgren, Glenn Strömberg, Olle Nordin, Tommy Holmgren (72 Anders Ahlberg), Torbjörn Nilsson.   Trainer: Sven-Göran Eriksson
Goal: Anastopoulos (69)

IFK GÖTEBORG v PANIONIOS ATHINA   2-0 (1-0)
Gamla Ullevi, Göteborg   7.11.1979
Referee: Sigfried Kirschen (E. GER)   Attendance: 16,000
IFK: Odd Lindberg, Ruben Svensson, Glenn Hysén, Conny Karlsson, Reine Olausson, Glenn Schiller (88 Reine Almqvist), Tord Holmgren, Glenn Strömberg, Olle Nordin, Tommy Holmgren (83 Anders Ahlberg), Torbjörn Nilsson.   Trainer: Sven-Göran Eriksson
PANIONIOS: Zafeiris Kakaris, Serafeim Zaharopoulos, Mihalis Beriel, Hristos Emboliadis (46 Harilaos Sofianos), Vasilis Moraitelis, Haralampos Saipas (70 Giannis Pathiakakis), Nikos Halkidis, Dimitris Maurikis, Nikos Anastopoulos, Kostas Vallidis, Giannis Grabanis.
Trainer: Z. Meltsik
Goals: Nordin (17), Tord Holmgren (48)

LOKOMOTÍVA KOŠICE v NK RIJEKA 2-0 (2-0)
Jeho-Cermell-Stadion, Košice 24.10.1979
Referee: Anatoli Milchenko (USSR)   Attendance: 5,000
LOKOMOTÍVA: Stanislav Seman, Jiří Repík, Jozef Suchánek, Vladimír Dobrovic, Gejza Farkas, Ján Kozák, Dušan Ujhely, Józef Moder (82 Pavol Pizur), Stanislav Strapek, Peter Fecko, Peter Lovacky (63 Peter Jacko).   Trainer: Jozef Jankech
NK RIJEKA: Mauro Ravnić, Sergio Makin, Miloš Hrstić, Nikica Cukrov, Zvjezdan Radin, Srećko Juričić, Bacvarević, Milan Radović (63 Bursac), Edmond Tomić, Milan Ruzić, Damir Desnica.   Trainer: Miroslav Blazević
Goals: Kozák (28, 38)

NK RIJEKA v LOKOMOTÍVA KOŠICE 3-0 (2-0)
Kantrida, Rijeka 7.11.1979
Referee: Bogdan Dochev (BUL)   Attendance: 18,000
NK RIJEKA: Mauro Ravnić, Milenković, Miloš Hrstić, Nikica Cukrov, Zvjezdan Radin, Srećko Juričić, Bacvarević, Željko Mijač, Milan Radović, Milan Ruzić, Damir Desnica.   Trainer: Miroslav Blazević
LOKOMOTÍVA: Stanislav Seman, Pavol Biros, Jozef Suchánek, Vladimír Dobrovic, Gejza Farkas, Ján Kozák, Peter Jacko, Józef Moder, Stanislav Strapek, Peter Fecko, Dušan Ujhely (62 Zdeno Kost).   Trainer: Jozef Jankech
Goals: Desnica (1 pen, 44, 75)

FC NANTES v STEAUA BUCUREȘTI 3-2 (0-0)
Marcel Saupin, Nantes 24.10.1979
Referee: Ronald Bridges (WAL)   Attendance: 13,000
FC NANTES: Jean-Paul Bertrand-Demanes; Maxime Bossis, Thierry Tusseau, Patrice Rio, Henri Michel; Enzo Trossero (77 José Touré), Victor Trossero, Oscar Muller, Eric Pécout, Gilles Rampillon, Loic Amisse.   Trainer: Jean Vincent
STEAUA: Vasile Iordache; Teodor Anghelini, Mario Agiu, Ștefan Sameș, Ion Nițu, Ion Dumitru, Tudorel Stoica, Anghel Iordănescu; Gabriel Zahiu, Adrian Ionescu, Marcel Răducanu.   Trainer: Gheorghe Constantin
Goals: Pécout (59, 73), M. Răducanu (63 pen, 68 pen), Touré (84)

STEAUA BUCUREȘTI v FC NANTES 1-2 (1-0)
Steaua, București 7.11.1979
Referee: Ernst Dörflinger (SWI)   Attendance: 25,000
STEAUA: Vasile Iordache; Mario Agiu, Ștefan Sameș, Florin Marin, Ion Nițu (89 Iosif Vigu); Anghel Iordănescu, Ion Dumitru, Tudorel Stoica; Marcel Răducanu, Adrian Ionescu, Constantin Zamfir (74 Gabriel Zahiu).   Trainer: G. Constantin
FC NANTES: Jean-Paul Bertrand-Demanes; Maxime Bossis, William Ayache, Patrice Rio, Henri Michel; Thierry Tusseau, Victor Trossero, Oscar Muller, Eric Pécout, Gilles Rampillon, Loic Amisse.   Trainer: Jean Vincent
Goals: A. Ionescu (16), Pécout (60), Amisse (83)

DINAMO MOSKVA v BOAVISTA FC 0-0
Dinamo, Moskva 24.10.1979
Referee: Svein Inge Thime (NOR)   Attendance: 5,000
DINAMO: Nikolai Gontar, Aleksandr Novikov, Sergei Nikulin, Aleksandr Makhovikov, Aleksandr Bubnov, Aleksei Petruschin, Nikolai Tolstikh (46 Nikolai Kolesov), Aleksandr Minaev, Yuri Reznik (75 Vadim Pavlenko), Aleksandr Maksimenkov, Valeri Gazzaev.
BOAVISTA: Luís Filipe da Cruz MATOS, Manuel José Ferreira da Silva BARBOSA, António Carlos Sousa Laranjeira "TAÍ", ELISEU Martins Ramalho, ADÃO da Silva, ARTUR Nogueira Ferreira, Antonio Manuel dos Santos ALMEIDA (72 Francisco JARBAS), ÓSCAR Vicente Martins Duarte (55 Mario Jorge MOINHOS de Matos), SALVADOR Luis Almeida, AILTON Ballesteros, JÚLIO Carlos da Costa Augusto.

BOAVISTA PORTO v DYNAMO MOSKVA 1-1 (1-1)
Estádio do Bessa, Porto 7.11.1979
Referee: Clive Bradley White (ENG)   Attendance: 27,000
BOAVISTA: Luís Filipe da Cruz MATOS, Manuel José Ferreira da Silva BARBOSA, António Carlos Sousa Laranjeira "TAÍ", ELISEU Martins Ramalho, ADÃO da Silva, ARTUR Nogueira Ferreira, Antonio Manuel dos Santos ALMEIDA (67 ÓSCAR Vicente Martins Duarte), Mario Jorge MOINHOS de Matos, JÚLIO Carlos da Costa Augusto, AILTON Ballesteros, Fernando Manuel Parada FOLHA (46 SALVADOR Luis Almeida)
DINAMO: Nikolai Gontar, Aleksandr Novikov, Sergei Nikulin, Aleksandr Makhovikov, Aleksandr Bubnov, Aleksei Petruschin, Nikolai Kolesov, Aleksandr Minaev, Yuri Reznik (85 Vadim Pavlenko), Aleksandr Maksimenkov, Valeri Gazzaev.
Goals: Minaev (26), Moinhos (34)

**BEROE STARA ZAGORA
v JUVENTUS TORINO 1-0** (0-0)
Gradski, Stara Zagora 24.10.1979
Referee: Walter Eschweiler (W. GER)   Attendance: 25,000
BEROE: Kosta Kostov; Mitkov, Dinko Dimitrov, Ilia Iliev, Tenio Minchev, Georgi Stoianov, Tanio Petrov, Stefan Stefanov, Petko Petkov, Stefan Naidenov (70 Tenio Tenev), Plamen Lipenski (46 Angel Yanev).   Trainer: Ivan Tanev
JUVENTUS: Dino Zoff, Antonello Cuccureddu, Antonio Cabrini, Giuseppe Furino, Sergio Brio, Claudio Gentile, Franco Causio, Marco Tardelli, Roberto Bettega, Vinicio Verza, Antonio Paolo Virdis (56 Roberto Tavola).
Trainer: Giovanni Trapattoni
Sent off: Minchev (82)
Goal: Stoianov (82 pen)

**JUVENTUS TORINO
v BEROE STARA ZAGORA 3-0** (1-0, 1-0) (AET)

Stadio Comunale, Torino   7.11.1979

Referee: Bruno Galler (SWI)   Attendance: 40,000

JUVENTUS: Dino Zoff, Antonello Cuccureddu, Claudio Gentile, Giuseppe Furino (62 Claudio Prandelli), Sergio Brio, Gaetano Scirea, Franco Causio, Marco Tardelli, Roberto Bettega (31 Pietro Fanna), Vinicio Verza, Domenico Marocchino.   Trainer: Giovanni Trapattoni

BEROE: Kosta Kostov, Hristo Beltchev, Dinko Dimitrov, Ilia Iliev, Mitkov, Georgi Stoianov, Tanio Petrov (104 Plamen Lipenski), Stefan Stefanov, Petko Petkov, Stefan Naidenov (72 Staiko Staikov), Tenio Tenev.   Trainer: Ivan Tanev

Goals: Scirea (7), Causio (103), Verza (109)

VALENCIA CF v GLASGOW RANGERS 1-1 (1-1)

Estadio Luis Casanova, Valencia   24.10.1979

Referee: Erich Linemayr (AUS)   Attendance: 45,000

VALENCIA CF: Carlos Santiago PEREIRA, Ángel CASTELLANOS Céspedes, José CERVERO San Braulio, Ricardo ARIAS Penella, Manuel BOTUBOT Pereira, Rainer Bonhof, Enrique SAURA Gil, Daniel SOLSONA Puig, Orlando Ramon JIMÉNEZ (71 José BALAGUER), Mario Alberto KEMPES Chiodi, Luis Dario FELMAN.
Trainer: Alfredo DI STEFANO Lahule

RANGERS: Peter McCloy, Alexander Miller, Alex Forsyth, William Jardine, Derek Johnstone, Kenneth Watson, Thomas McLean (77 Derek Parlane), Alexander MacDonald, William Urquhart, Gordon Smith, David Cooper (89 Alistair Dawson).   Manager: John Greig

Sent off: Pereira (71)

Goals: Kempes (23), McLean (44)

GLASGOW RANGERS v VALENCIA CF 1-3 (1-2)

Ibrox, Glasgow   7.11.1979

Referee: Charles Corver (HOL)   Attendance: 36,000

RANGERS: Peter McCloy, William Jardine, Alex Forsyth, Alexander Miller, Kenneth Watson, Alexander MacDonald, Thomas McLean, Gordon Smith, Derek Johnstone, William Urquhart (46 Derek Parlane), David Cooper (65 William Mackay).   Manager: John Greig

VALENCIA CF: José Luis Fernández MANZANEDO, José CERVERO San Braulio, Manuel BOTUBOT Pereira, Ricardo ARIAS Penella, Miguel TENDILLO Berenguer, Ángel CASTELLANOS Céspedes, Enrique SAURA Gil, Rainer Bonhof, Mario Alberto KEMPES Chiodi, Javier SUBIRATS Hernández, PABLO Rodríguez Flores.
Trainer: Alfredo DI STEFANO Lahule

Goals: Bonhof (15), Johnstone (23), Kempes (43, 77)

QUARTER-FINALS

ARSENAL LONDON v IFK GÖTEBORG 5-1 (3-1)

Arsenal Stadium Highbury, London   5.03.1980

Referee: Alojzy Jarguz (POL)   Attendance: 36,323

ARSENAL: Patrick Jennings, Brian Talbot, John Devine, Samuel Nelson, David O'Leary, William Young, Liam Brady (80 John Hollins), Alan Sunderland (48 Brian McDermott), Francis Stapleton, David Price, Graham Rix.
Manager: Terence Neill

IFK: Thorsteinn Ólafsson, Reine Olausson, Glenn Hysén, Conny Karlsson, Glenn Schiller, Olle Nordin, Tord Holmgren, Glenn Strömberg, Glenn Holm (75 Jerry Carlsson), Dan Corneliusson (60 Anders Ahlberg), Torbjörn Nilsson.
Trainer: Sven-Göran Eriksson

Goals: Nilsson (30), Sunderland (31, 43), Price (38), Brady (57), Young (64)

IFK GÖTEBORG v ARSENAL LONDON 0-0

Nya Ullevi, Göteborg   19.03.1980

Referee: Jan Redelfs (W. GER)   Attendance: 40,044

IFK: Thorsteinn Ólafsson, Reine Olausson, Conny Karlsson, Tord Holmgren, Glenn Hysén, Glenn Schiller, Glenn Strömberg (83 Reine Almqvist), Torbjörn Nilsson, Tommy Holmgren, Jerry Carlsson, Ruben Svensson.
Trainer: Sven-Göran Eriksson

ARSENAL: Patrick Jennings, John Devine, William Young, David O'Leary, Samuel Nelson, Brian Talbot, Liam Brady, David Price, Paul Vaessen, Francis Stapleton, Graham Rix.
Manager: Terence Neill

CF BARCELONA v VALENCIA CF 0-1 (0-0)

Camp Nou, Barcelona   5.03.1980

Referee: Georges Konrath (FRA)   Attendance: 75,000

CF BARCELONA: Pedro María ARTOLA Urrutia, Rafael Ignacio ZUVIRÍA Rodríguez, Antonio OLMO Ramírez, Miguel Bernardo Bianquetti "MIGUELI", Adjutorio SERRAT Giró, Jesús LANDABURU Sahuquillo, Julián RUBIO, José Vicente SÁNCHEZ Felip (66 Juan José ESTELLA Salas), Carlos REXACH Cerdá (66 Francisco José CARRASCO Hidalgo), ESTEBAN Vigo Benítez, Allan Simonsen.
Trainer: Joaquin RIFE Climent

VALENCIA CF: Carlos Santiago PEREIRA (89 José BALAGUER), José CARRETE de Julián, Manuel BOTUBOT Pereira, HIGINIO García Fernández, Miguel TENDILLO Berenguer, Enrique SAURA Gil, Daniel SOLSONA Puig, Rainer Bonhof, Javier SUBIRATS Hernández, Mario Alberto KEMPES Chiodi, PABLO Rodríguez Flores.
Trainer: Alfredo DI STEFANO Lahule

Goal: Pablo (50)

VALENCIA CF v CF BARCELONA 4-3 (2-2)
Estadio Luis Casanova, Valencia   19.03.1980
Referee: Alberto Michelotti (ITA)   Attendance: 50,000

VALENCIA CF: José Luis Fernández MANZANEDO, José CARRETE de Julián, Manuel BOTUBOT Pereira, Miguel TENDILLO Berenguer, Ricardo ARIAS Penella, Daniel SOLSONA Puig, Rainer Bonhof, Javier SUBIRATS Hernández, Enrique SAURA Gil, Mario Alberto KEMPES Chiodi, PABLO Rodríguez Flores.   Trainer: Alfredo DI STEFANO Lahule

CF BARCELONA: Pedro María ARTOLA Urrutia, Antonio OLMO Ramírez, José Antonio RAMOS Huete, Miguel Bernardo Bianquetti "MIGUELI", Jesús Antonio DE LA CRUZ Gallego, Jesús LANDABURU Sahuquillo, Carlos REXACH Cerdá, Francisco José CARRASCO Hidalgo (74 ESTEBAN Vigo Benítez), Allan Simonsen, José Cano "CANITO", Francisco MARTÍNEZ Díaz (69 Rafael Ignacio ZUVIRÍA Rodríguez).   Trainer: Helenio Herrera

Goals: Saura (10, 77), Cano (15, 89), Landaburu (26), Bonhof (29), Kempes (85 pen)

DINAMO MOSKVA v FC NANTES 0-2 (0-0)
Dinamo, Tbilisi   5.03.1980
Referee: Ulf Ericsson (SWE)   Attendance: 30,000

DINAMO: Nikolai Gontar, Evgeni Lovchev, Sergei Nikulin, Aleksandr Makhovikov, Aleksandr Bubnov, Aleksei Petruschin (61 Nikolai Latisch), Yuri Reznik, Aleksandr Minaev, Andrei Yakubik, Aleksandr Maksimenkov, Valeri Gazzaev.

FC NANTES: Jean-Paul Bertrand-Demanes; William Ayache, Thierry Tusseau, Patrice Rio (83 Michel Bibard), Enzo Trossero, Bruno Baronchelli, Victor Trossero, Henri Michel, Eric Pécout, Gilles Rampillon, Loic Amisse.
Trainer: Jean Vincent

Goals: Tusseau (57), Pécout (86)

FC NANTES v DINAMO MOSKVA 2-3 (1-2)
Marcel Saupin, Nantes   19.03.1980
Referee: Charles Corver (HOL)   Attendance: 25,000

FC NANTES: Jean-Paul Bertrand-Demanes; Maxime Bossis, Patrice Rio, Enzo Trossero, Thierry Tusseau, Henri Michel, Bruno Baronchelli, Oscar Muller, Victor Trossero (58 José Touré), Eric Pécout, Gilles Rampillon.   Trainer: Jean Vincent

DINAMO: Vladimir Pilgui, Evgeni Lovchev, Aleksandr Novikov (84 Andrei Yakubik), Sergei Nikulin, Aleksandr Makhovikov, Aleksandr Bubnov, Aleksandr Maksimenkov, Aleksei Petruschin, Aleksandr Minaev, Nikolai Kolesov, Valeri Gazzaev.

Goals: Minaev (21), Gazzaev (40), Michel (43), Touré (70), Kolesov (88)

NK RIJEKA v JUVENTUS TORINO 0-0
Fiume   5.03.1980
Referee: Jan Keizer (HOL)   Attendance: 25,000

NK RIJEKA: Mauro Ravnić, Miroslav Šugar, Miloš Hrstić, Milenković, Zvjezdan Radin (9 Bacvarević, 58 Petrović), Srećko Juričić, Sergio Makin, Milan Radović, Edmond Tomić, Milan Ruzić, Lukić.   Trainer: Miroslav Blazević

JUVENTUS: Dino Zoff, Claudio Gentile, Antonio Cabrini, Giuseppe Furino, Sergio Brio, Gaetano Scirea, Antonello Cuccureddu, Marco Tardelli, Domenico Marocchino, Claudio Prandelli, Roberto Bettega.   Trainer: Giovanni Trapattoni

JUVENTUS TORINO v NK RIJEKA 2-0 (1-0)
Stadio Comunale, Torino   19.03.1980
Referee: Talal Tokat (TUR)   Attendance: 55,000

JUVENTUS: Dino Zoff, Gaetano Scirea, Claudio Gentile, Sergio Brio, Antonio Cabrini, Franco Causio, Giuseppe Furino, Marco Tardelli, Domenico Marocchino, Roberto Bettega, Antonio Paolo Virdis (65 Claudio Prandelli).
Trainer: Giovanni Trapattoni

NK RIJEKA: Mauro Ravnić, Miroslav Šugar (86 Adrijano Fegić), Milenković, Ivan Jerolimov, Miloš Hrstić, Sergio Makin, Srećko Juričić, Milan Radović, Lukić (25 Edmond Tomić), Željko Mijač, Milan Ruzić.   Trainer: Miroslav Blazević

Goals: Causio (5), Bettega (72)

SEMI-FINALS

FC NANTES v VALENCIA CF 2-1 (1-0)
Marcel Saupin, Nantes   9.04.1980
Referee: Walter Eschweiler (W. GER)   Attendance: 22,000

FC NANTES: Jean-Paul Bertrand-Demanes; Henri Michel, Maxime Bossis, Patrice Rio, Thierry Tusseau, Enzo Trossero, Óscar Muller (76 Victor Trossero), Gilles Rampillon (72 José Touré), Bruno Baronchelli, Eric Pécout, Loic Amisse.
Trainer: Jean Vincent

VALENCIA CF: Carlos Santiago PEREIRA, José CARRETE de Julián, Ricardo ARIAS Penella, Miguel TENDILLO Berenguer, Manuel BOTUBOT Pereira, Daniel SOLSONA Puig, Rainer Bonhof, Ángel CASTELLANOS Céspedes, Enrique SAURA Gil, Mario Alberto KEMPES Chiodi, PABLO Rodríguez Flores.   Trainer: Alfredo DI STEFANO Lahule

Goals: Baronchelli (26, 80), Kempes (54)

VALENCIA CF v FC NANTES 4-0 (2-0)
Estadio Luis Casanova, Valencia   23.04.1980
Referee: Alexis Ponnet (BEL)   Attendance: 50,000

VALENCIA CF: Carlos Santiago PEREIRA, Ricardo ARIAS Penella, José CARRETE de Julián, Miguel TENDILLO Berenguer, Manuel BOTUBOT Pereira, Javier SUBIRATS Hernández, Rainer Bonhof, Daniel SOLSONA Puig, Enrique SAURA Gil (88 Pedro VILARRODA), Mario Alberto KEMPES Chiodi, PABLO Rodríguez Flores.
Trainer: Alfredo DI STEFANO Lahule

FC NANTES: Jean-Paul Bertrand-Demanes; Henri Michel, Maxime Bossis, Patrice Rio, Thierry Tusseau, Enzo Trossero, Óscar Muller, Gilles Rampillon, Bruno Baronchelli, Eric Pécout (65 José Touré), Loic Amisse.   Trainer: Jean Vincent

Goals: Bonhof (10), Michel (42 og), Kempes (59, 78 pen)

**ARSENAL LONDON
v JUVENTUS TORINO 1-1** (0-1)
Arsenal Stadium Highbury, London   9.04.1980
Referee: Charles Corver (HOL)   Attendance: 51,998

ARSENAL: Patrick Jennings, John Devine (86 Paul Vaessen), David O'Leary (23 Patrick Rice), William Young, Stephen Walford, Brian Talbot, Liam Brady, David Price, Alan Sunderland, Francis Stapleton, Graham Rix.
Manager: Terence Neill

JUVENTUS: Dino Zoff, Gaetano Scirea, Claudio Gentile, Sergio Brio, Antonio Cabrini, Antonello Cuccureddu, Giuseppe Furino, Franco Causio, Marco Tardelli, Roberto Bettega, Domenico Marocchino (46 Pietro Fanna).
Trainer: Giovanni Trapattoni

Sent off: Tardelli (33)

Goals: Cabrini (10), Bettega (85 og)

**JUVENTUS TORINO
v ARSENAL LONDON 0-1** (0-0)
Stadio Comunale, Torino   23.04.1980
Referee: Erich Linemayr (AUS)   Attendance: 66,386

JUVENTUS: Dino Zoff, Gaetano Scirea, Antonello Cuccureddu, Claudio Gentile, Antonio Cabrini, Giuseppe Furino, Claudio Prandelli (67 Domenico Marocchino), Roberto Tavola, Franco Causio, Roberto Bettega, Pietro Fanna.
Trainer: Giovanni Trapattoni

ARSENAL: Patrick Jennings, William Young, Patrick Rice, David O'Leary, John Devine, Brian Talbot (80 John Hollins), Liam Brady, David Price (78 Paul Vaessen), Alan Sunderland, Francis Stapleton, Graham Rix.   Manager: Terence Neill

Goal: Vaessen (88)

FINAL

VALENCIA CF v ARSENAL FC 0-0 (AET)
Stade du Heysel, Brussel   14.05.1980
Referee: Vojtěch Christov (CZE)   Attendance: 40,000

VALENCIA: Carlos Santiago PEREIRA, José CARRETE de Julián, Ricardo ARIAS Penella, Miguel TENDILLO Berenguer, Manuel BOTUBOT Pereira, Daniel SOLSONA Puig, Rainer Bonhof, Javier SUBIRATS Hernández (112 Ángel CASTELLANOS Céspedes), PABLO Rodríguez Flores, Enrique SAURA Gil, Mario Alberto KEMPES Chiodi.
Trainer: Alfredo DI STEFANO Lahule

ARSENAL: Patrick Jennings, Patrick Rice, David O'Leary, William Young, Samuel Nelson, Brian Talbot, William Brady, Alan Sunderland, David Price (106 John Hollins), Francis Stapleton, Graham Rix.   Trainer: Terence Neill

Penalties: 0-0 Kempes (saved), 0-0 Brady (saved), 1-0 Solsona, 1-1 Stapleton, 2-1 Pablo Rodríguez, 2-2 Sunderland, 3-2 Castellanos, 3-3 Talbot, 4-3 Bonhof, 4-4 Hollins, 5-4 Arias, 5-4 Rix (saved)

Goalscorers European Cup-Winners' Cup 1979-80:

9 goals: Mario Kempes (Valencia CF)

7 goals: Eric Pécout (FC Nantes)

4 goals: Sunderland (Arsenal), Krankl, Simonsen (FC Barcelona)

3 goals: Streich (FC Magdeburg), Young (Arsenal), Thygesen (B 1903 København), Júlio (Boavista Porto), Cano, Rexach (FC Barcelona), Causio (Juventus Torino), Kozák (Lokomotiva Košice), Desnica (NK Rijeka), Anastopoulos (Panionios Athina), Răducanu (Steaua București), Bonhof, Saura (Valencia CF)

2 goals: Hoffmann, Steinbach (FC Magdeburg), Schiltz (Aris Bonnevoie), Korynt (Arka Gdynia), Brady, Price (Arsenal), Kristiansen (B 1903 København), Petkov, Stoianov (Beroe Stara Zagora), Fortell (Sliema Wanderers), Liolios (Panionios Athina), Sameş (Steaua București), Moinhos (Boavista Porto), Johnstone, A.MacDonald, McLean (Glasgow Rangers), Tord Holmgren (IFK Göteborg), Carrasco, Heredia (FC Barcelona), Minaev (Dinamo Moskva), Radović (NK Rijeka), Baronchelli, Rampillon, Touré, V. Trossero (FC Nantes), Cabrini (Juventus Torino)

1 goal: Zwygart, Schönenberger (Young Boys Bern), Bos, Lindsted, Jol (Twente Enschede), Kwiatkowski (Arka Gdynia), Wenzel (Fortuna Düsseldorf), Póczik (Raba ETO Györ), McNeil, Fox, Buxton, Vinter, Hill (Wrexham), Pöll (SWW Innsbruck), Gzil (Beerschot), Hansen, Damm, Haarby, Larsen (B 1903 København), Tony Keane (Waterford FC), Pommerenke, Stahmann, Mewes (FC Magdeburg), Mathes, Colling (Aris Bonnevoie), Pathiakakis (Panionios Athina), Strapek, Jacko (Lokomotiva Košice), A.Ionescu, Stoica, Iordănescu, Niţu, Aelenei, Zahiu (Steaua Bucureşti), Ailton, Salvador, Folha, Oscar, Eliseu (Boavista Porto), Lipenski (Beroe Stara Zagora), Smith (Glasgow Rangers), Nilsson, Nordin, G.Holm (IFK Göteborg), Asensi, Landaburu (FC Barcelona), Gazzaev, Kolesov (Dinamo Moskva), Tusseau, Michel, Amisse, Rio (FC Nantes), Bettega, Scirea, Verza (Juventus Torino), Pablo Rodríguez, Felman, Arias, Castellanos (Valencia CF), Vaessen (Arsenal London)

Own goals: Furino (Juventus) for Raba ETO Györ, Pozsgai (Raba ETO Györ) for Juventus, Michel (FC Nantes) for Valencia CF, Bettega (Juventus Torino) for Arsenal

CUP WINNERS' CUP 1980-81

PRELIMINARY ROUND

CELTIC GLASGOW v DIÓSGYŐRI VTK 6-0 (0-0)

Celtic Park, Glasgow   20.08.1980

Referee: Widukind Hermann (E. GER)   Attendance: 28,000

CELTIC: Patrick Bonner; Alan Sneddon, Daniel McGrain, Robert Aitken, Thomas McAdam; Murdo MacLeod (68 John Doyle), David Provan (.. Charles Nicholas), Dominic Sullivan; Francis McGarvey, Thomas Burns, George McCluskey. Manager: William McNeill

DIÓSGYŐRI: László Szabó; Gabor Szántó, István Néder, Jánosz Kerekes, Lajos Kádár; Ferenc Oláh, Sándor Fükö, Borisz Teodoru I, János Görgei; Mihály Borostyán, Miklós Szlifka (71 Vaszilisz Teodoru II).

Goals: McGarvey (52, 65, 70), McCluskey (60, 79), Sullivan (71)

**DIÓSGYŐRI VASGYARAK TK
v CELTIC GLASGOW 2-1** (1-1)

Diósgyőr   3.09.1980

Referee: Josef Bucek (AUS)   Attendance: 8,000

DIÓSGYŐRI VTK: László Szabó; Gabor Szántó, István Néder, Jánosz Kerekes, Borisz Teodoru I; Ferenc Oláh, Sándor Fükö, János Görgei; Miklós Szlifka (62 Imre Czél), Balász Magyar (46 Vaszilisz Teodoru II), Mihály Borostyán.

CELTIC: Patrick Bonner; Alan Sneddon, Daniel McGrain, Robert Aitken, Thomas McAdam; Murdo MacLeod, David Provan, Dominic Sullivan; Francis McGarvey, Thomas Burns, Charles Nicholas.   Manager: William McNeill

Goals: Nicholas (24), Görgei (25, 66)

ALTAY IZMIR v BENFICA LISBOA 0-0

Atatürk, Izmir   20.08.1980

Referee: Iordan Zhezhov (BUL)   Attendance: 22,000

ALTAY: Sait; Sabahattin Erboga, Zafer Bilgitay, K. Dikmen, Bilal Yasar (40 Birol Ümit); Seref Incirmen (64 Oturmazer), Mustafa Kalpakaslan, Ondek, K. Kilik; Ahmet Turgat, Beic.

BENFICA: Manuel Galrinho BENTO; António José BASTOS LOPES, HUMBERTO Manuel Jesus COELHO, João Gonçalves LARANJEIRA, Minervino José Lopes PIETRA; António Augusto da Silva VELOSO (45 SHÉU Han), CARLOS MANUEL Correia dos Santos, João António Ferreira Resende ALVES, Fernando Albino de Sousa CHALANA, Tamagnini Manuel Gomes Baptista NENÉ, CÉSAR Martins de Oliveira (67 Francisco António Lucas VITAL). Trainer: Lajos Baroti (HUN)

BENFICA LISBOA v ALTAY IZMIR 4-0 (2-0)
Estádio da Luz, Lisboa   3.09.1980
Referee: Robert Wurtz (FRA)   Attendance: 60,000
BENFICA: Manuel Galrinho BENTO; António José BASTOS LOPES (80 FREDERICO Nobre Rosa), HUMBERTO Manuel Jesus COELHO, João Gonçalves LARANJEIRA, Minervino José Lopes PIETRA; CARLOS MANUEL Correia dos Santos, João António Ferreira Resende ALVES, SHÉU Han; Tamagnini Manuel Gomes Baptista NENÉ (80 Francisco António Lucas VITAL), CÉSAR Martins de Oliveira, Fernando Albino de Sousa CHALANA.   Trainer: Lajos Baroti
ALTAY: Sait; Kemal Eron, Sabahattin Erboga, Zafer Bilgitay, Lerei, Birol Ümit; Mustafa Kalpakaslan, Oner, B. Kemal; Vuriz (57 Bilal Yasar), B. Mustafa.
Goals: Chalana (22), Humberto Coelho (34), Nené (63), César (70)

FIRST ROUND

SLAVIA SOFIA v LEGIA WARSZAWA 3-1 (0-1)
Slavia, Sofia   16.09.1980
Referee: J. Veverka (CZE)   Attendance: 8,000
SLAVIA: Georgi Gugalov (46 Stoicho Stefanov), Rusi Ivanov, Ivan Haidarliev, Ivan Iliev, Milcho Evtimov (55 Botiu Malinov), Vanio Kostov, Andrei Jeliazkov, Ilia Aliev, Atanas Aleksandrov, Ilia Velichkov, Chavdar Tzvetkov.   Trainer: Aleksander Iliev
LEGIA: Jacek Kazimierski, Adam Topolski, Pawel Janas, Edward Zalezny, Stanislaw Sobczynski, Janusz Baran (85 Witold Sikorski), Henryk Miloszewicz, Stefan Majewski, Marek Kusto, Krzysztof Adamczyk, Miroslaw Okonski.
Goals: Miloszewicz (38), Tzvetkov (55 pen), Velichkov (73, 86)

LEGIA WARSZAWA v SLAVIA SOFIA 1-0 (0-0)
Wojska Polskiego, Warszawa   1.10.1980
Referee: Ian M.D. Foote (SCO)   Attendance: 15,000
LEGIA: Jacek Kazimierski, Adam Topolski, Waldemar Tuminski, Edward Zalezny, Stanislaw Sobczynski, Janusz Baran, Henryk Miloszewicz, Krzysztof Lason (46 Stefan Majewski), Marek Kusto, Krzysztof Adamczyk (46 Witold Sikorski), Miroslaw Okonski.
SLAVIA: Georgi Gugalov, Rusi Ivanov, Ivan Haidarliev, Ivan Iliev, Botiu Malinov, Ilia Aliev, Georgi Dermendjiev, Andrei Jeliazkov, Vanio Kostov, Atanas Aleksandrov, Chavdar Tzvetkov.   Trainer: Aleksander Iliev
Goal: Okonski (49 pen)

NEWPORT COUNTY v CRUSADERS BELFAST 4-0 (2-0)
Somerton Park, Newport   16.09.1980
Referee: George B. Smith (SCO)   Attendance: 6,285
COUNTY: Michael Dowler, Richard Walden, John Relish, David Bruton, Keith Oakes, Thomas Tynan, Nigel Vaughan, Stephen Lowndes, David Gwyther, John Aldridge (75 Karl Elsey), Kevin Moore.
CRUSADERS: Roy McDonald, Glenn Thompson, Geoff Gorman, Peter Mulhall, Robert Gillespie, Sammy Whiteside, Brian Jess, Roy Fellowes, Sean Byrne (.. Graham King), Alan Currie, Artie Rice (.. Garnett Cromie).
Goals: Gwyther (6), Moore (7), Aldridge (66), Bruton (68)

CRUSADERS BELFAST v NEWPORT COUNTY 0-0
Seaview, Belfast   1.10.1980
Referee: Alfred William Grey (ENG)   Attendance: 1,300
CRUSADERS: Roy McDonald, Alan Currie, Geoff Gorman, Peter Mulhall, Robert Gillespie, Glenn Thompson, Brian Jess (.. Sean Byrne), Roy Fellowes, Graham King, John McPolin (.. Sammy Whiteside), Artie Rice.
COUNTY: Gary Plumley, Richard Walden, John Relish (.. Karl Elsey), David Bruton (.. Grant Davies), Keith Oakes, Thomas Tynan, Nigel Vaughan, Stephen Lowndes, David Gwyther, John Aldridge, Kevin Moore.

SPORA LUXEMBOURG v SPARTA PRAHA 0-6 (0-2)
Stade Municipal Luxembourg   16.09.1980
Referee: Egbert Mulder (HOL)   Attendance: 1,000
SPORA: Zender, Pascal Rob (46 Wünsch), Baumert, Urbing, Schmidt (74 Brandt), Marco Molitor, Fiedler, Sauber, Petry, Pierre Hoscheid, Jean-Louis Berckes.
SPARTA: Miroslav Stárek, Zdenek Ščasný, František Straka, Jaroslav Kotek, Zdenek Caudr, Jaroslav Pollák, Josef Jarolím, Milan Vdovjak (65 Josef Raška), Jan Berger, Petr Slaný (65 Vratislav Chaloupka), Václav Kotal.   Trainer: Jiří Rubáš
Goals: Berger (33, 44), Kotek (62), Chaloupka (68, 81), Raška (68)

SPARTA PRAHA v SPORA LUXEMBOURG 6-0 (2-0)
Stadión na Letnej, Praha   1.10.1980
Referee: Klaus Peschell (E. GER)   Attendance: 4,000
SPARTA: Miroslav Koubek, Zdenek Ščasný (.. Zdenek Caudr), František Straka, Jaroslav Kotek, Jan Pospíšil, Josef Horváth, Josef Jarolím, Václav Kotal, Tomáš Stránsky, Petr Slaný (.. Milan Vdovjak), Jan Berger.   Trainer: Jiří Rubáš
SPORA: Zender (.. Joseph Mousel), R.Schmidt, Baumert (.. B.Schmidt), Urbing, Pascal Rob, Pierre Hoscheid, Fiedler, Marco Molitor, Alain Palgen, Petry, Jean-Louis Berckes.
Goals: Pospisil (25), Slaný (42), Jarolím (49, 80), Berger (54), Horváth (68)

208

HVIDOVRE IF v FRAM REYKJAVIK 1-0 (1-0)

Hvidovre stadion 17.09.1980

Referee: Ulf Eriksson (SWE)   Attendance: 1,636

HVIDOVRE: Curlei Nielsen, Finn Johansen, Jørgen Kirk, Michael Christensen, Steen Hansen, Jesper Petersen, Leroy Ambrose, Henrik Jensen, Michael Manniche, Jørgen Jacobsen (9 Steen Bybjerg), Jens Kurt Petersen.   Trainer: John Sinding

FRAM: Gudmundur Baldursson, Simon Kristjansson, Trausti Haraldsson, Gunnar Gudmundsson, Marteinn Geirsson, Jón Pétursson, Gustav Björnsson, Gudmundur Torfasson, Baldvin Elíasson, Gudmundur Steinsson, Hafthor Sveinjónsson.

Goal: Steen Hansen (22 pen)

FRAM REYKJAVIK v HVIDOVRE KØBENHAVN 0-2 (0-1)

Laugardalsvöllur, Reykjavik 28.09.1980

Referee: Kaare Lindbø (NOR)   Attendance: 6,000

FRAM: Gudmundur Baldursson, Simon Kristjansson, Trausti Haraldsson, Gunnar Gudmundsson, Marteinn Geirsson, Jón Pétursson, Gustav Björnsson, Gudmundur Torfasson, Larus Gretarsson (55 Gunnar Orrasson), Gudmundur Steinsson, Hafthor Sveinjónsson (80 Kristinn Atlasson).

HVIDOVRE: Curlei Nielsen, Finn Johansen, Jørgen Kirk, Michael Christensen, Steen Hansen, Gunter Lindahl, Leroy Ambrose, Henrik Jensen, Michael Manniche (83 Jens Petersen), Jørgen Jacobsen (61 Jesper Petersen), Jens Kurt Petersen.   Trainer: John Sinding

Goals: Ambrose (10), S. Hansen (50 pen)

MALMÖ FF v PARTIZANI TIRANA 1-0 (0-0)

Malmö Stadion 17.09.1980

Referee: Aleksander Suchanek (POL)   Attendance: 3,112

MALMÖ FF: Jan Möller, Roland Andersson, Kent Jönsson, Tim Parkin, Ingemar Erlandsson, Magnus Andersson, Robert Prytz, Roy Andersson, Jan-Olov Kinnvall, Thomas Sjöberg, Tommy Hansson (58 Paul McKinnon).

PARTIZANI: Perlat Musta, Sulejman Starova, K.Hysi, Ferid Rragami, Safet Berisha, A. Ahmeti, B. Hado, Haxhi Ballgjini, F. Breca, Ilir Lame, Sefedin Braho.

Goal: McKinnon (63)

PARTIZANI TIRANA v MALMÖ FF 0-0

Qemal Stafa, Tirana 1.10.1980

Referee: Sándor Kuti (HUN)   Attendance: 19,200

PARTIZANI: Perlat Musta, Sulejman Starova, K. Hysi, Ferid Rragami, Safet Berisha, Haxhi Ballgjini, Sefedin Braho, Ilir Lame, A. Ahmeti, B. Hado, M. Fagu (.. F.Breca)

MALMÖ FF: Jan Möller, Roland Andersson, Kent Jönsson, Tim Parkin, Ingemar Erlandsson, Rickard Strömbäck (68 Tommy Hansson), Robert Prytz, Roy Andersson, Jan-Olov Kinnvall (78 Mats Arvidsson), Thomas Sjöberg, Paul McKinnon.

FORTUNA DÜSSELDORF v SV AUSTRIA SALZBURG 5-0 (2-0)

Rheinstadion, Düsseldorf 17.09.1980

Referee: Georges Konrath (FRA)   Attendance: 10,000

FORTUNA: Jörg Daniel, Josef Weikl, Gerd Zewe, Egon Köhnen, Armand Theis, Heinz Wirtz, Rudi Bommer, Thomas Allofs, Rüdiger Wenzel (80 Ralf Dusend), Klaus Allofs, Wolfgang Seel (80 Günter Thiele).   Trainer: Otto Rehhagel

SV AUSTRIA: Herbert Rettensteiner (75 Hans Berger), Gerhard Roos, Gerhard Breitenberger, Johannes Winklbauer, Jaroslav Pirnus, Martin Öllerer, Klaus Schulze, Hans-Gerd Schildt, Ewald Gröss (68 Niels Haarbye), Leopold Lainer, Günther Kronsteiner.   Trainer: Rudolf Strittich

Goals: Köhnen (28,62), Wenzel (43), K.Allofs (78), Theis (90)

SV AUSTRIA SALZBURG v FORTUNA DÜSSELDORF 0-3 (0-1)

Lehen, Salzburg 1.10.1980

Referee: Enzo Barbaresco (ITA)   Attendance: 7,000

SV AUSTRIA: Hans Berger, Gerhard Roos, Martin Öllerer, Johannes Winklbauer, Jaroslav Pirnus, Günther Kronsteiner, Gerhard Breitenberger, Leopold Lainer (74 Hermann Stadler), Hans-Gerd Schildt (50 Klaus Schulze), Ewald Gröss, Gerhard Perlak.   Trainer: Rudolf Strittich

FORTUNA: Jörg Daniel, Josef Weikl, Gerd Zewe, Egon Köhnen, Armand Theis, Heinz Wirtz, Rudi Bommer, Thomas Allofs (61 Ralf Dusend), Rüdiger Wenzel, Klaus Allofs (70 Günter Thiele), Wolfgang Seel.   Trainer: Otto Rehhagel

Goals: Th. Allofs (43), Dusend (70, 88)

VALENCIA CF v AS MONACO 2-0 (0-0)

Estadio Luis Casanova, Valencia 17.09.1980

Referee: Günter Linn (W. GER)   Attendance: 40,000

VALENCIA CF: Carlos Santiago PEREIRA; Ricardo Penella ARIAS, Miguel TENDILLO Berenguer, Manuel BOTUBOT Perreira, Ángel CASTELLANOS Céspedes; Enrique SAURA Gil, Daniel SOLSONA Puig, Mario Alberto KEMPES Chiodi (69 Pedro VILLARODÁ); Luis Darío FELMAN, Fernando MORENA, PABLO Rodríguez Flores (53 Javier SUBIRATS Hernández).

Trainer: Bernardino Pérez Elizarán "PASIEGUITO"

AS MONACO: Jean-Luc Ettori; Daniel Zorzetto, Jacques Perais, Rolland Courbis, Claude Puel; Didier Christophe, Jean Petit, Umberto Barberis; Alain Couriol, Victor Trossero, Roger Ricort (57 Albert Emon).   Trainer: Gérard Banide

Sent off: Solsona (87)

Goals: Kempes (64), Morena (89 pen)

AS MONACO v VALENCIA CF 3-3 (2-1)

Louis II, Monaco 1.10.1980

Referee: Clive Bradley White (ENG)   Attendance: 6,666

AS MONACO: Jean-Luc Ettori; Daniel Zorzetto, Jacques Perais, Rolland Courbis, Claude Puel; Didier Christophe, Jean Petit, Umberto Barberis; Alain Couriol (76 Jean-Marc Valadier), Victor Trossero, Albert Emon.
Trainer: Gérard Banide

VALENCIA CF: José Manuel SEMPERE Maciá; José CARRETE de Julián, Ricardo Penella ARIAS, Miguel TENDILLO Berenguer, Manuel BOTUBOT Perreira; Ángel CASTELLANOS Céspedes, Javier SUBIRATS Hernández (87 Juan Cruz SOL Oria), Mario Alberto KEMPES Chiodi; Enrique SAURA Gil, Fernando MORENA, PABLO Rodríguez Flores (73 Luis Dario FELMAN).
Trainer: Bernardino Pérez Elizarán "PASIEGUITO"

Goals: Petit (7, 50), Barberis (21), Morena (36), Kempes (74), Felman (77)

**CASTILLA CF
v WEST HAM UNITED LONDON 3-1** (0-1)

Estadio Santiago Bernabéu, Madrid 17.09.1980

Referee: Alain Delmer (FRA)   Attendance: 40,000

CASTILLA: MIGUEL Recio Moya, Juan Antonio Felipe Gallego "JUANITO" (63 Miguel Porlan Noguera "CHENDO"), José Antonio SALGUERO García, José Manuel ESPINOSA Gómez, CASIMIRO Torres Ibáñez, Ricardo ÁLVAREZ de Mena, José SÁNCHEZ LORENZO, Miguel BERNAL Feito, Cristóbal Machín Fernández de la Puente "BALÍN", Francisco Machín Fernández de la Puente "PACO", Valentín CIDÓN Manso (82 Vicente BLANCO Brazales).
Trainer: Juan José García Santos "JUANJO"

WEST HAM UNITED: Phil Parkes, Raymond Stewart, Frank Lampard, William Bonds, Alvin Martin, Alan Devonshire (86 Paul Brush), Nicholas Morgan (73 David Barnes), Paul Goddard, David Cross, Trevor Brooking, Geoffrey Pike.
Manager: John Lyall

Goals: Cross (17), Paco (64), Balín (72), Cidón (77)

**WEST HAM UNITED LONDON
v CASTILLA CF 5-1** (3-0, 3-1) (AET)

Boleyn Ground Upton Park, London 1.10.1980

Referee: Jan N.I. Keizer (HOL)
Attendance: 262 (behind closed doors)

WEST HAM UNITED: Phil Parkes, Raymond Stewart, Frank Lampard, William Bonds, Alvin Martin, Alan Devonshire, Pat Holland (106 Paul Brush), Paul Goddard (91 Nicholas Morgan), David Cross, Trevor Brooking, Geoffrey Pike.
Manager: John Lyall

CASTILLA: MIGUEL Recio Moya, Miguel Porlan Noguera "CHENDO", José Manuel ESPINOSA Gómez, CASIMIRO Torres Ibáñez, José Antonio SALGUERO García, José SÁNCHEZ LORENZO, Cristóbal Machín Fernández de la Puente "BALÍN", Ricardo ÁLVAREZ de Mena, Francisco Machín Fernández de la Puente "PACO" (106 Francisco RAMÍREZ Brazales), Miguel BERNAL Feito, Valentín CIDÓN Manso (46 Vicente BLANCO Brazales).
Trainer: Juan José García Santos "JUANJO"

Goals: Pike (19), Cross (30, 102, 119), Goddard (39), Bernal (56)

**CELTIC GLASGOW
v POLITEHNICA TIMIŞOARA 2-1** (2-0)

Celtic Park, Glasgow 17.09.1980

Referee: Gerard Geurts (HOL)   Attendance: 30,000

CELTIC: Patrick Bonner; Alan Sneddon, Thomas McAdam, Robert Sime Aitken, Daniel Fergus McGrain; David Alexander Provan (82 John Doyle), Murdo MacLeod (65 Michael Conroy), Dominic Sullivan, Thomas Burns; George McCluskey, Charles Nicholas.   Manager: William McNeill

POLITEHNICA: Aurel Moise; Dumitru Nadu, Dan Păltinişan, Gheorghe Şerbănoiu, Aurel Şunda; Ion Dumitru, Adrian Manea, Viorel Vişan, Titi Nicolae (60 Emerich Dembrovski), Leonida Nedelcu, Gheorghe Cotec (88 Stelian Anghel).   Trainers: Ion Ionescu & Toma Dobândă

Goals: Nicholas (19, 43), Manea (78)

**POLITEHNICA TIMIŞOARA
v CELTIC GLASGOW 1-0** (0-0)

1 Mai, Timişoara 1.10.1980

Referee: Nikolaos Lagogiannis (GRE)   Attendance: 40,000

POLITEHNICA: Aurel Moise; Dumitru Nadu, Gheorghe Şerbănoiu, Dan Păltinişan, Aurel Şunda (70 Gheorghe Cotec); Adrian Manea, Ion Dumitru, Emerich Dembrovski (65 Titi Nicolae), Viorel Vişan; Stelian Anghel, Leonida Nedelcu.
Trainer: Ion Ionescu

CELTIC: Peter Latchford; Alan Snedonn, Rodney McDonald, Thomas McAdam, Daniel McGrain; Robert Sime Aitken, David Provan, Murdo MacLeod, Dominic Sullivan; Francis Peter McGarvey, Charles Nicholas.
Manager: William McNeill

Goal: Păltinişan (81)

AS ROMA v FC CARL ZEISS JENA 3-0 (2-0)

Stadio Olimpico, Roma   17.09.1980

Referee: Nikola M. Dudin (BUL)   Attendance: 72,578

AS ROMA: Franco Tancredi, Luciano Spinosi, Domenico Maggiora, Paulo Roberto Falcão, Vincenzo Romano, Maurizio Turone, Bruno Conti (65 Attilio Sorbi), Agostino di Bartolomei, Roberto Pruzzo (80 Roberto Scarnecchia), Romeo Benetti, Carlo Ancelotti.   Trainer: Nils Liedholm

FC CARL ZEISS: Hans-Ulrich Grapenthin, Wolfgang Schilling, Lothar Kurbjuweit, Gerhard Hoppe, Konrad Weise, Rüdiger Schnuphase, Jürgen Raab (71 Martin Trocha), Andreas Krause, Thomas Töpfer, Lutz Lindemann (58 Dietmar Sengewald), Eberhard Vogel.   Trainer: Hans-Joachim Meyer

Goals: Pruzzo (5), Ancelotti (28), Falcão (71)

HAUGAR HAUGESUND v FC SION 2-0 (1-0)

Haugesund stadion   1.10.1980

Referee: Erik Steen Jensen (DEN)   Attendance: 4,238

HAUGAR: Pål Schifloe; Jens Egil Vikanes, Åge Sørensen, Dennis Burnett, Terje Solberg (59 Kjell Hestvik), Olav Heimdal, Einar Straume, Roger Føleide, Dag Petter Christophersen, Tor Nilsen, Peter Osborne.

FC SION: Pierre-Marie Pittier; Edmond Isoz, Pierre-Alain Valentini, Alain Balet, Alain Geiger; Léonard Karlen (46 Marian Cernicky), Jean-Claude Richard, Georges Bregy; Jean-Paul Brigger, Fernand Luisier (69 Bernard Perrier), Christophe Saunier.   Trainer: Arce Oscar

Goals: T. Nilsen (40), D.P. Christophersen (47 pen)

FC CARL ZEISS JENA v AS ROMA 4-0 (2-0)

Ernst-Abbe-Sportfeld, Jena   1.10.1980

Referee: André Daina (SWI)   Attendance: 16,000

FC CARL ZEISS: Hans-Ulrich Grapenthin, Dietmar Sengewald, Lothar Kurbjuweit, Gerhard Hoppe, Konrad Weise, Rüdiger Schnuphase, Jürgen Raab, Andreas Krause (70 Andreas Bielau), Thomas Töpfer (70 Martin Trocha), Lutz Lindemann, Eberhard Vogel.   Trainer: Hans-Joachim Meyer

AS ROMA: Franco Tancredi, Luciano Spinosi, Domenico Maggiora, Paulo Roberto Falcão, Vincenzo Romano, Maurizio Turone, Bruno Conti (46 Roberto Scarnecchia), Agostino di Bartolomei, Roberto Pruzzo, Carlo Ancelotti, Maurizio Amenta (61 Francesco Rocca).   Trainer: Nils Liedholm

Sent off: Scarnecchia (50)

Goals: Krause (26), Lindemann (38), Bielau (71, 87)

KASTORIA v DINAMO TBILISI 0-0

Kautatzogleio, Thessaloniki   17.09.1980

Referee: Mircea Salomir (ROM)   Attendance: 20,000

KASTORIA: Thanasis Ermeidis, Giorgos Alexiadis, Lazaros Kalaitzidis, Antonis Kopanos, Giannis Siapanidis (63 Apostolos Pergaminos), Giorgos Parashos, Giannis Dintsikos (63 Andreas Voitsidis), Thomas Liolios, Pavlos Siantsis, Dimitris Tsironis, Grigoris Papavasileiou.   Trainer: Tzimas

DINAMO: Otar Gabeliya, Tamaz Kostava, Aleksandr Chivadze, Shota Khinchagashvili, Georgi Chilaia, Vitali Daraselia, Nugzar Kakilashvili, Tengiz Sulakvelidze, Revaz Chelebadze (77 Georgi Tavadze), David Kipiani, Ramaz Schengeliya (77 Guram Chkareuli).
Trainer: Nodari Akhalkatsi

FC SION v HAUGAR HAUGESUND 1-1 (0-1)

Stade de Tourbillon, Sion   17.09.1980

Referee: Jan Peters (HOL)   Attendance: 6,000

FC SION: Pierre-Marie Pittier; Edmond Isoz, Pierre-Alain Valentini, Alain Balet, Alain Geiger; Jean-Claude Richard, Bernard Perrier (85 Christophe Saunier), Georges Bregy; Marian Cernicky, Jean-Paul Brigger, Fernand Luisier. Trainer: Arce Oscar

HAUGAR: Pål Schifloe; Jens Egil Vikanes, Åge Sørensen, Dennis Burnett, Kjell Hestvik (46 Terje Solberg); Olav Heimdal (69 Harald Undahl), Roger Føleide, Dag Petter Christophersen, Einar Straume; Tor Nilsen, Peter Osborne.

Goals: P. Osborne (41), Brigger (65)

DINAMO TBILISI v KASTORIA 2-0 (0-0)

Dinamo, Tbilisi   1.10.1980

Referee: Dušan Maksimović (YUG)   Attendance: 30,000

DINAMO: Otar Gabeliya, David Mudzhiri, Aleksandr Chivadze, Nodar Khizanishvili, Georgi Tavadze, Vitali Daraselia, Nugzar Kakilashvili, Tengiz Sulakvelidze, Vladimir Gutsaev, David Kipiani (82 Vakhtang Koridze), Ramaz Schengeliya (85 Revaz Chelebadze).
Trainer: Nodari Akhalkatsi

KASTORIA: Thanasis Ermeidis, Giorgos Alexiadis, Lazaros Kalaitzidis, Andreas Voitsidis, Apostolos Pergaminos, Giorgos Parashos, Giannis Dintsikos, Grigoris Papavasileiou, Thomas Liolios, Zoran Babovic, Dimitris Tsironis.   Trainer: Tzimas

Goals: Schengeliya (52), Gutsaev (80)

HIBERNIANS PAOLA v WATERFORD 1-0 (0-0)
Gzira   17.09.1980
Referee: Gianfranco Menegali (ITA)   Attendance: 2,000
HIBERNIANS: A.Mizzi; Constantino Consiglio, Norman Buttigieg; Tony Zerafa, R.Mizzi, Paul Xuereb; Alfred Mallia, John Cauchi, Galea, Spiteri-Gonzi, Joe Curmi.
WATERFORD: Peter Thomas; Brian Gardiner, Noel McQuaid; Al Finucane, Tony Dunphy, Thomas Jackson; Paul Kirk, Mick Madigan, Mark Meagan, Vinny McCarthy, Larry Murray.
Goal: P. Xuereb (68)

KSV WATERSCHEI v OMONOIA NICOSIA 4-0 (1-0)
André Dumontstadion, Genk   1.10.1980
Referee: Paul Rion (LUX)   Attendance: 18,500
WATERSCHEI: Klaus Pudelko, Herman Houben, Pierre Plessers, Urbain Lespoix, Danny David; Jos Heyligen, Pierre Janssen, Ronny van Poucke; Heinz Gründel, Per Olav Ohlsson, Roland Janssen.
OMONOIA: Marios Praxitelous; Nikos Patikkis, Haralampos Kontogiorgos, Kleitos Erotokritou, Kostas Petsas (20 Sotiris Tsikos); Sotiris Kaiafas (68 Evagoras Hristofi), Andreas Kanaris, Petros Frixou, Hristakis Omirou "Mavris"; Filippos Dimitriou, Takis Miamiliotis.
Goals: R. Janssen (17), Plessers (65 pen), Van Poucke (68, 75)

WATERFORD v HIBERNIANS PAOLA 4-0 (3-0)
Kilcohan Park, Waterford   1.10.1980
Referee: Kenneth J. Hope (SCO)   Attendance: 5,000
WATERFORD: Peter Thomas; Ger O'Mahony (.. Noel McQuaid), Al Finucane; Tony Dunphy, Brian Gardiner, Mick Madigan; Thomas Jackson, Vinny McCarthy, Larry Murray (.. Mark Meagan), Gerald Fitzpatrick, Paul Kirk.
HIBERNIANS: A.Mizzi; Constantino Consiglio (.. John Campbell), Norman Buttigieg; Tony Zerafa, R.Mizzi, Paul Xuereb; Alfred Mallia, John Cauchi, Galea, Spiteri-Gonzi, Joe Curmi.
Goals: Kirk (32, 80), Finucane (40), Fitzpatrick (42)

DINAMO ZAGREB v SL BENFICA LISBOA 0-0
Maksimir, Zagreb   17.09.1980
Referee: Horst Brummeier (AUS)   Attendance: 52,500
DINAMO: Zeljko Stinčić; Ismet Hadzić, Branco Tucak, Džemal Mustenanagić, Marin Kurtela; Srecko Bogdan, Drago Dumbović (72 Marjanović), Bosnjak; Stjepan Deverić, Zlatko Kranjcar, Abid Kovačević.
BENFICA: Manuel Galrinho BENTO; António José BASTOS LOPES, HUMBERTO Manuel Jesus COELHO (30 Alberto BASTOS LOPES), João Gonçalves LARANJEIRA, FREDERICO Nobre Rosa; CARLOS MANUEL Correia dos Santos, João António Ferreira Resende ALVES, SHÉU Han, Fernando Albino de Sousa CHALANA; Tamagnini Manuel Gomes Baptista NENÉ, CÉSAR Martins de Oliveira (67 Francisco António Lucas VITAL).   Trainer: Lajos Baroti

OMONOIA NICOSIA v KSV WATERSCHEI 1-3 (0-1)
Makarion, Nicosia   17.09.1980
Referee: Ivan Iosifov (BUL)   Attendance: 17,000
OMONOIA: Marios Praxitelous (70 Loukas Andreou), Nikos Patikkis, Antonas Paraskeva, Kleitos Erotokritou, Haralampos Kontogiorgos, Kostas Petsas; Hristakis Omirou "Mavris", Filippos Dimitriou, Sotiris Kaiafas; Sotiris Tsikos (70 Evagoras Hristofi), Andreas Kanaris.
WATERSCHEI: Klaus Pudelko; Herman Houben, Pierre Plessers, Urbain Lespoix, Danny David; Pierre Janssen, Jos Heyligen (5 Danny Vandereycken), Eric Maes, Roland Janssen; Per Olav Ohlsson, Ronny van Poucke (59 Patrick Surinx).
Goals: Van Poucke (17), R. Janssen (69), Patikkis (82 og), Kanaris (88)

SL BENFICA LISBOA v DINAMO ZAGREB 2-0 (1-0)
Estádio da Luz, Lisboa   1.10.1980
Referee: Gianfranco Menegali (ITA)   Attendance: 50,000
BENFICA: Manuel Galrinho BENTO; FREDERICO Nobre Rosa, HUMBERTO Manuel Jesus COELHO (70 Alberto BASTOS LOPES), João Gonçalves LARANJEIRA, Minervino José Lopes PIETRA; CARLOS MANUEL Correia dos Santos, João António Ferreira Resende ALVES, SHÉU Han, Fernando Albino de Sousa CHALANA; Tamagnini Manuel Gomes Baptista NENÉ, CÉSAR Martins de Oliveira (74 Francisco António Lucas VITAL).   Trainer: Lajos Baroti
DINAMO: Zeljko Stinčić; Čedomir Jovičević, Kurtela, Srecko Bogdan, Branco Tucak; Bosnjak, Džemal Mustenanagić, Zlatko Kranjcar (75 Ivan Poljak); Borislav Cvetković (60 Drago Dumbović), Stjepan Deverić, Abid Kovačević.
Goals: Nené (17), César (56)

**ILVES TAMPERE
v FEYENOORD ROTTERDAM 1-3** (1-1)

Tammelan Pallokenttä, Tampere   17.09.1980

Referee: Miroslav Stupar (USSR)   Attendance: 6,000

ILVES: Seppo Sairanen, Risto Hurri, Seppo Räsänen, Jukka Heinonen, Erkki Vihtilä, Jukka Pirinen, Mika Vidgren, Raimo Kuulavainen, Seppo Lindström, Arto Uimonen, Esa Vuorinen.   Trainer: Pertti Mäkipää

FEYENOORD: Joop Hiele, Ben Wijnstekers, Luuk Balkestein, Ivan Nielsen, Stanley Brard, André Stafleu (67 Geo de Leeuw), René Notten, Wim van Til, Jan van Deinsen, Sjaak Troost, Pierre Vermeulen.   Trainer: Vaclav Jezek

Goals: Uimonen (9), Notten (37 pen), Van Deinsen (52), Troost (90)

**NEWPORT COUNTY
v HAUGAR HAUGESUND 6-0** (2-0)

Somerton Park, Newport   4.11.1980

Referee: C.G. McGrath (IRE)   Attendance: 8,855

COUNTY: Gary Plumley; Richard Walden, Neil Bailey, David Bruton, Keith Oakes, Thomas Tynan, Nigel Vaughan, Stephen Lowndes, David Gwyther, John Aldridge, Kevin Moore.

HAUGAR: Pål Schifloe; Jens Egil Vikanes, Åge Sørensen, Dennis Burnett, Terje Solberg (56 Harald Undahl), Olav Heimdal, Roger Føleide (85 Kjell Hestvik), Rune Larsen, Dag Petter Christoffersen, Tor Nilsen, Peter Osborne.

Goals: Gwyther (12), Lowndes (44), Aldridge (56), Tynan (61, 81), Moore (70)

**FEYENOORD ROTTERDAM
v ILVES TAMPERE 4-2** (1-1)

Feyenoord, Rotterdam   1.10.1980

Referee: Malcolm Moffat (NIR)   Attendance: 15,000

FEYENOORD: Joop Hiele, Ben Wijnstekers, Luuk Balkestein, Ivan Nielsen, Stanley Brard, André Stafleu, René Notten, Jan van Deinsen (46 Geo de Leeuw), Richard Budding, Karel Bouwens (65 Sjaak Troost), Pierre Vermeulen.   Trainer: Vaclav Jezek

ILVES: Seppo Sairanen, Risto Hurri, Seppo Räsänen, Markku Wacklin, Erkki Vihtilä, Jukka Pirinen, Mika Vidgren, Raimo Kuulavainen, Seppo Lindström (.. Timo Martinsen), Arto Uimonen, Esa Vuorinen.   Trainer: Pertti Mäkipää

Goals: Vermeulen (27), Pirinen (44 pen), Nielsen (55), Troost (70), Notten (79), Wacklin (88)

KSV WATERSCHEI v FORTUNA DÜSSELDORF 0-0

André Dumontstadion, Waterschei   22.10.1980

Referee: Victoriano Sánchez Arminio (SPA)   Att: 20,000

WATERSCHEI: Klaus Pudelko (14 Jean Thijs), Herman Houben, Pierre Plessers, Urbain Lespoix, Danny David, Jos Heyligen, Pierre Janssen, Ronny van Poucke (75 Patrick Surinx), Heinz Gründel, Per Olav Ohlsson, Roland Janssen.

FORTUNA: Jörg Daniel, Josef Weikl, Gerd Zewe, Egon Köhnen, Armand Theis, Heinz Wirtz (56 Günter Kuczinski), Rudi Bommer, Thomas Allofs, Rüdiger Wenzel, Klaus Allofs, Wolfgang Seel (71 Günter Thiele).   Trainer: Otto Rehhagel

SECOND ROUND

**HAUGAR HAUGESUND
v NEWPORT COUNTY 0-0**

Haugesund Stadion   22.10.1980

Referee: Hans Harrysson (SWE)   Attendance: 4,522

HAUGAR: Pål Schifloe; Jens Egil Vikanes, Åge Sørensen, Dennis Burnett, Kjell Hestvik (46 Harald Undahl), Olav Heimdal, Terje Solberg, Dag Petter Christophersen; Tor Nilsen, Peter Osborne, Roger Føleide.

COUNTY: Gary Plumley; Richard Walden, Neil Bailey, David Bruton, Keith Oakes, Karl Elsey, Nigel Vaughan, Stephen Lowndes, David Gwyther, John Aldridge, Kevin Moore.

**FORTUNA DÜSSELDORF
v KSV WATERSCHEI 1-0** (1-0)

Rheinstadion, Düsseldorf   5.11.1980

Referee: Jakob Baumann (SWI)   Attendance: 12,700

FORTUNA: Jörg Daniel, Josef Weikl, Gerd Zewe, Egon Köhnen, Armand Theis, Günther Bansemer, Rudi Bommer, Thomas Allofs (46 Ralf Dusend), Rüdiger Wenzel, Klaus Allofs, Wolfgang Seel.   Trainer: Otto Rehhagel

WATERSCHEI: Klaus Pudelko, Herman Houben, Pierre Plessers, Urbain Lespoix, Danny David, Jos Heyligen, Pierre Janssen, Eric Maes (75 Roland Janssen), Heinz Gründel, Per Olav Ohlsson, Patrick Surinx.

Goal: Bansemer (5)

FC CARL ZEISS JENA
v VALENCIA CF 3-1 (3-0)

Ernst-Abbe-Sportfeld, Jena 22.10.1980

Referee: Roger Schoeters (BEL)   Attendance: 15,000

FC CARL ZEISS: Hans-Ulrich Grapenthin; Dietmar Sengewald, Konrad Weise, Rüdiger Schnuphase, Lothar Kurbjuweit; Gerhard Hoppe, Lutz Lindemann, Andreas Krause; Martin Trocha, Jürgen Raab (72 Andreas Bielau), Eberhard Vogel (81 Thomas Töpfer).
Trainer: Hans-Joachim Meyer

VALENCIA CF: José Manuel SEMPERE Maciá; José CARRETE de Julián, Miguel TENDILLO Berenguer (85 Juan Cruz SOL Oria), Ricardo ARIAS Penella, Manuel BOTUBOT Perreira; Ángel CASTELLANOS Céspedes, Javier SUBIRATS Hernández, Mario Alberto KEMPES Chiodi (46 Luis Dario FELMAN); Enrique SAURA Gil, Fernando MORENA, PABLO Rodríguez Flores.
Trainer: Bernardino Pérez Elizarán "PASIEGUITO"

Goals: Sengewald (1), Schnuphase (9 pen), Trocha (31), Morena (69)

VALENCIA CF v FC CARL ZEISS JENA 1-0 (0-0)

Estadio Luís Casanova, Valencia 5.11.1980

Referee: Michel Vautrot (FRA)   Attendance: 35,000

VALENCIA CF: José Manuel SEMPERE Maciá; José CARRETE de Julián, Manuel BOTUBOT Perreira, Ricardo ARIAS Penella, José CERVERÓ San Braulio; Enrique SAURA Gil, Ángel CASTELLANOS Céspedes, Mario Alberto KEMPES Chiodi (46 Javier SUBIRATS Hernández); Luis Dario FELMAN (80 Orlando Ramón JIMÉNEZ), Fernando MORENA, PABLO Rodríguez Flores.
Trainer: Bernardino Pérez Elizarán "PASIEGUITO"

FC CARL ZEISS: Hans-Ulrich Grapenthin; Lothar Kurbjuweit, Konrad Weise, Rüdiger Schnuphase, Dietmar Sengewald; Gerhard Hoppe, Lutz Lindemann (70 Thomas Töpfer), Andreas Krause; Martin Trocha (75 Andreas Bielau), Jürgen Raab, Eberhard Vogel.   Trainer: Hans-Joachim Meyer

Goal: Botubot (61)

WATERFORD FC v DINAMO TBILISI 0-1 (0-0)

Kilcohan Park, Waterford 22.10.1980

Referee: Norbert Rolles (LUX)   Attendance: 5,000

WATERFORD FC: Peter Thomas, Ger O'Mahony (83 Gerald Fitzpatrick), Brian Gardiner, Al Finucane, Tony Dunphy, Thomas Jackson, Larry Murray, Mick Madigan, Paul Kirk, Vinny McCarthy (73 Brendan Carey), Mark Meagan.

DINAMO: Otar Gabeliya, Tamaz Kostava, Aleksandr Chivadze, Nodar Khizanishvili, David Mudzhiri, Vitali Daraselia, Tengiz Sulakvelidze, Vakhtang Koridze, Vladimir Gutsaev (20 Revaz Chelebadze), David Kipiani, Ramaz Schengeliya (63 Konstantin Kereselidze).
Trainer: Nodari Akhalkatsi

Goal: Schengeliya (50)

DINAMO TBILISI v WATERFORD FC 4-0 (0-0)

Dinamo, Tbilisi 5.11.1980

Referee: Iordan Zhezhov (BUL)   Attendance: 50,000

DINAMO: Otar Gabeliya; Tamaz Kostava, Aleksandr Chivadze, Nodar Khizanishvili, David Mudzniri (82 Georgi Chilaia), Vitali Daraselia, Tengiz Sulakvelidze, Vazha Zhvaniya (64 Gocha Dzhokhadze), Revaz Chelebadze, David Kipiani, Ramaz Schengeliya.   Trainer: Nodari Akhalkatsi

WATERFORD FC: Peter Thomas, Ger O'Mahony, Brian Gardiner, Al Finucane, Tony Dunphy, Thomas Jackson, Larry Murray, Mick Madigan, Paul Kirk, Vinny McCarthy, Mark Meagan.

Goals: Daraselia (66, 79), Chivadze (74), Chilaia (87)

WEST HAM UNITED LONDON
v POLITEHNICA TIMIŞOARA 4-0 (3-0)

Boleyn Ground Upton Park, London 22.10.1980

Referee: Heinz Fahnler (AUS)   Attendance: 27,157

WEST HAM UNITED: Phil Parkes; Raymond Stewart, William Bonds, Alvin Martin, Frank Lampard; Pat Holland, James Neighbour, Alan Devonshire; Paul Goddard (88 Nicholas Morgan), David Cross, Geoffrey Pike.
Manager: John Lyall

POLITEHNICA: Aurel Moise; Dumitru Nadu, Gheorghe Şerbănoiu, Dan Păltinişan, Aurel Şunda; Ion Dumitru, Emerich Dembrovski (69 Titi Nicolae), Gheorghe Cotec, Viorel Vişan; Stelian Anghel, Leonida Nedelcu.
Manager: Ion Ionescu

Goals: Bonds (25), Goddard (27), Stewart (30 pen), Cross (83)

POLITEHNICA TIMIŞOARA
v WEST HAM UNITED LONDON 1-0 (0-0)

1 Mai, Timişoara 5.11.1980

Referee: Riccardo Lattanzi (ITA)   Attendance: 25,000

POLITEHNICA: Aurel Moise; Viorel Vişan, Dan Păltinişan, Gheorghe Şerbănoiu, Nicolae Mircea Murar; Titi Nicolae (68 Ioan Palea), Emerich Dembrovski (36 Aurel Şunda), Ion Dumitru; Stelian Anghel, Leonida Nedelcu, Gheorghe Cotec.
Manager: Ion Ionescu

WEST HAM UNITED: Phil Parkes; Raymond Stewart (32 Paul Brush), Frank Lampard, William Bonds, Alvin Martin; Paul Allen, Pat Holland, Paul Goddard; James Neighbour (63 Trevor Brooking), David Cross, Geoffrey Pike.
Manager: John Lyall

Goal: Păltinişan (54)

**HVIDOVRE IF
v FEYENOORD ROTTERDAM 1-2** (1-1)

Idraettsparken, København 22.10.1980

Referee: Gwyn Piece Owen (WAL)   Attendance: 3,292

HVIDOVRE: Curlei Nielsen, Finn Johansen, Michael Christensen, Jens Kurt Petersen, Steen Hansen, Bjarne Vinsløv (78 Jesper Petersen), Jørgen Jacobsen, Henrik Jensen (56 Gunter Lindahl), Michael Manniche, Jørgen Kirk, Leroy Ambrose.   Trainer: John Sinding

FEYENOORD: Joop Hiele, Ben Wijnstekers, Ivan Nielsen, André Stafleu (46 Sjaak Troost), Stanley Brard, Karel Bouwens, Luuk Balkestein, René Notten, Richard Budding, Jan Peters (46 Geo de Leeuw), Pierre Vermeulen.   Trainer: Vaclav Jezek

Goals: Manniche (2), Wijnstekers (32), Bouwens (51)

**FEYENOORD ROTTERDAM
v HVIDOVRE IF 1-0** (1-0)

Feyenoord, Rotterdam 5.11.1980

Referee: Anders Mattson (FIN)   Attendance: 6,558

FEYENOORD: Hugo Van Houten, Ben Wijnstekers, André Stafleu (.. Luuk Balkestein), Sjaak Troost, Stanley Brard, Ivan Nielsen, Karel Bouwens, René Notten, Jan Peters (.. Richard Budding), Pierre Vermeulen, Geo de Leeuw.   Trainer: Vaclav Jezek

HVIDOVRE: Curlei Nielsen, Finn Johansen, Michael Christensen, Jens Kurt Petersen, Steen Hansen, Gunter Lindahl, Jørgen Jacobsen, Henrik Jensen (19 Jesper Petersen, 40 Steen Bybjerg), Michael Manniche, Jørgen Kirk, Leroy Ambrose.   Trainer: John Sinding

Goal: Nielsen (36)

MALMÖ FF v SL BENFICA LISBOA 1-0 (0-0)

Malmö Stadion 22.10.1980

Referee: Siegfried Kirschen (E. GER)   Attendance: 10,585

MALMÖ FF: Jan Möller, Roland Andersson, Tim Parkin, Kent Jönsson, Ingermar Erlandsson; Magnus Andersson, Robert Pritz, Roy Andersson; Tommy Hansson (65 Mats Arvidsson), Paul McKinnon, Jan-Olof Kinvall.

SL BENFICA: Manuel Galrinho BENTO; FREDERICO Nobre Rosa, António José BASTOS LOPES (45 JOSÉ LUÍS Lopes Costa e Silva), João Gonçalves LARANJEIRA, Minervino José Lopes PIETRA; SHÉU Han, CARLOS MANUEL Correia dos Santos (68 António Augusto da Silva VELOSO), João António Ferreira Resende ALVES, Tamagnini Manuel Gomes Baptista NENÉ; Francisco António Lucas VITAL, CÉSAR Martins de Oliveira.   Trainer: Lajos Baroti

Goal: M. Andersson (49)

SL BENFICA LISBOA v MALMÖ FF 2-0 (0-0)

Estádio da Luz, Lisboa 5.11.1980

Referee: Ian M.D. Foote (SCO)   Attendance: 70,000

SL BENFICA: Manuel Galrinho BENTO, António José BASTOS LOPES, HUMBERTO Manuel Jesus COELHO, João Gonçalves LARANJEIRA, Minervino José Lopes PIETRA; CARLOS MANUEL Correia dos Santos (77 JOSÉ LUÍS Lopes Costa e Silva), João António Ferreira Resende ALVES, SHÉU Han; CÉSAR Martins de Oliveira (80 António Augusto da Silva VELOSO), Tamagnini Manuel Gomes Baptista NENÉ, Fernando Albino de Sousa CHALANA.   Trainer: Lajos Baroti

MALMÖ FF: Jan Möller; Roland Andersson, Tim Parkin, Kent Jönsson, Ingemar Erlandsson; Magnus Andersson, Robert Pritz, Roy Andersson, Jan-Olov Kinnvall; Paul McKinnon, Tommy Hansson.

Goals: Nené (57 pen, 60 pen)

SPARTA PRAHA v SLAVIA SOFIA 2-0 (2-0)

Stadión na Letnej, Praha 22.10.1980

Referee: Clive Bradley White (ENG)   Attendance: 12,000

SPARTA: Miroslav Stárek; Zdenek Scasný, Zdenek Caudr, Jaroslav Kotek, František Straka, Jaroslav Pollák, Josef Jarolím, Milan Vdovjak, Vratislav Chaloupka, Jan Berger, Václav Kotal (.. Josef Raška).   Trainer: Jiří Rubáš

SLAVIA: Georgi Gugalov, Rusi Ivanov, Ivan Haidarliev, Milcho Evtimov, Ivan Iliev, Vanio Kostov, Atanas Aleksandrov (76 Georgi Minchev), Ilia Aliev, Andrei Jeliazkov, Georgi Dermendjiev (46 Ilia Velichkov), Botiu Malinov.   Trainer: Aleksander Iliev

Goals: Vdovjak (14, 45)

SLAVIA SOFIA v SPARTA PRAHA 3-0 (3-0)

Sofia 5.11.1980

Referee: Nicolae Rainea (ROM)   Attendance: 5,000

SLAVIA: Georgi Gugalov, Rusi Ivanov, Ivan Haidarliev, Milcho Evtimov, Ivan Iliev, Vanio Kostov, Atanas Aleksandrov, Ilia Aliev, Andrei Jeliazkov, Ilia Velichkov (73 Svetoslav Georgiev), Chavdar Tzvetkov (89 Georgi Dermendjiev).   Trainer: Aleksander Iliev

SPARTA: Miroslav Stárek, Zdenek Scasny, František Straka, Jaroslav Kotek, Jan Pospíšil, Jaroslav Pollák, Josef Jarolím (46 Petr Slaný), Milan Vdovjak, Vratislav Chaloupka, Jan Berger, Václav Kotal (58 Josef Raška).   Trainer: Jiří Rubáš

Goals: Velichkov (38), Jeliazkov (41), Tzvetkov (45)

QUARTER-FINALS

**WEST HAM UNITED LONDON
v DINAMO TBILISI 1-4** (0-2)
Boleyn Ground Upton Park, London   4.03.1980
Referee: Antonio José da Silva Garrido (POR)   Att: 34,957
WEST HAM UNITED: Phil Parkes, Raymond Stewart, Frank Lampard, William Bonds, Alvin Martin, Alan Devonshire (46 Paul Allen), James Neighbour, Paul Goddard, David Cross, Trevor Brooking, Geoffrey Pike.   Manager: John Lyall
DINAMO: Otar Gabeliya, Nodar Khizanishvili, Aleksandr Chivadze, Shota Khinchagashvili, Georgi Georgi Tavadze, Vitali Daraselia, Zaur Svanadze, Tengiz Sulakvelidze, Vladimir Gutsaev, David Kipiani, Ramaz Schengeliya.
Trainer: Nodari Akhalkatsi
Goals: Chivadze (24), Gutsaev (31), Cross (54), Schengeliya (55, 67)

DINAMO TBILISI v WEST HAM UNITED 0-1 (0-0)
Dinamo, Tbilisi   18.03.1981
Referee: Walter Eschweiler (W. GER)   Attendance: 90,000
DINAMO: Otar Gabeliya, Nodar Khizanishvili, Aleksandr Chivadze, Shota Khinchagashvili, Georgi Georgi Tavadze, Georgi Chilaia (77 David Mudzhiri), Zaur Svanadze, Tengiz Sulakvelidze, Vladimir Gutsaev, David Kipiani, Ramaz Schengeliya.   Trainer: Nodari Akhalkatsi
WEST HAM UNITED: Phil Parkes, Raymond Stewart, Frank Lampard, William Bonds, Alvin Martin, Paul Brush, James Neighbour, Paul Goddard (65 Stuart Pearson), David Cross, Trevor Brooking, Geoffrey Pike.   Manager: John Lyall
Goal: Pearson (87)

**FORTUNA DÜSSELDORF
v SL BENFICA LISBOA 2-2** (2-1)
Rheinstadion, Düsseldorf   4.03.1981
Referee: Eduard Sostarić (YUG)   Attendance: 32,000
FORTUNA: Jörg Daniel; Gerd Zewe, Heiner Baltes, Peter Löhr, Ralf Dusend; Josef Weikl, Rudi Bommer, Thomas Allofs, Wolfgang Seel; Klaus Allofs, Rüdiger Wenzel.
Trainer: Heinz Höher
SL BENFICA: Manuel Galrinho BENTO; António José BASTOS LOPES, HUMBERTO Manuel Jesus COELHO, FREDERICO Nobre Rosa, António Augusto da Silva VELOSO; CARLOS MANUEL Correia dos Santos, João António Ferreira Resende ALVES, SHÉU Han, Fernando Albino de Sousa CHALANA (79 JORGE GOMES da Silva Filho); Tamagnini Manuel Gomes Baptista NENÉ, Mauricio Zacarias REINALDO Gomes.   Trainer: Lajos Baroti
Goals: Wenzel (2), Carlos Manuel (35), Dusend (39), H. Coelho (77)

**SL BENFICA LISBOA
v FORTUNA DÜSSELDORF 1-0** (0-0)
Estádio Da Luz, Lisboa   18.03.1981
Referee: Jan Keizer (HOL)   Attendance: 80,000
SL BENFICA: Manuel Galrinho BENTO; António Augusto da Silva VELOSO, HUMBERTO Manuel Jesus COELHO, João Gonçalves LARANJEIRA, Minervino José Lopes PIETRA; CARLOS MANUEL Correia dos Santos (90 LORES), João António Ferreira Resende ALVES, SHÉU Han, Fernando Albino de Sousa CHALANA; Tamagnini Manuel Gomes Baptista NENÉ (65 JORGE GOMES da Silva Filho), Mauricio Zacarias REINALDO Gomes.   Trainer: Lajos Baroti
FORTUNA: Jörg Daniel; Gerd Zewe, Heiner Baltes, Peter Löhr, Ralf Dusend; Josef Weikl; Hubert Schmitz, Thomas Allofs, Wolfgang Seel, Klaus Allofs (61 Rudi Bommer), Rüdiger Wenzel.   Trainer: Heinz Höher
Goal: Chalana (87)

**SLAVIA SOFIA
v FEYENOORD ROTTERDAM 3-2** (1-1)
Sofia   4.03.1981
Referee: Paolo Bergamo (ITA)   Attendance: 7,000
SLAVIA: Georgi Gugalov, Ivan Chakarov, Ivan Haidierliev, Ivan Iliev (.. Georgi Dermendjiev), Milcho Evtimov, Botiu Malinov, Pavlin Dimitrov, Ilia Aliev, Ilia Velichkov, Georgi Minchev, Chavdar Tzvetkov.   Trainer: Aleksander Iliev
FEYENOORD: Joop Hiele, Ben Wijnstekers, Ivan Nielsen, Sjaak Troost, Stanley Brard, Wim van Til, René Notten, Luuk Balkestein (.. Karel Bouwens), Richard Budding (.. Hans Groenendijk), Petur Petursson, Pierre Vermeulen.
Trainer: Vaclav Jezek
Goals: Tzvetkov (8 pen, 63), Nielsen (20), Minchev (64), Vermeulen (78 pen)

**FEYENOORD ROTTERDAM
v SLAVIA SOFIA 4-0** (1-0)
Feyenoord, Rotterdam   18.03.1981
Referee: Siegfried Kirschen (E. GER)   Attendance: 25,000
FEYENOORD: Joop Hiele, Ben Wijnstekers, André Stafleu, Ivan Nielsen, Sjaak Troost, Wim van Til, René Notten, Jan van Deinsen, Richard Budding, Petur Petursson (65 Karel Bouwens), Pierre Vermeulen.   Trainer: Vaclav Jezek
SLAVIA: Georgi Gugalov (35 Stoicho Stefanov), Ivan Chakarov, Ivan Haidierliev, Ivan Iliev, Milcho Evtimov, Botiu Malinov, Pavlin Dimitrov, Ilia Aliev, Ilia Velichkov, Georgi Minchev (35 Atanas Aleksandrov), Chavdar Tzvetkov.
Trainer: Aleksander Iliev
Goals: Notten (18), Van Deinsen (48), Vermeulen (77, 85)

**FC CARL ZEISS JENA
v NEWPORT COUNTY 2-2** (1-1)

Ernst-Abbe-Sportfeld, Jena 4.03.1981

Referee: Reidar Bjørnestad (NOR)   Attendance: 15,000

FC CARL ZEISS: Hans-Ulrich Grapenthin, Gert Brauer, Rüdiger Schnuphase, Andreas Krause, Lothar Kurbjuweit, Wolfgang Schilling, Dietmar Sengewald (.. Gerhard Hoppe), Lutz Lindemann, Martin Trocha, Jürgen Raab, Eberhard Vogel (.. Andreas Bielau). Trainer: Hans-Joachim Meyer

COUNTY: Gary Plumley, Richard Walden, Grant Davies, Keith Oakes, John Relish, Thomas Tynan, Karl Elsey, Stephen Lowndes, Nigel Vaughan, David Gwyther, Kevin Moore.

Goals: Raab (23, 85), Tynan (40, 89)

**NEWPORT COUNTY
v FC CARL ZEISS JENA 0-1** (0-1)

Somerton Park, Newport 18.03.1981

Referee: Henning Lund-Sørensen (DEN)   Att: 18,000

COUNTY: Gary Plumley, Richard Walden, Grant Davies, Keith Oakes, John Relish, Thomas Tynan, Nigel Vaughan, Stephen Lowndes, David Gwyther, Karl Elsey, Kevin Moore.

FC CARL ZEISS: Hans-Ulrich Grapenthin, Gert Brauer, Wolfgang Schilling, Jörg Burow (60 Andreas Krause), Lothar Kurbjuweit, Rüdiger Schnuphase, Ullrich Oevermann, Dietmar Sengewald, Andreas Bielau, Jürgen Raab, Eberhard Vogel. Trainer: Hans-Joachim Meyer

Goal: Kurbjuweit (27)

SEMI-FINALS

**DINAMO TBILISI
v FEYENOORD ROTTERDAM 3-0** (2-0)

Dinamo, Tbilisi 8.04.1981

Referee: Erik Fredriksson (SWE)   Attendance: 80,000

DINAMO: Otar Gabeliya, Tamaz Kostava, Aleksandr Chivadze, Shota Khinchagashvili, Georgi Tavadze, Tengiz Sulakvelidze (61 Nodar Khizanishvili), Vitali Daraselia, Zaur Svanadze, Vladimir Gutsaev, David Kipiani, Ramaz Schengeliya (65 Vazha Zhvaniya). Trainer: Nodar Akhalkatsi

FEYENOORD: Joop Hiele, Ben Wijnstekers, Ivan Nielsen, André Stafleu, Sjaak Troost (17 Stanley Brard), Richard Budding, René Notten, Jan van Deinsen, Karel Bouwens, Petur Petursson (50 Geo de Leeuw), Pierre Vermeulen. Trainer: Vaclav Jezek

Goals: Sulakvelidze (23, 51), Gutsaev (30)

**FEYENOORD ROTTERDAM
v DINAMO TBILISI 2-0** (1-0)

Feyenoord, Rotterdam 22.04.1981

Referee: Franz Wöhrer (AUS)   Attendance: 24,000

FEYENOORD: Ton Van Engelen, Ivan Nielsen (81 Petur Petursson), Stanley Brard, Ben Wijnstekers, Wim van Til, Jan van Deinsen, René Notten, Karel Bouwens, Richard Budding (67 Geo de Leeuw), Jan Peters, Pierre Vermeulen. Trainer: Vaclav Jezek

DINAMO: Otar Gabeliya, Tamaz Kostava, Aleksandr Chivadze, Shota Khinchagashvili, Georgi Tavadze, Vitali Daraselia, Zaur Svanadze (75 Nugzar Kakilashvili), Tengiz Sulakvelidze, Vladimir Gutsaev, David Kipiani, Ramaz Schengeliya. Trainer: Nodari Akhalkatsi

Goals: Bouwens (43), Notten (56)

**FC CARL ZEISS JENA
v SL BENFICA LISBOA 2-0** (2-0)

Ernst-Abbe-Sportfeld, Jena 8.04.1981

Referee: Enzo Barbaresco (ITA)   Attendance: 18,000

FC CARL ZEISS: Hans-Ulrich Grapenthin; Gert Brauer, Ullrich Oevermann (80 Roland Kulb), Dietmar Sengewald, Lothar Kurbjuweit, Rüdiger Schnuphase, Andreas Krause, Lutz Lindemann, Andreas Bielau, Jürgen Raab, Eberhard Vogel (74 Thomas Töpfer). Trainer: Hans-Joachim Meyer

BENFICA: Manuel Galrinho BENTO; António José BASTOS LOPES, HUMBERTO Manuel Jesus COELHO, João Gonçalves LARANJEIRA (84 Mauricio Zacarias REINALDO Gomes), António Augusto da Silva VELOSO; JORGE GOMES da Silva Filho, CARLOS MANUEL Correia dos Santos, João António Ferreira Resende ALVES, SHÉU Han; Tamagnini Manuel Gomes Baptista NENÉ, Francisco António Lucas VITAL (64 CÉSAR Martins de Oliveira). Trainer: Lajos Baroti

Goals: Bielau (8), Raab (15)

**SL BENFICA LISBOA
v FC CARL ZEISS JENA 1-0** (0-0)

Estádio da Luz, Lisboa 22.04.1981

Referee: Patrick Partidge (ENG)   Attendance: 80,000

SL BENFICA: Manuel Galrinho BENTO; António Augusto da Silva VELOSO, António José BASTOS LOPES, HUMBERTO Manuel Jesus COELHO, Minervino José Lopes PIETRA; JORGE GOMES da Silva Filho (35 JOSÉ LUÍS Lopes Costa e Silva), CARLOS MANUEL Correia dos Santos, SHÉU Han (80 Francisco António Lucas VITAL), Fernando Albino de Sousa. Trainer: Lajos Baroti CHALANA; Tamagnini Manuel Gomes Baptista NENÉ, Mauricio Zacarias REINALDO Gomes. Trainer: Lajos Baroti

FC CARL ZEISS: Hans-Ulrich Grapenthin; Gert Brauer, Wolfgang Schilling, Ullrich Oevermann (75 Gerhard Hoppe), Lothar Kurbjuweit, Rüdiger Schnuphase, Andreas Krause, Dietmar Sengewald, Andreas Bielau, Jürgen Raab (20 Thomas Töpfer), Eberhard Vogel.   Trainer: Hans-Joachim Meyer
Goal: Reinaldo (59).

FINAL

DINAMO TBILISI
v FC CARL ZEISS JENA 2-1 (0-0)
Rheinstadion, Düsseldorf   13.05.1981
Referee: Riccardo Lattanzi (ITA)   Attendance: 4,750

DINAMO: Otar Gabeliya, Tamaz Kostava, Aleksandr Chivadze, Nodar Khizanishvili, Georgi Tavadze, Vitali Daraselia, Zaur Svanadze (67 Nugzar Kakilashvili), Tengiz Sulakvelidze, Vladimir Gutsaev, David Kipiani (Cap), Ramaz Schengeliya.   Trainer: Nodari Akhalkatsi

FC CARL ZEISS: Hans-Ulrich Grapenthin, Gert Brauer, Gerhard Hoppe (88 Ullrich Oevermann), Wolfgang Schilling, Lothar Kurbjuweit (Cap), Rüdiger Schnuphase, Andreas Krause, Lutz Lindemann, Andreas Bielau (76 Thomas Töpfer), Jürgen Raab, Eberhard Vogel.   Trainer: Hans-Joachim Meyer

Goals: Hoppe (63), Gutsaev (67), Daraselia (87)

1 goal: Miloszewicz, Okonski (Legia Warszawa), Barberis (AS Monaco), Bernal, Paco, Balin, Cidón (Castilla FC), Sullivan (Celtic Glasgow), Pruzzo, Ancelotti, Falcão (AS Roma), Brigger (FC Sion), P.Xuereb (Hibernians Paola), Kanaris (Omonoia Nicosia), Uimonen, Pirinen, Wacklin (Ilves Tampere), P.Osborne, T.Nilsen, D.P.Christophersen (Haugar Haugesund), Botubot, Felman (Valencia CF), Manea (Politehnica Timişoara), Manniche, Ambrose (Hvidovre), M.Andersson, McKinnon (Malmö FF), Pospisil, Slaný, Horváth, Kotek, Raška (Sparta Praha), Minchev, Jeliazkov (Slavia Sofia), Pearson, Bonds, Stewart, Pike (West Ham United), Bansemer, Th.Allofs, K.Allofs, Theis (Fortuna Düsseldorf), Lowndes, Bruton (Newport County), Wijnstekers (Feyenoord Rotterdam), Finucane, Fitzpatrick (Waterford), Reinaldo, Carlos Manuel (Benfica Lisboa), Hoppe, Kurbjuweit, Sengewald, Schnuphase, Trocha, Krause, Lindemann (FC Carl Zeiss Jena), Chilaia (Dinamo Tbilisi), Plessers (Waterschei)

Own goal: Patikkis (Omonia Nicosia) for Waterschei

Goalscorers European Cup-Winners' Cup 1980-81:

6 goals: David Cross (West Ham United)

4 goals: Vladimir Gutsaev, Ramaz Schengeliya (Dinamo Tbilisi), René Notten, Pierre Vermeulen (Feyenoord Rotterdam), Thomas Tynan (Newport County), Tamagnini Manuel Gomes Baptista NENÉ (Benfica Lisboa), Chavdar Tzvetkov (Slavia Sofia)

3 goals: McGarvey, Nicholas (Celtic Glasgow), Daraselia (Dinamo Tbilisi), Bielau, Raab (FC Carl Zeiss Jena), Nielsen (Feyenoord), Dusend (Fortuna Düsseldorf), Velichkov (Slavia Sofia), Berger (Sparta Praha), Morena (Valencia), Van Poucke (Waterschei)

2 goals: Petit (AS Monaco), McCluskey (Celtic Glasgow), Chivadze, Sulakvelidze (Dinamo Tbilisi), Görgei (Diosgyör VTK), Bouwens, Troost, van Deinsen (Feyenoord), Köhnen, Wenzel (Fortuna Düsseldorf), Hansen (Hvidovre København), Aldridge, Gwyther, Moore (Newport County), Păltinişan (Politehnica Timişoara), César, Chalana, Humberto Coelho (Benfica Lisboa), Chaloupka, Jarolím, Vdovjak (Sparta Praha), Kempes (Valencia CF), Kirk (Waterford AFC), Goddard (West Ham United), R. Janssen (Waterschei)

CUP WINNERS' CUP 1981-82

PRELIMINARY ROUND

**POLITEHNICA TIMIŞOARA
v 1.FC LOKOMOTIVE LEIPZIG 2-0** (2-0)

1 Mai, Timişoara   19.08.1981

Referee: Antonin Reznicek (CZE)   Attendance: 18,000

POLITEHNICA: Aurel Moise, Dumitru Nadu (88 Nicolae Murar), Dan Păltinişan (41 Vasile Nucă), Gheorghe Şerbănoiu, Viorel Vişan; Aurel Şunda, Ion Dumitru, Petre Vlătănescu; Stelian Anghel, Leonida Nedelcu, Gheorghe Cotec.
Trainer: Marcel Pigulea

LOKOMOTIVE: René Müller; Joachim Fritsche, Frank Baum, Thomas Dennstedt, Uwe Zötzsche; Andreas Roth (66 Hans-Jürgen Kinne), Peter Englisch, Matthias Liebers; Lutz Moldt, Peter Schöne, Dieter Kühn (80 Andreas Bornschein).
Trainer: Harro Miller

Goals: Anghel (19), Nedelcu (28)

**1.FC LOKOMOTIVE LEIPZIG
v POLITEHNICA TIMIŞOARA 5-0** (2-0)

Zentralstadion, Leipzig   26.08.1981

Referee: Josef Bucek (AUS)   Attendance: 17,500

LOKOMOTIVE: René Müller; Joachim Fritsche, Frank Baum, Thomas Dennstedt, Uwe Zötzsche; Lutz Moldt, Matthias Liebers, Hans-Jürgen Kinne; Volker Grossmann (85 Andreas Bornschein), Peter Schöne, Dieter Kühn.
Trainer: Harro Miller

POLITEHNICA: Aurel Moise; Aurel Şunda, Dan Păltinişan, Gheorghe Şerbănoiu, Viorel Vişan; Dumitru Manea, Ion Dumitru, Petre Vlătănescu; Stelian Anghel, Leonida Nedelcu, Vasile Nucă (65 Dumitru Nadu).   Trainer: Marcel Pigulea

Goals: Baum (22), Moldt (34), Zötzsche (62), Kühn (89, 90)

FIRST ROUND

JEUNESSE D'ESCH v VELEŽ MOSTAR 1-1 (0-0)

Stade de la Frontière, Esch-sur-Alzette   15.09.1981

Referee: Gerard J.M. Geurds (HOL)   Attendance: 5,000

JEUNESSE: Serge Roques; Carlo Jungbluth, Jean Noel, Gianni Di Pentima, Adrien Koster, André Zwally, Zieser, Léon Jang Mond, Jean-Pierre Barboni, Manou Scheitler, Simon.

VELEŽ: Enver Marić; Avdo Kalajdzić, Mirsad Mulahasanović, Dubravko Ledić, Vladimir Matijević, Veselin Djurasević, Dragan Okuka, Vladimir Skocajić, Dušan Bajević (.. Bijedić), Franjo Vladić, Momčilo Vukoje (.. Lucić).

Goals: Scheitler (71), Mulahasanović (88)

VELEŽ MOSTAR v JEUNESSE D'ESCH 6-1 (1-0)

Gradski, Mostar   30.09.1981

Referee: Sotos Afxentiou (CYP)   Attendance: 12,000

VELEŽ: Enver Marić; Avdo Kalajdzić, Mirsad Mulahasanović, Medvedović, Vladimir Matijević, Veselin Djurasević, Dragan Okuka, Vladimir Skocajić, Dušan Bajević, Franjo Vladić (.. Lucić), Momčilo Vukoje (.. Bijedić).

JEUNESSE: Serge Roques; Serge Pigat, Lucciarini, Gianni Di Pentima, Adrien Koster, Léon Jang Mond, Jean-Pierre Barboni (81 Romain Pavant), Carlo Jungbluth, Manou Scheitler, Simon (81 Catalina), André Zwally.

Goals: Okuka (28, 52), Skocajić (46), Matijević (53, 86), Bajević (67), Scheitler (80)

**AJAX AMSTERDAM
v TOTTENHAM HOTSPUR LONDON 1-3** (0-2)

Olympisch, Amsterdam   16.09.1981

Referee: Augusto Lamo Castillo (SPA)   Attendance: 21,742

AJAX: Piet Schrijvers, Keje Molenaar, Wim Jansen (20 Piet Wijnberg), Steen Ziegler, Peter Boeve, Dick Schoenaker, Edo Ophof (46 Gerald Vanenburg), Søren Lerby, Tscheu La Ling, Piet Hamberg, Jesper Olsen.   Trainer: Kurt Linder

TOTTENHAM: Raymond Clemence, Christopher Hughton, Paul Miller, Graham Roberts, Stephen Perryman, Osvaldo Ardiles, Anthony Galvin, Glenn Hoddle, Ricardo Villa, Steven Archibald, Mark Falco.   Manager: Keith Burkinshaw

Goals: Falco (19, 34), Villa (67), Lerby (68)

**TOTTENHAM HOTSPUR LONDON
v AJAX AMSTERDAM 3-0** (0-0)

White Hart Lane, London   29.09.1981

Referee: Adolf Prokop (E. GER)   Attendance: 34,606

TOTTENHAM: Raymond Clemence, Stephen Perryman, Graham Roberts (83 John Lacy), Paul Miller, Christopher Hughton, Glenn Hoddle, Osvaldo Ardiles, Ricardo Villa, Steven Archibald, Mark Falco, Anthony Galvin.
Manager: Keith Burkinshaw

AJAX: Hans Galjé, Keje Molenaar, Wim Jansen, Piet Wijnberg, Peter Boeve, Gerald Vanenburg, Dick Schoenaker, Søren Lerby, Piet Hamberg (67 Sonny Silooy), Wim Kieft, Jesper Olsen.
Trainer: Kurt Linder

Goals: Galvin (69), Falco (76), Ardiles (81)

**KOTKAN TYOVAEN PALLOILIJAT
v SÉC BASTIA 0-0**

Urheilukeskus, Kotka   16.09.1981

Referee: Kjell Johansson (SWE)   Attendance: 4,107

KTP: Jouko Kataja, Kalevi Eriksson, Juha Lehtinen, Arto Tolsa, Kari Bergqvist, Jouko Alila, Ari Alila, Oiva Ukkonen, Heikki Lampi, Vesa Nironen, Ari Tissari (46 Heikki Imonen).

SÉC BASTIA: Pierrick Hiard; Jean-Louis Cazes, Gerard Bacconier, Charles Orlanducci, Jose Pastinelli, Yves Ehrlacher, Alain Fiard, Claude Papi, Pascal Mariini, Roger Milla, Simei Ihily.   Trainer: Jean-Antoine Redin

**SÉC BASTIA
v KOTKAN TYOVAEN PALLOILIJAT 5-0** (2-0)

Stade Armand Césari, Bastia   30.09.1981

Referee: Antonio José da Silva Garrido (POR)   Att: 8,000

SÉC BASTIA: Pierrick Hiard; Jean-Louis Cazes, Gérard Fontana, Gerard Bacconier, Jose Pastinelli, Alain Fiard, Yves Ehrlacher, Claude Papi, Raimondo Ponte, Roger Milla, Simei Ihily.   Trainer: Jean-Antoine Redin

KTP: Jouko Kataja, Kari Bergqvist, Jouka Suronen, Arto Tolsa, Kalevi Eriksson, Jouko Alila, Heikki Imonen, Juha Vehvilainen (65 Ari Tissari), Ari Alila, Heikki Lampi, Vesa Nironen.

Goals: Cazes (25), Ihily (30, 51), Ponte (49), Milla (87)

**EINTRACHT FRANKFURT/MAIN
v PAOK THESSALONIKI 2-0** (1-0)

Waldstadion, Frankfurt am Main   16.09.1981

Referee: Robert B. Valentine (SCO)   Attendance: 22,000

EINTRACHT: Jürgen Pahl, Michael Sziedat, Bruno Pezzey, Karl-Heinz Körbel, Willi Neuberger, Ronald Borchers, Norbert Nachtweih, Bernd Nickel (88 Wolfgang Trapp), Ralf Falkenmayer, Bum-Kun Cha, Joachim Löw (57 Holger Anthes).   Trainer: Lothar Buchmann

PAOK: Panagiotis Pantelis, Giannis Gounaris, Theodoros Apostolidis, Thomas Siggas, Kostas Iosifidis, Giannis Damanakis, Vasilis Georgopoulos, Giorgos Koudas, Nikos Alavantas, Giorgos Kostikos, Stathis Triantafillidis.   Trainer: Heinz Heer

Goals: Pezzey (11), Körbel (78)

**PAOK THESSALONIKI v EINTRACHT
FRANKFURT/MAIN 2-0** (1-0, 2-0) (AET)

Toumpas, Thessaloniki   30.09.1981

Referee: Sándor Kuti (HUN)   Attendance: 35,000

PAOK: Panagiotis Pantelis, Giannis Gounaris, Theodoros Apostolidis, Thomas Siggas, Kostas Iosifidis, Giannis Damanakis, Stathis Triantafillidis (75 Hristos Dimopoulos), Vasilis Georgopoulos, Giorgos Koudas (91 Minervino Gkouerino), Giorgos Kostikos, Nikos Alavantas.   Trainer: Heinz Heer

EINTRACHT: Jürgen Pahl, Michael Sziedat, Bruno Pezzey, Karl-Heinz Körbel, Willi Neuberger, Werner Lorant, Stefan Lottermann (65 Norbert Otto), Norbert Nachtweih, Ralf Falkenmayer (91 Wolfgang Trapp), Ronald Borchers, Bum-Kun Cha.   Trainer: Lothar Buchmann

Goals: Kostikos (35, 60)

Penalties: 0-1 Lorant, 1-1 Kostikos, 1-2 Körbel, 2-2 Guerino, 2-3 Trapp, 3-3 Gounaris, 4-3 Nachtweih, 4-4 Damanakis, 4-5 Pezzey, Dimopoulos (miss)

DINAMO TBILISI v GRAZER AK 2-0 (1-0)

Dinamo, Tbilisi   16.09.1981

Referee: Rudolf Renggli (SWI)   Attendance: 59,900

DINAMO: Otar Gabeliya, Nodar Khizanishvili, Aleksandr Chivadze, Khinchagashvili, Georgi Tavadze, Vitali Daraselia, Zaur Svanadze, Tengiz Sulakvelidze, Vladimir Gutsaev, Vazha Zhvaniya, Ramaz Schengeliya.   Trainer: Nodari Akhalkatsi

GRAZER AK: Savo Ekmecic; Erich Marko, Erwin Hohenwarter, Harald Gamauf, Werner Maier, Mario Mohapp (46 Mario Zuenelli), Josef Moder, Johann Pigel, Josef Stering, Leo Weiss, Alfred Riedl (88 Klaus Spirk).   Trainer: Zlatko Čajkovski

Goals: Zhvaniya (42), Schengeliya (72 pen)

GRAZER AK v DINAMO TBILISI 2-2 (0-1)

Bundesstadion Liebenau, Graz   30.09.1981

Referee: Nicolaos Zlatanos (GRE)   Attendance: 7,000

GRAZER AK: Savo Ekmecic, Ewald Ratschnig, Erwin Hohenwarter, Werner Maier, Erich Marko, Paul Bajlitz (46 Leo Weiss, 70 Wolfgang Schwicker), Josef Moder, Harald Gamauf, Josef Stering, Johann Pigel, Alfred Riedl.   Trainer: Zlatko Čajkovski

DINAMO: Otar Gabeliya, Nodar Khizanishvili, Aleksandr Chivadze, Khinchagashvili, Georgi Tavadze, Vitali Daraselia, Zaur Svanadze, Tengiz Sulakvelidze, Vladimir Gutsaev, Vazha Zhvaniya (85 David Mudzhiri), Ramaz Schengeliya.   Trainer: Nodari Akhalkatsi

Goals: Schengeliya (41, 63 pen), Riedl (64), Schwicker (77)

FC BARCELONA v TRAKIA PLOVDIV 4-1 (3-0)
Camp Nou, Barcelona   16.09.1981
Referee: Kenneth J. Hope (SCO)   Attendance: 25,000

FC BARCELONA: Pedro María ARTOLA Urrutia, GERARDO Miranda Concepción (67 Bernardo Bianquetti Miguel "MIGUELI"), Antonio OLMO Ramírez, José Ramón ALESANCO Ventosa, José Manuel Martínez Toral "MANOLO", ESTEBAN Vigo Benítez, VÍCTOR Muñoz Manrique, Bernd Schuster, Juan José ESTELLA Salas (65 Enrique MORÁN Blanco), Allan Simonsen, Enrique Castro González "QUINI". Trainer: Udo Lattek

TRAKIA: Dimitar Vichev, Rumen Iurukov, Atanas Marinov, Dimitar Mladenov, Blagoi Blangev, Kosta Tanev (76 Petar Dimitrov), Georgi Slavkov, Petar Zehtinski (85 Trifon Pachev), Kostadin Kostadinov, Krasimir Manolov, Marin Bakalov. Trainer: Dinko Dermendjiev

Goals: Quini (25), Simonsen (27, 77 pen), Schuster (38), Slavkov (83)

LOKOMOTIVE LEIPZIG
v SWANSEA CITY 2-1 (2-0)
Zentralstadion, Leipzig   30.09.1981
Referee: Massimo Ciulli (ITA)   Attendance: 22,500

LOKOMOTIVE: René Müller, Frank Baum, Joachim Fritsche, Thomas Dennstedt, Uwe Zötzsche; Wolfgang Altmann, Lutz Moldt, Hans-Jürgen Kinne, Matthias Liebers, Dieter Kühn (79 Volker Grossmann), Andreas Bornschein (2 Peter Schöne). Trainer: Harro Miller

SWANSEA: David Davies, Ante Rajković, Brian Attley, Neil Robinson, Nigel Stevenson (46 Wyndham Evans), Džemal Hadziabdić, Robert James, Leighton James, Robert Latchford (69 David Giles), Jeremy Charles, Alan Curtis.

Goals: Kinne (14), Moldt (22), Charles (79)

TRAKIA PLOVDIV v FC BARCELONA 1-0 (1-0)
Hristo Botev, Plovdiv   30.09.1981
Referee: Roger Schoeters (BEL)   Attendance: 40,000

TRAKIA: Dimitar Vichev, Rumen Iurukov, Slavcho Horozov, Dimitar Mladenov, Blagoi Blangev, Kosta Tanev, Georgi Slavkov, Petar Zehtinski (70 Mitko Argirov), Kostadin Kostadinov, Krasimir Manolov (75 Trifon Pachev), Marin Bakalov.   Trainer: Dinko Dermendjiev

FC BARCELONA: Pedro María ARTOLA Urrutia, José Antonio RAMOS Huete, Antonio OLMO Ramírez, Juan Ramón ALESANCO Ventosa, José Manuel Martínez Toral "MANOLO", Juan José ESTELLA Salas, Bernd Schuster, VÍCTOR Muñoz Manrique, Allan Simonsen, Enrique Castro González "QUINI", ESTEBAN Vigo Benítez (66 José Vicente SÁNCHEZ Felip). Trainer: Udo Lattek

Goal: Slavkov (34)

VÅLERENGEN IF OSLO
v LEGIA WARSZAWA 2-2 (0-1)
Bislett, Oslo   16.09.1981
Referee: Magnus V. Petursson (ICE)   Attendance: 4,349

VÅLERENGEN: Tom R. Jacobsen; Petter Morstad, Ernst Pedersen, Stein Madsen, Tor Brevik; Tom Jacobsen, Stein Pedersen (68 Morten Haugen), Vidar Davidsen; Arnfinn Moen, Pål Jacobsen, Erik Foss.

LEGIA: Jacek Kazimierski; Adam Topolski, Pawel Janas, Edward Zalezny, Ryszard Milewski; Janusz Baran, Stefan Majewski, Henryk Miloszewicz; Marek Kusto (87 Bogdan Kwapisz), Krzysztof Adamczyk, Miroslaw Okonski.

Goals: Majewski (43), P. Jacobsen (55, 70), Okonski (62)

SWANSEA CITY
v LOKOMOTIVE LEIPZIG 0-1 (0-0)
Vetch Field, Swansea   16.09.1981
Referee: Joel Quiniou (FRA)   Attendance: 10,295

SWANSEA: David Davies, Neil Robinson, Džemal Hadziabdić, Ante Rajković, Nigel Stevenson, Brian Attley (61 Wyndham Evans), Robert James, John Mahoney, Robert Latchford, Alan Curtis, Leighton James (23 David Giles).

LOKOMOTIVE: René Müller; Frank Baum, Joachim Fritsche, Thomas Dennstedt, Uwe Zötzsche; Hans-Jürgen Kinne, Matthias Liebers, Wolfgang Altmann, Lutz Moldt; Peter Schöne, Dieter Kühn. Trainer: Harro Miller

Goal: Kinne (68)

LEGIA WARSZAWA
v VÅLERENGEN OSLO 4-1 (2-0)
Wojska Polskiego, Warszawa   30.09.1981
Referee: Mauri Laakso (FIN)   Attendance: 15,000

LEGIA: Jacek Kazimierski, Adam Topolski, Pawel Janas, Stefan Majewski, Ryszard Milewski; Janusz Baran, Waldemar Tuminski, Henryk Miloszewicz; Marek Kusto, Krzysztof Adamczyk, Miroslaw Okonski.

VÅLERENGEN: Tom R. Jacobsen; Petter Morstad, Ernst Pedersen, Dag Roar Austmo, Tor Brevik (70 Stein Madsen); Arnfinn Moen, Vidar Davidsen, Tom Jacobsen; Pål Jacobsen, Henning Bjarnøy (75 Morten Haugen), Erik Foss.

Goals: Baran (1), Adamczyk (6), Topolski (57), Moen (58), Miloszewicz (89)

SKA ROSTOV na DON v ANKARAGÜCÜ 3-0 (1-0)
Centralniy, Rostov   16.09.1981
Referee: Svein Inge Thime (NOR)   Attendance: 33,000
SKA: Viktor Radaev, Valeri Goncharov, Aleksandr Andriuschenko, Sergei Yashin, Aleksandr Barketov, Pavel Gusev, Vitali Popadopulo (46 Nikolai Romanchuk), Sergei Andreev, Aleksandr Zavarov, Igor Gamula (81 Yuri Schumlin), Aleksandr Vorobiev.
ANKARAGÜCÜ: Adil Eriç, Hikmet Hancioglu, Haluk Kargen, Fuat Akyuz, Kavak, Iskender Atasoy, Elölu (67 Kasar), Sadik Akgöz, Nazmi Erdenen, Halil Ibrahim Eren, Sahin (66 Kalagöl).
Goals: Zavarov (40, 56), Andreev (80)

**VASAS BUDAPEST
v PARALIMNI FAMAGUSTA 8-0** (1-0)
Fáy u, Budapest   30.09.1981
Referee: Jaromir Fausek (CZE)   Attendance: 4,000
VASAS: Imre Leboniczky; Péter Török, András Komjáti, István Halász (69 László Pecha), András Szabó (64 István Birinyi), András Szebegyinszki, Sándor Zombori, Géza Rixer; László Kiss, Ignác Izsó, Béla Váradi.
PARALIMNI: Antonis Kleftis, Loukis Louka, Mihalis Kafetzis, Andreas Kittos, Giorgos Kezos, George Oikonomou (69 Antonis Kalimeras), Giannis Hatzigiannis, Mihalis Goumenos, Dimitris Ecomou "Koudas", Kostas Tsierkezos, Pierakis Markoulis.
Goals: Váradi (33, 55 pen, 70 pen), Kiss (60, 84), Szebegyinszki (61), Izsó (63, 83)

ANKARAGÜCÜ v SKA ROSTOV na DON 0-2 (0-0)
19 Mayis Stadi, Ankara   30.09.1981
Referee: Aleksander Suchanek (POL)   Attendance: 17,000
ANKARAGÜCÜ: Adil Eriç, Iskender Atasoy, Hikmet Hancioglu, Fuat Akyuz, Ihsan, Cuneyt, Orhan, Geluk, Halil Ibrahim Eren, Mehmet, Sadik Akgöz.
SKA: Aleksei Chistiakov, Valeri Goncharov, Aleksandr Andriuschenko, Sergei Yashin, Aleksandr Barketov, Pavel Gusev, Nikolai Romanchuk, Sergei Andreev, Aleksandr Zavarov, Nail Kuriatnikov, Aleksandr Vorobiev.
Goals: Andreev (67), Vorobiev (71)

BALLYMENA UNITED v AS ROMA 0-2 (0-0)
The Showgrounds, Ballymena   16.09.1981
Referee: Michel Vautrot (FRA)   Attendance: 3,500
BALLYMENA UNITED: Dennis Matthews, George Beattie, Graham Fox, Anthony O'Doherty, Ronnie McCullough, Seamus McDowell (72 Thomas Huston), David Neill, John Sloan, Peter McCusker, Paul Malone, Frankie Moffatt (72 David Smyth).   Trainer: Campbell
AS ROMA: Franco Tancredi, Sebastiano Nela, Luciano Marangon, Paulo Roberto Falcão, Dario Bonetti, Maurizio Turone, Odoacre Chierico, Domenico Maggiora, Roberto Pruzzo, Carlo Ancelotti, Bruno Conti.   Trainer: Nils Liedholm
Goals: Chierico (56), Ancelotti (87)

**PARALIMNI FAMAGUSTA
v VASAS BUDAPEST 1-0** (0-0)
Paralimni, Famagusta   16.09.1981
Referee: Hiqmet Kuka (ALB)   Attendance: 3,000
PARALIMNI: Antonis Kleftis, Loukis Louka, Mihalis Kafetzis, Andreas Kittos, Giorgos Kezos, Giorgos Oikonomou, Nikos Krasias, Mihalis Goumenos, Dimitris Ecomou "Koudas", Kostas Tsierkezos, Pierakis Markoulis.
VASAS: Imre Leboniczky, Péter Török, Béla Hegedüs, István Halász, András Szabó; Tibor Balogh (60 András Komjáti), András Szebegyinszki, Sándor Zombori, Géza Rixer; László Kiss, Ignác Izsó (60 László Pecha).
Goal: Goumenos (57)

AS ROMA v BALLYMENA UNITED 4-0 (2-0)
Stadio Olimpico, Roma   30.09.1981
Referee: Edgar Azzopardi (MAL)   Attendance: 24,000
AS ROMA: Franco Tancredi, Sebastiano Nela, Luciano Marangon (62 Carlo Perrone), Paulo Roberto Falcão, Dario Bonetti, Luciano Spinosi, Odoacre Chierico, Paolo Giovanelli, Roberto Pruzzo, Carlo Ancelotti, Bruno Conti (66 Paolo Alberto Faccini).   Trainer: Nils Liedholm
BALLYMENA UNITED: Dennis Matthews, George Beattie, Thomas Huston, Anthony O'Doherty, Ronnie McCullough, Seamus McDowell, David Neill, John Sloan, Sammy McQuiston (63 Peter McCusker), Paul Malone, Graham Fox.   Trainer: Campbell
Goals: Spinosi (26), Pruzzo (42, 51), Giovannelli (55)

LAUSANNE SPORTS v KALMAR FF 2-1 (1-1)
Stade Olympique de la Pontaise, Lausanne 16.09.1981
Referee: Ángel Franco Martínez (SPA)   Attendance: 6,400
LAUSANNE SPORTS: Giuseppe Varquez; Stéphane Crescenzi, Pierre-Albert Chapuisat, Urs Bamert, Claude Ryf, Robert Lei-Ravello (46 Georges Diserens), Marcel Parietti, Gérard Castella, Robert Kok, Yves Mauron, Pierre-Albert Tachet. Trainer: Charles Hertig
KALMAR FF: Leif Friberg, Mikael Marko, Thomas Ström, Ulf Ohlsson, Peter Rydasp, Benno Magnusson (63 Tommy Berggren), Tony Persson, Alf Nilsson, Kurt-Arne Bergstrand, Jan-Åke Lundberg, Tomas Sunesson.
Goals: Parietti (7), Magnusson (35), Kok (83)

KALMAR FF v LAUSANNE SPORTS 3-2 (2-1)
Fredriksskans, Kalmar 30.09.1981
Referee's: Anatoli Kadetov; Lev Akseneviti, Valeriy Burtenko (USSR)   Attendance: 3,654
KALMAR FF: Leif Friberg, Mikael Marko, Ulf Ohlsson, Thomas Ström, Peter Rydasp (75 Tommy Berggren), Tony Persson, Kurt-Arne Bergstrand, Alf Nilsson, Benno Magnusson, Jan-Åke Lundberg, Tomas Sunesson.
LAUSANNE SPORTS: Jean-Claude Milani; Stéphane Crescenzi, Pierre-Albert Chapuisat, Urs Bamert, Claude Ryf, Robert Lei-Ravello (79 Christian Rytz), Marcel Parietti, Gérard Castella (56 Yves Mauron), Georges Diserens, Robert Kok, Pierre-Albert Tachet.   Trainer: Charles Hertig
Goals: Persson (10), Parietti (15), Ohlsson (42, 55), Kok (62)

FRAM REYKJAVIK v DUNDALK FC 2-1 (0-1)
Laugardalsvöllur, Reykjavik 16.09.1981
Referee: George B. Smith (SCO)   Attendance: 5,000
FRAM: Gudmundur Baldursson, Trausti Haraldsson, Agust Hauksson, Pétur Ormslev, Marteinn Geirsson, Gunnar Bjarnasson, Halldor Arason, Vidar Thorkelsson, Gunnar Gudmundsson, Gudmundur Torfasson, Hafthor Sveinjónsson.
DUNDALK FC: Richard Blackmore, Eamon Gregg, Martin Lawlor, Thomas McConville, Paddy Dunning, Leo Flanagan, Sean Byrne, Barry Kehoe, Michael Fairclough, Hilary Carlyle, John Archbold (.. Brian Duff).   Manager: Jim McLaughlin
Goals: Fairclough (35), Thorfasson (65), Sveinjónsson (82)

DUNDALK FC v FRAM REYKJAVIK 4-0 (2-0)
Oriel Park, Dundalk 30.09.1981
Referee: Torben Mansson (DEN)   Attendance: 3,500
DUNDALK FC: Richard Blackmore, Eamon Gregg, Martin Lawlor, Thomas McConville, Paddy Dunning, Leo Flanagan, Sean Byrne, Barry Kehoe, Michael Fairclough (.. John Archbold), Jimmy Reilly), Brian Duff, Hilary Carlyle.   Manager: Jim McLaughlin
FRAM: Gudmundur Baldursson, Trausti Haraldsson, Agust Hauksson, Pétur Ormslev, Marteinn Geirsson, Gunnar Bjarnasson, Halldor Arason, Vidar Thorkelsson, Gunnar Gudmundsson, Gudmundur Torfasson, Hafthor Sveinjónsson.
Goals: Flanagan (4 pen), Fairclough (23), Lawlor (49), Duff (62).

VEJLE BK v FC PORTO 2-1 (2-1)
Vejle Stadion 16.09.1981
Referee: Volker Roth (W. GER)   Attendance: 4,400
VEJLE BK: Alex Nielsen, Knud Sørensen, Per Jørgensen, Bjarne Schouw, Torben Sørensen, John Sivebaek, Gert Eg, Tommy Andersen, Poul Erik Østergaard (47 Lauridsen), Michael Rassmusen (30 Lars Pedersen), Steen Thychosen.
FC PORTO: João Francisco FONSECA dos Santos; GABRIEL Azevedo Mendes, FERNANDO Jorge da Costa Martins, Fernando José António FREITAS Alexandrino, Adelino de Jesús TEIXEIRA; RODOLFO Reis Fereira, JAIME Fernandes MAGALHAES (56 JAIME Moreira PACHECO), António Augusto Gomes de Silva "SOUSA", JACQUES Pereira (74 JÚLIO Carlos da Costa Augusto); ROMEU Fernando Fernandes da Silva, José Alberto COSTA.
Goals: Romeu (20), T. Andersen (23), Eg (42 pen)

FC PORTO v VEJLE BK 3-0 (0-0)
Estádio das Antas, Porto 30.09.1981
Referee: Emilio Carlos Guruceta Muro (SPA)   Att: 45,000
FC PORTO: João Francisco FONSECA dos Santos; GABRIEL Azevedo Mendes, FERNANDO Jorge da Costa Martins, Fernando José António FREITAS Alexandrino (87 Carlos António Fonseca SIMOES), Adelino de Jesús TEIXEIRA; JAIME Fernandes MAGALHAES, RODOLFO Reis Fereira, António Augusto Gomes de Silva "SOUSA" (81 JAIME Moreira PACHECO); Michael Walsh, JACQUES Pereira, José Alberto COSTA.
VEJLE BK: Alex Nielsen, Knud Sørensen, Per Jørgensen, Bjarne Schouw, Torben Sørensen (58 Ib Jacquet) Lauridsen (77 Johnny Madsen), Gert Eg, Poul Erik Østergaard, Tommy Andersen, John Sivebaek, Steen Thychosen.
Goals: Jaime Magalhaes (47, 49), Sousa (65)

DUKLA PRAHA v GLASGOW RANGERS 3-0 (1-0)
Štadión na Juliske, Praha   16.09.1981
Referee: Jan Redelfs (W. GER)   Attendance: 22,500
DUKLA: Jaroslav Netolicka; Ludek Macela, Josef Novák (39 Jiří Doležal), Jan Fiala, Petr Rada, Stanislav Pelc, Ladislav Vízek, Ján Kozák, Zdenek Nehoda, Tomáš Kříž, František Štambachr.   Trainer: Ladislav Novák
RANGERS: Peter McCloy, William Jardine, Alistair Dawson, Thomas Forsyth, Colin Jackson (39 Gregor Stevens), John McClelland, James Bett, Thomas McLean, Robert Russell, Colin McAdam, Derek Johnstone (85 Ian Redford).   Manager: John Greig
Goals: Rada (4), Štambachr (55), Nehoda (74)

STANDARD LIEGE v FLORIANA FC 9-0 (4-0)
Stade Maurice Dufrasne, Sclessin Liège   1.10.1981
Referee: Jean Koster (LUX)   Attendance: 10,000
STANDARD: Michel Preud'homme; Eric Gerets (58 Erhan Önal), Theo Poel, Walter Meeuws, John Dusbaba; Guy Vandersmissen, Gérard Plessers, Arendt Haan; Helmut Graf, Simon Tahamata, Eddy Voordeckers (58 Jean-Michel Lecloux).   Trainer: Raymond Goethals
FLORIANA: Robert Gatt; Falzon, Agius (76 Galea), John Holland, Edwin Farrugia; Joseph John Aquilina, Julian Holland, Raymond Xuereb; Salvu D'Emanuele, Buhagiar, T. Borg (63 Darmanin).
Goals: Voordeckers (12, 28, 56), Vandersmissen (31), Plessers (43, 58), Tahamata (63 pen), Graf (82), Haan (89)

GLASGOW RANGERS v DUKLA PRAHA 2-1 (2-1)
Ibrox, Glasgow   30.09.1981
Refere: Nicolae Rainea (ROM)   Attendance: 20,000
RANGERS: James Stewart, John McClelland (40 Ian Redford), William Jardine, Thomas Forsyth, Alistair Dawson, Robert Russell, David Cooper, James Bett, Colin McAdam (46 Derek Johnstone), John McDonald, William Johnston.   Manager: John Greig
DUKLA: Jaroslav Netolicka; Ján Kapko, Ludek Macela, Jan Fiala, Petr Rada, Oldrich Rott, Zdenek Nehoda, Ján Kozák (46 Jiří Doležal), František Štambachr, Ladislav Vízek, Tomáš Kríz.   Trainer: Ladislav Novák
Goals: Štambachr (23), Bett (43), McDonald (44)

SECOND ROUND

LEGIA WARSZAWA v LAUSANNE SPORTS 2-1 (2-1)
Wojska Polskiego, Warszawa   21.10.1981
Referee: Ib Nielsen (DEN)   Attendance: 12,000
LEGIA: Jacek Kazimierski (78 Krzysztof Sobieski), Adam Topolski, Pawel Janas, Edward Zalezny, Ryszard Milewski, Janusz Baran, Stefan Majewski, Henryk Miloszewicz, Marek Kusto, Krzysztof Adamczyk, Miroslaw Okonski.
LAUSANNE: Jean-Claude Milani; Stéphane Crescenzi, Pierre-Albert Chapuisat, Urs Bamert, Claude Ryf, Yves Mauron, Marcel Parietti, Gérard Castella, John Dario, Robert Kok, Pierre-Albert Tachet.   Trainer: Charles Hertig
Goals: Adamczyk (8), Kok (22), Baran (32)

FLORIANA FC v STANDARD LIEGE 1-3 (1-3)
Ta'Qali, Valletta   23.09.1981
Referee: Keith S. Hackett (ENG)   Attendance: 6,000
FLORIANA: Gauchi (46 Robert Gatt); George Ciantar, Galea (46 Buhagiar), John Holland, Edwin Farrugia; Joseph John Aquilina, Julian Holland, Agius; Salvu D'Emanuele, Raymond Xuereb, T. Borg.
STANDARD: Michel Preud'homme; Eric Gerets, Theo Poel (69 Erhan Önal), Walter Meeuws, John Dusbaba; Guy Vandersmissen, Gérard Plessers, Arendt Haan; Antony Englebert, Simon Tahamata (76 Helmut Graf), Eddy Voordeckers.   Trainer: Raymond Goethals
Goals: J.J. Aquilina (37), Meeuws (22), Voordeckers (26), Vandersmissen (30)

LAUSANNE SPORTS v LEGIA WARSZAWA 1-1 (0-0)
Stade Olympique de la Pontaise, Lausanne   4.11.1981
Referee: Oliver Donnely (NIR)   Attendance: 10,000
LAUSANNE: Jean-Claude Milani; Stéphane Crescenzi, Pierre-Albert Chapuisat, Urs Bamert, Claude Ryf, Gérard Castella, Marcel Parietti (23 Yves Mauron), Robert Lei-Ravello, John Dario, Robert Kok, Pierre-Albert Tachet.   Trainer: Charles Hertig
LEGIA: Krzysztof Sobieski, Adam Topolski, Pawel Janas, Edward Zalezny, Ryszard Milewski, Janusz Baran, Waldemar Tuminski, Henryk Miloszewicz, Marek Kusto (72 Witold Sikorski), Krzysztof Adamczyk, Miroslaw Okonski.
Goals: Baran (48), Lei-Ravello (85)

**SKA ROSTOV na DON
v EINTRACHT FRANKFURT 1-0** (0-0)

Centralniy, Rostov 21.10.1981

Referee: John Carpenter (IRE)   Attendance: 33,000

SKA: Viktor Radaev, Valeri Goncharov, Aleksandr Andriuschenko, Sergei Yashin, Aleksandr Barketov, Pavel Gusev, Nikolai Romanchuk, Sergei Andreev, Aleksandr Zavarov, Igor Gamula, Yuri Pilipko (46 Aleksandr Vorobiev).

EINTRACHT: Jürgen Pahl, Michael Sziedat, Bruno Pezzey, Karl-Heinz Körbel, Wolfgang Trapp (76 Norbert Otto, 85 Löw), Werner Lorant, Stefan Lottermann, Willi Neuberger, Ralf Falkenmayer, Bum-Kun Cha, Norbert Nachtweih. Trainer: Lothar Buchmann

Goal: Yashin (50)

FC BARCELONA v DUKLA PRAHA 4-0 (3-0)

Cam Nou, Barcelona   4.11.1981

Referee: Charles G.R. Corver (HOL)   Attendance: 90,000

FC BARCELONA: Pedro María ARTOLA Urrutia, José Antonio RAMOS Huete, Antonio OLMO Ramírez, José Ramón ALESANCO Ventosa, José Vicente SÁNCHEZ Felip (15 ESTEBAN Vigo Benítez), VÍCTOR Muñoz Manrique, Bernd Schuster, Juan José ESTELLA Salas, Allan Simonsen, Enrique Castro González "QUINI", Enrique MORÁN Blanco. Trainer: Udo Lattek

DUKLA: Jaroslav Netolicka, Ján Kapko (78 Jiří Chvojka), Ludek Macela, Jan Fiala, Petr Rada (50 Josef Novák), Ján Kozák, Oldrich Rott, Tomáš Kríz, Ladislav Vízek, Zdenek Nehoda, František Štambachr.   Trainer: Ladislav Novák

Goals: Morán (3), Sánchez (10), Alesanco (39), Schuster (89)

**EINTRACHT FRANKFURT
v SKA ROSTOV na DON 2-0** (1-0)

Waldstadion, Frankfurt   4.11.1981

Referee: John Hunting (ENG)   Attendance: 30,000

EINTRACHT: Jürgen Pahl, Bruno Pezzey, Michael Sziedat, Karl-Heinz Körbel, Willi Neuberger, Werner Lorant, Stefan Lottermann, Bernd Nickel (74 Norbert Nachtweih), Ralf Falkenmayer, Ronald Borchers (82 Löw), Bum-Kun Cha. Trainer: Lothar Buchmann

SKA: Viktor Radaev, Valeri Goncharov, Aleksandr Andriuschenko, Sergei Yashin, Aleksandr Barketov, Pavel Gusev, Nikolai Romanchuk, Sergei Andreev, Aleksandr Vorobiev, Nail Kuriatnikov, Yuri Pilipko.

Goals: Pezzey (3), Lorant (59 pen)

**DUNDALK FC
v TOTTENHAM HOTSPUR LONDON 1-1** (0-0)

Oriel Park, Dundalk   21.10.1981

Referee: Alain Delmer (FRA)   Attendance: 17,000

DUNDALK FC: Richard Blackmore, Eamon Gregg, Thomas McConville, Paddy Dunning, Martin Lawlor, Sean Byrne, Leo Flanagan, Barry Kehoe, Brian Duff (71 John Archbold), Michael Fairclough, Hilary Carlyle. Manager: Jim McLaughlin

TOTTENHAM: Raymond Clemence, Christopher Hughton, Paul Miller, Graham Roberts, Stephen Perryman, Michael Hazard, Osvaldo Ardiles, Steven Archibald, Anthony Galvin (76 Gordon Smith), Glenn Hoddle, Garth Crooks. Manager: Keith Burkinshaw

Goals: Crooks (63), Fairclough (82)

DUKLA PRAHA v FC BARCELONA 1-0 (1-0)

Štadión na Juliske, Praha   21.10.1981

Referee: Paolo Bergamo (ITA)   Attendance: 29,000

DUKLA: Jaroslav Netolicka, Ján Kapko, Ludek Macela, Jan Fiala, Petr Rada, Oldrich Rott, Stanislav Pelc, Ján Kozák, Ladislav Vízek, Zdenek Nehoda, Tomáš Kríz. Trainer: Ladislav Novák

FC BARCELONA: Pedro María ARTOLA Urrutia, José Antonio RAMOS Huete, Antonio OLMO Ramírez, José Ramón ALESANCO Ventosa, José Manuel Martínez Toral "MANOLO", José Vicente SÁNCHEZ Felip, Bernd Schuster, Juan José ESTELLA Salas, ESTEBAN Vigo Benítez, Enrique Castro González "QUINI", Allan Simonsen.   Trainer: Udo Lattek

Goal: Kozák (14)

**TOTTENHAM HOTSPUR LONDON
v DUNDALK FC 1-0** (0-0)

White Hart Lane, London   4.11.1981

Referee: Paul Rion (LUX)   Attendane: 33,455

TOTTENHAM: Raymond Clemence, Christopher Hughton, Paul Miller, Graham Roberts, Michael Hazard, Stephen Perryman, Osvaldo Ardiles, Steven Archibald, Anthony Galvin, Glenn Hoddle, Garth Crooks.   Manager: Keith Burkinshaw

DUNDALK FC: Richard Blackmore, Eamon Gregg, Martin Lawlor, Thomas McConville, Paddy Dunning, Leo Flanagan, Barry Kehoe, Sean Byrne, Michael Fairclough, Hilary Carlyle (75 Jimmy Reilly), Brian Duff (66 John Archbold). Manager: Jim McLaughlin

Goal: Crooks (63)

VASAS BUDAPEST v STANDARD LIÈGE 0-2 (0-0)
Fáy u, Budapest 21.10.1981
Referee: Josef Bucek (AUS)   Attendance: 8,000
VASAS: Imre Leboniczky; Péter Török, Gábor Hires, András Komjáti, András Szabó; András Szebegyinszki (69 István Birinyi), Sándor Zombori, Géza Rixer; László Kiss, Ignác Izsó (69 László Pecha), Béla Váradi.
STANDARD: Michel Preud'homme, Eric Gerets (80 Helmut Graf), Theo Poel, Walter Meeuws, John Dusbaba, Guy Vandersmissen, Arendt Haan, Jos Daerden, Gérard Plessers, Simon Tahamata (62 Jean-Michel Lecloux), Benny Wendt.
Trainer: Raymond Goethals
Goals: Tahamata (51, 60)

VELEŽ MOSTAR v 1.FC LOKOMOTIVE LEIPZIG 1-1 (1-0, 1-1)(AET)
Gradski, Mostar 4.11.1981
Referee: Antonio José da Silva Garrido (POR)   Att: 22,000
VELEŽ: Enver Marić; Vladimir Matijevic, Avdo Kalajdzić, Veselin Djurasević, Micić, Dubravko Ledić, Medvedović (70 Anel Karabeg), Franjo Vladić, Zoran Bingulac (60 Lucić), Dušan Bajević, Momčilo Vukoje.
1.FC LOKOMOTIVE: René Müller, Frank Baum, Joachim Fritsche (46 Volker Grossmann), Thomas Dennstedt, Uwe Zötzsche; Wolfgang Altmann, Lutz Moldt, Andreas Roth (89 Stephan Fritzsche), Matthias Liebers, Hans-Jürgen Kinne, Dieter Kühn.   Trainer: Harro Miller
Goals: Bajević (21), Zötzsche (74 pen)
Penalties: 0-1 Fritsche, Bajević (miss), 0-2 Zötzsche, Vladić (miss), 0-3 Liebers, Ledić (miss)

STANDARD LIÈGE v VASAS BUDAPEST 2-1 (1-0)
Stade Maurice Dufrasne Sclessin, Liège 4.11.1981
Referee: Siegfrid Kirschen (E. GER)   Attendance: 15,000
STANDARD: Michel Preud'homme, Eric Gerets, Theo Poel, Walter Meeuws, John Dusbaba (20 Helmut Graf), Jos Daerden, Arendt Haan, Gérard Plessers, Eddy Voordeckers, Jean-Michel Lecloux, Simon Tahamata (46 Guy Vandersmissen).
Trainer: Raymond Goethals
VASAS: Imre Leboniczky; Tibor Farkas, Gábor Hires, András Komjáti, András Szabó; András Szebegyinszki, Sándor Zombori, Géza Rixer; László Kiss, Ignác Izsó, Béla Váradi.
Goals: Voordeckers (9, 84), Hires (66)

SÉC BASTIA v DINAMO TBILISI 1-1 (0-0)
Stade Armand Césari, Bastia 21.10.1981
Referee: Augusto Lamo Castillo (SPA)   Att: 12,000
SÉC BASTIA: Pierrick Hiard; Jean-Louis Cazes, Charles Orlanducci, Louardi Badjika, Gerard Bacconnier, Alain Fiard, Simei Ihily, Claude Papi, Raimondo Ponte (74 Pascal Mariini), Roger Milla, Louis Marcialis.   Trainer: Jean-Antoine Redin
DINAMO: Otar Gabeliya, Nodar Khizanishvili, Aleksandr Chivadze, Khinchagashvili, David Mudzhiri, Vitali Daraselia, Zaur Svanadze, Tengiz Sulakvelidze, Vladimir Gutsaev (84 Georgi Tavadze), Nugzar Kakilashvili, Ramaz Schengeliya.
Trainer: Nodari Akhalkatsi
Goals: Gutsaev (56), Milla (65)

1.FC LOKOMOTIVE LEIPZIG v VELEŽ MOSTAR 1-1 (0-0)
Zentralstadion, Leipzig 21.10.1981
Referee: Valeri Butenko (USSR)   Attendance: 12,000
1.FC LOKOMOTIVE: René Müller, Frank Baum, Joachim Fritsche, Thomas Dennstedt, Uwe Zötzsche; Wolfgang Altmann, Lutz Moldt (46 Peter Schöne), Matthias Liebers, Volker Grossmann, Karl-Heinz Herrmann, Hans-Jürgen Kinne.   Trainer: Harro Miller
VELEŽ: Enver Marić; Vladimir Matijevic, Avdo Kalajdzić, Veselin Djurasević, Mirsad Mulahasanović, Dubravko Ledić, Medvedović, Franjo Vladić, Zoran Bingulac (73 Bijedić), Dušan Bajevic, Momčilo Vukoje.
Goals: Vukoje (49), Zötzsche (53 pen)

DINAMO TBILISI v SÉC BASTIA 3-1 (1-0)
Dinamo, Tbilisi 4.11.1981
Referee: Volker Roth (W. GER)   Attendance: 80,000
DINAMO: Otar Gabeliya, Nodar Khizanishvili, Aleksandr Chivadze (23 Vazha Zhvaniya, 86 Revaz Chelebadze), Khinchagashvili, David Mudzhiri, Vitali Daraselia, Zaur Svanadze, Tengiz Sulakvelidze, Vladimir Gutsaev, Nugzar Kakilashvili, Ramaz Schengeliya.   Trainer: Nodari Akhalkatsi
SÉC BASTIA: Pierrick Hiard; Jean-Louis Cazes, Charles Orlanducci, Louardi Badjika, Gerard Bacconnier, Alain Fiard, Simei Ihily, Yves Ehrlacher, Raimondo Ponte, Roger Milla, Louis Marcialis.   Trainer: Jean-Antoine Redin
Goals: Schengeliya (15, 74), Sulakvelidze (60), Milla (89)

FC PORTO v AS ROMA 2-0 (1-0)

Estádio das Antas, Porto   21.10.1981

Referee: Adolf Prokop (E. GER)   Attendance: 30.000

FC PORTO: João Francisco FONSECA dos Santos; GABRIEL Azevedo Mendes, Adelino de Jesús TEIXEIRA, RODOLFO Reis Fereira, Carlos António Fonseca SIMOES, Fernando José António FREITAS Alexandrino, JAIME Fernandes MAGALHAES, António Augusto Gomes de Silva "SOUSA", Michael Walsh (87 Julio), JACQUES Pereira, José Alberto COSTA.

AS ROMA: Franco Tancredi, Sebastiano Nela, Luciano Marangon, Paulo Roberto Falcão, Dario Bonetti, Maurizio Turone, Odoacre Chierico, Agostino di Bartolomei, Roberto Pruzzo, Carlo Ancelotti, Bruno Conti.   Trainer: Nils Liedholm

Goals: Walsh (41), Costa (46)

**EINTRACHT FRANKFURT
v TOTTENHAM HOTSPUR LONDON 2-1** (2-0)

Waldstadion, Frankfurt   17.03.1982

Referee: Antonio José da Silva Garrido (POR)   Att: 41,000

EINTRACHT: Jürgen Pahl, Michael Sziedat, Willi Neuberger, Stefan Lottermann (81 Michael Künast), Bruno Pezzey, Werner Lorant, Ralf Falkenmayer, Ronald Borchers, Norbert Nachtweih, Bernd Nickel, Bum-Kun Cha.
Trainer: Lothar Buchmann

TOTTENHAM: Raymond Clemence, Christopher Hughton, Paul Miller, Paul Price, Michael Hazard, Stephen Perryman, Osvaldo Ardiles (28 Graham Roberts), Steven Archibald, Anthony Galvin, Glenn Hoddle, Mark Falco (69 Ricardo Villa).
Manager: Keith Burtenshaw

Goals: Borchers (2), Cha Bum (15), Hoddle (80)

AS ROMA v FC PORTO 0-0

Stadio Olimpico, Roma   4.11.1981

Referee: Károly Palotai (HUN)   Attendance: 58,000

AS ROMA: Franco Tancredi, Luciano Spinosi (59 Paolo Giovanelli), Sebastiano Nela, Paulo Roberto Falcão, Dario Bonetti, Maurizio Turone, Odoacre Chierico, Agostino di Bartolomei, Roberto Pruzzo, Domenico Maggiora, Bruno Conti.   Trainer: Nils Liedholm

FC PORTO: João Francisco FONSECA dos Santos; GABRIEL Azevedo Mendes, António José LIMA PEREIRA, Adelino de Jesús TEIXEIRA, Carlos António Fonseca SIMOES, Fernando José António FREITAS Alexandrino, JAIME Fernandes MAGALHAES, António Augusto Gomes de Silva "SOUSA" (82 JACQUES Pereira), Michael Walsh (88 FERNANDO Jorge da Costa Martins), JAIME Moreira PACHECO, José Alberto COSTA.

LEGIA WARSZAWA v DINAMO TBILISI 0-1 (0-1)

Wojska Polskiego, Warszawa   3.03.1982

Referee: Ulf Eriksson (SWE)   Attendance: 25,000

LEGIA: Jacek Kazimierski, Adam Topolski, Pawel Janas, Ryszard Milewski, Stefan Majewski, Edward Zalezny, Henryk Miloszewicz, Krzysztof Adamczyk, Zbigniew Kakietek, Leszek Iwanicki (87 Witold Sikorski), Marek Kusto.

DINAMO: Otar Gabeliya, Nodar Khizanishvili, Aleksandr Chivadze, Khinchagashvili, David Mudzhiri, Vitali Daraselia, Zaur Svanadze (68 Nugzar Kakilashvili), Tengiz Sulakvelidze, Vladimir Gutsaev, David Kipiani, Ramaz Schengeliya.
Trainer: Nodari Akhalkatsi

Goal: Sulakvelidze (9)

QUARTER-FINALS

**TOTTENHAM HOTSPUR LONDON
v EINTRACHT FRANKFURT 2-0** (0-0)

White Hart Lane, London   3.03.1982

Referee: Nicolae Rainea (ROM)   Attendance: 38,172

TOTTENHAM: Raymond Clemence, Christopher Hughton, Paul Miller, Paul Price, Michael Hazard, Stephen Perryman, Osvaldo Ardiles, Steven Archibald, Anthony Galvin, Glenn Hoddle, Garth Crooks (60 Mark Falco).
Manager: Keith Burtenshaw

EINTRACHT: Joachim Jüriens, Michael Sziedat, Willi Neuberger, Karl-Heinz Körbel, Bruno Pezzey, Werner Lorant, Michael Künast (77 Helmut Gulich), Ralf Falkenmayer, Norbert Nachtweih, Bernd Nickel (85 Stefan Lottermann), Bum-Kun Cha.   Trainer: Lothar Buchmann

Goals: Miller (58), Hazard (81)

DINAMO TBILISI v LEGIA WARSZAWA 1-0 (1-0)

Dinamo, Tbilisi   17.03.1982

Referee: George Courtney (ENG)   Attendance: 80,000

DINAMO: Otar Gabeliya, Nodar Khizanishvili, Aleksandr Chivadze, Khinchagashvili, David Mudzhiri, Vitali Daraselia, Nugzar Kakilashvili (80 Zaur Svanadze), Tengiz Sulakvelidze, Vladimir Gutsaev, David Kipiani, Ramaz Schengeliya.
Trainer: Nodari Akhalkatsi

LEGIA: Jacek Kazimierski, Adam Topolski, Pawel Janas, Ryszard Milewski, Stefan Majewski, Edward Zalezny, Henryk Miloszewicz, Krzysztof Adamczyk, Zbigniew Kakietek, Leszek Iwanicki (69 Marek Szaniawski), Marek Kusto.

Goal: Schengeliya (30)

STANDARD LIEGE v FC PORTO 2-0 (1-0)
Stade Maurice Dufrasne Sclessin, Liège 3.03.1982
Referee: Rudolf Renggli (SWI)   Attendance: 27,000
STANDARD: Michel Preud'homme, Eric Gerets, Antony Englebert, Theo Poel, Walter Meeuws, Guy Vandersmissen, Simon Tahamata, Gérard Plessers, Arendt Haan, Benny Wendt (71 Jos Daerden), Eddy Voordeckers. Trainer: Raymond Goethals
FC PORTO: João Francisco FONSECA dos Santos; GABRIEL Azevedo Mendes, Carlos António Fonseca SIMOES (32 FERNANDO Jorge da Costa Martins), Fernando José António FREITAS Alexandrino, António José LIMA PEREIRA; Adelino de Jesús TEIXEIRA (78 JAIME Fernandes MAGALHAES), JACQUES Pereira, António Augusto Gomes de Silva "SOUSA", JAIME Moreira PACHECO, ROMEU Fernando Fernandes da Silva, José Alberto COSTA.
Goals: Englebert (31), Gabriel (67 og)

FC PORTO v STANDARD LIÈGE 2-2 (0-1)
Estádio das Antas, Porto 17.03.1982
Referee: Brian McGinlay (SCO)   Attendance: 60,000
FC PORTO: João Francisco FONSECA dos Santos; GABRIEL Azevedo Mendes, FERNANDO Jorge da Costa Martins, Fernando José António FREITAS Alexandrino (12 Adelino de Jesús TEIXEIRA), António José LIMA PEREIRA (59 ROMEU Fernando Fernandes da Silva); JAIME Fernandes MAGALHAES, JAIME Moreira PACHECO, António Augusto Gomes de Silva "SOUSA", Michael Walsh, JACQUES Pereira, José Alberto COSTA.
STANDARD: Michel Preud'homme, Eric Gerets, Antony Englebert, Theo Poel, Walter Meeuws, Guy Vandersmissen, Simon Tahamata, Gérard Plessers, Arendt Haan, Jos Daerden, Jean-Michel Lecloux (79 Roberto Sciascia). Trainer: Raymond Goethals
Goals: Lecloux (44), Jacques Pereira (56), Vandersmissen (68), Walsh (70)

1.FC LOKOMOTIVE LEIPZIG v FC BARCELONA 0-3 (0-0)
Zentralstadion, Leipzig 3.03.1982
Referee: Clive Bradley White (ENG)   Attendance: 68,500
1.FC LOKOMOTIVE: René Müller, Andreas Roth, Frank Baum, Thomas Dennstedt, Wolfgang Altmann, Ronald Kreer, Lutz Moldt, Matthias Liebers, Peter Englisch (66 Peter Schöne), Andreas Bornschein, Dieter Kühn. Trainer: Harro Miller

FC BARCELONA: Pedro María ARTOLA Urrutia, José Vicente SÁNCHEZ Felip, Antonio OLMO Ramírez, José Manuel Martínez Toral "MANOLO", GERARDO Miranda Concepción (70 José Antonio RAMOS Huete), José Ramón ALESANCO Ventosa, Allan Simonsen, Rafael Ignacio ZUVIRÍA Rodríguez, Enrique Castro González "QUINI" (86 José MORATALLA Claramunt), VÍCTOR Muñoz Manrique, Enrique MORÁN Blanco. Trainer: Udo Lattek
Goals: Quini (57), Morán (85), Simonsen (90)

FC BARCELONA v 1.FC LOKOMOTIVE LEIPZIG 1-2 (1-1)
Camp Nou, Barcelona 17.03.1982
Referee: Michel Vautrot (FRA)   Attendance: 61,000
FC BARCELONA: Pedro María ARTOLA Urrutia, José Vicente SÁNCHEZ Felip, Antonio OLMO Ramírez, José MORATALLA Claramunt, José Manuel Martínez Toral "MANOLO", José Ramón ALESANCO Ventosa, Allan Simonsen, Rafael Ignacio ZUVIRÍA Rodríguez, Enrique Castro González "QUINI" (56 Francisco José CARRASCO Hidalgo), Juan José ESTELLA Salas, Enrique MORÁN Blanco (85 José Antonio RAMOS Huete). Trainer: Udo Lattek
1.FC LOKOMOTIVE: René Müller, Wolfgang Altmann, Frank Baum, Thomas Dennstedt, Uwe Zötzsche, Ronald Kreer, Lutz Moldt, Matthias Liebers, Peter Schöne, Andreas Bornschein (84 Volker Grossmann), Dieter Kühn. Trainer: Harro Miller
Goals: Morán (16), Kühn (41), Bornschein (48)

SEMI-FINALS

DINAMO TBILISI v STANDARD LIEGE 0-1 (0-1)
Dinamo, Tbilisi 7.04.1982
Referee: Horst Brummeier (AUS)   Attendance: 88,600
DINAMO: Otar Gabeliya, Tengiz Sulakvelidze, Aleksandr Chivadze, Nodar Khizanishvili, Georgi Tavadze, Vitali Daraselia, Nugzar Kakilashvili, Georgi Tsaava, Vladimir Gutsaev (20 Vazha Zhvaniya, 64 Revaz Chelebadze), David Kipiani, Ramaz Schengeliya. Trainer: Nodari Akhalkatsi
STANDARD: Michel Preud'homme, Eric Gerets, Antony Englebert, Theo Poel, Walter Meeuws, Guy Vandersmissen, Simon Tahamata, Gérard Plessers, Arendt Haan, Jos Daerden, René Botteron. Trainer: Raymond Goethals
Goal: Daerden (40)

STANDARD LIEGE v DINAMO TBILISI 1-0 (1-0)
Stade Maurice Dufrasne Sclessin, Liège   21.04.1982
Referee: Jan Redelfs (W. GER)   Attendance: 40,000

STANDARD: Michel Preud'homme, Eric Gerets, Antony Englebert, Theo Poel, Walter Meeuws, Guy Vandersmissen, Simon Tahamata, Gérard Plessers, Arendt Haan, Benny Wendt, Jos Daerden.   Trainer: Raymond Goethals

DINAMO: Otar Gabeliya, Nodar Khizanishvili, Aleksandr Chivadze, Khinchagashvili, David Mudzhiri, Vitali Daraselia, Zaur Svanadze (46 Mikhail Meskhi), Tengiz Sulakvelidze, Nugzar Kakilashvili (72 Georgi Tsaava), David Kipiani, Ramaz Schengeliya.   Trainer: Nodari Akhalkatsi

Goal: Daerden (22)

**TOTTENHAM HOTSPUR LONDON
v FC BARCELONA 1-1** (0-0)
White Hart Lane, London   7.04.1982
Referee: Egbert Mulder (HOL)   Attendance: 41,555

TOTTENHAM: Raymond Clemence, Christopher Hughton, Paul Miller (75 Christopher Jones), Paul Price, Michael Hazard, Stephen Perryman, Graham Roberts, Ricardo Villa, Anthony Galvin, Glenn Hoddle, Garth Crooks.
Manager: Keith Burtenshaw

FC BARCELONA: Francisco Javier González URRUTIcoechea, José Vicente SÁNCHEZ Felip, Antonio OLMO Ramírez, José Antonio RAMOS Huete, José Manuel Martínez Toral "MANOLO", José Ramón ALESANCO Ventosa, Allan Simonsen, GERARDO Miranda Concepción, Francisco José CARRASCO Hidalgo, Juan José ESTELLA Salas, Enrique MORÁN Blanco (60 José MORATALLA Claramunt).
Trainer: Udo Lattek

Sent off: Estella (58)

Goals: Olmo (60), Roberts (84)

**FC BARCELONA
v TOTTENHAM HOTSPUR LONDON 1-0** (0-0)
Camp Nou, Barcelona   21.04.1982
Referee: Siegfried Kirschen (E. GER)   Attendance: 80,000

FC BARCELONA: Francisco Javier González URRUTIcoechea, José Antonio RAMOS Huete, Antonio OLMO Ramírez, José Manuel Martínez Toral "MANOLO", José Vicente SÁNCHEZ Felip, José Ramón ALESANCO Ventosa, Allan Simonsen (87 Rafael Ignacio ZUVIRIA Rodríguez), GERARDO Miranda Concepción, Enrique Castro González "QUINI" (76 ESTEBAN Vigo Benítez), José MORATALLA Claramunt, Francisco José CARRASCO Hidalgo.
Trainer: Udo Lattek

TOTTENHAM: Raymond Clemence, Christopher Hughton, Paul Price (82 Mark Falco), Graham Roberts, Michael Hazard, Stephen Perryman, Ricardo Villa, Steven Archibald, Anthony Galvin, Glenn Hoddle, Garth Crooks (.. Garry Brooke).
Manager: Keith Burtenshaw

Goal: Simonsen (47)

FINAL

FC BARCELONA v STANDARD LIEGE 2-1 (1-1)
Camp Nou, Barcelona   12.05.1982
Referee: Walter Eschweiler (W. GER)   Attendance: 100,066

FC BARCELONA: Francisco Javier González URRUTIcoechea, GERARDO Miranda Concepción, José Manuel Martínez Toral "MANOLO", José Vicente SÁNCHEZ Felip, Bernardo Bianquetti Miguel "MIGUELI", José Rámon ALESANCO Ventosa, Allan SIMONSEN, José MORATALLA Claramunt, Enrique Castro González QUINI, ESTEBAN Vigo Benítez, Francisco José CARRASCO Hidalgo.
Trainer: Udo Lattek

STANDARD: Michel Preud'homme, Eric Maria Gerets, Gérard Plessers, Guy Vandersmissen, Théo Poel, Walter Meeuws, Simon Tahamata, Jos Daerden, Benny Wendt, Arendt Haan, René Botteron.   Trainer: Raymond Goethals

Sent off: Meeuws (89)

Goals: Vandersmissen (8), Simonsen (45), Quini (63)

Goalscorers European Cup-Winners' Cup 1981-82:

6 goals: Ramaz Schengeliya (Dinamo Tbilisi), Eddy Voordeckers (Standard Liège)

5 goals: Allan Simonsen (FC Barcelona)

4 goals: Guy Vandersmissen (Standard Liège)

3 goals: Kühn, Zötzsche (Lokomotiv Leipzig), Fairclough (Dundalk AFC), Morán, Quini (FC Barcelona), Kok (Lausanne Sports), Baran (Legia Warszawa), Milla (SEC Bastia), Tahamata (Standard Liège), Falco (Tottenham), Váradi (Vasas Budapest)

2 goals: Ihily (SEC Bastia), Kinne, Moldt (Lokomotiv Leipzig), Pruzzo (AS Roma), Sulakvelidze (Dinamo Tbilisi), Štambachr (Dukla Praha), Pezzey (Eintracht Frankfurt), Schuster (FC Barcelona), Jaime Magalhães, Walsh (FC Porto), Scheitler (Jeunesse d'Esch), Ohlsson (Kalmar FF), Parietti (Lausanne Sports), Adamczyk (Legia Warszawa), Kostikos (PAOK Thessaloniki), Andreev, Zavarov (SKA Rostov), Daerden, Plessers (Standard Liège), Crooks (Tottenham), Slavkov (Trakia Plovdiv), P.Jacobsen (Vålerengens Oslo), Izsó, Kiss (Vasas Budapest), Bajević, Matijević, Okuka (Velež Mostar)

1 goal: Anghel, Nedelcu (Politehnica Timişoara), Lerby (Ajax Amsterdam), Riedl, Schwicker (Grazer AK), Charles (Swansea City), Moen (Vålerengen Oslo), Goumenos (Paralimni Famagusta), Magnusson, Persson (Kalmar FF), Thorfasson, Sveinjónsson (Fram Reykjavík), T.Andersen, Eg (Vejle BK), Bett, McDonald (Glasgow Rangers), J.J.Aquilina (Floriana FC), Lei-Ravello (Lausanne Sports), Yashin, Vorobiev (SKA Rostov), Kozák, Rada, Nehoda (Dukla Praha), Flanagan, Lawlor, Duff (Dundalk FC), Hires, Szebegyinszki (Vasas Budapest), Vukoje, Skocajić, Mulahasanović (Velež Mostar), Cazes, Ponte (SEC Bastia), Spinosi, Giovannini, Chierico, Ancelotti (AS Roma), Borchers, Cha Bum, Lorant, Körbel (Eintracht Frankfurt), Topolski, Miloszewicz, Majewski, Okonski (Legia Warszawa), Jacques Pereira, Costa, Romeu, Sousa (FC Porto), Bornschein, Baum (Lokomotive Leipzig), Gutsaev, Zhvaniya (Dinamo Tbilisi), Roberts, Miller, Hazard, Hoddle, Villa, Galvin, Ardiles (Tottenham), Olmo, Sánchez, Alesanco (FC Barcelona), Lecloux, Englebert, Graf, Haan, Meeuws (Standard Liège)

Own goal: Gabriel (FC Porto) for Standard Liège

CUP WINNERS' CUP 1982-83

PRELIMINARY ROUND

**SWANSEA CITY
v SPORTING CLUBE de BRAGA 3-0** (1-0)

Vetch Field, Swansea   17.08.1982

Referee: Albert Thomas (HOL)   Attendance: 10,641

SWANSEA: David Davies, Christopher Marustik, Džemal Hadziabdić, Colin Irwin, Raymond Kennedy, Ante Rajković, Robert James, Leighton James, Jeremy Charles, Nigel Stevenson (23 Maxwell Thompson), Robert Latchford (78 Ian Walsh).

SPORTING: HELDER Joaquim Maximo Catalão, ARTUR Soares Correia, João Soares CARDOSO, Manuel Gomes da Silva "NELITO", Manuel Fernando de Azevedo GUEDES, José Carvalho Gonçalves "SERRA", VÍTOR Manuel OLIVEIRA, António Cándido Duarte PARIS, JORGE GOMES da Silva Filho (..Fernando Manuel MALHEIRO Santos), MANOEL da Silva Costa, VITOR Manuel Lopes dos SANTOS.

Goals: Charles (42, 86), Cardoso (62 og)

**SPORTING CLUBE de BRAGA
v SWANSEA CITY 1-0** (0-0)

Estádio 1° Maio, Braga   25.08.1982

Referee: Jakob Baumann (SWI)   Attendance: 18,000

SPORTING: HELDER Joaquim Maximo Catalão, ARTUR Soares Correia, João Soares CARDOSO, António Cándido Duarte PARIS, Manuel Fernando de Azevedo GUEDES, José Carvalho Gonçalves "SERRA", VÍTOR Manuel OLIVEIRA, Adriano Santos SPENCER (69 Armando Gonçalves Medeiros FONTES), MANOEL da Silva Costa (..Fernando Manuel MALHEIRO Santos), JORGE GOMES da Silva Filho, VITOR Manuel Lopes dos SANTOS.

SWANSEA: David Davies, Christopher Marustik, Džemal Hadziabdić, Colin Irwin, John Mahoney, Ante Rajković, Leighton James, Robert James, Jeremy Charles, Garry Stanley, Robert Latchford.

Goal: Marustik (77 og)

FC ABERDEEN v FC SION 7-0 (4-0)

Pittodrie, Aberdeen   18.08.1982

Referee: Karl Heinz Tritschler (W. GER)   Att: 10,000

ABERDEEN: James Leighton, John McMaster, Stuart Kennedy, Neil Simpson, Alex McLeish, William Miller, Gordon Strachan, Eric Black (73 Peter Weir), Mark McGhee, Douglas Bell (59 Douglas Rougvie), John Hewitt.
Manager: Alex Ferguson

FC SION: Pierre-Marie Pittier; Jean-Yves Valentini, Jean-Claude Richard, Alain Balet, Pierre-Alain Valentini, Alvaro Lopez, Georges Bregy, Bernard Karlen, Marian Cernicky, Fernand Luisier (46 Franco Cucinotta), Dominique Cina.
Trainer: Jean-Claude Donzé

Goals: Black (2, 56), Strachan (21), Hewitt (23), Simpson (34), McGhee (63), Kennedy (82)

FC SION v FC ABERDEEN 1-4 (1-1)

Stade de Tourbillon, Sion   1.09.1982

Referee: Glazar (YUG)   Attendance: 2,400

FC SION: Pierre-Marie Pittier; Jean-Yves Valentini, Jean-Claude Richard, Christophe Moulin, Léonard Karlen, Marian Cernicky, Alvaro Lopez, Fernand Luisier (46 Bernard Karlen), Georges Bregy, Franco Cucinotta, Dominique Cina (69 Pierre-Albert Tachet).   Trainer: Jean-Claude Donzé

ABERDEEN: James Leighton; Neale Cooper, William Miller, Stuart Kennedy, John McMaster, Gordon Strachan (75 Eric Black), Douglas Bell (60 Alex McLeish), Neil Simpson, John Hewitt, Mark McGhee, Peter Weir.   Manager: Alex Ferguson

Goals: Hewitt (27), Bregy (27), Miller (61), McGhee (64, 72)

FIRST ROUND

ÍB VESTMANNAEYJAR
v LECH POZNAN 0-1 (0-1)

Kopavogsvöllur, Kopavogur   14.09.1982

Referee: Alan Snnody (NIR)   Attendance: 5,000

ÍBV: Páll Palmason, Vidar Elíasson, Orn Oskarsson, Thordur Hallgrimsson, Valthor Sigthórsson, Snorri Rúttsson, Omar Jóhansson, Jóhann Georgsson (70 Bergur Augustsson), Sigurlás Thorleifsson, Kári Thorleifsson, Sveinn Sveinsson.

LECH: Piotr Mowlik, Krzysztof Pawlak, Józef Szewczyk, Józef Adamiec, Hieronim Barczak, Leszek Partynski (65 Marek Skurczynski), Boguslaw Oblewski, Janusz Kupcewicz, Jerzy Krzyzanowski (75 Andrzej Strugarek), Jacek Bak, Miroslaw Okonski.

Goal: Partynski (28)

LECH POZNAN
v ÍB VESTMANNAEYJAR 3-0 (1-0)

Lech, Poznan   29.09.1982

Referee: Klaus Scheurell (E. GER)   Attendance: 20,000

LECH: Zbigniew Plesnierowicz, Krzysztof Pawlak, Józef Szewczyk, Józef Adamiec, Andrzej Strugarek, Jerzy Krzyzanowski, Leszek Partynski (55 Rafal Stroinski), Hieronim Barczak, Boguslaw Oblewski (60 Janusz Malek), Miroslaw Okonski, Mariusz Niewiadomski.

IBV: Páll Palmason, Snorri Rútsson, Thordur Hallgrimsson, Valthor Sigthórsson, Agust Einarsson, Bergur Augustsson, Orn Oskarsson, Sveinn Sveinsson, Sigurlás Thorleifsson, Kári Thorleifsson, Omar Jóhansson.

Goals: Okonski (6, 52), Niewiadowski (49)

LOKOMOTIV SOFIA
v PARIS ST.GERMAIN 1-0 (1-0)

Vasil Levski, Sofia   15.09.1982

Referee: Jan Redelfs (W. GER)   Attendance: 13,500

LOKOMOTIV: Nikolai Donev, Nasko Jelev, Vladimir Lalov, Georgi Bonev, Aleksandar Markov, Ventseslav Arsov (82 Rumen Stoianov), Nako Doichev, Petar Milanov, Boicho Velichkov, Valeri Damianov, Stoicho Stoev (67 Boris Iliev).

PARIS ST.GERMAIN: Dominique Baratelli; Philippe Col, Luis Fernandez, Jean-Marc Pilorget, Dominique Bathenay, Jean-Claude Lemoult, Yannick Guillochon, Pascal Zaremba, Kees Kist, Osvaldo Ardiles, Dominique Rocheteau (78 Nambatingue Toko).   Trainer: Georges Peyroche

Goal: Milanov (15)

PARIS ST.GERMAIN
v LOKOMOTIV SOFIA 5-1 (1-0)

Parc des Princes, Paris   28.09.1982

Referee: Horst Brummeier (AUS)   Attendance: 32,000

PARIS ST.GERMAIN: Dominique Baratelli; Yannick Guillochon, Luis Fernandez, Jean-Marc Pilorget, Dominique Bathenay, Jean-Claude Lemoult, Nambatingue Toko, Pascal Zaremba, Kees Kist, Osvaldo Ardiles, Michel N'Gom.   Trainer: Georges Peyroche

LOKOMOTIV: Nikolai Donev, Aleksandar Dudov (72 Stoicho Stoev), Vladimir Lalov, Aleksandar Markov (75 Stanislav Vasilev), Valeri Damianov, Ventseslav Arsov, Boris Iliev, Petar Milanov, Boicho Velichkov, Marko Bogdanov, Nako Doichev.

Goals: Toko (20, 81), Bogdanov (48), Bathenay (63), N'Gom (85), Lemoult (89)

FC COLERAINE
v TOTTENHAM HOTSPUR LONDON 0-3 (0-1)

The Showgrounds, Coleraine   15.09.1982

Referee: Francis Bastian (LUX)   Attendance: 12,000

COLERAINE: Vincent Magee, Ronnie McDowell, Eugene McNutt, Gerry O'Kane, John Shannon, Patrick Mullan, Raymond Henry (82 Roy McCreadie), Felix Healy, Raymond McCoy, Des Dickson (70 Mark Allan), Jackie McManus.   Trainer: Des Dickson

TOTTENHAM: Raymond Clemence, Christopher Hughton, Paul Price, John Lacy, Garry Brooke, Stephen Perryman, Gary Mabbutt (82 Michael Hazard), Steven Archibald, Anthony Galvin, Ricardo Villa, Garth Crooks.   Manager: Keith Burkinshaw

Goals: Archibald (12), Crooks (48, 84)

TOTTENHAM HOTSPUR LONDON
v FC COLERAINE 4-0 (1-0)

White Hart Lane, London   28.09.1982

Referee: Edgar Azzopardi (MAL)   Attendance: 20,925

TOTTENHAM: Raymond Clemence (60 Anthony Parks), Christopher Hughton, Paul Price, John Lacy, Garry Brooke, Stephen Perryman, Gary Mabbutt, Michael Hazard, Steven Archibald, Ricardo Villa, Garth Crooks (67 Terence Gibson).   Manager: Keith Burkinshaw

COLERAINE: Vincent Magee, Ronnie McDowell, Eugene McNutt (29 Roy McCreadie), Gerry O'Kane, John Shannon, Patrick Mullan, Raymond Henry, Felix Healy, Raymond McCoy, Des Dickson (62 Mark Allan), Jackie McManus.   Trainer: Des Dickson

Goals: Crooks (14), Mabbutt (52), Brooke (82), Gibson (85)

**LILLESTRØM SK
v CRVENA ZVEZDA BEOGRAD 0-4** (0-1)
Åråsen, Lillestrøm   15.09.1982
Referee: Oli Olsen (ICE)   Attendance: 4,877
LILLESTRØM: Arne Amundsen, Tor Inge Smedås, Frank Grønlund, Tore Kordahl, Ole Dyrstad, Erik Soler, Tom Frisvold Myklebust (65 Georg Hammer), Bård Bjerkeland, Juhani Himanka (85 Roger Skjåstad), Tom Lund, André Krogsaeter.
CRVENA ZVEZDA: Aleksandar Stojanović, Zlatko Krmpotić, Milan Jovin, Djordje Milovanović, Dragan Miletović, Milenko Rajković, Vladimir Petrović, Rajko Janjanin (67 Konstantin Djurić), Dušan Savić, Nedeljko Milosavljević, Ranko Djordjić.   Trainer: Stevan Ostojić
Goals: D. Savić (40, 71), Janjanin (57), Jovin (61)

**CRVENA ZVEZDA BEOGRAD
v LILLESTRØM SK 3-0** (2-0)
Crvena Zvezda, Beograd   29.09.1982
Referee: Erkan Göksel (TUR)   Attendance: 10,000
CRVENA ZVEZDA: Aleksandar Simeunović, Zlatko Krmpotić, Zoran Dimitrijević, Boško Djurovski, Dragan Miletović (46 Goran Milojević), Milenko Rajković, Vladimir Petrović, Dušan Savić, Konstantin Djurić, Ranko Djordjić (60 Rajko Janjanin), Milko Djurovski.   Trainer: Stevan Ostojić
LILLESTRØM: Arne Amundsen, Tor Inge Smedås (46 Georg Hammer), Frank Grønlund, Tore Kordahl, Ole Dyrstad, Erik Soler, Per Berg, Bård Bjerkeland, Juhani Himanka, Arne Erlandsen (72 Tom Frisvold Myklebust), André Krogsaeter.
Goals: M. Djurovski (3, 59), Djurić (13)

FC BARCELONA v APOLLON LIMASSOL 8-0 (3-0)
Estadio Camp Nou, Barcelona   15.09.1982
Referee: René Bindels (LUX)   Attendance: 26,600
FC BARCELONA: Pedro María ARTOLA Urrutia, GERARDO Miranda Concepción, Bernardo Bianquetti Miguel "MIGUELI", José Ramón ALESANCO Ventosa, José Manuel Martínez Toral "MANOLO", URBANO Ortega Cuadros, Bernd Schuster, VÍCTOR Muñoz Manrique, MARCOS Alonso Peña (63 Francisco José CARRASCO Hidalgo), Diego Armando MARADONA (67 ESTEBAN Vigo Benítez), Ángel "PICHI" ALONSO Herrera.   Trainer: Udo Lattek
APOLLON: Stavros Lambrou, Sotiris Gennaris, Kyriakos Kyriakou, Giannis Giagkoudakis, Giorgos Templar, Andreas Hristodoulou (76 Andreas Efrem), Giagkoudakis, Antonis Ilia "Antrelis", Giannis Ioannou, Walter Vevis, Dimitris Agas.   Trainer: Zdenek
Goals: Víctor (44), Maradona (45, 60, 64), Urbano (58), Schuster (35, 69), Alesanco (81)

APOLLON LIMASSOL v FC BARCELONA 1-1 (0-1)
Tsirion, Limassol   29.09.1982
Referee: Zivorad Vuksanović (YUG)   Attendance: 15,000
APOLLON: Thrasos Koniotis, Antonis Ilia "Antrelis", Giannis Giagkoudakis, Kyriakos Kyriakou, Giorgos Templar, Giagkoudakis, Giannis Ioannou, Andreas Efrem, Andreas Hristodoulou (72 Hristoforos Lambis), Dimitris Agas, Ted Storday (85 Walter Vevis).   Trainer: Zdenek
FC BARCELONA: Lorenzo AMADOR Lemos (56 Pedro María ARTOLA Urrutia), José Vicente SÁNCHEZ Felip, Antonio OLMO Ramírez, José MORATALLA Claramunt, José Manuel Martínez Toral "MANOLO", ESTEBAN Vigo Benítez, Miguel Ángel "PERICO" ALONSO Oyarbide, Juan José ESTELLA Salas, JULIO ALBERTO Moreno Casas, Francisco José CARRASCO Hidalgo (46 José Ramón ALESANCO Ventosa), MARCOS Alonso Peña.   Trainer: Udo Lattek
Goals: Moratalla (38), Hristodoulou (55)

**TORPEDO MOSKVA
v BAYERN MÜNCHEN 1-1** (1-0)
Moskva   15.09.1982
Referee: Rolf Ericsson (SWE)   Attendance: 31,750
TORPEDO: Viacheslav Chanov; Sergei Prigoda, Vladimir Pivtsov, Aleksandr Gostenin, Vasili Zhupikov, Aleksandr Polukarov, Valeri Petrakov, Nikolai Vasiliev (70 Andrei Redkous), Anatoli Soloviev (70 Vladimir Galaiba), Yuri Susloparov, Valentin Ivanov.
BAYERN: Jean-Marie Pfaff, Wolfgang Dremmler, Udo Horsmann, Wolfgang Grobe, Klaus Augenthaler, Norbert Nachtweih, Bernd Dürnberger, Dieter Hoeness, Paul Breitner, Karl Del'Haye, Karl-Heinz Rummenigge.   Trainer: Pál Csernai
Goals: Petrakov (40), Breitner (65)

BAYERN MÜNCHEN v TORPEDO MOSKVA 0-0
Olympiastadion, München   29.09.1982
Referee: John Carpenter (IRE)   Attendance: 19,000
BAYERN: Jean-Marie Pfaff, Wolfgang Dremmler, Udo Horsmann, Wolfgang Grobe, Klaus Augenthaler, Norbert Nachtweih, Bernd Dürnberger, Dieter Hoeness, Paul Breitner, Karl Del'Haye, Karl-Heinz Rummenigge.   Trainer: Pál Csernai
TORPEDO: Viacheslav Chanov, Sergei Prigoda, Aleksandr Polukarov, Aleksandr Gostenin, Vasili Zhupikov, Sergei Petrenko, Valeri Petrakov, Nikolai Vasiliev, Valentin Ivanov, Yuri Susloparov, Aleksandr Dozmorov.

FC BAIA MARE v REAL MADRID 0-0
23 August, Baia Mare   15.09.1982
Referee: Franz Wöhrer (AUS)   Attendance: 25,000
FC BAIA MARE: Vasile Moldovan; Imre Szepi, Ion Tătăran, Miron Borz, Alexandru Koller; Radu Pamfil, Marin Sabou, Lucian Bălan; Constantin Dragomirescu, Adalbert Rozsnyai (69 Viorel Buzgău), Cristian Ene.
Trainers: Paul Popescu & Nicolae Szabo
REAL: AGUSTIN Rodríguez Santiago; John Metgod (76 Alfonso FRAILE Sánchez), Francisco BONET Serrano, JUAN JOSÉ Jiménez Collar, José Antonio CAMACHO Alfaro; Ricardo GALLEGO Redondo, ÁNGEL de los Santos Cano, Ulrich Stielike, ISIDRO Díaz González; Juan Gómez González JUANITO, Carlos Alonso González SANTILLANA.
Trainer: Alfredo DI STÉFANO

REAL MADRID v FC BAIA MARE 5-2 (3-1)
Santiago Bernabeu, Madrid   29.09.1982
Referee: Stefanos Hatzistefanou (CYP)   Attendance: 45,000
REAL: AGUSTIN Rodríguez Santiago; JUAN JOSÉ Jiménez Collar, Francisco BONET Serrano, John Metgod, José Antonio CAMACHO Alfaro; Ricardo GALLEGO Redondo, ÁNGEL de los Santos Cano, Francisco GARCIA HERNÁNDEZ; Juan Gómez González JUANITO, Carlos Alonso González SANTILLANA (75 Andrés Alonso ITO), ISIDRO Díaz González (85 Juan Alberto ACOSTA).
Trainer: Alfredo DI STÉFANO
FC BAIA MARE: Vasile Moldovan; Vasile Ignat, Ioan Hotico, Ion Tătăran, Alexandru Koller; Radu Pamfil, Marin Sabou, Lucian Bălan; Constantin Dragomirescu (52 Viorel Buzgău), Gheorghe Tulba, Cristian Ene (52 Adalbert Rozsnyai).
Trainer: Paul Popescu
Goals: Koller (12), Juanito (16) Isidro (33), G. Hernández (45), Santillana (47), Metgod (71), Buzgău (89)

AUSTRIA WIEN v PANATHINAIKOS ATHINA 2-0 (2-0)
Prater, Wien   15.09.1982
Referee: Stjepan Glavina (YUG)   Attendance: 12,000
AUSTRIA: Friedrich Koncilia, Robert Sara, Erich Obermayer, Karl Daxbacher, Franz Zore; Johann Dihanich, Felix Gasselich (72 Harald Fürst), Ernst Baumeister, Alfred Drabits (65 Thomas Pfeiler), Gerhard Steinkogler, Anton Polster.
Trainer: Václav Halama
PANATHINAIKOS: Vasilis Konstantinou, Ilias Berios, Giannis Kyrastas, Anthimos Kapsis, Nikos Karoulias, Aggelos Anastasiadis, Spiros Livathinos, Grigoris Tsinos, Grigoris Papavasileiou, Grigoris Haralampidis, Tseu La Ling.
Trainer: Ştefan Kovacs
Goals: Polster (6), Steinkogler (10)

PANATHINAIKOS ATHINA v AUSTRIA WIEN 2-1 (1-0)
Apostolos Nikolaidis, Athina   29.09.1982
Referee: Antonio José da Silva Garrido (POR)   Att: 20,500
PANATHINAIKOS: Giorgos Dafkos, Ilias Berios, Giannis Kyrastas, Anthimos Kapsis, Nikos Karoulias, Spiros Livathinos (84 Theofilos Simaioforidis), Grigoris Tsinos (75 Dimitris Klis), Aggelos Anastasiadis, Tseu La Ling, Grigoris Haralampidis, Arne Dokken.   Trainer: Ştefan Kovacs
AUSTRIA: Friedrich Koncilia; Robert Sara, Erich Obermayer, Karl Daxbacher, Franz Zore; Johann Dihanich (74 Hans-Peter Buchleitner), Felix Gasselich, Thomas Pfeiler, Ernst Baumeister, Gerhard Steinkogler (88 Chavdar Tzvetkov), Anton Polster.   Trainer: Václav Halama
Goals: Anastasiadis (21), Polster (54), Haralampidis (78)

INTERNAZIONALE MILANO v SLOVAN BRATISLAVA 2-0 (0-0)
Stadio Giuseppe Meazza, Milano   15.09.1982
Referee: Viriato Graça Oliva (POR)   Attendance: 60,000
INTER: Ivano Bordon, Riccardo Ferri, Giuseppe Baresi, Gabriele Oriali, Fulvio Collovati, Graziano Bini (84 Giuseppe Bergomi), Salvatore Bagni, Antonio Sabato, Alessandro Altobelli, Evaristo Beccalossi (70 Roberto Bergamaschi), JUARY dos Santos filho Jorge.   Trainer: Rino Marchesi
SLOVAN: Milan Mana; Ján Nezhyba, Ján Hlavatý, Dušan Leško, Jozef Suchánek, Marián Takáč, Marián Masný (75 Bohuš Víger), Igor Frič, Pavol Bojkovský, Rudolf Bobek, Milan Luhový.   Trainer: Michal Vičan
Goals: Altobelli (78), Sabato (83)

SLOVAN BRATISLAVA v INTERNAZIONALE MILANO 2-1 (1-1)
Tehelné pole, Bratislava   29.09.1982
Referee: Georges Konrath (FRA)   Attendance: 35,000
SLOVAN: Milan Mana; Ján Nezhyba, Ján Hlavatý, Jozef Suchánek, Jozef Brňák, Pavol Bojkovský (79 Bohuš Víger), Rudolf Bobek (85 Dušan Leško,), Marián Takáč, Igor Frič, Marián Masný, Milan Luhový.   Trainer: Michal Vičan
INTER: Ivano Bordon, Giuseppe Bergomi, Fulvio Collovati, Graziano Bini, Giampiero Marini, Giuseppe Baresi, Hans Peter Müller (82 Evaristo Beccalossi), Salvatore Bagni, Antonio Sabato, JUARY dos Santos filho Jorge, Roberto Bergamaschi (57 Gabriele Oriali).   Trainer: Rino Marchesi
Goals: H. Müller (5 pen), Takáč (25), Bobek (78)

IFK GÖTEBORG
v ÚJPESTI DÓZSA BUDAPEST 1-1 (0-1)
Gamla Ullevi, Göteborg   15.09.1982
Referee: Klaus Peschell (E. GER)   Attendance: 18,000

IFK: Thomas Wernersson, Ruben Svensson, Glenn Hysen, Conny Karlsson, Stig Fredriksson, Tord Holmgren, Glenn Strömberg, Jerry Karlsson, Glenn Schiller, Dan Corneliusson, Håkan Sandberg.

ÚJPESTI DÓZSA: József Szendrei; Attila Herédi, József Kovács, József Kardos, József Tóth; András Szebegyinszki, András Töröcsik (71 Attila Balogh), Sándor Kisznyér, László Nagy; Lajos Arky, Sándor Kiss.   Trainer: Miklós Temesvári

Goals: J. Kovács (38), Strömberg (66)

B 93 KØBENHAVN
v DYNAMO DRESDEN 2-1 (0-1)
Idraetsparken, København   29.09.1982
Referee: Patrick Daly (IRE)   Attendance: 3,800

B 93: Bo Skovberg, Ole Petersen, Kim Hansen, Find Juhl Jensen, Mortensen, Jetzack (87 Lars Dalsborg), Kim Larsen, Keld Kristensen, Lars Hansen (62 Tonny Madsen), Jens Kolding, Lars Francker.

DYNAMO: Jörg Klimpel, Hans-Jürgen Dörner, Frank Schuster, Andreas Trautmann, Karsten Petersohn, Reinhard Häfner, Hans-Uwe Pilz, Matthias Döschner, Lutz Schülbe (83 Udo Schmuck), Ralf Minge, Torsten Gütschow.

Goals: Pilz (10), Larsen (71), Madsen (81)

ÚJPESTI DÓZSA BUDAPEST
v IFK GÖTEBORG 3-1 (3-1)
Megyeri út, Budapest   29.09.1982
Referee: Aron Schmidhuber (W. GER)   Attendance: 15,000

ÚJPESTI DÓZSA: József Szendrei; József Kardos, József Kovács, Attila Herédi, József Tóth; János Szűcs, Béla Kovács, Sándor Kisznyér, László Nagy (68 András Szabó); Sándor Kiss, András Töröcsik.   Trainer: Miklós Temesvári

IFK: Thomas Wernersson, Ruben Svensson, Glenn Hysen, Conny Karlsson, Stig Fredriksson, Tord Holmgren, Glenn Strömberg, Jerry Karlsson, Tommy Holmgren; Dan Corneliusson (69 Glenn Holm), Håkan Sandberg.

Goals: Töröcsik (5), Szendrei (10 og), Kiss (25, 35)

KSV WATERSCHEI
v RED BOYS DIFFERDANGE 7-1 (5-0)
André Dumontstadion, Genk   22.09.1982
Referee: John Moffat (SCO)   Attendance: 8,500

WATERSCHEI: Klaus Pudelko, Gyözö Martos, Pierre Plessers, Tony Bialousz, Adri van Kraay (65 Aimé Coenen), Willy Vliegen, Pierre Janssen, Leo Clijsters, Karl Berger, Larus Gudmundsson (46 Jos Coninx), Roland Janssen.

RED BOYS: Alain Valli; Romain Michaux, Herrin, Francis Kremer, Marcel Barthel, Luigi De Stephanis (25 Pascal Burger), René Muller, Romain Schreiner, Gilbert Hotton (85 Marco Heyar), William Bianchini, Marcel Di Domenico.

Goals: Gudmundsson (8, 19), Berger (15, 55), P. Janssen (22), Vliegen (37), Coninx (72), Di Domenico (80)

DYNAMO DRESDEN
v B 93 KØBENHAVN 3-2 (2-0)
Dynamo, Dresden   15.09.1982
Referee: Howard William King (WAL)   Attendance: 26,000

DYNAMO: Jörg Klimpel, Hans-Jürgen Dörner, Frank Schuster, Andreas Trautmann, Andreas Mittag, Reinhard Häfner, Andreas Schmidt, Hans-Uwe Pilz, Lutz Schülbe (63 Dirk Losert, 77 Torsten Gütschow), Ralf Minge, Matthias Döschner.

B 93: Bo Skovbjerg, Ole Petersen, Kim Hansen, Find Juhl Jensen, Mortensen, Kim Larsen, Lars Dalsborg, Lars Hansen (73 Jetzack), Keld Kristensen, Jens Kolding, Lars Francker (79 Tonny Madsen).

Goals: Trautmann (8, 16 pen), Francker (49), Pilz (80 pen), Madsen (90 pen)

RED BOYS DIFFERDANGE
v KSV WATERSCHEI 0-1 (0-0)
Stade Municipal, Differdange   29.09.1982
Referee: Joël Quiniou (FRA)   Attendance: 2,250

RED BOYS: Alain Valli; Romain Michaux, Herrin, Francis Kremer, Pascal Burger (76 Marco Heyar), Juan Sarrias, René Müller, Romain Schreiner, Gilbert Hotton, William Bianchini (87 Mosca), Marcel Di Domenico.

WATERSCHEI: Jean Thijs, Gyözö Martos (46 Aimé Coenen), Pierre Plessers, Adri van Kraay, Danny David, Willy Vliegen (75 Ivo Plessers), Pierre Janssen, Leo Clijsters, Constantinos Mbisdikis, Karl Berger, Larus Gudmundsson.

Goal: P. Janssen (56)

**GALATASARAY ISTANBUL
v KUUSYSI LAHTI 2-1** (2-1)
Ali Sami Yen, Istanbul   15.09.1982
Referee: Hiqmet Kuka (ALB)   Attendance: 37,000
GALATASARAY: Eser Özaltindere; Sefer Karaer, Ibrahim Akçay, Raşit Cetiner, Fatih Terim, Adnan Esen, Cengiz Yazicioglu (62 Ali Hamurcuoglu), Ahmet Keloglu, Mustafa Ergücü, Sinan Turhan, Bülent Alkiliç.
KUUSYSI: Ismo Korhonen, Ilkka Remes, Ilpo Talvio, Juha Saarikunnas, Timo Kautonen, Esa Pekonen, Keijo Kousa, Markus Törnvall, Raimo Kumpulainen, Petri Kurki (71 Jarmo Kaivonurmi), Juha Annunen.
Goals: Cetiner (21), Annunen (23), Ergücü (29)

**KUUSYSI LAHTI
v GALATASARAY ISTANBUL 1-1** (0-0)
Urheilukeskus, Lahti   29.09.1982
Referee: Kjell Johansson (SWE)   Attendance: 1,744
KUUSYSI: Ismo Korhonen, Ilkka Remes, Ilpo Talvio, Juha Saarikunnas, Timo Kautonen, Esa Pekonen, Keijo Kousa, Markus Törnvall (46 Jorma Kallio), Raimo Kumpulainen (58 Tapani Rantanen), Jarmo Kaivonurmi, Juha Annunen.
GALATASARAY: Eser Özaltindere; Ali Hamurcuoglu (35 Tarik Hodzic), Ahmet Keloglu, Raşit Cetiner, Fatih Terim, Mustafa Ergücü, Adnan Esen, Cengiz Yazicioglu, Mirsad Sejdić, Sinan Turhan, Bülent Alkiliç.
Goals: Hodzić (87), Kallio (89)

**SWANSEA CITY
v SLIEMA WANDERERS 12-0** (4-0)
Vetch Field, Swansea   15.09.1982
Referee: Gérard Biguet (FRA)   Attendance: 5,130
SWANSEA: David Davies, Christopher Marustik, Džemal Hadziabdić, Colin Irwin, Raymond Kennedy, Ante Rajković, James Loveridge (72 Leighton James), Robert James, Jeremy Charles, Nigel Stevenson, Robert Latchford (68 Ian Walsh).
SLIEMA WANDERERS: Alan Zammit, Oliver Losco, Gennaro Camilleri, Simon Tortell, Mario Schembri, Paul Portelli, John Caruana, Emanuel Fabri, Tony Tabone, John Buttigieg, Richard Aquilina.
Goals: Charles (16, 50), Loveridge (19, 54), Irwin (22), Latchford (42), Hadziabdić (60), Walsh (62, 68, 79), Rajković (75), Stevenson (85)

SLIEMA WANDERERS v SWANSEA CITY 0-5 (0-3)
Ta' Qali   29.09.1982
Referee: Enzo Barbaresco (ITA)   Attendance: 2,000
SLIEMA WANDERERS: Alan Zammit, Stephen Thewma, Gennaro Camilleri, Oliver Losco, Mario Schembri, Paul Portelli, John Buttigieg, Emanuel Fabri, Simon Tortell, Richard Aquilina, Onemo.
SWANSEA: Christopher Sander, Dudley Lewis, Džemal Hadziabdić, Jeremy Charles, Raymond Kennedy, Maxwell Thompson, Alan Curtis (78 John Toshack), Garry Stanley, Darren Gale, Christopher Marustik, James Loveridge.
Goals: Curtis (19, 45), Gale (38, 74), Toshack (89)

FC ABERDEEN v DINAMO TIRANA 1-0 (1-0)
Pittodrie, Aberdeen   15.09.1982
Referee: Louis Delsemme (BEL)   Attendance: 14,000
ABERDEEN: James Leighton, Stuart Kennedy (68 Eric Black), John McMaster, Douglas Bell (57 Neale Cooper), Douglas Rougvie, William Miller, Gordon Strachan, Neil Simpson, Mark McGhee, John Hewitt, Peter Weir.
Manager: Alex Ferguson
DINAMO: Ilir Luarasi, Durim Kuqi, Aleko Bregu, Muhedin Targaj, Ruci, Xhafa (84 Agron Duati), Halit Gega (89 Muasi), Agim Canaj, Vasillaq Zeri, Fagekugi, Sulejman Demollari.
Goal: Hewitt (8)

DINAMO TIRANA v FC ABERDEEN 0-0
Qemal Stafa, Tirana   29.09.1982
Referee: Bela Szabo (HUN)   Attendance: 19,000
DINAMO: Ilir Luarasi, Dautaj (61 Nago), Muhedin Targaj, Halit Gega, Durim Kuqi, Ruci, Dalia, Andrea Marko, Vasillaq Zeri, Agim Canaj, Sulejman Demollari (74 Roland Agalliu).
ABERDEEN: James Leighton, Stuart Kennedy, Neale Cooper (62 John McMaster), Douglas Rougvie, Alex McLeish, William Miller, Gordon Strachan, Neil Simpson, Mark McGhee (87 John Hewitt), Douglas Bell, Peter Weir.
Manager: Alex Ferguson

LIMERICK UNITED v AZ 67 ALKMAAR 1-1 (1-1)
Market's Field, Limerick   15.09.1982
Referee: Roger Schoeters (BEL)   Attendance: 3,000
LIMERICK: John Power, Patrick Nolan, Brendan Storan, Joe O'Mahony, Al Finucane, Liam Murphy (84 Gerry Duggan), James Nodwell, John Walsh, Liam Keane, Gary Hulmes, Jeremiah Dennehy (78 Desmond Kennedy).
AZ 67: Eddy Treijtel, Hans Reijnders, Peter Arntz, Henrik Eigenbrød, Gijs Steinmann, Richard Van der Meer, Ype Anema, Roelf-Jan Tiktak, Jos Jonker, Fokke Zwart, Kees Tol.
Trainer: Hans Eijkenbroek
Goals: Jonker (28), Nolan (40)

AZ 67 ALKMAAR v LIMERICK UNITED 1-0 (0-0)
Alkmaarderhout   30.09.1982
Referee: Raul Joaquín Fernandes Nazarre (POR)   Att: 4,068
AZ 67: Eddy Treijtel, Hans Reijnders, Hugo Hovenkamp, Henrik Eigenbrod, Gijs Steinmann, Peter Arntz, Richard Van der Meer, Jos Jonker, Roelf-Jan Tiktak, Rick Talan, Kees Tol (46 Fokke Zwart).   Trainer: Hans Eijkenbroek
LIMERICK: John Power, Patrick Nolan, Al Finucane, Joe O'Mahony, Brendan Storan, Liam Murphy (61 Gerry Duggan), James Nodwell, Gary Hulmes, Jeremiah Dennehy, John Walsh, Liam Keane (73 Desmond Kennedy).
Goal: Jonker (75)

CRVENA ZVEZDA BEOGRAD
v FC BARCELONA 2-4 (0-1)
Crvena Zvezda, Beograd   20.10.1982
Referee: Robert Valentine (SCO)   Attendance: 80,000
CRVENA ZVEZDA: Aleksandar Stojanović, Boško Djurovski, Milan Jovin, Djordje Milovanović (61 Rajko Janjanin), Milenko Rajković, Miroslav Šugar, Vladimir Petrović, Ranko Djordjić, Dušan Savić (61 Milko Djurovski), Nedeljko Milosavljević, Srebrenko Repčić.   Trainer: Stevan Ostojić
FC BARCELONA: Pedro María ARTOLA Urrutia, GERARDO Miranda Concepción, Bernardo Bernardo Bianquetti Miguel "MIGUELI", José Ramón ALESANCO Ventosa (67 José Manuel Martínez Toral "MANOLO"), JULIO ALBERTO Moreno Casas, Miguel Ángel "PERICO" ALONSO Oyarbide (60 José Vicente SÁNCHEZ Felip), VÍCTOR Muñoz Manrique, Bernd Schuster, Francisco José CARRASCO Hidalgo, Diego Armando MARADONA, MARCOS Alonso Peña.   Trainer: Udo Lattek
Goals: Maradona (36, 46), Schuster (65, 80), Janjanin (72, 73)

SECOND ROUND

B 93 KØBENHAVN
v KSV WATERSCHEI THOR 0-2 (0-0)
Idraetsparken, København   20.10.1982
Referee: Reidar Bjørnestad (NOR)   Attendance: 5,000
B 93: Bo Skorbjerg, Lars Dalsborg, Ole Petersen, Jetzack, Due, Keld Kristensen, Find Juhl Jensen, Mortensen, Jens Kolding, Lars Hansen (46 Tonny Madsen), Lars Francker (81 Nøravin).
WATERSCHEI: Klaus Pudelko, Aimé Coenen, Adri van Kraay, Pierre Plessers, Danny David, Willy Vliegen, Leo Clijsters, Pierre Janssen, Roland Janssen (75 Constantinos Mbisdikis), Karl Berger, Larus Gudmundsson (81 Tony Bialousz).
Goals: R. Janssen (66), Gudmundsson (72)

FC BARCELONA
v CRVENA ZVEZDA BELGRAD 2-1 (0-0)
Camp Nou, Barcelona   3.11.1982
Referee: Georges Konrath (FRA)   Attendance: 45,000
FC BARCELONA: Pedro María ARTOLA Urrutia, GERARDO Miranda Concepción, Antonio OLMO Ramírez, José Ramón ALESANCO Ventosa, José Manuel Martínez Toral "MANOLO", Miguel Ángel "PERICO" ALONSO Oyarbide (60 Enrique Castro González "QUINI"), Bernd Schuster, Diego Armando MARADONA, VÍCTOR Muñoz Manrique, Francisco José CARRASCO Hidalgo, MARCOS Alonso Peña (46 José Vicente SÁNCHEZ Felip).   Trainer: Udo Lattek
CRVENA ZVEZDA: Aleksandar Simeunović, Miladin Pesterac, Milan Jovin, Milenko Rajković, Boško Djurovski, Miroslav Šugar, Vladimir Petrović, Rajko Janjanin, Ranko Djordjić, Dušan Savić, Srebrenko Repčić (60 Nedeljko Milosavljević).   Trainer: Stevan Ostojić
Goals: B. Djurovski (54), Schuster (57), Alesanco (81)

KSV WATERSCHEI v B 93 KØBENHAVN 4-1 (2-1)
André Dumontstadion, Genk   3.11.1982
Referee: Widukind Herrmann (E. GER)   Att: 12,000
WATERSCHEI: Klaus Pudelko, Danny David, Pierre Plessers, Adri van Kraay, Aimé Coenen, Willy Vliegen, Pierre Janssen, Leo Clijsters (64 Tony Bialousz), Roland Janssen, Larus Gudmundsson (46 Jos Coninx), Eddy Voordeckers.
B 93: Bo Skorbjerg, Due, Ole Petersen, Lars Dalsborg, Kim Larsen, Mortensen, Find Juhl Jensen, Keld Kristensen, Jens Kolding (46 Jan Kreibke), Lars Hansen, Lars Francker (72 Jens Nørager).
Goals: P.Janssen (2), P. Plessers (25 pen), Gudmundsson (42), Vliegen (63), Dalsborg (88)

AZ 67 ALKMAAR
v INTERNAZIONALE MILANO 1-0 (1-0)
Alkmaarderhout   20.10.1982
Referee: Adolf Prokop (E. GER)   Attendance: 11,000
AZ 67: Eddy Treijtel, Hans Reijnders, Hugo Hovenkamp, Henrik Eigenbrød, Ype Anema, Richard Van der Meer, Peter Arntz, Jos Jonker (16 Gijs Steinmann), Roelf-Jan Tiktak, Rick Talan, Kees Tol (76 Fokke Zwart).   Trainer: Hans Eijkenbroek
INTER: Ivano Bordon, Giuseppe Bergomi, Riccardo Ferri, Fulvio Collovati, Giampiero Marini, Gabriele Oriali, Salvatore Bagni, Antonio Sabato, Evaristo Beccalossi (68 Roberto Bergamaschi), Alessandro Altobelli, JUARY dos Santos filho Jorge.   Trainer: Rino Marchesi
Goal: Tiktak (6)

INTERNAZIONALE MILANO
v AZ 67 ALKMAAR 2-0 (1-0)

Stadio Giuseppe Meazza, Milano   3.11.1982

Referee: Alojzy Jarguz (POL)   Attendance: 61,000

INTER: Ivano Bordon, Giuseppe Bergomi, Giuseppe Baresi, Gabriele Oriali, Fulvio Collovati, Giampiero Marini, Roberto Bergamaschi (85 Riccardo Ferri), Salvatore Bagni, Evaristo Beccalossi (60 Hans Peter Müller), Alessandro Altobelli, JUARY dos Santos filho Jorge.   Trainer: Rino Marchesi

AZ 67: Hans De Koning, Hans Reijnders, Hugo Hovenkamp, Henrik Eigenbrød, Gijs Steinmann, Peter Arntz, Richard Van der Meer, Jos Jonker, Roelf-Jan Tiktak, Rick Talan (76 Jan Gaasbeek), Kees Tol.   Trainer: Hans Eijkenbroek

Goals: Juary (4), Altobelli (66)

GALATASARAY SK ISTANBUL
v AUSTRIA WIEN 2-4 (2-1)

Ali Sami Yen, Istanbul   20.10.1982

Referee: Paolo Bergamo (ITA)   Attendance: 50,000

GALATASARAY: Eser Özaltindere; Adnan Esen, Ibrahim Akçay, Rasit Cetiner, Fatih Terim, Öner Kiliç (65 Murat Inan), Mustafa Ergücü, Bülent Alkiliç, Mirsad Sejdić, Tarik Hodzic, Sinan Turhan.

AUSTRIA: Friedrich Koncilia; Robert Sara, Erich Obermayer, Karl Daxbacher, Franz Zore; Johann Dihanich (70 Hans-Peter Buchleitner), Thomas Pfeiler, Felix Gasselich, Ernst Baumeister, Gerhard Steinkogler (70 Alfred Drabits), Anton Polster.   Trainer: Václav Halama

Goals: Sejdić (19, 34), Steinkogler (43), Polster (53, 74), Gasselich (77)

FC ABERDEEN v LECH POZNAN 2-0 (0-0)

Pittodrie, Aberdeen   20.10.1982

Referee: Egbert Mulder (HOL)   Attendance: 18,000

ABERDEEN: James Leighton, Neale Cooper, William Miller, Alex McLeish, Douglas Bell (70 Stuart Kennedy), Gordon Strachan, John McMaster, Neil Simpson, Mark McGhee, Eric Black (80 John Hewitt), Peter Weir.   Manager: Alex Ferguson

LECH: Zbigniew Plesnierowicz, Krzysztof Pawlak, Józef Szewczyk, Janusz Malek, Andrzej Strugarek (64 Jerzy Krzyzanowski), Janusz Kupcewicz (59 Mariusz Niewiadomski), Józef Adamiec, Boguslaw Oblewski, Hieronim Barczak, Jacek Bak, Miroslaw Okonski.

Goals: McGhee (54), Weir (56)

AUSTRIA WIEN
v GALATASARAY ISTANBUL 0-1 (0-0)

Franz Horr, Wien   3.11.1982

Referee: Nicolae Rainea (ROM)   Attendance: 7,500

AUSTRIA: Friedrich Koncilia, Robert Sara, Erich Obermayer, Karl Daxbacher, Hans-Peter Buchleitner,;Johann Dihanich, Ernst Baumeister, Felix Gasselich, Thomas Pfeiler; Gerhard Steinkogler (64 Alfred Drabits), Anton Polster.
Trainer: Václav Halama

GALATASARAY: Eser Özaltindere; Adnan Esen, Ahmet Keloglu, Rasit Cetiner, Fatih Terim, Fettah Dindar, Mustafa Ergücü, Bülent Alkiliç, Mirsad Sejdic, Tarik Hodzic, Sinan Turhan.

Goal: Ergücü (63)

LECH POZNAN v FC ABERDEEN 0-1 (0-0)

Lech, Poznan   3.11.1982

Referee: Talal Tokat (TUR)   Attendance: 25,000

LECH: Zbigniew Plesnierowicz, Krzysztof Pawlak, Józef Szewczyk (64 Jerzy Krzyzanowski), Józef Adamiec, Janusz Malek, Boguslaw Oblewski (88 Rafal Stroinski), Janusz Kupcewicz, Hieronim Barczak, Jacek Bak, Mariusz Niewiadomski, Miroslaw Okonski.

ABERDEEN: James Leighton, Stuart Kennedy, Alex McLeish, William Miller, Douglas Rougvie, Gordon Strachan, Neil Simpson (87 Andy Watson), John McMaster (57 Neale Cooper), Douglas Bell, Mark McGhee, Peter Weir.
Manager: Alex Ferguson

Goal: Bell (59)

SWANSEA CITY v PARIS ST.GERMAIN 0-1 (0-0)

Vetch Field, Swansea   20.10.1982

Referee: Ulf Eriksson (SWE)   Attendance: 9,505

SWANSEA: David Davies, Džemal Hadziabdić, Raymond Kennedy, Wyndham Evans, Christopher Marustik (72 Leighton James), Dudley Lewis, John Mahoney, Robert James, Alan Curtis, Robert Latchford (61 Ian Walsh), Garry Stanley.

PARIS ST.GERMAIN: Dominique Baratelli; Luis Fernandez, Jean-Marc Pilorget, Dominique Bathenay, Yannick Guillochon, Jean-Claude Lemoult, Pascal Zaremba, Osvaldo Ardiles, Mustapha Dahleb, Nambatingue Toko, Kees Kist.
Trainer: Georges Peyroche

Goal: Toko (71)

PARIS ST.GERMAIN v SWANSEA CITY 2-0 (1-0)
Parc des Princes, Paris   3.11.1982
Referee: Siegfried Kirschen (E. GER)   Attendance: 50,000
PARIS ST.GERMAIN: Dominique Baratelli; Philippe Col, Jean-Marc Pilorget, Dominique Bathenay, Yannick Guillochon, Jean-Claude Lemoult, Pascal Zaremba, Luis Fernandez, Mustapha Dahleb, Nambatingue Toko, Kees Kist (75 Michel N'Gom).   Trainer: Georges Peyroche
SWANSEA: David Davies, Džemal Hadžiabdić (49 Dudley Lewis), Nigel Stevenson, Ante Rajković, Garry Stanley, Robert James, Jeremy Charles, John Mahoney, Leighton James, Robert Latchford (65 Ian Walsh), Alan Curtis.
Goals: Kist (5), Fernandez (75)

**REAL MADRID
v ÚJPESTI DÓZSA BUDAPEST 3-1** (2-1)
Estadio Santiago Bernabéu, Madrid   20.10.1982
Referee: Rudolf Renggli (SWI)   Attendance: 60,000
REAL: AGUSTIN Rodríguez Santiago; JUAN JOSÉ Jiménez Collar, Francisco BONET Serrano, Johannes-Antonius METGOD (20 Alfonso FRAILE Sánchez), José Antonio CAMACHO Alfaro; Ricardo GALLEGO Redondo (89 José Antonio SALGUERO García), Ulrich Stielike, ÁNGEL de los Santos Cano; Juan Gomez González "JUANITO", Carlos Alonso González "SANTILLANA", ISIDRO Díaz González.   Trainer: Alfredo DI STÉFANO
ÚJPESTI DÓZSA: József Szendrei; János Szűcs, József Kardos, Béla Kovács, József Tóth; András Szebegyinszki, András Töröcsik (20 Lajos Arky), Sándor Kisznyér (73 László Polonyi), András Szabó; Attila Balogh, Sándor Kiss.   Trainer: Miklós Temesvári
Goals: Santillana (30, 90), Kiss (38), Juan José (40)

**ÚJPESTI DÓZSA BUDAPEST
v REAL MADRID 0-1** (0-0)
Megyeri út, Budapest   3.11.1982
Referee: Pietro d'Elia (ITA)   Attendance: 10,000
ÚJPESTI DÓZSA: József Szendrei; János Szűcs, József Kardos, József Tóth, Béla Kovács, Attila Herédi, Attila Balogh (75 Lajos Arky), Sándor Kiss, András Szabó, András Töröcsik (39 András Szebegyinszki), Sándor Kisznyér.   Trainer: Miklós Temesvári
REAL: AGUSTIN Rodríguez Santiago; JUAN JOSÉ Jiménez Collar, Johannes-Antonius METGOD, Francisco BONET Serrano, José Antonio CAMACHO Alfaro; Ricardo GALLEGO Redondo, ÁNGEL de los Santos Cano, Ulrich Stielike; Miguel Ángel PORTUGAL (72 Juan Gomez González "JUANITO"), Carlos Alonso González "SANTILLANA", ISIDRO Díaz González (89 Andrés Alonso ITO).   Trainer: Alfredo DI STÉFANO
Goal: Santillana (63)

**TOTTENHAM HOTSPUR LONDON
v BAYERN MÜNCHEN 1-1** (1-0)
White Hart Lane, London   20.10.1982
Referee: Luigi Agnolin (ITA)   Attendance: 36,488
TOTTENHAM: Raymond Clemence, Paul Price, Gary O'Reilly (78 Terence Gibson), Paul Miller, John Lacy, Michael Hazard, Garry Brooke, Steven Archibald (24 Mark Falco), Gary Mabbutt, Ricardo Villa, Garth Crooks.   Manager: Keith Burtenshaw
BAYERN: Jean-Marie Pfaff, Bernd Martin, Wolfgang Grobe, Udo Horsmann, Klaus Augenthaler, Wolfgang Kraus, Bernd Dürnberger, Paul Breitner, Dieter Hoeness, Karl-Heinz Rummenigge, Wolfgang Dremmler.   Trainer: Pál Csernai
Goals: Archibald (4), Breitner (53)

**BAYERN MÜNCHEN
v TOTTENHAM HOTSPUR LONDON 4-1** (1-0)
Olympiastadion, München   3.11.1982
Referee: André Daina (SWI)   Attendance: 55,000
BAYERN: Jean-Marie Pfaff, Wolfgang Dremmler, Udo Horsmann, Wolfgang Grobe, Klaus Augenthaler, Wolfgang Kraus, Paul Breitner, Bernd Dürnberger, Karl Del'Haye, Karl-Heinz Rummenigge, Dieter Hoeness.   Trainer: Pál Csernai
TOTTENHAM: Raymond Clemence, Paul Price, Christopher Hughton, Paul Miller (63 Stephen Perryman), John Lacy, Michael Hazard, Gary Mabbutt, Steven Archibald, Garry Brooke (57 Glenn Hoddle), Ricardo Villa, Garth Crooks.   Manager: Keith Burtenshaw
Goals: Hoeness (18), Horsmann (52), Breitner (73), Hughton (79), K.H. Rummenigge (80)

QUARTER-FINALS

**INTERNAZIONALE MILANO
v REAL MADRID 1-1** (1-0)
Stadio Giuseppe Meazza, Milano   2.03.1983
Referee: Talal Tokat (TUR)   Attendance: 75,248
INTER: Ivano Bordon, Giuseppe Bergomi, Giuseppe Baresi, Gabriele Oriali, Fulvio Collovati, Giampiero Marini, Salvatore Bagni, Hans Peter Müller, Alessandro Altobelli, Antonio Sabato, JUARY dos Santos filho Jorge.   Trainer: Rino Marchesi
REAL: AGUSTIN Rodríguez Santiago, JUAN JOSÉ Jiménez Collar, José Antonio CAMACHO Alfaro, Ricardo GALLEGO Redondo, Francisco BONET Serrano, Johannes-Antonius METGOD, Juan Gomez González "JUANITO" (88 Francisco PINEDA García), ÁNGEL de los Santos Cano, Carlos Alonso González "SANTILLANA", Ulrich Stielike, Alfonso FRAILE Sánchez.   Trainer: Alfredo DI STÉFANO
Goals: Oriali (15), Gallego (59)

**REAL MADRID
v INTERNAZIONALE MILANO 2-1** (0-1)

Estadio Santiago Bernabéu, Madrid   16.03.1983

Referee: Vojtěch Christov (CZE)   Attendance: 85,000

REAL: Mariano GARÇIA REMON, Isidoro SAN JOSÉ Pozo, José Antonio CAMACHO Alfaro, Johannes-Antonius METGOD, José Antonio SALGUERO García, Ricardo GALLEGO Redondo (30 JUAN JOSÉ Jiménez Collar), Juan Gomez González "JUANITO" (87 Vicente DEL BOSQUE González), ÁNGEL de los Santos Cano, Carlos Alonso González "SANTILLANA", Ulrich Stielike, Francisco PINEDA García.   Trainer: Alfredo DI STÉFANO

INTER: Ivano Bordon, Giuseppe Bergomi, Giuseppe Baresi, Riccardo Ferri, Fulvio Collovati, Graziano Bini, Salvatore Bagni, Hans Peter Müller (72 Roberto Bergamaschi), Alessandro Altobelli, Gabriele Oriali, JUARY dos Santos filho Jorge (66 Evaristo Beccalossi).   Trainer: Rino Marchesi

Goals: Altobelli (20), Salguero (51), Santillana (56)

**PARIS ST.GERMAIN
v KSV WATERSCHEI 2-0** (1-0)

Parc des Princes, Paris   2.03.1983

Referee: Bogdan Dochev (BUL)   Attendance: 49,407

PARIS ST.GERMAIN: Dominique Baratelli; Yannick Guillochon, Jean-Marc Pilorget, Thierry Bacconier, Dominique Bathenay, Jean-Claude Lemoult, Safet Sušić, Luis Fernandez, Kees Kist, Dominique Rocheteau, Mustapha Dahleb.   Trainer: Georges Peyroche

WATERSCHEI: Klaus Pudelko, Györö Martos, Pierre Plessers, Leo Clijsters, Danny David, Aimé Coenen (68 Jean-Paul Massignani), Adri van Kraay, Pierre Janssen, Roland Janssen, Karl Berger, Eddy Voordeckers.

Goals: Fernandez (43), Pilorget (57)

**KSV WATERSCHEI
v PARIS ST.GERMAIN 3-0** (1-0, 2-0) (AET)

André Dumontstadion, Genk   16.03.1983

Referee: Clive Thomas (WAL)   Attendance: 22,000

WATERSCHEI: Klaus Pudelko, Györö Martos, Leo Clijsters, Pierre Plessers, Danny David, Ivo Plessers, Adri van Kraay, Pierre Janssen, Roland Janssen, Larus Gudmundsson (72 Karl Berger), Eddy Voordeckers.

PARIS ST.GERMAIN: Dominique Baratelli; Saar Boubacar, Thierry Bacconier, Dominique Bathenay, Jean-Marc Pilorget, Jean-Claude Lemoult, Luis Fernandez, Safet Sušić (12 Dominique Rocheteau), Mustapha Dahleb, Nambatingue Toko, Kees Kist.   Trainer: Georges Peyroche

Goals: Gudmundsson (30), R. Janssen (67), P. Janssen (114)

AUSTRIA WIEN v FC BARCELONA 0-0

Prater, Wien   2.03.1983

Referee: Erik Fredriksson (SWE)   Attendance: 25,000

AUSTRIA: Friedrich Koncilia, Robert Sara, Erich Obermayer, Franz Zore, Josef Degeorgi; Džemal Mustedanagić, Felix Gasselich, Ernst Baumeister, István Magyar (70 Johann Dihanich); Anton Polster, Gerhard Steinkogler (77 Alfred Drabits).   Trainer: Václav Halama

FC BARCELONA: AMADOR Lorenzo Lemos, José Vicente SÁNCHEZ Felip, José Ramón ALESANCO Ventosa, Bernardo Bianquetti Miguel "MIGUELI", Juan José ESTELLA Salas; URBANO Ortega Cuadros, Bernd Schuster, Enrique MORÁN Blanco (75 ESTEBAN Vigo Benítez), VÍCTOR Muñoz Manrique, Ángel "PICHI" ALONSO Herrera, Francisco José CARRASCO Hidalgo.   Trainer: Udo Lattek

FC BARCELONA v AUSTRIA WIEN 1-1 (1-1)

Estadio Camp Nou, Barcelona   16.03.1983

Referee: Adolf Prokop (E. GER)   Attendance: 40,000

FC BARCELONA: AMADOR Lorenzo Lemos, José Vicente SÁNCHEZ Felip, Bernardo Bianquetti Miguel "MIGUELI", José Ramón ALESANCO Ventosa, Juan José ESTELLA Salas; Miguel Ángel "PERICO" ALONSO Oyarbide, Ángel "PICHI" ALONSO Herrera (61 Enrique MORÁN Blanco), Bernd Schuster (84 ESTEBAN Vigo Benítez), Diego Armando MARADONA; Enrique Castro González "QUINI", Francisco José CARRASCO Hidalgo.   Trainer: César Luis Menotti

AUSTRIA: Friedrich Koncilia; Robert Sara, Erich Obermayer, Franz Zore, Josef Degeorgi; Felix Gasselich, Džemal Mustedanagić, István Magyar (54 Johann Dihanich, 85 Karl Daxbacher), Ernst Baumeister; Anton Polster, Gerhard Steinkogler.   Trainer: Václav Halama

Goals: Steinkogler (37), Alesanco (44)

BAYERN MÜNCHEN v FC ABERDEEN 0-0

Olympiastadion, München   2.03.1983

Referee: Emilio Carlos Guruceta Muro (SPA)   Att: 28,000

BAYERN: Manfred Müller, Wolfgang Dremmler, Udo Horsmann, Wolfgang Grobe, Klaus Augenthaler, Wolfgang Kraus, Norbert Nachtweih, Paul Breitner, Dieter Hoeness, Karl Del'Haye, Karl-Heinz Rummenigge.   Trainer: Pál Csernai

ABERDEEN: James Leighton, Stuart Kennedy, Douglas Rougvie, Neale Cooper, Alex McLeish, William Miller, Eric Black (77 Gordon Strachan), Neil Simpson, Mark McGhee, Douglas Bell, Peter Weir.   Manager: Alex Ferguson

FC ABERDEEN v BAYERN MÜNCHEN 3-2 (1-1)

Pittodrie, Aberdeen 16.03.1983

Referee: Michel Vautrot (FRA)   Attendance: 24,000

ABERDEEN: James Leighton, Stuart Kennedy (66 John McMaster), Douglas Rougvie, Neale Cooper, Alex McLeish, Gordon Strachan, William Miller, Neil Simpson (76 John Hewitt), Mark McGhee, Eric Black, Peter Weir.
Manager: Alex Ferguson

BAYERN: Manfred Müller, Wolfgang Dremmler, Udo Horsmann, Wolfgang Grobe, Klaus Augenthaler, Wolfgang Kraus, Hans Pflügler (83 Reinhold Mathy), Dieter Hoeness, Paul Breitner, Karl Del'Haye, Karl-Heinz Rummenigge.
Trainer: Pál Csernai

Goals: Augenthaler (10), Simpson (39), Pflügler (61), McLeish (77), Hewitt (78)

AUSTRIA WIEN v REAL MADRID 2-2 (2-1)

Prater, Wien 6.04.1983

Referee: Alojzy Jarguz (POL)   Attendance: 40,000

AUSTRIA: Friedrich Koncilia; Robert Sara, Erich Obermayer, Franz Zore, Josef Degeorgi; Džemal Mustedanagić (70 Johann Dihanich), Ernst Baumeister, Felix Gasselich, István Magyar (79 Libor Radimec); Anton Polster, Gerhard Steinkogler.
Trainer: Václav Halama

REAL: Mariano GARCIA REMON (46 AGUSTIN Rodríguez Santiago); JUAN JOSÉ Jiménez Collar, José Antonio SALGUERO García, Johannes-Antonius METGOD, Francisco BONET Serrano, Vicente DEL BOSQUE González, Juan Gomez González "JUANITO" (84 Francisco PINEDA García), Ricardo GALLEGO Redondo, Carlos Alonso González "SANTILLANA", Ángel de Los Santos, Isidoro SAN JOSÉ Pozo.
Trainer: Alfredo DI STÉFANO

Goals: Polster (5), Santillana (6), Magyar (20), San José (55)

SEMI-FINALS

FC ABERDEEN v KSV WATERSCHEI 5-1 (2-0)

Pittodrie, Aberdeen 6.04.1983

Referee: Paolo Bergamo (ITA)   Attendance: 24,000

ABERDEEN: James Leighton, Stuart Kennedy, Douglas Rougvie, Douglas Bell (75 Neale Cooper), Alex McLeish, William Miller, Gordon Strachan, Neil Simpson, Mark McGhee, Eric Black (75 John Hewitt), Peter Weir.
Manager: Alex Ferguson

WATERSCHEI: Klaus Pudelko, Györzö Martos, Tony Bialousz, Leo Clijsters, Danny David, Adri van Kraay (71 Ivo Plessers), Aimé Coenen (76 Jos Coninx), Pierre Janssen, Roland Janssen, Eddy Voordeckers, Larus Gudmundsson.

Goals: Black (2), Simpson (4), McGhee (67, 83), Weir (69), Gudmundsson (74)

KSV WATERSCHEI v FC ABERDEEN 1-0 (0-0)

André Dumontstadion, Genk 19.04.1983

Referee: Adolf Prokop (E. GER)   Attendance: 20,000

WATERSCHEI: Klaus Pudelko, Györzö Martos, Leo Clijsters, Pierre Plessers, Danny David, Ivo Plessers, Pierre Janssen, Adri van Kraay, Roland Janssen, Larus Gudmundsson (37 Jean-Paul Massignani), Eddy Voordeckers.

ABERDEEN: James Leighton, Stuart Kennedy, Alex McLeish, William Miller, Douglas Rougvie, Neil Simpson (84 Ian Angus), John McMaster, Andy Watson, Mark McGhee (70 William Falconer), John Hewitt, Peter Weir.
Manager: Alex Ferguson

Goal: Voordeckers (64)

REAL MADRID v AUSTRIA WIEN 3-1 (1-0)

Estadio Santiago Bernabéu, Madrid 20.04.1983

Referee: Bogdan Dochev (BUL)   Attendance: 70,000

REAL: AGUSTIN Rodríguez Santiago, JUAN JOSÉ Jiménez Collar, Johannes-Antonius METGOD, José Antonio SALGUERO García, José Antonio CAMACHO Alfaro, Vicente DEL BOSQUE González, ÁNGEL de los Santos Cano, Isidoro SAN JOSÉ Pozo, ISIDRO Díaz González (60 Francisco PINEDA García), Juan Gomez González "JUANITO", Carlos Alonso González "SANTILLANA" (86 Francisco GARCIA HERNÁNDEZ).   Trainer: Alfredo DI STÉFANO

AUSTRIA: Friedrich Koncilia; Robert Sara, Erich Obermayer, Franz Zore, Josef Degeorgi; Džemal Mustedanagić (60 Johann Dihanich), Felix Gasselich, Ernst Baumeister, István Magyar; Anton Polster (54 Alfred Drabits), Gerhard Steinkogler.
Trainer: Václav Halama

Goals: Santillana (11, 83), Juan José (67 og), Juanito (71)

FINAL

FC ABERDEEN
v REAL MADRID 2-1 (1-1, 1-1) (AET)

Gamla Ullevi, Göteborg   11.05.1983

Referee: Gianfranco Menegali (ITA)   Attendance: 17,804

ABERDEEN: James Leighton, Alex McLeish, Douglas Rougvie, John McMaster, William Miller (Cap), Neale Cooper, Neil Simpson, Gordon Strachan, Eric Black (88 John Hewitt), Mark McGhee, Peter Weir.   Manager: Alex Ferguson

REAL: AGUSTIN Rodríguez Santiago, Johanes-Antonius METGOD, JUAN JOSE Jiménez Collar, Francisco BONET Serrano, José Antonio CAMACHO Alfaro (91 Isidoro SAN JOSE Pozo), Ricardo GALLEGO Redondo, ÁNGEL de los Santos Cano, Ulrich STIELIKE, Juan Gomez González JUANITO, Carlos Alonso González SANTILLANA (Cap), ISIDRO Díaz González (102 José Antonio SALGUERO García). Trainer: Alfredo DI STÉFANO

Goals: Black (7), Juanito (15 pen), Hewitt (112)

Haralampidis (Panathinaikos Athina), Takáč, Bobek (Slovan Bratislava), Strömberg (IFK Göteborg), Di Domenico (Red Boys Differdange), Annunen, Kallio (Kuusysi Lahti), Nolan (Limerick United), Dalsborg, Francker, Larsen (B 93 København), B.Djurovski, Djurić, Jovin (Crvena Zvezda), Tiktak (AZ 67 Alkmaar), Niewiadowski, Partynski (Lech Poznan), Hodzić, Cetiner (Galatasaray Istanbul), Toshack, Irwin, Latchford, Hadziabdić, Rajković, Stevenson (Swansea City), J.Kovács, Töröcsik (Újpesti Dózsa), Hughton, Mabbutt, Brooke, Gibson (Tottenham), Oriali, Juary, Sabato, H.Müller (Inter Milano), Pilorget, Kist, Bathenay, N'Gom, Lemoult (Paris St Germain), Moratalla, Víctor, Urbano (FC Barcelona), Augenthaler, Pflügler, Hoeness, Horsmann, K.H.Rummenigge (Bayern München), Voordeckers, P.Plessers, Coninx (KSV Waterschei), Magyar, Gasselich (Austria Wien), San José, Salguero, Gallego, Juan José, Isidro, G.Hernández, Metgod (Real Madrid), McLeish, Bell, Strachan, Kennedy, Miller (Aberdeen)

Own goals: Marustik (Swansea City) for Sporting Braga, Cardoso (Sporting Braga) for Swansea City, Szendrei (Újpesti Dózsa) for IFK Göteborg, Juan José (Real Madrid) for Austria Wien

Goalscorers European Cup-Winners' Cup 1982-83:

8 goals: Carlos Alonso González "Santillana" (Real Madrid)

6 goals: Mark McGhee (Aberdeen), Larus Gudmundsson (Waterschei)

5 goals: John Hewitt (Aberdeen), Diego Armando Maradona, Bernd Schuster (FC Barcelona), Anton Polster (Austria Wien)

4 goals: Eric Black (Aberdeen), Jeremy Charles (Swansea City), Pierre Janssen (Waterschei)

3 goals: Simpson (Aberdeen), Breitner (Bayern München), Janjanin (Crvena Zvezda), Alesanco (FC Barcelona), Steinkogler (Austria Wien), Altobelli (Inter Milano), Toko (Paris St. Germain), Juanito (Real Madrid), Walsh (Swansea City), Crooks (Tottenham), Kiss (Újpesti Dózsa Budapest)

2 goals: Weir (Aberdeen), Jonker (AZ 67 Alkmaar), Madsen (B 93 København), M.Djurovski, D.Savić (Crvena Zvezda Beograd), Pilz, Trautmann (Dynamo Dresden), Mustafa Ergücü, Sejdić (Galatasaray), Okonski (Lech Poznan), Fernandez (Paris St. Germain), Curtis, Gale, Loveridge (Swansea City), Archibald (Tottenham), Berger, R.Janssen, Vliegen (Waterschei)

1 goal: Bregy (FC Sion), Milanov, Bogdanov (Lokomotiv Sofia), Hristodoulou (Apollon Limassol), Petrakov (Torpedo Moskva), Koller, Buzgău (FC Baia Mare), Anastasiadis,

CUP WINNERS' CUP 1983-84

PRELIMINARY ROUND

SWANSEA CITY v 1.FC MAGDEBURG 1-1 (0-0)
Vetch Field, Swansea   24.08.1983
Referee: Erik Fredriksson (SWE)   Attendance: 6,500
SWANSEA: James Rimmer, Neil Robinson, Christopher Marustik, Jeremy Charles, Nigel Stevenson, Dudley Lewis, Alan Curtis (80 Ian Walsh), Garry Stanley, Huw Lake, Raymond Kennedy, Robert Latchford (85 Darren Gale).
FC MAGDEBURG: Dirk Heyne, Detlef Raugust (75 Detlef Schössler), Dirk Stahmann, Axel Wittke, Gerald Cramer, Siegmund Mewes, Jürgen Pommerenke, Wolfgang Steinbach, Joachim Streich, Damian Halata, Frank Frank Cebulla. Trainer: Klaus Kreul
Goals: Walsh (80), Streich (88)

1.FC MAGDEBURG v SWANSEA CITY 1-0 (1-0)
Ernst-Grube-Stadion, Magdeburg   31.08.1983
Referee: Georges Konrath (FRA)   Attendance: 25,000
FC MAGDEBURG: Dirk Heyne, Detlef Raugust (46 Detlef Schössler), Dirk Stahmann, Axel Wittke, Gerald Cramer, Siegmund Mewes, Jürgen Pommerenke, Wolfgang Steinbach, Joachim Streich, Damian Halata, Frank Windelbrand (83 Martin Hoffmann).   Trainer: Klaus Kreul
SWANSEA: James Rimmer, Neil Robinson, Christopher Marustik, Jeremy Charles, Nigel Stevenson, Dudley Lewis, Alan Curtis, Garry Stanley, Ian Walsh, Raymond Kennedy, Robert Latchford (88 Darren Gale).
Goal: Pommerenke (24)

FIRST ROUND

JUVENTUS TORINO v LECHIA GDANSK 7-0 (4-0)
Stadio Comunale, Torino   14.09.1983
Referee: Raul Joaquín Fernandes Nazare (POR)   Att: 32,000
JUVENTUS: Stefano Tacconi, Claudio Gentile, Antonio Cabrini (35 Nicola Caricola), Massimo Bonini, Sergio Brio, Gaetano Scirea, Domenico Penzo, Marco Tardelli, Paolo Rossi, Michel Platini (60 Beniamino Vignola), Zbigniew Boniek. Trainer: Giovanni Trapattoni
LECHIA: Tadeusz Fajfer, Zbigniew Kowalski, Lech Kulwicki, Aleksander Cybulski (67 Andrzej Marchel), Andrzej Salach, Dariusz Wójtowicz, Maciej Kaminski, Marek Kowalczyk, Jacek Grembocki, Ryszard Polak (55 Krzysztof Górski), Jerzy Kruszczynski.   Trainer: Jerzy Jastrzebowski
Goals: Platini (18, 26), Penzo (24, 28, 60, 67), Rossi (75)

LECHIA GDANSK v JUVENTUS TORINO 2-3 (0-1)
Armia, Gdansk   28.09.1983
Referee: Keith S. Hackett (ENG)   Attendance: 35,000
LECHIA: Tadeusz Fajfer, Andrzej Marchel, Lech Kulwicki, Zbigniew Kowalski, Andrzej Salach, Dariusz Wójtowicz, Maciej Kaminski (87 Roman Józefowicz), Marek Kowalczyk, Jacek Grembocki, Ryszard Polak (65 Dariusz Raczynski), Jerzy Kruszczynski.   Trainer: Jerzy Jastrzebowski
JUVENTUS: Stefano Tacconi, Nicola Caricola, Antonio Cabrini (55 Roberto Tavola), Massimo Bonini, Sergio Brio, Gaetano Scirea, Domenico Penzo, Claudio Prandelli (67 Michel Platini), Paolo Rossi, Beniamino Vignola, Zbigniew Boniek.   Trainer: Giovanni Trapattoni
Goals: Vignola (17), Kowalczyk (50), Kruszczynski (65 pen), Tavola (77), Boniek (83)

PARALIMNI FAMAGUSTA v SK BEVEREN 2-4 (1-2)
Paralimni, Famagusta   14.09.1983
Referee: Lajos Nemeth (HUN)   Attendance: 3,000
PARALIMNI: Antonis Kleftis, Mihalis Goumenos, Giorgos Kezos, Mihalis Kafetzis, Andreas Kittos, Mihalis Kittos (66 Antonis Kalimeras), Kostas Tsierkezos, Giorgos Savva, Panagiotis Manoli (.. Mihalis Oikonomou), Dimitris Oikonomou "Koudas", Tasos Zouvanis.
BEVEREN: Filip de Wilde, Eddy Jaspers, Philippe Garot, Paul Lambrichts, Marc Baecke, Patrick Stalmans, Heinz Schönberger (85 Danny Pfaff), Paul Theunis, Peter Crève (52 Armin Görtz), Marek Marek Kusto, Erwin Albert.
Goals: Zouvanis (12), Schönberger (16), Garot (29), Kusto (53), Tsierkezos (59), Stalmans (84)

SK BEVEREN v PARALIMNI FAMAGUSTA 3-1 (3-0)
Freethiel, Beveren   28.09.1983
Referee: Norbert Risch (LUX)   Attendance: 4,700
BEVEREN: Filip de Wilde, Eddy Jaspers, Philippe Garot, Paul Lambrichts, Armin Görtz, Patrick Stalmans, Heinz Schönberger (46 Marek Kusto), Paul Theunis, Ronny Martens, Erwin Albert, Peter Crève.
PARALIMNI: Antonis Kleftis, Mihalis Goumenos, Giorgos Kezos, Mihalis Kafetzis, Andreas Kittos, Mihalis Kittos, Tasos Zouvanis, Giorgos Savva, Antonis Kalimeras, Dimitris Oikonomou "Koudas", Pierakis Markoulis (46 Mihalis Oikonomou).
Goals: Theunis (27), Lambrichts (29), Stalmans (36), Kalimeras (64)

DINAMO ZAGREB v FC PORTO 2-1 (1-0)
Maksimir, Zagreb   14.09.1983
Referee: Talal Tokat (TUR)   Attendance: 40,000
DINAMO: Marjan Vlak, Milivoj Bracun, Zvezdan Cvetković, Ismet Hadzić, Velimir Zajec, B.Bosnjak, Borislav Cvetković (46 Vasil Ringov), Snjesko Cerin (68 Srecko Bogdan), Zlatko Kranjcar, Marko Mlinarić, Stjepan Deverić.
FC PORTO: José Alberto Teixeira Ferreirinha "ZÉ BETO", JOÃO Domingos Silva PINTO, Augusto Soares INÁCIO, António José LIMA PEREIRA, EURICO Monteiro Gomes; RODOLFO Reis Fereira, António Manuel FRASCO Vieira, Joaquim José Ferreirinha Moreira "QUINITO" (46 JAIME Fernandes MAGALHAES), Fernando Mendes Soares GOMES, António Augusto Gomes de Silva "SOUSA" (68 José Alberto COSTA), JAIME Moreira PACHECO.
Trainer: António Morais

Goals: Kranjcar (25 pen, 85), Gomes (65)

FC PORTO v DINAMO ZAGREB 1-0 (0-0)
Estádio das Antas, Porto   28.09.1983
Referee: Robert Valentine (SCO)   Attendance: 50,000
FC PORTO: José Alberto Teixeira Ferreirinha "ZÉ BETO", JOÃO Domingos Silva PINTO (59 JAIME Fernandes MAGALHAES), António José LIMA PEREIRA, EURICO Monteiro Gomes, Augusto Soares INÁCIO; RODOLFO Reis Fereira (46 José Alberto COSTA), António Manuel FRASCO Vieira, Michael Walsh, Fernando Mendes Soares GOMES, António Augusto Gomes de Silva "SOUSA", JAIME Moreira PACHECO.   Trainer: António Morais
DINAMO: Marjan Vlak, Milivoj Bracun, Dragan Bosnjak, Ismet Hadzić, Velimir Zajec, Srecko Bogdan, Zvezdan Cvetković, B.Bosnjak, Zlatko Kranjcar, Marko Mlinarić, Borislav Cvetković (46 Edi Krncević).

Goal: Gomes (85)

MERSIN ID. YK v SPARTAK VARNA 0-0
Mersin   14.09.1983
Referee: Aleksandr Mushkovetz (USSR)   Attendance: 6,000
MERSIN: Arif, Kerim, B.Metin Koyunçu, Ismail, Nasir, Isa Ertürk, Mahmut, Suat Akdereli (60 Zafer Altindag), K.Levent Arkidogan, Zekeriya, Mehmet Ali (46 Memik).
SPARTAK: Krasimir Zafirov, Niazim Ismailov, Vladimir Nikolchev, Iordan Vladimirov, Sasho Borisov, Borislav Giorev, Krasimir Venkov, Jivko Gospodinov, Ivan Kazakov (81 Stefan Stefanov), Emil Lichev, Georgi Aleksiev.
Trainer: Liudmil Goranov

SPARTAK VARNA v MERSIN ID. YK 1-0 (0-0)
Yuri Gagarin, Varna   28.09.1983
Referee: Radu Petrescu (ROM)   Attendance: 22,500
SPARTAK: Krasimir Zafirov, Niazim Ismailov, Sasho Borisov, Vladimir Nikolchev, Asen Mihailov, Rumen Dimov, Krasimir Venkov (81 Stefan Stefanov), Borislav Giorev, Emil Lichev (76 Georgi Aleksiev), Jivko Gospodinov, Ivan Kazakov.
Trainer: Liudmil Goranov
MERSIN: Arif, Mustafa Cimen, Ismail, Mehmet Ali, Nasir, Suat Akdereli, Güngör Günay, Isa Ertürk, Zafer Altindag (75 Mohamed), Zekeriya, Mehmet.

Goal: Kazakov (61)

FC VALLETTA v GLASGOW RANGERS 0-8 (0-6)
Ta' Qali, Valletta   14.09.1983
Referee: Milorad Vlajić (YUG)   Attendance: 18,213
FC VALLETTA: Frank Grima, David Buckingham, Francis Grioli, Hili, Paul Curmi, Dennis Fenech, Emanuel Farrugia, Melchior Cremona, Leonard Farrugia, Emanuel Seychell, Micallef.
RANGERS: Peter McCloy, Alistair Dawson, John McClelland, David McPherson, Craig Paterson, David MacKinnon, Robert Prytz, Alistair McCoist (59 William Davies), Sandy Clark (46 Derek Ferguson), John McDonald, David Cooper.

Goals: Paterson (8), McPherson (17, 34, 42, 48), McDonald (36), Prytz (37, 59 pen)

GLASGOW RANGERS v FC VALLETTA 10-0 (5-0)
Ibrox Park, Glasgow   28.09.1983
Referee: Gudmundur Haraldsson (ICE)   Attendance: 12,000
RANGERS: James Stewart; Alistair Dawson, John McClelland, David McPherson, Craig Paterson (46 Derek Ferguson), Ian Redford, Robert Prytz (46 William Mackay), William Davies, David Mitchell, John McDonald, David Cooper.
FC VALLETTA: Frank Grima (58 Raymond Mifsud), David Buckingham, Francis Grioli, Hili, Paul Curmi, Dennis Fenech, Emanuel Farrugia, Melchior Cremona, Leonard Farrugia, Emanuel Seychell, Micallef (.. Salebi).

Goals: Mitchell (1, 10), McDonald (6, 36, 62 pen), Dawson (16), McKay (52), Davies (67), Redford (55, 90)

**AEK ATHINA
v ÚJPESTI DÓZSA BUDAPEST 2-0** (0-0)
Nikos Gkoumas, Athina 14.09.1983
Referee: Keith S. Hackett (ENG)   Attendance: 20,000

AEK: Hristos Arvanitis, Paulos Papaioannou, Vaggelis Paraprastanitis, Stelios Manolas, Dimitris Karagkiozopoulos; Trevor Ross, Giannis Dintsikos, Kostas Ballis (59 Haralampos Akrivopoulos), Manolis Kottis, Vaggelis Vlahos (57 Hristos Ardizoglou), Thomas Mauros.   Trainer: Barngouel

ÚJPESTI DÓZSA: József Szendrei; János Szűcs, József Kovács, József Kardos, József Tóth; Attila Herédi, László Ambrus (88 András Sarlós), András Szebegyinszki (72 László Fekete), Sándor Kisznyér; András Töröcsik, Sándor Kiss. Trainer: Miklós Temesvári

Goals: Kottis (65), Ross (88)

HAKA VALKEAKOSKI v SLIGO ROVERS 3-0 (0-0)
Tehtaankenttä, Valkeakoski 28.09.1983
Referee: A. Milchenko (USSR)   Attendance: 1,253

HAKA: Olavi Huttunen, Esko Ranta, Risto Salonen, Teuvo Vilen, Reijo Vuorinen, Pekka Heikkilä (.. Jouko Pirinen), Heikki Huoviala, Mark Dziadulewicz, Endre Kolár (.. Timo Lehtinen), Jarmo Kujanpää, Pertti Nissinen. Trainer: Vakkyla

SLIGO: Colin Oakley, Mick Ferry (.. John Skeffington), Enda Scanlon, Tony Stenson, Michael Savage, Tony Fagan, Martin McDonnell, Harry McLoughlin, Gus Gilligan
(.. Chris Rutherford), Paul McGee, Paul Fielding.

Goals: Nissinen (52), Huoviala (54), Dziadulewicz (77)

**ÚJPESTI DÓZSA BUDAPEST
v AEK ATHINA 4-1** (3-1)
Megyeri út, Budapest 28.09.1983
Referee: Dieter Pauly (W. GER)   Attendance: 8,000

ÚJPESTI DÓZSA: József Szendrei; János Szűcs, József Kovács, András Sarlós; László Ambrus (67 András Szebegyinszki), József Kardos, Sándor Kisznyér, József Tóth; Sándor Kiss, Sándor Steidl (89 Béla Kovács), László Fekete. Trainer: Miklós Temesvári

AEK: Hristos Arvanitis, Paulos Papaioannou (46 Petros Ravousis), Dimitris Karagkiozopoulos, Stelios Manolas, Lissandros Georgamlis; Kostas Ballis, Trevor Ross (63 Hristos Ardizoglou), Vaggelis Vlahos, Haralampos Akrivopoulos; Giannis Dintsikos, Thomas Mauros.   Trainer: Barngouel

Goals: Kisznyer (10), Kiss (13), Vlahos (17), Kardos (39 pen, 74 pen)

**B 1901 NYKØBING FALSTER
v SHAKHTER DONETSK 1-5** (0-3)
Idraetspark, Nykøbing 14.09.1983
Referee: Klaus Peschel (E. GER)   Attendance: 1,892

B 1901: Rønnebro, F. Larsen, Johnny Bøgvad, K. Kristensen, Schmidt, V. Larsen, Nielsen, Rasmussen, N. Kristensen, Per Jensen (76 Sørensen), Jørgensen.

SHAKHTER: Valentin Elinskas, Aleksei Varnavski, Aleksandr Sopko, Vladimir Parkhomenko (60 Igor Petrov), Sergei Pokidin, Valeri Rudakov, Sergei Yaschenko (79 Oleg Smolianinov), Mihail Sokolovski, Anatoli Radenko, Sergei Morozov, Viktor Grachyev.

Goals: Radenko (43), Morozov (25, 53), Grachyev (32, 72), Bøgvad (50 pen)

SLIGO ROVERS v HAKA VALKEAKOSKI 0-1 (0-1)
The Showgrounds, Sligo 14.09.1983
Referee: Cornelis A. Bakker (HOL)   Attendance: 3,000

SLIGO: Colin Oakley, Paul Fielding, Enda Scanlon, Tony Fagan, Chris Rutherford, Tony Stenson, Harry McLoughlin, Michael Savage, John Skeffington, Gus Gilligan, Martin McDonnell.

HAKA: Olavi Huttunen, Teuvo Vilen, Endre Kolár, Reijo Vuorinen, Pertti Nissinen, Heikki Huoviala, Jouko Pirinen, Pekka Heikkilä (.. Jarmo Kujanpää), Ari Valvee (.. Olli Laakso), Risto Salonen, Mark Dziadulewicz.   Trainer: Vakkyla

Goal: Valvee (29)

**SHAKHTER DONETSK
v B 1901 NYKØBING FALSTER 4-2** (2-1)
Shakhter, Donetsk 28.09.1983
Referee: Ahmed Yasharov (BUL)   Attendance: 28,600

SHAKHTER: Valentin Elinskas, Aleksei Varnavski, Aleksandr Sopko, Igor Simonov, Sergei Morozov, Valeri Rudakov, Sergei Yaschenko, Mihail Sokolovski, Igor Petrov
(52 Igor Yurchenko), Oleg Smolianinov, Viktor Grachyev.

B 1901: Rønnebro, M. Kristensen, Johnny Bøgvad, Schmidt, F. Larsen, Rasmussen, Nielsen (46 Petersen), B. Larsen, Per Jensen (60 Gotvald), P. Kristensen, Jørgensen.

Goals: Morozov (25, 83), Sokolovski (37 pen), Jensen (43), Grachyev (80), Bøgvad (75)

ÍA AKRANES v FC ABERDEEN 1-2 (1-2)

Laugardalsvöllur, Reykjavík   14.09.1983

Referee: Patrick A. Daly (IRE)   Attendance: 5,577

ÍA AKRANES: Bjarni Sigurdsson, Gudjón Thordarson, Jón Askelsson, Sigurdur Lárusson, Sigurdur Haldórsson, Hordur Kári Jóhannesson (79 Julius Petur Ingólfsson), Sveinbjörn Hakonarsson, Sigurdur Jónsson, Sigthór Omarsson, Gudbjörn Tryggvason, Arni Sveinsson.

ABERDEEN: James Leighton, Brian Mitchell, Douglas Rougvie, Neale Cooper (46 John McMaster), Alex McLeish, William Miller, William Stark (64 Steve Cowan), Neil Simpson, Mark McGhee, Douglas Bell, John Hewitt. Manager: Alex Ferguson

Goals: Halldorsson (28), McGhee (30, 38)

FC ABERDEEN v ÍA AKRANES 1-1 (0-0)

Pittodrie, Aberdeen   28.09.1983

Referee: Rolf Nyhus (NOR)   Att: 8,000

ABERDEEN: James Leighton, Neale Cooper, John McMaster, Neil Simpson, Alex McLeish, William Miller, Gordon Strachan, William Stark (72 Ian Porteous), Mark McGhee, John Hewitt, Peter Weir (38 Douglas Bell).   Manager: Alex Ferguson

ÍA AKRANES: Bjarni Sigurdsson, Gudjón Thordarson, Jón Askelsson, Sigurdur Lárusson, Sigurdur Haldórsson, Hordur Kári Johannesson (59 Julius Petur Ingólfsson), Sveinbjörn Hakonarsson, Sigurdur Jónsson, Sigthór Omarsson, Gudbjörn Tryggvason, Arni Sveinsson.

Goals: Strachan (68 pen), Askelsson (89 pen)

SSW INNSBRUCK v FC KÖLN 1-0 (0-0)

Tivoli, Innsbruck   14.09.1983

Referee: Dušan Krchnak (CZE)   Attendance: 15,500

SSW: Fuad Djulic, Johann Dihanich, Hugo Hovenkamp, Robert Auer, Josef Kleinbichler, Manfred Linzmaier, Wesly Schenk, Andreas Gretschnig, Alfred Roscher, Ewald Gröss, Gerhard Steinkogler.   Trainer: Heinz Binder

FC KOLN: Harald Schumacher, Mathias Hönerbach, Gerd Strack, Paul Steiner, Holger Willmer, Herbert Zimmermann, Andreas Gielchen (79 Frank Hartmann), Uwe Haas, Pierre Littbarski, Klaus Fischer, Klaus Allofs.   Trainer: Hannes Löhr

Goal: Gröss (71)

FC KÖLN v SSW INNSBRUCK 7-1 (4-1)

Müngersdorfer Stadion, Köln   28.09.1983

Referee: André Daina (SWI)   Attendance: 19,000

FC KÖLN: Harald Schumacher, Mathias Hönerbach, Gerd Strack (77 Herbert Zimmermann), Paul Steiner, Dieter Prestin, Hans-Werner Reif, Frank Hartmann (70 Andreas Gielchen), Uwe Haas, Pierre Littbarski, Klaus Fischer, Klaus Allofs.   Trainer: Hannes Löhr

SSW: Fuad Djulic, Johann Dihanich, Hugo Hovenkamp, Robert Auer, Josef Kleinbichler, Manfred Linzmaier, Roland Hattenberger (65 Robert Idl), Wesly Schenk (39 Gerhard Steinkogler), Andreas Gretschnig, Ewald Gröss, Alfred Roscher.   Trainer: Heinz Binder

Goals: Strack (13, 60), Allofs (15, 53), Fischer (26, 49), Gröss (31), Steiner (44)

1.FC MAGDEBURG v FC BARCELONA 1-5 (0-2)

Ernst-Grube-Stadion, Magdeburg   14.09.1983

Referee: Luigi Agnolin (ITA)   Attendance: 32,000

FC MAGDEBURG: Dirk Heyne, Detlef Schössler, Dirk Stahmann, Siegmund Mewes, Axel Wittke, Gerald Cramer, Jürgen Pommerenke, Wolfgang Steinbach, Damian Halata, Joachim Streich, Martin Hoffmann.   Trainer: Klaus Kreul

FC BARCELONA: Pedro María ARTOLA Urrutia, José Vicente SÁNCHEZ Felip, Bernardo Bianquetti Miguel "MIGUELI", José Ramón ALESANCO Ventosa, JULIO ALBERTO Moreno Casas, Miguel Ángel "PERICO" ALONSO Oyarbide, Bernd Schuster, VÍCTOR Muñoz Manrique, ESTEBAN Vigo Benítez, Diego Armando MARADONA, Francisco José CARRASCO Hidalgo (85 Enrique MORÁN Blanco).   Trainer: César Luis MENOTTI

Goals: Schuster (3), Maradona (14, 76, 79 pen), Pommerenke (58), M. Alonso (66)

FC BARCELONA v 1.FC MAGDEBURG 2-0 (1-0)

Camp Nou, Barcelona   28.09.1983

Referee: Bruno Galler (SWI)   Attendance: 17,800

FC BARCELONA: Pedro María ARTOLA Urrutia, José Vicente SÁNCHEZ Felip, Bernardo Bianquetti Miguel "MIGUELI", José Ramón ALESANCO Ventosa, JULIO ALBERTO Moreno Casas, VÍCTOR Muñoz Manrique, Miguel Ángel "PERICO" ALONSO Oyarbide, Bernd Schuster (46 URBANO Ortega Cuadros), ESTEBAN Vigo Benítez, Enrique Castro González "QUINI", Francisco José CARRASCO Hidalgo (56 Enrique MORÁN Blanco).   Trainer: César Luis MENOTTI

FC MAGDEBURG: Dirk Heyne, Detlef Schössler, Dirk Stahmann, Siegmund Mewes, Axel Wittke (46 Gerald Cramer), Jürgen Pommerenke, Wolfgang Steinbach, Rolf Döbbelin, Damian Halata (77 Martin Hoffmann), Joachim Streich, Frank Windelbrand.   Trainer: Klaus Kreul

Goals: Quini (32, 78)

**MANCHESTER UNITED
v DUKLA PRAHA 1-1** (0-0)

Old Trafford, Manchester 14.09.1983

Referee: Adolf Prokop (E. GER)   Attendance: 39,765

MANCHESTER UNITED: Gary Bailey, Michael Duxbury, Arthur Albiston, Raymond Wilkins, Kevin Moran, Gordon McQueen, Bryan Robson (80 John Gidman), Arnold Mühren (73 Remi Moses), Francis Stapleton, Lou Macari, Arthur Graham.   Manager: Ron Atkinson

DUKLA: Karel Stromšik, Aleš Bažant (78 Ivo Staš), Josef Novák, Jan Fiala, Petr Rada, Stanislav Pelc, Ladislav Vízek, Luboš Urban, Václav Daněk, Tomáš Kriz (75 Bohuš Viger), František Štambachr.   Trainer: Ladislav Novák

Goals: Kríz (60), Wilkins (89 pen)

AVENIR BEGGEN v SERVETTE GENÈVE 1-5 (0-2)

Beggen 27.09.1983

Referee: Louis Delsemme (BEL)   Attendance: 650

AVENIR: Jeannot Moes; Rolf Jentgen, Jean Paul Girres, Thill, Patrick Thiry, André, Nico Wagner, Gilbert Dresch, Fred Schreiner, Armin Krings, Aldo Catani (57 Mertes).

SERVETTE: Philippe De Choudens; Rainer Hasler, Jean-François Henry (46 Gilbert Castella), Alain Geiger, Michel Renquin, Marc Schnyder, Guy Dutoit, Umberto Barberis, Angelo Elia (46 Manuel Mattioli), Jean-Paul Brigger, Laurent Jaccard.   Trainer: Guy Mathez

Goals: Elia (33), Brigger (43, 72), Dresch (51), Castella (62), Geiger (89)

**DUKLA PRAHA
v MANCHESTER UNITED 2-2** (1-1)

Stadión na Juliske, Praha 27.09.1983

Referee: Heinz Fähnler (AUS)   Attendance: 25,000

DUKLA: Karel Stromšik; Aleš Bažant, Josef Novák, Jan Fiala, Petr Rada, Stanislav Pelc, Ladislav Vízek, Luboš Urban, Václav Daněk, Tomáš Kríz, František Štambachr.   Trainer: Ladislav Novák

MANCHESTER UNITED: Gary Bailey, Michael Duxbury, Arthur Albiston, Raymond Wilkins, Kevin Moran, Gordon McQueen, Bryan Robson, Arnold Mühren, Francis Stapleton, Norman Whiteside, Arthur Graham.   Manager: Ron Atkinson

Goals: Štambachr (11), Robson (33), Stapleton (79), Daněk (83)

NEC NIJMEGEN v BRANN BERGEN 1-1 (1-0)

Goffert-stadion, Nijmegen 14.09.1983

Referee: Ángel Franco Martínez (SPA)   Attendance: 5,000

NEC: Wim Van Cuyk, Toon Willemse, Dick Mulderij, Sije Visser, Piet Hubers, John Van Geenen (75 Carlos Aalbers), Michel Mommertz, John Vievermans, Henk Grim, Frans Janssen, Danny Hoekman (75 Ronny De Groot).   Trainer: Pim van de Meent

BRANN: Dan Riisnes, Hans Brandtun, Arne Møller, Tore Strand, Asgeir Kleppa, Terje Risa, Anders Giske (87 Jarle Råum), Finn Einar Krogh (61 Oyvind Pettersen), Pål Fjeldstad, Ingvar Dalhaug, Kjell Rune Pedersen.

Goals: Frans Janssen (42), Krogh (67)

SERVETTE GENÈVE v AVENIR BEGGEN 4-0 (1-0)

Stade des Charmilles, Genève 14.09.1983

Referee: Georges Konrath (FRA)   Attendance: 7,000

SERVETTE: Philippe De Choudens; Jean-François Henry, Alain Geiger, Michel Renquin, Rainer Hasler, Umberto Barberis, Marc Schnyder, Laurent Jaccard, Angelo Elia, Jean-Paul Brigger, Manuel Mattioli.   Trainer: Guy Mathez

AVENIR: Jeannot Moes (81 Paul Koch); Paul Phillip, Schröder, Patrick Thiry, Rolf Jentgen, Jean Paul Girres, Thill, Nico Wagner, Gilbert Dresch, Fred Schreiner (69 Aldo Catani), Armin Krings.

Goals: Schnyder (25), Brigger (52), Elia (55), Barberis (75)

BRANN BERGEN v NEC NIJMEGEN 0-1 (0-1)

Brann, Bergen 28.09.1983

Referee: Ales Jacobsen (DEN)   Attendance: 11,247

BRANN: Dan Riisnes, Hans Brandtun, Arne Møller, Tore Strand, Asgeir Kleppa, Terje Risa, Anders Giske (.. Jarle Råum), Finn Einar Krogh (.. Oyvind Pettersen), Pål Fjeldstad, Ingvar Dalhaug, Kjell Rune Pedersen.

NEC: Wim Van Cuyk, Toon Willemse, Eric Van Rossum, Dick Mulderij, Sije Visser, Carlos Aalbers, Michel Mommertz, Ronny De Groot, John Vievermans, Henk Grim, Frans Janssen.   Trainer: Pim van de Meent

Goal: Mommertz (24)

HAMMARBY IF v 17 NENTORI TIRANA 4-0 (2-0)
Söderstadion, Hammarby 14.09.1983
Referee: Hugh Alexander (SCO) Attendance: 7,034
HAMMARBY: Anders Forsberg, Sulo Vaattovaara, Sten-Ove Ramberg, Björn Hedenström (59 Thom Åhlund), Klas Johansson, Per Holmberg, Mats Wahlberg (44 Thomas Lundin), Michael Andersson, Jonnie Efraimsson, Kenneth Ohlsson, Peter Gerhardsson.
17 NENTORI: Cumaku (46 Bujar Sharra), Millan Baçi, Skender Hodja, Arjan Bimo, Bedri Omuri, Leonard Liti, Ali Mema, Mirel Josa, Shkëlqim Muça, Arben Vila, Arben Minga.
Goals: Ohlsson (18, 46), Wahlberg (39), Lundin (58)

PARIS ST.GERMAIN
v GLENTORAN BELFAST 2-1 (0-1)
Parc des Princes, Paris 28.09.1983
Referee: Vitor Manuel FERNANDES CORREIA (POR)
Attendance: 20,000
PARIS ST.GERMAIN: Dominique Baratelli; Yannick Guillochon, Jean-Marc Pilorget, Dominique Bathenay, Franck Tanasi, Manuel Abreu, Pascal Zaremba, Alain Couriol, Safet Susić, Michel N'Gom, Mustapha Dahleb (43 Dominique Rocheteau). Trainer: Lucien Leduc
GLENTORAN: Alan Paterson, George Neill, Paul Dixon, Robert Strain, Thomas Connell, James Cleary, Robert Bowers, Ron Manley (69 Gary Blackledge), John Jameson, Gerry Mullan (87 Raymond Morrison), David Neill.
Goals: Mullan (20), Bathenay (48 pen), Susić (76)

17 NENTORI TIRANA v HAMMARBY IF 2-1 (0-0)
Qemal Stafa, Tirana 28.09.1983
Referee: Gerasimos Germanakos (GRE) Att: 19,000
17 NENTORI: Halim Durimi, Skender Hodja, Millan Baçi, Artur Lekbello, Bedri Omuri, Leonard Liti, Ali Mema, Mirel Josa, Arben Vila, Arben Minga, Shkëlqim Muça.
HAMMARBY: Anders Forsberg, Sten-Ove Ramberg, Thom Åhlund, Björn Hedenström, Klas Johansson, Thomas Dennerby, Sulo Vaattovaara, Michael Andersson, Kenneth Ohlsson (65 Thomas Lundin), Jonnie Efraimsson (76 Jörgen Sandell), Peter Gerhardsson.
Goals: Vila (47), Efraimsson (53), Mema (64)

SECOND ROUND

ÚJPESTI DÓZSA BUDAPEST v FC KÖLN 3-1 (2-0)
Megyeri út, Budapest 19.10.1983
Referee: Gerald Losert (AUS) Attendance: 7,000
ÚJPESTI DOZSA: József Szendrei; István Kozma, József Kovács, András Sarlós, József Tóth; Sándor Steidl, Sándor Kardos, Sándor Kisznyér; Sándor Kiss, András Töröcsik, László Fekete. Trainer: Miklós Temesvári
FC KÖLN: Harald Schumacher; Dieter Prestin, Gerd Strack, Paul Steiner, Mathias Hönerbach (76 Holger Willmer); Frank Hartmann, Hans-Werner Reif, Uwe Haas (54 Herbert Zimmermann); Pierre Littbarski, Klaus Fischer, Klaus Allofs. Trainer: Hannes Löhr
Goals: Kiss (38, 63), Kisznyér (43), Steiner (75)

GLENTORAN BELFAST
v PARIS ST.GERMAIN 1-2 (0-0)
The Oval, Belfast 14.09.1983
Referee: Alphonse Constantin (BEL) Attendance: 4,750
GLENTORAN: Alan Paterson, George Neill, Paul Dixon, Robert Strain, Thomas Connell, James Cleary, Robert Bowers, David Neill, John Jameson, Gary Blackledge (55 Gerry Mullan), Ron Manley.
PARIS ST.GERMAIN: Dominique Baratelli; Yannick Guillochon, Jean-Marc Pilorget, Dominique Bathenay, Franck Tanasi, Luis Fernandez, Pascal Zaremba, Mustapha Dahleb (46 Gérard Janvion), Alain Couriol, Safet Susić, Michel N'Gom. Trainer: Lucien Leduc
Goals: Jameson (75), Zaremba (78), N'Gom (84)

FC KÖLN v ÚJPESTI DÓZSA BUDAPEST 4-2 (2-1)
Müngersdorfer Stadion, Köln 2.11.1983
Referee: Svein Inge Thime (NOR) Attendance: 45,000
FC KÖLN: Harald Schumacher; Dieter Prestin, Gerd Strack, Paul Steiner, Mathias Hönerbach; Frank Hartmann, Uwe Haas (74 Holger Willmer), Stephan Engels; Pierre Littbarski, Klaus Fischer, Klaus Allofs. Trainer: Hannes Löhr
ÚJPESTI DOZSA: József Szendrei; István Kozma, József Kovács, András Sarlós, József Tóth; Sándor Steidl (86 András Szebegyinszki), József Kardos, Sándor Kisznyér; Sándor Kiss, András Töröcsik, László Fekete. Trainer: Miklós Temesvári
Goals: Strack (8 og, 17), Littbarski (43), K. Allofs (47, 88), Fekete (69)

SK BEVEREN v ABERDEEN FC 0-0
Freethiel, Beveren   19.10.1983

Referee: Dušan Krchnak (CZE)   Attendance: 17,100

SK BEVEREN: Filip de Wilde, Eddy Jaspers, Danny Pfaff, Paul Lambrichts, Marc Baecke, Patrick Stalmans (46 Armin Görtz), Heinz Schönberger, Erwin Albert, Paul Theunis, Ronny Martens, Peter Crève.

ABERDEEN: James Leighton, Douglas Rougvie, John McMaster, Neale Cooper, Alex McLeish, William Miller, John Hewitt, Neil Simpson, Mark McGhee, Douglas Bell (71 Gordon Strachan), Peter Weir.   Manager: Alex Ferguson

HAKA VALKEAKOSKI
v HAMMARBY IF 2-1 (1-1, 1-1) (AET)
Tehtaankenttä, Valkeakoski   2.11.1983

Referee: Aleksander Suchanek (POL)   Attendance: 3,891

HAKA: Olavi Huttunen, Teuvo Vilen, Risto Salonen, Reijo Vuorinen, Esko Ranta, Heikki Huoviala, Pertti Nissinen, Endre Kolár (102 Mikko Pakkanen), Timo Lehtinen (87 Petter Setälä), Jarmo Kujanpää, Ari Valvee.   Trainer: Vakkyla

HAMMARBY: Anders Markström, Thom Åhlund (93 Jörgen Sandell), Sten-Ove Ramberg, Björn Hederström, Klas Johansson, Thomas Dennerby, Per Holmberg, Michael Andersson, Jonnie Efraimsson (60 Billy Ohlsson), Kenneth Ohlsson, Peter Gerhardsson.

Goals: Holmberg (3), Nissinen (40), Kujanpää (109)

ABERDEEN FC v SK BEVEREN 4-1 (2-0)
Pittodrie, Aberdeen   2.11.1983

Referee: Henning Lund Sørensen (DEN)   Att: 24,500

ABERDEEN: James Leighton, Neale Cooper, Douglas Rougvie, Neil Simpson (77 Ian Angus), Alex McLeish, William Miller, Gordon Strachan, John Hewitt, Mark McGhee, Douglas Bell, Peter Weir (70 Eric Black).   Manager: Alex Ferguson

SK BEVEREN: Filip de Wilde, Eddy Jaspers, Philippe Garot, Paul Lambrichts, Marc Baecke, Danny Pfaff (67 Peter Crève), Heinz Schönberger, Erwin Albert, Paul Theunis, Ronny Martens, Marek Kusto (72 Patrick Stalmans).

Goals: Strachan (38 pen, 60), Simpson (44), Weir (69), Theunis (73)

SHAKHTER DONETSK
v SERVETTE GENÈVE 1-0 (0-0)
Shakhter, Donetsk   19.10.1983

Referee: Arto Ravander (FIN)   Attendance: 37,450

SHAKHTER: Valentin Elinskas; Anatoli Radenko, Valeri Rudakov, Aleksandr Sopko, Sergei Pokidin, Sergei Yaschenko, Mihail Sokolovski (63 Igor Petrov), Vladimir Parkhomenko, Igor Yurchenko, Sergei Morozov (35 Oleg Smolianinov), Viktor Grachyev.

SERVETTE: Philippe De Choudens; Rainer Hasler, Alain Geiger, Jean-François Henry, Pascal Cacciapaglia, Marc Schnyder, Michel Renquin, Umberto Barberis, Guy Dutoit, Laurent Jaccard (80 Angelo Elia), Jean-Paul Brigger.   Trainer: Guy Mathez

Goal: Grachyev (85)

HAMMARBY IF v HAKA VALKEAKOSKI 1-1 (0-1)
Söderstadion, Hammarby   19.10.1983

Referee: Egstein Gudmundsson (ICE)   Attendance: 5,995

HAMMARBY: Anders Markström, Per Holmberg, Sten-Ove Ramberg, Björn Hederström, Klas Johansson, Thomas Dennerby, Kenneth Ohlsson, Michael Andersson, Thomas Lundin (66 Billy Ohlsson), Jonnie Efraimsson, Peter Gerhardsson.

HAKA: Olavi Huttunen, Teuvo Vilen, Risto Salonen, Reijo Vuorinen, Esko Ranta, Jouko Pirinen, Endre Kolár (70 Pekka Heikkilä), Heikki Huoviala, Timo Lehtinen, Pertti Nissinen (78 Ari Valvee), Jarmo Kujanpää.   Trainer: Vakkyla

Goals: Kujanpää (33), Billy Ohlsson (75)

SERVETTE GENÈVE
v SHAKHTER DONETSK 1-2 (0-0)
Stade des Charmilles, Genève   1.11.1983

Referee: Alder Dante Silva dos Santos (POR)   Att: 16,000

SERVETTE: Erich Burgener; Rainer Hasler, Alain Geiger, Jean-François Henry, Guy Dutoit, Marc Schnyder (80 Alain Walder), Michel Renquin, Umberto Barberis, Laurent Jaccard, Angelo Elia, Jean-Paul Brigger.   Trainer: Guy Mathez

SHAKHTER: Valentin Elinskas; Vladimir Parkhomenko, Valeri Rudakov, Aleksandr Sopko, Sergei Pokidin, Aleksei Varnavski, Mihail Sokolovski (81 Anatoli Radenko), Sergei Yaschenko (60 Oleg Smolianinov), Igor Yurchenko, Viktor Grachyev, Sergei Morozov.

Goals: Varnavski (58, 61), Brigger (88)

**PARIS ST.GERMAIN
v JUVENTUS TORINO 2-2** (1-0)
Parc des Princes, Paris   19.10.1983
Referee: Vojtěch Christov (CZE)   Attendance: 48,776
PARIS ST.GERMAIN: Dominique Baratelli; Yannick Guillochon, Jean-Marc Pilorget, Dominique Bathenay (50 Mustapha Dahleb), Franck Tanasi, Pascal Zaremba, Manuel Abreu (65 Michel N'Gom), Luis Fernandez, Alain Couriol, Dominique Rocheteau, Safet Sušić.   Trainer: Lucien Leduc
JUVENTUS: Stefano Tacconi, Claudio Gentile, Sergio Brio, Gaetano Scirea, Antonio Cabrini, Nicola Caricola, Marco Tardelli, Michel Platini, Zbigniew Boniek, Domenico Penzo, Paolo Rossi (75 Massimo Bonini).
Trainer: Giovanni Trapattoni
Goals: Couriol (39), Boniek (62), Cabrini (76), N'Gom (90)

JUVENTUS TORINO v PARIS ST.GERMAIN 0-0
Stadio Comunale, Torino   2.11.1983
Referee: Volker Roth (W. GER)   Attendance: 53,610
JUVENTUS: Stefano Tacconi, Claudio Gentile, Antonio Cabrini, Massimo Bonini, Sergio Brio, Gaetano Scirea, Domenico Penzo, Marco Tardelli (63 Beniamino Vignola), Paolo Rossi, Michel Platini (57 Nicola Caricola), Zbigniew Boniek.   Trainer: Giovanni Trapattoni
PARIS SG: Dominique Baratelli; Manuel Abreu (46 Salah Assad), Franck Tanasi, Jean-Marc Pilorget, Pascal Zaremba (79 Mustapha Dahleb), Luis Fernandez, Alain Couriol, Gérard Janvion, Dominique Rocheteau, Safet Sušić, Michel N'Gom.
Trainer: Lucien Leduc

NEC NIJMEGEN v FC BARCELONA 2-3 (2-1)
Goffert-stadion, Nijmegen   19.10.1983
Referee: Heinz Fahnler (AUS)   Attendance: 28,200
NEC: Wim van Cuyk, Toon Willemse, Dick Mulderij, Eric van Rossum, Sije Visser, Carlos Aalbers, Ronny de Groot, Frans Janssen, Michel Mommertz, Henk Grim, Anton Janssen (59 John Vievermans).   Trainer: Pim van de Meent
FC BARCELONA: Francisco Javier González URRUTIcoechea, José Vicente SÁNCHEZ Felip, José Ramón ALESANCO Ventosa, Bernardo Bianquetti Miguel "MIGUELI", VÍCTOR Muñoz Manrique, Ángel "PICHI" ALONSO Herrera, JULIO ALBERTO Moreno Casas, ESTEBAN Vigo Benítez, URBANO Ortega Cuadros, MARCOS Alonso Peña (59 José MORATALLA Claramunt), Francisco José CARRASCO Hidalgo (73 Juan Carlos Pérez ROJO).
Trainer: César Luis MENOTTI
Sent off: Migueli (56)
Goals: A. Janssen (5), Mommertz (44), Migueli (45), Van Rossum (55 og), Urbano (70).

FC BARCELONA v NEC NIJMEGEN 2-0 (2-0)
Camp Nou, Barcelona   2.11.1983
Referee: Károly Palotai (HUN)   Attendance: 16,500
FC BARCELONA: Pedro María ARTOLA Urrutia, José Vicente SÁNCHEZ Felip, José Ramón ALESANCO Ventosa, José MORATALLA Claramunt, José Manuel Martínez Toral "MANOLO", Miguel Ángel "PERICO" ALONSO Oyarbide, URBANO Ortega Cuadros, VÍCTOR Muñoz Manrique (46 Juan Carlos Pérez ROJO), Francisco Javier CLOS Orozco, Ángel "PICHI" ALONSO Herrera, Francisco José CARRASCO Hidalgo (46 Enrique MORÁN Blanco).
Trainer: César Luis MENOTTI
NEC: Ben Klein Goldewijk, Toon Willemse, Dick Mulderij, Peter Selbach, Sije Visser, Carlos Aalbers, Ronny De Groot, John Vievermans (80 Michel Mommertz), Frans Janssen, John van Geenen (46 Danny Hoekman), Henk Grim.
Trainer: Pim van de Meent
Goals: M. Alonso (3), Clos (43)

GLASGOW RANGERS v FC PORTO 2-1 (1-0)
Ibrox, Glasgow   19.10.1983
Referee: Siegfried Kirschen (E. GER)   Attendance: 35,000
RANGERS: Peter McCloy, Alistair Dawson, Craig Paterson, David McPherson, John McClelland, Robert Russell, Robert Prytz (78 John McDonald), Ian Redford, Alistair McCoist, Sandy Clark, David Cooper (78 David Mitchell).
FC PORTO: José Alberto Teixeira Ferreirinha "ZÉ BETO", JOÃO Domingos Silva PINTO, António José LIMA PEREIRA, EURICO Monteiro Gomes, Augusto Soares INÁCIO; António Manuel FRASCO Vieira, RODOLFO Reis Fereira, JAIME Moreira PACHECO (75 JACQUES Pereira), José Alberto COSTA, Fernando Mendes Soares GOMES, Michael Walsh (46 JAIME Fernandes MAGALHAES).   Trainer: António Morais
Goals: Clark (35), Mitchell (84), Jacques (86)

FC PORTO v GLASGOW RANGERS 1-0 (0-0)
Estádio das Antas, Porto   2.11.1983
Referee: Pietro D'Elia (ITA)   Attendance: 60,000
FC PORTO: José Alberto Teixeira Ferreirinha "ZÉ BETO", JOÃO Domingos Silva PINTO, António José LIMA PEREIRA, EURICO Monteiro Gomes, Augusto Soares INÁCIO; RODOLFO Reis Fereira (46 António Augusto Gomes de Silva "SOUSA"), António Manuel FRASCO Vieira, JAIME Moreira PACHECO, José Alberto COSTA (46 JAIME Fernandes MAGALHAES); Fernando Mendes Soares GOMES, Michael Walsh.   Trainer: António Morais
RANGERS: Peter McCloy, David MacKinnon, Alistair Dawson, John McClelland, Craig Paterson, Robert Prytz (80 Alistair McCoist), Robert Russell, Ian Redford, David Cooper, Sandy Clark (77 David Mitchell), David McPherson.
Goals: Gomes (52)

SPARTAK VARNA
v MANCHESTER UNITED 1-2 (1-1)
Yuri Gagarin, Varna   19.10.1983
Referee: Walter Eschweiller (W. GER)   Attendance: 37,500

SPARTAK: Krasimir Zafirov, Niazim Ismailov, Sasho Borisov, Vladimir Nikolchev, Asen Mihailov, Rumen Dimov, Krasimir Venkov, Borislav Giorev, Emil Lichev, Jivko Gospodinov, Georgi Aleksiev (69 Ivan Kazakov).
Trainer: Liudmil Goranov

MANCHESTER UNITED: Gary Bailey, Michael Duxbury, Arthur Albiston, Raymond Wilkins, Kevin Moran, Gordon McQueen, Bryan Robson, Arnold Mühren, Francis Stapleton, Norman Whiteside, Arthur Graham.   Manager: Ron Atkinson

Goals: Robson (9), Dimov (11), Graham (48)

MANCHESTER UNITED
v SPARTAK VARNA 2-0 (2-0)
Old Trafford, Manchester   2.11.1983
Referee: Ulf Eriksson (SWE)   Attendance: 39,079

MANCHESTER UNITED: Gary Bailey, Michael Duxbury, Arthur Albiston, Remi Moses, Kevin Moran (55 Mark Dempsey), Gordon McQueen, Bryan Robson, Lou Macari, Francis Stapleton, Norman Whiteside (78 Mark Hughes), Arthur Graham.   Manager: Ron Atkinson

SPARTAK: Krasimir Zafirov, Niazim Ismailov, Sasho Borisov, Vladimir Nikolchev (60 Krasimir Venkov), Asen Mihailov, Rumen Dimov, Radi Radomirov, Borislav Giorev, Emil Lichev, Jivko Gospodinov (70 Georgi Aleksiev), Stefan Naidenov.
Trainer: Liudmil Goranov

Goals: Stapleton (1, 31)

QUARTER-FINALS

FC BARCELONA
v MANCHESTER UNITED 2-0 (1-0)
Estadio Camp Nou, Barcelona   7.03.1984
Referee: Michel Vautrot (FRA)   Attendance: 94,000

FC BARCELONA: Francisco Javier González URRUTIcoechea, GERARDO Miranda Concepción, José MORATALLA Claramunt, JULIO ALBERTO Moreno Casas, Juan Carlos Pérez ROJO, José Ramón ALESANCO Ventosa, Francisco José CARRASCO Hidalgo (71 Ángel "PICHI" ALONSO Herrera), Bernd Schuster, VÍCTOR Muñoz Manrique, Diego Armando MARADONA (71 Francisco Javier CLOS Orozco), MARCOS Alonso Peña.
Trainer: César Luis MENOTTI

MANCHESTER UNITED: Gary Bailey, Michael Duxbury, Arthur Albiston, Raymond Wilkins, Kevin Moran, Graeme Hogg, Bryan Robson, Arnold Mühren, Francis Stapleton, Mark Hughes (77 Arthur Graham), Remi Moses.
Manager: Ron Atkinson

Goals: Hogg (33 og), Rojo (89)

MANCHESTER UNITED
v FC BARCELONA 3-0 (1-0)
Old Trafford, Manchester   21.03.1984
Referee: Paolo Casarin (ITA)   Attendance: 58,350

MANCHESTER UNITED: Gary Bailey, Michael Duxbury, Arthur Albiston, Raymond Wilkins, Kevin Moran, Graeme Hogg, Bryan Robson, Arnold Mühren, Francis Stapleton, Norman Whiteside (70 Mark Hughes), Remi Moses.
Manager: Ron Atkinson

FC BARCELONA: Francisco Javier González URRUTIcoechea, GERARDO Miranda Concepción, José MORATALLA Claramunt, JULIO ALBERTO Moreno Casas, VÍCTOR Muñoz Manrique, José Ramón ALESANCO Ventosa, Miguel Ángel "PERICO" ALONSO Oyarbide (58 Francisco Javier CLOS Orozco), Bernd Schuster, Juan Carlos Pérez ROJO, Diego Armando MARADONA, MARCOS Alonso Peña.
Trainer: César Luis MENOTTI

Goals: Robson (23, 50), Stapleton (53)

FC PORTO v SHAKHTER DONETSK 3-2 (1-2)
Estádio das Antas, Porto   7.03.1984
Referee: John Carpenter (IRE)   Attendance: 62,500

FC PORTO: José Alberto Teixeira Ferreirinha "ZÉ BETO", JOÃO Domingos Silva PINTO, EURICO Monteiro Gomes, Manuel Fernando Silva Teixeira TEIXEIRINHA (28 JAIME Fernandes MAGALHAES), EDUARDO LUÍS Marques Kruss Gomes; Carlos Manuel Oliveiros Silva "VERMELHINHO", António Manuel FRASCO Vieira, António Augusto Gomes de Silva "SOUSA", Michael Walsh, JAIME Moreira PACHECO, José Alberto COSTA (34 JACQUES Pereira).
Trainer: António Morais

SHAKHTER: Valentin Elinskas, Igor Yurchenko (55 Anatoli Radenko, 66 Oleg Smolianinov), Sergei Kravchenko, Valeri Goschkoderia, Aleksei Varnavski, Mihail Sokolovski, Vladimir Parkhomenko, Sergei Pokidin, Viktor Grachyev, Sergei Morozov, Sergei Yaschenko.

Goals: Morozov (6), Sokolovski (37), Pacheco (41 pen), Frasco (47), Jacques (70)

SHAKHTER DONETSK v FC PORTO 1-1 (0-0)
Shakhter, Donetsk   21.03.1984
Referee: Franz Wöhrer (AUS)   Attendance: 40,000
SHAKHTER: Valentin Elinskas, Aleksei Varnavski, Valeri Goschkoderia, Anatoli Radenko, Vladimir Parkhomenko, Valeri Rudakov (58 Igor Petrov), Igor Yurchenko (82 Sergei Pokidin), Mihail Sokolovski, Sergei Kravchenko, Viktor Grachyev, Sergei Yaschenko.

FC PORTO: José Alberto Teixeira Ferreirinha "ZÉ BETO"; JOÃO Domingos Silva PINTO, EDUARDO LUÍS Marques Kruss Gomes, António José LIMA PEREIRA, EURICO Monteiro Gomes; JAIME Fernandes MAGALHAES, RODOLFO Reis Fereira (67 Michael Walsh), António Augusto Gomes de Silva "SOUSA", Fernando Mendes Soares GOMES (89 Augusto Soares INÁCIO), JAIME Moreira PACHECO, Carlos Manuel Oliveiros Silva "VERMELHINHO". Trainer: António Morais

Goals: Grachyev (63), Walsh (72)

HAKA VALKEAKOSKI
v JUVENTUS TORINO 0-1 (0-0)
Stade Meinau, Strasbourg   7.03.1984
Referee: Ib Nielsen (DEN)   Attendance: 19,000
HAKA: Olavi Huttunen, Teuvo Vilen, Timo Lehtinen (53 Petter Setälä), Risto Salonen, Esko Ranta, Endre Kolár, Heikki Leinonen (70 Mikko Pakkanen), Pertti Nissinen, Reijo Vuorinen, Jarmo Kujanpää, Ari Valvee.   Trainer: Vakkyla

JUVENTUS: Stefano Tacconi, Gaetano Scirea, Claudio Gentile, Sergio Brio, Antonio Cabrini, Massimo Bonini, Marco Tardelli, Michel Platini, Domenico Penzo (53 Beniamino Vignola), Paolo Rossi, Zbigniew Boniek.
Trainer: Giovanni Trapattoni

Goal: Vignola (90)

JUVENTUS TORINO
v HAKA VALKEAKOSKI 1-0 (1-0)
Stadio Comunale, Torino   21.03.1984
Referee: Ioan Igna (ROM)   Attendance: 22,135
JUVENTUS: Stefano Tacconi, Claudio Gentile, Antonio Cabrini, Massimo Bonini, Sergio Brio, Gaetano Scirea, Domenico Penzo, Marco Tardelli (74 Claudio Prandelli), Paolo Rossi, Beniamino Vignola, Zbigniew Boniek (81 Roberto Tavola).   Trainer: Giovanni Trapattoni

HAKA: Olavi Huttunen, Teuvo Vilen, Timo Lehtinen (70 Petter Setälä), Reijo Vuorinen, Esko Ranta, Endre Kolár, Pertti Nissinen, Heikki Huoviala (84 Mikko Pakkanen), Ari Valvee, Risto Salonen, Jarmo Kujanpää.   Trainer: Vakkyla

Goal: Tardelli (15)

ÚJPESTI DOZSA BUDAPEST
v ABERDEEN FC 2-0 (0-0)
Megyeri út, Budapest   7.03.1984
Referee: Talal Tokat (TUR)   Attendance: 30,000
ÚJPESTI DOZSA: József Szendrei; Béla Kovács, József Kovács, József Tóth; Sándor Steidl, Attila Herédi, József Kardos, Sándor Kisznyér; Sándor Kiss, András Töröcsik, László Fekete.   Trainer: Miklós Temesvári

ABERDEEN: James Leighton, Stewart McKimmie, William Miller, Alex McLeish, Douglas Rougvie; Gordon Strachan (80 Neil Simpson), Douglas Bell, Neale Cooper, Ian Angus; Mark McGhee, Eric Black (80 John Hewitt).
Manager: Alex Ferguson

Goals: Kisznyér (49), Herédi (78).

ABERDEEN FC
v ÚJPESTI DÓZSA BUDAPEST 3-0 (1-0, 2-0) (AET)
Pittodrie, Aberdeen   21.03.1984
Referee: Alexis Ponnet (BEL)   Attendance: 22,800
ABERDEEN: James Leighton, Neale Cooper, William Miller, Alex McLeish, Stewart McKimmie; Gordon Strachan, Neil Simpson, Douglas Bell (82 Ian Angus); Eric Black, Mark McGhee, John Hewitt (78 William Falconer).
Manager: Alex Ferguson

ÚJPESTI DOZSA: József Szendrei; Béla Kovács, József Kovács, József Kardos, József Tóth; Sándor Steidl, Attila Herédi, András Töröcsik, Sándor Kisznyér; Sándor Kiss, László Fekete (46 László Bodnár, 69 András Szebegyinszki). Trainer: Miklós Temesvári

Goals: McGhee (38, 85, 94)

SEMI-FINALS

MANCHESTER UNITED
v JUVENTUS TORINO 1-1 (1-1)
Old Trafford, Manchester   11.04.1984
Referee: Jan N.I. Keizer (HOL)   Attendance: 58,231
MANCHESTER UNITED: Gary Bailey, Michael Duxbury, Arthur Albiston, Kevin Moran, Graeme Hogg, Paul McGrath, Arthur Graham, Remi Moses, Francis Stapleton, Norman Whiteside, John Gidman (10 Alan Davies).
Trainer: Ron Atkinson

JUVENTUS: Stefano Tacconi, Gaetano Scirea, Claudio Gentile, Sergio Brio, Antonio Cabrini, Massimo Bonini, Claudio Prandelli, Zbigniew Boniek, Michel Platini, Marco Tardelli, Paolo Rossi.   Trainer: Giovanni Trapattoni

Goals: Rossi (14), Davies (35)

**JUVENTUS TORINO
v MANCHESTER UNITED 2-1** (1-0)

Stadio Comunale, Torino   25.04.1984

Referee: Alexis Ponnet (BEL)   Attendance: 54,555

JUVENTUS: Stefano Tacconi, Gaetano Scirea, Claudio Gentile, Sergio Brio, Antonio Cabrini, Massimo Bonini, Beniamino Vignola, Marco Tardelli (78 Claudio Prandelli), Michel Platini, Paolo Rossi, Zbigniew Boniek.
Trainer: Giovanni Trapattoni

MANCHESTER UNITED: Gary Bailey, Michael Duxbury, Arthur Albiston, Raymond Wilkins, Kevin Moran, Graeme Hogg, Paul McGrath, Remi Moses, Francis Stapleton (63 Norman Whiteside), Mark Hughes, Arthur Graham.
Trainer: Ron Atkinson

Goals: Boniek (13), Whiteside (70), Rossi (90)

FC PORTO v FC ABERDEEN 1-0 (1-0)

Estádio das Antas, Porto   11.04.1984

Referee: Ioan Igna (ROM)   Attendance: 62,500

FC PORTO: José Alberto Teixeira Ferreirinha "ZÉ BETO"; JOÃO Domingos Silva PINTO, Augusto Soares INÁCIO, António José LIMA PEREIRA, EDUARDO LUÍS Marques Kruss Gomes; JAIME Fernandes MAGALHAES, António Manuel FRASCO Vieira (74 Michael Walsh), António Augusto Gomes de Silva "SOUSA", Fernando Mendes Soares GOMES, JAIME Moreira PACHECO, José Alberto COSTA (82 Carlos Manuel Oliveiros Silva "VERMELHINHO").
Trainer: António Morais

ABERDEEN: James Leighton, Stewart McKimmie, Douglas Rougvie (77 Brian Mitchell), Neale Cooper, Alex McLeish, William Miller, Gordon Strachan, Eric Black, Mark McGhee, Neil Simpson, Douglas Bell (46 John Hewitt).
Manager: Alex Ferguson

Goal: Gomes (14)

FC ABERDEEN v FC PORTO 0-1 (0-0)

Pittodrie, Aberdeen   25.04.1984

Referee: Dušan Krchnak (CZE)   Attendance: 23,500

ABERDEEN: James Leighton, Stewart McKimmie (.. Neale Cooper), Douglas Rougvie, Neil Simpson, Alex McLeish, William Miller, Gordon Strachan, Eric Black, Mark McGhee, Douglas Bell, John Hewitt (65 Peter Weir).
Manager: Alex Ferguson

FC PORTO: José Alberto Teixeira Ferreirinha "ZÉ BETO"; JOÃO Domingos Silva PINTO, EDUARDO LUÍS Marques Kruss Gomes, António José LIMA PEREIRA, EURICO Monteiro Gomes; JAIME Fernandes MAGALHAES (69 José Alberto COSTA), António Manuel FRASCO Vieira (85 Joaquim José Ferreirinha Moreira "QUINITO"), António Augusto Gomes de Silva "SOUSA", Fernando Mendes Soares GOMES, JAIME Moreira PACHECO, Carlos Manuel Oliveiros Silva "VERMELHINHO".   Trainer: António Morais

Goal: Vermelhinho (76)

FINAL

JUVENTUS TORINO v FC PORTO 2-1 (2-1)

Sankt Jakob stadion, Basel   16.05.1984

Referee: Adolf Prokop (E. GER)   Attendance: 55,000

JUVENTUS: Stefano Tacconi, Gaetano Scirea, Claudio Gentile, Sergio Brio, Antonio Cabrini, Marco Tardelli, Massimo Bonini, Michel Platini, Beniamino Vignola (89 Nicola Caricola), Zbigniew Kazimierz Boniek, Paolo Rossi.
Trainer: Giovanni Trapattoni

FC PORTO: José Alberto Teixeira Ferreirinha "ZÉ BETO", EURICO Monteiro Gomes, António José LIMA PEREIRA, EDUARDO LUÍS Marques Kruss Gomes (82 José Alberto COSTA), JOÃO Domingos Silva PINTO, António Manuel FRASCO Vieira, JAIME Moreira PACHECO, António Augusto Gomes de Silva "SOUSA", JAIME Fernandes MAGALHAES (65 Michael Walsh), Fernando Mendes Soares GOMES, Carlos Manuel Oliveiros Silva "VERMELHINHO".
Trainer: António Morais

Goals: Vignola (13), Sousa (28), Boniek (41)

Goalscorers European Cup-Winners' Cup 1983-84:

5 goals: Mark McGhee (Aberdeen), Viktor Grachyev, Sergei Morozov (Shahtior Donetsk)

4 goals: Klaus Allofs (FC Köln), Fernando Gomes (FC Porto), John MacDonald, David McPherson (Glasgow Rangers), Zbigniew Boniek, Domenico Penzo (Juventus Torino), Bryan Robson, Stapleton (Manchester United), Jean Paul Brigger (Servette Genève)

3 goals: Strack (FC Köln), Strachan (Aberdeen), Maradona (FC Barcelona), Mitchell (Glasgow Rangers), Rossi, Vignola (Juventus Torino), Kiss, Kisznyér (Újpesti Dózsa)

2 goals: Kranjčar (Dinamo Zagreb), Bøgvad (B 1901 Nyköbing), Gröss (SSW Innsbruck), Pommerenke (FC Magdeburg), Stalmans, Theunis (Beveren), Fischer, Steiner (FC Köln), Alonso, Quini (FC Barcelona), Jacques (FC Porto), Elia (Servette Genève), N'Gom (Paris St Germain), Mommertz (NEC Nijmegen), Redford, Prytz (Glasgow Rangers), Kujanpää, Nissinen (Haka Valkeakoski), Sokolovski, Varnavski (Shahtior Donetsk), K.Ohlsson (Hammarby IF), Platini (Juventus Torino), Kardos (Újpesti Dózsa)

1 goal: Walsh (Swansea City), Kowalczyk, Kruszczynski (Lechia Gdansk), Zouvanis, Tsierkezos, Kalimeras (Paralimni Famagusta), Kottis, Ross, Vlahos (AEK Athina), Jensen (B 1901 Nyköbing), Askelsson, Halldorsson (ÍA Akranes), Streich (FC Magdeburg), Kríz, Štambachr, Daněk (Dukla Praha), Dresch (Avenir Beggen), Krogh (Brann Bergen), Vila, Mema (17 Nentori Tirana), Jameson, Mullan (Glentoran Belfast), Lambrichts, Schönberger, Garot, Kusto (Beveren), Littbarski (FC Köln), Castella, Geiger, Schnyder, Barberis (Servette Genève), Couriol, Bathenay, Sušić, Zaremba (Paris St Germain), A. Janssen, Frans Janssen (NEC Nijmegen), Clark, Dawson, McKay, Davies, Paterson (Glasgow Rangers), Dimov, Kazakov (Spartak Varna), Huoviala, Dziadulewicz, Valvee (Haka Valkeakoski), Rojo, Clos, Migueli, Urbano, Schuster (FC Barcelona), Radenko (Shahtior Donetsk), Billy Ohlsson, Holmberg, Wahlberg, Lundin, Efraimsson (Hammarby IF), Herédi, Fekete (Újpesti Dózsa), Davies, Graham, Whiteside, Wilkins (Manchester United), Sousa, Vermelhinho, Pacheco, Frasco, Walsh (FC Porto), Tardelli, Cabrini, Tavola (Juventus Torino), Simpson, Weir (Aberdeen)

Own goals: Strack (FC Köln) for Újpesti Dózsa, Van Rossum (NEC Nijmegen), Hogg (Manchester United) both for FC Barcelona

CUP WINNERS' CUP 1984-85

FIRST ROUND

RAPID WIEN v BEŞIKTAŞ ISTANBUL 4-1 (2-1)
Gerhard Hanappi, Wien   19.09.1984
Referee: Pietro d'Elia (ITA)   Attendance: 9,000
RAPID: Herbert Feurer, Leopold Lainer, Reinhard Kienast, Heribert Weber, Johann Pregesbauer; Antonin Panenka, Petar Brucic, Karl Brauneder (76 Rudolf Weinhofer); Zlatko Kranjcar, Johann Krankl, Peter Pacult.   Trainer: Otto Barić
BEŞIKTAŞ: Zafer Öger, Ulvi Gülveneroglu, Haluk Serenli, Samet Aybaba, Kadir Akbulut; Riza Çalimbay, Metin Tekin (76 Ali Gültiken), Fikret Demirer (76 Serdar Bali), Necdet Ergün, Mirsad Kovacević, Dzevad Secerbegović.
Goals: Kovacević (11), Panenka (12 pen, 56, 66 pen), Brucic (25)

BEŞIKTAŞ ISTANBUL v RAPID WIEN 1-1 (0-1)
Inönü, Istanbul   3.10.1984
Referee: Ion Igna (ROM)   Attendance: 33,000
BEŞIKTAŞ: Zafer Öger; Hüsamettin Gökçen, Ulvi Gülveneroglu, Samet Aybaba, Kadir Akbulut; Metin Tekin, Ali Gültiken (46 Ziya Dogan), Fikret Demirer (46 Sinan Ergin), Necdet Ergün; Mirsad Kovacević, Dzevad Secerbegović.
RAPID: Herbert Feurer; Kurt Garger, Heribert Weber, Reinhard Kienast, Johann Pregesbauer; Leopold Lainer, Antonin Panenka (67 Rudolf Weinhofer), Karl Brauneder, Petar Brucic; Zlatko Kranjcar (73 Peter Pacult), Johann Krankl.   Trainer: Otto Barić
Goals: Kranjcar (15), Metin (61)

**BALLYMENA UNITED
v HAMRUN SPARTANS 0-1** (0-1)
The Showgrounds, Ballymena   19.09.1984
Referee: Joseph Worrall (ENG)   Attendance: 3,800
BALLYMENA UNITED: Brian Hutchinson; Robert McCreery, Graham Fox, Alan Harrison, Brian Crockard, James Buchanan, Roy Smyth, John Sloan, Colin O'Neill, Alan Campbell (.. Jeff Wright), Don McAllister.
HAMRUN SPARTANS: Alan Zammit, Edwin Farrugia, Alex Azzopardi, George Xuereb, Marco Grech, Alfred Azzopardi, Leo Refalo, Robertson (.. Joe Zarb), Stegner, Raymond Xuereb, Michael Degiorgio.
Goal: R. Xuereb (19)

**HAMRUN SPARTANS
v BALLYMENA UNITED 2-1** (1-1)

Valletta 26.09.1984

Referee: Claudio Pieri (ITA)   Attendance: 12,000

HAMRUN SPARTANS: Alan Zammit, Edwin Farrugia, Alex Azzopardi, Marco Grech, George Xuereb, Alfred Azzopardi, Leo Refalo, Robertson, Stegner, Raymond Xuereb, Michael Degiorgio.

BALLYMENA UNITED: Brian Hutchinson; Robert McCreery (.. Don McAllister), Graham Fox, Alan Harrison, Brian Crockard, George Beattie, Roy Smyth, John Sloan, Colin O'Neill, Alan Campbell, Jeff Wright (.. James Buchanan).

Goals: Beattie (7), R. Xuereb (43, 86 pen)

**UNIVERSITY COLLEGE DUBLIN
v EVERTON LIVERPOOL 0-0**

Tolka Park, Dublin   19.09.1984

Referee: Keith Cooper (WAL)   Attendance: 9,750

UC DUBLIN: Alan O'Neill, Robert Lawlor, Ken O'Doherty, Paddy Dunning, Martin Moran, Robert Gaffney, Keith Dignam, Paul Roche, Donal Murphy, John Cullen, Joe Hanrahan.   Manager: Theo Dunne

EVERTON: Neville Southall, Gary Stevens, Derek Mountfield, Kevin Ratcliffe, John Bailey, Trevor Steven (71 Edward "Terry" Curran), Peter Reid, Paul Bracewell, Kevin Sheedy, Graeme Sharp, Adrian Heath.   Manager: Howard Kendall

**EVERTON LIVERPOOL
v UNIVERSITY COLLEGE DUBLIN 1-0** (1-0)

Goodison Park, Liverpool   2.10.1984

Referee: Frederick McKnight (NIR)   Attendance: 16,277

EVERTON: Neville Southall, Gary Stevens, John Bailey, Kevin Ratcliffe, Derek Mountfield, Peter Reid, Edward "Terry" Curran, Adrian Heath (77 Robert Wakenshaw), Graeme Sharp, Paul Bracewell, Trevor Steven.   Manager: Howard Kendall

UC DUBLIN: Alan O'Neill, Robert Lawlor, Martin Moran, Ken O'Doherty, Paddy Dunning, Robert Gaffney, Keith Dignam, Paul Roche (77 Paul Caffrey), Joe Hanrahan, John Cullen (88 Dudley Solan), Donal Murphy.   Manager: Theo Dunne

Goal: Sharp (10)

BAYERN MÜNCHEN v FK MOSS 4-1 (1-1)

Olympiastadion, München   19.09.1984

Referee: Krzysztof Czermarmazowicz (POL)   Att: 5,000

BAYERN: Raimond Aumann, Bernd Dürnberger, Klaus Augenthaler, Norbert Eder, Hans Pflügler; Karl Del'Haye, Ludwig Kögl, Lothar Matthäus, Norbert Nachtweih; Michael Rummenigge (74 Hans-Werner Grünwald), Roland Wohlfahrt.   Trainer: Udo Lattek

FK MOSS: Nils Espen Eriksen, Rune Gjestrumsbakken, Einar Jan Aas, Rune Tangen, Svein Grøndalen, Per HElíasz, Pål Grønstad, Lars Ragnar Kristiansen (54 Tore Gregersen), Geir Henaes, Tore Lahn Johannesen (46 Jan Rafn), Stein Kollshaugen.

Sent off: Matthäus (39)

Goals: Kollshaugen (2), Pflügler (31, 54), Wohlfarth (69), Nachtweih (77)

FK MOSS v BAYERN MÜNCHEN 1-2 (0-1)

Melløs, Moss   3.10.1984

Referee: Simo Ruokonen (FIN)   Attendance: 4,600

FK MOSS: Nils Espen Eriksen, Rune Gjestrumsbakken, Einar Jan Aas (67 Lars Ragnar Kristiansen), Rune Tangen, Svein Grøndalen, Per HElíasz, Pål Grønstad, Geir Henaes, Tore Lahn Johannesen (80 Ole Petter Jensen), Jan Kristian Fjaerestad, Stein Kollshaugen.

BAYERN: Raimond Aumann, Bernd Dürnberger, Klaus Augenthaler, Norbert Eder, Holger Willmer; Wolfgang Dremmler, Bertram Beierlorzer, Norbert Nachtweih, Ludwig Kögl (68 Karl Del'Haye); Roland Wohlfahrt, Michael Rummenigge (61 Dieter Hoeness).   Trainer: Udo Lattek

Goals: Wohlfarth (23), Rummenigge (48), Kollshaugen (87)

WREXHAM v FC PORTO 1-0 (0-0)

Racecourse Ground, Wrexham   19.09.1984

Referee: Jean-François Crucke (BEL)   Attendance: 4,935

WREXHAM: Stuart Parker, John King, Shaun Cunnington, Neil Salathiel, John Keay, Stephen Wright, Michael Williams (71 John Muldoon), Barry Horne, James Steel, David Gregory, Kevin Rogers.   Trainer: Roberts

FC PORTO: Petar Borota, JOÃO Domingos Silva PINTO, Augusto Soares INÁCIO, EDUARDO LUÍS Marques Kruss Gomes, EURICO Monteiro Gomes; JAIME Fernandes MAGALHAES (46 ADEMAR Moreira Marques), António Manuel FRASCO Vieira, Joaquim Carvalho Azevedo "QUIM", Fernando Mendes Soares GOMES, Paulo Jorge dos Santos FUTRE (71 Michael Walsh), Carlos Manuel Oliveiros Silva "VERMELHINHO".

Goal: Steel (77)

FC PORTO v WREXHAM 4-3 (3-2)

Estádio das Antas, Porto   3.10.1984

Referee: Albert Thomas (HOL)   Attendance: 35,000

FC PORTO: Petar Borota, JOÃO Domingos Silva PINTO (89 Michael Walsh), António José LIMA PEREIRA, EURICO Monteiro Gomes, Augusto Soares INÁCIO; JAIME Fernandes MAGALHAES, António Manuel FRASCO Vieira, Joaquim Carvalho Azevedo "QUIM", Fernando Mendes Soares GOMES, Carlos Manuel Oliveiros Silva "VERMELHINHO" (77 Joaquim José Ferreirinha Moreira "QUINITO"), Paulo Jorge dos Santos FUTRE.

WREXHAM: Stuart Parker, John King, John Keay, Stephen Wright, Neil Salathiel, Shaun Cunnington, Michael Williams (23 David Gregory), Andrew Edwards (76 John Muldoon), Barry Horne, Kevin Rogers, James Steel.

Goals: Gomes (5, 38 pen), J. Magalhaes (18), Futre (61), King (39, 43), Horne (89)

FC METZ v FC BARCELONA 2-4 (1-1)

Saint-Symphorien, Metz   19.09.1984

Referee: Jan Keizer (HOL)

FC METZ: Michel Ettore; Luc Sonor, Alain Colombo (62 Claude Lowitz), Fernando Zappia, Robert Barraja, Vincent Bracigliano, Jean-Philippe Rohr, Jean Paul Bernad, Zvonko Kurbos, Jules Bocande, Philippe Hinschberger (78 Michel Deza).   Trainer: Marcel Husson

FC BARCELONA: Francisco Javier González URRUTIcoechea, José Vicente SÁNCHEZ Felip, JULIO ALBERTO Moreno Casas, José Ramón ALESANCO Ventosa, José MORATALLA Claramunt, VÍCTOR Muñoz Manrique, Bernd Schuster, Ramón María CALDERÉ del Rey, Juan Carlos Pérez ROJO, Steven Archibald, Francisco José CARRASCO Hidalgo.   Trainer: Terry Venables

Goals: Sonor (12 og), Kurbos (44), Schuster (47), Calderé (53), Carrasco (64), Rohr (87 pen)

FC BARCELONA v FC METZ 1-4 (1-2)

Camp Nou, Barcelona   3.10.1984

Referee: Ronald Bridges (WAL)   Attendance: 24,000

FC BARCELONA: AMADOR Lorenzo Lemos, José Vicente SÁNCHEZ Felip (cap), Bernardo Bianquetti Miguel "MIGUELI", José Ramón ALESANCO Ventosa, JULIO ALBERTO Moreno Casas; VÍCTOR Muñoz Manrique, Bernd Schuster, Ramón María CALDERÉ del Rey (72 Francisco Javier CLOS Orozco), Juan Carlos Pérez ROJO (63 ESTEBAN Vigo Benítez); Steven Archibald, Francisco José CARRASCO Hidalgo.   Trainer: Terry Venables

FC METZ: Michel Ettore; Luc Sonor (52 Alain Colombo), Claude Lowitz, Robert Barraja (60 Thierry Pauk), Fernando Zappia; Vincent Bracigliano, Jean-Philippe Rohr, Jean-Paul Bernad (Cap), Philippe Hinschberger; Zvonko Kurbos, Jules Bocande.   Trainer: Marcel Husson

Goals: Carrasco (33), Kurbos (38, 65, 85), Sánchez (39 og)

DINAMO MOSKVA v HAJDUK SPLIT 1-0 (1-0)

Dinamo, Moskva   19.09.1984

Referee: Luigi Agnolin (ITA)   Attendance: 14,200

DINAMO: Aleksei Prudnikov, Igor Bulanov, Aleksandr Novikov, Vladimir Fomichiev, Aleksandr Golovnia, Aleksandr Khapsalis, Renat Ataulin, Yuri Pudischev, Sergei Argudiaev (86 Aleksandr Molodtsov), Vasili Karataev, Valeri Gazzaev.   Trainer: Aleksandr Savinov

HAJDUK: Ivan Pudar; Josko Spanjić, Darko Drazić, Ivan Gudelj, Stjepan Andrijasević, Dragutin Celić, Zlatko Vujović (77 Frane Bucan), Nenad Salov, Zoran Vujović, Aljosa Asanović, Dževad Prekazi (79 Vlaho Macan).

Goal: Argudiaev (9)

HAJDUK SPLIT v DINAMO MOSKVA 2-5 (1-1)

Gradski, Osijek   3.10.1984

Referee: Bogdan Dochev (BUL)   Attendance: 40,000

HAJDUK: Ivan Pudar; Stjepan Andrijasević, Zoran Vulić, Ivan Gudelj, Momir Bakrac (71 Josko Spanjić), Dragutin Celić, Zlatko Vujović, Blaz Slisković, Nenad Salov (71 Darko Drazić), Aljosa Asanović, Stjepan Deverić.

DINAMO: Aleksei Prudnikov, Igor Bulanov, Aleksandr Novikov, Vladimir Fomichiev, Aleksandr Golovnia, Aleksandr Khapsalis, Renat Ataulin, Yuri Pudischev (81 Sergei Silkin), Sergei Argudiaev (71 Mikhail Chesnokov), Vasili Karataev, Valeri Gazzaev.   Trainer: Aleksandr Savinov

Goals: Gazzaev (7, 57, 77 pen), Deverić (40), Zl. Vujović (50 pen), Bulanov (63), Khapsalis (80)

AS ROMA v STEAUA BUCUREȘTI 1-0 (0-0)

Stadio Olimpico, Roma   19.09.1984

Referee: Robert Wurtz (FRA)   Attendance: 50,000

AS ROMA: Franco Tancredi; Emidio Oddi, Ubaldo Righetti, Sebastiano Nela, Aldo Maldera; Bruno Conti, Ruben Buriani, Antonio Carlos Cerezo, Giuseppe Giannini (49 Odoacre Chierico); Roberto Pruzzo (70 Maurizio Iorio), Francesco Graziani.   Trainer: Sven-Göran Eriksson

STEAUA: Helmuth Duckadam; Nicolae Laurențiu, Ștefan Iovan, Adrian Bumbescu, Augustin Eduard; Marcel Pușcaș, Ștefan Petcu (80 Gavril Balint), Ion Tătăran, Mihail Majearu; Marius Mihai Lăcătuș, Victor Pițurcă (85 Marin Radu).   Trainer: Florin Halagian

Goal: Graziani (73)

STEAUA BUCUREŞTI v AS ROMA 0-0
Steaua Bucureşti   3.10.1984
Referee: Bruno Galler (SWI)   Attendance: 30,000
STEAUA: Helmuth Duckadam; Ilie Bărbulescu, Ştefan Iovan, Adrian Bumbescu, Augustin Eduard; Ştefan Petcu (64 Marin Radu), Ladislau Bölöni (57 Gavril Balint), Marcel Puşcaş, Mihail Majearu; Marius Mihai Lăcătuş, Victor Piţurcă. Trainer: Florin Halagian

AS ROMA: Franco Tancerdi; Dario Bonetti, Ubaldo Righetti, Sebastiano Nela, Emidio Oddi; Bruno Conti, Antonio Carlos Cerezo, Aldo Maldera, Giuseppe Giannini; Roberto Pruzzo, Francesco Graziani (22 Roberto Antonelli, 69 Odoacre Chierico).   Trainer: Sven-Göran Eriksson

KB KØBENHAVN v FORTUNA SITTARD 0-0
Frederiksberg, København   19.09.1984
Referee: Bernd Stumpf (E. GER)   Attendance: 1,900
KB: Ole Qvist, Henrik Hansen, Søren Busk, Torben Piechnik, Garly (46 Claus Windfeld), Thomassen, Petersen, Bo Fosgaard, Rene Hansen, Schøne (65 Sparring), Terkelsen.

FORTUNA: André Van Gerven, René Maessen, Chris Dekker, Wim Koevermans, Willy Boessen, Roger Reijners, Wilbert Suvrijn, Theo van Well (46 Anne Evers), Arthur Hoyer, Wout Holverda, Tiny Ruys.   Trainer: Bert Jacobs

FORTUNA SITTARD v KB KØBENHAVN 3-0 (1-0)
De Bandeert, Sittard   3.10.1984
Referee: José Rosa Dos Santos (POR)   Attendance: 11,386
FORTUNA: Chris Körver, René Maessen, Chris Dekker, Wim Koevermans, Willy Boessen, Mario Eleveld, Arthur Hoyer, Wilbert Suvrijn, Theo van Well (46 Tiny Ruys, 66 Anne Evers), Wout Holverda, Roger Reijners.   Trainer: Bert Jacobs

KB: Ole Qvist, Claus Windfeld, Søren Busk, Torben Piechnik, Garly, Thomassen, Petersen (.. Terkelsen), Bo Fosgaard (.. Henrik Hansen), Rene Hansen, Schøne, Stig Andersen.

Goals: Holverda (35, 73), Hoyer (68)

MALMÖ FF v DYNAMO DRESDEN 2-0 (1-0)
Malmö Stadion   19.09.1984
Referee: Aleksandr Mushkovets (USSR)   Attendance: 3,434
MALMÖ FF: Jan Möller, Mats Arvidsson, Magnus Andersson, Kent Jonsson, Ingemar Erlandsson, Mikael Rönnberg, Björn Nilsson, Hasse Borg, Torbjörn Persson, Anders Palmer, Mats Magnusson (87 Deval Eminovski).

DYNAMO: Bernd Jakubowski, Andreas Trautmann, Hans-Jürgen Dörner, Udo Schmuck, Matthias Döschner, Reinhard Häfner, Hans-Uwe Pilz, Jörg Stübner, Torsten Gütschow (77 Ulf Kirsten), Ralf Minge, Frank Lippmann.   Trainer: Sammer

Goals: Mats Magnusson (44, 64)

DYNAMO DRESDEN v MALMÖ FF 4-1 (2-0)
Dynamo Dresden   3.10.1984
Referee: Ulrich Nyffenegger (SWI)   Attendance: 36,000
DYNAMO: Bernd Jakubowski, Hans-Jürgen Dörner, Andreas Trautmann, Andreas Schmidt, Matthias Döschner, Reinhard Häfner, Jörg Stübner, Hans-Uwe Pilz, Torsten Gütschow (84 Ulf Kirsten), Ralf Minge, Frank Lippmann (85 Lutz Schülbe). Trainer: Sammer

MALMÖ FF: Jan Möller, Mats Arvidsson, Ingemar Erlandsson, Magnus Andersson, Kent Jonsson, Hasse Borg, Mikael Rönnberg, Björn Nilsson, Torbjörn Persson, Anders Palmer, Mats Magnusson.

Goals: Häfner (13 pen), Minge (29), Stübner (52), Pilz (63), Rönnberg (82 pen)

WISLA KRAKÓW v ÍB VESTMANNAEYJAR 4-2 (3-2)
Wisla Kraków   19.09.1984
Referee: Klaus Peschel (E. GER)   Attendance: 5,000
WISLA: Jerzy Zajda, Janusz Nawrocki, Krzysztof Budka, Piotr Skrobowski, Janusz Krupinski, Leszek Lipka, Jan Jalocha, Adam Nawalka, Marek Banaszkiewicz, Marek Swierczewski (82 Jaroslaw Giszka), Michal Wróbel.

ÍBV: H. Pálsson, Agust Einarsson, Elías Fridriksson, Thordur Hallgrimsson, Arnarsson, Tómas Pálsson (66 Hlynur Stéfansson), Vidar Elíasson, Jóhann Georgsson, Hedinn Saevarsson, Kári Thorleifsson, Bergur Augustsson.

Goals: Wrobel (19), Nawalka (20), Banaszkiewicz (31, 67), Elíasson (40), Georgsson (44 pen)

ÍB VESTMANNAEYJAR v WISLA KRAKÓW 1-3 (0-2)
Hásteinsvöllur Vestmannaeyjar   3.10.1984
Referee: George Smith (SCO)   Attendance: 1,000
ÍBV: H. Pálsson, Arnason, Thordur Hallgrimsson, Elías Fridriksson, Arnarsson, Jóhann Georgsson, Vidar Elíasson, Kári Thorleifsson, Bergur Augustsson, Tómas Pálsson, Sigurjon Kristinsson (71 Scheving).

WISLA: Robert Gaszynski, Janusz Nawrocki, Krzysztof Budka, Wojciech Gorgon, Jan Jalocha, Janusz Krupinski (46 Marek Banaszkiewicz), Adam Nawalka, Andrzej Targosz, Michal Wróbel (71 Jacek Mróz), Marek Swierczewski, Andrzej Iwan.

Goals: Iwan (26, 31), Georgsson (86), Banaszkiewicz (75)

TRAKIA PLOVDIV v US LUXEMBOURG 4-0 (0-0)
Stadion Deveti septembri, Plovdiv   19.09.1984
Referee: Hiqmet Kuka (ALB)   Attendance: 6,000
TRAKIA: Dimitar Vichev, Ianko Dinev (37 Georgi Georgiev), Dimitar Mladenov, Zaprian Ivanov, Slavcho Horozov, Marin Bakalov, Kostadin Kostadinov, Vasil Simov, Antim Pehlivanov (46 Ivailo Stoinov), Petar Zehtinski, Atanas Pashev.
US LUXEMBOURG: François Novak, Gilbert Schmit (82 Nico Bremer), Hans Lochen, Laurent Schonckert, Romain Delhalt, Fernand Heinisch, Luc Feiereisen, René Thines, Manou Scheitler, Nico Braun, Claude Grimberger (71 André Lamas).
Goals: Pashev (54), Stoinov (63), Georgiev (69), Kostadinov (77 pen)

LARISA v SIÓFOK BANYASZ 2-0 (1-0)
Alkazar, Larisa   3.10.1984
Referee: Ion Crăciunescu (ROM)   Attendance: 15,000
LARISA: Giorgos Plitsis, Dimitris Parafestas, Giorgos Mitsibonas, Giannis Gkalitsios (32 Kostas Kolomitrousis), Nikos Patsiavouras; Mihalis Ziogas, Anderoudis, Theodoros Voutiritsas; Krzysztof Adamczyk, Kazimir Kmiecik, Giannis Valaoras.   Trainer: Andrei Strejlau
SIÓFOK: László Horváth; Csaba Brettner, Károly Pardavi, László Takács, Ernő Virágh, Miklós Szajcz, Zoltán Bódi, Sándor Olajos; László Tieber, László Horváth, Sándor Jankovics (63 Mihály Boda).   Trainer: Mikos Szöke
Goals: Kmiecik (29), Valaoras (66)

US LUXEMBOURG v TRAKIA PLOVDIV 1-1 (0-1)
Luxembourg   3.10.1984
Referee: Karl-Josef Assenmacher (W. GER)   : 500
US LUXEMBOURG: François Novak, Gilbert Schmit, Hans Lochen, Laurent Schonckert, Romain Delhalt, Fernand Heinisch (70 René Thines), Luc Feiereisen, Nico Bremer (80 Carlo Lambert), Manou Scheitler, Nico Braun, Claude Grimberger.
TRAKIA: Dimitar Vichev, Kosta Tanev (64 Ianko Dinev), Dimitar Mladenov, Blagoi Blangev, Zaprian Ivanov, Georgi Georgiev (63 Marin Bakalov), Ivailo Stoinov, Vasil Simov, Antim Pehlivanov, Petar Zehtinski, Atanas Pashev
Goals: Stoinov (15), Thines (74)

K AA GENT v CELTIC GLASGOW 1-0 (0-0)
Jules Otten, Gent   19.09.1984
Referee: Alder Da Silva dos Santos (POR)   Att: 22,500
KAA GENT: André Lauryssen, Søren Busk, Luc Criel, Guy Hanssens, Michel De Wolf, Milan Ruzic, Hubert Cordiez, Willy Quipor (75 Benny de Kneef), Kees Schapendonck, Johan Van Looy (60 Jean-Claude Bouvy), Ronny Martens.
Trainer: Johan Grijzenhout
CELTIC: Patrick Bonner, Thomas McAdam, Robert Aitken, Mark Reid, Daniel McGrain, Peter Grant, Murdo MacLeod, Paul McStay, Brian McClair, Francis McGarvey, Thomas Burns.
Goal: Cordiez (73)

SIÓFOK BANYASZ v LARISA 1-1 (0-1)
Sóstói Székesfehérvár   19.09.1984
Referee: Wieslaw Karolak (POL)   Attendance: 8,000
SIÓFOK: László Horváth; Csaba Brettner, Tibor Onhausz (46 Károly Pardavi), Ernő Virágh; Péter Kiss (75 Miklós Szajcz), László Takács, Zoltán Bódi, Sándor Olajos; László Tieber, László Horváth, Sándor Jankovics.   Trainer: Mikos Szöke
LARISA: Giorgos Plitsis, Dimitris Parafestas, Giorgos Mitsibonas, Giannis Gkalitsios, Nikos Patsiavouras; Mihalis Ziogas (81 Lazaros Kirilidis), Hristos Andreoudis, Kazimir Kmiecik, Theodoros Voutiritsas; Krzysztof Adamczyk, Giannis Valaoras (75 Antonis Rigas).   Trainer: Andrei Strejlau
Goals: Adamczyk (29), Tieber (68)

CELTIC GLASGOW v K AA GENT 3-0 (1-0)
Celtic Park, Glasgow   3.10.1984
Referee: Egbert Mulder (HOL)   Attendance: 32,749
CELTIC: Patrick Bonner, Daniel McGrain, Murdo MacLeod, Robert Aitken, Thomas McAdam, Peter Grant, John Colquhoun (.. David Provan), Paul McStay, Brian McClair, Thomas Burns, Francis McGarvey.
KAA GENT: André Lauryssen; Guy Hanssens, Luc Criel, Søren Busk, Michel De Wolf, Hubert Cordiez, Benny De Kneef, Willy Quipor (55 Johan Van Looy), Ronny Martens, Kees Schapendonk, Jean-Claude Bouvy (76 Kiyiaki Tokodi).
Trainer: Johan Grijzenhout
Goals: McGarvey (41, 62), P. McStay (89)

APOEL NICOSIA v SERVETTE GENÈVE 0-3 (0-1)

Makarion, Nicosia 19.09.1984

Referee: Mircea Neşu (ROM)   Attendance: 10,000

APOEL: Stavros Stavrou, Petrakis Hatzithomas, Nikos Pantziaras, Koulis Pantziaras, Kostas Miamiliotis, Thomas Cassidy, Panagiotis Maragkos, Giannis Ioannou, Giangos Ioannides (40 Andreas Stylianou), Ian Moores, Dimitris Kleanthous (57 Marios Haralampous).

SERVETTE: Erich Burgener; Rainer Hasler, Michel Renquin, Alain Geiger, Guy Dutoit (85 Gilbert Castella), Marc Schnyder, Umberto Barberis, Lucien Favre, Michel Decastel, Jean-Paul Brigger, Robert Kok (87 Angelo Elia).   Trainer: Guy Mathez

Goals: Decastel (40), Brigger (79), Favre (84)

**KUUSYSI LAHTI
v INTERNACIONÁL SLOVNAFT BRATISLAVA 0-0**

Urheilukeskus Lahti 4.10.1984

Referee: Thorbjorn Aas (NOR)   Attendance: 2,639

KUUSYSI: Ismo Korhonen, Jyrki Hännikäinen, Kenneth Mitchel, Raimo Kumpulainen, Ilkka Remes, Jari Rinne, Esa Pekonen, Keijo Kousa, Ilpo Talvio, Ismo Lius (77 Jarmo Kaivonurmi), Keith Armstrong.   Trainer: Koijo Voutilainen

INTER: Dušan Maluniak; Radomír Hrotek, Jozef Barmoš, Pavol Šebo, Peter Fieber, Milan Krupcík, Peter Michalec, Libor Koník, Stanislav Moravec (82 Rudolf Ducký), Marián Tomcák (77 Jozef Reznák), Peter Mráz.   Trainer: Štefan Šimoncic

SECOND ROUND

SERVETTE GENÈVE v APOEL NICOSIA 3-1 (3-0)

Stade des Charmilles, Genève 3.10.1984

Referee: Paul Rion (LUX)   Attendance: 3,500

SERVETTE: Erich Burgener; Rainer Hasler, Michel Renquin, Alain Geiger, Guy Dutoit (62 Pascal Besnard), Gilbert Castella, Umberto Barberis, Marc Schnyder, Michel Decastel, Jean-Paul Brigger, Robert Kok.   Trainer: Guy Mathez

APOEL: Stavros Stavrou, Nikos Pantziaras, Koulis Pantziaras, Petrakis Hatzithomas, Kostas Miamiliotis, Giangos Ioannides (46 Andreas Stylianou), Thomas Cassidy, Panagiotis Maragkos, Ian Moores, Giannis Ioannou (73 Marios Giousellis), Dimitris Kleanthous.

Goals: Kok (6), Barberis (14), Brigger (31), Moores (82)

DYNAMO DRESDEN v FC METZ 3-1 (2-1)

Dynamo Dresden 24.10.1984

Referee: Neil Midgley (ENG)   Att: 30,000

DYNAMO: Bernd Jakubowski, Hans-Jürgen Dörner, Andreas Trautmann, Matthias Döschner, Frank Schuster; Jörg Stübner, Reinhard Häfner, Ralf Minge, Ulf Kirsten (74 Lutz Schülbe), Torsten Gütschow, Frank Lippmann.   Trainer: Sammer

FC METZ: Michel Ettore; Fernando Zappia, Luc Sonor, Robert Barraja, Claude Lowitz; Thierry Pauk, Vincent Bracigliano, Jean Paul Bernad (Cap), Jean-Philippe Rohr, Zvonko Kurbos (89 Carmelo Micciche), Philippe Hinschberger (69 Marco Morgante).   Trainer: Marcel Husson

Goals: Trautmann (9 og), Häfner (24 pen), Stübner (37), Gütschow (51)

**INTERNACIONÁL SLOVNAFT BRATISLAVA
v KUUSYSI LAHTI 2-1** (1-1)

Stadion na Pasienkoch, Bratislava 19.09.1984

Referee: Iordan Zhezhov (BUL)   Attendance: 2,100

INTER: Dušan Maluniak, Milan Krupcík, Jozef Barmoš, Pavol Šebo, Peter Fieber, Libor Koník, Peter Michalec (33 Marián Tomcák), Rudolf Ducký, Stanislav Moravec (88 Ján Lehnert), Karol Brezík, Peter Mráz.   Trainer: Štefan Šimoncic

KUUSYSI: Ismo Korhonen, Jyrki Hännikäinen, Kenneth Mitchel, Raimo Kumpulainen (37 Jarmo Kaivonurmi), Ilkka Remes, Jari Rinne, Esa Pekonen, Markus Törnvall, Ilpo Talvio, Ismo Lius (65 Keijo Kousa), Keith Armstrong.   Trainer: Koijo Voutilainen

Goals: Törnvall (4), Brezík (42), Moravec (65)

FC METZ v DYNAMO DRESDEN 0-0

Saint-Symphorien, Metz 7.11.1984

Referee: Zoran Petrović (YUG)   Attendance: 19,928

FC METZ: Michel Ettore; Fernando Zappia, Luc Sonor, Robert Barraja, Claude Lowitz (73 Thierry Pauk); Jean-Philippe Rohr, Jean Paul Bernad, Vincent Bracigliano; Philippe Hinschberger (59 Michel Deza), Jules Bocande, Carmelo Micchiche.   Trainer: Marcel Husson

DYNAMO: Bernd Jakubowski, Hans-Jürgen Dörner, Frank Schuster, Andreas Trautmann, Matthias Döschner, Reinhard Häfner (82 Udo Schmuck), Ralf Minge, Jörg Stübner, Ulf Kirsten (69 Steffen Büttner), Torsten Gütschow, Frank Lippmann.   Trainer: Sammer

FORTUNA SITTARD v WISLA KRAKÓW 2-0 (1-0)
De Bandeert, Sittard   24.10.1984
Referee: Patrick Daly (IRE)   Attendance: 12,282

FORTUNA: André Van Gerven, René Maessen, Chris Dekker, Wim Koevermans, Willy Boessen, Wilbert Suvrijn, Anne Evers, Mario Eleveld, Arthur Hoyer, Wout Holverda (63 Theo van Well), Roger Houtackers.   Trainer: Bert Jacobs

WISLA: Jerzy Zajda, Marek Motyka, Krzysztof Budka, Piotr Skrobowski, Janusz Nawrocki, Leszek Lipka, Adam Nawalka, Jan Jalocha, Janusz Krupinski (60 Michal Wróbel), Marek Swierczewski (69 Marek Banaszkiewicz), Andrzej Iwan.

Goals: Hoyer (21), Van Well (78)

WISLA KRAKÓW v FORTUNA SITTARD 2-1 (2-1)
Wisla Kraków   7.11.1984
Referee: Gerasimos Germanakos (GRE)   Att: 12,000

WISLA: Jerzy Zajda, Janusz Nawrocki, Krzysztof Budka, Marek Motyka, Jan Jalocha (54 Marek Swierczewski), Leszek Lipka, Adam Nawalka, Janusz Krupinski, Michal Wróbel, Andrzej Iwan, Marek Banaszkiewicz (78 Jaroslaw Giszka).

FORTUNA: André Van Gerven, René Maessen, Chris Dekker, Wim Koevermans, Willy Boessen, Mario Eleveld, Wilbert Suvrijn, Anne Evers (74 Theo van Well), Arthur Hoyer, Roger Reijners, Wout Holverda.   Trainer: Bert Jacobs

Goals: Hoyer (1), Iwan (6 pen), Wróbel (42)

INTERNACIONÁL SLOVNAFT BRATISLAVA v EVERTON LIVERPOOL 0-1 (0-1)
Stadion na Pasienkoch, Bratislava   24.10.1984
Referee: Jakob Baumann (SWI)   Attendance: 15,000

INTER: Dušan Maluniak, Radomír Hrotek, Milan Krupčík, Pavol Šebo, Peter Fieber, Libor Koník (77 Ján Lehnert), Peter Michalec (46 Marián Tomčiák), Rudolf Ducký, Stanislav Moravec, Karol Brezík, Peter Mráz.   Trainer: Štefan Šimoncic

EVERTON: Neville Southall, Gary Stevens, Derek Mountfield, Kevin Ratcliffe, John Bailey, Trevor Steven, Peter Reid, Paul Bracewell, Alan Harper, Adrian Heath, Graeme Sharp.

Goal: Bracewell (6)

EVERTON LIVERPOOL v INTERNACIONÁL SLOVNAFT BRATISLAVA 3-0 (2-0)
Goodison Park, Liverpool   7.11.1984
Referee: Egbert Mulder (HOL)   Attendance: 25,007

EVERTON: Neville Southall, Gary Stevens, John Bailey, Kevin Ratcliffe, Derek Mountfield, Peter Reid (69 Alan Harper), Trevor Steven, Adrian Heath, Graeme Sharp, Paul Bracewell, Kevin Sheedy (78 John Morissey).   Manager: Howard Kendall

INTER: Dušan Maluniak, Milan Krupčík, Jozef Barmoš, Peter Fieber, Rudolf Ducký, Pavol Šebo, Peter Mráz, Karol Brezík (64 Peter Michalec), Stanislav Moravec, Marián Tomcák, Libor Koník (46 Ján Lehnert).   Trainer: Štefan Šimoncic

Goals: Sharp (12), Sheedy (44), Heath (63)

DINAMO MOSKVA v HAMRUN SPARTANS 5-0 (2-0)
Dinamo Moskva   24.10.1984
Referee: Wieslaw Karolak (POL)   Attendance: 7,300

DINAMO: Aleksei Prudnikov, Igor Bulanov, Aleksandr Novikov, Vladimir Fomichiev, Aleksandr Golovnia, Aleksandr Khapsalis, Renat Ataulin, Yuri Pudischev (70 Valeri Matiunin), Sergei Argudiaev, Vasili Karataev, Valeri Gazzaev (70 Yuri Mentiukov).   Trainer: Aleksandr Savinov

HAMRUN SPARTANS: Alan Zammit, Edwin Farrugia, Alex Azzopardi, Marco Grech, D.Xuereb, Alfred Azzopardi (81 Joseph Salerno), Leo Refalo, Robertson, Stegner (53 Gejtu Refalo), Raymond Xuereb, Michael Degiorgio.

Goals: Gazzaev (6, 64), Karataev (43), Khapsalis (52), Bulanov (56)

HAMRUN SPARTANS v DINAMO MOSKVA 0-1 (0-1)
Hamrun   7.11.1984
Referee: Helmut Kohl (AUS)   Attendance: 7,000

HAMRUN SPARTANS: Alan Zammit, Edwin Farrugia, Alex Azzopardi, Marco Grech, d. Xuereb, Alfred Azzopardi, Leo Refalo, Gejtu Reffalo (46 Stegner), Michael Degiorgio, Robertson, Raymond Xuereb (80 Consiglio).

DINAMO: Aleksei Prudnikov, Valeri Matiunin, Aleksandr Novikov, Vladimir Fomichiev, Aleksandr Golovnia, Aleksandr Khapsalis (46 Igor Bulanov), Renat Ataulin, Yuri Pudischev, Mikhail Chesnokov, Vasili Karataev, Argudaiev (46 Aleksandr Borodiuk).   Trainer: Aleksandr Savinov

Goal: Chesnokov (12)

BAYERN MÜNCHEN v TRAKIA PLOVDIV 4-1 (2-1)
Olympiastadion, München   24.10.1984
Referee: Henning Lund Sørensen (DEN)   Attendance: 9500

BAYERN: Jean-Marie Pfaff, Bernd Martin (64 Karl Del'Haye), Klaus Augenthaler, Norbert Eder, Wolfgang Dremmler, Søren Lerby, Holger Willmer (64 Dieter Hoeness), Bernd Dürnberger, Ludwig Kögl, Michael Rummenigge, Roland Wohlfahrt.   Trainer: Udo Lattek

TRAKIA: Dimitar Vichev, Zaprian Ivanov, Dimitar Mladenov (74 Kostadin Kostadinov), Slavcho Horozov, Blagoi Blangev, Marin Bakalov (81 Rumen Bairev), Vasil Simov, Georgi Georgiev, Petar Zehtinski, Ivailo Stoinov, Atanas Pashev.

Goals: Mladenov (8 og), Wohlfarth (20, 76), Georgiev (40), Rummenigge (71)

**TRAKIA PLOVDIV
v BAYERN MÜNCHEN 2-0** (1-0)
Stadion Deveti septembri, Plovdiv   7.11.1984
Referee: Paolo Casarin (ITA)   Attendance: 30,000
TRAKIA: Dimitar Vichev, Slavcho Horozov (58 Dimitar Mladenov), Ianko Dinev, Blagoi Blangev, Zaprian Ivanov, Georgi Georgiev, Kostadin Kostandinov, Vasil Simov, Trifon Pachev (64 Marin Bakalov), Petar Zehtinski, Atanas Pashev.
BAYERN: Jean-Marie Pfaff, Klaus Augenthaler, Wolfgang Dremmler, Norbert Eder, Holger Willmer, Reinhold Mathy, Norbert Nachtweih, Bernd Dürnberger, Søren Lerby, Roland Wohlfahrt, Michael Rummenigge (46 Dieter Hoeness).
Trainer: Udo Lattek
Goals: Pashev (39), Kostandinov (51 pen)

AS ROMA v WREXHAM 2-0 (1-0)
Stadio Olimpico, Roma   24.10.1984
Referee: László Padar (HUN)   Attendance: 36,792
AS ROMA: Franco Tancredi, Emidio Oddi, Dario Bonetti (60 Giuseppe Giannini), Carlo Ancelotti, Ubaldo Righetti, Aldo Maldera (24 Odoacre Chierico), Bruno Conti, Antonino Carlos Cerezo, Roberto Pruzzo, Ruben Buriani, Maurizio Iorio. Trainer: Sven-Göran Eriksson
WREXHAM: Stuart Parker; John King, Shaun Cunnington, Neil Salathiel, John Keay, Stephen Wright, Andrew Edwards, Barry Horne, James Steel, David Gregory (60 John Muldoon), Kevin Rogers.
Goals: Pruzzo (37 pen), Cerezo (50)

WREXHAM v AS ROMA 0-1 (0-0)
Racecourse Ground, Wrexham   7.11.1984
Referee: Ángel Franco Martínez (SPA)   Attendance: 14,007
WREXHAM: Stuart Parker; John King, Shaun Cunnington, Neil Salathiel, John Muldoon, Stephen Wright, Andrew Edwards, Barry Horne, James Steel, David Gregory, Kevin Rogers.
AS ROMA: Franco Tancredi, Sebastiano Nela, Dario Bonetti, Ubaldo Righetti, Paulo Roberto Falcão, Aldo Maldera, Bruno Conti, Ruben Buriani, Francesco Graziani (75 Maurizio Iorio), Giuseppe Giannini, Odoacre Chierico (87 Antonio di Carlo). Trainer: Sven-Göran Eriksson
Goal: Graziani (67)

RAPID WIEN v CELTIC GLASGOW 3-1 (0-0)
Gerhard Hanappi, Wien   24.10.1984
Referee: Iordan Zhezhov (BUL)   Attendance: 15,700
RAPID: Herbert Feurer, Leopold Lainer, Heribert Weber, Reinhard Kienast (65 Kurt Garger), Johann Pregesbauer; Antonin Panenka, Petar Brucic, Karl Brauneder; Zlatko Kranjcar, Johann Krankl, Peter Pacult.   Trainer: Otto Barić
CELTIC: Patrick Bonner, Daniel McGrain, Robert Aitken, William McStay, Mark Reid, Peter Grant, David Provan, Paul McStay, Murdo MacLeod, Brian McClair, Francis McGarvey (34 Alan McInally).
Goals: Pacult (53), McClair (56), Lainer (66), Krankl (87)

CELTIC GLASGOW v RAPID WIEN 3-0 (2-0)
Celtic Park, Glasgow   7.11.1984
Referee: Kjell Johansson (SWE)   Attendance: 48,813
CELTIC: Patrick Bonner, William McStay, Thomas McAdam, Robert Aitken, Murdo MacLeod, Paul McStay, Peter Grant, Thomas Burns (10 Latchford), David Provan, Brian McClair, Francis McGarvey.
RAPID: Ehn; Kurt Garger, Heribert Weber, Reinhard Kienast, Johann Pregesbauer; Petar Brucic, Leopold Lainer, Karl Brauneder (50 Gerald Willfurth), Zlatko Kranjcar; Johann Krankl, Peter Pacult (65 Rudolf Weinhofer). Trainer: Otto Barić
Sent off: Kienast (73)
Goals: McClair (32), MacLeod (49), Burns (71)
A replay of this match was subsequently ordered by UEFA

CELTIC GLASGOW v RAPID WIEN 0-1 (0-1)
Old Trafford, Manchester   12.12.1984
Referee: Luigi Agnolin (ITA)   Attendance: 51,550
CELTIC: Patrick Bonner, Daniel McGrain, Murdo MacLeod, Robert Aitken, Thomas McAdam (67 John Colquhoun); Peter Grant, David Provan, Paul McStay, Francis McGarvey; Thomas Burns, Brian McClair.
RAPID: Herbert Feurer; Leopold Lainer, Kurt Garger, Rudolf Weinhofer, Heribert Weber; Karl Brauneder, Zlatko Kranjcar, Gerald Willfurth (89 Michael Keller), Johann Gröss (85 Leopold Rotter), Petar Brucic, Peter Pacult.
Trainer: Otto Barić
Goal: Pacult (18)

LARISA v SERVETTE GENÈVE 2-1 (0-1)

Alkazar, Larisa   24.10.1984

Referee: Bogdan Dochev (BUL)   Attendance: 13,000

LARISA: Giorgos Plitsis; Dimitris Parafestas, Giorgos Mitsibonas, Giannis Gkalitsios, Nikos Patsiavouras, Theodoros Voutiritsas, Kazimir Kmiecik (81 Lazaros Kirilidis), Hristos Andreoudis, Vasilsi Tsiolis (46 Mihalis Ziogas), Krzysztof Adamczyk, Giannis Valaoras.   Trainer: Andrei Strejlau

SERVETTE: Erich Burgener; Rainer Hasler, Alain Geiger, Michel Renquin, Guy Dutoit, Michel Decastel, Marc Schnyder, Umberto Barberis, Lucien Favre, Jean-Paul Brigger, Robert Kok.   Trainer: Guy Mathez

Goals: Kok (13), Patsiavouras (53), Kmiecik (65 pen)

**FORTUNA SITTARD
v EVERTON LIVERPOOL 0-2** (0-1)

De Baandert, Sittard   20.03.1985

Referee: Franz Wöhrer (AUS)   Attendance: 16,425

FORTUNA: Chris Körver, René Maessen, Chris Dekker (46 Anne Evers), Wim Koevermans, Gerrie Schrijnemakers, Wilbert Suvrijn, Frans Thijssen, Willy Boessen, Theo van Well, Arthur Hoyer, Rob Philippen (75 Roger Reijners).   Trainer: Bert Jacobs

EVERTON: Neville Southall, Gary Stevens, Derek Mountfield, Kevin Ratcliffe (62 Ian Atkins), Patrick van den Hauwe; Peter Reid, Trevor Steven, Alan Harper, Kevin Richardson, Edward "Terry" Curran, Graeme Sharp (76 Rob Wakenshaw).   Manager: Howard Kendall

Goals: Sharp (15), Reid (76)

SERVETTE GENÈVE v LARISA 0-1 (0-0)

Stade des Charmilles, Genève   7.11.1984

Referee: Vitor Fernandes Correia (POR)   Att: 12,500

SERVETTE: Erich Burgener; Alain Geiger, Michel Renquin, Rainer Hasler (74 Gilbert Castella), Jean-François Henry, Marc Schnyder, Umberto Barberis (77 Laurent Jaccard), Lucien Favre, Michel Decastel, Jean-Paul Brigger, Robert Kok.   Trainer: Guy Mathez

LARISA: Giorgos Plitsis; Dimitris Parafestas, Giorgos Mitsibonas, Giannis Gkalitsios, Nikos Patsiavouras, Theodoros Voutiritsas, Kazimir Kmiecik, Hristos Andreoudis, Mihalis Ziogas (88 Lazaros Kirilidis), Krzysztof Adamczyk (80 Antonis Rigas), Giannis Valaoras.   Trainer: Andrei Strejlau

Goal: Valaoras (60)

LARISA v DINAMO MOSKVA 0-0

Alkazar, Larisa   6.03.1985

Referee: Lajos Nemeth (HUN)   Attendance: 20,000

LARISA: Giorgos Plitsis, Dimitris Parafestas, Nikos Patsiavouras, Giorgos Mitsibonas, Giannis Gkalitsios, Theodoros Voutiritsas, Mihalis Ziogas (86 Giannis Alexoulis), Kazimir Kmiecik, Krzysztof Adamczyk, Hristos Andreoudis (80 Vassilis Hristodoulou), Giannis Valaoras.   Trainer: Andrei Strejlau

DINAMO: Aleksei Prudnikov, Sergei Silkin, Aleksandr Novikov, Vladimir Fomichiev, Aleksandr Golovnia, Viktor Vasiliev (80 Sergei Stukashov), Renat Ataulin, Yuri Pudischev, Aleksandr Borodiuk (63 Aleksandr Molodtsov), Vasili Karataev, Valeri Gazzaev.   Trainer: Aleksandr Savinov

QUARTER-FINALS

**EVERTON LIVERPOOL
v FORTUNA SITTARD 3-0** (0-0)

Goodison Park, Liverpool   6.03.1985

Referee: Eduard Sostarić (YUG)   Attendance: 25,782

EVERTON: Neville Southall, Gary Stevens, Kevin Ratcliffe, Derek Mountfield, Patrick van den Hauwe; Peter Reid (76 Kevin Richardson), Trevor Steven, Edward "Terry" Curran; Andrew Gray, Paul Bracewell, Kevin Sheedy.   Manager: Howard Kendall

FORTUNA: André Van Gerven, René Maessen, Wim Koevermans, Gerrie Schrijnemakers, Chris Dekker; Anne Evers, Wilbert Suvrijn, Frans Thijssen, Arthur Hoyer, Wout Holverda, Theo van Well.   Trainer: Bert Jacobs

Goals: Gray (48, 74, 75)

DINAMO MOSKVA v LARISA 1-0 (0-0)

Dinamo Tbilisi   20.03.1985

Referee: Robert Valentine (SCO)   Attendance: 16,200

DINAMO: Aleksei Prudnikov, Sergei Silkin, Aleksandr Novikov, Vladimir Fomichiev, Aleksandr Golovnia, Aleksandr Khapsalis, Sergei Stukashov (68 Yuri Pudischev), Renat Ataulin, Viktor Vasiliev, Vasili Karataev (86 Aleksandr Borodiuk), Valeri Gazzaev.   Trainer: Aleksandr Savinov

LARISA: Giorgos Plitsis, Dimitris Parafestas, Nikos Patsiavouras, Giorgos Mitsibonas, Giannis Gkalitsios, Theodoros Voutiritsas, Mihalis Ziogas (40 Thanasis Tsiolis, 68 Antonis Rigas), Kazimir Kmiecik, Krzysztof Adamczyk, Hristos Andreoudis, Giannis Valaoras.   Trainer: Andrei Strejlau

Goal: Fomichiev (60)

BAYERN MÜNCHEN v AS ROMA 2-0 (1-0)

Olympiastadion, München   6.03.1985

Referee: George Courtney (ENG)   Attendance: 60,000

BAYERN: Jean-Marie Pfaff, Wolfgang Dremmler, Klaus Augenthaler, Norbert Eder, Holger Willmer, Norbert Nachtweih, Dieter Hoeness, Lothar Matthäus, Søren Lerby, Reinhold Mathy (74 Ludwig Kögl), Roland Wohlfahrt.   Trainer: Udo Lattek

AS ROMA: Franco Tancredi, Dario Bonetti, Antonino Carlos Cerezo, Emidio Oddi, Ubaldo Righetti, Sebastiano Nela, Odoacre Chierico, Giuseppe Giannini, Carlo Ancelotti, Roberto Pruzzo, Antonio di Carlo (79 Maurizio Iorio).   Trainer: Sven-Göran Eriksson

Goals: Augenthaler (44), Hoeness (77)

AS ROMA v BAYERN MÜNCHEN 1-3 (0-1)

Stadio Olimpico, Roma   20.03.1985

Referee: Vojtěch Christov (CZE)   Attendance: 55,000

AS ROMA: Franco Tancredi, Emidio Oddi, Dario Bonetti (86 Giuseppe Giannini), Ubaldo Righetti, Sebastiano Nela, Antonino Carlos Cerezo, Carlo Ancelotti, Maurizio Iorio, Roberto Pruzzo (46 Francesco Graziani), Bruno Conti, Odoacre Chierico.   Trainer: Sven-Göran Eriksson

BAYERN: Jean-Marie Pfaff, Klaus Augenthaler, Wolfgang Dremmler, Norbert Eder, Holger Willmer, Norbert Nachtweih, Lothar Matthäus, Søren Lerby, Hans Pflügler, Reinhold Mathy, Dieter Hoeness (68 Ludwig Kögl).   Trainer: Udo Lattek

Goals: Matthäus (32 pen), Nela (79), Kögl (80)

DYNAMO DRESDEN v RAPID WIEN 3-0 (0-0)

Dynamo Dresden   6.03.1985

Referee: Ronald Bridges (WAL)   Attendance: 36,000

DYNAMO: Bernd Jakubowski; Hans-Jürgen Dörner, Matthias Döschner, Andreas Trautmann, Reinhard Häfner, Jörg Stübner, Hans-Uwe Pilz, Frank Schuster, Ulf Kirsten, Ralf Minge (81 Dirk Losert), Torsten Gütschow (65 Frank Lippmann).   Trainer: Sammer

RAPID: Herbert Feurer, Heribert Weber, Leopold Lainer, Kurt Garger, Karl Brauneder; Johann Gröss (62 Hermann Stadler), Zlatko Kranjcar, Petar Brucic, Gerald Willfurth; Johann Krankl, Peter Pacult.   Trainer: Otto Barić

Goals: Trautmann (47), Minge (57), Kirsten (82)

RAPID WIEN v DYNAMO DRESDEN 5-0 (3-0)

Gerhard Hanappi, Wien   20.03.1985

Referee: Alain Delmer (FRA)   Attendance: 15,000

RAPID: Herbert Feurer; Heribert Weber, Leopold Lainer, Kurt Garger, Karl Brauneder; Gerald Willfurth, Petar Brucic, Antonin Panenka; Zlatko Kranjcar, Johann Krankl, Peter Pacult.   Trainer: Otto Barić

DYNAMO: Bernd Jakubowski, Hans-Jürgen Dörner, Matthias Döschner, Andreas Trautmann, Frank Schuster; Reinhard Häfner, Jörg Stübner, Hans-Uwe Pilz (82 Dirk Losert); Ulf Kirsten, Ralf Minge, Torsten Gütschow (53 Frank Lippmann).   Trainer: Sammer

Goals: Pacult (4, 37), Lainer (17), Panenka (70 pen), Krankl (77)

SEMI-FINALS

RAPID WIEN v DINAMO MOSKVA 3-1 (0-1)

Gerhard Hanappi, Wien   10.04.1985

Referee: Vojtěch Christov (CZE)   Attendance: 20,000

RAPID: Michael Konsel; Leopold Lainer, Johann Pregesbauer (46 Peter Hrstic), Kurt Garger, Rudolf Weinhofer; Antonin Panenka (85 Hermann Stadler), Karl Brauneder, Gerald Willfurth; Zlatko Kranjcar, Johann Krankl, Peter Pacult.   Trainer: Otto Barić

DINAMO: Aleksei Prudnikov, Sergei Silkin, Igor Bulanov, Aleksandr Novikov, Boris Pozdniakov, Aleksandr Khapsalis (76 Aleksandr Borodiuk), Renat Ataulin, Viktor Vasiliev (67 Yuri Pudischev), Vasili Karataev, Sergei Stukashov, Valeri Gazzaev.   Trainer: Aleksandr Savinov

Goals: Karataev (26 pen), Lainer (68), Krankl (70 pen), Hrstic (72)

DINAMO MOSKVA v RAPID WIEN 1-1 (1-1)

Dinamo Moskva   24.04.1985

Referee: Marcel van Langenhove (BEL)   Attendance: 50,400

DINAMO: Aleksei Prudnikov, Igor Bulanov, Aleksandr Novikov, Boris Pozdniakov, Aleksandr Golovnia, Aleksandr Khapsalis (75 Valeri Matiunin), Renat Ataulin, Viktor Vasiliev, Vasili Karataev, Sergei Stukashov, Aleksandr Molodtsov (23 Yuri Pudischev).   Trainer: Aleksandr Savinov

RAPID: Michael Konsel; Leopold Lainer, Kurt Garger, Karl Brauneder, Heribert Weber, Reinhard Kienast, Zlatko Kranjcar, Antonin Panenka (67 Peter Hrstic), Johann Krankl, Petar Brucic, Peter Pacult (60 Gerald Willfurth).   Trainer: Otto Barić

Goals: Panenka (4), Pozdniakov (29)

BAYERN MÜNCHEN v EVERTON LIVERPOOL 0-0
Olympiastadion, München 10.04.1985
Referee: Paolo Bergamo (ITA)   Attendance: 67,000

BAYERN: Jean-Marie Pfaff, Wolfgang Dremmler, Klaus Augenthaler, Norbert Eder, Holger Willmer, Lothar Matthäus, Hans Pflügler, Søren Lerby, Michael Rummenigge, Dieter Hoeness, Ludwig Kögl.   Trainer: Udo Lattek

EVERTON: Neville Southall, Derek Mountfield, Gary Stevens, Kevin Ratcliffe, Patrick van den Hauwe, Peter Reid, Alan Harper, Paul Bracewell, Kevin Richardson, Trevor Steven, Graeme Sharp.   Manager: Howard Kendall

EVERTON v BAYERN MÜNCHEN 3-1 (0-1)
Goodison Park, Liverpool 24.04.1985
Referee: Erik Fredriksson (SWE)   Attendance: 49,476

EVERTON: Neville Southall, Derek Mountfield, Gary Stevens, Kevin Ratcliffe, Patrick van den Hauwe, Peter Reid, Peter Reid, Andrew Gray, Trevor Steven, Kevin Sheedy, Paul Bracewell, Graeme Sharp.   Manager: Howard Kendall

BAYERN: Jean-Marie Pfaff, Wolfgang Dremmler, Klaus Augenthaler, Norbert Eder (73 Michael Rummenigge), Holger Willmer (66 Bertram Beierlozer), Norbert Nachtweih, Lothar Matthäus, Søren Lerby, Hans Pflügler, Dieter Hoeness, Ludwig Kögl.   Trainer: Udo Lattek

Goals: Hoeness (38), Sharp (48), Gray (73), Steven (86)

FINAL

EVERTON LIVERPOOL v RAPID WIEN 3-1 (0-0)
Feyenoord, Rotterdam 15.05.1985
Referee: Paolo Casarin (ITA)   Attendance: 50,000

EVERTON: Neville Southall, Gary Stevens, Derek Mountfield, Kevin Ratcliffe, Patrick van den Hauwe, Trevor Steven, Peter Reid, Paul Bracewell, Kevin Sheedy, Andrew Gray, Graeme Sharp.   Trainer: Howard Kendall.

RAPID: Michael Konsel, Heribert Weber, Leopold Lainer, Kurt Garger, Karl Brauneder, Reinhard Kienast, Zlatko Kranjcar, Peter Hrstic, Rudolf Weinhofer (67 Antonin Panenka), Johann Krankl, Peter Pacult (61 Johann Gröss).   Trainer: Otto Barić

Goals: Gray (58), Steven (73), Krankl (85), Sheedy (86)

Goalscorers European Cup-Winners' Cup 1984-85:

5 goals: Valeri Gazzaev (Dinamo Moskva), Andrew Gray (Everton Liverpool), Antonin Panenka (Rapid Wien)

4 goals: Roland Wohlfahrt (Bayern München), Graeme Sharp (Everton Liverpool), Zvonko Kurbos (FC Metz), Johann Krankl, Peter Pacult (Rapid Wien)

3 goals: Arthur Hoyer (Fortuna Sittard), Raymond Xuereb (Hamrun Spartans), Leopold Lainer (Rapid Wien), Marek Banaszkiewicz, Andrzej Iwan (Wisła Kraków)

2 goals: Graziani (AS Roma), Hoeness, Pflügler, M. Rummenigge (Bayern München), McGarvey (Celtic Glasgow), Bulanov, Karataev, Khapsalis (Dinamo Moskva), Häfner, Minge, Stübner (Dynamo Dresden), Sheedy, Steven (Everton Liverpool), Carrasco (FC Barcelona), Gomes (FC Porto), Holverda (Fortuna Sittard), Georgsson (ÍB Vestmannaeyjar), Kmiecik, Valaoras (Larisa AE), Mats Magnusson (Malmö FF), Kollshaugen (Moss FK), Brigger, Kok (Servette Genève), Georgiev, Kostadinov, Pashev, Stoinov (Trakia Plovdiv), Wróbel (Wisła Kraków), King (West Ham United)

1 goal: Moores (Apoel Nicosia), Metin, Kovacević (Beşiktaş Istanbul), Beattie (Ballymena United), J.Magalhaes, Futre (FC Porto), Schuster, Caldere (FC Barcelona), Deverić, Zl.Vujović (Hajduk Split), Rönnberg (Malmö FF), Elíasson (ÍB Vestmannaeyjar), Thines (US Luxembourg), Tieber (Siófok), Cordiez (KAA Gent), Törnvall (Kuusysi Lahti), Nawalka (Wisła Kraków), Brezík, Moravec (Inter Bratislava), Horne, Steel (Wrexham United), McClair, P.McStay (Celtic Glasgow), Nela, Pruzzo, Cerezo (AS Roma), Trautmann, Kirsten, Gütschow, Pilz (Dynamo Dresden), Patsiavouras, Adamczyk (Larisa), Rohr (FC Metz), Barberis, Decastel, Favre (Servette Genève), Van Well (Fortuna Sittard), Hrstic, Kranjcar, Brucic (Rapid Wien), Matthäus, Kögl, Augenthaler, Nachtweih (Bayern München), Fomichiev, Chesnokov, Argudiaev (Dinamo Moskva), Reid, Heath, Bracewell (Everton Liverpool)

Own goals: Sonor (FC Metz) for FC Barcelona, Sánchez (FC Barcelona) for FC Metz, Trautmann (Dynamo Dresden) for FC Metz, Mladenov (Trakia Plovdiv) for Bayern München

CUP WINNERS' CUP 1985-86

FIRST ROUND

FC ZURRIEQ v BAYER UERDINGEN 0-3 (0-2)
Valletta 17.09.1985
Referee: Dan Petrescu (ROM)   Attendance: 5,000
FC ZURRIEQ: Anthony Pace, Tony Bonnici, Louis Cutajar, Pierre Brincat, R.Zahra (53 Alfons Camilleri), Adelmo Paris, Gilberto De Ponti, Francis Scicluna, Mario Farrugia, Raymond Falzon, mario Schembri (60 Oliver Cutajar).
BAYER: Werner Vollack, Matthias Herget, Karl-Heinz Wöhrlin, Michael Dämgen, Wolfgang Funkel (85 Dietmar Klinger), Norbert Brinkmann, Rudi Bommer, Friedhelm Funkel, Werner Buttgereit (76 Franz Raschid), Atli Edvaldsson, Larus Gudmundsson.   Trainer: Karlheinz Feldkamp
Goals: F. Funkel (8, 34), Gudmundsson (87)

BAYER UERDINGEN v FC ZURRIEQ 9-0 (5-0)
Grotenburg, Krefeld 2.10.1985
Referee: Krzysztof Czermarmazowicz (POL)   Att: 8,000
BAYER: Manfred Kubik, Matthias Herget (58 Dietmar Janssen), Norbert Brinkmann, Dietmar Klinger, Karl-Heinz Wöhrlin, Rudi Bommer, Friedhelm Funkel, Franz Raschid, Frank Kirchhhoff (63 Toni Puszamszies), Horst Feilzer, Peter Loontiens.   Trainer: Karlheinz Feldkamp
FC ZURRIEQ: Anthony Pace, Tony Bonnici, Louis Cutajar, Pierre Brincat, Alfons Camilleri, Adelmo Paris, Francis Scicluna (46 Paul Camilleri), Mario Farrugia, Oliver Cutajar (58 Charlie Muscat), Raymond Falzon, Mario Schembri.
Goals: Bommer (13 pen, 32), F. Funkel (22 pen), Raschid (29, 49), Loontiens (37, 82), Puszamszies (72), Feilzer (76)

AS MONACO v UNIVERSITATEA CRAIOVA 2-0 (1-0)
Louis II, Monaco 18.09.1985
Referee: Franz Wöhrer (AUS)   Attendance: 7,765
AS MONACO: Jean-Luc Ettori; Abdallah Liégeon, Nenad Stojkovic, Juan-Ernest Simon, Manuel Amoros; Daniel Bravo, Bernard Genghini, Claude Puel; Philippe Tibeuf (67 Marcel Dib), Youssouf Fofana (60 Philippe Anziani), Bruno Bellone.   Trainer: Lucien Muller
UNIVERSITATEA: Silviu Lung; Adrian Popescu, Nicolae Tilihoi, Costică Ştefănescu, Nicolae Ungureanu; Gheorghe Popescu, Vasile Mănăilă, Ion Căţoi; Pavel Badea (46 Sorin Cîrţu), Rodion Cămătaru, Marian Bîcu (71 Ion Geolgău).   Trainers: Mircea Rădulescu & Silviu Stănescu
Goals: Bellone (21), Genghini (72)

UNIVERSITATEA CRAIOVA v AS MONACO 3-0 (1-0)
Central, Craiova 2.10.1985
Referee: Aron Schmidhuber (W. GER)   Attendance: 40,000
UNIVERSITATEA: Silviu Lung; Nicolae Negrilă, Nicolae Tilihoi, Costică Ştefănescu, Nicolae Ungureanu; Adrian Popescu, Vasile Mănăilă, Ion Căţoi (46 Florin Cioroianu); Pavel Badea, Marian Bîcu, Ion Geolgău.   Trainer: Mircea Rădulescu
AS MONACO: Jean-Luc Ettori; Abdallah Liégeon, Nenad Stojkovic, Juan-Ernest Simon (84 Philippe Anziani), Manuel Amoros; Dominique Bijotat, Daniel Bravo, Claude Puel, Bernard Genghini; Youssouf Fofana, Bruno Bellone.   Trainer: Lucien Muller
Goals: Geolgău (19, 82), Bîcu (77 pen)

RAPID WIEN v TATABÁNYA BANYASZ 5-0 (1-0)
Gerhard Hanappi, Wien 18.09.1985
Referee: Ion Crăciunescu (ROM)   Attendance: 15,500
RAPID: Michael Konsel; Kurt Garger, Reinhard Kienast, Karl Brauneder, Leopold Lainer, Petar Brucic, Gerald Willfurth, Rudolf Weinhofer (46 Peter Hrstic, 69 Johann Pregesbauer), Zlatko Kranjcar, Johann Krankl, Sulejman Halilovic.   Trainer: Vlatko Marković
TATABÁNYA: Miklós Józsa, József Vincze, Károly Lakatos, László Szabó, József Szalma; István Schmidt (87 Ignác Tepszics), László Emmer, Sándor Hermann, István Vincze (72 Ervin Udvardi II); József Kiprich, Gyula Plotár.
Goals: Halilovic (18, 69, 72), Kienast (58), Krankl (62)

TATABÁNYA BÁNYÁSZ v RAPID WIEN 1-1 (0-0)
Bányász, Tatabánya 2.10.1985
Referee: Ángel Franco Martínez (SPA)   Attendance: 5,000
TATABÁNYA: Miklós Józsa; Ignác Tepszics, László Szabó, László Emmer (55 Endre Udvardi I); Sándor Herrmann, István Schmidt, István Vincze, József Vincze, Ervin Udvardi II; József Kiprich, Gyula Plotár (69 Tibor Simon).
RAPID: Michael Konsel; Leopold Lainer, Heribert Weber, Karl Brauneder; Petar Brucic, Zlatko Kranjcar (70 Peter Pacult), Reinhard Kienast (59 Kurt Garger), Rudolf Weinhofer, Gerald Willfurth; Johann Krankl, Sulejman Halilovic.   Trainer: Vlatko Marković
Goals: Schmidt (50), Weinhofer (59)

**GALATASARAY ISTANBUL
v WIDZEW LÓDZ 1-0** (1-0)

Ali Sami Yen, Istanbul   18.09.1985

Referee: Bernd Stumpf (E. GER)   Attendance: 35,000

GALATASARAY: Zoran Simović; Yusuf Altintas, Rasit Cetiner, Erhan Önal, Ahmet Ceylan; Arif Kocabiyik, Bülent Alkiliç, Dzevad Prekazi; Halil Ibrahim Akçay, Cüneyt Tanman, Erdal Keser.

WIDZEW: Henryk Bolesta; Krzysztof Kaminski, Roman Wójcicki, Marek Dziuba, Kazimierz Przybys; Tadeusz Swiatek (85 Tomasz Glowacki), Miroslaw Jaworski, Krzysztof Kajrys, Marek Podsiadlo, Wlodzimierz Smolarek, Wieslaw Cisek (61 Jerzy Leszczyk).   Trainer: Bronisław Waligóra

Goal: Erhan Onal (13 pen)

**WIDZEW LÓDZ
v GALATASARAY ISTANBUL 2-1** (1-0)

Widzew Lódz   2.10.1985

Referee: Alan Robinson (ENG)   Attendance: 17,000

WIDZEW: Henryk Bolesta; Kazimierz Przybys, Roman Wójcicki, Marek Dziuba, Krzysztof Kaminski; Krzysztof Kajrys, Miroslaw Jaworski, Marek Podsiadlo (75 Tadeusz Swiatek), Jerzy Leszczyk, Wieslaw Cisek (67 Wieslaw Wraga), Wlodzimierz Smolarek.   Trainer: Bronisław Waligóra

GALATASARAY: Zoran Simović, Yusuf Altintas, Erhan Önal, Ahmet Ceylan, Rasit Cetiner, Ismail Demiriz, Halil Ibrahim Akçay, Dzevad Prekazi, Erdal Keser (63 Bülent Alkiliç), Cüneyt Tanman, Arif Kocabiyik (83 Adnan Esen).

Goals: Cisek (1), Erdal (54), Leszczyk (90)

HJK HELSINKI v FLAMURTARI VLORË 3-2 (3-1)

Olympiastadion, Helsinki   18.05.1985

Referee: Michal Listkiewicz (POL)   Attendance: 2,166

HJK: Markku Palmroos, Reijo Linna, Erik Holmgren, Petteri Schutschkoff, Harri Koskinen, Jari Rantanen, Juha Dahllund, Erkki Valla (78 Kari Martonen), Mika Muhonen (82 Hannu Valtonen), Terry Lee, Markku Kanerva.

FLAMURTARI: Halim Durimi, Petro Ruci, Kreshnik Çipi, Rrapo Taho, Lushaj, Alfred Ferko, Shkëlkim Muça, Alfred Zijai, Sokol Kushta (85 Latif Gjondeda), Agim Bubeqi, Vasil Ruci (75 Eqerem Memushi).

Goals: Muhonen (8), Kanerva (25), Muça (26), Rantanen (34), Bubeqi (65)

FLAMURTARI VLORË v HJK HELSINKI 1-2 (1-2)

Flamurtari Vlorë   2.10.1985

Referee: Konstantinos Dimitriadis (GRE)   Att: 15,000

FLAMURTARI: Luan Birçe (33 Halim Durimi); Petro Ruci, Kreshnik Çipi, Rrapo Taho, Lushaj, Alfred Ferko, Shkëlkim Muça, Alfred Zijai, Sokol Kushta (62 Latif Gjondeda), Agim Bubeqi, Vasil Ruci.

HJK: Markku Palmroos, Reijo Linna, Erik Holmgren, Jyrki Nieminen, Hannu Valtonen, Petteri Schutschkoff, Mika Muhonen (46 Kari Martonen), Erkki Valla, Markku Kanerva, Terry Lee (89 Harri Koskinen), Jari Rantanen.

Goals: Valla (9, 30), V. Ruci (11)

**ATLÉTICO MADRID
v CELTIC GLASGOW 1-1** (1-0)

Estadio Vicente Calderón, Madrid   18.09.1985

Referee: Volker Roth (RFG)   Attendance: 60,000

ATLÉTICO: Ubaldo Matildo FILLOL, JULIO PRIETO Martín (73 Juan José RUBIO Jiménez), Pedro TOMÁS Reñones Crego, Juan Carlos ARTECHE Gómez, Miguel Ángel RUIZ García, Enrique "QUIQUE" SETIÉN Soler, Luis Mario CABRERA Molina, Enrique "QUIQUE" RAMOS González, Jorge Orosman DA SILVA Echevarría, Jesús LANDÁBURU Sahuquillo, Roberto Simón MARINA.   Trainer: LUIS Aragonés

CELTIC: Patrick Bonner, Daniel McGrain, Thomas Burns, Robert Aitken, Paul McGugan, Peter Grant, David Provan, Paul McStay, Maurice Johnston, Murdo MacLeod, Brian McClair.   Manager: David Hay

Goals: Setién (34), Johnston (69)

**CELTIC GLASGOW
v ATLÉTICO MADRID 1-2** (0-1)

Celtic Park, Glasgow   2.10.1985

Referee: Paolo Casarin (ITA)   Attendance: 200

CELTIC: Patrick Bonner, Daniel McGrain (78 Alan McInally), Thomas Burns, Robert Aitken, Paul McGugan, Peter Grant, David Provan, Paul McStay (69 Thomas McAdam), Maurice Johnston, Murdo MacLeod, Brian McClair.   Manager: David Hay

ATLÉTICO: Ubaldo Matildo FILLOL, Pedro TOMÁS Reñones Crego, CLEMENTE Villaverde Huelga, Juan Carlos ARTECHE Gómez, Miguel Ángel RUIZ García, Enrique "QUIQUE" SETIÉN Soler, Luis Mario CABRERA Molina (55 Juan José RUBIO Jiménez), Enrique "QUIQUE" RAMOS González, Jorge Orosman DA SILVA Echevarría, Jesús LANDÁBURU Sahuquillo, Roberto Simón MARINA (66 JULIO PRIETO Martín).   Trainer: LUIS Aragonés

Goals: Setién (39), Quique Ramos (72), Aitken (73)

FC UTRECHT v DINAMO KIEV 2-1 (1-0)
Nieuw Galgenwaard, Utrecht   18.09.1985
Referee: Raul Joaquín Fernandes Nazarre (POR)   Att: 18,000
FC UTRECHT: Jan Willem Van Ede, Herman Verrips, Wim Rijsbergen, Ton Du Chatinier, Edwin Godee (83 Gerrit Plomp), Jan Wouters, Gert Kruys, Frans Adelaar, Peter Van der Waart, John Van Loen, Johan Van der Hooft.
Trainer: Nol de Ruiter
DINAMO: Mikhail Mikhailov, Ivan Yaremchuk, Vladimir Bessonov, Oleg Kuznetsov, Anatoli Demianenko, Andrei Bal, Pavel Yakovenko, Aleksandr Zavarov, Vasili Rats, Vadim Evtuschenko, Oleg Blohin (73 Igor Belanov).
Trainer: Valeriy Lobanovskiy
Goals: Kruys (40), Van Loen (63), Demianenko (82)

DINAMO KIEV v FC UTRECHT 4-1 (2-1)
Republikanskiy, Kiev   2.10.1985
Referee: Talal Tokat (TUR)   Attendance: 100,062
DINAMO: Mikhail Mikhailov, Ivan Yaremchuk, Vladimir Bessonov, Oleg Kuznetsov, Anatoli Demianenko, Andrei Bal, Pavel Yakovenko (81 Sergei Baltacha), Aleksandr Zavarov, Vasili Rats, Vadim Evtuschenko, Oleg Blohin (71 Igor Belanov).   Trainer: Valeriy Lobanovskiy
FC UTRECHT: Jan Willem Van Ede, Herman Verrips, Wim Rijsbergen, Ton Du Chatinier, Gerrit Plomp, Jan Wouters, Ton De Kruyk, Frans Adelaar, Peter Van der Waart, John Van Loen, Johan Van der Hooft (46 Edwin Godee).
Trainer: Nol de Ruiter
Goals: De Kruyk (8), Blohin (9), Yaremchuk (19), Zavarov (55), Evtuschenko (60)

AIK SOLNA v RED BOYS DIFFERDANGE 8-0 (2-0)
Råsunda Solna   18.09.1985
Referee: Simo Ruokonen (FIN)   Attendance: 2,387
AIK: Bernt Ljung, Göran Göransson (73 Roger Sundin), Mats Olausson, Sven Dahlqvist, Björn Kindlund, Thomas Lundmark (73 Johan Johansson), Lars Zetterlund, Thomas Bergman, Mats Rohdin, Thomas Johansson, Thomas Andersson.
RED BOYS: Chèvremont, Daniel Kuffer, René Scheuer, Marc Thomé, Juan Sarrias (88 Manuel Schammo), Gilbert Hotton, Sauro Marinelli (86 Pascal Burger), Luigi de Stephanis, René Müller, Romain Michaux, Patrick Formica.
Goals: Andersson (9), Dahlqvist (35, 58), Bergman (47, 55), Lundmark (60), Zetterlund (77), T. Johansson (80)

RED BOYS DIFFERDANGE v AIK SOLNA 0-5 (0-3)
Differdange   2.10.1985
Referee: Manfred Neuner (W. GER)   Attendance: 341
RED BOYS: Chèvremont, Daniel Kuffer, René Scheuer, Marc Thomé, Manuel Schammo, Gilbert Hotton, René Müller, Juan Sarrias, Romain Schreiner (85 Ralph Hilgert), Fabrizio Bei (82 Pierrot Ferrari), Patrick Formica.
AIK: Bernt Ljung, Mats Rohdin, Kari Virtanen, Mats Olausson, Björn Kindlund, Thomas Bergman (65 Thomas Lundmark), Goran Göransson, Björn Johansson, Thomas Andersson, Lars Zetterlund (65 Thomas Johansson), Roger Sundin.
Goals: Sundin (11), Bergman (15), Göransson (27), Andersson (81), B. Johansson (88)

LARISA v SAMPDORIA GENOVA 1-1 (1-0)
Alkazar, Larisa   18.09.1985
Referee: Jan N.I. Keizer (HOL)   Attendance: 35,000
LARISA: Giorgos Plitsis, Dimitris Parafestas, Kostas Kolomitrousis, Giorgos Mitsibonas, Giannis Gkalitsios, Theodoros Voutiritsas, Janusz Kupcewicz, Thanasis Tsiolis (77 Filippos Stamos), Krzysztof Adamczyk, Hristos Andreoudis, Giannis Valaoras (77 Giorgos Agoragiannis).
Trainer: Andrej Strejlau
SAMPDORIA: Ivano Bordon, Moreno Mannini, Roberto Galia, Fausto Pari, Pietro Vierchowod, Luca Pellegrini, Alessandro Scanziani, Graeme Souness, Trevor Francis (58 Gianluca Vialli), Gianfranco Matteoli, Roberto Mancini.
Trainer: Eugenio Bersellini
Goals: Mitsibonas (39), Mancini (81)

SAMPDORIA GENOVA v LARISA 1-0 (1-0)
Luigi Ferraris, Genova   2.10.1985
Referee: Siegfried Kirschen (E. GER)   Attendance: 36,000
SAMPDORIA: Ivano Bordon, Moreno Mannini, Roberto Galia, Fausto Pari, Pietro Vierchowod, Luca Pellegrini, Alessandro Scanziani, Graeme Souness, Roberto Mancini (89 Fausto Salsano), Gianfranco Matteoli, Gianluca Vialli (85 Trevor Francis).   Trainer: Eugenio Bersellini
LARISA: Giorgos Plitsis, Dimitris Parafestas, Kostas Kolomitrousis, Giorgos Mitsibonas, Giannis Gkalitsios, Theodoros Voutiritsas, Mihalis Ziogas, Janusz Kupcewicz (79 Giannis Alexoulis), Krzysztof Adamczyk (51 Panagiotis Katholos), Hristos Andreoudis, Giannis Valaoras.
Trainer: Andrej Strejlau
Goal: Mancini (41)

AEL LIMASSOL v DUKLA PRAHA 2-2 (0-1)
Limassol   18.09.1985
Referee: Radu Petrescu (ROM)   Attendance: 10,000
AEL: Andreas Konstantinou, Panikos Orfanidis, Makis Sokratous, Giorgos Stylianou, Giorgos Anastasiou, Gejza Farkas, Josef Pesice (67 Aristos Aristotelous), Pavlos Savva, Giannis Ioannou, Loizos Mavroudis, Stelios Pelendritis (46 Hristos Koliantris).   Trainer: František Havránek
DUKLA: Karel Štromsik, Aleš Laušman, Josef Novák, Josef Klucký, Dušan Fitzel, Peter Fijalka, Stanislav Pelc, Miloš Belák, Milan Luhový, Pavel Korejcík, Tomáš Kríz.
Trainer: Jiří Lopata
Goals: Korejcík (36), Savva (55), Farkas (62), Pelc (78)

BANGOR CITY v FK FREDRIKSTAD 0-0
Farrar Road, Bangor   2.10.1985
Referee: Egbert Mulder (HOL)   Attendance: 4,000
BANGOR CITY: David Davies; Mark Cartwright, Phil Lunn, Gary Evans, Jerry Banks, Les Armor (71 Paul Whelan), Bruce Urquhart, Mark Palios, Viv Williams, Everton Williams, Neville Powell (65 Reg McGuire).   Trainer: John Mahoney
FREDRIKSTAD: Jan Erik Olsen; Lars Sørlie, Per Egil Ahlsen, Hans Deunk, Terje Jensen; Espen Engebretsen, Morten Thomassen (69 Vidar Boye Hansen), Jan Rafn (69 Vidar Kristoffersen), Steinar Baerøe Mathisen, Atle Kristoffersen, Vidar Hansen.

DUKLA PRAHA v AEL LIMASSOL 4-0 (1-0)
Stadión na Juliske, Praha   2.10.1985
Referee: Vladimir Kuznetsov (USSR)   Attendance: 6,000
DUKLA: Karel Štromsik, Dušan Fitzel, Josef Klucký, Josef Novák, Petr Rada, Ladislav Vízek, Stanislav Pelc (70 Aleš Laušman), Miloš Belák, Milan Luhový, Pavel Korejcík, Tomáš Kríz.   Trainer: Jiří Lopata
AEL: Andreas Konstantinou; Giannis Ioannou, Makis Sokratous, Hristos Hristoforou, Giorgos Anastasiou, Gejza Farkas, Josef Pesice, Aristos Aristotelous, Pavlos Savva (75 Hristos Genethliou), Loizos Mavroudis, Stelios Pelendritis (68 Hristos Koliantris).
Goals: Luhový (29), Pelc (49, 65), Vízek (60)

CERCLE BRUGGE v DYNAMO DRESDEN 3-2 (2-0)
Jan Breydelstadion, Brugge   18.09.1985
Referee: Gerald Losert (AUS)   Attendance: 9,000
CERCLE: Frank Mestdagh, Hans Van der Broek, Filip Schepens, Wim Kooiman, André Raes, Kari Ukkonen, Jef Vanthournout, Kurt Soenens (75 Karel Cornelissen), Zoran Bojovic, Paul Sanders, Edi Krncevic.
Trainer: Georges Leekens
DYNAMO: Bernd Jakubowski, Hans-Jürgen Dörner, Andreas Trautmann, Steffen Büttner, Reinhard Häfner, Roland Rüster, Ralf Minge, Hans-Uwe Pilz, Jörg Stübner, Ulf Kirsten, Frank Lippmann (46 Matthias Sammer).
Goals: Vanthournout (23), Raes (26), Trautmann (55), Kirsten (75), Krncevic (81)

FK FREDRIKSTAD v BANGOR CITY 1-1 (0-0)
Fredrikstad Stadion   18.09.1985
Referee: Egsteinn Gudmundsson (ICE)   Attendance: 2,611
FREDRIKSTAD: Jan Erik Olsen; Lars Sørlie, Per Egil Ahlsen, Hans Deunk, Espen Engebretsen; Morten Thomassen, Terje Jensen, Vidar Boye Hansen (28 Jan Rafn); Steinar Baerøe Mathisen, Atle Kristoffersen, Vidar Hansen.
BANGOR CITY: David Davies; Mark Cartwright, Phil Lunn, Gary Evans, Jerry Banks, Les Armor, Bruce Urquhart, Mark Palios, Viv Williams (68 Reg McGuire), Everton Williams, Neville Powell.   Trainer: John Mahoney
Goals: E. Williams (60), Deunk (87)

DYNAMO DRESDEN v CERCLE BRUGGE 2-1 (1-0)
Dynamo Dresden   2.10.1985
Referee: Håkan Lundgren (SWE)   Attendance: 35,000
DYNAMO: Bernd Jakubowski, Hans-Jürgen Dörner, Andreas Trautmann, Matthias Döschner, Reinhard Häfner, Jörg Stübner, Ralf Minge, Hans-Uwe Pilz (86 Roland Rüster), Ulf Kirsten, Matthias Sammer (77 Dirk Losert), Frank Lippmann.
CERCLE: Frank Mestdagh, Hans Van der Broek, Filip Schepens, Wim Kooiman, André Raes, Jef Vanthournout, Geert Broeckaert, Zoran Bojovic, Kari Ukkonen, Edi Krncevic, Paul Sanders (70 Peter Carly).   Trainer: Georges Leekens
Goals: Pilz (37), Krncević (47), Lippmann (49)

**CRVENA ZVEZDA BEOGRAD
v FC AARAU 2-0** (1-0)
Crvena Zvezda Beograd 18.09.1985
Referee: A.Milchenko (USSR)   Attendance: 37,700
CRVENA ZVEZDA: Živan Ljukovcan, Marko Elsner, Dragan Miletović, Slavko Radovanović, Milan Janković, Boško Djurovski, Milan Ivanović (46 Miroslav Šugar), Miralem Zjajo, Jovica Nikolić, Husref Musemić, Mitar Mrkela (85 Zoran Dimitrijević).

FC AARAU: Roberto Böckli; Rolf Osterwalder, Hans Rudolf Zahner, Markus Schärer, Hansruedi Schaer (32 Patrick Taudien), Roberto Fregno, Jens-Jörn Bertelsen, Alfred Herberth, Walter Iselin, Christophe Gilli, Erwin Meyer (89 Uwe Wassmer). Trainer: Ottmar Hitzfeld (GER)

Goals: Musemić (22), B. Djurovski (72)

GALWAY UNITED v LYNGBY IF 2-3 (0-2)
Sportsground, Galway 2.10.1985
Referee: Konstantinos Dimitriadis (GRE)   Att: 5,300
GALWAY UNITED: Richard Blackmore, Gerard Daly, Kevin Cassidy, Denis Bonner, Brian Gardiner, Jimmy Nolan, Eamonn Deacy, Micky McLoughlin (.. Rory Fahy), Martin McDonnell, Paul McGee, Malcolm McGonigle (46 Paul Murphy).

LYNGBY: Per Poulsen, Tom Olczyk, Lars Sørensen, Peter Packness, John Larsen, Michael Schäfer, Michael Lyng, Henrik Bo Larsen, Michael Christopherson, Flemming Christensen, Michael Spansborg.

Goals: F. Christensen (12), Schäfer (42), Murphy (51), Bonner (84), Lyng (86)

**FC AARAU
v CRVENA ZVEZDA BEOGRAD 2-2** (2-2)
Letzigrund, Zürich 2.10.1985
Referee: Robert Matusik (CZE)   Attendance: 12,000
FC AARAU: Roberto Böckli; Rolf Osterwalder, Hans Rudolf Zahner, Markus Schärer, Christophe Gilli, Jens-Jörn Bertelsen, Roberto Fregno (70 Uwe Wassmer), Alfred Herberth, Walter Iselin, Erwin Meyer (83 Hansruedi Metschl), Thomas Zwahlen. Trainer: Ottmar Hitzfeld

CRVENA ZVEZDA: Živan Ljukovčan; Dragan Miletović, Zlatko Krmpotić, Slavko Radovanović, Milan Janković, Boško Djurovski, Milan Ivanović, Marko Elsner, Jovica Nikolić (89 Miroslav Šugar), Husref Musemić, Mitar Mrkela.

Goals: Musemić (3), Meyer (7), Janković (17), Zwahlen (37)

**FRAM REYKJAVIK
v GLENTORAN BELFAST 3-1** (1-0)
Laugardalsvöllur, Reykjavik 1.09.1985
Referee: Rolf Ericsson (SWE)   Attendance: 1,382
FRAM: Fridrik Fridriksson, Thorsteinn Vilhjalmsson (..Orn Valdimarsson), Ormarr Örlygsson, Pétur Ormslev, Vidar Thorkelsson, Kristinn Rúnar Jónsson, Sverrir Einarsson, Gudmundur Steinsson, Omar Torfasson, Gudmundur Torfasson, Asgeir Elíasson.

GLENTORAN: Reg Hillen, George Neill, Thomas Connell, Robert Bowers, Paul Dixon, Raymond Morrison, John Jameson, David Mills, Ron Manley, Alfie Stewart, James Cowden (.. Gerry Mullan).

Goals: Bowers (2), Torfasson (49, 80), Thorkelsson (68)

LYNGBY IF v GALWAY UNITED 1-0 (1-0)
København 18.09.1985
Referee: Oli P. Olsen (ICE)   Attendance: 2,800
LYNGBY: Per Poulsen, Tom Olczyk, Lars Sørensen, Peter Packness, John Larsen, Michael Christophersen (90 John Andreasen), Henrik Bo Larsen, Michael Schäfer, Michael Spansborg, Flemming Christensen, Michael Lyng (66 Michael Gothenborg).

GALWAY UNITED: Richard Blackmore, Gerard Daly, Kevin Cassidy, Denis Bonner, Brian Gardiner, Jimmy Nolan, Eamonn Deacy, John Mannion, Martin McDonnell, Paul McGee, Malcolm McGonigle (77 Micky McLoughlin).

Goal: F. Christensen (36)

**GLENTORAN BELFAST
v FRAM REYKJAVIK 1-0** (0-0)
The Oval, Belfast 2.10.1985
Referee: Jan Damgaard (DEN)   Attendance: 5,000
GLENTORAN: Reg Hillen, George Neill, Thomas Connell, Robert Bowers, Terry Moore, James Cleary, John Jameson, Raymond Morrison, Ron Manley (.. Gary Blackledge), Gerry Mullan, Alfie Stewart (.. David Mills).

FRAM: Fridrik Fridriksson, Thorsteinn Vilhjalmsson, Ormarr Örlygsson, Pétur Ormslev, Vidar Thorkelsson, Kristinn Rúnar Jónsson, Sverrir Einarsson, Gudmundur Steinsson, Omar Torfasson, Gudmundur Torfasson, Steinn Gudjónsson.

Goal: Mullan (72)

SECOND ROUND

BAYER UERDINGEN
v GALATASARAY ISTANBUL 2-0 (1-0)
Grotenburg Krefeld   23.10.1985
Referee: Henning Lund Sørensen (DEN)   Att: 27,000
BAYER: Werner Vollack, Matthias Herget, Michael Dämgen, Norbert Brinkmann, Rudi Bommer, Horst Feilzer, Wolfgang Funkel, Werner Buttgereit, Friedhelm Funkel (85 Dietmar Klinger), Wolfgang Schäfer (75 Frank Kirchhhoff), Peter Loontiens.   Trainer: Karlheinz Feldkamp
GALATASARAY: Zoran Simović, Erhan Önal, Ismail Demiriz, Rasit Cetiner, Ahmet Ceylan (28 Eser), Ibrahim Akçay, Dzevad Prekazi, Arif Kocabiyik, Bülent Alkiliç, Erdal Keser (74 Erkan Ultanir), Cüneyt Tanman.

Goals: Schäfer (35), Bommer (85)

DINAMO KIEV
v UNIVERSITATEA CRAIOVA 3-0 (3-0)
Republikanskiy, Kiev   6.11.1985
Referee: Lajos Nemeth (HUN)   Attendance: 100,062
DINAMO: Mikhail Mikhailov; Vasili Evseev, Sergei Baltacha, Oleg Kuznetsov, Anatoli Demianenko; Vasili Rats, Ivan Yaremchuk, Andrei Bal, Aleksandr Zavarov; Igor Belanov (79 Aleksei Mikhailichenko), Oleg Blohin (71 Vadim Evtuschenko).   Trainer: Valeriy Lobanovskiy

UNIVERSITATEA: Silviu Lung; Nicolae Negrilă, Nicolae Tilihoi, Costică Ştefănescu, Nicolae Ungureanu; Gheorghe Popescu (46 Ion Căţoi), Adrian Popescu (67 Pavel Badea), Mircea Irimescu, Vasile Mănăilă; Ion Geolgău, Marian Bîcu.
Trainer: Mircea Rădulescu

Goals: Rats (5), Belanov (11), Demianenko (12)

GALATASARAY ISTANBUL
v BAYER UERDINGEN 1-1 (0-1)
Ali Sami Yen, Istanbul   5.11.1985
Referee: Bruno Galler (SWI)   Attendance: 23,777
GALATASARAY: Zoran Simović, Ismail Demiriz, Rasit Cetiner, Erhan Önal, Yusuf Altintas, Ahmet Ceylan (28 Adnan Esen), Dzevad Prekazi, Arif Kocabiyik (.. Semih Caliskan), Öner Kiliç, Cüneyt Tanman, Bülent Alkiliç.

BAYER: Werner Vollack, Karl-Heinz Wöhrlin, Wolfgang Funkel, Matthias Herget, Michael Dämgen, Dietmar Klinger, Horst Feilzer, Friedhelm Funkel, Rudi Bommer, Wolfgang Schäfer, Peter Loontiens (..Larus Gudmundsson).
Trainer: Karlheinz Feldkamp

Goals: Herget (26), Prekazi (55)

DUKLA PRAHA v AIK SOLNA 1-0 (1-0)
Stadión na Juliske, Praha   23.10.1985
Referee: Talal Tokat (TUR)   Attendance: 10,000
DUKLA: Petr Kostelník, Dušan Fitzel, Josef Novák, Petr Rada, Aleš Laušman (62 Günther Bittengel), Stanislav Pelc, Peter Fijalka, Miloš Belák, Milan Luhový, Pavel Korejcík, Tomáš Kríz.   Trainer: Jiří Lopata

AIK: Bernt Ljung, Johan Johansson, Sven Dahlqvist, Mats Olausson, Mats Rohdin, Thomas Lundmark, Kari Virtanen, Lars Zetterlund (44 Thomas Bergman), Göran Göransson, Thomas Johansson, Roger Sundin.

Goal: Korejcík (7)

UNIVERSITATEA CRAIOVA
v DINAMO KIEV 2-2 (1-2)
Central Craiova   23.10.1985
Referee: Iordan Zhezhov (BUL)   Attendance: 40,000
UNIVERSITATEA: Silviu Lung; Nicolae Negrilă, Nicolae Tilihoi, Costică Ştefănescu, Nicolae Ungureanu; Adrian Popescu (76 Gheorghe Popescu), Vasile Mănăilă, Ion Căţoi; Pavel Badea, Marian Bîcu, Ion Geolgău.
Trainer: Mircea Rădulescu

DINAMO: Mikhail Mikhailov; Vladimir Bessonov, Sergei Baltacha, Oleg Kuznetsov, Anatoli Demianenko; Vasili Rats, Pavel Iakovenko (15 Andrei Bal), Ivan Yaremchuk, Aleksandr Zavarov; Vadim Evtuschenko (68 Igor Belanov), Oleg Blohin.
Trainer: Valeriy Lobanovskiy

Goals: Bîcu (12, 82 pen), Zavarov (16, 24)

AIK SOLNA v DUKLA PRAHA 2-2 (1-1)
Råsunda, Solna   6.11.1985
Referee: David F.T. Syme (SCO)   Attendance: 8,500
AIK: Bernt Ljung; Johan Johansson, Kari Virtanen, Mats Olausson, Göran Göransson, Roger Sundin (55 Lars Zetterlund), Thomas Lundmark, Thomas Bergman, Mats Rohdin (76 Björn Johansson), Sven Dahlqvist, Thomas Johansson.

DUKLA: Petr Kostelník; Pavel Karoch, Josef Novák, Dušan Fitzel, Pet Rada, Ladislav Vízek, Günther Bittengel (80 Miloš Belák), Stanislav Pelc (88 Peter Fijalka), Tomáš Kríz, Milan Luhový, Pavel Korejcík.   Trainer: Jiří Lopata

Goals: Vízek (13, 60), Dahlqvist (14), Zetterlund (89)

**BENFICA LISBOA
v SAMPDORIA GENOVA 2-0** (0-0)
Estádio da Luz, Lisboa   23.10.1985
Referee: Vojtěch Christov (CZE)   Attendance: 92,500
BENFICA: Manuel Galrinho BENTO (Cap), SAMUEL António Silva Tavares Quina, António Henrique Jesus OLIVEIRA, António José BASTOS LOPES, ÁLVARO Monteiro Magalhaes, CARLOS Eduardo Deus PEREIRA (41 DIAMANTINO Manuel Miranda), SHÉU Han, JOSÉ LUÍS Lopes Costa e Silva, CARLOS MANUEL Correia dos Santos, Michael Manniche, Tamagnini Manuel Gomes Baptista NENÉ (75 José RUI Lopes AGUAS).   Trainer: John Mortimore
SAMPDORIA: Ivano Bordon, Moreno Mannini, Roberto Galia, Fausto Pari, Pietro Vierchowod, Luca Pellegrini, Alessandro Scanziani, Graeme Souness, Roberto Mancini, Fausto Salsano, Gianluca Vialli.   Trainer: Eugenio Bersellini
Goals: Diamantino (47), Rui Aguas (89).

**SAMPDORIA GENOVA
v BENFICA LISBOA 1-0** (0-0)
Luigi Ferraris, Genova   6.11.1985
Referee: Volker Roth (W. GER)   Attendance: 30,000
SAMPDORIA: Ivano Bordon, Moreno Mannini, Fausto Pari (85 Roberto Galia), Alessandro Scanziani, Pietro Vierchowod, Luca Pellegrini, Gianluca Vialli, Graeme Souness, Trevor Francis, Gianfranco Matteoli, Roberto Mancini (56 Giuseppe Lorenzo).   Trainer: Eugenio Bersellini
BENFICA: Manuel Galrinho BENTO (Cap), SAMUEL António Silva Tavares Quina, António Augusto da Silva VELOSO, António José BASTOS LOPES, António Henrique Jesus OLIVEIRA, ÁLVARO Monteiro Magalhaes, SHÉU Han (63 Adelino Carlos Morais NUNES), JOSÉ LUÍS Lopes Costa e Silva (88 Tamagnini Manuel Gomes Baptista NENÉ), CARLOS MANUEL Correia dos Santos, DIAMANTINO Manuel Miranda, Michael Manniche.   Trainer: John Mortimore
Goal: Lorenzo (62)

SK RAPID WIEN v FRAM REYKJAVIK 3-0 (1-0)
Gerhard Hanappi, Wien   23.10.1985
Referee: Stefanos Hatzistefanou (CYP)   Attendance: 14,500
RAPID: Michael Konsel; Leopold Lainer, Heribert Weber, Kurt Garger, Karl Brauneder; Zlatko Kranjcar, Petar Brucic, Rudolf Weinhofer (45 Franz Weber), Gerald Willfurth (66 Peter Pacult), Sulejman Halilovic, Johann Krankl. Trainer: Vlatko Markovic
FRAM: Fridrik Fridriksson, Thorsteinn Thorsteinsson, Vidar Thorkelsson, Ormarr Örlygsson, Pétur Ormslev, Sverrir Einarsson, Kristinn Rúnar Jónsson, Gudmundur Steinsson, Asgeir Elíasson, Omar Thorfasson, Gudmundur Torfasson.
Goals: Kranjcar (18), Pacult (80, 85).

FRAM REYKJAVIK v RAPID WIEN 2-1 (1-0)
Laugardalsvöllur, Reykjavik   6.11.1985
Referee: Frederick McKnight (NIR)   Attendance: 450
FRAM: Fridrik Fridriksson, Ormarr Örlygsson, Sverrir Einarsson, Thorsteinn Thorsteinsson, Vidar Thorkelsson, Omar Torfasson, Pétur Ormslev (78 Steinn Gudjónsson), Kristinn Rúnar Jónsson, Gudmundur Steinsson, Gudmundur Torfasson, Orn Valdimarsson (82 Asgeir Elíasson).
RAPID: Michael Konsel, Leopold Lainer, Heribert Weber, Kurt Garger, Johann Pregesbauer; Petar Brucic, Zlatko Kranjcar, Karl Brauneder, Franz Weber (55 Leopold Rotter), Sulejman Halilovic, Peter Pacult (83 Bernhard Brunner).
Trainer: Vlatko Marković
Goals: Jonsson (17), Pacult (66), Thorfasson (88 pen)

BANGOR CITY v ATLÉTICO MADRID 0-2 (0-2)
Farrar Road, Bangor   23.10.1985
Referee: Albert R. Thomas (HOL)   Attendance: 5,181
BANGOR CITY: David Davies, Mark Cartwright, Phil Lunn, Gary Evans, Jerry Banks, Les Armor, Bruce Urquhart (80 Paul Whelan), Mark Palios, Ian McMullen (65 Viv Williams), Everton Williams, Neville Powell.   Trainer: John Mahoney
ATLÉTICO: Ubaldo Matildo FILLOL (46 Ángel Jesús MEJÍAS Rodríguez), JULIO PRIETO Martín, Pedro TOMÁS Reñones Crego, Juan Carlos ARTECHE Gómez, Miguel Ángel RUIZ García, Enrique "QUIQUE" SETIÉN Soler, Luis Mario CABRERA Molina (46 Juan José RUBIO Jiménez), Enrique "QUIQUE" RAMOS González, Jorge Orosman DA SILVA Echevarría, Roberto Simón MARINA, Jesús LANDÁBURU Sahuquillo.   Trainer: LUIS Aragonés
Goals: Da Silva (5), Setién (25)

ATLÉTICO MADRID v BANGOR CITY 1-0 (1-0)
Estadio Vicente Calderón, Madrid   6.11.1985
Referee: Edgar Azzopardi (MAL)   Attendance: 20,000
ATLÉTICO: Ángel Jesús MEJÍAS Rodríguez, Pedro TOMÁS Reñones Crego (58 BALBINO García Puerto), Juan Carlos ARTECHE Gómez, SERGIO Elías Morgado Rodríguez, CLEMENTE Villaverde Huelga, Ricardo Ortega MÍNGUEZ, Jesús LANDÁBURU Sahuquillo, Roberto Simón MARINA, Enrique "QUIQUE" RAMOS González (46 Juan José RUBIO Jiménez), Luis Mario CABRERA Molina, Jorge Orosman DA SILVA Echevarría.   Trainer: LUIS Aragonés
BANGOR CITY: David Davies, Mark Cartwright, Phil Lunn, Gary Evans, Jerry Banks, Bruce Urquhart (55 Paul Whelan), Mark Palios, Les Armor, Neville Powell, Everton Williams, Viv Williams (64 Reg McGuire).   Trainer: John Mahoney
Goal: Landáburu (26)

HJK HELSINKI v DYNAMO DRESDEN 1-0 (0-0)
Olympiastadion, Helsinki   23.10.1985
Referee: Valeri Butenko (USSR)   Attendance: 3,454
HJK: Markku Palmroos, Jyrki Nieminen, Petteri Schutschkoff, Markku Kanerva, Erik Holmgren, Reijo Linna, Juha Dahllund, Mika Muhonen (63 Jari Parikka), Erkki Valla, Jari Rantanen (57 Kari Martonen), Terry Lee.
DYNAMO: Bernd Jakubowski, Hans-Jürgen Dörner, Roland Rüster, Andreas Trautmann, Matthias Döschner, Reinhard Häfner, Hans-Uwe Pilz, Jörg Stübner, Ulf Kirsten, Ralf Minge, Frank Lippmann (57 Matthias Sammer).
Goal: Lee (50)

CRVENA ZVEZDA BEOGRAD v LYNGBY 3-1 (1-0)
Crvena Zvezda Beograd   27.11.1985
Referee: Gerasimos Germanakos (GRE)
CRVENA ZVEZDA: Živan Ljukovčan, Miodrag Krivokapić, Milan Janković, Dragan Miletović, Marko Elsner, Miroslav Šugar, Jovica Nikolić, Boško Djurovski, Husref Musemić, Goran Milojević, Mitar Mrkela (22 Žarko Djurović).
LYNGBY: Per Poulsen, Tom Olczyk, Lars Sørensen, Henrik Larsen, Peter Packness, Michael Spangsborg (53 Michael Gothenborg), Michael Lyng (80 Dennis Foss Nielsen), Michael Schäfer, Flemming Christensen, Bent Christensen, Tom Vilmar.
Goals: Šugar (25), Nikolić (58), Vilmar (59), Djurović (84)

DYNAMO DRESDEN v HJK HELSINKI 7-2 (4-0)
Dynamo Dresden   6.11.1985
Referee: Einar Halle (NOR)   Attendance: 36,000
DYNAMO: Bernd Jakubowski, Hans-Jürgen Dörner, Steffen Büttner, Andreas Trautmann, Matthias Döschner, Reinhard Häfner, Hans-Uwe Pilz, Jörg Stübner, Ulf Kirsten, Matthias Sammer (53 Dirk Losert), Frank Lippmann.
HJK: Markku Palmroos, Juha Dahllund, Reijo Linna, Markku Kanerva, Petteri Schutschkoff, Jyrki Nieminen, Erik Holmgren, Harri Koskinen (46 Erkki Valla), Kari Martonen, Ari Valvee (74 Risto Puustinen), Terry Lee.
Goals: Sammer (19, 43), Lippmann (20, 69), Trautmann (40), Lee (48), Pilz (56), Valvee (61), Kirsten (90)

LYNGBY v CRVENA ZVEZDA BEOGRAD 2-2 (2-0)
København   23.10.1985
Referee: Arto Ravander (FIN)   Attendance: 48,000
LYNGBY: Per Poulsen, Tom Olczyk, Henrik Larsen, John Larsen, Peter Packness, Bent Christensen, Michael Spangsborg (55 Michael Gothenborg), Michael Schäfer, E.Kristensson, Michael Lyng (68 Henrik Bo Larsen), Tom Vilmar.
CRVENA ZVEZDA: Živan Ljukovčan, Slavisa Radanović, Milan Janković, Dragan Miletović, Zoran Dimitrijević, Marko Elsner, Jovica Nikolić, Boško Djurovski, Husref Musemić (84 Goran Milojević), MilkoDjurovski, Mitar Mrkela.
Goals: B. Christensen (4), Spangsborg (40), M. Djurovski (52), Mrkela (59)

QUARTER-FINALS

RAPID WIEN v DINAMO KIEV 1-4 (0-0)
Gerhard Hanappi, Wien   5.03.1986
Referee: Michel Vautrot (FRA)   Attendance: 13,000
RAPID: Michael Konsel, Heribert Weber, Leopold Lainer (75 Gerald Willfurth), Reinhard Kienast, Kurt Garger, Karl Brauneder, Zlatko Kranjcar, Petar Brucic, Rudolf Weinhofer, Sulejman Halilovic (63 Peter Hrstic), Peter Pacult. Trainer: Vlatko Markovic
DINAMO: Viktor Chanov, Vladimir Bessonov, Sergei Baltacha, Oleg Kuznetsov, Anatoli Demianenko, Vasili Rats, Pavel Yakovenko, Andrei Bal, Ivan Yaremchuk, Igor Belanov (77 Vadim Evtuschenko), Oleg Blohin. Trainer: Valeriy Lobanovskiy
Goals: Belanov (56, 61), Rats (68), Yakovenko (74), Willfurth (84)

DINAMO KIEV v RAPID WIEN 5-1 (4-1)
Republikanskiy, Kiev   19.03.1986
Referee: Ronald Bridges (WAL)   Attendance: 100,000
DINAMO: Viktor Chanov; Vladimir Bessonov, Sergei Baltacha, Oleg Kuznetsov, Anatoli Demianenko; Vasili Rats, Pavel Yakovenko, Ivan Yaremchuk, Aleksandr Zavarov (62 Vadim Evtuschenko); Igor Belanov, Oleg Blohin (74 Andrei Bal). Trainer: Valeriy Lobanovskiy
RAPID: Michael Konsel (46 Herbert Feurer); Heribert Weber, Kurt Garger, Leopold Rotter (46 Franz Weber), Reinhard Kienast, Rudolf Weinhofer, Gerald Willfurth, Karl Brauneder, Hermann Stadler, Zlatko Kranjcar, Sulejman Halilovic. Trainer: Vlatko Markovic
Goals: Yaremchuk (7, 32), Belanov (10 pen), Halilovic (39), Blohin (43), Evtuschenko (79)

DUKLA PRAHA v BENFICA LISBOA 1-0 (1-0)
Štadión na Juliske, Praha 5.03.1986
Referee: Marcel van Langenhove (BEL)   Attendance: 10,000
DUKLA: Petr Kostelník, Josef Klucký, Josef Novák, Jan Fiala, Petr Rada, Stanislav Pelc, Ladislav Vízek, Aleš Laušman (79 Tomáš Kríz), Pavel Korejcík, Aleš Bazant, Milan Luhový. Trainer: Jiří Lopata
BENFICA: Manuel Galrinho BENTO (Cap), SAMUEL António Silva Tavares Quina, António Augusto da Silva VELOSO, António José BASTOS LOPES, António Henrique Jesus OLIVEIRA, ÁLVARO Monteiro Magalhaes, SHÉU Han, DIAMANTINO Manuel Miranda, CARLOS MANUEL Correia dos Santos, Adelino Carlos Morais NUNES (86 José RUI Lopes AGUAS), Michael Manniche.   Trainer: John Mortimore

Goal: Luhovy (14)

BENFICA LISBOA v DUKLA PRAHA 2-1 (2-0)
Estádio da Luz, Lisboa 19.03.1986
Referee: Siegfried Kirschen (E. GER)   Attendance: 120,000
BENFICA: Manuel Galrinho BENTO (Cap), António Augusto da Silva VELOSO, SAMUEL António Silva Tavares Quina, António Henrique Jesus OLIVEIRA, ÁLVARO Monteiro Magalhaes (71 António José BASTOS LOPES), DIAMANTINO Manuel Miranda, SHÉU Han, CARLOS MANUEL Correia dos Santos, Geovânio Bonfim Sobrinho WANDO, José RUI Lopes AGUAS, Michael Manniche   Trainer: John Mortimore
DUKLA: Petr Kostelník, Josef Klucký, Josef Novák, Jan Fiala, Petr Rada, Stanislav Pelc, Ladislav Vízek (86 Aleš Laušman), Tomáš Kríz, Pavel Korejcík, Aleš Bazant, Milan Luhový. Trainer: Jiří Lopata

Goals: Carlos Manuel (20), Manniche (37 pen), Korejcík (65)

**DYNAMO DRESDEN
v BAYER UERDINGEN 2-0** (0-0)
Dynamo Dresden 5.03.1986
Referee: Joël Quiniou (FRA)   Attendance: 36,000
DYNAMO: Bernd Jakubowski, Hans-Jürgen Dörner, Steffen Büttner, Andreas Trautmann, Matthias Döschner, Reinhard Häfner, Jörg Stübner, Hans-Uwe Pilz, Ulf Kirsten, Matthias Sammer (69 Torsten Gütschow), Frank Lippmann.
BAYER: Werner Vollack, Matthias Herget, Karl-Heinz Wöhrlin, Friedhelm Funkel, Wolfgang Funkel, Michael Dämgen, Atli Edvaldsson (53 Franz Raschid), Dietmar Klinger, Werner Buttgereit (89 Norbert Brinkmann), Rudi Bommer, Wolfgang Schäfer.   Trainer: Karlheinz Feldkamp

Goals: Lippmann (50), Pilz (60)

**BAYER UERDINGEN
v DYNAMO DRESDEN 7-3** (1-3)
Grotenburg-Stadion, Krefeld 19.03.1986
Referee: Lajos Nemeth (HUN)   Attendance: 17,000
BAYER: Werner Vollack, Matthias Herget, Michael Dämgen, Wolfgang Funkel, Werner Buttgereit, Rudi Bommer, Franz Raschid (53 Dietmar Klinger), Horst Feilzer, Friedhelm Funkel, Larus Gudmundsson (74 Peter Loontiens), Wolfgang Schäfer.   Trainer: Karlheinz Feldkamp
DYNAMO: Bernd Jakubowski (46 Jens Ramme), Hans-Jürgen Dörner, Andreas Trautmann, Matthias Döschner, Reinhard Häfner, Ralf Minge, Jörg Stübner, Hans-Uwe Pilz, Ulf Kirsten, Matthias Sammer (28 Torsten Gütschow), Frank Lippmann.

Goals: Minge (1), W. Funkel (13, 57 pen, 79 pen), Lippmann (35), Bommer (42 og), Gudmundsson (62), Klinger (78), Schäfer (66, 87)

**CRVENA ZVEZDA BEOGRAD
v ATLÉTICO MADRID 0-2** (0-1)
Crvena Zvezda Beograd 5.03.1986
Referee: Luigi Agnolin (ITA)   Attendance: 65,000
CRVENA ZVEZDA: Živan Ljukovčan, Miodrag Krivokapić, Milan Janković, Dragan Miletović, Milan Ivanović, Goran Milojević (68 Žarko Djurović), Jovica Nikolić (79 Miroslav Šugar), Boško Djurovski, Husref Musemić, Milko Djurovski, Mitar Mrkela.
ATLÉTICO: Ubaldo Matildo FILLOL, Pedro TOMÁS Reñones Crego, CLEMENTE Villaverde Huelga, Juan Carlos ARTECHE Gómez, Miguel Ángel RUIZ García, Enrique "QUIQUE" SETIÉN Soler (73 Juan José RUBIO Jiménez), Luis Mario CABRERA Molina (62 Ricardo Ortega MÍNGUEZ), JULIO PRIETO Martín, Jorge Orosman DA SILVA Echevarría, Jesús LANDÁBURU Sahuquillo, Roberto Simón MARINA. Trainer: LUIS Aragonés

Sent off: M. Djurovski (74)

Goals: Da Silva (29, 90)

**ATLÉTICO MADRID
v CRVEA ZVEZDA BEOGRAD 1-1** (1-0)
Estadio Vicente Calderón, Madrid 19.03.1986
Referee: Robert Valentine (SCO)   Attendance: 42,000
ATLÉTICO: Ángel Jesús MEJÍAS Rodríguez, Pedro TOMÁS Reñones Crego, CLEMENTE Villaverde Huelga, Juan Carlos ARTECHE Gómez, Miguel Ángel RUIZ García; Enrique "QUIQUE" SETIÉN Soler (14 JULIO PRIETO Martín), Luis Mario CABRERA Molina, Ricardo Ortega MÍNGUEZ, Jorge Orosman DA SILVA Echevarría; Jesús LANDÁBURU Sahuquillo, Roberto Simón MARINA (30 Enrique "QUIQUE" RAMOS González).   Trainer: LUIS Aragonés

CRVENA ZVEZDA: Živan Ljukovčan, Miodrag Krivokapić, Zoran Dimitrijević, Dragan Miletović, Marko Elsner; Milan Ivanović, Žarko Djurović, Boško Djurovski, Husref Musemić; Miroslav Šugar, Mitar Mrkela.

Goals: Marina (7), Djurović (83)

BAYER: Werner Vollack, Matthias Herget, Michael Dämgen, Wolfgang Funkel, Atli Edvaldsson, Rudi Bommer, Horst Feilzer (87 Werner Buttgereit), Friedhelm Funkel, Dietmar Klinger, Franz Raschid, Larus Gudmundsson (63 Karl-Heinz Wöhrlin). Trainer: Karlheinz Feldkamp

Goal: Julio Prieto (78)

SEMI-FINALS

DINAMO KIEV v DUKLA PRAHA 3-0 (3-0)

Republikanskiy, Kiev 2.04.1986

Referee: José Rosa dos Santos (POR)   Attendance: 100,000

DINAMO: Viktor Chanov, Vladimir Bessonov, Sergei Baltacha, Oleg Kuznetsov, Anatoli Demianenko, Vasili Rats, Pavel Yakovenko, Ivan Yaremchuk, Aleksandr Zavarov, Igor Belanov, Oleg Blohin (73 Vadim Evtuschenko). Trainer: Valeriy Lobanovskiy

DUKLA: Petr Kostelník; Aleš Bazant, Josef Novák, Jan Fiala, Petr Rada, Aleš Laušman, Stanislav Pelc, Pavel Korejcík, Tomáš Kríz, Ladislav Vízek, Milan Luhový (66 Günther Bittengel). Trainer: Jiří Lopata

Goals: Blohin (7, 37), Zavarov (35).

DUKLA PRAHA v DINAMO KIEV 1-1 (0-0)

Juliska Stadión, Praha 16.04.1986

Referee: Ioan Igna (ROM)   Attendance: 22,000

DUKLA: Petr Kostelník; Jan Fiala, Aleš Bazant, Josef Novák, Petr Rada; Aleš Laušman, Stanislav Pelc, Dušan Fitzel; Tomáš Kríz, Pavel Korejcík, Milan Luhový.   Trainer: Jiří Lopata

DINAMO: Viktor Chanov (88 Mikhail Mikhailov); Ivan Yaremchuk, Sergei Baltacha, Oleg Kuznetsov, Anatoli Demianenko, Vasili Rats, Pavel Yakovenko, Andrei Bal, Aleksandr Zavarov (78 Vadim Evtuschenko), Igor Belanov, Oleg Blohin.   Trainer: Valeriy Lobanovskiy

Goals: Belanov (63 pen), Kríz (70)

ATLÉTICO MADRID v BAYER UERDINGEN 1-0 (0-0)

Estadio Vicente Calderón, Madrid 2.04.1986

Referee: Alexis Ponnet (BEL)   Attendance: 50,000

ATLÉTICO: Ubaldo Matildo FILLOL, Juan Carlos ARTECHE Gómez, JULIO PRIETO Martín, Miguel Ángel RUIZ García, CLEMENTE Villaverde Huelga, Pedro TOMÁS Reñones Crego, Roberto Simón MARINA, Jesús LANDÁBURU Sahuquillo, Enrique "QUIQUE" RAMOS González, Luis Mario CABRERA Molina (81 Juan Carlos Gómez PEDRAZA), Jorge Orosman DA SILVA Echevarría.   Trainer: LUIS Aragonés

BAYER UERDINGEN v ATLÉTICO MADRID 2-3 (0-2)

Grotenburg-Stadion, Krefeld 16.04.1986

Referee: Neil Midgley (ENG)   Attendance: 25,000

BAYER: Werner Vollack, Matthias Herget, Michael Dämgen, Wolfgang Funkel, Rudi Bommer, Dietmar Klinger, Atli Edvaldsson, Friedhelm Funkel, Franz Raschid, Wolfgang Schäfer (46 Peter Loontiens), Larus Gudmundsson (71 Horst Feilzer).   Trainer: Karlheinz Feldkamp

ATLÉTICO: Ángel Jesús MEJÍAS Rodríguez, Juan Carlos ARTECHE Gómez, Pedro TOMÁS Reñones Crego, Miguel Ángel RUIZ García, CLEMENTE Villaverde Huelga, JULIO PRIETO Martín, Roberto Simón MARINA, Jesús LANDÁBURU Sahuquillo, Enrique "QUIQUE" SETIÉN Soler (76 BALBINO García Puerto), Luis Mario CABRERA Molina, Juan José RUBIO Jiménez (71 Juan Carlos Gómez PEDRAZA).   Trainer: LUIS Aragonés

Goals: Rubio (16 pen), Cabrera (28), Herget (55), Prieto (58), Gudmundsson (64)

FINAL

DINAMO KIEV v ATLÉTICO MADRID 3-0 (1-0)

Stade de Gerland, Lyon 2.05.1986

Referee: Franz Wöhrer (AUS)   Attendance: 39,000

DINAMO: Viktor Chanov, Vladimir Bessonov, Sergei Baltacha (39 Andrei Bal), Oleg Kuznetsov, Anatoli Demianenko, Vasili Rats, Pavel Yakovenko, Ivan Yaremchuk, Aleksandr Zavarov (78 Vadim Evtuschenko), Igor Belanov, Oleg Blohin.   Trainer: Valeriy Lobanovskiy

ATLÉTICO: Ubaldo Matildo Fillol, Pedro TOMÁS Reñones Crego, CLEMENTE Villaverde Huelga, JULIO PRIETO Martin, Miguel Ángel RUIZ García, Juan Carlos ARTECHE Gómez, Luis Mario CABRERA Molina, Enrique "QUIQUE" RAMOS González, Jorge Orosman DA SILVA Echevarría, Jesus LANDÁBURU Sahuquillo (60 Enrique QUIQUE SETIÉN Solar), Roberto Simón MARINA.   Trainer: LUIS Aragonés

Goals: Zavarov (5), Blohin (84), Evtuschenko (87)

Goalscorers European Cup-Winners' Cup 1985-86:

5 goals: Igor Belanov, Oleg Blohin, Aleksandr Zavarov (Dinamo Kiev), Frank Lippmann (Dynamo Dresden)

4 goals: Sulejman Halilovic (Rapid Wien)

3 goals: Bergman, Dahlqvist (AIK Solna), da Silva, Quiqe Setién (Atlético Madrid), Bommer, F.Funkel, W.Funkel, Gudmundsson, Schäfer (Bayer Uerdingen), Evtuschenko, Yaremchuk (Dinamo Kiev), Korejcík, Pelc, Vízek (Dukla Praha), Pilz (Dynamo Dresden), Torfasson (Fram Reykjavík), Pacult (Rapid Wien), Bîcu (Universitatea Craiova)

2 goals: Krncevic (Cercle Brugge), Geolgău (Universitatea Craiova), Andersson, Zetterlund (AIK Solna), Mancini (Sampdoria Genova), Lee, Valla (HJK Helsinki), F.Christensen (Lyngby IF), Sammer, Trautmann, Kirsten (Dynamo Dresden), Djurović, Musemić (Crvena Zvezda), Luhový (Dukla Praha), Rats, Demianenko (Dinamo Kiev), Herget, Raschid, Loontiens (Bayer Uerdingen), Julio Prieto (Atlético Madrid)

1 goal: Bellone, Genghini (AS Monaco), Schmidt (Tatabánya Bányász), Cisek, Leszczyk (Widzew Lódz), Muça, Bubeqi, V.Ruci (Flamurtari Vlorë), Johnston, Aitken (Celtic Glasgow), De Kruyk, Kruys, Van Loen (FC Utrecht), Mitsibonas (Larisa), Savva, Farkas (AEL Limassol), Deunk (FK Fredrikstad), Vanthournout, Raes (Cercle Brugge), Meyer, Zwahlen (FC Aarau), Murphy, Bonner (Galway United), Bowers, Mullan (Glentoran Belfast), Prekazi, Erdal, Erhan Onal (Galatasaray Istanbul), Sundin, Göransson, B.Johansson, Lundmark, T.Johansson (AIK Solna), Lorenzo (Sampdoria), Jonsson, Thorkelsson (Fram Reykjavík), E.Williams (Bangor City), Valvee, Muhonen, Kanerva, Rantanen (HJK Helsinki), B.Christensen, Spangsborg, Vilmar, Schäfer, Lyng (Lyngby IF), Willfurth, Kranjcar, Kienast, Krankl, Weinhofer (Rapid Wien), Carlos Manuel, Manniche, Diamantino, Rui Aguas (Benfica Lisboa), Minge (Dynamo Dresden), Šugar, Nikolić, M. Djurovski, Mrkela, Janković, B.Djurovski (Crvena Zvezda), Kríz (Dukla Praha), Yakovenko (Dinamo Kiev), Klinger, Puszamszies, Feilzer (Bayer Uerdingen), Rubio, Cabrera, Marina, Landáburu, Quique Ramos (Atlético Madrid)

Own goal: Bommer (Bayer Uerdingen) for Dynamo Dresden

CUP WINNERS' CUP 1986-87

FIRST ROUND

B 1903 KØBENHAVN v VITOSHA SOFIA 1-0 (0-0)
København   16.09.1986
Referee: Manfred Neuner (W. GER)   Attendance: 4,593
BK 1903: Palle Petersen, Henrik Ibenfeldt, Lars Dalsborg, Jakob Friis-Hansen, Michael Kristensen, Søren Nygaard, Jens Sass Hansen, Jørgen Juul Jensen, Jens Rasmussen, Jens Nørager, Klaus Mathiesen.
VITOSHA: Borislav Mihailov, Krasimir Koev, Antoni Zdravkov, Petar Petrov, Nikolai Iliev,Dimitar Markov, Rusi Gochev, Nasko Sirakov, Emil Velev, Sasho Nachev (..Georgi Iordanov), Bojidar Iskrenov.   Trainer: Pavel Panov
Goal: Mathiesen (50)

VITOSHA SOFIA v B 1903 KØBENHAVN 2-0 (0-0)
Levski, Sofia   1.10.1986
Referee: Eduard Sostarić (YUG)   Attendance: 25,000
VITOSHA: Borislav Mihailov, Kalin Bankov, Krasimir Koev, Petar Petrov, Nikolai Iliev, Dimitar Markov, Rusi Gochev, Nasko Sirakov, Emil Velev, Georgi Iordanov, Bojidar Iskrenov. Trainer: Pavel Panov
BK 1903: Palle Petersen, Henrik Ibenfeldt, Lars Dalsborg, Jakob Friis-Hansen (61 Max Petersen), Michael Kristensen, Søren Nygard, Jens Sass Hansen, Jørgen Juul Hansen, Jens Rasmussen, Jens Nørager, Klaus Mathiesen.
Goals: Iskrenov (75), Sirakov (85)

FRAM REYKJAVIK v GKS KATOWICE 0-3 (0-1)
Laugardalsvöllur, Reykjavik   16.09.1986
Referee: Frangcon Roberts (WAL)   Attendance: 1,097
FRAM: Fridrik Fridriksson, Ormarr Orlygsson, Jón Thór Sveinsson, Thorsteinn Thorsteinsson (64 Arnljotur Davidsson), Vidar Thorkelsson; Steinn Gudjónsson, Gauti Laxdal (76 Jonas Bjornsson), Pétur Ormslev, Kristinn Rúnar Jónsson, Gudmundur Steinsson, Gudmundur Torfasson.
GKS: Robert Sek; Piotr Nazimek, Krzysztof Zajac (46 Wiktor Morcinek), Piotr Piekarczyk, Jerzy Kapias; Marek Biegun, Janusz Nawrocki, Zbigniew Krzyzos, Marek Koniarek, Jan Furtok, Miroslaw Kubisztal.   Trainer: Alojzy Lysko
Goals: Koniarek (25, 66), Kubisztal (85)

GKS KATOWICE v FRAM REYKJAVIK 1-0 (0-0)

GKS Katowice   2.10.1986

Referee: Yusuf Namoglu (TUR)   Attendance: 20,000

GKS: Robert Sek, Piotr Nazimek (63 Wiktor Morcinek), Piotr Piekarczyk, Marek Biegun, Jerzy Kapias, Krzysztof Rzeszutek, Janusz Nawrocki, Jerzy Wijas, Miroslaw Kubisztal, Jan Furtok, Marek Koniarek.   Trainer: Alojzy Lysko

FRAM: Fridrik Fridriksson, Ormarr Orlygsson, Gauti Laxdal (79 Arnljotur Davidsson), Jón Thór Sveinsson, Vidar Thorkelsson; Pétur Ormslev, Kristinn Rúnar Jónsson, Steinn Gudjónsson, Thorsteinn Thorsteinsson, Jonas Bjornsson (.. Orn Valdimarsson); Gudmundur Torfasson.

Goal: Koniarek (81)

RAPID WIEN v CLUB BRUGGE 4-3 (2-1)

Gerhard Hanappi, Wien   17.09.1986

Referee: André Daina (SWI)   Attendance: 11,000

RAPID: Michael Konsel; Leopold Lainer, Heribert Weber, Kurt Garger, Karl Brauneder; Zlatko Kranjcar, Gerald Willfurth, Reinhard Kienast, Petar Brucic; Sulejman Halilovic, Richard Niederbacher (70 Rudolf Weinhofer).
Trainer: Otto Baric

CLUB BRUGGE: Philippe Van de Walle, Luc Beyens, Franky Van der Elst, Hugo Broos, Dennis Van Wijk; Leo Van der Elst, Jan Ceulemans, Alex Querter, Kenneth Brylle, Peter Crève (55 Marc Degryse), Ronny Rosenthal.

Goals: Rosenthal (36), Kienast (44, 56), Brauneder (45), Willfurth (47), Beyens (61), Van Wijk (71)

**WATERFORD UNITED
v GIRONDINS de BORDEAUX 1-2** (0-1)

Kilcohan Park, Waterford   17.09.1986

Referee: Ales Jacobsen (DEN)   Attendance: 4,500

WATERFORD: David Flavin, Duncan Burns (17 Derek Grace), Noel Synnott, Kevin Power, Al Finucane, Paul Cashin, Anthony Macken, James Donnelly, Kieran McCabe (60 Ken O'Neill), Michael Bennett, Martin Reid.   Trainer: Hale

GIRONDINS: Dominique Dropsy; Gernot Rohr, Patrick Battiston, Léonard Specht, Jean-François Thouvenel, Jean Tigana, Philippe Vercruysse, René Girard, Zoran Vujović (64 Laurent Lassagne), Jean-Marc Ferreri, Zlatko Vujović.
Trainer: Aimé Jacquet

Goals: Girard (33), Vercruysse (62), Synnott (89)

CLUB BRUGGE v RAPID WIEN 3-3 (1-0)

Olympiapark, Brugge   1.10.1986

Referee: Werner Föckler (W. GER)   Attendance: 20,000

CLUB BRUGGE: Philippe Van de Walle, Luc Beyens, Franky Van der Elst, Hugo Broos, Dennis Van Wijk, Peter Crève (80 Henk Houwaart), Leo Van der Elst (62 Marc Degryse), Jan Ceulemans, Alex Querter, Kenneth Brylle, Ronny Rosenthal.

RAPID: Herbert Feurer, Leopold Lainer, Kurt Garger, Karl Brauneder, Heribert Weber; Reinhard Kienast, Richard Niederbacher, Franz Weber, Rudolf Weinhofer, Zlatko Kranjcar (89 Andreas Heraf), Sulejman Halilovic.   Trainer: Otto Baric

Goals: Brylle (41), Rosenthal (52), Kranjcar (53), Weinhofer (57), Halilovic (81), Van Wijk (88)

**GIRONDINS de BORDEAUX
v WATERFORD UNITED 4-0** (0-0)

Municipal, Bordeaux   30.09.1986

Referee: René Bindels (LUX)   Attendance: 8,800

GIRONDINS: Dominique Dropsy; Gernot Rohr, Léonard Specht, Patrick Battiston (80 Laurent Lassagne), Zoran Vujović, Jean Tigana, Jean-Marc Ferreri, René Girard, Philippe Vercruysse, Bernard Lacombe (80 Uwe Reinders), Zlatko Vujović.   Trainer: Aimé Jacquet

WATERFORD: David Flavin, Noel Bollard, Noel Synnott, Kevin Power (84 Terry Kearns), Al Finucane, Paul Cashin, Derek Grace, James Donnelly, John Burns, Michael Bennett, Reid.   Trainer: Hale

Goals: Zo. Vujović (79), Zl. Vujović (85), Reinders (86), Vercruysse (90)

AS ROMA v REAL ZARAGOZA 2-0 (1-0)

Stadio Olimpico, Roma   17.09.1986

Referee: Siegfried Kirschen (E. GER)   Attendance: 55,000

AS ROMA: Franco Tancredi, Marco Baroni, Manuel Gerolin, Zbigniew Boniek, Sebastiano Nela, Ubaldo Righetti (67 Settimio Lucci), Klaus Berggreen (46 Stefano Desideri), Giuseppe Giannini, Roberto Pruzzo, Carlo Ancelotti, Antonio di Carlo.   Trainer: Sven-Göran Eriksson

REAL ZARAGOZA: Andoni CEDRÚN Ibarra, Juan Martínez Martínez "CASUCO", Rafael GARCÍA CORTÉS (76 Francisco PINEDA García), Narciso JULIÁ Fontané, Alfonso FRAILE Sánchez, Francisco GÜERRI Ballarín, Patricio Nazario YÁÑEZ Candia, Juan Antonio SEÑOR Gómez, RUBÉN SOSA Aráiz, Pedro Miguel HERRERA Sancristóbal, JUAN CARLOS Justes Abiol (69 José Manuel MEJÍAS López).   Trainer: Luis Costa

Goals: Di Carlo (23), Gerolin (55)

REAL ZARAGOZA v AS ROMA 2-0 (1-0, 2-0) (AET)

La Romareda, Zaragoza   1.10.1986

Referee: George Courtney (ENG)   Attendance: 45,000

REAL ZARAGOZA: Andoni CEDRÚN Ibarra, Juan Martínez Martínez "CASUCO", Narciso JULIÁ Fontané, Alfonso FRAILE Sánchez, Rafael GARCÍA CORTÉS, Francisco GÜERRI Ballarín, Juan Antonio SEÑOR Gómez, Pedro Miguel HERRERA Sancristóbal, Patricio Nazario YÁÑEZ Candia, RUBÉN SOSA Aráiz (46 Mariano AYNETO Castro), Francisco PINEDA García (117 José Manuel MEJÍAS López).
Trainer: Luis Costa

AS ROMA: Franco Tancredi, Manuel Gerolin, Ubaldo Righetti, Marco Baroni, Sebastiano Nela, Stefano Desideri, Carlo Ancelotti, Zbigniew Boniek, Giuseppe Giannini, Antonio di Carlo (51 Klaus Berggreen), Roberto Pruzzo (62 Massimo Agostini).   Trainer: Sven-Göran Eriksson

Goals: Señor (44 pen, 47 pen)

Pen: García Cortés (saved), 0-1 Desideri, 1-1 Mejías, 1-2 Giannini, 2-2 Yáñez, 2-3 Baroni, 3-3 Ayneto, Boniek (saved), 4-3 Señor, Ancelotti (saved)

BENFICA LISBOA v LILLESTRØM SK 2-0 (1-0)

Estádio da Luz, Lisboa   17.09.1986

Referee: Roger Phillipi (LUX)   Attendance: 20,000

BENFICA: SILVINO Almeida Louro, António Augusto da Silva VELOSO, Eduardo José Camassele Mendes "DITO", António Henrique Jesus OLIVEIRA (80 Zvonko Zivkovic), ÁLVARO Monteiro Magalhaes; DIAMANTINO Manuel Miranda, CARLOS MANUEL Correia dos Santos, SHÉU Han (65 CÉSAR Gonçalves de BRITO), Adelino Carlos Morais NUNES; Michael Manniche, Francisco Carlos "CHIQUINHO".
Trainer: John Henry Mortimore

LILLESTRØM SK: Arne Amundsen; Ole Dyrstad, Tor Inge Smedås, Bård Bjerkeland, Gunnar Halle; Rune Richardsen, Kjetil Osvold, Tom Sundby, Arne Erlandsen; Sten Glenn Håberg, Joar Joar Vaadal.

Goals: Manniche (21), Chiquinho (54)

LILLESTRØM SK v BENFICA LISBOA 1-2 (1-1)

Åråsen, Lillestrøm   1.10.1986

Referee: Henning Lund Sørensen (DEN)   Attendance: 7,750

LILLESTRØM SK: Arne Amundsen; Ole Dyrstad, Bård Bjerkeland, Gunnar Halle; Rune Richardsen, Tom Sundby, Arne Erlandsen (69 Bjarne Sognnaes), Sten Glenn Håberg, Kjetil Osvold, Tor Inge Smedås, Joar Vaadal (69 André Krogsaeter).

BENFICA: SILVINO Almeida Louro, Eduardo José Camassele Mendes "DITO", António Augusto da Silva VELOSO, Antonio José BASTOS LOPES, António Henrique Jesus OLIVEIRA, ÁLVARO Monteiro Magalhaes; SHÉU Han, DIAMANTINO Manuel Miranda, Adelino Carlos Morais NUNES (17 Zvonko Zivkovic), CARLOS MANUEL Correia dos Santos; Michael Manniche (87 José RUI Lopes AGUAS).
Trainer: John Henry Mortimore

Goals: Sundby (2), Diamantino (25), Bjerkelund (76 og).

**17 NENTORI TIRANA
v DINAMO BUCUREŞTI 1-0** (0-0)

Qemal Stafa, Tirana   17.09.1986

Referee: Tadeusz Diakonowicz (POL)   Attendance: 19,000

17 NENTORI: Halim Mersini; Millan Baçi, Artur Lekbello, Skender Hodja, Arjan Bimo; Leonard Liti, Mirel Josa, Shkëlqim Muça, Bedri Omuri; Arben Minga, Agustin Kola.

DINAMO: Dumitru Moraru; Ioan Varga, Lică Movilă, Alexandru Nicolae, Nelu Stănescu; Mircea Rednic, Ioan Andonie, Iulian Mihăescu (65 Marin Dragnea), Ilie Balaci (82 Alexandru Suciu); Rodion Cămătaru, Marian Damaschin.
Trainer: Mircea Lucescu

Goal: Kola (86)

**DINAMO BUCUREŞTI
v 17 NENTORI TIRANA 1-2** (0-1)

Dinamo Bucureşti   1.10.1986

Referee: Sotos Afxentiou (CYP)   Attendance: 20,000

DINAMO: Dumitru Moraru, Ioan Varga (61 Alexandru Suciu), Lică Movilă, Alexandru Nicolae, Nelu Stănescu;, Mircea Rednic, Ioan Andonie (20 Marin Dragnea), Iulian Mihăescu, Ilie Balaci; Rodion Cămătaru, Marian Damaschin.
Trainer: Mircea Lucescu

17 NENTORI: Halim Mersini; Millan Baçi, Artur Lekbello, Skender Hodja, Arjan Bimo; Krenar Alimehmeti, Mirel Josa, Shkëlqim Muça (85 Sulejman Mema), Bedri Omuri; Arben Minga, Agustin Kola.

Goals: Minga (2), Cămătaru (80), Josa (90)

ABERDEEN FC v FC SION 2-1 (0-1)

Pittodrie, Aberdeen   17.09.1986

Referee: Einar Halle (NOR)   Attendance: 12,500

ABERDEEN: James Leighton; Stewart McKimmie, Brian Mitchell, William Stark, Alex McLeish, William Miller, John Hewitt, James Bett, Paul Wright (88 William Falconer), David Robertson, Peter Weir.   Manager: Alex Ferguson

FC SION: Pierre-Marie Pittier, Olivier Rey (85 François Rey), Slobodan Rojevic, Alain-Emile Balet, Michel Sauthier, Alvaro Lopez, Yves Debonnaire, Georges Bregy, Jean-Paul Brigger, Abdel Asiz Bouderbala, Christophe Bonvin (73 Dominique Cina).   Trainer: Jean-Claude Donzé

Goals: Debonnaire (40), Bett (73 pen), Wright (80)

FC SION v ABERDEEN FC 3-0 (2-0)

Stade de Tourbillon, Sion   1.10.1986

Referee: Albert Thomas (HOL)   Attendance: 11,800

FC SION: Pierre-Marie Pittier, Michel Sauthier, Alain-Emile Balet, François Rey, Slobodan Rojevic; Alvaro Lopez, Georges Bregy, Yves Debonnaire (46 Vincent Fournier); Abdel Asiz Bouderbala, Jean-Paul Brigger, Christophe Bonvin. Trainer: Jean-Claude Donzé

ABERDEEN: James Leighton; Brian Irvine, Alex McLeish, William Miller, Brian Mitchell (63 David Robertson); Stewart McKimmie, James Bett, Robert Connor, Peter Weir (67 Paul Wright); William Stark, John Hewitt. Manager: Alex Ferguson

Sent off: Bett (38)

Goals: Leighton (5 og), Bouderbala (29), Brigger (88)

MALMÖ FF v APOLLON LIMASSOL 6-0 (5-0)

Malmö Stadion   17.09.1986

Referee: Alan Snoddy (NIR)   Attendance: 5,683

MALMÖ FF: Jan Möller; Caspar Pauckstadt, Ingemar Erlandsson, Hasse Borg, Magnus Andersson (29 Mats Arvidsson), Leif Engqvist, Kent Jonsson, Björn Nilsson, Lars Larsson (70 Mats Magnusson), Anders Palmer, Torbjörn Persson. Trainer: Roy Hodgson

APOLLON: Thrasos Koniotis; Giannis Pieris, Haralampos Pittas, Akis Agiomamitis, Antonis Ilia, Ilias Hrisostomou, Andreas Sokratous, David Kenny, Teodor Barzov, Giannis Ioannou, Hristos Danos (32 Andreas Efrem)

Goals: Palmer (5, 85), Lasse Larsson (16, 30, 54), Björn Nilsson (44)

APOLLON LIMASSOL v MALMÖ FF 2-1 (2-1)

Tsirion, Limassol   1.10.1986

Referee: Petrescu (ROM)   Attendance: 7,000

APOLLON: Thrasos Koniotis; Ilias Hrysostomou (46 Giannis Pieris), Haralampos Pittas, Akis Agiomamitis, Antonis Ilia, Giannis Giagkoudakis, Andreas Hristodoulou (46 Andreas Sokratous), David Kenny, Teodor Barzov, Giannis Ioannou, Aggelos Tsolakis.

MALMÖ FF: Jan Möller; Caspar Pauckstadt, Ingemar Erlandsson, Hasse Borg, Magnus Andersson, Leif Engqvist, Kent Jonsson, Mats Magnusson, Håkan Lindman, Deval Eminovski (83 Jonas Thern), Torbjörn Persson. Trainer: Roy Hodgson

Goals: Lindman (12), Hristodoulou (42, 44)

BURSASPOR v AJAX AMSTERDAM 0-2 (0-0)

Atatürk Bursa   17.09.1986

Referee: Pavel Kuznetzov (USSR)   Attendance: 6,500

BURSASPOR: Eser Kardesler, Ahmet Suphi (61 Talip Ikikardesler), Atilla Kerekes, Esat Bayram, Salih Salimoglu; Dragi Kaliçanin, Yalçin Cemin, Taygun Erdem; Gürsel Hatlat, Beyhan Caliskan, Bülent Izgis (75 Djavid). Trainer: Toma Kaloperović

AJAX: Stanley Menzo, Sonny Silooy, Frank Rijkaard, Ronald Spelbos, Peter Boeve (46 John Bosman); Danny Blind, Aron Winter (82 Arnold Scholten), Jan Wouters; John van't Schip, Marco van Basten, Rob Witschge.   Trainer: Johan Cruijff

Goals: Bosman (72), Van Basten (85)

AJAX AMSTERDAM v BURSASPOR 5-0 (4-0)

Ajax Amsterdam   1.10.1986

Referee: Idelfonso Urizar Azpitarte (SPA)   Att: 18,044

AJAX: Stanley Menzo, Danny Blind, Frank Rijkaard (73 Aron Winter), Ronald Spelbos, Sonny Silooy, Jan Wouters, Arnold Mühren (64 Alistair Dick), John Bosman, John van't Schip, Marco van Basten, Rob Witschge.   Trainer: Johan Cruyff

BURSASPOR: Eser Kardesler, Salih Salimoglu, Turan Sen, Atilla Kerekes, Dragi Kaliçanin, Islam Ollan, Ibrahim Türkseven (68 Esat Bayram), Beyhan Caliskan (27 Memduh Fidan), Yalçin Cemin, Taner Taylan, Gürsel Hatlat. Trainer: Toma Kaloperović

Goals: Bosman (17, 21, 34, 90), Van Basten (24)

FC ZURRIEQ v WREXHAM FC 0-3 (0-1)

National Ta'Qali   17.09.1986

Referee: Konstantinos Dimitriadis (GRE)   Att: 8,000

FC ZURRIEQ: Eugenio Duca, C.Camilleri, Alfons Camilleri, Louis Cutajar, Mario A. Schembri, Pierre Brincat, Francis Scicluna (75 James Navarro), Raymond Falzon, Mario B. Schembri, Mario Farrugia, Charlie Micallef.

WREXHAM: Christopher Pearce, Neil Salathiel, Shaun Cunnington, Michael Williams, Joseph Cooke, Paul Comstive, Stephen Massey, Barry Horne (73 Roger Preece), James Steel (75 Stephen Buxton), Stephen Charles, Michael Conroy. Manager: Dixie McNeil

Goals: Massey (14), Charles (56), Conroy (65)

WREXHAM FC v FC ZURRIEQ 4-0 (3-0)
Racecourse Ground, Wrexham   1.10.1986
Referee: Oli Peter Olsen (SWE)   Attendance: 2,793
WREXHAM: Christopher Pearce, Neil Salathiel, Shaun Cunningham (.. Darren Wright), Michael Williams (.. Frank Jones), Joseph Cooke, Paul Comstive, Michael Conroy, Barry Horne, James Steel, Stephen Massey, Paul Emson. Manager: Dixie McNeil

FC ZURRIEQ: Anthony Pace, C.Camilleri, Alfons Camilleri, Louis Cutajar, Mario A.Schembri, Pierre Brincat, Tony Bonnici, Charlie Micallef, Mario B.Schembri, Mario Farrugia, Raymond Falzon.

Goals: Massey (10 pen, 39), Steel (35), Horne (87)

**OLYMPIAKOS PEIRAIAS
v US LUXEMBOURG 3-0** (1-0)
Olympiako Athina   17.09.1986
Referee: Plarent Kotherja (ALB)   Attendance: 28,543
OLYMPIAKOS: Dimitris Skounas, Petros Xanthopoulos, Giorgos Togias, Alexis Alexiou, Stratos Apostolakis, Giorgos Semertzidis, Jorge Barrios, Tasos Mitropoulos (70 Theodoros Zelilidis), Milos Sestic, Nikos Anastopoulos, Giorgos Kostikos (73 Vasilis Hardalias). Trainer: Antonis Georgiadis

US: Théo Zender, Romain Primc (72 Gilbert Schmit), Romain Delhalt, Laurent Schonckert, Nico Bremer, Marc Birsens, Fernand Heinisch, René Thines, Joël Groff, Luc Feiereisen, Claude Ganser (76 Johny Schleck). Trainer: Pis

Goals: Anastopoulos (2, 47 pen), Togias (57)

**HAKA VALKEAKOSKEN
v TORPEDO MOSKVA 2-2** (1-1)
Tehtaankenttä, Valkeakoski   17.09.1986
Referee: Manfred Rossner (E. GER)   Attendance: 1,900
HAKA: Olavi Huttunen, Petter Setälä (67 Jarmo Kujanpää), Heikki Leinonen, Reijo Vuorinen, Heikki-Jussi Laine, Markus Törnvall, Ilkka Mäkelä, Endre Kolár, Mika-Matti Paatelainen, Marko Myyry, Richard Wilson (82 Jouko Pirinen).

TORPEDO: Dmitri Kharin, Viktor Kruglov, Valentin Kovach, Sergei Prigoda, Valeri Schaveiko, Sergei Schavlo, Yuri Savichev (90 Nikolai Pisarev), Vladimir Kobzev, Nikolai Savichev, Aleksandr Gostenin, Valeri Plotnikov.
Trainer: Valentin Ivanov

Goals: Kobzev (21), Törnval (38), Nikolai Savichev (65), Paatelainen (82)

**US LUXEMBOURG
v OLYMPIAKOS PEIRAIAS 0-3** (0-0)
Achille Hammerel Municipal, Luxembourg   1.10.1986
Referee: Ignace Goris (BEL)   Attendance: 1,173
US: Théo Zender, Fernand Heinisch, Nico Bremer, Laurent Schonckert, Romain Delhalt, Marc Birsens, Johny Schleck (73 Gilbert Schmit), Luc Feiereisen, Joël Groff (73 Claude Ganser), Manou Scheitler, René Thines. Trainer: Pis

OLYMPIAKOS: Dimitris Skounas, Petros Xanthopoulos (71 Tasos Mitropoulos), Stratos Apostolakis, Giorgos Togias, Alexis Alexiou, Giorgos Semertzidis, Giorgos Kapouranis, Jorge Barrios (71 Theodoros Zelilidis), Nikos Anastopoulos, Vasilis Papahristou, Giorgos Kostikos.
Trainer: Antonis Georgiadis

Goals: Papahristou (53), Zelilidis (84), Anastopoulos (89)

**TORPEDO MOSKVA
v HAKA VALKEAKOSKEN 3-1** (2-0)
Moskva   1.10.1986
Referee: Bo Helén (SWE)   Attendance: 5,000
TORPEDO: Dmitri Kharin, Viktor Kruglov, Valentin Kovach, Sergei Prigoda, Valeri Schaveiko, Aleksandr Gostenin, Yuri Savichev, Vladimir Kobzev, Nikolai Savichev, Aleksandr Polukarov, Gennadi Grishin (69 Sergei Schavlo). Trainer: Valentin Ivanov

HAKA: Olavi Huttunen, Petter Setälä, Heikki Leinonen, Reijo Vuorinen, Heikki-Jussi Laine, Jouko Pirinen, Ilkka Mäkelä, Markus Törnvall, Mika-Matti Paatelainen, Marko.Myyry, Richard Wilson (46 Jarmo Kujanpää).

Goals: Y. Savichev (21), Kruglov (38), Gostenin (67), Prigoda (70 og)

VfB STUTTGART v SPARTAK TRNAVA 1-0 (0-0)
Neckarstadion, Stuttgart   17.09.1986
Referee: José Rosa Dos Santos (POR)   Attendance: 24,250
VfB: Eike Immel, Bertram Beierlorzer (46 Andreas Müller), Günther Schäfer, Guido Buchwald, Rainer Zietsch, Karl Allgöwer, Asgeir Sigurvinsson, Michael Schröder, Jürgen Klinsmann, Andreas Merkle, Predrag Pasić (64 Leo Bunk). Trainer: Egon Coordes

SPARTAK: Vlastimil Opálek, Libor Fašiang, Ivan Hucko, Alexander Cabanik, Marián Kopcan, František Klinovský, Vladimír Ekhardt, Vladimír Filo, Ján Gabriel, Atila Belanský (80 Ivan Kavecký), Peter Fijalka (90 František Broš).
Trainer: Stanislav Jarábek

Goal: Allgöwer (87 pen)

SPARTAK TRNAVA v VFB STUTTGART 0-0
Trnava Stadion   1.10.1986
Referee: Gerard Geurds (HOL)   Attendance: 17,500

SPARTAK: Vlastimil Opálek, Libor Fašiang, Alexander Cabanik, Vladimír Ekhardt, Marián Kopcan, František Klinovský, Vladimír Filo, Jozef Dian (88 František Broš), Ján Gabriel, Peter Fijalka (74 Michal Svrcek), Atila Belanský.
Trainer: Stanislav Jarábek

VfB: Eike Immel, Bertram Beierlorzer, Günther Schäfer, Guido Buchwald, Karl Allgöwer, Rainer Zietsch, Asgeir Sigurvinsson, Andreas Merkle, Michael Schröder, Jürgen Klinsmann (83 Andreas Müller), Leo Bunk (55 Jürgen Hartmann).   Trainer: Egon Coordes

VASAS BUDAPEST v VELEŽ MOSTAR 2-2 (1-1)
Fáy ú, Budapest   17.09.1986
Referee: Ioan Igna (ROM)   Attendance: 5,000

VASAS: László Kakas; Tibor Farkas, József Elekes, Tibor Balogh, János Csorba; István Szijjártó, László Rácz (70 Vaszilisz Teodoru), István Bodnár, Péter Galaschek; József Zvara (60 Mihály Borostyán), László Szabadi.

VELEŽ: Vukašin Petranović, Mili Hadžiabdić, Goran Jurić, Vladimir Matijević, Draženko Prskalo; Ivica Barbarić, Vladimir Skocajić, Anel Karabeg; Sead Kajtaz (80 Medvedović), Predrag Jurić, Semir Tuce (89 Vladimir Gudelj).

Goals: Bodnár (13), Tuce (23), Skocajić (60), Szabadi (70)

**GLENTORAN BELFAST
v 1.FC LOKOMOTIVE LEIPZIG 1-1** (1-0)
The Oval, Belfast   17.09.1986
Referee: Thorbjorn Aas (NOR)   Attendance: 8,000

GLENTORAN: Alan Paterson; Thomas Connell, James Smyth, Terry Moore, James Cowden, Raymond Morrison, Alfie Stewart, James Cleary, John Jameson (75 Robert Bowers), Paul Millar, Gary Macartney.

1.FC LOKOMOTIVE: René Müller, Frank Baum, Ronald Kreer, Matthias Lindner, Uwe Zötzsche, Matthias Liebers, Uwe Bredow, Peter Schöne, Hans-Jörg Leitzke (52 Wolfgang Altmann), Dieter Kühn (85 Olaf Marschall), Hans Richter.
Trainer: Hans-Ulrich Thomale

Goals: Cleary (42), Lindner (65)

VELEŽ MOSTAR v VASAS BUDAPEST 3-2 (0-0)
Gradski Mostar   1.10.1986
Referee: Franz Wöhrer (AUS)   Attendance: 30,000

VELEŽ: Vukašin Petranović, Mili Hadžiabdić, Vladimir Matijevic, Ivica Barbarić, Goran Jurić; Draženko Prskalo, Vladimir Skocajić (76 Medvedović), Anel Karabeg; Sead Kajtaz (70 Vladimir Gudelj), Predrag Jurić, Semir Tuce.

VASAS: László Kakas; József Elekes, László Rácz, Tibor Balogh, János Csorba; István Szijjártó, Tibor Farkas, Vaszilisz Teodoru, Péter Galaschek (60 István Bodnár); László Szabadi, Mihály Borostyán (76 László Gubucz).

Goals: P. Jurić (55, 73), Tuce (75), Csorba (80, 89)

SECOND ROUND

**1.FC LOKOMOTIVE LEIPZIG
v GLENTORAN BELFAST 2-0** (1-0)
Bruno-Plache stadion, Leipzig   1.10.1986
Referee: P. Karlsson (SWE)   Attendance: 7,200

1.FC LOKOMOTIVE: René Müller, Frank Baum, Ronald Kreer, Matthias Lindner, Uwe Bredow, Wolfgang Altmann, Matthias Liebers, Uwe Zötzsche, Hans-Jörg Leitzke (83 Peter Schöne), Hans Richter, Dieter Kühn (76 Heiko Scholz).
Trainer: Hans-Ulrich Thomale

GLENTORAN: Alan Paterson, Thomas Connell, James Smyth, Terry Moore, James Cowden, John Jameson, Raymond Morrison, James Cleary, Alfie Stewart, Paul Millar, Gary Macartney.

Goals: Bredow (35), Richter (90)

**RAPID WIEN
v 1.FC LOKOMOTIVE LEIPZIG 1-1** (0-1)
Gerhard Hanappi, Wien   22.10.1986
Referee: Gerard Geurds (HOL)   Attendance: 18,000

RAPID: Herbert Feurer; Heribert Weber, Leopold Lainer, Reinhard Kienast, Robert Pecl, Peter Hrstic, Zlatko Kranjcar (64 Andreas Heraf), Petar Brucic, Rudolf Weinhofer, Sulejman Halilovic, Richard Niederbacher (75 Hermann Stadler).
Trainer: Otto Baric

LOKOMOTIVE: René Müller, Uwe Zötzsche, Matthias Lindner, Frank Edmond, Uwe Bredow, Matthias Liebers, Wolfgang Altmann, Heiko Scholz, Hans-Jörg Leitzke (80 Olaf Marschall), Hans Richter, Dieter Kühn (57 Peter Schöne).
Trainer: Hans-Ulrich Thomale

Goals: Lindner (37), Kranjcar (61 pen)

**1.FC LOKOMOTIVE LEIPZIG
v RAPID WIEN 2-1** (0-0, 0-0) (AET)

Zentralstadion, Leipzig   5.11.1986

Referee: Claudio Pieri (ITA)   Attendance: 19,300

LOKOMOTIVE: René Müller, Uwe Zötzsche, Matthias Lindner, Frank Edmond, Uwe Bredow; Matthias Liebers, Wolfgang Altmann (91 Peter Schöne), Heiko Scholz; Hans-Jörg Leitzke, Olaf Marschall (70 Dieter Kühn), Hans Richter.   Trainer: Hans-Ulrich Thomale

RAPID: Herbert Feurer; Heribert Weber, Leopold Lainer, Kurt Garger (83 Robert Pecl), Karl Brauneder, Reinhard Kienast, Peter Hrstic (46 Andreas Heraf), Petar Brucic, Rudolf Weinhofer, Richard Niederbacher, Sulejman Halilovic.   Trainer: Otto Baric

Goals: Kienast (65), Richter (70), Leitzke (118)

REAL ZARAGOZA v WREXHAM FC 0-0

La Romareda, Zaragoza   22.10.1986

Referee: Gérard Biguet (FRA)   Attendance: 27,000

REAL ZARAGOZA: Manuel RUIZ Pérez, Juan Martínez Martínez "CASUCO", Narciso JULIÁ Fontané, Rafael GARCÍA CORTÉS, Francisco GÜERRI Ballarín, Juan Antonio SEÑOR Gómez, José Manuel MEJÍAS López, Pedro Miguel HERRERA Sancristóbal, Patricio Nazario YÁÑEZ Candia, Mariano AYNETO Castro (72 ROBERTO Elvira Estrany), RUBÉN SOSA Aráiz (85 JUAN CARLOS Justes Abiol).   Trainer: Luis Costa

WREXHAM: Christopher Pearce, Neil Salathiel, Michael Williams, Joseph Cooke, Shaun Cunnington, Paul Comstive, Barry Horne, Stephen Charles, Paul Emson, Stephen Massey (58 Stephen Buxton), James Steel.   Manager: Dixie McNeil

**WREXHAM FC
v REAL ZARAGOZA 2-2** (0-0, 0-0) (AET)

Racecourse Ground, Wrexham   5.11.1986

Referee: Ulf Eriksson (SWE)   Attendance: 14,550

WREXHAM: Christopher Pearce, Neil Salathiel, Michael Williams, Joseph Cooke, Shaun Cunnington, Paul Comstive, Barry Horne, Stephen Charles, Paul Emson (88 Stephen Buxton), Stephen Massey, James Steel.   Trainer: Dixie McNeil

REAL ZARAGOZA: Andoni CEDRÚN Ibarra, Juan Martínez Martínez "CASUCO", Alfonso FRAILE Sánchez, Tomás BLESA Noé, Narciso JULIÁ Fontané, Francisco GÜERRI Ballarín, Juan Antonio SEÑOR Gómez, Pedro Miguel HERRERA Sancristóbal, Francisco PINEDA García (108 JUAN CARLOS Justes Abiol), Mariano AYNETO Castro (81 Patricio Nazario YÁÑEZ Candia), RUBÉN SOSA Aráiz.   Trainer: Luis Costa

Goals: Yáñez (98, 104), Massey (102), Buxton (107)

VITOSHA SOFIA v VELEŽ MOSTAR 2-0 (0-0)

Levski, Sofia   22.10.1986

Referee: Aleksander Suchanek (POL)   Attendance: 40,000

VITOSHA: Borislav Mihailov, Kalin Bankov, Krasimir Koev, Stoil Georgiev, Nikolai Iliev, Dimitar Markov (74 Vlado Shalamanov), Rusi Gochev, Nasko Sirakov, Emil Velev, Georgi Iordanov, Bojidar Iskrenov.   Trainer: Pavel Panov

VELEŽ: Vukašin Petranović, Mili Hadžiabdić, Goran Jurić, Draženko Prskalo, Veselin Djurasović (50 Vladimir Matijević), Ivica Barbarić, Avdo Kalajdžić, Vladimir Skokajić (79 Vladimir Gudelj), Predrag Jurić, Anel Karabeg, Semir Tuce.

Goals: Iordanov (54 pen), Sirakov (67)

VELEŽ MOSTAR v VITOSHA SOFIA 4-3 (1-1)

Gradski, Mostar   5.11.1986

Referee: Yuri Savchenko (USSR)   Attendance: 30,000

VELEŽ: Vukašin Petranović, Mili Hadžiabdić, Goran Jurić, Draženko Prskalo, Vladimir Matijević, Avdo Kalajdžić, Sead Kajtaz (62 Medvedović), Vladimir Skokajić, Predrag Jurić, Anel Karabeg (46 Vladimir Gudelj), Semir Tuce.

VITOSHA: Borislav Mihailov, Kalin Bankov, Krasimir Koev, Petar Petrov, Nikolai Iliev, Dimitar Markov, Rusi Gochev, Nasko Sirakov, Emil Velev, Georgi Iordanov, Bojidar Iskrenov.   Trainer: Pavel Panov

Goals: Iskrenov (43), Tuce (44 pen, 85), Sirakov (67, 70), Gudelj (86), Matijević (89)

TORPEDO MOSKVA v VfB STUTTGART 2-0 (1-0)

Moskva   22.10.1986

Referee: Neil Midgley (ENG)   Attendance: 12,000

TORPEDO: Dmitri Kharin, Dmitri Chugunov, Valentin Kovach, Sergei Prigoda, Valeri Schaveiko, Nikolai Savichev (86 Viktor Kruglov), Vladimir Grechnev, Aleksandr Polukarov, Valeri Plotnikov (82 Sergei Schavlo), Yuri Savichev, Vladimir Kobzev.   Trainer: Valentin Ivanov

VfB: Eike Immel; Michael Schröder; Günther Schäfer, Guido Buchwald, Alexander Strehmel (54 Michael Nushöhr), Rainer Zietsch, Jürgen Hartmann, Asgeir Sigurvinsson, Andreas Merkle (80 Stefan Schmitt); Jürgen Klinsmann, Leo Bunk.   Trainer: Egon Coordes

Goals: N. Savichev (32), Y. Savichev (72)

VfB STUTTGART v TORPEDO MOSKVA 3-5 (2-4)
Neckarstadion, Stuttgart 5.11.1986
Referee: Henning Lund Sørensen (DEN)   Att: 30,100
VfB: Eike Immel, Günther Schäfer, Michael Nushöhr (29 Leo Bunk), Guido Buchwald, Michael Schröder, Rainer Zietsch (46 Jürgen Hartmann), Andreas Merkle, Andreas Müller; Jürgen Klinsmann, Asgeir Sigurvinsson, Predrag Pasić.
Trainer: Egon Coordes
TORPEDO: Dmitri Kharin, Dmitri Chugunov (69 Viktor Kruglov), Valentin Kovach, Sergei Prigoda, Valeri Schaveiko, Vladimir Grechnev, Yuri Savichev, Sergei Muschtruev, Nikolai Savichev, Aleksandr Polukarov, Valeri Plotnikov (75 Sergei Schavlo).   Trainer: Valentin Ivanov
Goals: N. Savichev (11, 88), Y. Savichev (13, 37), Klinsmann (17), Plotnikov (28), Pasić (31), Sigurvinsson (55)

GKS KATOWICE v FC SION 2-2 (2-0)
Slaski Chorzów 22.10.1986
Referee: Meletio Voutsaras (GRE)   Attendance: 10,000
GKS: Robert Sek, Piotr Nazimek, Piotr Piekarczyk, Krzysztof Zajac, Jerzy Kapias; Marek Biegun, Janusz Nawrocki, Jerzy Wijas; Miroslaw Kubisztal, Jan Furtok, Marek Koniarek.
Trainer: Alojzy Lysko
FC SION: Pierre-Marie Pittier; Olivier Rey, Alain-Emile Balet, Michel Sauthier, Vincent Fournier; Georges Bregy, Alvaro Lopez, Yves Debonnaire (70 Paul Brantschen); Abdel Asiz Bouderbala, Jean-Paul Brigger, Christophe Bonvin (60 Dominique Cina).   Trainer: Jean-Claude Donzé
Goals: Koniarek (9, 12), Brigger (74), Cina (78)

FC SION v GKS KATOWICE 3-0 (0-0)
Stade de Tourbillon, Sion 5.11.1986
Referee: Vitor Fernandes Correia (POR)   Att: 10,000
FC SION: Pierre-Marie Pittier, Michel Sauthier, Vincent Fournier, François, François Rey, Slobodan Rojevic, Alvaro Lopez, Georges Bregy, Yves Debonnaire; Abdel Asiz Bouderbala (70 Christophe Bonvin), Jean-Paul Brigger, Dominique Cina.   Trainer: Jean-Claude Donzé
GKS: Miroslaw Dreszer (58 Robert Sek); Piotr Piekarczyk, Marek Biegun, Krzysztof Zajac, Jerzy Kapias, Wiktor Morcinek, Janusz Nawrocki, Zbigniew Krzyzos, Jan Furtok, Marek Koniarek, Miroslaw Kubisztal (81 Krzysztof Hetmanski).   Trainer: Alojzy Lysko
Goals: Bregy (58 pen), Cina (61), Brigger (83)

**BENFICA LISBOA
v GIRONDINS de BORDEAUX 1-1** (1-1)
Estádio da Luz, Lisboa 22.10.1986
Referee: Franz Wöhrer (AUS)   Attendance: 80,000
BENFICA: SILVINO Almeida Louro, António Augusto da Silva VELOSO, Eduardo José Camassele Mendes "DITO", António Henrique Jesus OLIVEIRA (62 Geovânio Bonfim Sobrinho WANDO), ÁLVARO Monteiro Magalhaes, SHÉU Han, DIAMANTINO Manuel Miranda, CARLOS MANUEL Correia dos Santos, Adelino Carlos Morais NUNES, Michael Manniche (46 Francisco Carlos "CHIQUINHO"), José RUI Lopes AGUAS.   Trainer: John Henry Mortimore
GIRONDINS: Dominique Dropsy; Jean-François Thouvenel, Patrick Battiston, Léonard Specht, Alain Roche, Zoran Vujović, Jean Tigana, Philippe Vercruysse, René Girard, Jean-Marc Ferreri, Zlatko Vujović.   Trainer: Aimé Jacquet
Goals: Zl. Vujović (17), Rui Aguas (31)

**GIRONDINS de BORDEAUX
v BENFICA LISBOA 1-0** (1-0)
Municipal, Bordeaux 5.11.1986
Referee: Karl-Heinz Tritschler (W. GER)   Att: 24,000
GIRONDINS: Dominique Dropsy; Jean-François Thouvenel, Léonard Specht, Patrick Battiston, Zoran Vujović, Jean Tigana, René Girard, Gernot Rohr, Philippe Vercruysse, Jean-Marc Ferreri (70 Alain Roche), Zlatko Vujović.
Trainer: Aimé Jacquet
BENFICA: SILVINO Almeida Louro, António Augusto da Silva VELOSO, António Henrique Jesus OLIVEIRA, Eduardo José Camassele Mendes "DITO", ÁLVARO Monteiro Magalhaes, CARLOS MANUEL Correia dos Santos (66 Zvonko Zivkovic), Geovânio Bonfim Sobrinho WANDO, SHÉU Han (53 Francisco Carlos "CHIQUINHO"), Adelino Carlos Morais NUNES, José RUI Lopes AGUAS, DIAMANTINO Manuel Miranda.   Trainer: John Henry Mortimore
Goals: Vercruysse (44)

17 NENTORI TIRANA v MALMÖ FF 0-3 (0-0)
Qemal Stafa, Tirana 22.10.1986
Referee: Albert Thomas (HOL)   Attendance: 19,000
17 NENTORI: Halim Mersini; Millan Baçi, Skender Hodja, Artur Lekbello, Arjan Bimo; Leonard Liti, Sulejman Mema (46 Shkëlkim Muça), Mirel Josa, Bedri Omuri; Arben Minga, Augustin Kola.
MALMÖ FF: Jan Möller; Magnus Andersson, Ingemar Erlandsson, Hasse Borg, Torbjörn Persson, Kent Jonsson, Leif Engqvist, Deval Eminovski (75 Mats Arvidsson), Lars Larsson (70 Roger Ljung); Mats Magnusson, Anders Palmer.
Trainer: Roy Hodgson
Goals: Magnusson (47), Larsson (60), Persson (83 pen)

MALMÖ FF v 17 NENTORI TIRANA 0-0

Malmö Stadion 5.11.1986

Referee: Jiří Stiegler (CZE)   Attendance: 3,170

MALMÖ FF: Jan Möller; Torbjörn Persson, Ingemar Erlandsson, Hasse Borg, Magnus Andersson, Leif Engqvist (84 Håkan Lindman), Kent Jonsson, Deval Eminovski, Lars Larsson, Anders Palmer (74 Jonas Thern), Mats Magnusson. Trainer: Roy Hodgson

17 NENTORI: Halim Mersini; Millan Baçi, Mirel Josa, Arjan Bimo, Krenar Alimehmeti (70 Sulejman Mema), Skender Hodja, Artur Lekbello (89 Anesti Stoja), Shkelqim Muça, Bedri Omuri, Arben Minga, Augustin Kola.

AJAX AMSTERDAM v OLYMPIAKOS PEIRAIAS 4-0 (2-0)

Ajax Amsterdam 22.10.1986

Referee: Siegfried Kirschen (E. GER)   Attendance: 21,981

AJAX: Stanley Menzo, Danny Blind, Frank Rijkaard, Ronald Spelbos, Sonny Silooy, Jan Wouters, Arnold Mühren, John Bosman (81 Aron Winter), John van't Schip, Marco van Basten, Alistair Dick (46 Peter Boeve).   Trainer: Johan Cruijff

OLYMPIAKOS: Hristos Arvanitis, Petros Xanthopoulos, Alexis Alexiou, Giorgos Togias, Stratos Apostolakis, Giorgos Semertzidis, Theodoros Zelilidis (46 Milos Sestic), Tasos Mitropoulos, Giorgos Kokolakis (61 Giorgos Vaitsis), Giorgos Kostikos, Nikos Anastopoulos.   Trainer: Alketas Panagoulias

Goals: Bosman (7), Rijkaard (44), Van Basten (53), A. Mühren (84)

OLYMPIAKOS PEIRAIAS v AJAX AMSTERDAM 1-1 (0-0)

Olympiako Athina 5.11.1986

Referee: Ioan Igna (ROM)   Attendance: 21,000

OLYMPIAKOS: Dimitris Skounas, Vasilis Papahristou, Giorgos Togias, Alexis Alexiou, Stratos Apostolakis, Petros Xanthopoulos, Petros Mihos (15 Giorgos Kapouranis), Jorge Barrios, Giorgos Kostikos, Nikos Anastopoulos, Theodoros Zelilidis (37 Giorgos Vaitsis).   Trainer: Alketas Panagoulias

AJAX: Stanley Menzo, Danny Blind, Frank Rijkaard, Ronald Spelbos, Sonny Silooy, Jan Wouters, Arnold Mühren, John Bosman (36 Aron Winter), John van't Schip, Marco van Basten (77 Peter Boeve), Rob Witschge.   Trainer: Johan Cruijff

Goals: Kapouranis (58), Wouters (90)

QUARTER-FINALS

REAL ZARAGOZA v VITOSHA SOFIA 2-0 (0-0)

La Romareda, Zaragoza 4.03.1987

Referee: Marcel van Langenhove (BEL)   Attendance: 20,000

REAL ZARAGOZA: Andoni CEDRÚN Ibarra, Juan Martínez Martínez "CASUCO", Rafael GARCÍA CORTÉS, Manuel ABAD Francés (67 Tomás BLESA Noé), Alfonso FRAILE Sánchez; Francisco GÜERRI Ballarín, ROBERTO Elvira Estrany, José Manuel MEJÍAS López, RUBÉN SOSA Aráiz, JUAN CARLOS Justes Abiol, Francisco PINEDA García.   Trainer: Luis Costa

VITOSHA: Vlado Delchev (50 Borislav Mihailov), Kalin Bankov, Krasimir Koev, Petar Petrov, Nikolai Iliev, Stoil Georgiev (79 Sasho Nachev), Rusi Gochev, Nasko Sirakov, Vlado Shalamanov, Bojidar Iskrenov, Dimitar Markov. Trainer: Pavel Panov

Goals: Roberto (57), García Cortés (77)

VITOSHA SOFIA v REAL ZARAGOZA 0-2 (0-1)

Vasil Levski, Sofia 18.03.1987

Referee: Horst Brummeier (AUS)   Attendance: 50,000

VITOSHA: Borislav Mihailov, Antoni Zdravkov, Kalin Bankov, Nikolai Iliev, Petar Petrov, Rusi Gochev, Dimitar Markov, Georgi Iordanov, Bojidar Iskrenov, Emil Velev, Nasko Sirakov.   Trainer: Pavel Panov

REAL ZARAGOZA: Andoni CEDRÚN Ibarra, Tomás BLESA Noé, Juan Martínez Martínez "CASUCO", Alfonso FRAILE Sánchez, Manuel ABAD Francés, José Manuel MEJÍAS López (80 ROBERTO Elvira Estrany), Juan Antonio SEÑOR Gómez, JUAN CARLOS Justes Abiol, Rafael GARCÍA CORTÉS, RUBÉN SOSA Aráiz, Francisco PINEDA García (87 Mariano AYNETO Castro).   Trainer: Luis Costa

Goals: Mejías (33), Roberto (82)

1.FC LOKOMOTIVE LEIPZIG v FC SION 2-0 (0-0)

Zentralstadion, Leipzig 4.03.1987

Referee: Henning Lund Sørensen (DEN)   Att: 21,000

1.FC LOKOMOTIVE: René Müller; Frank Baum; Matthias Lindner, Ronald Kreer, Uwe Zötzsche; Heiko Scholz (57 Wolfgang Altmann), Matthias Liebers, Uwe Bredow; Olaf Marschall, Hans Richter, Dieter Kühn (64 Hans-Jörg Leitzke). Trainer: Hans-Ulrich Thomale

FC SION: Pierre-Marie Pittier; Michel Sauthier; Vincent Fournier (81 Olivier Rey), Alain-Emile Balet, François Rey, Alvaro Lopez, Georges Bregy, Yves Debonnaire; Dominique Cina (86 Abdel Asiz Bouderbala), Jean-Paul Brigger, Christophe Bonvin.   Trainer: Jean-Claude Donzé

Goals: Marschall (86), Richter (90)

FC SION v 1.FC LOKOMOTIVE LEIPZIG 0-0
Stade de Tourbillon, Sion   18.03.1987
Referee: Ioan Igna (ROM)   Attendance: 12,200
FC SION: Pierre-Marie Pittier; Michel Sauthier, Olivier Rey, Alain-Emile Balet, Slobodan Rojevic, Alvaro Lopez, Georges Bregy, Yves Debonnaire (85 Abdel Asiz Bouderbala), Dominique Cina, Jean-Paul Brigger, Christophe Bonvin. Trainer: Jean-Claude Donzé
1.FC LOKOMOTIVE: René Müller, Frank Baum, Matthias Lindner, Ronald Kreer, Uwe Zötzsche, Heiko Scholz, Uwe Bredow, Matthias Liebers, Hans-Jörg Leitzke, Hans Richter (59 Dieter Kühn), Olaf Marschall (88 Wolfgang Altmann). Trainer: Hans-Ulrich Thomale

GIRONDINS de BORDEAUX v TORPEDO MOSKVA 1-0 (0-0)
Municipal, Bordeaux   4.03.1987
Referee: Claudio Pieri (ITA)   Attendance: 35,000
GIRONDINS: Dominique Dropsy; Jean-François Thouvenel, Alain Roche (78 Gernot Rohr), Patrick Battiston, Zoran Vujović; Jean-Marc Ferreri, Jean Tigana, José Touré (87 Bernard Lacombe), René Girard; Philippe Fargeon, Zlatko Vujović.   Trainer: Aimé Jacquet
TORPEDO: Dmitri Kharin, Aleksandr Polukarov, Sergei Prigoda, Valeri Schaveiko, Vladimir Galaiba; Sergei Agashkov, Vladimir Grechnev (53 Sergei Schavlo), Sergei Muschtruev, Oleg Schirinbekov, Nikolai Savichev, Yuri Savichev (61 Vladimir Kobzev).   Trainer: Valentin Ivanov
Goal: Fargeon (57)

TORPEDO MOSKVA v GIRONDINS de BORDEAUX 3-2 (0-1)
Dinamo Tbilisi   18.03.1987
Referee: Bruno Galler (SWI)   Attendance: 60,000
TORPEDO: Dmitri Kharin, Sergei Prigoda, Aleksandr Polukarov, Valentin Kovach, Valeri Schaveiko, Sergei Schavlo (65 Gennadi Grishin), Yuri Savichev, Vladimir Galaiba (30 Valeri Plotnikov), Vladimir Kobzev, Sergei Agashkov, Oleg Schirinbekov.   Trainer: Valentin Ivanov
GIRONDINS: Dominique Dropsy; Patrick Battiston, Jean-François Thouvenel, Alain Roche, Zoran Vujović, Gernot Rohr, Jean Tigana, José Touré, René Girard, Jean-Marc Ferreri (81 Philippe Fargeon), Zlatko Vujović.   Trainer: Aimé Jacquet
Goals: Touré (39 pen, 60), Agashkov (49 pen, 71 pen), Schirinbekov (62)

MALMÖ FF v AJAX AMSTERDAM 1-0 (1-0)
Pilsdamm Park, Malmö   14.03.1987
Referee: George Smith (SCO)   Attendance: 20,186
MALMÖ FF: Jan Möller, Magnus Andersson, Hasse Borg, Kent Jönsson, Torbjörn Persson, Jonas Thern, Leif Enqvist, Ingemar Erlandsson, Anders Palmer, Lars Larsson, Mats Magnusson.   Trainer: Roy Hodgson
AJAX: Stanley Menzo, Danny Blind, Frank Rijkaard, Ronald Spelbos, Sonny Silooy, Aron Winter, Jan Wouters, Arnold Mühren, John Bosman (76 Dennis Bergkamp), Marco van Basten, John van't Schip.   Trainer: Johan Cruijff
Goal: Persson (43 pen)

AJAX AMSTERDAM v MALMÖ FF 3-1 (1-0)
Ajax Amsterdam   18.03.1987
Referee: Dieter Pauly (W. GER)   Attendance: 24,775
AJAX: Stanley Menzo, Danny Blind, Frank Rijkaard, Ronald Spelbos, Sonny Silooy, Jan Wouters, Arnold Mühren, John Bosman (46 Aron Winter), Dennis Bergkamp (89 Peter Boeve), Marco van Basten, John van't Schip. Trainer: Johan Cruijff
MALMÖ FF: Jan Möller; Magnus Andersson, Kent Jönsson, Hasse Borg, Torbjörn Persson, Mats Arvidsson (67 Deval Eminovski), Leif Enqvist, Ingemar Erlandsson, Anders Palmer, Håkan Lindman, Lars Larsson.   Trainer: Roy Hodgson
Goals: Van Basten (13, 72), Winter (61), Lindman (81)

SEMI-FINALS

REAL ZARAGOZA v AJAX AMSTERDAM 2-3 (1-1)
La Romareda, Zaragoza   8.04.1987
Referee: Zoran Petrović (YUG)   Attendance: 35,000
REAL ZARAGOZA: Andoni CEDRÚN Ibarra, Juan Martínez Martínez "CASUCO", Alfonso FRAILE Sánchez, JUAN CARLOS Justes Abiol, Rafael GARCÍA CORTÉS (66 ROBERTO Elvira Estrany), Francisco GÜERRI Ballarín, Juan Antonio SEÑOR Gómez, Manuel ABAD Francés, José Manuel MEJÍAS López, RUBÉN SOSA Aráiz, Francisco PINEDA García. Trainer: Luis Costa
AJAX: Stanley Menzo, Danny Blind, Frank Rijkaard, Aron Winter, Sonny Silooy, Jan Wouters, Arnold Mühren, John Bosman, John van't Schip, Marco van Basten, Rob Witschge (85 Peter Boeve).   Trainer: Johan Cruijff
Sent off: Güerri & Bosman (87)
Goals: Rubén Sosa (13), Rob Witschge (16), Bosman (47, 55), Señor (71 pen)

AJAX AMSTERDAM v REAL ZARAGOZA 3-0 (1-0)
Olympisch, Amsterdam 22.04.1987

Referee: Franz Wöhrer (AUS)   Attendance: 47,916

AJAX: Stanley Menzo, Sonny Silooy, Frank Rijkaard, Aron Winter, Peter Boeve, Jan Wouters, Arnold Scholten, Arnold Mühren, John van't Schip, Marco van Basten, Rob Witschge (74 Dennis Bergkamp).   Trainer: Johan Cruijff

REAL ZARAGOZA: Andoni CEDRÚN Ibarra, Juan Martínez Martínez "CASUCO", Tomás BLESA Noé, Alfonso FRAILE Sánchez, José Antonio CASAJÚS Mayén, JUAN CARLOS Justes Abiol, Juan Antonio SEÑOR Gómez, Rafael GARCÍA CORTÉS, ROBERTO Elvira Estrany (74 Mariano AYNETO Castro), José Manuel MEJÍAS López (67 Manuel ABAD Francés), Francisco PINEDA García.   Trainer: Luis Costa

Goals: Van't Schip (17), Rob Witschge (73), Rijkaard (90)

**GIRONDINS de BORDEAUX
v 1.FC LOKOMOTIVE LEIPZIG 0-1** (0-0)
Municipal, Bordeaux 8.04.1987

Referee: Horst Brummeier (AUS)   Attendance: 37,082

GIRONDINS: Dominique Dropsy; Patrick Battiston, Gernot Rohr, Léonard Specht, Zoran Vujović, René Girard (88 Laurent Lassagne), Jean Tigana, Jean-Marc Ferreri, José Touré, Philippe Fargeon (70 Philippe Vercruysse), Zlatko Vujović.   Trainer: Aimé Jacquet

1.FC LOKOMOTIVE: René Müller, Frank Baum, Ronald Kreer, Matthias Lindner, Uwe Zötzsche, Uwe Bredow, Frank Edmond, Matthias Liebers, Hans-Jörg Leitzke (66 Olaf Marschall), Hans Richter (85 Wolfgang Altmann), Heiko Scholz.   Trainer: Hans-Ulrich Thomale

Goal: Bredow (65)

**1.FC LOKOMOTIVE LEIPZIG
v GIRONDINS BORDEAUX 0-1** (0-1, 0-1) (AET)
Zentralstadion, Leipzi 22.04.1987

Referee: George Courtney (ENG)   Attendance: 73,000

1.FC LOKOMOTIVE: René Müller, Frank Baum, Ronald Kreer, Matthias Lindner, Uwe Zötzsche, Uwe Bredow, Heiko Scholz (95 Wolfgang Altmann), Matthias Liebers, Hans-Jörg Leitzke (66 Dieter Kühn), Hans Richter, Olaf Marschall.   Trainer: Hans-Ulrich Thomale

GIRONDINS: Dominique Dropsy; Alain Roche, Jean-François Thouvenel, Gernot Rohr, Zoran Vujović, René Girard, Jean Tigana, Jean-Marc Ferreri (80 Philippe Vercruysse), José Touré, Philippe Fargeon, Zlatko Vujović.   Trainer: Aimé Jacquet

Goal: Zl. Vujović (3)

Pen: 0-1 Touré, 1-1 Lindner, Vercruysse (miss), Liebers (miss), 1-2 Rohr, 2-2 Marschall, 2-3 Girard, 3-3 Zötzsche, 3-4 Roche, 4-4 Kühn, 4-5 Tigana, 5-5 Altmnann, Zoran Vujović (miss), 6-5 Müller

FINAL

**AJAX AMSTERDAM
v 1.FC LOKOMOTIVE LEIPZIG 1-0** (1-0)
Olympiako, Athina 13.05.1987

Referee: Luigi Agnolin (ITA)   Attendance: 35,017

AJAX: Stanley Menzo, Sonny Silooy, Frank Rijkaard, Frank Verlaat, Peter Boeve, Jan Wouters, Aron Winter, Arnold Mühren (82 Arnold Scholten), John van't Schip, Marco Van Basten, Rob Witschge (67 Dennis Bergkamp). Trainer: Johann Cruyff

1.FC LOKOMOTIVE: René Müller, Ronald Kreer, Frank Baum, Matthias Lindner, Uwe Zötzsche, Heiko Scholz, Uwe Bredow, Frank Edmond (54 Hans-Jörg Leitzke), Matthias Liebers (76 Dieter Kühn), Hans Richter, Olaf Marschall.   Trainer: Hans-Ulrich Thomale

Goal: Van Basten (21)

Goalscorers European Cup-Winners' Cup 1986-87:

8 goals: John Bosman (Ajax Amsterdam)

6 goals: Marco van Basten (Ajax Amsterdam)

5 goals: Marek Koniarek (GKS Katowice)

4 goals: Lasse Larsson (Malmö FF), Nikolai Savichev, Yuri Savichev (Torpedo Moskva), Semir Tuce (Velež Mostar), Nasko Sirakov (Vitosha Sofia), Stephen Massey (Wrexham)

3 goals: Richter (Lokomotiv Leipzig), Brigger (FC Sion), Anastopoulos (Olympiakos Peiraias), Señor (Real Zaragoza), Kienast (Rapid Wien), Vercruysse, Zl. Vujović (Girondins de Bordeaux)

2 goals: Rosenthal, Van Wijk (Club Brugge), Hristodoulou (Apollon Limassol), Csorba (Vasas Budapest), Kranjcar (Rapid Wien), P.Jurić (Velež Mostar), Iskrenov (Vitosha Sofia), Cina (FC Sion), Agashkov (Torpedo Moskva), Lindman, Palmer, Persson (Malmö FF), Roberto, Yáñez (Real Zaragoza), Touré (Girondins Bordeaux), Bredow, Lindner (Lokomotive Leipzig)

1 goal: Mathiesen (B 1903 København), Synnott (Waterford United), Brylle, Beyens (Club Brugge), Di Carlo, Gerolin (AS Roma), Sundby (Lillestrøm SK), Cămătaru (Dinamo București), Bett, Wright (Aberdeen), Törnval, Paatelainen (Haka Valkeakoski), Cleary (Glentoran Belfast), Bodnár, Szabadi (Vasas Budapest), Brauneder, Willfurth, Weinhofer, Halilovic (Rapid Wien), Buxton, Steel, Horne, Charles, Conroy (Wrexham United), Gudelj, Matijević, Skocajić (Velež Mostar), Klinsmann, Pasić, Sigurvinsson, Allgöwer (VfB Stuttgart), Kubisztal (GKS Katowice), Rui Aguas, Manniche,

Chiquinho, Diamantino (Benfica Lisboa), Minga, Josa, Kola (17 Nentori Tirana), Kapouranis, Papahristou, Togias, Zelilidis (Olympiakos Peiraias), Iordanov (Vitosha Sofia), Bregy, Debonnaire, Bouderbala (FC Sion), Schirinbekov, Plotnikov, Kobzev, Kruglov, Gostenin (Torpedo Moskva), Magnusson, Björn Nilsson (Malmö FF), Rubén Sosa, Mejías, García Cortés (Real Zaragoza), Fargeon, Girard, Zo.Vujović, Reinders (Girondins de Bordeaux), Marschall, Leitzke (Lokomotive Leipzig), Rijkaard, Rob Witschge (Ajax Amsterdam), Van't Schip, Winter, Wouters, A.Mühren (Ajax Amsterdam)

Own goals: Bjerkelund (Lillestrøm SK) for Benfica, Leighton (Aberdeen) for FC Sion, Prigoda (Torpedo Moskva) for Haka Valkeakoski

CUP WINNERS CUP 1987-88

PRELIMINARY ROUND

AEL LIMASSOL
v DAC DUNAJSKÁ STREDA 0-1 (0-0)

Limassol 23.08.1987

Referee: Heinz Holzmann (AUS)   Attendance: 10,000

AEL: Marios Onisiforou, Giannis Ioannou, Hristos Hristoforou, Hristos Hristodoulou, Giorgos Anastasiou (80 Kostas Konstantinou); Panikos Orfanidis, Loizos Mavroudis, Pavlos Savva, Hristos Koliantris (70 A. Hristodoulou); Ladislav Lauda, Aristos Aristotelous.   Trainer: Valerian Svec

DAC: Stanislav Vahala; Ján Kapko, Lubomír Šrámek, Dušan Liba, Tibor Szaban; Ján Hodúr (75 Peter Šoltés), Rudolf Pavlík, Peter Michalec, Petr Kašpar; Jozef Medgyes (87 Peter Bartoš), Juraj Majoros.   Trainer: Karol Pecze

Goal: Majoros (66)

DAC DUNAJSKÁ STREDA
v AEL LIMASSOL 5-1 (4-0)

DAC Dunajská Streda 27.08.1987

Referee: Stjepan Glavina (YUG)   Attendance: 5,000

DAC: Stanislav Vahala, Ján Kapko (46 Vladimír Brodziansky), Lubomír Šrámek, Dušan Liba, Tibor Szaban; Rudolf Pavlík, Peter Michalec, Petr Kašpar (59 Ján Hodúr); Tibor Micinec, Jozef Medgyes, Juraj Majoros.   Trainer: Karol Pecze

AEL: Marios Onisiforou, Hristos Hristoforou, Hristos Hristodoulou, Giorgos Stylianou, Makis Sokratous, Panikos Orfanidis, Loizos Mavroudis, Pavlos Savva, Giannis Ioannou (74 Giorgos Anastasiou), Ladislav Lauda (39 Aristos Aristotelous), Hristos Koliantris.   Trainer: Valerian Svec

Goals: Micinec (6, 39), Medgyes (20), Pavlík (27), Majoros (85 pen), Aristotelous (69).

FIRST ROUND

VLLAZNIA SHKODËR
v SLIEMA WANDERERS 2-0 (0-0)

Vojo Kushi Shkodër 13.09.1987

Referee: Vasilis Nikakis (GRE)   Attendance: 12,500

VLLAZNIA: Agim Maliqati, Hysen Zmijani, Vata, Hysen Dedja, Isak Pashaj; Ferid Rragami, Viktor Briza (4 Adrian Barbullushi), Fatbardh Jera, Adrian Bushati; Luan Vukatana (77 Arian Laçja), Faslli Fakja.   Trainer: Ramazan Ragami

SLIEMA WANDERERS: Pierre Calleja, Stephen Thewma, Oliver Losco, John Buttigieg, James Navarro, Emanuel Farrugia, Martin Gregory, George Zammit, John Caruana (82 Julian Magri Overend), Mario Gauci (68 Jonathan Magri Overend), Edmond Zammit.   Trainer: Lawrence Borg

Goals: Bushati (53), Jera (68)

SLIEMA WANDERERS
v VLLAZNIA SKHODËR 0-4 (0-1)

National Ta'Qali 29.09.1987

Referee: Soldatić (YUG)   Attendance: 1,500

SLIEMA WANDERERS: Pierre Calleja, Stephen Thewma, Oliver Losco, John Buttigieg, James Navarro, Emanuel Farrugia, Martin Gregory, George Zammit, Mario Gauci (66 Carlos Cluett), John Caruana, Edmond Zammit (81 Simon Grech).   Trainer: Lawrence Borg

VLLAZNIA: Agim Maliqati, Hysen Zmijani, Vata, Hysen Dedja, Fatbardh Jera (73 Arian Laçja), Isak Pashaj; Ferid Rragami, Viktor Briza, Adrian Bushati (62 Faslli Fakja), Adrian Barbullushi; Luan Vukatana.   Trainer: Ramazan Ragami

Goals: Pashaj (15), Vukatana (59), Ragami (70 pen), Fakja (83)

IA AKRANES v KALMAR FF 0-0

Akranesvöllur 15.09.1987

Referee: Thorodd Presberg (NOR)   Attendance: 2,108

IA AKRANES: Birkir Kristinsson, Adalsteinn Viglundsson, Sigurdur Lárusson, Orn Gunnarsson, Sigurdur B.Jónsson, Gudbjörn Tryggvason, Olafur Thordarson, Sveinbjörn Hákonarson, Heimir Gudmundsson, Valgeir Bardason (67 Haraldur Hinriksson), Haraldur Ingólfsson.
Trainer: Gudjon Thordarson

KALMAR FF: Jörgen Tellqvist, Håkan Jägerbrink, Torbjörn Arvidsson, Håkan Arvidsson, Magnus Arvidsson, Martin Holmberg, Mikael Marko, Peter Nilsson, Ergon (70 Björn Wigstedt), Billy Landsdowne (83 Stefan Alexandersson), Jan Jansson.   Trainer: Göran Andersson

KALMAR FF v ÍA AKRANES 1-0 (0-0, 0-0) (AET)
Fredriksskans, Kalmar 30.09.1987
Referee: Tadeusz Diakonowicz (POL)   Attendance: 1,067
KALMAR FF: Leif Friberg, Torbjörn Arvidsson, Håkan Arvidsson, Magnus Arvidsson, N.Ergon, Håkan Jägerbrink (74 Björn Wigstedt), Peter Nilsson, Martin Holmberg, Mikael Marko, Billy Landsdowne, Stefan Alexandersson.
Trainer: Göran Andersson
ÍA AKRANES: Birkir Kristinsson, Adalsteinn Viglundsson, Sigurdur Lárusson, Orn Gunnarsson (111 Thrandur Sigurdsson), Sigurdur B.Jónsson, Haraldur Hinriksson, Olafur Thordarson, Sveinbjörn Hákonarson, Heimir Gudmundsson, Valgeir Bardason, Haraldur Ingólfsson.
Trainer: Gudjon Thordarson
Goal: Alexandersson (102)

AVENIR BEGGEN v HAMBURGER SV 0-5 (0-2)
Stade de Beggen 15.09.1987
Referee: Alphonse Constantin (BEL)   Attendance: 2,000
AVENIR: Paul Koch, Gilbert Dresch, Alex Wilhelm, Thomas Wolf, Rolf Jentgen, Serge Jentgen, Léon Mond, Fred Schreiner, Martin Jank, Armin Krings, David Wynn.
Trainer: Jean-Marie Nurenberg
HAMBURGER SV: Mladen Pralija, Ditmar Jakobs (73 Carsten Kober), Manfred Kaltz, Dietmar Beiersdorfer, Thomas Kroth, Thomas von Heesen, Miroslaw Okonski, Uwe Bein, Thomas Hinz, Walter Laubinger (73 Lothar Dittmer), Bruno Labbadia.   Trainer: Josip Skoblar
Goals: Labbadia (9, 70), Laubinger (44), Okonski (58), Dittmer (83)

HAMBURGER SV v AVENIR BEGGEN 3-0 (1-0)
Volksparkstadion, Hamburg 30.09.1987
Referee: Jan Damgaard (DEN)   Attendance: 6,500
HAMBURGER SV: Richard Golz, Carsten Kober, Dietmar Beiersdorfer, Thomas Hinz, Manfred Kaltz, Harald Spörl, Uwe Bein (60 Josef Klos), Thomas Kroth, Thomas von Heesen, Bruno Labbadia, Miroslaw Okonski (46 Walter Laubinger).
Trainer: Josip Skoblar
AVENIR: Paul Koch, Léon Mond, Alex Wilhelm, Rolf Jentgen, Martin Jank, Jean Paul Girres, Hubert Meunier, Serge Jentgen, Gilbert Dresch, Jean-Jacques Robert (72 Goran Stankovic), Armin Krings (89 Floriani).   Trainer: Jean-Marie Nurenberg
Goals: Kroth (9), Kaltz (72), Labbadia (82)

**SPORTING LISBOA
v FC SWAROWSKI TIROL INNSBRUCK 4-0** (3-0)
Estadio José de Alvalade, Lisboa 15.09.1987
Referee: Marcel van Langenhove (BEL)   Att: 51,000
SPORTING: RUI Manuel da Silva CORREIA; JOÃO LUIS Barbosa, DUÍLIO Dias Júnior, Pedro Manuel Regateiro VENÂNCIO (Cap), VÍTOR Manuel Fernandes dos SANTOS (83 MÁRIO JORGE da Silva Pinho Fernandes), Jorge Paulo CADETE dos Santos Reis (74 MARLON Roniel Brandão), OCEANO Andrade da Cruz, MÁRIO Marques Coelho, Sílvio Paiva "SILVINHO", Tony Sealy, Paulo Roberto Vacinello "PAULINHO CASCAVEL".   Trainer: António Morais
FCS TIROL: Tomislav Ivkovic; Bruno Pezzey (Cap), Robert Auer, Ivica Kalinic, Gerald Messlender, Robert Wazinger, Manfred Linzmaier, Alfred Hörtnagl, Hansi Müller (33 Thomas Eder, 65 Peter Pacult), Arnold Koreimann; Alfred Roscher.   Trainer: Ernst Happel
Goals: Sealy (7, 41), Cascavel (24 pen, 83)

**FC SWAROWSKI TIROL INNSBRUCK
v SPORTING LISBOA 4-2** (1-0)
Tivoli, Innsbruck 30.09.1987
Referee: Paolo Casarin (ITA)   Attendance: 4,500
FCS TIROL: Tomislav Ivkovic; Robert Auer (23 Robert Wazinger), Gerald Messlender, Bruno Pezzey (Cap), Michael Streiter, Ivica Kalinic (71 Heinz Peischl), Manfred Linzmaier, Peter Pacult, Arnold Koreimann; Alfred Roscher, Rupert Marko.   Trainer: Ernst Happel
SPORTING: RUI Manuel da Silva CORREIA, António Maurício Farinha Henrique MORATO, DUÍLIO Dias Júnior, Pedro Manuel Regateiro VENÂNCIO (Cap), VÍTOR Manuel Fernandes dos SANTOS; OCEANO Andrade da Cruz, Luís Filipe Vieira Carvalha "LITOS", Tony Sealy, MÁRIO JORGE da Silva Pinho Fernandes; Paulo Roberto Vacinello "PAULINHO CASCAVEL", Sílvio Paiva "SILVINHO".
Trainer: António Morais
Goals: Marko (16), Roscher (53), Sealy (57), Cascavel (67), Pezzey (69), Linzmaier (85)

**ROVANIEMI PALLOSEURA
v GLENTORAN BELFAST 0-0**
Keskuskenttä, Rovaniemi 16.09.1987
Referee: Robert Holley Davidson (SCO)   Attendance: 3,978
PALLOSEURA: Ari Matinlassi, Arto Autti, Hannu Ollila, Miika Tolvanen, Jarmo Ilola, Heikki Hannola, Kari Virtanen (27 Hannu Honkanen), Markku Kallio, Pasi Tauriainen (24 Ari Tegelberg), Steven Polack, Paul Heaton.
Trainer: Graham Williams
GLENTORAN: Alan Paterson, Norman McGreevy, Alfie Stewart, Robert Bowers, Terry Moore, James Cleary, John Jameson, William Caskey, Gary Blackledge (57 David Montgomery), Gary McCartney, Alan Harrison.
Manager: Tommy Jackson

GLENTORAN BELFAST
v ROVANIEMI PALLOSURA 1-1 (0-0)

The Oval, Belfast 29.09.1987

Referee: Gudmundsson Haraldsson (ICE)   Att: 2,000

GLENTORAN: Alan Paterson, Norman McGreevy, Alfie Stewart, Robert Bowers, Terry Moore, James Cleary, David Montgomery (.. Patrick McCoy), William Caskey, Gerry Mullan, Gary McCartney (.. Gary Blackledge), John Jameson.   Manager: Tommy Jackson

PALLOSEURA: Ari Matinlassi, Arto Autti, Hannu Ollila, Miika Tolvanen, Jarmo Ilola, Markku Kallio, Vesa Tauriainen, Heikki Hannola, Pasi Tauriainen, Steven Polack, Paul Heaton.   Trainer: Graham Williams

Goals: Caskey (70), Kallio (65)

1.FC LOKOMOTIVE LEIPZIG
v OLYMPIQUE MARSEILLE 0-0

Zentralstadion, Leipzig 16.09.1987

Referee: Erik Fredriksson (SWE)   Attendance: 30,800

1.FC LOKOMOTIVE: René Müller, Ronald Kreer, Uwe Zötzsche, Frank Edmond, Torsten Kracht (80 Uwe Rösler), Uwe Bredow, Wolfgang Altmann, Matthias Liebers, Frank Pallgen (65 Frank Baum), Hans-Jörg Leitzke, Olaf Marschall.   Trainer: Hans-Ulrich Thomale

OLYMPIQUE: Joseph-Antoine Bell; Claude Lowitz, Karl-Heinz Förster, Yvon Le Roux, Jean-François Domergue; Franck Passi, Patrick Appriou, Bernard Genghini, Abdoulaye Diallo (75 Papa Abdourahmane Fall), Jean-Pierre Papin (82 Patrick Delamontagne), Klaus Allofs.   Trainer: Gérard Banide

DAC DUNAJSKÁ STREDA
v YOUNG BOYS BERN 2-1 (2-1)

DAC, Dunajská Streda 16.09.1987

Referee: Ignace van Swieten (HOL)   Attendance: 5,500

DAC: Stanislav Vahala, Ján Kapko, Lubomír Šrámek, Dušan Liba, Tibor Szaban; Rudolf Pavlík, Ján Hodúr (88 Július Simon), Petr Kašpar; Tibor Micinec, Jozef Medgyes (78 Peter Šoltés), Juraj Majoros.   Trainer: Karol Pecze

YOUNG BOYS: Peter Kobel, Jean-Marie Conz, Jürg Wittwer, Martin Weber, Alain Baumann (52 André Fimian), Hansruedi Baur, Hans Holmqvist, Albert Hohl, Erni Maissen, Björn Nilsson (60 Alain Sutter), Dario Zuffi.   Trainer: Alexander Mandziara

Goals: Micinec (9), Zuffi (22), Kašpar (37)

OLYMPIQUE MARSEILLE
v 1.FC LOKOMOTIVE LEIPZIG 1-0 (1-0)

Stade Vélodrôme, Marseille 30.09.1987

Referee: Franz Gächter (SWI)   Attendance: 23,680

OLYMPIQUE: Joseph-Antoine Bell; Claude Lowitz, Karl-Heinz Förster, Yvon Le Roux, Abdoulaye Diallo (81 Patrick Delamontagne), Franck Passi, Alain Giresse, Bernard Genghini, Jean-François Domergue, Jean-Pierre Papin, Klaus Allofs.   Trainer: Gérard Banide

1.FC LOKOMOTIVE: René Müller, Frank Baum, Ronald Kreer, Frank Edmond, Torsten Kracht, Wolfgang Altmann (65 Matthias Lindner), Uwe Bredow, Matthias Liebers, Uwe Zötzsche, Hans-Jörg Leitzke (72 Uwe Rösler), Olaf Marschall.   Trainer: Hans-Ulrich Thomale

Sent off: Kreer (72)

Goals: Allofs (8)

YOUNG BOYS BERN
v DAC DUNAJSKÁ STREDA 3-1 (0-0)

Wankdorf, Bern 30.09.1987

Referee: Wolf-Günther Wiesel (W. GER)   Attendance: 8,100

YOUNG BOYS: Peter Kobel, Jean-Marie Conz, Jürg Wittwer, Martin Weber, André Fimian, Hansruedi Baur, Hans Holmqvist (47 Erni Maissen), Albert Hohl, Björn Nilsson (78 Martin Jeitziner), Dario Zuffi, Alain Sutter.   Trainer: Alexander Mandziara

DAC: Stanislav Vahala; Lubomír Srámek, Vladimír Brodziansky, Dušan Liba, Tibor Szaban; Ján Hodúr, Peter Michalec (69 Peter Šoltés), Rudolf Pavlík, Petr Kašpar; Tibor Micinec, Juraj Majoros.   Trainer: Karol Pecze

Goals: Zuffi (63), Weber (67), Majoros (78), Maissen (88)

ÅLBORG BK v HAJDUK SPLIT 1-0 (0-0)

Ålborg Stadion 16.09.1987

Referee: Klaus Scheurell (E. GER)   Attendance: 12,000

ÅLBORG B: Henrik Hansen, Jens Steffensen, Søren Larsen, Steen Andersen, Søren Thorst; Henrik "KB" Hansen, Ib Simonsen, Henrik Vandet Kristensen, Torben Boye; Søren Dissing, Anders Sundstrup.   Trainer: Peter Rudbaek

HAJDUK: Zoran Varvodić, Dušan Vlaisavljević, Ante Miše, Dragutin Čelić, Zoran Vulić, Stjepan Andrijašević (60 Dragan Setinov), Zdenko Adamović (80 Frane Bucan), Branko Karačić, Jerko Tipurić, Robert Jarni; Miloš Bursać.   Trainer: Ivan Vutsov

Goal: Boye (63)

HAJDUK SPLIT v ÅLBORG BK 1-0 (1-0, 1-0) (AET)

Poljud Split 30.09.1987

Referee: Sadik Deda (TUR)   Attendance: 11,000

HAJDUK: Zoran Varvodić, Jerko Tipurić, Branko Miljuš, Dragutin Čelić, Zoran Vulić, Stjepan Andrijašević (68 Frane Bucan), Dragan Setinov, Branko Karačić (98 Franko Bogdan), Miloš Bursać, Aljoša Asanović, Darko Dražić.   Trainer: Ivan Vutsov

ÅLBORG B: Henrik Hansen, Jens Steffensen, Søren Larsen, Steen Andersen, Søren Thorst; Henrik "KB" Hansen, Ib Simonsen, Henrik Vandet Kristensen, Torben Boye; Søren Dissing, Jes Høgh.   Trainer: Peter Rudbaek

Goal: Asanović (43 pen)

Penalties: Hadjuk Split won 4-2 on penalties

AJAX AMSTERDAM v DUNDALK AFC 4-0 (0-0)

Ajax Amsterdam 16.09.1987

Referee: José María Enriquez Negreira (SPA)   Att: 15,712

AJAX: Stanley Menzo, Danny Blind, Frank Rijkaard, Ronald Spelbos, Peter Boeve, Jan Wouters, John Bosman (65 Aron Winter), Arnold Mühren, John van't Schip, Hennie Meijer (46 Frank Stapleton), Bryan Roy.   Trainer: Johan Cruijff

DUNDALK FC: Alan O'Neill, Gino Lawless, Harry McCue, Joey Malone, Mick Shelley; Larry Wyse, John Cleary, Martin Murray, Barry Kehoe; Terry Eviston (72 Dessie Gorman), Dave Newe.   Trainer: Turlough O'Connor

Goals: Rijkaard (65), Blind (73), Winter (81), Stapleton (85)

DUNDALK AFC v AJAX AMSTERDAM 0-2 (0-0)

Oriel Park, Dundalk 30.09.1987

Referee: Rune Larsson (SWE)   Attendance: 5,000

DUNDALK FC: Alan O'Neill, Gino Lawless, Harry McCue, Joey Malone, Mick Shelley; Larry Wyse, John Cleary, Martin Murray, Barry Kehoe; Dessie Gorman (75 Terry Eviston), Dave Newe.   Trainer: Turlough O'Connor

AJAX: Stanley Menzo, Danny Blind, Ronald Spelbos, Aron Winter, Jan Wouters, Arnold Scholten, John Bosman (65 Richard Witschge), Arnold Mühren, John van't Schip, Frank Stapleton (65 Hennie Meijer), Rob Witschge.   Trainer: Johan Cruyff

Goals: Newe (71 og), Meijer (87)

REAL SOCIEDAD SAN SEBASTIÁN v SLASK WROCLAW 0-0

Estadio San Mamés, Bilbao 16.09.1987

Referee: Carlo Longhi (ITA)   Attendance: 15,000

REAL SOCIEDAD: Luis Miguel ARCONADA Echarre, Joaquín URÍA Lekuona, Alberto GÓRRIZ Echarte, Agustín GAJATE Vidriales, Luis María LÓPEZ REKARTE, Santiago BAKERO Escudero, Manuel URBIETA Illarramendi (58 Juan María MUJIKA Izaguirre), Jesús María ZAMORA Ansorena, Aitor BEGUIRISTÁIN Mujika, Lorenzo Juarros García "LOREN", José María BAKERO Escudero.

SLASK: Janusz Jedynak, Waldemar Tesiorowski, Pawel Król, Modest Boguszewski (85 Ryszard Rosa), Janusz Góra; Stefan Machaj, Ryszard Tarasiewicz, Waldemar Prusik, Zbigniew Mandziejewicz, Dariusz Marciniak (83 Mariusz Stelmach), Kazimierz Mikolajewicz.   Trainer: Henryk Apostel

Note: Real Sociedad's stadium, Atotxa, didn't meet the requirements for a Cup Winners' Cup match so the game was played in Bilbao.

SLASK WROCLAW v REAL SOCIEDAD SAN SEBASTIÁN 0-2 (0-0)

Slask, Wroclaw 30.09.1987

Referee: Jan Keizer (HOL)   Attendance: 35,000

SLASK: Janusz Jedynak, Waldemar Tesiorowski, Pawel Król, Stefan Machaj, Janusz Góra, Zbigniew Mandziejewicz, Waldemar Prusik, Ryszard Tarasiewicz, Mirosław Gil, Kazimierz Mikołajewicz (70 Aleksandr Socha), Dariusz Marciniak (80 Mieczysław Łuszczynski).

REAL SOCIEDAD: Luis Miguel ARCONADA Echarre, Santiago BAKERO Escudero, Alberto GÓRRIZ Echarte, Agustín GAJATE Vidriales, Luis María LÓPEZ REKARTE, Juan Antonio LARRAÑAGA Gurruchaga, Juan MÚJIKA Izaguirre, Jesús María ZAMORA Ansorena, Aitor BEGUIRISTÁIN Mujika, José María BAKERO Escudero, Lorenzo Juarros García "LOREN" (84 Miguel Ángel FUENTES Azpiroz).   Trainer: John Toshack

Goals: Loren (76), Beguiristáin (82)

DINAMO MINSK v GENÇLERBIRLIĞI ANKARA 2-0 (0-0)

Dinamo Minsk 16.09.1987

Referee: Eero Aho (FIN)   Attendance: 25,000

DINAMO: Andrei Satsunkevich, Aleksandr Metlitski, Sergei Gomonov, Viktor Yanushevski, Sergei Shirokyi, Andrei Zigmantovich, Sergei Gotsmanov, Aleksandr Kisten (46 Pavel Rodnienok), Sergei Aleinikov, Andrei Schalimo (50 Viktor Sokol), Georgi Kondratiev.   Trainer: Ivan Savostikov

GENÇLERBIRLIĞI: Okan Gedikali, Ahmet Celikan, K.Hasan, Gökhan Itmeç, Sirin Berber; Zlatko, Avni Okumus (.. Hikmet), Agim, Muammer Ulug, Tuncay Mesci, Mehmet Sengüler (88 B. Metin Gökalp).   Trainer: Teoman Yamanlar

Goals: Zigmantovich (83), Gotsmanov (88)

**GENÇLERBIRLIĞI ANKARA
v DINAMO MINSK 1-2** (0-1)

19 Mayis Stadi Ankara 30.09.1987

Referee: Adrian Porumboiu (ROM)   Attendance: 7,445

GENÇLERBIRLIĞI: Okan Gedikali, Ahmet Celikan (74 Erkan Özeri), Sirin Berber, Gökhan Itmeç, K.Hasan, Avni Okumus, Mehmet Sengüler (74 Hayrettin Aksay), Zlatko, Muammer Ulug, Tuncay Mesci, Hikmet.
Trainer: Teoman Yamanlar

DINAMO: Andrei Satsunkevich, Sergei Borovski, Sergei Gomonov, Viktor Yanushevski, Viktor Sokol (62 Sergei Derkach), Andrei Zigmantovich, Sergei Gotsmanov, Sergei Pavliuchuk, Sergei Aleinikov, Andrei Schalimo (55 Georgi Kondratiev), Sergei Shirokyi.   Trainer: Ivan Savostikov

Goals: Tuncay (29), Derkach (69), Kondratiev (84)

ST. MIRREN PAISLEY v TROMSØ IL 1-0 (1-0)

St. Mirren Park, Paisley 16.09.1987

Referee: Ignace Goris (BEL)   Attendance: 7,797

ST.MIRREN: Campbell Money, Robert Dawson, David Winnie, William Abercromby, Peter Godfrey, Neil Cooper, Francis McGarvey (65 Norman McWhirter), Ian Ferguson, Paul Lambert (65 Paul Chalmers), Kenneth McDowall, Ian Cameron.   Manager: Alex Smith

TROMSØ: Bjarte Flem, Nils Solstad, Trond Steinar Albertsen, Tor Pedersen, Tore Nilsen, Morten Kraemer (85 Tom Ovesen), Bjørn Johansen, Truls Jenssen, Tore Rismo, Trond Johansen, Per Høgmo (89 Kjetil Olsen).   Trainer: Arne Andreassen

Goal: McDowall (3)

VITOSHA SOFIA v OFI IRAKLEIO 1-0 (0-0)

Levski, Sofia 16.09.1987

Referee: Helmut Kohl (AUS)   Attendance: 11,000

VITOSHA: Borislav Mihailov, Stoil Georgiev, Krasimir Koev, Petar Petrov, Dimitar Markov; Emil Velev, Sasho Nachev (83 Rosen Krumov), Nasko Sirakov, Emil Spasov (51 Petar Kurdov), Georgi Iordanov, Bojidar Iskrenov.
Trainer: Vasil Metodiev

OFI: Vaggelis Hosadas, Nikos Gkoulis, Grigoris Tsinos, Nikos Tsimpos, Miltiadis Andreanidis, Alexander Isis, Meletios Persias, Grigoris Papavasileiou, Grigoris Haralampidis (90 Hristos Kariotis), Nikos Nioplias (83 Giorgos Athanasiadis), Giannis Samaras.   Trainer: Eugenios Gerard

Goal: Sirakov (87 pen)

TROMSØ IL v ST. MIRREN PAISLEY 0-0

Alfheim, Tromsø 29.09.1987

Referee: Kurt Horsted (DEN)   Attendance: 5,114

TROMSØ: Bjarte Flem, Nils Solstad, Trond Steinar Albertsen, Tor Pedersen, Tore Nilsen, Sigmund Forfang (77 Kjetil Olsen), Bjørn Johansen, Lars Espejord, Tore Rismo (68 Eivind Andreassen), Trond Johansen, Per Høgmo.
Trainer: Arne Andreassen

ST.MIRREN: Campbell Money, Thomas Wilson, Peter Godfrey, Neil Cooper, David Winnie, Keith Walker, Ian Ferguson, William Abercromby (19 Anthony Fitzpatrick), Ian Cameron, Kenneth McDowall (76 Paul Chalmers), Paul Lambert.   Manager: Alex Smith

OFI IRAKLEIO v VITOSHA SOFIA 3-1 (1-0)

OFI Irakleio 30.09.1987

Referee: Bruno Galler (SWI)   Attendance: 12,000

OFI: Vaggelis Hosadas, Nikos Gkoulis, Nikos Tsimpos, Grigoris Tsinos, Miltiadis Andreanidis, Alexander Isis, Meletios Persias, Grigoris Papavasileiou (49 Manolis Patemtzis), Grigoris Haralampidis, Nikos Nioplias, Giannis Marinakis (76 Giorgos Athanasiadis).
Trainer: Eugenios Gerard

VITOSHA: Vlado Delchev, Stefan Kolev, Krasimir Koev, Stoil Georgiev, Nikolai Iliev, Dimitar Markov (80 Rosen Krumov), Emil Velev, Nasko Sirakov, Emil Spasov (55 Petar Kurdov), Georgi Iordanov, Bojidar Iskrenov.   Trainer: Vasil Metodiev

Goals: Tsimpos (26), Marinakis (48), Haralampidis (68), Kurdov (71)

**MERTHYR TYDFIL
v ATALANTA BERGAMO 2-1** (1-1)

Penydarren Park, Merthyr 16.09.1987

Referee: Charles Gilson (LUX)   Attendance: 8,000

MERTHYR TYDFIL: Gary Wager, David Tong, Chris Baird, Roger Mullen, Phil Evans, Kevin Rogers, Nigel French, Dave Webley, Chris Williams (87 Peter Jones), Andy Beattie, Ceri Williams.   Trainer: Lyn Jones

ATALANTA: Ottorino Piotti, Carmine Gentile, Luigino Pasciullo (46 Eligio Nicolini), Claudio Prandelli, Costanzo Barcella, Domenico Progna, Glenn Peter Strömberg, Andrea Icardi, Oliviero Garlini, Daniele Fortunato, Giuseppe Incocciati (75 Aldo Cantarutti).   Trainer: Emiliano Mondonico

Goals: Rogers (34), Progna (41), Ceri Williams (82)

**ATALANTA BERGAMO
v MERTHYR TYDFYLL 2-0** (2-0)
Stadio Communale, Bergamo 30.09.1987
Referee: Victor Mintoff (MAL)   Attendance: 14,000
ATALANTA: Ottorino Piotti, Claudio Prandelli, Carmine Gentile, Daniele Fortunato, Domenico Progna, Andrea Icardi, Glenn Peter Strömberg, Eligio Nicolini, Aldo Cantarutti, Giuseppe Incocciati (84 Costanzo Barcella), Oliviero Garlini.   Trainer: Emiliano Mondonico
MERTHYR TYDFIL: Gary Wager, David Tong, Chris Baird, Roger Mullen, Phil Evans, Kevin Rogers, Nigel French, Dave Webley, Ceri Williams (84 Steve Williams), Andy Beattie (87 Anthony Hopkins), Chris Williams.   Trainer: Lyn Jones
Goals: Garlini (16), Cantarutti (21)

**ÚJPESTI DÓZSA BUDAPEST
v FC DEN HAAG 1-0** (1-0)
Megyeri út, Budapest 16.09.1987
Referee: Karl-Heinz Tritschler (W. GER)   Attendance: 6,600
ÚJPESTI DÓZSA: László Kakas, István Schneider, József Varga, Zoltán Kecskés; István Kozma, László Szélpal, Attila Herédi, Ervin Kovács, Lajos Schróth (46 Sándor Rostás), Sándor Steidl (83 István Balogh), György Katona.   Trainer: János Göröcs
FC DEN HAAG: René Stam, Marco Van Alphen, Martin Jol, Joop Lankhaar, Albert Van Oosten, Karel Bouwens, Heini Otto, Frans Danen, Edwin Purvis, Ron De Roode, Bram Rontberg (88 John Van den Hoogenband)   Trainer: Pim van de Meent
Goal: Herédi (31 pen)

**FC DEN HAAG
v ÚJPESTI DÓZSA BUDAPEST 3-1** (2-0)
Zuiderpark, Den Haag 30.09.1987
Referee: Neil Midgley (ENG)   Attendance: 11,500
FC DEN HAAG: René Stam, Marco Van Alphen, Martin Jol, Joop Lankhaar, Edwin Purvis, Ron De Roode, Karel Bouwens, Heini Otto, John Van den Hoogenband, Peter Boere, Bram Rontberg.   Trainer: Pim van de Meent
ÚJPESTI DÓZSA: László Kakas, István Schneider (69 István Balogh), József Varga, Ervin Kovács, Zoltán Kecskés, Attila Herédi, László Szélpál (75 Viktor Mundi), György Kozma, Sándor Steidl, Sándor Rostás, György Katona.   Trainer: János Göröcs
Goals: Boere (22, 24), Varga (82 og), Rostás (89)

KV MECHELEN v DINAMO BUCUREŞTI 1-0 (0-0)
Achter de Caserne, Mechelen 16.09.1987
Referee: Ildefonso Urizar Aspitarte (SPA)   Att: 12,000
KV MECHELEN: Michel Preud'homme; Albert Cluytens, Leo Clijsters, Graeme Rutjes, Wim Hofkens; Paul Theunis, Erwin Koeman (80 Joachim Benfeld), Pascal De Wilde, Koen Sanders; Eli Ohana, Piet Den Boer.   Trainer: Aad de Mos
DINAMO: Dumitru Moraru; Iulian Mihăescu, Alexandru Nicolae, Lică Movilă, Ioan Varga (85 Gheorghe Dumitraşcu); Dănuţ Lupu, Dorin Mateuţ, Mircea Rednic, Costel Orac; Marian Damaschin, Rodion Cămătaru.
Trainer: Mircea Lucescu
Sent off: Movilă (45)
Goal: Den Boer (50)

DINAMO BUCUREŞTI v KV MECHELEN 0-2 (0-1)
Dinamo Bucureşti 30.09.1987
Referee: Pietro d'Elia (ITA)   Attendance: 20,000
DINAMO: Dumitru Moraru; Iulian Mihăescu, Alexandru Nicolae, Mircea Rednic, Ioan Varga; Ionuţ Lupescu, Dănuţ Lupu, Dorin Mateuţ, Costel Orac (61 Gheorghe Timiş); Marian Damaschin (46 Ilie Balaci), Rodion Cămătaru.   Trainer: Mircea Lucescu
KV MECHELEN: Michel Preud'homme; Albert Cluytens, Leo Clijsters, Graeme Rutjes, Wim Hofkens; Koen Sanders, Pascal De Wilde, Paul Theunis (34 Raymond Jaspers), Erwin Koeman; Eli Ohana (70 Joachim Benfeld), Piet Den Boer.   Trainer: Aad de Mos
Goals: Hofkens (39), Den Boer (71)

SECOND ROUND

KALMAR FF v SPORTING LISBOA 1-0 (0-0)
Fredriksskans, Kalmar 21.10.1987
Referee: Neil Midgley (ENG)   Attendance: 2,070
KALMAR FF: Jörgen Tellqvist, Hakan Jägerbrink, Billy Landsdowne, Håkan Arvidsson (Cap), Mikael Marko; Björn Wigstedt, Martin Holmberg, Torbjörn Arvidsson, Peter Nilsson, Johnny Erlandsson (83 Stefan Landberg), Jan Jansson.   Trainer: Göran Andersson
SPORTING: RUI Manuel da Silva CORREIA, JOÃO LUIS Barbosa, DUÍLIO Dias Júnior, António Maurício Farinha Henrique MORATO, FERNANDO Manuel Antunes MENDES, Luís Filipe Vieira Carvalha "LITOS" (58 CARLOS Jorge Marques Caldas XAVIER), OCEANO Andrade da Cruz (Cap), MÁRIO JORGE da Silva Pinho Fernandes, Tony Sealy, Paulo Roberto Vacinello "PAULINHO CASCAVEL" (71 MARLON Roniel Brandão), Sílvio Paiva "SILVINHO".
Trainer: António Morais
Goal: T. Arvidsson (88)

SPORTING LISBOA v KALMAR FF 5-0 (1-0)

Estádio José Alvalade, Lisboa   3.11.1987

Referee: George Smith (SCO)   Attendance: 45,000

SPORTING: Vítor Manuel Afonso DAMAS de Oliveira, JOÃO LUIS Barbosa, DUÍLIO Dias Júnior, António Maurício Farinha Henrique MORATO, VÍTOR Manuel Fernandes dos SANTOS, VIRGÍLIO Manuel Bagulho Lopes (/Cap), OCEANO Andrade da Cruz (Cap/) (19 Luís Filipe Vieira Carvalha "LITOS"), MÁRIO Marques Coelho, Tony Sealy, Sílvio Paiva "SILVINHO", Paulo Roberto Vacinello "PAULINHO CASCAVEL".   Trainer: António Morais

KALMAR FF: Jörgen Tellqvist, Håkan Jägerbrink (74 Stefan Alexandersson), Billy Landsdowne, Håkan Arvidsson (Cap), Mikael Marko, Kjell Johansson (46 Björn Wigstedt), Martin Holmberg, Torbjörn Arvidsson, Peter Nilsson, Johnny Erlandsson, Jan Jansson.   Trainer: Göran Andersson

Goals: Cascavel (34 pen, 53, 57), Sealy (62), Duílio (73)

HAMBURGER SV v AJAX AMSTERDAM 0-1 (0-0)

Volksparkstadion, Hamburg   21.10.1987

Referee: Franz Wöhrer (AUS)   Attendance: 24,600

HAMBURGER SV: Mladen Pralija, Manfred Kaltz, Ditmar Jakobs, Dietmar Beiersdorfer, Thomas Hinz, Harald Spörl, Thomas von Heesen, Thomas Kroth, Uwe Bein (56 Lothar Dittmer), Bruno Labbadia, Miroslaw Okonski.   Trainer: Josip Skoblar

AJAX: Stanley Menzo, Danny Blind, Ronald Spelbos, Frank Verlaat, John van't Schip, John Bosman (72 Arnold Scholten), Aron Winter, Arnold Mühren, Dennis Bergkamp, Hennie Meijer, Rob Witschge (85 Richard Witschge).   Trainer: Johan Cruyff

Goal: Meijer (52)

AJAX AMSTERDAM v HAMBURGER SV 2-0 (1-0)

Olympisch, Amsterdam   4.11.1987

Referee: George Courtney (ENG)   Attendance: 42,943

AJAX: Stanley Menzo, Danny Blind, Ronald Spelbos, Rob Witschge, John van't Schip, John Bosman, Aron Winter, Arnold Mühren, Dennis Bergkamp, Hennie Meijer, Bryan Roy (70 Richard Witschge).   Trainer: Johan Cruijff

HAMBURGER SV: Mladen Pralija, Manfred Kaltz, Ditmar Jakobs, Dietmar Beiersdorfer, Thomas Hinz, Thomas Kroth, Thomas von Heesen, Uwe Bein (46 Bruno Labbadia), Harald Spörl, Lothar Dittmer, Miroslaw Okonski.   Trainer: Josip Skoblar

Goals: A. Mühren (13), Meijer (83)

FC DEN HAAG v YOUNG BOYS BERN 2-1 (1-0)

Zuiderpark, Den Haag   21.10.1987

Referee: Luigi Agnolin (ITA)   Attendance: 9,337

FC DEN HAAG: René Stam, Marco Van Alphen, Joop Lankhaar, Martin Jol, Edwin Purvis, Karel Bouwens (70 Frans Danen), Heini Otto, John Van den Hoogenband, Bram Rontberg (80 Leo Schellevis), Peter Boere, Ron De Roode.   Trainer: Pim van de Meent

YOUNG BOYS: Peter Kobel, Jürg Wittwer, Jean-Marie Conz, Martin Weber, Albert Hohl, Hansruedi Baur, Hans Holmqvist, Martin Jeitziner, Alain Sutter (76 Björn Nilsson), Erni Maissen, Dario Zuffi.   Trainer: Alexander Mandziara

Goals: De Roode (3), Zuffi (62), Boere (71)

YOUNG BOYS BERN v FC DEN HAAG 1-0 (0-0)

Wankdorf, Bern   4.11.1987

Referee: Helmut Kohl (AUS)   Attendance: 6,400

YOUNG BOYS: Peter Kobel, Jean-Marie Conz, Jürg Wittwer, Martin Weber, André Fimian, Martin Jeitziner, Hansruedi Baur (82 Albert Hohl), Hans Holmqvist, Alain Sutter (89 Adam Mandziara), Dario Zuffi, Björn Nilsson.   Trainer: Alexander Mandziara

FC DEN HAAG: René Stam, Marco Van Alphen, Martin Jol, Joop Lankhaar, Albert Van Oosten, Edwin Purvis, Heini Otto, Karel Bouwens, John Van den Hoogenband (78 Bram Rontberg), Peter Boere, Ron De Roode (69 Leo Schellevis).   Trainer: Pim van de Meent

Goal: Fimian (66)

VLLAZNIA SHKODËR v PALLOSEURA ROVANIEMI 0-1 (0-1)

Vojo Kushi Shkodër   21.10.1987

Referee: Dimitar Dimitrov (BUL)   Attendance: 15,000

VLLAZNIA: Agim Maliqati, Hysen Zmijani, Hysen Dedja, Vata, Isak Pashaj; Ferid Rragami, Fatbardh Jera, Viktor Briza (71 Ilir Kepa), Adrian Barbullushi; Faslli Fakja, Luan Vukatana (77 Ardian Laçja).   Trainer: Ramazan Rragami

PALLOSEURA: Ari Matinlassi, Arto Autti, Hannu Honkanen, Steven Polack, Jarmo Ilola, Miika Tolvanen, Markku Kallio, Vesa Tauriainen (81 Ari Tegelberg), Heikki Hannola, Pasi Tauriainen, Paul Heaton.   Trainer: Graham Williams

Goal: Polack (27)

**PALLOSEURA ROVANIEMI
v VLLAZNIA SHKODËR 1-0** (0-0)

Keskuskenttä, Rovaniemi   4.11.1987

Referee: Bo Karlsson (SWE)   Attendance: 7,312

PALLOSEURA: Ari Matinlassi, Arto Autti, Hannu Ollila, Markku Kallio (28 Hannu Honkanen), Jarmo Ilola; Miika Tolvanen, Vesa Tauriainen, Heikki Hannola, Steven Polack, Ari Tegelberg (64 Pasi Tauriainen), Paul Heaton.
Trainer: Graham Williams

VLLAZNIA: Agim Maliqati, Kujtim Shaba, Hysen Dedja, Ferid Rragami, Ilir Kepa, Isak Pashaj; Fatbardh Jera, Viktor Briza, Adrian Barbullushi; Ardian Laçja, Luan Vukatana.
Trainer: Ramazan Ragami

Goal: Polack (47)

OFI IRAKLEIO v ATALANTA BERGAMO 1-0 (1-0)

Toumpas, Thessaloniki   21.10.1987

Referee: Aron Schmidhuber (W. GER)   Attendance: 9,500

OFI: Vaggelis Hosadas, Nikos Gkoulis, Nikos Tsimpos, Grigoris Tsinos, Miltiadis Andreanidis, Alexander Isis, Meletis Persias, Grigoris Papavasileiou, Grigoris Haralampidis (70 Giannis Marinakis), Nikos Nioplias, Giannis Samaras.
Trainer: Eugenios Gerard

ATALANTA: Ottorino Piotti, Giampaolo Rossi, Carmine Gentile, Domenico Progna, Costanzo Barcella, Claudio Prandelli, Glenn Peter Strömberg, Eligio Nicolini (88 Gian Mario Consonni), Andrea Icardi, Daniele Fortunato, Oliviero Garlini (83 Giuseppe Incocciati).
Trainer: Emiliano Mondonico

Goal: Persias (17)

ATALANTA BERGAMO v OFI IRAKLEIO 2-0 (1-0)

Stadio Comunale, Bergamo   4.11.1987

Referee: Gérard Biguet (FRA)   Attendance: 15,000

ATALANTA: Ottorino Piotti, Costanzo Barcella, Giampaolo Rossi, Daniele Fortunato, Claudio Prandelli, Andrea Icardi, Glenn Peter Strömberg, Eligio Nicolini, Gian Mario Consonni (75 Carmine Gentile), Walter Bonacina, Oliviero Garlini (86 Aldo Cantarutti).   Trainer: Emiliano Mondonico

OFI: Vaggelis Hosadas, Nikos Gkoulis, Nikos Tsimpos, Giannis Mihalitsios (79 Giannis Marinakis), Miltiadis Andreanidis, Alexander Isis, Meletis Persias, Grigoris Papavasileiou, Grigoris Haralampidis (46 Giorgos Athanasiadis), Nikos Nioplias, Giannis Samaras.
Trainer: Eugenios Gerard

Goals: Nicolini (22), Garlini (73)

**REAL SOCIEDAD SAN SEBASTIÁN
v DINAMO MINSK 1-1** (0-1)

Estadio Atotxa, San Sebastián   21.10.1987

Referee: Vitor FERNANDES CORREIA (POR)   Att: 25,000

REAL SOCIEDAD: Luis Miguel ARCONADA Echarre, Santiago BAKERO Escudero (70 Luciano ITTURINO Cenekorta), Luis María LÓPEZ REKARTE, Juan Antonio LARRAÑAGA Gurruchaga, Alberto GÓRRIZ Echarte, Agustín GAJATE Vidriales, Juan MÚJIKA Izaguirre (46 Joaquín URÍA Lekuona), José María BAKERO Escudero, Lorenzo Juarros García "LOREN", Jesús María ZAMORA Ansorena, Aitor BEGUIRISTÁIN Mujika.   Trainer: John Toshack

DINAMO: Andrei Satsunkevich, Sergei Borovski, Sergei Gomonov, Viktor Yanushevski, Viktor Sokol, Andrei Zigmantovich, Sergei Gotsmanov, Sergei Derkach (82 Andrei Schalimo), Sergei Aleinikov, Sergei Shirokyi (85 Sergei Pavliuchuk), Georgi Kondratiev.   Trainer: Ivan Savostikov

Goals: Kondratiev (5), Gajate (87)

**DINAMO MINSK
v REAL SOCIEDAD SAN SEBASTIÁN 0-0**

Dinamo Minsk   4.11.1987

Referee: Yusuf Namoğlu (TUR)   Attendance: 25,000

DINAMO: Andrei Satsunkevich, Sergei Borovski, Sergei Gomonov (85 Pavel Rodnienok), Viktor Yanushevski, Viktor Sokol, Andrei Zigmantovich, Sergei Shirokyi, Sergei Gotsmanov, Sergei Derkach (24 Aleksandr Kisten), Sergei Aleinikov, Georgi Kondratiev.   Trainer: Ivan Savostikov

REAL SOCIEDAD: Luis Miguel ARCONADA Echarre, Santiago BAKERO Escudero, Luis María LÓPEZ REKARTE, Juan Antonio LARRAÑAGA Gurruchaga, Alberto GÓRRIZ Echarte, Agustín GAJATE Vidriales, Juan María MÚJIKA Izaguirre (59 Joaquín URÍA Lekuona), José María BAKERO Escudero, Lorenzo Juarros García "LOREN", Jesús María ZAMORA Ansorena (70 Luciano ITTURINO Cenekorta), Aitor BEGUIRISTÁIN Mujika.   Trainer: John Toshack

KV MECHELEN v ST. MIRREN PAISLEY 0-0

Achter de Kazerne, Mechelen   21.10.1987

Referee: Lajos Hartmann (HUN)   Attendance: 6,146

KV MECHELEN: Michel Preud'homme, Albert Cluytens, Graeme Rutjes, Leo Clijsters, Erwin Koeman, Koen Sanders, Paul Theunis (46 Pascal de Wilde), Paul de Mesmaeker, Wim Hofkens, Piet den Boer, Eli Ohana.   Trainer: Aad de Mos

ST.MIRREN: Campbell Money, David Winnie, Peter Godfrey, Neil Cooper, Thomas Wilson, Keith Walker (77 Robert Dawson), Ian Cameron, Anthony Fitzpatrick (63 Brian Hamilton), Paul Chalmers, Paul Lambert, Ian Ferguson.
Manager: Alex Smith

ST. MIRREN PAISLEY v KV MECHELEN 0-2 (0-1)
St. Mirren Park, Paisley 4.11.1987
Referee: Einar Halle (NOR)   Attendance: 12,000
ST.MIRREN: Campbell Money, Robert Dawson, Thomas Wilson, Anthony Fitzpatrick, Peter Godfrey, Neil Cooper, Paul Lambert, Keith Walker (63 Brian Hamilton), Paul Chalmers, Kenneth McDowall (89 George Shaw), Ian Cameron.
Manager: Alex Smith
KV MECHELEN: Michel Preud'homme, Albert Cluytens, Raymond Jaspers, Graeme Rutjes, Wim Hofkens; Paul Theunis, Koen Sanders, Paul de Mesmaeker, Erwin Koeman; Eli Ohana, Piet den Boer.   Trainer: Aad de Mos
Goals: Ohana (34, 50)

**OLYMPIQUE MARSEILLE
v HAJDUK SPLIT 4-0** (1-0)
Stade Vélodrôme, Marseille 22.10.1987
Referee: Paolo Casarin (ITA)   Attendance: 28,313
OLYMPIQUE: Joseph-Antoine Bell; Yvon Le Roux, Jean-François Domergue, Karl-Heinz Förster, Claude Lowitz, Franck Passi, Bernard Genghini, Alain Giresse, Jean-Pierre Papin, Abdoulaye Diallo, Klaus Allofs.
Trainer: Gérard Banide
HAJDUK: Zoran Varvodić, Dušan Vlaisavljević, Ante Miše, Dragutin Čelić, Zoran Vulić, Stjepan Andrijašević, Zdenko Adamović (81 Miloš Bursać), Branko Miljuš, Dragan Setinov, Aljoša Asanović, Frane Bucan (66 Stjepan Deverić).
Trainer: Ivan Vutsov
Goals: Papin (30), Diallo (48), K. Allofs (69), Giresse (89)

**HAJDUK SPLIT
v OLYMPIQUE MARSEILLE 2-0** (1-0)
Poljud, Split 5.11.1987
Referee: Dieter Pauly (W. GER)   Attendance: 22,000
HAJDUK: Zoran Varvodić,, Dušan Vlaisavljević, Jerko Tipurić, Dragutin Čelić, Zoran Vulić, Stjepan Andrijašević, Dragan Setinov, Branko Miljuš, Miloš Bursać, Aljoša Asanović, Radovan Krstović (70 Frane Bucan).   Trainer: Ivan Vutsov
OLYMPIQUE: Joseph-Antoine Bell; Yvon Le Roux, Jean-François Domergue, Karl-Heinz Förster, Claude Lowitz, Franck Passi, Bernard Genghini, Alain Giresse, Jean-Pierre Papin (37 Abdoulaye Diallo), William Ayache, Klaus Allofs.
Trainer: Gérard Banide
Goals: Asanović (19 pen), Bursać (83)
Note: UEFA awarded the game 3-0 to Olympique Marseille

QUARTER-FINALS

**PALLOSEURA ROVANIEMI
v OLYMPIQUE MARSEILLE 0-1** (0-1)
Stadio Via del Mare, Lecce 1.03.1988
Referee: Velitchko Tsonchev (BUL)   Attendance: 1,631
PALLOSEURA: Ari Matinlassi, Miika Tolvanen, Steven Polack, Jarmo Ilola, Heikki Hannola, Hannu Honkanen, Markku Kallio, Pasi Tauriainen, Hannu Ollila, Vesa Tauriainen, Malcolm Dunkley (81 Petri Nieminen).
Trainer: Graham Williams
OLYMPIQUE: Joseph-Antoine Bell; Yvon Le Roux, Jean-François Domergue, Karl-Heinz Förster, Benoît Cauet (62 Papa Abdourahmane Fall), Alain Giresse, Bernard Genghini, Ayew Abedi Pelé, William Ayache, Jean-Pierre Papin, Klaus Allofs.   Trainer: Gérard Banide
Goal: Papin (26)

**OLYMPIQUE MARSEILLE
v PALLOSEURA ROVANIEMI 3-0** (2-0)
Stade Vélodrôme, Marseille 15.03.1988
Referee: Vitor Fernandes Correia (POR)   Att: 16,016
OLYMPIQUE: Joseph-Antoine Bell; William Ayache, Yvon Le Roux, Claude Lowitz, Jean-François Domergue, Karl-Heinz Förster, Alain Giresse (83 Abdoulaye Diallo), Ayew Abedi Pelé, Bernard Genghini (80 Benoît Cauet), Jean-Pierre Papin, Klaus Allofs.   Trainer: Gérard Banide
PALLOSEURA: Ari Matinlassi, Hannu Honkanen, Steven Polack, Hannu Ollila, Miika Tolvanen, Pasi Tauriainen, Petri Nieminen, Malcolm Dunkley (35 Ari Tegelberg), Vesa Tauriainen, Heikki Hannola, Markku Kallio.
Trainer: Graham Williams
Goals: Genghini (18), Allofs (22), Papin (76 pen)

KV MECHELEN v DINAMO MINSK 1-0 (0-0)
Achter de Kazerne, Mechelen 2.03.1988
Referee: Gerasimos Germanakos (GRE)   Attendance: 9,000
KV MECHELEN: Michel Preud'homme, Marc Emmers, Leo Clijsters, Graeme Rutjes, Wim Hofkens; Koen Sanders, Joachim Benfeld (19 Paul De Mesmaeker), Erwin Koeman; Pascal de Wilde; Eli Ohana, Piet den Boer.
Trainer: Aad de Mos
DINAMO: Andrei Satsunkevich, Pavel Rodnienok, Viktor Yanushevski, Sergei Gomonov, Viktor Sokol, Andrei Zigmantovich, Sergei Aleinikov, Sergei Gotsmanov, Andrei Schalimo, Sergei Derkach, Georgi Kondratiev.
Trainer: Ivan Savostikov
Sent off: Schalimo (81)
Goal: De Wilde (86)

DINAMO MINSK v KV MECHELEN 1-1 (0-1)

Dinamo Minsk 16.03.1988

Referee: Henning Lund Sørensen (DEN)   Att: 50,000

DINAMO: Andrei Satsunkevich, Pavel Rodnienok, Sergei Gomonov, Viktor Yanushevski, Sergei Shirokyi (26 Viktor Sokol), Andrei Zigmantovich, Sergei Gotsmanov, Aleksandr Kisten, Sergei Aleinikov, Sergei Derkach, Georgi Kondratiev.   Trainer: Ivan Savostikov

KV MECHELEN: Michel Preud'homme, Marc Emmers, Graeme Rutjes, Leo Clijsters, Erwin Koeman, Raymond Jaspers, Koen Sanders, Joachim Benfeld, Pascal de Wilde (60 Paul De Mesmaeker), Eli Ohana (89 Paul Theunis), Piet den Boer.   Trainer: Aad de Mos

Goals: Ohana (29), Kisten (59)

**ATALANTA BERGAMO
v SPORTING LISBOA 2-0** (1-0)

Stadio Comunale, Bergamo 2.03.1988

Referee: Siegfried Kirschen (E. GER)   Attendance: 25,000

ATALANTA: Ottorino Piotti (Cap), Giampaolo Rossi, Carmine Gentile, Daniele Fortunato, Domenico Progna, Walter Bonacina, Glenn Peter Strömberg (85 Andrea Salvadori), Eligio Nicolini, Aldo Cantarutti, Andrea Icardi, Ivano Bonetti (73 Gian Mario Consonni).   Trainer: Emiliano Mondonico

SPORTING: RUI Manuel da Silva CORREIA, JOÃO LUIS Barbosa, VIRGÍLIO Manuel Bagulho Lopes, DUÍLIO Dias Júnior, Pedro Manuel Regateiro VENÂNCIO (Cap), OCEANO Andrade da Cruz, CARLOS Jorge Marques Caldas XAVIER (75 MÁRIO JORGE da Silva Pinho Fernandes), Tony Sealy, Paulo Roberto Vacinello "PAULINHO CASCAVEL", MÁRIO Marques Coelho, MARLON Roniel Brandão (46 Sílvio Paiva "SILVINHO").   Trainer: António Morais

Goals: Nicolini (44 pen), Cantarutti (79)

**SPORTING LISBOA
v ATALANTA BERGAMO 1-1** (0-0)

Estádio José Alvalade, Lisboa 16.03.1988

Referee: Horst Brummeier (AUS)   Attendance: 55,000

SPORTING: Vítor Manuel Afonso DAMAS de Oliveira, JOÃO LUIS Barbosa (46 MÁRIO Marques Coelho), MÁRIO JORGE da Silva Pinho Fernandes, António Maurício Farinha Henrique MORATO, Pedro Manuel Regateiro VENÂNCIO (Cap), DUÍLIO Dias Júnior (64 CARLOS Jorge Marques Caldas XAVIER), OCEANO Andrade da Cruz, Peter Houtman, Paulo Roberto Vacinello "PAULINHO CASCAVEL", MARLON Roniel Brandão, Sílvio Paiva "SILVINHO".   Trainer: António Morais

ATALANTA: Ottorino Piotti (Cap), Andrea Salvadori, Costanzo Barcella, Daniele Fortunato, Domenico Progna, Walter Bonacina, Andrea Icardi, Eligio Nicolini, Aldo Cantarutti, Gian Mario Consonni (88 Carlo Osti), Ivano Bonetti.   Trainer: Emiliano Mondonico

Goals: Houtman (66), Cantarutti (82)

**YOUNG BOYS BERN
v AJAX AMSTERDAM 0-1** (0-1)

Wankdorf, Bern 9.03.1988

Referee: Emilio Soriano Aladren (SPA)   Attendance: 7,686

YOUNG BOYS: Urs Zurbuchen; Jürg Wittwer, Jean-Marie Conz, Martin Weber, Erich Hänzi (73 Ronnie Frederiksen), Martin Jeitzner (53 René Sutter), Alain Baumann, Hans Holmqvist, Erni Maissen, Dario Zuffi, Alain Sutter.   Trainer: Alexander Mandziara

AJAX: Stanley Menzo, Danny Blind, Peter Larsson, Ronald Spelbos, Danny Hesp; Jan Wouters, Aron Winter (70 Arnold Scholten), Arnold Mühren; John van't Schip (83 Dennis Bergkamp), John Bosman, Rob Witschge.   Trainers: Barry Hulshoff, Spitz Kohn & Bobby Haarms

Goal: Bosman (44)

**AJAX AMSTERDAM
v YOUNG BOYS BERN 1-0** (1-0)

Olympisch, Amsterdam 16.03.1988

Referee: Valeri Butenko (USSR)   Attendance: 28,000

AJAX: Stanley Menzo, Arnold Scholten, Peter Larsson, Ronald Spelbos, Frank Verlaat, Jan Wouters, Aron Winter (84 Dennis Bergkamp), Arnold Mühren, John van't Schip, John Bosman (86 Hennie Meijer), Rob Witschge.   Trainer: Barry Hulshoff

YOUNG BOYS: Urs Zurbuchen; Jürg Wittwer, Jean-Marie Conz, Martin Weber, Alain Baumann, Martin Jeitziner (76 Erich Hänzi), Erni Maissen, Hans Holmqvist, René Sutter (76 Ronnie Frederiksen), Dario Zuffi, Alain Sutter.   Trainer: Alexander Mandziara

Goal: Larsson (39)

SEMI-FINALS

**OLYMPIQUE MARSEILLE
v AJAX AMSTERDAM 0-3** (0-2)

Stade Vélodrôme, Marseille 6.04.1988

Referee: Ioan Igna (ROM)   Attendance: 42,584

OLYMPIQUE: Joseph-Antoine Bell; Papa Abdourahmane Fall (46 Abdoulaye Diallo), Yvon Le Roux (64 Eric Mura), Claude Lowitz, Jean-François Domergue; Karl-Heinz Förster, Alain Giresse, Bernard Genghini, Ayew Abedi Pelé; Jean-Pierre Papin, Klaus Allofs.   Trainer: Gérard Banide

AJAX: Stanley Menzo, Danny Blind, Peter Larsson, Jan Wouters, Frank Verlaat; Arnold Scholten, Aron Winter, Arnold Mühren; John van't Schip, John Bosman (85 Dennis Bergkamp), Rob Witschge.   Trainer: Barry Hulshoff

Goals: Rob Witschge (12, 42), Bergkamp (89)

**AJAX AMSTERDAM
v OLYMPIQUE MARSEILLE 1-2** (1-0)

Olympisch, Amsterdam   20.04.1988

Referee: Siegfried Kirschen (E. GER)   Attendance: 42,000

AJAX: Stanley Menzo, Danny Blind (67 Marcel Keizer), Peter Larsson, Jan Wouters, Frank Verlaat; Arnold Scholten, Aron Winter, Arnold Mühren; John van't Schip, John Bosman, Rob Witschge.   Trainer: Barry Hulshoff

OLYMPIQUE: Henri Stambouli; Franck Passi, Karl-Heinz Förster, Claude Lowitz, Benoît Cauet (83 Regina), Abdoulaye Diallo, Patrice Eyraud (57 Patrick Appriou), Alain Giresse, Ayew Abedi Pelé, Jean-Pierre Papin, Klaus Allofs.   Trainer: Gérard Banide

Goals: Larsson (23), Papin (67), Allofs (90)

**KV MECHELEN
v ATALANTA BERGAMO 2-1** (1-1)

Achter de Kazerne, Mechelen   6.04.1988

Referee: Emilio Soriano Aladren (SPA)   Attendance: 11,700

KV MECHELEN: Michel Preud'homme, Marc Emmers, Graeme Rutjes, Leo Clijsters, Wim Hofkens; Koen Sanders, Joachim Benfeld (72 Paul De Mesmaeker), Erwin Koeman, Pascal de Wilde; Piet den Boer, Eli Ohana.   Trainer: Aad de Mos

ATALANTA: Ottorino Piotti, Domenico Progna, Giampaolo Rossi, Carmine Gentile, Daniele Fortunato, Costanzo Barcella, Glenn Peter Strömberg (86 Gian Mario Consonni), Eligio Nicolini, Ivano Bonetti (78 Andrea Salvadori), Andrea Icardi, Oliviero Garlini.   Trainer: Emiliano Mondonico

Goals: Ohana (7), Strömberg (8), Den Boer (83)

**ATALANTA BERGAMO
v KV MECHELEN 1-2** (1-0)

Stadio Comunale, Bergamo   20.04.1988

Referee: Valeri Butenko (USSR)   Attendance: 40,000

ATALANTA: Ottorino Piotti, Costanzo Barcella, Carmine Gentile, Daniele Fortunato, Giampaolo Rossi (67 Aldo Cantarutti), Andrea Icardi (80 Giuseppe Compagno), Glenn Peter Strömberg, Eligio Nicolini, Ivano Bonetti, Walter Bonacina, Oliviero Garlini.   Trainer: Emiliano Mondonico

KV MECHELEN: Michel Preud'homme, Koen Sanders, Graeme Rutjes, Leo Clijsters, Geert Deferm, Marc Emmers, Wim Hofkens, Erwin Koeman, Paul De Mesmaeker (46 Piet den Boer), Eli Ohana, Pascal de Wilde (71 Raymond Jaspers).   Trainer: Aad de Mos

Goals: Garlini (39 pen), Rutjes (57), Emmers (80)

FINAL

KV MECHELEN v AJAX AMSTERDAM 1-0 (0-0)

Stade de la Meinau, Strasbourg   11.05.1988

Referee: Dieter Pauly (W. GER)   Attendance: 39,446

KV MECHELEN: Michel Preud'homme, Koenraad Sanders, Graeme Rutjes, Leo Clijsters, Geert Deferm; Wim Hofkens (73 Paul Theunis), Erwin Koeman, Marc Emmers, Pascal De Wilde (60 Paul De Mesmaeker); Piet Den Boer, Eli Ohana.   Trainer: Aad de Mos

AJAX: Stanley Menzo, Danny Blind, Frank Verlaat (73 Hennie Meijer), Jan Wouters, Peter Larsson; Arnold Scholten, Aron Winter, Arnold Mühren; John van't Schip (57 Dennis Bergkamp), John Bosman, Rob Witschge.   Trainer: Bernardus Hulshof.

Sent off: Blind (16)

Goal: Den Boer (53)

Goalscorers Cup-Winners' Cup 1987-88:

6 goals: Paulo Roberto Vacinello "PAULINHO" CASCAVEL (Sporting Lisboa)

4 goals: Piet den Boer, Eli Ohana (KV Mechelen), Klaus Allfos, Jean-Pierre Papin (Olympique Marseille), Tony Sealy (Sporting Lisboa)

3 goals: Meijer (Ajax), Cantarutti, Garlini (Atalanta), Majoros, Micinec (DAC Dunajska Streda), Boere (FC den Haag), Labbadia (Hamburger SV), Zuffi (Young Boys Bern),

2 goals: Larsson, Rob Witschge (Ajax), Nicolini (Atalanta), Kondratiev (Dinamo Minsk), Polack (Rovaniemi Palloseura), Caskey (Glentoran Belfast), Kašpar, Medgyes, Pavlík (DAC Dunajska Streda)

1 goal: Aristotelous (AEL Limassol), Marko, Roscher, Pezzey, Linzmaier (FCS Tirol Innsbruck), Boye (Ålborg BK), Tuncay (Gençlerbirliği Ankara), Sirakov, Kurdov (Vitosha Sofia), Rogers, Ceri Williams (Merthyr Tydfil), Rostás, Herédi (Újpesti Dózsa Budapest), T.Arvidsson, Alexandersson (Kalmar FF), Kroth, Kaltz, Laubinger, Okonski, Dittmer (Hamburger SV), De Roode (FC den Haag), Pashaj, Vukatana, Ragami, Fakja, Bushati, Jera (Vllaznia Shkodër), Persias, Tsimpos, Marinakis, Haralampidis (OFI Irakleio), Gajate, Loren, Beguiristáin (Real Sociedad), McDowall (St Mirren), Asanović (Hajduk Split), Kallio (Rovaniemi Palloseura), Kisten, Derkach, Zigmantovich, Gotsmanov (Dinamo Minsk), Houtman, Duílio (Sporting Lisboa), Fimian, Weber, Maissen (Young Boys Bern), Genghini, Diallo, Giresse (Olympique Marseille), Bergkamp, Bosman, A. Mühren, Rijkaard, Blind, Winter, Stapleton (Ajax Amsterdam), Strömberg, Progna (Atalanta), Rutjes, Emmers, De Wilde, Hofkens (KV Mechelen)

Own goals: Newe (Dundalk FC) for Ajax, Varga (Újpesti Dózsa) for FC den Haag

CUP WINNERS' CUP 1988-89

PRELIMINARY ROUND

**ELÖRE SPARTACUS BÉKÉSCSABA
v BRYNE IL 3-0** (3-0)

Békéscsabai stadion   10.08.1988

Referee: Wolf-Günter Wiesel (W. GER)   Attendance: 10,000

BÉKÉSCSABA: István Gulyás, Zoltán Szenti, Mihály Ottlakán, Sándor Csató, György Fabulya, Mihály Mracskó, Tibor Gruborovics, Miklós Csalánosi, László Horvath (60 Zoltán Kanál), Lajos Kvaszta (46 István Csernus), József Szekeres.   Trainer: János Csank

BRYNE: Lars Gaute Bø, Hugo Hansen, Ulf Karlsen, Leif Rune Salte, Geir Giljarhus (76 Trond Fylling), Erling Undheim (46 Roar Pedersen), Pål Fjeldstad, Nils Ove Hellvik, Stig Norheim, Børre Meinseth, Bjarne Lodden.   Trainer: Bjarne Berntsen

Goals: Gruborovics (4, 10), Csató (37)

**BRYNE IL
v ELÖRE SPARACUS BEKESCSABA 2-1** (1-1)

Bryne Stadion   24.08.1988

Referee: Kenneth Hope (SCO)   Attendance: 630

BRYNE: Lars Gaute Bø, Pål Fjeldstad, Ulf Karlsen, Leif Rune Salte, Geir Giljarhus (72 Bjarne Lodden), Hugo Hansen, Tor Fosse, Jan Madsen (72 Børre Meinseth), Nils Ove Hellvik, Stig Norheim, Paul Folkvord.   Trainer: Bjarne Berntsen

BÉKÉSCSABA: István Gulyás, Zoltán Szenti, Zoltán Kanál (58 Lajos Arky), György Fabulya, Tibor Gruborovics, Mihály Ottlakán, Mihály Mracskó (75 István Csernus), Sándor Csató, Lajos Kvaszta, Miklós Csalánosi, József Szekeres.   Trainer: János Csank

Goals: Kvaszta (35), Hellvik (45 pen), Meinseth (80 pen)

FIRST ROUND

**GRASSHOPPER ZÜRICH
v EINTRACHT FRANKFURT/MAIN 0-0**

Wankdorf, Basel   6.09.1988

Referee: George Smith (SCO)   Attendance: 13,600

GRASSHOPPER: Martin Brunner; Alex Imhof (74 Arne Stiel), Charly In-Albon, André Egli, Silvano Bianchi, Mats Gren, Martin Andermatt, Ciriaco Sforza, Alain Sutter, Paulo Cesar Camassuti (74 Necip Ugras), Wynton Rufer.   Trainer: Ottmar Hitzfeld

EINTRACHT: Ulrich Stein, Manfred Binz, Ralf Sievers, Dieter Schlindwein, Dietmar Roth, Peter Hobday, Dirk Bakalorz, Karl-Heinz Körbel, Stefan Studer, Janusz Turowski, Jørn Andersen (90 Thomas Klepper).   Trainer: Pál Csernai

**EINTRACHT FRANKFURT/MAIN v
GRASSHOPPER ZÜRICH 1-0** (1-0)

Waldstadion, Frankfurt/Main   4.10.1988

Referee: Dušan Krchnak (CZE)   Attendance: 13,280

EINTRACHT: Ulrich Stein, Manfred Binz, Karl-Heinz Körbel, Michael Kostner, Dietmar Roth, Dirk Heitkamp (32 Janusz Turowski), Peter Hobday, Dirk Bakalorz, Stefan Studer, Heinz Gründel, Jørn Andersen.   Trainer: Pál Csernai

GRASSHOPPER: Martin Brunner; André Egli, Charly In-Albon, Alex Imhof, Arne Stiel, Mats Gren, Martin Andermatt, Ciriaco Sforza (75 Paulo Cesar Camassuti), Alain Sutter (80 Luca Pedrotti), Necip Ugras, Wynton Rufer.   Trainer: Ottmar Hitzfeld

Sent off: Ugras (78)

Goal: Bakalorz (32)

**OMONOIA NICOSIA
v PANATHINAIKOS ATHINA 0-1** (0-1)

Makareio, Nicosia   6.09.1988

Referee: Dimitar Dimitrov (BUL)   Attendance: 21,182

OMONOIA: Andreas Haritou, Giannis Kalotheu, Sotiris Tsikkos, Giorgos Hristodoulou, Evagoras Hristofi, Kostas Petsas (16 Lefteris Mavros), Andreas Kantilos, Andreas Giatrou, Panagiotis Xiouroupas, Andreou Tsakis (75 Giannakis Kambouris), Giorgos Tsigov.   Trainer: Ioncho Arsov

PANATHINAIKOS: Nikos Sargkanis, Iakovos Hatziathanasiou, Nikos Vamvakoulas, Kostas Batsinilas, Kostas Mauridis, Lissandros Georgamlis, Hristos Kalatzis, Leonidas Hristodoulou, Vaggelis Vlahos, Dimitris Saravakos, Claus Nielsen.   Trainer: Gunder Bengtsson

Sent off: Saravakos (87)

Goal: Mauridis (13)

**PANATHINAIKOS ATHINA
v OMONOIA NICOSIA 2-0** (0-0)

Olympiako, Athina   5.10.1988

Referee: Namik Jareci (ALB)   Attendance: 11,798

PANATHINAIKOS: Giorgos Abadiotakis, Iakovos Hatziathanasiou, Nikos Vamvakoulas, Hristos Kalatzis (75 Juan Ramon Rocha), Nikos Kourbanas, Kostas Mauridis, Claus Nielsen, Leonidas Hristodoulou (63 Hristo Kolev), Hristos Dimopoulos, Vaggelis Vlahos, Lissandros Georgamlis.   Trainer: Gunder Bengtsson

OMONOIA: Andreas Haritou, Giannis Kalotheu, Sotiris Tsikkos, Giorgos Hristodoulou, Evagoras Hristofi, Kostas Petsas, Andreas Kantilos, Andreas Giatrou (71 Lefteris Mavros), Panagiotis Xiouroupas, Andreas Tsakis (79 Koulis Iakovou), Giorgos Tsigov.   Trainer: Ioncho Arsov

Sent off: Tsigov (70)

Goals: Dimopoulos (56), Nielsen (59)

FLORIANA VALLETTA v DUNDEE UNITED 0-0
Nazional Stadium, Tá Qali   6.09.1988
Referee: Vaso Vujović (YUG)   Attendance: 3,250
FLORIANA: David Cluett, Dennis Cauchi, George Xuereb, John Holland, Pierre Brincat, James Briscoe, Mark Miller, Joseph Aquilina, Michael Greeno, Mario Spiteri (88 Jerm Holland), Charles Magri.   Trainer: Hugh Caruana
DUNDEE UNITED: William Thomson, David Bowman, Maurice Malpas, James McInally, Paul Hegarty, Dave Narey, Mika-Matti Paatelainen, William McKinlay, Alexander Cleland, Kevin Gallacher, Raphael Meade (70 Hamish French). Manager: James McLean

DUNDEE UNITED v FLORIANA VALLETTA 1-0 (0-0)
Tannadice Park, Dundee   5.10.1988
Referee: Rodger Gifford (WAL)   Attendance: 6,000
DUNDEE UNITED: William Thomson, David Bowman, Maurice Malpas, Ian McPhee, John Clark, Paul Hegarty, Kevin Gallacher, William McKinlay (67 Hamish French), Mika-Matti Paatelainen (35 Raphael Meade), Ian Redford, Allan Preston. Manager: James McLean
FLORIANA: David Cluett, Dennis Cauchi, Vincent Darmanin, Patrick Delia, John Holland, Pierre Brincat, Charles Magri (82 Bernard Licari), Joseph Aquilina, Mark Miller, George Xuereb, Michael Greeno.   Trainer: Hugh Caruana
Goal: Meade (69)

KV MECHELEN v AVENIR BEGGEN 5-0 (0-0)
Achter de Kazerne, Mechelen   7.09.1988
Referee: Wim Egbertzen (HOL)   Attendance: 5,000
KV MECHELEN: Michel Preud'homme (Captain), Wim Hofkens, Graeme Rutjes, Erwin Koeman, Geert Deferm (34 Piet den Boer), Marc Emmers, Pascal de Wilde, Bruno Versavel, Marc Wilmots (56 Yves de Greef), John Bosman, Eli Ohana.   Trainer: Aad de Mos
AVENIR: Fernand Schaber, Hubert Meunier, Rodolphe Jentgen (85 Léon Mond), José Nora Favita, Alex Wilhelm, Josy Schmitz, Jean-Paul Girres, Gilbert Dresch, Fred Schreiner, Armin Krings, Markus Krahen (59 Claude Osweiller). Trainer: Louis Pilot
Goals: E. Koeman (59), Bosman (61 pen, 84), Den Boer (77), Ohana (88 pen)

AVENIR BEGGEN v KV MECHELEN 1-3 (0-1)
Stade de Beggen   28.09.1988
Referee: Jean-Marie Lartigot (FRA)   Attendance: 2,101
AVENIR: Jeannot Moës, Jean-Paul Girres, José Nora Favita, Gilbert Dresch, Hubert Meunier, Alex Wilhelm, Fred Schreiner, Serge Jentgen (76 Frank Goergen), Rodolphe Jentgen, Claude Osweiller, Markus Krahen (61 Armin Krings). Trainer: Louis Pilot
KV MECHELEN: Michel Preud'homme, Koen Sanders, Leo Clijsters (63 Raymond Jaspers), Graeme Rutjes, Geert Deferm, Marc Emmers (46 Frank Leen), John Bosman, Bruno Versavel, Paul de Mesmaeker, Marc Wilmots, Piet den Boer. Trainer: Aad de Mos
Goals: Bosman (34 pen), Den Boer (55), Versavel (62), Krings (66)

FC METZ v ANDERLECHT BRUSSE 1-3 (0-2)
Saint-Symphorien, Metz   7.09.1988
Referee: Victoriano Sánchez Arminio (SPA)   Att: 20,000
FC METZ: Jean-Marc Rodolphe; Serge Romano, Albert Cartier, Sylvain Kastendeuch, Antoine Pfrunner (70 Eric Denizart), Philippe Gaillot, Leo Van der Elst (80 Daniel Krawczyk), Philippe Hinschberger, Jean-Louis Zanon, Mario Relmy, Carmelo Micciche.   Trainer: Marcel Husson
ANDERLECHT: Jacky Munaron, Georges Grün, Stephen Keshi, Adri Van Tiggelen, Wim Kooiman, Henrik Andersen, Kari Ukkonen, Arnór Gudjohnsen, Michel de Groote, Luc Nilis (73 Patrick Vervoort), Edi Krncevic.
Trainer: Raymond Goethals
Goals: Pfrunner (2 og), Krncevic (26, 83), Zanon (87)

ANDERLECHT BRUSSEL v FC METZ 2-0 (0-0)
Constant vanden Stock, Brussel   5.10.1988
Referee: Siegfried Kirschen (E. GER)   Attendance: 12,000
ANDERLECHT: Filip De Wilde, Georges Grün, Adri Van Tiggelen, Stephen Keshi, Patrick Vervoort, Arnór Gudjohnsen, Wim Kooiman, Kari Ukkonen (74 Charles Musonda), Michel de Groote, Edi Krncevic, Luc Nilis.
Trainer: Raymond Goethals
METZ: Jean-Marc Rodolphe; Serge Romano, Albert Cartier, Thierry Pauk, Philippe Gaillot, Philippe Hinschberger, Leo Van der Elst, Jean-Louis Zanon, André Kana-Biyik (88 Daniel Krawczyk), Carmelo Micciche (75 Eddy Boncoeur), Mario Relmy.   Trainer: Marcel Husson
Goals: Krncevic (47), Van Tiggelen (73 pen)

FRAM REYKJAVIK v FC BARCELONA 0-2 (0-1)
Laugardalsvöllur, Reykjavík   7.09.1988
Referee: Patrick Kelly (IRE)   Attendance: 4,000

FRAM: Birkir Kristinsson, Thorsteinn Thorsteinsson, Pétur Anthorsson, Vidar Torkelsson, Omar Torfason, Pétur Ormslev, Kristin R. Jonsson, Kristjan Jonsson, Gudmundur Steinsson (65 Jón Sveinsson), Arnljotur Davidsson, Ormarr Örlygsson.   Trainer: Ásgeir Elíasson

FC BARCELONA: Andoni ZUBIZARRETA Urreta, URBANO Ortega Cuadros, Juan Ramón ALESANCO Ventosa (72 Ricardo Jesús SERNA Orozco), JULIO ALBERTO Moreno, Luis MILLA Aspas, EUSEBIO Sacristán Mena, ROBERTO Fernández Bonilla, Miguel SOLER Sararols, Francisco José CARRASCO (84 CRISTÓBAL Parralo), Julio SALINAS Fernández, Aitor BEGUIRISTÁIN Mujika.   Trainer: Johan Cruyff

Goals: Roberto (33, 62)

FC BARCELONA v FRAM REYKJAVIK 5-0 (2-0)
Camp Nou, Barcelona   5.10.1988
Referee: Michel Vautrot (FRA)   Attendance: 15,000

FC BARCELONA: Andoni ZUBIZARRETA Urreta, Luis María LÓPEZ REKARTE, Ricardo Jesús SERNA Orozco, Miguel SOLER Sararols, Luis MILLA Aspas (46 ROBERTO Fernández Bonilla), EUSEBIO Sacristán Mena, José María BAKERO Escudero, Francisco José CARRASCO, Gary Lineker (46 URBANO Ortega Cuadros), Julio SALINAS Fernández, Aitor BEGUIRISTÁIN Mujika.   Trainer: Johan Cruyff

FRAM: Birkir Kristinsson, Ormarr Örlygsson, Vidar Thorkelsson, Thorsteinn Thorsteinsson, Jón Sveinsson, Kristin Jonsson, Pétur Ormslev (44 Gudmundur Steinsson), Kristjan Jonsson, Pétur Anthorsson, Omar Torfasson, Arnljotur Davidsson (84 Jonas Gudjónsson).   Trainer: Ásgeir Elíasson

Goals: Lineker (9), Beguiristáin (23, 63), Roberto (66), Bakero (70)

DINAMO BUCUREŞTI v KUUSYSI LAHTI 3-0 (1-0)
Dinamo Bucureşti   7.09.1988
Referee: Stefanos Hatzistefanou (CYP)   Attendance: 18,000

DINAMO: Bogdan Stelea; Ioan Varga (46 Iulian Mihăescu), Mircea Rednic, Ioan Andonie, Marcel Sabou; Dorin Mateuţ, Ioan Lupescu, Ioan Ovidiu Sabău, Dănuţ Lupu; Claudiu Vaişcovici, Rodion Cămătaru (71 Florin Răducioiu).   Trainer: Mircea Lucescu

KUUSYSI: Ismo Korhonen; Sami Vehkakoski, Mika Viljanen, Hannu Jäntti, Ilkka Remes; Keijo Kousa, Sixten Boström (76 Timo Reinikainen), Juha Annunen, Kalle Lehtinen; Jari Rinne, Ismo Lius.   Trainers: Antti Muurinen & Penti Körkö

Goals: Jantti (12 og), Andonie (72), Vaişcovici (74)

KUUSYSI LAHTI v DINAMO BUCUREŞTI 0-3 (0-2)
Urheilukeskus, Lahti   5.10.1988
Referee: Alexandr Kokriakov (USSR)   Attendance: 960

KUUSYSI: Ismo Korhonen; Keijo Kousa, Mika Viljanen, Hannu Jäntti, Ilkka Remes (72 Timo Reinikainen); Sami Vehkakoski (72 Markku Tuominen), Jari Rinne, Sixten Bostrom; Juha Annunen, Ismo Lius, Kalle Lehtinen.   Trainers: Antti Muurinen & Penti Körkö

DINAMO: Bogdan Stelea; Iulian Mihăescu (46 Gheorghe Viscreanu), Mircea Rednic, Ioan Andonie, Ioan Varga; Ioan Ovidiu Sabău (64 Florin Răducioiu), Ioan Lupescu, Dănuţ Lupu, Dorin Mateuţ; Claudiu Vaişcovici, Rodion Cămătaru.   Trainer: Mircea Lucescu

Goals: Vaişcovici (11 pen), Kousa (34 og), Răducioiu (71 pen)

GLENAVON LURGAN v ÅRHUS GF 1-4 (1-1)
Mourneview Park, Lurgan   7.09.1988
Referee: Alphonse Constantin (BEL)   Attendance: 3,000

GLENAVON: Robert Beck, David Dennison, Andrew Russell, Paul Byrne, Duncan Lowry, Dessie McCann, Fintan McConville, Geoff Ferris, Gary Blackledge (55 James Gardiner), Stephen McBride, Martin Woodhead (70 Alan Jardine).   Trainer: Terry Nicholson

ÅRHUS GF: Troels Rasmussen, Bent Wachmann, Bjørn Kristensen, John Stampe, Marc Rieper, Thomas Andersen, Morten Donnerup, Jimmy Mørup (75 Per Beck Andersen), Karsten Christensen, Henrik Mortensen, Frank Pingel.   Trainer: Allan-Hebo Larsen

Goals: McCann (17), Mortensen (25), Pingel (52, 80), Rieper (65)

ÅRHUS GF v GLENAVON LURGAN 3-1 (1-0)
Århus stadion   5.10.1988
Referee: Tadeusz Diakonowicz (POL)   Attendance: 2,300

ÅRHUS: Troels Rasmussen, Bjørn Kristensen, Marc Rieper, John Stampe, Bent Wachmann, Karsten Christensen, Per Beck Andersen, Kenni Andersen (77 Jimmy Mørup), Morten Donnerup, Frank Pingel (62 Thomas Andersen), Henrik Mortensen.   Trainer: Allan-Hebo Larsen

GLENAVON: Robert Beck, David Dennison, Paul Byrne, Duncan Lowry, Andrew Russell, Martin Woodhead, Geoff Ferris (62 Fintan McConville), Alex Denver, Dessie McCann, Gary Blackledge, Stephen McBride.   Trainer: Terry Nicholson

Goals: Pingel (26), B. Kristensen (57), Stampe (87), McConville (89)

FLAMURTARI VLORE v LECH POZNAN 2-3 (1-1)
Flamurtari Vlore   7.09.1988
Referee: Georgos Koukoulakis (GRE)   Attendance: 12,000

FLAMURTARI: Perlat Sevo, Eqerem Memushi, Kreshnik Çipi, Roland Iljadhi (75 Thanas Gjyli), Rrapo Taho, Alfred Zijaj, Vasillaq Ziu, Latif Gjondeda, Viktor Daullja (79 Samir Haxhiu), Sokol Kushta, Vasil Ruci.   Trainer: Leonidha Çuri

LECH: Ryszard Jankowski, Marek Rzepka, Czeslaw Jakolcewicz, Waldemar Kryger, Damian Lukasik, Dariusz Kofnyt, Dariusz Skrzypczak (78 Przemyslaw Bereszynski), Jerzy Kruszczynski, Jaroslaw Araszkiewicz, Andrzej Juskowiak (82 Marian Glombiowski), Boguslaw Pachelski.
Trainer: Henryk Apostel

Goals Lukasik (32), V. Ruci (40, 76), Araszkiewicz (67), Glombiowski (89)

KREMSER SC v FC CARL ZEISS JENA 1-0 (1-0)
Wachau Stadion, Krems   5.10.1988
Referee: Pierluigi Magni (ITA)   Attendance: 2,500

KREMS: Thomas Kronsteiner; Günther Grundner, Slobodan Batricevic, Franz Miesbauer, Hannes Neumayer (75 Otto Hauptmann); Peter Netuschill, Erwin Höld, Andreas Studeny, Nedeljko Milosavljević; Thomas Janeschitz (67 Horst Baumgartner), Ronald Otto.   Trainer: Karl Daxbacher

FC CARL ZEISS: Perry Bräutigam; Heiko Peschke, Mario Röser, Thomas Ludwig, Jens Uwe Penzel; Stefan Böger (69 Oliver Merkel), Jürgen Raab, Michael Stolz, Stefan Meixner; Ralf Strässer, Heiko Weber (78 Henry Lesser).
Trainer: Lothar Kurbjuweit

Goal: Studeny (27)

LECH POZNAN v FLAMURTARI VLORE 1-0 (1-0)
Lech Poznan   5.10.1988
Referee: Esa Palsi (FIN)   Attendance: 18,000

LECH: Zbigniew Plesnierowicz, Marek Rzepka, Czeslaw Jakolcewicz, Damian Lukasik, Waldemar Kryger, Ryszard Rybak, Jerzy Kruszczynski, Piotr Romke, Dariusz Skrzypczak (81 Przemyslaw Bereszynski), Boguslaw Pachelski (86 Andrzej Juskowiak), Jaroslaw Araszkiewicz.   Trainer: Henryk Apostel

FLAMURTARI: Anesti Arapi, Petro Ruci, Kreshnik Çipi, Rrapo Taho, Roland Iljadhi, Agim Bubeqi, Eqerem Memushi, Alfred Zijaj, Latif Gjondeda (80 Viktor Daullja), Sokol Kushta, Vasil Ruci (6 Vasillaq Ziu).   Trainer: Leonidha Çuri

Goal: Araszkiewicz (25)

DERRY CITY v CARDIFF CITY 0-0
The Brandywell Ground, Derry   7.09.1988
Referee: John Blankenstein (HOL)   Attendance: 11,000

DERRY CITY: Timothy Dalton, Pascal Vaudequin, Kevin Brady, Paul Curran, Michael Neville, Paul Doolin, Paul Hegarty (46 Paul Carlyle), Noel Larkin, Jonathan Speak, Stuart Gauld, Felix Healy (84 Jack Keay).   Trainer: James McLaughlin

CARDIFF CITY: George Wood, Philip Bater, Nicholas Platnauer, Paul Wimbleton (88 Brian McDermott), Nigel Stevenson, Terence Boyle, Alan Curtis, Ian Walsh (75 Kevin Bartlett), James Gilligan, Jason Gummer, Mark Kelly.
Manager: Frank Burrows

FC CARL ZEISS JENA v KREMSER SC 5-0 (1-0)
Ernst Abbe Stadion, Jena   7.09.1988
Referee: Christian Van der Laar (HOL)   Attendance: 9,000

FC CARL ZEISS: Perry Bräutigam; Heiko Peschke, Mario Röser, Thomas Ludwig, Jens Uwe Penzel; Stefan Böger, Michael Stolz, Jürgen Raab, Oliver Merkel (90 Steffen Zipfel), Heiko Weber (87 Henry Lesser), Ralf Strässer.
Trainer: Lothar Kurbjuweit

KREMS: Horst Kirasitsch; Slobodan Batricevic, Peter Netuschill, Franz Miesbauer, Hannes Neumayer; Erwin Höld, Erwin Wolf (39 Thomas Pirkner), Johann Drabek (76 Horst Baumgartner), Nedeljko Milosavljević; Ronald Otto, Thomas Janeschitz.   Trainer: Karl Daxbacher

Goals: Weber (19), Strässer (48, 67), Merkel (53), Ludwig (78)

CARDIFF CITY v DERRY CITY 4-0 (1-0)
Ninian Park, Cardiff   5.10.1988
Referee: Egil Nervik (NOR)   Attendance: 6,933

CARDIFF CITY: George Wood, Philip Bater (75 Jason Perry), Nicholas Platnauer, Paul Wimbleton (50 Jonathan Morgan), Nigel Stevenson, Terence Boyle, Alan Curtis, Kevin Bartlett, James Gilligan, Brian McDermott, Mark Kelly.
Manager: Frank Burrows

DERRY CITY: Timothy Dalton, Jack Keay, Kevin Brady, Paul Curran, Michael Neville, Paul Doolin, Paul Carlyle (70 John Quigg), Larkin, Jonathan Speak, John Cunningham, Felix Healy.   Trainer: James McLaughlin

Goals: McDermott (20), Gillighan (47, 65, 76)

FK BORAC BANJA LUKA
v METALLIST HARKOV 2-0 (1-0)

Borac Banja Luka 7.09.1988

Referee: Vitor Fernandes Correia (POR)   Att: 22,500

BORAC: Ranko Jakovljević, Stoian Malbasić, Mario Mataja, Milorad Bilbija, Zvonko Lipovac, Damir Spica, Vladica Lemić (66 Zvonko Kalezic), Bozur Matejić, Suad Besirević, Zeljko Buvac (80 Sasa Knezevic), Senad Lupic.
Trainer: Husnija Fazlić

METALIST: Igor Kutepov, Boris Derkach, Ruslan Kolokolov, Nikolai Romanchuk, Ivan Panchischin, Oleg Derevinski (55 Aleksandr Ivanov), Aleksandr Baranov (81 Aleksandr Esipov), Yuri Tarasov, Guram Adzhoev, Sergei Raliuchenko, Igor Yakubovski.   Trainer: Evgeniy Lemescko

Goals: Lenić (43), Lipovac (85 pen)

METALIST HARKOV
v BORAC BANJA LUKA 4-0 (1-0)

Metalist Harkov 5.10.1988

Referee: Håkan Lundgren (SWE)   Attendance: 12,000

METALIST: Yuri Sivukha, Ruslan Kolokolov, Nikolai Romanchuk, Ivan Panchischin, Viktor Suslo, Aleksandr Ivanov, Guram Adzhoev (86 Viktor Yalevski), Sergei Raliuchenko, Igor Yakubovski, Yuri Tarasov (75 Aleksandr Esipov), Aleksandr Baranov.   Trainer: Evgeniy Lemescko

BORAC: Ranko Jakovljević, Stoian Malbasić, Mario Mataja, Milorad Bilbija, Zvonko Lipovac, Damir Spica, Albert Pobor, Bozur Matejić (55 Zvonko Kalezic), Suad Besirević, Zeljko Buvac (81 Sasa Knezevic), Senad Lupic.
Trainer: Husnija Fazlić

Sent off: Bilbija (80)

Goals: Tarasov (25, 62), Adsgoev (78 pen), Esipov (88).

RODA JC KERKRADE
v VITORIA GUIMARÃES 2-0 (0-0)

Gemerntelijk Sportpark Kaalheide, Kerkrade 7.09.1988

Referee: John Spillane (IRE)   Attendance: 16,000

RODA: Jan Nederburgh, Eugène Hanssen, Michel Boerebach, Henk Fräser, René Trost, Wilbert Suvrijn, Pierre Blätter (87 Michel Broeders), Silvio Diliberto (46 Alfons Groenendijk), Eric van de Luer, John van Loen, Frits Nöllgen.
Trainer: Jan Reker

VITORIA: Adelino Augusto Barros "NENO", Ângelo Fernando Conçeicao Santos "NANDO", GERMANO Joaquim Estêvão Santos, Ornedes Alves Santos "NENÉ", VÍTOR Manuel Fernandes dos SANTOS (89 Sílvio Paiva "SILVINHO"), N'DINGA Mbote, Rui António Cruz Ferreira "NASCIMENTO", BASILIO Fernandes Marques, José Mauel Guedes SOEIRO da Silva, ROLDÃO Moreira de Novais, Francisco Carlos "CHIQUINHO" (75 Ernest Ebongue).
Trainer: Eugénio Machado Souto "Geninho"

Goals: Nando (65 og), Van Loen (87)

VITORIA GUIMARÃES
v RODA JC KERKRADE 1-0 (1-0)

Estádio Municipal, Guimarães 5.10.1988

Referee: Heinz Holzmann (AUS)   Attendance: 15,000

VITORIA: Adelino Augusto Barros "NENO", Ângelo Fernando Conçeicao Santos "NANDO", Ornedes Alves Santos "NENÉ" (71 Benjamin Pereira Sobrinho "BENÉ"), GERMANO Joaquim Estêvão Santos, BASILIO Fernandes Marques, N'DINGA Mbote (68 Ernest Ebongue), ROLDÃO Moreira de Novais, António José Pereira de CARVALHO, RENÉ Carmo Kreuz, DÉCIO ANTÓNIO Corazza, Francisco Carlos "CHIQUINHO".   Trainer: Eugénio Machado Souto "Geninho" (Bra)

RODA: Jan Nederburgh, Eugène Hanssen, Ernie Brandts, Henk Fräser, René Trost, Pierre Blätter, Michel Boerebach, Wilbert Suvrijn, Frits Nöllgen, Eric van de Luer (83 Manuel Sánchez Torres), John van Loen.   Trainer: Jan Reker

Goal: Roldao (27)

INTERNATIONAL SLOVNAFT BRATISLAVA
v CFKA SREDETS SOFIA 2-3 (1-2)

Stadión na Pasienkoch, Bratislava 7.09.1988

Referee: Adrian Porumboiu (ROM)   Attendance: 4,144

INTER: Miroslav Mentel, Rudolf Rehák, Milan Bagin, Bartolomej Juraško, Emil Stranianek, Marián Kopca, Vladimír Weiss, Kazimír Gajdos (68 Ján Richter), Rudolf Kramoliš, Stanislav Moravec, Ján Lehnert (77 Ľubomír Luhový).
Trainer: Vladimír Hrivnác

SREDETS: Ilia Valov, Krasimir Bezinski, Emil Dimitrov, Trifon Ivanov, Stefan Bachev, Petar Vitanov, Ivailo Kirov, Georgi Georgiev (65 Kostadin Ianchev), Hristo Stoichkov, Emil Kostadinov (78 Plamen Getov), Liuboslav Penev.
Trainer: Dimitar Penev

Goals: Penev (36, 39 pen, 78), Moravec (45), Weiss (58 pen)

CFKA SREDETS SOFIA v INTERNATIONAL
SLOVNAFT BRATISLAVA 5-0 (5-0)

Narodna Armia, Sofia 5.10.1988

Referee: Zdravko Jokić (YUG)   Attendance: 10,000

SREDETS: Ilia Valov, Stefan Bachev, Trifon Ivanov, Krasimir Bezinski, Kiril Kachamanov, Petar Vitanov, Emil Kostadinov, Hristo Stoichkov (46 Kostadin Ianchev), Liuboslav Penev, Ivailo Kirov (73 Georgi Georgiev), Plamen Getov.
Trainer: Dimitar Penev

INTER: Miroslav Mentel (41 Jozef Hroš), Rafael Tománek, Karol Brezík, Emil Stranianek, Rudolf Rehák (80 Marián Kopca), Ľubomír Luhovy, Rudolf Kramoliš, Milan Bagin, Bartolomej Juraško, Stanislav Moravec, Vladimír Weiss.
Trainer: Vladimír Hrivnác

Sent off: Weiss (47)

Goals: Penev (1), Stoichkov (3), Kostadinov (13, 38), Getov (21)

SAKARYASPOR v
ELÖRE SPARTACUS BEKESCSABA 2-0 (1-0)

Atatürk, Adapazari 7.09.1988

Referee: Besnik Kaimi (ALB)   Attendance: 7,000

SAKARYASPOR: Engin Ipekoglu, Selçuk Yigitlik, Murat Dogansoy, Bierim Mula, Erol Kolcu, Yüksel Can (46 Ilker Yagcioglu), Dušan Pesic, Mustafa Golpinai, Senol Kaba, Yücel Çolak, Kemal Yildirim.   Trainer: Tamer Kaptan

BÉKÉSCSABA: István Gulyás, Zoltán Szenti, Miklós Csanolosi, Mihaly Ottlakan, Tibor Gruborovics, György Fabulya, Lajos Arky (85 Zoltán Kanál), Sándor Csato, László Horvath, Lajos Kvaszta (85 Zoltán Miklya), József Szekeres. Trainer: János Csank

Goals: Pesić (35), Yücel (50)

ELÖRE SPARTACUS BEKESCSABA
v SAKARYASPOR 1-0 (0-0)

Békéscsaba stadion 5.10.1988

Referee: Jiří Stiegler (CZE)   Attendance: 13,000

BEKESCSABA: István Gulyás, Zoltán Szenti, György Fabulya, László Horvath, János Banfi, Sándor Csato, Tibor Gruborovics (46 Zoltán Kanál), Mihaly Ottlakan, Miklós Csánolosi, Lajos Kvaszta (70 Attila Belvon), József Szekeres.
Trainer: János Csank

SAKARYASPOR: Engin Ipekoglu, Selçuk Yigitlik, Murat Dogansoy, Bierim Mula, Erol Kolcu, Mustafa Golpinai (89 Mehmet San), Senol Kaba, Rahim Zafer, Dušan Pesic, Yücel Çolak, Kemal Yildirim.   Trainer: Tamer Kaptan

Goal: Selçuk (49 og)

IFK NORRKÖPING
v SAMPDORIA GENOVA 2-1 (1-0)

Idrottsparken, Norrköping 7.09.1988

Referee: Allan Gunn (ENG)   Attendance: 13,216

IFK: Mats Johansson, Sulo Vaattovaara, Peter Lönn, Mats Almgren, Jan Kalen, Tor-Arne Fredheim, Jonas Lind, Ranko Djordjić (88 Lennart Weidenstolpe), Patrik Andersson, Göran Holter (74 Magnus Karlsson), Jan Hellström.
Trainer: Kent Karlsson

SAMPDORIA: Gianluca Pagliuca, Moreno Mannini (12 Marco Lanna), Amedeo Carboni, Fausto Pari, Pietro Vierchowod, Luca Pellegrini, Fulvio Bonomi, Antonio Carlos CEREZO, Gianluca Vialli, Roberto Mancini (Cap), Giuseppe Dossena (85 Fausto Salsano).   Trainer: Vujadin Boškov

Goals: P.Andersson (9), Carboni (51), Hellström (86)

SAMPDORIA GENOVA
v IFK NORRKÖPING 2-0 (1-0)

Giovanni Zini, Cremona 6.10.1988

Referee: Rolf Blattmann (SWI)   Attendance: 17,683

SAMPDORIA: Gianluca Pagliuca, Moreno Mannini, Amedeo Carboni, Fausto Pari, Pietro Vierchowod, Fausto Salsano (85 Fulvio Bonomi), VÍCTOR Muñoz Manrique, Antonio Carlos CEREZO, Gianluca Vialli (89 Loris Pradella), Roberto Mancini, Giuseppe Dossena.   Trainer: Vujadin Boškov

IFK: Mats Johansson, Sulo Vaattovaara, Peter Lönn, Lennart Weidenstolpe, Jan Kalen, Tor-Arne Fredheim, Jonas Lind, Ranko Djordjić, Patrik Andersson, Göran Holter, Jan Hellström.   Trainer: Kent Karlsson

Goals: Salsano (37), Vialli (82)

SECOND ROUND

KV MECHELEN
v ANDERLECHT BRUSSEL 1-0 (0-0)

Achter de Kazerne, Mechelen 26.10.1988

Referee: Michel Vautrot (FRA)   Attendance: 15,000

KV MECHELEN: Michel Preud'homme, Koen Sanders, Leo Clijsters, Graeme Rutjes, Bruno Versavel, Frank Leen (32 Eli Ohana), Erwin Koeman, Marc Emmers, John Bosman, Paul de Mesmaeker (55 Marc Wilmots), Piet den Boer.
Trainer: Aad de Mos

ANDERLECHT: Filip De Wilde, Georges Grün, Adri Van Tiggelen, Stephen Keshi, Henrik Andersen, Arnór Gudjohnsen (69 Charles Musonda), Wim Kooiman, Michel de Groote, Patrick Vervoort, Luc Nilis (7 Guy Marchoul), Edi Krncevic.
Trainer: Raymond Goethals

Goal: Wilmots (88)

ANDERLECHT BRUSSEL
v KV MECHELEN 0-2 (0-1)

Constant vandenstock, Brussel 9.11.1988

Referee: Karl-Heinz Tritschler (W. GER)   Att: 33,500

ANDERLECHT: Filip De Wilde, Georges Grün, Adri Van Tiggelen, Guy Marchoul, Michel de Groote, Charles Musonda, Wim Kooiman, Henrik Andersen, Patrick Vervoort (46 Kari Ukkonen), Edi Krncevic, Luc Nilis (75 Marc Wuyts).
Trainer: Raymond Goethals

KV MECHELEN: Michel Preud'homme, Wim Hofkens, Koen Sanders, Graeme Rutjes, Leo Clijsters (55 Pascal De Wilde), Geert Deferm, Marc Emmers, Erwin Koeman, Bruno Versavel (47 Paul de Mesmaeker), Eli Ohana, John Bosman.
Trainer: Aad de Mos

Goals: E. Koeman (17), Ohana (46)

DUNDEE UNITED
v DINAMO BUCUREŞTI 0-1 (0-0)

Tannadice Park, Dundee 26.10.1988

Referee: Guy Goethals (BEL)   Attendance: 10,594

UNITED: William Thomson; David Bowman, Maurice Malpas, James McInally (74 John Clark), Paul Hegarty, David Narey, Raphael Meade, David Beaumont, Mika-Matti Paatelainen, Ian McPhee (84 Ian Redford), Kevin Gallacher.   Manager: Jim McLean

DINAMO: Bogdan Stelea; Iulian Mihăescu, Ioan Varga, Mircea Rednic, Ioan Andonie; Ioan Ovidiu Sabău, Ioan Lupescu, Dorin Mateuţ, Dănuţ Lupu; Claudiu Vaişcovici, Rodion Cămătaru.   Trainer: Mircea Lucescu

Goal: Mateuţ (89)

DINAMO BUCUREŞTI
v DUNDEE UNITED 1-1 (0-0)

Dinamo Bucureşti 9.11.1988

Referee: Albert Thomas (HOL)   Attendance: 20,000

DINAMO: Bogdan Stelea; Iulian Mihăescu, Ioan Andonie, Mircea Rednic, Ioan Varga; Ioan Ovidiu Sabău, Ioan Lupescu, Dorin Mateuţ, Dănuţ Lupu (88 Gheorghe Viscreanu); Claudiu Vaişcovici (86 Florin Răducioiu), Rodion Cămătaru.   Trainer: Mircea Lucescu

UNITED: William Thomson; John Clark (58 David Bowman), Paul Hegarty, David Narey, Maurice Malpas; James McInally (82 Ian Redford), David Beaumont, Billy McKinlay; Raphael Meade, Allan Preston, Kevin Gallacher.   Manager: Jim McLean

Goals: Beaumont (79), Mateuţ (82)

FC BARCELONA v LECH POZNAN 1-1 (1-0)

Camp Nou, Barcelona 26.10.1988

Referee: Howard King (WAL)   Attendance: 25,000

FC BARCELONA: Andoni ZUBIZARRETA Urreta (Cap), URBANO Ortega Cuadros, Luis María LÓPEZ REKARTE, Ricardo Jesús SERNA Orozco, ALOÍSIO Pires Alves, Luis MILLA Aspas, José María BAKERO Escudero, ROBERTO Fernández Bonilla, Francisco José CARRASCO Hidalgo (46 Julio SALINAS Fernández), Gary Lineker, Aitor BEGUIRISTÁIN Mujika.   Trainer: Johan Cruyff

LECH: Ryszard Jankowski, Marek Rzepka, Czeslaw Jakolcewicz, Waldemar Kryger, Damian Lukasik, Dariusz Kofnyt, Piotr Romke, Jerzy Kruszczynski, Jaroslaw Araszkiewicz (90 Przemyslaw Bereszynski), Ryszard Rybak, Boguslaw Pachelski (82 Andrzej Slowakiewicz).   Trainer: Henryk Apostel

Goals: Roberto (26 pen), Pachelski (66)

LECH POZNAN
v FC BARCELONA 1-1 (1-1, 1-1) (AET)

Lech Poznan 9.11.1988

Referee: Sadik Deda (TUR)   Attendance: 30,000

LECH: Ryszard Jankowski, Marek Rzepka, Czeslaw Jakolcewicz, Damian Lukasik, Andrzej Slowakiewicz, Dariusz Kofnyt (94 Przemyslaw Bereszynski), Piotr Romke (72 Marian Glombiowski), Jerzy Kruszczynski, Ryszard Rybak, Boguslaw Pachelski, Jaroslaw Araszkiewicz.   Trainer: Henryk Apostel

FC BARCELONA: Andoni ZUBIZARRETA Urreta (Captain), Ricardo Jesús SERNA Orozco, ALOÍSIO Pires Alves, Luis María LÓPEZ REKARTE, Luis MILLA Aspas, EUSEBIO Sacristán Mena, José María BAKERO Escudero, ROBERTO Fernández Bonilla, Francisco José CARRASCO Hidalgo (77 Ernesto VALVERDE Tejedor), Gary Lineker (92 Juan Ramón ALESANCO Ventosa), Aitor BEGUIRISTÁIN Mujika.   Trainer: Johan Cruyff

Goals: Kruszczynski (28 pen), Roberto (37)

Penalties: 0-0 Roberto (saved), 1-0 Kruszczynski, 1-1 Beguiristáin, 2-1 Jakolcewicz, 2-2 Valverde, 3-2 Rzepka, 3-3 Eusebio, Araszkiewicz (miss), Alesanco (miss), Pachelski (saved), 4-3 Bakero, 4-4 Glombiowski, 5-4 ALOÍSIO, Lukasik (miss)

FC CARL ZEISS JENA
v SAMPDORIA GENOVA 1-1 (1-0)

Ernst-Abbe-Sportfeld, Jena 26.10.1988

Referee: Bo Karlsson (SWE)   Attendance: 13,500

FC CARL ZEISS: Perry Bräutigam, Mario Röser, Jens Uwe Penzel, Thomas Ludwig, Heiko Peschke, Steffen Zipfel (80 Matthias Pittelkow), Stefan Boger, Michael Stolz, Ralf Strässer, Jürgen Raab (73 Henry Lesser), Heiko Weber.

SAMPDORIA: Gianluca Pagliuca, Moreno Mannini, Amedeo Carboni, Fausto Pari, Pietro Vierchowod, Marco Lanna (89 Fulvio Bonomi), VÍCTOR Muñoz Manrique, Antonio Carlos CEREZO, Gianluca Vialli, Giuseppe Dossena, Roberto Mancini (Cap).   Trainer: Vujadin Boškov

Goals: Weber (38), Vialli (81 pen)

SAMPDORIA GENOVA
v FC CARL ZEISS JENA 3-1 (2-0)

Luigi Ferraris Genova 9.11.1988

Referee: Robert Valentine (SCO)   Attendance: 16,714

SAMPDORIA: Gianluca Pagliuca, Moreno Mannini, Fulvio Bonomi, Fausto Pari, Pietro Vierchowod, Luca Pellegrini, VÍCTOR Muñoz Manrique, Antonio Carlos CEREZO, Gianluca Vialli, Giuseppe Dossena, Roberto Mancini (Cap).   Trainer: Vujadin Boškov

FC CARL ZEISS: Perry Bräutigam, Mario Röser, Jens Uwe Penzel, Thomas Ludwig, Matthias Pittelkow, Henry Lesser (80 Oliver Merkel), Stefan Boger, Michael Stolz, Ralf Strässer, Jürgen Raab, Heiko Weber.   Trainer: Lothar Kurbjuweit

Goals: Vierchowod (25), Cerezo (43), Vialli (53), Raab (59)

**EINTRACHT FRANKFURT
v SAKARYASPOR 3-1** (3-0)

Waldstadion, Frankfurt 26.10.1988

Referee: John Spillane (IRE)   Attendance: 28,000

EINTRACHT: Ulrich Stein, Manfred Binz, Dietmar Roth, Karl-Heinz Körbel, Ralf Sievers, Peter Hobday, Frank Schulz (81 Maximilian Heidenreich), Ralf Balzis (77 JaroslavBiernat), Stefan Studer, Janusz Turowski, Jørn Andersen.
Trainer: Pál Csernai

SAKARYASPOR: Engin Ipekoglu, Bierim Mula, Murat Dogansoy, Erol Kolcu (84 Mehmet San), Selçuk Yigitlik, Mustafa Golpinai, Rahim Zafer, Dušan Pesić, Senol Kaba, Yücel Çolak (70 Nezet Muharrem), Kemal Yildirim.
Trainer: Tamer Kaptan

Goals: Sievers (9), Balzis (31), Studer (43), Kemal (85 pen)

**PANATHINAIKOS ATHINA
v CFKA SREDETS SOFIA 0-1** (0-0)

Stadio Olympiako Athina 9.11.1988

Referee: Keith Stuart Hackett (ENG)   Attendance: 61,500

PANATHINAIKOS: Nikos Sargkanis, Iakovos Hatziathanasiou, Giannis Kalitzakis, Hristos Kalatzis, Nikos Kourbanas, Kostas Mauridis, Dimitris Saravakos, Leonidas Hristodoulou (63 Hristo Kolev), Claus Nielsen, Vaggelis Vlahos (23 Hristos Dimopoulos), Lissandros Georgamlis.
Trainer: Gunder Bengtsson

SREDETS: Ilia Valov, Nedialko Mladenov, Trifon Ivanov, Krasimir Bezinski, Emil Dimitrov, Kostadin Ianchev, Emil Kostadinov, Hristo Stoichkov (89 Lachezar Tanev), Liuboslav Penev, Ivailo Kirov, Stefan Bachev.   Trainer: Dimitar Penev

Goal: Penev (85 pen)

**SAKARYASPOR
v EINTRACHT FRANKFURT 0-3** (0-2)

Atatürk Adapazari 9.11.1988

Referee: Hubert Forstinger (AUS)   Attendance: 12,500

SAKARYASPOR: Engin Ipekoglu, Rahim Zafer, Murat Dogansoy, Mehmet San, Selçuk Yigitlik, Faton Domi, Dušan Pesić, Mustafa Golpinai (81 Saban Yildirim), Ilker Yagcioglu, Yücel Çolak, Kemal Yildirim.   Trainer: Tamer Kaptan

EINTRACHT: Ulrich Stein, Manfred Binz, Dietmar Roth (81 Michael Kostner), Karl-Heinz Körbel, Thomas Klepper, Frank Schulz, Peter Hobday, Dirk Bakalorz, Ralf Sievers, Janusz Turowski (67 Ralf Balzis), Jørn Andersen.
Trainer: Pál Csernai

Goals: Sievers (5, 65), Binz (35)

CARDIFF CITY v ÅRHUS GF 1-2 (1-1)

Ninian Park, Cardiff 26.10.1988

Referee: Roger Phillipi (LUX)   Attendance: 6,155

CARDIFF CITY: George Wood, Nicholas Platnauer (79 Ian Rodgerson), Philip Bater, Paul Wimbleton, Nigel Stevenson, Terence Boyle, Brian McDermott, Kevin Bartlett, James Gilligan, Mark Kelly, Steven Lynex (63 Alan Curtis).   Manager: Frank Burrows

ÅRHUS: Troels Rasmussen, Bent Wachmann, Bjørn Kristensen, John Stampe, Marc Rieper, Thomas Andersen, Jimmy Mørup (56 Morten Donnerup), Per Beck Andersen, Karsten Christensen, Lars Lundkvist, Henrik Mortensen.
Trainer: Allan-Hebo Larsen

Goals: Kristensen (8, 73), Gilligan (42)

**CFKA SREDETS SOFIA
v PANATHINAIKOS ATHINA 2-0** (1-0)

Narodna Armia, Sofia 26.10.1988

Referee: José Rosa dos Santos (POR)   Attendance: 22,000

SREDETS: Ilia Valov, Nedialko Mladenov, Trifon Ivanov, Krasimir Bezinski, Stefan Bachev, Kostadin Ianchev, Ivailo Kirov (80 Petar Vitanov), Emil Kostadinov, Hristo Stoichkov, Liuboslav Penev, Plamen Getov (80 Doncho Donev).
Trainer: Dimitar Penev

PANATHINAIKOS: Giorgos Abadiotakis, Iakovos Hatziathanasiou, Kostas Batsinilas, Nikos Vamvakoulas, Nikos Kourbanas, Kostas Mauridis, Leonidas Hristodoulou (78 Juan Ramon Rocha), Hristos Kalatzis, Hristo Kolev (70 Vaggelis Vlahos), Claus Nielsen, Lissandros Georgamilis.
Trainer: Gunder Bengtsson

Goals: Stoichkov (45), Penev (90 pen)

ÅRHUS GF v CARDIFF CITY 4-0 (2-0)

Århus stadium 9.11.1988

Referee: Kaj John Natri (FIN)   Attendance: 3,700

ÅRHUS: Troels Rasmussen, Bent Wachmann, Bjørn Kristensen, John Stampe, Marc Rieper, Thomas Andersen, Claus Thomsen (70 Morten Donnerup), Per Beck Andersen, Karsten Christensen, Lars Lundkvist, Frank Pingel (64 Henrik Mortensen).   Trainer: Allan-Hebo Larsen

CARDIFF CITY: George Wood, Alan Rogers, Nicholas Platnauer, Paul Wimbleton, Gareth Abraham, Terence Boyle, Alan Curtis, Kevin Bartlett (70 Paul Wheeler), James Gilligan, Mark Kelly, Brian McDermott (59 Steven Lynex)   Manager: Frank Burrows

Goals: Pingel (15), P.B. Andersen (25, 75), Stampe (82 pen)

**RODA JC KERKRADE
v METALIST HARKO 1-0** (1-0)

Gemerntelijk Sportpark Kaalheide, Kerkrade   26.10.1988

Referee: Einar Halle (NOR)   Attendance: 10,000

RODA: Jan Nederburgh, Eugène Hanssen, Ernie Brandts, Henk Fräser, René Trost, Pierre Blätter, Michel Boerebach, Eric van de Luer, Manuel Sánchez Torres (80 Silvio Diliberto), John van Loen, Frits Nöllgen (62 Huub Smeets).
Trainer: Jan Reker

METALIST: Yuri Sivukha, Boris Derkach, Nikolai Romanchuk, Ivan Panchischin, Viktor Suslo, Oleg Derevinski, Aleksandr Baranov, Guram Adzhoev (81 Aleksandr Ivanov), Igor Yakubovski, Sergei Raliuchenko, Aleksandr Esipov (50 Yuri Tarasov).   Trainer: Evgeniy Lemescko

Goal: Van de Luer (43)

**KV MECHELEN
v EINTRACHT FRANKFURT/MAIN 1-0** (0-0)

Achter de Kazerne, Mechelen   15.03.1989

Referee: Alexei Spirin (USSR)   Attendance: 12,000

KV MECHELEN: Michel Preud'homme, Koen Sanders, Graeme Rutjes, Marc Emmers, Geert Deferm, Wim Hofkens, Bruno Versavel, Paul de Mesmaeker, Pascal de Wilde (18 Eli Ohana, 85 Yves De Greef), John Bosman, Marc Wilmots.
Trainer: Aad de Mos

EINTRACHT: Ulrich Stein, Dietmar Roth, Karl-Heinz Körbel, Manfred Binz, Thomas Klepper, Heinz Gründel, Ralf Sievers, Henry Lesser (74 Ralf Balzis), Dietmar Rompel (75 Jaroslav Biernat), Dirk Bakalorz, Jørn Andersen.
Trainer: Jörg Berger

Goal: Wilmots (67)

METALIST HARKOV v RODA JC KERKRADE 0-0

Metalist Harkov   9.11.1988

Referee: Gerassimos Germanakos (GRE)   Att: 40,000

METALIST: Igor Kutepov, Boris Derkach, Nikolai Romanchuk, Ivan Panchischin, Viktor Suslo, Oleg Derevinski, Igor Yakubovski (5 Aleksandr Ivanov), Sergei Raliuchenko, Guram Adzhoev, Aleksandr Baranov, Aleksandr Esipov (46 Yuri Tarasov).   Trainer: Evgeniy Lemescko

RODA: Jan Nederburgh, Eugène Hanssen, Ernie Brandts, Henk Fräser, René Trost, Wilbert Suvrijn, Michel Boerebach, Silvio Diliberto, Sánchez-Torres, John van Loen, Eric van de Luer.   Trainer: Jan Reker

**CFKA SREDETS SOFIA
v RODA JC KERKRADE 2-1** (1-0)

Narodna Armia, Sofia   1.03.1989

Referee: Kurt Röthlisberger (SWI)   Attendance: 30,000

SREDETS: Ilia Valov, Nedialko Mladenov, Trifon Ivanov, Emil Dimitrov, Stefan Bachev, Ivailo Kirov (90 Lachezar Tanev), Kostadin Ianchev, Georgi Georgiev, Emil Kostadinov, Liuboslav Penev, Hristo Stoichkov.   Trainer: Dimitar Penev

RODA: Jan Nederburgh, Michel Broeders, Michel Boerebach, Henk Fräser, René Trost, Wilbert Suvrijn, Alfons Groenendijk, Michel Van der Linden (70 Huub Smeets), Frits Nöllgen, Michel Haan, Eugène Hanssen.   Trainer: Jan Reker

Goals: Stoichkov (12), Kostadinov (65), Boerebach (83)

QUARTER-FINALS

**EINTRACHT FRANKFURT/MAIN
v KV MECHELEN 0-0**

Waldstadion, Frankfurt/Main   1.03.1989

Referee: Bo Karlsson (SWE)   Attendance: 20,000

EINTRACHT: Ulrich Stein, Manfred Binz, Dieter Schlindwein (68 Dietmar Rompel), Karl-Heinz Körbel, Dietmar Roth, Heinz Gründel, Thomas Lasser, Dirk Bakalorz, Stefan Studer, Janusz Turowski (29 Ralf Balzis), Jørn Andersen.   Trainer: Jörg Berger

KV MECHELEN: Michel Preud'homme, Marc Emmers, Koen Sanders, Graeme Rutjes, Geert Deferm, Erwin Koeman, Wim Hofkens, Pascal de Wilde, Paul de Mesmaeker, John Bosman (62 Eli Ohana), Piet den Boer.   Trainer: Aad de Mos

**RODA JC KERKRADE
v CFKA SREDETS SOFIA 2-1** (1-0, 2-1) (AET)

Gemerntelijk Sportpark, Kaalheide Kerkrade   15.03.1989

Referee: Peter Mikkelsen (DEN)   Attendance: 17,500

RODA: Jan Nederburgh, Michel Broeders, Michel Boerebach, Henk Fräser, René Trost, Eric van de Luer, Eugène Hanssen, Alfons Groenendijk, Michel Haan, John van Loen, Manuel Sánchez Torres (91 Huub Smeets).   Trainer: Jan Reker

SREDETS: Ilia Valov, Nedialko Mladenov, Trifon Ivanov, Emil Dimitrov, Stefan Bachev, Kostadin Ianchev (52 Georgi Georgiev), Krasimir Bezinski, Ivailo Kirov (62 Petar Vitanov), Emil Kostadinov, Liuboslav Penev, Hristo Stoichkov.
Trainer: Dimitar Penev

Goals: Haan (38), Van der Leur (50), Stoichkov (78)

Penalties: 1-0 Van de Leur, Penev (miss), 2-0 Hanssen, 2-1 Georgiev, Groenendijk (miss), 2-2 Ivanov, 3-2 Haan, 3-3 Mladenov, Boerebach (miss), 3-4 Stoichkov

DINAMO BUCUREŞTI v SAMPDORIA GENOVA 1-1 (1-0)

Dinamo Bucureşti   1.03.1989

Referee: Horst Brummeier (AUS)   Attendance: 20,000

DINAMO: Bogdan Stelea; Ioan Varga (58 Iulian Mihăescu), Mircea Rednic, Alexandru Nicolae, Michael Klein; Ioan Ovidiu Sabău, Dănuţ Lupu, Ioan Lupescu, Dorin Mateuţ; Claudiu Vaişcovici (68 Florin Răducioiu), Rodion Cămătaru. Trainer: Mircea Lucescu

SAMPDORIA: Gianluca Pagliuca; Moreno Mannini (18 13.Marco Lanna), Pietro Vierchowod, .Luca Pellegrini, Amedeo Carboni; Fausto Pari, VÍCTOR Muñoz Manrique, Carlos Antonio Cerezo, Giuseppe Dossena;Gianluca Vialli, Loris Pradella (54 Fausto Salsano).   Trainer: Vujadin Boškov

Sent off: Carboni (10)

Goals: Vaişcovici (16 pen), Vialli (90)

SAMPDORIA GENOVA v DINAMO BUCUREŞTI 0-0

Giovanni Zini, Cremona   15.03.1989

Referee: Lajos Nemeth (Ung)   Attendance: 17,652

SAMPDORIA: Gianluca Pagliuca; Marco Lanna, Pietro Vierchowod, Fausto Salsano, Luca Pellegrini; VÍCTOR Muñoz Manrique, Fausto Pari, Carlos Antonio Cerezo, Loris Pradella (83 Fulvio Bonomi), Roberto Mancini, Giuseppe Dossena. Trainer: Vujadin Boškov

DINAMO: Bogdan Stelea; Ioan Varga, Mircea Rednic, Ioan Andonie, Michael Klein; Ioan Lupescu, Ioan Ovidiu Sabău, Dorin Mateuţ, Dănuţ Lupu (72 Costel Orac); Claudiu Vaişcovici (46 Florin Răducioiu), Rodion Cămătaru. Trainer: Mircea Lucescu

ÅRHUS GF v FC BARCELONA 0-1 (0-0)

Århus Idraetspark   1.03.1989

Referee: Jiří Stiegler (CZE)   Attendance: 25,000

ÅRHUS: Troels Rasmussen, John Stampe, Karsten Christensen, Marc Rieper, Bent Wachmann (46 Thomas Andersen), Claus Thomsen (80 Anders Bjerre), Henrik Jespersen, Jimmy Mørup, Henrik Mortensen, Bjørn Kristensen, Lars Lundqvist.   Trainer: Jens Harmsen

FC BARCELONA: Andoni ZUBIZARRETA Urreta, Juan Ramón ALESANCO Ventosa (Cap) (82 JULIO ALBERTO Moreno), ALOÍSIO Pires Alves, Ricardo Jesús SERNA Orozco, EUSEBIO Sacristán Mena, Luis MILLA Aspas, ROBERTO Fernández Bonilla, José María BAKERO Escudero, Julio SALINAS Fernández, Gary Lineker, Guillermo AMOR Martínez (71 Aitor BEGUIRISTÁIN Mujika). Trainer: Johan Cruyff

Goal: Lineker (70)

FC BARCELONA v ÅRHUS GF 0-0

Nou Camp, Barcelona   15.03.1989

Referee: Gerassimos Germanakos (GRE)   Att: 7,000

FC BARCELONA: Andoni ZUBIZARRETA Urreta, ALOÍSIO Pires Alves, JULIO ALBERTO Moreno (60 SERGI López Segú), Ricardo Jesús SERNA Orozco, Luis MILLA Aspas, EUSEBIO Sacristán Mena, José María BAKERO Escudero, ROBERTO Fernández Bonilla, Guillermo AMOR Martínez (71 Francisco José CARRASCO Hidalgo), Gary Lineker, Aitor BEGUIRISTÁIN Mujika.   Trainer: Johan Cruyff

ÅRHUS GF: Troels Rasmussen, Bjørn Kristensen, John Stampe, Bent Wachmann, Marc Rieper, Henrik Jespersen (82 Karsten Christensen), Thomas Andersen, Søren Andersen (64 Claus Thomsen), Jimmy Mørup, Henrik Mortensen, Lars Lundqvist.   Trainer: Jens Harmsen

SEMI-FINALS

FC BARCELONA v CFKA SREDETS SOFIA 4-2 (2-1)

Nou Camp, Barcelona   4.04.1989

Referee: Siegfried Kirschen (E. GER)   Attendance: 22,000

FC BARCELONA: Andoni ZUBIZARRETA Urreta (Cap), ALOÍSIO Pires Alves, Ricardo Jesús SERNA Orozco, JULIO ALBERTO Moreno, Guillermo AMOR Martínez, EUSEBIO Sacristán Mena (75 Juan Ramón ALESANCO Ventosa), José María BAKERO Escudero, ROBERTO Fernández Bonilla, Julio SALINAS Fernández, Gary Lineker, Aitor BEGUIRISTÁIN Mujika (83 Francisco José CARRASCO Hidalgo). Trainer: Johan Cruyff

CFKA SREDETS: Ilia Valov (79 Rumen Apostolov), Nedialko Mladenov, Trifon Ivanov, Krasimir Bezinski, Emil Dimitrov, Ivailo Kirov, Petar Vitanov, Hristo Stoichkov, Stefan Bachev, Emil Kostadinov, Lachezar Tanev (77 Georgi Georgiev). Trainer: Dimitar Penev

Goals: Stoichkov (24, 67 pen), Lineker (36), Amor (37), Bakero (48), Salinas (72)

CFKA SREDETS SOFIA
v FC BARCELONA 1-2 (0-1)

Vasil Levski, Sofia 19.04.1989

Referee: Aron Schmidhuber (W. GER)   Attendance: 40,000

SREDETS: Ilia Valov, Nedialko Mladenov, Emil Dimitrov, Petar Vitanov, Krasimir Bezinski, Kostadin Ianchev, Emil Kostadinov, Hristo Stoichkov, Georgi Georgiev (81 Rumen Stoianov), Lachezar Tanev (79 Doncho Donev), Ivailo Kirov.   Trainer: Dimitar Penev

FC BARCELONA: Andoni ZUBIZARRETA Urreta (Captain), Luis María LÓPEZ REKARTE, ALOÍSIO Pires Alves, Ricardo Jesús SERNA Orozco, Luis MILLA Aspas (78 Miguel SOLER Sararols), Guillermo AMOR Martínez, EUSEBIO Sacristán Mena, Julio SALINAS Fernández, Gary Lineker, ROBERTO Fernández Bonilla, Aitor BEGUIRISTÁIN Mujika (87 URBANO Ortega Cuadros).   Trainer: Johan Cruyff

Goals: Lineker (25), Stoichkov (65), Amor (81)

KV MECHELEN
v SAMPDORIA GENOVA 2-1 (1-0)

Achter de Kazerne, Mechelen 5.04.1989

Referee: Bruno Galler (SWI)   Attendance: 14,500

KV MECHELEN: Michel Preud'homme (Cap), Koen Sanders (65 Geert Deferm), Marc Emmers, Graeme Rutjes, Erwin Koeman, Wim Hofkens, Pascal de Wilde, Paul de Mesmaekers, Bruno Versavel, John Bosman, Eli Ohana (49 Marc Wilmots).   Trainer: Aad de Mos

SAMPDORIA: Gianluca Pagliuca, Moreno Mannini (25 Stefano Pellegrini), Pietro Vierchowod, Luca Pellegrini (Cap), Marco Lanna, Fausto Pari, VÍCTOR Muñoz Manrique, Antonio Carlos CEREZO, Giuseppe Dossena, Gianluca Vialli, Roberto Mancini.   Trainer: Vujadin Boškov

Goals: Ohana (11), Deferm (68), Vialli (75)

SAMPDORIA GENOVA
v KV MECHELEN 3-0 (0-0)

Giovanni Zini, Cremona 19.04.1989

Referee: Jiří Stiegler (CZE)   Attendance: 18,419

SAMPDORIA: Gianluca Pagliuca, Pietro Vierchowod, Luca Pellegrini (Cap), Stefano Pellegrini (76 Marco Lanna), Fausto Salsano, Fausto Pari, VÍCTOR Muñoz Manrique, Antonio Carlos CEREZO, Giuseppe Dossena, Loris Pradella (65 Fulvio Bonomi), Roberto Mancini.   Trainer: Vujadin Boškov

KV MECHELEN: Michel Preud'homme (Cap), Geert Deferm, Graeme Rutjes, Erwin Koeman, Bruno Versavel, Paul De Mesmaeker (66 Marc Wilmots), Marc Emmers, Wim Hofkens, Pascal de Wilde, Eli Ohana, Piet den Boer.   Trainer: Aad de Mos

Goals: Cerezo (68), Dossena (85), Salsano (88)

FINAL

FC BARCELONA
v SAMPDORIA GENOVA 2-0 (1-0)

Wankdorf, Bern 10.05.1989

Referee: George Courtney (ENG)   Attendance: 42,707

FC BARCELONA: Andoni ZUBIZARRETA Urreta, Luis MILLA Aspas (61 Miguel SOLER Sararols), Juan Ramón ALESANCO Ventosa (Cap), ALOÍSIO Pires Alves, URBANO Ortega Cuadros, Guillermo AMOR Martínez, EUSEBIO Sacristán Mena, ROBERTO Fernández Bonilla, Gary Winston LINEKER, Julio SALINAS Fernández, Aitor BEGUIRISTÁIN Mujika (75 Luis María LÓPEZ REKARTE). Not used: Juan Carlos UNZÚE Lubianu, SERGI López, Francisco José CARRASCO Hidalgo.   Trainer: Johannes Hendrikus Cruyff

SAMPDORIA: Gianluca Pagliuca, Moreno Mannini (28 Stefano Pellegrini), Luca Pellegrini (Cap) (54 Fulvio Bonomi), Fausto Pari, Marco Lanna, Fausto Salsano, VÍCTOR Muñoz Manrique, Antonio Carlos CEREZO, Giuseppe Dossena, Gianluca Vialli, Roberto Mancini. Not used: Sergio Marcon, Loris Pradella.   Trainer: Vujadin Boškov

Goals: Salinas (4), López Rekarte (79)

Goalscorers European Cup-Winners' Cup 1988-89:

7 goals: Hristo Stoichkov (CFKA Sredets Sofia)

6 goals: Liuboslav Penev (CFKA Sredets)

5 goals: ROBERTO Fernández Bonilla (FC Barcelona), Gianluca Vialli (Sampdoria)

4 goals: Frank Pingel (Århus GF), James Gilligan (Cardiff City), Gary Lineker (FC Barcelona)

3 goals: Krncevic (Anderlecht), Kristensen (Århus GF), Kostadinov (CFKA Sredets), Vaişcovici (Dinamo Bucureşti), Sievers (Eintracht Frankfurt), Bosman, Ohana (KV Mechelen)

2 goals: P.B. Andersen, Stampe (Århus GF), Mateuţ (Dinamo Bucureşti), Gruborovics (Elöre Békéscsaba), Amor, Bakero, Beguiristáin, Julio Salinas (FC Barcelona), Strässer, Weber (FC Carl Zeiss Jena), V.Ruci (Flamurtari Vlorë), Den Boer, E. Koeman, Wilmots (KV Mechelen), Araszkiewicz (Lech Poznan), Tarasov (Metalist Harkov), van de Luer (Roda Kerkrade), Cerezo, Salsano (Sampdoria)

1 goal: Hellvik, Meinseth (Bryne IL), Krings (Avenir Beggen), Zanon (FC Metz), McCann, McConville (Glenavon Lurgan), Studeny (Kremser SC), Lenić, Lipovac (Borac Banja Luka), Roldao (Vitoria Guimarães), Moravec, Weiss (Inter Bratislava), Kvaszta, Csató (Elöre Békéscsaba), P.Andersson, Hellström (IFK Norrköping), Van Tiggelen (Anderlecht), Beaumont, Meade (Dundee United), Pachelski, Kruszczynski, Lukasik, Glombiowski (Lech Poznan), Raab, Merkel, Ludwig (FC Carl Zeiss Jena), Kemal, Pesić, Yücel (Sakaryaspor), Dimopoulos, Nielsen, Mauridis (Panathinaikos Athina), McDermott (Cardiff City), Adsgoev, Esipov (Metalist Harkov), Binz, Balzis, Studer, Bakalorz (Eintracht Frankfurt), Haan, Boerebach, Van Loen (Roda Kerkrade), Răducioiu, Andonie (Dinamo Bucureşti), Rieper, Mortensen (Århus GF), Getov (CFKA Sredets Sofia), López Rekarte (FC Barcelona), Deferm, Versavel (KV Mechelen), Dossena, Vierchowod, Carboni (Sampdoria Genova)

Own goal: Pfrunner (FC Metz) for Anderlecht, Jantti & Kousa (Kuusysi Lahti) for Dinamo Bucureşti, Nando (Vitória Guimarães) for Roda Kerkrade, Selçuk (Sakaryaspor) for Békéscsaba

CUP WINNERS' CUP 1989-90

PRELIMINARY ROUND

CHERNOMORETS BURGAS
v DINAMO TIRANA 3-1 (1-0)

Deveti Septembri, Burgas 16.08.1989

Referee: Roman Steindl (AUS)   Attendance: 9,000

CHERNOMORETS: Liubomir Sheitanov, Ivan Iovchev, Stoian Stoianov, Liubomir Liubenov, Krasimir Kostov, Zlatko Iankov, Ivan Aleksandrov, Stoian Pumpalov, Vladimir Stoianov, Dian Petkov (59 Valentin Ivanov), Simeon Chilibonov (76 Mihail Ganev).   Trainer: Ivan Vutov

DINAMO: Ilir Bozhiqi, Pjerin Noga, Arian Stafa, Ilir Daja, Rudi Vata, Agim Canaj, Viktor Briza (55 Ermal Tahiri), Alfred Ferko (88 Adrian Jançe), Josif Gjergji, Eduard Abazi, Sulejman Demollari.   Trainer: Baikush Beci

Goals: Petkov (25), V. Stoianov (53), Demollari (69), Pumpalov (71 pen)

DINAMO TIRANA
v CHERNOMORETS BURGAS 4-0 (0-0)

Qemal Stafa, Tirana 30.08.1989

Referee: Sándor Puhl; Geri, Nogi (HUN)   Attendance: 7,000

DINAMO: Foto Strakosha, Arian Stafa, Pjerin Noga, Rudi Vata, Naum Kove, Alfred Ferko (46 Adrian Jançe), Viktor Briza, Agim Canaj, Ermal Tahiri, Eduard Abazi, Sulejman Demollari.   Trainer: Baikush Beci

CHERNOMORETS: Plamen Nikolov, Rosen Petrov, Stoian Stoianov, Miroslav Kralev, Krasimir Kostov, Zlatko Iankov, Valentin Ivanov, Ivan Aleksandrov (75 Mihail Ganev), Vladimir Stoianov (46 Dian Petkov), Simeon Chilibonov, Ivan Iovchev.   Trainer: Ivan Vutov

Goals: Canaj (46), Abazi (62), Jance (68), Demollari (71)

FIRST ROUND

SLOVAN BRATISLAVA
v GRASSHOPPER ZÜRICH 3-0 (1-0)

Tehelné pole, Bratislava 12.09.1989

Referee: Sadik Deda (TUR)   Attendance: 12,817

SLOVAN: Stanislav Fisan; Tomáš Stúpala, Dušan Tittel, Vladimír Ekhardt, Jozef Juriga, Vladimír Kinier (Cap), Ladislav Pecko, Ladislav Repácik (89 Miroslav Chvíla), Eugen Varga, Vladimiír Vankovic (71 Ondrej Kristofik), Jaroslav Timko.   Trainer: Jozef Jankech

GRASSHOPPER: Martin Brunner; Mats Gren, Charly In-Albon, André Egli (Cap), Marcel Koller, Urs Meier, Adrian De Vicente (78 Thomas Wyss), Alain Sutter, Mark Strudal (75 André Wiederkehr), Thomas Bickel, André Halter.   Trainer: Ottmar Hitzfeld

Sent off: Halter (89)

Goals: Timko (35), Vankovic (53 pen), Tittel (88 pen)

GRASSHOPPER ZÜRICH
v SLOVAN BRATISLAVA 4-0 (1-0, 3-0) (AET)

Hardturm, Zürich 26.09.1989

Referee: Günther Habermann (E. GER)   Attendance: 3,100

GRASSHOPPER: Martin Brunner; Mats Gren, Charly In-Albon, André Egli (Cap), Marcel Koller (70 Thomas Wyss), Martin Andermatt, Urs Meier, Alain Sutter, Mark Strudal, Thomas Bickel, André Wiederkehr (75 Adrian De Vicente).   Trainer: Ottmar Hitzfeld

SLOVAN: Ivo Schmucker; Tomš Stúpala, Dušan Tittel, Vladimír Ekhardt, Jozef Juriga (52 Vladimír Vankovic), Vladimír Kinier (Cap), Ladislav Pecko (113 Ondrej Kristofik), Ladislav Repacik, Eugen Varga, Miroslav Chvila, Jaroslav Timko.   Trainer: Jozef Jankech

Sent off: Ekhardt (56)

Goals: Gren (10, 115), Egli (59 pen), Strudal (84)

307

**REAL VALLADOLID
v HAMRUN SPARTANS 5-0** (2-0)

Nuevo Zorrilla, Valladolid   12.09.1989

Referee: Vitor Manuel FERNANDES CORREIA (POR)
Attendance: 8,116

REAL: Mauro Ravnić; Branko Miljuš, José LEMOS Rodríguez, Enrique MORENO Bellver, Andoni AYARZA Zallo (72 GONZALO Arguiñano Lezkano), Luis Miguel Martínez DAMIAN, ROBERTO Valverde Maestre, Raul ALBISceascoechea, ALBERTO López Moreno, Luis Mariano MINGUELA Muñoz (Cap) (75 PATRIcio Sánchez Maures), Jésus HIDALGO Bermejo.   Trainer: Josip Skoblar

HAMRUN SPARTANS: Ian Leigh; John Micallef, Alex Azzopardi, Marco Grech, Raymond Vella (78 Marco Marlow), Gejtu Refalo, Anthony Morley (53 Julian Micallef), Brian Mundee, Noel Fenech, Michael Degiorgio (Cap), Stefan Sultana.   Trainer: Terenzio Polverini

Goals: Albis (22, 70), Roberto (38, 46), Ayarza (59)

**HAMRUN SPARTANS
v REAL VALLADOLID 0-1** (0-1)

National Ta'Qali   26.09.1989

Referee: Pier Luigi Magni (ITA)   Attendance: 1,188

HAMRUN SPARTANS: Ian Leigh; Julian Micallef, Alex Azzopardi, Marco Grech, Brian Mundee, Raymond Vella, Gejtu Refalo, John Micallef, Noel Fenech, Michael Degiorgio (Cap), Stefan Sultana.   Trainer: Terenzio Polverini

REAL: Mauro Ravnić; PATRIcio Sánchez Maures, José LEMOS Rodríguez, Luis Miguel Martínez DAMIAN, GONZALO Arguiñano Lezkano, Andoni AYARZA Zallo, Janko Janković, Raul ALBISceascoechea (46 Jesús Ángel LOPEZ González), ROBERTO Valverde Maestre, Luis Mariano MINGUELA Muñoz (Cap) (58 José Luis Pérez CAMINERO), Jésus HIDALGO Bermejo.   Trainer: Josip Skoblar

Goal: Hidalgo (37)

BELENENSES LISBOA v AS MONACO 1-1 (0-0)

Estádio do Restelo, Lisboa   12.09.1989

Referee: Ignace van Swieten (HOL)   Attendance: 6,200

BELENENSES: Borislav Mikhailov; João António Silva Duarte GALO, JOSÉ ANTONIO Prudencio Bargiela (Cap), EDMUNDO Joaquim Pascoal da Silva, "ZÉ MARIO" José Amaro Justino, "JUANICO" José Alberto Peixoto da Silva, "MACAÉ" Fernando Ferreira de Assis, Anio Sadkov (46 "ADÃO" Carlos Manuel Pereira Pinto), "CHICO" José Francisco FARIA, JORGE Manuel Correia Oliveira SILVA (75 Manuel Martins SAAVEDRA), "CHIQUINHO" Francisco Condé Junior. Trainer: Hristo Mladenov

AS MONACO: Jean-Luc Ettori (Captain); Claude Puel, Luc Sonor, Rémy Vogel, Patrick Blondeau, Fabrice Poullain, Jean-Marc Ferratge (79 José Touré), Fabrice Mège, George Weah, Ramón Díaz, Emmanuel Petit.   Trainer: Arsène Wenger

Goals: Chiquinho (55), Diaz (70)

AS MONACO v BELENENSES LISBOA 3-0 (3-0)

Stade Louis II, Monte Carlo   26.09.1989

Referee: Manfred Rossner (E. GER)   Attendance: 7,480

AS MONACO: Jean-Luc Ettori (Cap); Patrick Blondeau (41 Fabrice Poullain), Luc Sonor, Rémy Vogel (46 Emmanuel Petit), Roger Mendy, Claude Puel, Jean-Marc Ferratge, Marcel Dib, George Weah, Ramón Díaz, Fabrice Mège.   Trainer: Arsène Wenger

BELENENSES: Borislav Mikhailov; João António Silva Duarte GALO, JOSÉ ANTONIO Prudencio Bargiela (Cap), EDMUNDO Joaquim Pascoal da Silva, Carlos Manuel Cândido GROSSO (46 Manuel Martins SAAVEDRA), "JUANICO" José Alberto Peixoto da Silva, "MACAÉ" Fernando Ferreira de Assis, CARLOS Manuel Gonçalves RIBEIRO, "CHICO" José Francisco FARIA, "ADÃO" Carlos Manuel Pereira Pinto, "CHIQUINHO" Francisco Condé Junior (58 JAIME Jerónimo das Merces).   Trainer: Hristo Mladenov

Goals: Weah (30, 35), Mège (40)

US LUXEMBOURG v DJURGÅRDEN STOCKHOLM 0-0

Stade Achille Hammerel, Luxembourg   12.09.1989

Referee: Jacob Uilenberg (HOL)   Attendance: 429

US LUXEMBOURG: John van Rijswijck, Claude Ganser (87 Pierre Hoscheid), Marc Birsens, Laurent Schönckert (Cap), Thomas Wolf, Gérard Jeitz, Joël Groff, Luc Feiereisen, Denis Mogenot, Christian Joachim (85 Luc Lambert), Patrick Morocutti.   Trainer: Alex Pequeur

DJURGÅRDEN: Anders Almgren, Glenn Schiller, Stephan Kullberg (Cap), Lars Lundborg, Leif Nilsson, Christer Nordin, Niklas Karlström, Mikael Martinsson, Jens Fjellström, Steve Galloway (70 Glenn Myrthil), Peter Skoogh. Trainer: Tommy Söderberg

**DJURGÅRDEN STOCKHOLM
v US LUXEMBOURG 5-0** (0-0)

Råsunda, Solna   27.09.1989

Referee: Timo Keltanen (FIN)   Attendance: 1,180

DJURGÅRDEN: Anders Almgren, Glenn Schiller, Stephan Kullberg (Cap), Lars Lundborg, Christer Nordin, Niklas Karlström (50 Jonas Claesson), Mikael Martinsson, Leif Nilsson, Steve Galloway, Jens Fjellström, Peter Skoogh (80 Kefa Olsson).   Trainer: Tommy Söderberg

US LUXEMBOURG: John van Rijswijck, Claude Ganser, Thomas Wolf, Laurent Schönckert (Cap), Marc Birsens, Gérard Jeitz, Joël Groff, Luc Feiereisen, Patrick Morocutti, Denis Mogenot (85 Marc Chaussy), Luc Lambert (72 Fernand Heinisch).   Trainer: Alex Pequeur

Goals: Martinsson (54, 85), Nilsson (60), Galloway (80, 90)

PARTIZAN BEOGRAD
v CELTIC GLASGOW 2-1 (1-1)

Gradski, Mostar   12.09.1989

Referee: Helmut Kohl   Attendance: 8,500

PARTIZAN: Fahrudin Omerović (10 Goran Pandurović), Bajro Zupić, Darko Milanić, Miodrag Spasić, Gordan Petrić, Budimir Vujacić, Aleksandr Djordjević, Goran Milojević, Milan Djurdjević, Milko Djurovski (Cap), Goran Bogdanović (70 Milinko Pantić).   Trainer: Momčilo Vukotić

CELTIC: Patrick Bonner, Christopher Morris, Anton Rogan, Robert Aitken (Cap), Derek Whyte, Peter Grant, Michael Galloway, Paul McStay, Dariusz Dziekanowski (62 Andrew Walker), Thomas Coyne, Thomas Burns.
Manager: William McNeill

Goals: Milojević (21), Galloway (42), Djurdjević (55)

HAKA VALKEAKOSKI
v FERENCVÁROS BUDAPEST 1-1 (0-0)

Tehtaankenttä, Valkeakoski   27.09.1989

Referee: Bo Helen (SWE)   Attendance: 503

HAKA: Olavi Huttunen (Cap); Ari Tanttu, Kari Korkea-Aho, Jussi Rautiainen (63 Kimmo Hell), Rami Nieminen (40 Gary Rice), Mauri Holappa, Ilkka Makelä, Tommi Paavola, Tapio Lintunen, Ari Valvee, Mika Laiho.
Trainer: Jorma Kangasmaki

FERENCVÁROS: Miklós Jozsa; Tibor Simon, Attila Pinter, Jozsef Keller, Gyula Vaszil, András Kereszturi, Zsolt Paling (78 Flórián Albert), József Banki (Cap), László Wukovics, Antal Topor, Béla Dukon.   Trainer: Gyula Rákosi

Goals: Keller (47), Paavola (75)

CELTIC GLASGOW
v PARTIZAN BEOGRAD 5-4 (1-1)

Celtic Park, Glasgow   27.09.1989

Referee: Klaus Peschell (E. GER)   Attendance: 45,298

CELTIC: Patrick Bonner, Peter Grant, Anton Rogan, Robert Aitken (Cap), Paul Elliott, Derek Whyte, Michael Galloway, Paul McStay, Dariusz Dziekanowski, Andrew Walker, Joseph Miller.   Manager: William McNeill

PARTIZAN: Goran Pandurović, Vujadin Stanojković, Miodrag Spasić, Darko Milanić, Gordan Petrić, Budimir Vujacić, Aleksandr Djordjević (79 Miodrag Bajović), Goran Milojević, Sladjan Scepović, Milko Djurovski (Cap), Goran Bogdanović (62 Milan Djurdjević).
Trainer: Momčilo Vukotić

Goals: Vujacić (8), Dziekanowski (25, 47, 55, 80), Djordjević (50), Djurovski (61), Walker (65), Scepović (86)

DINAMO TIRANA
v DINAMO BUCUREŞTI 1-0 (0-0)

Qemal Stafa, Tirana   13.09.1989

Referee: Tadeusz Diakonowicz (POL)   Attendance: 13,000

DINAMO T: Foto Strakosha; Arian Stafa, Rudi Vata, 2.Pjerin Noga, Naum Kove; Agim Canaj, Ilir Daja (17 Josif Gjergji) Alfred Ferko, Sulejman Demollari (Cap); Eduard Abazi, Ermal Tahiri.   Trainer: Bekushi Birçe

DINAMO B: Bogdan Stelea; Iulian Mihăescu, Mircea Rednic, Ioan Andonie, Michael Klein (Cap); Ioan Ovidiu Sabău, Ioan Lupescu, Dorin Mateuţ, Daniel Timofte; Claudiu Vaişcovici (50 Cezar Zamfir), Florin Răducioiu.
Trainer: Mircea Lucescu

Goal: Canaj (52)

FERENCVÁROS BUDAPEST
v HAKA VALKEAKOSKI 5-1 (3-1)

Üllői ut Budapest   12.09.1989

Referee: Ihsan Ture (TUR)   Attendance: 15,865

FERENCVÁROS: Miklós Jozsa; Tibor Simon, Attila Pinter, Jozsef Keller, György Szeibert, Zsolt Limperger, László Wukovics (72 Zsolt Paling), József Banki, József Dzurjak, Sándor Kincses (Cap), András Kereszturi (80 Béla Dukon).
Trainer: Gyula Rákosi

HAKA: Olavi Huttunen (Cap); Ari Tanttu, Kari Korkea-Aho, Juha Lahtinen (86 Ari Valvee), Rami Nieminen, Mauri Holappa, Ilkka Makelä, Tommi Paavola, Tapio Lintunen, Sándor Lörincz, Mika Laiho.   Trainer: Jorma Kangasmaki

Goals: Kincses (1), Paavola (4), Limperger (10), Szeibert (29, 64), Dzurjak (80)

DINAMO BUCUREŞTI
v DINAMO TIRANA 2-0 (2-0)

Dinamo, Bucureşti   26.09.1989

Referee: Zoran Petrović (YUG)   Attendance: 25,000

DINAMO B: Bogdan Stelea; Iulian Mihăescu (55 Daniel Timofte), Mircea Rednic,Ioan Andonie (Cap), Michael Klein; Ioan Lupescu, Ioan Ovidiu Sabău, Dorin Mateuţ, Dănuţ Lupu; Claudiu Vaişcovici (74 Marian Damaschin), Florin Răducioiu.
Trainer: Mircea Lucescu

DINAMO T: Foto Strakosha; Pjerin Noga, Genci Ibro, Viktor Briza (30 Josif Gjergji), Rudi Vata, Agim Canaj, Naum Kove, Alfred Ferko, Ermal Tahiri (76 Ardjan Jançe), Eduard Abazi, Sulejman Demollari (Cap).   Trainer: Baikush Beci

Goals: Mateuţ (8), Mihăescu (13)

ADMIRA WACKER WIEN
v AEL LIMASSOL 3-0 (0-0)
Bundesstadion Südstadt, Maria Enzesdorf   13.09.1989

Referee: Adrian Porumboiu (ROM)   Attendance: 1,500

ADMIRA WACKER: Wolfgang Knaller, Dietmar Kuhbauer (46 Walter Knaller), Thomas Zingler, Helmut Graf, Michael Gruber, Fred Schaub, Ernst Baumeister, Peter Artner, Uwe Müller, Manfred Seber (46 Manfred Kern), Gerhard Rodax.   Trainer: Ernst Weber

AEL: Marios Onisiforou; Xenios Aristotelous (80 Pavlos Savva), Makis Sokratous, Kostas Konstantinou, Giorgos Anastasiou, Panikos Orfanidis (Cap) (31 Giorgos Stylianou), Miroslav Prilozny, Hristos Hristodoulou, Hristos Koliantris, Giannis Ioannou, Giorgos Sofokleous.   Trainer: Jiří Dunai

Goals: Schaub (80), Walter Knaller (86), Rodax (89)

AEL LIMASSOL
v ADMIRA WACKER WIEN 1-0 (1-0)
Tsirion, Limassol   27.09.1989

Referee: Mateo Beusan (YUG)   Attendance: 2,785

AEL: Marios Onisiforou; Xenios Aristotelous, Giorgos Stylianou (52 Marios Savva), Kostas Konstantinou, Giorgos Anastasiou (Cap), Marios Dimitriou, Jiří Shourek, Hristos Hristodoulou (23 Neofytos Neofytou), Hristos Koliantris, Loizos Mavroudis, Giorgos Sofokleous.   Trainer: Jiří Dunai

ADMIRA WACKER: Wolfgang Knaller; Gerald Bacher, Thomas Zingler, Helmut Graf, Michael Gruber, Peter Artner, Ernst Baumeister (87 Fred Schaub), Manfred Kern (77 Dietmar Kühbauer), Uwe Müller, Walter Knaller, Gerhard Rodax.   Trainer: Ernst Weber

Sent off: Bacher (60)

Goal: Sofokleous (43)

FC BARCELONA v LEGIA WARSZAWA 1-1 (0-1)
Camp Nou, Barcelona   13.09.1989

Referee: Rolf Blattmann (SWI)   Attendance: 30,000

FC BARCELONA: Andoni ZUBIZARRETA Urreta (Cap), Luis María LÓPEZ REKARTE, ALOÍSIO Pires Alves (46 SERGI López Segú), Ronald Koeman, Ricardo Jesús SERNA Orozco, EUSEBIO Sacristán Mena, Julio SALINAS Fernández, Guillermo AMOR Martínez (58 Jordi ROURA Sola), Michael Laudrup, ROBERTO Fernández Bonilla, Aitor BEGUIRISTÁIN Mujika.   Trainer: Johan Cruyff

LEGIA: Maciej Szczesny, Dariusz Kubicki, Juliusz Kruszankin, Dariusz Wdowczyk, Zbigniew Kaczmarek (Cap), Krzysztof Budka, Leszek Pisz (67 Marek Jozwiak), Roman Kosecki, Krzysztof Iwanicki, Andrzej Latka, Stanislaw Terlecki (77 Myeczislaw Pisz).   Trainer: Rudolf Kapera

Goals: Latka (25), R. Koeman (85 pen)

LEGIA WARSZAWA v FC BARCELONA 0-1 (0-1)
Wojska Polskiego, Warszawa   27.09.1989

Referee: Heinz Holzmann (AUS)   Attendance: 17,000

LEGIA: Maciej Szczesny, Dariusz Kubicki, Juliusz Kruszankin, Dariusz Wdowczyk, Zbigniew Kaczmarek (Cap), Jacek Bak, Jacek Cyzio (83 Marek Jozwiak), Krzysztof Iwanicki, Andrzej Latka, Roman Kosecki, Stanislaw Terlecki.   Trainer: Rudolf Kapera

FC BARCELONA: Andoni ZUBIZARRETA Urreta, Luis María LÓPEZ REKARTE, Juan Ramon ALESANCO Ventosa, Ronald Koeman, Ricardo Jesús SERNA Orozco, Miguel SOLER Sararols, Julio SALINAS Fernández, EUSEBIO Sacristán Mena (88 Luis MILLA Aspas), Michael Laudrup, ROBERTO Fernández Bonilla, Aitor BEGUIRISTÁIN Mujika (59 Guillermo AMOR Martínez).   Trainer: Johan Cruyff

Goal: M. Laudrup (11)

BEŞIKTAŞ ISTANBUL
v BORUSSIA DORTMUND 0-1 (0-1)
Inönü, Istanbul   13.09.1989

Referee: Kenneth Hope (SCO)   Attendance: 13,635

BEŞIKTAŞ: Engin Ipekoglu, Recep Çetin, Gökhan Keskin, Ulvi Guveneroglu, Kadir Akbulut, Mehmet Özdilek, Riza Çalimbay (Cap), Ian Wilson, Alan Walsh (59 Robert McDonald), Feyyaz Uçar, Ali Gultiken.   Trainer: Gordon Milne

BORUSSIA: Wolfgang de Beer, Michael Schulz, Robert Nikolic, Andreas Möller, Thomas Helmer, Murdo MacLeod, Michael Lusch, Michael Zorc (Cap), Jürgen Wegmann (73 Martin Driller), Michael Rummenigge (3 Thomas Kroth), Frank Mill.   Trainer: Horst Köppel

Goal: Mill (13)

BORUSSIA DORTMUND
v BEŞIKTAŞ ISTANBUL 2-1 (1-0)
Westfalenstadion, Dortmund   27.09.1989

Referee: John Blankenstein (HOL)   Attendance: 43,000

BORUSSIA: Wolfgang de Beer, Michael Schulz, Gunter Kutowski, Andreas Möller, Thomas Helmer, Murdo MacLeod, Michael Lusch, Michael Zorc (Cap), Martin Driller (79 Jürgen Wegmann), Michael Rummenigge, Frank Mill.   Trainer: Horst Köppel

BEŞIKTAŞ: Engin Ipekoglu, Recep Çetin, Kadir Akbulut, Gökhan Keskin, Ulvi Guveneroglu, Mehmet Özdilek, Feyyaz Uçar, Riza Çalimbay (Cap), Ian Wilson, Ali Gultiken, Metin Tekin.   Trainer: Gordon Milne

Goals: Driller (11), Ali (76), Wegmann (85)

VALUR REYKJAVIK v DYNAMO BERLIN 1-2 (1-0)
Laugardalsvöllur, Reykjavik 13.09.1989
Referee: John Purcell (IRE)   Attendance: 510
VALUR: Bjarni Sigurdsson; Thorgrimur Thrainsson (Cap), Steinar Adolfsson, Saevar Jonsson, Magni Blondal Petursson, Einar Pall Thomasson, Halldor Askelsson, Gudmundur Baldursson, Larus Gudmundsson, Baldur Bragasson, Ingvar Gudmundsson.   Trainer: Gudmundur Thorbjornsson
DYNAMO: Bodo Rudwaleit; Waldemar Ksienczyk, Bernd Schulz, Marco Köller, Burkhard Reich, Hendrik Herzog, Heiko Bonan, Thomas Doll, Jörg Fügner (60 Eike Küttner), Rainer Ernst (Cap), Andreas Thom.   Trainer: Helmut Jaschke
Goals: Askelsson (37), Bonan (70), Thom (75)

SWANSEA CITY
v PANATHINAIKOS ATHINA 3-3 (1-0)
Vetch Field, Swansea 27.09.1989
Referee: Henning Lund Sørensen (DEN)   Attendance: 8,276
SWANSEA: Lee Bracey, David Hough, Chris Coleman, Andrew Melville (Cap), Terence Boyle, Robert Mark James, Stewart Phillips, Andrew Legg (58 David D'Auria), Thomas Hutchinson, John Salako, Paul Raynor.   Manager: Ian Evans
PANATHINAIKOS: Giorgos Abadiotakis; Iakovos Hatziathanasiou, Nikos Kourbanas, Hristos Kalatzis, Giannis Kalitzakis, Kostas Mauridis, Dimitris Saravakos (Cap), Jason Sean Polack (57 Kostas Antoniou), Hristos Dimopoulos, Hristo Kolev, Lissandros Georgamlis.   Trainer: Günder Bengtsson
Goals: James (31 pen), Melville (46, 66), Dimopoulos (50), Saravakos (71 pen, 89)

DYNAMO BERLIN v VALUR REYKJAVIK 2-1 (1-0)
Friedrich-Ludwig-Jahn-Sportpark, Berlin 27.09.1989
Referee: Jan Damgaard (DEN)   Attendance: 9,500
DYNAMO: Bodo Rudwaleit; Waldemar Ksienczyk, Burkhard Reich, Marco Köller, Frank Rohde (Cap), Hendrik Herzog, Heiko Bonan (37 Jörn Lenz), Thomas Doll, Dirk Anders, Rainer Ernst, Andreas Thom.   Trainer: Helmut Jaschke
VALUR: Bjarni Sigurdsson; Thorgrimur Thrainsson (Cap), Steinar Adolfsson, Saevar Jonsson, Magni Blondal Petursson, Einar Pall Thomasson, Halldor Askelsson, Gudmundur Baldursson, Larus Gudmundsson, Ingvar Gudmundsson, Sigurjon Kristjansson.   Trainer: Gudmundur Thorbjornsson
Goals: Ernst (25), Kristjansson (53), Lenz (83)

ANDERLECHT BRUSSEL
v BALLYMENA UNITED 6-0 (3-0)
Constant Vanden Stock, Brussel 13.09.1989
Referee: Thorodd Presberg (NOR)   Attendance: 2,824
ANDERLECHT: Filip de Wilde; Guy Marchoul, Adri van Tiggelen (Cap), Kari Ukkonen, Henrik Andersen, Luc Nilis, Patrick Vervoort, Arnór Gudjohnsen, Marc Degryse, Milan Janković (28 Pär Zetterberg), Marc van der Linden (58 Airton Luis Barroso de OLIVEIRA).   Trainer: Aad de Mos
BALLYMENA: Damian Grant; Ian Hamilton, Michael Smyth (Cap), John Garrett, John Heron, Stephen Young, John McKee, Lindsay Curry (.. Desmond Loughery), Thomas Sloan, Paul Hardy, David Smyth (.. Richard Simpson).
Trainer: Alex McKee
Goals: Ukkonen (11), Nilis (16, 35), Van der Linden (47, 52), Gudjohnsen (85)

PANATHINAIKOS ATHINA
v SWANSEA CITY 3-2 (2-0)
Olympiako stadio "Spiros Louis", Athina 13.09.1989
Referee: Lajos Nemeth (HUN)   Attendance: 42,000
PANATHINAIKOS: Giorgos Abadiotakis; Iakovos Hatziathanasiou, Hristo Kolev, Hristos Kalatzis, Giannis Kalitzakis, Kostas Mauridis, Dimitris Saravakos (Cap), Kostas Antoniou, Hristos Dimopoulos (75 Leonidas Hristodoulou), Vaggelis Vlahos (64 Jason Sean Polack), Lissandros Georgamlis.   Trainer: Günder Bengtsson
SWANSEA: Lee Bracey, David Hough, Chris Coleman, Andrew Melville (Cap), Terence Boyle, Robert Mark James (62 Simon Davey), Gary Cobb, David D'Auria (55 Andrew Legg), Thomas Hutchinson, John Salako, Paul Raynor.
Manager: Ian Evans
Goals: Vlahos (4, 53), Saravakos (38), Raynor (63), Salako (80)

BALLYMENA UNITED
v ANDERLECHT BRUSSEL 0-4 (0-1)
The Showgrounds, Ballymena 27.09.1989
Referee: Eyjolfur Olafsson (ICE)   Attendance: 2,100
BALLYMENA: Joseph McErlean; Ian Hamilton, Michael Smyth, John Garrett, John Heron, Stephen Young, John McKee (80 James Scott), Desmond Loughery, William Pyper, Paul Hardy, Richard Simpson (78 David Smyth).
Trainer: Alex McKee
ANDERLECHT: Filip de Wilde; Arnór Gudjohnsen, Guy Marchoul, Adri van Tiggelen (Cap), Henrik Andersen, Kari Ukkonen, Patrick Vervoort, Luc Nilis, Marc Degryse, Milan Janković (62 Charles Musonda), Marc van der Linden (46 Airton Luis Barroso de OLIVEIRA).   Trainer: Aad de Mos
Goals: Vervoort (27, 87), Degryse (54), Gudjohnsen (83)

**SK BRANN BERGEN
v SAMPDORIA GENOVA 0-2** (0-1)

Brann Bergen 13.09.1989

Referee: William Crombie (SCO)   Attendance: 16,789

BRANN: Kjetil Elvenes; Henrik Bjornstad, Per Egil Ahlsen (Cap), Roy Wassberg, Lars Moldestad (60 Trond Nordeide), Einar Arne Roth, Atle Torvanger, Redouane Drici, Jan Erland Kruse, Olafur Thordarson, Tore Hadler Olsen (60 Per Hilmar Nybø).   Trainer: Teitur Thordarson

SAMPDORIA: Gianluca Pagliuca, Moreno Mannini, Srecko Katanec, Fausto Pari, Pietro Vierchowod, Luca Pellegrini (Cap), VÍCTOR Muñoz Manrique, Antonio Carlos CEREZO, Gianluca Vialli (64 Attilio Lombardo), Giuseppe Dossena, Roberto Mancini (46 Amedeo Carboni).
Trainer: Vujadin Boškov

Goals: Vialli (40), Mancini (55)

**SAMPDORIA GENOVA
v BRANN BERGEN 1-0** (0-0)

Luigi Ferraris, Genova   27.09.1989

Referee: Borislav Alexandrov (BUL)   Attendance: 9,460

SAMPDORIA: Gianluca Pagliuca, Amedeo Carboni, Srecko Katanec, Fausto Pari (81 Marco Lanna), Pietro Vierchowod, Luca Pellegrini (Cap), VÍCTOR Muñoz Manrique (63 Fausto Salsano), Giovanni Invernizzi, Gianluca Vialli, Giuseppe Dossena, Roberto Mancini.   Trainer: Vujadin Boškov

BRANN: Kjetil Elvenes; Henrik Bjornstad, Per Egil Ahlsen (Cap), Roy Wassberg, Lars Moldestad, Einar Arne Roth, Atle Torvanger (46 Gert Berentsen), Redouane Drici, Trond Nordeide, Olafur Thordarson, Tore Hadler Olsen (75 Per Hilmar Nybø).   Trainer: Teitur Thordarson

Goal: Katanec (75)

FC GRONINGEN v IKAST FS 1-0 (0-0)

Oosterpark, Groningen   13.09.1989

Referee: Thomas Donnely (NIR)   Attendance: 12,000

FC GRONINGEN: Patrick Lodewijks, Wim Koevermans, Claus Boekweg, Ulrich Wilson, Barend Beltman (68 Marco Koorman), Jan Van Dijk (Cap), Edwin Olde Riekerink, Jos Roossien, Hennie Meijer, Theo Ten Caat (80 Geon Weering), René Eijkelkamp.   Trainer: Hans Westerhof

IKAST: Mogens Krogh (Cap); Kim Eriksen, Rene Hansen, Torben Piechnik, Michael Larsen, Henning Larsen (63 Ejnar Rahbek), Sigurd Kristensen, Kent Hansen, Michael Pedersen, Ove Hansen (74 Jens Madsen), Jesper Thygesen.
Trainer: Anders Hust

Goal: Koevermans (49)

IKAST FS v FC GRONINGEN 1-2 (0-1)

Ikast stadion   27.09.1989

Referee: Egil Nervik (NOR)   Attendance: 3,639

IKAST: Mogens Krogh (Cap); Kim Eriksen, Henning Larsen, Torben Piechnik, Jan Larsen (58 Johnny Hansen), Jens Madsen, Sigurd Kristensen, Kent Hansen, Michael Pedersen, Jesper Thygesen, Mogens Kjeldsen (76 Michael Larsen).
Trainer: Anders Hust

FC GRONINGEN: Patrick Lodewijks, Wim Koevermans, Claus Boekweg, Ulrich Wilson, Marco Koorman, Jan Van Dijk (Cap), Harrie Sinkgraeven, Jos Roossien, Hennie Meijer, Theo Ten Caat, René Eijkelkamp.   Trainer: Hans Westerhof

Goals: Meijer (35), Eijkelkamp (70), Kristensen (83 pen)

TORPEDO MOSKVA v CORK CITY 5-0 (4-0)

Torpedo Moskva   13.09.1989

Referee: Ion Crăciunescu (ROM)   Attendance: 4,050

TORPEDO: Valeri Sarichev; Aleksandr Polukarov (Cap), Mikhail Soloviev, Dmitri Chugunov, Andrei Afanasiev, Vladimir Grechnev, Yuri Savichev, Aleksandr Gitselov (46 Andrei Rudakov), Nikolai Savichev, Oleg Schirinbekov (56 Sergei Zhukov), Gennadi Grishin.   Trainer: Valentin Ivanov

CORK: John Donnegan; Paul Bowdren, Philip Long, Noel Healy, Liam Murphy (Cap), Patrick Freyne, Cormac Cotter, Michael Conroy, Paul Bannon, Patrick Duggan (66 Kieran Hoare), John Caulfield.   Trainer: Noel O'Mahoney

Goals: Grechnev (24, 40 pen), Y. Savichev (27), Chugunov (34), Afanasiev (72)

CORK CITY v TORPEDO MOSKVA 0-1 (0-1)

Turner's Cross, Cork   27.09.1989

Referee: Jean-Marie Lartigot (FRA)   Attendance: 2,560

CORK: Philip Harrington; Paul Bowdren, Philip Long, Liam Murphy (Cap), Michael Conroy, Cormac Cotter, Dave Barry, Patrick Freyne, Kieran Nagle, Paul Bannon, John Caulfield.
Trainer: Noel O'Mahoney

TORPEDO: Valeri Sarichev; Aleksandr Polukarov, Valentin Kovach, Dmitri Chugunov, Vadim Rogovskoi, Vladimir Grechnev, Yuri Savichev, Andrei Rudakov, Nikolai Savichev, Oleg Schirinbekov (51 Mikhail Soloviev), Gennadi Grishin (30 Sergei Zhukov).   Trainer: Valentin Ivanov

Goal: Y. Savichev (12)

SECOND ROUND

ANDERLECHT BRUSSEL
v FC BARCELONA 2-0 (1-0)

Constant Vandenstock, Brussel 18.10.1989

Referee: Erik Fredriksson (SWE)   Attendance: 25,000

ANDERLECHT: Filip de Wilde; Georges Grün (Cap), Adri van Tiggelen, Stephen Keshi, Henrik Andersen, Charles Musonda (36 Luc Nilis), Patrick Vervoort, Arnór Gudjohnsen, Marc Degryse, Milan Janković, Marc van der Linden.   Trainer: Aad de Mos

FC BARCELONA: Andoni ZUBIZARRETA Urreta (Cap), URBANO Ortega Cuadros (46 Luis MILLA Aspas), ALOÍSIO Pires Alves, Ronald Koeman, Ricardo Jesús SERNA Orozco, José María BAKERO Escudero (75 JULIO ALBERTO Moreno Casas), Julio SALINAS Fernández, EUSEBIO Sacristán Mena, Michael Laudrup, ROBERTO Fernández Bonilla, Aitor BEGUIRISTÁIN Mujika.   Trainer: Johan Cruyff

Goals: Janković (12), Degryse (46)

FC BARCELONA
v ANDERLECHT BRUSSEL 2-1 (0-0, 2-0) (AET)

Camp Nou Barcelona 1.11.1989

Referee: Luigi Agnolin (ITA)   Attendance: 86,159

FC BARCELONA: Andoni ZUBIZARRETA Urreta (Cap); ALOÍSIO Pires Alves, JULIO ALBERTO Moreno Casas, Ronald Koeman, Luis MILLA Aspas, José María BAKERO Escudero, Ernesto VALVERDE Tejedor (46 ONÉSIMO Sánchez González), EUSEBIO Sacristán Mena, Julio SALINAS Fernández (74 Juan Ramón ALESANCO Ventosa), ROBERTO Fernández Bonilla, Aitor BEGUIRISTÁIN Mujika.

ANDERLECHT: Filip de Wilde; Georges Grün (Cap) (37 Luc Nilis), Adri van Tiggelen, Stephen Keshi, Henrik Andersen, Charles Musonda, Patrick Vervoort, Arnór Gudjohnsen, Marc Degryse (51 Guy Marchoul), Milan Janković, Marc van der Linden.   Trainer: Aad de Mos

Goals: Salinas (50), Beguiristáin (56), Van der Linden (97)

FC GRONINGEN
v PARTIZAN BEOGRAD 4-3 (2-2)

Oosterpark, Groningen 18.10.1989

Referee: Henning Lund Sørensen (DEN)   Att: 10,115

FC GRONINGEN: Patrick Lodewijks; Wim Koevermans, Claus Boekweg, Ulrich Wilson, Marco Koorman (74 Erik Groeleken), Jan Van Dijk (Cap), Harrie Sinkgraven, Jos Roossien, Hennie Meijer, Theo Ten Caat, René Eijkelkamp.

PARTIZAN: Fahrudin Omerović; Vujadin Stanojković, Milan Djurdjević (70 Miodrag Bajović), Predrag Spasić, Miloje Kljajević, Budimir Vujačić, Milorad Bajović, Goran Milojević, Sladjan Scepović (75 Jovica Kolb), Milko Djurovski (Cap), Goran Bogdanović   Trainer: Ivan Golac

Goals: Meijer (16), Milorad Bajović (32), Ten Caat (35), Djurovski (45, 83), Roosinen (48), Koevermans (74)

PARTIZAN BEOGRAD
v FC GRONINGEN 3-1 (1-0)

JNA Beograd 1.11.1989

Referee: Karl-Heinz Tritschler (W. GER)   Att: 55,000

PARTIZAN: Fahrudin Omerović; Vujadin Stanojković, Goran Jevtić (63 Jovica Kolb), Predrag Spasić, Gordan Petrić, Miloje Kljajević, Milorad Bajović (66 Milan Djurdjević), Goran Milojević, Sladjan Scepović, Milko Djurovski (Cap), Goran Bogdanović.   Trainer: Ivan Golac

FC GRONINGEN: Patrick Lodewijks; Wim Koevermans, Claus Boekweg, Ulrich Wilson, Marco Koorman, Jan Van Dijk (Cap), Harrie Sinkgraven (78 Erik Groeleken), Jos Roossien, Hennie Meijer, Theo Ten Caat, René Eijkelkamp.   Trainer: Hans Westerhof

Goals: Djurovski (16), Ten Caat (80), Milojević (83), Djurdjević (90)

ADMIRA WACKER WIEN
v FERENCVÁROS BUDAPEST 1-0 (0-0)

Bundesstadion Südstadt, Maria Enzesdorf 18.10.1989

Referee: Ignace van Swieten (HOL)   Attendance: 6,000

ADMIRA WACKER: Wolfgang Knaller; Thomas Zingler, Herbert Oberhofer, Helmut Graf, Gerhard Rodax (Cap), Walter Knaller, Michael Gruber, Peter Artner, Uwe Müller, Manfred Kern, Fred Schaub (85 Reinhard Zingler).   Trainer: Ernst Weber

FERENCVÁROS: Miklós Jozsa; Tibor Simon, Attila Pinter, József Keller, Gyula Vaszil, András Kereszturi, Zsolt Paling (78 László Wukovics), József Banki (Cap), József Dzurjak, Antál Topor, Zsolt Fonnyadt.   Trainer: Gyula Rákosi

Goal: Rodax (88)

FERENCVÁROS BUDAPEST
v ADMIRA WACKER WIEN 0-1 (0-0)

Szeged stadion 1.11.1989

Referee: Wolf-Günter Wiesel (W. GER)   Attendance: 2,000

FERENCVÁROS: Miklós Jozsa; Gyula Vaszil, Attila Pinter, József Keller, Antál Topor, Zsolt Limperger, Zsolt Paling (78 Béla Dukon), József Banki, József Dzurjak (66 László Wukovics), Sándor Kincses (Cap), Zsolt Fonnyadt.   Trainer: Gyula Rákosi

ADMIRA WACKER: Wolfgang Knaller; Thomas Zingler, Herbert Oberhofer, Helmut Graf, Gerald Bacher, Walter Knaller, Michael Gruber (88 Manfred Kern), Peter Artner, Uwe Müller, Gerhard Rodax, Fred Schaub (85 Manfred Seber).   Trainer: Ernst Weber

Goals: Oberhofer (48)

**BORUSSIA DORTMUND
v SAMPDORIA GENOVA 1-1** (0-0)

Westfalenstadion, Dortmund 17.10.1989

Referee: Alexei Spirin (USSR)   Attendance: 45,560

BORUSSIA: Wolfgang de Beer; Michael Schulz, Günter Kutowski, Thomas Kroth, Thomas Helmer, Murdo MacLeod, Michael Lusch, Michael Zorc (Cap), Martin Driller, Andreas Möller, Frank Mill (46 Jürgen Wegmann).
Trainer: Horst Köppel

SAMPDORIA: Gianluca Pagliuca; Moreno Mannini, Amedeo Carboni, Fausto Pari, Pietro Vierchowod, Luca Pellegrini (Cap), VÍCTOR Muñoz Manrique (73 Attilio Lombardo), Srecko Katanec, Gianluca Vialli, Roberto Mancini, Giuseppe Dossena (88 Fausto Salsano).   Trainer: Vujadin Boškov

Goals: Wegmann (64), Mancini (88)

**SAMPDORIA GENOVA
v BORUSSIA DORTMUND 2-0** (0-0)

Luigi Ferraris, Genova 1.11.1989

Referee: Marcel van Langenhove (BEL)   Attendance: 32,683

SAMPDORIA: Gianluca Pagliuca; Moreno Mannini, Fausto Salsano (88 Giovanni Invernizzi), Fausto Pari, Pietro Vierchowod, Luca Pellegrini (Cap), Attilio Lombardo, Antonio Carlos CEREZO, Gianluca Vialli, Roberto Mancini, Giuseppe Dossena (55 VÍCTOR Muñoz Manrique).
Trainer: Vujadin Boškov

BORUSSIA: Wolfgang de Beer; Michael Lusch, Günter Kutowski, Thomas Kroth (75 Martin Driller), Thomas Helmer, Murdo MacLeod, Andreas Möller, Michael Zorc (Cap), Jürgen Wegmann (75 Michael Schulz), Michael Rummenigge, Frank Mill.   Trainer: Horst Köppel

Goals: Vialli (74 pen, 88)

AS MONACO v DYNAMO BERLIN 0-0

Stade Louis II Monaco 17.10.1989

Referee: Hubert Forstinger (AUS)   Attendance: 6,648

AS MONACO: Jean-Luc Ettori (Cap); Claude Puel, Luc Sonor, Emmanuel Petit, Roger Mendy, Fabrice Poullain, Jean-Marc Ferratge, Marcel Dib, George Weah (46 Mark Hateley), Ramón Díaz (49 José Touré), Fabrice Mège.   Trainer: Arsène Wenger

DYNAMO: Bodo Rudwaleit; Waldemar Ksienczyk, Burkhardt Reich, Marco Köller, Frank Rohde (Cap), Hendrik Herzog, Heiko Bonan, Thomas Doll, Jörn Lenz (46 Eike Küttner), Rainer Ernst, Andreas Thom.   Trainer: Helmut Jaschke

**DYNAMO BERLIN
v AS MONACO 1-1** (0-0, 1-1) (AET)

Friedrich-Ludwig-Jahn-Sportpark, Berlin 1.11.1989

Referee: Guy Goethals (BEL)   Attendance: 6,250

DYNAMO: Bodo Rudwaleit; Waldemar Ksienczyk, Burkhardt Reich, Jens-Uwe Zophel, Frank Rohde (Cap), Hendrik Herzog, Heiko Bonan, Thomas Doll, Eike Küttner (116 Jörg Fügner), Rainer Ernst (97 Thomas Strecker), Andreas Thom.
Trainer: Helmut Jaschke

AS MONACO: Jean-Luc Ettori (Cap); Claude Puel, Patrick Blondeau, Luc Sonor, Roger Mendy, Fabrice Poullain, Jean-Marc Ferratge (106 Youssouf Fofana), Marcel Dib, Mark Hateley (79 José Touré), Ramón Díaz, Fabrice Mège.
Trainer: Arsène Wenger

Goals: Kuttner (110), Diaz (117)

**REAL VALLADOLID
v DJURGÅRDEN STOCKHOLM 2-0** (2-0)

Nuevo Zorilla, Valladolid 18.10.1989

Referee: Bruno Galler (SWI)   Attendance: 23,236

REAL: Mauro Ravnić; Andoni AYARZA Zallo, José LEMOS Rodríguez, Enrique MORENO Bellver, GONZALO Arguiñano Lezkano, Gabriel MOYA Sanz, ROBERTO Valverde Maestre (58 José Luis Pérez CAMINERO), Raul ALBISceascoechea, ALBERTO López Moreno (62 Janko Janković), Luis Mariano MINGUELA Muñoz, Jésus HIDALGO Bermejo.
Trainer: Josip Skoblar

DJURGÅRDEN: Anders Almgren; Glenn Schiller, Stephan Kullberg (Cap), Lars Lundborg, Leif Nilsson, Christer Nordin, Niklas Karlström, Mikael Martinsson (71 Jonas Claesson), Jens Fjellström, Steve Galloway, Peter Skoogh.
Trainer: Tommy Söderberg

Goals: Kullberg (30 og), Moya (33)

**DJURGÅRDEN STOCKHOLM
v REAL VALLADOLID 2-2** (1-0)

Råsunda Solna 1.11.1989

Referee: Manfred Rossner (E. GER)   Attendance: 3,166

DJURGÅRDEN: Anders Almgren; Glenn Schiller, Stephan Kullberg (Cap), Lars Lundborg, Jonas Claesson, Christer Nordin, Niklas Karlström, Mikael Martinsson (87 Steve Galloway), Jens Fjellström, Glenn Myrthill (87 Thomas Johansson), Peter Skoogh.   Trainer: Tommy Söderberg

REAL: Mauro Ravnić; PATRIcio Sánchez Maures, José LEMOS Rodríguez, Enrique MORENO Bellver, GONZALO Arguiñano Lezkano, Andoni AYARZA Zallo, Gabriel MOYA Sanz, Raul ALBISceascoechea, ALBERTO López Moreno (80 Janko Janković), Luis Mariano MINGUELA Muñoz (Cap), José Luis Pérez CAMINERO (56 Luis Miguel Martínez DAMIÁN).
Trainer: Pepe MORÉ

Goals: Skoogh (41), Martinsson (55), Moreno (65, 72)

**PANATHINAIKOS ATHINA
v DINAMO BUCUREŞTI 0-2** (0-0)

Olympiako stadio "Spiros Louis", Athina   18.10.1989

Referee: Dieter Pauli (W. GER)   Attendance: 38,444

PANATHINAIKOS: Nikos Sargkanis; Iakovos Hatziathanasiou, Giannis Samaras, Hristos Kalatzis, Giannis Kalitzakis, Kostas Mauridis, Dimitris Saravakos (Cap), Kostas Antoniou, Hristos Dimopoulos, Vaggelis Vlahos (75 Paris Georgakopoulos), Lissandros Georgamlis (81 Hristo Kolev). Trainer: Günder Bengtsson

DINAMO: Bogdan Stelea; Iulian Mihăescu, Mircea Rednic, Ioan Andonie, Michael Klein; Ioan Lupescu (Cap) (73 Daniel Timofte), Ioan Ovidiu Sabău, Dorin Mateuţ, Dănuţ Lupu; Claudiu Vaişcovici, Florin Răducioiu (85 Cezar Zamfir). Trainer: Mircea Lucescu

Goals: Răducioiu (57), Mateuţ (66)

**DINAMO BUCUREŞTI
v PANATHINAIKOS ATHINA 6-1** (3-1)

Dinamo Bucureşti   1.11.1989

Referee: Kurt Röthlisberger (SWI)   Attendance: 22,000

DINAMO: Bogdan Stelea; Iulian Mihăescu (65 Alpar Meszaros), Mircea Rednic, Ioan Andonie (Cap), Michael Klein; Daniel Timofte, Ioan Ovidiu Sabău, Dorin Mateuţ, Dănuţ Lupu; Claudiu Vaişcovici (74 Cezar Zamfir), Florin Răducioiu. Trainer: Mircea Lucescu

PANATHINAIKOS: Nikos Sargkanis; Iakovos Hatziathanasiou, Giannis Samaras, Hristos Kalatzis, Giannis Kalitzakis, Kostas Mauridis, Paris Georgakopoulos (46 Jason Sean Polack), Kostas Antoniou (Cap), Hristos Dimopoulos, Hristo Kolev (46 Vaggelis Vlahos), Lissandros Georgamlis. Trainer: Günder Bengtsson

Goals: Rednic (21), Mateuţ (31, 48), Samaras (34), Sabău (40, 50), Klein (89)

**TORPEDO MOSKVA
v GRASSHOPPER ZÜRICH 1-1** (1-0)

Torpedo Moskva   18.10.1989

Referee: Timo Keltanen (FIN)   Attendance: 4,000

TORPEDO: Valeri Sarichev; Aleksandr Polukarov (Cap), Valentin Kovach, Gennadi Grishin, Vadim Rogovskoi, Vladimir Grechnev, Yuri Savichev, Andrei Rudakov, Nikolai Savichev (46 Andrei Afanasiev), Oleg Schirinbekov, Sergei Agashkov.   Trainer: Valentin Ivanov

GRASSHOPPER: Martin Brunner; Urs Meier, Giorgios Nemtsoudis, André Egli (Cap), Marcel Koller, Martin Andermatt, Mats Gren, Alain Sutter (85 Markus Nyfeler), Mark Strudal, Thomas Bickel, André Wiederkehr. Trainer: Ottmar Hitzfeld

Goals: Y. Savichev (29), Strudal (88)

**GRASSHOPPER ZÜRICH
v TORPEDO MOSKVA 3-0** (2-0)

Hardturm, Zürich   1.11.1989

Referee: Kenneth Hope (SCO)   Attendance: 22,000

GRASSHOPPER: Martin Brunner; Urs Meier, Charly In-Albon, André Egli (Cap), Marcel Koller, Martin Andermatt, Mats Gren (86 Giorgios Nemtsoudis), Alain Sutter, Mark Strudal, Thomas Bickel, André Wiederkehr (82 Markus Nyfeler).   Trainer: Ottmar Hitzfeld

TORPEDO: Valeri Sarichev; Aleksandr Polukarov (Cap), Valentin Kovach, Mikhail Soloviev, Vadim Rogovskoi, Vladimir Grechnev, Yuri Savichev (68 Andrei Rudakov), Aleksandr Gitselov, Nikolai Savichev, Sergei Zhukov (46 Gennadi Grishin), Dmitri Chugunov. Trainer: Valentin Ivanov

Goals: Egli (33), Wiederkehr (35), Gren (79)

QUARTER-FINALS

**ANDERLECHT BRUSSEL
v ADMIRA WACKER WIEN 2-0** (2-0)

Constant van den Stock, Brussel   6.03.1990

Referee: Klaus Peschel (E. GER)   Attendance: 16,000

ANDERLECHT: Filip de Wilde; Georges Grün (Cap), Stephen Keshi, Adri van Tiggelen, Henrik Andersen, Charles Musonda, Milan Janković (77 Patrick Vervoort), Wim Kooiman, Marc Degryse, Luc Nilis, Marc van der Linden (79 Airton Luis Barroso de OLIVEIRA).   Trainer: Aad de Mos

ADMIRA WACKER: Wolfgang Knaller; Gerald Bacher, Herbert Oberhofer (Cap), Alexander Sperr, Helmut Graf (65 Alois Dotzl), Peter Artner, Gerhard Rodax, Andreas Gretschnig, Fred Schaub (75 Walter Knaller), Uwe Müller, Johannes Abfalterer.   Trainer: Ernst Weber

Goals: Degryse (32, 37)

**ADMIRA WACKER WIEN
v ANDERLECHT BRUSSEL 1-1** (0-0)

Bundesstadion Südstadt, Maria Enzersdorf   21.03.1990

Referee: Alexei Spirin (USSR)   Attendance: 7,000

ADMIRA WACKER: Wolfgang Knaller; Gerald Bacher, Herbert Oberhofer, Alexander Sperr (65 Michael Gruber), Alois Dötzl, Walter Knaller (Cap), Johannes Abfalterer, Peter Artner, Uwe Müller, Dietmar Kühbauer, Gerhard Rodax. Trainer: Ernst Weber

ANDERLECHT: Filip de Wilde; Georges Grün (Cap), Wim Kooiman (82 Patrick Vervoort), Adri van Tiggelen, Henrik Andersen, Arnór Gudjohnsen (37 Guy Marchoul), Stephen Keshi, Luc Nilis, Marc Degryse, Milan Janković, Marc van der Linden.   Trainer: Aad de Mos

Goals: Nilis (57), Rodax (65)

REAL VALLADOLID v AS MONACO 0-0
Nuevo Zorrilla, Valladolid 7.03.1990
Referee: Pietro d'Elia (ITA)   Attendance: 14,000
REAL: Mauro Ravnić; Andoni AYARZA Zallo (70 José Gangoso Gil "FANO"), José LEMOS Rodríguez, Enrique MORENO Bellver, GONZALO Arguiñano Lezkano, Manuel García Ardura „MANOLO", Gabriel MOYA Sanz, José Luis Pérez CAMINERO, Manuel PEÑA Escontrela, Luis Mariano MINGUELA Muñoz (Cap) (70 Gregorio FONSECA Recio), Janko Janković.   Trainer: Fernando REDONDO
AS MONACO: Jean-Luc Ettori (Cap); Patrick Valéry, Claude Puel, Emmanuel Petit, Roger Mendy, Eric Guerit, Jean-Marc Ferratge, Marcel Dib, George Weah (83 Luc Sonor), Fabrice Mège (78 José Touré), Benjamin Clément.
Trainer: Arsène Wenger

AS MONACO v REAL VALLADOLID 0-0 (AET)
Louis II, Monaco 20.03.1990
Referee: Wolf-Günter Wiesel (W. GER)   Attendance: 11,301
AS MONACO: Jean-Luc Ettori; Patrick Valéry, Claude Puel, Emmanuel Petit, Roger Mendy, Eric Guerit, Jean-Marc Ferratge (41 José Touré), Marcel Dib, George Weah, Ramón Díaz, Fabrice Mège (73 Youssouf Fofana).
Trainer: Arsène Wenger
REAL: Mauro Ravnić; PATRIcio Sánchez Maures, José LEMOS Rodríguez, Enrique MORENO Bellver (26 Manuel García Ardura „MANOLO"), Andoni AYARZA Zallo, José Luis Pérez CAMINERO, Gabriel MOYA Sanz, Jésus HIDALGO Bermejo (80 Raul ALBISceascoechea), Manuel PEÑA Escontrela, Luis Mariano MINGUELA Muñoz, Janko Janković.
Trainer: Fernando REDONDO
Penalties: Janković (saved), 1-0 Diaz, 1-1 Albis, Touré (miss), Moya (saved), 2-1 Fofana, Ayarza (saved), 3-1 Petit

DINAMO BUCUREŞTI
v PARTIZAN BEOGRAD 2-1 (1-0)
Dinamo Bucureşti 7.03.1990
Referee: Dušan Krchnak (CZE)   Attendance: 12,000
DINAMO: Bogdan Stelea; Iulian Mihăescu, Mircea Rednic, Ioan Andonie, Michael Klein (Cap); Daniel Timofte, Ioan Ovidiu Sabău, Dorin Mateuţ; Dănuţ Lupu, Claudiu Vaişcovici (51 Ioan Lupescu), Florin Răducioiu (85 Cezar Zamfir).
Trainer: Mircea Lucescu
PARTIZAN: Fahrudin Omerović; Vujadin Stanojković (71 Miodrag Bajović), Predrag Spasić, Aleksandar Djordjević, Gordan Petrić; Budimir Vujacić, Predrag Mijatović, Milan Djurdjević (75 Miliuko Pantić), Sladjan Scepović, Milko Djurovski (Cap), Goran Bogdanović.   Trainer: Ivan Golac
Goals: Răducioiu (18, 57), Spasić (68)

PARTIZAN BEOGRAD
v DINAMO BUCUREŞTI 0-2 (0-0)
FK Buducnost, Titograd 21.03.1990
Referee: José Rosa Dos Santos (POR)   Attendance: 15,000
PARTIZAN: Fahrudin Omerović; Vujadin Stanojković, Miodrag Bajović, Predrag Spasić, Gordan Petrić; Milan Djurdjević (59 Milorad Bajović), Predrag Mijatović, Goran Milojević, Sladjan Scepović (60 Goran Stevanović), Milko Djurovski (Cap), Goran Bogdanović.   Trainer: Ivan Golac
DINAMO: Bogdan Stelea; Iulian Mihăescu (82 Alpar Meszaros), Mircea Rednic, Ioan Andonie, Michael Klein (Cap); Ioan Lupescu, Daniel Timofte, Dorin Mateuţ, Dănuţ Lupu; Claudiu Vaişcovici (76 Cezar Zamfir), Florin Răducioiu.
Trainer: Mircea Lucescu
Goals: Lupescu (53), Răducioiu (70)

SAMPDORIA GENOVA
v GRASSHOPPER ZÜRICH 2-0 (1-0)
Stadio Comunale Luigi Ferraris, Genova 7.03.1990
Referee: Peter Mikkelsen (DEN)   Attendance: 31,323
SAMPDORIA: Gianluca Pagliuca; Moreno Mannini, Amedeo Carboni, Fausto Pari (Cap), Pietro Vierchowod, Giovanni Invernizzi, Attilio Lombardo, Srecko Katanec, Gianluca Vialli (64 Giuseppe Dossena), Roberto Mancini, Fausto Salsano.
Trainer: Vujadin Boškov
GRASSHOPPER: Martin Brunner; Urs Meier, Charly In-Albon, André Egli (Cap), Marcel Koller, Martin Andermatt (88 Adrian De Vicente), Mats Gren, Alain Sutter, Mark Strudal, Thomas Bickel, Giorgios Nemtsoudis (63 Harald Kohr).
Trainer: Ottmar Hitzfeld
Goals: Vierchowod (13), Meier (84 og)

GRASSHOPPER ZÜRICH
v SAMPDORIA GENOVA 1-2 (0-1)
Hardturm, Zürich 22.03.1990
Referee: Zoran Petrović (YUG)   Attendance: 30,000
GRASSHOPPER: Martin Brunner; Urs Meier, Giorgios Nemtsoudis, André Egli (Cap), Marcel Koller (65 Markus Nyfeler), Martin Andermatt, Mats Gren, Alain Sutter, Harald Kohr, Thomas Bickel, Mark Strudal (65 Thomas Wyss).
Trainer: Ottmar Hitzfeld
SAMPDORIA: Gianluca Pagliuca; Moreno Mannini, Amedeo Carboni, Fausto Pari (Cap), Pietro Vierchowod, Srecko Katanec, Attilio Lombardo, Antonio Carlos CEREZO (83 Marco Lanna), Giovanni Invernizzi (87 Fausto Salsano), Roberto Mancini, Giuseppe Dossena.
Trainer: Vujadin Boškov
Goals: Cerezo (43), Wyss (67), Lombardo (81)

SEMI-FINALS

AS MONACO v SAMPDORIA GENOVA 2-2 (1-0)

Stade Louis II, Monaco 3.04.1990

Referee: Siegfried Kirschen (E. GER)   Attendance: 23,000

AS MONACO: Jean-Luc Ettori; Patrick Valéry, Luc Sonor, Emmanuel Petit, Roger Mendy, Claude Puel, Jean-Marc Ferratge (76 Fabrice Mège), Marcel Dib, George Weah, Ramón Díaz, José Touré (76 Youssouf Fofana).
Trainer: Arsène Wenger

SAMPDORIA: Gianluca Pagliuca; Moreno Mannini, Giovanni Invernizzi, Fausto Pari (Cap), Pietro Vierchowod, VÍCTOR Muñoz Manrique (69 Fausto Salsano), Attilio Lombardo, Srecko Katanec, Gianluca Vialli, Roberto Mancini, Giuseppe Dossena.   Trainer: Vujadin Boškov

Goals: Weah (44), Vialli (75 pen, 78), Diaz (81)

SAMPDORIA GENOVA v AS MONACO 2-0 (1-0)

Stadio Comunale Luigi Ferraris, Genova   18.04.1990

Referee: José Rosa dos Santos (POR)   Attendance: 35,577

SAMPDORIA: Gianluca Pagliuca; Marco Lanna, Amedeo Carboni, Fausto Pari (Cap), Pietro Vierchowod, Giovanni Invernizzi, Attilio Lombardo, Srecko Katanec, Gianluca Vialli, Roberto Mancini, Giuseppe Dossena.
Trainer: Vujadin Boškov

AS MONACO: Jean-Luc Ettori; Patrick Valéry, Luc Sonor, Emmanuel Petit, Roger Mendy, Patrick Blondeau (46 Youssouf Fofana), Jean-Marc Ferratge, Marcel Dib, George Weah, Ramón Díaz, Fabrice Mège (62 Benjamin Clément).
Trainer: Arsène Wenger

Goals: Vierchowod (9), Lombardo (57)

ANDERLECHT BRUSSEL v DINAMO BUCUREȘTI 1-0 (0-0)

Constant van den Stock, Brussel   4.04.1990

Referee: Aron Schmidhuber (W. GER)   Attendance: 15,000

ANDERLECHT: Filip Alfons de Wilde; George Serge Grün (Cap), Wim Kooiman, Stephen Keshi (68 Guy Marchoul), Henrik Andersen, Arnór Gudjohnsen, Patrick Felix Vervoort, Luc Nilis, Marc Gabriel Degryse, Marc Angele Vanderlinden, Airton Luis Barroso de Oliveira.   Trainer: Aad de Mos

DINAMO: Bogdan Stelea; Anton Doboș, Mircea Rednic, Ioan Andonie, Michael Klein (Cap); Daniel Timofte, Ioan Ovidiu Sabău, Dorin Mateuț, Dănuț Lupu; Claudiu Vaișcovici (87 Cezar Zamfir), Florin Răducioiu.   Trainer: Mircea Lucescu

Sent off: Klein (67)

Goal: Nilis (66)

DINAMO BUCUREȘTI v ANDERLECHT BRUSSEL 0-1 (0-0)

Dinamo București   18.04.1990

Referee: John Blankenstein (HOL)   Attendance: 45,000

DINAMO: Bogdan Stelea; Iulian Mihăescu (71 Anton Doboș), Mircea Rednic, Ioan Andonie, Daniel Timofte; Ioan Lupescu, Ioan Ovidiu Sabău, Dorin Mateuț, Dănuț Lupu; Claudiu Vaișcovici (67 Cezar Zamfir), Florin Răducioiu.
Trainer: Mircea Lucescu

ANDERLECHT: Filip Alfons De Wilde; George Serge Grün (Cap) (12 Airton Luis Barroso de Oliveira), Guy Marchoul, Wim Kooiman, Henrik Andersen; Charles Musonda, Patrick Felix Vervoort, Luc Nilis, Marc Gabriel Degryse, Marc Angele Vanderlinden, Arnór Gudjohnsen.   Trainer: Aad de Mos

Sent off: Răducioiu (85)

Goal: Vanderlinden (60)

FINAL

SAMPDORIA GENOVA v ANDERLECHT BRUSSEL 2-0 (0-0, 0-0) (AET)

Gamla Ullevi, Göteborg   9.05.1990

Referee: Bruno Galler (SWI)   Attendance: 20,103

SAMPDORIA: Gianluca Pagliuca, Moreno Mannini, Amedeo Carboni, Fausto Pari, Pietro Vierchowod, Luca Pellegrini (Cap), Giovanni Invernizzi (55 Attilio Lombardo), Srecko Katanec (93 Fausto Salsano), Gianluca Vialli, Roberto Mancini, Giuseppe Dossena.   Trainer: Vujadin Boškov

ANDERLECHT: Filip Alfons De Wilde, George Serge Grün (Cap), Guy Marchoul, Stephen Keshi, Wim Kooiman, Charles Musonda, Patrick Felix Vervoort, Arnór Gudjohnsen, Marc Gabriel Degryse (102 Luc Nilis), Milan Janković (116 Airton Luis Barroso de OLIVEIRA), Marc Angele Vanderlinden.
Trainer: Aad de Mos

Goals: Vialli (104, 107)

Goalscorers European Cup-Winners' Cup 1989-90:

7 goals: Gianluca Vialli (Sampdoria Genova)

4 goals: Marc Degryse, Luc Nilis, Marc van der Linden (Anderlecht), Dariusz Dziekanowski (Celtic Glasgow), Dorin Mateuţ, Florin Răducioiu (Dinamo Bucureşti), Milko Djurovski (Partizan Beograd)

3 goals: Rodax (Admira Wacker Wien), Díaz, Weah (AS Monaco), Martinsson (Djurgårdens), Gren (Grasshopper Zürich), Saravakos (Panathinaikos Athina), Yuri Savichev (Torpedo Moskva)

2 goals: Gudjohnsen, Vervoort (Anderlecht), Wegmann (Borussia Dortmund), Sabău (Dinamo Buucreşti), Canaj, Demollari (Dinamo Tirana), Galloway (Djurgårdens), Koevermans, Meijer, Ten Caat (FC Groningen), Szeibert (Ferencváros), Egli, Strudal (Grasshopper), Paavola (Haka Valkeakoski), Vlahos (Panathinaikos), Djurdjević, Milojević (Partizan Beograd), Albis, Moreno, Roberto (Real Valladolid), Lombardo, Mancini, Vierchowod (Sampdoria), Melville (Swansea City), Grechnev (Torpedo Moskva)

1 goal: Knaller, Oberhofer, Schaub (Admira-Wacker Wien), Janković, Ukkonen (Anderlecht), Driller, Mill (Borussia Dortmund), Lupescu, Rednic, Klein, Mihăescu (Dinamo Bucureşti), Petkov, V.Stoianov, Pumpalov (Chernomorets Burgas), Abazi, Jance (Dinamo Tirana), Timko, Vankovic, Tittel (Slovan Bratislava), Chiquinho (Belenenses Lisboa), Roosinen, Eijkelkamp (FC Groningen), Wiederkehr, Wyss (Grasshopper), Walker, Galloway (Celtic Glasgow), Sofokleous (AEL Limassol), Latka (Legia Warszawa), Mège (AS Monaco), Ali Gültiken (Beşiktaş Istanbul), Nilsson, Skoogh (Djurgården), Askelsson, Kristjansson (Valur Reykjavík), Kuttner, Ernst, Lenz, Bonan, Thom (Dynamo Berlin), Salinas, Beguiristáin, M.Laudrup, R.Koeman (FC Barcelona), James, Raynor, Salako (Swansea City), Samaras, Dimopoulos (Panathinaikos), Keller, Kincses, Limperger, Dzurjak (Ferencváros), Kristensen (Ikast FS), Milorad Bajović, Vujacić, Djordjević, Scepović, Spasić (Partizan Beograd), Hidalgo, Moya, Ayarza (Real Valladolid), Cerezo, Katanec (Sampdoria), Chugunov, Afanasiev (Torpedo Moskva)

Own goals: Meier (Grasshopper) for Sampdoria, Kullberg (Djurgården) for Real Valladolid

CUP WINNERS' CUP 1990-91

PRELIMINARY ROUND

BRAY WANDERERS v TRABZONSPOR 1-1 (0-1)
Tolka Park, Dublin 22.08.1990
Referee: Michel Piraux (BEL)   Attendance: 5,000

BRAY WANDERERS: Joseph Moran; Anthony McKeever, Brian Cosgrave, Mick Doohan, Derek Judge, Colm Philips, Martin Nugent, Clem MacAuley (80 Richie Parsons), Alan Smyth, John Ryan, Derek Corcoran (57 Andy Lynch).
Trainer: Pat Devlin

TRABZONSPOR: Vukasin Petranović; Ogün Temizkanoglu, Hamdi Aslan, Kemal Serdar, Seyhmuz Suna, Orhan Çikrikçi, Ünal Karaman (46 Turgut Uçar), Goran Ivanovic, Soner Boz, Hami Mandirali, Milonja Djukić.   Trainer: Özkan Sümer

Goals: Djukić (2), Nugent (52)

TRABZONSPOR v BRAY WANDERERS 2-0 (0-0)
Avni Aker, Trabzon 5.09.1990
Referee: Adrian Porumboiu (ROM)   Attendance: 17,000

TRABZONSPOR: Levent Ümit; Seyhmuz Suna, Ogün Temizkanoglu, Kemal Serdar, Mehmet Arslan, Ünal Karaman, Soner Boz, Lemi Çelik (46 Orhan Çikrikçi), Hami Mandirali, Milonja Djukić (75 Turgut Uçar), Hamdi Aslan. Trainer: Özkan Sümer

BRAY WANDERERS: Joseph Moran; Anthony McKeever, Mick Doohan, Colm Philips, Brian Cosgrave, Alan Smyth, Kevin Reynolds (56 Richie Parsons), Derek Judge, Andy Lynch (88 Adrian Cairns), Martin Nugent, John Ryan.
Trainer: Pat Devlin

Goals: Djukić (48), Hamdi (63)

FIRST ROUND

SLIEMA WANDERERS v DUKLA PRAHA 1-2 (0-1)
National Ta'Qali 18.09.1990
Referee: Rosario Lo Bello (ITA)   Attendance: 850

SLIEMA WANDERERS: Michael Atsbury; John Caruana, Carlos Cluett, Edmond Zammit (78 Gordon Camenzuli), Stephen Thewma, Aldo Scardino, Jonathan Magri Overend, Michael Taliana, Hubert Suda, Roger Walker, Simon Grech.
Trainer: Lawrence Borg

DUKLA: Petr Kostelník; Roman Pivarník, Jan Suchopárek, Václav Rada, Marián Kopca, Jiří Zálesky, Ales Foldyna, Pavel Karoch, Radoslav Látal, Günter Bittengel, Tomás Krejcík (63 Jozef Kostelník).   Trainer: Ivo Viktor

Goals: V. Rada (32), Walker (54), J. Kostelník (87)

DUKLA PRAHA v SLIEMA WANDERERS 2-0 (0-0)
Štadión Na Julisce, Praha   3.10.1990
Referee: Ernest Kessler (LUX)   Attendance: 677
DUKLA: Josef Novák; Roman Pivarník, Jan Suchopárek, Václav Rada, Marián Kopca; Edvard Lasota (64 Pavel Karoch), Ales Foldyna, Jiří Zálesky, Radoslav Látal (76 Dušan Fitzel), Günter Bittengel, Jozef Kostelník.   Trainer: Ivo Viktor
SLIEMA WANDERERS: Michael Atsbury; John Caruana, Carlos Cluett, James Navarro, Stephen Thewma, Edmond Zammit, Aldo Scardino (84 Gordon Camenzuli), Edwin Gauci, Jonathan Magri Overend, Roger Walker, Hubert Suda.
Trainer: Lawrence Borg
Goals: Walker (47 og), Zálesky (73)

FRAM REYKJAVÍK
v DJURGÅRDENS IF STOCKHOLM 3-0 (0-0)
Laugardalsvöllur, Reykjavík   19.09.1990
Referee: Wilfred Wallace (Eir)   Attendance: 637
FRAM: Birkir Kristinsson; Jón Sveinsson, Vidar Thorkelsson, Kristján Jónsson; Steinar Gudgeirsson, Kristinn R. Jónsson, Anton Bjorn Markusson, Baldur Bjarnason (59 Pétur Arnthórsson), Pétur Ormslev, Jón Erling Ragnarsson (72 Haukur Pálmason), Ríkhardur Dadason.   Trainer: Asgeir Elíasson
DJURGÅRDENS: Anders Almgren; Kenneth Bergqvist, Stephan Kullberg, Leif Nilsson, Glenn Schiller, Ken Burwall (80 Peter Mörk), Jens Fjellström, Niklas Karlström (72 Krister Nordin), Thomas Lundmark, Mikael Martinsson, Peter Skoog.
Trainer: Lennart Wass
Goals: Ragnarsson (55, 57), Arnthorsson (89)

TRABZONSPOR v FC BARCELONA 1-0 (0-0)
Avni Aker, Trabzon   19.09.1990
Referee: Lajos Németh (HUN)   Attendance: 21,352
TRABZONSPOR: Levent Ümit; Şeyhmuz Suna, Ogün Temizkanoğlu, Kemal Serdar, Mehmet Arslan, Soner Boz, Ünal Karaman, Lemi Çelik, Orhan Çıkrıkçı, Hamdi Aslan (74 Ismail Gökçek), Milonja Djukić.   Trainer: Özkan Sümer
FC BARCELONA: Andoni ZUBIZARRETA Urreta; Fernando Muñoz García "NANDO", Ronald Koeman, Ricardo Jesús SERNA Orozco, EUSEBIO Sacristán Mena (82 Miquel SOLER Sarasols), Guillermo AMOR Martínez, Albert FERRER Llopis, Jon Andoni GOIKOETXEA, José María BAKERO Escudero, Aitor BEGUIRISTÁIN Mújica, Hristo Stoichkov (46 Julio SALINAS Fernández).   Trainer: Johan Cruyff
Goal: Hamdi (67)

DJURGÅRDENS IF STOCKHOLM
v FRAM REYKJAVÍK 1-1 (0-1)
Stockholm   3.10.1990
Referee: Eero Aho (FIN)   Attendance: 956
DJURGÅRDENS: Anders Almgren; Glenn Schiller, Stephan Kullberg, Kenneth Bergqvist, Leif Nilsson, Thomas Lundmark (75 Peter Mörk), Niklas Karlström (57 Mikael Martinsson), Ken Burwall, Jens Fjellström, Krister Nordin, Anders Nilsson.
Trainer: Lennart Wass
FRAM: Birkir Kristinsson; Jón Sveinsson, Vidar Thorkelsson, Kristján Jónsson; Ríkhardur Dadason, Steinar Gudgeirsson, Kristinn R. Jónsson, Pétur Arnthórsson, Pétur Ormslev, Anton Bjorn Markusson, Jón Erling Ragnarsson (67 Baldur Bjarnason).
Trainer: Asgeir Elíasson
Goals: Ormslev (9 pen), Martinsson (81)

FC BARCELONA v TRABZONSPOR 7-2 (5-1)
Camp Nou, Barcelona   3.10.1990
Referee: Joseph Bertram Worrall (ENG)   Att: 35,000
FC BARCELONA: Andoni ZUBIZARRETA Urreta; Fernando Muñoz García "NANDO", Ronald Koeman, Albert FERRER Llopis, Ricardo Jesús SERNA Orozco, José María BAKERO Escudero (46 Julio SALINAS Fernández), Jon Andoni GOIKOETXEA, Hristo Stoichkov, Michael Laudrup (67 Luis María LÓPEZ REKARTE), Guillermo AMOR Martínez, Aitor BEGUIRISTÁIN Mújica.   Trainer: Johan Cruyff
TRABZONSPOR: Vukašin Petranović; Şeyhmuz Suna, Ogün Temizkanoğlu (46 Ismail Gökçek), Kemal Serdar, Mehmet Arslan, Lemi Çelik, Soner Boz, Turgut Uçar, Orhan Çıkrıkçı, Hamdi Aslan (46 Goran Ivanović), Hami Mandirali.
Trainer: Özkan Sümer
Goals: Hamdi (7), Beguiristáin (13), Amor (29), R. Koeman (32, 40, 76 pen), Stoichkov (44, 87), Soner (68)

FC SLIVEN v JUVENTUS TORINO 0-2 (0-1)
Hadzhi Dimitar, Sliven   19.09.1990
Referee: Ignatius van Swieten (HOL)   Attendance: 19,000
SLIVEN: Dencho Iorgov; Kiril Kirilov, Ivan Mitev, Vasil Tinchev, Velian Parushev, Ivan Vasilev (75 Rumen Iliev), Zhivko Kelepov, Christian Penev (54 Valentin Stefanov), Iordan Lechkov, Panaiot Vandev, Valeri Valkov.   Trainer: Stoian Gurkov
JUVENTUS: Stefano Tacconi; Nicolo Napoli, JÚLIO CÉSAR Silva, Daniele Fortunato (81 Roberto Galia), Marco De Marchi, Luigi de Agostini, Thomas Hässler, Giancarlo Marocchi, Pierluigi Casiraghi (72 Paolo di Canio), Roberto Baggio, Salvatore Schillaci.   Trainer: Luigi Maifredi
Goals: Schillaci (26), R. Baggio (88 pen)

JUVENTUS TORINO v FC SLIVEN 6-1 (3-0)
Delle Alpi, Torino   3.10.1990
Referee: David Syme (SCO)   Attendance: 9,765
JUVENTUS: Stefano Tacconi; Gianluca Luppi, Dario Bonetti, Eugenio Corini, JÚLIO CÉSAR Silva, Luigi de Agostini, Thomas Hässler, Giancarlo Marocchi (58 Roberto Galia), Paolo di Canio, Roberto Baggio, Salvatore Schillaci (55 Massimo Orlando).   Trainer: Luigi Maifredi
SLIVEN: Dencho Iorgov; Valentin Stefanov, Ivan Mitev, Vasil Tinchev, Velian Parushev, Vitali Mutafchiev (46 Petar Ivanov), Zhivko Kelepov, Christian Penev, Iordan Lechkov, Panaiot Vandev (75 Rumen Iliev), Doncho Vasilev.
Trainer: Stoian Gurkov
Goals: R. Baggio (15 pen, 18), Schillaci (25), Corini (49), Bonetti (52), Júlio César (56), Kelepov (85)

**KUOPIO PALLOSEURA
v DYNAMO KIEV 2-2** (1-1)
Väinölänniemi, Kuopio   19.09.1990
Referee: Egil Nervik (NOR)   Attendance: 2,460
KuPS: Jyrki Rovio; Jyrki Houtsonen, Kari Tissari, Tuomo Hyvärinen, Markku Raatikainen (23 Janne Savolainen), Kai Nyyssönen (63 Yrjö Happonen), Kari Niskanen, Hannu Turunen, Timo Vesterinen, Marcus Gayle, Jukka Turunen.
Trainer: Martti Räsänen
DINAMO: Viktor Chanov; Sergei Shmatovalenko, Andrei Bal, Andrei Aleksanenkov, Anatoli Demianenko, Vasili Rats, Andrei Annenkov, Gennadi Litovchenko, Oleg Salenko, Sergei Kovalets, Sergei Yuran.   Trainer: Anatoli Puzach
Goals: Salenko (11), Nyyssönen (38), Yuran (66), Gayle (90)

VIKING STAVANGER v RFC LIÈGE 0-2 (0-1)
Stavanger stadium   19.09.1990
Referee: George Smith (SCO)   Atendancet: 1,845
VIKING: Lars Gaute Bø; Kent Christiansen, Ingve Henrik Bøe, Egil Fjetland, Roger Nilsen, Rune Gjerde, Trond Egil Soltvedt, Kenneth Storvik (78 Øivind Mellomstrand), Gunnar Aase (78 Endre Tangen), Alf Kåre Tveit, Gaute Johannessen.
Trainer: Benny Lennartsson
RFC LIÈGE: Jacky Munaron; Bernard Wégria, Frédéric Waseige, Boris Henry, Jean-François de Sart, Moreno Giusto, Danny Boffin (71 Luc Ernes), Didier Quain; Edi Krncevic, Cvijan Milosevic (86 Vincent Machiels), Nebojsa Malbasa.
Trainer: Robert Waseige
Goals: Boffin (15), Ernes (82)

**DYNAMO KIEV
v KUOPIO PALLOSEURA 4-0** (2-0)
Republikanskiy, Kiev   3.10.1990
Referee: Deda Sadik (TUR)   Attendance: 28,500
DINAMO: Viktor Chanov; Boris Derkach, Akhrik Tsveiba, Andrei Aleksanenkov, Sergei Shmatovalenko, Vasili Rats, Andrei Annenkov, Gennadi Litovchenko, Oleg Salenko, Sergei Kovalets, Sergei Yuran.   Trainer: Anatoli Puzach
KuPS: Jyrki Rovio; Jyrki Houtsonen, Kari Tissari, Tuomo Hyvärinen, Janne Savolainen (57 Yrjö Happonen), Harri Nyyssönen, Kari Niskanen, Hannu Turunen, Jukka Turunen, Timo Vesterinen (81 Jorma Väinikäinen), Marcus Gayle.
Trainer: Martti Räsänen
Goals: Salenko (14), Litovchenko (25, 54), Yuran (85)

RFC LIÈGE v VIKING STAVANGER 3-0 (2-0)
Jules George, Liège   3.10.1990
Referee: Josè Alberto Veiga Trigo (POR)   Attendance: 2,570
RFC LIÈGE: Jacky Munaron; Bernard Wégria (46 Luc Ernes), Jean-François de Sart, Moreno Giusto; Vincent Machiels, Cvijan Milosevic, Didier Quain, Jean-Marie Houben (73 Bernard Habrant), Danny Boffin, Edi Krncevic, Nebojsa Malbasa.   Trainer: Robert Waseige
VIKING: Lars Gaute Bø; Kent Christiansen, Ingve Henrik Bøe, Egil Fjetland, Roger Nilsen, Rune Gjerde, Trond Egil Soltvedt, Kenneth Storvik, Gunnar Aase, Knut Hammer Larsen (57 Kjell Jonevret), Gaute Johannessen.
Trainer: Benny Lennartsson
Goals: Boffin (22, 35, 88)

**GLENTORAN BELFAST
v STEAUA BUCUREŞTI 1-1** (0-0)
The Oval, Belfast   19.09.1990
Referee: Tore Hollung (NOR)   Attendance: 2,163
GLENTORAN: Dean Smyth; George Neill, Conor McCaffrey, John Devine, Terry Moore; Robert Bowers, Raymond Campbell, Johnny Jameson, Raymond Morrison (88 Billy Totten); Stephen Douglas, Ron Manley (68 Gary McCartney).
Managers: Tommy Jackson & Billy McCullough
STEAUA: Dumitru Stîngaciu ; Dan Petrescu, Adrian Bumbescu, Ştefan Iovan, Nicolae Ungureanu; Iulian Minea II (73 Constantin Pistol), Daniel Minea, Tony Sedecaru, Ilie Dumitrescu; Ovidiu Lazăr (89 Adrian Săvoiu), Ilie Stan.   Trainer: Costică Ştefănescu
Goals: Stan (47 pen), Douglas (84)

**STEAUA BUCUREŞTI
v GLENTORAN BELFAST 5-0** (3-0)

Steaua Bucureşti   3.10.1990

Referee: Arsen Hoxha (ALB)   Attendance: 7,000

STEAUA: Dumitru Stîngaciu; Dan Petrescu, Ştefan Iovan, Adrian Bumbescu, Nicolae Ungureanu; Tony Sedecaru, Daniel Minea, Ilie Stan (58 Constantin Pistol), Ilie Dumitrescu; Adrian Săvoiu (46 Iulian Minea), Ovidiu Lazăr.
Trainer: Costică Ştefănescu

GLENTORAN: Dean Smyth; George Neill, John Devine, Terry Moore, Conor McCaffrey; Raymond Morrison, William Caskey, Robert Bowers (46 Johnny Jameson), Raymond Campbell; Gary McCartney, Ron Manley.   Manager: Tommy Jackson

Sent off: Caskey (66)

Goals: Stan (21), Dumitrescu (37, 45), Petrescu (80, 88)

**LEGIA WARSZAWA
v SWIFT HESPERANGE 3-0** (0-0)

Wojska Polskiego, Warszawa   19.09.1990

Referee: Kaj Natri (FIN)   Attendance: 4,172

LEGIA: Maciej Szczesny; Miroslaw Modzelewski (69 Dariusz Czykier), Arkadiusz Gmur, Krzysztof Budka, Dariusz Kubicki, Jacek Bak, Leszek Pisz, Krzysztof Iwanicki, Jacek Cyzio (63 Andrzej Latka), Roman Kosecki, Albert Swietlik.
Trainer: Wladyslaw Stachurski

SWIFT: Alain Schumacher; Marc Lang, Marc Burggraf, Roby Cillien (80 Henri Wingert), John Schleck, Marc Brittner, Antoine Van Rijswick (75 Dragan Vrebac), Claude Mangen, Frank Deville, Robert Axmann, Laurent Deville.   Trainer: Jean Fiedler

Goals: Kosecki (48, 79), L. Pisz (90)

WREXHAM v LYNGBY BK 0-0

Racecourse Ground, Wrexham   19.09.1990

Referee: Frans van den Wijngaert (BEL)   Attendance: 3,417

WREXHAM: Mark Morris; Wayne Phillips, Nigel Beaumont, Gareth Owen, Mike Williams, Mark Sertori, Graham Cooper, Brian Flynn (65 Geoff Hunter), Andrew Preece, Gary Worthington, John Bowden.   Manager: Brian Flynn

LYNGBY: Jan Rindom; Hasse Kuhn, Morten Wieghorst, Michael Gothenborg, Claus Christiansen, John Larsen, John Helt, Michael Schäfer, Flemming Christensen, Steen Rode (46 Vetle Andersen), Allan Kuhn.   Trainer: Kim Lyshøj Sørensen

**SWIFT HESPERANGE
v LEGIA WARSZAWA 0-3** (0-0)

Stade de la Frontière, Esch-sur-Alzette   3.10.1990

Referee: Hans-Peter Dellwing (GER)   Attendance: 518

SWIFT: Alain Schumacher (80 Marc Muschter); Marc Lang, Roby Cillien, Marc Burggraf, Marc Brittner, Claude Mangen, Dragan Vrebac, Frank Deville (70 Gary Schmitz), Antoine Van Rijswick, Robert Axmann, Laurent Deville.
Trainer: Jean Fiedler

LEGIA: Maciej Szczesny; Dariusz Kubicki, Arkadiusz Gmur, Krzysztof Budka, Marek Józwiak, Dariusz Czykier (83 Artur Kupiec), Leszek Pisz, Krzysztof Iwanicki, Andrzej Latka, Roman Kosecki, Jacek Cyzio (76 Albert Swietlik).
Trainer: Wladyslaw Stachurski

Goals: Józwiak (60), Latka (82), Kosecki (88)

LYNGBY BK v WREXHAM 0-1 (0-1)

Lyngby stadium   3.10.1990

Referee: Jiří Stiegler (CZE)   Attendance: 1,548

LYNGBY: Jan Rindom; Hasse Kuhn, Morten Wieghorst, Michael Gothenborg, Claus Christiansen, John Larsen, John Helt, Steen Rode (65 Knut Clem), Flemming Christensen, Olav Kirchhoff (58 Kim Rasmussen), Allan Kuhn.
Trainer: Kim Lyshøj Sørensen

WREXHAM: Mark Morris; Wayne Phillips, Alan Kennedy, Gareth Owen, Mike Williams, Mark Sertori, Graham Cooper (45 Darren Wright), Brian Flynn, Christopher Armstrong, Gary Worthington, John Bowden.   Manager: Brian Flynn

Goal: Armstrong (10)

MANCHESTER UNITED v PÉCSI MSC 2-0 (2-0)

Old Trafford, Manchester   19.09.1990

Referee: Mario van der Ende (HOL)   Attendance: 28,411

MANCHESTER UNITED: Leslie Sealey, Dennis Irwin, Clayton Blackmore, Stephen Bruce, Mike Phelan, Gary Pallister, Neil Webb, Paul Ince (69 Lee Sharpe), Brian McClair, Mark Robins (79 Mark Hughes), Russell Beardsmore.
Manager: Alex Ferguson

PÉCSI MSC: László Bodnár; Mihály Kónya, Károly Braun, János Palaczky (82 Sándor Czérna), Zoltán Balog, Balázs Bérczy, Ferenc Lovász (74 Lajos Bojás), János Tomka, László Czéh, Károly Megyeri, István Lehota.   Trainer: József Garami

Goals: Blackmore (10), Webb (17)

PÉCSI MSC v MANCHESTER UNITED 0-1 (0-0)

PMSC Pécsi 3.10.1990

Referee: Zoran Petrović (YUG)   Attendance: 16,500

PÉCSI MSC: László Bodnár; Mihály Kónya, Sándor Czérna, János Palaczky, Zoltán Balog, Balázs Bérczy, Ferenc Lovász, Károly Braun, László Czéh, Károly Megyeri, István Lehota (72 Lajos Bojás).   Trainer: József Garami

MANCHESTER UNITED: Leslie Sealey; Vivian Anderson, Malachy Donaghy, Stephen Bruce, Mike Phelan, Gary Pallister, Neil Webb, Clayton Blackmore, Brian McClair, Mark Hughes, Lee Martin (86 Lee Sharpe).   Manager: Alex Ferguson

Goal: McClair (78)

PSV SCHWERIN v AUSTRIA WIEN 0-2 (0-2)

Dynamo Schwerin 19.09.1990

Referee: John Nielsen (DEN)   Attendance: 835

PSV SCHWERIN: Dirk Minklei; Gerbert Eggert, Peter Herzberg, Gunnar Bast (67 Frank Beutling), Mario Drews, Frank Prange, Olaf Hirsch, Ulrich Ruppach, Steffen Benthin, André Korth, Sven Buchsteiner (46 Steffen Baumgart). Trainer: Manfred Radtke

AUSTRIA: Franz Wohlfahrt; Ernst Aigner, Robert Frind, Walter Hörmann, Anton Pfeffer, Christian Prosenik, Peter Stöger (46 Thomas Flögel), Manfred Zsak, Evgeny Milewski, Hannes Pleva (79 Manfred Nastl), Ralph Hasenhüttl. Trainer: Herbert Prohaska

Goals: Milewski (34), Zsak (36)

**NEA SALAMIS FAMAGUSTA
v ABERDEEN FC 0-2** (0-0)

Antonis Papadopoulos, Larnaca 19.09.1990

Referee: Octavian Ştreng (ROM)   Attendance: 8,000

NEA SALAMIS: Hristakis Hristofi; Artemis Andreou, Kypros Tsingelis, Elisseos Psaras, Floros Nikolaou, Kenny Dyer, Pambis Andreou, Takis David (68 Stavrakis Efthymiou), Nigel McNeal (85 Vasos Mavros), Ilias Ilia, Vaggelis Adamou. Trainer: Bojil Kolev

ABERDEEN: Theo Snelders; Stewart McKimmie, David Robertson, Brian Grant, Alex McLeish, Brian Irvine, Peter Van de Ven, Paul Mason (85 Eoin Jess), James Bett, Scott Booth (72 Gregg Watson), Hans Gillhaus.
Trainers: Alex Smith & Jocky Scott

Goals: Mason (62), Gillhaus (81)

AUSTRIA WIEN v PSV SCHWERIN 0-0

Franz-Horr, Wien 3.10.1990

Referee: Zdravko Jokić (YUG)   Attendance: 1,500

AUSTRIA: Franz Wohlfahrt; Ernst Aigner, Robert Frind, Anton Pfeffer, Walter Hörmann, Christian Prosenik, Thomas Flögel, Manfred Zsak, Evgeny Milewski, Ralph Hasenhüttl (67 Günter Quantschnigg), Hannes Pleva.
Trainer: Herbert Prohaska

PSV SCHWERIN: Thomas Raatz; Gerbert Eggert, Gunnar Bast (32 Mario Drews), Lars Petereit, Frank Beutling, Frank Prange, Olaf Hirsch, Ulrich Ruppach, Steffen Benthin, André Korth (57 Dirk Gottschalk), Sven Buchsteiner.
Trainer: Manfred Radtke

**ABERDEEN FC
v NEA SALAMIS FAMAGUSTA 3-0** (2-0)

Pittodrie Park, Aberdeen 3.10.1990

Referee: Andrew Ritchie (NIR)   Attendance: 9,884

ABERDEEN: Theo Snelders; Stewart McKimmie, Alex McLeish (62 Peter Van de Ven), Brian Irvine, David Robertson, Craig Robertson, James Bett, Robert Connor, Eoin Jess, Paul Mason (73 Lee Gardner), Hans Gillhaus.
Trainers: Alex Smith & Jocky Scott

NEA SALAMIS: Giannakis Ioannou; Artemis Andreou, Kypros Tsingelis, Eliseos Giannaki, Floros Nikolaou, Kenny Dyer, Vaggelis Adamou, Vasos Mavros, Nigel McNeal (47 Pambis Andreou), Ilias Ilia, Hristakis Georgiou.
Trainer: Bojil Kolev

Goals: C. Robertson (13), Gillhaus (33), Jess (67)

**1.FC KAISERSLAUTERN
v SAMPDORIA GENOVA 1-0** (0-0)

Fritz-Walter-Stadion, Kaiserslautern 19.09.1990

Referee: John Blankenstein (HOL)   Attendance: 32,674

1.FC KAISERSLAUTERN: Gerald Ehrmann; Miroslav Kadlec, Kay Friedmann, Thomas Dooley, Uwe Scherr (56 Guido Hoffmann), Axel Roos, Marco Haber, Markus Kranz, Frank Lelle, Demir Hotić, Stefan Kuntz.
Trainer: Karl-Heinz Feldkamp

SAMPDORIA: Gianluca Pagliuca; Antônio Carlos "Toninho" CEREZO (42 Giovanni Invernizzi), Marco Lanna, Pietro Vierchowod, Giuseppe Dossena (80 Attilio Lombardo), Fausto Pari, Srečko Katanec, Aleksei Mikhailichenko, Ivano Bonetti, Roberto Mancini, Gianluca Vialli.   Trainer: Vujadin Boškov

Goal: Kuntz (75)

SAMPDORIA GENOVA
v FC KAISERSLAUTERN 2-0 (1-0)

Luigi Ferraris, Genova   3.10.1990

Referee: Neil Midgley (ENG)   Attendance: 29,994

SAMPDORIA: Gianluca Pagliuca; Moreno Mannini, Giovanni Invernizzi, Fausto Pari, Srečko Katanec, Luca Pellegrini, Aleksei Mikhailichenko, Attilio Lombardo, Marco Branca, Roberto Mancini, Giuseppe Dossena. Trainer: Vujadin Boškov

1.FC KAISERSLAUTERN: Gerald Ehrmann; Kay Friedmann, Thomas Dooley, Uwe Scherr, Miroslav Kadlec, Frank Lelle (80 Markus Kranz), Demir Hotić, Bjarne Goldbæk, Guido Hoffmann, Marco Haber (77 Rainer Ernst), Stefan Kuntz.   Trainer: Karl-Heinz Feldkamp

Goals: Mancini (6 pen), Branca (75)

OLYMPIAKOS PEIRAIAS
v FLAMURTARI VLORË 3-1 (2-0)

Karaiskaki, Peiraias   19.09.1990

Referee: Atanas Uzunov (BUL)   Attendance: 14,907

OLYMPIAKOS: Ilias Talikriadis; Theodoros Pahatouridis, Kiriakos Karataidis, Sotiris Maurommatis, Giorgos Hristodoulou, Panagiotis Tsalouhidis, Minas Hantzidis (78 Nikos Tsiantakis), Apostolos Drakopoulos (51 Nikos Nentidis), Nikos Anastopoulos, Savvas Kofidis, Tasos Mitropoulos. Trainer: Oleg Blohin

FLAMURTARI: Anesti Arapi; Gjergji Dema, Kreshnik Çipi, Roland Iliadhi, Rrapo Taho, Viktor Daullja (49 Vasillaq Ziu), Sokol Kushta, Eqerem Memushi, Alfred Zijai, Agim Bubeqi, Latif Gjondeda (67 Viktor Paço).   Trainer: Edmond Licaj

Goals: Anastopoulos (9, 69), Hantzidis (25), Ziu (75)

FLAMURTARI VLORË
v OLYMPIAKOS PEIRAIAS 0-2 (0-0)

Flamurtari Vlorë   3.10.1990

Referee: Laszlo Molnar (HUN)   Attendance: 5,000

FLAMURTARI: Anesti Arapi; Gjergji Dema, Kreshnik Çipi, Roland Iliadhi, Rrapo Taho, Dritan Sadedini (46 Viktor Paço), Sokol Kushta, Eqerem Memushi, Alfred Zijai (62 Vasillaq Ziu), Agim Bubeqi, Latif Gjondeda.   Trainer: Edmond Licaj

OLYMPIAKOS: Ilias Talikriadis; Theodoros Pahatouridis, Kiriakos Karataidis, Sotiris Maurommatis, Nikos Nentidis, Panagiotis Tsalouhidis, Giorgos Hristodoulou, Savvas Kofidis (83 Apostolos Drakopoulos), Nikos Anastopoulos, Nikos Tsiantakis (60 Minas Hantzidis), Tasos Mitropoulos. Trainer: Oleg Blohin

Goals: Hristodoulou (84), Mitropoulos (87)

CF ESTRELA da AMADORA
v NEUCHÂTEL XAMAX 1-1 (1-0)

Estrela da Amadora stadium, Amadora   19.09.1990

Referee: Alphonse Constantin (BEL)   Attendance: 6,000

ESTRELA: Jorge Manuel Domingos Maria VITAL; DUÍLIO Dias Junior, Francisco José de Matos AGATÃO, VALÉRIO Jorge Madeira Pereira, RUI Miguel Leal das NEVES, DIMAS Manuel Marques Teixeira, António Isaías Carvalho MIRANDA (66 PEDRO Alexandre Caldas XAVIER), PAULO Jorge Gomes BENTO, Afonso ABEL de Campos, Richard Daddy Owubokiri "RICKY", Carlos Idalécio Silva "BAROTI" (76 PAULO JORGE Roque Marques).
Trainer: MANUEL José Tavares FERNANDES

XAMAX: Marco Pascolo; André Egli, Peter Lönn, Régis Rothenbühler, Walter Fernandez, Philippe Perret, Martin Jeitziner, Didier Gigon (68 Francis Froidevaux), Christophe Bonvin, Beat Sutter, Frédéric Chassot.   Trainer: Roy Hodgson

Goals: Owubokiri (26), B. Sutter (57)

NEUCHÂTEL XAMAX
v CF ESTRELA da AMADORA 1-1 (0-0, 1-1) (AET)

Stade de la Maladière, Neuchâtel   3.10.1990

Referee: Dušan Krchnak (CZE)   Attendance: 12,400

XAMAX: Marco Pascolo; Régis Rothenbühler, André Egli, Robert Lüthi (56 Froidevaux), Walter Fernandez, Didier Gigon, Martin Jeitziner, Philippe Perret, Christophe Bonvin, Beat Sutter, Frédéric Chassot (76 Stefan Lindqvist). Trainer: Roy Hodgson

ESTRELA: Jorge Manuel Domingos Maria VITAL; DUÍLIO Dias Junior, VALÉRIO Jorge Madeira Pereira, ABEL Luís da Silva Costa Xavier (61 PAULO JORGE Roque Marques), RUI Miguel Leal das NEVES, DIMAS Manuel Marques Teixeira, PAULO Jorge Gomes BENTO, António Isaías Carvalho MIRANDA, Afonso ABEL de Campos, Carlos Idalécio Silva "BAROTI" (52 Richard Daddy Owubokiri "RICKY"), Mário Alexandre Vasconcelos "MARITO".
Trainer: MANUEL José Tavares FERNANDES

Goals: B. Sutter (49), Valério (82)

Penalties: 1-0 Sutter, 1-1 Valerio, 2-1 Gigon, 2-2 Rui Neves, 3-2 Fernandez, 3-3 Dimas, Froidevaux (miss), 3-4 Paulo Jorge, Egli (miss)

MONTPELLIER HSC v PSV EINDHOVEN 1-0 (0-0)

La Mosson, Montpellier 20.09.1990

Referee: Karl-Josef Assenmacher (GER) Att: 14,404

MONTPELLIER: Claude Barrabé; Pascal Baills (81 Stephane Blondeau), Laurent Blanc, Jean Manuel Thétis, Wilbert Suvrijn, Franck Lucchesi, Vincent Guérin, Jean Claude Lemoult, Carlos Valderrama, Daniel Xuereb (87 Kader Ferhaoui), Jacek Ziober. Trainer: Henri Kasperczak

PSV: Hans Van Breukelen; Jerry De Jong, Gheorghe Popescu, Addick Koot, Stan Valckx, Jan Heintze, Gerald Vanenburg, Erwin Koeman, Jozef Chovanec (81 Kalusha Bwalya), Romário de Souza Faria, John Bosman. Trainer: Bobby Robson

Goal: Ziober (54)

PSV EINDHOVEN v MONTPELLIER HSC 0-0

Philips, Eindhoven 3.10.1990

Referee: Aleksei Spirin (USSR) Attendance: 24,500

PSV: Hans Van Breukelen; Eric Gerets, Stan Valckx, Jerry De Jong, Jan Heintze, Gerald Vanenburg, Gheorghe Popescu (54 Kalusha Bwalya), Erwin Koeman, Juul Ellerman, John Bosman (78 Twan Scheepers), Romário de Souza Faria. Trainer: Bobby Robson

MONTPELLIER: Claude Barrabé; Pascal Baills, Laurent Blanc, Franck Lucchesi, Jean Manuel Thétis, Patrick Colleter, Vincent Guérin, Jean Claude Lemoult, Wilbert Suvrijn, Jacek Ziober, Daniel Xuereb (77 Kader Ferhaoui). Trainer: Henri Kasperczak

SECOND ROUND

MANCHESTER UNITED v WREXHAM 3-0 (2-0)

Old Trafford, Manchester 23.10.1990

Referee: Antonio Martin Navarrete (SPA) Att: 29,406

MANCHESTER UNITED: Leslie Sealey; Clayton Blackmore, Lee Martin, Stephen Bruce, Lee Sharpe, Gary Pallister, Neil Webb, Paul Ince (70 Russell Beardsmore), Brian McClair, Mark Hughes, David Wallace (60 Mark Robins). Manager: Alex Ferguson

WREXHAM: Mark Morris; Wayne Phillips, Alan Kennedy, Sean Reck, Nigel Beaumont, Mike Williams (61 Geoff Hunter), Brian Flynn, Gareth Owen, Christopher Armstrong, Graham Cooper, John Bowden. Manager: Brian Flynn

Goals: McClair (42), Bruce (44 pen), Pallister (59)

WREXHAM v MANCHESTER UNITED 0-2 (0-2)

Racecourse Ground, Wrexham 7.11.1990

Referee: Milton Nielsen (DEN) Attendance: 13,327

WREXHAM: Mark Morris; Andrew Thackeray, Philip Hardy, Geoff Hunter, Nigel Beaumont, Wayne Phillips, Brian Flynn (58 Joey Jones), Gareth Owen, Christopher Armstrong (66 Kevin Jones), Lee Jones, Graham Cooper. Manager: Brian Flynn

MANCHESTER UNITED: Leslie Sealey; Dennis Irwin, Clayton Blackmore, Stephen Bruce, Mike Phelan, Gary Pallister, Neil Webb, Paul Ince (67 Malachy Donaghy), Brian McClair (59 Lee Martin), Mark Robins, David Wallace. Manager: Alex Ferguson

Goals: Robins (31), Bruce (35)

FRAM REYKJAVÍK v FC BARCELONA 1-2 (0-1)

Laugardalsvöllur, Reykjavík 23.10.1990

Referee: Rodger Gifford (WAL) Attendance: 1,321

FRAM: Birkir Kristinsson; Kristján Jónsson, Thorsteinn Thorsteinsson, Jón Sveinsson, Pétur Arnthórsson, Anton Björn Markússon (81 Gudmundur Páll Gíslason), Kristinn R. Jónsson, Baldur Bjarnason, Steinar Gudgeirsson (77 Haukur Pálmason), Jón Erling Ragnarsson, Ríkhardur Dadason. Trainer: Ásgeir Elíasson

FC BARCELONA: Andoni ZUBIZARRETA Urreta; Fernando Muñoz García "NANDO", Luis María LÓPEZ REKARTE, José Ramón ALESANCO Ventosa, Aitor BEGUIRISTÁIN Mújica (46 URBANO Ortega Cuadros), Ronald Koeman, Guillermo AMOR Martínez, EUSEBIO Sacristán Mena, Michael Laudrup (60 Miquel SOLER Sarasols), Hristo Stoichkov, Julio SALINAS Fernández. Trainer: Johan Cruyff

Goals: J. Salinas (32), Dadason (60), Stoichkov (86)

FC BARCELONA v FRAM REYKJAVÍK 3-0 (2-0)

Camp Nou, Barcelona 7.11.1990

Referee: Stavros Zakestidis (GRE) Attendance: 17,300

FC BARCELONA: Andoni ZUBIZARRETA Urreta; Albert FERRER Llopis (66 Luis María LÓPEZ REKARTE), José Ramón ALESANCO Ventosa, Ricardo Jesús SERNA Orozco; Miquel SOLER Sarasols, EUSEBIO Sacristán Mena, Guillermo AMOR Martínez, Julio SALINAS Fernández, Hristo Stoichkov (51 Antonio PINILLA Miranda), Michael Laudrup, Aitor BEGUIRISTÁIN Mújica. Trainer: Johan Cruyff

FRAM: Birkir Kristinsson; Jón Sveinsson, Kristján Jónsson, Pétur Ormslev, Vidar Thorkelsson; Kristinn R. Jónsson, Pétur Arnthorsson (85 Haukur Pálmason), Jón Erling Ragnarsson (64 Anton Björn Markússon), Baldur Bjarnason, Steinar Gudgeirsson, Ríkhardur Dadason. Trainer: Ásgeir Elíasson

Goals: Eusebio (17), Beguiristáin (33), Pinilla (69)

DYNAMO KYIV v DUKLA PRAHA 1-0 (0-0)

Republikanskiy, Kiev 24.10.1990

Referee: Borislav Aleksandrov (BUL)   Attendances: 42,500

DINAMO: Viktor Chanov; Boris Derkach, Akhrik Tsveiba, Andrei Aleksanenkov, Sergei Shmatovalenko, Vasili Rats, Andrei Annenkov, Gennadi Litovchenko, Sergei Kovalets (60 Sergei Zaets), Ivan Yaremchuk, Oleg Salenko. Trainer: Anatoli Puzach

DUKLA: Josef Novák; Jan Suchopárek (79 Pavel Karoch), Václav Rada, Jiří Záleski, Ales Foldyna, Marián Kopca; Günter Bittengel, Edvard Lasota, Radoslav Látal, Jozef Kostelník (87 Daniel Smejkal), Dušan Fitzel.   Trainer: Ivo Viktor

Goal: Litovchenko (65)

SAMPDORIA GENOVA v OLYMPIAKOS PEIRAIAS 3-1 (2-0)

Luigi Ferraris, Genova 7.11.1990

Referee: Emilio Soriano Aladren (SPA)   Attendance: 23,745

SAMPDORIA: Gianluca Pagliuca; Moreno Mannini, Srečko Katanec, Fausto Pari, Pietro Vierchowod, Attilio Lombardo, Aleksei Mikhailichenko (69 Giovanni Invernizzi), Antônio Carlos "Toninho" CEREZO (43 Marco Lanna), Gianluca Vialli, Marco Branca, Giuseppe Dossena.   Trainer: Vujadin Boškov

OLYMPIAKOS: Ilias Talikriadis; Theodoros Pahatouridis, Kiriakos Karataidis, Sotiris Maurommatis, Nikos Nentidis (82 Panagiotis Sofianopoulos), Panagiotis Tsalouhidis, Nikos Tsiantakis, Savvas Kofidis, Nikos Anastopoulos, Minas Hantzidis (59 Apostolos Drakopoulos), Tasos Mitropoulos. Trainer: Oleg Blohin

Goals: Branca (17, 66), Lombardo (29), Drakopoulos (62)

DUKLA PRAHA v DYNAMO KYIV 2-2 (0-1)

Stadión na Julisce, Praha 7.11.1990

Referee: Piotr Werner (POL)   Attendance: 2,191

DUKLA: Josef Novák; Dušan Fitzel, Jiří Záleski, Václav Rada, Marián Kopca; Ales Foldyna, Pavel Karoch (90 Daniel Smejkal), Edvard Lasota (68 Jan Suchopárek), Radoslav Látal, Günter Bittengel, Jozef Kostelník.   Trainer: Ivo Viktor

DINAMO: Viktor Chanov; Boris Derkach, Akhrik Tsveiba, Andrei Aleksanenkov, Sergei Shmatovalenko, Ivan Yaremchuk (70 Sergei Zaets), Gennadi Litovchenko, Andrei Annenkov, Vasili Rats, Oleg Salenko (77 Sergei Kovalets), Sergei Yuran. Trainer: Anatoli Puzach

Goals: Yuran (6, 60), Foldyna (51), Bittengel (72)

MONTPELLIER HSC v STEAUA BUCUREŞTI 5-0 (1-0)

La Mosson, Montpellier 24.10.1990

Referee: Carlos Silva Valente (POR)   Attendance: 18,869

MONTPELLIER: Claude Barrabe; Pascal Bails, Michel Der Zakarian, Laurent Blanc, Franck Lucchesi; Jean Claude Lemoult, Wilbert Suvrijn, Kader Ferhaoui (11 Laurent Castro), Carlos Valderrama; Daniel Xuereb, Jacek Ziober. Trainer: Henri Kasperczak

STEAUA: Dumitru Stîngaciu; Dan Petrescu, Adrian Bumbescu, Ştefan Iovan, Dănuţ Munteanu; Daniel Minea, Tony Sedecaru, Ilie Stan, Ilie Dumitrescu (85 Iulian Minea); Marian Popa, Ovidiu Lazăr (59 Cornel Mirea).   Trainer: Costică Ştefănescu

Sent off: Popa (22), Petrescu (79)

Goals: Ziober (27, 62), Xuereb (51), Blanc (56 pen), Castro (81)

OLYMPIAKOS PEIRAIAS v SAMPDORIA GENOVA 0-1 (0-0)

Karaiskaki, Athina 24.10.1990

Referee: George Courtney (ENG)   Attendance: 14,289

OLYMPIAKOS: Ilias Talikriadis; Theodoros Pahatouridis, Kiriakos Karataidis, Sotiris Maurommatis, Giorgos Hristodoulou, Panagiotis Tsalouhidis, Nikos Tsiantakis (72 Minas Hantzidis), Savvas Kofidis, Nikos Anastopoulos, Ilias Savvidis, Tasos Mitropoulos.   Trainer: Oleg Blohin

SAMPDORIA: Gianluca Pagliuca; Moreno Mannini, Attilio Lombardo, Fausto Pari, Srečko Katanec, Luca Pellegrini, Aleksei Mikhailichenko, Antônio Carlos "Toninho" CEREZO (46 Giovanni Invernizzi), Marco Branca (83 Marco Lanna), Roberto Mancini, Giuseppe Dossena.   Trainer: Vujadin Boškov

Goal: Katanec (53)

STEAUA BUCUREŞTI v MONTPELLIER HSC 0-3 (0-0)

Steaua Bucureşti 7.11.1990

Referee: Erik Fredriksson (SWE)   Attendance: 4,000

STEAUA: Daniel Gherasim; Tony Sedecaru, Adrian Bumbescu, Ştefan Iovan, Dănuţ Munteanu; Daniel Minea, Ilie Dumitrescu, Constantin Pistol, Cornel Mirea (62 Sandu Beca); Ovidiu Lazăr, Adrian Săvoiu.   Trainer: Costică Ştefănescu

MONTPELLIER: Claude Barrabe; Michel Der Zakarian, Laurent Blanc, Franck Lucchesi, Patrick Colleter, Pascal Bails, Wilbert Suvrijn, Carlos Valderrama, Vincent Guérin (85 Rizzetto), Laurent Djaffo (67 Patrice Garande), Stéphane Blondeau.   Trainer: Henri Kasperczak

Goals: Colleter (52), Garande (71), Guérin (82)

RFC LIÈGE v CF ESTRELA da AMADORA 2-0 (1-0)

Stade Jules George, Liège 24.10.1990

Referee: Wieland Ziller (GER) Attendance: 4,809

RFC LIÈGE: Jacky Munaron; Bernard Wégria, Jean-François de Sart, Moreno Giusto, Jean-Marie Houben, Cvijan Milosevic, Didier Quain (56 Vincent Machiels), Danny Boffin, Luc Ernes, Edi Krncevic, Nebojsa Malbasa. Trainer: Robert Waseige

ESTRELA: Jorge Manuel Domingos Maria VITAL; RUI Miguel Leal das NEVES, DUÍLIO Dias Junior, VALÉRIO Jorge Madeira Pereira, DIMAS Manuel Marques Teixeira, António Isaías Carvalho MIRANDA, Afonso ABEL de Campos, Carlos Idalécio Silva "BAROTI" (70 PAULO JORGE Roque Marques), ABEL Luís da Silva Costa Xavier, PAULO Jorge Gomes BENTO, Mário Alexandre Vasconcelos "MARITO" (60 Richard Daddy Owubokiri "RICKY").
Trainer: MANUEL José Tavares FERNANDES

Goals: Malbasa (7), Milosevic (86)

CF ESTRELA da AMADORA v RFC LIÈGE 1-0 (1-0)

Estrela da Amadora stadium, Amadora 7.11.1990

Referee: John Spillane (IRE) Attendance: 10,000

ESTRELA: Joaquim Alberto Castanheira de MELO; DUÍLIO Dias Junior, ABEL Luís da Silva Costa Xavier, PAULO JORGE Roque Marques, Joaquim Gonçalves REBELO, Mário Alexandre Vasconcelos "MARITO", António Isaías Carvalho MIRANDA, PAULO Jorge Gomes BENTO, Afonso ABEL de Campos, Richard Daddy Owubokiri "RICKY", Carlos Idalécio Silva "BAROTI" (68 Sabino MENDES Vieira Saraiva). Trainer: MANUEL José Tavares FERNANDES

RFC LIÈGE: Jacky Munaron; Bernard Wégria, Jean-François de Sart, Moreno Giusto, Vincent Machiels, Jean-Marie Houben (73 Danny Boffin), Didier Quain, Cvijan Milosevic, Luc Ernes; Edi Krncevic, Nebojsa Malbasa. Trainer: Robert Waseige

Goal: Duilio (32)

ABERDEEN FC v LEGIA WARSZAWA 0-0

Pittodrie Park, Aberdeen 24.10.1990

Referee: José Francisco CONCEIÇÃO SILVA (POR) Attendance: 15,946

ABERDEEN: Michael Watt; Stewart McKimmie, David Robertson, Brian Grant, Alex McLeish, Brian Irvine, Peter Van de Ven (82 Craig Robertson), James Bett, Paul Mason, Robert Connor, Hans Gillhaus. Trainers: Alex Smith & Jocky Scott

LEGIA: Maciej Szczesny; Dariusz Kubicki, Arkadiusz Gmur, Marek Józwiak, Krzysztof Budka, Dariusz Czykier, Leszek Pisz (19 Miroslaw Modzelewski), Krzysztof Iwanicki, Andrzej Latka, Roman Kosecki, Jacek Cyzio.
Trainer: Wladyslaw Stachurski

LEGIA WARSZAWA v ABERDEEN FC 1-0

Wojska Polskiego, Warszawa 7.11.1990

Referee: Leif Sundell (SWE) Attendance: 5,665

LEGIA: Maciej Szczesny; Dariusz Kubicki, Arkadiusz Gmur, Marek Józwiak, Krzysztof Budka, Dariusz Czykier, Jacek Bak, Krzysztof Iwanicki, Miroslaw Modzelewski, Roman Kosecki, Jacek Cyzio. Trainer: Wladyslaw Stachurski

ABERDEEN: Michael Watt; Stewart McKimmie, Alex McLeish, Brian Irvine, David Robertson, Brian Grant, Peter Van de Ven, James Bett, Robert Connor, Paul Mason (83 Eoin Jess), Hans Gillhaus. Trainers: Alex Smith & Jocky Scott

Goal: Iwanicki (85)

AUSTRIA WIEN v JUVENTUS TORINO 0-4 (0-2)

Franz-Horr, Wien 24.10.1990

Referee: Guy Goethals (BEL) Attendance: 10,000

AUSTRIA: Franz Wohlfarth; Robert Frind, Ernst Aigner (73 Attila Sekerlioglu), Anton Pfeffer, Christian Prosenik, Manfred Zsak, Peter Stöger, Evgeny Milewski (64 Thomas Flögel), Walter Hörmann, Hannes Pleva, Ralph Hasenhüttl.
Trainer: Herbert Prohaska

JUVENTUS: Stefano Tacconi; Dario Bonetti, JÚLIO CÉSAR Silva, Daniele Fortunato, Marco De Marchi (43 Roberto Galia), Luigi de Agostini, Thomas Hässler, Giancarlo Marocchi (71 Angelo Alessio), Pierluigi Casiraghi, Roberto Baggio, Salvatore Schillaci. Trainer: Luigi Maifredi

Goals: Casiraghi (30, 45), R. Baggio (49), Schillaci (70 pen)

JUVENTUS TORINO v AUSTRIA WIEN 4-0 (2-0)

Delle Alpi, Torino 7.11.1990

Referee: Bruno Galler (SWI) Attendance: 12,082

JUVENTUS: Stefano Tacconi; Nicolo Napoli, Dario Bonetti, Eugenio Corini, JÚLIO CÉSAR Silva (64 Gianluca Luppi), Luigi de Agostini, Thomas Hässler (23 Roberto Galia), Angelo Alessio, Salvatore Schillaci, Roberto Baggio, Paolo di Canio. Trainer: Luigi Maifredi

AUSTRIA: Franz Wohlfarth; Ernst Aigner, Attila Sekerlioglu, Robert Frind, Manfred Zsak, Walter Hörmann, Hannes Pleva, Evgeny Milewski (63 Christian Prosenik), Harald Schneider, Peter Stöger, Ralph Hasenhüttl (63 Thomas Flögel).
Trainer: Herbert Prohaska

Goals: Alessio (3), R. Baggio (25 pen, 46, 52)

QUARTER-FINALS

MANCHESTER UNITED
v MONTPELLIER HSC 1-1 (1-1)
Old Trafford, Manchester   6.03.1991
Referee: Pierluigi Pairetto (ITA)   Attendance: 41,942
MANCHESTER UNITED: Leslie Sealey, Clayton Blackmore, Malachy Donaghy, Gary Pallister, Lee Martin (58 David Wallace), Mike Phelan, Bryan Robson, Paul Ince, Brian McClair, Mark Hughes, Lee Sharpe.   Manager: Alex Ferguson
MONTPELLIER: Claude Barrabé; Pascal Baills, Michel Der Zakarian, Laurent Blanc, Franck Lucchesi, Vincent Guérin, Jean Claude Lemoult, Wilbert Suvrijn (88 Régis Brouard), Patrick Colleter, Clément Garcia (84 Daniel Xuereb), Jacek Ziober.   Trainer: Henri Kasperczak
Goals: McClair (1), Martin (7 og)

MONTPELLIER HSC
v MANCHESTER UNITED 0-2 (0-1)
La Mosson, Montpellier   19.03.1991
Referee: Hubert Forstinger (AUS)   Attendance: 20,433
MONTPELLIER: Claude Barrabé; Wilbert Suvrijn, Jean Manuel Thétis, Laurent Blanc, Franck Lucchesi, Régis Brouard (52 Daniel Xuereb), Jean Claude Lemoult, Carlos Valderrama, Patrick Colleter, Clément Garcia, Jacek Ziober (66 Patrice Garande). Trainer: Henri Kasperczak
MANCHESTER UNITED: Leslie Sealey, Dennis Irwin, Stephen Bruce, Gary Pallister, Clayton Blackmore, Mike Phelan, Bryan Robson, Paul Ince (46 Lee Martin), Brian McClair, Mark Hughes, Lee Sharpe.   Manager: Alex Ferguson
Goals: Blackmore (45), Bruce (49 pen)

LEGIA WARSZAWA
v SAMPDORIA GENOVA 1-0 (1-0)
Wojska Polskiego, Warszawa   6.03.1991
Referee: Serge Muhmenthaler (SWI)   Attendance: 7,028
LEGIA: Maciej Szczesny; Dariusz Kubicki, Arkadiusz Gmur, Jacek Bak, Piotr Czachowski, Dariusz Czykier, Leszek Pisz, Krzysztof Iwanicki, Andrzej Latka (10 Artur Salamon, 45 Wojciech Kowalczyk), Jacek Sobczak, Jacek Cyzio. Trainer: Wladyslaw Stachurski
SAMPDORIA: Gianluca Pagliuca; Moreno Mannini, Marco Lanna, Pietro Vierchowod, Fausto Pari, Attilio Lombardo, Srećko Katanec, Antônio Carlos "Toninho" CEREZO, Marco Branca, Roberto Mancini, Giuseppe Dossena. Trainer: Vujadin Boškov
Goal: Czykier (44)

SAMPDORIA GENOVA
v LEGIA WARSZAWA 2-2 (0-1)
Luigi Ferraris, Genova   20.03.1991
Referee: Wieland Ziller (GER)   Attendance: 25,860
SAMPDORIA: Gianluca Pagliuca; Moreno Mannini, Fausto Pari, Pietro Vierchowod (46 Marco Branca), Attilio Lombardo, Marco Lanna, Antônio Carlos "Toninho" CEREZO, Aleksei Mikhailichenko (56 Ivano Bonetti), Giuseppe Dossena, Gianluca Vialli, Roberto Mancini.   Trainer: Vujadin Boškov
LEGIA: Maciej Szczesny; Dariusz Kubicki, Arkadiusz Gmur, Piotr Czachowski, Jacek Bak (69 Marek Józwiak), Leszek Pisz, Jacek Sobczak, Krzysztof Iwanicki, Dariusz Czykier, Wojciech Kowalczyk (78 Artur Kupiec), Jacek Cyzio. Trainer: Wladyslaw Stachurski
Goals: Kowalczyk (19, 54), Mancini (67), Vialli (88).

DYNAMO KYIV v FC BARCELONA 2-3 (1-2)
Republikanskiy, Kiev   6.03.1991
Referee: David Syme (SCO)   Attendance: 96,000
DINAMO: Aleksandr Zhidkov; Oleg Luzhny, Boris Derkach, Yuri Moroz, Akhrik Tsveiba, Stepan Betsa, Sergei Shmatovalenko, Sergei Zaets, Oleg Salenko, Nikolai Yurchenko (69 Oleg Matveev), Sergei Yuran.   Trainer: Anatoli Puzach
FC BARCELONA: Andoni ZUBIZARRETA Urreta; Sebastián HERRERA, José Ramón ALESANCO Ventosa, EUSEBIO Sacristán Mena, Ricardo Jesús SERNA Orozco, Guillermo AMOR Martínez, José María BAKERO Escudero, URBANO Ortega Cuadros, Hristo Stoichkov, Michael Laudrup (61 Alejandro García Casaña "ALEX"), Aitor BEGUIRISTÁIN Mújica (88 Luis María LÓPEZ REKARTE).
Trainer: Carles REXACH
Goals: Baquero (5), Zaets (33), Urbano (45), Stoichkov (63 pen), Salenko (81 pen)

FC BARCELONA v DYNAMO KYIV 1-1 (0-0)
Camp Nou, Barcelona   20.03.1991
Referee: Zoran Petrović (YUG)   Attendance: 60,000
FC BARCELONA: Andoni ZUBIZARRETA Urreta; Ricardo Jesús SERNA Orozco, Albert FERRER Llopis, Ronald Koeman, Fernando Muñoz García "NANDO", Guillermo AMOR Martínez, EUSEBIO Sacristán Mena, José María BAKERO Escudero, Aitor BEGUIRISTÁIN Mújica, Julio SALINAS Fernández (50 Jon Andoni GOIKOETXEA), Hristo Stoichkov (89 URBANO Ortega Cuadros).   Trainer: Carles REXACH
DINAMO: Aleksandr Zhidkov; Sergei Kovalets, Boris Derkach, Oleg Luzhnyi, Sergei Shmatovalenko, Viktor Moroz, Nikolai Yurchenko, Stepan Betsa, Sergei Zaets, Sergei Yuran, Oleg Salenko.   Trainer: Anatoli Puzach
Goals: Yuran (62), Amor (90)

RFC LIÈGE v JUVENTUS TORINO 1-3 (0-2)

Jules George, Liège   6.03.1991

Referee: Aron Schmidhuber (GER)   Attendance: 16,463

RFC LIÈGE: Jacky Munaron; Bernard Wégria, Jean-François de Sart, Vincent Machiels (46 Moreno Giusto), Frédéric Waseige, Luc Ernes, Didier Quain, Jean-Marie Houben, Danny Boffin (63 Ronald Foguenne), Edi Krncevic, Nebojsa Malbasa. Trainer: Robert Waseige

JUVENTUS: Stefano Tacconi; Gianluca Luppi, JÚLIO CÉSAR Silva, Marco De Marchi (46 Nicolo Napoli), Luigi de Agostini, Eugenio Corini, Giancarlo Marocchi (70 Angelo Alessio), Daniele Fortunato, Thomas Hässler, Roberto Baggio, Pierluigi Casiraghi.   Trainer: Luigi Maifredi

Goals: Wegria (32 og), R. Baggio (43), Júlio César (47), Houben (83)

MANCHESTER UNITED v LEGIA WARSZAWA 1-1 (1-0)

Old Trafford, Manchester   24.04.1991

Referee: Aron Schmidhuber (GER)   Attendance: 44,269

MANCHESTER UNITED: Gary Walsh; Dennis Irwin, Clayton Blackmore (71 Malachy Donaghy), Stephen Bruce, Mike Phelan, Gary Pallister, Bryan Robson, Neil Webb, Brian McClair, Mark Hughes, Lee Sharpe.   Manager: Alex Ferguson

LEGIA: Zbigniew Robakiewicz; Dariusz Kubicki, Arkadiusz Gmur, Jacek Bak, Piotr Czachowski, Dariusz Czykier, Leszek Pisz, Krzysztof Iwanicki, Wojciech Kowalczyk, Jacek Sobczak (77 Andrzej Latka), Jacek Cyzio.
Trainer: Wladyslaw Stachurski

Goals: Sharpe (29), Kowalczyk (56)

JUVENTUS TORINO v RFC LIÈGE 3-0 (3-0)

Delle Alpi, Torino   20.03.1991

Referee: Howard King (WAL)   Attendance: 25,000

JUVENTUS: Stefano Tacconi; Nicolo Napoli (61 Dario Bonetti), JÚLIO CÉSAR Silva, Roberto Galia, Gianluca Luppi, Thomas Hässler, Daniele Fortunato, Roberto Baggio, Giancarlo Marocchi (46 Angelo Alessio), Salvatore Schillaci, Pierluigi Casiraghi.   Trainer: Luigi Maifredi

RFC LIÈGE: Jacky Munaron; Bernard Wégria, Jean-François de Sart, Moreno Giusto, Frédéric Waseige; Luc Ernes (46 Didier Quain), Jean-Marie Houben, Danny Boffin, Nebojsa Malbasa, Edi Krncevic (65 Ronald Foguenne), Zvonko Varga. Trainer: Robert Waseige

Goals: Casiraghi (9), Houben (18 og), Hässler (22)

FC BARCELONA v JUVENTUS TORINO 3-1 (0-1)

Camp Nou, Barcelona   10.04.1991

Referee: Joël Quiniou (FRA)   Attendance: 110,000

FC BARCELONA: Andoni ZUBIZARRETA Urreta; Fernando Muñoz García "NANDO", Ricardo Jesús SERNA Orozco, Ronald Koeman, Albert FERRER Llopis, Guillermo AMOR Martínez, Michael Laudrup, Jon Andoni GOIKOETXEA, Hristo Stoichkov, Julio SALINAS Fernández (85 Miquel SOLER Sarasols), Aitor BEGUIRISTÁIN Mújica (46 EUSEBIO Sacristán Mena).   Trainer: Johan Cruyff

JUVENTUS: Stefano Tacconi; Nicolò Napoli, Gianluca Luppi, JÚLIO CÉSAR Silva, Luigi de Agostini, Thomas Hässler, Daniele Fortunato, Roberto Baggio, Giancarlo Marocchi, Salvatore Schillaci (87 Paolo di Canio), Pierluigi Casiraghi (70 Eugenio Corini).   Trainer: Luigi Maifredi

Goals: Casiraghi (13), Stoichkov (58, 61), Goikoetxea (77)

SEMI-FINALS

LEGIA WARSZAWA v MANCHESTER UNITED 1-3 (1-1)

Wojska Polskiego, Warszawa   10.04.1991

Referee: Alphonse Constantin (BEL)   Attendance: 19,000

LEGIA: Zbigniew Robakiewicz; Jacek Bak, Arkadiusz Gmur (61 Cezary Wójcik), Marek Józwiak, Piotr Czachowski, Dariusz Czykier, Leszek Pisz, Krzysztof Iwanicki, Wojciech Kowalczyk, Miroslaw Modzelewski, Jacek Cyzio.
Trainer: Wladyslaw Stachurski

MANCHESTER UNITED: Leslie Sealey; Dennis Irwin, Clayton Blackmore, Stephen Bruce, Mike Phelan (46 Malachy Donaghy), Gary Pallister, Neil Webb, Paul Ince, Brian McClair, Mark Hughes, Lee Sharpe.   Manager: Alex Ferguson

Goals: Cyzio (37), McClair (37), Hughes (54), Bruce (68)

JUVENTUS TORINO v FC BARCELONA 1-0 (0-0)

Delle Alpi, Torino   24.04.1991

Referee: Kurt Röthlisberger (SWI)   Attendance: 70,000

JUVENTUS: Stefano Tacconi; Nicolo Napoli, JÚLIO CÉSAR Silva, Daniele Fortunato, Luigi de Agostini, Roberto Galia, Giancarlo Marocchi, Thomas Hässler, Eugenio Corini (46 Paolo di Canio), Pierluigi Casiraghi (40 Salvatore Schillaci), Roberto Baggio.   Trainer: Luigi Maifredi

FC BARCELONA: Andoni ZUBIZARRETA Urreta; Albert FERRER Llopis, Ricardo Jesús SERNA Orozco, Ronald Koeman, Miquel SOLER Sarasols, Jon Andoni GOIKOETXEA, Guillermo AMOR Martínez, José María BAKERO Escudero, EUSEBIO Sacristán Mena, Michael Laudrup (66 Sebastián HERRERA Zamora), Hristo Stoichkov (71 Julio SALINAS Fernández).   Trainer: Johann Cruyff

Goal: R. Baggio (61)

FINAL

MANCHESTER UNITED
v **FC BARCELONA 2-1** (0-0)

Feyenoord, Rotterdam   15.05.1991

Referee: Bo Karlsson (SWE)   Attendance: 47,000

MANCHESTER UNITED: Leslie Sealey, Dennis Irwin, Stephen Bruce, Gary Pallister, Clayton Blackmore, Mike Phelan, Bryan Robson, Paul Ince, Brian McClair, Lee Sharpe, Mark Hughes.   Manager: Alex Ferguson

FC BARCELONA: Carlos BUSQUETS Barroso; Fernando Muñoz García "NANDO", José Ramón ALEXANCO Ventosa (74 Antonio PINILLA Miranda), Albert FERRER Llopis, EUSEBIO Sacristán Mena, Ronald Koeman, José María BAKERO Escudero, Aitor BEGUIRISTÁIN Mújica, Jon Andoni GOIKOETXEA, Julio SALINAS Fernández, Michael Laudrup.   Trainer: Johann Cruyff

Sent off: Nando (84)

Goals: Hughes (68, 75), R. Koeman (80)

Goalscorers European Cup-Winners' Cup 1990-91:

9 goals: Roberto Baggio (Juventus Torino)

6 goals: Hristo Stoichkov (FC Barcelona)

5 goals: Sergei Yuran (Dynamo Kyiv)

4 goals: Pierluigi Casiraghi (Juventus Torino), Stephen Bruce, Brian McClair (Manchester United), Danny Boffin (FC Liège), Ronald Koeman (Barcelona)

3 goals: Hamdi Aslan (Trabzonspor), Jacek Ziober (Montpellier), Marco Branca (Sampdoria), Oleg Salenko, Gennadi Litovchenko (Dynamo Kyiv), Kowalczyk (Legia Warszawa), Salvatore Schillaci (Juventus Torino), Mark Hughes (Manchester United)

2 goals: Djukić (Trabzonspor), B.Sutter (Xamax), Ragnarsson (Fram Reykjavík), Anastopoulos (Olympiakos), Stan, Dumitrescu, Petrescu (Steaua), Gillhaus (Aberdeen), Mancini (Sampdoria), Kosecki (Legia Warszawa), Júlio César (Juventus), Blackmore (Manchester United), Amor, Beguiristáin (FC Barcelona)

1 goal: Nugent (Bray Wanderers), Walker (Sliema), Soner (Trabzonspor), Martinsson (Djurgardens), Kelepov (Sliven), Nyyssönen, Gayle (Paloseura Kuopio), Douglas (Glentoran), Kuntz (FC Kaiserslautern), Ziu (Flamurtari), Armstrong (Wrexham), Dadason, Ormslev, Arnthorsson (Fram Reykjavík), Foldyna, Bittengel, V.Rada, J.Kostelnik, Zálesky (Dukla Praha), Hantzidis, Drakopoulos, Christodoulou, Mitropoulos (Olympiakos), Duilio, Owubokiri, Valério (Estrela de Amadora), Mason, Robertson, Jess (Aberdeen), Milewski, Zsak (Austria Wien), Xuereb, Blanc, Castro, Colleter, Garande, Guérin (Montpellier), Vialli, Katanec, Lombardo (Sampdoria), Zaets (Dynamo Kyiv), Houben, Malbasa, Milosevic, Ernes (RFC Liège), Cyzio, Czykier, Iwanicki, L.Pisz, Józwiak, Latka, Kupiec (Legia), Hässler, Alessio, Corini, Bonetti (Juventus), Sharpe, Robins, Pallister, Webb (Manchester United), Bakero, Goikoetxea, Urbano, J.Salinas, Eusebio, Pinilla (Barcelona)

Own goals: Walker (Sliema) for Dukla Praha, Martin (Manchester United) for Montpellier, Houben, Wégria (FC Liège) for Juventus

CUP WINNERS' CUP 1991-92

PRELIMINARY ROUND

GALWAY UNITED
v **ODENSE BOLDKLUB 0-3** (0-1)

Hurling Ground, Ballinderreen   21.08.1991

Referee: Egil Nervik (NOR)   Attendance: 4,750

UNITED: Declan McIntyre; Derek Carroll, Derek Rodgers, John Cleary, Jimmy Nolan, Gerry Mullen, Larry Wyse, Peter Carpenter, John Morris-Burke (57 Eamon O'Donoghue), Stephen Lally (73 Thomas Kearns), Noel Mernagh.   Manager: Joey Malone

OB ODENSE: Lars Høgh; Steen Nedergaard (75 Per Hjorth), Per Steffensen, Geoffrey Gray, Thomas Helveg, Søren Lund, Chris Margaard, Leon Hansen, Morten Donnerup, Keld Bordingaard, Lars Elstrup.   Trainer: Ronald Poulsen

Goals: Donnerup (38), Nedergaard (46), Elstrup (68)

ODENSE BOLDKLUB
v **GALWAY UNITED 4-0** (1-0)

Odense stadion   3.09.1991

Referee: Zygmunt Ziober (POL)   Attendance: 1,750

OB ODENSE: Lars Høgh; Per Steffensen, Chris Margaard, Per Hjorth, Leon Hansen (57 Morten Donnerup), Steen Nedergaard, Ulrik Moseby, Jens Melvang, Søren Lund, Brian Christensen (69 Jacob Harder), Jess Thorup.   Trainer: Ronald Poulsen

UNITED: Declan McIntyre; Jimmy Nolan (48 John Morris-Burke), John Cleary, Derek Rodgers, Peter Carpenter, Derek Carroll, Gerry Mullen, Larry Wyse, Ronan Killeen (70 Thomas Kearns), Eamon O'Donoghue, Stephen Lally.   Manager: Joey Malone

Goals: Nedergaard (35), L. Hansen (51), Harder (81), Thorup (90)

**SV STOCKERAU
v TOTTENHAM HOTSPUR LONDON 0-1** (0-1)

Prater Wien 21.08.1991

Referee: Gérard Biguet (FRA)   Attendance: 15,500

SV STOCKEREAU: Peter Zajicek; Jozef Mazura, Michael Keller, Michael Wenzel, Marek Ostrowski (18 Peter Flicker), Andreas Wacek, Ewald Jenisch, Peter Pospisil, Josef Marko (63 Alfred Augustin), Walter Binder, Grzegorz Waliczek. Trainer: Willi Kreuz

TOTTENHAM: Erik Thorstvedt; Terry Fenwick, Patrick van den Hauwe, Mohamed Nayim, Gordon Durie, David Howells, Gary Mabbutt, Paul Stewart, Vincent Samways (89 Ian Hendon), Gary Lineker, Paul Allen.   Manager: Peter Shreeves

Goal: Durie (40)

**TOTTENHAM HOTSPUR LONDON
v SV STOCKERAU 1-0** (1-0)

White Hart Lane, London 4.09.1991

Referee: Michel Piraux (BEL)   Attendance: 28,072

TOTTENHAM: Ian Walker; Terry Fenwick, Patrick van den Hauwe, Mohamed Nayim, David Howells (79 Stephen Sedgley), Gary Mabbutt, Paul Stewart, Gordon Durie, Vincent Samways, Gary Lineker (74 Paul Moran), Gudni Bergsson. Manager: Peter Shreeves

SV STOCKEREAU: Peter Zajicek; Jozef Mazura, Michael Keller, Michael Wenzel, Andreas Wacek (64 Michael Van Muysen), Ewald Jenisch, Peter Flicker, Peter Pospisil, Josef Marko (56 Alfred Augustin), Walter Binder, Grzegorz Waliczek.   Trainer: Willi Kreuz

Goal: Mabbutt (41)

FIRST ROUND

SWANSEA CITY v AS MONACO 1-2 (0-2)

Vetch Field, Swansea 17.09.1991

Referee: Kim Milton Nielsen (DEN)   Attendance: 6,208

CITY: Mark Kendall; Stephen Jenkins, Steve Thornber, Russell Coughlin, Mark Harris, Mark Davies, Simon Davey, Alan Davies, Christian McClean, Terry Connor, Andrew Legg. Manager: Terry Yorath

AS MONACO: Jean-Luc Ettori; John Sivebaek, Emmanuel Petit, Roger Mendy, Luc Sonor, Claude Puel, Marcel Dib, Gérald Passi, George Weah, RUI Gil Soares de BARROS (76 Youri Djorkaeff), Christophe Robert (76 Jerome Gnako). Trainer: Arsène Wenger

Goals: Passi (8 pen), Rui Barros (27), Legg (71)

AS MONACO v SWANSEA CITY 8-0 (5-0)

Louis II Monaco 1.10.1991

Referee: Serge Muhmenthaler (SWI)   Attendance: 7,000

AS MONACO: Jean-Luc Ettori; Patrick Blondeau; Emmanuel Petit, Roger Mendy, Luc Sonor, Claude Puel, Marcel Dib (65 Christophe Robert), Gérald Passi, RUI Gil Soares de BARROS (46 Youri Djorkaeff), George Weah, Youssouf Fofana. Trainer: Arsène Wenger

CITY: Mark Kendall; Stephen Jenkins, Steve Thornber, Russell Coughlin, Mark Davies, Mark Harris (88 Desmond Trick), Simon Davey (72 Shaun Chapple), Alan Davies, Jimmy Gilligan, Paul Raynor, Andrew Legg.   Manager: Terry Yorath

Goals: Weah (6, 85), Fofana (18), Rui Barros (30), Passi (31, 89), Harris (39 og), Djorkaeff (75)

VALUR REYKJAVÍK v FC SION 0-1 (0-0)

Laugardalsvöllur, Reykjavík 17.09.1991

Referee: Svend Erik Christensen (DEN)   Attendance: 761

VALUR: Bjarni Sigurdsson; Arnaldur Loftsson, Saevar Jónsson, Einar Páll Tómasson, Gunnlaugur Einarsson, Steinar Adolfsson, Thórdur Birgir Bogason (75 Davíd Gardarsson), Jón Helgason, Baldur Bragason, Anthony Karl Gregory, Jón Grétar Jónsson.   Trainer: Gudmundur Kjartansson

FC SION: Stefan Lehmann; Alain Geiger, Michel Sauthier, Jean-Paul Brigger, Sébastien Fournier, Alvaro López, Patrice Schüler, Reto Gertschen, Giuseppe Manfreda (89 Olivier Biaggi), Mirsad Baljic, David Orlando (79 Alexandre Rey). Trainer: Enzo Trossero

Goal: Rey (80)

FC SION v VALUR REYKJAVÍK 1-1 (0-0)

Tourbillon, Sion 2.10.1991

Referee: José Alberto Veiga Trigo (POR)   Atendance: 6,100

FC SION: Stefan Lehmann; Sébastien Fournier, Michel Sauthier, Jean-Paul Brigger, Alain Geiger; Blaise Piffaretti, Alvaro López, Reto Gertschen, Mirsad Baljic, Alexandre Rey (83 Giuseppe Manfreda), David Orlando.
Trainer: Enzo Trossero

VALUR: Bjarni Sigurdsson; Arnaldur Loftsson, Saevar Jónsson, Einar Páll Tómasson, Gunnlaugur Einarsson, Steinar Adolfsson, Thórdur Birgir Bogason (75 Davíd Gardarsson), Jón Helgason, Baldur Bragason, Anthony Karl Gregory, Jón Grétar Jónsson.   Trainer: Gudmundur Kjartansson

Sent off: Piffaretti (55), Saevar Jonsson (55)

Goals: Einarsson (67), Orlando (78)

GLENAVON LURGAN v ILVES TAMPERE 3-2 (1-1)
Mourneview Park, Lurgan   17.09.1991
Referee: Marnix Sandra (BEL)   Attendance: 2,029
GLENAVON: Robbie Beck; Michael McKeown, Tony Scappaticci, Dean McCullough, Paul Byrne, Michael Crowe, Raymond McCoy, Alan McCann, Glenn Ferguson, Stephen McBride, Stevie Conville.   Manager: Terry Nicholson
ILVES: Teuvo Moilanen; Janne Mäkelä (46 Seppo Nikkilä), Jari Aaltonen, Yuri Shevliakov, Mika Aaltonen, Miika Juntunen, Pekka Mattila, Mark Dziadulewicz, Ari Hjelm, Petri Ojala, Marek Czakon.   Trainer: Ian Crawford
Goals: J. Aaltonen (12), Ferguson (32), McBride (60 pen), Dziadulewicz (78), Conville (80)

TOTTENHAM HOTSPUR LONDON v HAJDUK SPLIT 2-0 (2-0)
White Hart Lane, London   2.10.1991
Referee: Erik Fredriksson (SWE)   Attendance: 24,297
TOTTENHAM: Erik Thorstvedt; Gudni Bergsson, Stephen Sedgley, Mohamed Nayim, David Tuttle, Paul Stewart, Gary Mabbutt, Gordon Durie, Vincent Samways, Gary Lineker (90 Ian Hendon), Paul Allen.   Manager: Peter Shreeves
HAJDUK: Bosko Bošković; Predrag Erak (65 Robert Vladislavić), Robert Jarni, Igor Stimac, Slaven Bilić, Jiří Jeslinek, Mario Novaković, Ante Miše, Goran Milanko, Goran Vučević (73 Edward Abazi), Adrian Kozniku.   Trainer: Stanko Poklepović
Goals: Tuttle (6), Durie (14)

ILVES TAMPERE v GLENAVON LURGAN 2-1 (1-0)
Tammelan Pallokenttä, Tampere   2.10.1991
Referee: Henning Lund-Sørensen (DEN)   Att: 5,000
ILVES: Mika Malinen; Janne Mäkelä, Seppo Nikkilä (65 Mika Aaltonen), Ari Munnukka, Pekka Mattila, Jari Aaltonen, Miika Juntunen, Mark Dziadulewicz (75 Yuri Shevliakov), Ari Hjelm, Petri Ojala, Marek Czakon.   Trainer: Ian Crawford
GLENAVON: Robbie Beck; Michael McKeown, Tony Scappaticci, Dean McCullough, Paul Byrne, Alan McCann (46 Geoff Ferris), Michael Crowe (46 Andy Russell), Raymond McCoy, Glenn Ferguson, Stephen McBride, Stevie Conville. Manager: Terry Nicholson
Goals: Mattila (39 pen, 70), McBride (78)

FC BACĂU v WERDER BREMEN 0-6 (0-3)
Municipal, Bacău   18.09.1991
Referee: Josef Marko (CZE)   Attendance: 3,000
FC BACĂU: Neculai Alexa; Sorin Condurache, Marius Gireadă, Constantin Arteni, Florin Ionescu; Gheorghe Burleanu, Daniel Mihăilă, Giani Olteanu (72 Robert Ghioane), Ionel Căpușă (61 Dorinel Dragomir), Florin Hodină, Neculai Haidău. Trainer: Mircea Nedelcu
WERDER: Oliver Reck; Rune Bratseth, Miroslav Votava, Dieter Eilts, Manfred Bockenfeld, Thomas Schaaf, Frank Neubarth, Thorsten Legat, Stefan Kohn, Wynton Rufer (62 Marco Bode), Klaus Allofs (64 Günter Hermann).   Trainer: Otto Rehhagel
Goals: Rufer (9, 13, 31), Bratseth (63), Votava (78), Neubarth (80)

HAJDUK SPLIT v TOTTENHAM HOTSPUR LONDON 1-0 (0-0)
Linzer Stadion   17.09.1991
Referee: Kurt Röthlisberger (SWI)   Attendance: 7,000
HAJDUK: Bosko Bošković; Predrag Erak, Robert Jarni, Igor Stimac, Jiří Jeslinek, Goran Milanko, Mario Novaković, Ante Miše, Ivica Mornar (67 Edward Abazi), Goran Vučević, Adrian Kozniku (84 Hari Vukas).   Trainer: Stanko Poklepović
TOTTENHAM: Ian Walker; Terry Fenwick, Patrick van den Hauwe, Mohamed Nayim, David Howells (57 Paul Allen), Gary Mabbutt, Paul Stewart, Gordon Durie, Vincent Samways, Gary Lineker (73 Stephen Sedgley), Gudni Bergsson.
Manager: Peter Shreeves
Goal: Novaković (53)

WERDER BREMEN v FC BACĂU 5-0 (3-0)
Weserstadion, Bremen   1.10.1991
Referee: Patrick Kelly (IRL)   Attendance: 3,021
WERDER: Oliver Reck; Rune Bratseth, Miroslav Votava, Ulrich Borowka (46 Günter Hermann), Thomas Schaaf, Manfred Bockenfeld, Dieter Eilts, Thorsten Legat, Stefan Kohn (46 Marco Bode); Wynton Rufer, Klaus Allofs.   Trainer: Otto Rehhagel
FC BACĂU: Neculai Alexa; Sorin Condurache, Marius Gireadă, Constantin Arteni, Florin Ionescu; Robert Ghioane, Florin Hodină (67 Dorinel Dragomir), Gheorghe Burleanu, Adrian Postolache, Neculai Haidău, Daniel Mihăilă (75 Ionel Căpușă).
Trainer: Mircea Nedelcu
Goals: Kohn (6, 17), Eilts (9), Bratseth (66), Bode (71)

LEVSKI SOFIA
v FERENCVÁROS BUDAPEST 2-3 (1-1)
Georgi Asparuhov, Sofia 18.09.1991
Referee: Gheorghe Constantin (ROM)　Attendance: 15,000
LEVSKI: Zdravko Zdravkov; Stoian Pumpalov, Valentin Dartilov, Kalin Bankov, Georgi Dimitrov, Ivan Todorov (34 Velko Iotov), Zlatko Iankov, Nasko Sirakov, Petar Khubchev, Yasen Petrov (69 Ilian Iliev), Valeri Valkov.　Trainer: Vasil Metodiev
FERENCVÁROS: Tamás Balogh; Tibor Simon, András Telek, József Keller, Sergei Kuznetsov, Péter Lipcsei, Flórián Albert (54 Vasili Rats), Gábor Schneider (40 Zsolt Nagy), Zsolt Páling, Csaba Patkós, Péter Deszatnik.　Trainer: Tibor Nyilasi
Goals: Deszatnik (7), Dartilov (36), Lipcsei (72, 81), Bankov (90)

CLUB BRUGGE KV
v OMONOIA NICOSIA 2-0 (0-0)
Olympiastadion, Brugge 2.10.1991
Referee: John Purcell (Irl)　Attendance: 11,885
CLUB BRUGGE: Hans Galje; Alex Querter, László Disztl, Rudy Cossey, Vital Borkelmans, Peter Crève, Lorenzo Staelens, Franky van der Elst (80 Marc Schaessens), Stéphane van der Heyden, Foeke Booy, Tomasz Dziubinski.
Trainer: Hugo Broos
OMONOIA: Andreas Haritou; Koulis Iacovou, Kostas Konstantinou, Kostas Petsas, Giorgos Mina, Nedim Tutic, Stelios Mavroftis, Sakis Andreou, Evagoras Hristofi, Kostas Malekos (79 Andreas Avlonitis), Hrysanthos Hrysanthou.
Trainer: Valdemar Cratsiano
Goals: Booy (65), Van der Heyden (85)

FERENCVÁROS BUDAPEST
v LEVSKI SOFIA 4-1 (2-0)
Üllöi út, Budapest 2.10.1991
Referee: Yusuf Namoglu (TUR)　Attendance: 8,000
FERENCVÁROS: Tamás Balogh; Tibor Simon, András Telek, József Keller, Sergei Kuznetsov, Péter Lipcsei, Flórián Albert (46 Sándor Szenes), Gábor Schneider, Zsolt Páling, Csaba Patkós, Péter Deszatnik.　Trainer: Tibor Nyilasi
LEVSKI: Dimitar Popov; Plamen Nikolov, Valentin Dartilov, Stoian Pumpalov (46 Valeri Valkov), Zlatko Iankov, Ilian Iliev, Kalin Bankov, Stanimir Stoilov, Georgi Dimitrov, Velko Iotov (75 Yasen Petrov), Petar Khubchev.　Trainer: Vasil Metodiev
Goals: Lipcsei (1, 90), Albert (28), Deszatnik (57), Dimitrov (73)

IFK NORRKÖPING v JEUNESSE D'ESCH 4-0 (1-0)
Norrköpings Idrottsparken 18.09.1991
Referee: Esa Palsi (FIN)　Attendance: 2,438
IFK: Lars Eriksson; Sulo Vaattovaara, Jan Eriksson, Jan Kalén, Jonas Lind (75 Jan Hedén), Niklas Kindvall, Jonny Rödlund, Magnus Karlsson, Magnus Samuelsson, Patrik Andersson (75 Mikael Hansson), Jan Hellström.　Trainer: Sanny Åslund
JEUNESSE: Christian Hoffmann; Jacques Müller, Pierre Petry, Roland Schaack, Marcel Bossi, Claude Ganser, Marc Thomé, Jean Wagner, Denis Scuto, Sauro Marinelli (82 Hazib Selimovic), Dany Theis.　Trainer: Vinicio Monacelli
Goals: Karlsson (45), J. Eriksson (49), Hellström (70), Vaattovaara (71 pen)

OMONOIA NICOSIA
v CLUB BRUGGE KV 0-2 (0-1)
Makarion, Nicosia 18.09.1991
Referee: Plarent Kotherja (ALB)　Attendance: 16,000
OMONOIA: Andreas Haritou; Koulis Iacovou, Kostas Konstantinou, Kostas Petsas, Giorgos Mina, Nedim Tutic, Evagoras Hristofi, Sakis Andreou, Hrysanthos Hrysanthou (71 Andreas Avlonitis), Kostas Malekos (68 Andreas Kantilos), Panikos Xiouroupas.　Trainer: Valdemar Cratsiano
CLUB BRUGGE: Danny Verlinden; Claude Verspaille, László Disztl, Rudy Cossey, Vital Borkelmans, Peter Crève, Lorenzo Staelens (79 Dominique van Maele), Franky van der Elst, Stéphane van der Heyden (46 Alex Querter), Foeke Booy, Tomasz Dziubinski.　Trainer: Hugo Broos
Goals: Dziubinski (3), Booy (48)

JEUNESSE D'ESCH v IFK NORKÖPPING 1-2 (0-2)
Stade de la Frontière, Esch-sur-Alzette 2.10.1991
Referee: Johannes Reygwart (HOL)　Attendance: 765
JEUNESSE: Christian Hoffmann; Jacques Müller, Pierre Petry, Jean Wagner, Claude Ganser, Marc Thomé (65 Patrick Meyers), Marcel Bossi, Sauro Marinelli, Denis Scuto, Dany Theis, Marco Heyar (72 Hazib Selimovic).
Trainer: Vinicio Monacelli
IFK: Lars Eriksson; Sulo Vaattovaara, Jan Eriksson (46 Mats Almgren), Jan Kalén, Jonas Lind, Mikael Hansson, Evgeny Kuznetsov, Jonny Rödlund (47 Magnus Karlsson), Jan Hedén, Niklas Kindvall, Patrik Andersson.　Trainer: Sanny Åslund
Goals: J. Eriksson (2), Kindvall (40), Marinelli (83)

GKS KATOWICE v MOTHERWELL 2-0 (1-0)

GKS Katowice 18.09.1991

Referee: Einar Halle (NOR)   Attendance: 6,000

GKS: Janusa Jojko; Krzysztof Maciejewski, Roman Szewczyk, Andrzej Lesiak, Dariusz Grzesik, Zdzislaw Strojek, Marek Szyminski (46 Piotr Swierczewski), Arkadiusz Wolowicz, Krzysztof Walczak (80 Dariusz Wolny), Gija Guruli, Dariusz Rzezniczek.   Trainer: Alojzy Lysko

MOTHERWELL: William Thomson; James Griffin, Luc Nijholt, James Dolan, John Philliben, Chris McCart, Robert Russell (88 James Gardner), Phil O'Donnell, Joe McLeod (80 Nick Cusack), Steve Kirk, David Cooper.
Manager: Tommy McLean

Goals: Szewczyk (42), Wolny (81)

**BANÍK OSTRAVA
v ODENSE BOLDKLUB 2-1** (0-1)

Stadión na Bazaloch, Ostrava 2.10.1991

Referee: Daniel Roduit (SWI)   Attendance: 2,596

BANÍK: Ivo Schmucker; Dušan Vrto, Roman Sialini, Petr Skarabela, Jiří Zálesky, Pavel Kubánek, Radim Necas, Jiří Casko, Jan Palínek (79 Radek Sloncík), Radomír Chylek, Roman Pavelka (46 Libor Zelnícek).   Trainer: Jaroslav Gürtler

OB ODENSE: Lars Høgh; Chris Margaard, Per Hjorth, Thomas Hurwitz, Leon Hansen, Steen Nedergaard, Ulrik Moseby, Per Steffensen, Jens Melvang (79 Morten Donnerup), Keld Bordingaard (71 Jacob Harder), Lars Elstrup.
Trainer: Ronald Poulsen

Sent off: Hjorth (54)

Goals: Bordingaard (8), Chylek (82), Steffensen (83 og)

MOTHERWELL v GKS KATOWICE 3-1 (1-0)

Fir Park, Motherwell 2.10.1991

Referee: Bernd Heynemann (GER)   Attendance: 10,032

MOTHERWELL: William Thomson; James Griffin, Luc Nijholt, Chris McCart (59 John Philliben), Ian Angus (55 Iain Ferguson), Robert Russell, James Dolan, Steve Kirk, Nick Cusack, David Cooper, Phil O'Donnell.
Manager: Tommy McLean

GKS: Janusa Jojko; Krzysztof Maciejewski, Andrzej Lesiak, Dariusz Grzesik, Zdzislaw Strojek, Piotr Swierczewski, Arkadiusz Wolowicz, Dariusz Wolny (46 Krzysztof Walczak), Marek Swierczewski, Dariusz Rzezniczek, Gija Guruli.
Trainer: Alojzy Lysko

Goals: Kirk (29, 89), Rzezniczek (68), Cusack (86)

**PARTIZANI TIRANA
v FEYENOORD ROTTERDAM 0-0**

Qemal Stafa, Tirana 18.09.1991

Referee: Sandor Puhl (HUN)   Attendance: 5,000

PARTIZANI: Artur Lekbello; Shahin Berberi (67 Astrit Sheta), Armand Damo, Andon Nikolla, Ilir Shulku, Alfons Muça, Adnan Ocelli, Marko Pelinxhi (75 Klarent Fejzolli), Fatmir Hasanpapa, Edmond Dosti, Besnik Prenga.   Trainer: Sulejman Starova

FEYENOORD: Ed de Goey; Arnold Scholten, Henk Fräser, John De Wolf, Ruud Heus, Peter Bosz, John Metgod, Robert Witschge, Gaston Taument, Marian Damaschin, Reginald Blinker.
Trainer: Hans Dorjee

**ODENSE BOLDKLUB
v BANÍK OSTRAVA 0-2** (0-1)

Odense stadium 18.09.1991

Referee: Cornelius Bakker (HOL)   Attendance: 2,377

OB ODENSE: Lars Høgh; Chris Margaard, Per Steffensen, Per Hjorth, Steen Nedergaard, Ulrik Moseby (83 Morten Donnerup), Leon Hansen, Søren Lund (72 Lars Jacobsen), Keld Bordingaard, Lars Elstrup, Jens Melvang.
Trainer: Ronald Poulsen

BANÍK: Ivo Schmucker; Jiří Zálesky, Roman Sialini, Tomás Repka, Dušan Vrto, Radek Sloncík, Petr Skarabela, Radim Necas, Jiří Casko (89 Milan Duhan), Radomír Chylek, Libor Zelnícek (83 Jan Palínek).   Trainer: Jaroslav Gürtler

Goals: Skarabela (41), Casko (82)

**FEYENOORD ROTTERDAM
v PARTIZANI TIRANA 1-0** (0-0)

Feyenoord, Rotterdam 2.10.1991

Referee: Rune Pedersen (NOR)   Attendance: 17,750

FEYENOORD: Ed de Goey; Arnold Scholten, John Metgod, John De Wolf, Ruud Heus, Peter Bosz, Henk Fräser, Robert Witschge, Gaston Taument, Marian Damaschin (71 József Kiprich), Reginald Blinker.   Trainer: Hans Dorjee

PARTIZANI: Artur Lekbello; Shahin Berberi, Armand Damo, Andon Nikolla, Ilir Shulku, Adnan Ocelli, Alfons Muça, Klarent Fejzolli (63 Astrit Sheta), Edmond Dosti, Fatmir Hasanpapa, Besnik Prenga.   Trainer: Sulejman Starova

Goal: Bosz (87)

**EISENHÜTTENSTADTER FC STAHL
v GALATASARAY ISTANBUL 1-2** (1-1)

Sportplatz der Hüttenwerker, Eisenhüttenstadt   18.09.1991

Referee: Jacob Uilenberg (HOL)   Attendance: 3,420

STAHL: Andreas Hawa; Ernest Podsiadlo (82 Jens Wittke), Ralf Sack, Manfred Hirsch, René Wenzel, Karl Pospich, Olaf Bitzka, Dragoslav Mujakovic, Olaf Schnürer, Frank Bartz, Tino Jerkovic (53 Karsten Schulz).   Trainer: Karl Trautmann

GALATASARAY: Hayrettin Demirbas; Bülent Korkmaz, Tugay Kerimoglu, Tayfun Hut, Ismail Demiriz, Mustafa Yücedag (79 Arif Erdem), Muhammet Altintas, Iosif Rotariu, Metin Yildiz (81 Dzevad Prekazi), Roman Kosecki, Erdal Keser.
Trainer: Mustafa Denizli

Goals: F.Bartz (40), Kosecki (45), Erdal (71)

**GALATASARAY ISTANBUL
v EISENHÜTTENSTADTER FC STAHL 3-0** (1-0)

Ali Sami Yen, Istanbul   2.10.1991

Referee: Lube Spasov (BUL)   Attendance: 14,528

GALATASARAY: Hayrettin Demirbas; Bülent Korkmaz, Yusuf Altintas, Tugay Kerimoglu, Ismail Demiriz, Muhammet Altintas, Ugur Tütüneker (74 Mustafa Yücedag), Dzevad Prekazi (67 Sevket Mustafer), Tayfun Hut, Roman Kosecki, Arif Erdem.
Trainer: Mustafa Denizli

STAHL: Andreas Hawa; Ernest Podsiadlo, Manfred Hirsch, Olaf Bitzka (31 Karsten Schulz), Ralf Sack, René Wenzel, Dragoslav Mujakovic, Karl Pospich, Olaf Schnürer, Frank Bartz, Tino Jerkovic.   Trainer: Karl Trautmann

Goals: Kosecki (20 pen), Arif (67), Mustafa (87)

**ATHINAIKOS ATHINA
v MANCHESTER UNITED 0-0**

Apostolos Nikolaidis, Athina   18.09.1991

Referee: Aron Schmidhuber (GER)   Attendance: 5,647

ATHINAIKOS: Nikos Sargkanis; Theodoros Boutzoukas, Giorgos Kapouranis, Anastasios Hatziaggelis, Evangelos Spiliotis, Kostas Theodorakos, Giannis Hatziraptis (69 Hristos Dimopoulos), Damir Spica, Miroslaw Bak, Hristo Kolev (82 Giannis Tapratzis), Vasilis Tzalakostas.   Trainer: Gerd Prokop

UNITED: Peter Schmeichel; Mike Phelan, Dennis Irwin, Stephen Bruce, Neil Webb, Gary Pallister, Mark Robins, Paul Ince, Brian McClair, Mark Hughes, Russel Beardsmore (74 David Wallace).   Manager: Alex Ferguson

**MANCHESTER UNITED v ATHINAIKOS
ATHINA 2-0** (0-0,0-0)

Old Trafford, Manchester   2.10.1991

Referee: Rosario Lo Bello (ITA)   Attendance: 35,023

UNITED: Peter Schmeichel; Mike Phelan, Lee Martin (85 Russel Beardsmore), Bryan Robson, Stephen Bruce, Andrei Kanchelskis, Gary Pallister, Paul Ince, Brian McClair, Mark Hughes, David Wallace (77 Mark Robins).
Manager: Alex Ferguson

ATHINAIKOS: Nikos Sargkanis; Theodoros Boutzoukas, Giorgos Kapouranis, Anastasios Hatziaggelis, Evangelos Spiliotis (46 Kostas Theodorakos, 66 Giorgos Zotalis), Giorgos Anastasiou, Giannis Hatziraptis, Damir Spica, Miroslaw Bak, Vasilis Tzalakostas, Giannis Tapratzis.   Trainer: Gerd Prokop

Goals: Hughes (109), McClair (111)

FYLLINGEN IL v ATLÉTICO MADRID 0-1 (0-1)

Brann Bergen   18.09.1991

Referee: Walter Keith Burge (WAL)   Attendance: 4,333

FYLLINGEN IL: Vidar Bahus; Terje Tviberg, Inge Ludvigsen, Per-Ove Ludvigsen, Tore Brogstad, Rolf Barmen, Paul Tengs (83 Åge Maridal), Håkon Knudsen, Asbjørn Helgeland, Tor Vikenes, Frode Hellesø (85 Henrik Jørgensen).
Trainer: Jørgen Augustsson

ATLÉTICO: ABEL Resino Gómez; TOMÁS Reñones Crego, Miquel SOLER Sarasols, Roberto SOLOZÁBAL Villanueva, Francisco "PATXI" FERREIRA Colmenero, Juan Francisco Rodríguez "JUANITO", Manuel Sánchez Delgado "MANOLO" (86 Juan SABAS Huertas), Juan VIZCAÍNO Morcillo, Bernd Schuster, Paulo Jorge dos Santos "FUTRE", Gabriel MOYA Sanz (68 Antonio Muñoz Gómez "TONI").
Trainer: Luis Aragonés Suárez

Goal: Manolo (28)

ATLÉTICO MADRID v FYLLINGEN IF 7-2 (4-0)

Vicente Calderón, Madrid   2.10.1991

Referee: Freddy Phillipoz (SWI)   Attendance: 15,000

ATLÉTICO: ABEL Resino Gómez (55 DIEGO Díaz Garrido); Francisco "PATXI" FERREIRA Colmenero, Juan Francisco Rodríguez "JUANITO", Roberto SOLOZÁBAL Villanueva, TOMÁS Reñones Crego, Bernd Schuster, Juan VIZCAÍNO Morcillo, Miquel SOLER Sarasols, Gabriel MOYA Sanz (46 Juan Carlos AGUILERA Martín), Manuel Sánchez Delgado "MANOLO", Paulo Jorge dos Santos "FUTRE".
Trainer: Luis Aragonés Suárez

FYLLINGEN IL: Vidar Bahus; Terje Tviberg, Inge Ludvigsen, Per-Ove Ludvigsen, Tore Brogstad, Rolf Barmen, Paul Tengs, Asbjørn Helgeland, Tor Vikenes, Håkon Knudsen (82 Dag Bergset), Frode Hellesö (77 Ola Lyngvaer).
Trainer: Jørgen Augustsson

Goals: Schuster (4, 89), Manolo (19, 34 pen, 86), Soler (40), Tengs (54, 68), Futre (81)

CSKA MOSKVA v AS ROMA 1-2 (0-0)

Lenin, Moskva 18.09.1991

Referee: Bo Karlsson (SWE)   Attendance: 50,000

CSKA: Dmitri Kharin; Dmitri Kuznetsov, Sergei Kolotovkin, Dmitri Bystrov, Sergei Fokin, Mikhail Kolesnikov (46 Sergei Dmitriev), Igor Korneev (75 Valeri Masalitin), Valeri Broschin, Oleg Sergeev, Vladimir Tatarchuk, Dmitri Galiamin.   Trainer: Pavel Sadyrin

AS ROMA: Giovanni Cervone; Marco Antonio De Marchi (46 Luigi Garzja), Amedeo Carboni, Giovanni Piacentini, ALDAIR dos Santos, Sebastiano Nela, Thomas Hässler, Fabrizio Di Mauro, Ruggiero Rizzitelli, Giuseppe Giannini, Walter Bonacina.   Trainer: Ottavio Bianchi

Goals: Fokin (46 og), Sergeev (52), Rizzitelli (73)

AS ROMA v CSKA MOSKVA 0-1 (0-1)

Stadio Olimpico, Roma 2.10.1991

Referee: Hubert Forstinger (AUS)   Attendance: 45,086

AS ROMA: Giovanni Cervone; Antonio Tempestilli, Amedeo Carboni, Stefano Pellegrini, ALDAIR dos Santos, Sebastiano Nela, Thomas Hässler, Fabrizio Di Mauro, Rudi Völler, Giuseppe Giannini (65 Luigi Garzja), Ruggiero Rizzitelli.   Trainer: Ottavio Bianchi

CSKA: Dmitri Kharin; Dmitri Kuznetsov, Sergei Kolotovkin, Dmitri Bystrov, Sergei Fokin, Mikhail Kolesnikov (83 Oleg Sergeev), Igor Korneev (68 Valeri Masalitin), Valeri Broschin, Dmitri Galiamin, Vladimir Tatarchuk, Sergei Dmitriev.   Trainer: Pavel Sadyrin

Goal: Dmitriev (13)

VALLETTA FC v FC PORTO 0-3 (0-2)

National Ta'Qali, Valletta 19.09.1991

Referee: Gerd Grahber (AUS)   Attendance: 1,129

VALLETTA FC: Reginald Cini; William Mackay, Kristian Laferla, Raymond Sciberras, Charlie Magri, Joe Camilleri, Raymond Briffa, Gilbert Agius (81 Robert Spiteri), Nicholas Saliba, Joe Zarb, Jesmond Zerafa.   Trainer: Euchar Grech

FC PORTO: VÍTOR Manuel Martins BAÍA; JOÃO Domingos Silva PINTO, FERNANDO Manuel Silva COUTO, ALOÍSIO Pires Alves, Mário Jorge Castro MORGADO, António dos Santos ANDRÉ, José Orlando Rocha SEMEDO (22 Alcides Rodrigues Tavares "KIKI"), JAIME Fernandes MAGALHÃES, Ion Timofte, Emile Lubtchov Kostadinov (46 Petar Sotirov Mihtarski), DOMINGOS José Paciencia Oliveira.   Trainer: Carlos Alberto Silva

Goals: Kostadinov (28), Timofte (37), Mihtarski (78)

FC PORTO v VALLETTA FC 1-0 (0-0)

Estádio das Antas, Porto 2.10.1991

Referee: Antonio Martin Navarrete (SPA)   Att: 5,000

FC PORTO: VÍTOR Manuel Martins BAÍA; JOÃO Domingos Silva PINTO, JOSÉ CARLOS Nascimento, FERNANDO Manuel Silva COUTO, Lubomir Vlk, António José Alves Ribeiro "TOZÉ", António dos Santos ANDRÉ, RUI FILIPE Tavares Bastos (46 JORGE ANDRADE de Guimarães), António José Santos FOLHA (64 RICARDO João Cunha Oliveira), Ion Timofte, Emile Kostadinov.   Trainer: Carlos Alberto Silva

VALLETTA FC: Reginald Cini; Raymond Briffa, Charlie Magri, Kristian Laferla, Osnir Populin, Joe Camilleri, Leo Refalo (65 Raymond Sciberras), Jesmond Zerafa (83 William Mackay), Gilbert Agius, Nicholas Saliba, Joe Zarb.   Trainer: Euchar Grech

Goal: Timofte (90)

SECOND ROUND

IFK NORRKÖPING v AS MONACO 1-2 (1-1)

Norrköpings Idrottsparken 22.10.1991

Referee: Hans-Peter Dellwig (GER)   Attendance: 4,627

IFK: Lars Eriksson; Sulo Vaattovaara, Jan Eriksson, Jan Kalén, Jonas Lind, Mikael Hansson (81 Patrik Andersson), Evgeny Kuznetsov, Jonny Rödlund, Göran Bergort (77 Magnus Samuelsson), Jan Hellström, Niklas Kindvall.   Trainer: Sanny Åslund

AS MONACO: Jean-Luc Ettori; Patrick Blondeau, Emmanuel Petit, Roger Mendy, Luc Sonor, Claude Puel, Marcel Dib, RUI Gil Soares de BARROS, Youri Djorkaeff (72 Gérald Passi), George Weah, Youssouf Fofana.   Trainer: Arsène Wenger

Goals: Mendy (18), Hellström (22), Weah (48)

AS MONACO v IFK NORRKÖPING 1-0 (1-0)

Louis II, Monaco 5.11.1991

Referee: Rosario Lo Bello (ITA)   Attendance: 4,000

AS MONACO: Jean-Luc Ettori; John Sivebaek, Lilian Thuram, Roger Mendy, Luc Sonor, Claude Puel, RUI Gil Soares de BARROS, Youri Djorkaeff (70 Gérald Passi), Marcel Dib, George Weah, Christophe Robert (73 Jerome Gnako).   Trainer: Arsène Wenger

IFK: Lars Eriksson; Sulo Vaattovaara (44 Magnus Karlsson), Jan Eriksson, Jonas Lind (60 Niklas Kindvall), Jan Kalén, Mikael Hansson, Evgeny Kuznetsov, Jonny Rödlund, Göran Bergort, Jan Hellström, Patrik Andersson.   Trainer: Sanny Åslund

Goal: Robert (26)

ATLÉTICO MADRID v MANCHESTER UNITED 3-0 (1-0)
Vicente Calderón, Madrid   23.10.1991

Referee: Bernd Heynemann (GER)   Atendancet: 52,000

ATLÉTICO: ABEL Resino Gómez; TOMÁS Reñones Crego, Francisco "PATXI" FERREIRA Colmenero, Juan Francisco Rodríguez "JUANITO", Roberto SOLOZÁBAL Villanueva, Miquel SOLER Sarasols, Manuel Sánchez Delgado "MANOLO", Bernd Schuster, Juan VIZCAÍNO Morcillo, Gabriel MOYA Sanz (72 Sebastián LOSADA Bestard), Paulo Jorge dos Santos "FUTRE".   Trainer: Luis Aragonés Suárez

UNITED: Peter Schmeichel; Paul Parker, Dennis Irwin, Gary Pallister, Stephen Bruce, Neil Webb, Paul Ince (52 Lee Martin), Bryan Robson, Brian McClair, Mark Hughes, Mike Phelan (75 Russell Beardsmore).   Manager: Alex Ferguson

Goals: Futre (32, 87), Manolo (88)

MANCHESTER UNITED v ATLÉTICO MADRID 1-1 (1-0)
Old Trafford, Manchester   6.11.1991

Referee: Guy Goethals (BEL)   Attendance: 39,654

UNITED: Gary Walsh; Paul Parker, Clayton Blackmore, Stephen Bruce, Neil Webb, Mike Phelan (89 Lee Martin), Bryan Robson, Mark Robins (64 Gary Pallister), Brian McClair, Mark Hughes, Ryan Giggs.   Manager: Alex Ferguson

ATLÉTICO: ABEL Resino Gómez (74 DIEGO Díaz Garrido); TOMÁS Reñones Crego, DONATO Gama da Silva, Roberto SOLOZÁBAL Villanueva, Juan Francisco Rodríguez "JUANITO", Antonio Muñoz Gómez "TONI", Juan VIZCAÍNO Morcillo, Bernd Schuster, Manuel Sánchez Delgado "MANOLO" (53 Miquel SOLER Sarasols), Gabriel MOYA Sanz, Paulo Jorge dos Santos "FUTRE".
Trainer: Luis Aragonés Suárez

Goals: Hughes (4), Schuster (68)

GKS KATOWICE v CLUB BRUGGE 0-1 (0-1)
GKS Katowice   23.10.1991

Referee: Hasan Ceylan (TUR)   Attendance: 3,856

GKS: Janusa Jojko; Zdzislaw Strojek (46 Krzysztof Walczak), Krzysztof Maciejewski, Andrzej Lesiak, Marek Szyminski, Dariusz Grzesik, Marek Swierczewski, Piotr Swierczewski, Dariusz Wolny, Gija Guruli, Dariusz Rzezniczek.   Trainer: Alojzy Lysko

CLUB BRUGGE: Danny Verlinden; Claude Verspaille, Alex Querter, Rudy Cossey, Vital Borkelmans, Peter Crève, Franky van der Elst, Lorenzo Staelens, Stéphane van der Heyden, Daniel Amokachi (75 Pascal Plovie), Tomasz Dziubinski.   Trainer: Hugo Broos

Goal: Staelens (22)

CLUB BRUGGE v GKS KATOWICE 3-0 (0-0)
Olympiastadion, Brugge   6.11.1991

Referee: Walter Keith Burge (WAL)   Attendance: 14,428

CLUB BRUGGE: Danny Verlinden; Claude Verspaille, Alex Querter, László Disztl, Vital Borkelmans, Peter Crève, Franky van der Elst, Lorenzo Staelens, Stéphane van der Heyden (76 Marc Schaessens), Daniel Amokachi (80 Jan Ceulemans), Tomasz Dziubinski.   Trainer: Hugo Broos

GKS: Janusa Jojko; Krzysztof Maciejewski, Roman Szewczyk, Andrzej Lesiak, Dariusz Grzesik (80 Adam Ksiazek), Zdzislaw Strojek (74 Dariusz Wolny), Piotr Swierczewski, Marek Swierczewski, Dariusz Rzezniczek, Gija Guruli, Krzysztof Walczak.   Trainer: Alojzy Lysko

Goals: Verspaille (50), Staelens (58), Schaessens (78)

ILVES TAMPERE v AS ROMA 1-1 (0-1)
Tammelan Pallokenttä, Tampere   23.10.1991

Referee: Michal Listkiewicz (POL)   Attendance: 8,727

ILVES: Mika Malinen; Janne Mäkelä, Mika Aaltonen, Jari Aaltonen, Yuri Shevliakov, Pekka Mattila, Miika Juntunen, Mark Dziadulewicz, Ari Hjelm, Petri Ojala, Marek Czakon.
Trainer: Ian Crawford

AS ROMA: Giovanni Cervone; Marco Antonio De Marchi, Amedeo Carboni, Stefano Pellegrini (75 Fausto Salsano), ALDAIR dos Santos, Sebastiano Nela, Thomas Hässler, Fabrizio Di Mauro, Rudi Völler, Andrea Carnevale, Giovanni Piacentini.   Trainer: Ottavio Bianchi

Goals: Carnevale (20), Czakon (65)

AS ROMA v ILVES TAMPERE 5-2 (3-0)
Olimpico, Roma   6.11.1991

Referee: Charles Agius (MAL)   Attendance: 24,810

AS ROMA: Giovanni Cervone; Marco Antonio De Marchi, Amedeo Carboni, Walter Bonacina, ALDAIR dos Santos, Sebastiano Nela, Thomas Hässler, Fabrizio Di Mauro, Ruggiero Rizzitelli (60 Fausto Salsano), Giuseppe Giannini, Roberto Muzzi (17 Andrea Carnevale).   Trainer: Ottavio Bianchi

ILVES: Teuvo Moilanen; Janne Mäkelä, Mika Aaltonen, Timo Korsumäki, Yuri Shevliakov, Pekka Mattila, Miika Juntunen, Jari Aaltonen, Ari Hjelm (60 Ari Munnukka), Petri Ojala (46 Kimmo Mörö), Marek Czakon.   Trainer: Ian Crawford

Goals: Giannini (1), Rizzitelli (3), Di Mauro (15), Carnevale (48, 77), Czakon (80, 89)

FC SION v FEYENOORD ROTTERDAM 0-0
Tourbillon, Sion 23.10.1991

Referee: Jozef Marko (CZE)   Attendance: 9,111

FC SION: Stefan Lehmann; Michel Sauthier, Jean-Paul Brigger, Alain Geiger, Yvan Quentin, Alvaro López, Gabriel Calderón, Reto Gertschen (58 Sébastien Fournier), Mirsad Baljic, Giuseppe Manfreda, Alexandre Rey (89 Emmanuel Dupraz).   Trainer: Enzo Trossero

FEYENOORD: Ed de Goey; Arnold Scholten, John Metgod, John De Wolf, Ruud Heus, Peter Bosz, Henk Fräser (85 Ulrich van Gobbel), Robert Witschge, Gaston Taument, Marian Damaschin (75 József Kiprich), Reginald Blinker. Trainer: Wim Jansen

FERENCVÁROS BUDAPEST v WERDER BREMEN 0-1 (0-0)
Üllöi út, Budapest 6.11.1991

Referee: Einar Halle (NOR)   Attendance: 25,000

FERENCVÁROS: Tamás Balogh; Tibor Simon, András Telek, József Keller, Sergei Kuznetsov, Zsolt Páling, Flórián Albert, Sándor Szenes, Péter Lipcsei, László Wukovics, Péter Deszatnik (77 Vasili Rats).   Trainer: Tibor Nyilasi

WERDER: Oliver Reck; Rune Bratseth, Miroslav Votava, Ulrich Borowka, Thomas Wolter, Uwe Harttgen (49 Thorsten Legat), Frank Neubarth, Dieter Eilts, Günter Hermann, Wynton Rufer, Marco Bode.   Trainer: Otto Rehhagel

Goal: Bode (48)

FEYENOORD ROTTERDAM v FC SION 0-0 (AET)
Feyenoord, Rotterdam 6.11.1991

Referee: Kim Milton Nielsen (DEN)   Attendance: 24,408

FEYENOORD: Ed de Goey; Arnold Scholten, John Metgod, John De Wolf, Ruud Heus, Peter Bosz, Henk Fräser, Robert Witschge (74 Ioan Ovidiu Sabău), Gaston Taument, Marian Damaschin (46 Ulrich van Gobbel), Reginald Blinker. Trainer: Hans Dorjee

FC SION: Stefan Lehmann; Michel Sauthier, Alain Geiger, Jean-Paul Brigger, Yvan Quentin, Mirsad Baljic, Reto Gertschen, Alvaro López, David Orlando (46 Alexandre Rey), Gabriel Calderón, Giuseppe Manfreda (100 Sébastien Fournier). Trainer: Enzo Trossero

Penalties: 1-0 Metgod, 1-1 Calderón, 2-1 Sabău, Sauthier (saved), 3-1 Fraser, 3-2 Geiger, 4-2 De Wolf, 4-3 Baljic, 5-3 Bosz

GALATASARAY ISTANBUL v BANÍK OSTRAVA 0-1 (0-0)
Ali Sami Yen, Istanbul 23.10.1991

Referee: José Rosa dos Santos (POR)   Attendance: 20,586

GALATASARAY: Hayrettin Demirbas; Ismail Demiriz, Bülent Korkmaz, Yusuf Altintas, Tugay Kerimoglu, Iosif Rotariu, Mustafa Yücedag (67 Dzevad Prekazi), Muhammet Altintas, Metin Yildiz, Selçuk Yula, Roman Kosecki (52 Arif Erdem). Trainer: Mustafa Denizli

BANÍK: Ivo Schmucker; Dušan Vrto, Petr Skarabela, Roman Sialini, Jiří Zálesky, Radim Necas, Radek Sloncík, Jiří Casko, Jan Palínek, Radomír Chylek (87 Tomáš Galásek), Libor Zelnícek (55 Zbynek Ollender).   Trainer: Jaroslav Gürtler

Goal: Ollender (68)

WERDER BREMEN v FERENCVÁROS BUDAPEST 3-2 (3-1)
Weserstadion, Bremen 23.10.1991

Referee: David Syme (SCO)   Attendance: 7,502

WERDER: Oliver Reck; Rune Bratseth, Miroslav Votava, Ulrich Borowka (52 Manfred Bockenfeld), Thomas Wolter, Dieter Eilts, Marco Bode, Thorsten Legat, Wynton Rufer, Frank Neubarth, Klaus Allofs.   Trainer: Otto Rehhagel

FERENCVÁROS: Tamás Balogh; Tibor Simon, András Telek, József Keller, Sergei Kuznetsov, Zsolt Páling (67 Csaba Patkós), Flórián Albert, Péter Lipcsei, Sándor Szenes, Gábor Schneider, Péter Deszatnik (72 László Wukovics).   Trainer: Tibor Nyilasi

Goals: Neubarth (28, 40), Allofs (33), Lipcsei (35, 73)

BANÍK OSTRAVA v GALATASARAY ISTANBUL 1-2 (1-2)
Stadión na Bazalech, Ostrava 6.11.1991

Referee: Mircea Salomir (ROM)   Attendance: 3,250

BANÍK: Tomáš Bernády; Tomáš Repka, Roman Sialini, Petr Skarabela, Tomáš Galásek, Jan Palínek, Jiří Casko, Radim Necas, Roman Pavelka (64 Libor Zelnícek), Radmoír Chylek, Zbynek Ollender.   Trainer: Jaroslav Gürtler

GALATASARAY: Hayrettin Demirbas; Bülent Korkmaz, Erhan Önal, Tayfun Hut, Ismail Demiriz, Yusuf Altintas, Muhammet Altintas, Mustafa Yücedag, Hamza Hamzaoglu, Arif Erdem (88 Metin Yildiz), Roman Kosecki.   Trainer: Mustafa Denizli

Goals: Ollender (31), Yusuf (41), Kosecki (44 pen)

**TOTTENHAM HOTSPUR LONDON
v FC PORTO 3-1** (2-0)

White Hart Lane, London   23.10.1991

Referee: Zoran Petrović (YUG)   Attendance: 23,621

TOTTENHAM: Erik Thorstvedt; Justin Edinburgh, Patrick van den Hauwe, Stephen Sedgley, Paul Walsh (56 Scott Houghton), Gary Mabbutt, Paul Stewart, Gordon Durie, Vincent Samways (83 Gudni Bergsson), Gary Lineker, Paul Allen.
Manager: Peter Shreeves

FC PORTO: VÍTOR Manuel Martins BAÍA; JOÃO Domingos Silva PINTO, FERNANDO Manuel Silva COUTO, ALOÍSIO Pires Alves, PAULO António Prado PEREIRA, António dos Santos ANDRÉ, RUI FILIPE Tavares Bastos, JAIME Fernandes MAGALHÃES (46 António José Alves Ribeiro "TOZÉ"), José Orlando Rocha SEMEDO, Ion Timofte (73 Alcides Rodrigues Tavares "KIKI"), Emile Kostadinov.

Goals: Lineker (14, 82), Durie (32), Kostadinov (52)

**FC PORTO
v TOTTENHAM HOTSPUR LONDON 0-0**

Estádio das Antas, Porto   7.11.1991

Referee: Peter Mikkelsen (DEN)   Attendance: 40,000

FC PORTO: VÍTOR Manuel Martins BAÍA; JOÃO Domingos Silva PINTO, ALOÍSIO Pires Alves, FERNANDO Manuel Silva COUTO, António dos Santos ANDRÉ, PAULO António Prado PEREIRA, José Orlando Rocha SEMEDO (81 JAIME Fernandes MAGALHÃES), António José Alves Ribeiro "TOZÉ", Ion Timofte, António José Santos FOLHA (54 JORGE ANDRADE de Guimarães), Emile Kostadinov.
Trainer: Carlos Alberto Silva

TOTTENHAM: Erik Thorstvedt; Justin Edinburgh, Patrick van den Hauwe, Gudni Bergsson, David Howells, Gary Mabbutt, Paul Stewart, Gordon Durie (85 Stephen Sedgley), Vincent Samways, Paul Allen, Gary Lineker (89 Paul Walsh).
Manager: Peter Shreeves

QUARTER-FINALS

**WERDER BREMEN
v GALATASARAY ISTANBUL 2-1** (0-1)

Weserstadion, Bremen   4.03.1992

Referee: Michal Listkiewicz (POL)   Attendance: 33,000

WERDER: Oliver Reck; Manfred Bockenfeld, Uwe Harttgen, Ulrich Borowka, Marco Bode, Günter Hermann (54 Marinus Bester), Dieter Eilts, Miroslav Votava, Frank Neubarth, Wynton Rufer (31 Stefan Kohn), Klaus Allofs.   Trainer: Otto Rehhagel

GALATASARAY: Hayrettin Demirbas; Ismail Demiriz, Tayfun Hut, Yusuf Altintas, Erhan Önal, Muhammet Altintas, Tugay Kerimoglu, Iosif Rotariu, Hamza Hamzaoglu, Roman Kosecki, Arif Erdem (82 Taner Alpak).
Trainer: Mustafa Denizli

Goals: Kosecki (33), Kohn (78), Bester (85)

**GALATASARAY ISTANBUL
v WERDER BREMEN 0-0**

Ali Sami Yen, Istanbul   18.03.1992

Referee: Kim Milton Nielsen (DEN)   Attendance: 27,357

GALATASARAY: Hayrettin Demirbas; Bülent Korkmaz, Yusuf Altintas, Tugay Kerimoglu, Muhammet Altintas, Erhan Önal (76 Taner Alpak), Iosif Rotariu, Hamza Hamzaoglu, Tayfun Hut, Roman Kosecki, Erdal Keser (70 Arif Erdem).
Trainer: Mustafa Denizli

WERDER: Oliver Reck; Manfred Bockenfeld (77 Marinus Bester), Rune Bratseth, Günter Hermann (83 Thorsten Legat), Ulrich Borowka, Thomas Wolter, Thomas Schaaf, Jonny Otten, Dieter Eilts, Frank Neubarth, Marco Bode.
Trainer: Otto Rehhagel

Sent off: Eilts (88)

**FEYENOORD ROTTERDAM
v TOTTENHAM HOTSPUR LONDON 1-0** (0-0)

Feyenoord, Rotterdam   4.03.1992

Referee: Pier Luigi Pairetto (ITA)   Attendance: 48,000

FEYENOORD: Ed de Goey; Henk Fräser, John De Wolf, John Metgod, Ruud Heus, Arnold Scholten, Ioan Ovidiu Sabău, Robert Witschge, Gaston Taument, József Kiprich, Reginald Blinker (73 Ulrich van Gobbel).   Trainer: Hans Dorjee

TOTTENHAM: Erik Thorstvedt; Terry Fenwick, Stephen Sedgley, Gary Mabbutt, Paul Allen, Paul Stewart, Patrick van den Hauwe, David Howells (74 Vincent Samways), Mohamed Nayim, Gordon Durie, Gary Lineker (85 Paul Walsh).
Manager: Peter Shreeves

Goal: Kiprich (56)

**TOTTENHAM HOTSPUR LONDON
v FEYENOORD ROTTERDAM 0-0**

White Hart Lane, London   18.03.1991

Referee: Kurt Röthlisberger (SWI)   Attendance: 29,834

TOTTENHAM: Erik Thorstvedt; Gudni Bergsson, Stephen Sedgley, Gary Mabbutt, Justin Edinburgh, Paul Allen, Paul Stewart, David Howells (63 Scott Houghton), Mohamed Nayim (72 Paul Walsh), Gary Lineker, Gordon Durie.
Manager: Peter Shreeves

FEYENOORD: Ed de Goey; Arnold Scholten, John De Wolf, John Metgod, Ruud Heus, Ioan Ovidiu Sabău (75 Ulrich van Gobbel), Peter Bosz, Henk Fräser, Robert Witschge, Gaston Taument, Reginald Blinker (63 József Kiprich).
Trainer: Hans Dorjee

ATLÉTICO MADRID v CLUB BRUGGE 3-2 (1-2)
Vicente Calderón, Madrid 4.03.1992
Referee: Bruno Galler (SWI)   Attendance: 38,000
ATLÉTICO: ABEL Resino Gómez; DONATO Gama da Silva (56 Juan Manuel LÓPEZ Martínez), Juan Francisco Rodríguez "JUANITO", Roberto SOLOZÁBAL Villanueva, TOMÁS Reñones Crego, Juan VIZCAÍNO Morcillo, Bernd Schuster, Antonio Muñoz Gómez "TONI", Gabriel MOYA Sanz, Manuel Sánchez Delgado "MANOLO", Paulo Jorge dos Santos "FUTRE".   Trainer: Luis Aragonés Suárez
CLUB BRUGGE: Danny Verlinden; Claude Verspaille, Pascal Plovie (67 Stéphane van der Heyden), Rudy Cossey, Lorenzo Staelens, Vital Borkelmans, Luc Beyens, Franky van der Elst, Peter Crève, Foeke Booy, Daniel Amokachi.
Trainer: Hugo Broos
Goals: Schuster (30), Verspaille (31), Beyens (43), Toni (47), Futre (57)

CLUB BRUGGE v ATLÉTICO MADRID 2-1 (1-1)
Olympiastadion, Brugge 18.03.1992
Referee: Rune Larsson (SWE)   Attendance: 21,000
CLUB BRUGGE: Danny Verlinden; Claude Verspaille, Alex Querter, Rudy Cossey, Vital Borkelmans, Peter Crève, Lorenzo Staelens, Luc Beyens, Stéphane van der Heyden (66 Pascal Plovie), Foeke Booy, Daniel Amokachi (80 Tomasz Dziubiński).
Trainer: Hugo Broos
ATLÉTICO: ABEL Resino Gómez; TOMÁS Reñones Crego (65 Juan Carlos AGUILERA Martín), Juan Manuel LÓPEZ Martínez, Juan Francisco Rodríguez "JUANITO", Roberto SOLOZÁBAL Villanueva, Antonio Muñoz Gómez "TONI", Juan VIZCAÍNO Morcillo, Bernd Schuster, Miquel SOLER Sarasols (54 Gabriel MOYA Sanz), Manuel Sánchez Delgado "MANOLO", Paulo Jorge dos Santos "FUTRE".
Trainer: Luis Aragonés Suárez
Goals: Futre (10), Querter (40 pen), Booy (62)

AS ROMA v AS MONACO 0-0
Stadio Olimpico, Roma 4.03.1992
Referee: Antonio Martin Navarrete (SPA)   Att: 40,336
AS ROMA: Giuseppe Zinetti; Marco Antonio De Marchi (46 Luigi Garzja), Amedeo Carboni, Walter Bonacina, ALDAIR dos Santos, Sebastiano Nela, Thomas Hässler, Fabrizio Di Mauro, Rudi Völler, Fausto Salsano (52 Andrea Carnevale), Ruggiero Rizzitelli.   Trainer: Ottavio Bianchi
AS MONACO: Jean-Luc Ettori; Patrick Valéry, Emmanuel Petit, Roger Mendy, Luc Sonor, Marcel Dib, Claude Puel, Gérald Passi (79 Youri Djorkaeff), RUI Gil Soares de BARROS, George Weah, Youssouf Fofana (70 Jerome Gnako).
Trainer: Arsène Wenger

AS MONACO v AS ROMA 1-0 (1-0)
Louis II, Monaco 18.03.1992
Referee: John Blankenstein (HOL)   Attendance: 15,000
AS MONACO: Jean-Luc Ettori; Patrick Valéry, Emmanuel Petit, Roger Mendy, Luc Sonor, Claude Puel, Marcel Dib, Gérald Passi (84 Lilian Thuram), RUI Gil Soares de BARROS, Youssouf Fofana (74 Jerome Gnako), George Weah.
Trainer: Arsène Wenger
AS ROMA: Giuseppe Zinetti; Luigi Garzja, Amedeo Carboni, Giovanni Piacentini (53 Giuseppe Giannini), ALDAIR dos Santos, Sebastiano Nela (46 Antonio Comi), Thomas Hässler, Walter Bonacina, Rudi Völler, Fabrizio Di Mauro, Ruggiero Rizzitelli.   Trainer: Ottavio Bianchi
Goal: Rui Barros (45)

SEMI-FINALS

**AS MONACO
v FEYENOORD ROTTERDAM 1-1** (1-1)
Louis II Monaco 1.04.1992
Referee: Brian McGinlay (SCO)   Attendance: 15,000
AS MONACO: Jean-Luc Ettori; Patrick Valéry, Lilian Thuram, Roger Mendy, Luc Sonor, Claude Puel, Gérald Passi, RUI Gil Soares de BARROS, Marcel Dib (73 Jerome Gnako), George Weah, Youssouf Fofana (60 Youri Djorkaeff).
Trainer: Arsène Wenger
FEYENOORD: Ed de Goey; Ulrich van Gobbel, John Metgod, Henk Fräser, Ruud Heus, Arnold Scholten, Sjaak Troost, Robert Witschge, Gaston Taument, József Kiprich (75 Stanislav Griga), Reginald Blinker.   Trainer: Hans Dorjee
Goals: Robert Witschge (9), Valéry (26)

**FEYENOORD ROTTERDAM
v AS MONACO 2-2** (1-1)
Feyenoord, Rotterdam 15.04.1992
Referee: Rune Larsson (SWE)   Attendance: 42,107
FEYENOORD: Ed de Goey; Ulrich van Gobbel, John Metgod, Henk Fräser, Ruud Heus (78 Marian Damaschin), Arnold Scholten, Peter Bosz, Robert Witschge, Gaston Taument, József Kiprich, Reginald Blinker.   Trainer: Hans Dorjee
AS MONACO: Jean-Luc Ettori; Patrick Valéry, Roger Mendy, Emmanuel Petit, Luc Sonor, Jerôme Gnako (77 Lilian Thuram), Marcel Dib, Claude Puel, RUI Gil Soares de BARROS, Youssouf Fofana (70 Gérald Passi), George Weah.
Trainer: Arsène Wenger
Goals: Weah (33), Rui Barros (49), Witschge (50), Damaschin (86)

CLUB BRUGGE v WERDER BREMEN 1-0 (1-0)
Olympiastadion, Brugge   1.04.1992

Referee: Lube Spasov (BUL)   Attendance: 21,000

CLUB BRUGGE: Danny Verlinden; Luc Beyens, Alex Querter, Pascal Plovie (53 Dominique van Maele), Rudy Cossey, Vital Borkelmans, Franky van der Elst, Lorenzo Staelens, Stéphane van der Heyden, Daniel Amokachi, Foeke Booy.   Trainer: Hugo Broos

WERDER: Oliver Reck (67 Jürgen Rollmann); Manfred Bockenfeld, Thorsten Legat, Rune Bratseth, Jonny Otten, Ulrich Borowka, Thomas Wolter, Miroslav Votava (77 Thomas Schaaf), Frank Neubarth, Marco Bode, Wynton Rufer.   Trainer: Otto Rehhagel

Goal: Amokachi (5)

WERDER BREMEN v CLUB BRUGGE 2-0 (1-0)
Weserstadion, Bremen   15.04.1992

Referee: Howard King (WAL)   Attendance: 35,000

WERDER: Oliver Reck; Thomas Wolter, Ulrich Borowka, Manfred Bockenfeld (88 Thomas Schaaf), Günter Hermann (70 Klaus Allofs), Rune Bratseth, Miroslav Votava, Wynton Rufer, Thorsten Legat, Marco Bode, Stefan Kohn.   Trainer: Otto Rehhagel

CLUB BRUGGE: Danny Verlinden; Rudy Cossey, Claude Verspaille, Alex Querter, László Disztl (73 Stéphane van der Heyden), Vital Borkelmans, Franky van der Elst, Peter Crève (46 Luc Beyens), Lorenzo Staelens, Daniel Amokachi, Foeke Booy.   Trainer: Hugo Broos

Sent off: Amokachi (76)

Goals: Bode (31), Bockenfeld (60)

FINAL

SV WERDER BREMEN v AS MONACO 2-0 (1-0)

Estadio Da Luz, Lisboa   6.05.1992

Referee: Pietro D'Elia (ITA)   Attendance: 15,000

WERDER: Jürgen Rollmann, Thomas Wolter (35 Thomas Schaaf), Rune Bratseth, Ulrich Borowka, Marco Bode, Manfred Bockenfeld, Miroslav Votava, Dieter Eilts, Wynton Rufer, Klaus Allofs, Frank Neubarth (75 Stefan Kohn).   Trainer: Otto Rehhagel

AS MONACO: Jean-Luc Ettori; Patrick Valéry (62 Youri Djorkaeff), Roger Mendy, Emmanuel Petit, Luc Sonor, Jérôme Gnako, RUI Gil Soares de BARROS, Marcel Dib, Gérald Passi, George Weah, Youssouf Fofana (59 Benjamin Clément).   Trainer: Arsène Wenger

Goals: Allofs (41), Rufer (55)

Goalscorers European Cup-Winners' Cup 1991-92:

6 goals: Péter Lipcsei (Ferencváros)

5 goals: Paulo Jorge dos Santos "FUTRE", Manuel Sánchez Delgado "Manolo" (Atlético Madrid)

4 goals: RUI Gil Soares de BARROS, George Weah (Monaco), Wynton Rufer (Werder Bremen), Roman Kosecki (Galatasaray), Bernd Schuster (Atlético Madrid)

3 goals: Marek Czakon (Ilves Tampere), Gordon Durie (Tottenham), Andrea Carnevale (Roma), Foeke Booy (Club Brugge), Gérald Passi (Monaco), Marco Bode, Stefan Kohn, Frank Neubarth (Werder Bremen)

2 goals: McBride (Glenavon), Kirk (Motherwell), Nedergaard (OB Odense), Tengs (Fyllingen IL), Hellström, J.Eriksson (IFK Norrköping), Hughes (Manchester United), Mattila (Ilves), Desznatnik (Ferencváros), Ollender (Baník), Kostadinov, Timofte (FC Porto), Lineker (Tottenham), Rizzitelli (Roma), Witschge (Feyenoord), Staelens, Verspaille (Club Brugge), Allofs, Bratseth (Werder Bremen)

1 goal: Legg (Swansea), Einarsson (Valur), Ferguson, Conville (Glenavon), Novakovic (Hajduk Split), Dartilov, Bankov, Dimitrov (Levski Sofia), Marinelli (Jeunesse), Cusack (Motherwell), Bordingaard, Donnerup, Harder, Elstrup, L.Hansen, Thorup (OB Odense), F.Bartz (Stahl), Sergheev, Dmitriev (CSKA Moskva), Karlsson, Vaattovaara, Kindvall (IFK Norrköping), McClair (Manchester United), Szewczyk, Wolny, Rzezniczek (GKS Katowice), J. Aaltonen, Dziadulewicz (Ilves), Rey, Orlando (FC Sion), Albert (Ferencváros), Skarabela, Casko, Chylek (Baník Ostrava), Mihtarski (FC Porto), Yusuf, Erdal, Arif, Mustafa (Galatasaray), Tuttle, Mabbutt (Tottenham), Toni, Soler (Atlético Madrid), Giannini, Di Mauro (Roma), Damaschin, Kiprich, Bosz (Feyenoord), Amokachi, Beyens, Querter, Schaessens, Dziubinski, Van der Heyden (Club Brugge), Valéry, Mendy, Robert, Fofana, Djorkaeff (Monaco), Bockenfeld, Bester, Votava, Eilts (Werder Bremen)

Own goals: Harris (Swansea) for Monaco, Steffensen (OB Odense) for Baník Ostrava, Fokin (CSKA Moskva) for Roma

CUP WINNERS' CUP 1992-93

PRELIMINARY ROUND

**MARIBOR BRANIK
v HAMRUN SPARTANS 4-0** (2-0)

Ljudski Vrt, Maribor   19.08.1992

Referee: Bernd Heynemann (GER)   Attendance: 4,200

BRANIK: Mladen Dabanović; Emil Sterbal, Bostjan Ratković, Zarko Tarana, Saso Lukić, Ales Krizan, Ante Simundza, Peter Binkovski, Mirsad Bicakcić (76 Saso Gajser), Marko Krizanić (80 Simon Dvorsak), Marijan Bakula. Trainer: Marian Bloudek

HAMRUN SPARTANS: Alan Zammit; Emanuel Brincat (56 Noel Fenech), Mario Gorla, Marco Grech, Joe Brincat, Raymond Vella, Ivan Zammit, Miguel Corbalan, Cesar Paiber, Michael Degiorgio (22 David Camilleri), Stefan Sultana. Trainer: Victor Tedesco

Goals: Simundza (16, 30), Tarana (49), Binkovski (77)

**HAMRUN SPARTANS
v MARIBOR BRANIK 2-1** (1-1)

National Stadium, Ta'Qali   2.09.1992

Referee: Arcangelo Pezzella (ITA)   Attendance: 850

HAMRUN SPARTANS: Alan Zammit; John Micallef, Mario Gorla, Marco Grech, Joe Brincat, David Camilleri, Ivan Zammit, Noel Fenech, Cesar Paiber (90 Miguel Corbalan), Michael Degiorgio (Cap), Stefan Sultana (86 Alex Azzopardi). Trainer: Lolly Debattista

BRANIK: Mladen Dabanović; Emil Sterbal, Bostjan Ratković, Zarko Tarana, Saso Lukić, Ales Krizan (Cap), Ante Simundza (83 Enver Cirić), Peter Binkovski, Mirsad Bicakcić, Marko Krizanić (74 Saso Gajser), Marijan Bakula. Trainer: Marian Bloudek

Goals: J. Brincat (34, 59), Tarana (38)

**STRØMSGODSET IF
v HAPOEL PETACH TIKVA 0-2** (0-0)

Marienlyst Drammen   19.08.1992

Referee: Wojciech Rudy (POL)   Attendance: 1,933

STRØMSGODSET: Eirik Arildset; Ståle Skau (46 Arne Gustavsen), Frode Johannessen, Vegard Hansen, Jan Wendelborg (64 Odd Johnsen), Halvor Storskogen (Cap), Trond Nordeide, Geir Andersen, Krister Åre Isaksen, Juro Kuvicek, Glenn Knutsen.   Trainer: Halvard Thoresen

HAPOEL: Rafi Cohen; Benny Kozoshvily, Carlos Oleran, Alex Bremcher, Noam Keissy, Yossi Levi, Avi Keissy, Oz Ilia, Ely Mahpoud (Cap), Nir Levin, Meny Basson. Trainer: Jan Pivarnik

Goals: Basson (48, 59)

**HAPOEL PETACH TIKVA
v STRØMSGODSET DRAMMEN 2-0** (1-0)

Municipal, Petach Tikva   2.09.1992

Referee: Loizos Loizou (CYP)   Attendance: 2,000

HAPOEL: Rafi Cohen; Benny Kozoshvily, Avi Keissy, Bahagat Udda, Carlos Oleran, Noam Keissy, Yossi Levi, Ely Mahpoud (Cap) (73 Offir Kopel), Nir Levin, Meny Basson, Oz Ilia (70 Uzi Ohaion).   Trainer: Jan Pivarnik

STRØMSGODSET: Eirik Arildset; Arne Gustavsen, Frode Johannessen, Vegard Hansen, Jan Wendelborg, Krister Åre Isaksen, Ulf Camitz, Geir Andersen, Glenn Knutsen, Odd Johnsen (Cap) (46 Ståle Skau), Juro Kuvicek. Trainer: Halvard Thoresen

Goals: Levin (17), Basson (68)

FC VADUZ v CHERNOMORETS ODESSA 0-5 (0-1)

National Vaduz   19.08.1992

Referee: Ernest Kesseler (LUX)   Attendance: 1,650

FC VADUZ: Peter Hartmann; Roland Moser (77 Daniel Hemmerle), Patrik Hefti, Daniel Moser, Heinrich Nigg, Alexander Quaderer, Franco Rotunno, Wolfgang Ospelt (Cap), Franz Schädler (46 Daniel Hasler), Beat Lohner, Harry Schädler.   Trainer: Hans-Joachim Abel

CHERNOMORETS: Oleg Suslov; Yuri Nikiforov (Cap), Sergei Protsiuk, Yuri Bukel, Vladimir Lebed, Dmytro Parfenov (55 Ruslan Romanchuk), Ilia Tsimbalar, Viktor Yablonski, Oleg Kosheliuk (55 Konstantin Kulik), Yuri Sak, Sergei Gusev. Trainer: Viktor Prokopenko

Goals: Tsimbalar (45), Lebed (47), Sak (52), Gusev (80, 82)

CHERNOMORETS ODESSA v FC VADUZ 7-1 (4-0)

Central Odessa   2.09.1992

Referee: Jozef Marko (CZE)   Attendance: 4,600

CHERNOMORETS: Oleg Suslov; Yuri Nikiforov (Cap), Sergei Protsiuk, Yuri Bukel, Vladimir Lebed, Dmytro Parfenov, Ilia Tsimbalar, Viktor Yablonski (46 Andrei Lozovski), Oleg Kosheliuk, Yuri Sak (46 Konstantin Kulik), Sergei Gusev. Trainer: Viktor Prokopenko

FC VADUZ: Peter Hartmann (69 Oliver Gassner); Daniel Hasler (69 Rigobert Wolff), Patrik Hefti, Beat Lohner, Heinrich Nigg, Alexander Quaderer, Franco Rotunno, Roland Moser (Cap), Christian Stöber, Franz Scädler, Harry Schädler. Trainer: Hans-Joachim Abel

Goals: Nikiforov (9, 49 pen, 78, 90), Yablonski (23), Tsimbalar (27), Lebed (77), Stöber (87)

**AVENIR BEGGEN
v BOLTFELAG 36 TÓRSHAVN 1-0** (1-0)
Stade de Beggen 19.08.1992

Referee: Marnix Sandra (BEL)   Attendance: 684

AVENIR: Paul Koch; Ralph Ferron, Théo Scholten, Jean Vanek, Alex Wilhelm, Jaba Moreira, Markus Krahen (75 Mario Nowak), Carlo Weis (Cap), Frank Goergen (81 Serge Jentgen), Armin Krings, Luc Holtz.   Trainer: Jean Lanners

B 36: Wiscek Zakrewski; Danjal Petur Johansen (67 Samal Hansen), Tummas Eli Hansen (Cap), Bogi Jacobsen, Rogvi Thorsteinsson, Jon Hardlei, Jakup Mørk, Jens Christian Hansen, Jan Poulsen, Kari Reynheim, Jakup Simonsen.

Goal: Krings (1)

**BOLTFELAG 36 TÓRSHAVN
v AVENIR BEGGEN 1-1** (1-1)
Gundadalur, Tórshavn 2.09.1992

Referee: Joseph Timmons (SCO)   Attendance: 665

B 36: Wiscek Zakrewski; Danjal Petur Johansen, Tummas Eli Hansen (Cap), Bogi Jacobsen, Rogvi Thorsteinsson, Samal Hansen, Jakup Mørk (67 Jon Hardlei), Jens Christian Hansen, Jan Poulsen (84 Frodi Madsen), Kari Reynheim, Jakup Simonsen.

AVENIR: Paul Koch; Ralph Ferron, Rolf Jentgen, Jean Vanek, Alex Wilhelm, Serge Jentgen, Markus Krahen (84 Mario Nowak), Carlo Weis (Cap), Théo Scholten, Armin Krings, Luc Holtz (89 Jaba Moreira).   Trainer: Jean Lanners

Goals: Reynheim (9), Krahen (28)

FIRST ROUND

AIK SOLNA v ÅRHUS GF 3-3 (0-2)
Råsunda, Solna 15.09.1992

Referee: Stephen Lodge (ENG)   Attendance: 3,976

AIK: Bernt Ljung; Krister Nordin, Björn Kindlund (Cap), Anders Hjelm, Peter Larsson, Michael Borgqvist, Vadim Yevtushenko, Kim Bergstrand, Pascal Simpson, Peter Hallström (75 Dick Lidman), Gary Sundgren.
Trainer: Tommy Söderberg

AGF: Troels Rasmussen; Claus Thomsen, Kent Nielsen (Cap), Jan Halvor Halvorsen, Lasse Skov, Claus Christiansen, Stig Tøfting, Jan Bartram, Torben Christensen (65 Ole Mortensen), Bo Harder, Søren Andersen (75 Palle Sørensen).
Trainer: Lars Lundqvist

Goals: Tøfting (15), Christensen (36, 54), Simpson (51), Hallström (56), Yevtushenko (85)

ÅRHUS GF v AIK SOLNA 1-1 (0-1)
Århus stadion 29.09.1992

Referee: Arturo Martino (SWI)   Attendance: 9,000

AGF: Troels Rasmussen; Claus Thomsen, Jan Halvor Halvorsen, Kent Nielsen (Cap), Lasse Skov (58 Palle Sørensen), Stig Tøfting, Claus Christiansen (71 Gunner Lind Pedersen), Jan Bartram, Bo Harder, Torben Christensen, Søren Andersen.
Trainer: Lars Lundqvist

AIK: Bernt Ljung; Gary Sundgren, Peter Larsson, Anders Hjelm, Björn Kindlund (Cap), Krister Nordin, Michael Borgqvist, Vadim Yevtushenko, Peter Hallström (75 Dick Lidman), Kim Bergstrand, Pascal Simpson.   Trainer: Tommy Söderberg

Goals: Simpson (20), Harder (67)

AIRDRIEONIANS v SPARTA PRAHA 0-1 (0-0)
Broomfield Park, Airdrie 15.09.1992

Referee: Rune Pedersen (NOR)   Attendance: 5,377

AIRDRIEONIANS: John Martin; Walter Kidd, Sandy Stewart, James Sandison (Cap), Chris Honor, Kenneth Black, Jimmy Boyle, Evan Balfour, Andy Smith, Alan Lawrence, Owen Coyle.
Manager: Alex McDonald

SPARTA: Petr Kouba; Jan Sopko, Lumír Mistr, Petr Vrabec, Michal Hornák, Michal Bílek, Jiří Němec, Jozef Chovanec (Cap), Viktor Dvirnik (70 Marek Trval), Roman Vonasek, Martin Frýdek (89 Pavel Nedvěd).   Trainer: Dušan Uhrin

Goal: Sopko (89)

SPARTA PRAHA v AIRDRIEONIANS 2-1 (2-0)
Štadión na Letnej, Praha 30.09.1992

Referee: Atanas Uzunov (BUL)   Attendance: 8,989

SPARTA: Petr Kouba; Jan Sopko, Lumír Mistr, Petr Vrabec, Michal Hornák, Michal Bílek, Jiří Němec, Jozef Chovanec (Cap), Roman Vonasek, Horst Siegl (89 Viktor Dvirnik), Martin Frýdek (87 Pavel Nedvěd).   Trainer: Dušan Uhrin

AIRDRIEONIANS: John Martin; Walter Kidd, Sandy Stewart (Cap), James Sandison, Gus Caesar (54 Davie Kirkwood), Kenneth Black, Jimmy Boyle (65 Alan Lawrence), Evan Balfour, Andy Smith, Owen Coyle, Chris Honor.
Manager: Alex McDonald

Goals: Vrabec (31), Vonasek (37), Black (56)

**GLENAVON LURGAN
v ROYAL ANTWERP FC 1-1** (1-0)
Mourneview Park, Lurgan   15.09.1992

Referee: Nemus Djurhuus (FAR)   Attendance: 2,556

GLENAVON: Robbie Beck; Trevor McMullan, Paul Byrne (Cap), Michael McKeown (89 Fintan McConville), Tony Scappatici, Colin Crawford, Sammy Smith, Brian Kennedy, Michael Crowe, Glenn Ferguson, Geoff Ferris.   Trainer: Peter Watson

ANTWERP: Ratko Svilar; Ronny Van Rethy, Nico Broeckaert, Geert Emmerechts, Rudy Smidts (Cap), Wim Kiekens, Didier Segers, Hans-Peter Lehnhoff, Patrick Van Veirdeghem, Dragan Jakovljevic, Alex Czerniatynski (76 Francis Severeyns).
Trainer: Walter Meeuws

Goals: Smith (45), Lehnhoff (46)

HANNOVER 96 v WERDER BREMEN 2-1 (2-1)
Niedersachsen, Hannover   30.09.1992

Referee: Mario Van der Ende (HOL)   Attendance: 27,436

HANNOVER: Jörg Sievers; Dejan Raickovic, Jörg-Uwe Klütz, Axel Sundermann, Martin Groth, Reinhold Daschner (75 André Breitenreiter), André Sirocks, Hakan Bicici, Jörg Kretschmar, Milos Djelmas, Uwe Jursch (62 Michael Koch).
Trainer: Eberhard Vogel

WERDER: Oliver Reck; Rune Bratseth, Miroslav Votava (Cap), Dietmar Beiersdorfer (28 Uwe Harttgen), Thomas Wolter, Manfred Bockenfeld, Andreas Herzog (58 Günter Hermann), Dieter Eilts, Marco Bode, Wynton Rufer, Klaus Allofs.   Trainer: Otto Rehhagel

Goals: Rufer (19 pen), Daschner (29, 33)

**ROYAL ANTWERP FC
v GLENAVON LURGAN 1-1** (0-0, 1-1) (AET)
Bosuil, Antwerp   30.09.1992

Referee: Heinz Holzmann (AUS)   Attendance: 4,000

ANTWERP: Ratko Svilar; Wim Kiekens, Nico Broeckaert, Geert Emmerechts, Rudy Smidts (Cap), Nourédine Moukrim, Ronny Van Rethy (108 Patrick Van Veirdeghem), Didier Segers, Francis Severeyns, Hans-Peter Lehnhoff, Alex Czerniatynski (78 Willy Vincent).   Trainer: Walter Meeuws

GLENAVON: Robbie Beck; Paul Byrne (Cap), Trevor McMullan, Tony Scappatici (75 Keith Percy), Michael McKeown, Brian Kennedy, Colin Crawford, Fintan McConville (77 Sammy Smith), Michael Crowe, Glenn Ferguson, Geoff Ferris.
Trainer: Peter Watson

Sent off: Crowe

Goals: Kiekens (65 pen), Ferris (80)

Penalties: 0-1 McMullan, Lehnhoff (miss), Crawford (miss), 1-1 Emmerechts, Ferguson (miss), 2-1 Vincent, Smith (miss), 3-1 Smidts

BOHEMIANS DUBLIN v STEAUA BUCUREŞTI 0-0
Dalymount Park, Dublin   16.09.1992

Referee: Gilles Veissière (FRA)   Attendance: 4,513

BOHEMIANS: Dave Henderson; Thomas Byrne, Paul Whelan (Cap), Robert Best, Declan Goechegan (82 Paul Byrne), Maurice O'Driscoll, Lee King, Pat Fenlon, Alan Byrne, Joe Lawless, David Tilson.   Manager: Eamon Gregg

STEAUA: Daniel Gherasim; Aurel Silviu Panait, Ştefan Iovan, Bogdan Bucur, Anton Doboş, Ilie Stan (11 Ion Sburlea), Basarab Panduru, Ionel Pîrvu, Ilie Dumitrescu (Cap), Ion Vlădoiu, Viorel Ion (76 Iulian Sebastian Filipescu).
Trainer: Anghel Iordănescu

WERDER BREMEN v HANNOVER 96 3-1 (3-1)
Weserstadium, Bremen   15.09.1992

Referee: David Elleray (ENG)   Attendance: 17,003

WERDER: Oliver Reck; Rune Bratseth, Miroslav Votava (Cap), Dietmar Beiersdorfer (30 Günter Hermann), Manfred Bockenfeld, Uwe Harttgen, Andreas Herzog, Dieter Eilts, Marco Bode, Wynton Rufer (69 Thomas Wolter), Klaus Allofs.
Trainer: Otto Rehhagel

HANNOVER: Jörg Sievers; Roman Wójcicki (Cap), Axel Sundermann, Jörg-Uwe Klütz, Bernd Heemsoth, Martin Groth, André Sirocks, Hakan Bicici, Michael Schönberg, Michael Koch (67 Jörg Kretschmar), Milos Djelmas (64 Reinhold Mathy).
Trainer: Eberhard Vogel

Sent off: Scönberg

Goals: Rufer (19, 28), Wojcicki (26 pen), Bratseth (45)

**STEAUA BUCUREŞTI
v BOHEMIANS DUBLIN 4-0** (3-0)
Steaua Bucureşti   29.09.1992

Referee: Friedrich Kaupe (AUS)   Attendance: 10,000

STEAUA: Daniel Gherasim; Aurel Silviu Panait, Anton Doboş, Bogdan Bucur, Ionel Pîrvu, Ionel Fulga (63 Viorel Ion), Ilie Stan, Basarab Panduru, Ilie Dumitrescu (Cap), Ion Vlădoiu, Alexandru Andrasi (67 Adrian State).
Trainer: Anghel Iordănescu

BOHEMIANS: Dave Henderson; Thomas Byrne, Paul Whelan (Cap), Robert Best, Declan Geoghegan, Maurice O'Driscoll (82 Mark Devlin), Anthony O'Connor, Pat Fenlon, Alan Byrne (73 Lee King), Joe Lawless, David Tilson.
Manager: Eamon Gregg

Goals: Andrasi (25, 34), Vlădoiu (45), V.Ion (85)

CARDIFF CITY
v ADMIRA WACKER WIEN 1-1 (0-1)

Ninian Park, Cardiff 16.09.1992

Referee: Jorge Monteiro Coroado (POR)   Attendance: 9,624

CITY: Mark Grew; Tony Bird (72 Andrew Gorman), Damon Searle, Lee Baddeley, Gareth Abraham, Derek Brazil, Paul Ramsey (Cap), Cohen Griffith, Chris Pike, Carl Dale, Nathan Blake.   Trainer: Eddie May

ADMIRA: Franz Gruber; Alois Dötzl, Thomas Zingler, Michael Gruber, Gerald Messlender, Johannes Abfalterer, Andreas Gutlederer (54 Gerald Bacher), Olaf Marschall, Peter Artner (Cap), Kurt Temm, Roger Ljung.
Trainer: Siegfried Held

Goals: Abfalterer (44), Pike (59)

ADMIRA WACKER WIEN
v CARDIFF CITY 2-0 (0-0)

Bundesstadion Südstadt Stadium Wien 29.09.1992

Referee: Lube Spasov (BUL)   Attendance: 4,700

ADMIRA: Franz Gruber; Alois Dötzl, Uwe Müller (65 Thomas Zingler), Michael Gruber, Gerald Messlender, Johannes Abfalterer, Gerald Bacher, Olaf Marschall, Peter Artner (Cap), Kurt Temm, Roger Ljung.
Trainer: Siegfried Held

CITY: Mark Grew; Robbie James, Damon Searle, Lee Baddeley, Gareth Abraham (49 Tony Bird), Derek Brazil, Paul Ramsey (Cap), Cohen Griffith, Chris Pike, Carl Dale, Nathan Blake.   Trainer: Eddie May

Goals: Marschall (47), Abfalterer (90)

LIVERPOOL FC v APOLLON LIMASSOL 6-1 (3-0)

Anfield, Liverpool 16.09.1992

Referee: José Alberto Veiga Trigo (POR)   Att: 12,769

LIVERPOOL: David James; Steve Harkness (58 Philip Charnock), David Burrows, Steve Nicol, Jamie Redknapp, Mark Wright (Cap), Mike Marsh, Paul Stewart (85 Ronny Rosenthal), Ian Rush, Jan Mølby, Mark Walters.
Manager: Graeme Souness

APOLLON: Mihalis Hristofi; Antonis Ilia "Antrellis", Haralampos Pittas, Dimitris Ioannou, David Kenny, Giannis Giagkoudakis (Cap), Giorgos Iosifides, Milenko Spoljaric, Hrysostomos Juras, Haralampos Hristofi (60 Andreas Sofokleous), Marios Haralampous.   Trainer: Minos Kakoulis

Sent off: Haralampous

Goals: Stewart (4, 38), Rush (39, 50, 55, 74), Spoljaric (84 pen)

APOLLON LIMASSOL v LIVERPOOL 1-2 (0-0)

Tsirion, Limassol 29.09.1992

Referee: Loris Stafoggia (ITA)   Attendance: 10,000

APOLLON: Mihalis Hristofi; Antonis Antrellis Ilia, Haralampos Pittas, Dimitris Ioannou, Haralampos Hristofi, Giannis Giagkoudakis (Cap), Giorgos Iosifides, Milenko Spoljaric, Hrysostomos Juras (6 Andreas Sofokleous), Aggelos Tsolakis (67 Avgoustinos Gennaris), David Kenny.
Trainer: Minos Kakoulis

LIVERPOOL: Bruce Grobbelaar; Mike Marsh, David Burrows, Nicky Tanner, Jamie Redknapp, Don Hutchison, Steve McManaman, Paul Stewart, Ian Rush, Jan Mølby (Cap), Mark Walters (81 Steve Harkness).
Manager: Graeme Souness

Sent off: Stewart

Goals: Spoljaric (60), Rush (62), Hutchison (68)

MIEDZ LEGNICA v AS MONACO 0-1 (0-1)

Miedz Legnica 16.09.1992

Referee: Hans-Peter Dellwig (GER)   Attendance: 4,800

MIEDZ: Dariusz Placzkiewicz; Grzegorz Kochanek, Bogdan Pisz, Andrzej Cymbala (78 Krzysztof Wojtkowski), Cezary Michalski (Cap), Mariusz Urbaniak, Artur Wójcik (78 Pawel Prima), Marcin Cilinski, Jaroslaw Gierejkiewicz, Dariusz Dziarmaga, Wojciech Górski.   Trainer: Ryszard Bozyczko

AS MONACO: Jean-Luc Ettori (Cap); Patrick Valéry, Lilian Thuram, Franck Dumas, Patrick Blondeau, Claude Puel, Jerôme Gnako, Luis Henrique, Youri Djorkaeff, RUI Gil Soares de BARROS (46 Sylvain Legwinski), Jürgen Klinsmann.
Trainer: Arsène Wenger

Goal: Djorkaeff (3)

AS MONACO v MIEDZ LEGNICA 0-0

Louis II, Monaco 30.09.1992

Referee: Manuel Diaz Vega (SPA)   Attendance: 4,538

AS MONACO: Jean-Luc Ettori (Cap); Patrick Blondeau, Lilian Thuram, Franck Dumas, Luc Sonor, Claude Puel, Jerôme Gnako, Luis Henrique (63 Youri Djorkaeff), Marcel Dib, Jürgen Klinsmann, Youssouf Fofana (83 Bruno Rodríguez).
Trainer: Arsène Wenger

MIEDZ: Dariusz Placzkiewicz; Bogdan Pisz, Andrzej Cymbala, Cezary Michalski (Cap), Piotr Przerywacz, Mariusz Urbaniak (62 Krzysztof Wojtkowski), Marcin Cilinski, Jaroslaw Gierejkiewicz, Wojciech Górski, Dariusz Dziarmaga (17 Tadeusz Gajdzis), Artur Wójcik.   Trainer: Ryszard Bozyczko

TRABZONSPOR
v PALLOSEURA TURKU 2-0 (0-0)
Avni Aker, Trabzon   16.09.1992

Referee: Kaj Østergaard (DEN)   Attendance: 22,000

TRABZONSPOR: Viktor Grishko; Hamdi Aslan, Ogün Temizkanoglu, Kemal Serdar (Cap), Jacek Cyzio (46 Soner Boz), Yuri Shelepnitski, Ünal Karaman (83 Ismail Gökçek), Turgut Uçar, Abdullah Ercan, Hami Mandirali, Orhan Çikrikçi. Trainer: Ronny Desmeot

TPS: Petri Jakonen; Lars Dalsborg, Jyrki Hännikäinen, Petri Sulonen, Ari Heikkinen (Cap), Jani Keula, Janne Lehtinen (61 Kim Lehtonen), Petteri Viljanen, Mika Lipponen (81 Jasse Jalonen), György Kajdy, Marko Rajamäki. Trainer: Raimo Toivanen

Goals: Hami (51, 65)

PALLOSEURA TURKU
v TRABZONSPOR 2-2 (1-1)
Kupitaan, Turkku   30.09.1992

Referee: Hugh Fulton Williamson (SCO)   Attendance: 1,376

TPS: Petri Jakonen; Ari Heikkinen, Petri Sulonen, Jyrki Hännikäinen, Petteri Viljanen, Lars Dalsborg, Mika Lipponen (82 Kim Lehtonen), Mika Aaltonen, Janne Lehtinen, György Kajdy, Marko Rajamäki.   Trainer: Raimo Toivanen

TRABZONSPOR: Viktor Grishko; Metin Altinay (84 Seyhmuz Suna), Kemal Serdar, Hamdi Aslan, Ogün Temizkanoglu, Jacek Cyzio, Yuri Shelepnitski (88 Ismail Gökçek), Turgut Uçar, Abdullah Ercan, Hami Mandirali, Orhan Çikrikçi.   Trainer: Ronny Desmeot

Goals: Kajdy (1), Hamdi (14), Orhan (60), Lehtonen (84)

MARIBOR BRANIK
v ATLÉTICO MADRID 0-3 (0-2)
Ljudski Vrt, Maribor   16.09.1992

Referee: Hasan Ceylan (TUR)   Attendance: 5,000

BRANIK: Mladen Dabanović; Emil Sterbal, Zarko Tarana, Saso Lukić, Bostjan Ratković, Ales Krizan (Cap), Peter Binkovski (60 Saso Gajser), Renato Kotnik, Ante Simundza, Marijan Bakula (73 Marko Krizanić), Ermin Susić. Trainer: Marian Bloudek

ATLÉTICO: ABEL Resino Gómez; Juan Carlos AGUILERA Martín, DONATO Gama da Silva, Roberto SOLOZÁBAL Villanueva, Francisco FERREIRA Colmenero, Antonio Muñoz Gómez "TONI" (46 Juan Francisco Rodríguez "JUANITO"), ALFREDO Santaelena Aguado, Juan VIZCAÍNO Morcillo, Bernd Schuster, Paulo Jorge dos Santos "FUTRE" (Cap) (52 Manuel ALFARO de la Torre), LUIS GARCÍA Postigo. Trainer: Luis Aragones

Goals: Alfredo (26), Luis García (42, 56)

ATLÉTICO MADRID
v MARIBOR BRANIK 6-1 (3-0)
Vicente Calderón, Madrid   30.09.1992

Referee: Gerhard Kapl (AUS)   Attendance: 6,500

ATLÉTICO: Ángel Jesús MEJÍAS Rodríguez; José Antonio "PIZO" GÓMEZ Romón, Juan Francisco Rodríguez "JUANITO", TOMÁS Reñones Crego (Cap), Francisco FERREIRA Colmenero, PEDRO González Martínez, Juan VIZCAÍNO Morcillo (51 Manuel Sánchez "MANOLO"), Antonio ACOSTA Rivera, Gabriel MOYA Sanz, Juan SABAS Huertas, Manuel ALFARO de la Torre (75 Juan Carlos AGUILERA Martín).   Trainer: Luis Aragones

BRANIK: Darko Dubravica; Peter Binkovski, Saso Lukić, Ales Krizan (Cap), Bostjan Ratković, Zarko Tarana, Ante Simundza, Renato Kotnik (66 Marko Krizanić), Marijan Bakula, Mirsad Bicakcić, Saso Gajser (49 Simon Dvorsak). Trainer: Marian Bloudek

Sent off: Simundžija (70)

Goals: Alfaro (17), Bicakcić (22), Juanito (45), Sabas (48 pen), Gómez (69), Aguilera (80), Tarana (85 og)

FEYENOORD ROTTERDAM
v HAPOEL PETACH TIKVA 1-0 (0-0)
Feyenoord, Rotterdam   16.09.1992

Referee: Ernest Kesseler (LUX)   Attendance: 19,359

FEYENOORD: Ed de Goey; Arnold Scholten (60 Mike Obiku), John Metgod (Cap), John De Wolf (75 Ulrich van Gobbel), Errol Refos, Peter Bosz, Henk Fräser, Rob Witschge, Gaston Taument, József Kiprich, Regi Blinker. Trainer: Willem Van Hanege

HAPOEL: Rafi Cohen; Benny Kozoshvily, Carlos Oleran, Bahagat Udda, Avi Keissy, Uzi Ohaion, Noam Keissy, Yossi Levi, Nir Levin, Ely Mahpoud (Cap), Mordachy Kakon. Trainer: Jan Pivarnik

Goal: Kiprich (89)

HAPOEL PETACH TIKVA
v FEYENOORD ROTTERDAM 2-1 (1-0)
Ramat Gan, Tel-Aviv   30.09.1992

Referee: Sándor Piller (HUN)   Attendance: 7,500

HAPOEL: Rafi Cohen; Benny Kozoshvily, Carlos Oleran, Bahagat Udda, Avi Keissy, Mordachy Kakon, Uzi Ohaion, Oz Ilia (85 Yossi Levi), Noam Keissy, Meny Basson (48 Ely Mahpoud), Nir Levin (Cap).   Trainer: Jan Pivarnik

FEYENOORD: Ed de Goey; Arnold Scholten, Henk Fräser, John Metgod (Cap), John De Wolf, Peter Bosz, Dean Gorre, Rob Witschge, Gaston Taument (88 Ulrich van Gobbel), József Kiprich (62 Mike Obiku), Regi Blinker. Trainer: Willem Van Hanegem

Goals: Levin (3), Kakon (49), Fräser (69)

SPARTAK MOSKVA v AVENIR BEGGEN 0-0

Luzhniki, Moskva   16.09.1992

Referee: Luben Angelov (BUL)   Attendance: 5,000

SPARTAK: Stanislav Cherchesov; Dmitriy Khlestov, Andrei Ivanov, Nikolai Pisarev (50 Vladimir Beschastnikh), Mikhail Rusiaev, Andrei Chernyshov, Viktor Onopko, Valeri Karpin (Cap), Andrei Piatnitski, Igor Lediakhov, Dmitri Radchenko. Trainer: Oleg Romanchev

AVENIR: Paul Koch; Ralph Ferron, Rolf Jentgen, Jean Vanek, Alex Wilhelm (74 Serge Jentgen), Jaba Moreira, Théo Scholten, Carlo Weis (Cap), Frank Goergen, Armin Krings (58 Markus Krahen), Luc Holtz.   Trainer: Michel Clement

FC LUZERN v LEVSKI SOFIA   1-0 (1-0)

Allmend, Luzern   30.09.1992

Referee: Joaquin Urio Velazquez (SPA)   Attendance: 12,000

FC LUZERN: Beat Mutter; Martin Rueda (Cap), René Van Eck, Urs Birrer, Urs Schönenberger, Oliver Camenzind, Roberto Fregno, Hanspeter Burri (89 Stefan Wolf), Peter Gmür, Urs Güntensperger (70 Brian Bertelsen), Semir Tuce. Trainer: Bertalan Bickskei

LEVSKI: Plamen Nikolov; Nikolai Iliev (Cap), Petar Khubchev (55 Nikolai Mitov), Valentin Dartilov, Krasimir Koev, Daniel Borimirov, Plamen Getov, Zlatko Iankov, Dimitar Vasilev, Ilian Iliev, Georgi Donkov (78 Valeri Valkov). Trainer: Ivan Vutov

Goal: Camenzind (24)

AVENIR BEGGEN v SPARTAK MOSKVA   1-5 (0-2)

Stade de Beggen   30.09.1992

Referee: Sten Johansson (SWE)   Attendance: 2,000

AVENIR: Paul Koch; Ralph Ferron, Théo Scholten (46 Gabriel Lopes), Jean Vanek, Jaba Moreira (77 Mario Novak), Serge Jentgen, Markus Krahen, Carlos Weis (Cap), Frank Goergen, Armin Krings, Luc Holtz.   Trainer: Michel Clement

SPARTAK: Stanislav Cherchesov; Dmitriy Khlestov, Andrei Ivanov (76 Oleg Kuzhlev), Dmitri Popov, Mikhail Rusiaev (26 Vladimir Beschastnikh), Andrei Chernyshov, Viktor Onopko, Valeri Karpin (Cap), Andrei Piatnitski, Igor Lediakhov, Dmitri Radchenko.   Trainer: Oleg Romanchev

Goals: Onopko (6), Piatnitski (9, 79), Radchenko (55), Popov (59), Novak (87)

PARMA v ÚJPESTI TE BUDAPEST   1-0 (0-0)

Ennio Tardini, Parma   16.09.1992

Referee: Michal Listkiewicz (POL)   Attendance: 11,603

PARMA: Claudio Taffarel; Antonio Benarrivo, Alberto di Chiara, Lorenzo Minotti, Luigi Apolloni, Georges Grün, Alessandro Melli, Daniele Zoratto (74 Giovanni Sorce), Marco Osio, Gabriele Pin (89 Ivo Pulga), Faustino Asprilla. Trainer: Nevio Scala

ÚJPESTI: Attila Gróf; János Tomka, Zoltán Aczél, Zoltán Szlezák, Balázs Bérczy, Tamás Szönyi, Zoltán Kecskés, Sándor Bácsi (55 Tamás Tiefenbach), Zoltán Miovecz, György Véber, Zsolt Füzesi (68 Csaba Hetesi).   Trainer: Ferenc Bene

Sent off: Bérczy (40)

Goal: Asprilla (48)

LEVSKI SOFIA v FC LUZERN   2-1 (0-1)

Levski Sofia   16.09.1992

Referee: Václav Krondl (CZE)   Attendance: 15,000

LEVSKI: Plamen Nikolov; Nikolai Iliev (Cap), Valentin Dartilov, Petar Khubchev, Daniel Borimirov, Zlatko Iankov, Plamen Getov, Georgi Slavchev (46 Vladko Shalamanov), Ilian Iliev, Rumen Stoianov, Ivailo Iotov (16 Nikolai Mitov). Trainer: Ivan Vutov

FC LUZERN: Beat Mutter; Martin Rueda (Cap), René Van Eck, Urs Birrer, Peter Gmür (40 Adalbert Koch), Hanspeter Burri, Roberto Fregno, Oliver Camenzind, Christophe Gilli, Urs Güntensperger (55 Stefan Wolf), Semir Tuce. Trainer: Bertalan Bickskei

Goals: Camenzind (9), Borimirov (53), Getov (70 pen)

ÚJPESTI TE BUDAPEST v PARMA   1-1 (0-0)

Megyeri út, Budapest   1.10.1992

Referee: Frans Van den Wijngaert (BEL)   Attendance: 8,000

ÚJPESTI: Attila Gróf; János Tomka, Zoltán Aczél, Zoltán Szlezák (Cap), Zoltán Miovecz, Tamás Szönyi, Zoltán Kecskés, János Zsinka (54 Sándor Bácsi), Tamás Tiefenbach, György Véber, Ferenc Lovász (56 Csaba Hetesi).   Trainer: Ferenc Bene

PARMA: Marco Ballotta; Ivo Pulga, Salvatore Matrecano, Lorenzo Minotti (Cap), Luigi Apolloni, Georges Grün, Alessandro Melli, Daniele Zoratto (60 Aldo Monza), Gabriele Pin, Stefano Cuoghi, Faustino Asprilla (82 Sergio Berti). Trainer: Nevio Scala

Goals: Grün (53), Hetesi (62)

**OLYMPIAKOS PEIRAIAS
v CHERNOMORETS ODESSA 0-1** (0-1)

Karaiskaki, Peiraias 17.09.1992

Referee: Brian Hill (ENG)   Attendance: 30,000

OLYMPIAKOS: Giorgos Mirtsos; Theodoros Pahatouridis (61 Ilias Savvidis), Kiriakos Karataidis, Giorgos Mitsibonas, Mihalis Vlahos, Panagiotis Tsalouhidis (Cap), Gennadi Litovchenko, Nikos Tsiantakis, Oleg Protasov, Vasilis Karapialis, Giorgos Vaitsis (46 Daniel Batista).
Trainer: Oleg Blohin

CHERNOMORETS: Oleg Suslov; Yuri Nikiforov (Cap), Sergei Protsiuk, Yuri Bukel, Vladimir Lebed, Dmytro Parfenov, Ilia Tsimbalar, Konstantin Kulik, Oleg Kosheliuk, Sergei Gusev, Yuri Sak.   Trainer: Viktor Prokopenko

Goal: Sak (4)

**CHERNOMORETS ODESSA
v OLYMPIAKOS PEIRAIAS 0-3** (0-2)

Central Odessa 30.09.1992

Referee: Gianni Beschin (ITA)   Attendance: 26,500

CHERNOMORETS: Oleg Suslov; Yuri Nikiforov, Sergei Protsiuk, Yuri Bukel, Dmytro Parfenov, Vladimir Lebed (79 Andrei Lozovski), Ilia Tsimbalar, Oleg Kosheliuk (72 Ruslan Romanchuk), Konstantin Kulik, Yuri Sak, Sergei Gusev.
Trainer: Viktor Prokopenko

OLYMPIAKOS: Giorgos Mirtsos; Theodoros Pahatouridis, Kiriakos Karataidis, Giorgos Mitsibonas, Mihalis Vlahos, Panagiotis Tsalouhidis, Nikos Tsiantakis, Gennadi Litovchenko, Oleg Protasov (85 Daniel Batista), Vasilis Karapialis (81 Ilias Savvidis), Giorgos Vaitsis.
Trainer: Oleg Blohin

Goals: Vaitsis (15), Mitsibonas (27), Protasov (80)

VALUR REYKJAVÍK v BOAVISTA PORTO 0-0

Laugardalsvöllur, Reykjavík 17.09.1992

Referee: Jef Van Vliet (HOL)   Attendance: 715

VALUR: Bjarni Sigurdsson; Jón Grétar Jónsson, Einar Páll Tomasson, Izudin Dervic, Jón Helgason, Baldur Bragason, Salih Porca, Steinar Adólfsson, Gunnlaugur Einarsson, Agúst Gylfason, Anthony Gregory (Cap).
Trainer: Ingi-Björn Albertsson

BOAVISTA: ALFREDO da Silva Castro; Rui Manuel Magalhães CASACA (Cap), José António Rocha GARRIDO, RUI Fernando Silva BENTO, José Fernando Gomes TAVARES, António de Oliveira CAETANO, Erwin SANCHEZ Freking, Mamadu BOBÓ Dialo, Manuel António Guimarães "NELO", MARLON Romel Brandao (38 António José Santos "TOZÉ"), Richard Daddy Owubokiri "RICKY".   Trainer: Manuel José

BOAVISTA PORTO v VALUR REYKJAVÍK 3-0 (2-0)

Dr Alves Vieira Stadium, Torres Novas 1.10.1992

Referee: Eric Blareau (BEL)   Attendance: 5,000

BOAVISTA: ALFREDO da Silva Castro; JAIME ALVES Magalhães, RUI Fernando Silva BENTO, José Fernando Gomes TAVARES, António de Oliveira CAETANO, António José NOGUEIRA Santos, Rui Manuel Magalhães CASACA (Cap), Manuel António Guimarães "NELO", Erwin SANCHEZ Freking (74 Mamadu BOBÓ Dialo), MARLON Romel Brandao, Richard Daddy Owubokiri "RICKY" (81 Luís António Soares Cassamá "BAMBO").   Trainer: Manuel José

VALUR: Bjarni Sigurdsson; Jón Grétar Jónsson, Einar Páll Tomasson, Izudin Dervic, Jón Helgason, Salih Porca (72 Gunnar Gunnarsson), Agúst Gylfason, Gunnlaugur Einarsson (66 Arnljótur Davídsson), Steinar Adólfsson, Baldur Bragason, Anthony Gregory (Cap).   Trainer: Ingi-Björn Albertsson

Goals: Marlon (14, 81), Owubokiri (26)

SECOND ROUND

**FC LUZERN
v FEYENOORD ROTTERDAM 1-0** (0-0)

Allmend, Luzern 21.10.1992

Referee: Loizos Loizou (CYP)   Attendance: 11,700

FC LUZERN: Beat Mutter; Martin Rueda (Cap), Peter Gmür, René Van Eck, Urs Birrer, Hanspeter Burri (68 Brian Bertelsen), Roberto Fregno, Oliver Camenzind, Christophe Gilli, Urs Güntensperger, Adalbert Koch (66 Peter Nadig).
Trainer: Bertalan Bickskei

FEYENOORD: Ed de Goey; Arnold Scholten, John De Wolf, John Metgod (Cap), Errol Refos, Peter Bosz, Henk Fräser, Rob Witschge, Gaston Taument, József Kiprich (64 Ulrich van Gobbel), Regi Blinker.   Trainer: Willem Van Hanegem

Sent off: De Wolf

Goal: Rueda (75)

**FEYENOORD ROTTERDAM
v FC LUZERN 4-1** (2-1)

Feyenoord, Rotterdam 4.11.1992

Referee: Alan Snoddy (NIR)   Attendance: 27,231

FEYENOORD: Ed de Goey; Ulrich van Gobbel, John Metgod (Cap), John De Wolf, Errol Refos, Peter Bosz, Dean Gorre (87 Orlando Trustfull), Rob Witschge, Gaston Taument (78 Mike Obiku), József Kiprich, Regi Blinker.

FC LUZERN: Beat Mutter; Peter Gmür (57 Christophe Gilli), Martin Rueda (Cap), René Van Eck, Urs Birrer, Brian Bertelsen, Roberto Fregno, Herbert Baumann, Urs Schönenberger, Peter Nadig (70 Adalbert Koch), Oliver Camenzind.   Trainer: Bertalan Bickskei

Sent off: Van Eck & Bertelsen

Goals: Taument (2), Nadig (12), Blinker (16), Kiprich (55, 83 pen)

AS MONACO v OLIMPIAKOS PEIRAIAS 0-1 (0-0)

Louis II, Monaco   21.10.1992

Referee: Michal Listkiewicz (POL)   Attendance: 5,612

AS MONACO: Jean-Luc Ettori (Cap); Patrick Valéry, Lilian Thuram, Franck Dumas, Luc Sonor, Jerôme Gnako, Luis Henrique, Youri Djorkaeff, Marcel Dib (62 Kelvin Sebwe), Jürgen Klinsmann, Christian Perez.   Trainer: Arsène Wenger

OLIMPIAKOS: Giorgos Mirtsos; Theodoros Pahatouridis, Giorgos Mitsibonas, Mihalis Vlahos (62 Ilias Savvidis), Kiriakos Karataidis, Panagiotis Tsalouhidis (Cap), Gennadi Litovchenko, Nikos Tsiantakis, Vasilis Karapialis (40 Daniel Batista), Minas Hantzidis, Giorgos Vaitsis.
Trainer: Oleg Blohin

Goal: Vaitsis (86)

OLIMPIAKOS PEIRAIAS v AS MONACO 0-0

Karaiskaki, Peiraias   4.11.1992

Referee: Alphonse Constantin (BEL)   Attendance: 30,500

OLIMPIAKOS: Giorgos Mirtsos; Theodoros Pahatouridis, Mihalis Vlahos, Giorgos Mitsibonas, Kiriakos Karataidis, Panagiotis Tsalouhidis (Cap), Nikos Tsiantakis, Ilias Savvidis (86 Oleg Protasov), Gennadi Litovchenko, Sotiris Maurommatis (52 Daniel Batista), Giorgos Vaitsis.
Trainer: Oleg Blohin

AS MONACO: Jean-Luc Ettori (Cap); Patrick Valéry (59 Youri Djorkaeff), Lilian Thuram, Franck Dumas, Patrick Blondeau, Marcel Dib (68 Youssouf Fofana), Claude Puel, Luis Henrique, Jerôme Gnako, Christian Perez, Jürgen Klinsmann.
Trainer: Arsène Wenger

ÅRHUS GF v STEAUA BUCUREŞTI 3-2 (2-0)

Århus stadium   21.10.1992

Referee: Aron Schmidhuber (GER)   Attendance: 17,500

AGF: Troels Rasmussen; Lasse Skov, Martin Nielsen, Claus Thomsen (Cap), Palle Sørensen, Gunner Lind Pedersen (73 Bo Harder), Jan-Halvor Halvorsen, Torben Christensen, Stig Tøfting, Jan Bartram (68 Claus Christensen), Søren Andersen.
Trainer: Lars Lundqvist

STEAUA: Daniel Gherasim (46 Dumitru Stîngaciu); Constantin Gâlcă, Ionel Pîrvu, Anton Doboş, Bogdan Bucur, Viorel Ion (64 Alexandru Andrasi), Ion Vlădoiu, Ilie Dumitrescu (Cap), Ion Sburlea, Basarab Panduru, Ilie Stan.
Trainer: Anghel Iordănescu

Goals: Andersen (10), T. Christensen (19), Vlădoiu (63), M. Nielsen (76 pen), Dumitrescu (85)

STEAUA BUCUREŞTI v ÅRHUS GF 2-1 (0-1)

Steaua Bucureşti   4.11.1992

Referee: Ahmed Çakar (TUR)   Attendance: 25,000

STEAUA: Dumitru Stîngaciu; Cornel Cristescu, Ion Sburlea, Bogdan Bucur, Ionel Pîrvu (63 Iulian Filipescu), Viorel Ion, Ilie Stan, Constantin Gâlcă, Ilie Dumitrescu (Cap), Ion Vlădoiu, Alexandru Andrasi (55 Ionel Fulga).
Trainer: Anghel Iordănescu

AGF: Troels Rasmussen; Lasse Skov, Martin Nielsen, Kent Nielsen (Cap), Claus Thomsen, Gunner Lind Pedersen, Jan-Halvor Halvorsen, Jan Bartram (72 Claus Christiansen), Stig Tøfting, Søren Andersen (80 Palle Sørensen), Torben Christensen.   Trainer: Lars Lundqvist

Goals: Christensen (11), Cristescu (83), Vlădoiu (90)

TRABZONSPOR v ATLÉTICO MADRID 0-2 (0-1)

Avni Aker, Trabzon   21.10.1992

Referee: Aleksei Spirin (RUS)   Attendance: 24,000

TRABZONSPOR: Viktor Grishko; Ogün Temizkanoglu, Kemal Serdar (Cap), Hamdi Aslan, Seyhmuz Suna (79 Lemi Çelik), Turgut Uçar, Ünal Karaman, Jacek Cyzio, Abdullah Ercan, Hami Mandirali, Orhan Çikrikçi (46 Soner Boz).
Trainer: George Leekens

ATLÉTICO: ABEL Resino Gómez; Juan Carlos AGUILERA Martín, Juan Manuel LÓPEZ Martínez, Roberto SOLOZÁBAL Villanueva, DONATO Gama da Silva, TOMÁS Reñones Crego, Manuel Sánchez "MANOLO" (52 ALFREDO Santaelena Aguado), Bernd Schuster, Juan VIZCAÍNO Morcillo, Paulo Jorge dos Santos "FUTRE" (Cap) (60 LUIS GARCÍA Postigo), Gabriel MOYA Sanz.   Trainer: Luis Aragones

Goals: Futre (38), Moya (59)

ATLÉTICO MADRID v TRABZONSPOR 0-0

Vicente Calderón, Madrid   4.11.1992

Referee: Rémy Harrel (FRA)   Attendance: 8,672

ATLÉTICO: DIEGO Díaz Garrido; TOMÁS Reñones Crego, PEDRO González Martínez, Roberto SOLOZÁBAL Villanueva, Juan Manuel LÓPEZ Martínez, Francisco FERREIRA Colmenero (8 Antonio ACOSTA Rivera), Gabriel MOYA Sanz, DONATO Gama da Silva, Juan VIZCAÍNO Morcillo, Paulo Jorge dos Santos "FUTRE" (Cap), LUIS GARCÍA Postigo (52 Juan SABAS Huertas).   Trainer: Luis Aragones

TRABZONSPOR: Viktor Grishko; Lemi Çelik, Ogün Temizkanoglu, Hamdi Aslan, Kemal Serdar (Cap), Abdullah Ercan, Jacek Cyzio, Turgut Uçar (72 Seyhmuz Suna), Ünal Karaman (88 Süleyman Usta), Soner Boz, Orhan Çikrikçi.
Trainer: George Leekens

Sent off: Abdullah (50)

**FC ADMIRA WACKER WIEN
v ROYAL ANTWERP FC 2-4** (2-1)

Bundesstadion Südstadt Wien   21.10.1992

Referee: Sergei Khusainov (RUS)   Attendance: 3,000

ADMIRA WACKER: Franz Gruber; Alois Dötzl, Thomas Zingler, Uwe Müller, Gerald Messlender, Gerald Bacher (60 Johannes Abfalterer), Michael Gruber, Peter Artner (Cap), Roger Ljung, Ernst Ogris, Olaf Marschall. Trainer: Siegfried Held

ANTWERP: Wim De Coninck; Wim Kiekens, Nico Broeckaert, Geert Emmerechts, Rudy Smidts (Cap), Didier Segers (83 Nourédine Moukrim), Ronny Van Rethy, Patrick Van Veirdeghem, Hans-Peter Lehnhoff, Francis Severeyns, Alex Czerniatynsky.   Trainer: Walter Meeuws

Goals: Marschall (24), Czerniatynski (33, 63, 74), Bacher (41), Segers (55)

**ROYAL ANTWERP FC
v FC ADMIRA WACKER WIEN 3-4** (2-0, 2-4) (AET)

Bosuil, Antwerp   4.11.1992

Referee: Zbigniew Przesmycki (POL)   Attendance: 6,000

ANTWERP: Ratko Svilar; Wim Kiekens, Geert Emmerechts, Rudy Smidts (Cap), Nico Broeckaert, Nourédine Moukrim (74 Willy Vincent), Ronny Van Rethy, Didier Segers (21 Patrick Van Veirdeghem), Kari Ukkonen, Francis Severeyns, Alex Czerniatynski.   Trainer: Walter Meeuws

ADMIRA WACKER: Wolfgang Knaller (Cap); Gerald Bacher, Thomas Zingler (106 Kurt Temm), Uwe Müller, Helmut Graf, Andreás Gutlederer (106 Ernst Ogris), Peter Artner, Michael Gruber, Roger Ljung, Olaf Marschall, Johannes Abfalterer. Trainer: Siegfried Held

Sent off: Marschall

Goals: Czerniatynski (21, 97), Severeyns (43), Bacher (46), Abfalterer (57), Ljung (63, 77)

WERDER BREMEN v SPARTA PRAHA 2-3 (0-2)

Weserstadion, Bremen   21.10.1992

Referee: Angelo Amendolia (ITA)   Attendance: 10,747

WERDER: Oliver Reck; Rune Bratseth, Miroslav Votava (Cap), Dietmar Beiersdorfer (46 Klaus Allofs), Thomas Wolter, Ulrich Borowka, Dieter Eilts, Andreas Herzog, Thorsten Legat (46 Frank Neubarth), Wynton Rufer, Marco Bode. Trainer: Otto Rehhagel

SPARTA: Petr Kouba; Jozef Chovanec (Cap), Michal Hornák, Jan Sopko, Petr Vrabec, Lumír Mistr, Michal Bílek (49 Martin Frýdek), Jiří Němec, Roman Vonasek, Horst Siegl, Viktor Dvirnik (88 Marek Trval).   Trainer: Dušan Uhrin

Sent off: Chovanec (47)

Goals: Sopko (25), Dvirnik (35), Neubarth (56), Rufer (80), Vonasek (90)

SPARTA PRAHA v WERDER BREMEN 1-0 (1-0)

Stadión na Letnej, Praha   4.11.1992

Referee: Egil Nervik (NOR)   Attendance: 29,704

SPARTA: Petr Kouba; Jan Sopko, Petr Vrabec (Cap), Michal Hornák, Lumír Mistr, Michal Bílek, Martin Frýdek, Jiří Němec, Viktor Dvirnik (89 Pavel Nedved), Horst Siegl, Roman Vonasek. Trainer: Dušan Uhrin

WERDER: Oliver Reck; Manfred Bockenfeld, Thomas Wolter, Rune Bratseth, Ulrich Borowka (46 Klaus Allofs), Miroslav Votava (Cap), Dieter Eilts, Thorsten Legat, Frank Neubarth, Marco Bode (80 Stefan Kohn), Wynton Rufer. Trainer: Otto Rehhagel

Sent off: Rufer (63)

Goal: Siegl (7)

AS PARMA v BOAVISTA PORTO 0-0

Ennio Tardini, Parma   21.10.1992

Referee: Jan Damgaard (DEN)   Attendance: 8,675

PARMA: Marco Ballotta; Gabriele Pin, Alberto di Chiara, Luigi Apolloni, Georges Grün (63 Salvatore Matrecano), Lorenzo Minotti (Cap), Daniele Zoratto, Marco Osio, Stefano Cuoghi, Alessandro Melli, Faustino Asprilla (55 Fausto Pizzi). Trainer: Nevio Scala

BOAVISTA: ALFREDO da Silva Castro; JAIME ALVES Magalhães, RUI Fernando Silva BENTO, António de Oliveira CAETANO (65 Rui Manuel Magalhães CASACA), António José NOGUEIRA Santos, Pedro Manuel Regateiro VENÂNCIO, Mamadu BOBÓ Dialo, MARLON Romel Brandao (89 José António Rocha GARRIDO), Manuel António Guimarães "NELO" (Cap), Richard Daddy Owubokiri "RICKY", José Fernando Gomes TAVARES.   Trainer: Manuel José

BOAVISTA PORTO v AS PARMA 0-2 (0-1)

Dr Alves Vieira Stadium, Torres Novas   4.11.1992

Referee: Hans-Jürgen Weber (GER)   Attendance: 2,980

BOAVISTA: ALFREDO da Silva Castro; RUI Fernando Silva BENTO, Pedro Manuel Regateiro VENÂNCIO, António José NOGUEIRA Santos, António de Oliveira CAETANO, JAIME ALVES Magalhães (32 António José Santos "TOZÉ"), Mamadu BOBÓ Dialo (Cap), José Fernando Gomes TAVARES, Erwin SANCHEZ Freking (46 Luís Filipe Carvalho "LITOS"), MARLON Romel Brandao, Richard Daddy Owubokiri "RICKY". Trainer: Manuel José

PARMA: Claudio Taffarel; Salvatore Matrecano, Lorenzo Minotti (Cap), Luigi Apolloni, Alberto di Chiara, Gabriele Pin, Daniele Zoratto, Stefano Cuoghi, Fausto Pizzi, Alessandro Melli (86 Cornelio Donati), Tomas Brolin (52 Gianluca Franchini). Trainer: Nevio Scala

Goals: Nogueira (12 og), Melli (78)

SPARTAK MOSKVA v LIVERPOOL FC 4-2 (1-0)
Lenin, Moskva 22.10.1992
Referee: Rune Larsson (SWE)   Attendance: 55,000
SPARTAK: Stanislav Cherchesov (Cap); Dmitriy Khlestov, Viktor Onopko, Andrei Chernyshov, Andrei Ivanov, Valeri Karpin, Andrei Piatnitski, Igor Lediakhov, Nikolai Pisarev, Vladimir Beschastnikh (54 Mikhail Rusiaev), Dmitri Radchenko.   Trainer: Oleg Romanchev
LIVERPOOL FC: Bruce Grobbelaar; Mike Marsh, Mark Wright (Cap), David Burrows, Rob Jones (78 Nicky Tanner), Steve McManaman, Michael Thomas, Jamie Redknapp, Don Hutchison, Mark Walters, Ian Rush (54 Ronny Rosenthal).   Manager: Graeme Souness
Sent off: Grobbelaar (82)
Goals: Pisarev (10), Karpin (69, 84 pen), Wright (66), McManaman (74), Lediakhov (89)

**SPARTAK MOSKVA
v FEYENOORD ROTTERDAM 3-1** (1-1)
Torpedo, Moskva 17.03.1993
Referee: Joël Quiniou (FRA)   Attendance: 15,250
SPARTAK: Stanislav Cherchesov (Cap); Dmitriy Khlestov (63 Ramiz Mamedov), Igor Lediakhov, Andrei Ivanov, Viktor Onopko, Valeri Karpin, Aleksandr Bondar, Andrei Piatnitski, Dmitri Popov, Dmitri Radchenko, Fiodor Cherenkov.   Trainer: Oleg Romanchev
FEYENOORD: Ed de Goey; Ulrich van Gobbel, John Metgod (Cap), John De Wolf, Ruud Heus, Orlando Trustfull, Arnold Scholten (34 dean Gorre), Rob Witschge, Gaston Taument, József Kiprich, Regi Blinker (75 Mike Obiku).   Trainer: Willem Van Hanegem
Sent off: Van Gobbel (85), Cherenkov (85)
Goals: Karpin (8, 81), Kiprich (14), Radchenko (90)

LIVERPOOL FC v SPARTAK MOSKVA 0-2 (0-0)
Anfield Road, Liverpool 4.11.1992
Referee: Manuel Diaz Vega (SPA)   Attendance: 37,993
LIVERPOOL FC: Mike Hooper; Rob Jones (55 Ronny Rosenthal), David Burrows, Steve Nicol, Mark Wright (Cap), Steve McManaman, Mike Marsh, Don Hutchison, Michael Thomas, Jamie Redknapp, Ian Rush.   Manager: Graeme Souness
SPARTAK: Stanislav Cherchesov (Cap); Dmitriy Khlestov, Andrei Ivanov, Nikolai Pisarev (64 Mikhail Rusiaev), Andrei Chernyshov, Viktor Onopko, Andrei Piatnitski, Igor Lediakhov (85 Vladimir Bakschev), Valeri Karpin, Dmitri Radchenko, Vladimir Beschastnikh.   Trainer: Oleg Romanchev
Sent off: Marsh (87)
Goals: Radchenko (63), Piatnitski (89)

SPARTA PRAHA v AC PARMA 0-0
Štadión na Letnej, Praha 3.03.1993
Referee: Alfred Wieser (AUS)   Attendance: 24,900
SPARTA: Petr Kouba; Pavel Nedved (82 Tomás Votava), Lumír Mistr, Petr Vrabec, Michal Hornák, Roman Vonasek, Jiří Němec, Jozef Chovanec (Cap), Viktor Dvirnik, Horst Siegl, Martin Frýdek.   Trainer: Dušan Uhrin
PARMA: Marco Ballotta; Antonio Benarrivo, Alberto di Chiara, Lorenzo Minotti (Cap), Luigi Apolloni, Georges Grün, Faustino Asprilla, Gabriele Pin, Tomas Brolin, Stefano Cuoghi, Fausto Pizzi.   Trainer: Nevio Scala

QUARTER-FINALS

**FEYENOORD ROTTERDAM
v SPARTAK MOSKVA 0-1** (0-1)
Feyenoord, Rotterdam 2.03.1993
Referee: Karl-Josef Assenmacher (GER)   Att: 33,187
FEYENOORD: Ed de Goey; Ulrich van Gobbel, John Metgod (Cap) (66 Mike Obiku), John De Wolf, Errol Refos, Arnold Scholten, Peter Bosz, Rob Witschge, Gaston Taument, József Kiprich, Regi Blinker.   Trainer: Willem Van Hanegem
SPARTAK: Stanislav Cherchesov; Dmitriy Khlestov, Andrei Chernyshov, Viktor Onopko, Andrei Ivanov, Valeri Karpin (Cap) (70 Nikolai Pisarev), Igor Lediakhov, Andrei Piatnitski, Dmitri Popov (89 Andrei Gashkin), Dmitri Radchenko, Vladimir Beschastnikh.   Trainer: Oleg Romanchev
Sent off: Chernyshov (89)
Goal: Piatnitski (36)

AC PARMA v SPARTA PRAHA 2-0 (2-0)
Ennio Tardini, Parma 17.03.1993
Referee: John Blankenstein (HOL)   Attendance: 17,942
PARMA: Marco Ballotta; Antonio Benarrivo, Lorenzo Minotti (Cap), Luigi Apolloni, Alberto di Chiara, Daniele Zoratto, Tomas Brolin (85 Gabriele Pin), Stefano Cuoghi, Georges Grün, Alessandro Melli (79 Fausto Pizzi), Faustino Asprilla.   Trainer: Nevio Scala
SPARTA: Petr Kouba; Jiří Novotný, Jozef Chovanec (Cap), Petr Vrabec, Michal Hornák, Jiří Němec, Michal Bílek, Roman Vonasek, Martin Frýdek (70 Lumír Mistr), Viktor Dvirnik (46 Pavel Nedved), Horst Siegl.   Trainer: Dušan Uhrin
Sent off: Hornák
Goals: Melli (10), Asprilla (33)

OLYMPIAKOS PEIRAIAS
v ATLÉTICO MADRID 1-1 (0-1)

Olympiako Spiros Louis, Athina   4.03.1993

Referee: Rune Larsson (SWE)   Attendance: 52,000

OLYMPIAKOS: Giorgos Mirtsos; Theodoros Pahatouridis, Giorgos Mitsibonas, Mihalis Vlahos (61 Ilias Savvidis), Panagiotis Tsalouhidis (Cap), Kiriakos Karataidis, Nikos Tsiantakis (76 Panagiotis Sofianopoulos), Sotiris Maurommatis, Vasilis Karapialis, Daniel Batista, Giorgos Vaitsis.   Trainer: T. Petrović

ATLÉTICO: ABEL Resino Gómez (Cap); Juan Manuel LÓPEZ Martínez, Juan Francisco Rodríguez "JUANITO", Roberto SOLOZÁBAL Villanueva, Francisco FERREIRA Colmenero, Antonio Muñoz Gómez "TONI", Bernd Schuster, Manuel ALFARO de la Torre (87 Antonio OREJUELA Ribero), ALFREDO Santaelena Aguado (84 TOMÁS Reñones Crego), Gabriel MOYA Sanz, LUIS GARCÍA Postigo.   Trainer: Omar José Pastoriza

Goals: Moya (10), Vaitsis (63)

ATLÉTICO MADRID
v OLYMPIAKOS PEIRAIAS 3-1 (1-0)

Vicente Calderón, Madrid   18.03.1993

Referee: James McCluskey (SCO)   Attendance: 50,000

ATLÉTICO: ABEL Resino Gómez (Cap); ALFREDO Santaelena Aguado, Francisco FERREIRA Colmenero, Juan Francisco Rodríguez "JUANITO", Antonio Muñoz Gómez "TONI", Manuel Sánchez "MANOLO", Roberto SOLOZÁBAL Villanueva, Bernd Schuster, Juan VIZCAÍNO Morcillo, LUIS GARCÍA Postigo (88 Juan SABAS Huertas), Gabriel MOYA Sanz (56 Manuel ALFARO de la Torre).   Trainer: Omar José Pastoriza

OLYMPIAKOS: Giorgos Mirtsos; Minas Hantzidis (69 Panagiotis Sofianopoulos), Giorgos Mitsibonas, Nikos Tsiantakis, Sotiris Maurommatis, Daniel Batista (76 Oleg Protasov), Ilias Savvidis, Panagiotis Tsalouhidis (Cap), Gennadi Litovchenko, Vasilis Karapialis, Giorgos Vaitsis.   Trainer: T. Petrović

Goals: Manolo (10, 58), Tsalouhidis (59), Alfaro (67)

ROYAL ANTWERP FC v STEAUA BUCUREŞTI 0-0

Bosuil, Antwerp   4.03.1993

Referee: Vadim Zhuk (BLS)   Attendance: 9,500

ANTWERPEN: Stevan Stojanovic; Wim Kiekens, Nico Broeckaert, Rudy Taeymans, Rudy Smidts (Cap); Didier Segers, Patrick Van Veirdeghem, Hans-Peter Lehnhoff, Dragan Jakovljevic; Francis Severeyns, Alex Czerniatynski.   Trainer: Walter Meeuws

STEAUA: Dumitru Stîngaciu; Aurel Panait, Anton Doboş, Bogdan Bucur, Daniel Prodan, Constantin Gâlcă; Ilie Stan, Basarab Panduru, Ilie Dumitrescu (Cap) (85 Daniel Iftodi); Ion Vlădoiu (61 Ion Sburlea), Iulian Filipescu.   Trainer: Anghel Iordănescu

Sent off: Bucur (60)

STEAUA BUCUREŞTI
v ROYAL ANTWERP FC 1-1 (1-0)

Steaua Bucureşti   17.03.1993

Referee: Leslie William Mottram (SCO)   Att: 30,000

STEAUA: Dumitru Stîngaciu; Daniel Prodan, Ion Sburlea, Aurel Panait, Ionel Pîrvu, Ionel Fulga, Basarab Panduru, Constantin Gâlcă, Ilie Dumitrescu (71 Daniel Iftodi), Iulian Filipescu, Ion Vlădoiu (81 Alexandru Andrasi).

ANTWERP: Stevan Stojanovic; Wim Kiekens, Nico Broeckaert, Rudy Taeymans, Rudy Smidts (Cap), Ronny Van Rethy (63 Dragan Jakovljevic), Didier Segers, Patrick Van Veirdeghem (83 Geert Emmerechts), Hans-Peter Lehnhoff, Francis Severeyns, Alex Czerniatynski.

Sent off: Fulga (56), Taeymans

Goals: Dumitrescu (19), Czerniatynski (81)

SEMI-FINALS

ATLÉTICO MADRID v AC PARMA 1-2 (1-0)

Vicente Calderón, Madrid   6.04.1993

Referee: Philip Don (ENG)   Attendance: 50,000

ATLÉTICO: ABEL Resino Gómez (Cap); Juan Manuel LÓPEZ Martínez, Antonio Muñoz Gómez "TONI", Roberto SOLOZÁBAL Villanueva, Juan VIZCAÍNO Morcillo, Juan Francisco Rodríguez "JUANITO" (75 Francisco FERREIRA Colmenero), Manuel Sánchez "MANOLO" (63 Juan SABAS Huertas), Bernd Schuster, Manuel ALFARO de la Torre, ALFREDO Santaelena Aguado, LUIS GARCÍA Postigo.   Trainer: Ramon Armando Heredia

PARMA: Marco Ballotta; Antonio Benarrivo, Alberto di Chiara, Lorenzo Minotti (Cap), Salvatore Matrecano, Georges Grün, Alessandro Melli (70 Fausto Pizzi), Daniele Zoratto, Tomas Brolin, Stefano Cuoghi, Faustino Asprilla.   Trainer: Nevio Scala

Goals: Luis García (44), Solozábal (57 og), Asprilla (61)

AC PARMA v ATLÉTICO MADRID 0-1 (0-0)

Ennio Tardini, Parma   22.04.1993

Referee: Aron Schmidhuber (GER)   Attendance: 21,915

PARMA: Marco Ballotta; Salvatore Matrecano, Antonio Benarrivo, Lorenzo Minotti (Cap), Luigi Apolloni, Georges Grün, Alessandro Melli (88 Gianluca Hervatin), Gabriele Pin, Marco Osio (76 Fausto Pizzi), Stefano Cuoghi, Tomas Brolin.   Trainer: Nevio Scala

ATLÉTICO: DIEGO Díaz Garrido; Juan Carlos AGUILERA Martín (58 Manuel ALFARO de la Torre), Antonio Muñoz Gómez "TONI", Roberto SOLOZÁBAL Villanueva, TOMÁS Reñones Crego (Cap), DONATO Gama da Silva, Juan SABAS Huertas, Bernd Schuster, Juan VIZCAÍNO Morcillo, ALFREDO Santaelena Aguado, LUIS GARCÍA Postigo (74 Juan Francisco Rodríguez "JUANITO").   Trainer: Ramon Heredia

Sent off: Juanito (88), Vizcaíno & Alfaro (after the match)

Goal: Sabas (78)

SPARTAK MOSKVA
v ROYAL ANTWERP FC 1-0 (1-0)
Lenin, Moskva   7.04.1993

Referee: Leif Sundell (SWE)   Attendance: 60,000

SPARTAK: Stanislav Cherchesov; Dmitriy Khlestov, Ramiz Mamedov, Andrei Chernyshov, Andrei Ivanov, Valeri Karpin (Cap), Andrei Piatnitski, Igor Lediakhov, Dmitri Popov, Vladimir Beschastnikh, Dmitri Radchenko (48 Nikolai Pisarev).   Trainer: Oleg Romanchev

ANTWERP: Stevan Stojanovic; Nourédine Moukrim, Nico Broeckaert, Wim Kiekens, Rudy Smidts (Cap), Hans-Peter Lehnhoff (88 Gerry De Graef), Ronny Van Rethy, Dragan Jakovljevic, Didier Segers, Francis Severeyns, Alex Czerniatynski.   Trainer: Walter Meeuws

Goal: Piatnitski (35)

ROYAL ANTWERP FC
v SPARTAK MOSKVA 3-1 (1-1)
Bosuil, Antwerp   22.04.1993

Referee: Jorge Monteiro Coroado (POR)   Att: 11,128

ANTWERP FC: Stevan Stojanovic; Patrick Van Veirdeghem (85 Nourédine Moukrim), Nico Broeckaert, Rudy Taeymans, Rudy Smidts (Cap), Hans-Peter Lehnhoff, Dragan Jakovljevic (82 Geert Emmerechts), Ronny Van Rethy, Didier Segers, Francis Severeyns, Alex Czerniatynski.
Trainer: Walter Meeuws

SPARTAK: Stanislav Cherchesov: Dmitriy Khlestov, Andrei Chernyshov, Andrei Ivanov, Viktor Onopko (Cap), Valeri Karpin, Igor Lediakhov, Andrei Piatnitski, Dmitri Popov (41 Andrei Gashkin), Nikolai Pisarev, Dmitri Radchenko (43 Vladimir Bakshev).   Trainer: Oleg Romanchev

Sent off: Onopko (77)

Goals: Radchenko (9), Czerniatynski (36), Jakovljevic (64), Lehnhoff (76 pen)

FINAL

PARMA AC v ROYAL ANTWERP FC 3-1 (2-1)
Wembley, London   12.05.1993

Referee: Karl-Josef Assenmacher (GER)   Att: 37,393

PARMA AC: Marco Ballotta; Antonio Benarrivo, Lorenzo Minotti (Cap), Georges Grün, Luigi Apolloni, Alberto di Chiara, Marco Osio (75 Fausto Pizzi), Stefano Cuoghi, Daniele Zoratto (26 Gabriele Pin), Alessandro Melli, Tomas Brolin.   Trainer: Nevio Scala

ANTWERP: Stevan Stojanovic; Wim Kiekens, Nico Broeckaert, Rudy Taeymans, Rudy Smidts (Cap), Hans-Peter Lehnhoff, Ronny Van Rethy, Dragan Jakovljevic (56 Patrick Van Veirdeghem), Didier Segers (83 Nourédine Moukrim), Francis Severeyns, Alex Czerniatynski.
Trainer: Walter Meeuws

Goals: Minotti (9), Severeyns (11), Melli (30), Cuoghi (84)

Goalscorers European Cup-Winners' Cup 1992-93:

7 goals: Alex Czerniatynski (Royal Antwerp FC)

5 goals: Andrei Piatnitski (Spartak Moskva), Ian Rush (Liverpool)

4 goals: Dmitri Radchenko, Valeri Karpin (Spartak Moskva), József Kiprich (Feyenoord), Torben Christensen (Aarhus), Wynton Rufer (Werder Bremen), Yuri Nikiforov (Chernomorets Odessa)

3 goals: Faustino Asprilla, Alessandro Melli (Parma), LUIS GARCÍA Postigo (Atlético Madrid), Ion Vlădoiu (Steaua București), Meny Basson (Hapoel Petach-Tikva), Johannes Abfalterer (Admira Wacker)

2 goals: J. Brincat (Hamrun Spartans), Simpson (AIK Stockholm), Daschner (Hannover 96), Spoljaric (Apollon Limassol), Levin (Hapoel Petach Tikva), Simundza, Tarana (Maribor Branik), Gusev, Lebed, Sak, Tsimbalar (Chernomorets Odessa), Camenzind (FC Luzern), Hami (Trabzonspor), Bacher, Ljung, Marschall (Admira Wacker Wien), Sopko, Vonasek (Sparta Praha), Marlon (Boavista), Stewart (Liverpool), Vaitsis (Olympiakos Peiraias), Dumitrescu, Andrasi (Steaua București), Alfaro, Manolo, Moya, Sabas (Atlético Madrid), Lehnhoff, Severeyns (Antwerp)

1 goal: Stöber (FC Vaduz), Reynheim (B 36 Tórshavn), Hellström, Yevtushenko (AIK Stockholm), Black (Airdrieonians), Smith, Ferris (Glenavon), Wojcicki (Hannover 96), Pike (Cardiff City), Kajdy, Lehtonen (Palloseura Turku), Bicakcic (Maribor Branik), Kakon (Hapoel Petach Tikva), Binkovski (Maribor Branik), Krings, Krahen, Novak (Avenir Beggen), Borimirov, Getov (Levski Sofia), Hetesi (Újpesti Budapest), Yablonski (Chernomorets Odessa), Rueda, Nadig (FC Luzern), Djorkaeff (Monaco), Andersen, Nielsen, Tøfting, Harder (Aarhus), Hamdi, Orhan (Trabzonspor), Dvirnik, Siegl, Vrabec (Sparta Praha), Neubarth, Bratseth (Werder Bremen), Owubokiri (Boavista), Wright, McManaman, Hutchison (Liverpool), Taument, Blinker, Fräser (Feyenoord), Tsalouhidis, Mitsibonas, Litovcenko, Protasov (Olympiakos Peiraias), Cristescu, V.Ion (Steaua București), Futre, Alfredo, Juanito, Gomez, Aguilera (Atlético Madrid), Pisarev, Lediakhov, Onopko, Popov (Spartak Moskva), Jakovljevic, Segers, Kiekens (Antwerp), Minotti, Cuoghi, Grün (Parma)

Own goals: Tarana (Maribor Branik) for Atlético Madrid, Nogueira (Boavista) for Parma, Solozábal (Atlético Madrid) for Parma

CUP WINNERS' CUP 1993-94

PRELIMINARY ROUND

FC BALZERS v ALBPETROL PATOSI 3-1 (1-1)
Balzers 15.08.1993
Referee: Roman Steindl (AUS)   Attendance: 1,600
FC BALZERS: Martin Brunhart; Heini Stocker, Christoph Frick, Reto Grunenfelder, Daniel Telser; Michael Nushöhr, Harri Benz, Martin Vogt, Modesto Haas (46 Bruno Vogt); Mario Frick, John Kuster (77 Markus Wille).
Trainer: Weidmann
ALBPETROL: Durim Velçani, Arben Beta, Adrian Prifti, Altin Lisi (72 Mihail Coba), Dashnor Poçi, Adriatik Kurti (62 Luan Ruci), Altin Jaupi, Ilir Caushllari, Arjan Hasa, Anesti Vito, Artjan Papa.   Trainer: Fatmir Dogani
Sent off: Haas (33)
Goals: Nushöhr (31), D. Poçi (39), M.Frick (53, 86)

ALBPETROL PATOSI v FC BALZERS 0-0
Qemal Stafa, Tirana 31.08.1993
Referee: Darko Jamsek (SVN)   Attendance: 1,250
ALBPETROL: Durim Velçani, Gentian Kripa, Ardian Poçi, Adrian Prifti (46 Altin Poçi), Brikenlav Shabani, Dashnor Poçi, Altin Jaupi, Luan Ruci, Ilir Caushllari, Anesti Vito, Artjan Papa.
Trainer: Fatmir Dogani
FC BALZERS: Martin Brunhart; Heini Stocker, Christoph Frick, Reto Grunenfelder, Daniel Telser; Michael Nushöhr (86 Daniel Broder), Harri Benz, Martin Vogt, Modesto Haas (37 Bruno Vogt); Mario Frick, John Kuster.   Trainer: Weidmann
Sent off: Ardian Poçi (88)

RAF JELGAVA v HAVNAR BOLTFELAG 1-0 (0-0)
Daugava, Riga 17.08.1993
Referee: Timo Keltanen (FIN)   Attendance: 500
RAF: Konstantin Igoshin; Alexandr Danilov, Gatis Erglis, Sergei Borisov, Vitaly Dolgopolov, Vadim Mikutsky, Valeri Bogdan (71 Alberts Shvans), Roman Sidorov, Igor Kozlov, Aivars Poznyak, Agris Zarinsh (60 Gints Krogeris).
Trainer: Vasili Ivanov
HB: Kaj Leo Johanssen; Hans Thomassen, Andreas Hansen, Jóannes Jakobsen, Jón Dahl, Albert Ari Thomassen, Rúni Nolsoe, Leivur Holm, Jan Dam (89 Niclas Johannesen), Uni Arge, Kári Reynheim.   Trainer: Sverri Jacobsen
Goal: Kozlov (79)

The second match was not played because the aeroplane containing the RAF team couldn't land for two consecutive days at the airport. Hafnar were awarded this second match with a 3-0 scoreline!   Referee: Piotr Werner (POL)

F91 DUDELANGE v MACCABI HAIFA 0-1 (0-1)
Jos Nosbaum, Dudelange 17.08.1993
Referee: Werner Miller (SWI)   Attendance: 1,363
F91: Serge Rohmann; Gérard Schintgen, Patrick Moretto, José Nora Favita, Antonio Sorcinelli, Serge Cardoni (75 Paolo Serrano), Gérard Urhausen, Frank Petitfrère, Marco Morgante, Enrico Cardoni, Stefano Fanelli.   Trainer: Claude Hausknecht
MACCABI: Rafi Cohen; Eitan Ahroni (79 Alon Harazi), Arik Benado, Roman Pets, Moshe Glam, Alon Hazan, Roni Levi, Sergei Kandaurov, Eyal Berkovich, Ivan Getsko, Alon Mizrahi.
Trainer: Giora Spiegel
Goal: Mizrahi (38)

MACCABI HAIFA v F91 DUDELANGE 6-1 (2-0)
Kiryat Eliezer, Haifa 1.09.1993
Referee: Loris Stafoggia (ITA)   Attendance: 3,500
MACCABI: Rafi Cohen; Eitan Ahroni, Roman Pets, Alon Harazi, Moshe Glam, Alon Hazan (61 Shai Holzman), Roni Levi, Eyal Berkovich (73 Avraham Abukarat), Reuben Atar, Sergei Kandaurov, Alon Mizrahi.   Trainer: Giora Spiegel
F91: Serge Rohmann; Patrick Moretto, Gérard Schintgen, José Nora Favita, Gérard Urhausen, Serge Cardoni, Enrico Cardoni, Angelo Fiorucci, Marco Morgante (89 Antonio Sorcinelli), Stefano Fanelli, Thorvic Amari.   Trainer: Claude Hausknecht
Goals: A. Mizrahi (26, 50 pen), Kandaurov (37), Atar (55), Holzman (75), Harazi (76), Urhausen (90)

KARPATY LVOV v SHELBOURNE FC 1-0 (0-0)
Ukraina Lvov 18.08.1993
Referee: Andreas Georgiou (CYP)   Attendance: 25,000
KARPATY: Bogdan Strontsitskiy; Olexandr Yevtushok, Aleksandr Chizhevski, Sergei Romanishin, Yuri Mokritski, Anatoli Petrik, Andriy Pokladok, Vasyl Kardash, Viktor Rafalchuk (46 Yuri Shuliatitski), Igor Plotko, Mikhail Stelmakh (76 Vladimir Reznik).   Trainer: Miron Markevich
SHELBOURNE: Jody Byrne; Michael Neville, Anto Whelan, Kevin Brady, Tommy Dunne, Brian Mooney, Paul Doolin, Mark Rutherford, Greg Costello, Vinny Arkins (83 Bobby Browne), Ken O'Doherty.   Trainer: Pat Byrne
Goal: Yevtushok (84)

SHELBOURNE FC v KARPATY LVOV 3-1 (1-0)
Tolka Park, Dublin   1.09.1993
Referee: Philippe Leduc (FRA)   Attendance: 7,000
SHELBOURNE: Jody Byrne; Brian Flood, Anto Whelan, Michael Neville, Kevin Brady, Brian Mooney, Greg Costello, Paul Doolin, Mark Rutherford, Padraig Dully (58 Antonio Izzi), Ken O'Doherty.   Trainer: Pat Byrne
KARPATY: Bogdan Strontsitskiy; Olexandr Yevtushok, Aleksandr Chizhevski, Dmitri Mazur, Yuri Mokritski, Anatoli Petrik, Andriy Pokladok, Vasyl Kardash (81 Yuri Shuliatitski), Vladimir Reznik, Igor Plotko, Mikhail Stelmakh (46 Viktor Rafalchuk).   Trainer: Miron Markevich
Goals: Costello (9), Mooney (67), Izzi (76), Reznik (86)

BANGOR CITY v APOEL NICOSIA 1-1 (1-1)
Clandeboye Park, Bangor   18.08.1993
Referee: Roelof Luinge (HOL)   Attendance: 2,000
CITY: Stephen Eachus; Tony Canning, Mark Glendinning, Ray McGuinness, Stephen Brown, John O'Connor, Raymond Hill, Marc Kenny, David McCallan (56 Michael Surgeon), Barry McCreadie (80 Jonathan Magee), Richard McEvoy.   Trainer: Nigel Best
APOEL: Andreas Petridis; Hristakis Pounas, Dimitris Kleanthous, Nikos Haralampous, Dimitri Goutinov, Aristos Aristokleous (80 Nicos Magnitis), Vesko Mihajlovic, Antros Sotiriou, Vasko Gunev, Giannis Ioannou (80 Willy Nwakama), Loukas Hatziloukas.   Trainer: Takis Antoniou
Goals: McEvoy (25), Sotiriou (44)

APOEL NICOSIA v BANGOR CITY 2-1 (1-1)
Makarios, Nicosia   1.09.1993
Referee: Itzhak Ben Itzhak (Isr)   Attendance: 15,000
APOEL: Andreas Petridis; Kostas Kosta, Dimitris Kleanthous, Dimitri Goutinov, Hristakis Pounas, Aristos Aristokleous (69 Nicos Magnitis), Vesko Mihajlovic, Antros Sotiriou, Willy Nwakama (86 Kostas Fasouliotis), Giannis Ioannou, Loukas Hatziloukas.   Trainer: Takis Antoniou
CITY: Stephen Eachus; Tony Canning, Mark Glendinning, Ray McGuinness, Stephen Brown, John O'Connor, Raymond Hill, Marc Kenny, David McCallan (71 Michael Surgeon), Michael Crowe (58 Reg Dornan), Richard McEvoy.   Trainer: Nigel Best
Goals: Glendinning (4), Mihajlovic (15), Pounas (69)

KNATTSPYRNUFÉLAG VALUR REYKJAVÍK v MyPa ANJALANKOSKI 3-1 (0-1)
Laugardalsvöllur, Reykjavík   18.08.1993
Referee: John Ferry (NIR)   Attendance: 409
VALUR: Bjarni Sigurdsson; Gunnar Gunnarsson (61 Milomir Gajic), Jón Helgason, Arnaldur Loftsson, Bjarki Stefánsson, Jón Grétar Jónsson, Agúst Gylfason, Steinar Adolfsson, Hördur Már Magnússon, Kristinn Lárusson (68 Sigurbjörn Hreidarsson), Anthony Karl Gregory.   Trainer: Kristinn Björnsson
MyPa: Mihail Biriukov; Janne Mäkelä, Mika Viljanen, Jukka Koskinen, Esa Pekonen, Janne Lindberg, Saku Laaksonen (71 Tomi Kinnunen), Yrjö Happonen (46 Sami Hyypiä), Anders Roth, Marko Rajamäki, Jukka Turunen.   Trainer: Harri Kampman
Goals: Rajamäki (33), Gregory (53, 58), Lárusson (63)

MyPa ANJALANKOSKI v KNATTSPYRNUFÉLAG VALUR REYKJAVÍK 0-1 (0-0)
Kisapuisto, Lahti   1.09.1993
Referee: Taras Bezoubiak (RUS)   Attendance: 800
MyPa: Mihail Biriukov; Janne Mäkelä, Mika Viljanen, Esa Pekonen, Ilpo Hellsten, Toni Huttunen, Anders Roth, Janne Lindberg, Marko Rajamäki (57 Mauri Keskitalo), Saku Laaksonen (71 Tomi Kinnunen), Jukka Turunen.   Trainer: Harri Kampman
VALUR: Bjarni Sigurdsson; Jón Grétar Jónsson, Saevar Jónsson, Jón Helgason, Bjarki Stefánsson, Steinar Adolfsson, Kristinn Lárusson (75 Sigurbjörn Hreidarsson), Agúst Gylfason, Hördur Már Magnússon, Arnljótur Davídsson (83 Gudmundur Brynjólfsson), Anthony Karl Gregory.   Trainer: Kristinn Björnsson
Goal: Lárusson (68)

FC VMK NIKOL TALLINN v SK LILLESTRØM 0-4 (0-4)
Tallinn stadium   18.08.1993
Referee: Hans-Peter Dellwing (GER)   Attendance: 900
NIKOL: Oleg Andreiev; Andrei Krasnopiorov, Aleksandr Borodin, Aleksei Kapustin, Igor Bakhmatski, Pavel Kazakov, Valeri Mozhukhin, Boris Kudriavtsev (46 Viktor Pasikuta), Igor Andreiev (64 Nikolai Arendash), Oleg Guzik, Evgeni Oleinikov.   Trainer: Viacheslav Smirnov
LILLESTRØM: Frode Grodas; Dennis Schiller (46 Bard Bjerkeland), Torgeir Bjarmann, Thomas Berntsen, Bjarne Sognnaes, Jan Ove Pedersen, Lars Bohinen, André Bergdølmo, Tom Gulbrandsen (64 Stuart McManus), Patrick Karlsson, Mons Ivar Mjelde.   Trainer: Ivar Hoff
Goals: Karlsson (6), T. Gulbrandsen (10), Schiller (39), Bjärmann (44)

SK LILLESTRØM v FC VMK TALLINN 4-1 (3-0)
Åråsen, Lillestrøm   1.09.1993
Referee: Andrew Wilson Waddell (SCO)   Attendance: 1,120
LILLESTRØM: Frode Grodås; Dennis Schiller, Torgeir Bjarmann, Thomas Berntsen, Bjarne Sognnaes, Jan Ove Pedersen, Lars Bohinen, Tom Gulbrandsen, André Bergdølmo (60 Tom Buer), Patrick Karlsson (62 Stuart McManus), Mons Ivar Mjelde.   Trainer: Ivar Hoff
NIKOL:Oleg Andreiev; Andrei Krasnopiorov, Aleksandr Borodin (46 Nikolai Arendash), Aleksei Kapustin, Igor Bakhmatski, Pavel Kazakov, Valeri Mozhukhin, Boris Kudriavtsev (65 Igor Andreiev), Yuri Lebret, Viktor Pasikuta, Evgeni Oleinikov.   Trainer: Viacheslav Smirnov
Goals: T. Gulbrandsen (35), Bergdølmo (38), Mjelde (40), Arendash (71), McManus (74)

FC LUGANO v NEMAN GRODNO 5-0 (1-0)
Stadium Comunale di Cornaredo, Lugano   18.08.1993
Referee: Rémy Harrel (FRA)   Attendance: 6,000
FC LUGANO: Philipp Walker; René Morf, Thomas Käslin, Mauro Galvão, Walter Fernández, Salvo Paradiso (76 Daniele Penzavalli), Antonio Esposito (89 Romeo Pelosi), Christian Colombo, Paulo Andrioli, Nestor Subiat, Martin Fink.
Trainer: Karl Engel
NEMAN: Yuri Svirkov; Sergei Miroshkin, Gennadi Mardas, Sergei Gurenko, Oleg Sisoyev, Aleksandr Zhiliuk (62 Yuri Mazurchik), Dmitri Trosko, Marat Beleziako (75 Sergei Kukalevich), Viktor Yuyko, Sergei Koroza, Sergei Solodovnikov.   Trainer: Stanislav Vlasevich
Goals: Andrioli (37, 83), Subiat (59), Fink (68), Penzavalli (85)

FC KOŠICE v ZALGIRIS VILNIUS 2-1 (2-1)
VSE Sportovi, Košice   18.08.1993
Referee: Adrian Porumboiu (ROM)   Attendance: 6,000
FC KOŠICE: Jaroslav Olejár; Slavomír Prúcny, Peter Furda, Ján Blahusiak, Erik Vágner, Peter Durica, Igor Kasana, Cyril Stachura, Ondrej Danko (49 Milos Belák), Viktor Pobegajev, Jaroslav Sovic.   Trainer: Ján Zachar
ZALGIRIS: Darius Spetyla; Tomas Ziukas, Darius Maciulevicius, Girius Kalvaitis, Grazvydas Mikulenas, Ramunas Stonkus, Valdas Urbonas, Andrius Tereskinas, Gintaras Rimkus (62 Arnas Balsevicius), Aurelijus Skarbalius (46 Donatos Vencevicius), Ricardas Zdancius.
Trainer: Benjaminas Zelkevicius
Goals: Danko (22), Pobegajev (36), Maciulevicius (82)

NEMAN GRODNO v FC LUGANO 2-1 (0-1)
Dinamo Minsk   1.09.1993
Referee: Václav Krondl (CZE)   Attendance: 2,000
NEMAN: Albert Rybak; Aleksandr Zhiliuk, Gennadi Mardas, Oleg Sisoyev, Aleksandr Znak, Sergei Gurenko, Dmitri Trosko, Sergei Kukalevich (58 Yuri Mazurchik), Marat Beleziako (68 Viktor Yuyko), Sergei Solodovnikov, Sergei Koroza.
Trainer: Stanislav Vlasevich
FC LUGANO: Philipp Walker; Patrick Englund, Salvo Paradiso, Mauro Galvão, René Morf, Eduardo Carrasco, Thomas Käslin, Paulo Andrioli, Walter Fernández (70 Christian Colombo), Martin Fink (82 Romeo Pelosi), Nestor Subiat.   Trainer: Karl Engel
Goals: Subiat (29), Solodovnikov (60), Mazurchik (69)

ZALGIRIS VILNIUS v FC KOŠICE 0-1 (0-1)
Zalgiris Vilnius   1.09.1993
Referee: Svend Erik Christensen (Den)   Attendance: 3,000
ZALGIRIS: Darius Spetyla; Tomas Ziukas, Darius Maciulevicius, Girius Kalvaitis, Ramunas Stonkus, Donatos Vencevicius, Valdas Urbonas, Andrius Tereskinas, Grazvydas Mikulenas (46 Gintaras Rimkus), Arnas Balsevicius (46 Aurelijus Skarbalius), Ricardas Zdancius.
Trainer: Benjaminas Zelkevicius
FC KOŠICE: Jaroslav Olejár; Slavomír Prúcny, Peter Furda, Ján Blahusiak, Imrich Babincák, Peter Durica (64 Cyril Stachura), Ondrej Danko, Milos Belák, Igor Kasana, Oleg Lipinski (81 Ivan Lapsansky), Viktor Pobegajev.
Trainer: Ján Zachar
Goal: Durica (13)

PUBLIKUM CELJE v ODENSE BK 0-1 (0-0)
Skalna Klet, Celje   18.08.1993
Referee: Freddy Philippoz (SWI)   Attendance: 2,500
PUBLIKUM: Branko Zupan; Ales Turk, Dejan Romih, Janez Zilnik, Gregor Blatnik, Stjepan Pranjić, Matjaz Stancar (87 Robert Cugmas), Joze Prelogar, Bojan Romih, Robert Pevnik, Andrej Gorsek.   Trainer: Janez Zavrl
OB: Lars Høgh; Steen Nedergaard, Michael Hemmingsen, Brian Steen Nielsen, Thomas Helveg, Allan Nielsen, Carsten Dethlefsen, John Damsted (52 Alphonse Tchami), Brian Skaarup, Jess Thorup, Lars Brøgger (74 Jens Melvang).
Trainer: Kim Brink
Goal: Nedergaard (83)

ODENSE BK v PUBLIKUM CELJE 0-0
Odense Stadion   1.09.1993
Referee: Léon Schelings (BEL)   Attendance: 2,525
OB: Lars Høgh; Torben Sangild, Thomas Helveg, Michael Hemmingsen, Steen Nedergaard, Jens Melvang (74 Lars Brøgger), Allan Nielsen, Brian Steen Nielsen, Brian Skaarup (80 Carsten Dethlefsen), Jess Thorup, Alphonse Tchami.   Trainer: Kim Brink
PUBLIKUM: Branko Zupan; Ales Turk, Dejan Romih, Janez Zilnik, Gregor Blatnik, Stjepan Pranjić, Matjaz Stancar, Joze Prelogar, Bojan Romih, Robert Pevnik, Andrej Gorsek (68 Dejan Car).   Trainer: Janez Zavrl

SLIEMA WANDERERS v DEGERFORS IF 1-3 (0-2)
Ta'Qali, Valletta   18.08.1993
Referee: Brian Hill (ENG)   Attendance: 1,438
SLIEMA WANDERERS: István Tárlosi; Joe Sant Fournier, Edmond Zammit, John Caruana (74 Jonathan Magri Overend), James Navarro, Kevan Smith, Martin Gregory, Sandro Zammit Fava, George Lawrence, Hubert Suda (77 Noel Turner), Aldo Scardino.   Trainer: Marcel Scicluna
DEGERFORS: Jesper Leu; Vujadin Stanojkovic, Peter Karlsson (88 Tommy Mohlin), Krister Ericsson, Ivan Djuric, Henrik Berger, Milenko Vukoevic, Dusko Radinovic, Dan Fröberg, Ulf Ottosson, Ola Svensson.   Trainer: Börje Andersson
Goals: Ottosson (7, 31), Fröberg (52), Gregory (67 pen)

DEGERFORS IF v SLIEMA WANDERERS 3-0 (2-0)
Stora Valla, Degerfors   2.09.1993
Referee: Karel Bohunek (CZE)   Attendance: 4,029
DEGERFORS: Jesper Leu; Vujadin Stanojkovic, Peter Karlsson, Krister Ericsson, Ivan Djuric, Dusko Radinovic, Henrik Berger, Milenko Vukoevic, Ola Svensson, Ulf Ottosson, Dan Fröberg.   Trainer: Börje Andersson
SLIEMA: István Tárlosi; John Caruana, Aldo Scardino, James Navarro, Carlos Cluett, Hubert Suda, Joe Sant Fournier, John Micallef, Sandro Zammit Fava (72 Jonathan Magri Overend), Noel Turner (.. Gordon Asciak), Martin Gregory.   Trainer: Marcel Scicluna
Goals: Ottosson (2), Fröberg (14), Eriksson (64 pen)

FIRST ROUND

DEGERFORS IF v AC PARMA 1-2 (0-0)
Stora Valla, Degerfors   14.09.1993
Referee: Ryszard Wójcik (POL)   Attendance: 10,482
DEGERFORS: Mats Johansson, Vujadin Stanojkovic, Peter Karlsson, Tommy Mohlin, Sebastian Henriksson, Henrik Berger, Milenko Vukcevic, Dusko Radinovic (82 Johan Ström), Dan Fröberg (54 Daniel Ericsson), Leif Olsson, Ola Svensson.   Trainer: Börje Andersson
PARMA: Luca Bucci; Antonio Benarrivo, David Balleri, Lorenzo Minotti, Luigi Apolloni, Georges Grün, Tomas Brolin, Daniele Zoratto (82 Alessandro Melli), Massimo Crippa, Gianfranco Zola, Faustino Asprilla.   Trainer: Nevio Scala
Goals: Berger (72), Asprilla (87, 88)

AC PARMA v DEGERFORS IF 2-0 (1-0)
Stadio Ennio Tardini, Parma   28.09.1993
Referee: Oguz Sarvan (TUR)   Attendance: 14,977
PARMA: Luca Bucci; David Balleri, Alberto di Chiara, Lorenzo Minotti, Luigi Apolloni, Georges Grün (69 Salvatore Matrecano), Gabriele Pin, Daniele Zoratto, Massimo Crippa, Tomas Brolin, Faustino Asprilla (64 Gianfranco Zola).   Trainer: Nevio Scala
DEGERFORS: Mats Johansson, Vujadin Stanojkovic, Peter Karlsson (46 Johan Ström), Krister Ericsson, Tommy Mohlin, Henrik Berger, Milenko Vukcevic, Sebastian Henriksson, Dan Fröberg (77 Daniel Ericsson), Leif Olsson, Ola Svensson.   Trainer: Börje Andersson
Goals: Balleri (3), Brolin (68)

**APOEL NICOSIA
v PARIS SAINT GERMAIN 0-1** (0-0)
Makarion, Nicosia   14.09.1993
Referee: Marnix Sandra (BEL)   Attendance: 12,000
APOEL: Andreas Petridis; Kostas Kosta, Hristakis Pounas, Dimitri Goutinov, Dimitris Kleanthous, Willy Nwakama (83 Aristos Aristokleous), Vesko Mihajlovic, Loukas Hatziloukas, Kostas Fasouliotis, Antros Sotiriou, Giannis Ioannou (20 Nikos Magnitis).   Trainer: Takis Antoniou
PSG: Bernard Lama; Jean-Luc Sassus, Antoine Kombouaré (33 José Cobos), Alain Roche, Francis Llacer, Paul le Guen, Vincent Guérin, Laurent Fournier, Daniel Bravo, Xavier Gravelaine (46 George Weah), David Ginola.   Trainer: Artur Jorge Braga
Goal: Sassus (78)

**PARIS SAINT GERMAIN
v APOEL NICOSIA 2-0** (2-0)
Parc des Princes, Paris 28.09.1993
Referee: Hartmut Strampe (GER)   Attendance: 13,500
PSG: Bernard Lama; Jean-Luc Sassus, Alain Roche, Ricardo Gomes, Patrick Colleter, Laurent Fournier (46 Daniel Bravo), Paul le Guen, Valdo Cândido Filho, Raí Oliveira (61 José Cobos), Xavier Gravelaine, David Ginola.   Trainer: Artur Jorge Braga
APOEL: Andreas Petridis; Kostas Kosta, Nikos Magnitis (75 Kostas Miamiliotis), Dimitri Goutinov, Dimitris Kleanthous, Willy Nwakama, Vesko Mihajlovic, Antros Sotiriou, Giannis Ioannou (46 Hristakis Pounas), Kostas Fasouliotis, Loukas Hatziloukas.   Trainer: Takis Antoniou
Goals: Le Guen (1), Gravelaine (31)

VALUR REYKJAVÍK v ABERDEEN FC 0-3 (0-2)
Laugardalsvöllur, Reykjavík 14.09.1993
Referee: Michel Piraux (BEL)   Attendance: 656
VALUR: Bjarni Sigurdsson; Bjarki Stefánsson, Jón Helgason, Saevar Jónsson, Arnljótur Davídsson, Jón Grétar Jónsson (82 Sigurbjörn Hreidarsson), Agúst Gylfason, Steinar Adolfsson, Anthony Karl Gregory (83 Tryggvi Valsson), Kristinn Lárusson, Hördur Már Magnússon.   Trainer: Kristinn Björnsson
ABERDEEN: Theo Snelders; Stewart McKimmie, Stephen Wright, Paul Kane, Alex McLeish, Brian Irvine, Joe Miller (85 Roy Aitken), James Bett (56 David Winnie), Eoin Jess, Duncan Shearer, Robert Connor.   Manager: Willie Miller
Goals: Shearer (8), Jess (29, 56)

BAYER LEVERKUSEN v FC BOBY BRNO 2-0 (1-0)
Ulrich Haberland stadion, Leverkusen 14.09.1993
Referee: Juan Ansuategui Roca (SPA)   Attendance: 6,100
BAYER: Rüdiger Vollborn; Franco Foda, Christian Wörns, Markus Happe, Andreas Fischer, Ioan Lupescu, Pavel Hapal, Martin Kree, Paulo Sérgio, Andreas Thom, Josef Nehl (75 René Rydlewicz).   Trainer: Dragoslav Stepanović
BOBY: René Twardzik; Petr Malér, Petr Krivanek, Frantisek Chovanec, Pavel Kobylka, Petr Kocman, Jiří Zalesky, Edvard Lasota, Libor Soldan (86 Vladimir Hekerle), René Wagner (79 Pavel Holomek), Jan Janostak.   Trainer: Josef Masopust
Goals: Hapal (30), Thom (66)

ABERDEEN FC v VALUR REYKJAVÍK 4-0 (0-0)
Pittodrie, Aberdeen 29.09.1993
Referee: Rune Pedersen (NOR)   Attendance: 10,000
ABERDEEN: Theo Snelders; Stewart McKimmie (69 David Winnie), Stephen Wright, Paul Kane, Brian Irvine, Gary Smith, Joe Miller (75 Andrew Gibson), James Bett, Eoin Jess, Lee Richardson, Mika-Matti Paatelainen.   Manager: Willie Miller
VALUR: Bjarni Sigurdsson; Jón Grétar Jónsson, Saevar Jónsson, Milomir Gajic, Jón Helgason, Arnljótur Davídsson (78 Saevar Pétursson), Agúst Gylfason, Hördur Már Magnússon, Steinar Adolfsson (68 Sigurbjörn Hreidarsson), Kristinn Lárusson, Anthony Karl Gregory.   Trainer: Kristinn Björnsson
Goals: Miller (51), Jess (60, 69), Irvine (65)

FC BOBY BRNO v BAYER LEVERKUSEN 0-3 (0-1)
Za Luzankami, Brno 29.09.1993
Referee: Stephen Lodge (ENG)   Attendance: 10,105
BOBY: René Twardzik; Petr Malér, Petr Krivanek, Frantisek Chovanec, Pavel Kobylka, Petr Kocman, Jiří Zalesky, Edvard Lasota, Libor Soldan, René Wagner, Jan Janostak.   Trainer: Josef Masopust
BAYER: Rüdiger Vollborn; Franco Foda, Christian Wörns, Markus Happe, Andreas Fischer, Ioan Lupescu, Pavel Hapal (29 Ralf Becker), Martin Kree, Paulo Sérgio (76 René Rydlewicz), Andreas Thom, Ulf Kirsten.   Trainer: Dragoslav Stepanović
Goals: Kirsten (16), Fischer (59), Wörns (79)

TORPEDO MOSKVA v MACCABI HAIFA 1-0 (0-0)
Torpedo Moskva 15.09.1993
Referee: Kaj John Natri (FIN)   Attendance: 3,150
TORPEDO: Aleksandr Podzhivalov, Andrei Kalaichev, Maksim Cheltsov, Andrei Afanasiev, Sergei Borisov, Sergei Chumachenko (78 Dmitri Prokopenko), Gennadi Grishin, Gennadi Filimonov (15 Dmitri Ulianov), Andrei Talalaev, Igor Chugainov, Ivan Pazemov.   Trainer: Yuri Mironov
MACCABI: Rafi Cohen; Marco Balbul (75 Daniel Zabar), Alon Harazi, Alon Hazan, Roman Pets, Sergei Kandaurov, Roni Levi, Moshe Glam, Eyal Berkovich, Reuven Atar (85 Ivan Getsko), Alon Mizrahi.   Trainer: Giora Spiegel
Goal: Borisov (88)

MACCABI HAIFA v TORPEDO MOSKVA 3-1 (1-1)
Kiryat Eliezer, Haifa   28.09.1993
Referee: Alfred Micallef (MAL)   Attendance: 9,500
MACCABI: Rafi Cohen; Marco Balbul (46 Shay Holzman), Alon Harazi, Alon Hazan, Roman Pets, Sergei Kandaurov, Roni Levi, Moshe Glam, Eyal Berkovich, Reuven Atar, Alon Mizrahi.   Trainer: Giora Spiegel
TORPEDO: Aleksandr Podzhivalov, Andrei Kalaichev (46 Nikolai Savichev), Maksim Cheltsov, Andrei Afanasiev, Dmitri Ulianov (82 Mikhail Soloviev), Sergei Shustikov, Gennadi Grishin, Boris Vostrosablin, Andrei Talalaev, Igor Chugainov, Sergei Borisov.   Trainer: Yuri Mironov
Goals: Mizrahi (6), Kalaichev (12), Pets (73), Holzman (85)

REAL MADRID v FC LUGANO 3-0 (1-0)
Estadio Santiago Bernabéu, Madrid   15.09.1993
Referee: Dick Jol (HOL)   Attendance: 37,600
REAL: Francisco BUYO Sánchez; LUIS ENRIQUE Martínez García, Manuel SANCHIS Hontiyuelo, Rafael ALKORTA Martínez, Miguel LASA Goikoetxea, Rafael MARTÍN VÁZQUEZ, Fernando Ruiz HIERRO, José Miguel González "MICHEL", Peter Dubovský, Emilio BUTRAGUEÑO Santos, Iván Luis ZAMORANO Zamora (62 ALFONSO Pérez Muñoz).   Trainer: Benito Floro
FC LUGANO: Philipp Walker; Salvo Paradiso, Patrick Englund (70 René Morf), Mauro Galvão, Walter Fernández, Paulo Andrioli, Thomas Käslin, Christian Colombo, Antonio Esposito (72 Eduardo Carrasco), Martin Fink, Nestor Subiat.   Trainer: Karl Engel
Goals: Dubovský (44), Michel (67 pen), Fernández (71 og)

STANDARD LIÈGE v CARDIFF CITY 5-2 (1-1)
Stade Maurice Dufrasne Sclessin Liège   15.09.1993
Referee: Eyjolfur Olafsson (ICE)   Attendance: 9,000
STANDARD: Gilbert Bodart; Axel Smeets, Guy Hellers, André Cruz, Philippe Léonard, Alain Bettagno (63 Michael Goossens), Sasha Richkov (82 Yves Sondan), Thierry Pister, Roberto Bisconti, Patrick Asselman, Marc Wilmots.   Trainer: Arie Haan
CITY: Phil Kite; Robbie James, Kevin Ratcliffe, Jason Perry, Lee Baddeley, Damon Searle, Nick Richardson, Anthony Bird, Nathan Blake, Cohen Griffith, Phil Stant (89 Terence Evans).   Manager: Eddie May
Goals: Bisconti (13), Bird (39, 62), Wilmots (63, 84), Cruz (71 pen), Asselman (76)

FC LUGANO v REAL MADRID 1-3 (0-1)
Letzigrund, Zürich   29.09.1993
Referee: Gerald Ashby (ENG)   Attendance: 8,000
FC LUGANO: Philipp Walker; René Morf, Thomas Käslin, Mauro Galvão, Christian Andreoli, Walter Fernández (46 Antonio Esposito), Paulo Andrioli (58 Romeo Pelosi), Daniele Penzavalli, Christian Colombo, Martin Fink, Nestor Subiat.   Trainer: Karl Engel
REAL: Francisco BUYO Sánchez; Manuel SANCHIS Hontiyuelo, Fernando Muñoz García "NANDO", Rafael ALKORTA Martínez, Miguel LASA Goikoetxea, José Miguel González "MICHEL", Fernando Ruiz HIERRO, Luis MILLA Aspas (69 Peter Dubovský), LUIS ENRIQUE Martínez García, Iván Luis ZAMORANO Zamora, ALFONSO Pérez Muñoz (55 Robert Prosinecki).   Trainer: Benito Floro
Goals: Hierro (41), Subiat (61), Zamorano (77, 88)

CARDIFF CITY v STANDARD LIÈGE 1-3 (0-2)
Ninian Park, Cardiff   28.09.1993
Referee: Graziano Cesari (ITA)   Attendance: 6,096
CITY: Steve Williams; Robbie James, Lee Baddeley, Kevin Ratcliffe, Damon Searle, Cohen Griffith, Jason Perry, Paul Millar (69 Kevin Bartley), Anthony Bird (69 Nathan Wigg), Phil Stant, Garry Thompson.   Manager: Eddie May
STANDARD: Gilbert Bodart (18 Jacky Munaron); Roberto Bisconti, Guy Hellers, André Cruz, Philippe Léonard, Mohamed Lashaf, Frans Van Rooy, Thierry Pister, Patrick Vervoort (46 Axel Smeets), Patrick Asselman, Marc Wilmots.   Trainer: Arie Haan
Goals: Wilmots (13), Lashaf (34), Bisconti (50), James (59)

CSKA SOFIA v FC BALZERS 8-0 (2-0)
Vasil Levski, Sofia   15.09.1993
Referee: Charles Agius (MAL)   Attendance: 10,000
CSKA: Antonio Ananiev; Zorko Machev, Milen Radukanov, Ljubco Markovski, Boban Babunski (60 Martin Goranov), Pavel Dochev, Anatoli Nankov, Sasa Ciric (46 Latchezar Tanev), Vanio Shishkov, Ivailo Andonov, Hristo Koilov.   Trainer: Asparukh Nikodimov
FC BALZERS: Martin Brunhart; Heini Stocker, Mario Gunsch (46 Modesto Haas), Reto Grunenfelder, Daniel Telser; Nushöhr, Harri Benz, Martin Vogt, Pascal Brötz; Mario Frick, Bruno Vogt.   Trainer: Weidmann
Goals: Shishkov (12, 21, 54, 69), Andonov (47, 50), Nankov (68 pen, 88)

FC BALZERS v CSKA SOFIA 1-3 (0-1)

Rheinau, Balzers 29.09.1993

Referee: George Mihanikos (CYP)   Attendance: 1,200

FC BALZERS: Stefan Wolfinger; Heini Stocker, Daniel Broder, Reto Grunenfelder, Daniel Telser; Nushöhr (73 Peter Thöny), Harri Benz, Martin Vogt, Christoph Frick; Mario Frick, John Kuster.   Trainer: Weidmann

CSKA: Antonio Ananiev; Radoslav Vidov, Milen Radukanov, Ljubco Markovski, Boban Babunski, Pavel Dochev, Latchezar Tanev, Anatoli Nankov (59 Aleks Aleksandrov), Vanio Shishkov, Ivailo Andonov (46 Sasa Ciric), Hristo Koilov.
Trainer: Asparukh Nikodimov

Goals: Andonov (32), L. Tanev (53), Kuster (63), Ciric (90)

BENFICA LISBOA v GKS KATOWICE 1-0 (0-0)

Estádio da Luz, Lisboa 15.09.1993

Referee: Karl Finzinger (AUS)   Attendance: 10,000

BENFICA: Adelino Augusto Barros NENO; ABEL Luís da Silva Costa XAVIER (64 José RUI Lopes ÁGUAS), José Carlos Nepomuceno MOZER, WILLIAM Amaral de Andrade, Hans Jurgen Stefan SCHWARZ, VÍTOR Manuel Araújo "PANEIRA", RUI Manuel César COSTA, JOÃO Manuel Vieira PINTO, ISAÍAS Marques Soares, CÉSAR Gonçalves BRITO Duarte, AILTON Delfino.
Trainer: António José Conceição Oliveira "TONI"

GKS: Janusz Jojko; Marek Swierczewski, Grzegorz Borawski, Krzysztof Maciejewski, Kazimierz Wegrzyn, Dariusz Rzezniczek, Zdzislaw Strojek, Marian Janoszka, Miroslaw Widuch, Adam Kucz, Dariusz Wolny.
Trainer: Piotr Piekarczyk

Goal: Rui Aguas (86)

PANATHINAIKOS ATHINA v SHELBOURNE FC 3-0 (2-0)

Olympiako Spiros Louis, Athina 15.09.1993

Referee: Bernd Heynemann (GER)   Attendance: 18,310

PANATHINAIKOS: Jozef Wandzik; Stratos Apostolakis, Giorgos H. Georgiadis, Leonidas Hristodoulou (62 Dimitris Markos), Giannis Kalitzakis, Kostas Mauridis, Dimitris Saravakos, Giorgos Donis, Krzysztof Warzycha, Kostas Frantzeskos, Spiros Maragkos (62 Asterios Giotsas).
Trainer: Ivica Osim

SHELBOURNE: Jody Byrne; Brian Flood, Anto Whelan, Kevin Brady, Karl Wilson (52 Bobby Browne), Brian Mooney, Greg Costello, Paul Doolin, Mark Rutherford, Stephen Cooney, Ken O'Doherty.   Trainer: Pat Byrne

Goals: Donis (1), Saravakos (39), Warzycha (48)

GKS KATOWICE v BENFICA LISBOA 1-1 (1-0)

GKS Katowice 29.09.1993

Referee: Aron Schmidhuber (GER)   Attendance: 7,000

GKS: Janusz Jojko; Marek Swierczewski, Grzegorz Borawski, Kazimierz Wegrzyn, Krzysztof Maciejewski, Dariusz Wolny (77 Arkadiusz Szczygiel), Miroslaw Widuch, Adam Kucz, Zdzislaw Strojek, Marian Janoszka, Dariusz Rzezniczek.
Trainer: Piotr Piekarczyk

BENFICA: Adelino Augusto Barros NENO; ABEL Luís da Silva Costa XAVIER, HÉLDER Marino Rodrigues Cristóvão, José Carlos Nepomuceno MOZER, António Augusto da Silva VELOSO, VÍTOR Manuel Araújo "PANEIRA", Hans Jurgen Stefan SCHWARZ, RUI Manuel César COSTA, JOÃO Manuel Vieira PINTO, José RUI Lopes ÁGUAS, ISAÍAS Marques Soares (87 CÉSAR Gonçalves BRITO Duarte).
Trainer: António José Conceição Oliveira "TONI"

Goals: Kucz (45), Vítor Paneira (70)

SHELBOURNE FC v PANATHINAIKOS ATHINA 1-2 (0-1)

Tolka Park, Dublin 29.09.1993

Referee: Mark Kowalczyk (POL)   Attendance: 2,000

SHELBOURNE: Jody Byrne; Brian Flood, Michael Neville, Anto Whelan, Kevin Brady, Brian Mooney, Greg Costello, Paul Doolin, Mark Rutherford (65 Bobby Browne), Ken O'Doherty, Padraig Dully (60 Stephen Cooney).   Trainer: Pat Byrne

PANATHINAIKOS: Jozef Wandzik; Stratos Apostolakis, Giorgos H. Georgiadis (60 Asterios Giotsas), Giorgos Donis (60 Kostas Frantzeskos), Giannis Kalitzakis, Kostas Mauridis, Dimitris Saravakos, Kostas Antoniou, Krzysztof Warzycha, Nikos Nioplias, Spiros Maragkos.   Trainer: Ivica Osim

Goals: Georgiadis (26), Saravakos (57), Cooney (86)

UNIVERSITATEA CRAIOVA v HAVNAR BOLTFELAG TÓRSHAVN 4-0 (0-0)

Central Craiova 15.09.1993

Referee: Serdar Cakman (TUR)   Attendance: 8,000

UNIVERSITATEA: Silviu Lung; Daniel Emil Mogoşanu, Corneliu Papură, Gheorghe Biţă (78 Gheorghe Bujor), Victor Cojocaru (72 Adrian Pigulea); Aurel Augustin Călin, Ion Olaru, Silvian Cristescu, Cristian Marius Vasc; Gheorghe Craioveanu, Ionel Tersinio Gane.   Trainer: Marian Bondrea

HB: Kaj Leo Johannessen; Kári Nielsen, Jóannes Jakobsen (Cap), Andreas F. Hansen, Albert Ari Thomassen; Jan Dam, Leivur Holm, Rúni Nolsöe, Kári Reynheim; Gunnar Mohr (59 Julian Johnsson), Uni Arge.   Trainer: Sverri Jakobsen

Goals: Craioveanu (47 pen), Gane (58, 70), Călin (81)

**HAVNAR BOLTFELAG TÓRSHAVN
v UNIVERSITATEA CRAIOVA 0-3** (0-2)
Svangaskard, Toftir 29.09.1993
Referee: Tore Hollung (NOR)   Attendance: 275

HB: Kaj Leo Johannessen; Hans Petur í Brekkunum, Kári Nielsen, Jóannes Jakobsen (Cap), Jón Dahl, Hans Thomassen; Sámal Erik Hentze, Julian Johnsson, Rúni Nolsöe; Gunnar Mohr (86 Sigfridur S.Clementsen), Uni Arge.
Trainer: Sverri Jacobsen

UNIVERSITATEA: Silviu Lung; Daniel Emil Mogoşanu, Corneliu Papură, Gheorghe Biţă, Victor Cojocaru; Aurel Augustin Călin (46 Cristian Marius Vasc), Ion Olaru, Silvian Cristescu (70 Adrian Pigulea), Ovidiu Stîngă; Gheorghe Craioveanu, Ionel Tersinio Gane.   Trainer: Marian Bondrea

Goals: Gane (27, 32), Vasc (70)

SK LILLESTRØM v AC TORINO 0-2 (0-1)
Åråsen, Lillestrøm 15.09.1993
Referee: Vladimir Ovchinnikov (RUS)   Attendance: 5,056

LILLESTRØM: Frode Grodås; Dennis Schiller, Torgeir Bjarmann, Thomas Berntsen, Bjarne Sognnaes, Jan Ove Pedersen, Lars Bohinen, Tom Gulbrandsen, André Bergdølmo, Stuart McManus, Rune Nordengen (46 Tom Buer).
Trainer: Ivar Hoff

AC TORINO: Giovanni Galli; Sandro Cois, Robert Jarni (82 Marco Sinigaglia), Roberto Mussi, Angelo Gregucci, Luca Fusi, Gianluca Sordo, Daniele Fortunato, Andrea Silenzi (74 Benito Carbone), Giorgio Venturin, Marco Osio.
Trainer: Emiliano Mondonico

Goals: Silenzi (26), Jarni (58)

**FC TIROL INNSBRUCK
v FERENCVÁROS TC BUDAPEST 3-0** (0-0)
Tivoli, Innsbruck 15.09.1993
Referee: Joël Quiniou (FRA)   Attendance: 6,505

FC TIROL: Milan Oraze; Kurt Russ (36 Jürgen Hartmann), Oliver Prudlo, Robert Wazinger, Andrzej Lesiak, Harald Schneider, Thomas Janeschitz (76 Roland Kirchler), Michael Baur, Václav Daněk, Marcello Carracedo, Christoph Westerthaler.   Trainer: Horst Köppel

FERENCVÁROS: József Szeiler; Tibor Simon, András Telek, József Keller, Tamás Szekeres, Péter Lipcsei, Zsolt Páling, Flórián Albert, József Kovács (75 Sorin Cigan), Lajos Détári, László Wukovics.   Trainer: Tibor Nyilasi

Goals: Daněk (48), Westerthaler (58), Carracedo (65)

AC TORINO v SK LILLESTRØM 1-2 (1-0)
Stadio Delle Alpi, Torino 29.09.1993
Referee: Leif Sundell (SWE)   Attendance: 6,323

AC TORINO: Giovanni Galli; Angelo Gregucci, Raffaele Sergio, Roberto Mussi, Daniele Delli Carri, Luca Fusi, Marco Sinigaglia, Daniele Fortunato, Andrea Silenzi (46 Benito Carbone), Giorgio Venturin, Paolo Poggi (69 Giulio Falcone).
Trainer: Emiliano Mondonico

LILLESTRØM: Frode Grodås; Dennis Schiller, Torgeir Bjarmann, Thomas Berntsen, André Bergdølmo, Jan Ove Pedersen, Lars Bohinen, Tom Gulbrandsen, Patrick Karlsson, Stuart McManus, Mons Ivar Mjelde.   Trainer: Ivar Hoff

Goals: Silenzi (45), Sinigaglia (48 og), Mjelde (58)

**FERENCVÁROS BUDAPEST
v FC TIROL INNSBRUCK 1-2** (0-1)
Üllöi út, Budapest 29.09.1993
Referee: Sergei Khusainov (RUS)   Attendance: 12,000

FERENCVÁROS: József Szeiler; Tibor Simon, András Telek, Péter Lipcsei, Zsolt Páling, Flórián Albert, Lajos Détári, József Keller (46 Tamás Szekeres), Zsolt Nagy, József Kovács, László Wukovics (66 József Gregor).   Trainer: Tibor Nyilasi

FC TIROL: Milan Oraze; Michael Streiter, Oliver Prudlo, Andrzej Lesiak, Jürgen Hartmann, Roland Kirchler (79 Thomas Janeschitz), Marcello Carracedo (60 Rudolf Gussnig), Robert Wazinger, Michael Baur, Christoph Westerthaler, Václav Daněk.   Trainer: Horst Köppel

Goals: Westerthaler (19, 90), Détári (48)

FC KOŠICE v BEŞIKTAŞ ISTANBUL 2-1 (0-1)
VSE Sportovi Stadion, Košice 15.09.1993
Referee: Veselin Bogdanov (BUL)   Attendance: 15,000

FC KOŠICE: Jaroslav Olejár; Erik Vágner, Peter Furda, Ján Blahusiak, Imrich Babincák, Rastislav Lazorík (53 Ivan Lapsansky), Peter Durica, Milos Belák, Jaroslav Sovic, Ondrej Danko, Viktor Pobegajev.   Trainer: Ján Zachar

BEŞIKTAŞ: Sener Kurtdemir; Recep Çetin, Gökhan Keskin, Ulvi Güveneroglu, Riza Çalimbay, Ali Günçar, Mehmet Özdilek, Sergen Yalçin (46 Oktay Derelioglu), Mutlu Topçu, Feyyaz Uçar, Fani Madida (72 Kadir Akbulut).
Trainer: Gordon Milne

Goals: Sergen Yalçin (2), Danko (71 pen, 78 pen)

BEŞIKTAŞ ISTANBUL v FC KOŠICE 2-0 (1-0)

Inönü, Istanbul   29.09.1993

Referee: Lajos Hartmann (HUN)   Attendance: 27,258

BEŞIKTAŞ: Sener Kurtdemir; Recep Çetin, Gökhan Keskin, Ali Günçar, Oktay Derelioglu, Riza Çalimbay, Mehmet Özdilek, Sergen Yalçin (73 Yusuf Tokaç), Mutlu Topçu, B.Metin Tekin, Feyyaz Uçar.   Trainer: Gordon Milne

FC KOŠICE: Jaroslav Olejár; Erik Vágner, Peter Furda, Ján Blahusiak, Milos Belák, Peter Durica, Slavomír Prúcny, Ondrej Danko, Imrich Babincák, Viktor Pobegajev, Oleg Lipinski (67 Ivan Lapsansky).   Trainer: Ján Zachar

Goals: Metin (45, 72)

HAJDUK SPLIT v AJAX AMSTERDAM 1-0 (1-0)

Olimpija, Ljubljana   17.09.1993

Referee: Fabio Baldas (ITA)   Attendance: 8,909

HAJDUK: Vatroslav Mihacić; Robert Vladislavić, Josko Spanjić, Mirsad Hibić, Mario Osibov, Stipe Andrijasević (89 Stipe Balajić), Ante Miše, Dejan Racunica, Nenad Pralija, Ardijan Kozniku (78 Milan Rapaić), Ivica Mornar. Trainer: Ivan Katalinić

AJAX: Edwin Van der Sar; Danny Blind, John Van den Brom, Frank De Boer, Michel Kreek, Frank Rijkaard, Jari Litmanen, Edgar Davids, Finidi George (81 Peter Van Vossen), Ronald De Boer (66 Stefan Pettersson), Marc Overmars.
Trainer: Louis Van Gaal

Goal: Mornar (44)

OB ODENSE v ARSENAL LONDON 1-2 (1-1)

Odense stadium   15.09.1993

Referee: Ahmet Cakar (TUR)   Attendance: 9,580

OB: Lars Høgh; Thomas Helveg, Michael Hemmingsen, Torben Sangild (80 Per Hjorth), Steen Nedergaard, Allan Nielsen, Brian Steen Nielsen, Brian Skaarup, Jess Thorup, Carsten Dethlefsen, Alphonse Tchami.   Trainer: Kim Brink

ARSENAL: David Seaman; Eddie McGoldrick, Andy Linighan, Martin Keown, Nigel Winterburn, Ian Selley, John Jensen, Paul Davis, Paul Merson, Kevin Campbell, Ian Wright (86 Alan Smith).   Trainer: George Graham

Goals: Keown (19 og), Wright (35), Merson (68)

AJAX AMSTERDAM v HAJDUK SPLIT 6-0 (2-0)

Olympisch, Amsterdam   29.09.1993

Referee: Patrick Kelly (IRE)   Attendance: 33,000

AJAX: Edwin Van der Sar; Danny Blind, John Van den Brom, Frank De Boer, Michel Kreek, Frank Rijkaard (66 Rob Alflen), Jari Litmanen, Edgar Davids, Finidi George, Ronald De Boer, Marc Overmars (57 Stefan Pettersson).
Trainer: Louis Van Gaal

HAJDUK: Vatroslav Mihacić; Robert Vladislavić, Josko Spanjić, Mario Osibov, Mirsad Hibić, Stipe Andrijasević (46 Milan Rapaić), Ante Miše, Dejan Racunica, Nenad Pralija, Ivica Mornar (68 Darko Butorović), Ardijan Kozniku.
Trainer: Ivan Katalinic

Goals: R. De Boer (11), Davids (37, 76), Litmanen (56), F. De Boer (61), Pettersson (73)

SECOND ROUND

ARSENAL LONDON v OB ODENSE 1-1 (0-0)

Highbury, London   29.09.1993

Referee: Hans-Jürgen Weber (GER)   Attendance: 25,689

ARSENAL: David Seaman; Lee Dixon, Nigel Winterburn, Paul Davis, Martin Keown, Tony Adams, John Jensen, Ian Wright (69 Alan Smith), Kevin Campbell, Paul Merson, Eddie McGoldrick.   Trainer: George Graham

OB: Lars Høgh; Steen Nedergaard, Michael Hemmingsen, Brian Steen Nielsen, Thomas Helveg, Allan Nielsen, Per Hjorth (53 Jens Melvang), Carsten Dethlefsen, Jess Thorup, Alphonse Tchami, Brian Skaarup (87 John Damsted).
Trainer: Kim Brink

Goals: Campbell (52), A. Nielsen (86)

AJAX AMSTERDAM v BEŞIKTAŞ ISTANBUL 2-1 (0-1)

Olympisch, Amsterdam   20.10.1993

Referee: Keith Burge (WAL)   Attendance: 42,000

AJAX: Edwin Van der Sar; Danny Blind, John Van den Brom (61 Martijn Reuser), Frank De Boer, Michel Kreek, Ronald De Boer, Frank Rijkaard, Jari Litmanen, Rob Alflen, Finidi George, Stefan Pettersson (76 Ignacio Tuhuteru).
Trainer: Louis Van Gaal

BEŞIKTAŞ: Zafer Öger; Recep Çetin, Alpay Özalan, Gökhan Keskin, Ali Günçar, Mutlu Topçu, Riza Çalimbay, Mehmet Özdilek, Sergen Yalçin, Feyyaz Uçar, Oktay Derelioglu.
Trainer: Gordon Milne

Goals: Mehmet Özdilek (40), Rijkaard (60), R. de Boer (81)

**BEŞIKTAŞ ISTANBUL
v AJAX AMSTERDAM 0-4** (0-1)
Inönü, Istanbul 2.11.1993
Referee: Manuel Diaz Vega (SPA)   Attendance: 27,115
BEŞIKTAŞ: Zafer Öger; Recep Çetin (55 Osvaldo Nartallo), Gökhan Keskin, Ali Günçar, Mutlu Topçu, Riza Çalimbay, Alpay Özalan (46 Metin Tekin), Mehmet Özdilek, Sergen Yalçin, Feyyaz Uçar, Oktay Derelioglu.
Trainer: Gordon Milne
AJAX: Edwin Van der Sar; Sonny Silooy, Danny Blind, Frank De Boer, Frank Rijkaard, Rob Alflen (79 John Van den Brom), Clarence Seedorf, Jari Litmanen, Finidi George, Ronald De Boer (74 Stefan Pettersson), Marc Overmars.
Trainer: Louis Van Gaal
Goals: Litmanen (19, 72, 75), Pettersson (78)

**PANATHINAIKOS ATHINA
v BAYER LEVERKUSEN 1-4** (1-1)
Olympiako Spiros Louis, Athina 20.10.1993
Referee: Gianni Beschin (ITA)   Attendance: 60,000
PANATHINAIKOS: Jozef Wandzik; Kostas Mauridis, Stratos Apostolakis, Giannis Kalitzakis, Giorgos Kapouranis, Giorgos H. Georgiadis, Spiros Maragkos, Nikos Nioplias (77 Kostas Frantzeskos), Kostas Antoniou (61 Giorgos Donis), Krzysztof Warzycha, Dimitris Saravakos.   Trainer: Ivica Osim
BAYER: Rüdiger Vollborn; Franco Foda, Christian Wörns, Markus Happe, Andreas Fischer, Ioan Lupescu, Pavel Hapal, Martin Kree, Andreas Thom, Ulf Kirsten, Paulo Sérgio.
Trainer: Dragoslav Stepanović
Goals: Sérgio (42), Warzycha (44), Thom (52), Kirsten (59), Hapal (72)

**BAYER LEVERKUSEN
v PANATHINAIKOS ATHINAI 1-2** (0-1)
Ulrich Haberland, Leverkusen 2.11.1993
Referee: Vadim Zhuk (BLS)   Attendance: 11,900
BAYER: Rüdiger Vollborn; Franco Foda, Christian Wörns, Markus Happe, Andreas Fischer, Ralf Becker (71 Heiko Scholz), Ioan Lupescu, Pavel Hapal, Martin Kree, Andreas Thom, Ulf Kirsten.   Trainer: Dragoslav Stepanović
PANATHINAIKOS: Jozef Wandzik; Kostas Mauridis, Giannis Kalitzakis, Kostas Antoniou, Stratos Apostolakis, Spiros Maragkos, Juan Borelli (84 Giorgos Donis), Nikos Nioplias, Giorgos H. Georgiadis, Krzysztof Warzycha, Dimitris Saravakos.   Trainer: Ivica Osim
Goals: Saravakos (6 pen), Georgiadis (66), Kirsten (82)

MACCABI HAIFA v AC PARMA 0-1 (0-0)
Kiryat Eliezer, Haifa 20.10.1993
Referee: Gheorghe Constantin (ROM)   Attendance: 13,973
MACCABI: Rafi Cohen; Marco Balbul (78 Shay Holzman), Alon Harazi, Arik Benado, Moshe Glam, Alon Hazan, Sergei Kandaurov, Roni Levi (89 Daniel Zabar), Reuben Atar, Eyal Berkovich, Alon Mizrahi.   Trainer: Giora Spiegel
PARMA: Luca Bucci; Antonio Benarrivo, Georges Grün, Lorenzo Minotti, Luigi Apolloni, David Balleri, Massimo Crippa, Gianfranco Zola (86 Daniele Zoratto), Alessandro Melli, Tomas Brolin, Faustino Asprilla.   Trainer: Nevio Scala
Goal: Brolin (90)

AC PARMA v MACCABI HAIFA 0-1 (0-0, 0-1) (AET)
Ennio Tardini, Parma 3.11.1993
Referee: Ahmet Cakar (TUR)   Attendance: 9,312
PARMA: Luca Bucci; Antonio Benarrivo (66 David Balleri), Lorenzo Minotti, Luigi Apolloni, Alberto di Chiara, Salvatore Matrecano, Gabriele Pin (80 Daniele Zoratto), Massimo Crippa, Gianfranco Zola, Faustino Asprilla, Tomas Brolin.
Trainer: Nevio Scala
MACCABI: Rafi Cohen; Marco Balbul (27 Arik Benado), Alon Harazi, Roman Pets, Moshe Glam, Sergei Kandaurov, Roni Levi (104 Shay Holzman), Ivan Getsko, Reuben Atar, Eyal Berkovich, Alon Mizrahi.   Trainer: Giora Spiegel
Goal: A. Mizrahi (51)
Penalties: A. Mizrahi (miss), 1-0 Crippa, 1-1 Glam, 2-1 Minotti, A. Harazi (miss), 3-1 Brolin, R. Atar (miss)

**FC TIROL INNSBRUCK
v REAL MADRID 1-1** (0-1)
Tivoli, Innsbruck 20.10.1993
Referee: Ryszard Wójcik (POL)   Attendance: 10,000
FC TIROL: Milan Oraze; Michael Streiter, Andrzej Lesiak, Robert Wazinger, Oliver Prudlo, Michael Baur, Marcello Carracedo (62 Thomas Janeschitz), Roland Kirchler (85 Rudolf Gussnig), Jürgen Hartmann, Václav Daněk, Christoph Westerthaler.   Trainer: Horst Köppel
REAL: Francisco BUYO Sánchez; LUIS ENRIQUE Martínez García, Manuel SANCHIS Hontiyuelo, Fernando Muñoz García "NANDO", Francisco José Pérez VILLARROYA, Peter Dubovský (64 Luis Miguel RAMIS Monfort), Robert Prosinecki (80 José Alberto TORIL Rodríguez), Rafael MARTIN VÁZQUEZ, José Miguel González "MICHEL", Emilio BUTRAGUEÑO Santos, ALFONSO Pérez Muñoz.
Trainer: Benito Floro
Goals: Alfonso (14), Streiter (69 pen)

**REAL MADRID
v FC TIROL INNSBRUCK 3-0** (1-0)
Estadio Santiago Bernabéu, Madrid   3.11.1993
Referee: Vasilis Nikakis (GRE)   Attendance: 19,000
REAL: Francisco BUYO Sánchez; Fernando Muñoz García "NANDO", Rafael ALKORTA Martínez, Manuel SANCHIS Hontiyuelo, LUIS ENRIQUE Martínez García, Fernando Ruiz HIERRO, José Miguel González "MICHEL" (66 Francisco José Pérez VILLARROYA), Robert Prosinecki, Peter Dubovský, ALFONSO Pérez Muñoz, Emilio BUTRAGUEÑO Santos (55 Luis MILLA Aspas).   Trainer: Benito Floro
FC TIROL: Milan Oraze; Roland Kirchler, Andrzej Lesiak, Michael Streiter, Robert Wazinger, Oliver Prudlo, Thomas Janeschitz, Michael Baur, Marcello Carracedo, Václav Daněk, Christoph Westerthaler (73 Rudolf Gussnig).
Trainer: Horst Köppel
Goals: Michel (6), Butragueño (46), Alfonso (65)

AC TORINO v ABERDEEN FC 3-2 (1-2)
Stadio Delle Alpi   20.10.1993
Referee: Václav Krondl (CZE)   Attendance: 19,410
AC TORINO: Giovanni Galli; Roberto Mussi, Angelo Gregucci (66 Marco Osio), Luca Fusi, Raffaele Sergio, Enrico Annoni, Daniele Fortunato, Benito Carbone (46 Juan Carlos AGUILERA Martín), Giorgio Venturin, Enzo Francescoli, Andrea Silenzi.   Trainer: Emiliano Mondonico
ABERDEEN: Theo Snelders; Stewart McKimmie, Gary Smith, Alex McLeish, Brian Irvine, Paul Kane, Lee Richardson, Brian Grant, Robert Connor, Eoin Jess (65 Stephen Wright), Mika-Matti Paatelainen (69 Scott Booth).   Manager: Willie Miller
Goals: Paatelainen (9), Jess (24), Sergio (45), Fortunato (51), Booth (89 og)

ABERDEEN FC v AC TORINO 1-2 (1-1)
Pittodrie, Aberdeen   3.11.1993
Referee: Markus Merk (GER)   Attendance: 21,655
ABERDEEN: Theo Snelders; Stewart McKimmie, Gary Smith (60 Robert Connor), Alex McLeish, Brian Irvine, Paul Kane, Lee Richardson, Brian Grant (75 Joe Miller), Eoin Jess, Mika-Matti Paatelainen, Duncan Shearer.   Manager: Willie Miller
AC TORINO: Giovanni Galli; Roberto Mussi (81 Sandro Cois), Angelo Gregucci (20 Giulio Falcone), Luca Fusi, Raffaele Sergio, Daniele Delli Carri, Daniele Fortunato, Benito Carbone, Giorgio Venturin, Marco Sinigaglia, Andrea Silenzi.
Trainer: Emiliano Mondonico
Goals: Richardson (12), Fortunato (40), Silenzi (53)

BENFICA LISBOA v CSKA SOFIA 3-1 (2-0)
Estádio Da Luz, Lisboa   20.10.1993
Referee: Patrick Kelly (IRE)   Attendance: 40,000
BENFICA: Adelino Augusto Barros NENO; ABEL Luís da Silva Costa XAVIER, HÉLDER Marino Rodrigues Cristóvão, José Carlos Nepomuceno MOZER, António Augusto da Silva VELOSO, VÍTOR Manuel Araújo "PANEIRA", Hans Jurgen Stefan SCHWARZ, RUI Manuel César COSTA, JOÃO Manuel Vieira PINTO, CÉSAR Gonçalves BRITO Duarte (63 Sergei Yuran), ISAÍAS Marques Soares.
Trainer: António José Conceição Oliveira "TONI"
CSKA: Antonio Ananiev; Boban Babunski, Pavel Dochev (67 Martin Goranov), Ljubco Markovski, Milen Radukanov, Hristo Koilov, Anatoli Nankov, Ivailo Kirov, Sasa Ciric (65 Ivailo Ilarionov), Latchezar Tanev, Ivailo Andonov.
Trainer: Djoko Hadjievski
Goals: Rui Costa (27, 37), Andonov (60), Schwarz (90)

CSKA SOFIA v BENFICA LISBOA 1-3 (0-1)
Vasil Levski, Sofia   3.11.1993
Referee: Rune Pedersen (NOR)   Attendance: 20,000
CSKA: Antonio Ananiev; Ljubco Markovski, Pavel Dochev, Milen Radukanov, Rosen Kirilov (46 Vanio Shishkov), Anatoli Nankov, Ivailo Kirov, Hristo Koilov, Latchezar Tanev (80 Hristo Marashliev), Sasa Ciric, Ivailo Andonov.
Trainer: Djoko Hadjievski
BENFICA: Adelino Augusto Barros NENO; ABEL Luís da Silva Costa XAVIER, José Carlos Nepomuceno MOZER, HÉLDER Marino Rodrigues Cristóvão, WILLIAM Amaral de Andrade, António Augusto da Silva VELOSO, VÍTOR Manuel Araújo "PANEIRA" (74 ISAÍAS Marques Soares), Hans Jurgen Stefan SCHWARZ, RUI Manuel César COSTA, JOÃO Manuel Vieira PINTO (78 José RUI Lopes ÁGUAS), Sergei Yuran.   Trainer: António José Conceição Oliveira "TONI"
Goals: Rui Costa (31), Andonov (56), João Pinto (73), Yuran (89)

**ARSENAL LONDON
v STANDARD LIÈGE 3-0** (1-0)
Arsenal Stadium Highbury, London   20.10.1993
Referee: Friedrich Kaupe (AUS)   Attendance: 25,258
ARSENAL: David Seaman; Lee Dixon, Martin Keown (82 Andy Linighan), Tony Adams, Nigel Winterburn, Eddie McGoldrick, Paul Merson, John Jensen, Paul Davis, Alan Smith, Ian Wright (82 Kevin Campbell).
Trainer: George Graham
STANDARD: Jacky Munaron; Régis Genaux, Guy Hellers, Mircea Rednic, Philippe Léonard, Patrick Vervoort, Mohamed Lashaf, Frans Van Rooy, Thierry Pister, Patrick Asselman (48 Michael Goossens), Marc Wilmots.   Trainer: Arie Haan
Goals: Wright (39, 64), Merson (51)

STANDARD LIÈGE
v ARSENAL LONDON 0-7 (0-4)

Stade Maurice Dufrasne, Sclessin Liège 3.11.1993

Referee: Kaj John Natri (FIN)   Attendance: 13,276

STANDARD: Jacky Munaron; Régis Genaux, André Cruz, Guy Hellers, Philippe Léonard, Roberto Bisconti, Thierry Pister, Frans Van Rooy, Patrick Asselman, Marc Wilmots, Michael Goossens.   Trainer: Arie Haan

ARSENAL: David Seaman; Lee Dixon, Tony Adams, Martin Keown (82 Steve Bould), Nigel Winterburn, Paul Davis, John Jensen, Ian Selley, Paul Merson, Kevin Campbell, Alan Smith (46 Eddie McGoldrick).   Trainer: George Graham

Goals: Smith (2), Selley (20), Adams (37), Campbell (41, 79), Merson (71), McGoldrick (81)

PARIS ST.GERMAIN
v UNIVERSITATEA CRAIOVA 4-0 (2-0)

Parc des Princes, Paris 20.10.1993

Referee: Leslie William Mottram (SCO)   Att: 11,364

PARIS SG: Bernard Lama, Jean-Luc Sassus, Patrick Colleter, Ricardo Gomes, Alain Roche, Paul le Guen, Raí Oliveira (66 Laurent Fournier), Vincent Guérin, Valdo Cândido Filho, Daniel Bravo (62 Xavier Gravelaine), David Ginola. Trainer: Artur Jorge Braga

UNIVERSITATEA: Silviu Lung; Daniel Mogoşanu, Corneliu Papură, Gheorghe Biţă, Victor Cojocaru, Ion Olaru, Aurel Augustin Călin (83 Ovidiu Tiberiu Dodu), Cristian Marius Vasc, Ovidiu Stîngă, Adrian Pigulea (62 Gheorghe Craioveanu), Ionel Tersinio Gane.   Trainer: Marian Bondrea

Goals: Guérin (12), Ginola (17 pen), Călin (60 og), Valdo (72)

UNIVERSITATEA CRAIOVA
v PARIS SAINT GERMAIN 0-2 (0-1)

Central Craiova 3.11.1993

Referee: John Blankenstein (HOL)   Attendance: 15,000

UNIVERSITATEA: Dorin Arcanu; Daniel Mogoşanu, Gheorghe Biţă, Corneliu Papură, Victor Cojocaru (80 Ovidiu Tiberiu Dodu), Aurel Augustin Călin, Ovidiu Stîngă, Cristian Marius Vasc, Ion Olaru, Gheorghe Craioveanu, Ionel Tersinio Gane (40 Adrian Pigulea).   Trainer: Marian Bondrea

PARIS SG: Bernard Lama, Jean-Luc Sassus, Ricardo Gomes, Alain Roche, Patrick Colleter, Raí Oliveira, Paul le Guen, Vincent Guérin (54 Francis Llacer), Laurent Fournier, George Weah, David Ginola (46 Daniel Bravo).
Trainer: Artur Jorge Braga

Goals: Guérin (29, 48)

QUARTER-FINALS

BENFICA LISBOA
v BAYER LEVERKUSEN 1-1 (0-0)

Estádio Da Luz, Lisboa 1.03.1994

Referee: Pierluigi Pairetto (ITA)   Attendance: 80,000

BENFICA: Adelino Augusto Barros NENO; ABEL Luís da Silva Costa XAVIER, HÉLDER Marino Rodrigues Cristóvão (61 ISAÍAS Marques Soares), José Carlos Nepomuceno MOZER, António Augusto da Silva VELOSO, WILLIAM Amaral de Andrade, VÍTOR Manuel Araújo "PANEIRA", JOÃO Manuel Vieira PINTO, Sergei Yuran, RUI Manuel César COSTA, AÍLTON Delfino (73 CÉSAR Gonçalves BRITO Duarte).   Trainer: António José Conceição Oliveira "TONI"

BAYER: Rüdiger Vollborn; Markus Happe, Jens Melzig, Ioan Lupescu, Christian Wörns, Ralf Becker (78 Andreas Fischer), Franco Foda, Pavel Hapal, Mario Tolkmitt, Andreas Thom (87 René Rydlewicz), Paulo Sérgio. Trainer: Dragoslav Stepanović

Goals: Happe (64), Isaías (90)

BAYER LEVERKUSEN
v BENFICA LISBOA 4-4 (1-0)

Ulrich Haberland Stadion, Leverkusen 15.03.1994

Referee: James McCluskey (SCO)   Attendance: 21,000

BAYER: Dirk Heinen; Christian Wörns, Markus Happe, Franco Foda, Ralf Becker (66 Andreas Fischer), Bernd Schuster, Ioan Lupescu, Pavel Hapal, Mario Tolkmitt (66 Paulo Sérgio), Andreas Thom, Ulf Kirsten.
Trainer: Dragoslav Stepanović

BENFICA: Adelino Augusto Barros NENO; ABEL Luís da Silva Costa XAVIER, WILLIAM Amaral de Andrade, HÉLDER Marino Rodrigues Cristóvão, Hans Jurgen Stefan SCHWARZ, VÍTOR Manuel Araújo "PANEIRA", Vasili Kulkov, RUI Manuel César COSTA (85 HERNÂNI Madruga Neves), ISAÍAS Marques Soares, JOÃO Manuel Vieira PINTO, Sergei Yuran (88 José RUI Lopes ÁGUAS).
Trainer: António José Conceição Oliveira "TONI"

Goals: Kirsten (24, 80), Schuster (58), Abel Xavier (58), João Pinto (59), Kulkov (77, 85), Hapal (82)

AC TORINO v ARSENAL LONDON 0-0

Stadio Delle Alpi, Torino 2.03.1994

Referee: Joël Quiniou (FRA)   Attendance: 32,480

AC TORINO: Giovanni Galli; Andrea Sottil (62 Marco Sinigaglia), Sandro Cois, Angelo Gregucci, Robert Jarni, Luca Fusi, Roberto Mussi, Daniele Fortunato, Giorgio Venturin, Andrea Silenzi (67 Benito Carbone), Enzo Francescoli.

ARSENAL: David Seaman; Lee Dixon, Steve Bould, Tony Adams, Nigel Winterburn, Paul Davis (83 Ian Selley), John Jensen, Alan Smith, Paul Merson, Kevin Campbell, David Hillier.   Trainer: George Graham

364

ARSENAL LONDON v AC TORINO 1-0 (0-0)

Arsenal Stadium Highbury, London   15.03.1994

Referee: John Blankenstein (HOL)   Attendance: 34,678

ARSENAL: David Seaman; Lee Dixon, Steve Bould, Tony Adams, Nigel Winterburn, John Jensen (87 Martin Keown), Paul Davis, David Hillier (15 Ian Selley), Paul Merson, Alan Smith, Ian Wright.   Trainer: George Graham

AC TORINO: Giovanni Galli; Roberto Mussi, Angelo Gregucci, Sandro Cois, Enrico Annoni, Daniele Fortunato, Luca Fusi, Marco Sinigaglia (72 Paolo Poggi), Giorgio Venturin (26 Robert Jarni), Andrea Silenzi, Enzo Francescoli. Trainer: Emiliano Mondonico

Goal: Adams (66)

**REAL MADRID
v PARIS SAINT-GERMAIN 0-1** (0-1)

Estadio Santiago Bernabéu, Madrid   3.03.1994

Referee: Bernd Heynemann (GER)   Attendance: 64,000

REAL: Francisco BUYO Sánchez; Miguel Porlan "CHENDO" Noguera, Rafael ALKORTA Martínez, Manuel SANCHIS Hontiyuelo (56 José Luis MORALES Martín), Miguel LASA Goikoetxea (82 Robert Prosinecki), José Miguel González "MICHEL", Luis Miguel RAMIS Monfort, Luis MILLA Aspas, Peter Dubovský, LUIS ENRIQUE Martínez García, Iván Luis ZAMORANO Zamora.   Trainer: Benito Floro

PSG: Bernard Lama; Jean-Luc Sassus, Alain Roche, Ricardo Gomes, Patrick Colleter, Laurent Fournier, Francis Llacer, Valdo Cândido Filho, Vincent Guérin, George Weah (85 Daniel Bravo), David Ginola (88 Xavier Gravelaine).
Trainer: Artur Jorge Braga

Goal: Weah (32)

**PARIS SAINT-GERMAIN
v REAL MADRID 1-1** (0-1)

Parc des Princes, Paris   15.03.1994

Referee: Vadim Zhuk (BLS)   Attendance: 45,000

PSG: Bernard Lama; Jean-Luc Sassus, Alain Roche, Ricardo Gomes, Patrick Colleter, Laurent Fournier, Paul le Guen, Valdo Cândido Filho, Vincent Guérin, George Weah (89 Xavier Gravelaine), David Ginola (76 Daniel Bravo).
Trainer: Artur Jorge Braga

REAL: Francisco BUYO Sánchez; Jesús Enrique VELASCO Muñoz, Rafael ALKORTA Martínez, Manuel SANCHIS Hontiyuelo, LUIS ENRIQUE Martínez García, José Miguel González "MICHEL", Fernando Ruiz HIERRO, Robert Prosinecki (60 Peter Dubovský), Rafael MARTIN VÁZQUEZ (74 Miguel LASA Goikoetxea), Emilio BUTRAGUEÑO Santos, Iván Luis ZAMORANO Zamora.
Trainer: Vicente DEL BOSQUE

Goals: Butragueño (20), Ricardo (51)

AJAX AMSTERDAM v AC PARMA 0-0

Olympisch, Amsterdam   3.03.1994

Referee: Philip Don (ENG)   Attendance: 42,000

AJAX: Edwin Van der Sar; Sonny Silooy, Danny Blind, Tarik Oulida, Frank De Boer, Frank Rijkaard, Jari Litmanen, Edgar Davids (72 Peter Van Vossen), Dan Petersen (63 Marc Overmars), Stefan Pettersson, Ronald de Boer.
Trainer: Louis Van Gaal

PARMA: Luca Bucci; Roberto Maltagliati (77 David Balleri), Gabriele Pin, Luigi Apolloni, Salvatore Matrecano, Tomas Brolin, Roberto Nestor Sensini, Gianfranco Zola, Massimo Crippa, Faustino Asprilla, Alessandro Melli.
Trainer: Nevio Scala

AC PARMA v AJAX AMSTERDAM 2-0 (1-0)

Ennio Tardini, Parma   16.03.1994

Referee: Frans Van den Wijngaert (BEL)   Att: 24,212

PARMA: Luca Bucci; Antonio Benarrivo, Roberto Nestor Sensini, Alberto di Chiara (80 David Balleri), Lorenzo Minotti, Roberto Maltagliati, Gabriele Pin (75 Daniele Zoratto), Massimo Crippa, Gianfranco Zola, Tomas Brolin, Faustino Asprilla.   Trainer: Nevio Scala

AJAX: Edwin Van der Sar; Sonny Silooy, Danny Blind, John Van der Brom (55 Dan Petersen), Frank De Boer, Frank Rijkaard (60 Ronald de Boer), Peter Van Vossen, Edgar Davids, Clarence Seedorf, Stefan Pettersson, Marc Overmars.
Trainer: Louis Van Gaal

Goals: Minotti (16), Brolin (49)

SEMI-FINALS

**PARIS SAINT GERMAIN
v ARSENAL LONDON 1-1** (0-1)

Parc des Princes, Paris   29.03.1994

Referee: Leif Sundell (SWE)   Attendance: 45,000

PSG: Bernard Lama; Francis Llacer (46 Daniel Bravo), Jean-Luc Sassus, Ricardo Gomes, Patrick Colleter, Laurent Fournier, Paul le Guen, Valdo Cândido Filho, Vincent Guérin, George Weah, David Ginola.   Trainer: Artur Jorge Braga

ARSENAL: David Seaman; Lee Dixon, Steve Bould, Tony Adams, Nigel Winterburn, John Jensen, Paul Davis (84 Martin Keown), Ian Selley, Paul Merson, Ian Wright, Alan Smith (84 Kevin Campbell).   Trainer: George Graham

Goals: Wright (35), Ginola (49)

**ARSENAL LONDON
v PARIS SAINT GERMAIN 1-0** (1-0)

Arsenal Stadium Highbury, London   12.04.1994

Referee: Peter Mikkelsen (DEN)   Attendance: 34,212

ARSENAL: David Seaman; Lee Dixon, Steve Bould, Tony Adams, Nigel Winterburn (88 Martin Keown), Paul Davis (76 David Hillier), John Jensen, Ian Selley, Kevin Campbell, Ian Wright, Alan Smith.   Trainer: George Graham

PSG: Bernard Lama; Jean-Luc Sassus (80 Francis Llacer), Ricardo Gomes, Alain Roche, Patrick Colleter, Laurent Fournier, Paul le Guen, Valdo Cândido Filho, Vincent Guérin, Raí Oliveira (78 Xavier Gravelaine), David Ginola.   Trainer: Artur Jorge Braga

Goal: Campbell (7)

BENFICA LISBOA v AC PARMA 2-1 (1-1)

Estádio Da Luz, Lisboa   29.03.1994

Referee: Bernd Heynemann (GER)   Attendance: 100,000

BENFICA: Adelino Augusto Barros NENO; ABEL Luís da Silva Costa XAVIER, José Carlos Nepomuceno MOZER, HÉLDER Marino Rodrigues Cristóvão, António Augusto da Silva VELOSO (44 Daniel KENEDY Pimentel Mateus dos Santos), Vasili Kulkov, VÍTOR Manuel Araújo "PANEIRA", ISAÍAS Marques Soares, RUI Manuel César COSTA, JOÃO Manuel Vieira PINTO, Sergei Yuran.
Trainer: António José Conceição Oliveira "TONI"

PARMA: Luca Bucci; Antonio Benarrivo, Lorenzo Minotti, Luigi Apolloni, Alberto di Chiara, Roberto Nestor Sensini, Tomas Brolin, Gabriele Pin (85 Daniele Zoratto), Massimo Crippa, Gianfranco Zola, Faustino Asprilla.
Trainer: Nevio Scala

Goals: Isaías (7), Zola (13), Rui Costa (60)

AC PARMA v BENFICA LISBOA 1-0 (0-0)

Ennio Tardini, Parma   13.04.1994

Referee: Mario Van der Ende (HOL)   Attendance: 21,488

PARMA: Luca Bucci; Antonio Benarrivo (30 David Balleri), Georges Grün (65 Roberto Colacone), Roberto Nestor Sensini, Alberto di Chiara, Gabriele Pin, Luigi Apolloni, Daniele Zoratto, Massimo Crippa, Tomas Brolin, Gianfranco Zola.
Trainer: Nevio Scala

BENFICA: Adelino Augusto Barros NENO; ABEL Luís da Silva Costa XAVIER, José Carlos Nepomuceno MOZER, Daniel KENEDY Pimentel Mateus dos Santos (83 CÉSAR Gonçalves BRITO Duarte), WILLIAM Amaral de Andrade, VÍTOR Manuel Araújo "PANEIRA", Vasili Kulkov, JOÃO Manuel Vieira PINTO, Hans Jurgen Stefan SCHWARZ, ISAÍAS Marques Soares (76 HERNÂNI Madruga Neves), RUI Manuel César COSTA.   Trainer: António José Conceição Oliveira "TONI"

Goal: Sensini (78)

FINAL

ARSENAL FC LONDON v AC PARMA 1-0 (1-0)

Idraetsparken, København   4.05.1994

Referee: Václav Krondl (CZE)   Attendance: 33,765

ARSENAL: David Seaman; Lee Dixon, Tony Adams, Steve Bould, Nigel Winterburn, Paul Davis, Steve Morrow, Ian Selley, Kevin Campbell, Alan Smith, Paul Merson (86 Eddie McGoldrick).   Trainer: George Graham

AC PARMA: Luca Bucci; Antonio Benarrivo, Lorenzo Minotti, Luigi Apolloni, Alberto di Chiara, Roberto Nestor Sensini, Gabriele Pin (71 Alessandro Melli), Gianfranco Zola, Massimo Crippa, Tomas Brolin, Faustino Asprilla.   Trainer: Nevio Scala

Goal: Smith (19)

Goalscorers European Cup-Winners' Cup 1993-94:

5 goals: Alon Mizrahi (Maccabi Haifa), Eoin Jess (Aberdeen), Ivailo Andonov (CSKA Sofia), Ulf Kirsten (Bayer Leverkusen)

4 goals: Vanio Shishkov (CSKA Sofia), Ionel Tersinio Gane (Universitatea Craiova), Jari Litmanen (Ajax Amsterdam), Rui Costa (Benfica), Kevin Campbell, Ian Wright (Arsenal)

3 goals: Ottosson (Degerfors IF), Wilmots (Standard Liège), Subiat (FC Lugano), Westerthaler (FC Tirol), Danko (FC Košice), Saravakos (Panathinaikos), Silenzi (Torino), Wright, Merson (Arsenal), Guérin (Paris St.Germain), Brolin (Parma), Hapal (Bayer Leverkusen)

2 goals: M. Frick (FC Balzers), Gregory, Lárusson (Valur Reykjavík), T.Gulbrandsen, Mjelde (SK Lillestrøm), Andrioli (FC Lugano), Fröberg (Degerfors IF), Asprilla (Parma), Holzman (Maccabi Haifa), Bird (Cardiff City), Bisconti (Standard Liège), Zamorano, Alfonso, Michel, Butragueño (Real Madrid), Nankov (CSKA Sofia), Georgiades (Panathinaikos), Mooney (Shelbourne), Fortunato (Torino), Metin (Beşiktaş), Davids, R.De Boer, Petterson (Ajax), Thom (Bayer Leverkusen), João Pinto, Kulkov, Isaías (Benfica), T.Adams, A.Smith (Arsenal), Ginola (Paris St.Germain)

1 goal: Igor Kozlov (RAF Jelgava), Kandaurov, Atar, A.Harazi, Pets (Maccabi Haifa), Urhausen (F91 Dudelange), D.Poçi (Albpetrol Patosi), Nushöhr, Kuster (FC Balzers), Ievtushok, Reznik (Karpati Lvov), Costello, Izzi (Shelbourne), Sotiriou, Mihajlovic, Pounas (Apoel Nicosia), McEvoy, Glendinning (Bangor City), Rajamäki (MyPa), Karlsson, Schiller, Bjärmann, Bergdølmo, McManus (SK Lillestrøm), Arendash (Nikol Tallinn), Durica, Pobegayev (FC Košice), Maciulevicius (Zalgiris), Fink, Penzavalli (FC Lugano), Mazurchik, Solodovnikov (Neman Grodno), Nedergaard, A.Nielsen (BK Odense), Gregory (Sliema), Berger, Eriksson (Degerfors IF), Balleri, Minotti, Sensini, Zola (Parma), Gravelaine, Le Guen, Ricardo, Sassus, Valdo, Weah (Paris SG), Fischer, Happe, Schuster, Sérgio, Wörns (Bayer Leverkusen), Irvine, Miller, Paatelainen, Richardson, Shearer (Aberdeen), Borisov, Kalaichev (Torpedo Moskva), Asselman, Cruz, Lashaf (Standard Liège), James (Cardiff City), Dubovský, Fernández, Hierro (Real Madrid), Ciric, Tanev (CSKA Sofia), Donis, K.Warzycha, R.Warzycha (Panathinaikos), Abel Xavier, Rui Aguas, Yuran, Vítor Paneira, Schwarz (Benfica), Kucz (GKS Katowice), Călin, Craioveanu, Vasc (Universitatea Craiova), Carracedo, Daněk, Streiter (FC Tirol), Détári (Ferencváros), Jarni, Sergio (Torino), Sergen Yolgin, Mehmet Özdilek (Beşiktaş), Selley, McGoldrick (Arsenal), Mornar (Hajduk), F.de Boer, Rijkaard (Ajax)

Own goal: Sinigaglia (Torino) for Lillestrøm, Keown (Arsenal) for BK Odense, Both (Aberdeen) for Torino, Călin (Universitatea Craiova) for Paris SG

CUP WINNERS CUP 1994-95

PRELIMINARY ROUND

PIRIN BLAGOEVGRAD v FC SCHAAN 3-0 (2-0)

Vasil Levski, Sofia 11.08.1994

Referee: Andreas Georgiou (CYP)   Attendance: 1,200

PIRIN: Miroslav Mitev (Cap), Kostadin Trendafilov, Georgi Petrov, Krasimir Bezinski, Radoslav Kresnichki (46 Konstantin Hadzhiin), Stefan Goshev, Blagoi Latinov, Anton Bachev, Boris Ianev, Malin Orachev (85 Stefan Sotirov), Georgi Bachev. Trainer: Iordan Kostov

FC SCHAAN: Martin Heeb (Cap), Nedeljko Mlikota, Ralf Ackermann, Hermann Neusüss, Bersad Jehic (46 Herbert Bicker), Ratko Milojević, Meyzhit Memeti, Michael Kindle, Hansi Lingg, Marcel Seger, Markus Wille (89 Fabio Büchel). Trainer: Dragan Bogojević

Goals: Orachev (18), Ianev (28), Petrov (60 pen)

FC SCHAAN v PIRIN BLAGOEVGRAD 0-1 (0-1)

Sportplatz Rheinwiese, Schaan 24.08.1994

Referee: Stefan Tivold (SVN)   Attendance: 1,150

FC SCHAAN: Martin Heeb (Cap), Nedeljko Mlikota, Ralf Ackermann, Hermann Neusüss, Herbert Bicker, Meyzhit Memeti, Hansi Lingg (84 Marc Walser), Michael Kindle, Marcel Seger, Markus Wille, Ratko Milojević (82 Marcel Jehle). Trainer: Dragan Bogojević

PIRIN: Kiril Stoikov, Kostadin Trendafilov, Georgi Petrov, Stefan Goshev, Blagoi Latinov, Krasimir Bezinski (Cap), Stefan Sotirov, Malin Orachev, Anton Bachev, Boris Ianev, Georgi Bachev. Trainer: Iordan Kostov

Goal: Ianev (2)

SANDOYAR ITROTTARFELAG B 71 v HJK HELSINKI 0-5 (0-2)

Toftir stadium 11.08.1994

Referee: Dermot Gallagher (ENG)   Attendance: 462

B 71: Waldemar Nowicki; Runi Soylu, Ib Mohr Olsen (46 John Sörensen), Niclas Joensen, Bjarki Mohr, Eli Hentze, Joan Petur Clementsen, Piotr Krakowski (Cap), Sofus Clementsen (77 Jøgvang Jon Petersen), Pall a Reynatugvu, Torbjörn Jensen. Trainer: Piotr Krakowski

HJK: Antti Niemi; Aki Hyryläinen, Marko Helin, Antti Heinola, Tommi Grönlund, Mika Lehkosuo, Rami Rantanen, Markku Kanerva (62 Pekka Onttonen), Pasi Tauriainen, Ismo Lius (83 Janne Murtomäki), Jari Vanhala. Trainer: Jari-Pekka Keurulainen

Goals: Vanhala (3, 86), Lius (20, 68), Heinola (80)

HJK HELSINKI v SANDOYAR ITROTTARFELAG B 71 2-0 (1-0)

Olympic Helsinki 24.08.1994

Referee: Algirdas Diubinskas (LIT)   Attendance: 1,257

HJK: Markku Palmroos; Aki Hyryläinen, Pekka Onttonen, Antti Heinola, Jari Europaeus (Cap), Tommi Grönlund (46 Janne Suokonautio), Marko Helin, Vasili Karatayev, Mika Lehkosuo, Janne Saarinen, Mika Kottila. Trainer: Jari-Pekka Keurulainen

B 71: Waldemar Nowicki, Runi Soylu (76 Frankie Jensen), John Sörensen, Piotr Krakowski (Cap), Ib Mohr Olsen, Bjarki Mohr, Pall a Reynatugvu, Jøgvang Jon Petersen, Eli Hentze, Joan Petur Clementsen (62 Julian Thomsen), Torbjörn Jensen. Trainer: Piotr Krakowski

Goals: Kottila (1), Suokonautio (79)

NORMA TALLINN v MARIBOR BRANIK 1-4 (0-0)
Tallinn stadium 11.08.1994
Referee: Mika Peltola (FIN)   Attendance: 1,000
NORMA: Ain Tammus; Rafig Adigazalov (Cap), Juri Tsurilkin, Hans Näks, Veiko Murumaa (74 Alik Karajev), Terjo Tirel, Aleksandras Koroljovas, Maksim Rotskov, Arunas Gylys (62 Igor Sööt), Janek Meet, Urmas Kaal.
Trainer: Mati Kebina
BRANIK: Mladen Dabanović; Milan Sterbal, Blagoje Milevski, Renato Kotnik, Marinko Galić, Ales Krizan (Cap), Ante Simundza, Peter Binkovski (66 Amir Karić), Milko Djurovski (77 Danijel Sirec), Kliton Bozgo, Ingemar Bloudek.
Trainer: Marijan Bloudek
Goals: Galić (52), Milevski (62), Djurovski (68), Rostkov (83), Simundza (90)

KS TIRANA v FANDOK BOBRUISK 3-0 (1-0)
Qemal Stafa, Tirana 25.08.1994
Referee: Hermann Albrecht (GER)   Attendance: 6,000
KS TIRANA: Elton Kasmi; Afrim Tole, Nevil Dede, Sajmir Malko, Alpin Gallo, Dritan Baholli, Ardian Mema (61 Artan Kukli), Klarent Fejzolli, Sokol Prenga, Auron Miloti, Indrit Fortuzi.   Trainer: Shkëlkim Muça
FANDOK: Andrei Svirkov; Igor Shustikov, Sergei Razumovich, Andrei Khripach, Oleg Cherepnev, Kiril Savostikov, Vladimir Konovalov, Viktor Kukar, Roman Meleshko (62 Igor Gradoboyev), Sergei Omelyusik (81 Andrei Khlebosolov), Sergei Yaromko (Cap).
Trainer: Evgenyi Shabunya
Goals: Fortuzi (45, 75, 90)

**MARIBOR BRANIK
v NORMA TALLINN 10-0** (8-0)
Ljudski vrt, Maribor 25.08.1994
Referee: Ladislav Gádosi (SVK)   Attendance: 4,500
BRANIK: Mladen Dabanović (68 Darko Dubravica), Peter Binkovski, Ingemar Bloudek, Marinko Galić, Saso Lukić, Ales Krizan (Cap), Ante Simundza, Gregor Zidan, Milko Djurovski (55 Renato Kotnik), Kliton Bozgo, Goran Gutalj (55 Amir Karić).   Trainer: Marijan Bloudek
NORMA: Ain Tammus; Rafig Adigazalov (Cap), Juri Tsurilkin, Hans Näks, Terjo Tirel (46 Veiko Murumaa), Jorma Karolin (60 Priit Simson), Aleksandras Koroljovas, Maksim Rotskov, Arunas Gylys, Janek Meet, Urmas Kaal.
Trainer: Mati Kebina
Goals: Djurovski (4, 9), Gutalj (20, 45), Bozgo (21, 23, 42, 81), Simundza (39, 83)

**TILIGUL TIRASPOL
v OMONOIA NICOSIA 0-1** (0-1)
Republican, Chişinău 11.08.1994
Referee: Gunther Benkö (AUS)   Attendance: 4,000
TILIGUL: Vasili Coşelev; Serghei Secu, Petr But, Valeri Pogorelov, Vladimir Gaidamaşciuc (60 Vadim Sereda), Serghei Stroenco (Cap), Andrei Stroenco, Eric Ococo (46 Anatoli Luchiancicov), Vladimir Kosse, Serghei Belous, Igor Oprea.
Trainer: Efim Grigorevich.
OMONOIA: Andreas Haritou; Kostas Konstantinou, Athos Hrisanthou, Sakis Andreou; Andreas Kantilos, Giorgos Hristodoulou, Evagoras Hristofi (Cap); Gocha Gogrichiani (24 David Kizilashvili), Giorgos Savvidis, Nedim Tutic (55 Kostas Kaiafas), Kostas Malekos.   Trainer: Gerd Prokop
Goal: Gogrichiani (17)

FANDOK BOBRUISK v KS TIRANA 4-1 (2-0)
Minsk 11.08.1994
Referee: Nikolai Levnikov (RUS)   Attendance: 5,000
FANDOK: Andrei Svirkov; Igor Shustikov, Sergei Razumovich, Andrei Khripach, Oleg Cherepnev, Kiril Savostikov, Vladimir Konovalov, Viktor Kukar, Roman Meleshko (63 Sergei Omelyusik), Vladimir Skorobogatyi, Sergei Yaromko (Cap) (63 Andrei Khlebosolov).
Trainer: Evgenyi Shabunya
KS TIRANA: Thoma Kokuri; Afrim Tole, Nevil Dede, Sajmir Malko, Alpin Gallo, Dritan Baholli, Ardian Mema, Artan Kukli, Auron Miloti, Indrit Fortuzi, Klarent Fejzolli (55 Anesti Stoja).
Trainer: Shkëlkim Muça
Goals: Yaromko (1, 5), Khripach (65), Miloti (60), Savostikov (72)

**OMONOIA NICOSIA
v TILIGUL TIRASPOL 3-1** (3-1)
Makarios, Nicosia 25.08.1994
Referee: Chaim Lipkovitch (ISR)   Attendance: 12,500
OMONOIA: Hristos Hristou; Giannis Kalotheou, Giorgos Hristodoulou, Kostas Konstantinou, Evagoras Hristofi (Cap), Sakis Andreou, Andreas Kantilos, Giorgos Savvidis, Kostas Kaiafas, Nedim Tutic (70 David Kizilashvili), Kostas Malekos (30 Panikos Xiourouppas).   Trainer: Gerd Prokop
TILIGUL: Vasili Coşelev; Serghei Secu, Petr But, Valeri Pogorelov, Vladimir Gaidamaşciuc; Serghei Stroenco (Cap), Andrei Stroenco (61 Serghei Kuznetsov); Vadim Sereda (23 Igor Oprea), Serghei Belous, Vladimir Kosse, Yuri Culiş.
Trainer: Efim Skolnikov
Goals: Kantilos (5 pen), Tutic (45), Belous (50), Savvidis (89)

FERENCVÁROS BUDAPEST v F 91 DUDELANGE 6-1 (3-1)

Üllöi út, Budapest   11.08.1994

Referee: Adrian Moroianu-Geamăn (ROM)   Att: 13,825

FERENCVÁROS: József Szeiler; András Telek; Tibor Simon, Tamás Szekeres, Zsolt Páling, Péter Lipcsei, Flórián Albert, László Czéh, József Keller (Cap); Kenneth Christiansen, Eugen Neagoe.   Trainer: Dezsö Novák

F 91: Serge Rohmann; Jerry Hutmacher, José Nora Favita (46 Gérard Urhausen), Manuel Gomes, Marco Galli, Enrico Cardoni, Angelo Fiorucci (Cap), Joël Groff, Stefano Fanelli, Thorvic Amari (67 Pedro Borrega), Serge Cardoni.   Trainer: Philippe Guérard

Goals: Neagoe (2), Szekeres (18, 75), Páling (45), Lipcsei (55), Albert (78), Fanelli (83)

F 91 DUDELANGE v FERENCVÁROS BUDAPEST 1-6 (0-3)

Jos Nosbaum, Dudelange   25.08.1994

Referee: Marc Batta (FRA)   Attendance: 750

F 91: Serge Rohmann; Serge Cardoni, Jerry Hutmacher (78 Toni Sorcinelli), Gérard Urhausen, Marco Morgante, Marco Galli, Enrico Cardoni, Angelo Fiorucci (Cap) (74 Pedro Borrega), Joël Groff, Frank Petitfrère, Stefano Fanelli.   Trainer: Philippe Guérard

FERENCVÁROS: József Szeiler; András Telek; Tibor Simon (Cap), Tamás Szekeres, Zsolt Páling, Péter Lipcsei, Flórián Albert (46 Mihály Szűcs), Krisztián Lisztes, László Czéh; Kenneth Christiansen, Eugen Neagoe (67 Gábor Zavadszky).   Trainer: Dezsö Novák

Goals: Lisztes (6), Páling (18), Morgante (21), Lipcsei (39, 70), Christiansen (56), Zavadszky (89)

FLORIANA FC v SLIGO ROVERS 2-2 (0-2)

National Ta'Qali   11.08.1994

Referee: Garcia Redondo Celino (SPA)   Attendance: 2,030

FLORIANA: David Cluett; Dennis Cauchi, Kim Wright (46 Mark Marlow), Jesmond Delia (Cap), Jeffrey Farrugia, John Buttigieg, Albert Busuttil, Igor Stefanović, Charles Sciberras, Mario Caruana, Richard Buhagiar.   Trainer: George Busuttil

SLIGO: Mark McLean; David Reid, Robert Brunton, Declan Boyle, Gavin Dykes (Cap), John Kenny, Will Hastie, Gerry Carr, John Brennan, Mark Reid, Padraig Moran (77 Martin McDonnell).   Manager: Chris Rutherford

Goals: Moran (12), M. Reid (30), Stefanović (52, 90)

SLIGO ROVERS v FLORIANA FC 1-0 (0-0)

The Showgrounds, Sligo   25.08.1994

Referee: Antonio José Almeida Marcal (POR)   Att: 3,058

SLIGO: Mark McLean; David Reid, Declan Boyle, Gavin Dykes (Cap), Martin McDonnell, John Kenny (82 Aidan Rooney), Will Hastie, Gerry Carr, John Brennan, Mark Reid, Padraig Moran.   Manager: Chris Rutherford

FLORIANA: David Cluett; Dennis Cauchi, Jeffrey Farrugia (36 Mario Caruana), Jesmond Delia (Cap), Joe Brincat, John Buttigieg, Albert Busuttil, Igor Stefanović, Charles Sciberras, Mark Marlow (73 Jonathan Buhagiar), Richard Buhagiar.   Trainer: George Busuttil

Goal: Brennan (72)

BARRY TOWN v ZALGIRIS VILNIUS 0-1 (0-0)

Ninian Park, Cardiff   11.08.1994

Referee: Roy Helge Olsen (NOR)   Attendance: 1,914

BARRY TOWN: Glenn Livingstone, Ashley Griffiths, Phillip Williams, Mark Davies (Cap) (46 Garfield Leask), Terrence Boyle, Andrew Ellis, Paul Giles, Evran Wright (46 Ian Mitchell), David D'Auria, Richard Jones, Morrys Scott.   Manager: Andy Beattie

ZALGIRIS: Darius Spetyla, Dainius Suliauskas, Darius Maciulevicius, Virginijus Baltusnikas (Cap), Ramunas Stonkus, Sergejus Novikovas, Vytautas Karvelis (30 Donatos Vencevicius), Andrius Tereskinas, Aidas Preiksaitis, Edgaras Jankauskas, Eimantas Poderis (77 Gintaras Rimkus).   Trainer: Benjaminas Zelkevicius

Sent off: D'Auria (64)

Goal: Vencevicius (77)

ZALGIRIS VILNIUS v BARRY TOWN 6-0 (2-0)

Zalgiris Vilnius   25.08.1994

Referee: Dick Jol (HOL)   Attendance: 2,900

ZALGIRIS: Darius Spetyla (77 Alvydas Koncevicius), Dainius Suliauskas, Ramunas Stonkus, Sergejus Novikovas, Andrius Tereskinas, Virginijus Baltusnikas (Cap), Vytautas Karvelis (53 Edgaras Jankauskas), Aidas Preiksaitis (68 Valdas Urbonas), Darius Maciulevicius, Donatos Vencevicius, Eimantas Poderis.   Trainer: Benjaminas Zelkevicius

BARRY TOWN: Glenn Livingstone, Ashley Griffiths, Dean Threlfall (46 Morrys Scott), Terrence Boyle (Cap), Garfield Leask, Andrew Ellis, Paul Giles, Alan Curtis, Paul Sanderson, Richard Jones, Ian Mitchell.   Manager: Andy Beattie

Goals: Karvelis (18, 50), Baltusnikas (40), Poderis (48), Maciulevicius (68), Jankauskas (89)

FK BODØ GLIMT v OLYMPIA RIGA 6-0 (1-0)
Aspmyra, Bodø 11.08.1994
Referee: Sten Johanson (SWE)   Attendance: 2,290
FK BODØ: Ronny Westad; Thor Mikalsen, Trond Sollied, Charles Berstad (69 Tommy Hansen), Andreas Evjen, Runar Berg (Cap), Tom Kare Staurvik (65 Jan Egil Brekke), Ørjan Berg, Aasmund Björkan, Bent Inge Johnsen, Arild Berg.   Trainer: Trond Sollied
OLYMPIA: Leonid Dvorkin, Andrei Abzhinov, Igor Korablyov, Sergei Semionov (Cap), Mihail Lisyakov, Vladislav Skorodikhin (57 Andrei Pumpa), Artur Shketov, Alexandr Dibrivny, Boris Korotkevitch, Nikolai Polyakov, Andrei Shtolcers (85 Vitali Ryabinin).   Trainer: Genady Shitik
Goals: Berstad (5), R. Berg (53, 89), Björkan (70), Johnsen (72, 82)

**IFK NORRKÖPING
v VIKTORIA ZIZKOV 3-3** (1-0)
Norrköpings Idrottsparken 25.08.1994
Referee: Zbigniew Przesmycki (POL)   Attendance: 3,060
IFK: Lars Eriksson, Erik Norrby, Sulo Vaattovaara (Cap), Jonas Lind, Mikael Blomberg (71 Donny Sundell), Mikael Hansson, Göran Bergort (81 Tony Martinsson), Jan Jansson, Patrik Sandström, Patrik Andersson, Göran Holter. Trainer: Sören Cratz
VIKTORIA: Oldřich Parizek (38 Daniel Zitka), Jiří Casko, Miloslav Kordule, Petr Gabriel, Michal Petrous, Petr Holota, Michal Bilek (Cap), Petr Vrabec, Karel Poborsky, Jozef Majoros (46 Tomas Krejcik), Marek Trval (73 Tibor Jancula). Trainer: Jiří Kotrba
Goals: Hansson (40, 71), Trval (52), Kordule (56), Vrabec (86 pen), Vaattovaara (90 pen)

OLYMPIA RIGA v FK BODØ GLIMT 0-0
University Riga 25.08.1994
Referee: Finn Lambek (DEN)   Attendance: 500
OLYMPIA: Leonid Dvorkin, Andrejs Baumanis, Igor Korablyov, Sergey Semionov (Cap), Mihail Lisyakov, Alexander Zverugo, Vladislav Skorodikhin, Boris Korotkevich (57 Vladimir Verbitsky), Alexandr Dibrivny, Nikolai Polyakov, Andrei Shtolcers.   Trainer: Genady Shitik
FK BODØ: Ronny Westad, Ola Haldorsen (Cap), Trond Sollied (46 Petter Solli), Charles Berstad, Andreas Evjen, Runar Berg, Tom Kare Staurvik, Ørjan Berg, Tommy Hansen (60 Thor Mikalsen), Kyrre Nilsen, Jan Egil Brekke. Trainer: Trond Sollied

IB KEFLAVÍK v MACCABI TEL AVIV 1-2 (0-1)
Keflavíkurvöllur, Keflavík 11.08.1994
Referee: Richard O'Hanlon (Eire)   Attendance: 1,914
KEFLAVÍK: Ólafur Gottskálsson; Gestur Gylfason, Kristinn Gudbrandsson, Sigurdur Björgvinsson, Jóhann Magnússon, Ragnar Steinarsson, Gunnar Oddsson (Cap), Marko Tanasic, Ragnar Margeirsson, Kjartan Einarsson, Oli Thór Magnússon. Trainer: Pétur Pétursson
MACCABI: Aleksandr Uvarov; Avi Cohen, Gadi Brumer, Amir Shelach, Yaacov Hilel, Noam Shoam, Nir Klinger (Cap), Alon Brumer, Yuri Shukanov, Avi Nimni, Eli Driks. Trainer: Avraham Grant
Goals: Klinger (35), Tanasic (75), Nimni (82)

**VIKTORIA ZIZKOV
v IFK NORRKÖPING 1-0** (0-0)
Praha 11.08.1994
Referee: László Vagner (HUN)   Attendance: 1,905
VIKTORIA: Oldřich Parizek, Jiří Casko, Miloslav Kordule, Petr Gabriel, Michal Petrous, Petr Holota, Michal Bilek (Cap), Petr Vrabec, Karel Poborsky, Jozef Majoros (57 Tibor Jancula), Marek Trval (63 Daniel Masek).   Trainer: Jiří Kotrba
IFK: Lars Eriksson; Mikael Hansson, Sulo Vaattovaara (Cap), Jonas Lind, Mikael Blomberg, Patrik Sandström (87 Tony Martinsson), Göran Bergort, Jan Jansson, Göran Holter (76 Patrik Andersson), Jan Hellström, Niklas Kindvall. Trainer: Sören Cratz
Goal: Poborsky (72)

MACCABI TEL AVIV v IB KEFLAVÍK 4-1 (3-1)
Ramat Gan, Tel Aviv 25.08.1994
Referee: Roger Philippi (LUX)   Attendance: 8,125
MACCABI: Aleksandr Uvarov; Avi Cohen, Gadi Brumer, Amir Shelach, Yaacov Hilel, Noam Shoam, Nir Klinger (Cap) (73 Guy Nachman), Alon Brumer, Yuri Shukanov, Avi Nimni, Eli Driks (68 Alon Mizrahi).   Trainer: Avraham Grant
KEFLAVÍK: Ólafur Gottskálsson; Karl Finnbogason, Jóhann Magnússon, Gestur Gylfason, Kristinn Gudbrandsson, Gunnar Oddsson (Cap), Ragnar Steinarsson, Marko Tanasic, Georg Birgisson, Oli Thór Magnússon (60 Ragnar Margeirsson), Kjartan Einarsson (71 Sverrir Thór Sverrisson). Trainer: Pétur Pétursson
Goals: A. Brumer (14), G. Brumer (17 pen), Klinger (26), Tanasic (36), Driks (69)

FC BANGOR v TATRAN PREŠOV 0-1 (0-0)

Clandeboye Park, Bangor   11.08.1994

Referee: Gylfi Orrason (ICE)   Attendance: 1,200

BANGOR: Timothy Dalton, Mark Glendinning, Gary Ferguson (69 Reg Dornan), Conor McCaffrey, Stephen Brown, Nigel Melly, Raymond Hill (Cap), Peter Batey, David McCallan, Jonathan Magee (83 Gary Wilkinson), Richard McEvoy. Trainer: Nigel Best

TATRAN: Peter Jakubech, Lubomir Bajtos, Robert Kocis, Stanislav Varga, Vladimir Nenadic, Peter Hlusko, Marian Skalka (Cap), Richard Höger, Jaroslav Kentos, Vladislav Zvara, Rudolf Matta.   Trainer: Igor Novák

Sent off: Batey (81)

Goal: Nenadic (73)

TATRAN PREŠOV v FC BANGOR 4-0 (2-0)

Tatran Prešov   25.08.1994

Referee: Mateo Beusan (CRO)   Attendance: 4,792

TATRAN: Peter Jakubech, Lubomir Bajtos, Robert Kocis, Stanislav Varga, Vladimir Nenadic, Peter Hlusko, Marian Skalka (Cap) (60 Kennedy Chihuri), Richard Höger, Jaroslav Kentos, Vladislav Zvara, Rudolf Matta.   Trainer: Igor Novák

FC BANGOR: Timothy Dalton, Mark Glendinning, Gary Ferguson, Conor McCaffrey, Stephen Brown (46 Eddie Spiers), Nigel Melly, Raymond Hill (Cap), Gary Wilkinson (89 Michael Surgeon), David McCallan, Jonathan Magee, Richard McEvoy. Trainer: Nigel Best

Goals: Kocis (13, 49), Matta (41), Höger (55)

FIRST ROUND

MACCABI TEL AVIV v WERDER BREMEN 0-0

Ramat Gan, Tel Aviv   13.09.1994

Referee: Daniel Roduit (SWI)   Attendance: 10,000

MACCABI: Aleksandr Uvarov, Nir Klinger (Cap), Gadi Brumer, Amir Shelach, Yaacov Hilel, Alon Brumer, Noam Shoam, Yuri Belkin (76 Nir Sivilia), Avi Nimni, Yuri Shukanov (87 Amit Levi), Alon Mizrahi.   Trainer: Avraham Grant

WERDER: Oliver Reck (Cap), Hany Ramzy, Uli Borowka, Miroslav Votava, Michael Schulz, Mario Basler, Dieter Eilts, Wynton Rufer, Marco Bode (46 Thomas Wolter), Bernd Hobsch, Vladimir Beschastnîh.   Trainer: Otto Rehhagel

WERDER BREMEN v MACCABI TEL AVIV 2-0 (0-0)

Weserstadion, Bremen   29.09.1994

Referee: Juha Hirviniemi (FIN)   Attendance: 22,431

WERDER: Oliver Reck (Cap), Hany Ramzy, Michael Schulz, Thomas Wolter, Mario Basler, Miroslav Votava, Dieter Eilts, Andreas Herzog, Andree Wiedener, Wynton Rufer (82 Gunnar Sauer), Marco Bode.   Trainer: Otto Rehhagel

MACCABI: Aleksandr Uvarov, Nir Klinger (Cap), Amir Shelach, Gadi Brumer, Amit Levi (74 Nir Sivilia), Yuri Shukanov, Alon Brumer, Avi Nimni, Yuri Belkin, Yaacov Hilel, Alon Mizrahi (80 Eli Driks).   Trainer: Avraham Grant

Goals: Bode (51), Basler (81)

FK BODØ GLIMT v SAMPDORIA GENOVA 3-2 (2-0)

Aspmyra, Bodø   15.09.1994

Referee: Stephen Lodge (ENG)   Attendance: 2,015

FK BODØ: Ronny Westad, Ola Haldorsen (Cap), Charles Berstad (76 Kristján Jónsson), Andreas Evjen, Trond Sollied, Runar Berg, Tom Kare Staurvik, Ørjan Berg, Bent Inge Johnsen, Aasmund Björkan (80 Tommy Hansen), Arild Berg. Trainer: Trond Sollied

SAMPDORIA: Walter Zenga, Moreno Mannini (Cap), Riccardo Ferri, Stefano Sacchetti, Michele Serena, Attilio Lombardo, David Platt, Vladimir Jugovic (46 Giovanni Invernizzi), Alberigo Evani, Riccardo Maspero, Mauro Bertarelli.   Trainer: Sven Göran Eriksson

Goals: Staurvik (2), Johnsen (32, 58), Bertarelli (47), Platt (67)

SAMPDORIA GENOVA v FK BODØ GLIMT 2-0 (2-0)

Luigi Ferraris, Genova   29.09.1994

Referee: Vladimir Hrinak (SVK)   Attendance: 28,656

SAMPDORIA: Walter Zenga, Michele Serena, Riccardo Ferri, Pietro Vierchowod (Cap), Sinisa Mihajlovic, Attilio Lombardo, Vladimir Jugovic, David Platt (29 Fausto Salsano), Alberigo Evani, Alessandro Melli, Mauro Bertarelli (4 Riccardo Maspero).   Trainer: Sven Göran Eriksson

FK BODØ: Ronny Westad, Ola Haldorsen (Cap), Trond Sollied, Charles Berstad, Andreas Evjen, Runar Berg (49 Thor Mikalsen), Tom Kare Staurvik, Ørjan Berg, Arild Berg, Aasmund Björkan, Bent Inge Johnsen. Trainer: Trond Sollied

Goals: Platt (13), Lombardo (37)

OMONOIA NICOSIA
v ARSENAL LONDON 1-3 (0-1)

Makarion, Nicosia   15.09.1994

Referee: Antonio José Almeida Marcal (POR)   Att: 13,954

OMONOIA: Hristos Hristou, Giorgos Hristodoulou, Panagiotis Panagiotou, Kostas Konstantinou, Evagoras Hristofi (Cap), Sakis Andreou, Andreas Kantilos (55 David Kizilashvili), Giorgos Savvidis, Gocha Gogrichiani, Kostas Malekos, Panikos Xiourouppas (66 Kostas Kaiafas). Trainer: Gerd Prokop

ARSENAL: David Seaman, Lee Dixon, Andy Linighan, Martin Keown, Nigel Winterburn (Cap), John Jensen, Ray Parlour, Hans Jurgen Stefan SCHWARZ (82 Stephen Morrow), Paul Merson, Ian Wright, Alan Smith.
Manager: George Graham

Goals: Merson (37, 80), Wright (49), Malekos (73)

ARSENAL LONDON
v OMONOIA NICOSIA 3-0 (2-0)

Highbury, London   29.09.1994

Referee: Juan Ansuategui Roca (SPA)   Attendance: 24,165

ARSENAL: David Seaman, Lee Dixon, Nigel Winterburn, Hans Jurgen Stefan SCHWARZ, Andy Linighan, Tony Adams (Cap), John Jensen (74 David Hillier), Ian Wright, Alan Smith, Paul Merson (74 Kevin Campbell), Ray Parlour. Manager: George Graham

OMONOIA: Hristos Hristou, Giannis Kalotheou, Panagiotis Panagiotou, Kostas Konstantinou, Evagoras Hristofi (Cap), Sakis Andreou, Andreas Kantilos (70 Kostas Kaiafas), Giorgos Savvidis, Giorgos Hristodoulou, Kostas Malekos, Panikos Xiourouppas (57 Nedim Tutic).   Trainer: Gerd Prokop

Goals: Wright (9, 70), Schwarz (31)

FC PORTO v LKS LÓDZ 2-0 (0-0)

Estádio Das Antas, Porto   15.09.1994

Referee: Sándor Piller (HUN)   Attendance: 17,000

FC PORTO: VÍTOR Manuel Martins BAÍA, JORGE Paulo COSTA Almeida, João Paulo Santos "PAULINHO SANTOS", Carlos Alberto Oliveira SECRETÁRIO, EMERSON Moisés Costa, António dos Santos ANDRÉ (Cap) (57 Ljubinko Drulovic), RUI JORGE de Sousa Dias Macedo de Oliveira, JORGE António Pinto COUTO (69 Ronald Pablo BARONI), António José Santos FOLHA, RUI Gil Soares de BARROS, DOMINGOS José Paciência Oliveira.
Trainer: Robert William Bobby Robson

LKS: Jerzy Zajda, Marek Chojnacki (Cap), Witold Bendkowski, Rafal Pawlak, Grzegorz Krysiak (76 Dariusz Nowacki), Tomasz Lenart, Artur Kosciuk, Tomasz Wieszczycki, Zdzislaw Leszczynski, Tomasz Cebula, Jacek Pluciennik (86 Dariusz Matusiak).   Trainer: Ryszard Polak

Goals: Domingos (71), Rui Barros (76)

LKS LÓDZ v FC PORTO 0-1 (0-1)

LKS Lódz   29.09.1994

Referee: Martin Bodenham (ENG)   Attendance: 6,113

LKS: Jerzy Zajda, Marek Chojnacki (Cap), Grzegorz Krysiak, Rafal Pawlak (86 Jaroslaw Soszynski), Witold Bendkowski, Tomasz Lenart, Artur Kosciuk (65 Dariusz Nowacki), Zdzislaw Leszczynski, Tomasz Cebula, Tomasz Wieszczycki, Jacek Pluciennik.   Trainer: Ryszard Polak

FC PORTO: VÍTOR Manuel Martins BAÍA, Carlos Alberto Oliveira SECRETÁRIO, ALOÍSIO Pires Alves, JORGE Paulo COSTA Almeida, RUI JORGE de Sousa Dias Macedo de Oliveira, EMERSON Moisés Costa, João Paulo Santos "PAULINHO SANTOS", JORGE António Pinto COUTO (34 Fernando Oscar BANDEIRINHA Barbosa), RUI Gil Soares de BARROS (46 António dos Santos ANDRÉ), Ljubinko Drulovic, DOMINGOS José Paciência Oliveira (Cap).
Trainer: Robert William "Bobby" Robson.

Sent off: Domingos (31)

Goal: Drulović (44)

CHELSEA LONDON
v VIKTORIA ZIZKOV 4-2 (2-2)

Stamford Bridge, London   15.09.1994

Referee: Christer Fällström (SWE)   Attendance: 22,036

CHELSEA: Dmitri Kharin, Eddie Newton, Erland Johnsen, Frank Sinclair, Scott Minto, David Rocastle (89 Graham Rix), Nigel Spackman, Gavin Peacock, Dennis Wise (Cap), John Spencer, Paul Furlong.   Manager: Glenn Hoddle

VIKTORIA: Daniel Zitka, Miloslav Kordule, Jiří Casko, Petr Gabriel, Michal Petrous, Karel Poborsky, Michal Bilek (Cap), Petr Vrabec, Jozef Majoros, Marek Trval (67 Tomas Krejcik), Tibor Jancula (85 Daniel Masek).   Trainer: Jiří Kotrba

Goals: Furlong (3), Sinclair (4), Majoros (35, 42), Rocastle (53), Wise (68)

VIKTORIA ZIZKOV v CHELSEA LONDON 0-0

FK Viktoria Zizkov   29.09.1994

Referee: Gianni Beschin (ITA)   Attendance: 5,176

VIKTORIA: Michal Silhavy, Miloslav Kordule, Tibor Notin, Petr Gabriel, Michal Petrous, Karel Poborsky, Michal Bilek (Cap), Jozef Majoros (61 Daniel Masek), Petr Vrabec (61 Marek Trval), Tibor Jancula, Jiří Casko.   Trainer: Jiří Kotrba

CHELSEA: Dmitri Kharin, Steve Clarke, Anthony Barness, Eddie Newton, Erland Johnsen, Frank Sinclair, Graham Rix, David Rocastle, Paul Furlong, Gavin Peacock, Dennis Wise (Cap).
Manager: Glenn Hoddle

SLIGO ROVERS v CLUB BRUGGE 1-2 (1-1)
The Showgrounds, Sligo 15.09.1994
Referee: Robert Sedlacek (AUS) Attendance: 5,000
SLIGO ROVERS: Mark McLean, Gerry Kelly, Declan Boyle, Gavin Dykes (Cap), John Kenny, Will Hastie, Gerard Carr, Robert Brunton, Ger Houlahan (84 David McDermott), Eddie Annand, Padraig Moran (63 Aidan Rooney). Manager: Chris Rutherford
CLUB BRUGGE: Danny Verlinden; Dirk Medved, Pascal Plovie, Paul Okon, Vital Borkelmans, Gert Verheyen, Franky van der Elst (Cap), Lorenzo Staelens, Stefan Van der Heyden, Sven Vermant, René Eykelkamp. Trainer: Hugo Broos
Goals: Vermant (10), Kenny (44), Verheyen (62)

CLUB BRUGGE v SLIGO ROVERS 3-1 (1-1)
Olympiapark, Brugge 29.09.1994
Referee: Lars Gerner (DEN) Attendance: 6,281
CLUB BRUGGE: Jurgen Belpaire, Dirk Medved, Pascal Plovie, Paul Okon, Vital Borkelmans, Gert Verheyen, Franky van der Elst (Cap), Lorenzo Staelens, Stefan Van der Heyden, Sven Vermant (72 Tjorven de Brul), René Eykelkamp (72 Jan Van Tieghem). Trainer: Hugo Broos
SLIGO ROVERS: Mark McLean, Gerry Kelly, Martin McDonnell (60 Padraig Moran), Declan Boyle, Gavin Dykes (Cap), John Kenny, Will Hastie, Gerard Carr, Ian Lynch, Ger Houlahan (60 Eddie Annand), Aidan Rooney. Manager: Chris Rutherford
Goals: Staelens (3, 45 pen), Rooney (8), Eykelkamp (60)

**CSKA MOSKVA
v FERENCVÁROS BUDAPEST 2-1** (0-0)
Dinamo Moskva 15.09.1994
Referee: Veselin Bogdanov (BUL) Attendance: 6,000
CSKA: Andrei Novosadov, Vladislav Radimov, Sergei Kolotovkin, Denis Mashkarin, Sergei Mamchur, Dmitri Shukov (62 Sergei Semak), Yuri Antonovich, Valeri Broschin (Cap), Mikhail Sinev, Vladimir Tatarchuk (46 Oleg Sergeev), Ilshat Faizulin. Trainer: Aleksandr Tarkhanov
FERENCVÁROS: Tamás Balogh; Tibor Simon, Mihály Szűcs, József Keller (Cap), Tamás Szekeres, Péter Lipcsei, Krisztián Lisztes, Flórián Albert, Kenneth Christiansen, László Czéh (46 Zsolt Nagy), Eugen Neagoe (88 János Hrutka). Trainer: Dezsö Novák
Goals: Mamchur (50), Christiansen (60), Sergeev (74)

**FERENCVÁROS BUDAPEST
v CSKA MOSKVA 2-1** (2-1, 2-1) (AET)
Üllöi út, Budapest 29.09.1994
Referee: Wieland Ziller (GER) Attendance: 20,000
FERENCVÁROS: Tamás Balogh, Tibor Simon (Cap), András Telek, János Hrutka, Tamás Szekeres, Péter Lipcsei, Zsolt Nagy (112 Gábor Zavadszky), Mihály Szűcs, Kenneth Christiansen, Krisztián Lisztes, Eugen Neagoe (91 József Gregor). Trainer: Dezsö Novák
CSKA: Andrei Novosadov, Vladislav Radimov, Sergei Kolotovkin, Dmitri Bystrov, Sergei Mamchur, Denis Mashkarin (46 Evgeni Bushmanov), Mikhail Sinev (75 Andrei Demchenko), Valeri Broschin (Cap), Valeri Minko, Dmitri Shukov, Ilshat Faizulin. Trainer: Aleksandr Tarkhanov
Goals: Radimov (15, 36 og), Neagoe (45)
Penalties: 1-0 Gregor, 1-1 Bystrov, 2-1 Lisztes, 2-2 Bushmanov, 3-2 Christiansen, 3-3 Demchenko, 4-3 Szekeres, 4-4 Mamchur, 5-4 Lipcsei, 5-5 Minko, 6-5 Zavadszky, 6-6 Broschin, 7-6 Hrutka, Kolotovkin (miss)

BRØNDBY IF v KS TIRANA 3-0 (1-0)
Brøndby stadion 15.09.1994
Referee: Gylfi Orrason (ICE) Attendance: 6,035
BRØNDBY: Mogens Krogh; Søren Colding, Marc Rieper, Brian Jensen, Jens Risager, Ole Bjur (71 Kim Daugaard), Henrik Jensen (Cap), Jesper Kristensen, Thomas Thøgersen, Mark Strudal, Bo Hansen (81 Dan Eggen). Trainer: Ebbe Skovdahl
KS TIRANA: Elton Kasmi; Sajmir Malko, Nevil Dede, Alpin Gallo, Klarent Fejzolli, Afrim Tole, Dritan Baholli, Ardian Mema (Cap), Sokol Prenga (60 Frenkli Dhales), Auron Miloti, Indrit Fortuzi (87 Artan Kukli). Trainer: Shkëlqim Muça
Goals: B. Jensen (20 pen), Bo Hansen (57), Malko (66 og)

KS TIRANA v BRØNDBY IF 0-1 (0-1)
Qemal Stafa, Tirana 29.09.1994
Referee: Marc Batta (FRA) Attendance: 4,650
KS TIRANA: Blendi Nallbani; Sajmir Malko, Nevil Dede, Alpin Gallo, Klarent Fejzolli, Afrim Tole, Dritan Baholli, Ardian Mema (Cap), Sokol Prenga, Auron Miloti, Indrit Fortuzi. Trainer: Shkëlkim Muça
BRØNDBY: Mogens Krogh; Sören Colding, Marc Rieper, Dan Eggen, Jens Risager, Ole Bjur, Kim Vilfort (Cap), Henrik Jensen (72 Jes Högh), Thomas Thögersen (57 Brian Jensen), Mark Strudal, Bo Hansen. Trainer: Ebbe Skovdahl
Goal: Strudal (29)

ZALGIRIS VILNIUS
v FEYENOORD ROTTERDAM 1-1 (0-1)

Zalgiris Vilnius   15.09.1994

Referee: Roy Helge Olsen (NOR)   Attendance: 9,000

ZALGIRIS: Alvydas Koncevicius, Sergejus Novikovas, Darius Maciulevicius, Virginijus Baltusnikas (Cap), Ramunas Stonkus, Donatos Vencevicius, Gintaras Rimkus, Andrius Tereskinas, Aidas Preiksaitis (75 Vytautas Karvelis), Edgaras Jankauskas, Eimantas Poderis.
Trainer: Benjaminas Zelkevicius

FEYENOORD: Ed de Goey; Ulrich van Gobbel, John de Wolf (Cap), Henk Fräser, Ruud Heus, Peter Bosz, Arnold Scholten, Gaston Taument (66 József Kiprich), Henrik Larsson, Rob Witschge (81 Rob Maas), Regi Blinker.
Trainer: Wim van Hanegem

Goals: Larsson (9), Tereskinas (87 pen)

AUSTRIA WIEN
v NK MARIBOR BRANIK 3-0 (1-0)

Ernst Happel, Wien   29.09.1994

Referee: Loizos Loizou (CYP)   Attendance: 5,014

AUSTRIA: Franz Wohlfahrt; Stojan Belajic, Manfred Zsak (Cap), Walter Kogler, Anton Pfeffer, Thomas Flögel, Christian Prosenik, Michael Wagner, Andreas Ogris (74 Jürgen Kauz), Mons Ivar Mjelde (61 Goran Djuricin), Andrzej Kubica.
Trainer: Egon Coordes

BRANIK: Mladen Dabanović, Saso Lukić, Gregor Zidan, Marinko Galić, Ales Krizan (Cap), Peter Binkovski, Renato Kotnik (61 Milan Sterbal), Goran Gutalj (61 Danijel Sirec), Amir Karić, Kliton Bozgo, Ante Simundza.   Trainer: Marijan Bloudek

Goals: Flögel (18), Kubica (53, 56)

FEYENOORD ROTTERDAM
v ZALGIRIS VILNIUS 2-1 (0-0)

Feyenoord, Rotterdam   29.09.1994

Referee: István Vad (HUN)   Attendance: 17,682

FEYENOORD: Ed de Goey; Ulrich van Gobbel, John de Wolf (Cap), Henk Fräser, Ruud Heus, Rob Maas, Arnold Scholten (72 Orlando Trustfull), Gaston Taument, Henrik Larsson, Rob Witschge, Regi Blinker (72 József Kiprich).
Trainer: Wim van Hanegem

ZALGIRIS: Alvydas Koncevicius, Sergejus Novikovas, Dainius Suliauskas (75 Edgaras Jankauskas), Virginijus Baltusnikas (Cap), Ramunas Stonkus, Donatos Vencevicius, Gintaras Rimkus, Andrius Tereskinas, Vytautas Karvelis, Darius Maciulevicius, Eimantas Poderis.
Trainer: Benjaminas Zelkevicius.

Sent off: Novikovas (66)

Goals: Larsson (54), Heus (65 pen), Vencevicius (89)

DUNDEE UNITED v TATRAN PREŠOV 3-2 (1-2)

Tannadice Park, Dundee   15.09.1994

Referee: Leon Schellings (BEL)   Attendance: 9,454

DUNDEE UNITED: Alan Main, James McInally, Maurice Malpas (Cap), David Hannah, Gordan Petric, Brian Welsh, David Bowman, William McKinlay, Dragutin Ristic (52 Andy McLaren), Craig Brewster (63 Christian Dailly), Jerren Nixon.   Trainer: Ivan Golac

TATRAN: Peter Jakubech, Lubomir Bajtos, Kennedy Chihuri (73 Robert Kocis), Stanislav Varga, Vladimir Nenadic, Peter Hlusko, Marian Skalka (Cap), Richard Höger, Jaroslav Kentos (90 Robert Petrus), Vladislav Zvara, Rudolf Matta.   Trainer: Igor Novák

Goals: Skalka (10), Petric (16), Zvara (41 pen), Nixon (66), Hannah (69)

NK MARIBOR BRANIK
v AUSTRIA WIEN 1-1 (0-1)

Ljudski vrt, Maribor   15.09.1994

Referee: Sergey Shmolik (BLS)   Attendance: 15,000

BRANIK: Mladen Dabanović, Saso Lukić, Blagoje Milevski, Ales Krizan (Cap), Peter Binkovski, Goran Gutalj (77 Amir Karić), Marinko Galić, Gregor Zidan, Kliton Bozgo, Renato Kotnik (74 Danijel Sirec), Ante Simundza.
Trainer: Marijan Bloudek

AUSTRIA: Franz Wohlfahrt; Manfred Zsak (Cap), Walter Kogler, Stojan Belajic, Manfred Schmid, Christian Prosenik, Attila Sekerlioglu, Michael Zechner (63 Andrzej Kubica), Thomas Flögel, Mons Ivar Mjelde (86 Goran Djuricin), Andreas Ogris.   Trainer: Egon Coordes.

Sent off: Sekerlioglu (86)

Goals: Prosenik (23), Bozgo (46 pen)

TATRAN PREŠOV v DUNDEE UNITED 3-1 (2-1)

Tatran Prešov   29.09.1994

Referee: Serdar Cakman (TUR)   Attendance: 8,184

TATRAN: Peter Jakubech, Lubomir Bajtos, Jaroslav Kentos, Martin Lukac, Robert Petrus, Peter Hlusko, Marian Skalka (Cap), Richard Höger, Robert Kocis (85 Adrian Lesko), Vladislav Zvara, Rudolf Matta (71 Lubomir Puhak).   Trainer: Igor Novák

DUNDEE UNITED: Alan Main, Alec Cleland (46 David Craig), Maurice Malpas (Cap), David Hannah, Gordan Petric, Brian Welsh, Christian Dailly, William McKinlay, Andy McLaren (60 Craig Brewster), James McInally, Jerren Nixon.   Trainer: Ivan Golac

Goals: Nixon (3), Zvara (11, 77), Kocis (20)

**PIRIN BLAGOEVGRAD
v PANATHINAIKOS ATHINA 0-2** (0-0)
Hristo Botev, Blagoevgrad 15.09.1994
Referee: Yuri Chebotarev (RUS)   Attendance: 11,972
PIRIN: Miroslav Mitev (Cap); Kostadin Trendafilov, Georgi Petrov, Blagoi Latinov (57 Boris Ianev), Ivo Trenchev, Stefan Goshev, Ivan Stoichev, Anton Bachev, Nikolai Petrunov, Malin Orachev, Georgi Bachev.   Trainer: Iordan Kostov
PANATHINAIKOS: Jozef Wandzik, Stratos Apostolakis (Cap), Giorgos H.Georgiadis, Marinos Ouzounidis, Thanasis Kolitsidakis, Giorgos Donis (78 Kostas Antoniou), Juan Borelli, Nikos Nioplias, Krzysztof Warzycha, Spiros Maragkos, Dimitris Markos (66 Alexandros Alexoudis).   Trainer: Juan Ramón Rocha
Goals: Nioplias (70), Alexoudis (84)

**PANATHINAIKOS ATHINA
v PIRIN BLAGOEVGRAD 6-1** (3-1)
Olympiako Spiros Louis, Athina 29.09.1994
Referee: Svend Erik Christensen (DEN)   Att: 22,230
PANATHINAIKOS: Jozef Wandzik (80 Antonis Nikopolidis), Stratos Apostolakis (Cap), Giorgos H.Georgiadis, Marinos Ouzounidis, Giannis Kalitzakis, Thanasis Kolitsidakis, Juan Borelli, Dimitris Markos, Krzysztof Warzycha, Spiros Maragkos (74 Giorgos Donis), Alexandros Alexoudis (78 Anastasios Mitropoulos).   Trainer: Juan Ramón Rocha
PIRIN: Miroslav Mitev (Cap) (81 Kiril Stoikov), Kostadin Trendafilov, Georgi Petrov, Blagoi Latinov, Ivo Trenchev, Stefan Goshev, Ivan Stoichev (68 Radoslav Kresnichki), Anton Bachev, Nikolai Petrunov, Malin Orachev, Georgi Bachev (76 Boris Ianev).   Trainer: Iordan Kostov
Goals: Alexoudis (7, 17), Warzycha (30, 87, 90), Orachev (44), Borelli (65)

BEŞIKTAŞ ISTANBUL v HJK HELSINKI 2-0 (2-0)
Inönü, Istanbul 15.09.1994
Referee: Keith Burge (WAL)   Attendance: 23,256
BEŞIKTAŞ: Sener Kurtdemir, Recep Çetin, Gökhan Keskin, K.Ali Günçar, Fani Madida, Eyjólfur Sverisson, Riza Çalimbay (Cap), Sergen Yalçin (76 B.Metin Tekin), Mutlu Topcu, Oktay Derelioglu, Ertugrul Saglam (85 Mehmet Özdilek).   Trainer: Christoph Daum
HJK HELSINKI: Antti Niemi, Aki Hyryläinen, Marko Helin, Antti Heinola, Jari Europaeus (Cap), Janne Suokonautio (46 Jari Vanhala), Rami Rantanen, Markku Kanerva, Pasi Tauriainen, Ismo Lius (82 Mika Lehkosuo), Janne Saarinen.   Trainer: Jari-Pekka Keurulainen
Goals: Oktay (27), Ertugrul (35 pen)

HJK HELSINKI v BEŞIKTAŞ ISTANBUL 1-1 (0-0)
Olympic Helsinki 29.09.1994
Referee: Hugh Dallas (SCO)   Attendance: 2,390
HJK HELSINKI: Antti Niemi, Aki Hyryläinen, Antti Heinola, Pekka Onttonen (Cap) (77 Mika Lehkosuo), Janne Suokonautio, Rami Rantanen, Janne Murtomäki, Pasi Tauriainen, Janne Saarinen, Mika Kottila, Jari Vanhala.   Trainer: Jari-Pekka Keurulainen
BEŞIKTAŞ: Sener Kurtdemir, Recep Çetin, Gökhan Keskin, K.Ali Günçar, Fani Madida (72 Alpay Özalan), Eyjólfur Sverisson, Riza Çalimbay (Cap), Mehmet Özdilek, Mutlu Topcu, Oktay Derelioglu, Sertan Eser (77 B.Metin Tekin).   Trainer: Christoph Daum
Goals: Rantanen (68), Oktay (88)

**GRASSHOPPER ZÜRICH
v CHORNOMORETS ODESSA 3-0** (1-0)
Hardturm Zürich 15.09.1994
Referee: Jiří Ulrich (CZE)   Attendance: 3,600
GRASSHOPPER: Roberto Böckli, Harald Gämperle, Mats Gren, Ramon Vega, Pascal Thüler, Massimo Lombardo (88 Bernd Kilian), Thomas Bickel, Marcel Koller (Cap), Murat Yakin, Nestor Subiat, Ron Willems (82 Joël Magnin).   Trainer: Christian Gross
CHORNOMORETS: Oleg Suslov, Andri Telesnenko (Cap), Yuri Bukel, Yuri Smotrich (51 Viacheslav Skish), Ihor Zhabchenko (46 Vitali Parakhnevich), Igor Korniets, Dmytro Parfenov, Aleksandr Gorshkov, Ruslan Romanchuk, Aleksandr Nikiforov, Timerlan Guseinov.   Trainer: Leonid Buriak.
Sent off: Nikiforov (75)
Goals: Bickel (41), Koller (52), Subiat (85)

**CHORNOMORETS ODESSA
v GRASSHOPPER ZÜRICH 1-0** (1-0)
Central Odessa 29.09.1994
Referee: Hermann Albrecht (GER)   Attendance: 12,000
CHORNOMORETS: Oleg Suslov, Andri Telesnenko (Cap), Viacheslav Skish (46 Aleksandr Gorshkov), Yuri Bukel, Ihor Zhabchenko, Dmytro Parfenov, Ruslan Romanchuk, Igor Korniets, Konstantin Kulik (69 Viacheslav Yeremeev), Timerlan Guseinov, Vitali Parakhnevich.   Trainer: Leonid Buriak
GRASSHOPPER: Pascal Zuberbühler, Harald Gämperle, Ramon Vega, Mats Gren, Pascal Thüler, Massimo Lombardo (70 Bernd Kilian), Marcel Koller (Cap), Thomas Bickel, Murat Yakin, Ron Willems, Nestor Subiat (82 Joël Magnin).   Trainer: Christian Gross
Goal: Guseinov (10)

GLORIA BISTRIŢA v REAL ZARAGOZA 2-1 (0-1)

Gloria Bistriţa   15.09.1994

Referee: Ahmet Çakar (TUR)   Attendance: 12,000

GLORIA: Costel Câmpeanu (Cap), Dorel Ioan Zegrean, Gabriel Cristea, Simion Mironaş, Valer Săsărman, Marius Răduţă, Florin Stancu, Mihai Tararache, Cornel Sevastiţa, Ilie Lazăr (23 Mihai Lungu, 67 Ion Balaur), Dănuţ Matei. Trainer: Constantin Cîrstea

REAL ZARAGOZA: Andoni CEDRÚN Ibarra, Alberto BELSUÉ Arias, Javier AGUADO Companys, Fernando Gabriel CÁCERES, Íñigo LIZARRALDE Lazcano, Miguel PARDEZA Pichardo (Cap) (71 ÓSCAR Luis Celada), DARÍO Javier FRANCO Gatti, Santiago ARAGÓN Martínez, Ángel de Juana García "GELI", Juan Eduardo ESNÁIDER Esnáider, Francisco HIGUERA Fernández (77 Mohamed Ali Amar "NAYIM"). Trainer: Víctor Fernández

Sent off: Franco (70), Săsărman (87)

Goals: Esnáider (44), M. Răduţă (51), Lungu (52)

REAL ZARAGOZA v GLORIA BISTRIŢA 4-0 (2-0)

Estadio Luis Casanova, Valencia   29.09.1994

Referee: Andrew Waddell (SCO)   Attendance: 5,000

REAL ZARAGOZA: Andoni CEDRÚN Ibarra, Alberto BELSUÉ Arias, Fernando Gabriel CÁCERES, Javier AGUADO Companys, Jesús Ángel SOLANA Bermejo, Mohamed Ali Amar "NAYIM", Miguel PARDEZA Pichardo (Cap), Santiago ARAGÓN Martínez (53 ÓSCAR Luis Celada), Gustavo POYET Domínguez, Juan Eduardo ESNÁIDER Esnaider (73 Ángel de Juana García "GELI"), Francisco HIGUERA Fernández. Trainer: Víctor Fernández

GLORIA: Costel Cîmpeanu (Cap), Dorel Ioan Zegrean, Simion Mironaş, Sorin Moraru (46 Mihai Lungu), Gabriel Cristea, Adrian Fekete Cocan (65 Ion Balaur), Cornel Sevastiţa, Florin Stancu, Marius Răduţă, Mihai Tararache, Dănuţ Matei. Trainer: Constantin Cîrstea

Goals: Pardeza (12), Aguado (42), Poyet (49, 57)

CROATIA ZAGREB v AJ AUXERRE 3-1 (2-1)

Maksimir, Zagreb   15.09.1994

Referee: Marcello Nicchi (ITA)   Attendance: 20,000

CROATIA: Drazen Ladić, Jozo Gaspar, Zvonimir Soldo, Slavko Istvanić (Cap), Zoran Mamić, Josko Jelicić (83 Fuad Sasivarević), Dzevad Turković (80 Elvis Skoria), Sead Halilović, Vjekoslav Skrinjar, Igor Pamić, Igor Cvitanović. Trainer: Ivan Bedi

AJ AUXERRE: Lionel Charbonnier; Alain Goma, Franck Silvestre, Frank Verlaat, Stéphane Mahé; Moussa Saib, Raphäel Guerreiro, Corentin Martins (Cap), Bernard Diomède (78 Taribo West), Sabri Lamouchi, Lilian Laslandes. Trainer: Guy Roux.

Sent off: Silvestre (80)

Goals: Jelicić (1), Diomède (20), Soldo (40), Pamić (65)

AJ AUXERRE v CROATIA ZAGREB 3-0 (1-0)

Stade Abbé-Deschamps, Auxerre   29.09.1994

Referee: Roelof Luinge (HOL)   Attendance: 13,874

AJ AUXERRE: Lionel Charbonnier, Alain Goma (50 Franck Rabarivony), Taribo West, Frank Verlaat, Stéphane Mahé, Moussa Saib, Corentin Martins (Cap), Raphäel Guerreiro, Sabri Lamouchi, Lilian Laslandes, Bernard Diomède.

CROATIA: Drazen Ladić, Dzevad Turković, Zvonimir Soldo, Slavko Istvanić (Cap), Zoran Mamić (36 Damir Lesjak), Vjekoslav Skrinjar, Sead Halilović, Jozo Gaspar, Josko Jelicić, Igor Pamić (46 Dario Simić), Igor Cvitanović.

Goals: Diomède (41), Mahé (75), Lamouchi (89)

SECOND ROUND

FC PORTO v FERENCVÁROS BUDAPEST 6-0 (3-0)

Estádio Das Antas, Porto   20.10.1994

Referee: Marnix Sandra (BEL)   Attendance: 15,880

FC PORTO: VÍTOR Manuel Martins BAÍA, JOÃO Domingos Silva PINTO (Cap), JORGE Paulo COSTA Almeida, ALOÍSIO Pires Alves, Fernando Oscar BANDEIRINHA Barbosa, EMERSON Moisés Costa, João Paulo Santos "PAULINHO SANTOS", Carlos Alberto Oliveira SECRETÁRIO, RUI Gil Soares de BARROS (66 António José Santos FOLHA), Ljubinko Drulovic (83 Ronald Pablo BARONI), DOMINGOS José Paciência Oliveira. Trainer: Robert William "Bobby" Robson

FERENCVÁROS: Tamás Balogh, Mihály Szűcs, András Telek, József Keller (Cap) (79 Norbert Bubcsó), László Czéh, János Hrutka, Kenneth Christiansen, Krisztian Lisztes, Flórián Albert, József Gregor, Gábor Zavadszky.   Trainer: Dezsö Novák

Goals: Jorge Costa (14), Rui Barros (15), Drulovic (40, 58), Domingos (85), Aloísio (87)

FERENCVÁROS BUDAPEST v FC PORTO 2-0 (1-0)

Üllöi út, Budapest   3.11.1994

Referee: Alfredo Trentalange (ITA)   Attendance: 9,385

FERENCVÁROS: Tamás Balogh, András Telek, Tibor Simon (Cap), János Hrutka, Tamás Szekeres, Flórián Albert (84 Zsolt Nagy), Péter Lipcsei, Mihály Szűcs (66 Zoltán Kecskés), Gábor Zavadszky, Eugen Neagoe, Kenneth Christiansen. Trainer: Dezsö Novák

FC PORTO: VÍTOR Manuel Martins BAÍA, JORGE Paulo COSTA Almeida, Fernando Oscar BANDEIRINHA Barbosa, ALOÍSIO Pires Alves, JORGE António Pinto COUTO (69 JOÃO Domingos Silva PINTO), EMERSON Moisés Costa, João Paulo Santos "PAULINHO SANTOS", José Orlando Rocha SEMEDO (Cap) (69 JOSÉ CARLOS Nascimento), RUI JORGE de Sousa Dias Macedo de Oliveira, DOMINGOS José Paciência Oliveira, António José Santos FOLHA.   Trainer: Robert William "Bobby" Robson

Sent off: Bandeirinha (52)

Goals: Zavadszky (27), Neagoe (60)

CLUB BRUGGE
v PANATHINAIKOS ATHINA 1-0 (1-0)
Olympiapark, Brugge 20.10.1994

Referee: Marc Batta (FRA)   Attendance: 14,760

CLUB BRUGGE: Danny Verlinden, Dirk Medved, Pascal Renier, Paul Okon, Vital Borkelmans, Gert Verheyen, Lorenzo Staelens, Franky van der Elst (Cap), Stefan Van der Heyden, Sven Vermant, René Eykelkamp.   Trainer: Hugo Broos

PANATHINAIKOS: Jozef Wandzik, Stratos Apostolakis, Giorgos H.Georgiadis, Marinos Ouzounidis, Giannis Kalitzakis (Cap), Thanasis Kolitsidakis, Juan Borelli, Nikos Nioplias, Krzysztof Warzycha, Spiros Maragkos, Dimitris Markos (46 Giorgos Donis, 80 Alexandros Alexoudis).   Trainer: Juan Ramón Rocha

Goal: Staelens (5 pen)

GRASSHOPPER ZÜRICH
v SAMPDORIA GENOVA 3-2 (1-2)
Hardturm, Zürich 3.11.1994

Referee: John Blankenstein (HOL)   Attendance: 12,100

GRASSHOPPER: Pascal Zuberbühler, Giorgios Nemtsoudis, Pascal Thüler, Mats Gren, Murat Yakin, Marcel Koller (Cap), Bernd Kilian, Harald Gämperle, Thomas Bickel, Nestor Subiat (80 Joël Magnin), Ron Willems.   Trainer: Christian Gross

SAMPDORIA: Walter Zenga, Moreno Mannini (53 Marco Rossi), Riccardo Ferri, Pietro Vierchowod (Cap), Sinisa Mihajlovic, Giovanni Invernizzi, Michele Serena, Alberigo Evani, Attilio Lombardo, David Platt, Alessandro Melli (78 Fausto Salsano).   Trainer: Sven Göran Eriksson

Goals: Willems (13), Melli (17), Lombardo (40), Bickel (52), Koller (55)

PANATHINAIKOS ATHINA v CLUB BRUGGE 0-0
Olympiako Spiros Louis, Athina 3.11.1994

Referee: Bernd Heynemann (GER)   Attendance: 67,133

PANATHINAIKOS: Jozef Wandzik; Stratos Apostolakis, Giannis Kalitzakis (Cap), Thanasis Kolitsidakis, Giorgos H.Georgiadis (73 Giorgos Donis), Giorgos Kapouranis, Juan Borelli, Nikos Nioplias, Spiros Maragkos (61 Dimitris Markos), Krzysztof Warzycha, Alexandros Alexoudis.   Trainer: Juan Ramón Rocha

CLUB BRUGGE: Danny Verlinden, Vital Borkelmans, Pascal Renier, Paul Okon, Tjorven de Brul (40 Rudy Cossey), Dirk Medved, Stefan Van der Heyden, Franky van der Elst (Cap), Lorenzo Staelens, Sven Vermant, Gert Verheyen.   Trainer: Hugo Broos

Sent off: Kolitsidakis (90)

BEŞIKTAŞ ISTANBUL v AJ AUXERRE 2-2 (2-0)
Inönü, Istanbul 20.10.1994

Referee: Peter Mikkelsen (DEN)   Attendance: 20,936

BEŞIKTAŞ: Sener Kurtdemir, Recep Çetin, Gökhan Keskin, K.Ali Günçar (11 Alpay Özalan), Mutlu Topcu, Eyjólfur Sverisson (70 B.Metin Tekin), Oktay Derelioglu, Riza Çalimbay (Cap), Ertugrul Saglam, Mehmet Özdilek, Sergen Yalçin.   Trainer: Christoph Daum

AJ AUXERRE: Lionel Charbonnier, Alain Goma, Taribo West, Frank Verlaat, Stéphane Mahé, Raphäel Guerreiro, Sabri Lamouchi, Corentin Martins (Cap), Moussa Saib, Lilian Laslandes, Bernard Diomède.   Trainer: Guy Roux

Goals: Mehmet (40), Ertugrul (43), Saib (54), Martins (59)

SAMPDORIA GENOVA
v GRASSHOPPER ZÜRICH 3-0 (1-0)
Luigi Ferraris, Genova 20.10.1994

Referee: Ryszard Wójcik (POL)   Attendance: 25,316

SAMPDORIA: Walter Zenga, Moreno Mannini (62 Fausto Salsano), Riccardo Ferri (86 Marco Rossi), Pietro Vierchowod (Cap), Michele Serena, Sinisa Mihajlović, Attilio Lombardo, Giovanni Invernizzi, Riccardo Maspero, Alessandro Melli, Alberigo Evani.   Trainer: Sven Göran Eriksson

GRASSHOPPER: Pascal Zuberbühler, Harald Gämperle, Mats Gren, Ramon Vega, Pascal Thüler, Marcel Koller (Cap), Murat Yakin, Massimo Lombardo, Bernd Kilian, Nestor Subiat, Joël Magnin (70 Ron Willems).   Trainer: Christian Gross

Goals: Melli (45), Mihajlovic (76), Maspero (83)

AJ AUXERRE v BEŞIKTAŞ ISTANBUL 2-0 (1-0)
Stade Abbé-Deschamps, Auxerre 3.11.1994

Referee: Manuel Diaz Vega (SPA)   Attendance: 21,140

AJ AUXERRE: Lionel Charbonnier, Alain Goma, Taribo West, Frank Verlaat, Stéphane Mahé, Raphäel Guerreiro, Corentin Martins (Cap), Moussa Saib, Sabri Lamouchi, Lilian Laslandes (88 Gérald Baticle), Bernard Diomède (80 Franck Rabarivony).   Trainer: Guy Roux

BEŞIKTAŞ: Raimond Aumann, Recep Çetin, Gökhan Keskin (75 Ertugrul Saglam), Alpay Özalan, Fani Madida, Riza Çalimbay (Cap), Mehmet Özdilek, Sergen Yalçin, Mutlu Topcu, Eyjólfur Sverisson, Metin B. Tekin (62 Oktay Derelioglu).   Trainer: Christoph Daum

Goals: Lamouchi (45, 49)

**FEYENOORD ROTTERDAM
v WERDER BREMEN 1-0** (0-0)

Feyenoord, Rotterdam 20.10.1994

Referee: Bo Karlsson (SWE)   Attendance: 35,624

FEYENOORD: Ed de Goey; Ulrich van Gobbel, John de Wolf (Cap), Henk Fräser, Ruud Heus, Arnold Scholten, Peter Bosz, Rob Witschge, Gaston Taument, Henrik Larsson, Regi Blinker. Trainer: Wim van Hanegem

WERDER: Oliver Reck (Cap), Hany Ramzy, Andree Wiedener, Michael Schulz, Thomas Wolter, Mario Basler, Miroslav Votava, Andreas Herzog (58 Frank Neubarth), Dieter Eilts, Wynton Rufer, Marco Bode.   Trainer: Otto Rehhagel

Goal: Larsson (63)

**WERDER BREMEN
v FEYENOORD ROTTERDAM 3-4** (1-2)

Weserstadion, Bremen 3.11.1994

Referee: Pierluigi Pairetto (ITA)   Attendance: 31,118

WERDER: Oliver Reck (Cap), Frank Neubarth, Thomas Wolter, Hany Ramzy (78 Marinus Bester), Michael Schulz, Mario Basler, Miroslav Votava, Dieter Eilts, Andreas Herzog, Vladimir Beschastnîh, Marco Bode.   Trainer: Otto Rehhagel

FEYENOORD: Ed de Goey, Henk Fräser, John de Wolf (Cap), Orlando Trustfull, Ruud Heus, Arnold Scholten, Peter Bosz, Rob Witschge, Gaston Taument (87 Dean Gorré), Henrik Larsson, Regi Blinker (74 Rob Maas).
Trainer: Wim van Hanegem

Sent off: Scholten (70)

Goals: Beschastnîh (12, 60), Larsson (21, 34, 67 pen), Heus (56 pen), Basler (90)

CHELSEA LONDON v AUSTRIA WIEN 0-0

Stamford Bridge, London 20.10.1994

Referee: Atanas Uzunov (BUL)   Attendance: 22,560

CHELSEA: Dmitri Kharin, Nigel Spackman, Jakob Kjeldbjerg, Erland Johnsen, Frank Sinclair (14 Anthony Barness, 75 Graham Rix), Neil Shipperley, Eddie Newton, David Rocastle, Gavin Peacock (Cap), Paul Furlong, Dennis Wise. Manager: Glenn Hoddle

AUSTRIA: Franz Wohlfahrt; Anton Pfeffer, Attila Sekerlioglu, Manfred Schmid, Walter Kogler, Manfred Zsak (Cap), Stojan Belajic, Christian Prosenik, Thomas Flögel, Mons Ivar Mjelde (70 Michael Zechner), Andreas Ogris (52 Arminas Narbekovas).   Trainer: Egon Coordes

Sent off: Schmid (68)

AUSTRIA WIEN v CHELSEA LONDON 1-1 (0-1)

Ernst Happel, Wien 3.11.1994

Referee: Frans Van den Wijngaert (BEL)   Att: 18,000

AUSTRIA: Franz Wohlfahrt; Manfred Zsak (Cap), Anton Pfeffer, Walter Kogler, Stojan Belajic, Thomas Flögel, Attila Sekerlioglu, Michael Zechner (52 Michael Wagner), Christian Prosenik, Arminas Narbekovas, Mons Ivar Mjelde. Trainer: Egon Coordes

CHELSEA: Dmitri Kharin, Gareth Hall (46 Scott Minto), Nigel Spackman (Cap), Erland Johnsen, Anthony Barness, David Rocastle (77 Glenn Hoddle), Dennis Wise, Eddie Newton, Andy Myers, John Spencer, Neil Shipperley.
Manager: Glenn Hoddle

Goals: Spencer (40), Narbekovas (73)

BRØNDBY IF v ARSENAL LONDON 1-2 (0-2)

Brøndby stadium 20.10.1994

Referee: Werner Müller (SWI)   Attendance: 13,406

BRØNDBY: Mogens Krogh; Sören Colding (71 Jes Høgh), Marc Rieper, Dan Eggen, Jens Risager, Ole Bjur, Kim Vilfort (Cap), Henrik Jensen (81 Jesper Kristensen), Thomas Thøgersen, Bo Hansen, Mark Strudal.
Trainer: Ebbe Skovdahl

ARSENAL: David Seaman, Lee Dixon, Tony Adams (Cap), Steve Bould, Nigel Winterburn, Ray Parlour, John Jensen, Stefan Schwarz, Kevin Campbell, Ian Wright, Alan Smith. Manager: George Graham

Goals: Wright (16), Smith (18), Strudal (53)

ARSENAL LONDON v BRØNDBY IF 2-2 (2-1)

Highbury, London 3.11.1994

Referee: Sergei Khusainov (RUS)   Attendance: 32,290

ARSENAL: David Seaman, Lee Dixon (67 Steve Bould), Tony Adams (Cap), Martin Keown, Nigel Winterburn, Ray Parlour, Ian Selley, John Jensen, Paul Merson, Ian Wright (64 Kevin Campbell), Alan Smith.   Manager: George Graham

BRØNDBY: Mogens Krogh, Jes Høgh, Marc Rieper, Dan Eggen, Ole Bjur, Kim Vilfort (Cap), Thomas Thøgersen, Brian Jensen (46 Søren Colding), Jesper Kristensen, Bo Hansen, Mark Strudal (85 Ruben Bagger).   Trainer: Ebbe Skovdahl

Goals: Bo Hansen (2), Wright (25 pen), Selley (46), Eggen (69)

TATRAN PREŠOV v REAL ZARAGOZA 0-4 (0-2)

Tatran Prešov   20.10.1994

Referee: José João Mendes Pratas (POR)   Att: 12,105

TATRAN: Peter Jakubech; Lubomir Bajtos (46 Martin Lukac), Jaroslav Kentos, Stanislav Varga, Peter Hlusko, Rudolf Matta, Marian Skalka (Cap), Vladislav Zvara, Richard Höger, Kennedy Chihuri, Vladimir Nenadic (66 Robert Kocis). Trainer: Igor Novák

REAL ZARAGOZA: Andoni CEDRÚN Ibarra, Alberto BELSUÉ Arias, Fernando Gabriel CÁCERES, Javier AGUADO Companys, Jesús Ángel SOLANA Bermejo (46 Jesús GARCÍA SANJÚAN), Mohamed Ali Amar "NAYIM", Santiago ARAGÓN Martínez, Gustavo POYET Domínguez, Ángel de Juana García "GELI", Francisco HIGUERA Fernández (Cap) (60 José Luis Rodríguez LORETO), Juan Eduardo ESNÁIDER Esnaider. Trainer: Víctor Fernández

Sent off: Hlusko (35)

Goals: Poyet (26), Varga (43 og), Esnáider (50, 88)

REAL ZARAGOZA v TATRAN PREŠOV 2-1 (1-1)

Estadio Luis Casanova, Valencia   3.11.1994

Referee: Dermot Gallagher (ENG)   Attendance: 2,500

REAL ZARAGOZA: Juan Miguel García Inglés "JUANMI", Íñigo LIZARRALDE Lazcano, Fernando Gabriel CÁCERES, Javier AGUADO Companys, Ángel de Juana García "GELI", ÓSCAR Luis Celada, Mohamed Ali Amar "NAYIM", Jesús GARCÍA SANJÚAN, Gustavo POYET Domínguez (Cap) (58 Miguel PARDEZA Pichardo), Juan Eduardo ESNÁIDER Esnaider, José Luis Rodríguez LORETO. Trainer: Víctor Fernández

TATRAN: Peter Jakubech, Rudolf Matta, Adrian Lesko, Stanislav Varga, Tomas Gerich; Vladislav Zvara, Vladimir Nenadic, Marian Skalka (Cap), Robert Kocis, Richard Höger, Kennedy Chihuri (74 Radovan Kocurek). Trainer: Belo Malaga

Goals: Esnáider (6), Kocis (38), Óscar (56)

QUARTER-FINALS

CLUB BRUGGE v CHELSEA LONDON 1-0 (0-0)

Olympiastadion, Brugge   28.02.1995

Referee: Serge Muhmenthaler (SWI)   Attendance: 16,145

CLUB BRUGGE: Danny Verlinden, Dirk Medved, Paul Okon, Pascal Renier, Franky van der Elst (Cap) (81 Tjorven de Brul), Gert Verheyen, Vital Borkelmans, Lorenzo Staelens, Sven Vermant, Yves Buelinckx, René Eykelkamp. Trainer: Hugo Broos

CHELSEA: Kevin Hitchcock, Steve Clarke, Scott Minto, Nigel Spackman, Erland Johnsen, Frank Sinclair, John Spencer, Eddie Newton, Paul Furlong, Gavin Peacock, Dennis Wise (Cap) (85 David Rocastle).   Manager: Glenn Hoddle

Goal: Verheyen (82)

CHELSEA LONDON v CLUB BRUGGE 2-0 (2-0)

Stamford Bridge, London   14.03.1995

Referee: Pierluigi Pairetto (ITA)   Attendance: 28,661

CHELSEA: Kevin Hitchcock, Steve Clarke, Scott Minto (55 Gareth Hall), Nigel Spackman, Erland Johnsen, Frank Sinclair, Craig Burley, Mark Stein, Paul Furlong, Gavin Peacock (Cap), David Rocastle (74 David Lee).   Manager: Glenn Hoddle

CLUB BRUGGE: Danny Verlinden (81 Jurgen Belpaire), Dirk Medved (74 Sven Vermant), Franky van der Elst (Cap), Gert Verheyen, Vital Borkelmans, Yves Buelinckx (46 Stefan Van der Heyden), Paul Okon, Tjorven de Brul, Lorenzo Staelens, René Eykelkamp, Pascal Renier.   Trainer: Hugo Broos

Goals: Stein (16), Furlong (38)

**FEYENOORD ROTTERDAM
v REAL ZARAGOZA 1-0** (0-0)

Feyenoord, Rotterdam   2.03.1995

Referee: Ilkka Koho (FIN)   Attendance: 41,920

FEYENOORD: Ed de Goey (Cap); Errol Refos, Peter Bosz, Orlando Trustfull, Rob Maas, Ruud Heus, Henk Fräser, Rob Witschge, Regi Blinker (87 Harvey Esajas), József Kiprich, Henrik Larsson (82 John van Loen). Trainer: Wim van Hanegem

REAL ZARAGOZA: Andoni CEDRÚN Ibarra, Alberto BELSUÉ Arias, Fernando Gabriel CÁCERES, Javier AGUADO Companys, Jesús Ángel SOLANA Bermejo (62 Íñigo LIZARRALDE Lazcano), Jesús GARCÍA SANJÚAN, Santiago ARAGÓN Martínez, Gustavo POYET Domínguez, Ángel de Juana García "GELI" (82 Mohamed Ali Amar "NAYIM"), Juan Eduardo ESNÁIDER Esnaider, Francisco HIGUERA Fernández (Cap).   Trainer: Víctor Fernández

Sent off: R. Witschge (86)

Goal: Larsson (61)

**REAL ZARAGOZA
v FEYENOORD ROTTERDAM 2-0** (0-0)

Estadio la Romareda, Zaragoza   16.03.1995

Referee: Markus Merk (GER)   Attendance: 36,000

REAL ZARAGOZA: Juan Miguel García Inglés "JUANMI", Alberto BELSUÉ Arias, Javier AGUADO Companys, Fernando Gabriel CÁCERES, Santiago ARAGÓN Martínez, Mohamed Ali Amar "NAYIM", Miguel PARDEZA Pichardo (Cap) (90 Ángel de Juana García "GELI"), Jesús GARCÍA SANJÚAN, Gustavo POYET Domínguez, Francisco HIGUERA Fernández (75 ÓSCAR Luis Celada), Juan Eduardo ESNÁIDER Esnaider. Trainer: Víctor Fernández

FEYENOORD: Ed de Goey (Cap); Ulrich van Gobbel, Errol Refos, Henk Fräser, Rob Maas, József Kiprich, Peter Bosz, Orlando Trustfull, Arnold Scholten, Henrik Larsson, Regi Blinker (68 Mike Obiku).   Trainer: Wim van Hanegem

Sent off: Bosz (85), Kiprich (89)

Goals: Pardeza (58), Esnáider (71)

SAMPDORIA GENOVA v FC PORTO 0-1 (0-0)

Stadio Luigi Ferraris, Genova   2.03.1995

Referee: David Elleray (ENG)   Attendance: 21,004

SAMPDORIA: Walter Zenga, Moreno Mannini, Alberigo Evani, Pietro Vierchowod (69 Marco Rossi), Michele Serena, Sinisa Mihajlovic, Vladimir Jugovic, Attilio Lombardo, David Platt, Roberto Mancini (Cap), Claudio Bellucci (61 Fausto Salsano).   Trainer: Sven Göran Eriksson

FC PORTO: VÍTOR Manuel Martins BAÍA, JOÃO Domingos Silva PINTO (Cap), João Paulo Santos "PAULINHO SANTOS", ALOÍSIO Pires Alves, JOSÉ CARLOS Nascimento, EMERSON Moisés Costa, Carlos Alberto Oliveira SECRETÁRIO, Russel Nigel Latapy, DOMINGOS José Paciência Oliveira (75 António José Santos FOLHA), Sergei Yuran, RUI Gil Soares de BARROS (85 RUI JORGE de Sousa Dias Macedo de Oliveira). Trainer: Robert William "Bobby" Robson

Goal: Yuran (64)

**FC PORTO
v SAMPDORIA GENOVA 0-1** (0-0, 0-1) (AET)

Estádio Das Antas, Porto   16.03.1995

Referee: Marc Batta (FRA)   Attendance: 35,076

FC PORTO: VÍTOR Manuel Martins BAÍA, JOÃO Domingos Silva PINTO (Cap), ALOÍSIO Pires Alves, JOSÉ CARLOS Nascimento, João Paulo Santos "PAULINHO SANTOS", Carlos Alberto Oliveira SECRETÁRIO (91 RUI JORGE de Sousa Dias Macedo de Oliveira), EMERSON Moisés Costa, Russel Nigel Latapy, RUI Gil Soares de BARROS (75 António José Santos FOLHA), Sergei Yuran, DOMINGOS José Paciência Oliveira. Trainer: Robert William "Bobby" Robson

SAMPDORIA: Walter Zenga, Michele Serena, Stefano Sacchetti, Marco Rossi (93 Riccardo Maspero), Sinisa Mihajlovic, Fausto Salsano, Giovanni Invernizzi, David Platt, Alberigo Evani (71 Vladimir Jugovic), Attilio Lombardo, Roberto Mancini.   Trainer: Sven Göran Eriksson

Sent off: Platt (117)

Goal: Mancini (50)

Penalties: 0-1 Mihajlović, 1-1 Emerson, 1-2 Jugović, Latapy (miss), 1-3 Maspero, 2-3 Domingos, 2-4 Salsano, 3-4 Folha, 3-5 A. Lombardo

ARSENAL LONDON v AJ AUXERRE 1-1 (0-0)

Highbury, London   2.03.1995

Referee: Leif Sundell (SWE)   Attendance: 35,208

ARSENAL: David Seaman, Lee Dixon, Tony Adams (Cap), Steve Bould, Nigel Winterburn, Eddie McGoldrick (46 John Hartson), John Jensen, Stefan Schwarz, Paul Merson, Ian Wright, Chris Kiwomya (79 Ray Parlour).
Manager: George Graham

AJ AUXERRE: Fabien Cool; Alain Goma, Taribo West, Frank Verlaat, Franck Rabarivony (79 Christophe Rémy), Sabri Lamouchi, Philippe Violeau, Corentin Martins (Cap), Stéphane Mahé, Lilian Laslandes, Pascal Vahirua (81 Christophe Cocard).   Trainer: Guy Roux

Goals: Wright (59 pen), Verlaat (63)

AJ AUXERRE v ARSENAL LONDON 0-1 (0-1)

Stade Abbé-Deschamps, Auxerre   16.03.1995

Referee: Vadim Zhuk (BLS)   Attendance: 22,000

AJ AUXERRE: Fabien Cool, Alain Goma, Franck Silvestre, Frank Verlaat, Stéphane Mahé, Moussa Saib, Corentin Martins (Cap), Franck Rabarivony (68 Christophe Cocard), Sabri Lamouchi, Lilian Laslandes, Pascal Vahirua (77 Gérald Baticle).   Trainer: Guy Roux

ARSENAL: David Seaman, Lee Dixon, Steve Bould, Tony Adams (Cap), Nigel Winterburn, Martin Keown, Ray Parlour, Stefan Schwarz, Paul Merson, John Hartson (77 Stephen Morrow), Ian Wright.   Manager: George Graham

Goal: Wright (16)

SEMI-FINALS

**ARSENAL LONDON
v SAMPDORIA GENOVA 3-2** (2-0)

Highbury, London   6.04.1995

Referee: Jacobus Uilenberg (HOL)   Attendance: 38,089

ARSENAL: David Seaman, Lee Dixon, Steve Bould, Tony Adams (Cap), Nigel Winterburn, Ray Parlour, David Hillier, Stefan Schwarz, Paul Merson (85 Stephen Morrow), Ian Wright (85 Chris Kiwomya), John Hartson.
Manager: George Graham

SAMPDORIA: Walter Zenga, Moreno Mannini, Stefano Sacchetti, Marco Rossi, Michele Serena, Fausto Salsano, Giovanni Invernizzi (76 Riccardo Maspero), Vladimir Jugovic, Alberigo Evani, Attilio Lombardo, Roberto Mancini (Cap). Trainer: Sven Göran Eriksson

Goals: Bould (34, 36), Jugovic (52, 77), Wright (69)

SAMPDORIA GENOVA
v ARSENAL LONDON 3-2 (1-0, 3-2) (AET)
Stadio Luigi Ferraris, Genova   20.04.1995
Referee: Gerd Grabher (AUS)   Attendance: 34,353

SAMPDORIA: Walter Zenga, Moreno Mannini, Riccardo Ferri (75 Claudio Bellucci), Pietro Vierchowod, Michele Serena, Riccardo Maspero, Vladimir Jugovic, Alberigo Evani (60 Giovanni Invernizzi), Sinisa Mihajlovic, Attilio Lombardo, Roberto Mancini (Cap).   Trainer: Sven Göran Eriksson

ARSENAL: David Seaman, Lee Dixon, Steve Bould, Tony Adams (Cap), Nigel Winterburn, Martin Keown, David Hillier (55 Eddie McGoldrick), Stefan Schwarz, Paul Merson, John Hartson, Ian Wright (81 Chris Kiwomya).
Manager: George Graham

Goals: Mancini (14), Wright (60), Belucci (83, 86), Schwarz (87)

Penalties: 0-1 Dixon, Mihajlović (miss), McGoldrick (miss), Jugović (miss), 0-2 Hartson, 1-2 Maspero, 1-3 Adams, 2-3 Mannini, Merson (miss), Lombardo (miss)

CHELSEA LONDON v REAL ZARAGOZA 3-1 (1-0)
Stamford Bridge, London   20.04.1995
Referee: Jorge Emanuel Monteiro Coroado (POR)
Attendance: 26,456

CHELSEA: Kevin Hitchcock, Steve Clarke, Erland Johnsen (61 Glenn Hoddle), Frank Sinclair, Scott Minto; David Rocastle (46 John Spencer), Nigel Spackman, David Lee, Mark Stein, Paul Furlong, Gavin Peacock (Cap).
Manager: Glenn Hoddle

REAL ZARAGOZA: Juan Miguel García Inglés "JUANMI", Alberto BELSUÉ Arias, Fernando Gabriel CÁCERES, ÓSCAR Luis Celada, Jesús Ángel SOLANA Bermejo, Marcos Evangelista de Moraes "CAFU", Miguel PARDEZA Pichardo (Cap), Santiago ARAGÓN Martínez, Mohamed Ali Amar "NAYIM", Juan Eduardo ESNÁIDER Esnaider (83 José Luis Rodríguez LORETO), Francisco HIGUERA Fernández (67 Ángel de Juana García "GELI").   Trainer: Víctor Fernández

Goals: Furlong (30), Aragón (53), Sinclair (62), Stein (86)

REAL ZARAGOZA v CHELSEA LONDON 3-0 (2-0)
Estadio la Romareda, Zaragoza   6.04.1995
Referee: Leif Sundell (SWE)   Attendance: 37,000

REAL ZARAGOZA: Juan Miguel García Inglés "JUANMI", Alberto BELSUÉ Arias, Fernando Gabriel CÁCERES, Javier AGUADO Companys, Jesús Ángel SOLANA Bermejo; Mohamed Ali Amar "NAYIM", Santiago ARAGÓN Martínez (80 Jesús GARCÍA SANJÚAN), Gustavo POYET Domínguez, Miguel PARDEZA Pichardo (Cap) (64 ÓSCAR Luis Celada), Juan Eduardo ESNÁIDER Esnaider, Francisco HIGUERA Fernández.   Trainer: Víctor Fernández

CHELSEA: Kevin Hitchcock, Steve Clarke, Erland Johnsen, Frank Sinclair, Scott Minto, David Rocastle (64 Glenn Hoddle), Nigel Spackman, Andy Myers, Gavin Peacock (Cap), John Spencer (46 Mark Stein), Paul Furlong.
Manager: Glenn Hoddle

Goals: Pardeza (7), Esnáider (25, 56)

FINAL

REAL ZARAGOZA
v ARSENAL LONDON 2-1 (0-0, 1-1) (AET)
Parc des Princes, Paris   10.05.1995
Referee: Piero Ceccarini (ITA)   Attendance: 42,424

REAL ZARAGOZA: Andoni CEDRÚN Ibarra, Alberto BELSUÉ Arias, Fernando Gabriel CÁCERES, Javier AGUADO Companys, Jesús Ángel SOLANA Bermejo; Miguel PARDEZA Pichardo (Cap), Gustavo POYET Domínguez, Santiago ARAGÓN Martínez, Mohamed Ali Amar "NAYIM", Juan Eduardo ESNÁIDER Esnaider, Francisco HIGUERA Fernández (67 Jesús GARCÍA SANJÚAN, 114 Ángel de Juana García "GELI").   Trainer: Víctor Fernández

ARSENAL: David Seaman, Lee Dixon, Andy Linighan, Tony Adams (Cap), Nigel Winterburn (46 Stephen Morrow), Martin Keown (46 David Hillier), Ray Parlour, Stefan Schwarz, Paul Merson, Ian Wright, John Hartson.   Manager: Stewart Houston

Goals: Esnáider (68), Hartson (76), Nayim (120)

Goalscorers European Cup-Winners' Cup 1994-95:

9 goals: Ian Wright (Arsenal)
8 goals: Juan Eduardo ESNÁIDER Esnaider (Real Zaragoza)
7 goals: Henrik Larsson (Feyenoord)
5 goals: Kliton Bozgo (Maribor Branik)
4 goals: Bent Inge Johnsen (FK Bodø Glimt); Robert Kocis (Tatran Prešov),
3 goals: Fortuzi (KS Tirana), Djurovski, Simundza (Maribor Branik), Lipcsei, Neagoe (Ferencváros), Alexoudis, Warzycha (Panathinaikos), Staelens (Club Brugge), Lamouchi (Auxerre), Furlong (Chelsea), Zvara (Tatran Prešov), Poyet, Pardeza (Zaragoza)
2 goals: Yaromko (Fandok Bobruisk), Hansson (IFK Norrkøping), Tanasic (Keflavvk), Klinger (Maccabi Tel Aviv), R.Berg (Bodø Glimt), Majoros (Viktoria Zizkov), Vencevicius, Karvelis (Zalgiris Vilnius), Nixon (Dundee United), Orachev, Ianev (Pirin Blagoevgrad), Vanhala, Lius (HJK Helsinki), Gutalj (Maribor Branik), Christiansen, Zavadszky, Szekeres, Páling (Ferencváros), Bickel, Koller (Grasshopper), Ertugrul, Oktay (Beşiktaş), Beschastnîh, Basler (Werder Bremen), Kubica (Austria Wien), Strudal, Bo Hansen (Brøndby IF), Verheyen (Club Brugge), Heus (Feyenoord), Rui Barros, Drulovic, Domingos (FC Porto), Diomède (Auxerre), Jugovic, Belucci, Mancini, Melli, Lombardo, Platt (Sampdoria), Sinclair, Stein (Chelsea), Merson, Schwarz, Bould (Arsenal)
1 goal: Rostkov (Norma Tallin), Khripach, Savostikov (Fandok Bobruisk), Belous (Tiligul Tiraspol), Fanelli, Morgante (F 91 Dudelange), Stefanovic (Floriana), Vaattovaara (IFK Norrköping), Nimni, A.Brumer, G.Brumer, Driks (Maccabi Tel Aviv), Staurvik, Berstad, Björkan (Bodø Glimt), Malekos, Gogrichiani, Kantilos, Tutic, Savvidis (Omonoia Nicosia), Poborsky, Trval, Kordule, Vrabec (Viktoria Zizkov), Kenny, Rooney, Moran, D.Reid, Brennan (Sligo Rovers), Radimov, Mamchur, Sergeev (CSKA Moskva), Miloti (KS Tirana), Tereskinas, Baltusnikas, Poderis, Maciulevicius, Jankauskas (Zalgiris Vilnius), Bozgo (Maribor Branik), Petric, Hannah (Dundee United), Heinola, Kottila, Suokonautio, Rantanen (HJK Helsinki), Petrov (Pirin Blagoevgrad), Guseinov (Chornomorets Odessa), Galic, Milevski (Maribor Branik), M.Răduţă, Lungu (Gloria Bistriţa), Jelicic, Soldo, Pamic (Croatia Zagreb), Albert, Lisztes (Ferencváros), Nioplias, Borelli (Panathinaikos), Willems, Subiat (Grasshopper), Mehmet (Beşiktaş), Bode (Werder Bremen), Narbekovas, Prosenik, Flögel (Austria Wien), Eggen, B.Jensen (Brøndby IF), Skalka, Nenadic, Matta, Höger (Tatran Prešov), Vermant, Eykelkamp (Club Brugge), Yuran, Jorge Costa, Aloísio, Drulovic (FC Porto), Verlaat, Saib, Martins, Mahé (Auxerre), Mihajlovic, Maspero, Bertarelli (Sampdoria), Spencer, Rocastle, Wise (Chelsea), Hartson, Smith, Selley (Arsenal), Nayim, Aragón, Oscar, Aguado (Zaragoza)
Own goals: Radimov (CSKA Moskva) for Ferencváros, Malko (KS Tirana) for Brøndby IF, Varga (Tatran Prešov) for Zaragoza

CUP WINNERS' CUP 1995-96

PRELIMINARY ROUND

CS GREVENMACHER v KR REYKJAVÍK 3-2 (1-0)
Op Flohr, Luxembourg 9.08.1995
Referee: José Enrique Rubio Valdivieso (SPA) Att: 1,025
CS GREVENMACHER: Paul Koch; Laurent Giesser, Thomas Wolf, Pierre Petry, Jörg Lauer, Nico Funck, Jerry Jungblut (80 Adelino Dias), Marc Thomé (Cap), Sacha Schneider, Achim Wilbois, Lidio Alves Silva. Trainer: Alfons Jochem
KR: Kristján Finnbogason; Sigurdur Örn Jónsson (46 Hilmar Björnsson), Thormódur Egilsson (Cap), Oskar Thorvaldsson, Brynjar Gunnarsson, Izudin Dadi Dervic; Salih Heimir Porca (65 Magnús Orri Schram), Heimir Gudjónsson, Einar Thór Daníelsson; Mihajlo Bibercic, Gudmundur Benediktsson. Trainer: Gudjón Thórdarson
Goals: Jungblut (8, 52), Bibercic (50), Alves Silva (58), Egilsson (80)

KR REYKJAVÍK v CS GREVENMACHER 2-0 (1-0)
Laugardalsvöllur, Reykjavík 22.08.1995
Referee: John Ferry (NIR) Attendance: 932
KR: Kristján Finnbogason; Sigurdur Örn Jónsson, Steinar Adolfsson, Thormódur Egilsson (Cap), Izudin Dadi Dervic; Hilmar Björnsson, Salih Heimir Porca, Heimir Gudjónsson (89 Brynjar Gunnarsson), Einar Thór Daníelsson; Mihajlo Bibercic, Asmundur Haraldsson (68 Gudmundur Benediktsson). Trainer: Gudjón Thórdarson
CS GREVENMACHER: Paul Koch; Elmar Klodt, Thomas Wolf, Laurent Giesser (46 Adelino Dias), Pierre Petry, Nico Funck, Jerry Jungblut, Marc Thomé (Cap), Sacha Schneider, Achim Wilbois, Lidio Alves Silva. Trainer: Alfons Jochem
Goals: Biberic (45), Porca (67)

TILIGUL TIRASPOL v FC SION 0-0
Republican, Chişinău 10.08.1995
Referee: Veselin Bogdanov (BUL) Attendance: 5,000
TILIGUL: Evgheni Ivanov; Serghei Secu, Anatoli Luchiancicov (69 Alexandru Cotlear), Vladimir Gaidamaşciuc (76 Vladimir Dovghii), Valeri Pogorelov, Serghei Stroenco, Andrei Stroenco (46 Nicolae Mincev), Serghei Parhomenco, Serghei Belous, Vladimir Kosse, Igor Oprea. Trainer: Nikolai Mandrichenko
FC SION: Stephan Lehmann; Patrick Sylvestre, Yvan Quentin, Antoine Kombouaré, Dominique Herr, Raphaël Wicky, Jean-Pierre La Placa (61 Mirandinha Isailton), Sébastien Fournier, Frédéric Chassot, Philippe Vercruysse, Christophe Bonvin (80 Heinz Moser). Trainer: Michel Decastel

FC SION v TILIGUL TIRASPOL 3-2 (3-0)

Stade de Tourbillon, Sion 23.08.1995

Referee: Theodoros Kefalas (GRE)   Attendance: 12,000

FC SION: Stephan Lehmann; Patrick Sylvestre, Yvan Quentin (72 Patrick Bühlmann), Antoine Kombouaré, Dominique Herr, Raphäel Wicky, Heinz Moser, Sébastien Fournier (64 Gaetano Giallanza), Frédéric Chassot (67 Mirandinha Isailton), Philippe Vercruysse, Christophe Bonvin.
Trainer: Michel Decastel

TILIGUL: Evgheni Ivanov; Serghei Secu, Anatoli Luchiancicov, Valeri Pogorelov, Vladimir Gaidamaşciuc (76 Igor Ţîtîc), Serghei Stroenco, Andrei Stroenco (70 Alexandru Popovici), Nicolae Mincev, Serghei Belous, Vladimir Kosse, Igor Oprea.   Trainer: Nikolai Mandrichenko

Goals: Moser (23), Herr (29), Bonvin (45), Oprea (79), Popovici (90)

VÁC FC SAMSUNG v SILEKS KRATOVO 1-1 (0-0)

Városi, Vác 10.08.1995

Referee: Zygmunt Ziober (POL)   Attendance: 5,400

SAMSUNG: István Hámori; Tibor Nagy (Cap), István Kasza, Gábor Puglits; József Nyikos (34 Izedunor Austin), Csaba Vojtekovszki, Péter Vig (64 Tamás Sándor), Zoltán Schwarcz, János Romanek; Csaba Andrássy, István Borgulya (62 Béla Hanyecz).   Trainer: Dénes Tóth

SILEKS: Kiro Trajcev (Cap), Jovance Bizimoski, Marjan Nikolov, Arse Andovski (81 Igor Duzelov), Nedzmedin Memed, Vlatko Ljusev, Ljubodrag Milosević, Srdjan Zaharievski, Rade Karanfilovski (89 Trajca Senev), Ilco Borov, Toni Micevski (80 Zoran Angelović), Srdjan Zaharievski.
Trainer: Zoran Smilevski

Goals: Micevski (57), Romanek (90)

SILEKS KRATOVO v VÁC FC SAMSUNG 3-1 (1-1)

Kratovo 24.08.1995

Referee: Karl Finzinger (AUS)   Attendance: 10,200

SILEKS: Kiro Trajcev (Cap), Marjan Nikolov, Jovance Bizimovski (69 Igor Duzelov), Ljubodrag Milosević, Arse Andovski, Nedzmedin Memed, Vlatko Ljusev, Ilco Borov, Rade Karanfilovski, Srdjan Zaharievski (87 Zoran Angelović), Toni Micevski (68 Sreten Milosovski).   Trainer: Zoran Smilevski

SAMSUNG: István Hámori; Tibor Nagy (Cap), Gábor Puglits (49 Vladimir Siago), István Kasza; Csaba Vojtekovszki, Zoltán Schwarcz, Péter Vig, János Romanek (70 Tamás Sándor), József Nyikos; István Borgulya, Izedunor Austin (46 Csaba Andrássy).   Trainer: Dénes Tóth

Goals: Memed (15, 67), Borgulya (21), Borov (36)

JALKAPALLO TPS TURKU v FC TEUTA DURRËS 1-0 (1-0)

Kupittaa, Turku 10.08.1995

Referee: Nikolai Levnikov (RUS)   Attendance: 2,985

TPS: Panu Toivonen; Marco Casagrande, Jani Keula, Petri Sulonen (Cap), Janne Oinas, John Allen (88 Janne Savolainen), Mika Wallden, Jasse Jalonen, Tom Enberg, Jani Pylkäs, Jonatan Johansson (79 Tommi Virtanen).   Trainer: Juha Malinen

TEUTA: Xhevair Kapllani; Ardian Abazi (Cap), Marenglen Xhai, Nesti Qendro, Artan Koka, Mikel Furrxhi, Ilir Alliu, Artan Vila, Enkelejd Dobi (71 Alban Mehmeti), Elton Koça, Ardian Bushi.   Trainer: Bashkim Koka

Goal: Wallden (29 pen)

FC TEUTA DURRËS v JALKAPALLO TPS TURKU 3-0 (2-0)

Qemal Stafa, Tirana 24.08.1995

Referee: Stefan Tivold (SVN)   Attendance: 2,800

TEUTA: Xhevair Kapllani; Artan Koka, Ardian Abazi (Cap), Mikel Furrxhi, Nesti Qendro, Ilir Alliu, Artan Vila, Enkelejd Dobi (86 Gentjan Begeja), Ardian Dashi (83 Alban Mehmeti), Elton Koça, Ardian Bushi (83 Gazmend Çanaku).
Trainer: Bashkim Koka

TPS: Panu Toivonen; Marco Casagrande, Jani Keula, Petri Sulonen (Cap), Kimmo Miettinen, John Allen, Janne Savolainen (46 Jasse Jalonen), Mika Wallden (69 Tommi Virtanen), Tom Enberg, Jani Pylkäs, Jonatan Johansson (84 Jani Peltola).   Trainer: Juha Malinen

Goals: Vila (8), Koça (19), Bushi (55)

FC VADUZ v SK HRADEC KRALOVE 0-5 (0-3)

Sportpark, Eschen/Mauren 10.08.1995

Referee: Mateo Beusan (CRO)   Attendance: 1,170

FC VADUZ: Martin Heeb; Jürg Ritter, Hugo Hasler, Daniel Hasler (Cap), Daniel Moser, Eduard Kindle (62 Jürgen Ospelt), Andrea Beeli, Harry Zech, Marco Perez, Matek Nikolic (46 Thomas Hanselmann); Daniele Polverino (75 Frank Fremuth).
Trainer: Hans-Ruedi Fässler

SK HRADEC KRALOVE: Stanislav Vahala; Jaroslav Vrabel, Tomas Urban, Karel Urbanek, Ivo Ulich, Milan Ptacek, Ales Hynek (69 Petr Drozd), Pavel Cerny, Michal Smarda (Cap), Petr Samec (75 Daniel Masek), Marek Kincl (58 Radim Holub).   Trainer: Ludek Zajic

Goals: Cerny (15), Samec (30, 49, 59), Ptacek (37)

SK HRADEC KRALOVE v FC VADUZ 9-1 (5-1)

Všesportovní Hradec, Kralové 24.08.1995

Referee: Vladimir Pianních (Ucr)   Attendance: 3,558

SK HRADEC KRALOVE: Tomas Postulka; Rudolf Rehák, Tomas Urban, Jaroslav Vrabel (64 Bohuslav Pilny), Ivo Ulich, Josef Dzubara, Milan Ptacek, Pavel Cerny, Michal Smarda (Cap) (58 Petr Drozd), Petr Samec (71 Daniel Masek), Radim Holub.   Trainer: Ludek Zajic

FC VADUZ: Oliver Gassner; Daniel Moser, Hugo Hasler, Daniel Hasler (Cap), Andreas Birchler; Jürg Ritter (85 Foser), Thomas Hanselmann (46 Daniel Hemmerle), Andrea Beeli, Harry Zech, Jürgen Ospelt (76 Jürgen Frick); Daniele Polverino.   Trainer: Hans-Ruedi Fässler

Goals: Samec (4, 9, 30, 53), Urban (15, 82 pen), Ritter (27), Vrabel (37), Smarda (50 pen), Ptacek (63)

WREXHAM FC v PETROLUL PLOIEȘTI 0-0

Racecourse Ground, Wrexham 10.08.1995

Referee: Finn Lambek (DEN)   Attendance: 4,308

WREXHAM: Andy Marriott; Deryn Brace, Barry Hunter, Barry Jones, Phil Hardy (Cap), Wayne Phillips, Steve Futcher, Gareth Owen, Kieron Durkan; Karl Connolly, Steve Watkin. Trainer: Brian Flynn

PETROLUL: Ștefan Gabriel Preda; Daniel Chiriță, Gheorghe Adrian Bălăceanu, Valeriu Răchită (Cap), Gheorghe Aurelian Leahu, Octavian Grigore, Mihai Pîrlog (81 Daniel Eugen Baștină), Marcel Cristian Abăluță, Cristian Zmoleanu, Adrian Orlin Toader (87 Marian Mihai), Daniel Zafiris (70 Ion Claudiu Andreicuț).   Trainer: Ion Marin

APOEL NICOSIA v NEFTCHI BAKU 3-0 (2-0)

Makarion, Nicosia 10.08.1995

Referee: Ceri Richards (WAL)   Attendance: 12,600

APOEL: Andreas Petridis; Aristos Aristokleous, Nikos Haralampous, Giorgos Hristodoulou, Toza Sapuric, István Kozma, Antonis Antoniou, Kálmán Kovács (65 Alexis Alexandrou), Antros Sotiriou, Giannis Ioannou (Cap) (82 Hristakis Pounas), Loukas Hatziloukas (88 Xenios Aristotelous).   Trainer: Hristo Bonev

NEFTCHI: Elhan Hasanov; Vugar Ismaylov, Mekhman Yunusov, Mirza Asadullaev, Vyacheslav Lychkin, Mirbagir Isayev (41 Mais Azimov), Yunis Huseynov (Cap), Yashar Vahabzade, Bakhtiar Musayev, Nazim Aliyev (75 Kamil Bairamov), Samir Alekberov.   Trainer: Vaguif Sadhikov

Goals: Antoniou (18), Ioannou (44, 66)

PETROLUL PLOIEȘTI v WREXHAM FC 1-0 (0-0)

Petrolul Ploiești 24.08.1995

Referee: Oguz Sarvan (TUR)   Attendance: 9,000

PETROLUL: Ștefan Gabriel Preda; Daniel Chiriță, Gheorghe Aurelian Leahu, Gheorghe Adrian Bălăceanu, Octavian Grigore, Valeriu Răchită (Cap), Mihai Pîrlog, Marcel Cristian Abăluță, Daniel Zafiris (65 Adrian Orlin Toader), Cristian Zmoleanu (89 Daniel Eugen Baștină), Ion Claudiu Andreicuț (87 Lucian Balaban).   Trainer: Ion Marin

WREXHAM: Andy Marriott; Andrew Thomas, Phil Hardy (Cap), Wayne Phillips, Barry Hunter, Barry Jones, Steve Futcher (72 Richard Barnes), Gareth Owen, Karl Connolly, Steve Watkin, Jonathan Cross.   Trainer: Brian Flynn

Goal: Pîrlog (59)

NEFTCHI BAKU v APOEL NICOSIA 0-0

Tofig Bakhramov, Baku 24.08.1995

Referee: Dan Drago̦s Crăciun (ROM)   Attendance: 3,600

NEFTCHI: Elhan Hasanov; Vugar Ismaylov, Mekhman Yunusov, Arif Asadov, Vyacheslav Lychkin, Mais Azimov, Yunis Huseynov (Cap), Yashar Vahabzade, Bakhtiar Musayev (61 Kamil Bairamov), Nazim Aliyev (46 Mirbagir Isayev), Samir Alekberov.   Trainer: Vaguif Sadhikov

APOEL: Andreas Petridis; Aristos Aristokleous (70 Nikos Timotheou), Nikos Haralampous, Giorgos Hristodoulou, Toza Sapuric, István Kozma, Antonis Antoniou (62 Hristakis Pounas), Kálmán Kovács, Antros Sotiriou (78 Alexis Alexandrou), Giannis Ioannou (Cap), Loukas Hatziloukas. Trainer: Hristo Bonev

VALLETTA FC v INTER BRATISLAVA 0-0

National Ta'Qali 10.08.1995

Referee: Branimir Babarogić (YUG)   Attendance: 1,084

FC VALLETTA: Reggie Cini; Robert Spiteri, Jeffrey Chetcuti, Joe Camilleri, Darren Debono, Ivan Zammit, Gilbert Agius, Ragab Sazentati, Danilo Doncic (85 Ivan Woods), Joe Zarb (Cap), Jeremy Agius (66 Stefan Giglio).
Trainer: Edward Aquilina

INTER: Miroslav Hyll; Lubos Tomko, Boris Kitka, Martin Sevela, Martin Kuna (74 Jozef Dojcan); Dušan Rupec, Roman Greguska, Martin Obsitnik (Cap), Karol Schulz; Radovan Vasik (65 Lubos Luhovy), Tomas Medved.   Trainer: Jozef Adamec

INTER BRATISLAVA v VALLETTA FC 5-2 (3-0)
Inter Bratislava 24.08.1995
Referee: Valeri Onufer (UKR)   Attendance: 2,374
INTER: Miroslav Hyll; Lubos Tomko, Martin Sevela, Martin Kuna (10 Ivan Schulcz, 75 Jozef Dojcan), Karol Schulz; Dušan Rupec, Roman Greguska, Martin Obsitnik (Cap); Radovan Vasik, Tomas Medved, Lubos Luhovy (71 Rolf Landerl). Trainer: Jozef Adamec
FC VALLETTA: Reggie Cini; Joe Camilleri, Jeffrey Chetcuti, Kristian Laferla (Cap), Darren Debono, Ivan Zammit, Gilbert Agius, Nicky Saliba, Danilo Doncic, Joe Zarb, Stefan Giglio (55 Robert Spiteri).   Trainer: Edward Aquilina
Sent off: Camilleri (62)
Goals: Rupec (10), Tomko (15, 58), Doncic (61), Greguska (79), Zarb (84), Landerl (85)

**ZALGIRIS VILNIUS
v NK MURA MURSKA SOBOTA 2-0** (0-0)
Zalgiris Vilnius 10.08.1995
Referee: Sergo Kvaratskhelia (Geo)   Attendance: 1,800
ZALGIRIS: Alvydas Koncevicius; Rimas Skirmantas (51 Tomas Zvirgzdauskas), Gintaras Rimkus, Dainius Suliauskas, Ramunas Stonkus, Donatos Vencevicius, Vytautas Karvelis (44 Grazvydas Mikulenas), Andrius Tereskinas, Aidas Preiksaitis, Virginijus Baltusnikas (Cap), Edgaras Jankauskas. Trainer: Benjaminas Zelkevicius
MURA: Stefan Cernjavić; Vladimir Kokol, Simon Baranja, Peter Breznik, Miroslav Stampfer, Haris Alihodzić, Janez Kardos, Damjan Gajser, Robert Belec (80 Bojan Rous), Marijan Bakula (Cap), Mikhail Hlebalin (74 Marko Kmetec). Trainer: Marin Kovacić
Goals: Baltusnikas (53), Tereskinas (67)

**SHAKHTAR DONETSK
v FC LINFIELD BELFAST 4-1** (3-0)
Shakhtar Donetsk 10.08.1995
Referee: Lubos Michel (SVK)   Attendance: 27,600
SHAKHTAR: Dmytro Shutkov; Volodymyr Pyatenko, Olexandr Koval, Giorgi Chikhradze, Sergiy Kochvar, Olexandr Spivak, Hennadiy Orbu, Serhiy Atelkin (14 Andriy Fedkov, 75 Alexander Voskoboinik), Igor Petrov (Cap), Valeriy Kriventsov, Oleh Matveyev.   Trainer: Volodymyr Salkov
LINFIELD: Wesley Lamont; Peter Crothers, John Easton, Alan Ewing, Stuart McLean, Stephen Beatty, Raymond Campbell, Paul McGee, Darren Erskine, Jeff Spiers, Noel Bailie (Cap).   Trainer: Trevor Anderson
Goals: Atelkin (10), Matveyev (18), Orbu (28, 90), Ewing (47)

**NK MURA MURSKA SOBOTA v ZALGIRIS
VILNIUS 2-1** (1-0)
Fazanerija, Murska Sobota 24.08.1995
Referee: Georgios Bikas (GRE)   Attendance: 2,950
MURA: Stefan Cernjavić; Simon Baranja, Vladimir Kokol, Franc Cifer, Andrej Poljsak, Haris Alihodzić, Danijel Brezić (61 Marko Kmetec), Damjan Gajser, Peter Breznik, Marijan Bakula (Cap), Miroslav Stampfer (69 Ingmar Bloudek).   Trainer: Marin Kovacić
ZALGIRIS: Alvydas Koncevicius; Andrius Tereskinas, Virginijus Baltusnikas (Cap), Tomas Zvirgzdauskas, Dainius Suliauskas, Ramunas Stonkus (85 Arunas Pukelevicius), Aidas Preiksaitis, Donatos Vencevicius, Gintaras Rimkus, Grazvydas Mikulenas, Edgaras Jankauskas.   Trainer: Benjaminas Zelkevicius
Goals: Kokol (15), Vencevicius (73), Alihodzić (89)

**FC LINFIELD BELFAST
v SHAKHTAR DONETSK 0-1** (0-0)
Windsor Park, Belfast 24.08.1995
Referee: Juha Hirviniemi (FIN)   Attendance: 2,360
LINFIELD: Wesley Lamont; Alan Dornan, John Easton, Alan Ewing (77 Ian McCoosh), Jeff Spiers, Stephen Beatty (58 Ryan McLaughlin), Raymond Campbell, Dessie Gorman, Darren Erskine, Pat Fenlon, Noel Bailie (Cap).
Trainer: Trevor Anderson
SHAKHTAR: Andriy Nikitin; Volodymyr Pyatenko, Olexandr Koval, Giorgi Chikhradze, Serhiy Popov, Sergiy Kochvar, Hennadiy Orbu, Alexander Voskoboinik, Igor Petrov (Cap) (46 Dmytro Shutkov), Valeriy Kriventsov (78 Ihor Leonov), Oleh Matveyev (86 Andriy Fedkov).   Trainer: Volodymyr Salkov
Sent off: Nikitin (45)
Goal: Voskoboinik (86)

GKS KATOWICE v ARARAT EREVAN 2-0 (2-0)
GKS Katowice 10.08.1995
Referee: Rune Pedersen (NOR)   Attendance: 2,700
GKS: Janusz Jojko; Adam Ledwon, Marek Swierczewski (Cap), Kazimierz Wegrzyn, Grzegorz Borawski, Miroslaw Widuch, Dariusz Marzec, Slawomir Wojciechowski, Adam Kucz (63 Wojciech Szala), Bartosz Karwan (46 Grzegorz Pawluszek), Arkadiusz Bilski (79 Krzysztof Walczak).   Trainer: Orest Lenczyk
ARARAT: Harutyun Abrahamyan (58 Armen Petrosyan); Armen Shahgeldyan, Tigran Gsepyan, Aramais Tonoyan (Cap), Levon Stepanyan, Araik Nigoyan (82 Karen Barsegyan), Akop Mkyran, Akop Ter-Petrosyan, Hamlet Mkhitaryan, Sevada Arzumanyan, Karen Mikaelyan (46 Artur Kocharyan).
Trainer: Samuel Darbinyam
Goals: Bilski (26), Karwan (29)

**ARARAT EREVAN
v GKS KATOWICE 2-0** (2-0, 2-0) (AET)

Razdan, Erevan 24.08.1995

Referee: Gennadi Yakubovski (BLS)   Attendance: 3,000

ARARAT: Armen Petrosyan; Armen Shahgeldyan, Tigran Gsepyan, Aramais Tonoyan (Cap), Levon Stepanyan, Araik Nigoyan, Erik Ayrapetyan, Akop Ter-Petrosyan (61 Artur Kocharyan), Hamlet Mkhitaryan, Sevada Arzumanyan (26 Haik Harutyunyan), Aram Voskanyan.   Trainer: Samuel Darbinyam

GKS: Janusz Jojko; Adam Ledwon, Marek Swierczewski (Cap), Kazimierz Wegrzyn, Grzegorz Borawski (46 Bartosz Karwan), Miroslaw Widuch, Dariusz Marzec (46 Wojciech Szala), Slawomir Wojciechowski, Adam Kucz, Zdzislaw Strojek, Arkadiusz Bilski (115 Grzegorz Pawluszek).   Trainer: Orest Lenczyk

Goals: Gsepyan (23), Tonoyan (26 pen)

Ararat Erevan won 5-4 on penalties

**FK OBILIC BEOGRAD
v DINAMO BATUMI 0-1** (0-0)

"Milos Obilić", Beograd 10.08.1995

Referee: Roland Beck (Liec)   Attendance: 418

OBILIC: Aleksandr Sarić; Sesa Zorić (Cap), Jovo Aranitović, Ratko Vukcević, Darko Nović, Blagota Vilotijević (7 Daniel Marković), Branko Rasić, Davor Tasić, Petar Puaca (72 Sladjan Spasić), Dragan Sarac, Veselin Popović.
Trainer: Branko Nikolić

DINAMO: Aslan Baladze; Soso Malania, Valeri Shanidze, Rostom Torgashvili (65 Amiran Mudjiri), Tengiz Sichinava, Gela Shekiladze, Malkhaz Makharadze (Cap), Paata Machutadze, David Ujmajuridze, Temur Tugushi, Zurab Mindadze (81 Avtandil Glonti).
Trainer: Valerian Chkhartishvili

Goal: Machutadze (71)

**DINAMO BATUMI
v FC OBILIC BELGRAD 2-2** (0-2)

Central Batumi 24.08.1995

Referee: Leif Sundell (SWE)   Attendance: 18,000

DINAMO: Aslan Baladze; Soso Malania (46 Avtandil Glonti), Valeri Shanidze (78 Aleksandre Kantidze), Tengiz Sichinava (46 Amiran Mudjiri), Gela Shekiladze, Rostom Torgashvili, Malkhaz Makharadze (Cap), Paata Machutadze, David Ujmajuridze, Temur Tugushi, Zurab Mindadze.
Trainer: Valerian Chkhartishvili

OBILIC: Aleksandr Sarić; Sesa Zorić (Cap), Daniel Marković, Darko Nović (67 Dragan Steković), Ratko Vukcević, Blagota Vilotijević, Sladjan Spasić, Branko Rasić (56 Nenad Kostić), Dragan Sarac, Veselin Popović, Davor Tasić (80 Jovo Aranitović).   Trainer: Branko Nikolić

Goals: Sarac (8), Popović (35), Machutadze (65), Mudjiri (82 pen)

**DERRY CITY LONDONDERRY
v LOKOMOTIV SOFI 1-0** (1-0)

Brandywell Derry 10.08.1995

Referee: Marnix Sandra (BEL)   Attendance: 4,860

DERRY: Tony O'Dowd; Pascal Vaudequin, Paul McLaughlin (Cap), Harry McCourt, Paul Curran, Paul Carlyle, Paul Doolin, Sandy Fraser, Stuart Gauld, Liam Coyle, Tom Mohan (60 Gary Heaney).   Trainer: Felix Healy

LOKOMOTIV: Rumen Apostolov, Anton Velkov (Cap), Valeri Iochev, Iordan Marinov, Adalbert Zafirov, Dian Angelov, Dian Petkov, Boris Khvoinev (55 Georgi Borisov), Ivan Radivojevic, Hristo Koilov, Doncho Donev.   Trainer: Grigor Petkov

Goal: McCourt (43)

**LOKOMOTIV SOFIA
v DERRY CITY LONDONDERRY 2-0** (2-0)

Lokomotiv Sofia 24.08.1995

Referee: Anastasios Papaioannou (CYP)   Attendance: 3,600

LOKOMOTIV: Rumen Apostolov, Anton Velkov (Cap), Hristo Koilov, Georgi Borisov (84 Iordan Marinov), Adalbert Zafirov, Ivo Slavchev, Dian Angelov, Boris Khvoinev, Ivan Radivojevic, Dian Petkov (88 Georgi Antonov), Doncho Donev.   Trainer: Grigor Petkov

DERRY: Tony O'Dowd; Pascal Vaudequin, Paul McLaughlin (Cap), Peter Hutton, Paul Curran, Paul Carlyle, Paul Doolin, Harry McCourt (65 Anthony Tohill), Liam Coyle, Stuart Gauld, Tom Mohan.   Trainer: Felix Healy

Goals: Slavchev (6), Khvoinev (29)

**MACCABI HAIFA v KLAKSVIKAR
ÍTROTTARFELAG KLAKKSVIK 4-0** (2-0)

Kiriat Eliezer, Haifa 10.08.1995

Referee: Vencel Toth (HUN)   Attendance: 7,200

MACCABI: Rafi Cohen; Avishai Zano, Alon Harazi, Roman Pets, Moshe Glam; Alon Hazan (Cap), Sergei Kandaurov (76 Haim Silvas), Roni Levi, Haim Revivo (61 Offer Shitrit), Eyal Berkovich; Alon Mizrahi.   Trainer: Avraham Aboukarat

KÍ: Jon William Joensen; Samal Eydfinn Poulsen, Arnold Joensen, Jan Andreasen (Cap), Simun Waag Högnesen (65 Finn Baldvinsson), Josvein Jacobsen, Olgar Danielsen (85 Gunnar a Steig), Jan Joensen, Allan Mörköre, John Hansen, Harley Bertholdsen.   Trainer: Sverri Jacobsen

Sent off: Jon Joensen (85)

Goals: Mizrahi (9, 36, 84 pen), Shitrit (67)

KLAKSVIKAR ÍTROTTARFELAG KLAKKSVIK v MACCABI HAIFA 3-2 (0-1)

Svangaskard, Toftir 24.08.1995

Referee: Richard O'Hanlon (EIRE) Attendance: 295

KÍ: Gunnar a Steig; Samal Eydfinn Poulsen, Allan Joensen, Harley Bertholdsen, Jan Andreasen (Cap), John Hansen, Jan Joensen, Allan Mörköre (88 Simun Eliasen), Simun Waag Högnesen, Johan Lutzen (46 Olgar Danielsen), Hedin a Lakjuni (46 Arnold Joensen). Trainer: Sverri Jacobsen

MACCABI: Rafi Cohen; Avishai Zano, Alon Harazi, Roman Pets, Moshe Glam (46 Marco Balbul); Eyal Berkovich (75 Offer Shitrit), Haim Revivo, Roni Levi, Alon Hazan (Cap), Sergei Kandaurov; Alon Mizrahi. Trainer: Avraham Aboukarat

Goals: Revivo (32), Danielsen (53, 63, 70), Shitrit (82)

DINAMO 93 MINSK v MOLDE FK 1-1 (1-0)

Dinamo Minsk 10.08.1995

Referee: Claude Detruche (SWI) Attendance: 8,700

DINAMO 93: Alexandr Evnevich; Sergei Pavlyuchuk (Cap), Vadim Lasovski (68 Oleg Avgul), Andrei Dovnar, Andrei Lavrik, Andrei Shilo (57 Igor Tarlovski), Sergei Shushkevich, Sergei Gotsmanov (72 Fedor Sikorski), Vadim Skripchenko, Pavel Shavrov, Andrei Lobanov. Trainer: Viktor Sokol

MOLDE: Morten Bakke; Trond Andersen, José Glaria "Flaco", Petter Christian Singsaas, Knut Anders Fostervold (6 Bjarte Skuseth); Daniel Berg Hestad, Petter Rudi (Cap), Tarje Nordstrand Jacobsen, Arild Stavrum, Ole Gunnar Solskjaer, Ole Björn Sundgot. Trainer: Age Hareide

Goals: Lobanov (37), Solskjaer (85)

MOLDE FK v DINAMO 93 MINSK 2-1 (1-1)

Nya Molde 24.08.1995

Referee: Jürgen Aust (GER) Attendance: 2,989

MOLDE: Morten Bakke; Trond Andersen, Sindre Rekdal, José Glaria "Flaco", Knut Anders Fostervold; Daniel Berg Hestad, Petter Rudi (Cap), Tarje Nordstrand Jacobsen (60 Bjarte Skuseth), Arild Stavrum, Ole Gunnar Solskjaer, Ole Björn Sundgot. Trainer: Age Hareide

DINAMO 93: Alexandr Evnevich; Oleg Avgul, Sergei Gotsmanov, Andrei Dovnar, Sergei Pavlyuchuk, Fedor Sikorski (Cap), Sergei Shushkevich, Igor Tarlovski (79 Dmitri Bespanski), Vadim Skripchenko, Pavel Shavrov, Andrei Lobanov (68 Andrei Turchinovich). Trainer: Viktor Sokol

Goals: Solskjaer (4), Skripchenko (19), A. Stavrum (67)

DAG LIEPAYA v FC LANTANA TALLINN 1-2 (1-1)

Daugava, Riga 10.08.1995

Referee: Tomasz Mikulski (POL) Attendance: 1,200

DAG: Erik Grigyan; Andrei Osichenko, Yonas Kibartas, Janis Rimkus (30 Roman Kalyuzhny, 56 Ainars Bukovsky), Valeri Movko, Rolands Kragliks, Victor Dobretsov, Victor Baskakov, Janis Intenbergs, Ainars Linards (Cap), Tagir Fasakhov (50 Maxim Kasyan). Trainer: Victor Nesterenko

FC LANTANA: Sergei Ussoltsev; Andrei Krasnopjorov, Igor Bahmatski, Igor Prins (Cap), Juri Lebret, Urmas Hepner, Sergei Bragin (86 Juri Tsurilkin), Andris Lapsa, Andrei Borisov, Andrei Lapuskin, Sergei Leontjev (42 Maksim Gruznov, 84 Dmitri Nalivaiko). Trainer: Anatoli Belov

Goals: Dobretsev (6), Lapsa (18), Borisov (75)

FC Lantana fielded an ineligible player. The match was awarded 3-0 to DAG Liepaya.

FC LANTANA TALLINN v DAG LIEPAYA 0-0

Kadriorg, Tallinn 24.08.1995

Referee: Bohdan Benedikt (SVK) Attendance: 340

FC LANTANA: Sergei Ussoltsev; Andrei Krasnopjorov, Igor Bahmatski, Igor Prins (Cap), Juri Lebret, Urmas Hepner, Sergei Bragin, Andris Lapsa, Maksim Gruznov (37 Oleg Gorjatsov), Andrei Lapuskin, Sergei Leontjev (66 Dmitri Nalivaiko). Trainer: Anatoli Belov

DAG: Erik Grigyan; Andrei Osichenko (84 Andrei Stepanov), Yonas Kibartas, Janis Rimkus (66 Roman Kalyuzhny), Valeri Movko, Rolands Kragliks, Maxim Kasyan, Victor Baskakov, Ainars Bukovsky (72 Victor Dobretsov), Ainars Linards (Cap), Normunds Zile. Trainer: Victor Nesterenko

FIRST ROUND

DAG LIEPAYA v FEYENOORD ROTTERDAM 0-7 (0-1)

Daugava Liepaya 14.09.1995

Referee: Sven Kjelbrot (NOR) Attendance: 3,150

DAG: Erik Grigyan; Normunds Zile, Rolands Kragliks, Yonas Kibartas, Andrei Osichenko, Janis Rimkus, Valeri Movko (73 Vladlen Osipov), Victor Baskakov (55 Roman Kalyuzhny), Maxim Kasyan, Ainars Linards (Cap), Tagir Fasakhov (46 Victor Dobretsov). Trainer: Victor Nesterenko

FEYENOORD: Ed de Goey; George Boateng, Ronald Koeman (Cap), Ulrich van Gobbel, Ruud Heus, Gaston Taument, Rob Maas, Orlando Trustfull, Giovanni van Bronckhorst, Henrik Larsson (64 Aurelio Vidmar), Regi Blinker (64 Mike Obiku). Trainer: Willem van Hanegem

Goals: Larsson (2, 61), Blinker (47, 58, 62), R. Koeman (78), Obiku (88)

**FEYENOORD ROTTERDAM
v DAG LIEPAYA 6-0** (2-0)

Feyenoord, Rotterdam 28.09.1995

Referee: Brendan Shorte (IRE) Attendance: 10,746

FEYENOORD: Ed de Goey (Cap); Errol Refos, Rob Maas (46 Mike Obiku), Ulrich van Gobbel, Ruud Heus, Gaston Taument, GLÁUCIO DE Jesus Carvalho (72 Chaly Jones), Orlando Trustfull, Giovanni van Bronckhorst, Aurelio Vidmar, Regi Blinker. Trainer: Willem van Hanegem

DAG: Erik Grigyan; Roman Kalyuzhny, Rolands Kragliks, Normunds Zile, Ainars Bukovsky, Victor Baskakov (12 Victor Dobretsov, 81 Janis Intenbergs), Maxim Kasyan, Janis Rimkus, Yonas Kibartas, Ainars Linards (Cap), Tagir Fasakhov (46 Vladlen Osipov). Trainer: Victor Nesterenko

Goals: Heus (37 pen), Trustfull (43), Obiku (57, 63, 65), Gláucio (61)

DINAMO BATUMI v CELTIC GLASGOW 2-3 (1-2)

Central Batumi 14.09.1995

Referee: Amit Klein (Isr) Attendance: 15,200

DINAMO: Aslan Baladze; Soso Malania (46 Aleksandre Kantidze), Valeri Shanidze (86 Badri Putkaradze), Amiran Mudjiri, Gela Shekiladze, Rostom Torgashvili, Malkhaz Makharadze (Cap), Paata Machutadze, Temur Tugushi (85 Avtandil Glonti), David Ujmajuridze (46 David Makharadze), Zurab Mindadze. Trainer: Valerian Chkhartishvili

CELTIC: Gordon Marshall; Thomas Boyd, Tosh McKinlay, Rudi Vata, John Hughes, Peter Grant, Phil O'Donnell, Simon Donnelly (75 William Falconer), Andy Walker (89 Brian McLaughlin), Andreas Thom, John Collins (Cap).
Manager: Tommy Burns

Goals: Machutadze (11), Thom (21, 87), Donnelly (39), Tugushi (68)

CLUB BRUGGE v SHAKHTAR DONETSK 1-0 (0-0)

Olympiastadion, Brugge 14.09.1995

Referee: Vitor Manuel MELO PEREIRA (POR) Attendance: 7,520

CLUB BRUGGE: Danny Verlinden, Tjörven de Brul, Dirk Medved, Pascal Renier, Vital Borkelmans, Sven Vermant, Günther Verjans (56 Gert Verheyen), Franky van der Elst (Cap), Robert Špehar, Gert Claessens, Mario Stanić.
Trainer: Hugo Broos

SHAKHTAR: Dmytro Shutkov; Giorgi Chikhradze, Sergiy Kochvar, Olexandr Koval, Alexander Martyuk, Alexander Voskoboinik (69 Serhiy Onopko), Igor Petrov (Cap), Serhiy Popov, Olexandr Spivak, Hennadiy Orbu, Andriy Fedkov.
Trainer: Valeri Rudakov

Goal: Špehar (88)

CELTIC GLASGOW v DINAMO BATUMI 4-0 (2-0)

Celtic Park Glasgow 28.09.1995

Referee: Gylfi Thor Orasson (ICE) Attendance: 31,969

CELTIC: Gordon Marshall; Thomas Boyd, Tosh McKinlay, Rudi Vata, John Hughes, Peter Grant, Simon Donnelly (56 Chris Hay), Paul McStay (Cap), Pierre Van Hooijdonk (62 Andy Walker), Andreas Thom (70 Stuart Gray), Brian McLaughlin. Manager: Tommy Burns

DINAMO: Nikoloz Togonidze; Valeri Shanidze, Badri Putkaradze (60 Avtandil Glonti), Amiran Mudjiri, Gela Shekiladze, Rostom Torgashvili, Malkhaz Makharadze, Aleksandre Kantidze (46 David Makharadze), Temur Tugushi, David Ujmajuridze, Zurab Mindadze.
Trainer: Valerian Chkhartishvili

Goals: Thom (18, 20), Donnelly (46), Walker (90)

SHAKHTAR DONETSK v CLUB BRUGGE 1-1 (0-0)

Shakhtar Donetsk 28.09.1995

Referee: Gheorghe Constantin (ROM) Attendance: 37,600

SHAKHTAR: Dmytro Shutkov; Giorgi Chikhradze, Sergiy Kochvar, Olexandr Koval (Cap), Mikhailo Starostyak, Alexander Voskoboinik (68 Hennadiy Zubov), Igor Petrov, Ihor Leonov (74 Volodymyr Pyatenko), Olexandr Spivak, Hennadiy Orbu, Andriy Fedkov. Trainer: Valeri Rudakov

CLUB BRUGGE: Danny Verlinden, Tjörven de Brul, Dirk Medved, Pascal Renier, Vital Borkelmans, Gert Verheyen (87 Nzelo Lembi), Lorenzo Staelens, Franky van der Elst (Cap), Sven Vermant, Gert Claessens (81 Stéphane van der Heyden), Mario Stanić. Trainer: Hugo Broos

Goals: Stanić (60), Voskoboinik (61)

**SK HRADEC KRALOVE
v FC KØBENHAVN 5-0** (2-0)

Všesportovni, Hradec Kralove 14.09.1995

Referee: Ilka Koho (FIN) Attendance: 4,532

SK HRADEC KRALOVE: Stanislav Vahala; Rudolf Rehák, Tomas Urban, Karel Urbanek, Josef Dzubara, Ales Hynek, Pavel Cerny, Ivo Ulich (89 Milan Ptacek), Michal Smarda (Cap), Petr Samec (90 Radim Holub), Daniel Masek (86 Daniel Kaplan). Trainer: Ludek Zajic

FC KØBENHAVN: Algimantas Briaunys; Ole Tobiasen, Diego Tur, Carsten Vagn Jensen, Lars-Højer Nielsen (46 Morten Falch), Christian Lønstrup (59 Martin Johansen), Michael "Mio" Nielsen (Cap), Iørn Uldbjerg, Morten Nielsen, Per Frandsen, Michael Johansen (59 Thomas Schønnemann).
Trainer: Michael Schäfer

Goals: Samec (32, 76), Hynek (39), Cerny (53), Ptacek (90)

**FC KØBENHAVN
v SK HRADEC KRALOVE 2-2** (1-2)

Parken, København   28.09.1995

Referee: John Ferry (NIR)   Attendance: 4,432

FC KØBENHAVN: Karim Zaza; Thomas Schønnemann, Diego Tur, Per Frandsen (82 Jesper Sørensen), Lars-Højer Nielsen, Christian Lønstrup, Michael "Mio" Nielsen (Cap), Morten Nielsen (72 Kenny Thorup), Rene Tengstedt, Martin Johansen, Michael Johansen (46 Carsten Vagn Jensen). Trainer: Michael Schäfer

SK HRADEC KRALOVE: Stanislav Vahala; Rudolf Rehák, Tomas Urban (Cap), Jaroslav Vrabel, Josef Dzubara, Ivo Ulich, Ales Hynek, Pavel Cerny, Karel Urbanek (82 Milan Ptacek), Petr Samec (40 Daniel Masek), Daniel Kaplan (88 Petr Drozd). Trainer: Ludek Zajic

Goals: Urbanek (10), Rehák (12), Tengstedt (28), Tur (72)

LOKOMOTIV SOFIA v HALMSTADS BK 3-1 (2-1)

Lokomotiv Sofia   14.09.1995

Referee: Kurt Zuppinger (SWI)   Attendance: 2,008

LOKOMOTIV: Vladimir Manolkov, Anton Velkov (Cap) (75 Georgi Antonov), Iordan Marinov, Valentin Naidenov (72 Hristo Koilov), Adalbert Zafirov, Ivo Slavchev, Doncho Donev, Boris Khvoinev, Ivan Radivojevic, Dian Petkov (86 Georgi Borisov), Simeon Chilibonov.   Trainer: Grigor Petkov

HALMSTADS BK: Håkan Svensson; Joel Borgstrand, Torbjörn Arvidsson (63 Peter Vougt), Tommy Andersson (Cap), Fredrik Andersson, Jesper Mattsson, Anders Johansson-Smith, Magnus Svensson, Niklas Gudmundsson, Niclas Alexandersson (43 Fredrik Ljungberg), Robert Andersson. Trainer: Mats Jingbladh

Goals: M. Svensson (33), Marinov (41), Petkov (43 pen), Donev (57)

HALMSTADS BK v LOKOMOTIV SOFIA 2-0 (1-0)

Örjans Vall, Halmstad   28.09.1995

Referee: Vasili Melnichuk (Ucr)   Attendance: 3,145

HALMSTADS BK: Håkan Svensson; Joel Borgstrand, Torbjörn Arvidsson, Tommy Andersson (Cap), Fredrik Andersson, Jesper Mattsson, Anders Johansson-Smith, Magnus Svensson, Niklas Gudmundsson, Niclas Alexandersson (63 Fredrik Ljungberg), Robert Andersson (70 Peter Vougt).   Trainer: Mats Jingbladh

LOKOMOTIV: Rumen Apostolov, Anton Velkov (Cap) (75 Georgi Antonov), Iordan Marinov, Valentin Naidenov, Adalbert Zafirov, Ivo Slavchev, Doncho Donev (58 Hristo Koilov), Simeon Chilibonov, Ivan Radivojevic, Dian Petkov (65 Dian Angelov), Iasen Petrov.   Trainer: Grigor Petkov

Sent off: Ivanov (95)

Goals: R. Andersson (23), T. Andersson (75)

**KR REYKJAVÍK
v EVERTON LIVERPOOL 2-3** (1-1)

KR-völlur, Reykjavík   14.09.1995

Referee: Roger Phillipi (LUX)   Attendance: 5,956

KR REYKJAVÍK: Kristján Finnbogasson; Steinar Adolfsson, Izudin Dadi Dervic, Thormódur Egilsson (Cap), Sigurdur Örn Jónsson, Salih Heimir Porca, Hilmar Björnsson, Einar Thór Daníelsson, Mihajlo Bibercic, Heimir Gudjönsson, Gudmundur Benediktsson.   Trainer: Gudjón Thórdarson

EVERTON: Neville Southall; Matthew Jackson (61 Paul Holmes), Gary Ablett, David Unsworth, Dave Watson (Cap), Andy Hinchcliffe, Daniel Amokachi, Joe Parkinson, Paul Rideout, John Ebbrell, Anders Limpar (63 Tony Grant). Trainer: Joe Royle

Goals: Ebbrell (22), Bibercic (36 pen, 67 pen), Unsworth (56 pen), Amokachi (88)

**EVERTON LIVERPOOL
v KR REYKJAVÍK 3-1** (0-1)

Goodison Park, Liverpool   28.09.1995

Referee: Ladislav Gadosi (SVK)   Attendance: 18,422

EVERTON: Neville Southall (Cap); Earl Barrett, Andy Hinchcliffe, David Unsworth, Craig Short, John Ebbrell, Tony Grant, Joe Parkinson, Anders Limpar, Daniel Amokachi (38 Graham Stuart), Paul Rideout.   Trainer: Joe Royle

KR REYKJAVÍK: Kristján Finnbogasson; Steinar Adolfsson, Izudin Dadi Dervic, Thormódur Egilsson, Sigirdur Örn Jónsson, Brynjar Gunnarsson, Hilmar Björnsson, Einar Thór Daníelsson, Mihajlo Bibercic (82 Salih Heimir Porca), Heimir Gudjónsson, Gudmundur Benediktsson (81 Asmundur Haraldsson).   Trainer: Gudjón Thórdarson

Goals: Danielsson (22), Stuart (56), Grant (65), Rideout (87)

**INTER BRATISLAVA
v REAL ZARAGOZA 0-2** (0-1)

Stadión na Pasienkoch, Bratislava   14.09.1995

Referee: Periklis Vasilakis (GRE)   Attendance: 2,700

INTER: Miroslav Hyll; Jozef Dojcan, Lubos Tomko, Karol Schulz, Dušan Rupec, Roman Greguska (61 Milan Malatinsky), Martin Kuna, Martin Obsitnik (Cap), Vladimir Prokop (74 Boris Kitka), Lubos Luhovy, Rolf Landerl (70 Tomas Medved).   Trainer: Jozef Adamec

REAL ZARAGOZA: Juan Miguel García Inglés "JUANMI"; Alberto BELSÚE Arias, Xavier AGUADO Companys, Fernando Gabriel CÁCERES, Francisco Veza Fragoso "PAQUI", Mohamed Ali Hamar "NAYIM" (64 José Aurelio GAY López), ÓSCAR Luis Celada, Gustavo POYET Domínguez, Sergio Ángel BERTI (68 Miguel PARDEZA Pichardo), Daniel García Lara "DANI", Fernando MORIENTES Sánchez (74 Jesús GARCÍA SANJUÁN).   Trainer: Víctor Fernández Braulio

Goals: Morientes (42), Óscar (60)

REAL ZARAGOZA
v INTER BRATISLAVA 3-1 (1-0)
La Romareda, Zaragoza 28.09.1995
Referee: Gilles Veissière (FRA)   Attendance: 12,600
REAL ZARAGOZA: Juan Miguel García Inglés "JUANMI"; Alberto BELSÚE Arias (74 Jesús Ángel SOLANA Bermejo), Xavier AGUADO Companys, Fernando Gabriel CÁCERES, Francisco Veza Fragoso "PAQUI", Mohamed Ali Hamar "NAYIM", ÓSCAR Luis Celada, Gustavo POYET Domínguez (60 Daniel García Lara "DANI"), Sergio Ángel BERTI (46 Santiago ARAGÓN Martínez), Francisco HIGUERA Fernández, Miguel PARDEZA Pichardo (Cap).
Trainer: Víctor Fernández Braulio
INTER: Miroslav Hyll; Lubos Tomko; Dušan Rupec (79 Ivan Schulcz), Martin Kuna, Martin Sevela; Vladimir Prokop, Roman Greguska, Martin Obsitnik (Cap), Milan Malatinsky (68 Radovan Vasik), Lubos Luhovy, Tomas Medved (46 Rolf Landerl).   Trainer: Jozef Adamec
Goals: Poyet (12), Higuera (64), Dani (72), Obsitnik (77 pen)

RAPID WIEN v PETROLUL PLOIEŞTI 3-1 (1-0)
Gerhard-Hanappi, Wien 14.09.1995
Referee: Loizos Loizou (CYP)   Attendance: 9,979
RAPID: Michael Konsel (Cap); Peter Schöttel, Trifon Ivanov, Michael Hatz, Peter Guggi, Peter Stöger, Roman Pivarnik (77 Prvoslav Jovanovic), Zoran Barisic, Stefan Marasek, Christian Stumpf (71 Carsten Jancker), Andreas Heraf.
Trainer: Ernst Dokupil
PETROLUL: Ştefan Gabriel Preda; Daniel Chiriţă, Octavian Grigore, Valeriu Răchită (Cap), Mihai Pîrlog, Gheorghe Aurelian Leahu; Daniel Eugen Baştină, Daniel Zafiris (62 Adrian Orlin Toader), Marcel Cristian Abăluţă, Cristian Zmoleanu, Ion Claudiu Andreicuţ (81 Marian Grama).
Trainer: Ion Marin
Goals: Barisic (45, 90 pen), Ivanov (59), Toader (65)

PETROLUL PLOIEŞTI v RAPID WIEN 0-0
Petrolul Ploieşti 28.09.1995
Referee: Manuel Diaz Vega (SPA)   Attendance: 11,000
PETROLUL: Ştefan Gabriel Preda; Daniel Eugen Baştină, Gheorghe Adrian Bălăceanu, Valeriu Răchită (Cap), Gheorghe Aurelian Leahu; Marian Grama (66 Marian Mihai), Octavian Grigore, Marcel Cristian Abăluţă, Cristian Zmoleanu; Adrian Orlin Toader (75 Mihai Pîrlog), Ion Claudiu Andreicuţ (46 Daniel Zafiris).   Trainer: Ion Marin
RAPID: Michael Konsel (Cap); Trifon Ivanov, Peter Schöttel, Michael Hatz, Roman Pivarnik, Andreas Heraf, Peter Stöger (88 Zoran Barisic), Dietmar Kühbauer, Peter Guggi (62 Prvoslav Jovanovic), Stefan Marasek, Christian Stumpf (89 Rene Haller).   Trainer: Ernst Dokupil

FK MOLDE
v PARIS SAINT-GERMAIN FC 2-3 (0-0)
Molde stadion 14.09.1995
Referee: John Rowbotham (SCO)   Attendance: 3,379
MOLDE: Morten Bakke; Odd Petter Lyngstad, Sindre Rekdal (Cap), Ole Erik Stavrum (82 Ronald Wenaas), Trond Andersen (54 Per Olav Saetre), Knut Anders Fostervold, Petter Rudi, Daniel Berg Hestad, Ole Björn Sundgot, Arild Stavrum, Ole Gunnar Solskjaer.   Trainer: Age Hareide
PARIS SG: Richard Dutruel; José Cobos (68 Francis Llacer), Bruno N'Gotty, Oumar Dieng, Patrick Colleter, Laurent Fournier (80 Bernard Allou), Vincent Guérin (Cap), Youri Djorkaeff, Paul le Guen, Julio César DELY VALDÉS, Xavier Gravelaine (60 Pascal Nouma).   Trainer: Luis Fernández
Goals: Solskjaer (56), Le Guen (76), Djorkaeff (78 pen), A. Stavrum (81), Dely Valdes (84)

PARIS SAINT-GERMAIN FC
v FK MOLDE 3-0 (2-0)
Parc des Princes, Paris 28.09.1995
Referee: Sándor Piller (HUN)   Attendance: 18,898
PARIS SG: Richard Dutruel; Francis Llacer, Bruno N'Gotty, Oumar Dieng, Patrick Colleter (56 Stéphane Mahé), Vincent Guérin (46 Laurent Fournier), Daniel Bravo (72 Bernard Allou), Youri Djorkaeff, Paul le Guen, Pascal Nouma, Patrice Loko.   Trainer: Luis Fernández
MOLDE: Morten Bakke; Odd Petter Lyngstad, Sindre Rekdal, Ole Erik Stavrum (46 Petter Christian Singsaas), Knut Anders Fostervold; Petter Rudi, Ronald Wenaas (72 Tor Gunnar Johnsen, 86 José Glaria "Flaco"), Daniel Berg Hestad, Ole Björn Sundgot, Arild Stavrum, Ole Gunnar Solskjaer.
Trainer: Age Hareide
Goals: Nouma (7, 13), Djorkaeff (77)

DINAMO MOSKVA v ARARAT EREVAN 3-1 (1-0)
Dinamo Moskva 14.09.1995
Referee: Robert Sedlacek (AUS)   Attendance: 7,100
DINAMO: Andrei Smetanin (Cap); Erik Yakhimovich, Sergei Schulgin, Sergei Kolotovkin, Ravil Sabitov (80 Yuri Tishkov), Andrei Kobelev (55 Aleksandr Grishin), Oleg Samatov, Dmitri Cheryshev (62 Vitali Safronov), Sergei Nekrasov, Yuri Kuznetsov, Oleg Teryokhin.   Trainer: Konstantin Beskov
ARARAT: Armen Petrosyan; Armen Shahgeldyan, Tigran Gsepyan, Aramais Tonoyan, Levon Stepanyan, Haik Harutyunyan, Akop Mkyran, Akop Ter-Petrosyan (83 Rafik Nazaryan), Hamlet Mkhitaryan, Artour Kotcharyan, Aram Voskanyan.   Trainer: Samuel Darbinyam
Goals: Teryokhin (45, 90), Stepanyan (71), Safronov (73)

ARARAT EREVAN v DINAMO MOSKVA 0-1 (0-0)

Razdan, Erevan   28.09.1995

Referee: Jan Wegereef (HOL)   Attendance: 12,700

ARARAT: Armen Petrosyan; Armen Shahgeldyan, Tigran Gsepyan, Aramais Tonoyan (Cap), Levon Stepanyan (65 Haik Harutyunyan), Araik Nigoyan, Akop Mkyran, Akop Ter-Petrosyan, Hamlet Mkhitaryan, Erik Ayrapetyan, Aram Voskanyan (46 Artour Kotcharyan).
Trainer: Samuel Darbinyam

DINAMO: Valeri Kleimenov; Aleksandr Grishin (85 Andrei Kobelev), Yuri Kovtun, Sergei Kolotovkin, Sergei Schulgin, Yuri Kuznetsov, Oleg Samatov, Dmitri Cheryshev, Sergei Nekrasov (85 Vitali Safronov), Sergei Podpalyi (Cap), Oleg Teryokhin.   Trainer: Konstantin Beskov

Goal: Teryokhin (66)

**BORUSSIA MÖNCHENGLADBACH
v FC SILEKS KRATOVO 3-0** (2-0)

Bökelberg, Mönchengladbach   14.09.1995

Referee: Sándor Varga (HUN)   Attendance: 13,750

BORUSSIA: Jörg Kaessmann; Thomas Hoersen, Michael Klinkert, Patrik Andersson, Jörg Neun, Christian Hochstätter, Stefan Effenberg (Cap), Karlheinz Pflipsen (90 Michael Frontzeck), Peter Wynhoff (61 Max Huiberts), Martin Dahlin, Michael Sternkopf (74 Martin Schneider).   Trainer: Bernd Krauss

SILEKS: Kiro Trajcev (Cap); Marjan Nikolov, Arse Andovski (71 Marijan Nacev), Igor Duzelov, Jovance Bizimoski, Nedzmedin Memed, Milosević, Zoran Boškovski (54 Toni Micevski), Rade Karanfilovski, Ilco Borov, Srdjan Zaharievski (76 Vlatko Ljusev).
Trainer: Zoran Smilevski

Goals: Pflipsen (6), Effenberg (19), Klinkert (87)

AEK ATHINA v FC SION 2-0 (1-0)

Nikos Gkoumas, Athina   14.09.1995

Referee: Frans van den Wijngaert (BEL)   Att: 20,740

AEK: Ilias Atmatzidis; Mihalis Vlahos, Stelios Manolas (Cap), Hristos Maladenis, Nikos Kostenoglou, Vasilis Borbokis (88 Haralampos Kopitsis), Temur Ketsbaia, Toni Savevski, Mihalis Kasapis, Hristos Kostis (66 Vasilis Tsiartas), Daniel Batista (90 Vasilis Dimitriadis).   Trainer: Dušan Bajević

FC SION: Stephan Lehmann; Raphaël Wicky, Patrick Sylvestre, Dominique Herr (Cap), Antoine Kombouaré, Yvan Quentin, Sébastien Fournier, Philippe Vercruysse, Heinz Moser, Jean-Pierre La Placa (77 Christophe Bonvin), Mirandinha Isailton (83 Gaetano Giallanza).
Trainer: Michel Decastel

Goals: Vlahos (45), Borbokis (70)

**FC SILEKS KRATOVO
v BORUSSIA MÖNCHENGLADBACH 2-3** (0-1)

City, Skopje   28.09.1995

Referee: Fernand Meese (BEL)   Attendance: 9,000

SILEKS: Kiro Trajcev (Cap); Marjan Nikolov, Arse Andovski (61 Marijan Nacev), Vlatko Ljusev, Igor Duzelov, Nedzmedin Memed, Ljubodrag Milosević, Rade Karanfilovski, Zoran Boškovski, Srdjan Zaharievski, Toni Micevski (63 Zoran Angelović, 66 Mite Nacevski).   Trainer: Zoran Smilevski

BORUSSIA: Jörg Kaessmann; Thomas Kastenmaier, Michael Klinkert, Patrik Andersson, Jörg Neun, Christian Hochstätter, Peter Nielsen, Stefan Effenberg (Cap), Peter Wynhoff, Martin Dahlin, Michael Sternkopf.   Trainer: Bernd Krauss

Goals: Effenberg (29), Memed (52), Dahlin (54), Boškovski (60), Nielsen (80)

FC SION v AEK ATHINA 2-2 (1-0)

Stade de Tourbillon, Sion   28.09.1995

Referee: Loris Stafoggia (ITA)   Attendance: 6,900

FC SION: Stephan Lehmann; Patrick Sylvestre, Dominique Herr (Cap), Antoine Kombouaré, Yvan Quentin, Raphaël Wicky, Jean-Pierre La Placa (63 Heinz Moser), Sébastien Fournier, Patrick Bühlmann (78 Gaetano Giallanza), Christophe Bonvin, Frédéric Chassot (83 Josephus Yenay).
Trainer: Michel Decastel

AEK: Ilias Atmatzidis; Mihalis Vlahos, Stelios Manolas (Cap), Nikos Kostenoglou, Vasilis Borbokis (78 Haralampos Kopitsis), Hristos Maladenis, Temur Ketsbaia, Mihalis Kasapis, Refik Sabanadzović (73 Toni Savevski), Vasilis Tsiartas (55 Dimitris Saravakos), Daniel Batista.   Trainer: Dušan Bajević

Goals: Bonvin (20), Ketsbaia (82), Giallanza (85), Batista (87)

FC TEUTA DURRËS v AC PARMA 0-2 (0-0)

Qemal Stafa, Tirana   14.09.1995

Referee: Dimitar Momirov (BUL)   Attendance: 8,100

TEUTA: Xhevair Kapllani; Ardian Abazi (Cap), Ilir Alliu (83 Indrit Estrefi), Artan Vila, Gentjan Begeja (44 Ardian Dashi), Marenglen Xhai, Artan Koka, Elton Koça, Mikel Furrxhi, Alban Mehmeti, Nesti Qendro.   Trainer: Bashkim Koka

PARMA: Luca Bucci; Fabio Cannavaro, Roberto Mussi (84 Alberto di Chiara), Luigi Apolloni (Cap), Antonio Benarrivo, Tomas Brolin, Gabriele Pin, Néstor Sensini, Hristo Stoichkov, Alessandro Melli (72 Filippo Inzaghi), Gianfranco Zola.
Trainer: Nevio Scala

Goals: Zola (82, 85)

AC PARMA v FC TEUTA DURRËS 2-0 (1-0)
Ennio Tardini, Parma   28.09.1995
Referee: Milan Mitrović (SVN)   Attendance: 10,291
PARMA: Luca Bucci; Antonio Benarrivo, Luigi Apolloni (Cap), Néstor Sensini, Alberto di Chiara, Massimo Crippa (72 Tarcisio Catanese), FERNANDO Manuel Silva COUTO (42 Fabio Cannavaro), Massimo Brambilla, Alessandro Melli (46 Gianfranco Zola), Tomas Brolin, Filippo Inzaghi.   Trainer: Nevio Scala
TEUTA: Xhevair Kapllani; Ardian Abazi, Nesti Qendro, Artan Koka (88 Ardian Bushi), Artan Vila, Mikel Furrxhi, Ilir Alliu, Marenglen Xhai, Enkelejd Dobi, Alban Mehmeti, Elton Koça. Trainer: Bashkim Koka
Goals: Melli (8), Inzaghi (90)

ZALGIRIS VILNIUS v TRABZONSPOR 2-2 (1-1)
Zalgiris Vilnius   14.09.1995
Referee: Finn Lambek (DEN)   Attendance: 2,500
ZALGIRIS: Darius Spetyla; Dainius Suliauskas, Virginijus Baltusnikas (Cap), Tomas Zvirgzdauskas (46 Grazvydas Mikulenas), Sergejus Novikovas, Donatos Vencevicius, Andrius Tereskinas (71 Arunas Pukelevicius), Ramunas Stonkus, Aidas Preiksaitis, Gintaras Rimkus, Edgaras Jankauskas.
Trainer: Benjaminas Zelkevicius
TRABZONSPOR: Metin Mert; Ogün Temizkanoglu, Cengiz Atilla, Iskender Eroglu, Lemi Çelik, Tolunay Kafkas, Unal Karaman (89 Archil Arveladze), Fatih Tekke, Abdullah Ercan, Hami Mandirali (88 Orhan Çikrikçi), Shota Arveladze (Cap). Trainer: Senol Güneş
Goals: Tereskinas (7), S. Arveladze (25), Abdullah (54), Mikulenas (67)

TRABZONSPOR v ZALGIRIS VILNIUS 1-0 (1-0)
Avni Aker, Trabzon   28.09.1995
Referee: Sergey Shmolik (BLS)   Attendance: 22,600
TRABZONSPOR: Nihat Tümkaya; Ogün Temizkanoglu, Cengiz Atilla, Osman Özköylü, Lemi Çelik (83 Hamdi Aslan), Tolunay Kafkas, Unal Karaman, Archil Arveladze (88 Soner Boz), Abdullah Ercan, Hami Mandirali, Shota Arveladze (Cap) (62 Fatih Tekke).   Trainer: Senol Güneş
ZALGIRIS: Darius Spetyla; Dainius Suliauskas, Virginijus Baltusnikas (Cap), Tomas Zvirgzdauskas, Sergejus Novikovas, Ramunas Stonkus (78 Arunas Pukelevicius), Andrius Tereskinas (28 Grazvydas Mikulenas), Aidas Preiksaitis, Donatos Vencevicius, Gintaras Rimkus, Edgaras Jankauskas.
Trainer: Benjaminas Zelkevicius
Goal: Hami (37)

SPORTING LISBOA v MACCABI HAIFA 4-0 (2-0)
José Alvalade, Lisboa   14.09.1995
Referee: Keith Burge (WAL)   Attendance: 31,800
SPORTING: Paulo Rebelo COSTINHA; Fernando NÉLSON Jesus Alves, Noureddine NAYBET, MARCO AURÉLIO Cunha Santos, NUNO Jorge Pereira Silva VALENTE, OCEANO Andrade Cruz (Cap), PEDRO Rui da Mota Vieira MARTINS (85 José Luís da Cruz VIDIGAL), Ricardo Manuel SÁ PINTO, PEDRO Alexandre dos Santos BARBOSA (75 PAULO Lourenço Martins ALVES), Emanuel AMUNIKE, Ahmed OUATTARA (63 José Manuel Martins DOMINGUEZ).
Trainer: CARLOS Manuel Brito Leal QUEIRÓS
MACCABI: Rafi Cohen; Avishai Zano, Alon Harazi, Roman Pets, Sergei Kandaurov, Roni Levi (50 Edgardo Adinolfi), Alon Hazan (Cap), Eyal Berkovich, Marco Balbul, Haim Revivo; Alon Mizrahi (60 Offer Shitrit).   Trainer: Giora Spiegel
Goals: Pedro Barbosa (7, 10, 47), Sá Pinto (88)

MACCABI HAIFA v SPORTING LISBOA 0-0
Kiriat Eliezer, Haifa   28.09.1995
Referee: Taras Bezoubiak (RUS)   Attendance: 6,100
MACCABI: Rafi Cohen; Avishai Zano, Alon Harazi (44 Marco Balbul), Roman Pets, Moshe Glam, Roni Levi (70 Alon Mizrahi, Sergei Kandaurov, Alon Hazan (Cap) (59 Edgardo Adinolfi), Offer Shitrit, Haim Revivo, Eyal Berkovich.
Trainer: Giora Spiegel
SPORTING: Paulo Rebelo COSTINHA; Fernando NÉLSON Jesus Alves, Noureddine NAYBET, MARCO AURÉLIO Cunha Santos, NUNO Jorge Pereira Silva VALENTE, OCEANO Andrade Cruz (Cap), PEDRO Rui da Mota Vieira MARTINS (75 José Luís da Cruz VIDIGAL), Ricardo Manuel SÁ PINTO, PEDRO Alexandre dos Santos BARBOSA (45 José Manuel Martins DOMINGUEZ), Emanuel AMUNIKE, Ahmed OUATTARA (62 PAULO Lourenço Martins ALVES).
Trainer: CARLOS Manuel Brito Leal QUEIRÓS

APOEL NICOSIA v DEPORTIVO LA CORUÑA 0-0
Makarion, Nicosia   14.09.1995
Referee: Marcello Nicchi (ITA)   Attendance: 5,850
APOEL: Andreas Petridis, Giorgos Hristodoulou, Nikos Timotheou, Hristakis Pounas, Alexis Alexandrou (62 Kostas Fasouliotis), István Kozma, Giannis Ioannou (Cap) (85 Giorgos Papadopoulos), Antonis Antoniou, Antros Sotiriou, Kálmán Kovács (87 Kostas Skapoullis), Loukas Hatziloukas. Trainer: Hristo Bonev
DEPORTIVO: Juan Garrido CANALES; Salvador González Marco "VORO", Miroslav Djukić (Cap), Francisco Jémez Martín "PACO", Fernando Martínez Perales "NANDO", Juan Luis CASCALLAR Tiago, MAURO da SILVA Gomes, Adolfo ALDANA Torres, Aitor BEGUIRISTÁIN Mújika (77 DAVID Fernández Miramontes), Javier MANJARÍN Perea (84 Pedro RIESCO Herrera), Dmitri Radchenko (46 Emilio José VIQUEIRA Moure).   Trainer: John Toshack

DEPORTIVO LA CORUÑA
v APOEL NICOSIA 8-0 (5-0)

Riazor, La Coruña 28.09.1995

Referee: Alfred Micallef (MAL)   Attendance: 13,500

DEPORTIVO: Juan Garrido CANALES; Javier MANJARÍN Perea (57 Adolfo ALDANA Torres), Salvador González Marco "VORO", Miroslav Djukić (64 Emilio José VIQUEIRA Moure), Francisco Jémez Martín "PACO", Fernando Martínez Perales "NANDO", DONATO Gama da Silva, Francisco Javier González Pérez "FRAN" (Cap), Aitor BEGUIRISTÁIN Mújika, Dmitri Radchenko, Roberto Gama de Oliveira "BEBETO" (46 ALFREDO Santaelena Aguado).   Trainer: John Toshack

APOEL: Andreas Petridis, Aristos Aristokleous, Nikos Timotheou (61 Kostas Fasouliotis), Hristakis Pounas, Giorgos Hristodoulou (24 Nikos Haralampous), István Kozma, Giannis Ioannou (Cap), Loukas Hatziloukas, Kálmán Kovács (65 Alexis Alexandrou), József Kiprich, Antros Sotiriou.
Trainer: Hristo Bonev

Goals: Bebeto (16, 21, 44), Radchenko (28, 66), Beguiristáin (42), Donato (60), Aldana (78)

SECOND ROUND

SPORTING LISBOA v RAPID WIEN 2-0 (2-0)

José Alvalade, Lisboa 19.10.1995

Referee: Alain Hamer (LUX)   Attendance: 40,500

SPORTING: Paulo Rebelo COSTINHA; Fernando NÉLSON Jesus Alves, Noureddine NAYBET, MARCO AURÉLIO Cunha Santos, Budimir VUJACIC, OCEANO Andrade Cruz (Cap), PEDRO Rui da Mota Vieira MARTINS, Ricardo Manuel SÁ PINTO (85 AFONSO Paulo MARTINS da Agra), Roberto ASSIS Moreira (73 Daniel Cruz Carvalho "DANI"), José Manuel Martins DOMINGUEZ, PAULO Lourenço Martins ALVES (89 PEDRO Alexandre dos Santos BARBOSA).
Trainer: CARLOS Manuel Brito Leal QUEIRÓS

RAPID: Michael Konsel (Cap); Trifon Ivanov, Roman Pivarnik, Michael Hatz, Prvoslav Jovanovic, Stefan Marasek, Peter Stöger (72 Peter Guggi), Zoran Barisic, Andreas Heraf, Dietmar Kühbauer, Christian Stumpf (52 Sergei Mandrenko).
Trainer: Ernst Dokupil

Goals: Sá Pinto (13), Paulo Alves (25)

RAPID WIEN
v SPORTING LISBOA 4-0 (1-0, 2-0) (AET)

Ernst Happel, Wien 2.11.1995

Referee: Werner Müller (SWI)   Attendance: 22,500

RAPID: Michael Konsel (Cap): Trifon Ivanov, Roman Pivarnik, Peter Schöttel, Prvoslav Jovanovic (64 Rene Haller), Peter Guggi, Andreas Heraf (58 Zoran Barisic), Dietmar Kühbauer, Peter Stöger, Christian Stumpf, Carsten Jancker.
Trainer: Ernst Dokupil

SPORTING: Paulo Rebelo COSTINHA; Fernando NÉLSON Jesus Alves, Noureddine NAYBET, MARCO AURÉLIO Cunha Santos, Budimir VUJACIC, OCEANO Andrade Cruz (Cap), PEDRO Rui da Mota Vieira MARTINS, José Manuel Martins DOMINGUEZ (75 PEDRO Alexandre dos Santos BARBOSA), Ricardo Manuel SÁ PINTO, Emanuel AMUNIKE (66 Daniel Cruz Carvalho "DANI"), PAULO Lourenço Martins ALVES (87 CARLOS Jorge Marques Caldas XAVIER).
Trainer: CARLOS Manuel Brito Leal QUEIRÓS

Goals: Kühbauer (25), Stumpf (90, 105), Jancker (110)

DINAMO MOSKVA
v SK HRADEC KRALOVE 1-0 (0-0)

Dinamo Moskva 19.10.1995

Referee: Richard O'Hanlon (EIRE)   Attendance: 8,700

DINAMO: Valeri Kleimenov; Yuri Kuznetsov, Yuri Kovtun, Sergei Nekrasov, Sergei Schulgin, Andrei Kobelev (46 Aleksandr Grishin), Oleg Samatov, Dmitri Cheryshev, Vitali Safronov, Sergei Podpalyi (Cap), Yuri Tishkov (78 Aleksei Kutsenko).   Trainer: Konstantin Beskov

SK HRADEC KRALOVE: Stanislav Vahala; Rudolf Rehák (76 Jaroslav Vrabel), Tomas Urban, Karel Urbanek, Josef Dzubara, Ales Hynek, Milan Ptacek (78 Petr Drozd), Pavel Cerny, Michal Smarda (Cap), Daniel Masek, Daniel Kaplan (64 Radim Holub).   Trainer: Ludek Zajic

Goal: Kuznetsov (59)

SK HRADEC KRALOVE
v DINAMO MOSKVA 1-0 (1-0, 1-0) (AET)

Letná, Praha 2.11.1995

Referee: Roy Helge Olsen (NOR)   Attendance: 11,530

SK HRADEC KRALOVE: Stanislav Vahala; Rudolf Rehák, Tomas Urban (Cap), Karel Urbanek, Josef Dzubara, Ivo Ulich, Ales Hynek, Pavel Cerny, Petr Drozd, Radim Holub, Daniel Kaplan (73 Daniel Zoubek, 117 Milan Ptacek).
Trainer: Ludek Zajic

DINAMO: Andrei Smetanin; Yuri Kuznetsov, Sergei Kolotovkin, Yuri Kovtun, Erik Yakhimovich, Aleksandr Grishin, Oleg Samatov, Dmitri Cheryshev (120 Andrei Kobelev), Vitali Safronov (70 Yuri Tishkov), Sergei Podpalyi (Cap), Oleg Teryokhin.   Trainer: Konstantin Beskov

Goal: Kaplan (14)

Penalties: Drozd (miss), 0-1 Kobelev, Cerny (miss), Teryokhin (miss), Dzubara (miss), 0-2 Samatov, 1-2 Holub, 1-3 Kovtun

HALMSTADS BK v AC PARMA 3-0 (2-0)
Örjans Vall, Halmstad   19.10.1995
Referee: Bernd Heynemann (GER)   Attendance: 9,306
HALMSTADS BK: Håkan Svensson; Tommy Andersson (C), Torbjörn Arvidsson, Joel Borgstrand, Fredrik Ljungberg, Niklas Gudmundsson, Jesper Mattsson, Anders Johansson-Smith, Magnus Svensson, Niclas Alexandersson, Robert Andersson.   Trainer: Mats Jingbladh
PARMA: Luca Bucci; Antonio Benarrivo (75 Roberto Mussi), Fabio Cannavaro, Luigi Apolloni (Cap), Alberto di Chiara, Dino Baggio, Tomas Brolin (58 Filippo Inzaghi), Néstor Sensini, Massimo Crippa, Hristo Stoichkov, Gianfranco Zola (46 Alessandro Melli).   Trainer: Nevio Scala
Goals: Gudmundsson (7, 31), R. Andersson (76)

**CELTIC GLASGOW
v PARIS SAINT-GERMAIN FC 0-3** (0-2)
Celtic Park, Glasgow   2.11.1995
Referee: Kurt Rothlisberger (SWI)   Attendance: 34,822
CELTIC: Gordon Marshall; Rudi Vata (46 Simon Donnelly), Tosh McKinlay, Thomas Boyd, John Hughes, Peter Grant, Andy Walker, Paul McStay (Cap), John Collins, Pierre Van Hooijdonk (63 Brian McLaughlin), Andreas Thom.   Manager: Tommy Burns
PARIS SG: Bernard Lama (Cap); José Cobos, Patrick Colleter, Paul le Guen, Stéphane Mahé (28 Oumar Dieng), Laurent Fournier (68 Francis Llacer), Vincent Guérin, Daniel Bravo, Raí Souza de Oliveira, Youri Djorkaeff, Patrice Loko (59 Pascal Nouma).   Trainer: Luis Fernández
Goals: Loko (36, 42), Nouma (68)

AC PARMA v HALMSTADS BK 4-0 (2-0)
Ennio Tardini, Parma   2.11.1995
Referee: Finn Lambek (DEN)   Attendance: 13,053
PARMA: Luca Bucci; Antonio Benarrivo, FERNANDO Manuel Silva COUTO, Néstor Sensini, Fabio Cannavaro, Alberto di Chiara (70 Roberto Mussi), Dino Baggio, Gabriele Pin (Cap), Hristo Stoichkov, Gianfranco Zola (88 Massimo Brambilla), Filippo Inzaghi (74 Massimo Crippa).   Trainer: Nevio Scala
HALMSTADS BK: Håkan Svensson; Joel Borgstrand, Jesper Mattsson, Tommy Andersson (Cap), Fredrik Andersson, Fredrik Ljungberg, Anders Johansson-Smith, Niclas Alexandersson, Magnus Svensson, Peter Vougt (85 Tomas Stierna), Robert Andersson.   Trainer: Mats Jingbladh
Goals: Inzaghi (1), Baggio (28), Stoichkov (53), T. Andersson (59 og)

REAL ZARAGOZA v CLUB BRUGGE 2-1 (2-0)
La Romareda, Zaragoza   19.10.1995
Referee: Stephen John Lodge (ENG)   Attendance: 24,850
REAL ZARAGOZA: Juan Miguel García Inglés "JUANMI"; Alberto BELSÚE Arias, Fernando Gabriel CÁCERES, Jesús Ángel SOLANA Bermejo, Luis Carlos CUARTERO Laforga, Gustavo POYET Domínguez, Santiago ARAGÓN Martínez, Mohamed Ali Hamar "NAYIM", Daniel García Lara "DANI", Francisco HIGUERA Fernández (Cap) (58 Sergio Ángel BERTI), Fernando MORIENTES Sánchez (46 Miguel PARDEZA Pichardo, 88 ÓSCAR Luis Celada).   Trainer: Víctor Fernández Braulio
CLUB BRUGGE: Danny Verlinden, Vital Borkelmans, Paul Okon, Pascal Renier, Dirk Medved, Franky van der Elst (Cap), Lorenzo Staelens, Stéphane van der Heyden, Sven Vermant, Robert Špehar, Mario Stanić.   Trainer: Hugo Broos
Sent off: Renier (60), Nayim (69)
Goals: Aragón (28 pen), Dani (33), Staelens (73 pen)

**PARIS SAINT-GERMAIN FC
v CELTIC GLASGOW 1-0** (0-0)
Parc des Princes, Paris   19.10.1995
Referee: Günther Benkö (AUS)   Attendance: 30,010
PSG: Bernard Lama (Cap); José Cobos, Paul le Guen, Patrick Colleter, Laurent Fournier (80 Francis Llacer), Daniel Bravo, Vincent Guérin, Youri Djorkaeff (88 Bernard Allou), Stéphane Mahé, Raí Souza de Oliveira (81 Pascal Nouma), Patrice Loko.   Trainer: Luis Fernández
CELTIC: Gordon Marshall; Rudi Vata, John Hughes, Thomas Boyd, Tosh McKinlay, Peter Grant, Paul McStay, John Collins, Phil O'Donnell (69 Simon Donnelly), Andreas Thom, Pierre Van Hooijdonk.   Manager: Tommy Burns
Goal: Djorkaeff (76)

CLUB BRUGGE v REAL ZARAGOZA 0-1 (0-0)
Olympiapark, Brugge   2.11.1995
Referee: Dimitar Momirov (BUL)   Attendance: 16,613
CLUB BRUGGE: Danny Verlinden, Dirk Medved (75 Gert Verheyen), Paul Okon, Tjörven de Brul, Vital Borkelmans, Lorenzo Staelens, Franky van der Elst (Cap), Robert Špehar, Sven Vermant, Stéphane van der Heyden, Mario Stanić.   Trainer: Hugo Broos
REAL ZARAGOZA: Juan Miguel García Inglés "JUANMI"; Alberto BELSÚE Arias, Fernando Gabriel CÁCERES, Xavier AGUADO Companys, Jesús Ángel SOLANA Bermejo (46 Francisco Veza Fragoso "PAQUI"), Santiago ARAGÓN Martínez, ÓSCAR Luis Celada, Gustavo POYET Domínguez, Sergio Ángel BERTI (73 Jesús GARCÍA SANJUÁN), Francisco HIGUERA Fernández (Cap) (56 Daniel García Lara "DANI"), Fernando MORIENTES Sánchez.   Trainer: Víctor Fernández Braulio
Goal: Dani (90)

**BORUSSIA MÖNCHENGLADBACH
v AEK ATHINA 4-1** (0-0)

Bökelberg, Mönchengladbach 19.10.1995

Referee: Jorge Emanuel MONTEIRO COROADO (POR) Attendance: 18,700

BORUSSIA: Uwe Kamps; Thomas Kastenmaier (76 Thomas Hoersen), Patrik Andersson, Martin Schneider, Jörg Neun (87 Max Huiberts), Michael Klinkert, Michael Frontzeck, Stefan Effenberg (Cap), Karlheinz Pflipsen, Peter Wynhoff, Martin Dahlin. Trainer: Bernd Krauss

AEK: Ilias Atmatzidis; Giorgos Koutoulas, Mihalis Vlahos, Refik Sabanadzović, Nikos Kostenoglou, Hristos Maladenis, Mihalis Kasapis, Temur Ketsbaia (76 Haralampos Kopitsis), Vasilis Borbokis (61 Dimitris Saravakos), Toni Savevski, Daniel Batista (67 Vasilis Tsiartas). Trainer: Dušan Bajević

Goals: Dahlin (51, 90), Pflipsen (55), Wynhoff (67), Maladenis (79)

**AEK ATHINA
v BORUSSIA MÖNCHENGLADBACH 0-1** (0-0)

Nikos Gkoumas, Athina 2.11.1995

Referee: William Leslie Mottram (SCO) Att: 22,600

AEK: Ilias Atmatzidis; Vasilis Borbokis, Mihalis Vlahos, Stelios Manolas (Cap), Mihalis Kasapis, Hristos Maladenis, Refik Sabanadzović, Hristos Kostis (53 Temur Ketsbaia), Toni Savevski (53 Vasilis Dimitriadis), Vasilis Tsiartas (71 Haralampos Kopitsis), Dimitris Saravakos.
Trainer: Dušan Bajević

BORUSSIA: Uwe Kamps; Thomas Kastenmaier, Michael Klinkert, Patrik Andersson, Jörg Neun, Martin Schneider, Karlheinz Pflipsen (65 Christian Hochstätter), Stefan Effenberg (Cap) (87 Thomas Eichin), Peter Wynhoff, Martin Dahlin (72 Dirk Wolf), Michael Sternkopf.
Trainer: Bernd Krauss

Goal: Effenberg (71)

**EVERTON LIVERPOOL
v FEYENOORD ROTTERDAM 0-0**

Goodison Park, Liverpool 19.10.1995

Referee: Hans-Jürgen Weber (GER) Attendance: 27,526

EVERTON: Neville Southall; Matthew Jackson (82 Stuart Barlow), Earl Barrett, Craig Short, David Unsworth, Gary Ablett, Barry Horne (Cap), Vinny Samways, Anders Limpar (82 Paul Holmes), Paul Rideout, Graham Stuart.
Trainer: Joe Royle

FEYENOORD: Ed de Goey; Ulrich van Gobbel, Ronald Koeman (Cap), George Boateng, Clemens Zwijnenberg (61 Ruud Heus), Rob Maas, Rob Witschge, Giovanni van Bronckhorst, Henrik Larsson (81 Tomasz Iwan), Mike Obiku, Regi Blinker (61 Orlando Trustfull). Trainer: Arie Haan

FEYENOORD v EVERTON 1-0 (1-0)

Feyenoord, Rotterdam 2.11.1995

Referee: Marcelo Nicchi (ITA) Attendance: 40,289

FEYENOORD: Ed de Goey; Ulrich van Gobbel, Ronald Koeman (Cap), George Boateng, Tomasz Iwan, Peter Bosz, Orlando Trustfull (72 Clemens Zwijnenberg), Ruud Heus, Mike Obiku, Henrik Larsson (61 Gaston Taument), Regi Blinker (84 Rob Witschge). Trainer: Arie Haan

EVERTON: Neville Southall; Matthew Jackson, Andy Hinchcliffe, Dave Watson, Craig Short, John Ebbrell (64 Tony Grant), Gary Ablett (67 Stuart Barlow), Barry Horne, Graham Stuart, Paul Rideout, Daniel Amokachi. Trainer: Joe Royle

Sent off: Short (90)

Goal: Blinker (40)

**TRABZONSPOR
v DEPORTIVO LA CORUÑA 0-1** (0-0)

Avni Aker, Trabzon 19.10.1995

Referee: Frans van den Wijngaert (BEL) Att: 24,700

TRABZONSPOR: Nihat Tümkaya; Ogün Temizkanoglu, Osman Özköylü, Cengiz Atilla, Lemi Çelik, Tolunay Kafkas (79 Soner Boz), Unal Karaman (Cap)(70 Fatih Tekke), Hami Mandirali, Abdullah Ercan (82 Orhan Çikrikçi), Archil Arveladze, Shota Arveladze (Cap).

DEPORTIVO: Francisco LIAÑO Fernández; ALFREDO Santaelena Aguado, Salvador González Marco "VORO", Miroslav Djukić, José Luis RIBERA Uranga, Fernando Martínez Perales "NANDO", Adolfo ALDANA Torres (85 Javier MANJARÍN Perea), DONATO Gama da Silva, Francisco Javier González Pérez "FRAN" (Cap) (73 Aitor BEGUIRISTÁIN Mújika), Francisco Javier Pérez VILLARROYA (89 Emilio José VIQUEIRA Moure), Dmitri Radchenko.
Trainer: John Toshack

Goal: Donato (60)

**DEPORTIVO LA CORUÑA
v TRABZONSPOR 3-0** (2-0)

Riazor, La Coruña 2.11.1995

Referee: Gheorghe Constantin (ROM) Attendance: 27,500

DEPORTIVO: Francisco LIAÑO Fernández; ALFREDO Santaelena Aguado (46 Luis María LÓPEZ REKARTE), Salvador González Marco "VORO", Miroslav Djukić, Francisco Jémez Martín "PACO", Francisco Javier Pérez VILLARROYA (69 Fernando Martínez Perales "NANDO"), Javier MANJARÍN Perea, DONATO Gama da Silva (80 Adolfo ALDANA Torres), Francisco Javier González Pérez "FRAN" (Cap), Aitor BEGUIRISTÁIN Mújika, Roberto Gama de Oliveira "BEBETO".

TRABZONSPOR: Nihat Tümkaya; Lemi Çelik, Okan Özke, Osman Özköylü, Cengiz Atilla, Abdullah Ercan, Shota Arveladze (60 Soner Boz), Unal Karaman (Cap), Fatih Tekke, Hami Mandirali (69 Hasan Özer), Orhan Çikrikçi (83 Hamdi Aslan). Trainer: Turgay Semercioglu

Goals: Donato (22), Bebeto (39, 80)

QUARTER-FINALS

DINAMO MOSKVA v RAPID WIEN 0-1 (0-1)
Dinamo Moskva   7.03.1996

Referee: Bernd Heynemann (GER)   Attendance: 5,900

DINAMO: Andrei Smetanin (Cap); Erik Yakhimovich, Yuri Kovtun, Sergei Schulgin (63 Aleksei Kutsenko), Sergei Nekrasov, Andrei Kobelev, Oleg Samatov, Dmitri Cheryshev (40 Yuri Tishkov), Yuri Kuznetsov, Vitali Safronov (38 Aleksandr Grishin), Oleg Teryokhin.
Trainer: Konstantin Beskov

RAPID: Michael Konsel (Cap); Michael Hatz, Peter Schöttel, Trifon Ivanov, Peter Guggi, Peter Stöger, Stefan Marasek, Prvoslav Jovanovic, Andreas Heraf, Christian Stumpf, Carsten Jancker.   Trainer: Ernst Dokupil

Goal: Stumpf (35)

RAPID WIEN v DINAMO MOSKVA 3-0 (0-0)
Gerhard-Hanappi, Wien   21.03.1996

Referee: Marc Batta (FRA)   Attendance: 42,700

RAPID: Michael Konsel (Cap); Michael Hatz, Trifon Ivanov, Peter Schöttel, Peter Guggi, Andreas Heraf, Peter Stöger, Prvoslav Jovanovic, Stefan Marasek, Christian Stumpf, Carsten Jancker.   Trainer: Ernst Dokupil

DINAMO: Andrei Smetanin (Cap); Erik Yakhimovich, Yuri Kovtun, Sergei Schulgin (59 Vitali Safronov), Sergei Nekrasov, Andrei Kobelev, Oleg Samatov (65 Sergei Lemeshko), Dmitri Cheryshev, Sergei Podpalyi, Aleksandr Grishin (55 Yuri Tishkov), Oleg Teryokhin.   Trainer: Konstantin Beskov

Goals: Jancker (49, 74), Stoger (61 pen)

AS PARMA v PARIS SAINT-GERMAIN FC 1-0 (0-0)
Ennio Tardini, Parma   7.03.1996

Referee: Sándor Puhl (HUN)   Attendance: 12,447

PARMA: Luca Bucci; Antonio Benarrivo, Fabio Cannavaro, Néstor Sensini, Luigi Apolloni (Cap), Roberto Mussi, Dino Baggio (75 Massimo Crippa), Gabriele Pin (89 Lorenzo Minotti), Massimo Brambilla, Gianfranco Zola (26 Filippo Inzaghi), Hristo Stoichkov.   Trainer: Nevio Scala

PARIS SG: Bernard Lama (Cap); José Cobos (76 Francis Llacer), Bruno N'Gotty, Paul le Guen, Patrick Colleter, Youri Djorkaeff (42 Pascal Nouma), Daniel Bravo, Raí Souza de Oliveira, Stéphane Mahé, Julio César DELY VALDÉS, Patrice Loko.   Trainer: Luis Fernández

Goal: Stoichkov (58)

PARIS SAINT-GERMAIN FC v AC PARMA 3-1 (2-1)
Parc des Princes, Paris   21.03.1996

Referee: Leif Sundell (SWE)   Attendance: 43,686

PARIS SG: Bernard Lama (Cap); Bruno N'Gotty, Alain Roche, Paul le Guen, Laurent Fournier (75 Stéphane Mahé), Daniel Bravo, Raí Souza de Oliveira, Patrick Colleter (67 Vincent Guérin), Pascal Nouma (69 Francis Llacer), Julio César DELY VALDÉS, Patrice Loko.   Trainer: Luis Fernández

PARMA: Luca Bucci; Roberto Mussi (83 Alberto di Chiara), Fabio Cannavaro, Néstor Sensini, Luigi Apolloni (Cap), Antonio Benarrivo, Dino Baggio, Gabriele Pin (77 Massimo Crippa), Massimo Brambilla, Alessandro Melli, Hristo Stoichkov (64 Filippo Inzaghi).   Trainer: Nevio Scala

Goals: Raí (9 pen, 69 pen), Melli (26), Loko (38)

DEPORTIVO LA CORUÑA v REAL ZARAGOZA 1-0 (0-0)
Riazor, La Coruña   7.03.1996

Referee: Gerd Grabher (AUS)   Attendance: 13,800

DEPORTIVO: Francisco LIAÑO Fernández; Francisco Jémez Martín "PACO", Miroslav Djukić, Salvador González Marco "VORO", Francisco Javier Pérez VILLARROYA, Emilio José VIQUEIRA Moure, DONATO Gama da Silva, Aitor BEGUIRISTÁIN Mújika (67 Adolfo ALDANA Torres), Javier MANJARÍN Perea (58 DAVID Fernández Miramontes), Francisco Javier González Pérez "FRAN" (Cap), Dmitri Radchenko (72 Branko Milovanović).
Trainer: John Benjamin Toshack

REAL ZARAGOZA: José Francisco BELMAN González; Alberto BELSÚE Arias, Fernando Gabriel CÁCERES, Xavier AGUADO Companys, Jesús GARCÍA SANJUÁN, Gustavo POYET Domínguez, Daniel García Lara "DANI" (80 Miguel PARDEZA Pichardo), Mohamed Ali Hamar "NAYIM" (78 Gustavo LÓPEZ), Santiago ARAGÓN Martínez, Francisco HIGUERA Fernández (Cap) (53 José Aurelio GAY López), Fernando MORIENTES Sánchez.
Trainer: Víctor Fernández Braulio

Goal: David (69)

REAL ZARAGOZA v DEPORTIVO LA CORUÑA 1-1 (1-0)
La Romareda, Zaragoza   21.03.1996

Referee: Guy Goethals (BEL)   Attendance: 31,900

REAL ZARAGOZA: José Francisco BELMAN González; Alberto BELSÚE Arias, Jesús Ángel SOLANA Bermejo, Luis Carlos CUARTERO Laforga, Jesús GARCÍA SANJUÁN, Mohamed Ali Hamar "NAYIM" (67 Miguel PARDEZA Pichardo), Gustavo POYET Domínguez, Santiago ARAGÓN Martínez, Daniel García Lara "DANI" (62 ÓSCAR Luis Celada), Francisco HIGUERA Fernández (Cap), Fernando MORIENTES Sánchez.   Trainer: Víctor Fernández Braulio

DEPORTIVO: Francisco LIAÑO Fernández; Salvador González Marco "VORO", Miroslav Djukić, Francisco Jémez Martín "PACO", Luis María LÓPEZ REKARTE, Francisco Javier Pérez VILLARROYA, MAURO da SILVA Gomes (5 DONATO Gama da Silva), Adolfo ALDANA Torres, Javier MANJARÍN Perea (77 ALFREDO Santaelena Aguado), Francisco Javier González Pérez "FRAN" (Cap), José Roberto Gama de Oliveira "BEBETO". Trainer: John Benjamin Toshack

Goals: Morientes (37), Bebeto (63)

BORUSSIA MÖNCHENGLADBACH
v FEYENOORD ROTTERDAM 2-2 (2-2)

Rheinstadion, Düsseldorf   7.03.1996

Referee: László Vagner (HUN)   Attendance: 54,000

BORUSSIA: Uwe Kamps; Thomas Kastenmaier, Joachim Stadler, Patrik Andersson, Jörg Neun, Martin Schneider (61 Thomas Eichin), Stefan Effenberg (Cap), Karlheinz Pflipsen, Peter Wynhoff, Peter Nielsen, Martin Dahlin (4 Michael Sternkopf).   Trainer: Bernd Krauss

FEYENOORD: Ed de Goey; Rob Maas, Bernard Schuiteman, Ronald Koeman (Cap), Ruud Heus (21 George Boateng), Peter Bosz, Jean-Paul Van Gastel, Giovanni Van Bronckhorst, Gaston Taument (80 Tomasz Iwan), Henrik Larsson, Henk Vos. Trainer: Arie Haan

Goals: Wynhoff (4), Van Gastel (34), Kastenmaier (43 pen), R. Koeman (45 pen)

FEYENOORD ROTTERDAM
v BORUSSIA MÖNCHENGLADBACH 1-0 (0-0)

Feyenoord, Rotterdam   21.03.1996

Referee: Kim Milton Nielsen (DEN)   Attendance: 43,080

FEYENOORD: Ed de Goey; Peter Bosz, Ronald Koeman (Cap), Bernard Schuiteman, George Boateng, Jean-Paul Van Gastel, Rob Maas, Giovanni van Bronckhorst, Gaston Taument (75 Orlando Trustfull), Henrik Larsson (80 Mike Obiku), Henk Vos (77 Tomasz Iwan).   Trainer: Arie Haan

BORUSSIA: Uwe Kamps; Michael Klinkert, Thomas Eichin (73 Christian Hochstätter), Patrik Andersson, Dirk Wolf (46 Max Huiberts), Martin Schneider, Thomas Kastenmaier, Stefan Effenberg, Peter Wynhoff, Peter Nielsen (46 Karlheinz Pflipsen), Michael Sternkopf.   Trainer: Bernd Krauss

Goal: Trustfull (85)

SEMI-FINALS

FEYENOORD ROTTERDAM
v RAPID WIEN 1-1 (0-0)

Feyenoord, Rotterdam   4.04.1996

Referee: Ryszard Wójcik (POL)   Attendance: 41,241

FEYENOORD: Ed de Goey; George Boateng, Ronald Koeman, Bernard Schuiteman, Peter Bosz (Cap), Giovanni van Bronckhorst, Jean-Paul Van Gastel, Henrik Larsson (79 Orlando Trustfull), Gaston Taument, Henk Vos (76 Mike Obiku), Tomasz Iwan.   Trainer: Arie Haan

RAPID: Michael Konsel (Cap); Trifon Ivanov, Roman Pivarnik, Michael Hatz, Peter Guggi, Andreas Heraf, Peter Schöttel, Peter Stöger (79 Zoran Barisic), Stefan Marasek, Christian Stumpf, Carsten Jancker (87 Rene Haller). Trainer: Ernst Dokupil

Goals: Koeman (53 pen), Jancker (67)

RAPID WIEN
v FEYENOORD ROTTERDAM 3-0 (3-0)

Gerhard-Hanappi, Wien   18.04.1996

Referee: Sergej Khusainov (RUS)   Attendance: 49,800

RAPID: Michael Konsel (Cap); Trifon Ivanov, Michael Hatz, Peter Schöttel, Peter Guggi, Andreas Heraf, Dietmar Kühbauer (86 Rene Haller), Peter Stöger (86 Sergei Mandrenko), Stefan Marasek, Christian Stumpf, Carsten Jancker. Trainer: Ernst Dokupil

FEYENOORD: Ed de Goey; George Boateng, Ronald Koeman, Bernard Schuiteman, Peter Bosz (Cap), Giovanni van Bronckhorst, Jean-Paul Van Gastel, Henrik Larsson, Gaston Taument, Henk Vos, Tomasz Iwan (46 Mike Obiku). Trainer: Arie Haan

Goals: Jancker (2, 35), Stumpf (32)

DEPORTIVO LA CORUÑA
v PARIS SAINT-GERMAIN 0-1 (0-0)

Riazor, La Coruña   4.04.1996

Referee: Markus Merk (GER)   Attendance: 21,100

DEPORTIVO: Francisco LIAÑO Fernández; Salvador González Marco "VORO", Miroslav Djukić, Francisco Jémez Martín "PACO" (63 DAVID Fernández Miramontes), ALFREDO Santaelena Aguado; DONATO Gama da Silva, Luis María LÓPEZ REKARTE, Adolfo ALDANA Torres (69 Emilio José VIQUEIRA Moure), Francisco Javier González Pérez "FRAN" (Cap); Javier MANJARÍN Perea (80 Aitor BEGUIRISTÁIN Mújika), Roberto Gama de Oliveira "BEBETO".   Trainer: John Toshack

PARIS SG: Bernard Lama (Cap); Bruno N'Gotty, Alain Roche, Paul le Guen, Laurent Fournier (85 Stéphane Mahé), Daniel Bravo, Vincent Guérin, Patrick Colleter, Patrice Loko (47 Francis Llacer), Julio César DELY VALDÉS (80 Youri Djorkaeff), Pascal Nouma.   Trainer: Luis Fernández

Goal: Djorkaeff (90)

**PARIS SAINT-GERMAIN
v DEPORTIVO LA CORUÑA 1-0** (0-0)

Parc des Princes, Paris 18.04.1996

Referee: Alfredo Trentalange (ITA)   Attendance: 43,965

PARIS SG: Bernard Lama (Cap); Bruno N'Gotty, Alain Roche, Paul le Guen, Laurent Fournier (81 Francis Llacer), Daniel Bravo, Vincent Guérin, Patrick Colleter, Patrice Loko, Youri Djorkaeff (79 Julio César DELY VALDÉS), Pascal Nouma (57 Raí Souza de Oliveira).   Trainer: Luis Fernández

DEPORTIVO: Francisco LIAÑO Fernández; Salvador González Marco "VORO", Francisco Jémez Martín "PACO", José Luis RIBERA Uranga, ALFREDO Santaelena Aguado (50 Adolfo ALDANA Torres); Emilio José VIQUEIRA Moure (58 Aitor BEGUIRISTÁIN Mújika), DONATO Gama da Silva (Cap), Francisco Javier Pérez VILLARROYA, Javier MANJARÍN Perea; Roberto Gama de Oliveira "BEBETO", Dmitri Radchenko (62 Rafael MARTÍN VÁZQUEZ). Trainer: John Toshack

Goal: Loko (59)

FINAL

**PARIS SAINT-GERMAIN FC
v RAPID WIEN 1-0** (1-0)

Stade "Roi Baldouin" Brussels, 8.05.1996

Referee: Pierluigi Pairetto (ITA)   Attendance: 37,500

PARIS SG: Bernard Lama (Cap); Bruno N'Gotty, Alain Roche, Paul le Guen, Laurent Fournier (77 Francis Llacer), Daniel Bravo, Vincent Guérin, Patrick Colleter, Patrice Loko, Youri Djorkaeff, Raí Souza de Oliveira (11 Julio César DELY VALDÉS).   Trainer: Luis Fernández

RAPID: Michael Konsel (Cap); Trifon Ivanov, Michael Hatz, Peter Schöttel, Peter Guggi, Peter Stöger, Andreas Heraf, Dietmar Kühbauer, Stefan Marasek; Christian Stumpf (46 Zoran Barisic), Carsten Jancker.   Trainer: Ernst Dokupil

Goal: N'Gotty (29)

Goalscorers European Cup-Winners' Cup 1995-96:

9 goals: Petr Samec (SK Hradec Kralove)

6 goals: Carsten Jancker (Rapid Wien); José Gama de Oliveira Bebeto (Deportivo La Coruña)

4 goals: Youri Djorkaeff, Patrice Loko (Paris St.Germain), Mike Obiku, Regi Blinker (Feyenoord), Andreas Thom (Celtic), Christian Stumpf (Rapid Wien), Mihajlo Bibercic (KR Reykjavík)

3 goals: Donato Gama da Silva (Deportivo La Coruña), Ronald Koeman (Feyenoord), Martin Dahlin, Stefan Effenberg (Borussia), Daniel Garcia Lara "Dani" (Real Zaragoza), Oleg Teryokhin (Dinamo Moskva), Pedro Barbosa (Sporting Lisboa), Olgar Danielsen (Klaksvikar Itrottarfelag), Paata Machutadze (Dinamo Batumi), Ole Gunnar Solskjaer (Molde FK), Nadzmedin Memed (Sileks Kratovo), Alon Mizrahi (Maccabi Haifa), Milan Ptacek (SK Hradec Kralove), Pascal Nouma (Paris St.Germain)

2 goals: Jungblut (Grevenmacher), Orbu, Voskoboinik (Shakhtar Donetsk), Tomko (Inter Bratislava), A. Stavrum (Molde FK), Bonvin (FC Sion), Tereskinas (Zalgiris Vilnius), Shitrit (Maccabi Haifa), Ioannou (Apoel Nicosia), Sá Pinto (Sporting Lisboa), Cerny, Urban (SK Hradec Kralove), Gudmundsson, R.Andersson (Halmstads BK), Stoichkov, Melli, Zola, Inzaghi (AC Parma), Morientes (Real Zaragoza), Pflipsen, Wynhoff (Borussia), Trustfull, Larsson (Feyenoord), Donnelly (Celtic), Radchenko (Deportivo La Coruña), Raí (Paris St.Germain), Barisic (Rapid Wien)

1 goal: Vila, Koça, Bushi (Teuta Durres), Alves Silva (Grevenmacher), Oprea, Popovici (Tiligul), Borgulya, Romanek (Vác Samsung), Wallden (TPS Turku), Ritter (FC Vaduz), Doncic, Zarb (FC Valletta), Ewing (Linfield Belfast), Bilski, Karwan (GKS Katowice), Kokol, Alihodzic (NK Mura Murska Sobota), Sarac, Popovic (Obilic Beograd), McCourt (Derry City), Lobanov, Skripchenko (Dinamo 93 Minsk), Atelkin, Matveyev (Shakhtar Donetsk), Tugushi, Mudjiri (Dinamo Batumi), Tengstedt, Tur (FC København), Marinov, Petkov, Donev, Slavchev, Khvoinev (Lokomotiv Sofia), Danielsson, Egilsson, Porca (KR Reykjavík), Obsitnik, Rupec, Greguska, Landerl (Inter Bratislava), Toader, Pîrlog (Petrolul Ploieşti), Stepanyan, Gsepyan, Tonoyan (Ararat Erevan), Giallanza, Moser, Herr (FC Sion), Borov, Micevski, Boškovski (Sileks Kratovo), Mikulenas, Vencevicius, Baltusnikas (Zalgiris Vilnius), Revivo (Maccabi Haifa), Antoniou (Apoel Nicosia), Paulo Alves (Sporting Lisboa), Kaplan, Hynek, Urbanek, Rehák, Vrabel, Smarda (SK Hradec Kralove), M.Svensson, T.Andersson (Halmstads BK), Staelens, Špehar, Stanić (Club Brugge), Maladenis, Vlahos, Borbokis, Ketsbaia, Batista (AEK Athina), Ebbrell, Unsworth, Amokachi, Stuart, Grant, Rideout (Everton), S.Arveladze, Abdullah, Hami (Trabzonspor), Kuznetsov, Stafronov (Dinamo Moskva), Baggio (AC Parma), Aragón, Oscar, Poyet, Nayim (Real Zaragoza), Kastenmaier, Klinkert, Nielsen (Borussia), Van Gastel, Heus, Gláucio (Feyenoord), Walker (Celtic), David, Beguiristáin, Aldana (Deportivo La Coruña), N'Gotty, Le Guen, Dely Valdes (Paris St.Germain), Stoger, Kühbauer, Ivanov (Rapid Wien)

Own goal: T. Andersson (Halmstads BK) for AC Parma

CUP WINNERS' CUP 1996-97

PRELIMINARY ROUND

MPKC MOZYR v KR REYKJAVÍK 2-2 (0-0)
Yunost, Mozyr 8.08.1996
Referee: Armand Ancion (BEL)   Attendance: 4,800
MPKC: Yuri Svirkov; Alexander Sednev, Vyacheslav Levchuk, Viktor Kukar, Oleg Sisoyev, Yuri Maleyev, Boris Gorovoi (53 Dmitri Denisyuk), Vladimir Konovalov (46 Sergei Gomonov), Alexander Kulchi, Andrei Skorobogatko, Sergei Yaromko (Cap) (79 Sergei Terikhov).   Trainer: Anatoli Yurevich
KR: Kristján Finnbogason; Thormódur Egilsson (Cap), Thorsteinn Gudjónsson, Brynjar Gunnarsson, Sigurdur Örn Jónsson (28 Oskar Thorvaldsson); Hilmar Björnsson, Heimir Gudjónsson, Ólafur Kristjánsson, Einar Thór Daníelsson (74 Asmundur Haraldsson); Thorsteinn Jónsson, Ríkhardur Dadason.   Trainer: Lúkas Kostic
Goals: Yaromko (51), Skorobogatko (73), Dadason (84), Th. Jónsson (90)

KR REYKJAVÍK v MPKC MOZYR 1-0 (0-0)
Laugardalsvöllur, Reykjavík 21.08.1996
Referee: Sven Kjelbrott (NOR)   Attendance: 1,722
KR: Kristján Finnbogason; Thormódur Egilsson (Cap), Oskar Thorvaldsson, Brynjar Gunnarsson, Ólafur Kristjánsson; Hilmar Björnsson, Heimir Gudjónsson, Sigurdur Örn Jónsson, Thorsteinn Jónsson, Einar Thór Daníelsson (90 Asmundur Haraldsson); Ríkhardur Dadason (74 Gudmundur Benediktsson).   Trainer: Lúkas Kostic
MPKC: Yuri Svirkov; Alexander Sednev, Vyacheslav Levchuk, Vladimir Golmak (46 Andrei Lukashevich), Sergei Gomonov, Oleg Sisoyev, Alexander Kulchi, Boris Gorovoi (70 Dmitri Denisyuk), Yuri Maleyev (46 Vladimir Konovalov), Andrei Skorobogatko, Sergei Yaromko (Cap).
Trainer: Anatoli Yurevich
Goal: Daníelsson (90)

CHEMLON HUMENNE v FLAMURTARI VLORË 1-0 (0-0)
Chemlon Humenne 8.08.1996
Referee: Robert Sedlacek (AUS)   Attendance: 12,000
CHEMLON: Juraj Bucek; Niksa Boljat, Peter Dzurik (Cap), Frantisek Hanc; Jaroslav Sovic, Vladimir Sivy (65 Marek Lukac), Jozef Valkucak, Igor Sukennik, Lubomir Mati, Ruslan Lubarsky, Rastislav Tomovcik.   Trainer: Ondrej Danko
FLAMURTARI: Anesti Arapi (Cap); Ilir Alliu, Geri Çipi, Viktor Daullja, Ardian Behari, Devi Muka, Ervin Fakaj (72 Erjon Mëhilli), Sokol Prenga, Leonard Preloshi, Anesti Vito (88 Robert Bajrami), Sokol Kushta.   Trainer: Leonidha Çurri
Goal: Lubarsky (72)

FLAMURTARI VLORË v CHEMLON HUMENNE 0-2 (0-0)
Flamurtari Vlorë 22.08.1996
Referee: Attila Juhos (HUN)   Attendance: 4,500
FLAMURTARI: Anesti Arapi (Cap) (61 Julian Gjeloshi); Erjon Mëhilli, Viktor Daullja, Geri Çipi, Ardian Behari (61 Jorgaq Diamanti), Devi Muka (70 Robert Bajrami), Sokol Prenga, Ilir Alliu, Sokol Kushta, Anesti Vito, Leonard Preloshi.   Trainer: Leonidha Çurri
CHEMLON: Juraj Bucek; Niksa Boljat, Peter Dzurik (Cap), Frantisek Hanc; Jaroslav Sovic, Vladimir Sivy (85 Marek Gadzo), Jozef Valkucak, Milan Sciranka; Rastislav Tomovcik, Ruslan Lubarsky, Lubomir Mati (67 Marek Lukac, 77 Vojtech Kiss).   Trainer: Ondrej Danko
Goals: Lubarsky (48), Valkucak (53)

FC SION v KAREDA SIAULIAI 4-2 (3-0)
Stade de Tourbillon, Sion 8.08.1996
Referee: Ylvi Kollari (ALB)   Attendance: 6,200
FC SION: Stephan Lehmann; Alain Gaspoz, Antoine Kombouaré, Raphaël Wicky (46 Christian Colombo), Patrick Bühlmann, Patrick Sylvestre, Philippe Vercruysse, Luiz Milton, Christophe Bonvin (Cap); Frédéric Chassot (50 Mirandinha Isailton), Darko Pancev (80 Sébastien Zambaz).   Trainer: Michel Decastel
KAREDA: Vaidotas Zutautas; Tomas Ziukas, Arvydas Korsakovas, Tomas Kancelskis (51 Zilvinas Zudys), Irmantas Stumbrys, Egidijus Zukauskas, Vidas Dancenka, Stasys Baranauskas, Saulius Mikalajunas, Remigijus Pocius (Cap) (42 Audrius Zuta), Rimas Zvingilas (65 Deimantas Bicka).
Trainer: Algimantas Liubinskas
Sent off: Kombouaré (47)
Goals: Chassot (14), Bonvin (27), Pancev (35 pen), Branauskas (72 pen), Dancenka (86), Vercruysse (88)

KAREDA SIAULIAI v FC SION 0-0
Siauliai 22.08.1996
Referee: Lars Gerner (DEN)   Attendance: 2,500
KAREDA: Vaidotas Zutautas; Zilvinas Zudys, Arvydas Korsakovas, Tomas Kancelskis, Irmantas Stumbrys (75 Rimas Zvingilas), Stasys Baranauskas, Vidas Dancenka, Rolandas Vaineikis, Saulius Mikalajunas (68 Deimantas Bicka), Arturas Fomenka, Remigijus Pocius (Cap) (55 Audrius Zuta).   Trainer: Algimantas Liubinskas
FC SION: Fabrice Borer; Luiz Milton, Raphaël Wicky (Cap), Yvan Quentin, Alain Gaspoz; Patrick Sylvestre, Philippe Vercruysse, Christian Colombo, Patrick Bühlmann; Vladan Lukic (80 Frédéric Chassot), Christophe Bonvin (55 Sébastien Zambaz).   Trainer: Michel Decastel

OLIMPIJA LJUBLJANA v LEVSKI SOFIA 1-0 (0-0)
Bezigrad, Ljubljana   8.08.1996
Referee: Marek Kowalczyk (POL)   Attendance: 2,500
OLIMPIJA: Nihad Pejković (Cap); Erik Krzisnik, Aleksander Knavs, Safet Hadžić, Enver Adrović, Igor Benedejcić, Dejan Djuranović, Damjan Gajser, Kliton Bozgo, Edmond Dosti (77 Ermin Raković), Sebastijan Cimerotić.
Trainer: Petar Nadoveza
LEVSKI: Dimitar Ivankov; Georgi Petrov, Georgi Popivanov, Radostin Rusev, Ivan Vasilev, Vladimir Ionkov, Borislav Iliev (78 Todor Zaitsev), Viktorio Pavlov, Marian Hristov, Nikolai Todorov (Cap), Rumen Ivanov (77 Ilian Simeonov).
Trainer: Georgi Tsvbetkov
Goal: Bozgo (51)

**LEVSKI SOFIA
v OLIMPIJA LJUBLJANA 1-0** (0-0, 1-0) (AET)
Georgi Asparuchov, Sofia   22.08.1996
Referee: Bohdan Benedik (SVK)   Attendance: 25,000
LEVSKI: Dimitar Ivankov; Emil Kremenliev, Georgi Petrov, Radostin Rusev (41 Todor Zaitsev), Ivan Vasilev, Vladimir Ionkov, Viktorio Pavlov (88 Borislav Iliev), Marian Hristov, Ilian Simeonov, Nikolai Todorov (Cap), Anatoli Tonov (83 Rumen Ivanov).   Trainer: Georgi Tsvbetkov
OLIMPIJA: Nihad Pejković (Cap); Robert Englaro, Erik Krzisnik, Samir Zulić, Safet Hadžić, Enver Adrović, Dejan Djuranović, Damjan Gajser (84 Ermin Raković), Azrudin Valentić (80 Milenko Acimović), Sebastijan Cimerotić (100 Virginio Velkoski), Kliton Bozgo.   Trainer: Petar Nadoveza
Goal: Simeonov (58)
Penalties: 0-1 Bozgo, Zatsev (miss), 0-2 Acimović, 1-2 Ionkov, 1-3 Velkoski, Todorov (miss), Djuranović (miss), 2-3 Simeonov, 2-4 Zulić

**CRVENA ZVEZDA BEOGRAD
v HEART OF MIDLOTHIAN EDINBURGH 0-0**
Crvena Zvezda, Beograd   8.08.1996
Referee: Herrmann Albrecht (GER)   Attendance: 13,646
CRVENA ZVEZDA: Zvonko Milojević (Cap); Bratislav Zivković, Goran Djorović, Zoran Njegus, Predrag Stanković, Vinko Marinović, Perica Ognjenović, Miodrag Pantelić (65 Dragan Vulević), Zoran Jovicić, Dejan Stanković (65 Nenad Vanić), Darko Anić.   Trainer: Vladimir Petrović
HEARTS: Gilles Rousset; Stephen Frail (55 Allan McManus), David Weir, David McPherson (Cap), Paul Ritchie, Neil Pointon, Jeremy Goss, Pasquale Bruno, Gary Mackay, Colin Cameron, John Colquhoun (72 Kevin Thomas).
Manager: Jim Jefferies

**HEART OF MIDLOTHIAN EDINBURGH
v CRVENA ZVEZDA BEOGRAD 1-1** (1-0)
Tynecastle Park, Edinburgh   22.08.1996
Referee: Karl-Erik Nilsson (SWE)   Attendance: 15,062
HEARTS: Gilles Rousset; Colin Cameron, John Colquhoun, Pasquale Bruno (78 Kevin Thomas), Neil Pointon, Steve Fulton, Gary Mackay (84 John Robertson), Neil McCann, David McPherson (Cap), Paul Ritchie, David Weir.
Manager: Jim Jefferies
CRVENA ZVEZDA: Zvonko Milojević (Cap); Bratislav Zivković, Goran Djorović, Zoran Njegus, Predrag Stanković, Vinko Marinović, Perica Ognjenović (76 Nenad Sakić), Darko Anić, Zoran Jovicić, Dejan Stanković (85 Nenad Vanić), Goran Bošković (46 Dragan Vulević).   Trainer: Vladimir Petrović
Goals: McPherson (44), Marinović (59)

KARABAKH AGDAM v MYLLYKOSKEN PALLO-47 ANJALANKOSKI 0-1 (0-0)
Agdam   8.08.1996
Referee: Georgios Fassolis (GRE)   Attendance: 11,500
KARABAKH: Djamaladdin Aliyev; Mais Azimov, Elshad Akhmedov, Aslan Kerimov (83 Yashar Huseynov), Tabriz Hasanov, Bakhtiyar Musayev (46 Emin Salmanov), Satlar Aliyev, Mirbagir Isayev, Tarlan Akhmedov, Mushvik Huseynov (Cap), Nazim Aliyev.   Trainer: Elbrus Abbasov
MyPa: Miki Lehtonen; Jukka Koskinen, Toni Huttunen, Mika Viljanen (Cap), David Moore, Tommi Kautonen (54 Jarkko Koskinen), Sami Mahlio, Antti Pohja (62 Mika Hernesniemi), Tom Enberg, Niclas Grönholm (75 Juuso Kangaskorpi), John Allen.   Trainer: Harri Kampman
Goal: Mahlio (85 pen)

**MYLLYKOSKEN PALLO-47 ANJALANKOSKI v
KARABAKH AGDAM 1-1** (0-1, 0-1) (AET)
Saviniemi, Anjalankoski   22.08.1996
Referee: Terje Hauge (NOR)   Attendance: 2,493
MyPa: Petri Jakonen; Toni Huttunen, Mika Viljanen (Cap), David Moore, Jukka Koskinen, Sami Mahlio, Jarkko Koskinen, Antti Pohja (90 Jasse Jalonen), Juuso Kangaskorpi (73 Mauri Keskitalo), Tom Enberg, Mika Hernesniemi (22 John Allen).
Trainer: Harri Kampman
KARABAKH: Djamaladdin Aliyev; Elshad Akhmedov, Mais Azimov (118 Emin Salmanov), Tarlan Akhmedov, Aslan Kerimov, Tabriz Hasanov, Mirbagir Isayev, Bakhtiyar Musayev, Elmir Khankishiev, Mushvik Huseynov (Cap), Satlar Aliyev.
Trainer: Elbrus Abbasov
Goals: Musayev (28), Keskitalo (120)

KOTAYK ABOVYAN v AEK LARNACA 1-0 (0-0)
Abovyan 8.08.1996
Referee: Sergejs Braga (LAT)   Attendance: 5,000
KOTAYK: Armen Hovhannisyan; Albert Afyan, Gagik Manukyan, Gagik Hovhannisyan (Cap), Robert Mirzoyan, Vahram Hovhannisyan, Sevada Arzumanyan, Levon Sargsyan, Mkrtich Hovhannisyan, Henrik Berberyan, Artur Abazyan (65 Karen Khachatryan).   Trainer: Samuel Petrosyan

AEK: Andreas Mavris; Giorgos Theodotou, Hristos Bakaris, Giorgos Konstantinou, Neophytos Larkou (Cap), Aggelos Misos, Louis Stefani, Pavlos Markou, Zoran Kuntic (69 Eleytherios Elefyheriou), Milenko Kovacevic (86 Andreas Panagiotou), Klimis Alexandrou.
Trainer: Andreas Mouskalis

Goal: Berberyan (80)

AEK LARNACA v KOTAYK ABOVYAN 5-0 (2-0)
Zenon, Larnaca 22.08.1996
Referee: Amit Klein (Isr)   Attendance: 2,037
AEK: Andreas Mavris; Giorgos Theodotou (66 Andreas Panagiotou), Giorgos Konstantinou (76 Stelios Stylianidis), Neophytos Larkou (Cap), Aggelos Misos, Louis Stefani, Hristos Bakaris, Zoran Kuntic (58 Pavlos Markou), Goran Kopunovic, Milenko Kovacevic, Klimis Alexandrou.
Trainer: Andreas Mouskalis

KOTAYK: Armen Hovhannisyan (62 Edik Yeritsyan); Albert Afyan, Gagik Manukyan, Gagik Hovhannisyan (Cap), Karen Khachatryan (34 Vahan Arzumanyan), Vahram Hovhannisyan (71 Vardan Israelyan), Sevada Arzumanyan, Levon Sargsyan, Mkrtich Hovhannisyan, Henrik Berberyan, Artur Abazyan.
Trainer: Samuel Petrosyan

Sent off: Berberyan (40), M. Hovhannisyan (70)

Goals: Kuntic (28), Alexandrou (42), Kovacevic (58 pen), Kopunovic (82), Markou (86)

**CONSTRUCTORUL CHIŞINĂU
v HAPOEL IRONY RISHON LEZION 1-0** (1-0)
Republican, Chişinău 8.08.1996
Referee: Metin Tokat (TUR)   Attendance: 6,000
CONSTRUCTORUL: Serghei Dinov, Igor Filip, Ivan Tabanov (Cap), Gennadiy Skidan (35 Igor Cuciuc), Oleg Tverdohlebov, Vasile Apachiţei, Oleg Şişchin, Alexander Tarabrin (57 Serghei Prohorov), Iulian Bursuc, Alexandru Scrupschi, Serghei Rogaciov.
Trainer: Alexandru Maţiura

HAPOEL: Sagie Shtraus; Moshe Sabag, Yaron Ben Dov, Oded Tzahi, Dan Albert, Meir Azran (Cap), Alexandre Bogaichuk (27 Avi Pitusi), Sharon Marziano, Avi Oved (60 Nissan Kapeta), Tomasz Cebula, Tal Benaya (56 Nir Shikva).   Trainer: Victor Hadad

Goal: Rogaciov (20)

**HAPOEL IRONY RISHON LEZION
v CONSTRUCTORUL CHIŞINĂU 3-2** (2-1)
New Municipal, Rishon Lezion 22.08.1996
Referee: Juan Ansuategui Roca (SPA)   Attendance: 5,000
HAPOEL: Sagie Shtraus; Moshe Sabag, Yaron Ben Dov, Oded Tzahi (30 Oren Tassa), Dan Albert, Meir Azran (Cap), Sharon Marziano, Nissan Kapeta (30 Nir Shikva), Abuddi (52 Avi Pitusi), Tomasz Cebula, Tal Benaya.   Trainer: Victor Hadad

CONSTRUCTORUL: Vladimir Ceban; Igor Filip, Ivan Tabanov (Cap), Oleg Tverdohlebov, Vasile Apachiţei, Igor Cuciuc, Oleg Şişchin, Alexander Tarabrin (70 Gennadiy Skidan), Victor Comlionoc (62 Iulian Bursuc), Yuri Martâniuc (46 Alexandru Scrupschi), Serghei Rogaciov.   Trainer: Alexandru Maţiura

Goals: Sabag (10), Kapeta (28), Rogaciov (41), Cebula (60), Skidan (88)

VALLETTA FC v GLORIA BISTRIŢA 1-2 (0-0)
National Ta'Qali 8.08.1996
Referee: William Young (SCO)   Attendance: 2,500
FC VALLETTA: Reggie Cini; Drasko Braunovic, Jeffrey Chetcuti, Darren Debono, Ivan Zammit, Kristian Laferla (Cap), Gilbert Agius, Nicky Saliba, Joe Zarb, Danilo Doncic, Vesko Petrović.
Trainer: Edward Aquilina

GLORIA: Costel Câmpeanu (Cap); Ioan Miszti, Emil Gavril Dăncuş, Gabriel Cristea, Valer Săsărman, Radu Sabo (46 Eugen Voica), Dorel Purdea, Marius Răduţă (54 Dumitru Halostă), Daniel Iftodi, Ilie Lazăr (67 Marian Năstase), Dănuţ Matei.
Trainer: Remus Vlad

Goals: Matei (52), Dăncuş (67), Doncic (75)

GLORIA BISTRIŢA v VALLETTA FC 2-1 (1-1)
Gloria Bistriţa 22.08.1996
Referee: Jiří Ulrich; Bohoslav Legierski, Milan Brabec (CZE)   Attendance: 8,000
GLORIA: Costel Câmpeanu (Cap); Ioan Miszti (46 Eugen Voica), Dorel Purdea, Gabriel Cristea, Valer Săsărman, Radu Sabo (87 Marian Năstase), Marius Răduţă (63 Cornel Sevastiţa), Emil Gavril Dăncuş, Daniel Iftodi, Ilie Lazăr, Dănuţ Matei.
Trainer: Remus Vlad

VALLETTA FC: Reggie Cini; Drasko Braunovic, Jeffrey Chetcuti, Kristian Laferla (Cap) (20 Jeremy Agius), Darren Debono, Vesko Petrović (80 Andrea Bonnici), Ivan Zammit, Joe Zarb, Nicky Saliba, Lino Galea (85 Stefan Giglio), Danilo Doncic.
Trainer: Edward Aquilina

Goals: J. Agius (23), Lazăr (33), Voica (82)

**SHELBOURNE DUBLIN
v SK BRANN BERGEN 1-3** (1-2)

Tolka Park, Dublin 8.08.1996

Referee: Vitor Manuel Melo Pereira (POR)   Att: 3,010

SHELBOURNE: Alan Gough; Greg Costello, Michael Neville (Cap), David Campbell, Pascal Vaudequin, John O'Rourke (88 Donal Golden), Brian Flood, Declan Geoghegan, Anthony Sheridan, Mark Rutherford (68 David Smith), Stephen Geoghegan.   Manager: Damien Richardson

BRANN: Birkir Kristinsson; Geirmund Brendesaether, Claus Eftevaag (Cap), Claus Lundekvam, Morten Pedersen; Jan Ove Pedersen, Per-Ove Ludvigsen (87 Geir Hasund), Roger Helland, Lars Bakkerud; Mons Ivar Mjelde (79 Magnus Johansson), Tore André Flo (83 Eivind Karlsbakk).   Trainer: Kjell Tennfjord

Sent off: Campbell

Goals: Mjelde (28), M. Pedersen (31), S. Geoghegan (43), Eftevaag (69 pen)

**SK BRANN BERGEN
v SHELBOURNE DUBLIN 2-1** (1-1)

Brann Bergen 22.08.1996

Referee: Keimpe Zuidema (HOL)   Attendance: 2,189

BRANN: Birkir Kristinsson; Geirmund Brendesaether, Claus Eftevaag, Claus Lundekvam (Cap), Roger Helland, Jan Ove Pedersen, Lars Bakkerud, Morten Pedersen, Tore André Flo (87 Eivind Karlsbakk), Mons Ivar Mjelde, Agúst Gylfason.   Trainer: Kjell Tennfjord

SHELBOURNE: Alan Gough; Greg Costello, Declan Geoghegan, Michael Neville (Cap), Mark Rutherford, Pascal Vaudequin, Brian Flood, John O'Rourke, Anthony Sheridan, Stephen Geoghegan, David Tilson.   Manager: Damien Richardson

Goals: Rutherford (5), Mjelde (10), J.O. Pedersen (72)

**LLANSANTFFRAID FC
v RUCH CHORZOW 1-1** (0-1)

Racecourse Ground, Wrexham 8.08.1996

Referee: Eyjolfur Olafsson (ICE)   Attendance: 1,558

LLANSANTFFRAID: Andrew Mulliner; John Whelan, Gary Curtiss, Michael Brown, Arwel Jones, Leslie Thomas, Adrian Jones, Gary Evans (Cap), Thomas Morgan (78 Michael Davies), Andrew Edwards (84 Christopher Whelan), Simon Abercrombie.   Manager: Graham Breeze

RUCH: Ryszard Kolodziejczyk; Dariusz Fornalak, Dariusz Grzesik, Bogdan Pieniazek, Piotr Rowicki (67 Witold Wawrzyczek), Miroslaw Jaworski, Arkadiusz Bak, Dariusz Gesior, Miroslaw Mosor (Cap), Miroslaw Bak, Mariusz Srutwa (78 Maciej Mizia).   Trainer: Jerzy Wyrobek

Goals: Gesior (6), Thomas (83)

**RUCH CHORZOW
v LLANSANTFFRAID FC 5-0** (1-0)

Ruch Chorzow 22.08.1996

Referee: Dragutin Karlo Poljak (CRO)   Attendance: 6,700

RUCH: Piotr Lech; Dariusz Gesior, Arkadiusz Bak, Miroslaw Mosor, Arkadiusz Gaca (63 Piotr Rowicki), Jerzy Gasior, Mariusz Srutwa, Dariusz Grzesik, Miroslaw Bak (74 Witold Wawrzyczek), Bogdan Pieniazek, Maciej Mizia (46 Piotr Zaba).   Trainer: Jerzy Wyrobek

LLANSANTFFRAID: Andrew Mulliner, John Whelan (61 Christopher Whelan), Gary Curtiss, Michael Brown (57 Michael Davies), Arwel Jones, Leslie Thomas, Adrian Jones, Gary Evans, Thomas Morgan (61 Gary Jones), Andrew Edwards, Simon Abercrombie.   Manager: Graham Breeze

Goals: A. Bak (1, 57), Srutwa (48), M. Bak (64, 65)

**KISPEST-HONVÉD BUDAPEST
v SLOGA JUGOMAGNAT SKOPJE 1-0** (1-0)

József Bozsik stadion, Budapest 8.08.1996

Referee: Sergei Tatulian (UKR)   Attendance: 5,500

KISPEST: Ádám Vezér; Arpád Hahn (Cap), Attila Plókai, Krisztián Gabala; János Dubecz, Béla Kovács, István Urbányi, Zsolt Bárányos, Attila Piroska; Mirko Jovanovic (71 István Urbán), Mihály Tóth (82 István Faragó).   Trainer: Péter Török

SLOGA: Fuad Osmanagić; Husein Beganović, Zoran Vasevski, Esad Colaković, Dragan Siljanovski, Dejan Demjanski (75 Zoran Miserdovski), Feim Beganović, Janevski, Ernad Kovacević, Sead Kolasinac (59 Fikret Alomerović), Antonio Tasev (11 Goran Stankovski).   Trainer: Vanco Balevski.

Sent off: H. Beganovic (36)

Goal: Tóth (11)

**SLOGA JUGOMAGNAT SKOPJE
v KISPEST HONVÉD BUDAPEST 0-1** (0-0)

Skopje 22.08.1996

Referee: Marcello Nicchi (ITA)   Attendance: 1,000

SLOGA: Fuad Osmanagić; Dragan Siljanovski (83 Risto Petkov), Feim Beganović (Cap), Zoran Vasevski, Esad Colaković, Dejan Demjanski, Janevski, Sead Kolasinac (75 Goran Stankovski), Ardzend Beciri, Zoran Miserdovski, Fikret Alomerović.   Trainer: Vanco Balevski

KISPEST: Ádám Vezér; Gábor Hungler; Attila Plókai, János Mátyus; János Dubecz, Attila Forrai (81 Béla Kovács), István Urbányi (Cap), Krisztián Gabala; Zsolt Bárányos, Attila Piroska (71 Attila Ghinda), Mihály Tóth (85 Mirko Jovanovic).   Trainer: Péter Török

Goal: Ghindă (80)

VARTEKS VARAZDIN
v UNION LUXEMBOURG 2-1 (1-0)
Varteks Varazdin 8.08.1996
Referee: Josef Krula (CZE)   Attendance: 4,500

VARTEKS: Ivica Solomun; Krunoslav Gregorić, Goran Borović (46 Mario Ivanković), Krunoslav Beli, Mesud Duraković, Drazen Madunović, Drazen Besek (Cap), Robert Tezacki (72 Damir Maretić), Zoran Brlenić, Miljenko Mumlek (69 Damir Cvetko), Davor Vugrineć.
Trainer: Predrag Stilinović

UNION: Alija Besic; Laurent Deville (Cap), Eugène Afrika, Virgilio Bracigliano, Claude Mangen (68 Patrick Grettnich), Marc Kunen, Serge Makoumbou, Benoît Lahéry, Mustapha Kharoubi (88 Laurent Carème), Didier Pierrel (73 Dany Schammel), Luc Feiereisen.   Trainer: Gilbert Neumann

Sent off: Schammel (75)

Goals: Mumlek (41 pen), Maretić (80), Grettnich (87)

UNION LUXEMBOURG
v VARTEKS VARAZDIN 0-3 (0-0)
Luxembourg 22.08.1996
Referee: Roland Beck (Lie)   Attendance: 543

UNION: Alija Besic; Laurent Deville (Cap), Eugène Afrika, Virgilio Bracigliano, Laurent Pellegrino, Didier Pierrel, Luc Feiereisen, Serge Makoumbou, Benoît Lahéri (87 Martin Nosbusch), Mustapha Kharoubi (68 Laurent Carème), Patrick Grettnich (76 Jérôme Hochard).   Trainer: Gilbert Neumann

VARTEKS: Ivica Solomun; Krunoslav Gregorić, Goran Borović (60 Miljenko Mumlek), Samir Toplak (89 Krunoslav Beli), Damir Maretić, Drazen Madunović, Drazen Besek (Cap), Robert Tezacki, Davor Vugrinec, Zoran Brlenić, Mario Ivanković (81 Damir Cvetko).   Trainer: Predrag Stilinović

Goals: Besek (64), Mumlek (77 pen), Cvetko (88)

UNIVERSITATE RIGA v FC VADUZ 1-1 (1-1)
Riga 8.08.1996
Referee: Merab Malagouradze (Geo)   Attendance: 500

UNIVERSITATE: Andrei Oleinik; Vasily Ivanov, Vladimir Dragun, Valeri Bogdan, Vitaly Dolgopolov, Dmitri Travin (65 Victor Mastyanitsa), Igor Kril, Oleg Boiko (46 Alexander Tkachuk), Valentin Dubina (76 Denis Murin), Mikhail Sergeev, Agris Zarinsh (Cap).   Trainer: Victor Nesterenko

FC VADUZ: Martin Heeb; Erkan Erdogan, Daniel Hasler (Cap), Markus Weber, Harry Zech; Fulvio Cimino (71 Patrik Hefti), Tomas Daumantas (46 Peter Krainz), Marcel Müller, Marco Perez, Alexander Quaderer; Christian Kubli (59 Daniele Polverino).   Trainer: Hans Rudi Fässler

Goals: Perez (43), Zarinsh (43)

FC VADUZ
v UNIVERSITATE RIGA 1-1 (0-0, 1-1) (AET)
Gemeindersportplatz, Vaduz 22.08.1996
Referee: Krsto Danilovski (Mac)   Attendance: 1,100

FC VADUZ: Martin Heeb; Patrik Hefti, Erkan Erdogan, Markus Weber, Fulvio Cimino (62 Daniele Polverino), Marcel Müller, Marco Perez (88 Antonio Pietrafesa), Tomas Daumantas, Alexander Quaderer, Peter Krainz (46 Christian Kubli), Daniel Hasler (Cap).   Trainer: Hans Rudi Fässler

UNIVERSITATE: Andrei Oleinik; Vladimir Dragun, Valeri Bogdan, Vitaly Dolgopolov, Dmitri Travin (102 Alexander Kondratenko), Igor Kril, Valentin Dubina, Andrei Fadeyechev (71 Alberts Shvans), Mikhail Sergeev, Agris Zarinsh (Cap), Armandas Zeiberlinsh.   Trainer: Victor Nesterenko

Goals: Zarinsh (49), Polverino (90)

FC Vaduz won 4-2 on penalties.

GLENTORAN BELFAST
v SPARTA PRAHA 1-2 (0-0)
The Oval, Belfast 8.08.1996
Referee: Lawrence Sammut (MAL)   Attendance: 2,200

GLENTORAN: Neil Armstrong; Andy Mathieson, John Devine (Cap), Chris Walker, Michael Smyth, Pete Batey, Darren Parker, Darren Finlay, Glen Little, Justin McBride (81 Derek Cook), Trevor Smith (77 Andy Kirk).
Manager: Tommy Cassidy

SPARTA: Michal Caloun; Jiří Novotný, Michal Hornak, Tomas Votava, Vlastimil Svoboda (63 Vratislav Lokvenc), Zdenek Svoboda (Cap), Jiří Jarosik, Petr Gabriel, Lumir Mistr, Martin Frýdek (84 Josef Obajdin), Horst Siegl.
Trainer: Vlastimil Petrzela

Goals: Siegl (49), Little (53), Lokvenc (90)

SPARTA PRAHA
v GLENTORAN BELFAST 8-0 (4-0)
Štadión na Letnej, Praha 22.08.1996
Referee: Miroslav Radoman (YUG)   Attendance: 5,500

SPARTA: Ivan Ondruska; Michal Hornak, Petr Gabriel, Tomas Repka, Jiří Novotný, Lumir Mistr (61 Vlastimil Svoboda), Martin Frýdek (80 Jiří Jarosik), Zdenek Svoboda (Cap), Peter Gunda, Vratislav Lokvenc (71 Josef Obajdin), Horst Siegl.   Trainer: Vlastimil Petrzela

GLENTORAN: Neil Armstrong; James Quigley (85 Stuart Elliot), Michael Smyth, Darren Parker, John Devine, Chris Walker (57 Jonathan Houston), Darren Finlay, Andy Mathieson, Trevor Smith, Pete Batey, Justin McBride (68 Andy Kirk).   Manager: Tommy Cassidy

Sent off: Finlay (29)

Goals: Gunda (1, 25), Mistr (19), Siegl (24, 48, 80), Z. Svoboda (78), Gabriel (86)

DINAMO BATUMI
v HAVNAR BOLTFELAG TÓRSHAVN 6-0 (3-0)
Dinamo Batumi   8.08.1996

Referee: Juri Saar (Est)   Attendance: 6,400

DINAMO: Nikoloz Togonidze (66 David Gvaramadze); Tengiz Sichinava, Zurab Mindadze, Aleksandre Kantidze (60 Paata Machutadze), Gela Shekiladze, Rostom Torgashvili (Cap) (78 David Chichveishvili), Malkhaz Makharadze, Avtandil Glonti, Temur Tugushi, David Ujmajuridze, Amiran Mudjiri.   Trainer: Shota Cheishvili

HB: Kaj Leo Johannesen; Eydfinn Davidsen, Hans a Lag, Niclas Joensen (69 Gunnar Mohr), Bjarki Mohr, Petur Slyne, Ingi Rasmussen, Runi Nolsø (Cap), Mikkjal Thomassen, Johannes Joensen (46 Hans Thomassen), Uni Arge (73 Hallur Danielsen).   Trainer: Johan Nielsen

Goals: Tugushi (9, 22, 54), Ujmajuridze (26, 69), Davidsen (87 og)

HAVNAR BOLTFELAG TÓRSHAVN
v DINAMO BATUMI 0-3 (0-2)
Toftir stadion   22.08.1996

Referee: Juha Pulkinen (FIN)   Attendance: 800

HB: Kaj Leo Johannesen; Eydfinn Davidsen, Hans a Lag, Niclas Joensen, Bjarki Mohr, Petur Slyne (46 Hallur Danielsen), Ingi Rasmussen, Runi Nolsø (Cap) (78 Andrew Av Flotum), Mikkjal Thomassen, Gunnar Mohr (70 Bogi Midjørd), Uni Arge.   Trainer: Johan Nielsen

DINAMO: Nikoloz Togonidze; Tengiz Sichinava, Malkhaz Makharadze (Cap), Gela Shekiladze (46 Valeri Shanidze), Zurab Mindadze, Avtandil Glonti, Rostom Torgashvili, Aleksandre Kantidze, David Makharadze, David Ujmajuridze, Amiran Mudjiri (46 Paata Machutadze).   Trainer: Shota Cheishvili

Goals: Glonti (20, 21), Ujmajuridze (63)

TALLINNA SADAM
v NYVA VYNNYTSYA 2-1 (1-0)
Tallin   8.08.1996

Referee: Asim Hudiev (AZE)   Attendance: 700

SADAM: Sergei Pareiko; Mark Shvets (81 Sergei Terehov), Urmas Kaal, Vladimir Urjupin (Cap), Urmas Liivamaa, Konstantin Kolbasenko, Dalius Staleliunas, Andrei Krölov, Dmitri Ustritski, Artur Shketov, Igor Slesarchuk (69 Kristen Viikmäe).   Trainer: Uno Piir

NYVA: Volodymyr Tsytkin; Leonid Gaidarzhi (Cap), Viktor Brovchenko (84 Dmytro Lelyuk), Vyacheslav Zaporozhchenko, Yuri Solovienko, Alexander Guzun, Alexander Laktionov (67 Vasyl Maliuta), Ruslan Romanchuk, Olexiy Ryabtsev (71 Alexander Chervonyi), Pavlo Parshin, Alexander Lyubynskyi.   Trainer: Pasha Kasanov

Goals: Krölov (25 pen), Viikmäe (74), Romanchuk (77)

NYVA VYNNYTSYA
v TALLINNA SADAM 1-0 (0-0)
Central Vynnytsya   22.08.1996

Referee: Slavik Kazarian (ARM)   Attendance: 15,000

NYVA: Volodymyr Tsytkin; Leonid Gaidarzhi (Cap), Viktor Brovchenko, Vyacheslav Zaporozhchenko, Yuri Solovienko, Vasyl Maliuta (59 Oleg Bessarab), Alexander Chervonyi (65 Volodymyr Braila), Ruslan Romanchuk, Olexiy Ryabtsev, Alexander Guzun, Alexander Lyubynskyi (74 Dmytro Lelyuk).   Trainer: Pasha Kasanov

SADAM: Sergei Pareiko; Mark Shvets, Urmas Kaal, Urmas Liivamaa (63 Vladimir Urjupin), Konstantin Kolbasenko, Dalius Staleliunas, Andrei Krölov (Cap), Maksim Rötshkov, Dmitri Ustritski, Artur Shketov (41 Sergei Terehov), Igor Slesarchuk (81 Kristen Viikmäe).   Trainer: Uno Piir

Goal: Romanchuk (65)

FIRST ROUND

OLYMPIQUE NÎMES
v KISPEST HONVÉD BUDAPEST 3-1 (0-0)
Les Costières, Nîmes   12.09.1996

Referee: Richard O'Hanlon (EIRE)   Attendance: 7,948

NÎMES: Stanislaw Karwat; Franck Touron (58 Grégory Meilhac), Anthony Vosahlo, Johnny Ecker (69 Eric Auffret); Cyril Jeunechamp (75 Christophe Zugna), Antoine Preget, Omar Belbey, Mehmed Bazdarevic, Antoine Di Fraya (Cap); Eric Sabin, Nicolas Marx.   Trainer: Pierre Mosca

KISPEST: Ádám Vezér; Attila Plókai (Cap), János Mátyus, Gábor Hungler; Philip Tarlue, János Dubecz, Attila Piroska (65 Béla Kovács), Szabolcs Herczku (46 Krisztián Gabala), Attila Forrai; Zsolt Bárányos (82 Attila Ghindă), Mihály Tóth. Trainer: Péter Török

Sent off: Tarlue (44)

Goals: Jeunechamp (65), Tóth (70), Préget (75), Meilhac (86)

KISPEST HONVÉD BUDAPEST
v OLYMPIQUE NÎMES 1-2 (0-2)
"József Bozsik", Budapest   26.09.1996

Referee: Vladimir Antonov (MOL)   Attendance: 5,000

KISPEST: Ádám Vezér; Gábor Hungler, Attila Plókai, Krisztián Gabala; János Dubecz, Attila Forrai (35 Béla Kovács), István Urbányi (Cap) (46 Péter Kabát), Zsolt Bárányos, Attila Piroska; Mirko Jovanovic (71 Attila Ghindă), Mihály Tóth.   Trainer: Péter Török

NÎMES: Stanislaw Karwat; Franck Touron, Johnny Ecker, Antoine Preget, Cyril Jeunechamp, Omar Belbey, Mehmed Bazdarevic, Antoine Di Fraya (Cap), Anthony Vosahlo (65 Christophe Zugna), Eric Sabin (78 Eric Auffret), Nicolas Marx (71 Grégory Meilhac).   Trainer: Pierre Mosca

Goals: Ecker (6), Sabin (38), Piroska (61)

SK STURM GRAZ v SPARTA PRAHA 2-2 (1-0)

Arnold Schwarzenegger-Stadion, Graz   12.09.1996

Referee: Karl-Erik Nilsson (SWE)   Attendance: 3,208

STURM: Roland Goriupp; Mario Posch, Pål Lydersen, Günther Neukirchner, Martin Hiden, Herbert Grassler (83 Hannes Reinmayr), Marek Swierczewski, Roman Mählich, Marcus Pürk (62 Enzo Gambaro), Ivica Vastic (Cap), Giuseppe Giannini (62 Mario Haas).   Trainer: Ivica Osim

SPARTA: Ivan Ondruska; Tomas Repka, Jiří Novotný, Petr Gabriel, Michal Hornak, Vlastimil Svoboda, Martin Frýdek (85 Lumir Mistr), Zdenek Svoboda (Cap), Peter Gunda, Horst Siegl, Josef Obajdin (70 Vratislav Lokvenc).
Trainer: Vlastimil Petrzela

Goals: Vastic (8), Repka (57), Lokvenc (72), Mählich (85)

SPARTA PRAHA v STURM GRAZ 1-1 (0-0)

Stadion na Letnej, Praha   26.09.1996

Referee: Juan Antonio Fernandez Marin (SPA)   Att: 8000

SPARTA: Ivan Ondruska; Michal Hornak (Cap), Jiří Novotný, Tomas Repka, Lumir Mistr (88 Tomas Votava), Zdenek Svoboda, Martin Frýdek (90 Antonin Plachy), Vlastimil Svoboda, Peter Gunda (81 Josef Obajdin), Vratislav Lokvenc, Horst Siegl.   Trainer: Vlastimil Petrzela

STURM: Roland Goriupp; Mario Posch, Pål Lydersen, Marek Swierczewski, Martin Hiden, Herbert Grassler (70 Hannes Reinmayr), Giuseppe Giannini, Roman Mählich, Günther Neukirchner (59 Marcus Pürk), Mario Haas (86 Darko Milanic), Ivica Vastic (Cap).   Trainer: Ivica Osim

Goals: Novotný (77 og), Hornak (86)

CONSTRUCTORUL CHIŞINĂU v GALATASARAY ISTANBUL 0-1 (0-0)

Republican, Chişinău   12.09.1996

Referee: Kostadin Guerguinov (BUL)   Attendance: 7,000

CONSTRUCTORUL: Serghei Dinov; Vasile Apachiţei, Vladimir Dovghii, Gennadi Skidan, Iurie Platon (84 Ghenadie Puşca), Igor Cuciuc (Cap), Oleg Şişchin, Alexander Tarabrin, Iulian Bursuc, Serghei Rogaciov (77 Yuri Martâniuc), Victor Comlionoc (60 Serghei Prohorov).
Trainer: Alexandru Maţiura

GALATASARAY: Hayrettin Demirbas; Ulrich van Gobbel, Bülent Korkmaz (Cap), Vedat Inceefe (22 Bekir Gür), Feti Okuroglu; Arif Erdem (86 Okan Buruk), Hakan Ünsal, Hakan Şükür, Evren Turhan, Tugay Kerimoglu, Ümit Davala (67 Adrian Knup).   Trainer: Fatih Terim

Goal: Knup (73)

GALATASARAY ISTANBUL v CONSTRUCTORUL CHIŞINĂU 4-0 (0-0)

Ali Sami Yen, Istanbul   26.09.1996

Referee: Miroslav Radoman (YUG)   Attendance: 16,695

GALATASARAY: Hayrettin Demirbas; Bülent Korkmaz (Cap), Feti Okuroglu, Vedat Inceefe, Ulrich van Gobbel (78 Alp Küçükvardar), Ümit Davala, Tugay Kerimoglu, Gheorghe Hagi, Hakan Ünsal (82 Ergün Penbe); Hakan Şükür, Adrian Knup (46 Arif Erdem).   Trainer: Fatih Terim

CONSTRUCTORUL: Serghei Dinov; Igor Filip, Vasile Apachiţei, Oleg Tverdohlebov, Iurie Platon, Oleg Şişchin, Gennadi Skidan, Igor Cuciuc (Cap), Vladimir Dovghii (59 Serghei Prohorov), Victor Comlionoc (83 Ghenadie Puşca), Alexandru Scrupschi (53 Alexander Tarabrin).
Trainer: Alexandru Maţiura

Sent off: Platon (47)

Goals: Hakan Şükür (49, 80), Arif (73), Hagi (75)

FC KAISERSLAUTERN v CRVENA ZVEZDA BEOGRAD 1-0 (0-0)

Fritz-Walter-Stadion, Kaiserslautern   12.09.1996

Referee: Kenneth William Clark (SCO)   Attendance: 25,719

FC KAISERSLAUTERN: Andreas Reinke; Harry Koch, Andreas Brehme (Cap), Oliver Schäfer, Axel Roos, Frank Greiner, Uwe Wegmann, "Ratinho" Rodrigues, Thomas Riedl, Pavel Kuka, Jürgen Rische.   Trainer: Otto Rehhagel

CRVENA ZVEZDA: Zvonko Milojević (Cap); Vinko Marinović, Goran Djorović, Predrag Stanković, Nenad Sakić (90 Aleksandar Bratić), Zoran Njegus, Darko Anić, Nenad Vanić, Darko Ljubojević, Dejan Stanković (81 Goran Bošković), Zoran Jovicić.   Trainer: Vladimir Petrović

Goal: Wegmann (59)

CRVENA ZVEZDA BEOGRAD v FC KAISERSLAUTERN 4-0 (0-0, 1-0) (AET)

Crvena Zvezda Beograd   26.09.1996

Referee: Eric Blareau (BEL)   Attendance: 42,568

CRVENA ZVEZDA: Zvonko Milojević (Cap); Nenad Sakić, Goran Djorović, Nenad Vanić, Bratislav Zivković, Darko Anić, Zoran Njegus, Darko Ljubojević (46 Dejan Stanković), Predrag Stanković, Zoran Jovicić, Perica Ognjenović (84 Miodrag Pantelić).   Trainer: Vladimir Petrović

FC KAISERSLAUTERN: Andreas Reinke; Harry Koch (77 Thomas Riedl), Miroslav Kadlec, Oliver Schäfer, "Ratinho" Rodrigues, Frank Greiner, Thomas Franck (81 Jürgen Rische), Uwe Wegmann, Martin Wagner, Andreas Brehme (Cap), Pavel Kuka (90 Marco Reich).   Trainer: Otto Rehhagel

Goals: D. Stanković (55, 96), Njegus (107), Pantelić (120)

**MYLLYKOSKEN PALLO-47 ANJALANKOSKI
v LIVERPOOL FC 0-1** (0-0)

Saviniemi, Anjalankoski   12.09.1996

Referee: Gylfi Orrason (ICE)   Attendance: 4,767

MyPa: Petri Jakonen; Sami Mahlio, Mika Viljanen (Cap), David Moore, Jukka Koskinen, Antti Pohja, Mika Hernesniemi, Mauri Keskitalo (69 Tom Enberg), Toni Huttunen, John Allen (80 Juuso Kangaskorpi), Niclas Grönholm (74 Jasse Jalonen).   Trainer: Harri Kampman

LIVERPOOL FC: David James; Dominic Matteo, Phil Babb, Mark Wright, Jason McAteer, Michael Thomas, John Barnes (Cap), Stig Inge Bjørnebye, Steve McManaman, Stan Collymore, Robbie Fowler.   Manager: Roy Evans

Goal: Bjørnebye (61)

**LIVERPOOL FC v MYLLYKOSKEN PALLO-47
ANJALANKOSKI 3-1** (1-0)

Anfield, Liverpool   26.09.1996

Referee: Sergei Shmolik (BLS)   Attendance: 39,013

LIVERPOOL FC: David James; Jason McAteer, Mark Wright (19 John Scales), Phil Babb, Steve McManaman, Stan Collymore, John Barnes (Cap), Patrik Berger (79 Jamie Redknapp), Michael Thomas, Stig Inge Bjørnebye, Dominic Matteo (79 Neil Ruddock).   Manager: Roy Evans

MyPa: Petri Jakonen; Tommi Kautonen, Mika Viljanen (Cap), David Moore, Sami Mahlio, Antti Pohja, Mauri Keskitalo (75 Tom Enberg), Niclas Grönholm (63 Juuso Kangaskorpi), Jukka Koskinen, Toni Huttunen, John Allen (46 Jasse Jalonen).   Trainer: Harri Kampman

Goals: Berger (18), Collymore (59), Keskitalo (64), Barnes (78)

FC SION v NYVA VYNNYTSYA 2-0 (0-0)

Stade de Tourbillon, Sion   12.09.1996

Referee: Andreas Georgiou (CYP)   Attendance: 6,500

FC SION: Stephan Lehmann; Luiz Milton, Raphaël Wicky, Yvan Quentin (Cap); Alain Gaspoz, Patrick Sylvestre (84 Johann Lonfat), Ottó Vincze, Christophe Bonvin, Christian Colombo; Frédéric Chassot (63 Mirandinha Isailton), Vladan Lukic.   Trainer: Michel Decastel

NYVA: Volodymyr Tsytkin; Dmytro Lelyuk, Leonid Gaidarzhi (Cap), Anatoliy Balatskyi, Viktor Brovchenko, Yuri Solovienko, Vyacheslav Zaporozhchenko, Alexander Lyubynskyi (61 Pavlo Parshin), Volodymyr Braila (46 Alexander Laktionov), Olexiy Ryabtsev (89 Alexander Chervonyi), Ruslan Romanchuk.   Trainer: Pasha Kasanov

Goals: Colombo (50), Bonvin (85)

NYVA VYNNYTSYA v FC SION 0-4 (0-2)

Central Vynnytsya   26.09.1996

Referee: Manfred Schüttengruber (AUS)   Att: 12,000

NYVA: Volodymyr Tsytkin; Leonid Gaidarzhi (Cap), Viktor Brovchenko, Yuri Solovienko, Vyacheslav Zaporozhchenko, Anatoliy Balatskyi (46 Volodymyr Braila), Alexander Laktionov (46 Vasyl Maliuta), Ruslan Romanchuk, Olexiy Ryabtsev, Pavlo Parshin (67 Oleg Bessarab), Alexander Lyubynskyi.   Trainer: Pasha Kasanov

FC SION: Stephan Lehmann; Luiz Milton, Alain Gaspoz (55 Patrick Bühlmann), Raphaël Wicky, Yvan Quentin (Cap), Christian Colombo; Sébastien Zambaz, Philippe Vercruysse (68 Ottó Vincze), Johann Lonfat; Christophe Bonvin, Vladan Lukic (46 Frédéric Chassot).   Trainer: Michel Decastel

Goals: Lukic (3), Vercruysse (10, 63), Milton (49)

ÅRHUS GF v OLIMPIJA LJUBLJANA 1-1 (1-0)

Århus stadion   12.09.1996

Referee: Mikko Vuorela (FIN)   Attendance: 5,900

ÅRHUS: Lars Windfeld (Cap); Lennart Bak (81 Allan Jepsen), Gunner Lind, Torben Piechnik (46 Kern Lyhne), John Sivebaek, Johnny Vilstrup, Martin Jørgensen, Stig Tøfting, Håvard Flo, Thomas Thorningen (77 Lars Lambaek), Michael Nonbo.   Trainer: Peter Rudbaek

OLIMPIJA: Nihad Pejković; Robert Englaro (Cap), Samir Zulić, Erik Krzisnik, Safet Hadžić, Dejan Djuranović, Damjan Gajser (65 Azrudin Valentić), Igor Benedejcić, Milenko Acimović, Kliton Bozgo, Sebastijan Cimerotić (73 Edmond Dosti).   Trainer: Petar Nadoveza

Goals: Bak (15), Bozgo (57)

OLIMPIJA LJUBLJANA v ÅRHUS GF 0-0

Bezigrad, Ljubljana   26.09.1996

Referee: Sotirios Vorgias (GRE)   Attendance: 1,433

OLIMPIJA: Nihad Pejković; Robert Englaro (Cap), Safet Hadžić, Erik Krzisnik, Samir Zulić, Dejan Djuranović (89 Selvad Kujović), Igor Benedejcić, Milenko Acimović (70 Ermin Raković), Enver Adrović, Kliton Bozgo, Sebastijan Cimerotić (89 Edmond Dosti).   Trainer: Petar Nadoveza

ÅRHUS: Lars Windfeld (Cap); Lennart Bak (58 Lars Lambaek), Torben Piechnik, John Sivebaek, Michael Nonbo (86 Mads Rieper), Johnny Vilstrup, Martin Jørgensen, Stig Tøfting, Peter Degn (58 Kern Lyhne), Håvard Flo, Thomas Thorningen.   Trainer: Peter Rudbaek

CERCLE BRUGGE v SK BRANN BERGEN 3-2 (3-1)
Olympiastadion, Brugge   12.09.1996
Referee: John Ashman (WAL)   Attendance: 4,500
CERCLE: Yves Feys (Cap); Bert Lamaire, Alex Camerman, Dominique Van Maele, Musi Ajao (68 Giovanni De Keyser), Kofi M'Beah, Kurt Soenens (82 Frode Fermann), Ilie Stan, Björn Renty, Gábor Torma, Michael Gernsø (74 Anthony Annicaert).   Trainer: Jerko Tipuric
BRANN: Vidar Bahus; Geirmund Brendesaether, Claus Eftevaag (Cap), Per-Ove Ludvigsen, Morten Pedersen, Lars Bakkerud (78 Magnus Johansson), Jan Ove Pedersen, Roger Helland, Agúst Gylfason, Mons Ivar Mjelde, Tore André Flo.   Trainer: Kjell Tennfjord
Goals: Gernsö (5), Van Maele (26), Camerman (31), Flo (38), Eftevaag (89 pen)

**VARTEKS VARAZDIN
v LOKOMOTIV MOSKVA 2-1** (0-1)
Varteks Varazdin   26.09.1996
Referee: Georg Dardenne (GER)   Attendance: 8,500
VARTEKS: Ivica Solomun; Goran Borović, Mario Kovacević (43 Mario Ivanković), Drazen Madunović, Elvis Plantak, Zoran Ivancić (43 Damir Cvetko), Mladen Posavec, Robert Tezacki (66 Goran Dasović), Zoran Brlenić, Miljenko Mumlek, Davor Vugrinec (Cap).   Trainer: Predrag Stilinović
LOKOMOTIV: Sergei Ovchinnikov; Andrei Solomatin, Sarkis Hovhannisyan, Igor Chugainov, Aleksei Kosolapov (Cap), Sergei Gurenko, Zaza Janashia (80 Aleksei Snigiryev), Vladimir Maminov (86 Yuri Drozdov), Oleg Garas (63 Oleg Yelyshev), Igor Cherevchenko, Oleg Pashinin.   Trainer: Yuri Syomin
Goals: Kosolapov (41), Vugrinec (62, 79)

SK BRANN BERGEN v CERCLE BRUGGE 4-0 (1-0)
Brann Bergen   26.09.1996
Referee: Valeri Onufer (UKR)   Attendance: 6,104
BRANN: Birkir Kristinsson; Claus Eftevaag (Cap), Roger Helland, Geirmund Brendesaether, Morten Pedersen, Agúst Gylfason, Per-Ove Ludvigsen, Jan Ove Pedersen, Lars Bakkerud; Tore André Flo, Mons Ivar Mjelde.   Trainer: Kjell Tennfjord
CERCLE: Yves Feys (Cap); Thierry Siquet, Dominique Van Maele, Alex Camerman, Kofi M'Beah (75 Musi Ajao), Bert Lamaire, Kurt Soenens, Ilie Stan (46 Davy Cooreman), Björn Renty, Frode Fermann (46 Michael Gernsø), Gábor Torma.   Trainer: Jerko Tipuric
Goals: Mjelde (5, 80), Eftevaag (78), Helland (86)

KR REYKJAVÍK v AIK SOLNA 0-1 (0-0)
Laugardalsvöllur, Reykjavík   12.09.1996
Referee: Tore Hollung (NOR)   Attendance: 3,500
KR: Kristján Finnbogason; Thormódur Egilsson (Cap), Oskar Thorvaldsson, Brynjar Gunnarsson, Sigurdur Örn Jónsson; Hilmar Björnsson, Heimir Gudjónsson, Thorsteinn Jónsson (46 Gudmundur Benediktsson), Ólafur Kristjánsson, Einar Thór Daníelsson; Ríkhardur Dadason.   Trainer: Lúkas Kostic
AIK: Magnus Hedman; Pär Millqvist, Gary Sundgren (Cap), Michael Brundin, Pierre Gallo, Krister Nordin, Johan Mjällby, Ola Andersson, Marco Ciardi (68 Thomas Lagerlöf), Cesar Pacha (68 Patrik Fredholm), Pascal Simpson.   Trainer: Erik Hamrén
Goal: Nordin (78)

**LOKOMOTIV MOSKVA
v VARTEKS VARAZDIN 1-0** (1-0)
Lokomotiv Moskva   12.09.1996
Referee: Jacek Granat (POL)   Attendance: 5,000
LOKOMOTIV: Sergei Ovchinnikov; Yuri Drozdov, Igor Cherevchenko (87 Aleksei Arifullin), Evgeniy Kharlachov, Igor Chugainov, Aleksei Kosolapov (Cap), Sergei Gurenko, Oleg Yelyshev, Zaza Janashia, Oleg Garin (56 Aleksei Snigiryev, 75 Vladimir Maminov), Oleg Pashinin.   Trainer: Yuri Syomin
VARTEKS: Ivica Solomun; Krunoslav Beli (84 Mario Kovacević), Krunoslav Gregorić, Damir Maretić, Elvis Plantak, Goran Borović, Drazen Madunović, Robert Tezacki (89 Zoran Ivancić), Zoran Brlenić, Davor Vugrinec (Cap), Mario Ivanković (77 Goran Dasović).   Trainer: Predrag Stilinović
Sent off: Kharlachov (61)
Goal: Cherevchenko (12)

AIK SOLNA v KR REYKJAVÍK 1-1 (0-0)
Råsunda, Solna   26.09.1996
Referee: Stephen John Lodge (ENG)   Attendance: 3,267
AIK: Magnus Hedman; Pär Millqvist, Gary Sundgren (Cap), Michael Brundin, Pierre Gallo, Krister Nordin, Johan Mjällby, Ola Andersson, Marco Ciardi (59 Mattias Johansson), Cesar Pacha (66 Patrik Fredholm), Pascal Simpson.   Trainer: Erik Hamrén
KR: Kristján Finnbogason; Thormódur Egilsson (Cap), Brynjar Gunnarsson, Thorsteinn Gudjónsson, Ólafur Kristjánsson (65 Gudmundur Benediktsson); Hilmar Björnsson (77 Arnar Jón Sigurgeirsson), Sigurdur Örn Jónsson, Thorsteinn Jónsson, Einar Thór Daníelsson; Ríkhardur Dadason (80 Arni Inge Pjetursson), Bjarni Thorsteinsson.   Trainer: Lúkas Kostic
Goal: Simpson (79), Benediktsson (87)

FC BARCELONA v AEK LARNACA 2-0 (1-0)
Camp Nou, Barcelona 12.09.1996

Referee: Roland Beck (Lie)   Attendance: 35,000

FC BARCELONA: VÍTOR Manuel Martins BAÍA; LUIS ENRIQUE Martínez García, ABELARDO Fernández Antuña, Laurent Blanc, SERGI Barjuan Esclusa; Luis Filipe Madeira Caeiro FIGO (72 Angel Manuel CUELLAR Llanos), Gheorghe Popescu (Cap) (72 Josep GUARDIOLA Sala), Robert Prosinecki (72 ROGER García Junyent), GIOVANNI Silva de Oliveira; Juan Antonio PIZZI Torroja, RONALDO Luiz Nazario da Lima.   Trainer: Bobby Robson

AEK: Andreas Mavris; Giorgos Theodotou (78 Nikolas Georgiou), Neophytos Larkou (Cap), Giorgos Konstantinou, Aggelos Misos, Louis Stefani, Pavlos Markou, Milenko Kovacevic (84 Stelios Stylianidis), Zoran Kuntic (70 Andreas Panagiotou), Klimis Alexandrou, Goran Kopunovic.   Trainer: Andreas Mouskalis

Goals: Ronaldo (19, 77)

AEK LARNACA v FC BARCELONA 0-0
Zenon, Larnaca 26.09.1996

Referee: Claude Colombo (FRA)   Attendance: 6,000

AEK: Andreas Mavris; Aggelos Misos, Pavlos Markou, Giorgos Konstantinou, Neophytos Larkou (Cap), Louis Stefani, Nikolas Georgiou (64 Dimitris Panagiotou), Hristos Bakaris (61 Lazaros Iacovou), Milenko Kovacevic, Andreas Panagiotou (50 Stelios Stylianidis), Zoran Kuntic.   Trainer: A. Mouskalis

FC BARCELONA: VÍTOR Manuel Martins BAÍA; Albert CELADES López, Laurent Blanc, ABELARDO Fernández Antuña; LUIS ENRIQUE Martínez García, Luis Filipe Madeira Caeiro FIGO (78 Angel Manuel CUELLAR Llanos), Gheorghe Popescu (Cap), Robert Prosinecki (71 ROGER García Junyent), Guillermo AMOR Martínez, Iván DE LA PEÑA (73 José María BAKERO Escudero), GIOVANNI Silva de Oliveira.

BENFICA LISBOA v RUCH CHORZOW 5-1 (3-0)
Estádio da Luz, Lisboa 12.09.1996

Referee: Herrmann Albrecht (GER)   Attendance: 17,000

BENFICA: Michel Georges Jean Ghislain PREUD'HOMME; José António CALADO da Silva, Jorge Hernan BERMUDEZ Morales, HÉLDER Marino Rodrigues Cristóvão, DIMAS Manuel Marques Teixeira (60 Luís GUSTAVO Carvalho Soares), JAMIR Adriano Paz Gomes, BRUNO Ricardo Mendonça de CAIRES (71 HASSAN Nader), VALDO Cândido Filho, Basarab Nica Panduru (84 Tahar EL KHALEJ), JOÃO Manuel Vieira PINTO (Cap), Osmar DONIZETE Cândido.   Trainer: Paulo Autuori

RUCH: Piotr Lech; Jerzy Gasior, Marcin Baszczynski, Miroslaw Jaworski, Arkadiusz Bak, Miroslaw Mosor (Cap) (78 Witold Wawryczek), Dariusz Gesior, Mariusz Srutwa (59 Maciej Mizia), Piotr Rowicki, Bogdan Pieniazek, Miroslaw Bak (70 Adam Katolik).   Trainer: Jerzy Wyrobek

Goals: Donizete (24), João V. Pinto (26), Jamir (31), Valdo (68, 90), Gesior (71)

RUCH CHORZOW v BENFICA LISBOA 0-0
Ruch Chorzow 26.09.1996

Referee: Mika Peltola (FIN)   Attendance: 4,547

RUCH: Piotr Lech; Witold Wawrzyczeck (64 Miroslaw Bak), Dariusz Fornalak, Dariusz Gesior, Marcin Baszczynski, Piotr Rowicki (57 Arkadiusz Gaca), Maciej Mizia, Bogdan Pieniazek, Miroslaw Mosor (Cap), Arkadiusz Bak, Mariusz Srutwa (88 Adam Katolik).   Trainer: Jerzy Wyrobek

BENFICA: Michel Georges Jean Ghislain PREUD'HOMME; Mário Teixeira da Costa "MARINHO" (46 HASSAN Nader), Jorge Hernan BERMUDEZ Morales, HÉLDER Marino Rodrigues Cristóvão, PEDRO Ricardo Quintela HENRIQUES, Tahar El Khalej, JAMIR Adriano Paz Gomes, VALDO Cândido Filho (74 Ilian Dimov ILIEV), Basarab Nica Panduru, JOÃO Manuel Vieira PINTO (Cap) (86 Alves Paulo António "PAULÃO"), Osmar DONIZETE Cândido.   Trainer: Paulo Autuori

AEK ATHINA v CHEMLON HUMENNE 1-0 (0-0)
Nikos Goumas, Athina 12.09.1996

Referee: Yuri Chebotarev (RUS)   Attendance: 15,141

AEK: Ilias Atmatzidis; Vasilis Borbokis (80 Haralampos Kopitsis), Anton Doboş (46 Stelios Manolas), Nikos Kostenoglou, Mihalis Kasapis (Cap); Temur Ketsbaia, Hristos Maladenis, Hristos Kostis, Toni Savevski, Themistoklis Nikolaidis (68 MARCELO Veridiano), Daniel Batista.   Trainer: Petros Ravousis

CHEMLON: Juraj Bucek; Peter Dzurik (Cap), Niksa Boljat, Frantisek Hanc; Vladimir Sivy, Jozef Valkucak (60 Pavel Dina), Igor Sukennik, Rastislav Tomovcik (84 Marek Lukac), Jaroslav Sovic, Ruslan Lubarsky, Vojtech Kiss (60 Lubomir Mati).   Trainer: Ondrej Danko

Goal: Batista (48)

CHEMLON HUMENNE v AEK ATHINA 1-2 (1-2)
Chemlon Humenne 26.09.1996

Referee: Mateo Beusan (CRO)   Attendance: 14,600

CHEMLON: Juraj Bucek; Marek Gadzo (67 Vojtech Kiss), Peter Dzurik (Cap), Niksa Boljat (67 Milan Sciranka), Frantisek Hanc, Jozef Valkucak, Igor Sukennik (49 Lubomir Mati), Pavel Dina, Vladimir Sivy, Ruslan Lubarsky, Rastislav Tomovcik.   Trainer: Ondrej Danko

AEK: Ilias Atmatzidis; Vasilis Borbokis, Nikos Kostenoglou, Mihalis Vlahos, Mihalis Kasapis (Cap), Hristos Kostis (46 Hristos Maladenis), Stelios Manolas, Temur Ketsbaia (73 Haralampos Kopitsis), Toni Savevski, Daniel Batista, Themistoklis Nikolaidis.   Trainer: Petros Ravousis

Goals: Dina (1), Nikolaidis (17), Batista (44)

**GLORIA BISTRIȚA
v AC FIORENTINA FIRENZE 1-1** (1-0)

Gloria Bistrița   12.09.1996

Referee: Christer Fällström (SWE)   Attendance: 10,000

GLORIA: Costel Câmpeanu (Cap); Eugen Voica (83 Marian Năstase), Valer Săsărman, Emil Gavril Dăncuș, Gabriel Cristea, Dorel Purdea, Ioan Miszti, Marius Răduță (43 Cornel Sevastița), Ilie Lazăr, Dănuț Matei, Radu Sabo (70 Gheorghe Bogdan Nicolae).   Trainer: Remus Vlad

FIORENTINA: Francesco Toldo; Daniele Carnasciali, Giovanni Piacentini (72 Francesco Baiano), Lorenzo Amoruso, Giulio Falcone (62 Vittorio Pusceddu), Aldo Firicano, Stefan Schwarz, Rui Costa, Emiliano Bigica (83 Sandro Cois); Gabriel Batistuta (Cap), Anselmo Robbiati.   Trainer: Claudio Ranieri

Goals: Lazăr (3), Batistuta (47)

PSV EINDHOVEN v DINAMO BATUMI 3-0 (1-0)

Philips, Eindhoven   26.09.1996

Referee: Stuart Dougall (SCO)   Attendance: 14,200

PSV: Ronald Waterreus; Marcos Batista Vampeta, Jaap Stam, Stan Valckx, Arthur Numan (Cap), Marciano Vink (46 Boudewijn Zenden), Win Jonk, Marc Degryse, Philip Cocu, Luc Nilis (66 Marcello Silva Ramos), René Eijkelkamp (80 Zeljko Petrović).   Trainer: Dick Advocaat

DINAMO: Nikoloz Togonidze; Tengiz Sichinava (53 Valeri Shanidze), Zurab Mindadze, David Chichveishvili, Gela Shekiladze, Rostom Torgashvili, Malkhaz Makharadze (Cap), Temur Tugushi, Paata Machutadze, David Ujmajuridze, Amiran Mudjiri.   Trainer: Shota Cheishvili

Goals: Nilis (15 pen), Eijkelkamp (57), Marcelo (86)

**AC FIORENTINA FIRENZE
v GLORIA BISTRIȚA 1-0** (1-0)

Artemio Franchi, Firenze   26.09.1996

Referee: Ladislav Gadosi (SVK)   Attendance: 18,607

FIORENTINA: Francesco Toldo; Daniele Carnasciali, Lorenzo Amoruso, Aldo Firicano, Vittorio Pusceddu; Emiliano Bigica, Rui Costa (46 Francesco Baiano), Stefan Schwarz; Luis Oliveira (85 Anselmo Robbiati), Gabriel Batistuta (Cap), Massimo Orlando (73 Giovanni Piacentini).
Trainer: Claudio Ranieri

GLORIA: Costel Câmpeanu (Cap), Aurelian Ioan Șomotecan, Gabriel Cristea, Cornel Sevastița, Dumitru Halostă, Valer Săsărman, Eugen Voica, Emil Gavril Dăncuș, Radu Sabo, Dănuț Matei, Ilie Lazăr (79 Marian Năstase).
Trainer: Remus Vlad

Goal: Orlando (23)

FC VADUZ v PARIS SAINT-GERMAIN 0-4 (0-3)

Gemeindersportplatz, Vaduz   12.09.1996

Referee: Romans Lajuks (LAT)   Attendance: 3,900

FC VADUZ: Martin Heeb; Markus Weber, Harry Zech, Daniel Hasler (Cap), Erkan Erdogan; Marcel Müller, Marco Perez, Alexander Quaderer (67 Patrik Hefti), Tomas Daumantas; Fulvio Cimino (70 Lobli), Daniele Polverino (76 Peter Krainz).   Trainer: Hans Rudi Fässler

PSG: Bernard Lama (Cap); Laurent Fournier, Alain Roche (46 Romeo Calenda), Paul le Guen (46 José Cobos), Daniel Kenedy; Bruno Ngotty, Benoît Cauet, Jérôme Leroy, LEONARDO Nascimento de Araújo; Patrick Mboma (67 Bernard Allou), Julio César DELY VALDÉS.
Trainer: Ricardo Gomes

Goals: Le Guen (13), Dely Valdes (41), Leonardo (45), Allou (72)

DINAMO BATUMI v PSV EINDHOVEN 1-1 (1-1)

Dinamo Batumi   12.09.1996

Referee: Kurt Zuppinger (SWI)   Attendance: 14,000

DINAMO: Nikoloz Togonidze; Tengiz Sichinava, Zurab Mindadze, David Chichveishvili (87 Valeri Shanidze), Gela Shekiladze, Rostom Torgashvili, Malkhaz Makharadze, Paata Machutadze (73 Avtandil Glonti), Temur Tugushi, David Ujmajuridze, Amiran Mudjiri.   Trainer: Shota Cheishvili

PSV: Ronald Waterreus; Chris Van der Weerden, Stan Valckx, Jaap Stam, Arthur Numan, Marciano Vink, Win Jonk, Marc Degryse (80 Boudewijn Zenden), Philip Cocu, Luc Nilis, René Eijkelkamp (70 Marcelo Silva Ramos).
Trainer: Dick Advocaat

Goals: Mudjiri (23), Nilis (42 pen)

PARIS SAINT-GERMAIN v FC VADUZ 3-0 (2-0)

Parc des Princes, Paris   26.09.1996

Referee: Bujar Pregia (ALB)   Attendance: 15,973

PSG: Vincent Fernandez; José Cobos, Alain Roche, Paul le Guen (Cap), Didier Domi; Bruno Ngotty (61 Laurent Fournier), Romeo Calenda, Vincent Guérin, Jérôme Leroy (73 RAÍ Souza Vieira de Oliveira); Bernard Allou, Patrick Mboma.   Trainer: Ricardo Gomes

FC VADUZ: Martin Heeb; Markus Weber, Patrik Hefti, Daniel Hasler, Harry Zech, Erkan Erdogan, Marcel Müller (73 Patrick Albrecht), Marco Perez, Tomas Daumantas, Fulvio Cimino (46 Peter Krainz), Christian Kubli (79 Daniele Polverino).
Trainer: Hans Rudi Fässler

Goals: Allou (22), Roche (40), Mboma (50)

SECOND ROUND

**BENFICA LISBOA
v LOKOMOTIV MOSKVA 1-0** (1-0)
SL Benfica Lisboa 17.10.1996
Referee: Alain Sars (FRA)   Attendance: 8,090
BENFICA: Michel Georges Jean Ghislain PREUD'HOMME; José António CALADO da Silva, HÉLDER Marino Rodrigues Cristóvão, JAMIR Adriano Paz Gomes, DIMAS Manuel Marques Teixeira, Basarab Nicǎ Panduru, BRUNO Ricardo Mendonça de CAIRES (55 EDGAR Patrício Carvalho Pacheco), VALDO Cândido Filho, Jorge Hernan BERMUDEZ Morales, HASSAN Nader (55 Tahar El Khalej), JOÃO Manuel Vieira PINTO (Cap).   Trainer: Paulo Autuori
LOKOMOTIV: Sergei Ovchinnikov; Sergei Gurenko, Igor Chugainov, Igor Cherevchenko, Oleg Pashinin, Aleksei Kosolapov (Cap), Sarkis Hovhannisyan, Evgeniy Kharlachov, Yuri Drozdov, Oleg Garas (70 Vitaliy Veselov), Vladimir Maminov (59 Alexander Smirnov).   Trainer: Yuri Syomin
Goal: João V. Pinto (8)

**LOKOMOTIV MOSKVA
v BENFICA LISBOA 2-3** (1-0)
Lokomotiv Moskva 31.10.1996
Referee: Knud Erik Fisker (DEN)   Attendance: 6,500
LOKOMOTIV: Sergei Ovchinnikov; Sergei Gurenko, Igor Chugainov, Igor Cherevchenko, Andrei Solomatin, Aleksei Kosolapov (Cap), Oleg Pashinin, Evgeniy Kharlachov, Yuri Drozdov, Oleg Garas (75 Vitaliy Veselov), Vladimir Maminov. Trainer: Yuri Syomin
BENFICA: Michel Georges Jean Ghislain PREUD'HOMME; Tahar El Khalej, HÉLDER Marino Rodrigues Cristóvão, JAMIR Adriano Paz Gomes (39 Basarab Nicǎ Panduru), DIMAS Manuel Marques Teixeira, José António CALADO da Silva, Jorge Hernan BERMUDEZ Morales, VALDO Cândido Filho, Ilian Dimov ILIEV (81 JORGE Manuel Guerreiro SOARES), Osmar DONIZETE Cândido (81 MAURO Gabriel AIREZ Airez), JOÃO Manuel Vieira PINTO (Cap).
Trainer: Paulo Autuori
Sent off: Gurenko (28)
Goals: Solomatin (9), Panduru (48), Garas (59), Donizete (63), João V. Pinto (89)

OLYMPIQUE NÎMES v AIK SOLNA 1-3 (0-2)
Les Costières, Nîmes 17.10.1996
Referee: Leslie John Irvine (NIR)   Attendance: 15,049
NÎMES: Stanislaw Karwat; Franck Touron (81 Grégory Meilhac), Johnny Ecker, Antoine Preget, Anthony Vosahlo (65 Christophe Zugna); Cyril Jeunechamp, Omar Belbey, Mehmed Baždarević, Antoine Di Fraya (Cap); Eric Sabin (59 Sébastien Fidani), Nicolas Marx.   Trainer: Pierre Mosca

AIK: Magnus Hedman; Thomas Lagerlöf, Pär Millqvist, Michael Brundin, Johan Mjällby, Krister Nordin, Ola Andersson (Cap), Marco Ciardi (46 Mattias Johansson), Pierre Gallo, Pascal Simpson, Cesar Pacha.   Trainer: Erik Hamrén
Goals: Simpson (9), Pacha (12), M. Johansson (70), Fidani (88)

AIK SOLNA v OLYMPIQUE NÎMES 0-1 (0-0)
Råsunda, Solna 31.10.1996
Referee: Lubos Michel (SVK)   Attendance: 5,620
AIK: Magnus Hedman; Pär Millqvist, Thomas Lagerlöf, Michael Brundin, Gary Sundgren (Cap), Patrik Fredholm (75 Alexander Östlund), Pierre Gallo, Marco Ciardi, Mattias Johansson, Cesar Pacha, Pascal Simpson.   Trainer: E. Hamrén
NÎMES: Stanislaw Karwat; Franck Touron (Cap), Anthony Vosahlo, Cyril Jeunechamp, Laurent De Palmas, Christophe Zugna; Omar Belbey, Mohamed Benyachou, Mehmed Baždarević; Nicolas Marx, Eric Sabin (53 Sébastien Gervais).   Trainer: Pierre Mosca
Goal: Brundin (69 og)

OLIMPIJA LJUBLJANA v AEK ATHINA 0-2 (0-1)
Bezigrad, Ljubljana 17.10.1996
Referee: Atanas Uzunov (BUL)   Attendance: 4,000
OLIMPIJA: Nihad Pejković; Safet Hadžić, Samir Zulić, Robert Englaro (Cap), Enver Adrović (67 Virginio Velkoski), Igor Benedejcić, Dejan Djuranović, Damjan Gajser, Erik Krzisnik (76 Azrudin Valentić), Kliton Bozgo, Sebastijan Cimerotić (67 Ermin Raković).   Trainer: Petar Nadoveza
AEK: Ilias Atmatzidis; Vasilis Borbokis, Stelios Manolas (84 Anton Doboş), Nikos Kostenoglou, Mihalis Kasapis (Cap), Hristos Maladenis, Mihalis Vlahos, Toni Savevski (80 Vaios Karagiannis), Hristos Kostis, Temur Ketsbaia, Themistoklis Nikolaidis (73 Haralampos Kopitsis). Trainer: Petros Ravousis
Goals: Kostis (12), Ketsbaia (49)

AEK ATHINA v OLIMPIJA LJUBLJANA 4-0 (2-0)
Nikos Goumas, Athina 31.10.1996
Referee: Herrmann Albrecht (GER)   Attendance: 14,482
AEK: Ilias Atmatzidis; Vasilis Borbokis (48 Temur Ketsbaia), Mihalis Kasapis (Cap), Stelios Manolas (84 Anton Doboş), Nikos Kostenoglou, Mihalis Vlahos, Daniel Batista, Toni Savevski (80 Vaios Karagiannis), Hristos Maladenis, Hristos Kostis, Themistoklis Nikolaidis (69 Haralampos Kopitsis). Trainer: Petros Ravousis
OLIMPIJA: Nihad Pejković; Robert Englaro (Cap), Samir Zulić, Safet Hadžić, Erik Krzisnik, Enver Adrović, Dejan Djuranović (45 Milenko Acimović), Damjan Gajser, Igor Benedejcić (77 Azrudin Valentić), Kliton Bozgo, Sebastijan Cimerotić (80 Ermin Raković).   Trainer: Petar Nadoveza
Goals: Savevski (4 pen), Batista (20), Maladenis (80), Kostis (85)

**GALATASARAY ISTANBUL
v PARIS SAINT-GERMAIN 4-2** (3-2)

Ali Sami Yen, Istanbul 17.10.1996

Referee: Pier Luigi Collina (ITA)   Attendance: 23,000

GALATASARAY: Hayrettin Demirbas; Bekir Gür, Vedat Inceefe, Ergün Penbe, Bülent Korkmaz (Cap); Ümit Davala, Tugay Kerimoglu, Gheorghe Hagi (87 Mert Korkmaz), Hakan Ünsal (79 Suat Kaya); Arif Erdem (85 Okan Buruk), Hakan Şükür. Trainer: Fatih Terim

PSG: Vincent Fernandez; José Cobos, Alain Roche, Paul le Guen (Cap), Daniel Kenedy; Jérôme Leroy, Vincent Guérin, RAí Souza Vieira de Oliveira (60 Laurent Fournier), Benoît Cauet; Julio César DELY VALDÉS (74 Patrick Mboma), Patrice Loko (63 Nicolas Anelka). Trainer: Ricardo Gomes

Goals: Hakan Şükür (5, 31), Tugay (13), Le Guen (18), Dely Valdes (19), Hakan Ünsal (53)

**PARIS SAINT-GERMAIN
v GALATASARAY ISTANBUL 4-0** (2-0)

Parc des Princes, Paris 31.10.1996

Referee: Karol Ihring (SVK)   Attendance: 34,032

PSG: Bernard Lama (Cap); Jimmy Algérino (72 Laurent Fournier), Alain Roche, Paul le Guen, Benoît Cauet; Vincent Guérin (63 Daniel Kenedy), Bruno Ngotty, RAí Souza Vieira de Oliveira (87 Jérôme Leroy), LEONARDO Nascimento de Araújo; Julio César DELY VALDÉS, Patrice Loko. Trainer: Ricardo Gomes

GALATASARAY: Hayrettin Demirbas; Bekir Gür, Vedat Inceefe, Bülent Korkmaz (Cap), Ümit Davala (60 Evren Turhan), Ergün Penbe, Mert Korkmaz (46 Okan Buruk), Gheorghe Hagi, Hakan Ünsal (65 Adrian Knup); Arif Erdem, Hakan Şükür. Trainer: Fatih Terim

Goals: Leonardo (10), Dely Valdes (23), Loko (59), Rai (78)

FC SION v LIVERPOOL FC 1-2 (1-1)

Stade de Tourbillon, Sion 17.10.1996

Referee: Antonio Jesús López Nieto (SPA)   Att: 16,500

FC SION: Stephan Lehmann; Alain Gaspoz, Raphaël Wicky, Luiz Milton, Yvan Quentin (Cap); Patrick Sylvestre, Sébastien Zambaz (67 Frédéric Chassot), Philippe Vercruysse, Johann Lonfat; Christophe Bonvin (80 Ottó Vincze), Vladan Lukic. Trainer: Michel Decastel

LIVERPOOL FC: David James; John Scales, Dominic Matteo, Phil Babb, Jason McAteer, John Barnes (Cap), Michael Thomas, Steve McManaman, Stig Inge Bjørnebye, Patrik Berger, Robbie Fowler (67 Jamie Redknapp). Manager: Roy Evans

Goals: Bonvin (11), Fowler (24), Barnes (60)

LIVERPOOL FC v FC SION 6-3 (1-2)

Anfield, Liverpool 31.10.1996

Referee: Hartmut Strampe (GER)   Attendance: 38,514

LIVERPOOL FC: David James; John Scales (60 Jamie Redknapp), Phil Babb, Dominic Matteo, Jason McAteer, John Barnes (Cap), Michael Thomas, Steve McManaman, Stig Inge Bjørnebye, Patrik Berger, Robbie Fowler. Manager: Roy Evans

FC SION: Stephan Lehmann; Patrick Sylvestre, Luiz Milton, Yvan Quentin (Cap); Alain Gaspoz (76 Patrick Bühlmann), Johann Lonfat (46 Sébastien Zambaz), Christian Colombo, Philippe Vercruysse, Raphaël Wicky; Christophe Bonvin (76 Ottó Vincze), Frédéric Chassot. Trainer: Michel Decastel

Goals: Chassot (19, 64), Bonvin (23), McManaman (28), Bjørnebye (54), Barnes (65), Fowler (71, 72), Berger (90)

SK BRANN BERGEN v PSV EINDHOVEN 2-1 (2-0)

Brann Bergen 17.10.1996

Referee: Alain Hamer (LUX)   Attendance: 7,842

BRANN: Birkir Kristinsson; Lars Bakkerud, Roger Helland, Claus Eftevaag (Cap), Geirmund Brendesaether, Per-Ove Ludvigsen, Jan Ove Pedersen (84 Magnus Johansson), Agúst Gylfason, Morten Pedersen; Tore André Flo, Mons Ivar Mjelde. Trainer: Kjell Tennfjord

PSV: Ronald Waterreus; Marcos Batista Vampeta, Jaap Stam, Stan Valckx, Arthur Numan (Cap), Björn Van der Doelen (38 Chris Van der Weerden), Zeljko Petrović (60 Boudewijn Zenden), Marc Degryse, Luc Nilis, René Eijkelkamp, Philip Cocu. Trainer: Dick Advocaat

Goals: Mjelde (29, 34 pen), Cocu (90)

PSV EINDHOVEN v SK BRANN BERGEN 2-2 (0-1)

Philips, Eindhoven 31.10.1996

Referee: Philippe Leduc (FRA)   Attendance: 19,000

PSV: Ronald Waterreus; Marcos Batista Vampeta, Jaap Stam, Arthur Numan (Cap), Stan Valckx (63 Marcello Silva Ramos), Win Jonk, Marciano Vink (79 Zeljko Petrović), Philip Cocu, Boudewijn Zenden, René Eijkelkamp, Luc Nilis. Trainer: Dick Advocaat

BRANN: Birkir Kristinsson; Roger Helland, Claus Eftevaag (Cap), Jan Ove Pedersen, Morten Pedersen (86 Asbjørn Tenden), Eirik Skjaelaaen, Magnus Johansson (90 Erik Johannessen), Geir Hasund (76 Cato Guntveit), Geirmund Brendesaether; Mons Ivar Mjelde, Tore André Flo. Trainer: Kjell Tennfjord

Goals: Hasund (35), Flo (60), Eijkelkamp (75), Zenden (82)

**FIORENTINA FIRENZE
v SPARTA PRAHA 2-1** (1-0)

Artemio Franchi, Firenze 17.10.1996

Referee: Serge Muhmenthaler (SWI)   Attendance: 22,400

FIORENTINA: Francesco Toldo; Daniele Carnasciali, Aldo Firicano, Lorenzo Amoruso, Vittorio Pusceddu; Sandro Cois (84 Luis Oliveira), Emiliano Bigica (55 Anselmo Robbiati), Rui Costa, Stefan Schwarz; Gabriel Batistuta (Cap), Francesco Baiano (74 Giulio Falcone).   Trainer: Claudio Ranieri

SPARTA: Michal Caloun; Tomas Repka, Michal Hornak, Tomas Votava, Petr Gabriel (65 Vratislav Lokvenc), Lumir Mistr, Jiří Novotný, Zdenek Svoboda (Cap) (84 Peter Gunda), Vlastimil Svoboda (76 Josef Obajdin), Horst Siegl, Martin Frýdek.   Trainer: Vlastimil Petrzela

Goals: Batistuta (5), Schwarz (56), Siegl (80)

**SPARTA PRAHA
v AC FIORENTINA FIRENZE 1-1** (1-0)

Štadión na Letnej, Praha 31.10.1996

Referee: David Roland Elleray (ENG)   Attendance: 16,021

SPARTA: Michal Caloun; Michal Hornak, Tomas Votava, Tomas Repka, Lumir Mistr (72 Josef Obajdin), Zdenek Svoboda (Cap), Jiří Novotný, Martin Frýdek, Vlastimil Svoboda (82 Petr Gabriel), Horst Siegl, Vratislav Lokvenc.
Trainer: Vlastimil Petrzela

FIORENTINA: Francesco Toldo; Daniele Carnasciali, Aldo Firicano, Pasquale Padalino, Vittorio Pusceddu; Sandro Cois, Stefan Schwarz, Rui Costa (90 Massimo Orlando), Anselmo Robbiati (76 Giovanni Piacentini), Gabriel Batistuta (Cap), Luis Oliveira (89 Francesco Baiano).
Trainer: Claudio Ranieri

Goals: Lokvenc (5), Robbiati (63)

**FC BARCELONA
v CRVENA ZVEZDA BEOGRAD 3-1** (2-1)

Camp Nou, Barcelona 17.10.1996

Referee: Rémy Harrel (FRA)   Attendance: 73,000

FC BARCELONA: VÍTOR Manuel Martins BAÍA; LUIS ENRIQUE Martínez García, ABELARDO Fernández Antuña, Laurent Blanc, SERGI Barjuan Esclusa; Luis Filipe Madeira Caeiro FIGO, Josep GUARDIOLA Sala, Gheorghe Popescu (Cap), Hristo Stoichkov (73 Robert Prosinecki), GIOVANNI Silva de Oliveira, Juan Antonio PIZZI Torroja (67 Iván DE LA PEÑA).   Trainer: Bobby Robson

CRVENA ZVEZDA: Zvonko Milojević (Cap); Nenad Sakić, Vinko Marinović, Goran Djorović, Predrag Stanković, Zoran Njegus, Nenad Vanić, Bratislav Zivković, Dejan Stanković, Miodrag Pantelić (60 Perica Ognjenović), Zoran Jovicić.
Trainer: Vladimir Petrović

Goals: Zivković (21), Giovanni (34, 36), Figo (54)

**CRVENA ZVEZDA BEOGRAD
v FC BARCELONA 1-1** (1-0)

Crvena Zvezda Beograd 31.10.1996

Referee: Gerd Grabher (AUS)   Attendance: 44,694

CRVENA ZVEZDA: Zvonko Milojević (Cap); Bratislav Zivković, Predrag Stanković, Zoran Njegus, Goran Djorović, Nenad Vanić, Perica Ognjenović, Goran Bošković (46 Miodrag Pantelić), Zoran Jovicić, Darko Anić, Darko Ljubojević.
Trainer: Vladimir Petrović

FC BARCELONA: VÍTOR Manuel Martins BAÍA; ABELARDO Fernández Antuña, Miguel Angel NADAL Homar, Laurent Blanc, SERGI Barjuan Esclusa, LUIS ENRIQUE Martínez García; Gheorghe Popescu (Cap), Josep GUARDIOLA Sala; Hristo Stoichkov (83 ROGER García Junyent), GIOVANNI Silva de Oliveira (87 Guillermo AMOR Martínez), RONALDO Luiz Nazario da Lima (76 Juan Antonio PIZZI Torroja).   Trainer: Bobby Robson

Goals: Jovicić (47), Giovanni (48)

QUARTER-FINALS

SK BRANN BERGEN v LIVERPOOL FC 1-1 (0-1)

Brann Bergen 6.03.1997

Referee: Nikolai Levnikov (RUS)   Attendance: 12,700

BRANN: Vidar Bahus; Stefan Paldan, Claus Eftevaag (Cap), Per-Ove Ludvigsen, Roger Helland, Morten Pedersen; Eirik Skjaelaaen, Agúst Gylfasson, Arne Vidar Moen (46 Mons Ivar Mjelde), Geir Hasund; Tore André Flo.
Trainer: Kjell Tennfjord

LIVERPOOL FC: David James; Dominic Matteo, Neil Ruddock, Steve Harkness, Jason McAteer, Jamie Redknapp, Steve McManaman, John Barnes (Cap), Stig Inge Bjørnebye, Robbie Fowler, Patrik Berger.   Manager: Roy Evans

Goals: Fowler (10), Hasund (48)

LIVERPOOL FC v SK BRANN BERGEN 3-0 (1-0)

Anfield, Liverpool 20.03.1997

Referee: Alfredo Trentalange (ITA)   Attendance: 40,326

LIVERPOOL FC: David James; Jason McAteer, Steve Harkness, Mark Wright, Dominic Matteo (46 Phil Babb), Stig Inge Bjørnebye, John Barnes (Cap), Jamie Redknapp, Steve McManaman, Patrik Berger (59 Stan Collymore), Robbie Fowler.   Manager: Roy Evans

BRANN: Vidar Bahus; Claus Eftevaag (46 Agúst Gylfason), Roger Helland, Eirik Skjaelaaen (86 Erik Johannessen), Geir Hasund (65 Cato Guntveit), Per-Ove Ludvigsen, Morten Pedersen, Stefan Paldan, Arne Vidar Moen; Mons Ivar Mjelde, Tore André Flo.   Trainer: Kjell Tennfjord

Goals: Fowler (26 pen, 77), Collymore (60)

PARIS SAINT-GERMAIN v AEK ATHINA 0-0

Parc des Princes, Paris   6.03.1997

Referee: Urs Meier (SWI)   Attendance: 21,952

PSG: Bernard Lama; Laurent Fournier, Bruno Ngotty, Paul le Guen, Daniel Kenedy; Benoît Cauet, RAÍ Souza Vieira de Oliveira (Cap), LEONARDO Nascimento de Araújo, Bernard Allou; Julio César DELY VALDÉS (75 Cyrille Pouget), Patrice Loko.   Trainer: Ricardo Gomes

AEK: Ilias Atmatzidis; Vasilis Borbokis, Stelios Manolas, Nikos Kostenoglou, Mihalis Kasapis (Cap), Temur Ketsbaia, Triantafilos Mahairidis (73 Anton Doboş), Mihalis Vlahos, Toni Savevski (89 Haralampos Kopitsis), Themistoklis Nikolaidis (82 MARCELO Veridiano), Daniel Batista.   Trainer: Petros Ravousis

AEK ATHINA v PARIS SAINT-GERMAIN 0-3 (0-2)

Nikos Goumas, Athina   20.03.1996

Referee: Antonio Jesús Lopez Nieto (SPA)   Att: 33,000

AEK: Ilias Atmatzidis; Vasilis Borbokis, Stelios Manolas, Mihalis Vlahos (58 Vaios Karagiannis), Mihalis Kasapis, Temur Ketsbaia, Triantafilos Mahairidis (73 MARCELO Veridiano), Toni Savevski, Themistoklis Nikolaidis, Daniel Batista (55 Hristos Maladenis), Hristos Kostis.   Trainer: Petros Ravousis

PSG: Bernard Lama; Laurent Fournier (84 Jimmy Algérino); Bruno Ngotty, Paul le Guen, Daniel Kenedy; Jérôme Leroy, RAÍ Souza Vieira de Oliveira (Cap), Vincent Guérin, Benoît Cauet; Patrice Loko, LEONARDO Nascimento de Araújo (82 Cyrille Pouget).   Trainer: Ricardo Gomes

Goals: Loko (22, 44, 81)

FC BARCELONA v AIK SOLNA 3-1 (1-1)

Camp Nou, Barcelona   6.03.1997

Referee: David Roland Elleray (ENG)   Attendance: 60,000

FC BARCELONA: Carlos BUSQUETS Barroso; Albert FERRER Llopis (46 GIOVANNI Silva de Oliveira), Miguel Angel NADAL Homar, Laurent Blanc, SERGI Barjuan Esclusa; LUIS ENRIQUE Martínez García, Josep GUARDIOLA Sala, Gheorghe Popescu (Cap) (70 Iván DE LA PEÑA), Luis Filipe Madeira Caeiro FIGO; RONALDO Luiz Nazario da Lima, Hristo Stoichkov (70 Juan Antonio PIZZI Torroja).   Trainer: Bobby Robson

AIK: Magnus Hedman; Pär Millqvist, Michael Brundin, Johan Mjällby, Gary Sundgren, Krister Nordin, Mattias Johansson (85 Dick Lidman), Ola Andersson (Cap), Pierre Gallo, Nebojsa Novakovic (71 Cesar Pacha), Pascal Simpson.   Trainer: Erik Hamrén

Sent off: Blanc (75), Nordin (75)

Goals: Simpson (1), Popescu (2), Ronaldo (55), Pizzi (81)

AIK SOLNA v FC BARCELONA 1-1 (0-1)

Råsunda, Solna   20.03.1997

Referee: Gilles Veissière (FRA)   Attendance: 35,049

AIK: Magnus Hedman; Pär Millqvist, Michael Brundin, Johan Mjällby, Gary Sundgren, Nebojsa Novakovic, Ola Andersson (Cap), Thomas Lagerlöf (45 Mattias Johansson), Pierre Gallo (88 Patrik Fredholm), Pascal Simpson, Cesar Pacha (68 Dick Lidman).   Trainer: Erik Hamrén

FC BARCELONA: VÍTOR Manuel Martins BAÍA; Albert FERRER Llopis, FERNANDO Manuel Silva COUTO, Miguel Angel NADAL Homar, SERGI Barjuan Esclusa; Gheorghe Popescu (Cap), Josep GUARDIOLA Sala (68 Guillermo AMOR Martínez), Luis Filipe Madeira Caeiro FIGO (63 GIOVANNI Silva de Oliveira), Iván DE LA PEÑA; RONALDO Luiz Nazario da Lima (74 Juan Antonio PIZZI Torroja), Hristo Stoichkov.   Trainer: Bobby Robson

Goals: Ronaldo (12), Simpson (73)

**BENFICA LISBOA
v AC FIORENTINA FIRENZE 0-2** (0-1)

SL Benfica Lisboa   6.03.1997

Referee: Hellmut Krug (GER)   Attendance: 58,000

BENFICA: Michel Georges Jean Ghislain PREUD'HOMME; José António CALADO da Silva (44 Basarab Nica Panduru), Tahar El Khalej, Jorge Hernan BERMUDEZ Morales, JORGE Manuel Guerreiro SOARES, BRUNO Ricardo Mendonça de CAIRES (75 Ilian Dimov ILIEV), JAMIR Adriano Paz Gomes, MAURO Gabriel AIREZ (34 EDGAR Patrício Carvalho Pacheco), Abdelkrim El Hadrioui, JOÃO Manuel Vieira PINTO (Cap), HASSAN Nader.   Trainer: Paulo Autuori

FIORENTINA: Francesco Toldo; Lorenzo Amoruso, Pasquale Padalino, Giulio Falcone, Michele Serena; Sandro Cois, Rui Costa (78 Anselmo Robbiati), Stefan Schwarz; Luis Oliveira (46 Giovanni Piacentini), Gabriel Batistuta (Cap), Francesco Baiano (88 Vittorio Pusceddu).   Trainer: Claudio Ranieri

Goals: Baiano (45), Batistuta (90)

413

**AC FIORENTINA FIRENZE
v BENFICA LISBOA 0-1** (0-1)

Artemio Franchi, Firenze   20.03.1997

Referee: Mario Van der Ende (HOL)   Attendance: 35,071

FIORENTINA: Francesco Toldo; Daniele Carnasciali, Giulio Falcone, Pasquale Padalino, Lorenzo Amoruso, Michele Serena; Giovanni Piacentini, Rui Costa (70 Anselmo Robbiati), Stefan Schwarz; Gabriel Batistuta (Cap), Francesco Baiano (80 Luis Oliveira).   Trainer: Claudio Ranieri

BENFICA: Michel Georges Jean Ghislain PREUD'HOMME; JORGE Manuel Guerreiro SOARES, Jorge Hernan BERMUDEZ Morales, Tahar El Khalej (77 Ilian Dimov ILIEV), Mário Teixeira da Costa "MARINHO", JAMIR Adriano Paz Gomes (77 BRUNO Ricardo Mendonça de CAIRES), VALDO Cândido Filho, PEDRO Ricardo Quintela HENRIQUES, JOÃO Manuel Vieira PINTO (Cap), EDGAR Patrício Carvalho Pacheco, Alves Paulo António "PAULÃO" (77 Basarab Nica Panduru).   Trainer: Paulo Autuori

Goal: Edgar (22)

**AC FIORENTINA FIRENZE
v FC BARCELONA 0-2** (0-2)

Artemio Franchi, Firenze   24.04.1997

Referee: Anders Frisk (SWE)   Attendance: 43,588

FIORENTINA: Francesco Toldo; Daniele Carnasciali, Pasquale Padalino, Lorenzo Amoruso, Michele Serena (82 Vittorio Pusceddu); Luis Oliveira, Rui Costa (Cap), Sandro Cois (88 Aldo Firicano), Stefan Schwarz, Anselmo Robbiati, Francesco Baiano (88 Emiliano Bigica).   Trainer: Claudio Ranieri

FC BARCELONA: VÍTOR Manuel Martins BAÍA; Albert FERRER Llopis, FERNANDO Manuel Silva COUTO, Miguel Angel NADAL Homar (Cap), SERGI Barjuan Esclusa; LUIS ENRIQUE Martínez García (81 Guillermo AMOR Martínez), Iván DE LA PEÑA, Josep GUARDIOLA Sala, Luis Filipe Madeira Caeiro FIGO (83 Hristo Stoichkov), GIOVANNI Silva de Oliveira (83 ABELARDO Fernández Antuña), RONALDO Luiz Nazario da Lima.   Trainer: Bobby Robson

Sent off: Oliveira (48), Nadal (83)

Goals: Couto (30), Guardiola (35)

SEMI-FINALS

**FC BARCELONA
v AC FIORENTINA FIRENZE 1-1** (1-0)

Camp Nou, Barcelona   10.04.1997

Referee: Bernd Heynemann (GER)   Attendance: 100,000

FC BARCELONA: VÍTOR Manuel Martins BAÍA; Albert FERRER Llopis, Fernado Couto, Miguel Angel NADAL Homar, ROGER García Junyent; Guillermo AMOR Martínez, Gheorghe Popescu (Cap), Luis Filipe Madeira Caeiro FIGO, GIOVANNI Silva de Oliveira; RONALDO Luiz Nazario da Lima, Hristo Stoichkov (75 Juan Antonio PIZZI Torroja).   Trainer: Bobby Robson

FIORENTINA: Francesco Toldo; Giulio Falcone, Sandro Cois, Lorenzo Amoruso, Michele Serena, Rui Costa, Pasquale Padalino, Anselmo Robbiati, Vittorio Pusceddu, Gabriel Batistuta (Cap), Luis Oliveira.   Trainer: Claudio Ranieri

Goals: Nadal (42), Batistuta (62)

**PARIS SAINT-GERMAIN
v LIVERPOOL FC 3-0** (2-0)

Parc des Princes, Paris   10.04.1997

Referee: Hellmut Krug (GER)   Attendance: 35,142

PSG: Bernard Lama; Laurent Fournier, Bruno Ngotty, Paul le Guen, Didier Domi (41 Jimmy Algérino); RAÍ Souza Vieira de Oliveira (Cap), Jérôme Leroy (86 Bernard Allou), Vincent Guérin, Benoît Cauet; Patrice Loko (83 Cyrille Pouget), LEONARDO Nascimento de Araújo.   Trainer: Ricardo Gomes

LIVERPOOL FC: David James; Jason McAteer, Dominic Matteo, Mark Wright, Steve Harkness, Stig Inge Bjørnebye, Jamie Redknapp, John Barnes (Cap), Steve McManaman, Robbie Fowler, Stan Collymore (46 Michael Thomas).   Manager: Roy Evans

Goals: Leonardo (11), Cauet (43), Leroy (84)

**LIVERPOOL FC
v PARIS SAINT-GERMAIN 2-0** (1-0)

Anfield Road, Liverpool   24.04.1997

Referee: Rune Pedersen (NOR)   Attendance: 38,984

LIVERPOOL FC: David James; Jason McAteer, Mark Wright, Neil Ruddock, Stig Inge Bjørnebye, Steve McManaman, Jamie Redknapp, Michael Thomas, Patrik Berger (69 Mark Kennedy), Robbie Fowler, Stan Collymore.   Manager: Roy Evans

PSG: Bernard Lama; Laurent Fournier, Bruno Ngotty, Paul le Guen, Jimmy Algérino; Jérôme Leroy, Vincent Guérin, RAÍ Souza Vieira de Oliveira (Cap), Benoît Cauet; Patrice Loko (57 Cyrille Pouget), LEONARDO Nascimento de Araújo (83 Daniel Kenedy).   Trainer: Ricardo Gomes

Goals: Fowler (12), Wright (79)

FINAL

**FC BARCELONA
v PARIS SAINT-GERMAIN 1-0** (1-0)

Feyenoord, Rotterdam 14.05.1997

Referee: Markus Merk (GER)   Attendance: 45,000

FC BARCELONA: VÍTOR Manuel Martins BAÍA; Albert FERRER Llopis, ABELARDO Fernández Antuña, FERNANDO Manuel Silva COUTO, SERGI Barjuan Esclusa; Josep GUARDIOLA Sala, Gheorghe Popescu (Cap) (46 Guillermo AMOR Martínez), Luis Filipe Madeira Caeiro FIGO, Iván DE LA PEÑA (84 Hristo Stoichkov); LUIS ENRIQUE Martínez García (88 Juan Antonio PIZZI Torroja), RONALDO Luiz Nazario da Lima.
Trainer: Bobby Robson

PSG: Bernard Lama; Laurent Fournier (57 Jimmy Algérino), Bruno Ngotty, Paul le Guen, Didier Domi; Vincent Guérin (68 Julio César DELY VALDÉS), RAÍ Souza Vieira de Oliveira (Cap), Jérôme Leroy, Benoît Cauet; Patrice Loko (77 Cyrille Pouget), LEONARDO Nascimento de Araújo.   Trainer: Ricardo Gomes

Goal: Ronaldo (36 pen)

Goalscorers European Cup-Winners' Cup 1996-97:

7 goals: Robbie Fowler (Liverpool)

6 goals: Mons Ivar Mjelde (SK Brann)

5 goals: RONALDO Luiz Nazario da Lima (FC Barcelona), Horst Siegl (Sparta Praha)

4 goals: Gabriel Batistuta (Fiorentina), Patrice Loko (Paris SG), Hakan Şükür (Galatasaray), Pascal Simpson (AIK Solna), Christophe Bonvin (FC Sion)

3 goals: Dely Valdes, Leonardo (PSG), Tugushi, Ujmajuridze (Dinamo Batumi), Chassot, Vercruysse (FC Sion), Eftevaag (Brann), Lokvenc (Sparta Praha), João V.Pinto (Benfica), Batista (AEK Athina), Barnes (Liverpool), Giovanni (FC Barcelona)

2 goals: Zarinsh (Universitate Riga), Tóth (Kispest), Rogaciov (Constructorul Chişinău), Keskitalo (MyPa-47), Romanchuk (Nyva Vynnytsya), Mumlek, Vugrinec (Varteks Varazdin), Gesior, A.Bak, M.Bak (Ruch), Lubarsky (Chemlon Humenne), Lazar (Gloria Bistrita), Glonti (Dinamo Batumi), Bozgo (Olimpija Ljubljana), Flo, Hasund (Brann), Nilis, Eijkelkamp (PSV Eindhoven), Gunda (Sparta Praha), D.Stankovic (Crvena Zvezda), Donizete, Valdo (Benfica), Kostis (AEK Athina), Berger, Bjørnebye, Collymore (Liverpool), Le Guen, Allou (PSG)

1 goal: Yaromko, Skorobogatko (MPKC Mozyr), Branauskas, Dancenko (Kareda Siauliai), Simeonov (Levski Sofia), McPherson (Hearts), Musayev (Karabakh Agdam), Barberyan (Kotayk Abovyan), Sabag, Kapeta, Cebula (Hapoel), Doncic, J.Agius (Valletta FC), S.Geoghegan, Rutherford (Shelbourne), Thomas (Llansantffraid), Grettnich (Union), Little (Glentoran), Krölov, Viikmäe (Tallinna Sadam), Ghinda, Piroska (Kispest), Vastic, Mählich (Sturm Graz), Skidan (Constructorul Chişinău), Wegmann (FC Kaiserslautern), Mahlio (MyPa-47), Bak (Aarhus GF), Gernsö, Van Maele, Camerman (Cercle Brugge), Maretic, Besek, Cvetko (Varteks Varazdin), Benediktsson, Dadason, Th.Jónsson, Daníelsson (KR Reykjavík), Kuntic, Alexandrou, Kovacevic, Kopunovic, Markou (AEK Larnaca), Srutwa (Ruch), Dina, Valkucak (Chemlon Humenne), Matei, Dancus, Voica (Gloria Bistriţa), Mudjiri (Dinamo Batumi), Perez, Polverino (FC Vaduz), Solomatin, Garas, Cherevchenko, Kosolapov (Lokomotiv Moskva), Fidani, Jeunechamp, Préget, Meilhac, Ecker, Sabin (Nîmes), Tugay, Hakan Ünsal, Knup, Arif, Hagi (Galatasaray), Colombo, Lukic, Milton, Pancev (FC Sion), Helland, M.Pedersen, J.O.Pedersen (Brann), Cocu, Zenden, Marcelo (PSV Eindhoven), Repka, Hornak, Mistr, Z.Svoboda, Gabriel (Sparta Praha), Zivkovic, Jovicic, Njegus, Pantelic, Marinovic (Crvena Zvezda Beograd), Pacha, M.Johansson, Nordin (AIK Solna), Edgar, Panduru, Jamir (Benfica), Baiano, Robbiati, Schwarz, Orlando (Fiorentina), Ketsbaia, Savevski, Maladenis, Nikolaidis (AEK Athina), Wright, McManaman (Liverpool), Nadal, Couto, Guardiola, Popescu, Pizzi, Figo (FC Barcelona), Cauet, Leroy, Rai, Roche, Mboma (Paris Saint-Germain)

Own goals: Davidsen (HB Tórshavn) for Dinamo Batumi, Novotný (Sparta Praha) for Sturm Graz, Brundin (AIK Solna) for Nîmes

CUP WINNERS' CUP 1997-98

QUALIFYING ROUND

HAVNAR BOLTFELAG TÓRSHAVN
v APOEL NICOSIA 1-1 (1-1)

Toftir stadium 13.08.1997

Referee: Oleg Timofeyev (EST)   Attendance: 200

HB: Kaj Leo Johannesen (Cap); Mikkjal Thomassen, Hans Frodi Hansen, Jan Dam, Andreas F.Hansen, Hallur Danielsen (83 Jøgvan Hegga Samuelsen), Runi Nolsø, Ingi Rasmussen (77 Gunnar Mohr), Allan Mørkøre, Jens Erik Rasmussen, Uni Arge. Trainer: Odbjörn Joensen

APOEL: Andreas Petridis; Kostas Kosta, Giorgos Hristodoulou, Nikos Haralampous, Giannis Ioannou (Cap), Kostas Konstantinou, Nikos Timotheou, Kostas Fasouliotis, Alexis Alexandrou, Christoph Westerthaler, Alfred Hörtnagl. Trainer: Kurt Jara

Goals: Alexandrou (19), Arge (40)

APOEL NICOSIA
v HAVNAR BOLTFELAG TÓRSHAVN 6-0 (2-0)

Makarion, Nicosia 28.08.1997

Referee: Konrad Plautz (AUS)   Attendance: 3,498

APOEL: Andreas Petridis; Kostas Kosta, Aristos Aristokleous (67 Nikos Haralampous), Kostas Konstantinou, Nikos Timotheou (54 Hristakis Pounas), Alfred Hörtnagl, Antros Sotiriou (62 Kostas Fasouliotis), Giannis Ioannou (Cap), Alexis Alexandrou, Giorgos Hristodoulou, Christoph Westerthaler. Trainer: Kurt Jara

HB: Kaj Leo Johannesen (Cap); Allan Mørkøre, Hans Frodi Hansen, Jan Dam, Andreas F.Hansen, Hallur Danielsen (67 Bjarki Mohr), Runi Nolsø, Ingi Rasmussen (77 Gunnar Mohr), Jens Erik Rasmussen (67 Andrew a Flotum), Uni Arge (84 Niels Poulsen), Mikkjal Thomassen. Trainer: Odbjörn Joensen

Goals: Hörtnagl (14, 21), Sotiriou (30), Ioannou (77, 81), Fasouliotis (83)

HIBERNIANS AFC PAOLA
v ÍB VESTMANNAEYJAR 0-1 (0-0)

National Ta'Qali 14.08.1997

Referee: Stuart Dougall (SCO)   Attendance: 631

HIBERNIANS: Ruben Debono; Lawrence Attard, Roderick Baldacchino, Silvio Vella, Jesmond Delia (66 Chukunyere Ndubisi), Michael Spiteri (Cap), Charlie Scerri, Alan Mifsud (87 Malcolm Tirchett), David Carabott, Darren Attard, Robert Walley (51 Fadel Ben Ammar). Trainer: Mark Miller

ÍBV: Gunnar Sigurdsson; Ivar Bjarklind, Hlynur Stefánsson (Cap), Zoran Miljkovic, Gudni Rúnar Helgason; Sverrir Sverrisson, Kristinn Haflidason, Sigurvin Olafsson, Steingrímur Jóhannesson, Leifur Geir Hafsteinsson (75 Bjarnólfur Lárusson), Tryggvi Gudmundsson. Trainer: Bjarni Jóhansson

Goal: T. Gudmundsson (70)

ÍB VESTMANNAEYJAR
v HIBERNIANS AFC PAOLA 3-0 (2-0)

Hásteinsvöllur, Vestmannaeijarre 27.08.1997

Referee: Juha Hirviniemi (FIN)   Attendance: 1,000

ÍBV: Gunnar Sigurdsson; Ivar Bjarklind (82 Ingi Sigurdsson), Hlynur Stefánsson (Cap), Zoran Miljkovic, Hjalti Jóhanesson, Gudni Rúnar Helgason, Sigurvin Olafsson, Sverrir Sverrisson (68 Bjarnólfur Lárusson), Kristinn Haflidason, Steingrímur Jóhannesson (77 Leifur Geir Hafsteinsson), Tryggvi Gudmundsson. Trainer: Bjarni Jóhansson

HIBERNIANS: Ruben Debono; Lawrence Attard, Martin Borg (89 Roderick Baldacchino), Silvio Vella, Kenneth Abela (46 Jesmond Delia), Michael Spiteri (Cap), Charlie Scerri, Alan Mifsud, David Carabott, Darren Attard, Robert Walley. Trainer: Mark Miller

Sent off: Attard (70)

Goals: Helgasson (21), Gudmundsson (33,90)

GLENAVON LURGAN
v LEGIA WARSZAWA 1-1 (0-1)

Mourneview Park, Lurgan 14.08.1997

Referee: Juan Antonio Fernandez Marin (SPA)   Att: 1,075

GLENAVON: Dermot O'Neill; John Gregg, Paul Peter Byrne, Nigel Quigley, Mark Glendinning, Darren Murphy (46 James McCartan), Jonathan Prizeman, Stephen Caffrey, Lee Doherty (Cap), Glenn Ferguson, Tony Grant. Trainer: Nigel Best

LEGIA: Grzegorz Szamotulski; Pawel Skrzypek, Jacek Bednarz, Jacek Zielinski (Cap), Sylwester Czereszewski, Jacek Kacprzak, Marcin Mieciel, Tomasz Sokolowski, Piotr Wlodarczyk, Dariusz Solnica (74 Andrzej Sazanowicz), Jacek Magiera. Trainer: Miroslaw Jablonski

Sent off: Mieciel (79)

Goals: Sokolowski (32), Grant (59)

LEGIA WARSZAWA
v GLENAVON LURGAN 4-0 (0-0)
Wojska Polskiego, Warszawa   28.08.1997
Referee: Loizos Loizou (CYP)   Attendance: 4,000
LEGIA: Grzegorz Szamotulski; Jacek Magiera, Jacek Bednarz, Sylwester Czereszewski, Jacek Zielinski (Cap), Jacek Kacprzak, Kenneth Zeigbo, Pawel Skrzypek, Piotr Wlodarczyk (68 Dariusz Solnica), Tomasz Sokolowski, Bartosz Karwan.   Trainer: Miroslaw Jablonski
GLENAVON: Dermot O'Neill; Stephen Caffrey, Mark Glendinning, Nigel Quigley (72 Colin Russell), Paul Peter Byrne, Lee Doherty (Cap) (38 Jonathan Prizeman), James McCartan (64 Raymond McCoy), John Gregg, Glenn Ferguson, Tony Grant, Gary Smyth.   Trainer: Nigel Best
Goals: Kacprzak (73), Sokolowski (76, 89 pen), Skrzypek (86)

CWMBRAN TOWN
v FC NAŢIONAL BUCUREŞTI 2-5 (0-1)
Cwmbran stadium   14.08.1997
Referee: Sergei Shmolik (BLS)   Attendance: 1,500
CWMBRAN TOWN: Patrick O'Hagan (50 Jim Speare); Mark Parfitt, Roger Gibbins, Jim Blackie (Cap), Adam Moore, Richard Carter (72 John Powell), Phil James, Andy Jones, Chris Watkins; Richard Townsend, Simon Dyer (72 Nathan Johnson).   Manager: Tony Wilcokx
FC NAŢIONAL: Paul Ştefănescu; Tinel Petre, Ion Sburlea (73 Gabriel Vochin), Liviu Ciobotariu, Cătălin Necula, Petre Marin; Stelian Carabaş (62 Cătălin Nicolae Liţă), Adrian Ion Pigulea, Cristian Marius Vasc; Radu Niculescu (76 Cristian Albeanu), Marin Dună (Cap).   Trainer: Florin Halagian
Goals: Vasc (32), R. Niculescu (46, 61), Parfitt (75 pen), Liţă (77, 79), Townsend (82)

FC NAŢIONAL BUCUREŞTI
v CWMBRAN TOWN 7-0 (4-0)
Cotroceni, Bucureşti   28.08.1997
Referee: Roger Philippi (LUX)   Attendance: 6,000
FC NAŢIONAL: Paul Ştefănescu; Tinel Petre (52 Cătălin Nicolae Liţă), Liviu Ciobotariu (Cap), Cătălin Necula, Ion Sburlea (46 Gabriel Vochin), Petre Marin; Stelian Carabaş, Adrian Ion Pigulea, Cristian Marius Vasc; Cristian Albeanu (46 Marian Savu), Radu Niculescu.   Trainer: Florin Halagian
CWMBRAN TOWN: Jim Speare; Jim Blackie (Cap), Mark Parfitt, Roger Gibbins (46 Phil James), Andy Jones; Paul Walker (65 Chris Watkins), Wayne Goodridge, Adam Moore, John Powell; Simon Dyer, Richard Townsend (65 Mattie Davies).   Manager: Roger Gibbins
Goals: Niculescu (15), Pigulea (21, 41, 75), Albeanu (30, 38), Savu (47)

ZALGIRIS VILNIUS v HAPOEL BEER SHEVA 0-0
Zalgiris Vilnius   14.08.1997
Referee: Morgan Norman (SWE)   Attendance: 2,000
ZALGIRIS: Algimantas Briaunys (Cap); Andrius Skerla, Viaceslavas Sukristovas, Nerijus Radzius, Sergejus Novikovas, Dainius Suliauskas, Deividas Semberas, Igoris Stesko (78 Arturas Stesko), Arunas Pukelevicius (75 Dainius Saulenas), Tomas Ramelis (88 Nerijus Vasiliauskas), Igoris Morinas.   Trainer: Eugeniuszs Riabovas
HAPOEL: Shaul Smadga; Sharon Rafael, Alexander Zakharov, Sharon Bochnik, Nigel Quigley, Shimon Biton (Cap), Yossi Benayoun (76 Ilan Vaknin), Gyula Zsivótzky, Dudu Hefer (85 Sergei Gusev), David Moial, Oren Sagron, Sharon Avitan (52 Rami Eliaho).   Trainer: Benni Tabac

HAPOEL BEER SHEVA
v ZALGIRIS VILNIUS 2-1 (0-0, 0-0) (AET)
Municipal, Beer Sheva   28.08.1997
Referee: Attila Juhos (HUN)   Attendance: 9,000
HAPOEL: Shaul Smadga; Sharon Rafael, Alexander Zakharov, Sharon Bochnik, David Moial, Shimon Biton (Cap) (91 Rami Eliaho), Csaba Horváth (46 Oren Sagron), Dudu Hefer (91 Amir Avigdor), Yossi Benayoun, Gyula Zsivótzky (63 Ilan Vaknin), Yair Simhon.   Trainer: Benni Tabac
ZALGIRIS: Algimantas Briaunys (Cap); Andrius Skerla, Viaceslavas Sukristovas, Nerijus Radzius, Darius Zutautas, Sergejus Novikovas (91 Arturas Stesko), Dainius Suliauskas, Deividas Semberas, Arunas Pukelevicius (95 Igoris Stesko), Tomas Ramelis (105 Dainius Saulenas), Igoris Morinas.   Trainer: Eugeniuszs Riabovas
Sent off: Radzius (99), Suliauskas (118)
Goals: Radzius (96), Benayoun (105 pen), Bochnik (116)

ZIMBRU CHIŞINĂU
v SHAKHTAR DONETSK 1-1 (0-1)
Republican, Chişinău   14.08.1997
Referee: Taras Bezoubiak (RUS)   Attendance: 8,000
ZIMBRU: Denis Romanenco; Oleg Fistican, Ion Testimiţanu, Radu Rebeja (Cap), Marin Spânu, Iuri Miterev, Serghei Cleşcenco, Dinu Caras (77 Vitali Culibaba), Serghei Zgură, Igor Oprea, Vadim Boreţ.   Trainer: Semion Altman
SHAKHTAR: Dmytro Shutkov; Ihor Zhabchenko, Mikhailo Starostyak, Olexandr Babiy (87 Serhiy Onopko), Olexandr Koval, Yuri Seleznev, Hennadiy Orbu, Mikhail Potskhveria (72 Olexandr Spivak), Hennadiy Zubov, Valeriy Kriventsov (Cap), Serhiy Atelkin.   Trainer: Valeri Yaremchenko
Goals: Atelkin (45), Zgură (75)

**SHAKHTAR DONETSK
v ZIMBRU CHIȘINĂ 3-0** (2-0)

Skhakhter, Donetsk   28.08.1997

Referee: Dan Dragoș Crăciun (ROM)   Attendance: 21,000

SHAKHTAR: Dmytro Shutkov; Ihor Leonov, Mikhailo Starostyak (65 Ihor Zhabchenko), Olexandr Babiy, Olexandr Koval, Yuri Seleznev, Hennadiy Orbu, Serhiy Kovalev, Hennadiy Zubov (78 Olexandr Spivak), Valeriy Kriventsov (Cap), Serhiy Atelkin.   Trainer: Valeri Yaremchenko

ZIMBRU: Denis Romanenco; Oleg Fistican, Ion Testimițanu, Radu Rebeja (Cap), Iuri Miterev, Serghei Savcenko, Serghei Cleșcenco (60 Boris Cebotari), Dinu Caras, Serghei Zgură, Igor Oprea, Vadim Boreț.   Trainer: Semion Altman

Goals: Orbu (28), Atelkin (43), Kriventsov (82)

**DINABURG DAUGAVPILS
v KAPAZ GANJA 1-0** (1-0)

Tseltnieks, Daugavpils   14.08.1997

Referee: Alan Howells (WAL)   Attendance: 1,100

DINABURG: Vyacheslav Dusmanov; Alexander Isakov, Nikita Shmikov, Alexander Glazov (Cap), Georgy Shebarshin, Mikhail Zizilev, Sergey Isayev (57 Kirill Kurbatov), Edgar Burlakov, Vitaly Pinyaskin, Sergey Tarasov, Vladimir Zhavoronkov (70 Sergey Pogodin).
Trainer: Dmitri Kuzminchev

KAPAZ: Nizami Sadigov; Fizuli Allakhverdiev (55 Tofik Mamedov), Fazil Parvarov, Sakit Aliyev, Faik Jabbarov, Elhan Shakhniyarov, Goshkar Gadjiev (46 Rovshan Akhmedov), Khalid Mardanov (Cap), Firuz Gulami, Imamiar Suleymanov (46 Bakhram Shakhguliev), Makhmud Kurbanov.
Trainer: Mekhman Allakhverdiyev

Goal: Tarasov (35)

**KAPAZ GANJA
v DINABURG DAUGAVPILS 0-1** (0-0)

Ganja   28.08.1997

Referee: Milan Mitrovic (SVN)   Attendance: 10,286

KAPAZ: Nizami Sadigov; Sakit Aliyev, Fazil Parvarov (57 Imamiar Suleymanov), Tofik Mamedov, Faik Jabbarov (Cap), Elhan Shakhniyarov (85 Ulfat Madatov), Goshkar Gadjiev, Makhmud Kurbanov, Firuz Gulami (46 Bakhram Shakhguliev), Yadigar Suleymanov, Rovshan Akhmedov.
Trainer: Mekhman Allakhverdiyev

DINABURG: Vyacheslav Dusmanov; Alexander Glazov (Cap), Nikita Shmikov, Alexander Isakov, Georgy Shebarshin, Edgar Burlakov (73 Valeri Bogdan), Mikhail Zizilev, Alexander Fedotov, Vitaly Pinyaskin (65 Sergey Isayev), Sergey Tarasov (30 Kirill Kurbatov), Yuri Karashauskas.
Trainer: Dmitri Kuzminchev

Goal: Isayev (71 pen)

**KILMARNOCK FC
v SHELBOURNE DUBLIN 2-1** (0-1)

Rugby Park, Kilmarnock   14.08.1997

Referee: Vasiliy Melnichuk (UKR)   Attendance: 9,041

KILMARNOCK: Dragoje Lekovic; Angus MacPherson, Martin Baker, Ray Montgomerie (Cap), Kevin McGowne, Mark Reilly, Ally Mitchell (58 Pat Nevin), Willie Findlay, Paul Wright, Jim McIntyre (57 Jérôme Vareille), Alex Burke.
Manager: Bobby Wiliamson

SHELBOURNE: Alan Gough; Pascal Vaudequin (79 Greg Costello), Declan Geoghegan, Michael Neville (Cap) (65 Tony McCarthy), David Campbell, Patrick Scully, Desmond Baker (81 Stephen Geoghegan), Anthony Sheridan, Mark Rutherford, Patrick Fenlon, David Smith.
Manager: Damien Richardson

Goals: Rutherford (12), Wright (65 pen, 90)

**SHELBOURNE DUBLIN
v KILMARNOCK FC 1-1** (1-1)

Tolka Park, Dublin   28.08.1997

Referee: Jorge Monteiro Coroado (POR)   Attendance: 8,100

SHELBOURNE: Alan Gough; David Smith, Patrick Scully, David Campbell, Declan Geoghegan, Anthony Sheridan, Pascal Vaudequin (64 Stephen Geoghegan), Patrick Fenlon (89 Dean Fitzgerald), Michael Neville (Cap) (80 Tony McCarthy), Mark Rutherford, Desmond Baker.
Manager: Damien Richardson

KILMARNOCK: Dragoje Lekovic; Angus MacPherson, Ray Montgomerie (Cap), Kevin McGowne, Ally Mitchell, Martin Baker, Willie Findlay, Pat Nevin (84 Jérôme Vareille), Jim McIntyre, David Bagan, Mark Reilly.
Manager: Bobby Wiliamson

Goals: McIntyre (21), D. Baker (39)

**HJK HELSINKI
v CRVENA ZVEZDA BEOGRAD 1-0** (0-0)

Olympiastadion, Helsinki   14.08.1997

Referee: Hugh Dallas (SCO)   Attendance: 5,140

HJK: Tommi Koivistoinen; Hannu Tihinen, Ville Nylund, Jarmo Saastamoinen, Mika Lehkosuo, Jarkko Wiss (Cap), Markku Kanerva, Vesa Vasara (82 RODRIGO Martins Vaz), Petri Helin, Aki Riihilahti (46 Mika Kottila), Shefki Kuqi (66 RAFAEL Pires Vieira).   Trainer: Antti Muurinen

CRVENA ZVEZDA: Dragoslav Jevrić; Bratislav Zivković, Nikoslav Bjegović, Darko Krstevski, Zoran Njegus, Goran Bunjevcević, Dalibor Skorić (63 Jovan Gojković), Miodrag Pantelić (83 Goran Drulić), Zoran Jovićić (Cap), Dejan Stanković, Srdjan Pecelj.   Trainer: Milorad Kosanović

Goal: Helin (58)

CRVENA ZVEZDA BEOGRAD
v HJK HELSINKI 3-0 (2-0)

Crvena Zvezda Beograd   28.08.1997

Referee: Antony Boggi (ITA)   Attendance: 24,375

CRVENA ZVEZDA: Dragoslav Jevrić; Bratislav Zivković, Srdjan Pecelj, Zoran Njegus, Darko Krstevski, Goran Bunjevcević, Blaze Georgievski (46 Nikoslav Bjegović), Miodrag Pantelić (46 Dejan Ilić), Zoran Jovicić (Cap), Dejan Stanković, Perica Ognjenović (87 Dragan Micić). Trainer: Milorad Kosanović

HJK: Tommi Koivistoinen; Hannu Tihinen (46 Vesa Vasara), Aarno Turpeinen, Ville Nylund, Jarmo Saastamoinen, Mika Lehkosuo, Jarkko Wiss (Cap), Markku Kanerva, Aki Riihilahti (46 RODRIGO Martins Vaz), Petri Helin (57 Kalle Lehtinen), Mika Kottila.   Trainer: Antti Muurinen

Sent off: Saastamoinen (70)

Goals: Stanković (6, 26), Njegus (90 pen)

SLOGA JUGOMAGNAT SKOPJE
v NK ZAGREB 1-2 (0-0)

Eairu, Skopje   14.08.1997

Referee: Andreas Schluchter (SWI)   Attendance: 4,000

SLOGA: Lazo Liposki, Saso Zdravevski, Husein Beganović, Sener Tuna (46 Halim Hodai), Esad Colaković, Nedzmedin Memedi (Cap), Dejan Demjanski (46 Risto Petkov), Feim Beganović, Albert Imer, Zoran Miserdovski (71 Iskender Jonuzi), Goran Stankovski.

NK ZAGREB: Sandro Tomić; Jasenko Sabitović, Drazen Biskup (Cap), Mario Osibov, Sunaj Keqi, Admir Adzem, Zeljko Sopić (70 Mario Cizmek), Marin Lalić, Vjekoslav Skrinjar, Mate Baturina (75 Darko Vukić), Elvis Scoria (46 Nino Bule). Trainer: Branko Tucak

Goals: Petkov (60), Bule (76), Cizmek (90)

NK ZAGREB
v SLOGA JUGOMAGNAT SKOPJE 2-0 (2-0)

Kranjcevica Zagreb   28.08.1997

Referee: Eric Blareau (BEL)   Attendance: 2,000

NK ZAGREB: Sandro Tomić; Jasenko Sabitović, Drazen Biskup (Cap), Mario Osibov, Sunaj Keqi, Darko Vukić (69 Jaksa Jurković), Zeljko Sopić (61 Marinko Galić), Marin Lalić, Vjekoslav Skrinjar, Mate Baturina (72 Darko Perić), Nino Bule. Trainer: Branko Tucak

SLOGA: Lazo Liposki; Risto Petkov, Esad Colaković, Husein Beganović, Bujar Muca, Nedzmedin Memedi (Cap), Halim Hodai (56 Albert Imer), Zoran Miserdovski, Sead Kolasinac (81 Arsim Abazi), Goran Stankovski, Iskender Jonuzi (70 Masar Omeragić).

Goals: Sopić (2), Bule (7)

FC BALZERS
v BVSC-ZUGLÓ BUDAPEST 1-3 (1-0)

Balzers   14.08.1997

Referee: Ante Kulusic (CRO)   Attendance: 660

FC BALZERS: Jürg Nüesch; Heini Stocker, Daniel Telser, Beat Lohner (Cap); Martin Telser, Thomas Hanselmann, Michael Nushöhr, Urs Wörnhard, Michael Zeder (83 Remo Tschumper); Daniel Frick (86 Marco Büchel), Franz Schädler (69 Alexander Scädler).   Trainer: Michael Nushöhr

BVSC: János Koszta (Cap); Csaba László, Ádám Komlósi, Ákos Csiszár (77 János Zováth), Ákos Füzi, Dénes Rósa (25 József Duró), Krisztián Csillag, Károly Erös, Daniel Usvat, Zoltán Bükszegi, István Kiss (63 Csaba Csordás). Trainer: György Mezey

Goals: Wörnhard (6), Telser (57 og), Füzi (76), Csordas (84)

BVSC-ZUGLÓ BUDAPEST
v FC BALZERS 2-0 (1-0)

Szönyi út, Budapest   28.08.1997

Referee: Richard O'Hanlon (IRE)   Attendance: 1,500

BVSC: János Koszta (Cap); Csaba László, Ádám Komlósi, Ákos Csiszár (46 Dénes Rósa), Csaba Barna (61 József Duró), Krisztián Csillag, János Zováth, Daniel Usvat, Ákos Füzi, Zoltán Bükszegi, István Kiss (46 Csaba Csordas). Trainer: György Mezey

FC BALZERS: Jürg Nüesch; Heini Stocker, Beat Lohner (Cap), Thomas Hanselmann; Martin Telser, Daniel Telser (70 Christoph Wille), Urs Wörnhard, Franz Schädler (46 Alexander Schädler), Michael Nushöhr (35 Marco Büchel), Michael Zeder; Daniel Frick.   Trainer: Michael Nushöhr

Goals: Komlósi (12), Bükszegi (90)

TALLINA SADAM
v BELSHINA BOBRUISK 1-1 (0-1)

Kadriorg, Tallinn   14.08.1997

Referee: Leslie John Irvine (NIR)   Attendance: 500

SADAM: Sergei Pareiko; Mark Shvets, Igor Prins, Urmas Liivamaa, Konstantin Kolbasenko, Maksim Rotshkov, Andrei Krolov (Cap), Toomas Krom, Indro Olumets, Dmitri Ustritski, Ivan O'Konnel-Bronin (70 Aleksander Olerski). Trainer: Vladimir Kolbasenko

BELSHINA: Andrei Svirkov; Eduard Apalkov (54 Igor Kovalevich), Evgeniy Timofeyev, Igor Shustikov, Dmitriy Balashov (89 Vyacheslav Derban), Igor Gradoboyev (Cap), Eduard Gradoboyev (54 Alexandr Borisik), Andrei Khripach, Vasiliy Smirnykh, Andrei Khlebosolov, Vladimir Putrash. Trainer: Oleg Volokh

Goals: Smirnykh (21), Olumets (50)

**BELSHINA BOBRUISK
v TALLINA SADAM 4-1** (1-0)

Dinamo Minsk 28.08.1997

Referee: Ladislav Gadosi (SVK)   Attendance: 3,000

BELSHINA: Andrei Svirkov; Igor Kovalevich, Andrei Khripach (46 Sergei Razumovich), Evgeniy Timofeyev, Igor Shustikov, Dmitriy Balashov, Igor Gradoboyev (Cap), Eduard Gradoboyev, Vasiliy Smirnykh (62 Vyacheslav Derban), Andrei Khlebosolov, Vladimir Putrash.   Trainer: Oleg Volokh

SADAM: Sergei Pareiko; Dalius Staleliunas, Igor Prins, Urmas Liivamaa, Konstantin Kolbasenko (63 Aleksander Olerski), Maksim Rotshkov, Andrei Krolov (Cap), Toomas Krom, Indro Olumets, Mark Shvets (75 Dmitri Ustritski), Ivan O'Konnel-Bronin.   Trainer: Vladimir Kolbasenko

Sent off: Krolov (61)

Goals: Smirnykh (3), Timofeyev (57), Rotshkov (69 pen), Khlebosolov (73), Putrash (75)

**PRIMORJE AJDOVSCINA
v UNION SPORTIVE LUXEMBOURG 2-0** (1-0)

Primorje Ajdovscina 14.08.1997

Referee: Roland Beck (LIE)   Attendance: 2,000

PRIMORJE: Robert Volk; Valter Sabadin, Andrej Poljsak, Sefik Mulahmetović, Edmond Gunjac, Anton Zlogar (42 Andrej Zelko, 50 Ales Kodelja), Alen Sculac, Aljko Rastoder (80 Igor Pandza), Borivoje Lucić (Cap), Patrik Ipavec, Mladen Rudonja.   Trainer: Marin Kovacić

US: Alija Besic; Laurent Pellegrino, Laurent Deville, Eugène Afrika, Marc Birsens, David Borbiconi (Cap), Marc Kunen, Serge Makombou, Roby Langers (64 Mustapha Kharoubi), Benoît Lahéry (84 Joé Flick), Jörg Lauer (78 Lauret Carème).   Trainer: Gilbert Neumann

Sent off: Ipavec (73), Besic (84)

Goals: Sabadin (37), Sculac (85 pen)

**UNION SPORTIVE LUXEMBOURG
v PRIMORJE AJDOVSCINA 0-1** (0-0)

Luxembourg 28.08.1997

Referee: Vanco Kocev (MAK)   Attendance: 1,000

US: Joé Flick; Laurent Pellegrino, Laurent Deville, Marc Birsens (46 Roby Langers), David Borbiconi (Cap), Jörg Lauer, Marc Kunen (80 Claude Wolter), Eugène Afrika, Serge Makoumbou, Benoît Lahéry, Laurent Carème.   Trainer: Gilbert Neumann

PRIMORJE: Robert Volk; Andrej Poljsak, Sefik Mulahmetovic, Alen Sculac, Edmond Gunjac, Andrej Zelko (80 Sabadin), Ales Kodelja, Aljko Rastoder, Borivoje Lucic (Cap), Mladen Rudonja, Uros Stanić (56 Anton Zlogar).   Trainer: Marin Kovacić

Goal: Rudonja (18)

LEVSKI SOFIA v SLOVAN BRATISLAVA 1-1 (1-0)

Georgi Asparuchov, Sofia 14.08.1997

Referee: Juan Ansuategui Roca (SPA)   Attendance: 25,000

LEVSKI: Dimitar Ivankov; Vladimir Ivanov, Stanimir Gospodinov, Veselin Vachev, Vladimir Ionkov, Aleksandar Aleksandrov, Nikolai Todorov (Cap), Viktorio Pavlov, Iordan Marinov (61 Milen Radukanov), Georgi Ivanov (84 Ilian Simeonov), Hristo Iovov (51 Georgi Borisov).   Trainer: Stefan Grozdanov

SLOVAN: Miroslav König; Ladislav Pecko (75 Marian Timko), Milos Glonek (Cap), Jozef Antalovic, Zsolt Hornyak, Robert Novak, Milos Sobona (81 Peter Gunda), Robert Tomaschek, Roland Moder (46 Jozef Muzlay), András Keresztúri, Sergiy Borisenko.   Trainer: Jozef Prochotsky

Goals: G. Ivanov (18), Novak (65)

SLOVAN BRATISLAVA v LEVSKI SOFIA 2-1 (1-1)

Tehelné pole, Bratislava 28.08.1997

Referee: Claude Detruche (SWI)   Attendance: 6,850

SLOVAN: Miroslav König; Milos Glonek (Cap), Ladislav Pecko, Jozef Antalovic, Peter Gunda; Robert Novak, Milos Sobona (66 Roland Moder), Robert Tomaschek, András Keresztúri, Jozef Muzlay (82 Zsolt Hornyak), Sergiy Borisenko (89 Marian Timko).   Trainer: Jozef Prochotsky

LEVSKI: Dimitar Ivankov; Stanimir Gospodinov, Vladimir Ionkov, Ivan Vasilev, Milen Radukanov, Vladimir Ivanov (80 Asen Nikolov), Nikolai Todorov (Cap), Viktorio Pavlov, Aleksandar Aleksandrov (68 Ilian Simeonov), Georgi Ivanov, Georgi Borisov (51 Hristo Iovov).   Trainer: Stefan Grozdanov

Goals: Todorov (2), Novak (15), Muzlay (53)

DINAMO BATUMI v ARARAT EREVAN 4-2 (2-0)

Central, Batumi 15.08.1997

Referee: Manfred Schüttengruber (AUS)   Attendance: 8,000

DINAMO: Nikoloz Togonidze; Ivane Makharadze, Zurab Mindadze, Tengiz Sichinava, Gela Shekiladze, Rostom Torgashvili (75 Shalva Apkhazava), Valeri Shanidze, Avtandil Glonti, Temur Tugushi, Jumber Chukhua (88 Gocha Kulejishvili), David Sologashvili (Cap).   Trainer: Shota Cheishvili

ARARAT: Harutyun Abrahamyan (Cap); Artur Asoyan, Tigran Gsepyan (46 Artur Minasyan), Rafik Nazaryan, Arsen Ayvazyan, Vigen Abrahamyan, Araik Nigoyan, Armenak Galstyan, Hovakim Hovakimyan (46 Akop Ter-Petrosyan), Arshak Amiryan (66 Mher Gasparyan), Sedrak Babayan.   Trainer: Arsen Andreassian

Goals: Chukhua (23, 31), Ter-Petrosyan (59), Glonti (77), Nazaryan (81), Shekiladze (90)

Ararat Erevan were awarded the game 3-0 because Dinamo Batumi fielded an ineligible player.

ARARAT EREVAN v DINAMO BATUMI 0-2 (0-2)
Razdan, Erevan 28.08.1997
Referee: Marek Kowalczyk (POL)   Attendance: 5,000
ARARAT: Harutyun Abrahamyan; Artur Asoyan, Tigran Gsepyan, Armenak Galstyan, Arsen Ayvazyan, Araik Nigoyan (50 Rafik Nazaryan), Sedrak Babayan (60 Hovakim Hovakimyan), Robert Tamrazyan (68 Hayk Babayan), Akop Ter-Petrosyan (Cap), Artur Minasyan, Vigen Abrahamyan.   Trainer: Arsen Andreassian
DINAMO: Nikoloz Togonidze; Ivane Makharadze, Zurab Mindadze, Tengiz Sichinava, Gela Shekiladze, Rostom Torgashvili (75 Valeri Shanidze), Malkhaz Makharadze (Cap), Avtandil Glonti, David Chichveishvili, Jumber Chukhua, Gocha Kulejishvili (69 Shalva Apkhazava).   Trainer: Shota Cheishvili
Goals: Togashvili (2), I. Makharadze (38)

FIRST ROUND

KOCAELISPOR IZMIT v FC NAŢIONAL BUCUREŞTI 2-0 (2-0)
Ismetpaşa Izmit 18.09.1997
Referee: Claus Bo Larsen (DEN)   Attendance: 15,000
KOCAELISPOR: Dumitru Stângaciu; Turan Uzun (Cap), Misko Mirkovic, Mert Korkmaz; Soner Boz, Evren Turhan (59 Engin Öztonga), Zeki Önatli, John Moshoeu, Nuri Çolak; Faruk Yigit (82 Taskin Aksoy), Mustafa Özkan (29 Erhan Albayrak).   Trainer: Holger Osieck
FC NAŢIONAL: Ioan Pap Deac (46 Paul Ştefănescu); Tinel Petre, Liviu Ciobotariu (Cap), Cătălin Necula, Ion Sburlea, Remus Traian Ganea; Stelian Carabaş (64 Cătălin Nicolae Liţă), Adrian Ion Pigulea (46 Gabriel Vochin), Cristian Marius Vasc; Cristian Albeanu, Radu Niculescu.   Trainer: Florin Halagian
Goals: Erhan (41), Moshoeu (45)

FC NAŢIONAL BUCUREŞTI v KOCAELISPOR IZMIT 0-1 (0-0)
Cotroceni, Bucureşti 2.10.1997
Referee: Stephen John Lodge (ENG)   Attendance: 8,000
FC NAŢIONAL: Paul Ştefănescu; Tinel Petre (72 Stelian Carabaş), Gabriel Vochin, Cătălin Necula (Cap), Ion Sburlea, Petre Marin; Cătălin Liţă, Adrian Ion Pigulea (50 Ambrozie Cristian Coroian), Cristian Marius Vasc (80 Gigel Coman); Radu Niculescu, Cristian Albeanu.   Trainer: Florin Halagian
KOCAELISPOR: Dumitru Stîngaciu; Misko Mirkovic, Osman Çakir (Cap), Turan Uzun, Zeki Önatli, Evren Turhan (46 Ahmet Dursun), Faruk Yigit (82 Roman Dabrowski), John Moshoeu, Nuri Çolak, Soner Boz (89 Taskin Alsoy), Mert Korkmaz.   Trainer: Holger Osieck
Goal: Nuri (80)

APOEL NICOSIA v SK STURM GRAZ 0-1 (0-0)
Makarion, Nicosia 18.09.1997
Referee: Romans Lajuks (LAT)   Attendance: 3,700
APOEL: Andreas Petridis; Kostas Kosta, Marinos Satsias (79 Hristakis Pounas), Giorgos Hristodoulou, Kostas Konstantinou, Kostas Fasouliotis (65 Alexis Alexandrou), Antros Sotiriou, Loukas Hatziloukas (73 Nikos Timotheou), Alfred Hörtnagl, Aristos Aristokleous, Giannis Ioannou (Cap).   Trainer: Kurt Jara
STURM: Kazimierz Sidorczuk; Franco Foda; Darko Milanic, Ranko Popovic; Günther Neukirchner, Hannes Reinmayr, Roman Mählich (67 Tomislav Kocijan), Markus Schupp, Gilbert Prilasnig; Ivica Vastic (Cap), Mario Haas (63 Joseph Spiteri).   Trainer: Ivica Osim
Goal: Spiteri (81)

STURM GRAZ v APOEL NICOSIA 3-0 (3-0)
Arnold Schwarzenegger, Graz 2.10.1997
Referee: Haim Lipkovich (ISR)   Attendance: 11,500
STURM: Kazimierz Sidorczuk; Franco Foda; Darko Milanic, Ranko Popovic (69 Wolfgang Hopfer); Günther Neukirchner, Roman Mählich, Hannes Reinmayr, Markus Schupp (46 Mario Posch), Gilbert Prilasnig; Ivica Vastic (Cap), Mario Haas (69 Joseph Spiteri).   Trainer: Ivica Osim
APOEL: Andreas Petridis; Aristos Aristokleous, Kostas Kosta (88 Nikos Haralampous), Kostas Konstantinou, Nikos Timotheou (82 Giorgos Aloneftis), Giorgos Hristodoulou, Marinos Satsias (72 Alexis Alexandrou), Alfred Hörtnagl, Giannis Ioannou (Cap), Antros Sotiriou, Loukas Hatziloukas.   Trainer: Kurt Jara
Goals: Reinmayr (3), Vastic (29), Haas (42)

ÍB VESTMANNAEYJAR v VfB STUTTGART 1-3 (1-2)
Laugardalsvöllur, Reykjavík 18.09.1997
Referee: John Ashman (WAL)   Attendance: 3,148
ÍBV: Gunnar Sigurdsson; Gudni Rúnar Helgason (80 Ingi Sigurdsson), Hlynur Stefánsson (Cap), Zoran Miljkovic, Hjalti Jóhannesson, Sigurvin Olafsson, Sverrir Sverrisson, Kristinn Haflidason (73 Bjarnólfur Lárusson), Ivar Bjarklind, Steingrímur Jóhannesson (76 Leifur Geir Hafsteinsson), Tryggvi Gudmundsson.   Trainer: Bjarni Jóhansson
VfB: Marc Ziegler; Jochen Endress, Frank Verlaat (Cap), Thomas Schneider (73 Matthias Hagner), Marco Haber, Zvonimir Soldo, Krasimir Balakov, Gerhard Poschner, Florin Răducioiu (83 Murat Yakin), Fredi Bobic, Jonathan Akpoborie.   Trainer: Joachim Löw
Goals: Bobic (9, 12), Olafsson (39), Akpoborie (70)

**VfB STUTTGART
v ÍB VESTMANNAEYJAR 2-1** (0-0)

Gottlieb-Daimler-Stadion, Stuttgart   2.10.1997

Referee: Marek Kowalczyk (POL)   Attendance: 12,483

VfB: Franz Wohlfahrt; Marco Haber, Frank Verlaat (Cap), Jochen Endress, Matthias Hagner, Zvonimir Soldo, Gerhard Poschner, Kristijan Djordjevic (62 Matthias Becker), Krasimir Balakov (82 Krisztián Lisztes), Florin Răducioiu (46 Jonathan Akpoborie), Fredi Bobic.   Trainer: Joachim Löw

ÍBV: Gunnar Sigurdsson; Gudni Rúnar Helgason (Cap) (90 Björn Jakobsson), Zoran Miljkovic, Hlynur Stefánsson, Hjalti Johánnesson, Sigurvin Olafsson, Sverrir Sverisson, Ingi Sigurdsson (72 Bjarnólfur Lárusson), Ivar Bjarklind, Tryggvi Gudmundsson, Steingrímur Jóhannesson (85 Leifur Geir Hafsteinsson).

Goals: Akpoborie (73, 76), Larusson (80)

**BOAVISTA PORTO
v SHAKHTAR DONETSK 2-3** (2-1)

Estádio do Bessa, Porto   18.09.1997

Referee: Luc Huyghe (BEL)   Attendance: 5,000

BOAVISTA: RICARDO Alexandre Soares Pereira; PAULO Jorge Ferreira de SOUSA (Cap), Carlos Manuel de Oliveira Magalhães "LITOS", ISAÍAS Silva Aragao (75 José Fernando Gomes TAVARES), William Quevedo (69 Romeo Wouden), HÉLDER Manuel Elias Domingos Baptista, RUI Fernando da Silva Calapez BENTO, LUÍS CARLOS de Oliveira, Sasa Simic (57 Ion Timofte), Kwame Ayew, RUI MIGUEL Magal.   Trainer: Mario Reis

SHAKHTAR: Dmytro Shutkov; Mikhailo Starostyak, Ihor Leonov, Olexandr Koval, Olexandr Babiy (87 Ihor Zhabchenko), Yuri Seleznev (79 Andriy Vorobei), Hennadiy Orbu, Serhiy Kovalev, Hennadiy Zubov, Valeriy Kriventsov (Cap), Serhiy Atelkin (83 Vladyslav Novikov).   Trainer: Valeri Yaremchenko

Goals: Zubov (23), Rui Miguel (34), Litos (43), Atelkin (61, 63)

**SHAKHTAR DONETSK
v BOAVISTA PORTO 1-1** (0-0)

Shakhtar Donetsk   2.10.1997

Referee: Claude Detruche (SWI)   Attendance: 25,000

SHAKHTAR: Dmytro Shutkov; Ihor Leonov, Mikhailo Starostyak, Olexandr Babiy, Olexandr Koval, Hennadiy Orbu, Serhiy Kovalev, Hennadiy Zubov (83 Olexandr Spivak), Valeriy Kriventsov (Cap) (65 Mikhail Potskhveria), Serhiy Atelkin, Oleh Shelayev (46 Vladyslav Novikov).   Trainer: Valeri Yaremchenko

BOAVISTA: RICARDO Alexandre Soares Pereira; PAULO Jorge Ferreira de SOUSA (Cap), José Fernando Gomes TAVARES, HÉLDER Manuel Elias Domingos Baptista, LUÍS CARLOS de Oliveira, Kwame Ayew (69 Romeo Wouden), Carlos Manuel de Oliveira Magalhães "LITOS", MÁRIO Fernandes Magalhães da SILVA Fernando, JORGE António Pinto do COUTO, RUI MIGUEL Magal (75 Russel Latapy), PEDRO EMANUEL dos Santos M.Silva (55 Ion Timofte).   Trainer: Mario Reis

Sent off: Hélder (87)

Goals: Potskhveria (80), Latapy (87)

**GERMINAL EKEREN
v CRVENA ZVEZDA BEOGRAD 3-2** (1-0)

Veltwijckstadion, Ekeren   18.09.1997

Referee: Atanas Uzunov (BUL)   Attendance: 3,750

GERMINAL: Jan Moons; Tom Vandervee, Nick Descamps, Mike Verstraeten, Ervin Kovács (72 Rudy Moury), Laurent Dauwe, Manu Karagiannis, Ronny Van Geneugden, Edwin Van Ankeren (64 Tomasz Radzinski), Gunther Hofmans (Cap) (80 Cvijan Milosevic), Thierry Siquet.   Trainer: Herman Helleputte

CRVENA ZVEZDA: Dragoslav Jevrić; Bratislav Zivković, Nikoslav Bjegović, Zoran Njegus, Vinko Marinović, Goran Bunjevcević, Dalibor Skorić (88 Dejan Ilić), Goran Bošković, Zoran Jovicić (Cap), Dejan Stanković, Perica Ognjenović. Trainer: Milorad Kosanović

Goals: Kovács (17), Hofmans (57), Ognjenović (59), Stanković (63), Dauwe (71)

**CRVENA ZVEZDA BEOGRAD
v GERMINAL EKEREN 1-1** (1-0)

Crvena Zvezda Beograd   2.10.1997

Referee: Karol Ihring (SVK)   Attendance: 48,000

CRVENA ZVEZDA: Dragoslav Jevrić; Bratislav Zivković, Zoran Njegus (70 Dragan Micić), Goran Bunjevcević, Miodrag Pantelić, Dejan Stanković (Cap), Jovan Gojković (78 Goran Bošković), Vinko Marinović, Dalibor Skorić, Goran Drulić, Ivan Dudić.   Trainer: Milorad Kosanović

GERMINAL: Jan Moons; Tom Vandervee (58 Marc Schaessens), Thierry Siquet, Mike Verstraeten, Nick Descamps, Ervin Kovács, Manu Karagiannis, Laurent Dauwe (68 Mihály Tóth), Cvijan Milosevic (77 Rudy Moury), Tomasz Radzinski, Gunther Hofmans (Cap).   Trainer: Herman Helleputte

Sent off: Verstraeten (50), Drulić (50)

Goals: Drulić (18), Radzinski (66)

AIK SOLNA v PRIMORJE AJDOVSCINA 0-1 (0-0)

Råsunda, Solna   18.09.1997

Referee: Vladimir Hrinak (SVK)   Attendance: 4,100

AIK: Anders Almgren; Tomas Gustafsson, Thomas Lagerlöf, Patrick Englund (Cap), Michael Brundin, Pierre Gallo (66 Claes Green), Johan Mjällby, Mattias Johansson, Nebojsa Novakovic (58 Gonçalves Oliveira PIRACAÍA); Cesar Pacha (58 Patrik Fredholm), Pascal Simpson.
Trainer: Erik Hamrén

PRIMORJE: Robert Volk; Andrej Poljsak, Sefik Mulahmetović, Alen Sculac, Ales Kodelja, Borivoje Lucić (Cap) (86 Zlatko Cerimović), Anton Zlogar, Edmond Gunjac, Andrej Zelko (89 Matej Mavrić), Aljko Rastoder (89 Valter Sabadin), Mladen Rudonja.   Trainer: Marin Kovacić

Sent off: Almgren (65)

Goal: Rudonja (85)

**PRIMORJE AJDOVSCINA
v AIK SOLNA 1-1** (0-1, 1-1) (AET)
Primorje Ajdovscina 2.10.1997
Referee: Sotirios Vorgias (GRE)   Attendance: 3,000
PRIMORJE: Robert Volk; Andrej Poljsak, Sefik Mulahmetović, Alen Sculac, Edmond Gunjac, Andrej Zelko (114 Simon Gregorić), Ales Kodelja, Anton Zlogar, Aljko Rastoder (91 Zlatko Cerimović), Borivoje Lucić (Cap) (69 Valter Sabadin), Mladen Rudonja.   Trainer: Marin Kovacić

AIK: Claes Green; Tomas Gustafsson, Michael Brundin, Patrick Englund, Thomas Lagerlöf; Krister Nordin (74 Andreas Yngvesson), Ola Andersson (Cap), Johan Mjällby, Nebojsa Novakovic, Patrik Fredholm (71 Gonçalves Oliveira PIRACAÍA), Pascal Simpson (82 Cesar Pacha).

Sent off: Englund (66), Mjällby (100)

Goals: Novakovic (77), Rudonja (120)

**AEK ATHINA
v DINABURG DAUGAVPILS 5-0** (2-0)
Nikos Gkoumas, Athina   18.09.1997
Referee: Hans-Jürgen Weber (GER)   Attendance: 10,587
AEK: Ilias Atmatzidis (Cap); Haralampos Kopitsis, Mihalis Kasapis, Giannis Kalitzakis, Anton Doboş (69 Nikos Kostenoglou), Triantafilos Mahairidis, Evripidis Katsavos, Hristos Maladenis (64 Arnar Grétarsson), Toni Savevski, Daniel Batista (21 MARCELO Veridiano), Hristos Kostis.   Trainer: Dumitru Dumitriu

DINABURG: Vyacheslav Dusmanov; Alexander Glazov (Cap), Alexander Isakov (34 Victor Spole), Georgy Shebarshin (75 Alexander Zagorodin), Edgar Burlakov, Mikhail Zizilev, Kirill Kurbatov, Vitaly Pinyaskin, Sergey Isayev (89 Sergey Pogodin), Alexander Fedotov, Yuri Karashauskas.
Trainer: Dmitri Kuzminchev   **Sent off:** Dusmanov (34)

Goals: Kopitsis (36, 45 pen), Katsavos (63), Kalitzakis (66), Marcelo (77)

**DINABURG DAUGAVPILS
v AEK ATHINA 2-4** (1-1)
Daugava, Riga   2.10.1997
Referee: Tom Henning Øvrebø (NOR)   Attendance: 1,500
DINABURG: Victor Spole; Alexander Glazov (Cap), Nikita Shmikov, Alexander Isakov, Alexander Zagorodin, Mikhail Zizilev, Kirill Kurbatov, Yuri Karashauskas, Vitaly Pinyaskin, Sergey Isayev (84 Edgar Burlakov), Alexander Fedotov.
Trainer: Dmitri Kuzminchev

AEK: Ilias Atmatzidis; Haralampos Kopitsis, Mihalis Kasapis, Nikos Kostenoglou (Cap), Giannis Kalitzakis (49 Hristos Maladenis), Anton Doboş (83 MARCELO Veridiano), Toni Savevski, Evripidis Katsavos (46 Arnar Grétarsson), Mihalis Vlahos, Hristos Kostis, Themistoklis Nikolaidis.
Trainer: Dumitru Dumitriu

Goals: Fedotov (34), Nikolaidis (35, 80), Vlahos (50), Isayev (62), Kostis (72)

SLAVIA PRAHA v FC LUZERN 4-2 (2-1)
Dr. Vacka "Eden", Praha   18.09.1997
Referee: Fiorenzo Treossi (ITA)   Attendance: 5,614
SLAVIA: Jan Stejskal (Cap); Lubos Kozel, Sladjan Asanin, Petr Vlcek, Edvard Lasota, Ivo Ulich, Jiří Lerch, Tomas Kuchar (81 Lukas Jarolim), Vladimir Labant; Karel Vacha (86 Tomas Kucera), Robert Vagner (86 Samir Pinjo).
Trainer: František Cipro

FC LUZERN: Stephan Lehmann; Heinz Moser, Markus Brunner, René Van Eck (Cap); Manfred Joller, Raffaele Izzo, Thomas Wyss (46 Ibrahim Muri), Ludwig Kögl, Hristo Koilov; Agent Sawu (72 Herbert Baumann), Petar Aleksandrov.
Trainer: Kudi Müller

Goals: Asanin (5), Aleksandrov (7), Vacha (14), Vagner (49), Labant (54), Koilov (76)

FC LUZERN v SLAVIA PRAHA 0-2 (0-0)
Allmend, Luzern   2.10.1997
Referee: Miko Vuorela (FIN)   Attendance: 5,000
FC LUZERN: Stephan Lehmann; Heinz Moser, Markus Brunner (80 Gürkan Sermeter), René Van Eck (Cap), Manfred Joller; Raffaele Izzo, Hristo Koilov (64 Ibrahim Muri), Ludwig Kögl, Igor Trninic (64 Agent Sawu); Martin Fink, Petar Aleksandrov.   Trainer: Kudi Müller

SLAVIA: Jan Stejskal (Cap); Jiří Lerch, Lubos Kozel, Sladjan Asanin, Petr Vlcek, Ivo Ulich (87 Pavel Rehák), Edvard Lasota, Karel Vacha (82 Samir Pinjo), Pavel Horvath (76 Tomas Kuchar), Robert Vagner, Martin Hysky.
Trainer: František Cipro

Goals: Koilov (55 og), Vagner (74)

**HAPOEL BEER SHEVA
v RODA KERKRADE 1-4** (0-4)
Municipal, Beer Sheva   18.09.1997
Referee: Arturo Dauden Ibanez (SPA)   Attendance: 6,500
HAPOEL: Shaul Smadga; Sharon Bochnik (46 Ilan Vaknin), Shimon Biton (Cap), Gyula Zsivótzky, Csaba Horváth; Alexander Zakharov, Alon Rif (59 Amir Avigdor), Dudu Hefer (46 Yossi Benayoun), David Moial; Oren Sagron, Sharon Avitan.   Trainer: Benni Tabac

RODA: Nikolaj Damjanac; Stephan t'Hart, Gerry Senden (Cap) (65 Igor Tomasic), Regilio Vrede, Ramon Van Haaren; Eric Van de Luer, André Ooijer, Arno Doomernik, Garba Lawal; Peter Van Houdt (71 Bob Peeters), Gábor Torma (86 Jan-Pieter Martens).   Trainer: Martin Jol

Goals: Van Houdt (15, 31), Torma (18, 35), Benayoun (63 pen)

**RODA KERKRADE
v HAPOEL BEER SHEVA 10-0** (3-0)

Gemeentelijk Sportpark Kaalheide, Kerkrade 2.10.1997

Referee: Roland Beck (LIE)   Attendance: 5,010

RODA: Nikolaj Damjanac; Gerry Senden (Cap), Regilio Vrede, André Ooijer, Arno Doomernik, Eric Van de Luer, Peter Van Houdt, Arie Obdam, Stephan t'Hart (73 Edwin Grünholz), Gábor Torma, Garba Lawal.   Trainer: Martin Jol

HAPOEL: Shaul Smadga; Oren Sagron, Shimon Biton (Cap), Csaba Horváth, Sharon Refael, David Moial, Sharon Avitan (76 Ilan Vaknin), Alon Rif, Yossi Benayoun, Yair Simhon, Sergei Gusev (74 Rami Eliaho).   Trainer: Benni Tabac

Goals: Van Houdt (19, 32, 70), Lawal (41, 63), Ooijer (49, 85 pen), Vrede (53), Torma (72, 90).

NK ZAGREB v TROMSØ IL 3-2 (1-0)

Kranjcevica, Zagreb 18.09.1997

Referee: Attila Juhos (HUN)   Attendance: 5,000

NK ZAGREB: Sandro Tomić; Marinko Galić, Sunaj Keqi, Darko Vukić, Jasenko Sabitović, Mario Osibov, Zeljko Sopić (70 Ivo Milić), Mario Cizmek (Cap), Mate Baturina (65 Hari Vukas), Marin Lalić, Nino Bule (85 Darko Perić).   Trainer: Branko Tucak

TROMSØ: Tor André Grenersen; Svein Morten Johansen, Steinar Nilsen, Jonny Hanssen, Morten Kraemer (Cap); Robin Berntsen, Bjørn Johansen, Roar Christensen, Frode Fermann (54 Ulrik Balling), Rune Lange, Berg Johansen (54 Ole Martin Årst).   Trainer: Håkan Sandberg

Goals: Lalić (44), Sopić (50), Baturina (52), B. Johansen (56), Årst (80)

TROMSØ IL v NK ZAGREB 4-2 (1-0, 3-2) (AET)

Alfheim, Tromsø 2.10.1997

Referee: Andreas Schluchter (SWI)   Attendance: 3,893

TROMSØ: Tor André Grenersen; Svein Morten Johansen, Steinar Nilsen, Jonny Hanssen, Morten Kraemer (Cap); Robin Berntsen (68 Ulrik Balling), Bjørn Johansen, Roar Christensen, Frode Fermann (37 Thomas Hafstad, 80 Berg Johansen), Ole Martin Årst, Rune Lange.   Trainer: Håkan Sandberg

NK ZAGREB: Sandro Tomić; Drazen Biskup, Jasenko Sabitović, Mario Osibov, Sunaj Keqi, Darko Vukić, Zeljko Sopić, Vjekoslav Skrinjar (80 Ivan Kurtović), Mario Cizmek (46 Fuad Sasivarević), Mate Baturina, Nino Bule (Cap) (87 Zeljko Domjanić).   Trainer: Branko Tucak

Goals: Sabitović (13 og), Vukić (53), Bule (57), Årst (74), S.M. Johansen (90), Lange (115)

FC KØBENHAVN v ARARAT EREVAN 3-0 (1-0)

Parken, København 18.09.1997

Referee: Konrad Plautz (AUS)   Attendance: 7,563

FC KØBENHAVN: Karim Zaza; Michael "Mio" Nielsen, Diego Tur, Carsten Vagn Jensen, Lars Højer Nielsen, Carsten Hemmingsen, Henrik Larsen (Cap), Bjarne Goldbæk, Peter Nielsen, David Nielsen (73 Stefan Kofoed Hansen), Todi Jonsson.   Trainer: Kent Karlsson

ARARAT: Harutyun Abrahamyan (Cap); Artur Asoyan (51 Hovakim Hovakimyan), Rafik Nazaryan, Vigen Abrahamyan, Armenak Galstyan, Araik Nigoyan, Arshak Amiryan (68 Hayk Babayan), Artur Minasyan, Aram Sevan Voskanyan (59 Sedrak Babayan), Robert Tamrazyan, Mher Gasparyan.   Trainer: Arsen Andreassian

Sent off: Tamrazyan (52)

Goals: Jonsson (17), L.H. Nielsen (53), Tur (87)

ARARAT EREVAN v FC KØBENHAVN 0-2 (0-0)

Razdan, Erevan 2.10.1997

Referee: Ladislav Gadosi (SVK)   Attendance: 700

ARARAT: Harutyun Abrahamyan (Cap); Armenak Galstyan, Arshak Amiryan (86 Georgi Andriasyan), Rafik Nazaryan, Vigen Abrahamyan, Araik Nigoyan (87 Artur Asoyan), Artur Minasyan, Hovakim Hovakimyan, Sedrak Babayan (60 Karen Barsegyan), Hayk Babayan, Aram Sevan Voskanyan.   Trainer: Arsen Andreassian

FC KØBENHAVN: Karim Zaza; Michael "Mio" Nielsen, Diego Tur, Carsten Vagn Jensen, Lars Højer Nielsen, Carsten Hemmingsen (74 Morten Nielsen), Henrik Larsen (Cap), Bjarne Goldbæk, Peter Nielsen (79 Stefan Kofoed Hansen), David Nielsen (74 Mate Sestan), Martin Nielsen.   Trainer: Kent Karlsson

Goals: Mo. Nielsen (87), Sestan (89)

**BELSHINA BOBRUISK
v LOKOMOTIV MOSKVA 1-2** (1-0)

Dinamo Minsk 18.09.1997

Referee: Kostadin Guerguinov (BUL)   Attendance: 7,000

BELSHINA: Andrei Svirkov; Igor Shustikov, Evgeniy Timofeyev, Igor Kovalevich, Andrei Khripach, Igor Gradoboyev (Cap), Vasiliy Smirnykh (69 Alexandr Borisik), Eduard Gradoboyev, Dmitriy Balashov, Andrei Khlebosolov, Vladimir Putrash (63 Oleg Kovtun).   Trainer: Oleg Volokh

LOKOMOTIV: Aleksandr Podzhivalov; Andrei Solomatin, Aleksei Arifullin, Igor Chugainov, Igor Cherevchenko, Yuri Drozdov, Evgeniy Kharlachov, Dmitriy Loskov, Aleksandr Smirnov, Aleksandr Borodyuk, Zaza Janashia (78 Dmitriy Bulykin).   Trainer: Yuri Syomin

Goals: Khlebosolov (14 pen), Loskov (49), Borodyuk (71)

**LOKOMOTIV MOSKVA
v BELSHINA BOBRUISK 3-0** (2-0)
Lokomotiv Moskva 2.10.1997
Referee: Stuart Dougall (SCO)   Attendance: 3,000
LOKOMOTIV: Khasambi Bidzhiev; Igor Chugainov (Cap), Andrei Solomatin, Aleksei Arifullin, Igor Cherevchenko (75 Oleg Pashinin), Yuri Drozdov, Dmitriy Loskov, Aleksandr Smirnov (64 Albert Sarkisyan), Zaza Janashia (69 Vitaliy Veselov), Evgeniy Kharlachov, Vladimir Maminov.
Trainer: Yuri Syomin
BELSHINA: Andrei Svirkov; Eduard Apalkov, Evgeniy Timofeyev, Andrei Khripach (46 Oleg Kovtun), Sergei Razumovich, Igor Kovalevich, Igor Gradoboyev (Cap), Eduard Gradoboyev, Vasiliy Smirnykh (46 Vladimir Putrash), Dmitriy Balashov (66 Alexandr Borisik), Andrei Khlebosolov.
Trainer: Oleg Volokh
Goals: Maminov (23), Kharlachov (41), Loskov (74)

**CHELSEA LONDON
v SLOVAN BRATISLAVA 2-0** (1-0)
Stamford Bridge, London 18.09.1997
Referee: Antony Boggi (ITA)   Attendance: 23,067
CHELSEA: Ed de Goey; Paul Hughes, Frank Leboeuf, Michael Duberry, Danny Granville, Dan Petrescu, Roberto Di Matteo, Gustavo Poyet, Dennis Wise (Cap), Gianluca Vialli, Gianfranco Zola.   Trainer: Ruud Gullit
SLOVAN: Miroslav König; Milos Glonek (Cap), Jozef Antalovic, Ladislav Pecko, Milos Sobona, Peter Gunda; Robert Tomaschek, Zsolt Hornyak, Andras Keresztúri (81 Roland Moder), Sergiy Borisenko (62 Jozef Muzlay), Robert Novak (50 Marian Timko).   Trainer: Jozef Prochotsky
Goals: Di Matteo (6), Granville (80)

**SLOVAN BRATISLAVA
v CHELSEA LONDON 0-2** (0-1)
Tehelné pole, Bratislava 2.10.1997
Referee: Alain Hamer (LUX)   Attendance: 15,000
SLOVAN: Miroslav König; Peter Gunda, Ladislav Pecko, Robert Tomaschek (Cap), Jozef Muzlay, Jozef Pukalovic (65 Marian Puchner), Roland Moder, Zsolt Hornyak, András Keresztúy, Sergiy Borisenko (60 Tamás Nagy), Robert Novak.
Trainer: Jozef Prochotsky
CHELSEA: Ed de Goey; Frank Sinclair, Bernard Lambourde, Frank Leboeuf, Graeme Le Saux (65 Danny Granville), Dan Petrescu (72 Mark Nicholls), Roberto Di Matteo, Dennis Wise (Cap), Gustavo Poyet (46 Celestine Babayaro), Tore André Flo, Gianluca Vialli.   Trainer: Ruud Gullit
Goals: Vialli (28), Di Matteo (60)

OGC NICE v KILMARNOCK FC 3-1 (1-0)
Stade du Ray, Nice 18.09.1997
Referee: Sarvan Oguz (TUR)   Attendance: 10,000
OGC NICE: Robin Huc; Goran Kartalija, Didier Angan, Ludovic Stefano, Zoran Milinkovic, Dominique Aulanier, Henri Savini (76 Pierre Aubameyang), Mickael Rol; Didier Angibeaud, Franck Vandecasteele (Cap), Stefan Kohn.
Trainer: Silvester Takac
KILMARNOCK: Colin Meldrum; Angus MacPherson (Cap), Kevin McGowne, Ray Montgomerie, Martin Baker, Ally Mitchell, Willie Findlay (87 Martin O'Neill), Mark Reilly, Pat Nevin (65 David Bagan), Paul Wright, Jérôme Vareille (83 Mark Roberts).   Manager: Bobby Wiliamson
Sent off: Baker (73)
Goals: Kohn (12, 48), Wright (77 pen), Rol (79)

KILMARNOCK FC v OGC NICE 1-1 (1-0)
Rugby Park, Kilmarnock 2.10.1997
Referee: Juha Hirviniemi (FIN)   Attendance: 8,402
KILMARNOCK: Dragoje Lekovic; Angus MacPherson (Cap), Kevin McGowne, Neil Whitworth, Dylan Kerr, David Bagan (51 John Henry), Mark Reilly, Ally Mitchell (80 Pat Nevin), Alex Burke, Paul Wright, Jérôme Vareille (80 Mark Roberts).   Manager: Bobby Wiliamson
OGC NICE: Robin Huc; Didier Angan, Goran Kartalija, Ludovic Stefano (59 Pierre Aubameyang), Zoran Milinkovic, Henri Savini, Mickael Rol, Franck Vandecasteele (Cap), Dominique Aulanier, Didier Angibeaud, Stefan Kohn (9 Franck Pottier).   Trainer: Silvester Takac
Goals: Reilly (31), Milinkovic (76)

**REAL BETIS SEVILLA
v BVSC-ZUGLO BUDAPEST 2-0** (0-0)
Benito Villamarin, Sevilla 18.09.1997
Referee: Dany Koren (ISR)   Attendance: 15,000
BETIS: Antoni PRATS Servera; Jorge OTERO Bouzas (80 Nenad Bjelica), Hristo Vidakovic, Roberto SOLOZÁBAL Villanueva, Albert Nadj, ALEXIS Trujillo Oramas (Cap), Juan MERINO Ruiz, Robert Jarni, ALFONSO Pérez Muñoz, Oliverio Jesús Alvarez González "OLI" (64 IVÁN Pérez Muñoz), FERNANDO Sánchez Cipitria (90 LUIS Fernández Gutiurrez).
Trainer: Luis Aragonés
BVSC: János Koszta (Cap); Csaba László, Ádám Komlósi, Aleksandr Bondarenko, Ákos Csiszár (90 Dénes Rósa), Ákos Fózi, Krisztián Csillag, Károly Erös, Daniel Usvat (71 János Zováth), Zoltán Bókszegi, Zsolt Aubel (46 Csaba Csordás).
Trainer: György Mezey
Goals: Alfonso (58, 73)

425

**BVSC-ZUGLO BUDAPEST
v REAL BETIS SEVILLA 0-2** (0-1)

Szönyi út, Budapest   2.10.1997

Referee: Kazimir Znaydinsky (BLS)   Attendance: 1,000

BVSC: János Koszta (Cap); Csaba László, Aleksandr Bondarenko, Ákos Fózi, Krisztián Csillag (67 Csaba Barna), János Zováth, Daniel Usvat, Imre Szín, Károly Erös, Zoltán Bókszegi (46 László Cseke), Károly Potemkin.
Trainer: György Mezey

BETIS: Antoni PRATS Servera; Jorge OTERO Bouzas (Cap), Hristo Vidakovic, Roberto SOLOZÁBAL Villanueva; George Finidi, ALEXIS Trujillo Oramas (75 Albert Nadj), Juan MERINO Ruiz, FERNANDO Sánchez Cipitria (59 Juan José CAÑAS), Robert Jarni; ALFONSO Pérez Muñoz (64 IVÁN Pérez Muñoz), Oliverio Jesús Alvarez González "OLI".
Trainer: Luis Aragonés

Goals: Alexis (8), Alfonso (48)

VICENZA v LEGIA WARSZAWA 2-0 (2-0)

Romeo Menti, Vicenza   18.09.1997

Referee: Hermann Albrecht (GER)   Attendance: 10,081

VICENZA: Pierluigi Brivio; Gustavo Méndez, Giacomo Dicara, Davide Belotti, Francesco Coco; Marco Schenardi (86 Fabio Firmani), Fabio Viviani, Domenico Di Carlo (Cap), Gabriele Ambrosetti (67 Massimo Beghetto); Pasquale Luiso, Arturo Di Napoli (79 Lamberto Zauli).
Trainer: Francesco Guidolin

LEGIA: Grzegorz Szamotulski; Jacek Magiera (66 Piotr Wlodarczyk), Jacek Zielinski (Cap), Jacek Bednarz, Sylwester Czereszewski, Dariusz Czykier, Jacek Kacprzak, Pawel Skrzypek (16 Artur Kupiec), Dariusz Solnica (73 Andrzej Sazanowicz), Tomasz Sokolowski, Kenneth Zeigbo.
Trainer: Miroslaw Jablonski

Goals: Luiso (11), Ambrosetti (24)

LEGIA WARSZAWA v VICENZA 1-1 (0-0)

Wojska Polskiego, Warszawa   2.10.1997

Referee: Milan Mitrovic (SVN)   Attendance: 7,000

LEGIA: Grzegorz Szamotulski; Jacek Zielinski (Cap), Jacek Bednarz, Jacek Magiera, Bartosz Karwan, Dariusz Czykier, Sylwester Czereszewski, Tomasz Sokolowski, Jacek Kacprzak, Ryszard Staniek, Artur Kupiec (80 Dariusz Solnica).
Trainer: Miroslaw Jablonski

VICENZA: Pierluigi Brivio; Davide Belotti, Giacomo Dicara, Ricardo Canals, Massimo Beghetto; Gustavo Méndez (88 Fabio Firmani), Domenico Di Carlo (Cap), Fabio Viviani, Gabriele Ambrosetti (65 Massimo Ambrosini); Pasquale Luiso, Arturo Di Napoli (65 Lamberto Zauli).
Trainer: Francesco Guidolin

Goals: Kacprzak (56), Zauli (87)

SECOND ROUND

GERMINAL EKEREN v VfB STUTTGART 0-4 (0-1)

Veltwijckstadion, Ekeren   23.10.1997

Referee: Knud Erik Fisker (DEN)   Attendance: 2,704

GERMINAL: Jan Moons; Tom Vandervee, Rudy Moury, Ervin Kovács, Manu Karagiannis (66 Laurent Dauwe), Thierry Siquet, Gunther Hofmans (Cap), Tomasz Radzinski, Marc Schaessens (75 Edwin Van Ankeren), Alex Camerman, Cvijan Milosevic (61 Ronny Van Geneugden).
Trainer: Herman Helleputte

VfB: Franz Wohlfahrt; Frank Verlaat (Cap), Marco Haber, Matthias Hagner (87 Matthias Becker), Zvonimir Soldo (77 Michael Bochtler), Krasimir Balakov, Murat Yakin, Danny Schwarz, Gerhard Poschner, Jonathan Akpoborie, Fredi Bobic (82 Florin Răducioiu).   Trainer: Joachim Löw

Goals: Bobic (43, 62), Akpoborie (56, 75)

VfB STUTTGART v GERMINAL EKEREN 2-4 (2-2)

Gottlieb-Daimler-Stadion, Stuttgart   6.11.1997

Referee: Pierluigi Pairetto (ITA)   Attendance: 10,000

VfB: Franz Wohlfahrt; Thomas Schneider, Frank Verlaat (Cap), Thomas Berthold, Marco Haber, Danny Schwarz, Krisztián Lisztes (77 Jochen Endress), Murat Yakin, Gerhard Poschner (59 Matthias Hagner), Fredi Bobic, Jonathan Akpoborie (86 Kristijan Djordjevic).   Trainer: Joachim Löw

GERMINAL: Jan Moons; Ervin Kovács, Thierry Siquet, Alex Camerman, Marc Schaessens, Gunther Hofmans (Cap), Laurent Dauwe (40 Manu Karagiannis), Ronny Van Geneugden, Rudy Moury (54 Tom Vandervee), Edwin Van Ankeren, Mihály Tóth (67 Tomasz Radzinski).
Trainer: Herman Helleputte

Sent off: Yakin (45)

Goals: Verlaat (13), Poschner (35), Van Ankeren (44, 83), Van Geneugden (45), Karagiannis (77)

TROMSØ IL v CHELSEA LONDON 3-2 (2-0)

Alfheim, Tromsø   23.10.1997

Referee: Jacek Granat (POL)   Attendance: 6,438

TROMSØ: Tor André Grenersen; Svein Morten Johansen, Steinar Nilsen, Jonny Hanssen, Morten Kraemer (Cap); Robin Berntsen, Bjørn Johansen (64 Thomas Hafstad), Roar Christensen, Frode Fermann (69 Ulrik Balling), Ole Martin Årst, Rune Lange.   Trainer: Håkan Sandberg

CHELSEA: Ed de Goey; Frank Sinclair, Frank Leboeuf (85 Andy Myers), Steve Clarke, Danny Granville (46 Mark Hughes), Roberto Di Matteo, Dennis Wise (Cap), Eddie Newton, Celestine Babayaro, Gianfranco Zola, Gianluca Vialli.
Trainer: Ruud Gullit

Goals: S. Nilsen (6), Fermann (19), Vialli (85, 89), Årst (86)

CHELSEA LONDON v TROMSØ IL 7-1 (3-1)
Stamford Bridge, London 6.11.1997
Referee: Vasiliy Melnichuk (UKR)   Attendance: 29,363

CHELSEA: Ed de Goey; Frank Sinclair, Frank Leboeuf, Andy Myers, Celestine Babayaro, Dan Petrescu, Eddie Newton (70 Steve Clarke), Roberto Di Matteo (81 Bernard Lambourde), Dennis Wise (Cap), Gianfranco Zola, Gianluca Vialli (87 Tore André Flo).   Trainer: Ruud Gullit

TROMSØ: Tor André Grenersen; Svein Morten Johansen, Steinar Nilsen, Jonny Hanssen, Morten Kraemer (Cap); Robin Berntsen, Bjørn Johansen, Roar Christensen, Frode Fermann (58 Thomas Hafstad), Ole Martin Årst (70 Berg Johansen), Rune Lange.   Trainer: Håkan Sandberg

Sent off: Hanssen (53)

Goals: D. Petrescu (12, 86), Vialli (23, 60, 76), B. Johansen (38), Zola (42), Leboeuf (53 pen)

LOKOMOTIV MOSKVA v KOCAELISPOR IZMIT 2-1 (1-0)
Lokomotiv Moskva 23.10.1997
Referee: Georg Dardenne (GER)   Attendance: 3,500

LOKOMOTIV: Khasambi Bidzhiev; Andrei Solomatin, Yuri Drozdov (89 Oleg Pashinin), Evgeniy Kharlachov, Igor Chugainov (Cap), Sergei Gurenko, Igor Cherevchenko, Vitaliy Veselov (46 Aleksandr Smirnov), Vladimir Maminov (82 Albert Sarkisyan), Zaza Janashia, Dmitriy Loskov.   Trainer: Yuri Syomin

KOCAELISPOR: Dumitru Stîngaciu; Misko Mirkovic, Osman Çakir (Cap), Mert Korkmaz, Turan Uzun, Zeki Önatli, Evren Turhan, Nuri Çolak, Soner Boz, John Moshoeu, Faruk Yigit (46 Mustafa Özkan).   Trainer: Holger Osieck

Goals: Kharlachov (32), Turan (73), Janashia (82)

KOCAELISPOR IZMIT v LOKOMOTIV MOSKVA 0-0
Ismetpaşa, Izmit 6.11.1997
Referee: Fernand Meese (BEL)   Attendance: 12,000

KOCAELISPOR: Dumitru Stîngaciu; Osman Çakir (Cap) (65 Evren Turhan), Misko Mirkovic, Mert Korkmaz, Soner Boz (83 Ahmet Dursun), Zeki Önatli, Turan Uzun, John Moshoeu, Nuri Çolak, Mustafa Özkan, Faruk Yigit (54 Roman Dabrowski).   Trainer: Holger Osieck

LOKOMOTIV: Khasambi Bidzhiev; Andrei Solomatin, Igor Chugainov (Cap), Evgeniy Kharlachov, Vitaliy Veselov (73 Vladimir Maminov), Sergei Gurenko, Oleg Pashinin, Aleksei Arifullin, Dmitriy Loskov, Aleksandr Smirnov (78 Albert Sarkisyan), Yuri Drozdov.   Trainer: Yuri Syomin

SHAKHTAR DONETSK v VICENZA 1-3 (0-1)
Shakhtar Donetsk 23.10.1997
Referee: Pascal Garibian (FRA)   Attendance: 30,000

SHAKHTAR: Dmytro Shutkov; Olexandr Babiy (75 Volodymyr Yaksmanytskyi), Ihor Leonov, Serhiy Kovalev (81 Oleh Shelayev), Ihor Zhabchenko, Hennadiy Orbu, Valeriy Kriventsov (Cap), Yuri Seleznev, Hennadiy Zubov, Mikhail Potskhveria, Olexandr Koval.   Trainer: Valeri Yaremchenko

VICENZA: Pierluigi Brivio; Davide Belotti, Ricardo Canals, Giacomo Dicara, Francesco Coco; Massimo Beghetto, Marco Schenardi (66 Fabio Firmani), Domenico Di Carlo (Cap), Fabio Viviani, Massimo Ambrosini; Pasquale Luiso.   Trainer: Francesco Guidolin

Goals: Luiso (1, 90), Beghetto (55), Zubov (63)

VICENZA v SHAKHTAR DONETSK 2-1 (1-0)
Romeo Menti, Vicenza 6.11.1997
Referee: Roy Helge Olsen (NOR)   Attendance: 12,000

VICENZA: Pierluigi Brivio; Ricardo Canals, Davide Belotti, Giacomo Dicara, Francesco Coco; Marco Schenardi (72 Fabio Firmani), Domenico Di Carlo (Cap), Fabio Viviani, Massimo Ambrosini, Gabriele Ambrosetti (63 Gustavo Méndez); Pasquale Luiso (85 Arturo Di Napoli).   Trainer: Francesco Guidolin

SHAKHTAR: Dmytro Shutkov; Ihor Leonov, Mikhailo Starostyak, Olexandr Koval (72 Volodymyr Yaksmanytskyi), Ihor Zhabchenko (56 Mikhail Potskhveria), Hennadiy Zubov, Serhiy Kovalev, Yuri Seleznev, Hennadiy Orbu, Valeriy Kriventsov (Cap) (80 Olexandr Spivak), Serhiy Atelkin.   Trainer: Valeri Yaremchenko

Goals: Luiso (24), Atelkin (60), Viviani (71)

REAL BETIS SEVILLA v FC KØBENHAVN 2-0 (2-0)
Benito Villamarin, Sevilla 23.10.1997
Referee: Leslie John Irvine (NIR)   Attendance: 7,800

BETIS: Antoni PRATS Servera; Juan Antonio González UREÑA (Cap), Hristo Vidakovic, Roberto SOLOZÁBAL Villanueva; Robert Jarni, George Finidi, ALEXIS Trujillo Oramas (75 Nenad Bjelica), Juan José CAÑAS, FERNANDO Sánchez Cipitria (65 LUIS Fernández Gutiérrez); ALFONSO Pérez Muñoz, Oliverio Jesús Alvarez González "OLI" (59 JAIME Quesada Chavarría).   Trainer: Luis Aragonés

FC KØBENHAVN: Karim Zaza; Martin Nielsen, Michael "Mio" Nielsen, Carsten Vagn Jensen, Diego Tur, Lars Højer Nielsen (77 Morten Nielsen), Carsten Hemmingsen, Bjarne Goldbæk, Peter Nielsen, Henrik Larsen (Cap), David Nielsen (59 Mate Sestan).   Trainer: Kent Karlsson

Goals: Oli (25), Cañas (38)

**FC KØBENHAVN
v REAL BETIS SEVILLA 1-1 (0-0)**

Parken, København 6.11.1997

Referee: William Smith Young (SCO)   Attendance: 10,140

FC KØBENHAVN: Karim Zaza; Morten Falch, Michael "Mio" Nielsen, Morten Nielsen (50 Carsten Vagn Jensen), Diego Tur, Lars Højer Nielsen, Carsten Hemmingsen (Cap), Bjarne Goldbæk, Peter Nielsen, Henrik Larsen, Mate Sestan (80 David Nielsen).   Trainer: Kent Karlsson

BETIS: Antoni PRATS Servera; Juan Antonio González UREÑA (Cap), Roberto SOLOZÁBAL Villanueva, Tomás OLÍAS Gutiérrez; Robert Jarni (46 LUIS Fernández Gutiérrez), George Finidi (18 Albert Nadj), Juan José CAÑAS, ALEXIS Trujillo Oramas (84 JAIME Quesada Chavarría), Juan MERINO Ruiz, ALFONSO Pérez Muñoz, Oliverio Jesús Alvarez González "OLI".   Trainer: Luis Aragonés

Goals: Peter Nielsen (60 pen), Ureña (80)

AEK ATHINA v SK STURM GRAZ 2-0 (0-0)

Nikos Gkoumas, Athina 23.10.1997

Referee: Alfredo Trentalange (ITA)   Attendance: 13,000

AEK: Ilias Atmatzidis; Haralampos Kopitsis, Nikos Kostenoglou (Cap), Anton Doboş, Mihalis Kasapis, Giannis Kalitzakis, Mihalis Vlahos (67 Daniel Batista), Evripidis Katsavos (46 Arnar Grétarsson), Toni Savevski, Hristos Kostis (43 MARCELO Veridiano), Themistoklis Nikolaidis.   Trainer: Dumitru Dumitriu

STURM: Kazimierz Sidorczuk; Franco Foda; Darko Milanic (12 Mario Posch), Ranko Popovic; Günther Neukirchner, Roman Mählich, Markus Schupp, Hannes Reinmayr, Gilbert Prilasnig; Ivica Vastic (Cap) (79 Tomislav Kocijan), Mario Haas.   Trainer: Ivica Osim

Goals: Batista (75), Marcelo (85)

SK STURM GRAZ v AEK ATHINA 1-0 (0-0)

Arnold Schwarzenegger, Graz 6.11.1997

Referee: Atanas Uzunov (BUL)   Attendance: 15,400

STURM: Kazimierz Sidorczuk; Franco Foda; Mario Posch, Günther Neukirchner (71 Georg Bardel); Wolfgang Hopfer (73 Joseph Spiteri); Hannes Reinmayr, Roman Mählich, Markus Schupp (54 Tomislav Kocijan), Gilbert Prilasnig; Ivica Vastic (Cap), Mario Haas.   Trainer: Ivica Osim

AEK: Ilias Atmatzidis; Anton Doboş, Haralampos Kopitsis, Nikos Kostenoglou (Cap), Giannis Kalitzakis, Mihalis Kasapis, Arnar Grétarsson (90 Daniel Batista), Mihalis Vlahos, Toni Savevski, MARCELO Veridiano (58 Hristos Maladenis, 61 Triantafilos Mahairidis), Themistoklis Nikolaidis.   Trainer: Dumitru Dumitriu

Goal: Spiteri (82)

OGC NICE v SLAVIA PRAHA 2-2 (1-2)

Stade du Ray, Nice 23.10.1997

Referee: Celino Gracia Redondo (SPA)   Attendance: 14,274

OGC NICE: Bruno Valencony; Youssef Salimi (68 Ludovic Stefano), Goran Kartalija, Didier Angan, Mickael Rol, Pierre Aubameyang (46 Henri Savini), Dominique Aulanier, Zoran Milinkovic, Franck Vandecasteele (Cap), Didier Angibeaud, Franco Vignola (73 Franck Pottier).   Trainer: Silvester Takac

SLAVIA: Jan Stejskal (Cap); Sladjan Asanin, Lubos Kozel, Petr Vlcek, Martin Hysky (71 Jiří Lerch), Tomas Kuchar (74 Pavel Rehák), Ivo Ulich, Pavel Horvath, Edvard Lasota, Karel Vacha, Robert Vagner (83 Samir Pinjo).   Trainer: František Cipro

Goals: Aulanier (6 pen, 77), Vacha (14, 35)

SLAVIA PRAHA v OGC NICE 1-1 (0-0)

Dr. Vacka "Eden", Praha 6.11.1997

Referee: Lutz Michael Fröhlich (GER)   Attendance: 7,312

SLAVIA: Jan Stejskal (Cap); Sladjan Asanin, Radek Krejcik, Lubos Kozel, Edvard Lasota, Ivo Ulich (90 Pavel Rehák), Tomas Kuchar, Pavel Horvath, Vladimir Labant, Karel Vacha (86 Jiří Lerch), Robert Vagner (72 Samir Pinjo).   Trainer: František Cipro

OGC NICE: Bruno Valencony; Goran Kartalija, Didier Angan, Youssef Salimi, Frédéric Martin (59 Mickael Rol), Bruno Calegari, Roberto Onorati, Zoran Milinkovic, Franco Vignola, Franck Vandecasteele (Cap), Franck Pottier (67 Didier Angibeaud, 76 Dominique Aulanier).   Trainer: Silvester Takac

Goals: Vandecasteele (75), Labant (79)

**PRIMORJE AJDOVSCINA
v RODA KERKRADE 0-2 (0-1)**

Primorje Adjovscina 23.10.1997

Referee: Metin Tokat (TUR)   Attendance: 1,250

PRIMORJE: Bostjan Ziberna; Edmond Gunjac, Simon Gregorić, Sefik Mulahmetović, Andrej Poljsak, Valter Sabadin, Anton Zlogar, Andrej Zelko, Aljko Rastoder, Borivoje Lucić (Cap) (53 Igor Pandza), Patrik Ipavec.
Trainer: Marin Kovacić

RODA: Jörg Kaessmann; Stephan t'Hart, Gerry Senden (Cap), Regilio Vrede, Arie Obdam, Eric Van de Luer, André Ooijer, Arno Doomernik, Garba Lawal (83 Rastislav Mores), Peter Van Houdt, Bob Peeters (73 Gábor Torma).
Trainer: Martin Jol

Goals: Lawal (15), Van Houdt (68)

**RODA KERKRADE
v PRIMORJE AJDOVSCINA 4-0** (1-0)
Gemeentelijk Sportpark Kaalheide, Kerkrade 6.11.1997
Referee: Lucilio Cardoso Cortez Batista (POR)
Attendance: 5,000

RODA: Nikolaj Damjanac; Gerry Senden (Cap) (75 Stephan t'Hart), Regilio Vrede, Arie Obdam, Joos Valgaeren, Eric Van de Luer, André Ooijer (75 Melvin Plet), Arno Doomernik, Garba Lawal, Peter Van Houdt, Bob Peeters (70 Davy Zafarin). Trainer: Martin Jol

PRIMORJE: Uros Rutar; Andrej Poljsak, Sefik Mulahmetović, Alen Sculac, Andrej Zelko, Simon Gregorić (80 Valter Sabadin), Borivoje Lucić (Cap) (89 Elis Filipić), Edmond Gunjac, Aljko Rastoder, Anton Zlogar, Patrik Ipavec. Trainer: Marin Kovacić

Goals: Van de Luer (45), Peeters (50), Zafarin (75), Valgaeren (85)

QUARTER-FINALS

SLAVIA PRAHA v VfB STUTTGART 1-1 (1-0)
Dr. Vacka "Eden", Praha 5.03.1998
Referee: Rune Pedersen (NOR)   Attendance: 10,000

SLAVIA: Jan Stejskal (Cap) (74 Radek Cerny); Vladimir Labant, Radek Krejcik, Lubos Kozel, Libor Koller, Edvard Lasota; Ivo Ulich, Tomas Kuchar, Petr Vlcek; Karel Vacha (70 Samir Pinjo), Robert Vagner. Trainer: František Cipro

VfB: Marc Ziegler; Thomas Berthold, Frank Verlaat (Cap), Martin Spanring; Kristijan Djordjevic (90 Jochen Endress), Marco Haber, Mitko Stojkovski, Zvonimir Soldo, Gerhard Poschner; Jonathan Akpoborie (16 Sreto Ristic), Krasimir Balakov. Trainer: Joachim Löw

Goals: Vacha (39), Poschner (51)

VfB STUTTGART v SLAVIA PRAHA 2-0 (1-0)
Gottlieb-Daimler-Stadion, Stuttgart 19.03.1998
Referee: José Maria Garcia-Aranda Encinar (SPA)
Attendance: 18,921

VfB: Franz Wohlfahrt; Thomas Schneider, Frank Verlaat (Cap), Thomas Berthold; Kristijan Djordjevic, Murat Yakin, Zvonimir Soldo, Krasimir Balakov, Gerhard Poschner; Fredi Bobic (74 Krisztián Lisztes), Sreto Ristic (89 Martin Spanring). Trainer: Joachim Löw

SLAVIA: Radek Cerny; Lubos Kozel (Cap), Petr Vlcek, Libor Koller (77 Karel Vacha), Vladimir Labant; Edvard Lasota, Ivo Ulich, Pavel Horvath, Tomas Kuchar; Radek Krejcik (80 Jiří Lerch), Robert Vagner. Trainer: František Cipro

Goals: Balakov (10, 90)

RODA KERKRADE v VICENZA 1-4 (0-3)
Gemeentelijk Sportpark Kaalheide, Kerkrade 5.03.1998
Referee: Martin Krondl (AUS)   Attendance: 10,000

RODA: Gregory Delwarte; Gerry Senden (Cap), Joos Valgaeren (46 Stephan t'Hart), Regilio Vrede, Ramon Van Haaren (66 Rastislav Mores); Mariusz Kukielka, Eric Van de Luer, Davy Zafarin; Garba Lawal (56 Bob Peeters), Peter Van Houdt, Bernard Tchoutang. Trainer: Martin Jol

VICENZA: Pierluigi Brivio; Gustavo Méndez, Davide Belotti, Lorenzo Stovini, Marco Schenardi (46 Fabio Firmani); Lamberto Zauli, Fabio Viviani, Domenico Di Carlo (78 Roberto Baronio), Massimo Ambrosini; Pasquale Luiso, Marcelo Otero (69 Gabriele Ambrosetti). Trainer: Francesco Guidolin

Goals: Luiso (17, 40), Belotti (28), Otero (67), Peeters (73)

VICENZA v RODA KERKRADE 5-0 (4-0)
Romeo Menti, Vicenza 19.03.1998
Referee: Hugh Dallas (SCO)   Attendance: 19,319

VICENZA: Pierluigi Brivio; Lorenzo Stovini, Fabio Viviani, Giacomo Dicara (65 Ricardo Canals), Francesco Coco; Gustavo Méndez (46 Massimo Beghetto), Fabio Firmani, Massimo Ambrosini, Lamberto Zauli; Pasquale Luiso, Gabriele Ambrosetti (46 Roberto Baronio). Trainer: Francesco Guidolin

RODA: Jörg Kaessmann; Stephan t'Hart (Cap) (46 Melvin Plet), Gerry Senden, Regilio Vrede, Ramon Van Haaren; Eric Van de Luer, Joos Valgaeren, Mariusz Kukielka (62 Arie Obdam), Garba Lawal; Peter Van Houdt, Bob Peeters (46 Davy Zafarin). Trainer: Martin Jol

Goals: Luiso (5), Firmani (24), Méndez (38), Ambrosetti (42), Zauli (47)

AEK ATHINA v LOKOMOTIV MOSKVA 0-0
Nikos Goumas, Athina 5.03.1998
Referee: Dick Jol (HOL)   Attendance: 30,000

AEK: Ilias Atmatzidis (Cap); Vaios Karagiannis, Stelios Manolas, Haralampos Kopitsis (61 Kelvin Sebwe), Mihalis Kasapis; Arnar Grétarsson, Hristos Maladenis, Triantafilos Mahairidis (67 Anton Doboş), Toni Savevski; MARCELO Veridiano, Themistoklis Nikolaidis. Trainer: Dumitru Dumitriu

LOKOMOTIV: Ruslan Nigmatullin; Igor Chugainov (Cap), Aleksei Arifullin, Yuri Drozdov, Andrei Solomatin; Igor Cherevchenko, Aleksei Kosolapov, Sergei Gurenko, Aleksandr Borodyuk (69 Aleksandr Smirnov); Garas (46 Zaza Janashia), Dmitriy Loskov (46 Vladimir Maminov). Trainer: Yuri Syomin

Sent off: Doboş (75), Karagiannis (90)

LOKOMOTIV MOSKVA v AEK ATHINA 2-1 (0-0)

Lokomotiv Moskva 19.03.1998

Referee: Markus Merk (GER)   Attendance: 20,000

LOKOMOTIV: Ruslan Nigmatullin; Igor Chugainov (Cap), Aleksei Arifullin, Andrei Solomatin; Igor Cherevchenko, Aleksei Kosolapov, Evgeniy Kharlachov, Vladimir Maminov, Dmitriy Loskov (25 Zaza Janashia); Oleg Garas, Sergei Gurenko.   Trainer: Yuri Syomin

AEK: Ilias Atmatzidis; Haralampos Kopitsis, Mihalis Kasapis, Stelios Manolas (Cap), Giannis Kalitzakis; Arnar Grétarsson, Triantafilos Mahairidis, Nikos Kostenoglou, Toni Savevski (66 Kelvin Sebwe); Themistoklis Nikolaidis, Hristos Maladenis (88 Vagelis Kefalas).   Trainer: Dumitru Dumitriu

Goals: Kharlachov (55), Kopitsis (68 pen), Chugainov (90)

**REAL BETIS SEVILLA
v CHELSEA LONDON 1-2** (0-2)

Benito Villamarin, Sevilla 5.03.1998

Referee: Atanas Uzunov (BUL)   Attendance: 19,300

BETIS: Antoni PRATS Servera; Juan MERINO Ruiz, Tomás OLÍAS Gutiérrez, Roberto SOLOZÁBAL Villanueva; ALEXIS Trujillo Oramas (Cap), Hristo Vidakovic (46 Luis MÁRQUEZ Martín), Juan José CAÑAS (65 Oliverio Jesús Alvarez González "OLI"), Robert Jarni; George Finidi, ALFONSO Pérez Muñoz, FERNANDO Sánchez Cipitria.   Trainer: Luis Aragonés

CHELSEA: Ed de Goey; Steve Clarke, Michael Duberry, Frank Leboeuf, Eddie Newton; Dan Petrescu, Dennis Wise (Cap), Roberto Di Matteo, Frank Sinclair; Tore André Flo (84 Mark Hughes), Gianfranco Zola (77 Mark Nicholls).   Trainer: Ruud Gullit

Goals: Flo (8, 12), Alfonso (46)

**CHELSEA LONDON
v REAL BETIS SEVILLA 3-1** (1-1)

Stamford Bridge, London 19.03.1998

Referee: Bernd Heynemann (GER)   Attendance: 32,300

CHELSEA: Ed de Goey; Steve Clarke, Frank Leboeuf, Michael Duberry; Dan Petrescu (88 Bernard Lambourde), Eddie Newton, Roberto Di Matteo, Dennis Wise, Frank Sinclair; Gianfranco Zola, Gianluca Vialli.   Trainer: Ruud Gullit

BETIS: Antoni PRATS Servera; Juan MERINO Ruiz, Tomás OLÍAS Gutiérrez, José Tomás Valdomino "JOSETE"; Luis MÁRQUEZ Martín, Juan José CAÑAS (63 Oliverio Jesús Alvarez González "OLI"), ALEXIS Trujillo Oramas (Cap), LUIS Fernández Gutiérrez (73 Angel Manuel CUÉLLAR Llanos), Robert Jarni; George Finidi, ALFONSO Pérez Muñoz.   Trainer: Luis Aragonés

Goals: Finidi (20), Sinclair (30), Di Matteo (50), Zola (90)

SEMI-FINALS

VICENZA v CHELSEA LONDON 1-0 (1-0)

Romeo Menti, Vicenza 2.04.1998

Referee: Manuel Diaz Vega (SPA)   Attendance: 19,319

VICENZA: Pierluigi Brivio; Fabio Viviani, Davide Belotti, Giacomo Dicara, Gustavo Méndez; Lamberto Zauli (87 Fabio Firmani), Domenico Di Carlo (Cap), Marco Schenardi (73 Massimo Beghetto), Massimo Ambrosini; Pasquale Luiso, Gabriele Ambrosetti (73 Lorenzo Stovini).   Trainer: Francesco Guidolin

CHELSEA: Ed de Goey; Steve Clarke, Frank Leboeuf, Michael Duberry, Eddie Newton; Dan Petrescu (60 Tore André Flo), Dennis Wise (Cap), Roberto Di Matteo, Graeme Le Saux; Gianluca Vialli, Gianfranco Zola (89 Jody Morris).   Trainer: Ruud Gullit

Goal: Zauli (16)

CHELSEA LONDON v VICENZA 3-1 (1-1)

Stamford Bridge, London 16.04.1998

Referee: Marc Batta (FRA)   Attendance: 33,810

CHELSEA: Ed de Goey; Steve Clarke, Frank Leboeuf, Michael Duberry; Eddie Newton (70 Laurent Charvet), Jody Morris (70 Mark Hughes), Gustavo Poyet, Dennis Wise (Cap), Graeme Le Saux; Gianluca Vialli, Gianfranco Zola (82 Andy Myers).   Trainer: Ruud Gullit

VICENZA: Pierluigi Brivio; Gustavo Méndez, Giacomo Dicara, Davide Belotti, Fabio Viviani (61 Lorenzo Stovini); Marco Schenardi (82 Arturo Di Napoli), Massimo Ambrosini, Domenico Di Carlo (Cap) (82 Marcelo Otero), Gabriele Ambrosetti; Lamberto Zauli, Pasquale Luiso.   Trainer: Francesco Guidolin

Sent off: Ambrosini (88).

Goals: Luiso (32), Poyet (35), Zola (52), M. Hughes (76)

**VfB STUTTGART
v LOKOMOTIV MOSKVA 2-1** (1-1)

Gottlieb-Daimler-Stadion, Stuttgart 2.04.1998

Referee: Vítor Manuel Melo Pereira (POR)   Att: 14,416

VfB: Franz Wohlfahrt; Martin Spanring, Thomas Berthold, Frank Verlaat (Cap), Gerhard Poschner; Krasimir Balakov, Marco Haber, Murat Yakin (69 Krisztián Lisztes), Mitko Stojkovski (46 Matthias Hagner); Fredi Bobic, Jonathan Akpoborie.   Trainer: Joachim Löw

LOKOMOTIV: Ruslan Nigmatullin; Sergei Gurenko, Aleksei Arifullin, Igor Chugainov (Cap), Igor Cherevchenko; Yuri Drozdov, Evgeniy Kharlachov, Andrei Solomatin, Aleksei Kosolapov (53 Vladimir Maminov), Zaza Janashia, Garas (53 Aleksandr Smirnov).   Trainer: Yuri Syomin

Goals: Janashia (23), Akpoborie (43), Bobic (90)

LOKOMOTIV MOSKVA
v VfB STUTTGART 0-1 (0-1)
Lokomotiv Moskva 16.04.1998

Referee: Kim Milton Nielsen (DEN)   Attendance: 22,000

LOKOMOTIV: Ruslan Nigmatullin; Andrei Solomatin, Evgeniy Kharlachov, Igor Chugainov (Cap), Aleksei Arifullin; Sergei Gurenko, Aleksandr Smirnov (73 Sarkis Hovhannisyan), Aleksei Kosolapov, Vladimir Maminov; Dmitriy Loskov (60 Vitaliy Veselov), Zaza Janashia. Trainer: Yuri Syomin

VfB: Franz Wohlfahrt; Martin Spanring, Thomas Berthold, Frank Verlaat, Gerhard Poschner (90 Thomas Schneider); Marco Haber, Krasimir Balakov, Zvonimir Soldo, Mitko Stojkovski; Jonathan Akpoborie (84 Jochen Endress), Fredi Bobic. Trainer: Joachim Löw

Goal: Bobic (25)

FINAL

CHELSEA LONDON v VfB STUTTGART 1-0 (0-0)
Råsunda, Solna 13.05.1998

Referee: Stefano Braschi (ITA)   Attendance: 30,216

CHELSEA: Ed de Goey; Steve Clarke, Frank Leboeuf, Michael Duberry, Danny Granville; Dan Petrescu, Dennis Wise (Cap), Roberto Di Matteo, Gustavo Poyet (81 Eddie Newton); Gianluca Vialli, Tore André Flo (71 Gianfranco Zola). Manager: Gianluca Vilalli

VfB: Franz Wohlfahrt; Thomas Schneider (55 Jochen Endress), Thomas Berthold, Murat Yakin, Gerhard Poschner; Marco Haber (75 Kristijan Djordjevic), Zvonimir Soldo, Krasimir Balakov, Matthias Hagner (79 Sreto Ristic); Fredi Bobic (Cap), Jonathan Akpoborie. Trainer: Joachim Löw

Sent off: Petrescu (84), Poschner (90)

Goal: Zola (71)

Goalscorers European Cup-Winners' Cup 1997-98:

8 goals: Pasquale Luiso (Vicenza)

6 goals: Peter Van Houdt (Roda Kerkrade), Jonathan Akpoborie, Fredi Bobic (VfB Stuttgart), Gianluca Vialli (Chelsea London)

5 goals: Sergei Atelkin (Shakhtar Donetsk)

4 goals: Karel Vacha (Slavia Praha), Gábor Torma (Roda Kerkrade), ALFONSO Perez Muñoz (Betis Sevilla), Gianfranco Zola (Chelsea London)

3 goals: Niculescu, Pigulea (FC Naţional Bucureşti), Gudmundsson (ÍB Vestmannaeyjar), Stanković (Crvena Zvezda Beograd), Bule (NK Zagreb), Wright (FC Kilmarnock), Sokolowski (Legia Warszawa), Årst (Tromsø IL), Rudonja (Primorje Ajdovscina), Lawal (Roda Kerkrade), Kopitsis (AEK Athina), Zauli (Vicenza), Kharlachov (Lokomotiv Moskva), Di Matteo (Chelsea London)

2 goals: Liţă, Albeanu (FC Naţional Bucureşti), Hörtnagl, Ioannou (Apoel Nicosia), Isayev (Dinaburg Daugavpils), Benayoun (Hapoel Beer Sheva), Sopić (NK Zagreb), Khlebosolov, Smirnykh (Belshina Bobruisk), Novak (Slovan Bratislava), Kacprzak (Legia Warszawa), Van Ankeren (Germinal Ekeren), B.Johansen (Tromsø IL), Spiteri (Sturm Graz), Aulanier, Kohn (OGC Nice), Labant, Vagner (Slavia Praha), Ooijer, Peeters (Roda Kerkrade), Marcelo, Nikolaidis (AEK Athina), Ambrosetti (Vicenza), Janashia, Loskov (Lokomotiv Moskva), Balakov (VfB Stuttgart), Flo (Chelsea London)

1 goal: Grant (Glenavon Lurgan), Parfitt, Townsend (Cwmbran Town), Radzius (Zalgiris Vilnius), Zgură (Zimbru Chişinău), Rutherford, D.Baker (Shelbourne), Helin (HJK Helsinki), Petkov (Sloga Jugomagnat Skopje), Wörnhard (FC Balzers), Olumets, Rotshkov (Tallina Sadam), G.Ivanov, Todorov (Levski Sofia), Arge (HB Thórshavn), Vasc, Savu (FC Naţional Bucureşti), Alexandrou, Sotiriou, Fasouliotis (Apoel Nicosia), Olafsson, Larusson, Helgasson (ÍB Vestmannaeyjar), Rui Miguel, Litos, Latapy (Boavista Porto), Ognjenović, Drulić, Njegus (Crvena Zvezda), Novakovic (AIK Solna), Fedotov, Tarasov (Dinaburg Daugavpils), Aleksandrov, Koilov (FC Luzern), Bochnik (Hapoel Beer Sheva), Lalić, Baturina, Vukić, Cizmek (NK Zagreb), Timofeyev, Putrash (Belshina Bobruisk), Muzlay (Slovan Bratislava), Reilly, McIntyre (FC Kilmarnock), Komlósi, Bükszegi, Füzi, Csordas (BVSC Budapest), Skrzypek (Legia Warszawa), Van Geneugden, Karagiannis, Radzinski, Kovács, Hofmans, Dauwe (Germinal Ekeren), S.Nilsen, Fermann, S.M.Johansen, Lange (Tromsø IL), Turan, Nuri, Erhan, Moshoeu (Kocaelispor), Zubov, Potskhveria, Zubov, Orbu, Kriventsov (Shakhtar Donetsk), Togashvili, I.Makharadze (Dinamo Batumi), Peter Nielsen, Mo.Nielsen, Sestan, Jonsson, L.H.Nielsen, Tur (FC København), Reinmayr, Vastic, Haas (Sturm Graz), Vandecasteele, Milinkovic, Rol (OGC Nice), Sabadin, Sculac (Primorje Ajdovscina), Asanin (Slavia Praha), Van de Luer, Zafarin, Valgaeren, Vrede (Roda Kerkrade), Batista, Vlahos, Kostis, Katsavos, Kalitzakis (AEK Athina), Finidi, Ureña, Oli, Cañas, Alexis (Betis Sevilla), Belotti, Otero, Firmani, Méndez, Beghetto, Viviani (Vicenza), Chugainov, Maminov, Borodyuk (Lokomotiv Moskva), Verlaat (VfB Stuttgart), Poyet, M.Hughes, Sinclair, Leboeuf, Granville (Chelsea London)

Own goals: Telser (FC Balzers) for BVSC Budapest, Koilov (FC Luzern) for Slavia Praha, Sabitović (NK Zagreb) for Tromsø

CUP WINNERS' CUP 1998-99

QUALIFYING ROUND

**RUDAR VELENJE
v CONSTRUCTORUL CHIŞINĂU 2-0** (1-0)

Ob jezeru, Velenje 13.08.1998

Referee: Manfred Schüttengruber (AUS)   Attendance: 1,500

RUDAR: Mladen Dabanović (Cap); Goran Granić, Almir Sulejmanović, Samir Balagić, Ilir Caushllari, Danijel Brezić (60 Simon Pirc), Saso Gajser, Niko Podvinski, Jernej Javornik (78 Peter Sumnik), Zoran Pavlović, Zivojin Vidojević.   Trainer: Drago Jostanjsek

CONSTRUCTORUL: Serghei Dinov; Dumitru Tricolici, Ivan Tabanov (Cap), Ghenadie Puşca, Vasile Apachiţei, Emil Caras (46 Eric Ococo), Oleg Şişchin (46 Victor Comlionoc), Iurie Osipenco, Aurel Druţă (46 Alexandru Scrupschi), Igor Filip, Vladimir Dovghii.   Trainer: Valeri Rotari

Sent off: Dinov (64).

Goals: Vidojević (31), Sumnik (90).

**CONSTRUCTORUL CHIŞINĂU
v RUDAR VELENJE 0-0**

Republican, Chişinău 27.08.1998

Referee: Giorgos Fassolis (GRE)   Attendance: 4,500

CONSTRUCTORUL: Andrian Bogdan; Dumitru Tricolici, Ivan Tabanov (Cap), Vasile Apachiţei, Ghenadie Puşca (46 Igor Filip), Iurie Osipenco, Oleg Şişchin, Emil Caras (46 Aurel Druţă), Iuri Ciorici (46 Victor Comlionoc), Vladimir Dovghii, Alexandru Scrupschi.   Trainer: Valeri Rotari

RUDAR: Mladen Dabanović (Cap); Goran Granić, Almir Sulejmanović, Samir Balagić, Simon Pirc, Ilir Caushllari, Saso Gajser, Niko Podvinski (80 Peter Sumnik), Danijel Brezić (64 Damjan Jesenicnik), Jernej Javornik, Zoran Pavlović (87 Klemen Lavrić).   Trainer: Drago Jostanjsek

FC VADUZ v HELSINGBORGS IF 0-2 (0-1)

Gemeindersportplatz, Vaduz 13.08.1998

Referee: Gerard Perry (IRE)   Attendance: 950

FC VADUZ: Kurt Sieber; Olivier Bossi, Markus Weber, Daniel Keel, Martin Stocklasa, Roger Stilz, Dieter Alge, Daniel Hasler, Marcel Müller (Cap), Daniele Polverino (89 Hanno Hasler), Roman Hafner.   Trainer: Alfons Doble

HELSINGBORGS: Sven Andersson (Cap), Per-Ola Ljung (46 Ola Nilsson), Andreas Jacobsson, Zoran Jovanovski, Erik Edman, Peter Wibrån, Marcus Lantz, Kenneth Storvik, Arild Stavrum (72 Ulrik Jansson), Magnus Powell (36 Erik Wahlstedt), Christoffer Andersson.   Trainer: Åge Hareide

Goals: Stavrum (9), Wibrån (70).

HELSINGBORGS IF v FC VADUZ 3-0 (1-0)

Olympia, Helsingborg 27.08.1998

Referee: Andrei Butenko (RUS)   Attendance: 3,600

HELSINGBORGS: Sven Andersson; Per-Ola Ljung, Andreas Jacobsson, Zoran Jovanovski, Ulrik Jansson, Peter Wibrån, Erik Wahlstedt (78 Christoffer Andersson), Erik Edman (72 Ola Nilsson), Kenneth Storvik (46 Magnus Powell), Marcus Lantz, Arild Stavrum.   Trainer: Åge Hareide

FC VADUZ: Kurt Sieber; Markus Weber (85 Jürgen Ospelt), Bossi, Martin Stocklasa, Daniel Keel, Erkan Erdogan, Marcel Müller (Cap), Roger Stilz, Daniele Polverino, Dieter Alge, Roman Hafner.   Trainer: Alfons Dobler

Goals: Wibrån (43), Edman (57), Powell (67).

**LAUSANNE SPORTS
v TSEMENT ARARAT 5-1** (1-1)

Stade Olympique de La Pontaise, Lausanne 13.08.1998

Referee: Stefan Ormandjiev (BUL)   Attendance: 3,500

LAUSANNE: Martin Brunner (Cap); Marc Hottiger, Daniel Puce, Oscar Londono, Erich Hänzi; Christophe Ohrel (79 Serge Gogoua), Blaise Piffaretti, Fabio Celestini (85 Vincent Cavin), Philippe Douglas; Saso Udovic, Armen Shahgeldyan (66 Léonard Thurre).   Trainer: Georges Bregy

TSEMENT: Garnik Hovhannisyan; Vahan Arzumanyan, Tigran Gsepyan, Vahram Hovhannisyan, Norik Hokhoyan (60 Aram Ayrapetyan), Artur Voskanyan, Tigran Hovhannisyan, Haik Harutyunyan (76 Karen Asatryan), Gagik Manukyan, Aram Sargsyan (64 Armen Sargsyan), Shirak Sarikyan.   Trainer: Varouzhan Soukiasyan

Goals: Celestini (29 pen, 47, 59, 70), T. Hovhannisyan (36), Cavin (87).

**TSEMENT ARARAT
v LAUSANNE SPORTS 1-2** (1-0)

Tsement Ararat 27.08.1998

Referee: Frank De Bleeckere (BEL)   Attendance: 2,000

TSEMENT: Ashot Dadamyan; Aram Ayrapetyan (46 Gagik Manukyan), Vahan Arzumanyan, Tigran Gsepyan, Sargsyan Aram (57 Haik Harutyunyan), Shirak Sarikyan, Tigran Hovhannisyan, Artur Voskanyan, Vahram Hovhannisyan, Karen Asatryan, Romeo Dzenebyan (75 Abraham Abrahamyan).   Trainer: Varouzhan Soukiasyan

LAUSANNE: Martin Brunner (Cap); Marc Hottiger, Christophe Ohrel, Oscar Londono, Stefan Rehn, Erich Hänzi, Léonard Thurre, Daniel Puce, Fabio Celestini (71 Vincent Cavin), Paolo Diogo (62 Philippe Douglas), Armen Shahgeldyan (78 Artur Minasyan).   Trainer: Georges Bregy

Goals: Asatryan (39), Douglas (66), Hottiger (89).

CORK CITY v CSKA KYIV 2-1 (2-0)

Turner's Cross, Cork   13.08.1998

Referee: Dominique Tavel (SWI)   Attendance: 2,575

CORK: Noel Mooney; Declan Daly (Cap), Derek Coughlan, David Hill, Gareth Cronin, Greg O'Halloran (81 John Caulfield), Kelvin Flanagan, Patrick Freyne, Brian Barry-Murphy (75 Mark Herrick), Oliver Cahill, Noel Hartigan (71 Jason Kabia).   Trainer: Dave Barry

CSKA: Vitaliy Reva; Vitaliy Levchenko, Serhiy Revut, Vitaliy Daraselia (57 Dmytro Korenev), Dmytro Semchuk, Serhiy Bezhenar, Olexiy Oleynik, Pavlo Shkapenko, Serhiy Zakarlyuka (33 Olexandr Olexiyenko), Viktor Leonenko (73 Andriy Karyaka), Eduard Tsykhmeistruk (Cap).
Trainer: Volodymyr Bessonov

Goals: Flanagan (20 pen), Coughlan (31), Revut (90)

CSKA KYIV v CORK CITY 2-0 (1-0)

Kyiv   27.08.1998

Referee: Zeljko Siric (CRO)   Attendance: 6,000

CSKA: Vitaliy Reva; Valentyn Gregul, Serhiy Revut, Viktor Ulyanytskyi, Dmytro Semchuk, Serhiy Bezhenar, Andriy Karyaka (31 Dmytro Korenev), Pavlo Shkapenko, Serhiy Zakarlyuka, Viktor Leonenko (62 Vitaliy Daraselia), Eduard Tsykhmeistruk (Cap).   Trainer: Volodymyr Bessonov

CORK: Noel Mooney; Declan Daly (Cap), Gareth Cronin, David Hill, Derek Coughlan, Patrick Freyne, Oliver Cahill, Kelvin Flanagan (80 John Caulfield), Noel Hartigan (55 Jason Kabia), Brian Barry-Murphy (55 Gerald Dobbs), Greg O'Halloran.   Trainer: Dave Barry

Goals: Tsykhmeistruk (40), Leonenko (56)

**EKRANAS PANEVEZYS
v APOLLON LIMASSOL 1-2** (1-1)

Aukstaitija, Panevezys   13.08.1998

Referee: Thomas Michael McCurry (SCO)   Att: 4,000

EKRANAS: Imantas Satas; Darius Butkus, Dainius Gleveckas (Cap), Andrius Staliunas, Povilas Luksys (58 Kestutis Zeniauskas), Raimondas Vileniskis (69 Zilvinas Cenys), Vitalijus Danilicevas, Irmantas Stumbrys, Raimondas Petrukaitis, Mindaugas Gardzijauskas, Egidijus Varnas.
Trainer: Virginijus Liubsys

APOLLON: Alexandros Mihail; Haralampos Pittas (Cap), Filippos Filippou, Marios Haralampous, Ion Sburlea, Milenko Spoljaric, Florin Cârstea (74 Giorgos Kavazis), Paolo Da Silva (58 Stefanos Voskaridis), Xenios Kyriakou, Giorgos Kais (53 Nikodimos Papavasileiou), Nebojsa Mladenovic.
Trainer: Dumitru Dumitriu

Goals: Cârstea (17), Stumbrys (38), Pittas (90)

**APOLLON LIMASSOL
v EKRANAS PANEVEZYS 3-3** (0-2)

Tsirion, Limassol   27.08.1998

Referee: Bernard Saules (FRA)   Attendance: 8,000

APOLLON: Alexandros Mihail; Haralampos Pittas (Cap), Filippos Filippou (35 Giorgos Kais), Marios Haralampous, Ion Sburlea (78 Theodorors Aresti), Milenko Spoljaric, Florin Cârstea (66 Hrysostomos Juras), Marios Themistokleous, Xenios Kyriakou, Nebojsa Mladenovic, Giorgos Kavazis.
Trainer: Dumitru Dumitriu

EKRANAS: Imantas Satas; Darius Butkus (60 Vaidotas Sarkis), Dainius Gleveckas (Cap), Andrius Staliunas, Povilas Luksys (65 Deividas Cesnauskis), Raimondas Vileniskis, Vitalijus Danilicevas (72 Kestutis Zeniauskas), Irmantas Stumbrys, Raimondas Petrukaitis, Mindaugas Gardzijauskas, Egidijus Varnas.
Trainer: Virginijus Liubsys

Goals: Vileniskis (6, 9), Spoljaric (51, 88), Kavazis (60), Varnas (90)

APOLONIA FIER v KRC GENK 1-5 (1-3)

Qemal Stafa, Tirana   13.08.1998

Referee: Attila Hanacsek (HUN)   Attendance: 2500

APOLONIA: Arben Sinani; Dashnor Bita (Cap), Elidor Çobani (58 Fatos Sulaj), Artan Poçi, Gëzim Buziu (46 Elidon Demiri), Robert Nuredini (89 Vaskë Ruko), Alket Zeqo, Artan Bare, Dashnor Poçi, Romeo Haxhiaj, Arben Jahiqi.
Trainer: Dhimitër Papuçiu

KRC GENK: István Brockhauser; Daniel Kimoni, Domenico Olivieri (Cap), Marc Vangronsveld, Marc Hendrickx (46 Mike Origi), Besnik Hasi, Wilfried Delbroek, Thórdur Gudjónsson, ROGÉRIO de Oliveira, Branko Strupar (83 Edmilson Dos Santos), Souleymane Oulare (75 Ferenc Horváth).
Trainer: Aimé Antheunis

Goals: Vangronsveld (25 og), Strupar (33), Hendrickx (40), Oulare (37 pen, 68), Horváth (79)

KRC GENK v APOLONIA FIER 4-0 (1-0)

Thyl Geyselinck, Genk   27.08.1998

Referee: John Ashman (WAL)   Attendance: 3,982

KRC GENK: István Brockhauser; Juha Reini (58 Mike Origi), Daniel Kimoni, Wilfried Delbroek, Besnik Hasi, Souleymane Oulare (72 Ferenc Horváth), Thórdur Gudjónsson, Branko Strupar, Marc Hendrickx, Marc Vangronsveld (Cap), Chris Van Geem (62 Ngoy N'Sumbu).   Trainer: Aimé Antheunis

APOLONIA: Arben Sinani; Dashnor Bita (Cap), Elidor Çobani (68 Vaskë Ruko), Artan Poçi, Elidon Demiri, Robert Nuredini, Alket Zeqo, Fatos Sulaj, Dashnor Poçi, Romeo Haxhiaj, Arben Jahiqi (83 Endri Yzeiri).   Trainer: Dhimitër Papuçiu

Goals: Oulare (4), N'Sumbu (86), Strupar (87, 90)

BANGOR CITY v HAKA VALKEAKOSKI 0-2 (0-1)
Farrar Road, Bangor   13.08.1998
Referee: Gennadi Yakubovsky (BLS)   Attendance: 1,429
BANGOR: Lee Williams; Gareth Williams, Michael Fox, Mark Allen, Mick McLoughlin, Noel Horner, Darren Hildtich, Jamie Taylor (83 Paul Langley), Sammy Ayorinde, Chris Sharratt (Cap), Danny McGoona (54 Neil Wenham).   Manager: John King
HAKA: András Vilnrotter; Ari Heikkinen (Cap), Harri Ylönen, Janne Salli, Jouni Räsänen, Lasse Karjalainen, Janne Mäkelä, Oleg Ivanov (78 Jarkko Okkonen), Marlon Harewood (82 Tommi Torrkeli), Valeri Popovits, Jari Niemi (71 Jukka Ruhanen).   Trainer: Keith Armstrong
Goals: Niemi (40), Salli (60)

HAKA VALKEAKOSKI v BANGOR CITY 1-0 (1-0)
Tehtaankenttä, Valkeakoski   27.08.1998
Referee: Sergejs Braga (LAT)   Attendance: 2,451
HAKA: András Vilnrotter; Ari Heikkinen (Cap) (78 Jarkko Okkonen), Lasse Karjalainen, Janne Salli, Jouni Räsänen, Janne Mäkelä, Oleg Ivanov, Jukka Ruhanen (66 Tommi Torrkeli), Valeri Popovits, Harri Ylönen, Jari Niemi (85 Jukka Rantala).   Trainer: Keith Armstrong
BANGOR: Lee Williams; Paul Mooney (90 Phil Gibney), Michael Fox, Mark Allen, Arthur Lloyd, Noel Horner, Darren Hildtich, Jamie Taylor, Sammy Ayorinde, Chris Sharratt (Cap), Paul Langley.   Manager: John King
Goal: Ruhanen (29)

LEVSKI SOFIA
v LOKOMOTIV-96 VITEBSK 8-1 (5-1)
Vasil Levski, Sofia   13.08.1998
Referee: Kyros Vasaras (GRE)   Attendance: 15,000
LEVSKI: Dimitar Ivankov; Zakhari Sirakov, Asen Nikolov (56 Aleksandar Aleksandrov), Krasimir Dimitrov, Ivan Vasilev (46 Milen Radukanov), Vladimir Ionkov, Doncho Donev, Stanimir Stoilov, Georgi Ivanov, Nikolai Todorov (Cap), Georgi Borisov.   Trainer: Stefan Grozdanov
LOKOMOTIV: Andrei Lyubchenko (Cap); Vasiliy Dyatlov (56 Sergei Eremeyev), Yuri Konoplev (46 Vitaliy Sigov), Gennadiy Kashkar, Vitaliy Rogozhkin, Sergei Chernyshov, Vyacheslav Gormash, Andrei Sivkov (46 Viktor Malyavko), Eduard Demenkovets, Sergei Kulanin, Sergei Vekhtev.   Trainer: Vyacheslav Akshayev
Sent off: Dimitrov (78)
Goals: Ivanov (8, 32), Demenkovets (18 pen), Borisov (23, 44, 88), Donev (42), Radukanov (52), Todorov (85)

LOKOMOTIV-96 VITEBSK
v LEVSKI SOFIA 1-1 (0-0)
Dinamo Minsk   27.08.1998
Referee: Vladimir Hrinak (SVK)   Attendance: 2,000
LOKOMOTIV: Andrei Lyubchenko (Cap); Vasiliy Dyatlov, Gennadiy Kashkar, Vitaliy Rogozhkin, Sergei Chernyshov, Andrei Sivkov, Eduard Demenkovets (63 Alexei Soldatov), Sergei Kulanin, Sergei Eremeyev, Viktor Malyavko, Sergei Vekhtev.   Trainer: Vyacheslav Akshayev
LEVSKI: Dimitar Ivankov; Zakhari Sirakov (61 Zvetomir Chipev), Stanimir Gospodinov, Milen Radukanov, Igor Harkovchenko (60 Veselin Vachev), Vladimir Ionkov, Doncho Donev, Aleksandar Aleksandrov, Petar Shopov, Nikolai Todorov (Cap) (78 Elin Topuzakov), Zdravko Lazarov.   Trainer: Stefan Grozdanov
Goals: Lazarov (50), Sivkov (90)

METALURGS LIEPAYA v IB KEFLAVÍK 4-2 (0-0)
Daugava, Liepaya   13.08.1998
Referee: Leif Sundell (SWE)   Attendance: 4,500
METALURGS: Algimantas Bryaunis; Daryus Magdisauskas, Dzintars Zirnis, Victor Yuiko, Andrei Osichenko (Cap), Vladimir Dragun, Rolandas Vaineikis (75 Maris Verpakovsky), Victor Dobretsov (69 Svayunas Chernyauskas), Rolands Boulders, Oleg Rudenko, Saulius Atmanavicius.   Trainer: Yuri Popkov
IB KEFLAVÍK: Bjarki Gudmundsson; Snorri Már Jónsson, Georg Birgisson (72 Róbert Sigurdsson), Kristinn Gudbrandsson (Cap), Gestur Gylfason, Karl Finnbogason, Gunnar Odsson (60 Gudmundur Odsson), Marko Tanasic, Thórarinn Kristjánsson (75 Adolf Sveinsson), Eysteinn Hauksson, Sasa Pavic.   Trainer: Gunnar Oddsson & Sigurdur Björgvinsson
Goals: Kristjánsson (60), Boulders (61, 87, 88), Magdisauskas (89), Gylfason (90)

IB KEFLAVÍK v METALURGS LIEPAYA 1-0 (0-0)
Keflavíkurvöllur, Keflavík   27.08.1998
Referee: Jon Skjervold (NOR)   Attendance: 503
IB KEFLAVÍK: Bjarki Gudmundsson; Snorri Már Jónsson, Georg Birgisson (69 Róbert Sigurdsson), Kristinn Gudbrandsson (Cap) (83 Gudmundur Steinarsson), Gestur Gylfason, Karl Finnbogason, Gunnar Odsson, Marko Tanasic, Thórarinn Kristjánsson, Eysteinn Hauksson (85 Ólafur Ingólfsson), Sasa Pavic.   Trainers: Gunnar Oddsson & Sigurdur Björgvinsson
METALURGS: Algimantas Bryaunis; Daryus Magdisauskas, Dzintars Zirnis, Mikhail Lisyakov, Andrei Osichenko (Cap), Vladimir Dragun (79 Victor Yuiko), Rolandas Vaineikis (61 Eduard Kudryashov), Victor Dobretsov, Rolands Boulders, Oleg Rudenko, Saulius Atmanavicius.   Trainer: Yuri Popkov
Goal: Hauksson (58)

**CLUB SPORTIF GREVENMACHER
v RAPID BUCUREȘTI 2-6** (1-1)

Op Flohr, Grevenmacher   13.08.1998

Referee: Dejan Delević (YUG)   Attendance: 500

CS GREVENMACHER: Karl-Heinz Lohmer; 1Thierry Pauk, Erik Schröder, Théo Scholten (Cap), Laurent Giesser (56 Lidio Alves Silva), Bernhard Heinz; Serge Thill, Christian Alverdi, Mario Mendoza, Sacha Schneider (77 Damian Stoklosa); Markus Krahen (86 Daniel Huss).   Trainer: Harald Kohr

RAPID: Bogdan Lobonț; Bogdan Andone (55 Dorel Mutică), Cristian Dulca, Vasile Nicolae Popa, Nicolae Stanciu (Cap), Mugur Cristian Bolohan; Marius Constantin Măldărășanu (58 Daniel Gabriel Pancu), Dănuț Lupu, Ioan Ovidiu Sabău; Ovidiu Maier, Marius Ninel Șumudică (46 Sergiu Marian Radu).   Trainer: Mircea Lucescu

Goals: Sabău (13), Krahen (39, 72), Pancu (62), Dulca (65), Stanciu (70), Lupu (76), Mutică (82)

**RAPID BUCUREȘTI
v CS GREVENMACHER 2-0** (0-0)

Giulești, București   27.08.1998

Referee: Lawrence Sammut (MAL)   Attendance: 7,160

RAPID: Marius Bratu; Dorel Mutică, Vasile Nicolae Popa, Mihai Adrian Iencsi; Bogdan Ioan Andone, Zeno Marius Bundea, Narcis Mario Bugeanu (53 Dănuț Lupu), Marius Constantin Măldărășanu (58 Ovidiu Maier), Cezar Iulius Zamfir (61 Mugur Cristian Bolohan); Daniel Gabriel Pancu (Cap), Sergiu Marian Radu.   Trainer: Mircea Lucescu

CS GREVENMACHER: Oliver Köpke; Erik Schröder (58 Steve Birtz), Théo Scholten (Cap), Laurent Giesser (73 Lidio Alves Silva); Adelino Dias, Thierry Pauk, Claude Dublin, Mario Mendoza, Damian Stoklosa; Serge Thill, Markus Krahen (53 Daniel Huss).   Trainer: Harald Kohr

Goals: Pancu (54, 88)

**FC LANTANA TALLINN v HEART OF
MIDLOTHIAN EDINBURGH 0-1** (0-1)

Kadriorg, Tallinn   13.08.1998

Referee: Michal Benes (CZE)   Attendance: 1,000

LANTANA: Sergei Ussoltsev; Andrei Krasnopjorov, Andrei Kalimullin, Oleg Kolotsei, Igor Bahmatski, Andrei Mitjunov, Andrei Borisov (Cap), Vitali Leitan, Vitali Valuiski (80 Vladimir Tshelnokov), Oleg Gorjatsov (78 Dmitri Kulikov), Sergei Kulichenko.   Trainer: Anatoli Belov

HEARTS: Gilles Rousset; Gary Naysmith, David Weir, Stefano Salvatori, Paul Ritchie, Neil McCann, Stéphane Adam (86 José Quitongo), Jim Hamilton (86 Grant Murray), Gary Locke (Cap), Thomas Flögel, Lee Makel.   Trainer: James Jefferies

Goal: Makel (21)

**HEART OF MIDLOTHIAN EDINBURGH
v LANTANA TALLINN 5-0** (3-0)

Tynecastle Park, Edinburgh   27.08.1998

Referee: Jan Wegreef (HOL)   Attendance: 15,053

HEARTS: Gilles Rousset; David Weir, Paul Ritchie, Neil McCann, Steve Fulton, Stéphane Adam (60 José Quitongo), Jim Hamilton (60 Thomas Flögel), Gary Locke (Cap), Lee Makel (76 Derek Holmes), Robert McKinnon, Steven Pressley.   Trainer: James Jefferies

LANTANA: Sergei Ussoltsev (Cap); Andrei Krasnopjorov, Oleg Kolotsei, Igor Bahmatski, Andrei Mitjunov, Dmitri Kulikov, Vitali Leitan, Vitali Valuiski (80 Vladimir Tshelnokov), Oleg Gorjatsov, Sergei Kulichenko, Andrei Tjunin.   Trainer: Anatoli Belov

Goals: Hamilton (18), Fulton (29), McCann (41), Flögel (75), Holmes (90)

**AMICA WRONKI
v HIBERNIANS PAOLA 4-0** (1-0)

Amica Wronki   13.08.1998

Referee: Igor Yaremchuk (UKR)   Attendance: 4,600

AMICA: Jaroslaw Strozynski; Zbigniew Malachowski, Grzegorz Motyka, Pawel Kryszalowicz, Grzegorz Matlak, Bartosz Bosacki (68 Miroslaw Siara), Dariusz Jackiewicz, Tomasz Sokolowski (85 Piotr Kasperski), Marek Bajor (Cap), Andrzej Przerada, Grzegorz Krol (58 Remigiusz Sobocinski).   Trainer: Wojciech Wasikiewicz

HIBERNIANS: Mario Muscat; Lawrence Attard, Roderick Baldacchino (71 Claude Mangion), Essien Mbong, Roger Walker, Michael Spiteri (Cap), Egiro Kologbo (63 Darren Attard), Alan Mifsud, David Carabott, Chukunyere Ndubisi, Pavel Mraz (85 Charles Scerri).   Trainer: Mark Miller

Goals: Kryszalowicz (38), Prerada (56), Sobocinski (62, 75)

**HIBERNIANS PAOLA
v AMICA WRONKI 0-1** (0-0)

Corradino, Paola   27.08.1998

Referee: Graham Barber (ENG)   Attendance: 113

HIBERNIANS: Mario Muscat; Kevin Noteman, Martin Borg (76 Charles Scerri), Essien Mbong, Roger Walker, Michael Spiteri (Cap), Darren Attard (61 Egiro Kologbo), Alan Mifsud, David Carabott, Chukunyere Ndubisi, Pavel Mraz (76 Roderick Baldacchino).   Trainer: Mark Miller

AMICA: Jaroslaw Strozynski; Zbigniew Malachowski, Ireneusz Koscielniak (21 Grzegorz Motyka), Pawel Kryszalowicz, Tomasz Dawidowski, Bartosz Bosacki, Remigiusz Sobocinski (70 Grzegorz Krol), Dariusz Jackiewicz, Tomasz Sokolowski, Marek Bajor (Cap), Andrzej Przerada (80 Miroslaw Kalita).   Trainer: Wojciech Wasikiewicz

Goal: Kryszalowicz (70)

GOTU ÍTROTTARFELAG
v MTK HUNGÁRIA BUDAPEST 1-3 (1-2)

Toftir stadion 13.08.1998

Referee: Kristinn Jakobsson (ICE)   Attendance: 340

GÍ GOTU: Sunnvard Joensen; Simun Petur Justinussen, Pol Ennigard, Svenn Olsen (85 Samson Nesa), Runi Justinussen, Søren Skov Jørgensen (60 Joan Petur Olsen), Magni Jarnskor (Cap), Pauli Jarnskor (65 Magni Jacobsen), Suni Olsen, Henning Jarnskor, Samal Joensen.   Trainer: Johan Nielsen

MTK: Gábor Babos; Emil Lörincz (Cap), Zoltán Molnár, Ádám Komlósi, Tamás Szamosi, Károly Erös, Gábor Halmai, Béla Illés, Csaba Madar (46 Tamás Szekeres), Sándor Preisinger (74 Iván Balaskó), Krisztián Kenesei. Trainer: Sándor Egervári

Goals: Su. Olsen (8), Kenesei (17), Preisinger (19), Szekeres (90)

MTK HUNGÁRIA BUDAPEST
v GOTU ÍTROTTARFELAG 7-0 (3-0)

Hungária, Budapest 27.08.1998

Referee: Otar Guntadze (GEO)   Attendance: 1,500

MTK: Gábor Babos; Zoltán Molnár, Tamás Szekeres, Emil Lörincz (Cap), Csaba Madar, Károly Erös, Béla Illés (73 Csaba Csordás), Gábor Halmai (64 Iván Balaskó), Tamás Szamosi, Krisztián Kenesei, Sándor Preisinger (64 Péter Czvitkovics). Trainer: Sándor Egervári

GÍ GOTU: Sunnvard Joensen; Svenn Olsen, Henning Jarnskor, Magni Jacobsen, Søren Skov Jørgensen, Joan Petur Olsen, Magni Jarnskor (Cap), Pauli Jarnskor, Suni Olsen, Samal Joensen (46 Erland Tvorfoss), Runi Justinussen (85 Leivur Hansen).   Trainer: Johan Nielsen

Goals: Kenesei (16, 71, 76), Preisinger (34), Halmai (37), Illés (62), Balaskó (73)

GLENTORAN BELFAST
v MACCABI HAIFA 0-1 (0-1)

The Oval, Belfast 13.08.1998

Referee: Tom Henning Øvrebø (NOR)   Attendance: 2,000

GLENTORAN: Wayne Russell; Colin Nixon, John Kennedy, Chris Walker, John Devine (Cap), Paul Leeman, Philip Mitchell (80 James Quigley), Rory Hamill (90 David Rainey), Andy Kirk (65 David McCallan), Pete Batey, Stuart Elliot. Manager: Roy Coyle

MACCABI: Nir Davidovich; Serhiy Balanchuk, Alon Harazi, Arik Benado (Cap), Adoram Keissy, Eliron Elkayam, Offir Kopel, Ibrahim Duro (84 Haim Silvas), Avishai Jano, Alon Mizrahi (90 Liron Vilner), Radovan Hromadko (62 Yossi Benayoun).   Trainer: Dušan Uhrin

Goal: Mizrahi (23)

MACCABI HAIFA
v GLENTORAN BELFAST 2-1 (1-1)

Kiriat Eliezer, Haifa 27.08.1998

Referee: Sergyi Tatulyan (UKR)   Attendance: 4,250

MACCABI: Nir Davidovich; Serhiy Balanchuk, Alon Harazi, Arik Benado (Cap), Adoram Keissy, Eliron Elkayam, Offir Kopel (63 Haim Silvas), Ibrahim Duro (77 Yossi Benayoun), Alon Mizrahi, Radovan Hromadko, Avishai Jano. Trainer: Dušan Uhrin

GLENTORAN: Wayne Russell; Colin Nixon, John Kennedy, Chris Walker, John Devine (Cap), Paul Leeman, Philip Mitchell, Rory Hamill, David Rainey (77 Stuart Elliott), Pete Batey (83 Stephen Livingstone), Justin McBride (83 Andy Kirk).   Manager: Roy Coyle

Goals: Mizrahi (16 pen, 81 pen), Batey (42)

VARDAR SKOPJE v SPARTAK TRNAVA 0-1 (0-0)

Gradski, Skopje 13.08.1998

Referee: Charles Agius (MAL)   Attendance: 9,700

VARDAR: Muarem Zekir (Cap); Goran Jovanovski, Zlatko Todorovski, Igorce Stojanov, Vanco Trajcev, Ilco Djorgjioski (71 Dejan Demjanski), Nikola Avramovski, Ljupco Dimitkovski, Goran Karadzov, Toni Eftimov (76 Aleksandar Bajevski), Sasko Krstev (58 Dragan Nacevski). Trainer: Gore Jovanovski

SPARTAK: Kamil Susko; Miroslav Karhan, Vladimir Leitner, Jaroslav Hrabal, Igor Balis (Cap), Dušan Tittel, Marek Ujlaky, Jaroslav Timko (81 Lubomir Talda), Ondrej Kristofik, Jaroslav Macak (46 Robert Formanko), Fábio Luís Gomes. Trainer: Dušan Galis

Sent off: Hrabal (68)

Goal: Ujlaky (76)

SPARTAK TRNAVA v VARDAR SKOPJE 2-0 (0-0)

Spartak Trnava 27.08.1998

Referee: Romans Lajuks (LAT)   Attendance: 10,400

SPARTAK: Kamil Susko; Dušan Tittel, Miroslav Karhan, Vladimir Leitner, Igor Balis (Cap), Lubomir Talda (70 Jaroslav Macak), Ondrej Kristofik, Sergej Jakirovic (83 Marcel Horky), Marek Ujlaky; Jaroslav Timko (46 Rastislav Tomovcik), Fábio Luís Gomes.   Trainer: Dušan Galis

VARDAR: Muarem Zekir (Cap); Ljupco Dimitkovski, Goran Jovanovski, Saso Janev, Igorce Stojanov, Zlatko Todorovski, Goran Karadzov, Nikola Avramovski, Vanco Trajcev, Aleksandar Bajevski (65 Dragan Nacevski), Sasko Krstev. Trainer: Gore Jovanovski

Sent off: Janev (79)

Goals: Tittel (83), Gomes (85)

FC KØBENHAVN v KARABAKH AGDAM 6-0 (6-0)
Idraetsparken, København   13.08.1998
Referee: Vladimir Antonov (Mol)   Attendance: 5,672
FC KØBENHAVN: Michael Stensgaard; Martin Nielsen (62 Martin Bill Larsen), Morten Falch, Carsten Hemmingsen, Bjarne Goldbæk (46 Kenneth Jensen), Piotr Haren, David Nielsen (74 Claus Nielsen), Peter Nielsen (Cap), Thomas Thorninger, Michael "Mio" Nielsen, Niclas Jensen.   Trainer: Kent Karlsson
KARABAKH: Djamalladin Aliyev; Elshad Akhmedov, Vadar Nuriyev, Zaur Karaev, Rufat Kuliyev (59 Mais Azimov), Mirbagir Isayev (80 Satlar Aliyev), Tabriz Hasanov, Mushvik Huseynov (Cap), Bakhtiyar Musayev, Rinat Abdashev, Emil Pashayev.   Trainer: Agaselim Mirkavadov
Goals: Ma. Nielsen (2), Thorninger (6), P. Nielsen (13, 40), Goldbæk (20), Falch (26)

KARABAKH AGDAM v FC KØBENHAVN 0-4 (0-0)
Baku   27.08.1998
Referee: Henri Diederich (LUX)   Attendance: 1,500
KARABAH: Djamalladin Aliyev; Satlar Aliyev, Elshad Akhmedov, Zaur Karaev, Rufat Kuliyev, Mirbagir Isayev (79 Kanan Makhmudov), Mais Azimov, Tabriz Hasanov, Mushvik Huseynov (Cap) (68 Jalcin Bagirov), Emil Pashayev, Veli Huseynov.   Trainer: Agaselim Mirkavadov
FC KØBENHAVN: Michael Stensgaard; Michael "Mio" Nielsen, Carsten Hemmingsen, Bjarne Goldbæk (46 David Nielsen), Piotr Haren, Peter Nielsen (Cap), Todi Jonsson (56 Claus Nielsen), Thomas Thorninger, Martin Nielsen (71 Newroz Dogan), Niclas Jensen, Kim Madsen.   Trainer: Kent Karlsson
Sent off: Azimov (10)
Goals: N. Jensen (64), P. Nielsen (68), D. Nielsen (75, 84)

PARTIZAN BEOGRAD
v DINAMO BATUMI 2-0 (2-0)
Partizan Beograd   13.08.1998
Referee: Dick Van Egmond (HOL)   Attendance: 8,500
PARTIZAN: Nikola Damjanac; Vuk Rasović, Igor Duljaj, Zoltan Sabo, Marjan Gerasimovski, Goran Trobok (71 Ljubisa Ranković), Nenad Bjeković (73 Mateja Kezman), Dragan Stojisavljević, Goran Obradović, Vladimir Ivić (64 Aleksandar Vuković), Sasa Ilić (Cap).   Trainer: Ljubisa Tumbaković
DINAMO: Nikoloz Togonidze; Zurab Mindadze (46 Avtandil Glonti), Tengiz Sichinava, Aleksandre Kantidze (57 Temur Gadelia), Dmitri Veremchuk, Malkhaz Makharadze (Cap), David Chichveishvili, Paata Machutadze, Temur Tugushi, Mamuka Rusia, Zviad Papidze.   Trainer: Shota Cheishvili
Goals: Bjeković (17), Ilić (33)

DINAMO BATUMI
v PARTIZAN BEOGRAD 1-0 (1-0)
Central Batumi   27.08.1998
Referee: Pasquale Rodomonti (ITA)   Att: 10,300
DINAMO: Nikoloz Togonidze; Tengiz Sichinava, Aleksandre Kantidze (46 David Makatsaria), Dmitri Veremchuk, Malkhaz Makharadze (Cap), Paata Machutadze, Temur Tugushi, Temur Gadelia (84 Shalva Apkhazava), Avtandil Glonti, Gocha Kulejishvili, Zviad Papidze.   Trainer: Shota Cheishvili
PARTIZAN: Nikola Damjanac; Vuk Rasović, Branko Savić, Igor Duljaj, Zoltan Sabo (31 Milan Stojanoski), Goran Trobok, Dragan Stojisavljević, Goran Obradović, Vladimir Ivić (68 Darko Tesović), Sasa Ilić (Cap), Ljubisa Ranković (50 Mateja Kezman).   Trainer: Ljubisa Tumbaković
Goal: Sichinava (28)

FIRST ROUND

RUDAR VELENJE
v VARTEKS VARAZDIN 0-1 (0-0)
Ob jezeru, Velenje   17.09.1998
Referee: Tomasz Mikulski (POL)   Attendance: 850
RUDAR: Mladen Dabanović (Cap); Goran Granić, Almir Sulejmanović, Samir Balagić, Ilir Caushllari, Danijel Brezić, Saso Gajser, Niko Podvinski (80 Peter Sumnik), Jernej Javornik, Zoran Pavlović, Zivojin Vidojević.   Trainer: Drago Jostanjsek
VARTEKS: Ivica Solomun; Drazen Besek, Andrija Balajić (74 Danijel Hrman), Drazen Madunović, Krunoslav Gregorić, Zlatko Dalić, Damir Muzek, Veldin Karić (83 Paul Matas), Silvester Sabolcki, Faik Kamberović, Mladen Posavec (63 Miljenko Mumlek).   Trainer: Drazen Besek
Sent off: Gajser (86)
Goal: Matas (90)

VARTEKS VARAZDIN
v RUDAR VELENJE 1-0 (1-0)
Varteks Varazdin   1.10.1998
Referee: Adrian Stoica (ROM)   Attendance: 2,850
VARTEKS: Ivica Solomun; Drazen Besek, Drazen Madunović, Krunoslav Gregorić, Danijel Hrman, Zlatko Dalić (76 Zoran Kastel), Damir Muzek (70 Mladen Posavec), Miljenko Mumlek, Veldin Karić (87 Mario Ivanković), Faik Kamberović, Andrija Balajić.   Trainer: Drazen Besek
RUDAR: Mladen Dabanović (Cap); Goran Granić, Almir Sulejmanović, Samir Balagić, Aleš Purg (58 Klemen Lavrić), Ilir Caushllari, Danijel Brezić (81 Peter Sumnik), Niko Podvinski, Jernej Javornik, Zoran Pavlović, Zivojin Vidojević.   Trainer: Drago Jostanjsek
Goal: Kamberović (7)

PANIONIOS ATHINA
v HAKA VALKEAKOSKI 2-0 (1-0)
Neas Smirnis, Athina   17.09.1998

Referee: Charles Agius (MAL)   Attendance: 4,222

PANIONIOS: Foto Strakosha; Jan Erlend Kruse, Vasilis Ioannidis, Dimitrios Bougas, Mark Robins (88 Vasilis Kouvalis), Garry Haylock (89 Dimitrios Nalitzis), Andonis Sapountzis (Cap) (65 Konstantinos Kafalis), Giorgos Mitsopoulos, Panagiotis Fissas, Anastasios Zahopoulos, Theofilos Karasavvidis.   Trainer: Ronnie Whelan

HAKA: András Vilnrotter; Ari Heikkinen (Cap), Lasse Karjalainen, Janne Salli, Jouni Räsänen (69 Janne Hyökyvaara), Janne Mäkelä, Oleg Ivanov, Jukka Ruhanen (72 Jukka Rantala), Valeri Popovits, Harri Ylönen, Jari Niemi (80 Tommi Torrkeli).   Trainer: Keith Armstrong

Goals: Haylock (36), Robins (54)

HAKA VALKEAKOSKI
v PANIONIOS ATHINA 1-3 (0-2)
Tehtaankenttä, Valkeakoski   1.10.1998

Referee: Konrad Plautz (AUS)   Attendance: 1,750

HAKA: András Vilnrotter; Janne Mäkelä, Janne Salli, Harri Ylönen, Ari Heikkinen (Cap) (76 Janne Hyökyvaara), Jouni Räsänen, Lasse Karjalainen (28 Jarkko Okkonen), Oleg Ivanov, Jukka Rantala (61 Tommi Torrkeli), Valeri Popovits, Jari Niemi.   Trainer: Keith Armstrong

PANIONIOS: Foto Strakosha; Jan Erlend Kruse (73 Giannis Kamitsis), Giorgos Mitsopoulos, Anastasios Zahopoulos (84 Athanasios Gazis), Vasilis Ioannidis, Theofilos Karasavvidis, Dimitrios Bougas, Panagiotis Fissas, Vasilis Kouvalis, Andonis Sapountzis (Cap), Garry Haylock (58 Mark Robins).   Trainer: Ronnie Whelan

Goals: Fissas (32), Kouvalis (45), Sapountzis (56), Popovits (75)

SV RIED v MTK HUNGÁRIA BUDAPEST 2-0 (1-0)
Rieder Stadion, Ried   17.09.1998

Referee: Yuri Baskakov (RUS)   Attendance: 4,500

SV RIED: Ronald Unger; Günter Steininger, Boris Kitka, Oliver Glasner, Manfred Rothbauer, Michael Angerschmid (62 Stefan Hartl), Goran Stanisavljevic, Michael Anicic (73 Jacek Berensztajn), Helmut Zeller; Ronald Brunmayr (82 Maciej Sliwowski), Gerald Strafner (Cap).   Trainer: Klaus Roitinger

MTK: Gábor Babos; Zoltán Molnár, Ádám Komlósi, Tamás Szekeres, Tamás Szamosi; Károly Erös (82 Csaba Csordás), Gábor Halmai, Béla Illés, Csaba Madar, Iván Balaskó (57 Ferenc Orosz), Krisztián Kenesei (73 Sándor Preisinger).   Trainer: Sándor Egervári

Goals: Strafner (19), Komlósi (65 og)

MTK HUNGÁRIA BUDAPEST v SV RIED 0-1 (0-1)
Hungária, Budapest   1.10.1998

Referee: Martin Ingvarsson (SWE)   Attendance: 2,500

MTK: Gábor Babos; Zoltán Molnár (46 Károly Erös), Ádám Komlósi, Tamás Szekeres, Tamás Szamosi, Csaba Csordás, Gábor Halmai, Béla Illés, Csaba Madar, Krisztián Kenesei, Sándor Preisinger (46 Iván Balaskó).
Trainer: Sándor Egervári

SV RIED: Ronald Unger; Günter Steininger, Boris Kitka, Oliver Glasner, Manfred Rothbauer (60 Alexander Jank), Michael Angerschmid, Goran Stanisavljevic, Michael Anicic, Helmut Zeller (81 Wolfgang Hacker), Gerald Strafner (Cap), Ronald Brunmayr (67 Maciej Sliwowski).
Trainer: Klaus Roitinger

Goal: Strafner (10)

LEVSKI SOFIA v FC KØBENHAVN 0-2 (0-1)
Vasil Levski, Sofia   17.09.1998

Referee: Dick Van Egmond (HOL)   Attendance: 2,350

LEVSKI: Dimitar Ivankov; Zakhari Sirakov, Stanimir Gospodinov, Milen Radukanov, Asen Nikolov (35 Veselin Vachev), Vladimir Ionkov, Doncho Donev (13 Krasimir Dimitrov), Stanimir Stoilov, Georgi Ivanov, Nikolai Todorov (Cap), Georgi Borisov (81 Aleksandar Aleksandrov).
Trainer: Stefan Grozdanov

FC KØBENHAVN: Michael Stensgaard; Martin Nielsen, Morten Falch, Bjarne Goldbæk, Piotr Haren, David Nielsen (83 Kenneth Jensen), Peter Nielsen (Cap), Todi Jonsson (64 Thomas Thorninger), Michael "Mio" Nielsen, Niclas Jensen, Kim Madsen.   Trainer: Kent Karlsson

Goals: Goldbæk (33), Thorninger (76)

FC KØBENHAVN v LEVSKI SOFIA 4-1 (1-0)
Idraetsparken, København   1.10.1998

Referee: Thomas Michael McCurry (SCO)   Att: 6,354

FC KØBENHAVN: Michael Stensgaard; Martin Nielsen, Morten Falch, Lars Højer Nielsen (84 Carsten Vagn Jensen), Bjarne Goldbæk, Piotr Haren, Peter Nielsen (Cap) (76 Claus Nielsen), Todi Jonsson (74 Martin Bill Larsen), Thomas Thorninger, Michael "Mio" Nielsen, Niclas Jensen.
Trainer: Kent Karlsson

LEVSKI: Dimitar Ivankov; Krasimir Dimitrov, Veselin Vachev (70 Martin Goranov), Milen Radukanov, Ivan Vasilev, Stanimir Stoilov, Doncho Donev (65 Aleksandar Aleksandrov), Aleksei Iakimenko, Georgi Ivanov, Nikolai Todorov (Cap), Georgi Borisov (54 Zdravko Lazarov).   Trainer: Stefan Grozdanov

Goals: Ma. Nielsen (18), L.H. Nielsen (49), Thorninger (59, 76), Lazarov (85)

SC HEERENVEEN v AMICA WRONKI 3-1 (2-0)

Abe Lenstra, Heerenveen 17.09.1998

Referee: John McDermott (IRE)   Attendance: 12,100

SC HEERENVEEN: Hans Vonk; Arek Radomski, Tieme Klompe, Johan Hansma (Cap), Dumitru Mitriţă, Jeffrey Talan, Boudewijn Pahlplatz, Gerard de Nooijer (64 Ronnie Pander), Jan De Visser, Dennis De Nooijer (81 Radu Mugur Gusatu), Radoslav Samardzic (87 Ivan Tzvetkov).
Trainer: Foppe De Haan

AMICA: Jaroslaw Strozynski; Zbigniew Malachowski, Ireneusz Koscielniak, Pawel Kryszalowicz, Grzegorz Matlak (62 Tomasz Dawidowski), Bartosz Bosacki, Dariusz Jackiewicz, Tomasz Sokolowski (80 Grzegorz Motyka), Marek Bajor (Cap), Andrzej Przerada, Grzegorz Krol (64 Remigiusz Sobocinski).
Trainer: Wojciech Wasikiewicz

Goals: Talan (38), Mitriţă (45), Krol (63), Pahlplatz (66)

AMICA WRONKI v SC HEERENVEEN 0-1 (0-1)

Amica Wronki 1.10.1998

Referee: Gylfi Thor Orasson (ICE)   Attendance: 3,000

AMICA: Jaroslaw Strozynski; Andrzej Przerada (84 Miroslaw Kalita), Ireneusz Koscielniak, Zbigniew Malachowski, Marek Bajor (Cap), Dariusz Jackiewicz (64 Miroslaw Siara), Tomasz Dawidowski, Bartosz Bosacki, Tomasz Sokolowski (77 Remigiusz Sobocinski), Pawel Kryszalowicz, Grzegorz Krol.
Trainer: Wojciech Wasikiewicz

SC HEERENVEEN: Hans Vonk; Arek Radomski, Tieme Klompe, Johan Hansma (Cap), Dumitru Mitriţă, Boudewijn Pahlplatz (63 Max Houttuin), Gerard de Nooijer (84 Ronnie Pander), Jan De Visser, Jeffrey Talan, Dennis De Nooijer, Radoslav Samardzic (75 Emanuel Ebiede).
Trainer: Foppe De Haan

Goal: D. de Nooijer (30)

HEART of MIDLOTHIAN EDINBURGH v REAL CLUB DEPORTIVO MALLORCA 0-1 (0-1)

Tynecastle Park, Edinburgh 17.09.1998

Referee: Alfredo Trentalange (ITA)   Attendance: 13,573

HEARTS: Gilles Rousset; David McPherson, Gary Naysmith, David Weir, Stefano Salvatori, Paul Ritchie, Neil McCann, Stéphane Adam, Jim Hamilton (84 Derek Holmes), Gary Locke (Cap), Steven Pressley.   Trainer: James Jefferies

RCD MALLORCA: Carlos Roa; Miquel SOLER Sarasols, Gustavo Lionel SIVIERO, Vicente ENGONGA Maté, LAUREN Bisan Etama-Mayer, Jovan Stankovic (86 Lluís CARRERAS Ferrer), MARCELINO Elena Sierra, Javier OLAIZOLA Rodríguez (Cap), Oscar ARPÓN Ochoa (88 Fernando NIÑO Bejereno), Daniel García Lara "DANI", Ariel LÓPEZ (71 CARLOS Domínguez).   Trainer: Héctor Raúl Cúper

Goal: Marcelino (17)

REAL CD MALLORCA v HEART of MIDLOTHIAN EDINBURGH 1-1 (0-0)

San Moix, Palma de Mallorca 1.10.1998

Referee: Hermann Albrecht (GER)   Attendance: 8,717

RCD MALLORCA: CÉSAR GÁLVEZ Espinar; Javier OLAIZOLA Rodríguez, MARCELINO Elena Sierra, Gustavo Lionel SIVIERO, Miquel SOLER Sarasols (Cap); LAUREN Bisan Etama-Mayer, Francisco SOLER Atencia (86 Lluís CARRERAS Ferrer), Oscar ARPÓN Ochoa (80 Fernando NIÑO Bejereno), Jovan Stankovic; Daniel García Lara "DANI", Ariel LÓPEZ (82 Leonardo Angel BIAGINI).
Trainer: Héctor Raúl Cúper

HEARTS: Gilles Rousset; Gary Locke (Cap), David Weir, Paul Ritchie, Gary Naysmith, Neil McCann (53 Derek Holmes), Stefano Salvatori, Steven Pressley, Lee Makel (84 David McPherson), Stéphane Adam, Jim Hamilton.
Trainer: James Jefferies

Goals: López (50), Hamilton (76)

CHELSEA LONDON v HELSINGBORGS IF 1-0 (1-0)

Stamford Bridge, London 17.09.1998

Referee: Juan Ansuategui Roca (SPA)   Attendance: 17,714

CHELSEA: Dmitri Kharin; Albert Ferrer, Frank Leboeuf, Marcel Desailly, Graeme Le Saux, Brian Laudrup, Dennis Wise (Cap), Roberto Di Matteo, Celestine Babayaro (62 Gustavo Poyet), Gianluca Vialli (83 Mark Nicholls), Tore André Flo (54 Pierluigi Casiraghi).   Trainer: Gianluca Vialli

HELSINGBORGS: Sven Andersson; Ola Nilsson, Andreas Jacobsson, Zoran Jovanovski, Erik Edman, Arild Stavrum (65 Erik Wahlstedt), Peter Wibrån, Marcus Lantz, Kenneth Storvik (90 Per-Ola Ljung), Stig Johansen (73 Mattias Jonsson), Magnus Powell.   Trainer: Åge Hareide

Goal: Leboeuf (43)

HELSINGBORGS IF v CHELSEA LONDON 0-0

Olympia, Helsingborg 1.10.1998

Referee: Vladimir Hrinak (SVK)   Attendance: 12,348

HELSINGBORGS: Sven Andersson; Ola Nilsson, Andreas Jacobsson, Zoran Jovanovski, Peter Wibrån, Magnus Powell, Mattias Jonsson (72 Erik Wahlstedt), Erik Edman (82 Christoffer Andersson), Kenneth Storvik, Marcus Lantz, Arild Stavrum (61 Stig Johansen).   Trainer: Åge Hareide

CHELSEA: Ed de Goey; Celestine Babayaro, Frank Leboeuf (Cap), Michael Duberry, Graeme Le Saux, Albert Ferrer, Roberto Di Matteo, Marcel Desailly, Gustavo Poyet, Gianluca Vialli (90 Pierluigi Casiraghi), Tore André Flo.   Trainer: Gianluca Vialli

MSV DUISBURG v KRC GENK 1-1 (0-0)

Wedaustadion, Duisburg   17.09.1998

Referee: Václav Krondl (CZE)   Attendance: 10,602

MSV: Thomas Gill; Slobodan Komljenovic, Stefan Emmerling, Tomasz Hajto, Thomas Hoersen (44 Carsten Wolters), Lubomir Moravcik, Torsten Wohlert (Cap), Stig Tøfting (78 Marcus Wedau), Jörg Neun, Markus Beierle, Uwe Spies (68 Erik Bo Andersen).   Trainer: Friedhelm Funkel

KRC GENK: István Brochkauser; Chris Van Geem, Domenico Olivieri (Cap), Daniel Kimoni, Juha Reini, Besnik Hasi, Thórdur Gudjónsson, Wilfried Delbroek, Marc Hendrickx, Branko Strupar (89 Marc Vangronsveld), Souleymane Oulare (85 Mike Origi).   Trainer: Aimé Antheunis

Sent off: Hendrickx (57)

Goals: Reini (61), Wedau (83)

KRC GENK v MSV DUISBURG 5-0 (2-0)

Brussel   1.10.1998

Referee: Karl Erik Nilsson (SWE)   Attendance: 17,200

KRC GENK: István Brochkauser; Chris Van Geem, Domenico Olivieri (Cap), Daniel Kimoni, Juha Reini, Besnik Hasi, Thórdur Gudjónsson (89 Mike Origi), Wilfried Delbroek, ROGÉRIO de Oliveira, Souleymane Oulare (84 Ferenc Horváth), Branko Strupar (89 Marc Vangronsveld).   Trainer: Aimé Antheunis

MSV: Thomas Gill; Torsten Wohlert (Cap), Stefan Emmerling, Tomasz Hajto, Thomas Hoersen, Stig Tøfting (61 Thomas Vana), Marcus Wedau, Slobodan Komljenovic (75 Dietmar Hirsch), Jörg Neun, Uwe Spies, Markus Beierle.   Trainer: Friedhelm Funkel

Goals: Oulare (12, 48), Strupar (31), Gudjónsson (71, 78)

BEŞIKTAŞ ISTANBUL v SPARTAK TRNAVA 3-0 (2-0)

Inönün Istanbul   17.09.1998

Referee: Tom Henning Øvrebø (NOR)   Attendance: 20,580

BEŞIKTAŞ: Hakan Caliskan; Erkan Avseren, Alpay Özalan, Tayfur Havutçu, Ali Eren Beserler, Mehmet Özdilek (Cap) (85 Ertugrul Saglam), Hikmet Çapanoglu (70 Jamal Sellami), Alvarez Del Solar, Serdar Topraktepe, Oktay Derelioglu, Christopher Ohen (79 Ayhan Akman).   Trainer: John Toshack

SPARTAK: Kamil Susko (Cap); Miroslav Karhan, Vladimir Leitner, Jaroslav Hrabal, Igor Balis (71 Jaroslav Macak), Dušan Tittel, Marek Ujlaky, Jaroslav Timko, Ondrej Kristofik (60 Peter Bugar), Sergej Jakirovic, Fábio Luís Gomes.   Trainer: Dušan Galis

Goals: Mehmet (11), Oktay (22), Ohen (50)

SPARTAK TRNAVA v BEŞIKTAŞ ISTANBUL 2-1 (0-1)

Spartak Trnava   1.10.1998

Referee: Sergyi Tatulyan (UKR)   Attendance: 6,246

SPARTAK: Kamil Susko; Miroslav Karhan (73 Sergej Jakirovici), Marcel Horky, Jaroslav Hrabal, Igor Balis (Cap) (64 Lubomir Talda), Dušan Tittel, Marek Ujlaky, Vladimir Leitner, Robert Formanko, Fábio Luís Gomes, Jaroslav Macak (81 Rastislav Tomovcik).   Trainer: Dušan Galis

BEŞIKTAŞ: Fevzi Tuncay; Ali Eren Beserler, Rahim Zafer, Alpay Özalan, Erkan Avseren (84 Ertugrul Saglam), Jamal Sellami, Alvarez Del Solar, Tayfur Havutçu, Serdar Topraktepe (46 Yasin Sülün), Mehmet Özdilek (Cap) (66 Daniel Amokachi), Oktay Derelioglu.   Trainer: John Toshack

Goals: Oktay (45), Formanko (49), Timko (71)

RAPID BUCUREŞTI v VÅLERENGA IF OSLO 2-2 (0-0)

Giuleşti, Bucureşti   18.09.1998

Referee: Zoran Arsić (YUG)   Attendance: 4,150

RAPID: Bogdan Lobonţ; Nicolae Stanciu (Cap) (67 Mugur Bolohan), Dorel Mutică, Mircea Rednic, Cristian Dulca, Ştefan Dumitru Nanu; Ioan Ovidiu Sabău, Dănuţ Lupu, Marius Măldărăşanu (58 Zeno Bundea); Marius Şumudică (75 Sergiu Radu), Ovidiu Maier.   Trainer: Mircea Lucescu

VÅLERENGA: Tore Krogstad (Cap); Joachim Walltin, Knut Henry Haraldsen, Fredrik Kjølner, Hai Ngoc Tran; Kjell Roar Kaasa (46 Juro Kuvicek), Bjørn Viljugrein (69 Espen Musaeus), Bjørn Arild Levernes, Tom Henning Hovi (87 Fredrik Thorsen), Espen Haug; John Carew.   Trainers: Egil Olsen & Lars Tjernaas

Goals: Şumudică (52), Carew (53, 88), Bundea (76)

VÅLERENGEN IF OSLO v RAPID BUCUREŞTI 0-0

Ullevaal, Oslo   1.10.1998

Referee: Roman Lajuks (LAT)   Attendance: 6,257

VÅLERENGA: Tore Krogstad (Cap); Joachim Walltin, Knut Henry Haraldsen, Fredrik Kjølner, Hai Ngoc Tran; Jon Eirik Ødegaard (87 Kjell Roar Kaasa), Bjørn Viljugrein, Bjørn Arild Levernes, Espen Haug (78 Fredrik Thorsen), Tom Henning Hovi; John Carew.   Trainers: Egil Olsen & Lars Tjernaas

RAPID: Bogdan Lobonţ; Mihai Adrian Iencsi (85 Mugur Bolohan), Nicolae Stanciu (Cap), Mircea Rednic, Dorel Mutică, Ştefan Dumitru Nanu; Zeno Bundea, Dănuţ Lupu, Ovidiu Maier (60 Marius Măldărăşanu); Marius Şumudică (85 Sergiu Radu), Daniel Pancu.   Trainer: Mircea Lucescu

APOLLON LIMASSOL v SK JABLONEC 2-1 (1-1)
Tsirion, Limassol   17.09.1998
Referee: Claude Detruche (SWI)   Attendance: 3,000
APOLLON: Sofronis Avgousti; Hrysostomos Juras, Haralampos Pittas (Cap), Filippos Filippou, Marios Haralampous, Florin Cârstea (84 Hrysostomos Hristofi), Marios Themistokleous (72 Stefanos Voskaridis), Xenios Kyriakou, Nebojsa Mladenovic, Hristos Germanos, Giorgos Kavazis.   Trainer: Dumitru Dumitriu
JABLONEC: Zdenek Janos; Roman Skuhravy, Martin Vejprava, Robert Neumann, Pavel Penicka, Milan Barteska, Pavel Jirousek (65 Jaromir Navratil), Radim Necas (Cap), Radim Holub (79 Jiří Vavra), Martin Prochazka (62 Ales Kohout), Milan Fukal.   Trainer: Jiří Kotrba
Goals: Fukal (38), Kavazis (46), Cârstea (67)

**PARTIZAN BEOGRAD
v NEWCASTLE UNITED 1-0** (0-0)
Partizan Beograd   1.10.1998
Referee: Manuel Diaz Vega (SPA)   Attendance: 26,700
PARTIZAN: ikola Damjanac; Vuk Rasović, Branko Savic, Mladen Krstajić (46 Dragan Stojisavljević), Milan Stojanoski, Goran Trobok, Vladimir Ivić, Sasa Ilić (Cap), Djordje Tomić, Nenad Bjeković (79 Darko Tesović), Mateja Kezman (66 Predrag Pazin).   Trainer: Ljubisa Tumbaković
UNITED: Shay Given; Andy Griffin (73 Philippe Albert), Stephen Glass, Stuart Pearce, Nolberto Solano, David Batty, Temur Ketsbaia, Laurent Charvet, Nikos Dabizas, Gary Speed, Alan Shearer (Cap).   Manager: Ruud Gullit
Goal: Rasović (53 pen)

**SK JABLONEC
v APOLLON LIMASSOL 2-1** (2-0, 2-1) (AET)
Strelnice, Jablonec   1.10.1998
Referee: Dermot Gallagher (ENG)   Attendance: 3,100
JABLONEC: Zdenek Janos; Roman Skuhravy, Jan Sopko, Pavel Penicka, Milan Barteska, Pavel Jirousek, Radim Necas (Cap), Radim Holub (69 Ales Kohout, 106 Milan Fukal), Jaromir Navratil (80 Tomas Cizek), Josef Just, Martin Prochazka.   Trainer: Jiří Kotrba
APOLLON: Sofronis Avgousti; Hrysostomos Juras, Filippos Filippou, Milenko Spoljaric (Cap), Marios Themistokleous (66 Hrysostomos Hristofi), Theodoros Aresti, Xenios Kyriakou, Stefanos Voskaridis (74 Nikodimos Papavasileiou), Giorgos Kais, Nebojsa Mladenovic (70 Hristos Germanos), Giorgos Kavazis.   Trainer: Dumitru Dumitriu
Goals: Prochazka (25, 45), Themistokleous (59)
Apollon Limassol won 4-3 on penalties.

LAZIO ROMA v LAUSANNE SPORTS 1-1 (1-0)
Stadio Olimpico, Roma   17.09.1998
Referee: Dani Koren (ISR)   Attendance: 22,659
LAZIO: Luca Marchegiani (Cap); FERNANDO Manuel Silva COUTO, Giovanni Lopez, Sinisa Mihajlovic, Giuseppe Pancaro (60 Stefano Lombardi), Dejan Stankovic, Giorgio Venturin, Iván De La Peña (23 Sérgio Conceição), Pavel Nedved, Marcelo Salas (81 Guerino Gottardi), Roberto Mancini.
Trainer: Sven Göran Eriksson
LAUSANNE: Martin Brunner (Cap); Marc Hottiger, Daniel Puce, Oscar Londono, Erich Hänzi (79 Ricardo Iglesias), Fabio Celestini, Stefan Rehn, Blaise Piffaretti, Philippe Douglas, Saso Udovic (58 Léonard Thurre), Armen Shahgeldyan (65 Andres Gerber).
Trainer: Georges Bregy
Sent off: D. Stankovic (2)
Goals: Nedved (37), Douglas (54)

**NEWCASTLE UNITED
v PARTIZAN BEOGRAD 2-1** (1-0)
St. James' Park, Necastle   17.09.1998
Referee: Dick Jol (HOL)   Attendance: 26,599
UNITED: Shay Given; Steve Watson, Nikos Dabizas, Laurent Charvet, Stuart Pearce, Gary Speed, Robert Lee (Cap), Stephen Glass, Andreas Andersson (46 Nolberto Solano), Temur Ketsbaia, Alan Shearer.   Manager: Ruud Gullit
PARTIZAN: Nikola Damjanac; Vuk Rasović, Branko Savić, Mladen Krstajić, Goran Trobok, Vladimir Ivić (73 Predrag Pazin), Sasa Ilić (Cap), Djordje Tomić, Milan Stojanoski, Nenad Bjeković (86 Dragan Stojisavljević), Goran Obradović.
Trainer: Ljubisa Tumbaković
Goals: Shearer (12), Rasović (69 pen), Dabizas (71)

LAUSANNE SPORTS v LAZIO ROMA 2-2 (1-2)
Stade Olympique de La Pontaise, Lausanne   1.10.1998
Referee: Kyros Vassaras (GRE)   Attendance: 12,500
LAUSANNE: Martin Brunner (Cap); Marc Hottiger, Oscar Londono, Ricardo Iglesias (46 Daniel Puce), Erich Hänzi, Fabio Celestini (64 Andres Gerber), Blaise Piffaretti, Stefan Rehn, Philippe Douglas, Saso Udovic (75 Armen Shahgeldyan), Léonard Thurre.   Trainer: Georges Bregy
LAZIO: Luca Marchegiani; Giuseppe Pancaro, FERNANDO Manuel Silva COUTO, Sinisa Mihajlovic, Giuseppe Favalli (Cap) (89 Giovanni Lopez), Sérgio Conceição (84 Guerino Gottardi), Giorgio Venturin, Matias Almeyda (73 Roberto Baronio), Pavel Nedved, Roberto Mancini, Marcelo Salas.
Trainer: Sven Göran Eriksson
Goals: Salas (8), Douglas (10), Sérgio Conceição (25), Rehn (84)

**PARIS SAINT-GERMAIN
v MACCABI HAIFA 1-1** (0-0)

Parc des Princes, Paris 17.09.1998

Referee: Herbert Fandel (GER)   Attendance: 28,183

PSG: Bernard Lama; Jimmy Algérino, Alain Goma, Christian Wörns, Didier Domi; Bruno Carotti, Augustine Okocha, Igor Yanovskiy (87 Yann Lachuer), Adailton Martins (46 Patrice Loko); Nicolas Ouédec, Marco Simone (Cap).   Trainer: Alain Giresse

MACCABI: Nir Davidovich; Eliron Elkayam, Serhiy Balanchuk (25 Avishai Jano), Arik Benado (Cap), Alon Harazi, Haim Silvas (80 Shuki Nagar), Adoram Keissy, Offir Kopel, Yossi Benayoun, Radovan Hromadko (89 Ibrahim Duro), Alon Mizrahi.
Trainer: Dušan Uhrin

Goals: Simone (82 pen), Benayoun (87)

**MACCABI HAIFA
v PARIS SAINT-GERMAIN 3-2** (0-0)

Kiriat Eliezer, Haifa 1.10.1998

Referee: Fernand Meese (BEL)   Attendance: 10,500

MACCABI: Nir Davidovich; Avishai Jano, Eliron Elkayam, Alon Harazi, Arik Benado (Cap), Adoram Keissy, Ibrahim Duro (75 Yaniv Katan), Offir Kopel, Yossi Benayoun (90 Shuki Nagar), Radovan Hromadko, Alon Mizrahi (90 Guy Melamed).
Trainer: Dušan Uhrin

PSG: Bernard Lama; Nicolas Laspalles, Alain Goma, Eric Rabesandratana, Jimmy Algérino; Yann Lachuer (86 Patrice Loko), Pierre Ducrocq, Augustine Okocha, Igor Yanovskiy (75 Jérôme Leroy); Nicolas Ouédec, Marco Simone (Cap).
Trainer: Alain Giresse

Goals: Keissy (59), Ouédec (73), Mizrahi (78, 90), Okocha (87)

METALURGS LIEPAYA v SPORTING BRAGA 0-0

Daugava, Liepaya 17.09.1998

Referee: Milan Mitrovic (SVN)   Attendance: 5,150

METALURGS: Algimantas Bryaunis; Daryus Magdisauskas, Dzintars Zirnis, Victor Yuiko, Andrei Osichenko (Cap), Vladimir Dragun, Rolandas Vaineikis, Victor Dobretsov (58 Eduard Kudryashov), Rolands Boulders, Oleg Rudenko (46 Janis Rimkus), Saulius Atmanavicius. Trainer: Yuri Popkov

SPORTING: PAULO Jorge Matos MORAIS; JOSÉ NUNO da Silva AZEVEDO (Cap), ODAIR D'Arc Borges, IDALÉCIO Silvestre Lopes Rosa, Rui Miguel Baptista Araújo "MOZER", ELPÍDIO Pereira da SILVA Filho, Vítor Ilídio CASTANHEIRA Penas, Paulo Rui LINO Borges, Mladen Karoglan (63 Costa Silva LUÍS MIGUEL), Adelino José Martins Baptista "JORDÃO" (80 António José Faria FORMOSO), Jorge Manuel Nunes GAMBOA (71 António Dinis Duarte "TONI").
Trainer: VÍTOR Manuel OLIVEIRA

**SPORTING BRAGA
v METALURGS LIEPAYA 4-0** (2-0)

1o de Maio, Braga 1.10.1998

Referee: Roland Beck (Lie)   Attendance: 8,750

SPORTING: PAULO Jorge Matos MORAIS; JOSÉ NUNO da Silva AZEVEDO (Cap), ODAIR D'Arc Borges, IDALÉCIO Silvestre Lopes Rosa, Paulo Rui LINO Borges, Adelino José Baptista "JORDÃO" (55 Vítor Ilídio CASTANHEIRA Penas), Rui Miguel Baptista Araújo "MOZER", BRUNO Alexandre Vaz Ferreira, Costa Silva LUÍS MIGUEL (21 ELPÍDIO Pereira da SILVA Filho), António Dinis Duarte "TONI", Mladen Karoglan (79 Reginaldo Rosenberg de Carvalho "DÉ").
Trainer: VÍTOR Manuel OLIVEIRA

METALURGS: Algimantas Bryaunis; Andrei Osichenko (Cap), Daryus Magdisauskas, Saulius Atmanavicius, Mikhail Lisyakov (26 Victor Dobretsov), Rolandas Vaineikis (74 Maris Verpakovsky), Dzintars Zirnis, Oleg Rudenko (52 Eduard Kudryashov), Janis Rimkus, Victor Yuiko, Rolands Boulders.

Goals: Bruno (13 pen, 61), Karoglan (35), Elpídio Silva (86)

CSKA KYIV v LOKOMOTIV MOSKVA 0-2 (0-1)

Kyiv 17.09.1998

Referee: Eyal Zur (ISR)   Attendance: 4,500

CSKA: Vitaliy Reva; Vitaliy Levchenko, Vitaliy Balytskyi, Viktor Ulyanytskyi, Valentyn Gregul, Serhiy Bezhenar, Olexiy Oleynik (78 Vasyl Novokhatskyi), Ruslan Kostyshyn (25 Olexandr Olexiyenko), Serhiy Zakarlyuka (53 Vitaliy Daraselia), Viktor Leonenko, Eduard Tsykhmeistruk (Cap).
Trainer: Volodymyr Bessonov

LOKOMOTIV: Ruslan Nigmatullin; Oleg Pashinin, Yuri Drozdov, Evgeniy Kharlachov, Andrei Lavrik, Igor Chugainov (Cap), Andrei Solomatin, Sergei Gurenko, Zaza Janashia (90 Dmitriy Bulykin), Aleksandr Borodyuk (80 Oleg Garas), Aleksei Arifullin.   Trainer: Yuri Syomin

Goals: Kharlachov (24), Janashia (51)

LOKOMOTIV MOSKVA v CSKA KYIV 3-1 (1-1)

Lokomotiv Moskva 1.10.1998

Referee: Robert Sedlacek (AUS)   Attendance: 4,850

LOKOMOTIV: Ruslan Nigmatullin; Aleksei Arifullin (74 Igor Cherevchenko), Yuri Drozdov (57 Dmitriy Loskov), Evgeniy Kharlachov, Andrei Lavrik, Igor Chugainov (Cap), Andrei Solomatin, Sergei Gurenko, Zaza Janashia, Aleksandr Borodyuk, Dmitriy Bulykin (73 Oleg Pashinin).
Trainer: Yuri Syomin

CSKA: Vitaliy Reva; Vitaliy Levchenko, Vitaliy Balytskyi, Serhiy Bezhenar, Valentyn Gregul, Vasyl Novokhtarskyi (46 Serhiy Revut), Andriy Karyaka (75 Vitaliy Daraselia), Pavlo Shkapenko, Serhiy Zakarlyuka, Viktor Leonenko (46 Dmytro Korenev), Eduard Tsykhmeistruk (Cap).
Trainer: Volodymyr Bessonov   **Sent off**: Levchenko (34)

Goals: Bezhenar (13), Bulykin (19, 53), Janashia (70)

SECOND ROUND

VÅLERENGA IF OSLO v BEŞIKTAŞ ISTANBUL 1-0 (0-0)

Ullevaal, Oslo   22.10.1998

Referee: Sándor Puhl (HUN)   Attendance: 6,284

VÅLERENGA: Tore Krogstad (Cap); Fredrik Kjølner, Bjørn Arild Levernes, Hai Ngoc Tran, Dag Riisnaes (88 Jon Eirik Ødegaard), Kjell Roar Kaasa (58 Espen Haug), Joachim Walltin, Bjørn Viljugrein (85 Juro Kuvicek), Knut Henry Haraldsen, Tom Henning Hovi, John Carew.   Trainers: Egil Olsen & Lars Tjernaas

BEŞIKTAŞ: Fevzi Tuncay; Tayfur Havutçu, Alvarez Del Solar, Alpay Özalan, Erkan Avseren, Christopher Ohen (70 Daniel Amokachi), Mehmet Özdilek (Cap) (75 Ertugrul Saglam), Oktay Derelioglu, Jamal Sellami, Ali Eren Beserler, Hikmet Çapanoglu (83 Ayhan Akman).   Trainer: John Toshack

Goal: Levernes (49)

BEŞIKTAŞ ISTANBUL v VÅLERENGA IF OSL 3-3 (3-0)

Inönü, Istanbul   5.11.1998

Referee: Edgar Steinborn (GER)   Attendance: 25,000

BEŞIKTAŞ: Fevzi Tuncay; Tayfur Havutçu, Jamal Sellami, Alpay Özalan (75 Nihat Kahveci), Alvarez Del Solar, Ali Eren Beserler, Mehmet Özdilek (Cap), Aydin Tuna (28 Erkan Avseren), Ertugrul Saglam, Oktay Derelioglu, Christopher Ohen (65 Serdar Topraktepe).   Trainer: John Toshack

VÅLERENGA: Tore Krogstad (Cap); Tom Henning Hovi, Knut Henry Haraldsen, Fredrik Kjølner, Hai Ngoc Tran, Joachim Walltin, Bjørn Viljugrein, Bjørn Arild Levernes (89 Fredrik Thorsen), Espen Haug (85 Juro Kuvicek), Dag Riisnaes (46 Kjell Roar Kaasa), John Carew.   Trainers: Egil Olsen & Lars Tjernaas

Goals: Oktay (7, 42), Tayfur (38), Haraldsen (62), Kaasa (66), Carew (73)

KRC GENK v REAL CD MALLORCA 1-1 (0-0)

Brussel   22.10.1998

Referee: Konrad Plautz (AUS)   Attendance: 24,046

GENK: István Brockhauser; Chris Van Geem, Domenico Olivieri (Cap), Daniel Kimoni, Wilfried Delbroek, Juha Reini, Besnik Hasi, Mike Origi, ROGIRIO de Oliveira (61 Ngoy N'Sumbu), Souleymane Oulare, Branko Strupar.   Trainer: Aimé Antheunis

RCD MALLORCA: Carlos Roa; Javier OLAIZOLA Rodrvguez (Cap), MARCELINO Elena Sierra, Gustavo Lionel SIVIERO, Miquel SOLER Sarasols; LAUREN Bisan Etama-Mayer, Vicente ENGONGA Maté, Veljko Paunovic (79 Fernando NIÑO Bejereno), Jovan Stankovic; Daniel García Lara "DANI" (86 Lluís CARRERAS Ferrer), Leonardo Angel BIAGINI (81 CARLOS Domínguez).   Trainer: Héctor Raúl Cúper

Sent off: J. Stankovic (84)

Goals: Dani (56), Oulare (71)

REAL CD MALLORCA v RK GENK 0-0

San Moix, Palma de Mallorca   5.11.1998

Referee: Rémi Harrel (FRA)   Attendance: 15,000

RCD MALLORCA: Carlos Roa; Javier OLAIZOLA Rodrvguez (Cap), Gustavo Lionel SIVIERO, MARCELINO Elena Sierra, Miquel SOLER Sarasols; Lluís CARRERAS Ferrer, Vicente ENGONGA Maté (62 Fernando NIÑO Bejereno), LAUREN Bisan Etama-Mayer, Ariel Miguel IBAGAZA (80 Oscar ARPÓN Ochoa); Daniel García Lara "DANI", Leonardo Angel BIAGINI (90 Ariel LÓPEZ).   Trainer: Héctor Raúl Cúper

RK GENK: István Brockhauser (Cap); Daniel Kimoni, Domenico Olivieri, Chris Van Geem, ROGIRIO de Oliveira (73 Ngoy N'Sumbu), Mike Origi, Wilfried Delbroek, Juha Reini, Branko Strupar (83 Edmilson Dos Santos), Thórdur Gudjønsson, Souleymane Oulare.   Trainer: Aimé Antheunis

LAZIO ROMA v PARTIZAN BEOGRAD 0-0

Stadio Olimpico, Roma   22.10.1998

Referee: Renı Temmink (HOL)   Attendance: 24,966

LAZIO: Luca Marchegiani; Giuseppe Pancaro, FERNANDO Manuel Silva COUTO, Sinisa Mihajlovic, Giuseppe Favalli (Cap); Sérgio Conceição, Giorgio Venturin, Matias Almeyda, Pavel Nedved, Guerino Gottardi (70 Marcolin), Roberto Mancini.   Trainer: Sven Göran Eriksson

PARTIZAN: Nikola Damjanac; Branko Savić, Vuk Rasović, Milan Stojanoski, Mladen Krstajić, Vladimir Ivić (76 Predrag Pazin), Goran Trobok, Sasa Ilić (Cap), Djordje Tomić, Mateja Kezman, Goran Obradović (63 Ivica Ilijev).   Trainer: Ljubisa Tumbaković

PARTIZAN BEOGRAD v LAZIO ROMA 2-3 (1-1)

Partizan Beograd   5.11.1998

Referee: Fritz Stuchlik (AUS)   Attendance: 32,000

PARTIZAN: Nikola Damjanac; Vuk Rasović, Branko Savić, Marjan Gerasimovski, Goran Trobok, Mateja Kezman (70 Nenad Bjeković), Goran Obradović (50 Dragan Stojisavljević), Vladimir Ivić (66 Ivica Ilijev), Mladen Krstajić, Sasa Ilić (Cap), Djordje Tomić.   Trainer: Ljubisa Tumbaković

LAZIO: Luca Marchegiani; Giuseppe Favalli (Cap), FERNANDO Manuel Silva COUTO, Sinisa Mihajlović, Giuseppe Pancaro, Sérgio Conceição (53 Dejan Stanković), Giorgio Venturin, Matias Almeyda, Pavel Nedved, Marcelo Salas (82 Alen Boksic), Roberto Mancini (89 Roberto Baronio).   Trainer: Sven Göran Eriksson

Goals: Krstajić (18), Salas (43 pen, 76), Stanković (67), Ilijev (85)

**LOKOMOTIV MOSKVA
v SPORTING BRAGA 3-1 (2-0)**

Lokomotiv Moskva 22.10.1998

Referee: Charles Agius (MAL)   Attendance: 12,000

LOKOMOTIV: Ruslan Nigmatullin; Igor Cherevchenko, Yuri Drozdov, Evgeniy Kharlachov (80 Albert Sarkisyan), Andrei Solomatin, Igor Chugainov (Cap), Aleksandr Borodyuk, Sergei Gurenko, Zaza Janashia, Dmitriy Loskov (88 Andrei Lavrik), Dmitriy Bulykin.   Trainer: Yuri Syomin

SPORTING: PAULO Jorge Matos MORAIS; ODAIR D'Arc Borges, JOSÉ NUNO da Silva AZEVEDO, SÉRGIO Manuel Freitas Abreu, Paulo Rui LINO Borges, Rui Miguel Baptista Araújo "MOZER", Adelino José Martins Baptista "JORDÃO", ARTUR JORGE Araújo Amorim (Cap) (74 Vítor Ilídio CASTANHEIRA Penas), BRUNO Alexandre Vaz Ferreira, Mladen Karoglan (74 António Dinis Duarte "TONI"), ELPÍDIO Pereira da SILVA Filho (87 Joaquim Manuel Silva "QUIM").   Trainer: VÍTOR OLIVEIRA

Sent off: Paulo Morais (87)

Goals: Bulykin (21, 35), Odair (47), Chugainov (59 pen)

**SPORTING BRAGA
v LOKOMOTIV MOSKVA 1-0 (1-0)**

1o de Maio, Braga 5.11.1998

Referee: Alfredo Trentalange (ITA)   Attendance: 15,000

SPORTING: Joaquim Manuel Silva "QUIM"; JOSÉ NUNO da Silva AZEVEDO, ARTUR JORGE Araújo Amorim (Cap) (80 SÉRGIO Manuel Freitas Abreu), ODAIR D'Arc Borges, Paulo Rui LINO Borges (67 António José Faria FORMOSO), BRUNO Alexandre Vaz Ferreira, Rui Miguel Baptista Araújo "MOZER", Adelino José Martins Baptista "JORDÃO", Jorge Manuel Nunes GAMBOA (59 António Dinis Duarte "TONI"), ELPÍDIO Pereira da SILVA Filho, Mladen Karoglan.   Trainer: VÍTOR OLIVEIRA

LOKOMOTIV: Ruslan Nigmatullin; Igor Cherevchenko, Igor Chugainov (Cap), Yuri Drozdov (31 Andrei Lavrik), Dmitriy Loskov, Sergei Gurenko, Evgeniy Kharlachov (65 Albert Sarkisyan), Andrei Solomatin, Aleksandr Borodyuk, Zaza Janashia (87 Aleksei Arifullin), Dmitriy Bulykin.   Trainer: Yuri Syomin

Goal: Karoglan (11)

**SC HEERENVEEN
v VARTEKS VARAZDIN 2-1 (0-0)**

Abe Lenstra, Heerenveen 22.10.1998

Referee: Dani Koren (Isr)   Attendance: 12,000

SC HEERENVEEN: Hans Vonk; Arek Radomski, Gerard de Nooijer, Tieme Klompe, Dumitru Mitriţă, Max Houttuin (71 Radu Mugur Gusatu), Johan Hansma (Cap), Jan De Visser, Boudewijn Pahlplatz (46 Ali El Khattabi), Dennis De Nooijer, Radoslav Samardzic.   Trainer: Foppe De Haan

VARTEKS: Ivica Solomun; Mladen Posavec, Drazen Besek, Drazen Madunović, Silvester Sabolcki, Andrija Balajić, Damir Muzek, Zlatko Dalić, Mario Ivanković (71 Zoran Kastel), Veldin Karić (90 Paul Matas), Miljenko Mumlek (Cap).   Trainer: D. Besek

Goals: D. de Nooijer (56), Mumlek (63), Hansma (89)

**VARTEKS VARAZDIN
v SC HEERENVEEN 4-2 (0-1,2-1)**

Varteks Varazdin 5.11.1998

Referee: Kyros Vassaras (GRE)   Attendance: 6,000

VARTEKS: Ivica Solomun; Mladen Posavec, Drazen Besek (42 Krunoslav Beli), Drazen Madunović, Silvester Sabolcki (59 Faik Kamberović), Andrija Balajić, Damir Muzek, Krunoslav Gregorić, Miljenko Mumlek (Cap), Veldin Karić, Mario Ivanković (46 Danijel Hrman).   Trainer: Drazen Besek

SC HEERENVEEN: Hans Vonk; Max Houttuin (105 Ali El Khattabi), Tieme Klompe, Johan Hansma (Cap), Ronnie Pander, Arek Radomski, Gerard de Nooijer, Jan De Visser, Jeffrey Talan, Dennis De Nooijer (78 Radu Mugur Guşatu), Radoslav Samardzić (91 Boudewijn Pahlplatz).   Trainer: Foppe De Haan

Goals: Samardzić (18), Mumlek (65, 117), Kamberović (80, 99), De Visser (114)

SV RIED v MACCABI HAIFA 2-1 (1-1)

Rieder Stadion 22.10.1998

Referee: Adrian Stoica (ROM)   Attendance: 5,000

SV RIED: Ronald Unger; Goran Stanisavljevic, Manfred Rothbauer, Maciej Sliwowski (70 Ronald Brunmayr), Boris Kitka, Helmut Zeller, Michael Angermschid (81 Wolfgang Hacker), Gónter Steininger, Oliver Glasner (66 Alexander Jank), Gerald Strafner (Cap), Michael Anicic.   Trainer: Klaus Roitinger

MACCABI: Nir Davidovich; Serhiy Balanchuk, Alon Harazi, Adoram Keissy, Offir Kopel, Ibrahim Duro (46 Assi Kalman), Alon Mizrahi (Cap), Radovan Hromadko, Shuki Nagar, Guy Melamed, Yaniv Katan.   Trainer: Dušan Uhrin

Goals: A. Mizrahi (13), Sliwowski (22), Strafner (88)

MACCABI HAIFA v SV RIED 4-1 (1-0)

Kiriat Eliezer, Haifa 5.11.1998

Referee: Zeljko Siric (CRO)   Attendance: 17,500

MACCABI: Nir Davidovich; Guy Melamed, Arik Benado, Alon Harazi, Adoram Keissy, Offir Kopel, Radovan Hromadko, Shuki Nagar, Yossi Benayoun, Yaniv Katan (85 Ibrahim Duro), Alon Mizrahi (Cap).   Trainer: Dušan Uhrin

SV RIED: Milan Oraze; Oliver Glasner, Boris Kitka, Gónter Steininger, Manfred Rothbauer (78 Faruk Hujdurovic), Michael Angermschid, Goran Stanisavljevic, Michael Anicic, Helmut Zeller (81 Wolfgang Hacker); Gerald Strafner (Cap), Maciej Sliwowski (76 Ronald Brunmayr).   Trainer: Klaus Roitinger

Sent off: Kopel (8), Steininger (11), Hujdurovic (90)

Goals: Mizrahi (33), Keissy (62), Anicic (70), Benayoun (75), Duro (90)

CHELSEA LONDON v FC KØBENHAVN 1-1 (0-0)

Stamford Bridge, London 22.10.1998

Referee: Metin Tokat (TUR)   Attendance: 21,207

CHELSEA: Ed de Goey; Albert Ferrer (69 Dan Petrescu), Frank Leboeuf, Marcel Desailly, Graeme Le Saux, Brian Laudrup, Gustavo Poyet, Roberto Di Matteo, Dennis Wise (Cap), Gianfranco Zola, Pierluigi Casiraghi (68 Tore André Flo).   Trainer: Gianluca Vialli

FC KØBENHAVN: Michael Stensgaard; Lars Højer Nielsen (84 Morten Falch), Carsten Hemmingsen, Bjarne Goldbæk, Piotr Haren, David Nielsen, Peter Nielsen (Cap), Thomas Thorninger (80 Todi Jonsson), Michael "Mio" Nielsen, Niclas Jensen, Thomas Rytter (73 Kim Madsen).   Trainer: Kim Brink

Goals: Goldbæk (81), Desailly (90)

FC KØBENHAVN v CHELSEA LONDON 0-1 (0-1)

Idraetsparken, København 5.11.1998

Referee: Claude Colombo (FRA)   Attendance: 25,000

FC KØBENHAVN: Michael Stensgaard; Lars Højer Nielsen, Carsten Hemmingsen, Bjarne Goldbæk, Piotr Haren (88 Martin Bill Larsen), David Nielsen, Peter Nielsen (Cap), Thomas Thorninger (56 Todi Jonsson), Michael "Mio" Nielsen, Niclas Jensen, Thomas Rytter.   Trainer: Kim Brink

CHELSEA: Ed de Goey; Celestine Babayaro, Frank Leboeuf, Marcel Desailly, Albert Ferrer, Roberto Di Matteo, Dennis Wise (Cap), Brian Laudrup (67 Dan Petrescu), Graeme Le Saux, Pierluigi Casiraghi (89 Gustavo Poyet), Gianfranco Zola (76 Tore André Flo).   Trainer: Gianluca Vialli

Goal: Laudrup (32)

PANIONIOS ATHINA v APOLLON LIMASSOL 3-2 (2-2)

Neas Smirnis, Athinai 22.10.1998

Referee: Roy Helge Olsen (NOR)   Attendance: 10,000

PANIONIOS: Foto Strakosha (/Cap); Panagiotis Fissas, Jan Erlend Kruse, Vasilis Ioannidis, Kent Bergersen; Antonis Sapountzis (Cap/) (46 Konstandinos Kafalis), Giorgos Mitsopoulos, Anastasios Zahopoulos (81 Dimitrios Nalitzis), Theofilos Karasavvidis; Mark Robins, Garry Haylock.   Trainer: Ronald Whelan

APOLLON: Sofronis Avgousti (46 Alexandros Mihail); Hrysostomos Juras, Haralampos Pittas (Cap), Filippos Filippou, Marios Haralampous, Milenko Spoljaric, Florin Cârstea (65 Nikodimos Papavasileiou), Marios Themistokleous, Xenios Kyriakou (72 Giorgos Kais), Nebojsa Mladenovic, Giorgos Kavazis.   Trainer: Dumitru Dumitriu

Sent off: Filippou (64)

Goals: Spoljaric (14, 43), Sapountzis (22), Haylock (39), Robins (57)

APOLLON LIMASSOL v PANIONIOS ATHINAI 0-1 (0-1)

Tsirion, Limassol 5.11.1998

Referee: Jan Wegereef (HOL)   Attendance: 8,000

APOLLON: Alexandros Mihail; Hrysostomos Juras (78 Hrysostomos Hristofi), Haralampos Pittas (Cap), Giorgos Kavazis, Marios Haralampous, Hristos Germanos, Milenko Spoljaric, Florin Cârstea, Nikodimos Papavasileiou, Marios Themistokleous (57 Stefanos Voskaridis), Giorgos Kais.   Trainer: Dumitru Dumitriu

PANIONIOS: Foto Strakosha; Vasilis Ioannidis, Dimitrios Bougas, Garry Haylock (65 Dimitrios Nalitzis), Andonis Sapountzis (Cap), Giorgos Mitsopoulos, Panagiotis Fissas (90 Dimitrios Markezinis), Anastasios Zahopoulos (85 Konstandinos Kafalis), Theofilos Karasavvidis, Giannis Kamitsis, Kent Bergersen.   Trainer: Ronald Whelan

Goal: Sapountzis (18)

QUARTER-FINALS

CHELSEA LONDON v VÅLERENGA IF OSLO 3-0 (2-0)

Stamford Bridge, London 4.03.1999

Referee: Günter Benkö (AUS)   Attendance: 34,177

CHELSEA: Ed de Goey; Albert Ferrer, Marcel Desailly, Bernard Lambourde, Graeme Le Saux, Dan Petrescu, Dennis Wise (Cap), Roberto Di Matteo, Celestine Babayaro, Gianluca Vialli, Gianfranco Zola (46 Tore André Flo).   Trainer: Gianluca Vialli

VÅLERENGA: Mikko Juhani Kaven; Knut Henry Haraldsen, Hai Ngoc Tran, Thomas Berntsen, Fredrik Kjølner (Cap); Bjørn Arild Levernes (85 Pascal Simpson), Dag Riisnaes, Joachim Walltin, Tom Henning Hovi, John Carew, Espen Haug (56 Kjell Roar Kaasa).   Trainers: Egil Olsen & Lars Tjernaas

Goals: Babayaro (9), Zola (30), Wise (85)

VÅLERENGA IF OSLO v CHELSEA LONDON 2-3 (2-3)

Ulleval, Oslo 18.03.1999

Referee: Armand Ancion (BEL)   Attendance: 17,934

VÅLERENGA: Mikko Juhani Kaven; Thomas Berntsen, Knut Henry Haraldsen, Fredrik Kjølner (Cap), Hai Ngoc Tran; Joachim Walltin, Tom Henning Hovi (77 Espen Haug), Bjørn Arild Levernes, Dag Riisnaes, Pascal Simpson (70 Fredrik Thorsen), John Carew (86 Espen Musaeus).   Trainers: Egil Olsen & Lars Tjernaas

CHELSEA: Ed de Goey; John Terry, Bernard Lambourde, Michael Duberry, Graeme Le Saux, Dan Petrescu, Roberto Di Matteo, Dennis Wise (Cap) (46 Eddie Newton), Celestine Babayaro (46 Andy Myers), Gianluca Vialli, Tore André Flo (46 Mark Nicholls).   Trainer: Gianluca Vialli

Goals: Vialli (13), Lambourde (15), Kjølner (26), Flo (32), Carew (42)

**LOKOMOTIV MOSKVA
v MACCABI HAIFA 3-0** (0-0)

Lokomotiv Moskva 4.03.1999

Referee: Lubos Michel (SVK)   Attendance: 20,000

LOKOMOTIV: Ruslan Nigmatullin; Aleksei Arifullin (36 Igor Cherevchenko), Albert Sarkisyan (60 Evgeniy Kharlachov), Andrei Solomatin (43 Andrei Lavrik), Yuri Drozdov, Aleksei Smertin, Igor Chugainov (Cap), Sergei Gurenko, Dmitriy Loskov, Zaza Janashia, Dmitriy Bulykin.   Trainer: Yuri Syomin

MACCABI: Nir Davidovich; Alon Harazi, Arik Benado (Cap), Adoram Keissy, Radovan Hromadko (62 Ibrahim Duro), Shuki Nagar, Yossi Benayoun (85 Haim Silvas), Avishai Jano, Guy Melamed, Ronen Harazi (76 Victor Paço), Jerzy Brzeczek.   Trainer: Dušan Uhrin

Goals: Janashia (47, 77, 90)

**REAL CD MALLORCA
v VARTEKS VARAZDIN 3-1** (0-0)

San Moix, Palma de Mallorca 18.03.1999

Referee: Ryszard Wójcik (POL)   Attendance: 16,109

RCD MALLORCA: Carlos Roa; Javier OLAIZOLA Rodríguez, MARCELINO Elena Sierra, Gustavo Lionel SIVIERO, Miquel SOLER Sarasols (Cap); LAUREN Bisan Etama-Mayer, Vicente ENGONGA Maté, Ariel Miguel IBAGAZA (73 Francisco SOLER Atencia), Veljko Paunovic; Daniel García Lara "DANI" (81 CARLOS Domínguez), Leonardo Angel BIAGINI (64 Alberto LUQUE Martos).   Trainer: Héctor Raúl Cúper

VARTEKS: Marijan Mrmić; Drazen Madunović (46 Silvester Sabolcki), Zoran Kastel, Andrija Balajić, Krunoslav Gregorić, Damir Muzek, Mario Ivanković, Zlatko Dalić (59 Mladen Posavec), Miljenko Mumlek (Cap), Danijel Hrman, Veldin Karić (73 Faik Kamberović).   Trainer: Strucni Stozer

Goals: Ibagaza (53), Paunović (55), Dani (75), Balajić (88)

**MACCABI HAIFA
v LOKOMOTIV MOSKVA 0-1** (0-0)

Kiriat Eliezer, Haifa 18.03.1999

Referee: Stuart Dougal (SCO)   Attendance: 12,074

MACCABI: Nir Davidovich; Avishai Jano, Alon Harazi, Arik Benado (Cap), Adoram Keissy; Offir Kopel, Shuki Nagar (75 Ibrahim Duro), Jerzy Brzeczek, Yossi Benayoun, Ronen Harazi (32 Yaniv Katan), Victor Paço (69 Radovan Hromadko).   Trainer: Dušan Uhrin

LOKOMOTIV: Ruslan Nigmatullin; Aleksei Arifullin, Igor Chugainov (Cap), Yuri Drozdov, Vladimir Maminov (81 Albert Sarkisyan), Andrei Lavrik, Aleksei Smertin, Sergei Gurenko, Dmitriy Loskov (46 Evgeniy Kharlachov), Zaza Janashia, Dmitriy Bulykin (68 Aleksandr Borodyuk).   Trainer: Yuri Syomin

Goal: Chugainov (72 pen)

PANIONIOS ATHINA v LAZIO ROMA 0-4 (0-2)

Neas Smirnis, Athina 4.03.1999

Referee: Graham Poll (ENG)   Attendance: 10,175

PANIONIOS: Foto Strakosha; Anastasios Zahopoulos, Athanasios Gazis, Vasilis Ioannidis, Theofilos Karasavvidis (63 Mark Robins), Paul Tisdale, Andonis Sapountzis (Cap), Dimitrios Bougas, Lars Bakkerud, Garry Haylock, Gareth Roberts.
Trainer: Ronald Whelan

LAZIO: Luca Marchegiani; Paolo Negro (27 Stefano Lombardi), Alessandro Nesta (Cap), Sinisa Mihajlovic (65 Roberto Baronio), Giuseppe Pancaro; Attilio Lombardo, Dejan Stankovic, FERNANDO Manuel Silva COUTO, Pavel Nedved; Christian Vieri (75 Guerino Gottardi), Marcelo Salas.
Trainer: Sven Göran Eriksson

Goals: Stankovic (3, 60), Salas (14), Nedved (63)

VARTEKS VARAZDIN v REAL CD MALLORCA 0-0

Varteks Varazdin 4.03.1999

Referee: Karl Erik Nilsson (SWE)   Attendance: 8,970

VARTEKS: Marijan Mrmić; Zoran Kastel, Drazen Madunović, Krunoslav Gregorić, Danijel Hrman, Zlatko Dalić, Damir Muzek, Miljenko Mumlek (Cap) (89 Mario Ivanković), Andrija Balajić, Veldin Karić (75 Paul Matas), Faik Kamberović (70 Mladen Posavec).   Trainer: Strucni Stozer

RCD MALLORCA: Carlos Roa; Gustavo Lionel SIVIERO, MARCELINO Elena Sierra, Javier OLAIZOLA Rodríguez, Miquel SOLER Sarasols (Cap); LAUREN Bisan Etama-Mayer, Lluís CARRERAS Ferrer, Francisco SOLER Atencia, Veljko Paunovic; Daniel García Lara "DANI", Leonardo Angel BIAGINI (81 Ariel LÓPEZ).   Trainer: Héctor Raúl Cúper

LAZIO ROMA v PANIONIOS ATHINA 3-0 (0-0)

Stadio Olimpico, Roma 18.03.1999

Referee: Bernd Heynemann (GER)   Attendance: 20,488

LAZIO: Marco Ballotta; Attilio Lombardo, Alessandro Nesta (Cap), Sinisa Mihajlovic (70 Federico Crovari), Stefano Lombardi; Guerino Gottardi, Iván De La Peña, FERNANDO Manuel Silva COUTO, Roberto Baronio, Pavel Nedved, Dejan Stanković.
Trainer: Sven Göran Eriksson

PANIONIOS: Foto Strakosha; Giorgos Mitsopoulos, Giannis Kamitsis, Gareth Roberts, Athanasios Gazis, Lars Bakkerud (70 Dimitrios Bougas), Paul Tisdale, Anastasios Zahopoulos (46 Vasilis Ioannidis), Mark Robins (61 Garry Haylock), Andonis Sapountzis (Cap), Theofilos Karasavvidis.   Trainer: Ronald Whelan

Goals: Nedved (70), Stanković (77), De la Peña (82)

SEMI-FINALS

CHELSEA LONDON v REAL MALLORCA 1-1 (0-1)
Stamford Bridge, London   8.04.1999
Referee: Dick Jol (HOL)   Attendance: 32,524
CHELSEA: Ed de Goey; Albert Ferrer (80 Bernard Lambourde), Marcel Desailly, Frank Leboeuf, Graeme Le Saux, Dan Petrescu, Dennis Wise (Cap), Jody Morris, Celestine Babayaro (46 Tore André Flo), Gianluca Vialli, Gianfranco Zola (60 Gustavo Poyet).
Trainer: Gianluca Vialli
RCD MALLORCA: Carlos Roa; Javier OLAIZOLA Rodríguez, Gustavo Lionel SIVIERO, MARCELINO Elena Sierra, Miquel SOLER Sarasols (Cap); LAUREN Bisan Etama-Mayer, Vicente ENGONGA Maté, Ariel Miguel IBAGAZA (61 Lluís CARRERAS Ferrer), Veljko Paunovic; Leonardo Angel BIAGINI (85 Francisco SOLER Atencia), Daniel García Lara "DANI".
Trainer: Héctor Raúl Cúper
Goals: Dani (31), Flo (50)

REAL MALLORCA v CHELSEA LONDON 1-0 (0-0)
San Moix, Palma de Mallorca   22.04.1999
Referee: Heinz Hellmut Krug (GER)   Attendance: 18,848
RCD MALLORCA: Carlos Roa; Javier OLAIZOLA Rodríguez, MARCELINO Elena Sierra, Gustavo Lionel SIVIERO (46 Lluís CARRERAS Ferrer), Miquel SOLER Sarasols (Cap); LAUREN Bisan Etama-Mayer, Vicente ENGONGA Maté, Jovan Stankovic (80 Oscar ARPÓN Ochoa), Veljko Paunovic; Daniel García Lara "DANI", Leonardo Angel BIAGINI (67 Francisco SOLER Atencia).
Trainer: Héctor Raúl Cúper
CHELSEA: Ed de Goey; Albert Ferrer, Marcel Desailly, Frank Leboeuf, Graeme Le Saux (46 Celestine Babayaro), Dan Petrescu (77 Jody Morris), Roberto Di Matteo, Gustavo Poyet, Dennis Wise (Cap), Tore André Flo, Gianfranco Zola.   Trainer: Gianluca Vialli
Goal: Biagini (14)

LOKOMOTIV MOSKVA v LAZIO ROMA 1-1 (0-0)
Lokomotiv Moskva   8.04.1999
Referee: Gilles Veissière (FRA)   Attendance: 21,812
LOKOMOTIV: Ruslan Nigmatullin; Aleksei Arifullin, Igor Cherevchenko, Igor Chugainov (Cap), Yuri Drozdov, Aleksei Smertin (46 Dmitriy Loskov), Dmitriy Bulykin (85 Aleksandr Borodyuk), Sergei Gurenko, Andrei Lavrik, Zaza Janashia, Evgeniy Kharlachov (85 Vladimir Maminov).   Trainer: Yuri Syomin
LAZIO: Luca Marchegiani; Giuseppe Pancaro, Paolo Negro, Sinisa Mihajlovic, Giuseppe Favalli (Cap); Attilio Lombardo, Iván De La Peña, Matias Almeyda, Dejan Stankovic, Christian Vieri (65 Alen Boksic), Marcelo Salas (73 Roberto Mancini).
Trainer: Sven Göran Eriksson
Goals: Janashia (61), Boksic (77)

LAZIO ROMA v LOKOMOTIV MOSKVA 0-0
Stadio Olimpico, Roma   22.04.1999
Referee: Anders Frisk (SWE)   Attendance: 32,016
LAZIO: Luca Marchegiani; Paolo Negro, Alessandro Nesta (Cap), Sinisa Mihajlovic, Giuseppe Pancaro; Attilio Lombardo, FERNANDO Manuel Silva COUTO (46 Matias Almeyda), Dejan Stankovic, Pavel Nedved; Christian Vieri (87 Alen Boksic), Roberto Mancini (76 Iván De La Peña).   Trainer: Sven Göran Eriksson
LOKOMOTIV: Ruslan Nigmatullin; Aleksei Arifullin, Igor Cherevchenko, Igor Chugainov (Cap), Dmitriy Loskov, Aleksei Smertin, Andrei Lavrik, Sergei Gurenko, Dmitriy Bulykin, Zaza Janashia, Evgeniy Kharlachov (66 Vladimir Maminov, 83 Aleksandr Borodyuk).   Trainer: Yuri Syomin

FINAL

**LAZIO ROMA
v REAL CLUB DEPORTIVO MALLORCA 2-1** (1-1)
Villa Park, Birmingham   19.05.1999
Referee: Günter Benkö (AUS)   Attendance: 33,021
LAZIO: Luca Marchegiani; Giuseppe Favalli, Alessandro Nesta (Cap), Sinisa Mihajlovic, Giuseppe Pancaro; Matias Almeyda, Dejan Stankovic (55 Sérgio Conceição), Roberto Mancini (90 FERNANDO Manuel Silva COUTO), Pavel Nedved (83 Attilio Lombardo); Marcelo Salas, Christian Vieri.
Trainer: Sven Göran Eriksson
RCD MALLORCA: Carlos Roa; Miquel SOLER Sarasols, Gustavo Lionel SIVIERO, MARCELINO Elena Sierra; Daniel García Lara "DANI", Ariel Miguel IBAGAZA, Jovan Stankovic, LAUREN Bisan Etama-Mayer, Javier OLAIZOLA Rodríguez (Cap); Leonardo Angel BIAGINI (73 Veljko Paunovic), Vicente ENGONGA Maté.
Trainer: Héctor Raúl Cúper
Goals: Vieri (7), Dani (11), Nedved (81)

Lazio Roma won the trophy outright

Goalscorers European Cup-Winners' Cup 1998-99:

7 goals: Alon Mizrahi (Maccabi Haifa)

6 goals: Zaza Janashia (Lokomotiv Moskva), Souleymane Oulare (KRC Genk)

4 goals: Dmitri Bulykin (Lokomotiv Moskva), John Carew (Vålerengen Oslo), Fabio Celestini (Lausanne Sports), Krisztián Kenesei (MTK Budapest), Oktay Derelioglu (Beşiktaş Istanbul), Pavel Nedved, Marcelo Salas, Dejan Stanković (Lazio Roma), Milenko Spoljarić (Apollon Limassol), Branko Strupar (KRC Genk), Thomas Thorninger (FC København), Daniel Garcia Lara "DANI" (Real Mallorca),

3 goals: Georgi Borisov (Levski Sofia), Rolands Bulders (Metalurgs Liepaja), Philippe Douglas (Lausanne Sports), Gerald Strafner (SV Ried), Bjarne Goldbæk, Peter Nielsen (FC København), Faik Kamberovic, Miljenko Mumlek (Varteks Varazdin), Daniel Gabriel Pancu (Rapid Bucureşti), Antonis Sapountzis (Panionios Athina),

2 goals: Vileniskis (Ekranas Panevezys), Krahen (CS Grevenmacher), Preisinger (MTK Hungária Budapest), Lazarov (Levski Sofia), Kryszalowicz, Sobocinski (Amica Wronki), Hamilton (Heart of Midlothian Edinburgh), Wibrån (Helsingborgs IF), Prochazka (SK Jablonec), Rasović (Partizan Beograd), Gudjónsson (KRC Genk), Karoglan, Bruno (Sporting Braga), D. de Nooijer (SC Heerenveen), D.Nielsen, Ma.Nielsen (FC København), Kavazis, Cârstea (Apollon Limassol), Keissy, Benayoun (Maccabi Haifa), Flo (Chelsea London), Chugainov (Lokomotiv Moskva), Haylock, Robins (Panionios Athina)

1 goal: T.Hovhannisyan, Asatryan (Tsement Ararat), Flanagan, Coughlan (Cork City), Stumbrys, Varnas (Ekranas Panevezys), Demenkovets, Sivkov (Lokomotiv-96 Vitebsk), Hauksson, Kristjánsson, Gylfason (IB Keflavík), Su.Olsen (GI Gotu), Batey (Glentoran Belfast), Sichinava (Dinamo Batumi), Vidojević, Sumnik (Rudar Velenje), Popovits, Ruhanen, Niemi, Salli (Haka Valkeakoski), Halmai, Illés, Balaskó, Szekeres (MTK Hungária Budapest), Donev, Radukanov, Todorov (Levski Sofia), Krol, Prerada (Amica Wronki), Fulton, McCann, Flögel, Holmes, Makel (Hearts), Edman, Powell, Stavrum (Helsingborgs IF), Wedau (MSV Duisburg), Formanko, Karhan, Tittel, Gomes, Ujlaky (Spartak Trnava), Şumudică, Bundea, Săbău, Dulca, Stanciu, Lupu, Mutică (Rapid Bucureşti), Fukal (SK Jablonec), Krstajić, Ilijev, Bjeković, Ilić (Partizan Beograd), Rehn, Hottiger, Cavin (Lausanne Sports), Simone, Ouédec, Okocha (Paris St. Germain), Magdisauskas (Metalurgs Liepaya), Bezhenar, Tsykhmeistruk, Leonenko, Revut (CSKA Kyiv), Tayfur, Mehmet, Ohen (Beşiktaş Istanbul), Reini, N'Sumbu, Hendrickx, Horváth (KRC Genk), Odair, Elpídio Silva (Sporting Braga), Hansma, Samardzić, De Visser, Talan, Mitriţă, Pahlplatz (SC Heerenveen), Sliwowski, Anicic (SV Ried), L.H.Nielsen, N.Jensen, Falch (FC København), Themistokleous, Pittas (Apollon Limassol), Kjølner, Levernes, Haraldsen, Kaasa (Vålerenga Oslo), Duro (Maccabi Haifa), Balajić, Matas (Varteks Varazdin), Vialli, Lambourde, Babayaro, Zola, Wise, Laudrup, Desailly, Leboeuf (Chelsea London), Fissas, Kouvalis (Panionios Athina), Shearer, Dabizas (Newcastle United), Biagini, Ibagaza, Paunović, López, Marcelino (RCD Mallorca), Vieri, Boksić, De la Peña, Sérgio Conceição (Lazio Roma)

Own goals: Vangronsveld (KRC Genk) for Apolonia Fier, Komlósi (MTK Budapest) for SV Ried

---

Also available from Soccer Books Limited in the same series:

The Complete Results & Line-ups of the European Champion Clubs' Cup 1955-1991 – The Knockout Years
(ISBN 1-86223-089-7)   *Softback Price £28.00*

The Complete Results & Line-ups of the European Champions League 1991-2004   (ISBN 1-86223-114-1)   *Softback Price £27.50*

The Complete Results & Line-ups of the European Fairs Cup 1955-1971
(ISBN 1-86223-085-4)   *Softback Price £22.50*

The Complete Results & Line-ups of the UEFA Cup 1971-1991
(ISBN 1-86223-109-5)   *Softback Price £29.50*

The Complete Results & Line-ups of the UEFA Cup 1991-2004
(ISBN 1-86223-115-X)   *Softback Price £29.50*

The Complete Results & Line-ups of the European Football Championships 1958-2004   (ISBN 1-86223-108-7)   *Softback Price £24.50*

The Complete Results & Line-ups of the Olympic Football Tournaments 1900-2004   (ISBN 1-86223-088-9)   *Softback Price £18.95*